Robert Jamieson

The Pentateuch and the Book of Joshua

Robert Jamieson

The Pentateuch and the Book of Joshua

ISBN/EAN: 9783337734381

Printed in Europe, USA, Canada, Australia, Japan

Cover: Foto ©Lupo / pixelio.de

More available books at **www.hansebooks.com**

THE

PENTATEUCH

AND

THE BOOK OF JOSHUA.

WITH AN ORIGINAL AND COPIOUS CRITICAL AND
EXPLANATORY COMMENTARY.

BY THE

REV. ROBERT JAMIESON, D.D.

MINISTER OF ST. PAUL'S PARISH, GLASGOW, SCOTLAND.

PHILADELPHIA:
WILLIAM S. & ALFRED MARTIEN.
No. 606 CHESTNUT STREET.
1860.

LIST OF CONTRACTIONS.

Arab. Arabic version.
Beng. Bengel.
Bo. Bochart's Hierozoicon.
Cal. Calvin's Commentary.
Cf. Confer, compare.
Cocc. Cocceius.
De W. De Wette.
Eich. Eichhorn.
E. V. English version.
Ex. gr. For example.
Fig. Figuratively.
Ges. Gesenius.
Grand. Grandpierre's Essais sur la Pentateuque.
Heng. Hengstenberg's Christology, and the Books of Moses.
Hess. Hess's Geschichte der Patriarchen.
Hitch. Hitchcock's Geology.
La. Laborde's Commentaire Géogr.
Le. Leclerc's Commentary.
Lit. Literally.
LXX. The Septuagint Greek version.

Maurer. Maurer of Heiligstadt.
Mich. Michaelis.
Nom. Nominative.
Noy. Noyes.
N. S. E. W. North, South, East, West.
N. T. New Testament.
O. T. Old Testament.
Pax. Paxton's Illustrations of Scripture.
Plur. Plural.
P. Smith. Pye Smith's Scripture Geology.
Rawl. Rawlinson.
Rob. Robinson's Researches in Palestine.
Ros. Rosenmüller's Scholia.
Sch. Schultens.
Sing. Singular.
Syr. Syriac version.
Transl. Translate, Translation.
Umbr. Umbreit.
Vul. Vulgate Latin edition.
Wilk. Wilkinson's Ancient Egyptians.

NUMBER OF YEARS FROM THE CREATION TO THE FLOOD.

	Lived before Birth of Eldest Son.		After the Birth of Eldest Son.		Total Length of Life.	
	Heb.	Sept.	Heb.	Sept.	Heb.	Sept.
Adam,	130	230	800	700	930	930
Seth,	105	205	807	707	912	912
Enos,	90	190	815	715	905	905
Cainan,	70	170	840	740	910	910
Mahalaleel,	65	165	830	730	895	895
Jared,	162	162	800	800	962	962
Enoch,	65	165	300	200	365	365
Methuselah,	187	187	782	782	969	969
Lamech,	182	188	595	595	777	753
Noah, at the Flood,	600	600				
	1656	2262				

PATRIARCHS AFTER THE FLOOD.
YEAR OF THE FLOOD.

According to the Hebrew. According to Septuagint

A.M.	B.C.			A.M.	B.C.
1656.	2349.	Noah, ... 950.	Noah, ... 950.	2262.	3245.
		Shem, ... 602.	Shem, ... 602.		
		500, ... 2.	500, ... 2.		
		Arphaxad, 438.	Arphaxad, 538.		
		403, ... 35.	403, ... 135.		
		Salah, ... 433.	Cainan, .. 460.		
		403, ... 30.	330, ... 130.		
		Eber, ... 464.	Salah, ... 433.		
		4..0, ... 34.	303, ... 130.		
		Peleg, ... 239.	Eber, ... 404.		
		209, ... 30.	330, ... 134.		
		Reu, ... 239.	Peleg, ... 339.		
		207, ... 32.	209, ... 130.		
		Serug, ... 239.	Reu, ... 339.		
		200, ... 30.	207, ... 132.		
		Nahor, ... 148.	Serug, ... 330.		
		119, ... 29.	200, ... 130.		
		Terah, ... 205.	Nahor, ... 148.		
		135, ... 70.	69, ... 79.		
2150.	1848.	Abraham, 175.	Terah, ... 205.		
		75, ... 100.	75, ... 130.	3462.	2015.
			Abraham, 175.		
			75, ... 100.		

The figures after the names denote the whole period of life. Those on the right, when they became fathers; and those under each name, the number of years they lived after.

There is a difference of six hundred years between the Septuagint and the Hebrew Bible now in use. According to that Text, as it stands at present, the period that elapsed between the Creation and the Flood is much shorter than appears to have been in the ancient Hebrew copies of the Scriptures from which the LXX. made their version, the one generally quoted by our Lord and the Apostles, and corresponding generally in its chronology with that of Josephus. There is good reason to suspect that this alteration was designedly effected by the Masoreti Jews in the second century of the Christian era.

THE JOURNEYS OF ABRAHAM.

The following may be considered a pretty correct account of the extent of the Patriarch's Travels.

			Miles.
1	From	Ur in Chaldea to Haran	370
2	—	Haran to Sichem	400
3	—	Sichem to Mamre	28
4	—	Mamre to Egypt	240
5	—	Egypt to Mamre	240
6	—	Mamre to the plain near Hebron	32
7	—	The Plain of Mamre to Dan, (where Lot was rescued)	124
8	—	Dan, he pursued the defeated kings to Hobah	80
9	—	Hobah back to Sodom	160
10	—	Sodom to the plain of Mamre	40
11	—	Mamre to Gerar	6
12	—	Gerar to Beersheba	12
13	—	Beersheba to Moriah	40
14	—	Moriah to Beeersheba	40
15	—	Beersheba to Mamre	16
			1,834

From Bunting's Travels of the Patriarchs.

THE FIRST BOOK OF MOSES, CALLED

GENESIS.

CHAPTER I.

1 The creation of heaven and earth, 3 of the light, 6 of the firmament: 9 the earth separated from the waters, 11 and made fruitful. 14 The creation of the sun, moon, and stars. 20 of the fish and fowl, 24 of beasts and cattle. 26 Creation of man in the image of God; and his blessing. 29 The appointment of food.

IN *a* the beginning *b* God created the heaven and the earth.

2 And the earth was *c* without form, and void; and darkness was upon the face of the deep. *d* And the Spirit of God moved upon the face of the waters.

3 ¶ *e* And God said, Let there be light: and there was light.

4 And God saw the light, that it was good: and God divided the ¹ light from the darkness.

5 And God called the light *f* Day, and the darkness he called Night. ² And the evening and the morning were the first day.

6 ¶ And God said, *g* Let there be a ³ firmament in the midst of the waters, and let it divide the waters from the waters.

7 And God made the firmament, and divided the waters which were under the firmament from the waters which were above the firmament: and it was so.

8 And God called the firmament Heaven. And the evening and the morning were the second day.

9 ¶ And God said, *h* Let the waters under the heaven be gathered together unto one place, and let the dry land appear: and it was so.

10 And God called the dry land Earth; and the gathering together of the waters called he Seas: and God saw that it was good.

11 And God said, *i* Let the earth bring forth ⁴ grass, the herb yielding seed, and the fruit tree yielding *j* fruit after his kind, whose seed is in itself, upon the earth: and it was so.

12 And the earth brought forth grass, and herb yielding seed after his kind, and the tree yielding fruit, whose seed was in itself, after his kind: and God saw that it was good.

13 And the evening and the morning were the third day.

14 ¶ And God said, *k* Let there be lights in the firmament of the heaven to divide *b* the day from the night; and let them be for signs, and for seasons, and for days, and years:

15 And let them be for lights in the firmament of the heaven to give light upon the earth: and it was so.

16 And God made two great lights; the greater light ⁶ to rule the day, and the lesser light to rule the night: he made the stars also.

17 And God *l* set them in the firmament of the heaven to give light upon the earth,

18 And to rule over the day and over the night, and to divide the light from the darkness: and God saw that it was good.

19 And the evening and the morning were the fourth day.

B. C. 4004.

CHAP. I.
a Jn. 1, 1-3.
Heb. 1, 10.
b Job 38, 4.
Isa. 44, 24.
Ro. 1, 20.
Col. 1, 16.
Heb. 11, 3.
Rev. 4, 11.
c Jer. 4, 23.
d Is. 40, 12.
e Ps. 33, 9.
1 between the light and between the darkness.
e Ps. 74, 16.
2 And the evening was, and the morning was.
g Job 37, 11.
Ps. 136, 5.
Ps. 33, 6.
Jer. 10, 12.
3 expansion.
h Job 26, 10.
Job 38, 8.
Ps. 33, 7.
Ps. 95, 5.
i Heb. 6, 7.
4 tender grass.
j Luke 6, 44.
k De. 4, 19.
Job 25, 3. 5.
Ps. 74, 16.
Ps. 136, 7.
5 between the day and between the night.
6 for the rule of the day, etc.
l Ps. 8, 1.
m Ps. 104, 24.
7 or, creeping.
8 soul.
9 let fowl fly.
10 face of the firmament of heaven.
n Ps. 104, 18-23.
o Ps. 100, 3.
p Eph. 4, 24.
Ja. 3, 9.
q Ps. 8, 6.
r 1 Cor. 11, 7.
s Mal. 2, 15.
t Ps. 127, 3.
1 Ti. 4, 3.
11 creepeth.
12 seeding seed.
13 a living soul.

CHAP. 2.
a Ex. 31, 17
b Ex. 16, 23-30
1 created to make.

20 ¶ And God said, *m* Let the waters bring forth abundantly the ⁷ moving creature that hath ⁸ life, and ⁹ fowl that may fly above the earth in the ¹⁰ open firmament of heaven.

21 And God created great whales, and every living creature that moveth, which the waters brought forth abundantly, after their kind, and every winged fowl after his kind: and God saw that it was good.

22 And God blessed them, saying, Be fruitful, and multiply, and fill the waters in the seas, and let fowl multiply in the earth.

23 And the evening and the morning were the fifth day.

24 ¶ And God said, *n* Let the earth bring forth the living creature after his kind, cattle, and creeping thing, and beast of the earth after his kind: and it was so.

25 And God made the beast of the earth after his kind, and cattle after their kind, and every thing that creepeth upon the earth after his kind: and God saw that it was good.

26 ¶ And God said, *o* Let us make man *p* in our image, after our likeness: and let them have *q* dominion over the fish of the sea, and over the fowl of the air, and over the cattle, and over all the earth, and over every creeping thing that creepeth upon the earth.

27 So God created man in his own image, in the *r* image of God created he him; *s* male and female created he them.

28 And *t* God blessed them, and God said unto them, Be fruitful, and multiply, and replenish the earth, and subdue it; and have dominion over the fish of the sea, and over the fowl of the air, and over every living thing that ¹¹ moveth upon the earth.

29 ¶ And God said, Behold, I have given you every herb ¹² bearing seed, which is upon the face of all the earth, and every tree, in the which is the fruit of a tree yielding seed; to you it shall be for meat.

30 And to every beast of the earth, and to every fowl of the air, and to every thing that creepeth upon the earth, wherein there is ¹³ life, I have given every green herb for meat: and it was so.

31 And God saw every thing that he had made, and, behold, it was very good. And the evening and the morning were the sixth day.

CHAPTER II.

1 The first sabbath. 8 The garden of Eden. 17 The tree of knowledge forbidden. 19 The creatures named. 21 The making of woman, and institution of marriage.

THUS the heavens and the earth were finished, and all the host of them.

2 *a* And on the seventh day God ended his work which he had made; and he rested on the seventh day from all his work which he had made.

3 And God *b* blessed the seventh day, and sanctified it; because that in it he had rested from all his work which God ¹ created and made.

THE FIRST BOOK OF MOSES, CALLED
GENESIS.

CHAPTER I.

Ver. 1--2. The Creation of Heaven and Earth. In the beginning—a period of remote and unknown antiquity, hid in the depths of eternal ages; and so the phrase is used in Pro. 8. 22, 23; also Marg. Ref. **God**—the name of the Supreme Being, signifying in Hebrew, "Strong," "Mighty." It is expressive of omnipotent power; and by its use here in the plural form, is obscurely taught at the opening of the Bible a doctrine clearly revealed in other parts of it, viz., that though God is one, there is a plurality of persons in the Godhead—Father, Son, and Spirit, who were engaged in the creative work Pro. 8. 27; Jo. 1. 3, 10; Eph. 3. 9; Heb. 1. 2; Job 26. 13.) **created**—not formed from any pre-existing materials, but made out of nothing. **the heaven and the earth**—the universe. This first verse is a general introduction to the inspired volume, declaring the great and important truth, that all things had a beginning; that nothing throughout the wide extent of nature, existed from eternity, originated by chance, or from the skill of any inferior agent; but that the whole universe was produced by the creative power of God (A. 17. 21; Ro. 11, 36.). After this preface, the narrative is confined to the earth. 2. **without form and void**—or in "confusion and emptiness" as the words are rendered in Is. 34. 11. This globe, at some undescribed period, having been convulsed and broken up, was a dark and watery waste for ages perhaps, till out of this chaotic state, the present fabric of the world was made to arise. **moved**—lit. continued brooding over it, as a fowl does, when hatching eggs. The immediate agency of the Spirit, by working on the dead and discordant elements, combined, arranged, and ripened them into a state adapted for being the scene of a new creation. The account of this new creation properly begins at the end of this second verse; and the details of the process are described in the natural way an onlooker would have done, who beheld the changes that successively took place.

3--5. The First Day. God said—This phrase, which occurs so repeatedly in the account means—willed, decreed, appointed; and the determining will of God was followed in every instance by an immediate result. Whether the sun was created at the same time with, or long before, the earth, the dense accumulation of fogs and vapours which enveloped the chaos, had covered the globe with a settled gloom. But by the command of God, light was rendered visible; the thick murky clouds were dispersed, broken or rarefied, and light diffused over the expanse of waters. The effect is described in the name DAY, which in Hebrew signifies *warmth*, *heat*; while the name Night signifies a ROLLING UP, as night wraps all things in a shady mantle. **divided the light from darkness**—refers to the alternation or succession of the one to the other, produced by the daily revolution of the earth round its axis. **first day**—a natural day, as the mention of its two parts clearly determines; and Moses reckons, according to Oriental usage, from sunset to sunset, saying, not day and night as we do, but evening and morning.

6--8. Second Day. firmament—an expanse —a beating out as a plate of metal:—a name given to the atmosphere from its appearing to an observer to be the *vault* of heaven, supporting the weight of the *watery clouds*. By the creation of an atmosphere, the lighter parts of the waters which overspread the earth's surface were drawn up and suspended in the visible heavens, while the larger and heavier mass remained below. The air was thus "in the midst of the waters," *i. e.* separated them; and this being the apparent use of it, is the only one mentioned, although the atmosphere serves other uses, as a medium of life and light.

9--13. Third Day. let the waters, &c.—The world was to be rendered a terraqueous globe, and this was effected by a volcanic convulsion on its surface, the upheaving of some parts, the sinking of others, and the formation of vast hollows, into which the waters impetuously rushed, as is graphically described. (Ps. 104. 6-9.) [HITCH.] Thus a large part of the Earth was left "dry land," and thus were formed oceans, seas, lakes, and rivers which, though each having their own beds, or channels, are all connected with the sea (Job, 38. 10; Ecc. 1. 7.). **let the earth bring forth**—The bare soil was clothed with verdure, and it is noticeable that the trees, plants, and grasses—the three great divisions of the vegetable kingdom, here mentioned, were not called into existence in the same way as the light and the air; they were made to grow, and they grew as they do still out of the ground—not, however, by the slow process of vegetation, but through the Divine Power, without rain, dew, or any process of labour—sprouting up and flourishing in a single day.

14--19. Fourth Day. let there be light—The atmosphere being completely purified—the sun, moon, and stars were for the first time unveiled in all their glory in the cloudless sky; and they are described as "in the firmament" which to the eye they appear to be, though we know they are really at vast distances from it. **two great lights**—In consequence of the day being reckoned as commencing at even—the moon, which would be seen first in the horizon, would appear "a great light" compared with the little twinkling stars; while its pale benign radiance would be eclipsed by the dazzling splendour of the sun; when his resplendent orb rose in the morning and gradually attained its meridian blaze of glory, it would appear "the greater light" that ruled the day. Both these lights may be said to be "made" on the fourth day—not created, indeed, for it is a different word that is here used, but constituted, appointed to the important and necessary office of serving as luminaries to the world, and regulating by their motions and their influence the progress and divisions of time.

20--23. Fifth Day. The signs of animal life appeared in the waters and in the air. **moving creature**—all oviparous animals, both

4 ¶ These *are* the generations of the heavens and of the earth when they were created, in the day that the LORD God made the earth and the heavens,

5 And every plant of the field before it was in the earth, and every herb of the field before it grew: for the ᵈ LORD God had not caused it to rain upon the earth, and *there was* not a man to till the ground.

6 But ² there went up a mist from the earth, and watered the whole face of the ground.

7 And the LORD God formed man ³ *of* the dust of the ground, and breathed into his nostrils the breath of life; and man became a living soul.

8 ¶ And the LORD God planted ⁴ a garden eastward in Eden; and there he put the man whom he had formed.

9 And out of the ground made the LORD God to ᶠ grow every tree that is pleasant to the sight and good for food; ᵍ the tree of life also in the midst of the garden, and the tree of knowledge of good and evil.

10 And ʰ a river went out of Eden to water the garden; and from thence it was parted, and became into four heads.

11 The name of the first *is* Pison: that *is* it which compasseth the whole land of ⁱ Havilah, where *there is* gold;

12 And the gold of that land *is* good: there *is* bdellium and the onyx stone.

13 And the name of the second river *is* Gihon: the same *is* it that compasseth the whole land of ⁴ Ethiopia.

14 And the name of the third river *is* ʲ Hiddekel: that *is* it which goeth ⁵ toward the east of Assyria. And the fourth river *is* Euphrates.

15 And the LORD God took ⁶ the man, and put him into the garden of Eden to dress it and to keep it.

16 And the LORD God commanded the man, saying, Of every tree of the garden ⁷ thou mayest freely eat:

17 But of the tree of the knowledge of good and evil, thou shalt not eat of it: for in the day that thou eatest thereof ⁸ thou shalt surely die.

18 ¶ And the LORD God said, *It is* not good that the man should be alone; I will make him an help ⁹ meet for him.

19 And out of the ground the LORD God formed every beast of the field, and every fowl of the air; and ᵏ brought *them* unto Adam to see what he would call them: and whatsoever ¹⁰ Adam called every living creature, that *was* the name thereof.

20 And Adam ¹¹ gave names to all cattle, and to the fowl of the air, and to every beast of the field: but for Adam there was not found an help meet for him.

21 And the LORD God caused a ˡ deep sleep to fall upon Adam, and he slept: and he took one of his ribs, and closed up the flesh instead thereof;

22 And the rib, which the LORD God had taken from man, ¹² made he a woman, and ᵐ brought her unto the man.

23 And Adam said, This is now ⁿ bone of my bones, and flesh of my flesh: she shall be called ¹³ Woman, because she was taken out of ¹⁴ Man.

24 ᵒ Therefore shall a man leave his father and his mother, and shall cleave unto his wife: and ᵖ they shall be one flesh.

25 And they were both naked, the man and his wife, and were not ashamed.

CHAPTER III.

1 *The serpent deceiveth Eve.* 6 *Man's fall;* 9 *God arraigneth them.* 14 *The serpent cursed; his overthrow by the woman's seed.* 16 *Mankind's punishment; and loss of paradise.*

NOW the serpent was more ᵃ subtil than any beast of the field which the LORD God had made. And he said unto the woman, Yea, ¹ hath God said, Ye shall not eat of every tree of the garden?

2 And the woman said unto the serpent, We may eat of the fruit of the trees of the garden:

3 ᵇ But of the fruit of the tree which *is* in the midst of the garden, God hath said, Ye shall not eat of it, neither shall ye touch it, lest ye die.

4 And the serpent said unto the woman, ᶜ Ye shall not surely die:

5 For God doth know that in the day ye eat thereof, then your eyes shall be opened, and ye shall be as gods, knowing good and evil.

6 And when the woman saw that the tree *was* good for food, and that it *was* ² pleasant to the eyes, and a tree to be desired to make *one* wise, she took of the fruit thereof, and did eat, and gave also unto her husband with her; ᵈ and he did eat.

7 And the eyes of them both were opened, and they knew that they *were* naked; and they sewed fig leaves together, and made themselves ³ aprons.

8 And they heard the voice ᵉ of the LORD God walking in the garden in the ⁴ cool of the day: and Adam and his wife ᶠ hid themselves from the presence of the LORD God amongst the trees of the garden.

9 And the LORD God called unto Adam, and said unto him, ᵍ Where *art* thou?

10 And he said, I heard thy voice in the garden, and ʰ I was afraid, because I *was* naked; and I hid myself.

11 And he said, Who told thee that thou *wast* naked? Hast thou eaten of the tree, whereof I commanded thee that thou shouldest not eat?

12 And the man said, The woman whom thou gavest *to be* with me, she gave me of the tree, and I did eat.

13 And the LORD God said unto the woman, What *is* this *that* thou hast done? And the woman said, The serpent beguiled me, and I did eat.

14 And the LORD God said unto the serpent, Because thou hast done this, thou *art* cursed above all cattle, and above every beast of the field: upon thy belly shalt thou go, and ʲ dust shalt thou eat all the days of thy life:

15 And I will put ᵏ enmity between thee and the woman, and between thy seed and her seed; ˡ it shall bruise thy head, and thou shalt bruise his heel.

16 Unto the woman he said, I will greatly multiply thy sorrow and thy conception; in ᵐ sorrow thou shalt bring forth children; and thy desire *shall be* ⁵ to thy husband, and he shall rule over thee.

17 And unto Adam he said, Because thou hast hearkened unto the voice of thy wife, and hast eaten of the tree, of which I commanded thee, saying, Thou shalt not eat of it: cursed *is* the ground for thy sake; ⁿ in sorrow shalt thou eat *of* it all the days of thy life;

18 Thorns also and thistles shall it ⁶ bring

among the finny and the feathery tribes—remarkable for their rapid and prodigious increase. fowl—means every flying thing: The word rendered "whales," includes also sharks, crocodiles, &c.; so that from the countless shoals of small fish to the great sea monsters, from the tiny insect to the king of birds, the waters and the air were made suddenly to swarm with creatures formed to live and sport in their respective elements.

24-30. SIXTH DAY. A farther advance was made by the creation of terrestrial animals, all the various species of which are included in three classes—viz., cattle, the herbivorous kind capable of labour or domestication. beasts of the earth—*i. e.* wild animals, whose ravenous natures were then kept in check, and all the various forms of creeping things—from the huge reptiles to the insignificant caterpillars. 26. The last stage in the progress of creation being now reached—God said, Let us make man—words, which shew the peculiar importance of the work to be done, the formation of a creature, who was to be God's representative, clothed with authority and rule as visible head and monarch of the world. In our image, after our likeness—This was a peculiar distinction—the value attached to which appears in the words being twice mentioned. And in what did this image of God consist?—not in the erect form or features of man, not in his intellect; for the devil and his angels are, in this respect, far superior—not in his immortality; for he has not, like God, a past as well as a future eternity of being; but in the moral dispositions of his soul, commonly called *original righteousness*, (Ecc. 7. 29.) As the new creation is only a restoration of this image, the history of the one throws light on the other; and we are informed that it is renewed after the image of God in knowledge, righteousness, and true holiness, Col. 3. 10; Eph. 4. 24.) 28. Be fruitful, &c. The human race in every country and age have been the offspring of the first pair. Amid all the varieties found amongst men, some black as negroes, others copper-coloured, as well as white, the researches of modern science lead to a conclusion, fully accordant with the sacred history that they are all of one species and of one family (A. 17. 26.). What power in the word of God. "He spake and it was done, He commanded and all things stood fast." "Great and manifold are thy works, Lord God Almighty!—in wisdom hast thou made them all." We admire that wisdom—not only in the regular progress of creation, but in its perfect adaptation to the end. God is represented as pausing at every stage to look at his work. No wonder he contemplated it with complacency. Every object was in its right place, every vegetable process going on in its season, every animal in its structure and instincts suited to its mode of life, and its use in the economy of the world: he saw everything that he had made answering the plan which his eternal wisdom had conceived; and "BEHOLD IT WAS VERY GOOD."

CHAPTER II.

Ver. 1. THE NARRATIVE OF THE SIX DAYS' CREATION CONTINUED. The course of the narrative being improperly broken by the division of the chapter. the heavens—the firmament or atmosphere. host—a multitude, a numerous array—usually connected in Scripture with heaven only, but here with the earth also, meaning all that they contain. were finished—brought to completion—no permanent change has ever since been made on the course of the world, no new species of animals been formed, no law of nature repealed or added to. They could have been finished in a moment as well as in six days, but the work of creation was gradual for the instruction of man, as well, perhaps, as of higher creatures (Job, 38. 7.)

2-7. THE FIRST SABBATH. 2. rested—not to repose from exhaustion with labour (see Is. 50. 28), but ceased from working, an example equivalent to a command, that we also should cease from labour of every kind. 3. blessed and sanctified the seventh day—a peculiar distinction put upon it above the other six days, and showing it was devoted to sacred purposes. The institution of the Sabbath is as old as creation, giving rise to that weekly division of time which prevailed in the earliest ages. It is a wise and beneficent law, affording that regular interval of rest which the physical nature of man and the animals employed in his service requires, and the neglect of which brings both to premature decay. Moreover, it secures an appointed season for religious worship, and if it was necessary in a state of primeval innocence, how much more so now, when mankind have a strong tendency to forget God and his claims? 4. these are the generations of the heavens and the earth—the history or account of their production. Whence did Moses obtain this account so different from the puerile and absurd fictions of the heathen? not from any human source; for man was not in existence to witness it—not from the light of nature or reason; for though they proclaim the eternal power and Godhead by the things which are made, they cannot tell *how* they were made. None but the Creator himself could give this information, and therefore it is through faith we understand that the worlds were framed by the word of God (Heb. 11. 3.). rain, mist—See on ch. 1. 12. 7. Here the sacred writer supplies a few more particulars about the first pair. formed—had FORMED MAN OUT OF THE DUST OF THE GROUND. Science has proved that the substance of his flesh, sinews, and bones, consists of the very same elements as the soil which forms the crust of the earth, and the limestone that lies embedded in its bowels. But from that mean material what an admirable structure has been reared in the human body (Ps. 139. 14.). breath of life—*lit.*, of lives—not only animal but spiritual life. If the body is so admirable, how much more the soul with all its varied faculties. breathed into his nostrils—not that the Creator literally performed this act, but respiration being the medium and sign of life, this phrase is used to show that man's life originated in a different way from his body—being implanted directly by God (Eccl. 12. 7), and hence in the new creation of the soul Christ breathed on his disciples (Jo. 20. 22.).

8-17. THE GARDEN OF EDEN. 8. Eden—was probably a very extensive region in Mesopotamia, it is thought, distinguished for its natural beauty and the richness and variety of its produce. Hence its name signifying

forth to thee; and thou shalt eat the herb of the field;

19 In the sweat of thy face shalt thou eat bread, till thou return unto the ground; for out of it wast thou taken: for dust thou *art*, *o* and unto dust shalt thou return.

20 And Adam called his wife's name 7 Eve; because she was the mother of all living.

21 Unto Adam also and to his wife did the LORD God make coats of skins, and clothed them.

22 ¶ And the LORD God said, *p* Behold, the man is become as one of us, to know good and evil: and now, lest he put forth his hand, and take also of the tree of life, and eat, and live for ever:

23 Therefore the LORD God sent him forth from the garden of Eden, to till the ground from whence he was taken.

24 So he drove out the man; and he placed at the east of the garden of Eden cherubim, and a flaming sword which turned every way, 7 to keep the way of the tree of life.

CHAPTER IV.

1 *The birth of Cain and Abel.* 8 *The murder of Abel.* 11 *The curse of Cain.* 17 *Enoch, the first city, built.* 19 *Lamech and his two wives.* 25 *Seth and Enos born.*

AND Adam knew Eve his wife; and she conceived, and bare 1 Cain, and said, I have gotten a man from the LORD.

2 And she again bare his brother 2 Abel. And Abel was a 3 keeper of sheep, but Cain was a tiller of the ground.

3 And 4 in process of time it came to pass, that Cain brought of the fruit of the ground an offering unto the LORD.

4 And Abel, he also brought of the *a* firstlings of his 5 flock and of the fat thereof. And the LORD *b* had respect unto Abel and to his offering:

5 But *c* unto Cain and to his offering he had not respect. And Cain was very wroth, and his countenance fell.

6 And the LORD said unto Cain, Why art thou wroth? and why is thy countenance fallen?

7 If thou doest well, shalt thou not 6 be accepted? and if thou doest not well, sin lieth at the door. And 7 unto thee *shall* be his desire, and thou shalt rule over him.

8 And Cain talked with Abel his brother: and it came to pass, when they were in the field, that Cain rose up against Abel his brother, and *d* slew him.

9 And the LORD said unto Cain, Where *is* Abel thy brother? And he said, I know not: *Am* I my brother's keeper?

10 And he said, What hast thou done? the voice of thy brother's 8 blood *e* crieth unto me from the ground.

11 And now *art* thou *f* cursed from the earth, which hath opened her *g* mouth to receive thy brother's blood from thy hand;

12 When thou tillest the ground, it shall not henceforth yield unto thee her strength; a fugitive and a vagabond shalt thou be in the earth.

13 And Cain said unto the LORD, 9 My punishment *is* greater than I can bear.

14 Behold, thou hast driven me out this day from the face of the earth; and from thy face shall I be hid; and I shall be a fugitive and a vagabond in the earth: and it shall come to pass, *that* every one that findeth me shall slay me.

15 And the LORD said unto him, Therefore whosoever slayeth Cain, vengeance shall be taken on him sevenfold. And the LORD *h* set a mark upon Cain, lest any finding him should kill him.

16 ¶ And Cain went out from the *i* presence of the LORD, and dwelt in the land of Nod, on the east of Eden.

17 And Cain knew his wife; and she conceived, and bare 10 Enoch: and he builded a city, and *j* called the name of the city, after the name of his son, Enoch.

18 And unto Enoch was born Irad: and Irad begat Mehujael: and Mehujael begat Methusael: and Methusael begat 11 Lamech.

19 ¶ And Lamech took unto him two wives: the name of the one *was* Adah, and the name of the other Zillah.

20 And Adah bare Jabal: he was the father of such as dwell in tents, and *of such as have* cattle.

21 And his brother's name *was* Jubal: he was the father of all such as handle the harp and organ.

22 And Zillah, she also bare Tubal-cain, an 12 instructor of every artificer in brass and iron: and the sister of Tubal-cain *was* Naamah.

23 And Lamech said unto his wives, Adah and Zillah, hear my voice; ye wives of Lamech, hearken unto my speech: for 13 I have slain a man to my wounding, and a young man 14 to my hurt:

24 If Cain shall be avenged sevenfold, truly Lamech seventy and sevenfold.

25 ¶ And Adam knew his wife again; and she bare a son, and called his name 15 Seth: For God, *said she*, hath appointed me another seed instead of Abel, whom Cain slew.

26 And to Seth, to him also there was born a son; and he called his name 16 Enos: then began men to 17 call upon the name of the LORD.

CHAPTER V.

1 *The genealogy, age, and death of the patriarchs, from Adam unto Noah.* 24 *The godliness and translation of Enoch.*

THIS *is* *a* the book of the generations of Adam. In the day that God created man, *b* in the likeness of God made he him;

2 Male and female created he them; and blessed them, and called their name Adam, in the day when they were created.

3 ¶ And Adam lived an hundred and thirty years, and begat *a son* in his own likeness, after his image; and called his name Seth:

4 And the days of Adam after he had begotten Seth were eight hundred years: and he begat sons and daughters:

5 And all the days that Adam lived were nine hundred and thirty years: *c* and he died.

6 ¶ And Seth lived an hundred and five years, and begat Enos:

7 And Seth lived after he begat Enos eight hundred and seven years, and begat sons and daughters:

8 And all the days of Seth were nine hundred and twelve years: and he died.

9 ¶ And Enos lived ninety years, and begat 1 Cainan:

10 And Enos lived after he begat Cainan eight hundred and fifteen years, and begat sons and daughters:

pleasantness. God planted a garden eastward—an extensive park—a paradise, in which the man was put to be trained under the paternal care of his Maker to piety and usefulness. tree of life—so called from its symbolic character as a sign and seal of immortal life. Its prominent position "in the midst of the garden," where it must have been an object of daily observation and interest, was admirably fitted to keep them habitually in mind of God and futurity. 9. tree of the knowledge of good and evil—so called because it was a *test* of obedience by which our first parents were to be tried, whether they would be good or bad, obey God or break his commands. 17. shalt not eat of it—no reason assigned for the prohibition, but death was to be the punishment of disobedience. A positive command like this was not only the simplest and easiest, but the only trial to which their fidelity could be exposed. 15. put the man .. to dress it—not only to give him a pleasant employment, but to place him on his probation, and as the title of this garden, the garden of the Lord (Gen.13.10; Ez.28.13.), indicates—it was in fact a temple in which he worshipped God, and was daily employed in offering the sacrifices of thanksgiving and praise.

18-25. THE MAKING OF WOMAN. AND INSTITUTION OF MARRIAGE. 18. not good for man to be alone—In the midst of plenty and delights, he was conscious of feelings he could not gratify. To make him sensible of his wants. 19. God brought unto Adam—not all the animals in existence, but those chiefly in his immediate neighbourhood, and to be subservient to his use. whatever Adam called—His powers of perception and intelligence were supernaturally enlarged to know the characters, habits, and uses of each species that was brought to him. 20. but for Adam, &c.—The design of this singular scene was to show him that none of the living creatures he saw were on an equal footing with himself, and that while each class came with its mate of the same nature, form and habits, he alone had no companion. Besides, in giving names to them he was led to exercise his powers of speech, and prepare for social intercourse with his partner, a creature yet to be formed. 21. deep sleep—probably an ecstacy or trance like that of the prophets, when they had visions and revelations of the Lord, for the whole scene was probably visible to the mental eye of Adam, and hence his rapturous exclamation. took one of his ribs—"She was not made out of his head to surpass him, nor from his feet to be trampled on, but from his side to be equal to him, and near his heart to be dear to him." 23. —woman. *i. e.* in Heb.—man-Ess. one flesh—the human pair differed from all other pairs, that by the peculiar formation of Eve, they were one. And this passage is appealed to by our Lord as the divine institution of marriage (Matt. 19. 4. 5; Eph. 5. 28.) Thus Adam appears as a creature formed after the image of God—shewing his *knowledge* by giving names to the animals, his *righteousness* by his approval of the marriage relation, and his *holiness* by his principles and feelings—finding their gratification in the service and enjoyment of God.

CHAPTER III.

Ver. 1-5. THE TEMPTATION. the serpent—The fall of man was effected by the seductions of a serpent. That it was a real serpent is evident from the plain and artless style of the history; and from the many allusions made to it in the N. T. But the material serpent was the instrument or tool of a higher agent,—Satan or the Devil.—to whom the sacred writers apply from this incident the reproachful name of "the Serpent"—"the old Dragon." Though Moses makes no mention of this wicked spirit—giving only the history of the visible world—yet in the fuller discoveries of the Gospel, it is distinctly intimated that Satan was the author of the plot (Jo. 8. 44; 2 Cor. 11. 3; 1 Jo. 3. 8; 1 Tim. 2. 13; Rev. 20. 2. more subtile—serpents are proverbial for wisdom (Matt. 10. 16.). But these reptiles were at first, probably, far superior in beauty as well as in sagacity to what they are in their present state. He said—There being in the pure bosoms of the first pair, no principle of evil to work upon, a solicitation to sin could come only from *without*, as in the analogous case of Jesus Christ, (Matt.4.3 ; and as the tempter could not assume the human form—there being only Adam and Eve in the world—the agency of an inferior creature had to be employed. The Dragon-serpent [Bo.] seemed the fittest for the vile purpose; and the Devil was allowed by Him who permitted the trial, to bring articulate sounds from its mouth. unto the woman—the object of attack, from his knowledge of her frailty, of her having been but a short time in the world—her limited experience of the animal tribes, and, above all, her being alone, unfortified by the presence and counsels of her husband. Though sinless and holy, she was a free agent, liable to be tempted and seduced. yea, hath God said—Is it true that he hath restricted you in using the fruits of this delightful place? This is not like one so good and kind. Surely there is some mistake. He insinuated a doubt as to her sense of the divine will and appeared as "an angel of light" (2 Cor. 11. 14,) offering to lead her to the true interpretation. It was evidently from her regarding him as specially sent on that errand—that, instead of being startled by the reptile's speaking—she received him as a heavenly messenger. 2. the woman said, we may eat—'In her answer, Eve extolled the large extent of liberty they enjoyed in ranging at will amongst all the trees—one only excepted—with respect to which, she declared there was no doubt, either of the prohibition or the penalty. But there is reason to think that she had already received an injurious impression; for in using the words—"lest ye die," instead of "ye shall surely die"—she spoke as if the tree had been forbidden from some poisonous quality of its fruit. The tempter, perceiving this, became bolder in his assertions. 4. ye shall not surely die—He proceeded—not only to assure her of perfect impunity; but to promise great benefits from partaking of it. your eyes shall be opened—his words meant more than met the ear. In one sense their eyes were opened; for they acquired a direful experience of "good and evil"—of the happiness of a holy, and the misery of a sinful condition. But he studiously concealed this result from Eve, who fired with a tenerous desire for knowledge, thought only of rising to the rank and privileges of her angel inhabitants.

11 And all the days of Enos were nine hundred and five years: and he died.

12 ¶ And Cainan lived seventy years, and begat [2] Mahalaleel:

13 And Cainan lived after he begat Mahalaleel eight hundred and forty years, and begat sons and daughters:

14 And all the days of Cainan were nine hundred and ten years: and he died.

15 ¶ And Mahalaleel lived sixty and five years, and begat Jared:

16 And Mahalaleel lived after he begat [3] Jared eight hundred and thirty years, and begat sons and daughters:

17 And all the days of Mahalaleel were eight hundred ninety and five years: and he died.

18 ¶ And Jared lived an hundred sixty and two years, and he begat [d] Enoch:

19 And Jared lived after he begat Enoch eight hundred years, and begat sons and daughters:

20 And all the days of Jared were nine hundred sixty and two years: and he died.

21 ¶ And Enoch lived sixty and five years, and begat [4] Methuselah:

22 And Enoch [e] walked with God after he begat Methuselah three hundred years, and begat sons and daughters:

23 And all the days of Enoch were three hundred sixty and five years:

24 And Enoch walked with God: and he was not; [f] for God took him.

25 ¶ And Methuselah lived an hundred eighty and seven years, and begat [5] Lamech:

26 And Methuselah lived after he begat Lamech seven hundred eighty and two years, and begat sons and daughters:

27 And all the days of Methuselah were nine hundred sixty and nine years: and he died.

28 ¶ And Lamech lived an hundred eighty and two years, and begat a son:

29 And he called his name [6] Noah, saying, This same shall comfort us concerning our work and toil of our hands, because of the ground which the LORD hath [g] cursed.

30 And Lamech lived after he begat Noah five hundred ninety and five years, and begat sons and daughters:

31 And all the days of Lamech were seven hundred seventy and seven years: and he died.

32 ¶ And Noah was five hundred years old: and Noah begat Shem, Ham, and Japheth.

CHAPTER VI.

1 *The wickedness of the world, which provoketh God's wrath, and causeth the flood.* 8 *Noah findeth grace.* 14 *The order, form, and use of the ark.*

AND it came to pass, when men began to multiply on the face of the earth, and daughters were born unto them,

2 That [a] the sons of God saw the daughters of men that they were fair; and they [b] took them wives of all which they chose.

3 And the LORD said, [c] My Spirit shall not always strive with man, [d] for that he also is flesh: yet his days shall be an hundred and twenty years.

4 There were giants in the earth in those days; and also after that, when the sons of God came in unto the daughters of men, and they bare *children* to them, the same *became* mighty men which *were* of old, men of renown.

5 ¶ And [c] God saw that the wickedness of man *was* great in the earth, and *that* [1] every [f] imagination of the thoughts of his heart *was* only evil [2] continually.

6 And it [g] repented the LORD that he had made man on the earth, and it [h] grieved him at his heart.

7 And the LORD said, I will destroy man whom I have created from the face of the earth; [3] both man, and beast, and the creeping thing, and the fowls of the air; for it repenteth me that I have made them.

8 But Noah [i] found grace in the eyes of the LORD.

9 ¶ These *are* the generations of Noah: Noah was a just man *and* [4] perfect in his generations, *and* Noah walked with God.

10 And Noah begat three sons, Shem, Ham, and Japheth.

11 The earth also was corrupt before God, and the earth was filled with violence.

12 And God looked [j] upon the earth, and, behold, it was corrupt; for all flesh had corrupted his way upon the earth.

13 And God said unto Noah, [k] The end of all flesh is come before me; for the earth is filled with violence through them; and, behold, I will destroy them [5] with the earth.

14 Make thee an ark of gopher wood; [6] rooms shalt thou make in the ark, and shalt pitch it within and without with pitch.

15 And this *is the fashion* which thou shalt make it *of:* The length of the ark *shall be* three hundred cubits, the breadth of it fifty cubits, and the height of it thirty cubits.

16 A window shalt thou make to the ark, and in a cubit shalt thou finish it above; and the door of the ark shalt thou set in the side thereof; *with* lower, second, and third *stories* shalt thou make it.

17 [l] And, behold, I, even I, do bring a flood of waters upon the earth, to destroy all flesh, wherein *is* the breath of life, from under heaven; *and* every thing that *is* in the earth [m] shall die.

18 But with thee will I establish my covenant; and thou shalt come into the ark, thou, and thy sons, and thy wife, and thy sons' wives with thee.

19 And of every living thing of all flesh, two of every *sort* shalt thou bring into the ark, to keep *them* alive with thee; they shall be male and female.

20 Of fowls after their kind, and of cattle after their kind, of every creeping thing of the earth after his kind, two of every *sort* shall come unto thee, to keep *them* alive.

21 And take thou unto thee of [n] all food that is eaten, and thou shalt gather *it* to thee; and it shall be for food for thee, and for them.

22 [o] Thus did Noah; [p] according to all that God commanded him, so did he.

CHAPTER VII.

1 *Noah, with his family, and the living creatures, enter into the ark.* 17 *The beginning, increase, and continuance of the flood.* 21 *All flesh destroyed.*

AND the LORD said unto Noah, [a] Come thou and all thy house into the ark:

6-9. THE FALL. and when the woman saw—Her imagination and feelings were completely won; and the fall of Eve was soon followed by that of Adam. The history of every temptation, and of every sin, is the same: the outward object of attraction—the inward commotion of mind—the increase and triumph of passionate desire; ending in the degradation, slavery, and ruin of the soul Ja. 1. 15; 1 Jo. 11. 16.) 8. voice of the Lord God walking—The divine Being appeared in the same manner as formerly—uttering the well-known tones of kindness, walking in some visible form—not running hastily, as one impelled by the influence of angry feelings. How beautifully expressive are these words of the familiar and condescending manner in which He had hitherto held intercourse with the first pair. in the cool of the day—*lit.* the breeze of the day—the evening. hid themselves amongst the trees—Shame, remorse, fear—a sense of guilt—feelings to which they had hitherto been strangers, disordered their minds, and led them to shun him whose approach they used to welcome. How foolish to think of eluding His notice Ps. 139. 1-12.;

10-13. THE EXAMINATION. 10. afraid because-naked—apparently, a confession—the language of sorrow; but it was evasive—no signs of true humility and penitence—each tries to throw the blame on another. **12.** the woman gave me—He blames God. [CAL.] As the woman had been given him for his companion and help, he had eaten of the tree from love to her; and perceiving she was ruined, was determined not to survive her (M'Knt.) **13.** beguiled—cajoled by flattering lies. This sin of the first pair was heinous and aggravated—it was not simply eating an apple, but a love of self, dishonour to God, ingratitude to a benefactor, disobed ence to the best of Masters—a preference of the creature to the Creator.

14-24. THE SENTENCE. unto the serpent—The Judge pronounces a doom first—on the material serpent, which is cursed above all creatures; from being a model of grace and elegance in form—it has become the type of all that is odious, disgusting, and low [LE. ROS.]; or the curse has converted its natural condition into a punishment; it is now branded with infamy, and avoided with horror; next, on the spiritual Serpent—the seducer. Already fallen, he was to be still more degraded, and his power wholly destroyed, by the offspring of those he had deceived. **15.** thy seed—not only evil spirits, but wicked men. seed of the woman—the Messiah, or His Church. [CAL. HENG.] I will put enmity—God can only be said to do so by leaving "the Serpent and his seed to the influence of their own corruption; and by those measures which, pursued for the salvation of men, fill Satan and his angels with envy and rage." thou shalt bruise his heel—The serpent wounds the heel that crushes him; and so Satan would be permitted to afflict the humanity of Christ, and bring suffering and persecution on his people. it shall bruise thy head—the serpent's poison is lodged in its head; and a bruise on that part is fatal. Thus, fatal shall be the stroke which Satan shall receive from Christ; though, it is probable, he did not first understand the nature and extent of his doom. **16.** unto the woman greatly .. multiply—she was doomed as a wife and mother, to suffer pain of body and distress of mind. From being the help meet of man and the partner of his affections, her condition would henceforth be that of humble subjection. **17-19.** unto Adam he said—made to gain his livelihood by tilling the ground; but what before his fall he did with ease and pleasure, was not to be accomplished after it without painful and persevering exertion. return unto the ground—man became mortal; although he did not die the moment he ate the forbidden fruit—his body underwent a change, and that would lead to dissolution—the union subsisting between his soul and God having already been dissolved, he had become liable to all the miseries of this life, and to the pains of hell for ever. What a mournful chapter this is in the history of man. It gives the only true account of the origin of all the physical and moral evils that are in the world—upholds the moral character of God; shews that man, made upright, fell from not being able to resist a slight temptation; and becoming guilty and miserable, plunged all his posterity into the same abyss (Ro. 5. 12.). How astonishing the grace which at that moment gave promise of a Saviour: and conferred on her who had the disgrace of introducing sin—the future honour of introducing that Deliverer 1 Tim. 2. 15.) **20.** called wife's name Eve—probably in reference to her being a mother of the promised Saviour, as well as of all mankind. **21.** God gave coats of skins—taught them to make these for themselves. This implies the institution of animal sacrifice, which was undoubtedly of Divine appointment, and instruction in the only acceptable mode of worship for sinful creatures, through faith in a Redeemer Heb. 9. 22.) **22.** Behold the man is become—not spoken in irony as is generally supposed, but in deep compassion. The words should be rendered, "behold what has become by sin of the man who was as one of us!" formed at first, in our image to know good and evil—how sad his condition now. and now lest .. take of the tree of life—This tree being a pledge of that immortal life with which obedience should be rewarded, he lost, on his fall, all claim to this tree; and therefore, that he might not eat of it, or delude himself with the idea, that eating of it would restore what he had forfeited, the Lord sent him forth from the garden. **24.** placed .... cherubim—the passage should be rendered thus:—" And he dwelt between the Cherubim at the East of the Garden of Eden, and a fierce fire or Shechinah unfolding itself to preserve the way of the tree of life." This was the mode of worship now established, to show God's anger at sin, and teach the mediation of a promised Saviour, as the way of life, as well as of access to God. They were the same figures as were afterwards in the tabernacle and temple; and now, as then, God said, "I will commune with thee from between the cherubim" Ex. 25. 22.).

CHAPTER IV.

Ver. 1-2. BIRTH OF CAIN AND ABEL. Eve said, I have gotten a man from the Lord —*i. e.* "by the help of the Lord"—an expression of pious gratitude—and she called him Cain, *i. e.* "a possession as if valued

for thee have I seen *b* righteous before me in this generation.

2 Of every *c* clean beast thou shalt take to thee by ¹ sevens, the male and his female: and of beasts that *are* not clean by two, the male and his female.

3 Of fowls also of the air by sevens, the male and the female; to keep seed alive upon the face of all the earth.

4 For yet seven days, and *d* I will cause it to rain upon the earth forty days and forty nights; and every living substance that I have made will I ² destroy from off the face of the earth.

5 And Noah did according unto *e* all that the LORD commanded him.

6 And Noah *was* six hundred years old when the flood of waters was upon the earth.

7 And *f* Noah went in, and his sons, and his wife, and his sons' wives with him, into the ark, because of the waters of the flood.

8 Of clean beasts, and of beasts that *are* not clean, and of fowls, and of every thing that creepeth upon the earth,

9 There went in two and two unto Noah into the ark, the male and the female, as God had commanded Noah.

10 And it came to pass ³ after seven days, that the waters of the flood were upon the earth.

11 In the six hundredth year of Noah's life, in the second month, the seventeenth day of the month, the same day were all the *g* fountains of the great deep broken up, and the *h* ⁴ windows of heaven were opened.

12 And the rain was upon the earth forty days and forty nights.

13 In the selfsame day entered Noah, and Shem, and Ham, and Japheth, the sons of Noah, and Noah's wife, and the three wives of his sons with them, into the ark;

14 They, and every beast after his kind, and all the cattle after their kind, and every creeping thing that creepeth upon the earth after his kind, and every fowl after his kind, every bird of every ⁵ sort.

15 And they went in unto Noah into the ark, two and two of all flesh, wherein *is* the breath of life.

16 And they that went in, went in male and female of all flesh, as God had commanded him: and the LORD *i* shut him in.

17 And the flood was forty days upon the earth; and the waters increased, and bare up the ark, and it was lift up above the earth.

18 And the waters prevailed, and were increased greatly upon the earth; *j* and the ark went upon the face of the waters.

19 And the waters prevailed exceedingly upon the earth; *k* and all the high hills that *were* under the whole heaven were covered.

20 Fifteen cubits upward did the waters prevail; and the mountains were covered.

21 And *l* all flesh died that moved upon the earth, both of fowl, and of cattle, and of beast, and of every creeping thing that creepeth upon the earth, and every man:

22 All in whose *m* nostrils *was* ⁶ the breath of life, of all that *was* in the dry land, died.

23 And every living substance was destroyed which was upon the face of the ground, both man, and cattle, and the

B. C. 2349.

CHAP. 7.
b ch. 6, 9.
Psalm 33, 18, 19.
2 Pet. 2, 9.
c Lev. 11.
1 seven sevens.
d Job 22, 16. 2 Pet. 2, 5.
2 blot out.
e ch. 6, 22.
Ps. 119, 6.
f Heb. 6, 18.
3 or, on the seventh day.
g ch. 8, 2.
Prov. 8, 28.
Ex. 26, 19.
h Ps. 78, 23.
Isa. 24, 18.
Mal. 3 10.
4 or, floodgates.
5 wing.
i Psalm 91.
Psalm 17,8.
Psalm 145, 20.
1 Pet. 1, 5.
j Ps. 104, 26.
k Ps. 104, 6.
l ch. 6, 13,17.
Job 22, 16.
Mat. 24, 39.
Luke 17,27.
2 Pet. 3, 6.
m ch. 2, 7.
6 the breath of the spirit of life.
n Ex. 14, 14.
Mal. 3, 17, 18.
He. 11, 7.
1 Pet. 3, 20.
2 Pe. 2, 5.
o ch. 8, 3, 4, compared with ver. 11 of this chapter.

CHAP. 8.
a ch. 19, 29.
Ex. 2, 24.
1 Sam. 1, 19.
Psalm 105, 42.
Ps 136,23.
b Ex. 14, 21.
Ex. 15, 10.
Ps. 104, 7.
c ch. 7, 11.
d 1 Ki. 8, 35.
Job. 38, 37.
1 in going and returning.
e ch. 7, 24.
2 were in going and decreasing.
f ch. 8, 16.
g 1 Ki 17, 4.
3 in going forth and returning.
h Dou. 28,65.
4 caused her to come.
i Luke 2, 14.
j ch. 7, 13.
Ps. 121, 8.
k ch. 1, 22.

creeping things, and the fowl of the heaven; and they were destroyed from the earth: and *n* Noah only remained alive, and they that *were* with him in the ark.

24 *o* And the waters prevailed upon the earth an hundred and fifty days.

CHAPTER VIII.

1 *The waters asswage.* 4 *The ark resteth on Ararat.* 13 *The earth dried.* 15 *Noah goeth forth of the ark,* 21 *buildeth an altar, and offereth sacrifices.* 21 *God promiseth to curse the earth no more.*

AND *a* God remembered Noah, and every living thing, and all the cattle that *was* with him in the ark: and God *b* made a wind to pass over the earth, and the waters asswaged;

2 The *c* fountains also of the deep and the windows of heaven were stopped, and the *d* rain from heaven was restrained;

3 And the waters returned from off the earth ¹ continually: and after the end of *e* the hundred and fifty days the waters were abated.

4 And the ark rested in the seventh month, on the seventeenth day of the month, upon the mountains of Ararat.

5 And the waters ² decreased continually until the tenth month: in the tenth *month*, on the first *day* of the month, were the tops of the mountains seen.

6 ¶ And it came to pass at the end of forty days, that Noah opened the *f* window of the ark which he had made:

7 And he sent forth *g* a raven, which went forth ³ to and fro, until the waters were dried up from off the earth.

8 Also he sent forth a dove from him, to see if the waters were abated from off the face of the ground;

9 But the dove *h* found no rest for the sole of her foot, and she returned unto him into the ark, for the waters *were* on the face of the whole earth: then he put forth his hand, and took her, and ⁴ pulled her in unto him into the ark.

10 And he stayed yet other seven days; and again he sent forth the dove out of the ark;

11 And the dove came in to him in the evening; and, lo, in her mouth *was* an *i* olive leaf pluckt off: so Noah knew that the waters were abated from off the earth.

12 And he stayed yet other seven days; and sent forth the dove; which returned not again unto him any more.

13 ¶ And it came to pass in the six hundredth and first year, in the first *month*, the first *day* of the month, the waters were dried up from off the earth: and Noah removed the covering of the ark, and looked, and, behold, the face of the ground was dry.

14 And in the second month, on the seven and twentieth day of the month, was the earth dried.

15 ¶ And God spake unto Noah, saying,

16 *j* Go forth of the ark, thou, and thy wife, and thy sons, and thy sons' wives with thee.

17 Bring forth with thee every living thing that *is* with thee, of all flesh, *both* of fowl, and of cattle, and of every creeping thing that creepeth upon the earth; that they may breed abundantly in the earth, and *k* be fruitful, and multiply upon the earth.

18 And Noah went forth, and his sons,

above everything else; while the arrival of another son reminding her of the misery she had entailed on her offspring, led to the name Abel, *i. e.* either weakness, vanity, (Ps. 39. 5.) or grief, lamentation. Cain and Abel were probably twins; and it is thought that, at this early period, children were born in pairs, ch. 5. 4. [CAL.] keeper of sheep—*lit.* "feeder of a flock, which, in Oriental countries, always includes goats as well as sheep. Abel, though the younger, is mentioned first, probably on account of the pre-eminence of his religious character. 3. in process of time—Heb. "at the end of days;" probably on the Sabbath. brought an offering unto the Lord—Both manifested by the very act of offering their faith in the being of God, and in his claims to their reverence and worship; and had the kind of offering been left to themselves, what more natural than the one should bring "of the fruits of the ground;" that the other should bring "of the firstlings of his flock and the fat thereof." respect unto Abel, not unto Cain, &c. —the words "had respect to" signify in Hebrew—to look at anything with a keen earnest glance; which has been translated— "kindle into a fire," so that the divine approval of Abel's offering was shewn in its being consumed by fire see Gen. 15. 17; Jud. 13. 15.) 7. If thou dost well .. shalt thou not be accepted?—in the Marg. it is "shalt thou not have the excellency?" which is the true sense of the words referring to the high privileges and authority belonging to the first-born in patriarchal times. sin lieth at the door—sin, *i. e.* a sin-offering—a common meaning of the word in Scripture—as in Ho. 4. 8; 2 Cor. 5. 21; Heb. 9. 28. The purport of the Divine rebuke to Cain was this, "Why art thou angry, as if unjustly treated? If thou doest well, *i. e.* wert innocent and sinless—a thank-offering would have been accepted as a token of thy dependence as a creature. But as thou doest not well, *i. e.* art a sinner—a sin-offering is necessary, by bringing which thou wouldst have met with acceptance, and retained the honours of thy birth-right." This language implies that previous instructions had been given as to the mode of worship; Abel offered through faith, Heb. 11. 4. unto thee shall be his desire—The high distinction conferred by priority of birth is described, ch. 27. 29; and it was Cain's conviction, that this honour had been withdrawn from him by the rejection of his sacrifice, and conferred on his younger brother—hence the secret flame of jealousy, which kindled into a settled hatred, and fell-revenge. 8. and Cain talked—Under the guise of brotherly familiarity, he concealed his premeditated purpose till a convenient time and place occurred for the murder (1 Jo. 3. 12; 9-10.) the voice of thy brother's blood—Cain, to lull suspicion, had probably been engaging in the solemnities of religion, where he was challenged directly from the Shechinah itself. I know not—a falsehood. One sin leads to another. 11-12. cursed ... earth—A curse superadded to the general one denounced on the ground for Adam's sin. a fugitive—condemned to perpetual exile—a degraded outcast—the miserable victim of an accusing conscience. 13-14. my punishment is greater than I can bear— What an overwhelming sense of misery; but no sign of penitence, nor cry for pardon.

every one that findeth me shall slay me—This shows that the population of the world was now considerably increased. 15. Whosoever slayeth Cain—By a special act of Divine forbearance, the *life* of Cain was to be spared in the then small state of the human race. set a mark—not any visible mark or brand on his forehead, but some *sign* or *token* of assurance that his life would be preserved. This sign is thought by the best writers to have been a wild ferocity of aspect, that rendered him an object of universal horror and avoidance. 16. presence of the Lord—the appointed place of worship at Eden. Leaving it, he not only severed himself from his relatives, but forsook the ordinances of religion, probably casting off all fear of God from his eyes, so that the last end of this man is worse than the first (Matt. 12. 45.) land of Nod—of flight or exile—thought by many to have been Arabia Petræa—which was cursed to sterility on his account. 17-22. builded a city—It has been in cities that the human race has ever made the greatest social progress; and several of Cain's descendants distinguished themselves by their inventive genius in the arts. 19. Lamech ... two wives—This is the first transgression of the law of marriage on record, and the practice of polygamy, like all other breaches of God's institutions, has been a fruitful source of corruption and misery. 23, 24. Lam ... said unto .. wives— This speech is in a poetical form, probably the fragment of an old poem, transmitted to the time of Moses. It seems to indicate that Lamech had slain a man in self-defence, and its drift is to assure his wives, by the preservation of Cain; that an UNINTENTIONAL homicide, as he only was, could be in no danger. 26. men began to call upon the name of the Lord—rather, by the name of the Lord. God's people, a name probably applied to them in contempt by the world.

CHAPTER V.

Ver. 1-32. GENEALOGY OF THE PATRIARCHS. 1. Book of the generations—See ch. 11. 4. Adam—used here either as the name of the first man, or of the human race generally. 5. all the days Adam lived—The most striking feature in this catalogue is the longevity of Adam and his immediate descendants. Ten are enumerated in direct succession whose lives far exceed the ordinary limits with which we are familiar —the shortest being 365, and the longest 930. It is useless to enquire whether and what secondary causes may have contributed to this protracted longevity—vigorous constitutions, the nature of their diet, the temperature and salubrity of the climate; or, finally, as this list comprises only the true worshippers of God—whether their great age might be owing to the better government of their passions, and the quiet even tenor of their lives. Since we cannot obtain satisfactory evidence on these points, it is wise to resolve the fact into the sovereign will of God. We can, however, trace some of the important uses to which, in the early economy of Providence, it was subservient. It was the chief means of preserving a knowledge of God, of the great truths of religion, as well as the influence of genuine piety. So that, as their knowledge was obtained by tradition, they would be in a condition to preserve it in the greatest purity. 24.

and his wife, and his sons' wives with him.

19 Every beast, every creeping thing, and every fowl, *and* whatsoever creepeth upon the earth, after their [5] kinds, went forth out of the ark.

20 ¶ And Noah builded an altar unto the LORD; and took of every [l] clean beast, and of every clean fowl, and offered burnt offerings on the altar.

21 And the LORD smelled a [6] sweet savour; and the LORD said in his heart, I will not again [m] curse the ground any more for man's sake; [7] for the [n] imagination of man's heart *is* evil from his youth; neither will I again [o] smite any more every thing living, as I have done.

22 [8] While the earth remaineth, seedtime and harvest, and cold and heat, and summer and winter, and [p] day and night shall not cease.

CHAPTER IX.

1 *God blesseth Noah.* 4 *Blood and murder are forbidden.* 8 *God's covenant,* 13 *signified by the rainbow.* 23 *Noah is drunken, and mocked by Ham;* 25 *he pronounceth a curse on Canaan, and blessings on Shem and on Japheth;* 29 *he dieth.*

AND [a] God blessed Noah and his sons, and said unto them, Be fruitful, and multiply, and replenish the earth.

2 And [b] the fear of you and the dread of you shall be upon every beast of the earth, and upon every fowl of the air, upon all that moveth upon the earth, and upon all the fishes of the sea; into your hand are they delivered.

3 Every moving thing that liveth shall be [c] meat for you; even as the green herb have I given you all things.

4 But flesh with [d] the life thereof, *which is* the blood thereof, shall ye not eat.

5 And surely your blood of your lives will I require; at the hand of [e] every beast will I require it, and at the hand of [f] man; at the hand of every man's [g] brother will I require the life of man.

6 [h] Whoso sheddeth man's blood, by man shall his blood be shed: for in the [i] image of God made he man.

7 And you, be ye fruitful, and multiply; bring forth abundantly in the earth, and multiply therein.

8 ¶ And God spake unto Noah, and to his sons with him, saying,

9 And I, behold, I establish my covenant with you, and with your seed after you;

10 And with [j] every living creature that is with you, of the fowl, of the cattle, and of every beast of the earth with you; from all that go out of the ark, to every beast of the earth.

11 And I will establish my covenant with you; neither shall all flesh be cut off any more by the waters of a flood; neither shall there any more be a [k] flood to destroy the earth.

12 And God said, This *is* the [l] token of the covenant which I make between me and you and every living creature that is with you, for perpetual generations:

13 I do set my bow in the cloud, and it shall be for a token of a covenant between me and the earth.

14 And it shall come to pass, when I bring a cloud over the earth, that the bow shall be seen in the cloud:

15 And I will remember my covenant,

B. C. 2348.

CHAP. 8.
5 families.
l Lev. 11.
6 *savour of rest.*
Lev. 1, 9.
Ex. 20, 41.
2 Cor. 2, 15.
Eph. 5, 2.
m Is. 54, 9.
7 *or, though.*
n ch. 6, 5.
Ps. 51, 5.
Jer. 17, 9.
Rom. 1, 21.
Ep. 2, 1-3.
o ch. 9, 15.
8 *As yet all the days of the earth.*
p Jer. 33, 20, 25.

CHAP. 9.
a ch. 1, 28.
b Hos. 2, 18.
Ja. 3, 7.
c De. 12, 15.
De. 14, 3.
d Le. 17, 10.
Le. 19, 26.
De. 12, 23.
1 Sa. 14, 34.
Acts, 15, 20, 29.
e Ex. 21, 28, 29.
f Nu. 35, 31.
g Acts, 17, 26.
h Ex. 21, 12, 14.
Le. 24, 17.
Mat. 26, 52.
Rev. 13, 10.
i ch. 1, 27.
1 Cor. 11, 7.
j ch. 8, 1.
k 2 Pet. 3, 5.
l Mat. 26, 26-28.
m Ex. 18, 12.
Lev. 26, 42, 45.
Ex. 16, 60.
m Is. 54, 9.
n ch. 17, 13, 19.
2 Sa. 23, 5.
o ch. 10, 6.
1 Chenaan.
f ch. 10, 32.
q ch. 8, 19.
r ch. 19, 32, 36.
Pro. 20, 1.
Eph. 5, 18.
s Ex. 20, 12.
Gal. 6, 1.
t De. 27, 16.
Mat. 25, 41.
u Josh. 9, 23.
1 Ki. 9, 21.
2 *or, servant to them.*
3 *or, persuade.*
v Eph. 2, 13, 14.
Eph. 3, 6.

CHAP. 10.
a 1 Ch. 1, 5-7.
1 *or, Chittim.*
2 *or, Rodanim.*

which *is* between me and you and every living creature of all flesh; [m] and the waters shall no more become a flood to destroy all flesh.

16 And the bow shall be in the cloud; and I will look upon it, that I may remember the [n] everlasting covenant between God and every living creature of all flesh that *is* upon the earth.

17 And God said unto Noah, This *is* the token of the covenant, which I have established between me and all flesh that *is* upon the earth.

18 ¶ And the sons of Noah, that went forth of the ark, were Shem, and Ham, and Japheth: and Ham is the [o] father of 1 Canaan.

19 These *are* the three sons of Noah: and [p] of them was the whole earth overspread.

20 ¶ And Noah began to be an [q] husbandman, and he planted a vineyard:

21 And he drank of the wine, and [r] was drunken; and he was uncovered within his tent.

22 And Ham, the father of Canaan, saw the nakedness of his father, and told his two brethren without.

23 And [s] Shem and Japheth took a garment, and laid *it* upon both their shoulders, and went backward, and covered the nakedness of their father; and their faces *were* backward, and they saw not their father's nakedness.

24 And Noah awoke from his wine, and knew what his younger son had done unto him.

25 And he said, [t] Cursed *be* Canaan; a servant of [u] servants shall he be unto his brethren.

26 And he said, Blessed *be* the LORD God of Shem; and Canaan shall be [2] his servant.

27 God shall [3] enlarge Japheth, and he shall [v] dwell in the tents of Shem; and Canaan shall be his servant.

28 And Noah lived after the flood three hundred and fifty years:

29 And all the days of Noah were nine hundred and fifty years: and he died.

CHAPTER X.

1 *The generations of Noah.* 2 *The sons of Japheth,* 6 *and of Ham.* 8 *Nimrod the first monarch.* 15 *The descendants of Canaan.* 21 *The sons of Shem.*

NOW these *are* the generations of the sons of Noah; Shem, Ham, and Japheth: and unto them were sons born after the flood.

2 The [a] sons of Japheth; Gomer, and Magog, and Madai, and Javan, and Tubal, and Meshech, and Tiras.

3 And the sons of Gomer; Ashkenaz, and Riphath, and Togarmah.

4 And the sons of Javan; Elishah, and Tarshish, [1] Kittim, and [2] Dodanim.

5 By these were the isles of the Gentiles divided in their lands; every one after his tongue, after their families, in their nations.

6 ¶ And the sons of Ham; Cush, and Mizraim, and Phut, and Canaan.

7 And the sons of Cush; Seba, and Havilah, and Sabtah, and Raamah, and Sabtecha: and the sons of Raamah; Sheba, and Dedan.

8 And Cush begat Nimrod: he began to be a mighty one in the earth.

9 He was a mighty hunter before the

walked with God—A common phrase in eastern countries denoting constant and familiar intercourse. was not; for God took him—In He. 11. 3. we are informed that he was translated to heaven—a mighty miracle, designed to effect what ordinary means of instruction had failed to accomplish—gave a palpable proof to an age of almost universal unbelief that the doctrines which he had taught Ju. 14, 15.) were true, and that his devotedness to the cause of God, and righteousness in the midst of opposition, was highly pleasing to the mind of God. 21. Enoch begat Methuselah—This name signifies "He dieth, and the sending forth," so that Enoch gave it as prophetical of the flood. It is computed that Methusaleh died in the year of that catastrophe. Lamech—a different person from the one mentioned in preceding chapter. Like his namesake, however, he also spoke in numbers on occasion of the birth of Noah—i.e., "rest" or "comfort." 'The allusion is, undoubtedly, to the penal consequences of the fall in earthly toils and sufferings, and to the hope of a Deliverer, excited by the promise made to Eve. That this expectation was founded on a divine communication we infer from the importance attached to it and the confidence of its expression,' [P. SMITH.] 32. Noah was 500 years old and begat—That he and the other patriarchs were advanced in life ere children were born to them, is a difficulty accounted for probably from the circumstance that Moses does not here record their first-born sons, but only the succession from Adam through Seth to Abraham.

CHAPTER VI.

Ver. 1-4. WICKEDNESS OF THE WORLD. 2. Sons of God, daughters of men—By the former is meant the family of Seth, who were professedly religious, by the latter, the descendants of apostate Cain. Mixed marriages between parties of opposite principles and practice were necessarily sources of extensive corruption. The women, irreligious themselves, would, as wives and mothers, exert an influence fatal to the existence of religion in their household, and consequently the people of that later age sank to the lowest depravity. flesh—utterly, hopelessly debased. 3. My spirit shall not always strive—Christ, who had by His Spirit inspiring Enoch, Noah, and perhaps other prophets (1 Pe. 3. 9; 2 Pe. 2. 5; Ju. 14.), preached repentance to the antediluvians; but they were incorrigible. yet their days shall be 120 years—It is probable that the corruption of the world, which had now reached its height, had been long and gradually increasing, and this idea receives support from the long respite granted. 4. giants—The term in Heb. implies not so much the idea of great stature as of reckless ferocity, impious and daring characters, who spread devastation and carnage far and wide. 5, 6. God saw it, repented—grieved—God cannot change (Mal. 3. 6; Ja. 1. 17.); but, by language suited to our nature and experience, He is described as about to alter His visible procedure towards mankind—from being merciful and long-suffering, He was about to show Himself a God of judgment; and, as that impious race had filled up the measure of their iniquities, He was about to introduce a terrible display of His justice (Ecc. 8. 11.). 8. But Noah found grace—favour. What an awful state of things when only one man or one family of piety and virtue was now existing among the professed sons of God! 9. Noah just and perfect—not absolutely; for since the fall of Adam no man has been free from sin except Jesus Christ. But as living by faith he was just (Gal. 3. 2; Heb. 11. 7.) and perfect—i.e., sincere in his desire to do God's will. 11. the earth was filled with violence—In the absence of any well-regulated government it is easy to imagine what evils would arise. Men did what was right in their own eyes, and having no fear of God, destruction and misery were in their ways. 13. And God said unto Noah—How startling must have been the announcement of the threatened destruction! There was no outward indication of it. The course of nature and experience seemed against the probability of its occurrence. The public opinion of mankind would ridicule it. The whole world would be ranged against him. Yet, persuaded the communication was from God, through faith (He. 11. 7,) he set about preparing the means for preserving himself and family from the impending calamity. 14. Make thee an ark—ark, a hollow chest (Ex. 2. 3.). gopher wood—probably cypress, remarkable for its durability, and abounding on the Armenian mountains. rooms—cabins or small cells. pitch it within and without—mineral pitch, asphalt, naphtha, or some bituminous substance, which, when smeared over and become hardened, would make it perfectly water-tight. 15. And this is the fashion—according to the description, the ark was not a ship, but an immense house in form and structure like the houses in the east, designed not to sail; but only float. Assuming the cubit to be 21,888 inches, the ark would be 547 feet long, 91 feet 2 inches wide, and 47 feet 2 inches high—that is, three times the length of a first-rate man of war in the British navy. 16. a window—probably a skylight, formed of some transparent substance unknown. in a cubit shalt thou finish it above—a direction to raise the roof in the middle, seemingly to form a gentle slope for letting the water run off. 17-22. And, behold, I, even I, do bring a flood—The repetition of the announcement was to establish its certainty (ch. 41. 22.). Whatever opinion may be entertained as to the operation of natural laws and agencies in the deluge, it was brought on the world by God as a punishment for the enormous wickedness of its inhabitants. 18. But with thee will I establish my covenant—a special promise of deliverance, called a covenant, to convince him of the confidence to be reposed in it. The substance and terms of this covenant are related between v. 19. and 21. 22. Thus did Noah—He began without delay to prepare the colossal fabric, and in every step of his progress faithfully followed the divine directions he had received.

CHAPTER VII.

Ver. 1-16. ENTRANCE INTO THE ARK. And the Lord said unto Noah, Come, &c.—The ark was finished; and he now, in the spirit of implicit faith, which had influenced his whole conduct, waited for directions from God. 2, 3. of every clean beast . . . fowls—pairs of every species of animals except the tenants of the deep were to be taken for the preservation of their respective kinds. This was the general rule of admission, only with regard to those animals which are styled

LORD: wherefore it is said, Even as Nimrod the mighty hunter [b] before the LORD.

10 And the beginning of his [3] kingdom was [3] Babel, and Erech, and Accad, and Calneh, in the land of Shinar.

11 Out of that land [4] went forth Asshur, and builded Nineveh, and [5] the city Rehoboth, and Calah,

12 And Resen between Nineveh and Calah: the same *is* a great city.

13 And Mizraim begat Ludim, and Anamim, and Lehabim, and Naphtuhim,

14 And Pathrusim, and Casluhim, (d out of whom came Philistim,) and Caphtorim.

15 ¶ And Canaan begat [6] Sidon his firstborn, and Heth,

16 And the Jebusite, and the Amorite, and the Girgasite,

17 And the Hivite, and the Arkite, and the Sinite,

18 And the Arvadite, and the Zemarite, and the Hamathite: and afterward were the families of the Canaanites spread abroad.

19 [e] And the border of the Canaanites was from Sidon, as thou comest to Gerar, unto [7] Gaza; as thou goest, unto Sodom, and Gomorrah, and Admah, and Zeboim, even unto Lasha.

20 These *are* the sons of Ham, after their families, after their tongues, in their countries, *and* in their nations.

21 ¶ Unto Shem also, the father of all the children of Eber, the brother of Japheth the elder, even to him were *children* born.

22 The [f] children of Shem; Elam, and Asshur, and [8] Arphaxad, and Lud, and Aram.

23 And the children of Aram; Uz, and Hul, and Gether, and Mash.

24 And Arphaxad begat [9] [g] Salah; and Salah begat Eber.

25 [h] And unto Eber were born two sons: the name of one *was* [10] Peleg; for in his days was the earth divided; and his brother's name *was* Joktan.

26 And Joktan begat Almodad, and Sheleph, and Hazarmaveth, and Jerah,

27 And Hadoram, and Uzal, and Diklah,

28 And Obal, and Abimael, and Sheba,

29 And Ophir, and Havilah, and Jobab: all these *were* the sons of Joktan.

30 And their dwelling was from Mesha, as thou goest, unto Sephar, a mount of the east.

31 These *are* the sons of Shem, after their families, after their tongues, in their lands, after their nations.

32 [i] These *are* the families of the sons of Noah after their generations, in their nations: [j] and by these were the nations divided in the earth after the flood.

CHAPTER XI.

1 *One language in the world.* 3 *The building of Babel, and confusion of tongues.* 10 *The generations of Shem.* 27 *and of Terah.* 31 *Terah goeth from Ur to Haran.*

AND the whole earth [a] was of one [1] language, and of one [2] speech.

2 And it came to pass, as they journeyed [3] from the east, that they found a plain in the land of [b] Shinar; and they dwelt there.

3 And [c] they said one to another, Go to, let us make brick, and [5] burn them throughly. And they had brick for stone, and slime had they for mortar.

4 And they said, Go to, let us build us a city, and a tower whose top [6] *may reach* [c] unto heaven; and let us make us [d] a name, lest we be [e] scattered abroad upon the face of the whole earth.

5 [f] And the LORD came down to see the city and the tower, which the children of men builded.

6 And the LORD said, Behold, the people *is* one, and they have all one language; and this they begin to do: and now nothing will be restrained from them, which they have [g] imagined to do.

7 Go to, [h] let us go down, and there confound their language, that they may [i] not understand one another's speech.

8 So the LORD scattered them abroad from thence [j] upon the face of all the earth: and they left off to build the city.

9 Therefore is the name of it called [7] Babel; [k] because the LORD did there confound the language of all the earth: and from thence did the LORD scatter them abroad upon the face of all the earth.

10 ¶ These *are* the generations of Shem: [l] Shem *was* an hundred years old, and begat Arphaxad two years after the flood:

11 And Shem lived after he begat Arphaxad five hundred years, and begat sons and daughters.

12 And Arphaxad lived five and thirty years, and begat [m] Salah:

13 And Arphaxad lived after he begat Salah four hundred and three years, and begat sons and daughters.

14 And Salah lived thirty years, and begat Eber:

15 And Salah lived after he begat Eber four hundred and three years, and begat sons and daughters.

16 And [n] Eber lived four and thirty years, and begat [8] Peleg:

17 And Eber lived after he begat Peleg four hundred and thirty years, and begat sons and daughters.

18 And Peleg lived thirty years, and begat [9] Reu:

19 And Peleg lived after he begat Reu two hundred and nine years, and begat sons and daughters.

20 And Reu lived two and thirty years, and begat [10] Serug:

21 And Reu lived after he begat Serug two hundred and seven years, and begat sons and daughters.

22 And Serug lived thirty years, and begat Nahor:

23 And Serug lived after he begat Nahor two hundred years, and begat sons and daughters.

24 And Nahor lived nine and twenty years, and begat [11] Terah:

25 And Nahor lived after he begat Terah an hundred and nineteen years, and begat sons and daughters.

26 And Terah lived seventy years, and begat [o] Abram, Nahor, and Haran.

27 ¶ Now these *are* the generations of Terah: Terah begat Abram, Nahor, and Haran; and Haran begat [p] Lot.

28 And Haran died before his father Terah in the land of his nativity, in Ur of the Chaldees.

29 And Abram and Nahor took them wives: the name of Abram's wife *was* [q] Sarai; and the name of Nahor's wife, [r] Milcah, the daughter of Haran, the father of Milcah, and the father of Iscah.

"clean," three pairs were to be taken, whether of beasts or birds; and the reason was that their rapid multiplication was a matter of the highest importance, when the earth should be renovated from their utility either as articles of food, or as employed in the service of man. But what was the use of the seventh? It was manifestly reserved for sacrifice; and so that both during Noah's residence in the ark and after his return to dry land, provision was made for celebrating the rites of worship according to the religion of fallen man. He did not, like many, leave religion behind. He provided for it during his protracted voyage. for yet seven days—a week for a world to repent! What a solemn pause. Did they laugh and ridicule his folly still? He whose eyes saw, and whose heart felt the full amount of human iniquity and perverseness, has told us of their reckless disregard (L. 17. 27.). 9. There went in two and two—Doubtless they were led by a divine impulse. The number would not be so large as at first sight one is apt to imagine. It has been calculated that there are not more than three hundred distinct species of beasts and birds, the immense varieties in regard to form, size, and colour being traceable to the influence of climate and other circumstances. 16. And the Lord shut him in—*lit.* "covered him round about." The "shutting him in" intimated that he had become the special object of divine care and protection, and that to those without the season of grace was over (M. 25. 10.). 17-24. the waters increased and bare up the ark—it seems to have been raised so gradually as, perhaps, to be scarcely perceptible to the inmates. 20. fifteen cubits upward . . . mountains covered—twenty-two and a-half feet above the summits of the highest hills. The language is not consistent with the theory of a partial deluge. 21. all flesh died—fowl, cattle, and creeping thing—It has been a uniform principle in the divine procedure, when judgments were abroad on the earth, to include everything connected with the sinful objects of His wrath ch. 19. 25; Ex. 9. 6.). Besides, now that the human race were reduced to one single family, it was necessary that the beasts should be proportionally diminished, otherwise by their numbers they would have acquired the ascendancy, and overmastered the few that were to re-people the world. Thus goodness was mingled with severity; the Lord exercises judgment in wisdom, and in wrath remembers mercy. 24. a hundred and fifty days—a period of five months. Though long before that every living creature must have been drowned, such a lengthened continuance of the flood was designed to manifest God's stern displeasure at sin and sinners. Think of Noah during such a crisis. We learn (Ez. 14. 14.) that he was a man who lived and breathed habitually in an atmosphere of devotion; and having in the exercise of this high-toned faith made God his refuge, he did not fear "though the waters roared and were troubled; though the mountains shook with the swelling thereof."

CHAPTER VIII.

Ver. 1-14. ASSUAGING OF THE WATERS. God remembered Noah — The Divine purpose in this awful dispensation had been accomplished, and the world had undergone those changes necessary to fit it for becoming the residence of man under a new economy of providence, every living thing . . . in the ark—A beautiful illustration of M. 10. 20. made a wind to pass over—Though the Divine will could have dried up the liquid mass in an instant—the agency of a wind was employed (Ps. 104. 4.)—probably a *hot* wind, which, by rapid evaporation, would again absorb one portion of the waters into the atmosphere; and by which, the other would be gradually drained off by outlets beneath. 4. seventh month—of the year—not of the flood—which lasted only five months. rested—evidently indicating a calm and gentle motion. upon the mountains of Ararat—or Armenia, as the word is rendered (2 Ki. 19. 37; Is. 37. 38.). The mountain which tradition points to, as the one on which the ark rested, is now called Ara Dagh—the finger mountain. Its summit consists of two peaks—the higher of which is 17,750 feet, and the other 13,420 above the level of the sea. 5. And the waters decreased continually—The decrease of the waters was for wise reasons exceedingly slow and gradual—the period of their return being nearly twice as long as that of their rise. 6. At the end of forty days It is easy to imagine the ardent longing Noah and his family must have felt to enjoy again the sight of land as well as breathe the fresh air; and it was perfectly consistent with faith and patience to make enquiries, whether the earth was yet ready. 7. sent forth a raven—the smell of carrion would allure it to remain if the earth were in a habitable state. But it kept hovering about the spot, and being a solitary bird, probably perched on the covering. 8-11. also he sent forth a dove—A bird flying low and naturally disposed to return to the place of her abode. 10. again he sent forth the dove—Her flight, judging by the time she was abroad, was pursued to a great distance, and the newly-plucked olive leaf, she no doubt, by supernatural impulse, brought in her bill, afforded a welcome proof that the declivities of the hills were clear. 12. he sent forth the dove, which returned not any more. In these results, we perceive a wisdom and prudence far superior to the inspiration of instinct—we discern the agency of God guiding all the movements of this bird for the instruction of Noah, and reviving the hopes of his household. other seven days—a strong presumptive proof that Noah observed the Sabbath during his residence in the ark. 13, 14. Noah removed the covering—probably only as much of it as would afford him a prospect of the earth around. Yet for about two months he never stirred from his appointed abode till he had received the express permission of God. We should watch the leading of Providence to direct us in every step of the journey of life.

15-22. DEPARTURE FROM THE ARK. And God said, Go forth—They went forth in the most orderly manner—the human inmates first—then each species "after their kinds" *lit.* according to their families, implying that there had been an increase in the ark. 20. Noah builded an altar—*lit.* "a high place"—probably a mound of earth, on which a sacrifice was offered. There is something exceedingly beautiful and interesting to know that the first care of this devout patriarch was to return thanks for the signal instance of mercy and goodness which he and his family had experienced. took of every clean beast

30 But Sarai was *barren; she *had* no child.
31 And Terah took Abram his son, and Lot the son of Haran his son's son, and Sarai his daughter-in-law, his son Abram's wife; and they ᵗ went forth with them from Ur of the Chaldees, to go into the land of ᵘ Canaan; and they came unto ¹² Haran, and dwelt there.
32 And the days of Terah were two hundred and five years: and Terah died in Haran.

CHAPTER XII.

1 *God calleth Abram, and blesseth him with a promise of Christ:* 4 *he departs from Haran*, 6 *Canaan promised*.

NOW the ᵃ Lord had said unto Abram, Get thee out of thy country, and from thy kindred, and from thy father's house, unto a land that I will show thee:
2 And I will make of thee ᵇ a great nation, and I will bless thee, and make thy name great; and thou shalt be a blessing:
3 And I will ᶜ bless them that bless thee, and curse him that curseth thee: and ᵈ in thee shall all families of the earth be blessed.
4 So Abram departed, as the Lord had spoken unto him; and Lot went with him: and Abram *was* seventy and five years old when he departed out of Haran.
5 And Abram took Sarai his wife, and Lot his brother's son, and all their substance that they had gathered, and the souls that they had gotten in ᵉ Haran; and they went forth to go ᶠ into the land of Canaan; and into the land of Canaan they came.
6 ¶ And Abram passed through the land unto the place of ¹ Sichem, unto the plain of ᵍ Moreh. And the Canaanite *was* then in the land.
7 And the Lord ʰ appeared unto Abram, and said, ⁱ Unto thy seed will I give this land: and there builded he an ʲ altar unto the Lord, who appeared unto him.
8 And he removed from thence unto a mountain on the east of Beth-el, and pitched his tent, *having* Beth-el on the west, and ² Hai on the east: and there he builded an altar unto the Lord, and called upon the name of the Lord.
9 And Abram journeyed, ³ going ᵏ on still toward the south.
10 ¶ And there was ˡ a famine in the land: and Abram ᵐ went down into Egypt to sojourn there; for the famine *was* ⁿ grievous in the land.
11 And it came to pass, when he was come near to enter into Egypt, that he said unto Sarai his wife, Behold now, I know that thou *art* ᵒ a fair woman to look upon:
12 Therefore it shall come to pass, when the Egyptians shall see thee, that they shall say, This *is* his wife: and they ᵖ will kill me, but they will save thee alive.
13 ᵠ Say, I pray thee, ʳ thou *art* my sister: that it may be well with me for thy sake; and my soul shall live because of thee.
14 ¶ And it came to pass, that, when Abram was come into Egypt, the Egyptians beheld the woman, that she was very fair.
15 ˢ The princes also of Pharaoh saw her, and commended her before Pharaoh: and the woman was taken into Pharaoh's house.
16 And he entreated Abram well for her

sake: and he had sheep, and oxen, and he-asses, and men-servants, and maid-servants, and she-asses, and camels.
17 And the Lord ᵗ plagued Pharaoh and his house with great plagues because of Sarai, Abram's wife.
18 And Pharaoh called Abram, and said, ᵘ What *is* this *that* thou hast done unto me? why didst thou not tell me that she *was* thy wife?
19 Why saidst thou, She *is* my sister? so I might have taken her to me to wife now therefore behold thy wife, take *her*, and go thy way.
20 And ᵛ Pharaoh commanded *his* men concerning him: and they sent him away, and his wife, and all that he had.

CHAPTER XIII.

1 *Abram and Lot return from Egypt;* 7 *they part asunder*, 10 *Lot goes to Sodom*. 14 *God's promise renewed to Abram*. 18 *He goeth to Hebron, and there builds an altar*.

AND Abram went up out of Egypt, he, and his wife, and all that he had, and Lot with him, into the south.
2 And Abram *was* ᵃ very rich in cattle, in silver, and in gold.
3 And he went on his journeys from the south even to Beth-el, unto the place where his tent had been at the beginning, between Beth-el and Hai;
4 Unto the place of the ᵇ altar, which he had made there at the first: and there Abram called on the name of the Lord.
5 ¶ And Lot also, which went with Abram, had flocks, and herds, and tents.
6 And the land was ᶜ not able to bear them, that they might dwell together: for their substance was great, so that they could not dwell together.
7 And there was a ᵈ strife between the herdmen of Abram's cattle and the herdmen of Lot's cattle. And the Canaanite and the Perizzite dwelt then in the land.
8 And Abram said unto Lot, ᵉ Let there be no strife, I pray thee, between me and thee, and between my herdmen and thy herdmen; for we be ¹ brethren.
9 ᶠ *Is* not the whole land before thee? Separate thyself, I pray thee, from me: ᵍ if *thou wilt take* the left hand, then I will go to the right; or if *thou depart* to the right hand, then I will go to the left.
10 And Lot lifted up his eyes, ʰ and beheld all the ⁱ plain of Jordan, that it *was* well watered every where, before the Lord ʲ destroyed Sodom and Gomorrah, even as the garden of the Lord, like the land of Egypt, as thou comest unto ᵏ Zoar.
11 Then Lot chose him all the plain of Jordan; and Lot journeyed east: and they separated themselves the one from the other.
12 Abram dwelt in the land of Canaan, and Lot dwelt in the ˡ cities of the plain, and pitched *his* tent toward Sodom.
13 But ᵐ the men of Sodom *were* wicked and ⁿ sinners before the Lord exceedingly.
14 ¶ And the Lord said unto Abram, after that Lot was separated from him, ᵒ Lift up now thine eyes, and look from the place where thou *art* ᵖ northward, and southward, and eastward, and westward;
15 For all the land which thou seest, to thee will I give it, and to thy ᵠ seed for ever.

and fowl—For so unparalleled a deliverance, a special acknowledgment was due. 21. the Lord smelled a sweet savour—The sacrifice offered by a righteous man like Noah in faith, was acceptable as the most fragrant incense. Lord said in his heart—same as "I have sworn that the waters of Noah should no more go over the earth" (Is. 54. 9.), "f..r"— *i.e.*, "though the imagination is evil;" instead of inflicting another destructive flood, I shall spare them—to enjoy the blessings of grace, through a Saviour. 22. While the earth remaineth—The consummation as intimated in 2 Pet. 3. 7, does not frustrate a promise which held good only during the continuance of that system. There will be no flood between this and that day, when the earth therein shall be burnt up. [CHALMERS.]

CHAPTER IX.

Ver. 1-7. COVENANT. And God blessed Noah—Here is republished the law of nature that was announced to Adam, consisting as it originally did of several parts. be fruitful, &c.—the first part relates to the transmission of life, the original blessing being re-announced in the very same words in which it had been promised at first. 2. and the fear of you and dread of you—the second re-establishes man's dominion over the inferior animals; it was now founded not as at first in love and kindness, but in terror; this dread of man prevails among all the stronger as well as the weaker members of the animal tribes, and keeps away from his haunts all but those employed in his service. 3. every moving thing ... meat for you—the third part concerns the means of *sustaining* life; man was for the first time, it would seem, *allowed* the use of animal food, but the grant was accompanied with one restriction. 4. but flesh ... the blood—the sole intention of this prohibition was to prevent all excesses of cannibal ferocity in eating flesh of living animals, to which men in the earlier ages of the world were liable. 5. surely your blood of your lives will I require—The fourth part establishes a new power for *protecting* life—the institution of the civil magistrate Ro. 13. 4, armed with public and official authority to repress the commission of violence and crime. Such a power had not previously existed in patriarchal society. 6. whoso sheddeth ... for in the image of God—it is true that image has been injured by the fall, but it is not lost. In this view, a high value is attached to the life of every man, even the poorest and humblest, and an awful criminality is involved in the destruction of it.

8-29. RAINBOW. I do set my bow—Set, *i.e.* constitute or appoint. This common and familiar phenomenon being made the pledge of peace, its appearance when showers began to fall would be welcomed with the liveliest feelings of joy. 20. planted a vineyard—Noah had been probably bred to the culture of the soil, and resumed that employment on leaving the ark. 21. drank of the wine—perhaps at the festivities of the vintage season. This solitary stain on the character of so eminently pious a man must, it is believed, have been the result of age and inadvertency. 24. This incident could scarcely have happened till twenty years after the flood; for Canaan, whose conduct was more offensive than that even of his father, was not born till after that event. It is probable that there is a long interval included between these verses, and that this prophecy, like that of Jacob on his sons, was not uttered till near the close of Noah's life, when the prophetic spirit came upon him; this presumption is strengthened by the mention of his death immediately after. 25. cursed be Canaan—this doom has been fulfilled in the destruction of the Canaanites—in the degradation of Egypt and the slavery of the Africans, the descendants of Ham. 26. blessed be the Lord God of Shem—rather "blessed of Jehovah, my God, be Shem"—an intimation that the descendants of Shem should be peculiarly honoured in the service of the true God—His Church being for ages established amongst them the Jews, and of them concerning the flesh Christ came. They got possession of Canaan, the people of that land being made their "servants" either by conquest, or like the Gibeonites by submission. 27. God shall enlarge Japhet—pointing to a vast increase in posterity and possessions. Accordingly his descendants have been the most active and enterprising, spread over the best and largest portion of the world, all Europe and a considerable part of Asia. he shall dwell in the tents of Shem—a prophecy being fulfilled at the present day, as in India British government is established, and the Anglo-Saxons being in the ascendant from Europe to India, from India over the American continent. What a wonderful prophecy in a few verses! Is. 46, 10; 1 Pe. 1. 25; 2 Pe. 1. 19.

CHAPTER X.

Ver. 1-32. GENEALOGIES. Sons of Noah—The historian has not arranged this catalogue according to seniority of birth; for the account begins with the descendants of Japhet, and the line of Ham is given before that of Shem, though he is expressly said to be the youngest or younger son of Noah; and Shem was the elder brother of Japhet (*v.* 21.), the true rendering of that passage. generations, &c.—the narrative of the settlement of nations existing in the time of Moses, perhaps only the principal ones; for though the list comprises the sons of Shem, Ham, and Japhet, *all their descendants* are not enumerated. Those descendants, with one or two exceptions, are described by names indicative of tribes and nations, and ending in the Heb. *im.* or the Eng. *ite*. 5. The isles of the Gentiles—a phrase by which the Hebrews described all countries which were accessible by sea (Is. 11. 11, 20. 6; Jer. 25. 22.). Such in relation to them were the countries of Europe, the peninsula of Lesser Asia, and the region lying on the east of the Euxine. Accordingly, it was in these quarters the early descendants of Japhet had their settlements. 6. Sons of Ham—emigrated southward, and their settlements were—that of Cush in Arabia, of Canaan in the country known by his name, and Mizraim in Egypt Upper and Lower. It is generally thought that his father accompanied him, and personally superintended the formation of the settlement, whence Egypt was called "the land of Ham." 8. Nimrod—mentioned as eclipsing all his family in renown. He early distinguished himself by his daring and successful prowess in hunting wild beasts. By those useful services he earned a title to public gratitude; and having established a permanent ascendancy over the people, he founded the first kingdom in the world. 10.

16 And I will make thy seed as the *r* dust of the earth: so that if a man can number the dust of the earth, *then* shall thy seed also be numbered.
17 Arise, walk through the land, in the length of it, and in the breadth of it; for I will give it unto thee.
18 Then Abram removed *his* tent, and came and dwelt in the ² plain of Mamre, which *is* in Hebron, and built there an altar unto the LORD.

CHAPTER XIV.

1 *The battle of four kings against five.* 12 *Lot taken prisoner,* 14 *is rescued by Abram.* 18 *Melchizedek blesseth Abram;* 20 *Abram giveth him tithes.*

AND it came to pass in the days of Amraphel king of *a* Shinar, Arioch king of Ellasar, Chedorlaomer king of *b* Elam, and Tidal king of nations;
2 That these *c* made war with Bera king of Sodom, and with Birsha king of Gomorrah, Shinab king of *d* Admah, and Shemeber king of Zeboiim, and the king of Bela, which is *e* Zoar.
3 All these were joined together in the vale of Siddim, *f* which is the salt sea.
4 Twelve years they served Chedorlaomer, and in the thirteenth year they rebelled.
5 And in the fourteenth year came Chedorlaomer, and the kings that *were* with him, and smote the Rephaims in Ashteroth Karnaim, and the Zuzims in Ham, and the Emims in ¹ Shaveh Kiriathaim,
6 And the Horites in their mount Seir, unto ² El-paran, which *is* by the wilderness.
7 And they returned, and came to Enmishpat, which is *g* Kadesh, and smote all the country of the Amalekites, and also the Amorites, that dwelt in Hazezon-tamar.
8 And there went out the king of Sodom, and the king of Gomorrah, and the king of Admah, and the king of Zeboiim, and the king of Bela, (the same *is* Zoar;) and they joined battle with them in the vale of Siddim;
9 With Chedorlaomer the king of Elam, and with Tidal king of nations, and Amraphel king of Shinar, and Arioch king of Ellasar; four kings with five.
10 And the vale of Siddim *was full of* *h* slimepits; and the kings of Sodom and Gomorrah fled, and fell there; and they that remained fled to the *i* mountain.
11 And they took all the goods of Sodom and Gomorrah, and all their victuals, and went their way.
12 And they took Lot, Abram's *j* brother's son, *k* who dwelt in Sodom, and his goods, and departed.
13 ¶ And there came one that had escaped, and told Abram the Hebrew; for he dwelt in the plain of Mamre the Amorite, brother of Eshcol, and brother of Aner: and *l* these *were* confederate with Abram.
14 And when Abram heard that *m* his brother was taken captive, he ³ armed his ⁴ trained *servants,* *n* born in his own house, three hundred and eighteen, and pursued *them* unto Dan.
15 And he divided himself against them, he and his servants, by night, and *o* smote them, and pursued them unto Hobah, which *is* on the left hand of Damascus.
16 And *p* he brought back all the goods, and also brought again his brother Lot, and his goods, and the women also, and the people.

B.C. 1917.

CHAP. 13.
r ch. 26, 4.
Ex. 32, 13.
Nu. 23, 10.
De. 1. 10.
1 Ch.27,23.
Je. 33, 22.
Ro. 4, 16.
He. 11, 12.
² plains.

CHAP. 14.
a ch. 10, 10.
b Is. 11, 11.
c Ja. 4, 1.
d De. 29, 23.
e ch. 19, 22.
f De. 3, 17.
Nu. 34, 12.
Josh. 3, 16.
Ps. 107, 34.
¹ or, the plain of Kiriathaim.
² or, the plain of Paran.
g Nu. 13, 3.
h ch. 11, 3.
i ch. 19, 17, 30.
j ch. 11, 31.
k ch. 13, 12.
Jer. 2, 17-19.
l ver. 24.
m ch. 13, 8.
³ or, led forth.
⁴ or, instructed.
n ch. 17, 27.
Ec. 2, 7.
o Isa. 41, 2.
p 1 Sa. 30, 8, 18, 19.
q 2 Sa. 18,18.
r Heb. 7, 2.
s Ps. 110, 4.
Heb. 7, 10-22.
t Heb. 7, 4.
⁵ souls.
u Dan. 12, 7.
Rev. 10, 5.
v Ps. 24, 1.
w Esther 9, 15, 16.
2 Cor. 11, 9-12.

CHAP. 15.
a ch. 46, 2.
b Isa. 41, 10.
c Ps. 58, 11.
Ps. 84, 9, 11.
Heb. 11, 6.
d ch. 17, 16.
2 Sa. 7, 12.
e Ps. 147, 4.
f Ex. 32, 13.
He. 11, 12.
g Ro. 4, 3-6, 20-25.
h Ps. 106, 31.
Gal. 3, 6.
i Acts 7, 2.
j Judges 6, 36-40.
1 Sam. 14, 9, 10.
2 Ki. 20, 8.
Luke 1, 18.
k ch. 2, 21.
l Ex. 1, 1.
m Ex. 1, 11.
n Ex. 12, 40.

17 ¶ And the king of Sodom went out to meet him after his return from the slaughter of Chedorlaomer, and of the kings that *were* with him, at the valley of Shaveh, which is the *q* king's dale.
18 And *r* Melchizedek king of Salem brought forth bread and wine: and he *was* *s* the priest of the most high God.
19 And he blessed him, and said, Blessed be Abram of the most high God, possessor of heaven and earth:
20 And blessed *be* the most high God, which hath delivered thine enemies into thy hand. And he gave him *t* tithes of all.
21 And the king of Sodom said unto Abram, Give me the ⁵ persons, and take the goods to thyself.
22 And Abram said to the king of Sodom, *u* I have lift up mine hand unto the LORD, the most high God, *v* the possessor of heaven and earth,
23 That *w* I will not *take* from a thread even to a shoelatchet, and that I will not take any thing that *is* thine, lest thou shouldest say, I have made Abram rich:
24 Save only that which the young men have eaten, and the portion of the men which went with me, Aner, Eshcol, and Mamre; let them take their portion.

CHAPTER XV.

1 *God encourageth Abram;* 4 *promiseth him a son and a numerous seed;* 6 *he is justified by faith.* 7 *Canaan is again promised, and confirmed by a sign and a vision.*

AFTER these things the word of the LORD came unto Abram *a* in a vision, saying, *b* Fear not, Abram: I *am* thy shield, *and* thy *c* exceeding great reward.
2 And Abram said, Lord GOD, what wilt thou give me, seeing I go childless, and the steward of my house *is* this Eliezer of Damascus?
3 And Abram said, Behold, to me thou hast given no seed: and, lo, one born in my house is mine heir.
4 And, behold, the word of the LORD *came* unto him, saying, This shall not be thine heir; but he that *d* shall come forth out of thine own bowels shall be thine heir.
5 And he brought him forth abroad, and said, Look now toward heaven, and *e* tell the stars, if thou be able to number them: and he said unto him, *f* So shall thy seed be.
6 And *g* he believed in the LORD; and he *h* counted it to him for righteousness.
7 And he said unto him, I *am* the LORD that *i* brought thee out of Ur of the Chaldees, to give thee this land to inherit it.
8 And he said, Lord GOD, *j* whereby shall I know that I shall inherit it?
9 And he said unto him, Take me an heifer of three years old, and a she-goat of three years old, and a ram of three years old, and a turtledove, and a young pigeon.
10 And he took unto him all these, and divided them in the midst, and laid each piece one against another: but the birds divided he not.
11 And when the fowls came down upon the carcases, Abram drove them away.
12 And when the sun was going down, a *k* deep sleep fell upon Abram; and, lo, an horror of great darkness fell upon him.
13 And he said unto Abram, Know of a surety that *l* thy seed shall be a stranger in a land *that is* not theirs, and shall serve them; and they shall *m* afflict them *n* four hundred years;

the beginning of his kingdom—This kingdom, of course, though then considered great, would be comparatively limited in extent, and the towns but small forts. 11. Out of that land went forth Asshur—or, as the mar. has it, "he Nimrod) at the head of his army went for.h into Assyria," *i.e.*, he pushed his conquests into that country, and builded Nineveh—opposite the town of Mosul, on the Tigris, and the other towns were near it. This raid into Assyria was an invasion of the territories of Shem, and hence the name "Nimrod," signifying "rebel," is supposed to have been conferred on him from his daring revolt against the divine distribution. 21. unto Shem—The historian introduces him with marked distinction as "the father of Eber," the ancestor of the Hebrews. 23. unto Aram—In the general division of the earth the countries of Armenia, Mesopotamia, and Syria fell to his descendants. 24. Arphaxad—The settlement of his posterity was in the extensive valley of Shinar, on the Tigris, towards the southern extremity of Mesopotamia, including the country of Eden and the region on the east side of the river. 25. Peleg; for in his days was the earth divided—After the flood (ch. 11. 10-16.) the descendants of Noah settled at pleasure, and enjoyed the produce of the undivided soil. But according to divine instruction, made probably through Eber, who seems to have been distinguished for piety or a prophetic character, the earth was divided, and his son's name "Peleg" was given in memory of that event. See De. 32. 8; A. 17. 20. 32. after their generations, in their nations, &c.—This division was made in the most orderly manner; and the inspired historian evidently intimates that the sons of Noah were ranged according to their nations, and every nation ranked by its families, so that every nation had its assigned territory, and in every nation the tribes, and in every tribe the families were located by themselves.

CHAPTER XI.

Ver. 1-31. CONFUSION OF TONGUES. 1. one language—the descendants of Noah, united by the strong bond of a common language, had not separated, and notwithstanding the divine command to replenish the earth, were unwilling to separate. The more pious and well-disposed would of course obey the divine will; but a numerous body—seemingly the aggressive horde mentioned ch. 10. 10,) determined to please themselves by occupying the fairest region they came to. 2. land of Shinar—the fertile valley watered by the Euphrates and Tigris was chosen as the centre of their union and the seat of their power. 3. brick—there being no stone in that quarter, brick is and was the only material used for building, as appears in the mass of ruins which at the Birs Nimroud may have been the very town formed by those ancient rebels. Some of these are sun-dried—others burnt in the kiln and of different colours. slime—batumen, a mineral pitch, which, when hardened, forms a strong cement, commonly used in Assyria to this day, and forming the mortar found on the burnt-brick remains of antiquity. 4. tower ... reach unto heaven—a common figurative expression for great height. (Deut. 1. 28; 9. 1-6.) now nothing will be restrained—an apparent admission that the design was practicable, and would have been executed but for the divine interposition. lest we be scattered—to build a city and a town was no crime; but to do this, to defeat the counsels of heaven by attempting to prevent emigration, was foolish, wicked, and justly offensive to God. 7. confound their language—*lit.* their lip, it was a failure in utterance, occasioning a difference in dialect which was intelligible only to those of the same tribe. Thus easily by God their purpose was defeated, and they were compelled to the dispersion they had combined to prevent. It is only from the Scriptures we learn the true origin of the different nations and languages of the world. By one miracle of tongues men were dispersed, and gradually fell from true religion. By another, national barriers were broken down—that all men might be brought back to the family of God. 28. Ur—(now Orfa), *i.e.* light, or fire. Its name probably derived from its being devoted to the rites of fire-worship. Terah and his family were equally infected with that idolatry as the rest of the inhabitants. (Josh. 24. 15.) 31. Sarai, his daughter-in-law—the same as Iscah, grand daughter of Terah probably by a second wife, and by early usages considered marriageable to her uncle Abraham. came to Haran—two days' journey S.S.E. from Ur, in the direct road to the ford of the Euphrates at Rakka, the nearest and most convenient route to Palestine.

CHAPTER XII.

Ver. 1-20. CALL TO ABRAHAM. 1. now the Lord had said—it pleased God, who has often been found of them who sought him not, to reveal himself to Abraham perhaps by a miracle; and the conversion of Abraham is one of the most remarkable in Bible history. get thee out of thy country—his being brought to the knowledge and worship of the true God had probably been a considerable time before. This call included two promises: the first, showing the land of his future posterity; and the second, that in his posterity all the earth was to be blessed. Abraham obeyed, and it is frequently mentioned in the N. T. as a striking instance of his faith (Heb. 10. 8.) 5. into the land of Canaan they came—With his wife and an orphan nephew. Abram reached his destination in safety, and thus the first promise was made good. 6. the place of Sichem—or Shechem, a pastoral valley then unoccupied (cf. ch. 33. 18.). plain of Moreh—rather the "terebinth tree" of Moreh, very common in Palestine, remarkable for its wide-spreading branches and its dark green foliage. It is probable that in Moreh there was a grove of these trees, whose inviting shade led Abram to choose it for an encampment. 7. unto thy seed ... give this land—God was dealing with Abram not in his private and personal capacity merely, but with a view to high and important interests in future ages. That land his posterity was for centuries to inhabit as a peculiar people; the seeds of divine knowledge were to be sown there for the benefit of all mankind; and consid red in its geographical situation, it was chosen in divine wisdom the fittest of all lands to serve as the cradle of a divine revelation designed for the whole world. builded an altar—By this solemn act of devotion he made an open profession of his religion, established the worship of the true God, and declared his faith in the promise. 10. famine ... went down to Egypt—did not go back to the place

14 And also ᵒ that nation, whom they shall serve, will I judge: and afterward shall they come out with great substance.
15 And thou shalt go to thy fathers in peace; thou shalt be ᵖ buried in a good old age.
16 But in the fourth generation they shall come hither again: for the iniquity of the Amorites ᑫ is not yet full.
17 And it came to pass, that, when the sun went down, and it was dark, behold a smoking furnace, and ¹ a burning lamp that passed between those pieces.
18 In that same day the LORD made a covenant with Abram, saying, Unto thy seed ʳ have I given this land, from the river of Egypt unto the great river, the river Euphrates:
19 The Kenites, and the Kenizzites, and the Kadmonites,
20 And the Hittites, and the Perizzites, and the Rephaims,
21 And the Amorites, and the Canaanites, and the Girgashites, and the Jebusites.

CHAPTER XVI.

1 *Sarai, being barren, giveth Hagar to Abram.* 6 *Hagar fleeth from her mistress,* 9 *is sent back by an angel to submit to her,* 15 *Ishmael is born.*

NOW Sarai, Abram's wife, ᵃ bare him no children: and she had an handmaid, an Egyptian, whose name *was* ¹ Hagar.

2 And Sarai said unto Abram, Behold now, the LORD hath ᵇ restrained me from bearing: I pray thee, go in unto my maid; it may be that I may ² obtain children by her. And Abram hearkened to the voice of Sarai.

3 And Sarai, Abram's wife, took Hagar her maid, the Egyptian, after Abram had dwelt ten years in the land of Canaan, and gave her to her husband Abram to be his wife.

4 And he went in unto Hagar, and she conceived: and when she saw that she had conceived, her mistress was ᶜ despised in her eyes.

5 And Sarai said unto Abram, My wrong *be* upon thee: I have given my maid into thy bosom; and when she saw that she had conceived, I was despised in her eyes: ᵈ the LORD judge between me and thee.

6 But Abram said unto Sarai, Behold, thy maid *is* in thy hand; do to her ³ as it pleaseth thee. And when Sarai ⁴ dealt hardly with her, she fled from her face.

7 ¶ And the angel of the LORD found her by a fountain of water in the wilderness, by the fountain in the way to ᵉ Shur.

8 And he said, Hagar, Sarai's maid, whence camest thou? and whither wilt thou go? And she said, I flee from the face of my mistress Sarai.

9 And the angel of the LORD said unto her, Return to thy mistress, and ᶠ submit thyself under her hands.

10 And the ᵍ angel of the LORD said unto her, I will ʰ multiply thy seed exceedingly, that it shall not be numbered for multitude.

11 And the angel of the LORD said unto her, Behold, thou *art* with child, and shalt bear a son, and shalt call his name ⁵ Ishmael; because ⁱ the LORD hath heard thy affliction.

12 And he will be a wild man; his hand *will be* against every man, and every man's hand against him; and he ʲ shall dwell in the presence of all his brethren.

13 And she called the name of the LORD

B. C. 1913.

CHAP. 15.
ᵒ Ex. 6, 6.
Ez. 7, 14.
ᵖ ch. 25, 8.
Job 5, 26.
He. 11, 13.
ᑫ Mat. 23, 32.
1 Th. 2, 16.
ⁿ Pet. 3, 8, 9.
1 a lamp of fire.
ʳ ch. 17, 8.
Deut. 1, 7.
Nu. 34, 3.
2 Ch. 9, 26.
Neh. 9, 8.
Ps. 107, 11.

CHAP. 16.
ᵃ Ju. 13, 2.
Lu. 1, 7.
1 or, *Agar,* Gal. 4, 24.
ᵇ ch. 30, 2.
2 be builded by her.
Ruth 4, 11.
ᶜ Pro. 30, 23.
ᵈ Ex. 5, 21.
3 that which is good in thine eyes.
4 afflicted her.
ᵉ ch. 25, 18.
ᶠ Ep. 6, 5-9.
ᵍ ch. 22, 15-18.
Mal. 3, 1.
ʰ ch. 25, 12.
5 i. e. God shall hear.
ⁱ Ex. 2, 23, 24.
ʲ ch. 25, 18.
ᵏ Ps. 139, 1-12.
6 i. e. the well of him that liveth and seeth me.

CHAP. 17.
ᵃ ch. 5, 2.
ᵇ Job 1, 1.
1 or, *upright, or, sincere.*
ᶜ Gal. 3, 17, 18.
ᵈ Ex. 3, 6.
2 multitude of nations.
3 i. e. father of a great multitude.
ᵉ He. 11, 16.
Ro. 9, 7-9.
4 of thy sojournings.
ᶠ Ps. 48, 14.
ᵍ Ps. 25, 10.
ʰ Gal. 6, 15.
5 a son of eight days.
ⁱ Ex. 4, 24.
Josh. 5, 2-7.
6 i. e. Princess.
ʲ ch. 18, 10.
7 she shall become nations.
ᵏ ch. 18, 12.
ch. 21, 6.

that spake unto her, ᵏ Thou God seest me: for she said, Have I also here looked after him that seeth me?

14 Wherefore the well was called ⁶ Beer-lahai-roi; behold, *it is* between Kadesh and Bered.

15 And Hagar bare Abram a son: and Abram called his son's name, which Hagar bare, Ishmael.

16 And Abram *was* fourscore and six years old when Hagar bare Ismael to Abram.

CHAPTER XVII.

1 *The covenant is renewed.* 5 *Abram's name changed.* 9 *Circumcision instituted.* 16 *Isaac with a numerous issue is promised.*

AND when Abram was ninety years old and nine, the LORD appeared to Abram, and said unto him, I *am* the Almighty God; ᵃ walk before me, and be thou ᵇ ¹ perfect.

2 And I will make my ᶜ covenant between me and thee, and will multiply thee exceedingly.

3 And Abram ᵈ fell on his face: and God talked with him, saying,

4 As for me, behold, my covenant *is* with thee, and thou shalt be a father of ² many nations.

5 Neither shall thy name any more be called Abram, but thy name shall be ³ Abraham; for a father of many nations have I made thee.

6 And I will make thee exceeding fruitful, and I will make nations of thee, and kings shall come out of thee.

7 And I will establish my covenant between me and thee and thy seed after thee in their generations for an everlasting covenant, to be ᵉ a God unto thee, and to thy seed after thee.

8 And I will give unto thee, and to thy seed after thee, the land ⁴ wherein thou art a stranger, all the land of Canaan, for an everlasting possession; and ᶠ I will be their God.

9 ¶ And God said unto Abraham, ᵍ Thou shalt keep my covenant therefore, thou, and thy seed after thee in their generations.

10 This *is* my covenant, which ye shall keep, between me and you and thy seed after thee; Every man-child among you shall be circumcised.

11 And ʰ ye shall circumcise the flesh of your foreskin; and it shall be a token of the covenant betwixt me and you.

12 And ⁵ he that is eight days old shall be circumcised among you, every man-child in your generations, he that is born in the house, or bought with money of any stranger, which *is* not of thy seed.

13 He that is born in thy house, and he that is bought with thy money, must needs be circumcised: and my covenant shall be in your flesh for an everlasting covenant.

14 And the uncircumcised man-child, whose flesh of his foreskin is not circumcised, that soul shall be ⁱ cut off from his people; he hath broken my covenant.

15 ¶ And God said unto Abraham, As for Sarai thy wife, thou shalt not call her name Sarai, but ⁶ Sarah *shall* her name *be.*

16 And I will bless her, and ʲ give thee a son also of her: yea, I will bless her, and she shall ⁷ be *a mother* of nations; kings of people shall be of her.

17 Then Abraham fell upon his face, and ᵏ laughed, and said in his heart, Shall *child* be born unto him that is an hundr

of his nativity, as regretting his pilgrimage and despising the promised land (Heb. 11. 15., but withdrew for a while into a neighbouring country. **11-13.** Sarai's complexion, coming from a mountainous country, would be fresh and fair compared with the faces of Egyptian women which were sallow. The counsel of Abram to her was true in words, but it was a deception, intended to give an impression that she was no more than his sister. His conduct was culpable and inconsistent with his character as a servant of God; it shewed a reliance on worldly policy more than a trust in the promise; and he not only sinned himself, but tempted Sarai to sin also. **14. was come into Egypt**—It appears from the monuments of that country that at the time of Abram's visit a monarchy had existed for several centuries. The seat of government was in the Delta, the most northern part of the country, the very quarter in which Abram must have arrived. They were a race of shepherd kings, in close alliance with the people of Canaan. **15. The woman was taken into Pharaoh's house**—Eastern kings have for ages claimed the privilege of taking to their harem an unmarried woman whom they like. The father or brother may deplore the removal as a calamity, but the royal right is never resisted nor questioned. **16. entreated well for her sake**—The presents are just what one pastoral chief would give to another. **18-20.** Here is a most humiliating rebuke, and Abram deserved it. Had not God interfered he might have been tempted to stay in Egypt, and forget the promise (Ps. 105. 13, 15.). Often still does God rebuke His people and remind them through enemies that this world is not their rest.

CHAPTER XIII.

Ver. 1-18. RETURN FROM EGYPT. 1. went up ... south—Palestine being a highland country, the entrance from Egypt by its southern boundary is a continual ascent. **2. very rich**—compared with the pastoral tribes to which Abraham belonged. An Arab sheick is considered rich who has a hundred or two hundred tents, from sixty to a hundred camels, a thousand sheep and goats respectively. And Abraham being very rich, must have far exceeded that amount of pastoral property. "Gold and silver" being rare among these people, his probably arose from the sale of his produce in Egypt. **3. went on his journeys**—his progress would be by slow marches and frequent encampments, as he had to regulate his movements by the prospect of water and pasturage. **3. unto the place between Beth-el and Ai**—"a conspicuous hill—its topmost summit resting on the rocky slopes below, and distinguished by its olive groves—offering a natural base for the altar and a fitting shade for the tent of the patriarch." [STANLEY.] there Abraham called—he felt a strong desire to re-animate his faith and piety on the scene of his former worship: it might be to express humility and penitence for his misconduct in Egypt, or thankfulness for deliverance from perils—to embrace the first opportunity on returning to Canaan of leading his family to renew allegiance to God, and offer the typical sacrifices which pointed to the blessings of the promise. **7-10. and there was a strife**—Abraham's character appears here in a most amiable light. Having a strong sense of religion, he was afraid of doing anything that might tend to injure its character or bring discredit on its name, and he rightly judged that such unhappy effects would be produced if two persons whom nature and grace had so closely connected should come to a rupture. Waiving his right to dictate, he gave the freedom of choice to Lot. The conduct of Abraham was not only disinterested and peaceable, but generous and condescending in an extraordinary degree, exemplifying the Scripture precepts, Matt. 6. 32; Ro. 12. 10, 11; Phil. 2. 4. **10. Lot lifted up his eyes**—travellers describe that from the top of this hill, a little "to the east of Bethel," they can see the Jordan, the broad meadows on either bank, and the waving line of verdure which marks the course of the stream. **11. then Lot chose him all the plain**—a choice excellent in a worldly point of view, but most inexpedient for his best interests. He seems, though a good man, to have been too much under the influence of a selfish and covetous spirit; and how many, alas! imperil the good of their souls for the prospect of worldly advantage. **14. lift their eyes ... all the land which thou seest**—so extensive a survey of the country, *in all directions*, can be obtained from no other point in the neighbourhood; and those plains and hills, then lying desolate before the eyes of the solitary patriarch, were to be peopled with a mighty nation "like the dust of the earth in number," as they were in Solomon's time (1 Kings. 4. 20. . **18. plain of Mamre ... built an altar**—grove of Mamre—the renewal of the promise was acknowledged by Abram by a fresh tribute of devout gratitude.

CHAPTER XIV.

Ver. 1-24. WAR. And it came to pass—This chapter presents Abram in the unexpected character of a warrior. The occasion was this: the king of Sodom and the kings of the adjoining cities, after having been tributaries for twelve years to the king of Elam, combined to throw off his yoke. To chastise their rebellion, as he deemed it, Chedorlaomer, with the aid of three allies, invaded the territories of the refractory princes—defeated them in a pitched battle, where the nature of the ground favoured his army, (v. 10 and hastened in triumph on his homeward march, with a large amount of captives and booty, though merely a stranger. **they took Lot, &c.**—how would the conscience of that young man now upbraid him for his selfish folly and ingratitude in withdrawing from his kind and pious relative! Whenever we go out of the path of duty, we put ourselves away from God's protection, and cannot expect that the choice we make will be for our lasting good. **13. then came one that had escaped**—Abram might have excused himself from taking any active concern in his "brother," *i. e.* nephew, who little deserved that he should incur trouble or danger on his account. But Abram, far from rendering evil for evil, resolved to take immediate measures for the rescue of Lot. **14. he armed his trained servants**—domestic slaves, such as are common in Eastern countries still, and are considered and treated as members of the family. If Abram could spare three hundred and eighteen slaves and leave a sufficient number to take care of his flocks, what a large establishment he must have had. **15, 16. he divided himself, by**

years old? and shall ¹ Sarah, that is ninety years old, bear?

18 And Abraham said unto God, O that Ishmael might live before thee!

19 And God said, ᵐ Sarah thy wife shall bear thee a son indeed; and thou shalt call his name Isaac: and I will establish my covenant with him for an everlasting covenant, *and* with his seed after him.

20 And as for Ishmael, I have heard thee: Behold, I have blessed him, and will make him fruitful, and will ⁿ multiply him exceedingly; ᵒ twelve princes shall he beget, and I will make him a ᵖ great nation.

21 But my covenant will I establish with Isaac, which ᑫ Sarah shall bear unto thee at this set time in the next year.

22 And he left off ʳ talking with him, and God went up from Abraham.

23 ¶ And Abraham took Ishmael his son, and all that were born in his house, and all that were bought with his money, every male among the men of Abraham's house, and circumcised the flesh of their foreskin in the selfsame day, as God ˢ had said unto him.

24 And Abraham *was* ninety years old and nine when he was circumcised in the flesh of his foreskin.

25 And Ishmael his son *was* thirteen years old when he was circumcised in the flesh of his foreskin.

26 In ᵗ the selfsame day was Abraham circumcised, and Ishmael his son.

27 And all the men of his ᵘ house, born ᵛ in the house, and bought with money of the stranger, were circumcised with him.

CHAPTER XVIII.

1 *Abraham entertaineth three angels.* 9 *Sarah reproved.* 17 *Destruction of Sodom revealed to Abraham:* 23 *he intercedes for it.*

AND the LORD ᵃ appeared unto him in the plains of Mamre: and he sat in the tent door in the heat of the day;

2 And he lift up his eyes and looked, and, lo, ᵇ three men stood by him: and, when he saw *them*, he ᶜ ran to meet them from the tent door, and bowed himself toward the ground,

3 And said, My Lord, if now I have found favour in thy sight, pass not away, I pray thee, from thy servant:

4 Let a little water, I pray you, be fetched, and ᵈ wash your feet, and rest yourselves under the tree:

5 And I will fetch a morsel of bread, and ¹ comfort ye your hearts; after that ye shall pass on: for therefore ² are ye come to your servant. And they said, So do, as thou hast said.

6 And Abraham hastened into the tent unto Sarah, and said, ³ Make ready quickly three measures of fine meal, knead *it*, and make cakes upon the hearth.

7 And Abraham ran unto the herd, and fetched a calf tender and good, and gave *it* unto a young man; and he hasted to dress it.

8 And he took butter, and milk, and the calf which he had dressed, and set *it* before them; and he stood by them under the tree, and they did eat.

9 ¶ And they said unto him, Where *is* Sarah thy wife? And he said, Behold, ᵉ in the tent.

10 And he said, I will certainly return unto thee according to the time of life; and, lo, Sarah thy wife ᶠ shall have a son.

And Sarah heard *it* in the tent door, which *was* behind him.

11 Now Abraham and Sarah *were* ᵍ old and well stricken in age; *and* it ceased to be with Sarah after the ʰ manner of women.

12 Therefore Sarah laughed within herself, saying, ¹ After I am waxed old shall I have pleasure, my ʲ lord being old also?

13 And the LORD said unto Abraham, Wherefore did Sarah laugh, saying, Shall I of a surety bear a child, which am old?

14 Is any thing ᵏ too hard for the LORD? At the time appointed I will return unto thee, according to the time of life, and Sarah shall have a son.

15 Then Sarah denied, saying, I laughed not; for she was afraid. And he said, Nay; but thou didst laugh.

16 ¶ And the men rose up from thence, and looked toward Sodom: and Abraham went with them to bring them on the way.

17 And the LORD said, ˡ Shall I hide from Abraham that thing which I do;

18 Seeing that Abraham shall surely become a great and mighty nation, and all the nations of the earth shall ᵐ be blessed in him?

19 For I know him, that he ⁿ will command his children and his household after him, and they shall keep the way of the LORD, to do justice and judgment; that the LORD may bring upon Abraham that which he hath spoken of him.

20 And the LORD said, Because ᵒ the cry of Sodom and Gomorrah is great, and because their sin is very grievous,

21 I will go down now, ᵖ and see whether they have done altogether according to the cry of it, which is come unto me; and if not, I will know.

22 And the men turned their faces from thence, and went toward Sodom: but Abraham stood yet before the ᑫ LORD.

23 ¶ And Abraham drew near, and said, ʳ Wilt thou also destroy the righteous with the wicked?

24 Peradventure there be ˢ fifty righteous within the city: wilt thou also destroy and not spare the place for the fifty righteous that *are* therein?

25 That be far from thee to do after this manner, to slay the righteous with the wicked: and that the ᵗ righteous should be as the wicked, that be far from thee: ᵘ Shall not the Judge of all the earth do right?

26 And the LORD said, ᵛ If I find in Sodom fifty righteous within the city, then I will spare all the place for their sakes.

27 And Abraham answered and said, ʷ Behold now, I have taken upon me to speak unto the Lord which *am but* ˣ dust and ashes:

28 Peradventure there shall lack five of the fifty righteous: wilt thou destroy all the city for *lack of* five? And he said, If I find there forty and five, I will not destroy *it*.

29 And he spake unto him yet ʸ again, and said, Peradventure there shall be forty found there. And he said, I will not do *it* for forty's sake.

30 And he said *unto him*, ᶻ Oh let not the Lord be angry, and I will speak. Peradventure there shall thirty be found there. And he said, I will not do *it* if I find thirty there.

31 And he said, Behold now, ᵃ I have taken upon me to speak unto the Lord: Peradventure there shall be twenty found there.

night—this war between the petty princes of ancient Canaan is exactly the same as the frays and skirmishes between Arab chiefs in the present day. When a defeated party resolve to pursue the enemy, they wait till they are fast asleep—then, as they have no idea of posting sentinels, they rush upon them from different directions, strike down the tent poles—if there is any fight at all, it is the fray of a tumultuous mob—a panic commonly ensues, and the whole contest is ended with little or no loss on either side. **18. Melchisedec**—this victory conferred a public benefit on that part of the country; and Abram, on his return, was treated with high respect and consideration, particularly by the king of Sodom and Melchisedec, who seems to have been one of the few native princes, if not the only one who knew and worshipped "the Most High God," whom Abram served. This king, who was a type of the Saviour, (Heb. 7. 1) came to bless God for the victory which had been won, and in the name of God to bless Abram, by whose arms it had been achieved—a pious acknowledgment which we should imitate on succeeding in any lawful enterprise. **20. he gave him tithes of all**—here is an evidence of Abram's piety, as well as of his valour; for it was to a priest or official mediator between God and him, that Abram gave a tenth of the spoil—a token of his gratitude and in honour of a divine ordinance (Pro. 11. 9). **21. the king of Sodom... give... persons**—according to the war customs still existing among the Arab tribes, Abram might have retained the recovered goods—and his right was acknowledged by the king of Sodom. But with honest pride, and a generosity unknown in that part of the world, he replied with strong phraseology common to the East, "I have lifted up mine hand, *i. e.*, I have sworn unto the Lord that I will not take from a thread even to a sandal-thong—that I will not take anything that is thine, lest thou shouldest say, I have made Abram rich."

CHAPTER XV.

Ver. 1-21. DIVINE ENCOURAGEMENT. **After these things**—the conquest of the invading kings. **the word of the Lord**—a phrase used, when connected with a vision, to denote a prophetic message. **Fear not, Abram**—When the excitement of the enterprise was over he had become a prey to despondency and terror at the probable revenge that might be meditated against him. To dispel his fear, he was favoured with this gracious announcement. Having such a promise, how well did it become him, and all God's people who have the same promise, to dismiss their fears, and cast their burdens on the Lord Ps. 27. 3.). **2. Lord God, what wilt thou give?**—to his mind the declaration, "I am thy exceeding great reward," had but one meaning, or was viewed but in one particular light, as bearing on the fulfilment of the promise, and he was still experiencing the sickness of hope deferred. **Eliezer, of Damascus, mine heir**—according to the usage of Nomadic tribes, his chief confidential servant would be heir to his possessions and honours. But this man could have become his son only by adoption; and how sadly would that have come short of the parental hopes he had been encouraged to entertain! His language betrayed a latent spirit of fretfulness, or perhaps a temporary failure in the very virtue for which he is so renowned—an absolute submission to God's time as well as way of accomplishing His promise. **4. This shall not be thine heir**—To the first part of his address no reply was given; but having renewed it in a spirit of more becoming submission, "whereby shall I know that I shall inherit it," he was delighted by a most explicit promise of Canaan, which was immediately confirmed by a remarkable ceremony. **9-12. Take... an heifer, &c.**—On occasions of great importance, when two or more parties join in a compact, they either observe precisely the same rites as Abram did, or, where they do not, they invoke the lamp as their witness. According to these ideas, which have been from time immemorial engraven on the minds of eastern people, the Lord himself condescended to enter into covenant with Abram. The patriarch did not pass between the sacrifice, and the reason was that in this transaction he was bound to nothing. He asked a sign, and God was pleased to give him a sign, by which, according to eastern ideas, he bound himself. In like manner God has entered into covenant with us; and in the glory of the Only Begotten Son, who passed through between God and us, all who believe have, like Abram, a sign or pledge in the gift of the Spirit, whereby they may know that they shall inherit the heavenly Canaan.

CHAPTER XVI.

Ver. 1-16. BESTOWMENT OF HAGAR. **Now Sarai... had a handmaid**—a female slave—one of those obtained in Egypt. **3. Sarai gave her to... Abram to wife**—wife is here used to describe an inferior, though not degrading relation, in countries where polygamy prevails. In the case of these female slaves, which are the personal property of his lady, being purchased before her marriage or given as a special present to herself—no one can become the husband's secondary wife without her mistress' consent or permission. This usage seems to have prevailed in patriarchal times; and Hagar, the slave of Sarai, of whom she had the entire right of disposing, was given by her mistress' spontaneous offer, to be the secondary wife of Abram, in the hope of obtaining the long-looked for heir. It was a wrong step—indicating a want of simple reliance on God—and Sarah was the first to reap the bitter fruits of her device. **5. And Sarai said, My wrong, &c.**—Bursts of temper, or blows, as the original may bear, took place, till at length Hagar, perceiving the hopelessness of maintaining the unequal strife, resolved to escape from what had become to her in reality, as well as in name, a house of bondage. **7. And the angel... found her by a fountain**—This well, pointed out by tradition, lay on the side of the caravan road, in the midst of Shur, a sandy desert on the west of Arabia Petræa, to the extent of 150 miles, between Palestine and Egypt. By taking that direction, she seems to have intended to return to her relatives in that country. Nothing but pride, passion, and sullen obstinacy, could have driven any solitary person to brave the dangers of such an inhospitable wild; and she must have died, had not the timely appearance and words of the angel recalled her to reflection and duty. **11. Ishmael**—Like other Hebrew names, this had a signification, and it is made up of two words—"God hears." The reason is

And he said, I will not destroy it for twenty's sake.

32 And he said, *b* Oh let not the Lord be angry, and I will speak yet but this once! Peradventure ten shall be found there. And he said, *c* I will not destroy it for ten's sake.

33 And the LORD went his way, as soon as he had left communing with Abraham: and Abraham returned unto his place.

CHAPTER XIX.

1 *Lot entertaineth two angels;* 4 *The vicious Sodomites stricken with blindness.* 17 *He is directed to flee to the mountain.* 24 *Sodom and Gomorrah destroyed.* 26 *Lot's wife punished.* 31 *Origin of Moab and Ammon.*

AND there came *a* two angels to Sodom at even; and Lot sat in the gate of Sodom: and Lot seeing them rose up to meet them; and he bowed himself with his face toward the ground;

2 And he said, Behold now, my lords, *b* turn in, I pray you, into your servant's house, and tarry all night, and wash your feet, and ye shall rise up early, and go on your ways. And they said, Nay; *c* but we will abide in the street all night.

3 And he pressed upon them greatly; and they turned in unto him, and entered into his house; *d* and he made them a feast, and did bake unleavened bread, and they did eat.

4 ¶ But, before they lay down, the men of the city, even the men of Sodom, compassed the house round, both old and young, all the people from every quarter:

5 *e* And they called unto Lot, and said unto him, *f* Where are the men which came in to thee this night? bring them out unto us, that we may know them.

6 And *g* Lot went out at the door unto them, and shut the door after him,

7 And said, I pray you, brethren, do not so wickedly.

8 Behold now, I have two daughters which have not known man; let me, I pray you, bring them out unto you, and do ye to them as is good in your eyes: only unto these men do nothing; for *h* therefore came they under the shadow of my roof.

9 And they said, Stand back. And they said again, *i* This one fellow came in to sojourn, and he will needs be a judge: now will we deal worse with thee than with them. And they pressed sore upon the man, even Lot, and came near to break the door.

10 But the men put forth their hand, and pulled Lot into the house to them, and shut to the door.

11 And they smote the men that were at the door of the house with *j* blindness, both small and great; so that they wearied themselves to find the door.

12 ¶ And the men said unto Lot, *k* Hast thou here any besides? son-in-law, and thy sons, and thy daughters, and whatsoever thou hast in the city, *l* bring them out of this place:

13 For we will destroy this place, because the cry of them is waxen great before the face of the LORD; and the LORD hath *m* sent us to destroy it.

14 And Lot went out, and spake unto his sons-in-law, *n* which married his daughters, and said, *o* Up, get you out of this place; for the LORD will destroy this city. But he seemed *p* as one that mocked unto his sons-in-law.

15 ¶ And when the morning arose, then the angels hastened Lot, saying, Arise, take thy wife, and thy two daughters, which 1 are here; lest thou be consumed in 2 the iniquity of the city.

16 And, while he lingered, the men laid hold upon his hand, and upon the hand of his wife, and upon the hand of his two daughters; *q* the LORD being merciful unto him: and they brought him forth, and set him without the city.

17 And it came to pass, when they had brought them forth abroad, that he said, *r* Escape for thy life; *s* look not behind thee, neither stay thou in all the plain; escape to the mountain, lest thou be consumed.

18 And Lot said unto them, Oh! not so, *t* my lord:

19 Behold now, thy servant hath found grace in thy sight, and *u* thou hast magnified thy mercy, which thou hast shewed unto me in saving my life; and I cannot escape to the mountain, lest some evil take me, and I die:

20 Behold now, this city is near to flee unto, and it is a little one: Oh! let me escape thither, (is it not a little one?) and my soul shall live.

21 And he said unto him, See, I have accepted *3* thee concerning this thing also, that I will not overthrow this city, for the which thou hast spoken.

22 Haste thee, escape thither; for I cannot do any thing till thou be come thither. Therefore the name of the city was *u* called *4* Zoar.

23 The sun was *5* risen upon the earth when Lot entered into Zoar.

24 Then *v* the LORD rained upon Sodom and upon Gomorrah brimstone and fire from the LORD out of heaven;

25 And he overthrew those cities, and all *w* the plain, and all the inhabitants of the cities, and that which grew upon the ground.

26 But his wife *x* looked back from behind him, and she became a pillar of salt.

27 And Abraham gat up early in the morning to the place where *y* he stood before the LORD:

28 And he looked toward Sodom and Gomorrah, and toward all the land of the plain, and beheld, and, lo, *z* the smoke of the country went up as the smoke of a furnace.

29 ¶ And it came to pass, when God destroyed the cities of the plain, that God *a* remembered Abraham, and sent Lot out of the midst of the overthrow, when he overthrew the cities in the which Lot dwelt.

30 ¶ And Lot went up out of Zoar, and *b* dwelt in the mountain, and his two daughters with him; for he feared to dwell in Zoar: and he dwelt in a cave, he and his two daughters.

31 And the first-born said unto the younger, Our father is old, and there is not a man in the earth *c* to come in unto us after the manner of all the earth:

32 Come, *d* let us make our father drink wine, and we will lie with him, *e* that we may preserve seed of our father.

33 And they made their father drink wine that night; and the first-born went in, and lay with her father; and he perceived not when she lay down, nor when she arose.

explained. **12. a wild man**—*lit. a wild ass man*, expressing how the wildness of Ishmael and his descendants resembles that of the wild ass. **His hand shall be against every man,** and every man's hand against him—descriptive of the rude, turbulent and plundering character of the Arabs. **dwell in the presence of all his brethren**—dwell, *i. e.* pitch tents; and the meaning is that they maintain their independence in spite of all attempts to extirpate or subdue them. **13. called the name**—common in ancient times to name places from circumstances; and the name given to this well was a grateful recognition of God's gracious appearance in the hour of her distress.

CHAPTER XVII.

Ver. 1-20. RENEWAL OF THE COVENANT. Abram ninety and nine years old—Thirteen years after the birth of Ishmael. During that interval he had enjoyed the comforts of communion with God, but had been favoured with no special revelation as formerly, probably on account of his hasty and blameable marriage with Hagar. **The Lord appeared**—some visible manifestation of the divine presence, probably the shechinah or radiant glory of overpowering effulgence. **I am the Almighty God**—the name by which He made himself known to the patriarchs, Ex. 6. 3, designed to convey the sense of "all-sufficient" Ps. 16. 5, 6; 73. 25.). **walk ... and be perfect**—upright, sincere, Ps. 41. 6, in heart, speech, and behaviour. **3.** Abram fell on his face—the attitude of profoundest reverence assumed by eastern people. It consists in the prostrate body resting on the hands and knees, with the face bent till the forehead touches the ground. It is an expression of conscious humility and profound reverence. **4. My covenant is with thee**—renewed mention is made of it as the foundation of the communication that follows. It is the covenant of grace made with all who believe in the Saviour. **5. name shall be Abraham**—In eastern countries a change of name is an advertisement of some new circumstance in the history, rank, or religion of the individual who bears it. The change is made variously, by the old name being entirely dropped for the new, or by conjoining the new with the old, or sometimes only a few letters are inserted, so that the altered form may express the difference in the owner's state or prospects. It is surprising how soon a new name is known and its import spread through the country. In dealing with Abraham and Sarai, God was pleased to adopt His procedure to the ideas and customs of the country and age. Instead of Abram, "a high father," he was to be called Abraham, father of a multitude of nations Rev. 2. 17.). **6-8. I will give ... the land**—It had been previously promised to Abraham and his posterity (ch. 15. 18.). Here it is promised as an "everlasting possession," and was, therefore, a type of heaven, "the better country" (Heb. 11. 16.). **10. Every man-child ... circumcised** —This was the sign in the O. T. Church as baptism is in the N., and hence the covenant is called "covenant of circumcision" (A. 7. 8; R. 4. 11.). The terms of the covenant were these—on the one hand Abraham and his seed were to observe the rite of circumcision; and on the other, God promised, in the event of such observance, to give them Canaan for a perpetual possession, to be a God to him and his posterity, and that in him and his seed all nations should be blessed. **15 19. As for Sarai ... a son**—God's purposes are gradually made known. A son had been long ago promised to Abraham. Now, at length, for the first time he is informed that it was to be a child of Sarai. **17. Abraham fell on his face, and laughed**—It was not the sneer of unbelief, but a smile of delight at the improbability of the event (R. 4. 20.). **18. O that Ishmael**—natural solicitude of a parent. But God's thoughts are not as man's thoughts. **19-20.** The blessings of the covenant are reserved for Isaac, but common blessings were abundantly promised to Ishmael; and though the visible Church did not descend from his family, yet personally he might, and it is to be hoped *did*, enjoy its benefits.

CHAPTER XVIII.

Ver. 1-8. ENTERTAINMENT OF ANGELS. the Lord appeared—another manifestation of the divine presence, more familiar than any yet narrated; and more like that in the fulness of time, when the Word was made flesh. **plains of Mamre**—rather terebinth or oak of Mamre—a tall-spreading tree or grove of trees. **sat in the tent door**—the tent itself being too close and sultry at noon, the shaded open front is usually resorted to for the air that may be stirring. **2. lift up his eyes, and lo, three men**—travellers in that quarter start at sunrise and continue till mid day, when they look out for some resting-place. **ran to meet them**—when the visitor is an ordinary person, they merely rise; but if of superior rank, the custom is to advance a little towards the stranger, and after a very low bow, turn and lead him to the tent—putting an arm round his waist, or tapping him on the shoulder as they go, to assure him of welcome. **3. My Lord, if now I have found favour**—the hospitalities offered are just of the kind that are necessary and most grateful, the refreshment of water for feet exposed to dust and heat by the sandals being still the first observed amongst the pastoral people of Hebron. **5. for therefore are ye come**—no questions were asked. But Abraham knew their object by the course they took—approaching directly in *front* of the chief shieck's tent, which is always distinguishable from the rest, and thus showing their wish to be his guests. **6. Abraham hastened unto Sarah ... make cakes upon the hearth**—bread is baked daily and no more than is required for family use, and always by the women, commonly the wife. It is a short process. Flour mixed with water is made into dough, and being rolled out into cakes, it is placed on the earthen floor, previously heated by a fire. The fire being removed, the cakes are laid on the ground, and being covered over with hot embers, are soon baked, and eaten the moment they are taken off. **7. Abraham ran unto the herd, and fetched a calf**—animal food is never provided except for visitors of a superior rank, when a kid or lamb is killed. A calf is still a higher stretch of hospitality, and it would probably be cooked as is usually done when haste is required—either by roasting it whole or by cutting it up into small pieces and broiling them on skewers over the fire. It is always eaten along with boiled corn swimming in *butter* or melted fat, into which every morsel of meat, laid

34 And it came to pass on the morrow, that the first-born said unto the younger, Behold, I lay yesternight with my father: let us make him drink wine this night also; and go thou in, *and* lie with him, that we may preserve seed of our father.
35 And they made their father drink wine that night also: and the younger arose, and lay with him; and he perceived not when she lay down, nor when she arose.
36 Thus were both the daughters of Lot with child by their father.
37 And the first-born bare a son, and called his name Moab: the *f* same *is* the father of the Moabites unto this day.
38 And the younger, she also bare a son, and called his name Ben-ammi: the *g* same is the father of the children of Ammon unto this day.

CHAPTER XX.

1 *Abraham denieth his wife, and Abimelech taketh her:* 14 *he restoreth her with presents.*

AND Abraham journeyed from *a* thence toward the south country, and dwelled between Kadesh and Shur, and sojourned in *b* Gerar.
2 And *c* Abraham said of Sarah his wife, She *is* my sister: and Abimelech king of Gerar sent and *d* took Sarah.
3 But God *e* came to Abimelech *f* in a dream by night, and said to him, Behold, thou *art but g* a dead man, for the woman which thou hast taken; for she *is* ¹ a man's wife.
4 But Abimelech had not come near her: and he said, Lord, *h* wilt thou slay also a righteous nation?
5 Said he not unto me, She *is* my sister? and she, even she herself said, He *is* my brother: in the ² integrity of my heart, and innocency of my hands, have I done this.
6 And God said unto him in a dream, Yea, I know that thou didst this in the integrity of thy heart; for I also *i* withheld thee from sinning against me: therefore suffered I thee not to touch her.
7 Now therefore restore the man *his* wife; for he *is* a prophet, and *j* he shall pray for thee, and thou shalt live: and if thou restore *her* not, know thou that thou shalt surely die, thou, and all that *are* thine.
8 Therefore Abimelech rose early in the morning, and called all his servants, and told all these things in their ears: and the men were sore afraid.
9 Then Abimelech called Abraham, and said unto him, What hast thou done unto us? and what have I offended thee, that thou hast brought on me and on my kingdom *k* a great sin? thou hast done deeds unto me that ought not to be done.
10 And Abimelech said unto Abraham, What sawest thou, that thou hast done this thing?
11 And Abraham said, Because I thought, *l* Surely the fear of God *is* not in this place; and they will slay me for my wife's sake.
12 And *m* yet indeed she *is* my sister; she *is* the daughter of my father, but not the daughter of my mother; and she became my wife.
13 And it came to pass, when *n* God caused me to wander from my father's house, that I said unto her, This *is* thy kindness which thou shalt show unto me; at every place whither we shall come, say of me, *o* He *is* my brother

14 And Abimelech took *p* sheep, and oxen, and men-servants, and women-servants, and gave *them* unto Abraham, and restored him Sarah his wife.
15 And Abimelech said, *q* Behold, my land *is* before thee: dwell ³ where it pleaseth thee.
16 And unto Sarah he said, Behold, I have given thy *r* brother a thousand *pieces* of silver: behold, he *is* to thee a covering of the eyes, unto all that *are* with thee, and with all *other:* thus she was reproved.
17 So Abraham *s* prayed unto God: and God healed Abimelech, and his wife, and his maid-servants; and they bare *children.*
18 For the LORD had *t* fast closed up all the wombs of the house of Abimelech because of Sarah, Abraham's wife.

CHAPTER XXI.

2 *Isaac is born.* 9 *Hagar and Ishmael cast forth:* 17 *an angel comforteth her.* 22 *Abimelech makes a covenant with Abraham.*

AND the LORD *a* visited Sarah as he had said, and the LORD did unto Sarah *b* as he had spoken.
2 For Sarah conceived, *c* and bare Abraham a son in his old age, at the set time of which God had spoken to him.
3 And Abraham *d* called the name of his son that was born unto him, whom Sarah bare to him, Isaac.
4 And Abraham *e* circumcised his son Isaac being eight days old, as God had commanded him.
5 And Abraham was an hundred years old when his son Isaac was born unto him.
6 And Sarah said, *f* God hath made me to laugh, *so that* all that hear will *g* laugh with me.
7 And she said, Who would have said unto Abraham, that Sarah should have given children suck? *h* for I have born *him* a son in his old age.
8 And the child grew, and was weaned: and Abraham made a great feast the same day that Isaac was weaned.
9 ¶ And Sarah saw the *i* son of Hagar the Egyptian, which she had born unto Abraham, *j* mocking.
10 Wherefore she said unto Abraham, *k* Cast out this bond-woman and her son: for the son of this bond-woman shall not be heir with my son, *even* with Isaac.
11 And the thing was very *l* grievous in Abraham's sight because of his son.
12 And God said unto Abraham, Let it not be grievous in thy sight because of the lad, and because of thy bond-woman; in all that Sarah hath said unto thee, hearken unto her voice; for *m* in Isaac shall thy seed be called.
13 And also *n* of the son of the bond-woman will I make a nation, because he *is* thy seed.
14 And Abraham rose up early in the morning, and took bread and a bottle of water, and gave *it* unto Hagar, putting *it* on her shoulder, and the child, and *o* sent her away. And she departed, and wandered in the wilderness of Beer-sheba.
15 And *p* the water was spent in the bottle, and she cast the child under one of the shrubs.
16 And she went, and sat her down over against *him* a good way off, as it were a bow-shot; for she said, *q* Let me not see the death of the child. And she sat over against *him,* and lift up her voice, and wept.

upon a piece of bread, is dipped, before being conveyed by the fingers to the mouth. milk—a bowl of camel's milk ends the repast. he stood by them under the tree—the host himself, even though he has a number of servants, deems it a necessary act of politeness to *stand* while his guests are at their food, and Abraham evidently did this before he was aware of the real character of his visitors.

9-15. REPROOF OF SARAH. An inquiry about his wife, so surprising in strangers—the subject of conversation, and the fulfilment of the fondly-cherished promise within a specified time, showed Abraham that he had been entertaining more than ordinary travellers (Heb. 13. 2.). 10. Sarah... tent... door... behind—the women's apartment is in the back of the tent, divided by a thin partition from the men's. 12. laughed within herself—long delay seems to have weakened faith. Sarah treated the announcement as incredible, and when taxed with the silent sneer, she added falsehood to distrust. It was an aggravated offence (Acts 5. 4), and nothing but grace saved her (Ro. 9. 18.).

16-22. DISCLOSURE OF SODOM'S DOOM. men rose . . Abraham went with them—it is customary for a host to escort his guests a little way. 17. the Lord said, Shall I hide—the chief stranger—no other than the Lord disclosed to Abraham the awful doom about to be inflicted on Sodom and the cities of the plain for their enormous wickedness. 20. I will go down and see—language used after the manner of men. These cities were to be made ensamples to all future ages of God's severity; and therefore ample proof given that the judgment was neither rash nor excessive (Ez. 18. 23; Jer. 18. 7.).

23-33. ABRAHAM'S INTERCESSION. Abraham drew near, &c.—the scene described is full of interest and instruction—showing in an unmistakeable manner the efficacy of prayer and intercession. (See also Pro. 15. 8; Ja. 5. 16.) Abraham reasoned justly as to the rectitude of the divine procedure (Ro. 3. 5, 6.), and many guilty cities and nations have been spared on account of God's people (Matth. 5. 13; Matth. 24. 22.). 33. the Lord left communing, and Abraham returned to his place—why did Abraham cease to carry his intercessions farther? Either because he fondly thought that he was now sure of the cities being preserved (Luke 13.9.), or because the Lord restrained his mind from farther intercession (Jer. 7. 16; 11. 14.). But there were not ten "righteous persons." There was only one, and he might without injustice have perished in the general overthrow (Eccl. 9. 2.). But a difference is sometimes made, and on this occasion the grace of God was manifested in a signal manner for the sake of Abraham. What a blessing to be connected with a saint of God!

CHAPTER XIX.

Ver. 1-38. LOT'S ENTERTAINMENT. There came two angels—most probably two of those that had been with Abraham commissioned to execute the divine judgment against Sodom. Lot sat in the gate—In eastern cities it is the market, the seat of justice, of social intercourse and amusement, especially a favourite lounge in the evenings, the arched roof affording a pleasant shade. turn in... tarry all night—offer of the same generous hospitalities as described in the preceding chapter, and which are still spontaneously practised in the small towns. Nay; but we will abide in the street all night—Where there are no inns, and no acquaintance, it is not uncommon for travellers to sleep in the street wrapped up in their cloaks. 4. the house—On removing to the plain, Lot intended at first to live in his tent apart from the people. But he was gradually drawn in, dwelt in the city, and he and his family were connected with the citizens by marriage ties. 4. men of Sodom compassed the house—appalling proofs are here given of their wickedness. It is evident that evil communications had corrupted good manners, otherwise Lot would never have acted as he did. 12-14. Hast thou here any besides?.... we will destroy this place—apostolic authority has declared Lot was "a righteous man" (2 Pe. 2. 8), at bottom good, though he contented himself with lamenting the sins that he saw, instead of acting on his own convictions, and withdrawing himself and family from such a sink of corruption. But favour was shewn him: and even his bad relatives had, for his sake, an offer of deliverance, which was ridiculed and spurned (2 Pe. 3. 4.). 15-23. The kindly interest the angels took in the preservation of Lot is beautifully displayed. But he "lingered." Was it from sorrow at the prospect of losing all his property, the acquisition of many years? or was it that his benevolent heart was paralysed by thoughts of the awful crisis? This is the charitable way of accounting for a delay that must have been fatal but for the friendly violence and urgency of the angel. 19. Lot said, Oh! not so my lord ... I cannot escape to the mountain—what a strange want of faith and fortitude, as if He who had interfered for his rescue would not have protected him in the mountain solitude. 21. See, I have accepted thee concerning this also—his request was granted him, the prayer of faith availed, and to convince him, from his own experience, that it would have been best and safest at once to follow implicitly the divine directions. 22. Haste . . for I cannot do any thing till thou be come thither—The ruin of Sodom was suspended till he was secure. What care does God take of His people Re. 7. 3.)—what a proof of the love which God bore to a good though weak man! 24. Then the Lord rained brimstone and fire from heaven—God, in accomplishing His purposes, acts immediately or mediately through the agency of means; and there are strong grounds for believing that it was in the latter way he effected the overthrow of the cities of the plain—that it was, in fact, by a volcanic eruption. The raining down of fire and brimstone from heaven is perfectly accordant with this idea, since those very substances being raised into the air by the force of the volcano, would fall in a fiery shower on the surrounding region. This view seems countenanced by Job. Whether it was miraculously produced, or the natural operation employed by God, it is not of much consequence to determine: it was a divine judgment, foretold and designed for the punishment of those who were sinners exceedingly. 25. Lot was accompanied by his wife and two daughters. But whether it was from irresistible curiosity or perturbation of feeling, or she was about to return to save something, his wife lingered, and while thus disobeying the parting counsel "to look not back, nor stay in all the plain,"

17 And God heard the voice of the lad; and the angel of God called to Hagar out of heaven, and said unto her, What aileth thee, Hagar? fear not; for God hath heard the voice of the lad where he is.

18 Arise, lift up the lad, and hold him in thine hand; for I will make him a great nation.

19 And God opened her eyes, and she saw a well of water; and she went and filled the bottle with water, and gave the lad drink.

20 And God was with the lad; and he grew, and dwelt in the wilderness, and became an archer.

21 And he dwelt in the wilderness of Paran: and his mother took him a wife out of the land of Egypt.

22 ¶ And it came to pass at that time, that Abimelech and Phichol the chief captain of his host spake unto Abraham, saying, God is with thee in all that thou doest:

23 Now therefore swear unto me here by God, that thou wilt not deal falsely with me, nor with my son, nor with my son's son: but according to the kindness that I have done unto thee, thou shalt do unto me, and to the land wherein thou hast sojourned.

24 And Abraham said, I will swear.

25 And Abraham reproved Abimelech because of a well of water, which Abimelech's servants had violently taken away.

26 And Abimelech said, I wot not who hath done this thing; neither didst thou tell me, neither yet heard I of it, but to-day.

27 And Abraham took sheep and oxen, and gave them unto Abimelech; and both of them made a covenant.

28 And Abraham set seven ewe lambs of the flock by themselves.

29 And Abimelech said unto Abraham, What mean these seven ewe lambs which thou hast set by themselves?

30 And he said, For these seven ewe lambs shalt thou take of my hand, that they may be a witness unto me, that I have digged this well.

31 Wherefore he called that place Beer-sheba; because there they sware both of them.

32 Thus they made a covenant at Beer-sheba: then Abimelech rose up, and Phichol the chief captain of his host, and they returned into the land of the Philistines.

33 ¶ And Abraham planted a grove in Beer-sheba, and called there on the name of the LORD, the everlasting God.

34 And Abraham sojourned in the Philistines' land many days.

CHAPTER XXII.

1 *Abraham, offering Isaac, 11 is stayed by the Angel: 15 he is blessed again. 20 Generation of Nahor unto Rebekah.*

AND it came to pass after these things that God did tempt Abraham, and said unto him, Abraham: and he said, Behold, here I am.

2 And he said, Take now thy son, thine only son Isaac, whom thou lovest, and get thee into the land of Moriah; and offer him there for a burnt offering upon one of the mountains which I will tell thee of.

3 And Abraham rose up early in the morning, and saddled his ass, and took two of his young men with him, and Isaac his son, and clave the wood for the burnt offering, and rose up, and went unto the place of which God had told him.

4 Then on the third day Abraham lifted up his eyes, and saw the place afar off.

5 And Abraham said unto his young men, Abide ye here with the ass; and I and the lad will go yonder and worship, and come again to you.

6 And Abraham took the wood of the burnt offering, and laid it upon Isaac his son; and he took the fire in his hand, and a knife; and they went both of them together.

7 And Isaac spake unto Abraham his father, and said, My father: and he said, Here am I, my son. And he said, Behold the fire and the wood; but where is the lamb for a burnt offering?

8 And Abraham said, My son, God will provide himself a lamb for a burnt offering: so they went both of them together.

9 And they came to the place which God had told him of; and Abraham built an altar there, and laid the wood in order, and bound Isaac his son, and laid him on the altar upon the wood.

10 And Abraham stretched forth his hand, and took the knife to slay his son.

11 And the angel of the LORD called unto him out of heaven, and said, Abraham, Abraham: and he said, Here am I.

12 And he said, Lay not thine hand upon the lad, neither do thou any thing unto him: for now I know that thou fearest God, seeing thou hast not withheld thy son, thine only son, from me.

13 And Abraham lifted up his eyes, and looked, and behold behind him a ram caught in a thicket by his horns: and Abraham went and took the ram, and offered him up for a burnt offering in the stead of his son.

14 And Abraham called the name of that place Jehovah-jireh: as it is said to this day, In the mount of the LORD it shall be seen.

15 And the angel of the LORD called unto Abraham out of heaven the second time,

16 And said, By myself have I sworn, saith the LORD: for because thou hast done this thing, and hast not withheld thy son, thine only son;

17 That in blessing I will bless thee, and in multiplying I will multiply thy seed as the stars of the heaven, and as the sand which is upon the sea shore; and thy seed shall possess the gate of his enemies;

18 And in thy seed shall all the nations of the earth be blessed; because thou hast obeyed my voice.

19 So Abraham returned unto his young men, and they rose up and went together to Beer-sheba; and Abraham dwelt at Beer-sheba.

20 ¶ And it came to pass after these things, that it was told Abraham, saying, Behold, Milcah, she hath also born children unto thy brother Nahor;

21 Huz his first-born, and Buz his brother, and Kemuel the father of Aram,

22 And Chesed, and Hazo, and Pildash, and Jidlaph, and Bethuel.

23 And Bethuel begat Rebekah: these eight Milcah did bear to Nahor, Abraham's brother.

24 And his concubine, whose name was Reumah, she bare also Tebah, and Gaham, and Thahash, and Maachah.

the torrent of liquid lava enveloped her, so that she became the victim of her supine indolence or sinful rashness. 27. Abraham gat up early in the morning, &c.—Abraham was at this time in Mamre, near Hebron, and a traveller last year verified the truth of this passage. 'From the height which overlooks Hebron, where the patriarch stood, the observer at the present day has an extensive view spread out before him towards the Dead Sea. A cloud of smoke rising from the plain would be visible to a person at Hebron now, and could have been, therefore, to Abraham as he looked toward Sodom on the morning of its destruction by God.' [HACK.] It must have been an awful sight, and is frequently alluded to in Scripture Deu. 29. 23; Is. 13, 19; Jude 7.'. 'The plain which is now covered by the Salt or Dead Sea shews in the great difference of level between the bottoms of the northern and southern ends of the lake—the latter being 13 feet and the former 1,300—that the southern end was of recent formation, and submerged at the time of the fall of the cities.' [LYNCH.] 29. when God destroyed the cities, &c.—This is most welcome and instructive after so painful a narrative. It shews if God is a "consuming fire" to the wicked, He is the friend of the righteous. He "remembered" the intercessions of Abraham, and what confidence should not this give us that He will remember the intercessions of a greater than Abraham in our behalf.

CHAPTER XX.

Ver. 1-18. ABRAHAM'S DENIAL OF HIS WIFE. Journeyed from thence and dwelt between Kedesh and Shur—Leaving the encampment, he migrated to the southern border of Canaan. In the neighbourhood of Gerar was a very rich and well-watered pasture land. 2. Abraham said of Sarah, She is my sister—fear of the people amongst whom he was tempted him to equivocate. His conduct was highly culpable. It was deceit deliberate and premeditated—there was no sudden pressure upon him—it was the second offence of the kind—it was a distrust of God every way surprising, and it was calculated to produce injurious effects on the heathen around. Its mischievous tendency was not long in being developed. Abimelech (father-king) sent and took Sarah—to be one of his wives. In the exercise of a privilege claimed by Eastern sovereigns, already explained, ch. 12. 19. 3-8. But God came to Abimelech in a dream—in early times a dream was often made the medium of communicating important truths; and this method was adopted for the preservation of Sarah. 9. then Abimelech called Abraham and said, What hast thou done?—in what a humiliating plight does the patriarch now appear—he, a servant of the true God, rebuked by a heathen prince. Who would not rather be in the place of Abimelech than of the honoured but sadly offending patriarch! What a dignified attitude is that of the king—calmly and justly reproving the sin of the prophet, but respecting his person, and heaping coals of fire on his head by the liberal presents made to him. 10, 11. Abraham said, I thought surely the fear of God is not—from the horrible vices of Sodom he seems to have taken up the impression, that all other cities of Canaan were equally corrupt. There might have been few or none who feared God, but what a sad thing when men of the world show a higher sense of honour and a greater abhorrence of crimes than a true worshipper! 12. yet indeed she is my sister—See on ch. 11. 31. What a poor defence Abraham made. The statement ab solved him from the charge of direct and absolute falsehood, but he had told a moral untruth, because there was an intention to deceive, cf. ch. 12. 11-13. "Honesty is always the best policy." Abraham's life would have been as well protected without the fraud as with it: and what shame to himself—what distrust of God—what dishonour to religion might have been prevented! "Let us speak truth every man to his neighbour."

CHAPTER XXI.

Ver. 1-13. BIRTH OF ISAAC. The Lord visited Sarah—The language of the historian seems designedly chosen to magnify the power of God as well as his faithfulness to his promise. It was God's grace that brought about that event, as well as the raising of spiritual children to Abraham, of which the birth of this son was typical, [CAL.] 3, 4. Abraham called ... circumcised—God was acknowledged in the name which, by divine command, was given for a memorial (cf. ch. 17. 19., and also in the dedication of the child by administering the seal of the covenant cf. 17. 10-12.). 8. the child grew, &c.—children are suckled longer in the East than in Europe—boys usually for two or three years. Abraham made a great feast, &c.—in Eastern countries this is always a season of domestic festivity, and the newly-weaned child is formally brought, in presence of the assembled relatives and friends, to partake of some simple viands. Isaac, attired in the symbolic robe—the badge of birthright—was then admitted heir of the tribe. [ROS.] 9. Sarah saw, &c.—Ishmael was aware of the great change in his prospects, and under the impulse of irritated or resentful feelings, in which he was probably joined by his mother, treated the young heir with derision and probably some violence (Gal. 4, 20.). 10. cast out this bondwoman—nothing but the expulsion of both could now preserve harmony in the household. Abraham's perplexity was relieved by an announcement of the divine will, which in every thing, however painful to flesh and blood, all who fear God and are walking in his ways will, like him, promptly obey. This story, as the Apostle tells us, is "an allegory," and the "persecution" by the son of the *Egyptian* was the commencement of the four hundred years' affliction of Abraham's seed by the *Egyptians*. in all that Sarah hath said—it is called the Scripture (Gal. 4, 30.). 13. also of the son of the bondwoman, &c.—thus Providence overruled a family brawl to give rise to two great and extraordinary peoples.

14. EXPULSION OF ISHMAEL. Abraham rose up early, &c.—early, that the wanderers might reach an asylum before noon. Bread includes all sorts of victuals—bottle, a leathern vessel, formed of the entire skin of a lamb or kid sewed up, with the legs for handles, usually carried over the shoulder. Ishmael was a lad of seventeen years, and it is quite customary for Arab chiefs to send out their sons at such an age to do for themselves: often with nothing but a few days' provisions in a bag. 14. wandered in the wilderness, &c.—in the southern border of Palestine, but out of the common direction, a wide-extending desert, where they missed the track. 15. the

CHAPTER XXIII.

1 Sarah's age and death. 3 The purchase of Machpelah. 19 where Sarah was buried.

AND Sarah was an hundred and seven and twenty years old: *these were* the years of the life of Sarah.

2 And Sarah died in Kirjath-arba; the same *is* Hebron in the land of Canaan: and Abraham came *a* to mourn for Sarah, and to weep for her.

3 ¶ And Abraham stood up from before his dead, and spake unto the sons of Heth, saying,

4 I *am* *b* a stranger and a sojourner with you: give me a possession of *c* a burying-place with you, that I may bury my dead out of my sight.

5 And the children of Heth answered Abraham, saying unto him,

6 Hear us, my lord: Thou *art* ¹ a mighty *d* prince among us: in the choice of our sepulchres bury thy dead; none of us shall withhold from thee his sepulchre, but that thou mayest bury thy dead.

7 And Abraham stood up, and *e* bowed himself to the people of the land, *even* to the children of Heth.

8 And he communed with them, saying, If it be your mind that I should bury my dead out of my sight, hear me, and entreat for me to Ephron the son of Zohar,

9 That he may give me the cave of Machpelah, which he hath, which *is* in the end of his field; for ² as much money as it is worth he shall give it me for a possession of a burying-place amongst you.

10 And Ephron dwelt among the children of Heth. And Ephron the Hittite answered Abraham in the ³ audience of the children of Heth, *even* of all that went in at *f* the gate of his city, saying,

11 *g* Nay, my lord, hear me: the field give I thee, and the cave that *is* therein, I give it thee; in the presence of the sons of my people give I it thee: bury thy dead.

12 And Abraham bowed down himself before the people of the land.

13 And he spake unto Ephron in the audience of the people of the land, saying, But if thou *wilt give it*, I pray thee, hear me: *h* I will give thee money for the field; take *it* of me, and I will bury my dead there.

14 And Ephron answered Abraham, saying unto him,

15 My lord, hearken unto me: the land *is worth* four hundred *i* shekels of silver; what *is* that betwixt me and thee? bury therefore thy dead.

16 And Abraham hearkened unto Ephron; and Abraham *j* weighed to Ephron the silver, which he had named in the audience of the sons of Heth, four hundred shekels of silver, current *money* with the merchant.

17 And *k* the field of Ephron, which *was* in Machpelah, which *was* before Mamre, the field, and the cave which *was* therein, and all the trees that *were* in the field, that *were* in all the borders round about, were made sure

18 Unto Abraham for a possession in the presence of the children of Heth, before all that went in at the gate of his city.

19 And after this, *l* Abraham buried Sarah his wife in the cave of the field of Machpelah before Mamre: the same *is* Hebron in the land of Canaan.

20 And the field, and the cave that *is* therein, were *m* made sure unto Abraham for a possession of a burying-place by the sons of Heth.

CHAPTER XXIV.

1 Abraham sendeth his servant to get a wife for his son Isaac: 10 he obtaineth Rebekah: 62 Isaac meeteth her.

AND Abraham *a* was old, *and* ¹ well stricken in age: and the LORD had *b* blessed Abraham in all things.

2 And Abraham said *c* unto his eldest servant of his house, that *d* ruled over all that he had, *e* Put, I pray thee, thy hand under my thigh:

3 And I will make thee swear by the LORD, the God of heaven, and the God of the earth, that thou *f* shalt not take a wife unto my son of the daughters of the Canaanites, among whom I dwell:

4 But thou shalt go *g* unto my country, and to my kindred, and take a wife unto my son Isaac.

5 And the servant said unto him, Peradventure the woman will not be willing to follow me unto this land: must I needs bring thy son again unto the land from whence thou camest?

6 And Abraham said unto him, *h* Beware thou that thou bring not my son thither again.

7 The LORD God of heaven, which *i* took me from my father's house, and from the land of my kindred, and which spake unto me, and that sware unto me, saying, *j* Unto thy seed will I give this land; he shall send *k* his angel before thee, and thou shalt take a wife unto my son from thence.

8 And if the woman will not be willing to follow thee, then thou shalt *l* be clear from this my oath: only bring not my son thither again.

9 And the servant put his hand under the thigh of Abraham his master, and sware to him concerning that matter.

10 ¶ And the servant took ten camels of the camels of his master, and departed; ² for all the goods of his master *were* in his hand: and he arose, and went to Mesopotamia, unto the *m* city of Nahor.

11 And he made his camels to kneel down without the city by a well of water at the time of the evening, *even* the time ³ that women *n* go out to draw *water*.

12 And he said, *o* O LORD God of my master Abraham, *p* I pray thee, send me good speed this day, and show kindness unto my master Abraham.

13 Behold, I stand *here* by the well of water; and the daughters of the men of the city come out to draw water:

14 And let it come to pass, that the damsel to whom I shall say, Let down thy pitcher, I pray thee, that I may drink; and she shall say, Drink, and I will give thy camels drink also: *let the same be* she *q that* thou hast appointed for thy servant Isaac; and ⁴ thereby shall I know that thou hast showed kindness unto my master.

15 ¶ And it came to pass, *s* before he had done speaking, that, behold, Rebekah came out, who was born to Bethuel, son of *t* Milcah, the wife of Nahor, Abraham's brother, with her pitcher upon her shoulder.

16 And the damsel *was* ⁵ very ⁴ fair to look upon, a virgin, neither had any man known her: and she went down to the well, and filled her pitcher, and came up.

water, &c.—Ishmael sunk exhausted from fatigue and thirst—his mother laid his head under one of the bushes to smell the damp, while she herself, unable to witness his distress, sat down at a little distance in hopeless sorrow. 17-19. God opened her eyes—had she forgotten the promise? (ch. 16. 11.) Whether she looked to God or not, He regarded her and directed her to a fountain close beside her, but probably hid amid brushwood, by the waters of which her almost expiring son was revived. 20, 21. God was with the lad, &c.—Paran, *i. e.*, Arabia, where his posterity have ever dwelt (cf. 16. 12; also Isa. 48. 19; 1 Pe. 1. 25.). his mother took him a wife—on a father's death, the mother looks out for a wife for her son, however young; and as Ishmael was now virtually deprived of his father, his mother set about forming a marriage connection for him, it would seem, amongst her relatives. 22-24. COVENANT. Abimelech and Phichol —here a proof of the promise (ch. 12. 2.) being fulfilled, in a native prince wishing to form a solemn league with Abraham. The proposal was reasonable and agreed to. 25-31. Abraham reproved . . . because of a well—wells were of great importance to a pastoral chief, and on the successful operation of sinking a new one, the owner was solemnly infeft in person. If, however, they were allowed to get out of repair, the restorer acquired a right to them. In unoccupied lands the possession of wells gave a right of property in the land, and dread of this had caused the offence for which Abraham reproved Abimelech. Some describe four, others five wells in Beer-sheba. 33. Abraham planted a grove —*Heb.* of tamarisks, in which sacrificial worship was offered, as in a roofless temple, Abraha n sojourned, &c.—a picture of pastoral and an emblem of Christian life.

CHAPTER XXII.

Ver. 1-13. OFFERING ISAAC. God did tempt Abraham — not incite to sin (Ja. 1. 13.) but try, prove—give occasion for the development of his faith (1 Pe. 1. 7.). called Abraham, and he said, &c.—ready at a moment's warning for God's service. 2. Take now thy son, &c.—Every circumstance mentioned was calculated to give a deeper stab to the parental bosom. To lose his only son, and by an act of his own hand, too !—what a host of conflicting feelings must the order have raised; but he heard and obeyed without a murmur (Gal. 1. 16; L. 14. 26.). 3. Abraham rose early, &c.—That there might be no appearance of delay or reluctance on his part, he made every preparation for the sacrifice before setting out—the materials, the knife, the servants to convey them—from Beer-sheba to Moriah, being a journey of two days; he had the painful secret pent up in his bosom all that time: and as so distant a place must have been chosen for some important reason, it is generally thought that "the place of which God had told him" was one of the hills of Jerusalem, on which the Great Sacrifice was afterwards offered. 4. on the third day Abraham lifted up his eyes, &c.—Leaving the servants at the foot, the father and son ascended the hill—the one bearing the knife; the other, the wood for consuming the sacrifice. But there was no victim; and to the question so naturally put by Isaac, Abraham contented himself with replying, "My son, God will provide himself a lamb for a burnt-offering." It has been supposed, that the design of this extraordinary transaction was to show him, by action instead of words, the way in which all the families of the earth should be blessed; and that in his answer to Isaac, he anticipated some substitution. It is more likely that his words were spoken evasively to his son —in ignorance of the issue—yet in unbounded confidence that that son, though sacrificed, would, in some miraculous way, be restored (Heb. 11. 19.). 9. Abraham built an altar, &c.—Had not the patriarch been sustained by the full consciousness of acting in obedience to God's will, the effort must have been too great for human endurance; and had not Isaac—then upwards of twenty years of age displayed equal faith in submitting—this great trial could not have been gone through. 11-12. The Angel called, &c. —The sacrifice was virtually offered—the intention, the purpose to do it, was shown in all sincerity and fulness. The Omniscient witness likewise declared his acceptance in the highest terms of approval; and the apostle speaks of it as actually made (Heb. 11. 17; Ja. 2. 21.). 13. Behold a ram, &c.— No method was more admirably calculated to give the patriarch a distinct idea of the purpose of grace, than this scenic representation: and hence our Lord's allusion to it (Jo. 8. 56.).

CHAPTER XXIII.

Ver. 1-2. AGE AND DEATH OF SARAH.— Sarah was 120 years old, &c.—the only woman in Scripture whose age, death, and burial are mentioned, probably to do honour to the venerable mother of the Hebrew people. Abraham came to mourn for Sarah, &c.—he came from his own tent to take his station at the door of Sarah's. The "mourning" describes his conformity to the customary usage of sitting on the ground for a time; while the "weeping" indicates the natural outburst of his sorrow. 3-18. PURCHASE OF A BURYING PLACE. Abraham stood up, &c.—Eastern people are always provided with family burying-places; but Abraham's life of faith—his pilgrim state—had prevented him acquiring even so small a possession A. 7. 5.). spake unto the sons of Heth—he bespoke their kind offices to aid him in obtaining possession of a cave that belonged to Ephron—a wealthy neighbour. 9. Machpelah — the *double* cave. 10. Ephron dwelt—*lit.* was "sitting" among the children of Heth in the gate of the city where all business was transacted. But, though a chief man among them, he was probably unknown to Abraham. 11-15. Ephron answered, Nay, my lord, &c. — Here is a great show of generosity—but it was only a show; for while Abraham wanted only the cave— he joins "the field and the cave;" and though he offered them both as free gifts—he, of course, expected some costly presents in return—with which, he would not have been easily satisfied. The patriarch, knowing this, wished to make a purchase, and asked the terms. 15. The land is worth 400 shekels, &c.—as if Ephron had said, Since you wish to know the value of the property, it is so and so; but that is a trifle, which you may pay or not as it suits you. They spoke in the common forms of Arab civility, and this indifference was mere affectation. 16. Abraham weighed the silver—The money, amount-

17 And the servant ran to meet her, and said, ⁿ Let me, I pray thee, drink a little water of thy pitcher.

18 And she said, ʷ Drink, my lord: and she hasted, and let down her pitcher upon her hand, and gave him drink.

19 And when she had done giving him drink, she said, I will draw *water* for thy camels also, until they have done drinking.

20 And she hasted, and emptied her pitcher into the trough, and ran again unto the well to draw *water*, and drew for all his camels.

21 And the man ˣ wondering at her held his peace, to wit whether the LORD had made his journey prosperous or not.

22 And it came to pass, as the camels had done drinking, that the man took a golden ⁵ earring ʸ of half a shekel weight, and two bracelets for her hands of ten *shekels* weight of gold;

23 And said, Whose daughter *art* thou? tell me, I pray thee: is there room *in* thy father's house for us to lodge in?

24 And she said unto him, I *am* the daughter of Bethuel the son of Milcah, which she bare unto Nahor.

25 She said moreover unto him, ᶻ We have both straw and provender enough, and room to lodge in.

26 And the man ᵃ bowed down his head, and worshipped the LORD.

27 And he said, ᵇ Blessed *be* the LORD God of my master Abraham, who hath not left destitute my master of ᶜ his mercy and his truth: I *being* in the way, ᵈ the LORD led me to the house of my master's brethren.

28 And the damsel ran, and told *them of* her mother's house these things.

29 ¶ And Rebekah had a brother, and his name *was* ᵉ Laban: and Laban ran out unto the man, unto the well.

30 And it came to pass, when he saw the earring, and bracelets upon his sister's hands, and when he heard the words of Rebekah his sister, saying, Thus spake the man unto me, that he came unto the man; and, behold, he stood by the camels at the well.

31 And he said, Come in, ᶠ thou blessed of the LORD; wherefore standest thou without? for I have prepared the house, and room for the camels.

32 And the man came into the house: and he ungirded his camels, and ᵍ gave straw and provender for the camels, and water to wash his feet, and the men's feet that *were* with him.

33 And there was set *meat* before him to eat: but he said, ʰ I will not eat, until I have told mine errand. And he said, Speak on.

34 And he said, I *am* Abraham's servant.

35 And the LORD hath ⁱ blessed my master greatly; and he is become great: and he hath given him ʲ flocks, and herds, and silver, and gold, and men-servants, and maid-servants, and camels, and asses.

36 And Sarah my master's wife ᵏ bare a son to my master when she was old: and ˡ unto him hath he given all that he hath.

37 And my master ᵐ made me swear, saying, Thou shalt not take a wife to my son of the daughters of the Canaanites, in whose land I dwell:

38 But thou shalt go unto my father's house, and to my kindred, and take a wife unto my son.

B. C. 1857.

CHAP. 24.
ᵛ Jn. 4, 9.
ʷ 1 Pe. 3, 8.
1 Pe. 4. 9.
ˣ Lu. 2, 19, 51.
5 or, jewel for the forehead.
ʸ Ex. 32, 2, 3.
Isa. 3, 19, 20.
1 Pe. 3, 3.
ᶻ 1 Po. 4, 9.
ᵃ ver. 52.
Ex. 4, 31.
ᵇ Ex. 18, 10.
Ruth 4, 14.
1 Sam. 25, 32.
2 Sam. 18, 28.
Luke 1, 68.
ᶜ ch. 32, 10.
Ps. 98, 3.
ᵈ ver. 48.
Prov. 3, 6.
ᵉ ch. 29, 5.
ᶠ ch. 26, 29.
Jud. 17, 2.
Ru. 3, 10.
Ps. 115, 15.
ᵍ ch. 43, 24.
Jud. 19, 21.
ʰ Job 23, 12.
John 4, 34.
Eph. 6, 5-7.
ⁱ ver. 1.
ch. 13, 2.
ʲ Job 1, 3.
ᵏ ch. 21, 2.
ˡ ch. 21, 10.
ch. 25, 5.
ᵐ ver. 3.
ⁿ ver. 7.
ᵒ ch. 5, 22-24.
ch. 17, 1.
ᵖ Ex. 23, 20.
ᵠ ver. 8.
ʳ 1 Kings 1, 30.
Acts 10, 7, 8, 22.
ˢ No. 1, 11.
Ps. 90, 17.
Ro. 1, 10.
ᵗ ver. 13.
ᵘ He. 13, 2.
ᵛ ver. 15.
ʷ 1 Sam. 1, 13.
Is. 65, 24.
ˣ Ezek. 16, 11, 12.
ʸ ver. 26.
ᶻ Ps. 32, 8.
Ps. 48, 14.
Ps. 107, 7.
Is. 48, 17.
ᵃ ch. 47, 29.
Josh. 2, 14.
ᵇ Ps. 118, 23.
Mat. 21, 42.
Mark 12, 11.
ᶜ ch. 20, 15.
ᵈ Ex. 3, 22.
Ex. 11, 2.
Ex. 12, 35.
6 vessels.
ᵉ 2 Ch. 21, 3.
Ezra 1, 6.
ᶠ vers. 55, 59.
7 or, a full year, or, ten months.
ᵍ ver. 40.

39 And I said unto my master, Peradventure the woman will not follow me.

40 And ⁿ he said unto me, The LORD, before whom ᵒ I walk, will send his ᵖ angel with thee, and prosper thy way; and thou shalt take a wife for my son of my kindred, and of my father's house:

41 ᵠ Then shalt thou be clear from *this* my oath, when thou comest to my kindred; and if they give not thee *one*, thou shalt be clear from my oath.

42 And I came this day unto the well, and said, ʳ O LORD God of my master Abraham, if now thou do ˢ prosper my way which I go:

43 ᵗ Behold, I stand by the well of water; and it shall come to pass, that when the virgin cometh forth to draw *water*, and I say to her, Give me, I pray thee, a little water of thy pitcher to drink;

44 And she say to me, ᵘ Both drink thou, and I will also draw for thy camels: *let* the same *be* the woman whom the LORD hath appointed out for my master's son.

45 And ᵛ before I had done ʷ speaking in mine heart, behold, Rebekah came forth with her pitcher on her shoulder; and she went down unto the well, and drew *water:* and I said unto her, Let me drink, I pray thee.

46 And she made haste, and let down her pitcher from her *shoulder*, and said, Drink, and I will give thy camels drink also: so I drank, and she made the camels drink also.

47 And I asked her, and said, Whose daughter *art* thou? And she said, The daughter of Bethuel, Nahor's son, whom Milcah bare unto him: and I put the ˣ earring upon her face, and the bracelets upon her hands.

48 And I ʸ bowed down my head, and worshipped the LORD, and blessed the LORD God of my master Abraham, which had ᶻ led me in the right way to take my master's brother's daughter unto his son.

49 And now if ye will ᵃ deal kindly and truly with my master, tell me: and if not, tell me; that I may turn to the right hand, or to the left.

50 Then Laban and Bethuel answered and said, ᵇ The thing proceedeth from the LORD: we cannot speak unto thee bad or good.

51 Behold, Rebekah is ᶜ before thee, take her, and go, and let her be thy master's son's wife, as the LORD hath spoken.

52 And it came to pass, that, when Abraham's servant heard their words, he worshipped the LORD, *bowing himself* to the earth.

53 And the servant brought forth ᵈ jewels of silver, and ⁶ jewels of gold, and raiment, and gave *them* to Rebekah: he gave also to her brother and to her mother ᵉ precious things.

54 And they did eat and drink, he and the men that *were* with him, and tarried all night: and they rose up in the morning; and he said, ᶠ Send me away unto my master.

55 And her brother and her mother said, Let the damsel abide with us ⁷ *a few days*, at the least ten; after that she shall go.

56 And he said unto them, Hinder me not, seeing the LORD hath ᵍ prospered my way; send me away that I may go to my master.

57 And they said, We will call the damsel, and enquire at her mouth.

58 And they called Rebekah, and said unto

ing to L 50, was paid in presence of the assembled witnesses; and it was weighed. The practice of weighing money, which is often in lumps or rings, stamped each with their weight, is still common in many parts of the East; and every merchant at the gates or the bazaar has his scales at his girdle. 19. Abraham buried Sarah—Thus he got possession of Machpelah, and deposited the remains of his lamented partner in a family vault, which was the only spot of ground he owned.

CHAPTER XXIV.
Ver. 1-9. A MARRIAGE COMMISSION. And Abraham was old... take a wife—His anxiety to see his son married was natural to his position as a pastoral chief interested in preserving the honour of his tribe, and still more as a patriarch who had regard to the divine promise of a numerous posterity. 3. thou shalt not take a wife, &c.—Among the pastoral tribes the matrimonial arrangements are made by the parents, and a youth must marry, not among strangers, but in his own tribe—custom giving him a claim, which is seldom or never resisted, to the hand of his first cousin. But Abraham had a far higher motive—a fear least if his son married into a Canaanitish family he might be gradually led away from the true God. said unto his eldest servant—Abraham being too old, and as the heir of the promise not being at liberty to make even a temporary visit to his native land, was obliged to entrust this delicate mission to Eliezer, whom, although putting entire confidence in him, he on this occasion bound by a solemn oath. A pastoral chief in the present day would take the same plan if he could not go himself.

10-63. THE JOURNEY. 10. The servant took ten camels, &c.—So great an equipage was to give the embassy an appearance worthy of the rank and wealth of Abraham; to carry provisions; to bear the marriage presents, which as usual would be distributed over several beasts; besides one or two spare camels in case of emergency. went to Mesopotamia, &c. —A stranger in those regions, who wishes to obtain information, stations himself at one of the wells in the neighbourhood of a town, and he is sure to learn all the news of the place from the women who frequent them every morning and evening. Eliezer followed this course, and letting his camels rest, he waited till the evening time of water-drawing. 12. And he said, O Lord God of my master—The servant appears worthy of the master he served. He resolves to follow the leading of Providence; and while he shews good sense in the tokens he fixes upon of ascertaining the temper and character of the future bride, never doubts but that in such a case God will direct him. 15-21. Before he had done speaking—as he anticipated, a young woman unveiled, as in pastoral regions, appeared with her pitcher on her shoulder. Her comely appearance, her affable manners, her obliging courtesy in going down the steps to fetch water not only to him, but to pour it into the trough for his camels, afforded him the most agreeable surprise. She was the very person his imagination had pictured, and he proceeded to reward her civility. 22. the man took a golden earring, &c.—The ring was not for the ear, but the nose, and the armlets such as young women in Syria and Arabia still appear daily at wells decked in. They are worn from the elbow to the wrist, commonly made of silver, copper, brass, or horn. 23-31. He said, Whose daughter art thou?—After telling her name and family, the kindhearted damsel hastened home to give notice of a stranger's arrival. 28. She told them of her mother's house—the female apartments. This family were in an advanced stage of pastoral life, dwelling in a settled place and a fixed habitation. 30-31. Rebekah... brother ... Laban ran out—from what we know of his character, there is reason to believe that the sight of the dazzling presents increased both his haste and his invitation. 32. The man came into the house—What a beautiful picture of piety, fidelity, and disinterestedness in a servant! He declined all attention to his own comforts till he had told his name and his errand. 50. Then Laban and Bethuel answered—The brothers conduct all the marriage negotiations, their father being probably dead, and without consulting their sister. Their language seems to indicate they were worshippers of the true God. 53. Jewels of silver and gold—These are the usual articles, with money, that form a woman's dowry among the pastoral tribes. Rebekah was betrothed, and accompanied the servant to Canaan. 64. she alighted from her camel—If Isaac was walking it would have been most unmannerly for her to have continued seated; an inferior, if riding, always alight in presence of a person of rank, no exception being made for women. 65. she took a veil and covered herself—The veil is an essential part of female dress. In country places it is often thrown aside, but on the appearance of a stranger it is drawn over the face, so as to conceal all but the eyes. In a bride it was a token of her reverence and subjection to her husband. 67. Brought her into his mother's tent—thus establishing her at once in the rights and honours of a wife before he had seen her features. Disappointments often take place, but when Isaac saw his wife "he loved her."

CHAPTER XXV.
Ver. 1-6. SONS OF ABRAHAM. Abraham took a wife—rather, *had taken*; for Keturah is called Abraham's concubine, or secondary wife (1 Chron. 1. 32); and, as, from her bearing six sons to him, it is improbable that he married after Sarah's death; and also as he sent them all out to seek their own independence, during his life-time, it is clear that this marriage is related here out of its chronological order, merely to form a proper winding up of the patriarch's history. 5, 6. gave unto Isaac... unto the sons of the concubines—While the chief part of the inheritance went to Isaac—the other sons, Ishmael included, migrated to "the East country," *i. e.* Arabia—received each a portion of the patrimony, perhaps in cattle and other things; and this settlement of Abraham's must have given satisfaction, since it is still the rule followed among the pastoral tribes.

7-11. DEATH OF ABRAHAM. These are the days of Abraham—His death is here related, though he lived till Isaac and Esau were fifteen years, just one hundred years after coming to Canaan, "the father of the faithful," "the friend of God," died; and even in his death, the promises were fulfilled (ct. 15. 15.). We might have wished some memorials of his death-bed experience; but the Spirit of God has withheld them—nor was it necessary; for (see M. 7 16., from earth he passed

her, Wilt thou go with this man? And she said, I will go.

59 And they sent away Rebekah their sister, and her nurse, and Abraham's servant, and his men.

60 And they blessed Rebekah, and said unto her, Thou *art* our sister, be thou *the mother of* thousands of millions, and let thy seed possess the gate of those which hate them.

61 ¶ And Rebekah arose, and her damsels, and they rode upon the camels, and followed the man; and the servant took Rebekah, and went his way.

62 And Isaac came from the way of the well Lahai-roi; for he dwelt in the south country.

63 And Isaac went out to meditate in the field at the eventide: and he lifted up his eyes, and saw, and, behold, the camels *were* coming.

64 And Rebekah lifted up her eyes, and when she saw Isaac, she lighted off the camel.

65 For she had said unto the servant, What man *is* this that walketh in the field to meet us? And the servant had said, It *is* my master: therefore she took a veil, and covered herself.

66 And the servant told Isaac all things that he had done.

67 And Isaac brought her into his mother Sarah's tent, and took Rebekah, and she became his wife; and he loved her: and Isaac was comforted after his mother's death.

CHAPTER XXV.

1 *The sons of Abraham by Keturah.* 7 *his age and death.* 12 *The generations of Ishmael.* 21 *The birth of Esau and Jacob.* 29 *Esau selleth his birthright.*

THEN again Abraham took a wife, and her name *was* Keturah.

2 And she bare him Zimran, and Jokshan, and Medan, and Midian, and Ishbak, and Shuah.

3 And Jokshan begat Sheba and Dedan. And the sons of Dedan were Asshurim, and Letushim, and Leummim.

4 And the sons of Midian; Ephah, and Epher, and Hanoch, and Abidah, and Eldaah. All these *were* the children of Keturah.

5 And Abraham gave all that he had unto Isaac.

6 But unto the sons of the concubines, which Abraham had, Abraham gave gifts, and sent them away from Isaac his son, while he yet lived, eastward, unto the east country.

7 And these *are* the days of the years of Abraham's life which he lived, an hundred threescore and fifteen years.

8 Then Abraham gave up the ghost, and died in a good old age, an old man, and full of years; and was gathered to his people.

9 And his sons Isaac and Ishmael buried him in the cave of Machpelah, in the field of Ephron the son of Zohar the Hittite, which *is* before Mamre;

10 The field which Abraham purchased of the sons of Heth: there was Abraham buried, and Sarah his wife.

11 And it came to pass after the death of Abraham, that God blessed his son Isaac: and Isaac dwelt by the well Lahai-roi.

12 ¶ Now these *are* the generations of Ishmael, Abraham's son, whom Hagar the Egyptian, Sarah's handmaid, bare unto Abraham:

13 And these *are* the names of the sons of Ishmael, by their names, according to their generations: the first-born of Ishmael, Nebajoth; and Kedar, and Adbeel, and Mibsam,

14 And Mishma, and Dumah, and Massa,

15 Hadar, and Tema, Jetur, Naphish, and Kedemah:

16 These *are* the sons of Ishmael, and these *are* their names, by their towns, and by their castles; twelve princes according to their nations.

17 And these *are* the years of the life of Ishmael, an hundred and thirty and seven years: and he gave up the ghost and died, and was gathered unto his people.

18 And they dwelt from Havilah unto Shur, that *is* before Egypt, as thou goest toward Assyria: *and* he died in the presence of all his brethren.

19 ¶ And these *are* the generations of Isaac, Abraham's son: Abraham begat Isaac:

20 And Isaac was forty years old when he took Rebekah to wife, the daughter of Bethuel the Syrian of Padan-aram, the sister to Laban the Syrian.

21 And Isaac entreated the LORD for his wife, because she *was* barren: and the LORD was entreated of him, and Rebekah his wife conceived.

22 And the children struggled together within her; and she said, If *it be* so, why am I thus? And she went to enquire of the LORD.

23 And the LORD said unto her, Two nations *are* in thy womb, and two manner of people shall be separated from thy bowels; and *the* one people shall be stronger than *the* other people; and the elder shall serve the younger.

24 And when her days to be delivered were fulfilled, behold, *there were* twins in her womb.

25 And the first came out red, all over like an hairy garment; and they called his name Esau.

26 And after that came his brother out, and his hand took hold on Esau's heel; and his name was called Jacob: and Isaac *was* threescore years old when she bare them.

27 And the boys grew: and Esau was a cunning hunter, a man of the field; and Jacob *was* a plain man, dwelling in tents.

28 And Isaac loved Esau, because he did eat of *his* venison: but Rebekah loved Jacob.

29 And Jacob sod pottage: and Esau came from the field, and he *was* faint:

30 And Esau said to Jacob, Feed me, I pray thee, with that same red *pottage;* for I *am* faint: therefore was his name called Edom.

31 And Jacob said, Sell me this day thy birthright.

32 And Esau said, Behold, I *am* at the point to die: and what profit shall this birthright do to me?

33 And Jacob said, Swear to me this day; and he sware unto him: and he sold his birthright unto Jacob.

34 Then Jacob gave Esau bread and pottage of lentiles; and he did eat and drink and rose up, and went his way: thus Esau despised *his* birthright.

into heaven (L. 16. 22.). Though dead he yet liveth (M. 22. 32.). **9, 10.** his sons buried him—Death often puts an end to strife—reconciles those who have been alienated; and brings rival relations, as in this instance — to mingle tears over a father's grave.

12-18. DESCENDANTS OF ISHMAEL. Before passing to the line of the promised seed, the historian gives a brief notice of Ishmael, to show that the promises respecting that son of Abraham, were fulfilled—first in the GREATNESS of his posterity (cf. 17. 20); and, secondly, in their independence. **18.** he died—rather, "it their lot) fell in the presence of their brethren" (cf. 16. 12.).

19-34. HISTORY OF ISAAC. These are the generations—account of the leading events in his life. **21.** entreated the Lord for his wife—Though tried in a similar way to his father, he did not follow the same crooked policy. Twenty years he continued unblessed with offspring, whose seed was to be "as the stars." But in answer to their mutual prayers (1 Pe. 3. 7.) Rebekah was divinely informed, that she was to be the mother of twins, who should be the progenitors of two independent nations; that the descendants of the younger should act the more powerful and subdue those of the other (Ro. 9. 12; 2 Chron. 21. 8.). **27.** the boys grew—from the first opposite to each other in character, manners, and habits. **28.** The parents were divided in their affection; and while the grounds, at least, of the father's partiality, were weak—the distinction made between the children led, as such conduct always does, to unhappy consequences. **29.** Jacob sod pottage—made of lentiles or small beans, which are common in Egypt and Syria. It is probable that it was made of Egyptian beans, which Jacob had procured as a dainty; for Esau was a stranger to it. It is very palatable; and to the weary hunter, faint with hunger, its odour must have been irresistibly tempting. **31.** Jacob said, Sell my thy birthright—*i. e.* the rights and privileges of the first-born—which were very important—the chief being that they were the family priests (Ex. 4. 22 ; and had a double portion of the inheritance Deut. 21. 17.). **32.** Esau said, I am at the point to die—*i. e.* I am running daily risk of my life; and of what use will the birth-right be to me: so he despised or cared little about it, in comparison of gratifying his appetite—he threw away his religious privileges for a trifle; and thence he is styled—"a profane person" (He. 12. 10; also Job. 31. 7, 16; 6. 13; Phil. 3. 19. "There was never any meat, except the forbidden fruit, so dear bought, as this broth of Jacob."
[BISHOP HALL.]

CHAPTER XXVI.
Ver. 1-35. SOJOURN IN GERAR. Famine ... Isaac went unto Gerar—The pressure of famine in Canaan forced Isaac with his family and flocks to migrate into the land of the Philistines, where he was exposed to personal danger, as his father had been on account of his wife's beauty; but through the seasonable interposition of Providence he was preserved (Ps. 105. 14, 15.). **12.** Then Isaac sowed—During his sojourn in that district he farmed a piece of land, which, by the blessing of God on his skill and industry, was very productive (Isa. 65. 13; Ps. 37. 19.), and by his plentiful returns he increased so rapidly in wealth and influence, that the Philistines, afraid or envious of his prosperity, obliged him to leave the place (Pro. 27. 4; Eccles. 4. 4.). This may receive illustration from the fact that many Syrian shepherds at this day settle for a year or two in a place, rent some ground, in the produce of which they trade with the neighbouring market, till the people, through jealousy of their growing substance refuse to renew their lease, and compel them to remove elsewhere. **15. wells ... Philistines had stopped,** &c.—the same base stratagem for annoying those against whom they have taken an umbrage is practised still by choking the wells with sand or stones, or defiling them with putrid carcases. **17. valley of Gerar**—torrent-bed or wady, a vast undulating plain, unoccupied and affording good pasture. **18-22.** Isaac digged again—the naming of wells by Abraham, and the hereditary right of his family to the property—the change of the names by the Philistines to obliterate the traces of their origin—the restoration of the names by Isaac, and the contests between the respective shepherds to the exclusive possession of the water, are circumstances that occur amongst the natives in those regions as frequently in the present day as in the time of Isaac. **26-33. then Abimelech went unto him**—as there was a lapse of ninety years between the visit of Abraham and of Isaac, the Abimelech and Phichol spoken of must have been different persons' official titles. Here is another proof of the promise (12. 2.) being fulfilled, in an overture of peace being made to him by the king of Gerar. By whatever motive the proposal was dictated—whether fear of his growing power, or regret for the bad usage they had given him, the king and two of his courtiers paid a visit to the tent of Isaac (Pro. 16. 7.). His timid and passive temper had submitted to the annoyances of his rude neighbours—but now that they wish to renew the covenant, he evinces deep feeling at their conduct, and astonishment at their assurance, or artifice, in coming near him. Being, however, of a pacific disposition, he forgave their offence, accepted their proposals, and treated them to the banquet by which the ratification of a covenant was usually crowned. **34.** Esau took to wife—if the pious feelings of Abraham recoiled from the idea of Isaac forming a matrimonial connection with a Canaanitish woman, that devout patriarch himself would be equally opposed to such a union on the part of his children ; and we may easily imagine how much his pious heart was wounded and the family peace destroyed, when his favourite but wayward son brought no less than two idolatrous wives among them—an additional proof that Esau neither desired the blessing nor dreaded the curse of God. These wives never gained the affections of his parents, and this estrangement was overruled by God for keeping the chosen family aloof from the dangers of heathen influence.

CHAPTER XXVII.
Ver. 1-27. INFIRMITY OF ISAAC. When Isaac was old and eyes dim — He was in his 137th ear; and apprehending death to be near, he prepared to make his last will—an act of the gravest importance, especially as it included the conveyance through a prophetic spirit of the patriarchal blessing. **4. make savoury meat**—perhaps to revive and strength-

CHAPTER XXVI.

1 Isaac because of famine goeth to Gerar: 23 God appeareth to him at Beer-sheba, and blesseth him. 26 Abimelech's covenant with him. 34 Esau's wives.

AND there was a famine in the land, besides *a* the first famine that was in the days of Abraham. And Isaac went unto *b* Abimelech king of the Philistines u to Gerar.

2 And the LORD appeared unto him, and said, Go not down into Egypt; dwell in the *c* land which I shall tell thee of:

3 *d* Sojourn in this land, and *e* I will be with thee, and *f* will bless thee: for unto thee, and unto thy seed, *g* I will give all these countries; and I will perform *h* the oath which I sware unto Abraham thy father;

4 And *i* I will make thy seed to multiply as the stars of heaven, and will give unto thy seed all these countries; and *j* in thy seed shall all the nations of the earth be blessed;

5 *k* Because that Abraham obeyed my voice, and kept my charge, my commandments, my statutes, and my laws.

6 ¶ And Isaac dwelt in Gerar:

7 And the men of the place asked him of his wife; and he said, *l* She is my sister: for *m* he feared to say, She is my wife; lest, said he, the men of the place should kill me for Rebekah; because she was *n* fair to look upon.

8 And it came to pass, when he had been there a long time, that Abimelech king of the Philistines looked out at a window, and saw, and, behold, Isaac *was* sporting with Rebekah his wife.

9 And Abimelech called Isaac, and said, Behold, of a surety she *is* thy wife; and how saidst thou, She *is* my sister? And Isaac said unto him, Because I said, Lest I die for her.

10 And Abimelech said, What *is* this thou hast done unto us? one of the people might lightly have lien with thy wife, and *o* thou shouldest have brought guiltiness upon us.

11 And Abimelech charged all *his* people, saying, He that *p* toucheth this man or his wife shall surely be put to death.

12 Then Isaac sowed in that land, and 1 received in the same year *q* an hundredfold: and the LORD *r* blessed him:

13 And the man *s* waxed great, and 2 went forward, and grew until he became very great:

14 For he had possession of flocks, and possession of herds, and great store of 3 servants: and the Philistines *t* envied him.

15 For all the wells *u* which his father's servants had digged in the days of Abraham his father, the Philistines had stopped them, and filled them with earth.

16 And Abimelech said unto Isaac, Go from us; for *v* thou art much mightier than we.

17 ¶ And Isaac departed thence, and pitched his tent in the valley of Gerar, and dwelt there.

18 And Isaac digged again the wells of water which they had digged in the days of Abraham his father; for the Philistines had stopped them after the death of Abraham: *w* and he called their names after the names by which his father had called them.

19 And Isaac's servants digged in the valley, and found there a well of 4 springing water.

20 And the herdmen of Gerar *x* did strive with Isaac's herdmen, saying, The water *is* ours: and he called the name of the well 5 Esek; because they strove with him.

21 And they digged another well, and strove for that also: and he called the name of it 6 Sitnah.

22 And he removed from thence, and digged another well; and for that they strove not: and he called the name of it 7 Rehoboth; and he said, For now the LORD hath made room for us, and we shall be *y* fruitful in the land.

23 And he went up from thence to Beer-sheba.

24 And the LORD appeared unto him the same night, and said, *z* I *am* the God of Abraham thy father: *a* fear not, for *b* I *am* with thee, and will bless thee, and multiply thy seed, for my servant Abraham's sake.

25 And he *c* builded an altar there, and *d* called upon the name of the LORD, and pitched his tent there: and there Isaac's servants digged a well.

26 ¶ Then Abimelech went to him from Gerar, and Ahuzzath one of his friends, and Phichol the chief captain of his army.

27 And Isaac said unto them, Wherefore come ye to me, seeing *e* ye hate me, and have sent me away from you?

28 And they said, *g* We saw certainly that the LORD *f* was with thee: and we said, Let there be now an oath betwixt us, *even* betwixt us and thee, and let us make a covenant with thee;

29 9 That thou wilt do us no hurt, as we have not touched thee, and as we have done unto thee nothing but good, and have sent thee away in peace: *thou art* now the blessed of the LORD.

30 And *h* he made them a feast, and they did eat and drink.

31 And they rose up betimes in the morning, and *i* sware one to another: and Isaac sent them away, and they departed from him in peace.

32 And it came to pass the same day, that Isaac's servants came, and told him concerning the well which they had digged, and said unto him, We have found water.

33 And he called it 10 Shebah: *j* therefore the name of the city *is* 11 Beer-sheba unto this day.

34 ¶ *k* And Esau was forty years old when he took to wife Judith the daughter of Beeri the Hittite, and Bashemath the daughter of Elon the Hittite:

35 Which *l* were 12 a grief of mind unto Isaac and to Rebekah.

CHAPTER XXVII.

1 Isaac sendeth Esau for venison. 6 Jacob, instructed by Rebekah, obtaineth the blessing: 34 Esau's complaint: 41 he threateneth Jacob's life. 42 Rebekah sendeth Jacob to Laban.

AND it came to pass, that when Isaac was old, *a* his eyes were dim, so that he could not see, he called Esau his eldest son, and said unto him, My son: and he said unto him, Behold, here am I.

2 And he said, Behold now, I am old, *b* I know not the day of my death.

3 *c* Now therefore take, I pray thee, thy weapons, thy quiver and thy bow, and go out to the field, and 1 take me *some* venison;

en him for the duty, or rather "as eating and drinking," were used on all religious occasions, he could not convey the right, till he had eaten of the meat provided for the purpose by him who was to receive the blessing, [A. CLARKE], (cf. 18. 7.). **that my soul may bless thee**—It is difficult to imagine him ignorant of the divine purpose (cf. 20. 23.). But natural affection, prevailing through age and infirmity, prompted him to entail the honours and powers of the birthright on his eldest son; and, perhaps, he was not aware of what Esau had done (25. 34.). **5-10. Rebekah spake unto Jacob**—she prized the blessing as invaluable—she knew that God intended it for the younger son; and in her anxiety to secure its being conferred on the right object—on one who cared for religion—she acted in the sincerity of faith; but in crooked policy—with unenlightened zeal; on the false principle that the end would sanctify the means. **11, 12. Jacob said, Esau . . . a hairy man**—It is remarkable that his scruples were founded not on the evil of the act; but the risk and consequences of deception. **13-17. Rebekah said, Upon me be thy curse**—His conscience being soothed by his mother—preparations were hastily made for carrying out the device; consisting, first, of a kid's flesh, which, made into a ragout, spiced with salt, onions, garlic, and lemon-juice, might easily be passed off on a blind old man, with blunted senses, as game; secondly, of pieces of goat's skin bound on his hands and neck, its soft silken hair resembling that on the cheek of a young man; thirdly, of the long white robe—the vestment of the first-born, which, transmitted from father to son, and kept in a chest among fragrant herbs and perfumed flowers, used much in the East to keep away moths—his mother provided for him. **18-27. he came unto his father**—The scheme planned by the mother was to be executed by the son in the father's bed-chamber; and it is painful to think of the deliberate falsehoods, as well as daring profanity, he resorted to. The disguise, though wanting in one thing, which had nearly upset the whole plot, succeeded in misleading Isaac; and while giving his paternal embrace, the old man was roused into a state of high satisfaction and delight. **27. the smell . . . is as of a field**—The aromatic odours of the Syrian fields and meadows, often impart a strong fragrance to the person and clothes, as has been noticed by many travellers. **28-40. THE BLESSING. God give thee of the dew**—To an Oriental mind, this phraseology implied the highest flow of prosperity. The copious fall of dew is indispensable to the fruitfulness of lands, which would be otherwise arid and sterile through the violent heat; and it abounds most in hilly regions—such as Canaan—hence called the fat land (Neh. 9. 25, 35. . **plenty of corn and wine**—Palestine was famous for vineyards, and it produced varieties of corn, viz. wheat, barley, oats, and rye. **Let people serve thee**—fulfilled in the discomfiture of the hostile tribes that opposed the Israelites in the wilderness; and in the pre-eminence and power they attained after their national establishment in the promised land. This blessing was not realised to Jacob, but to his descendants; and the temporal blessings promised, were but a shadow of those spiritual ones, which formed the grand distinction of JACOB'S POSTERITY. **30-35. Esau came in from his hunting**—scarcely had the former scene been concluded, when the fraud was discovered. The emotions of Isaac, as well as Esau, may easily be imagined—the astonishment, alarm, and sorrow of the one—the disappointment and indignation of the other. But a moment's reflection convinced the aged patriarch that the transfer of the blessing was "of the Lord," and now irrevocable. The importunities of Esau, however, overpowered him; and as the prophetic afflatus was upon the patriarch, he added what was probably as pleasing to a man of Esau's character, as the other would have been. **39, 40. Behold thy dwelling**—The first part is a promise of temporal prosperity, made in the same terms as Jacob's—the second refers to the roving life of hunting freebooters, which he and his descendants should lead. Though Esau was not personally subject to his brother, his posterity were tributary to the Israelites, till the reign of Joram—when they revolted, and established a king of their own (2 Ki. 8. 20; 2 Chr. 21. 8-10.). **41. Esau hated Jacob**—It is scarcely to be wondered at—that Esau resented the conduct of Jacob, and vowed revenge. **The days of mourning for my father**—a common Oriental phrase for the death of a parent. **42-45. words of Esau were told Rebekah**—Poor woman; she now early begins to reap the bitter fruits of her fraudulent device; she is obliged to part with her son, for whom she planned it, never, probably, seeing him again; and he felt the retributive justice of heaven fall upon him heavily in his own future family. **why should I be deprived of you both**—This refers to the law of Goelism, by which the nearest of kin would be obliged to avenge the death of Jacob upon his brother. **46. Rebekah said to Isaac**—Another pretext her cunning had to devise to obtain her husband's consent to Jacob's journey to Mesopotamia; and she succeeded by touching the aged patriarch in a tender point, afflicting to his pious heart—the proper marriage of their younger son.

CHAPTER XXVIII.

Ver. 1-19. JACOB'S DEPARTURE. 1. Isaac called Jacob—He entered fully into Rebekah's feelings—and the burden of his parting counsel to his son was, to avoid a marriage alliance with any but the Mesopotamian branch of the family. At the same time he gave him a solemn blessing—pronounced before unwittingly, now designedly, and with a cordial spirit. It is more explicitly and fully given, and Jacob was thus acknowledged "the heir of the promise." **6-9. when Esau saw, &c.**—desirous to humour his parents, and if possible get the last will revoked, he became wise when too late (see Matth. 25. 10.), and hoped by gratifying his parents in one thing to atone for all his former delinquencies. But he only made bad worse, and though he did not marry a "wife of the daughters of Canaan," he married into a family which God had rejected—it shewed a partial reformation, but no repentance, for he gave no proofs of abating his vindictive purposes against his brother, nor cherishing that pious spirit that would have gratified his father—he was like Micah (see Jud. 17. 13.). **10. Jacob went out, &c.**—his departure from his father's house was an igno-

4 And make me savoury meat, such as I love, and bring *it* to me, that I may eat; that my soul may bless thee before I die.

5 And Rebekah heard when Isaac spake to Esau his son. And Esau went to the field to hunt *for* venison, *and* to bring *it.*

6 ¶ And Rebekah spake unto Jacob her son, saying, Behold, I heard thy father speak unto Esau thy brother, saying,

7 Bring me venison, and make me savoury meat, that I may eat, and bless thee before the LORD before my death.

8 Now therefore, my son, obey my voice according to that which I command thee.

9 Go now to the flock, and fetch me from thence two good kids of the goats; and I will make them savoury meat for thy father, such as he loveth:

10 And thou shalt bring *it* to thy father, that he may eat, and that he may bless thee before his death.

11 And Jacob said to Rebekah his mother, Behold, Esau my brother *is* a hairy man, and I *am* a smooth man:

12 My father peradventure will feel me, and I shall seem to him as a deceiver; and I shall bring a curse upon me, and not a blessing.

13 And his mother said unto him, Upon me *be* thy curse, my son: only obey my voice, and go fetch me *them.*

14 And he went, and fetched, and brought *them* to his mother: and his mother made savoury meat, such as his father loved.

15 And Rebekah took goodly raiment of her eldest son Esau, which *were* with her in the house, and put them upon Jacob her younger son:

16 And she put the skins of the kids of the goats upon his hands, and upon the smooth of his neck:

17 And she gave the savoury meat and the bread, which she had prepared, into the hand of her son Jacob.

18 ¶ And he came unto his father, and said, My father: and he said, Here *am* I; who *art* thou, my son?

19 And Jacob said unto his father, I *am* Esau thy first-born; I have done according as thou badest me: arise, I pray thee, sit and eat of my venison, that thy soul may bless me.

20 And Isaac said unto his son, How *is it* that thou hast found *it* so quickly, my son? And he said, Because the LORD thy God brought *it* to me.

21 And Isaac said unto Jacob, Come near, I pray thee, that I may feel thee, my son, whether thou *be* my very son Esau or not.

22 And Jacob went near unto Isaac his father; and he felt him, and said, The voice *is* Jacob's voice, but the hands *are* the hands of Esau.

23 And he discerned him not, because his hands were hairy, as his brother Esau's hands: so he blessed him.

24 And he said, *Art* thou my very son Esau? And he said, I *am.*

25 And he said, Bring *it* near to me, and I will eat of my son's venison, that my soul may bless thee. And he brought *it* near to him, and he did eat: and he brought him wine, and he drank.

26 And his father Isaac said unto him, Come near now, and kiss me, my son.

27 And he came near, and kissed him: and he smelled the smell of his raiment, and blessed him, and said, See, the smell of my son *is* as the smell of a field which the LORD hath blessed:

28 Therefore God give thee of the dew of heaven, and the fatness of the earth, and plenty of corn and wine:

29 Let people serve thee, and nations bow down to thee: be lord over thy brethren, and let thy mother's sons bow down to thee: cursed *be* every one that curseth thee, and blessed *be* he that blesseth thee.

30 ¶ And it came to pass, as soon as Isaac had made an end of blessing Jacob, and Jacob was yet scarce gone out from the presence of Isaac his father, that Esau his brother came in from his hunting.

31 And he also had made savoury meat, and brought it unto his father, and said unto his father, Let my father arise, and eat of his son's venison, that thy soul may bless me.

32 And Isaac his father said unto him, Who *art* thou? And he said, I *am* thy son, thy first-born, Esau.

33 And Isaac trembled very exceedingly, and said, Who? where *is* he that hath taken venison, and brought *it* me, and I have eaten of all before thou camest, and have blessed him? yea, *and* he shall be blessed.

34 And when Esau heard the words of his father, he cried with a great and exceeding bitter cry, and said unto his father, Bless me, even me also, O my father!

35 And he said, Thy brother came with subtilty, and hath taken away thy blessing.

36 And he said, Is not he rightly named Jacob? for he hath supplanted me these two times: he took away my birthright; and, behold, now he hath taken away my blessing. And he said, Hast thou not reserved a blessing for me?

37 And Isaac answered and said unto Esau, Behold, I have made him thy lord, and all his brethren have I given to him for servants; and with corn and wine have I sustained him: and what shall I do now unto thee, my son?

38 And Esau said unto his father, Hast thou but one blessing, my father? bless me, even me also, O my father! And Esau lifted up his voice, and wept.

39 And Isaac his father answered and said unto him, Behold, thy dwelling shall be the fatness of the earth, and of the dew of heaven from above;

40 And by thy sword shalt thou live, and shalt serve thy brother; and it shall come to pass when thou shalt have the dominion, that thou shalt break his yoke from off thy neck.

41 ¶ And Esau hated Jacob because of the blessing wherewith his father blessed him: and Esau said in his heart, The days of mourning for my father are at hand; then will I slay my brother Jacob.

42 And these words of Esau her elder son were told to Rebekah: and she sent and called Jacob her younger son, and said unto him, Behold, thy brother Esau, as touching thee, doth comfort himself, *purposing* to kill thee.

43 Now therefore, my son, obey my voice; and arise, flee thou to Laban my brother to Haran;

minious flight: and for fear of being pursued or waylaid by his vindictive brother, he did not take the common road, but went by lonely and unfrequented paths, which increased the length and dangers of the journey. 11. he lighted, &c.—by a forced march he had reached Beth-el, about forty-eight miles from Beer-sheba, and had to spend the night in the open field. he took of the stones, &c.—"the nature of the soil is an existing comment on the record of the stony territory where Jacob lay." [CLARKE'S TRAV.] 12. he dreamed... a ladder — some writers are of opinion that it was not a literal ladder that is meant, as it is impossible to conceive any imagery stranger and more unnatural than that of a ladder, whose base was on earth, while its top reached heaven, without having anything on which to rest its upper extremity. They suppose that the little heap of stones, on which his head reclined for a pillow, being the miniature model of the object that appeared to his imagination, the ladder was a gigantic mountain pile, whose sides, indented in the rock, gave it the appearance of a scaling ladder. There can be no doubt that this use of the original term was common among the early Hebrews: as Josephus, describing the town of Ptolemais (Acre,) says it was bounded by a mountain, which, from its projecting sides, was called "the ladder;" and the stairs that led down to the city are, in the original, termed a ladder (Neh. 3,) though they were only a flight of steps cut in the side of the rock. But whether the image presented to the mental eye of Jacob were a common ladder, or such a mountain pile as has been described, the design of this vision was to afford comfort, encouragement, and confidence to the lonely fugitive, both in his present circumstances and as to his future prospects. His thoughts during the day must have been painful—he would be his own self-accuser that he had brought exile and privation upon himself—and above all, that though he had obtained the forgiveness of his father, he had much reason to fear lest God might have forsaken him? Solitude affords time for reflection; and it was now that God began to bring Jacob under a course of religious instruction and training. To dispel his fears and allay the inward tumult of his mind, nothing was better fitted than the vision of the gigantic ladder, which reached from himself to heaven, and on which the angels were continually ascending and descending from God himself on their benevolent errands (Jo.1.51.) 13. the Lord stood, &c.—that Jacob might be at no loss to know the purport of the vision, he heard the Divine voice; and the announcement of His name, together with a renewal of the covenant, and an assurance of personal protection, produced at once the most solemnizing and inspiriting effect on his mind. 16. Jacob awoke, &c.—His language and his conduct were alike that of a man whose mind was pervaded by sentiments of solemn awe, of fervent piety, and lively gratitude (Jer. 31, 36.). 18, 19. Jacob set up a stone, &c.—the mere setting up of the stone might have been as a future memorial to mark the spot; and this practice is still common in the East, in memory of a religious vow or engagement. But the pouring oil upon it was a consecration. Accordingly he gave it a new name, Beth el, "the house of God" (Hos. 12. 4.); and it will not appear a thing forced or unnatural to call a stone a house, when one considers the common practice in warm countries of sitting in the open air by or on a stone, as are those of this place, "broad sheets of bare rock, some of them standing like the cromlechs of Druidical monuments." [STANLEY.]

20-22. JACOB'S VOW. Jacob vowed a vow—His words are not to be considered as implying a doubt, far less as stating the condition or terms on which he would dedicate himself to God. Let "if" be changed into "since," and the language will appear a proper expression of Jacob's faith—an evidence of his having truly embraced the promise. How edifying often to meditate on Jacob at Beth-el!

CHAPTER XXIX.

Ver. 1-35. THE WELL OF HARAN. 1. Then Jacob went, &c.—*Heb.*, lifted up his feet. He resumed his way next morning with a light heart and elastic step after the vision of the ladder: for tokens of the divine favour tend to quicken the discharge of duty (Neh. 8. 10.), and came into the land, &c.—Mesopotamia and the whole region beyond the Euphrates are by the sacred writers designated "the east" (Jud. 6. 3; 1 Kings 4. 32; Job 1. 3.). Between the first and the second clause of this verse is included a journey of four hundred miles. 2. And he looked, &c.—as he approached the place of his destination, he, according to custom, repaired to the well adjoining the town where he would obtain an easy introduction to his relatives. 3. three flocks... and a stone, &c.—In Arabia, owing to the shifting sands, and in other places, owing to the strong evaporation, the mouth of a well is generally covered, especially when it is private property. Over many is laid a broad, thick, flat stone, with a round hole cut in the middle, forming the mouth of the cistern. This hole is covered with a heavy stone which it would require two or three men to roll away. Such was the description of the well at Haran. 4. Jacob said, My brethren — Finding from the shepherds who were reposing there with flocks, and who all belonged to Haran, that his relatives in Haran were well, and that one of the family was shortly expected, he enquired why they were idling the best part of the day there instead of watering their flocks, and sending them back to pasture? 8. They said, We cannot, until—In order to prevent the consequences of too frequent exposure in places where water is scarce, it is not only covered, but it is customary to have all the flocks collected round the well before the covering is removed in presence of the owner or one of his representatives; and it was for this reason that those who were reposing at the well of Haran with the three flocks were waiting the arrival of Rachel. 9-11. While he yet spake, Rachel came—among the pastoral tribes the young unmarried daughters of the greatest sheicks tend the flocks, going out at sunrise, and continuing to watch their fleecy charge till sunset. Watering them, which is done twice a-day, is a work of time and labour, and Jacob rendered no small service in volunteering his aid to the young shepherdess. The interview was affecting, the reception welcome, and Jacob forgot all his toils in the society of his Mesopotamian relatives. Can we doubt that he returned thanks to God for His goodness by the way?

44 And tarry with him a few days, until thy brother's fury turn away;

45 Until thy brother's anger turn away from thee, and he forget *that* which thou hast done to him: then I will send and fetch thee from thence: why should I be deprived also of you both in one day?

46 And Rebekah said to Isaac, I am weary of my life because of the daughters of Heth: if Jacob take a wife of the daughters of Heth, such as these *which are* of the daughters of the land, what good shall my life do me?

CHAPTER XXVIII.

1 *Jacob is blessed, and sent to Padan-aram:* 10 *his vision, and God's promise in a dream.* 18 *The stone at Beth-el.* 20 *Jacob's vow.*

AND Isaac called Jacob, and blessed him, and charged him, and said unto him, Thou shalt not take a wife of the daughters of Canaan.

2 Arise, go to Padan-aram, to the house of Bethuel thy mother's father; and take thee a wife from thence of the daughters of Laban thy mother's brother.

3 And God Almighty bless thee, and make thee fruitful, and multiply thee, that thou mayest be a multitude of people;

4 And give thee the blessing of Abraham, to thee, and to thy seed with thee; that thou mayest inherit the land wherein thou art a stranger, which God gave unto Abraham.

5 And Isaac sent away Jacob: and he went to Padan-aram unto Laban, son of Bethuel the Syrian, the brother of Rebekah, Jacob's and Esau's mother.

6 ¶ When Esau saw that Isaac had blessed Jacob, and sent him away to Padan-aram, to take him a wife from thence; and that, as he blessed him, he gave him a charge, saying, Thou shalt not take a wife of the daughters of Canaan;

7 And that Jacob obeyed his father and his mother, and was gone to Padan-aram;

8 And Esau seeing that the daughters of Canaan pleased not Isaac his father;

9 Then went Esau unto Ishmael, and took unto the wives which he had Mahalath the daughter of Ishmael, Abraham's son, the sister of Nebajoth, to be his wife.

10 ¶ And Jacob went out from Beer-sheba, and went toward Haran.

11 And he lighted upon a certain place, and tarried there all night, because the sun was set; and he took of the stones of that place, and put *them for* his pillows, and lay down in that place to sleep.

12 And he dreamed, and behold a ladder set up on the earth, and the top of it reached to heaven: and behold the angels of God ascending and descending on it.

13 And, behold! the LORD stood above it, and said, I am the LORD God of Abraham thy father, and the God of Isaac: the land whereon thou liest, to thee will I give it, and to thy seed;

14 And thy seed shall be as the dust of the earth; and thou shalt spread abroad to the west, and to the east, and to the north, and to the south: and in thee and in thy seed shall all the families of the earth be blessed.

15 And, behold, I am with thee, and will keep thee in all *places* whither thou goest, and will bring thee again into this land; for I will not leave thee, until I have done *that* which I have spoken to thee of.

16 ¶ And Jacob awaked out of his sleep, and he said, Surely the LORD is in this place; and I knew it not.

17 And he was afraid, and said, How dreadful *is* this place! this *is* none other but the house of God, and this *is* the gate of heaven.

18 And Jacob rose up early in the morning, and took the stone that he had put *for* his pillows, and set it up *for* a pillar, and poured oil upon the top of it.

19 And he called the name of that place Beth-el: but the name of that city *was* called Luz at the first.

20 And Jacob vowed a vow, saying, If God will be with me, and will keep me in this way that I go, and will give me bread to eat, and raiment to put on,

21 So that I come again to my father's house in peace, then shall the LORD be my God:

22 And this stone, which I have set *for* a pillar, shall be God's house: and of all that thou shalt give me I will surely give the tenth unto thee.

CHAPTER XXIX.

1 *Jacob, coming to the well of Haran,* 9 *meeteth Rachel, and is entertained by Laban:* 15 *he covenanteth for her,* 21 *but is deceived with Leah.* 28 *Rachel also given him to wife on a new agreement.* 31 *Leah beareth Reuben, Simeon, Levi, and Judah.*

THEN Jacob went on his journey, and came into the land of the people of the east.

2 And he looked, and behold a well in the field, and, lo, there were three flocks of sheep lying by it; for out of that well they watered the flocks: and a great stone *was* upon the well's mouth.

3 And thither were all the flocks gathered: and they rolled the stone from the well's mouth, and watered the sheep, and put the stone again upon the well's mouth in his place.

4 And Jacob said unto them, My brethren, whence be ye? And they said, Of Haran *are* we.

5 And he said unto them, Know ye Laban the son of Nahor? And they said, We know him.

6 And he said unto them, *Is* he well? And they said, *He is* well: and, behold, Rachel his daughter cometh with the sheep.

7 And he said, Lo, *it is* yet high day, neither *is it* time that the cattle should be gathered together: water ye the sheep, and go *and* feed *them.*

8 And they said, We cannot, until all the flocks be gathered together, and *till* they roll the stone from the well's mouth; then we water the sheep.

9 ¶ And while he yet spake with them, Rachel came with her father's sheep; for she kept them.

10 And it came to pass, when Jacob saw Rachel the daughter of Laban his mother's brother, and the sheep of Laban his mother's brother, that Jacob went near, and rolled the stone from the well's mouth, and watered the flock of Laban his mother's brother.

11 And Jacob kissed Rachel, and lifted up his voice, and wept.

12 And Jacob told Rachel that he *was* her father's brother, and that he *was* Rebekah's son: and she ran and told her father.

12. Jacob told Rachel, &c.—according to the practice of the East, the term "brother" is extended to remote degrees of relationship, as uncle, cousin, or nephew. **14-20. he abode a month**—Among pastoral people a stranger is freely entertained for three days; on the fourth he is expected to tell his name and errand and if he prolongs his stay after that time, he must set his hand to work in some way, as may be agreed upon. A similar rule obtained in Laban's establishment, and the wages for which his nephew engaged to continue in his employment was the hand of Rachel. **17. Leah tender-eyed**—*i.e.*, soft blue eyes—thought a blemish. **Rachel beautiful and well-favoured**—*i.e.*, comely and handsome in form. The latter was Jacob's choice. **18. I will serve seven years**—a proposal of marriage is made to the father without the daughter being consulted, and the match is effected by the suitor either bestowing costly presents on the family, or by giving cattle to the value the father sets upon his daughter, or else by giving personal services for a specified period. The last was the course necessity imposed on Jacob; and there for seven years he submitted to the drudgery of a hired shepherd, with the view of obtaining Rachel. The time went rapidly away; for even severe and difficult duties become light when love is the spring of action. **21. Jacob said, Give me my wife**—At the expiry of the stipulated term the marriage festivities were held. But an infamous fraud was practised on Jacob, and on his shewing a righteous indignation, the usage of the country was pleaded in excuse. No plea or kindred should ever be allowed to come in opposition to the claim of justice. But this is often overlooked by the selfish mind of man, and fashion or custom rules instead of the will of God. This was what Laban did, as he said, "it must not be so done in our country, to give the younger before the first-born." But, then, if that were the prevailing custom of society at Haran, he should have apprized his nephew of it at an early period and in an honourable manner. This, however, is too much the way with the people of the East still. The duty of marrying an elder daughter before a younger, the tricks which parents take to get off an elder daughter that is plain or deformed, and in which they are favoured by the long bridal veil that entirely conceals her features all the wedding day, and the prolongation for a week of the marriage festivities among the greater shiecks, are accordant with the habits of the people in Arabia and Armenia in the present day. **28. gave him Rachel also**—It is evident that the marriage of both sisters took place nearly about the same time, and that such a connexion was then allowed, though afterwards prohibited (Lev. 18. 18.). **29. gave to Rachel . . . Bilhah for her maid**—A father in good circumstances still gives his daughter from his household a female slave, over whom the young wife, independently of her husband, has the absolute control. **31. Leah hated**—*i.e.*, not loved so much as she ought to have been. Her becoming a mother ensured her rising in the estimation both of her husband and of society. **32-35. son . . . called his name**—names were always significant; and those which Leah gave to her sons were expressive of her varying feelings of thankfulness or joy, or allusive to circumstances in the history of the family. There was piety and wisdom in attaching a signification to names, as it tended to keep the bearer in remembrance of his duty and the claims of God.

CHAPTER XXX.

Ver. 1--24. **DOMESTIC JEALOUSIES. 1. Rachel envied her sister**—The maternal relation confers a high degree of honour in the East, and the want of that status is felt as a stigma, and deplored as a grievous calamity. **else I die**—either be reckoned as good as dead, or pine away from vexation. The intense anxiety of Hebrew women for children arose from the hope of giving birth to the promised seed. Rachel's conduct was sinful, and contrasts unfavourably with that of Rebekah (cf. 25. 22.) and of Hannah (1 Sam. 1, 11,). **3-9. Bilhah, Zilpah**—following the example of Sarah with regard to Hagar, an example which is not seldom imitated still, she adopted the children of her maid. Leah took the same course. A bitter and intense rivalry existed between them, all the more from their close relationship as sisters; and although they occupied separate apartments, with their families, as is the uniform custom where a plurality of wives obtains, and the husband and father spends a day with each in regular succession, that did not allay their mutual jealousies. The evil lies in the system, which being a violation of God's original ordinance, cannot yield happiness. **20. Leah said, . . . good dowry**—the birth of a son is hailed with demonstrations of joy, and the possession of several sons confers upon the mother an honour and respectability proportioned to their number. The husband attaches a similar importance to the possession, and it forms a bond of union which renders it impossible for him ever to forsake or to be cold to a wife who has borne him sons. This explains the happy anticipations Leah founded on the possession of her six sons. **21. afterwards, a daughter**—the inferior value set on a daughter is displayed in the bare announcement of the birth.

25-43. **JACOB'S COVENANT WITH LABAN. When Rachel had born Joseph**—Shortly after the birth of this son, Jacob's term of servitude expired, and feeling anxious to establish an independence for his family, he probably, from knowing that Esau was out of the way, announced his intention of returning to Canaan (Heb. 13. 14.). In this resolution the faith of Jacob was remarkable, for as yet he had nothing to rely on but the promise of God (cf. 28. 15.). **27. Laban said, . . . I have learned**—his selfish uncle was averse to a separation, not from warmth of affection either for Jacob or his daughters, but from the damage his own interests would sustain. He had found, from long observation, that the blessing of heaven rested on Jacob, and that his stock had wonderfully increased under Jacob's management. This was a remarkable testimony that good men are blessings to the places where they reside. Men of the world are often blessed with temporal benefits on account of their pious relatives, though they have not always, like Laban, the wisdom to discern, or the grace to acknowledge it. **28. appoint me thy wages**—the Eastern shepherds receive for their hire not money, but a certain amount of the increase or produce of the flock; but Laban would at the time have done anything to secure the continued services of his nephew, and make a show of liberality, which Jacob

CHAPTER XXX.

1 Rachel's grief for her barrenness: 5 Bilhah beareth Dan and Naphtali: 9 Zilpah beareth Gad and Asher: 17 Leah beareth Issachar, Zebulun and Dinah: 22 Rachel beareth Joseph. 25 Jacob's new covenant with Laban: 37 his policy to become rich.

13 And it came to pass, when Laban heard the tidings of Jacob his sister's son, that he ran to meet him, and embraced him, and kissed him, and brought him to his house. And he told Laban all these things.

14 And Laban said to him, ‘Surely thou *art* my bone and my flesh. And he abode with him the space of a month.

15 ¶ And Laban said unto Jacob, Because thou *art* my brother, shouldest thou therefore serve me for nought? tell me, what shall thy wages *be?*

16 And Laban had two daughters: the name of the elder *was* Leah, and the name of the younger *was* Rachel.

17 Leah *was* tender-eyed; but Rachel was beautiful and well favoured.

18 And Jacob loved Rachel; and said, I will serve thee seven years for Rachel thy younger daughter.

19 And Laban said, *It is* better that I give her to thee, than that I should give her to another man: abide with me.

20 And Jacob served seven years for Rachel; and they seemed unto him *but* a few days, for the love he had to her.

21 ¶ And Jacob said unto Laban, Give me my wife, for my days are fulfilled, that I may go in unto her.

22 And Laban gathered together all the men of the place, and made a feast.

23 And it came to pass in the evening, that he took Leah his daughter, and brought her to him; and he went in unto her.

24 And Laban gave unto his daughter Leah Zilpah his maid *for* an handmaid.

25 And it came to pass, that in the morning, behold, it *was* Leah: and he said to Laban, What *is* this thou hast done unto me? did not I serve with thee for Rachel? wherefore then hast thou beguiled me?

26 And Laban said, It must not be so done in our country, to give the younger before the first-born.

27 Fulfil her week, and we will give thee this also for the service which thou shalt serve with me yet seven other years.

28 And Jacob did so, and fulfilled her week: and he gave him Rachel his daughter to wife also.

29 And Laban gave to Rachel his daughter Bilhah his handmaid to be her maid.

30 And he went in also unto Rachel, and he loved also Rachel more than Leah, and served with him yet seven other years.

31 ¶ And when the LORD saw that Leah *was* hated, he opened her womb: but Rachel *was* barren.

32 And Leah conceived, and bare a son, and she called his name Reuben: for she said, Surely the LORD hath looked upon my affliction; now therefore my husband will love me.

33 And she conceived again, and bare a son; and said, Because the LORD hath heard that I *was* hated, he hath therefore given me this *son* also: and she called his name Simeon.

34 And she conceived again, and bare a son; and said, Now this time will my husband be joined unto me, because I have born him three sons: therefore was his name called Levi.

35 And she conceived again, and bare a son: and she said, Now will I praise the LORD: therefore she called his name Judah: and left bearing.

CHAPTER XXX.

1 Rachel's grief for her barrenness: 5 Bilhah beareth Dan and Naphtali: 9 Zilpah beareth Gad and Asher: 17 Leah beareth Issachar, Zebulun and Dinah: 22 Rachel beareth Joseph. 25 Jacob's new covenant with Laban: 37 his policy to become rich.

AND when Rachel saw that she bare Jacob no children, Rachel envied her sister; and said unto Jacob, Give me children, or else I die.

2 And Jacob's anger was kindled against Rachel: and he said, *Am* I in God's stead, who hath withheld from thee the fruit of the womb?

3 And she said, Behold my maid Bilhah, go in unto her; and she shall bear upon my knees, that I may also have children by her.

4 And she gave him Bilhah her handmaid to wife: and Jacob went in unto her.

5 And Bilhah conceived, and bare Jacob a son.

6 And Rachel said, God hath judged me, and hath also heard my voice, and hath given me a son: therefore called she his name Dan.

7 And Bilhah, Rachel's maid, conceived again, and bare Jacob a second son.

8 And Rachel said, With great wrestlings have I wrestled with my sister, and I have prevailed: and she called his name Naphtali.

9 When Leah saw that she had left bearing, she took Zilpah her maid, and gave her Jacob to wife.

10 And Zilpah, Leah's maid, bare Jacob a son.

11 And Leah said, A troop cometh: and she called his name Gad.

12 And Zilpah, Leah's maid, bare Jacob a second son.

13 And Leah said, Happy am I, for the daughters will call me blessed: and she called his name Asher.

14 ¶ And Reuben went in the days of wheat harvest, and found mandrakes in the field, and brought them unto his mother Leah. Then Rachel said to Leah, Give me, I pray thee, of thy son's mandrakes.

15 And she said unto her, *Is it* a small matter that thou hast taken my husband? and wouldest thou take away my son's mandrakes also? And Rachel said, Therefore he shall lie with thee to-night for thy son's mandrakes.

16 And Jacob came out of the field in the evening, and Leah went out to meet him, and said, Thou must come in unto me; for surely I have hired thee with my son's mandrakes. And he lay with her that night.

17 And God hearkened unto Leah, and she conceived, and bare Jacob the fifth son.

18 And Leah said, God hath given me my hire, because I have given my maiden to my husband: and she called his name Issachar.

19 And Leah conceived again, and bare Jacob the sixth son.

20 And Leah said, God hath endued me *with* a good dowry; now will my husband dwell with me, because I have born him six sons: and she called his name Zebulun.

21 And afterwards she bare a daughter, and called her name Dinah.

well knew was constrained. 31. Jacob said, Thou shalt not give, &c.—a new agreement was made, the substance of which was, that he was to receive remuneration in the usual way, but on certain conditions which Jacob specified. 32. I will pass through, &c.—Eastern sheep being generally white, the goats black, and spotted or speckled ones comparatively few and rare. Jacob proposed to remove all existing ones of that description from the flock, and to be content with what might appear at the next lambing-time. The proposal seemed so much in favour of Laban, that he at once agreed to it. But Jacob has been accused of taking advantage of his uncle, and though it is difficult to exculpate him from practising some degree of dissimulation, he was only availing himself of the results of his great skill and experience in the breeding of cattle. But it is evident from the next chapter, 5-13, that there was something miraculous, and that the means he had employed had been suggested by a divine intimation. 37. Jacob took rods, &c.—there are many varieties of the hazel, some of which are more erect than the common hazel, and it was probably one of the varieties Jacob employed. The styles are of a bright red colour, when peeled; and along with them he took wands of other shrubs, which, when stripped of the bark, had white streaks. These, kept constantly before the eyes of the female at the time of gestation, his observation had taught him would have an influence, through the imagination, on the future offspring. 38. watering troughs—usually a long stone block hollowed out, from which several sheep could drink at once, but sometimes so small as to admit of one only drinking at a time.

CHAPTER XXXI.

Ver. 1-21. ENVY OF LABAN AND SONS. He heard the words of Laban's sons—It must have been from rumour that Jacob got knowledge of the invidious reflections cast upon him by his cousins; for they were separated at the distance of three days' journey. 2. And Jacob beheld the countenance of Laban—*lit.* was not the same as yesterday, and the day before; —a common Oriental form of speech. The insinuations against Jacob's fidelity by Laban's sons, and the sullen reserve, the churlish conduct, of Laban himself, had made Jacob's situation, in his uncle's establishment, most trying and painful. It is always one of the vexations attendant on worldly prosperity, that it excites the envy of others (Eccl. 4. 4; and that, however careful a man is to maintain a good conscience, he cannot always reckon on maintaining a good name, in a censorious world. This, Jacob experienced; and it is probable that, like a good man, he had asked direction and relief in prayer. 3. the Lord said, Return—Notwithstanding the ill usage he had received, Jacob might not have deemed himself at liberty to quit his present sphere, under the impulse of passionate fretfulness and discontent. Having been conducted to Haran by God (28. 15); and having got a promise that the same heavenly Guardian would bring him again into the land of Canaan—he might have thought he ought not to leave it, without being clearly persuaded as to the path of duty. So ought we to set the Lord before us, and to acknowledge him in all our ways, our journeys, our settlements and plans in life. 4. Jacob sent and called Rachel and Leah—His wives and family were in their usual residence; and whether he wished them to be present at the festivities of sheep-shearing, as some think; or, because he could not leave his flock, he called them both to come to him, in order that, having resolved on immediate departure, he might communicate his intentions, Rachel and Leah only were called, for the other two wives, being secondary, and still in a state of servitude, were not entitled to be taken into account. Jacob acted the part of a dutiful husband in telling them his plans; for husbands, that love their wives, should consult with them, and trust in them (Prov. 31. 1.). 6. Ye know that I have served— Having stated his strong grounds of dissatisfaction with their father's conduct, and the ill requital he had got, for all his faithful services—he informed them of the blessing of God, that had made him rich notwithstanding Laban's design to ruin him; and finally, of the command from God he had received to return to his own country, that they might not accuse him of caprice, or disaffection to their family; but be convinced, that in resolving to depart, he acted from a principle of religious obedience. 14. Rachel and Leah answered—Having heard his views, they expressed their entire approval; and from grievances of their own, were fully as desirous of a separation as himself. They display not only conjugal affection, but piety in following the course described—'whatsoever God hath said unto thee, do." "Those that are really their husbands' helps meet, will never be their hindrances in doing that to which God calls them." [HENRY.] 17. Then Jacob rose up—Little time is spent by pastoral people in removing. The striking down the tents and poles, and stowing them among their other baggage; the putting their wives and children in *houdas* like cradles, on the backs of camels, or in panniers on asses; and the ranging of the various parts of the flock under the respective shepherds; all this is a short process. A plain that is covered in the morning with a long array of tents, and with browsing flocks, may, in a few hours, appear so desolate, that not a vestige of the encampment remains, except the holes in which the tent-poles had been fixed. 20. Jacob stole away—The result showed the prudence and necessity of departing secretly; otherwise, Laban might have detained him by violence or artifice. 18. he carried the cattle of his getting—*i. e.*, his own and nothing more. He did not indemnify himself for his many losses by carrying off any thing of Laban's, but was content with what Providence had given him. Some may think that due notice should have been given; but when a man feels himself in danger—the law of self-preservation prescribes the duty of immediate flight, if it can be done consistently with conscience.

22-52. LABAN PURSUETH JACOB—THEIR COVENANT AT GALEED. 22. It was told Laban on the third day—No sooner did the intelligence reach Laban than he set out in pursuit, and he being not encumbered, advanced rapidly; whereas Jacob, with a young family and numerous flocks, had to march slowly, so that he overtook the fugitives after seven days' journey, as they lay encamped on the brow of mount Gilead, an extensive range of hills forming the eastern boundary of Canaan.

22 ¶ And God remembered Rachel, and God hearkened to her, and opened her womb.
23 And she conceived, and bare a son; and said, God hath taken away my reproach:
24 And she called his name Joseph; and said, The LORD shall add to me another son.
25 ¶ And it came to pass, when Rachel had born Joseph, that Jacob said unto Laban, Send me away, that I may go unto mine own place, and to my country.
26 Give me my wives and my children, for whom I have served thee, and let me go: for thou knowest my service which I have done thee.
27 And Laban said unto him, I pray thee, if I have found favour in thine eyes, tarry: for I have learned by experience that the LORD hath blessed me for thy sake.
28 And he said, Appoint me thy wages, and I will give it.
29 And he said unto him, Thou knowest how I have served thee, and how thy cattle was with me.
30 For it was little which thou hadst before I came, and it is now increased unto a multitude; and the LORD hath blessed thee since my coming: and now when shall I provide for mine own house also?
31 And he said, What shall I give thee? And Jacob said, Thou shalt not give me any thing. If thou wilt do this thing for me, I will again feed and keep thy flock:
32 I will pass through all thy flock to-day, removing from thence all the speckled and spotted cattle, and all the brown cattle among the sheep, and the spotted and speckled among the goats: and of such shall be my hire.
33 So shall my righteousness answer for me in time to come, when it shall come for my hire before thy face: every one that is not speckled and spotted among the goats, and brown among the sheep, that shall be counted stolen with me.
34 And Laban said, Behold, I would it might be according to thy word.
35 And he removed that day the he-goats that were ringstraked and spotted, and all the she-goats that were speckled and spotted, and every one that had some white in it, and all the brown among the sheep, and gave them into the hand of his sons.
36 And he set three days' journey betwixt himself and Jacob: and Jacob fed the rest of Laban's flocks.
37 ¶ And Jacob took him rods of green poplar, and of the hazel and chesnut tree; and pilled white strakes in them, and made the white appear which was in the rods.
38 And he set the rods which he had pilled before the flocks in the gutters in the watering troughs when the flocks came to drink, that they should conceive when they came to drink.
39 And the flocks conceived before the rods, and brought forth cattle ringstraked, speckled, and spotted.
40 And Jacob did separate the lambs, and set the faces of the flocks toward the ringstraked and all the brown in the flock of Laban; and he put his own flocks by themselves, and put them not unto Laban's cattle.
41 And it came to pass, whensoever the stronger cattle did conceive, that Jacob laid the rods before the eyes of the cattle in the gutters, that they might conceive among the rods.
42 But when the cattle were feeble, he put them not in: so the feebler were Laban's, and the stronger Jacob's.
43 And the man increased exceedingly, and had much cattle, and maid-servants, and men-servants, and camels, and asses.

CHAPTER XXXI.

1 Jacob departeth secretly from Laban: 19 Rachel stealeth away her father's images. 22 Laban pursueth Jacob: 44 their covenant at Galeed.

AND he heard the words of Laban's sons, saying, Jacob hath taken away all that was our father's; and of that which was our father's hath he gotten all this glory.
2 And Jacob beheld the countenance of Laban, and, behold, it was not toward him as before.
3 And the LORD said unto Jacob, Return unto the land of thy fathers, and to thy kindred; and I will be with thee.
4 And Jacob sent and called Rachel and Leah to the field unto his flock,
5 And said unto them, I see your father's countenance, that it is not toward me as before; but the God of my father hath been with me.
6 And ye know that with all my power I have served your father.
7 And your father hath deceived me, and changed my wages ten times; but God suffered him not to hurt me.
8 If he said thus, The speckled shall be thy wages; then all the cattle bare speckled: and if he said thus, The ringstraked shall be thy hire; then bare all the cattle ringstraked.
9 Thus God hath taken away the cattle of your father, and given them to me.
10 And it came to pass at the time that the cattle conceived, that I lifted up mine eyes, and saw in a dream, and, behold, the rams which leaped upon the cattle were ringstraked, speckled, and grisled.
11 And the angel of God spake unto me in a dream, saying, Jacob: and I said, Here am I.
12 And he said, Lift up now thine eyes and see, all the rams which leap upon the cattle are ringstraked, speckled, and grisled: for I have seen all that Laban doeth unto thee.
13 I am the God of Beth-el, where thou anointedst the pillar, and where thou vowedst a vow unto me: now arise, get thee out from this land, and return unto the land of thy kindred.
14 And Rachel and Leah answered and said unto him, Is there yet any portion or inheritance for us in our father's house?
15 Are we not counted of him strangers? for he hath sold us, and hath quite devoured also our money.
16 For all the riches which God hath taken from our father, that is ours, and our children's: now then, whatsoever God hath said unto thee, do.
17 ¶ Then Jacob rose up, and set his sons and his wives upon camels;
18 And he carried away all his cattle, and all his goods which he had gotten, the cattle of his getting, which he had gotten in Padan-aram, for to go to Isaac his father in the land of Canaan.
19 And Laban went to shear his sheep:

Being accompanied by a number of his people, he might have used violence had he not been divinely warned in a dream to give no interruption to his nephew's journey. How striking and sudden a change! For several days he had been full of rage, and was now in eager anticipation that his vengeance would be fully wreaked, when, lo! his hands are tied by invisible power (Ps. 76. 10.). He durst not touch Jacob, but there was a war of words. 25-42. Laban said, What hast thou done?—Not a word is said of the charge, v. 1. His reproaches were of a different kind. His first charge was for depriving him of the satisfaction of giving Jacob and his family the usual salutations at parting. In the East it is customary, when any are setting out to a great distance, for their relatives and friends to accompany them a considerable way with music and valedictory songs. Considering the past conduct of Laban, his complaint on this ground was hypocritical cant. But his second charge was a grave one—the carrying off his gods—Heb. Teraphim, small images of human figure, used not as idols or objects of worship, but as talismans, for superstitious purposes. 32. Jacob said, With whomsoever, &c. —Conscious of his own innocence, and little suspecting the misdeed of his favourite wife, he boldly challenged a search, and denounced the heaviest penalty on the culprit. A personal scrutiny was made by Laban, who examined every tent; and having entered Rachel's last, would have infallibly discovered the stolen images had not Rachel made an appeal to him which prevented further search. 34. had put them in the camel's furniture, and sat upon them—the common packsaddle is often used as a seat or a cushion, against which a person squatted on the floor may lean. 36-43. Jacob was wroth—Recrimination on his part was natural in the circumstances, and, as usual, when passion is high, the charges took a wide range. He rapidly enumerated his grievances for twenty years, and in a tone of unrestrained severity described the niggard character and vexatious exactions of his uncle, together with the hardships of various kinds he had patiently endured. the rams have I not eaten—Eastern people seldom kill the females for food except they are barren. That which was torn of beasts—The shepherds are strictly responsible for losses in the flock, unless they can prove these were occasioned by wild beasts. 40. in the day drought, and the frost by night—the temperature changes often in twenty-four hours from the greatest extremes of heat and cold, most trying to the shepherd who has to keep watch by his flocks. Much allowance must be made for Jacob. Great and long-continued provocations ruffle the mildest and most disciplined tempers. It is difficult to "be angry and sin not." But these two relatives, after having given utterance to their pent up feelings, came at length to a mutual understanding, or rather, God influenced Laban to make reconciliation with his injured nephew (Pro. 16. 7.). 44. Come, let us make a covenant—The way in which this covenant was ratified was by a heap of stones being laid in a circular pile, to serve as seats, and in the centre of this circle a large one was set up perpendicularly for an altar. It is probable that a sacrifice was first offered, and then that the feast of reconciliation was partaken of by both parties seated on the stones around it. To this day heaps of stones, which have been used as memorials, are found abundantly in the region where this transaction took place. 52. This heap be a witness—Objects of nature were frequently thus spoken of. But over and above, there was a solemn appeal to God; and it is observable that there was a marked difference in the religious sentiments of the two. Laban spake of the God of Abraham and Nahor, their common ancestors; but Jacob, knowing that idolatry had crept in among that branch of the family, swore by the Fear of Isaac. They who have one God should have one heart; they who are agreed in religion should endeavour to agree in every thing else.

CHAPTER XXXII.

Ver. 1, 2. VISION OF ANGELS. angels of God met—It is not said whether this angelic manifestation was made in a vision by day, or a dream by night. There is an evident allusion, however, to the appearance upon the ladder cf. 28. 12,) and this occurring to Jacob on his return to Canaan, was an encouraging pledge of the continued presence and protection of God (Ps. 34. 7; Heb. 1. 14.). 2. Mahanaim—two hosts or camps. The place was situated between mount Gilead and the Jabbok—near the banks of that brook.

3-32. MISSION TO ESAU. sent messengers —i. e. had sent. It was a prudent precaution to ascertain the present temper of Esau, as the road, on approaching the eastern confines of Canaan, lay near the wild district where his brother was now established. the land of Seir—A highland country on the east and south of the Dead Sea, inhabited by the Horites, who were dispossessed by Esau, or his posterity (Deut. 11. 12.). When, and in what circumstances he had emigrated thither—whether the separation arose out of the undutiful conduct and idolatrous habits of his wives, which had made them unwelcome inmates in the tent of his parents, or whether his roving disposition had sought a country from his love of adventure and the chase, he was living in a state of power and affluence, and this settlement on the outer borders of Canaan, though made of his own free-will — was overruled by Providence to pave the way for Jacob's return to the promised land. 4. Thus shall ye say—The purport of the message was that, after a residence of twenty years in Mesopotamia, he was now returning to his native land—that he did not need anything, for he had abundance of pastoral wealth—but that he could not pass without notifying his arrival to his brother, and paying the homage of his respectful obeisance. Acts of civility tend to disarm opposition, and soften hatred (Eccl. 10. 4.). Thy servant Jacob—He had been made lord over his brethren (cf. 27, 29.). But it is probable he thought this referred to a spiritual superiority; or if to temporal, that it was to be realised only to his posterity. At all events, leaving it to God to fulfil that purpose, he deemed it prudent to assume the most kind and respectful bearing. 6. The messengers returned—Their report left Jacob in painful uncertainty as to what was his brother's views and feelings. Esau's studied reserve, gave him reason to dread the worst. Jacob was naturally timid; but his conscience told him that there was much

and Rachel had stolen the ³ images ᵗ that were her father's.

20 And Jacob stole away ⁴ unawares to Laban the Syrian, in that he told him not that he fled.

21 So he fled with all that he had; and he rose up, and passed over the river, and ᵘ set his face toward the mount Gilead.

22 And it was told Laban on the third day that Jacob was fled.

23 And he took his ᵛ brethren with him, and pursued after him seven days' journey; and they overtook him in the mount Gilead.

24 And God ʷ came to Laban the Syrian in a dream by night, and said unto him, Take heed that thou ˣ speak not to Jacob ⁵ either good or bad.

25 ¶ Then Laban overtook Jacob. Now Jacob had pitched his tent in the mount: and Laban with his brethren pitched in the mount of Gilead.

26 And Laban said to Jacob, What hast thou done, that thou hast stolen away unawares to me, and ʸ carried away my daughters, as captives taken with the sword?

27 Wherefore didst thou flee away secretly, and ⁶ steal away from me; and didst not tell me, that I might have sent thee away with mirth, and with songs, with tabret, and with harp?

28 And hast not suffered me ᶻ to kiss my sons and my daughters? ᵃ Thou hast now done foolishly in so doing.

29 It is in the power of my hand to do you hurt: but the ᵇ God of your father spake unto me ᶜ yesternight, saying, Take thou heed that thou speak not to Jacob either good or bad.

30 And now, though thou wouldest needs be gone, because thou sore longedst after thy father's house, yet wherefore hast thou ᵈ stolen my gods?

31 And Jacob answered and said to Laban, Because I was afraid: for I said, Peradventure thou wouldest take by force thy daughters from me.

32 With whomsoever thou findest thy gods, ᵉ let him not live: before our brethren discern thou what is thine with me, and take it to thee. For Jacob knew not that Rachel had stolen them.

33 And Laban went into Jacob's tent, and into Leah's tent, and into the two maidservants' tents; but he found them not. Then went he out of Leah's tent, and entered into Rachel's tent.

34 Now Rachel had taken the images, and put them in the camel's furniture, and sat upon them. And Laban ᶠ searched all the tent, but found them not.

35 And she said to her father, Let it not displease my lord that I cannot ᶠ rise up before thee; for the custom of women is upon me. And he searched, but found not the ᵍ images.

36 ¶ And Jacob ʰ was wroth, and chode with Laban: and Jacob answered and said to Laban, What is my trespass? what is my sin, that thou hast so hotly pursued after me?

37 Whereas thou hast ⁸ searched all my stuff, what hast thou found of all thy household stuff? ⁱ set it here before my brethren and thy brethren, that they may judge betwixt us both.

38 This twenty years have I been with thee; thy ewes and thy she-goats have not cast their young, and the rams of thy flock have I not eaten.

39 ʲ That which was torn of beasts I brought not unto thee; I bare the loss of it; of ᵏ my hand didst thou require it, whether stolen by day, or stolen by night.

40 Thus I was; in the day the drought consumed me, and the frost by night; and my sleep departed from mine eyes.

41 Thus have I been twenty years in thy house; I ˡ served thee fourteen years for thy two daughters, and six years for thy cattle: and ᵐ thou hast changed my wages ten times.

42 ⁿ Except the God of my father, the God of Abraham, and the ᵒ Fear of Isaac, had been with me, surely thou hadst sent me away now empty. ᵖ God hath seen mine affliction and the labour of my hands, and ᵠ rebuked thee yesternight.

43 ¶ And Laban answered and said unto Jacob, These daughters are my daughters, and these children are my children, and these cattle are my cattle, and all that thou seest is mine: and what can I do this day unto these my daughters, or unto their children which they have born?

44 Now therefore come thou, ʳ let us make a covenant, I and thou; ˢ and let it be for a witness between me and thee.

45 And Jacob ᵗ took a stone, and set it up for a pillar.

46 And Jacob said unto his brethren, Gather stones; and they took stones, and made an heap: and they did eat there upon the heap.

47 And Laban called it ⁹ Jegar-sahadutha: but Jacob called it ¹⁰ Galeed.

48 And Laban said, ᵘ This heap is a witness between me and thee this day. Therefore was the name of it called Galeed;

49 And ᵛ Mizpah; for he said, The LORD watch between me and thee, when we are absent one from another.

50 If thou shalt afflict my daughters, or if thou shalt take other wives besides my daughters, no man is with us; see, God is witness betwixt me and thee.

51 And Laban said to Jacob, Behold this heap, and behold this pillar, which I have cast betwixt me and thee;

52 This heap be witness, and this pillar be witness, that I will not pass over this heap to thee, and that thou shalt not pass over this heap and this pillar unto me, for harm.

53 The God of Abraham, and the God of Nahor, the God of their father, ʷ judge betwixt us. And Jacob ˣ sware by ʸ the Fear of his father Isaac.

54 Then Jacob ¹² offered sacrifice upon the mount, and called his brethren to eat bread: and they did eat bread, and tarried all night in the mount.

55 And early in the morning Laban rose up, and kissed his sons and his daughters, and ᶻ blessed them: and Laban departed, and ᵃ returned unto his place.

CHAPTER XXXII.

1 Jacob's vision at Mahanaim; 3 his message to Esau. 6 He is afraid of Esau's coming; and prayeth for deliverance; 13 he sendeth a present to Esau; 24 he wrestleth with an Angel at Peniel, and is called Israel. 31 He halteth.

AND Jacob went on his way, and ᵃ the angels of God met him.

2 And when Jacob saw them, he said, This

ground for apprehension, and his distress was all the more aggravated that he had to provide for the safety of a large and helpless family. **9-12. Jacob said, O God**—In this great emergency, he had recourse to prayer. This is the first recorded example of prayer in the Bible. It is short, earnest, and bearing directly on the occasion. The appeal is made to God, as standing in a covenant-relation to his family, just as we ought to put our hopes of acceptance with God in Christ. It pleads the special promise made to himself of a safe return; and after a most humble and affecting confession of unworthiness, breathes an earnest desire for deliverance from the impending danger. It was the prayer of a kind husband, an affectionate father, a firm believer in the promises. **13-23. Took a present**—Jacob combined active exertions with earnest prayer; and this teaches us that we must not depend upon the aid and interposition of God in such a way as to supersede the exercise of prudence and foresight. Superiors are always approached with presents, and the respect expressed is estimated by the quality and amount of the gift. The present of Jacob consisted of 550 head of cattle, of different kinds, such as would be most prized by Esau. It was a most magnificent present, skilfully arranged and proportioned. The milch camels alone were of immense value; for the she-camels form the principal part of Arab wealth; their milk is a chief article of diet; and in many other respects, they are of the greatest use. **16. every drove by themselves**—There was great prudence in this arrangement: for the present would thus have a more imposing appearance; Esau's passion would have time to cool as he passed each successive company; and if the first was refused, the others would hasten back to convey a timely warning. **he commanded the foremost**—The messengers were strictly commanded to say the same words, that Esau might be more impressed, and that the uniformity of the address might appear more clearly to have come from Jacob himself. **21. himself lo'ged**—not the whole night, but only a part of it. **22. ford of Jabbok**—now the *Zerka*—a stream that rises among the mountains of Gilead, and running from east to west, enters the Jordan, about forty miles south of the Sea of Tiberias. At the ford it is ten yards wide. It is sometimes forded with difficulty; but in summer, very shallow. **he rose up and took**—Unable to sleep, he waded the ford in the night-time by himself; and having ascertained its safety, he returned to the north bank, and sent over his family and attendants—remaining behind, to seek anew, in solitary prayer, the divine blessing on the means he had set in motion. **24-30. There wrestled a man with him**—This mysterious person is called an angel (Hos. 12. 5,) and God, (*v*. 28, 30; Hos. 12. 4); and the opinion that is most supported is, that he was "the angel of the covenant," who, in a visible form, appeared to animate the mind, and sympathize with the distress of his pious servant. It has been a subject of much discussion whether the incident described was an actual conflict, or a visionary scene. Many think that as the narrative makes no mention in express terms either of sleep, or dream or vision, it was a real transaction; while others, considering the bodily exhaustion of Jacob, his great mental anxiety, the kind of aid he supplicated, as well as the analogy of former manifestations with which he was favoured—such as the ladder—have concluded that it w... a vision. [CAL., HESS., HENG.] The moral design of it was to revive the sinking spirit of the patriarch, and to arm him with confidence in God, while anticipating the dreaded scenes of the morrow. To us it is highly instructive; showing, that, to encourage us valiantly to meet the trials to which we are subjected, God allows us to ascribe to the efficacy of our faith and prayers, the victories which His grace alone enables us to make. **26. I will not let thee go**, &c.—It is evident that Jacob was aware of the character of Him with whom he wrestled; and, believing that his power, though by far superior to human, was yet limited by his promise to do him good, he determined not to lose the golden opportunity of securing a blessing. And nothing gives God greater pleasure than to see the hearts of his people firmly adhering to him. **28. Thy name no more ... Jacob**—The old name was not to be abandoned; but, referring as it did to a dishonourable part of the patriarch's history—it was to be associated with another descriptive of his now sanctified and eminently devout character. **29. Jacob asked, Tell me thy name**—The request was denied, that he might not be too elated with his conquest, nor suppose that he had obtained such advantage over the angel as to make him do what he pleased. **31, 32. halted on his thigh**—As Paul had a thorn in the flesh given to humble him, lest he should be too elevated by the abundant revelations granted him; so Jacob's lameness was to keep him mindful of this mysterious scene, and that it was in gracious condescension the victory was yielded to him. In the greatest of these spiritual victories, which, through faith, any of God's people obtain, there is always something to humble them. **32. the sinew which shrank**—the nerve that fastens the thigh-bone in its socket. The practice of the Jews in abstaining from eating this in the flesh of animals, is not founded on the law of Moses, but is merely a traditional usage. The sinew is carefully extracted; and, where there are no persons skilled enough for that operation, they do not make use of the hind legs at all.

CHAPTER XXXIII.

Ver. 1-11. KINDNESS OF JACOB AND ESAU. Behold, Esau and four hundred men—Jacob having crossed the ford, and ranged his wives and children in order—the dearest last, that they might be the least exposed to danger—awaited the expected interview. His faith was strengthened and his fears gone (Ps. 27. 3.). Having had power to prevail with God, he was confident of the same power with man, according to the promise (cf. 32. 28.). **3. he bowed himself seven times**—The manner of doing this is by looking towards a superior and bowing with the upper part of the body brought parallel to the ground, then advancing a few steps and bowing again, and repeating this obeisance till, at the seventh time, the suppliant stands in the immediate presence of his superior. The members of his family did the same. This was a token of profound respect, and, though very marked, it would appear natural; for Esau being the

is God's *b* host: and he called the name of that place ¹ Mahanaim.

3 And Jacob sent messengers before him to Esau his brother, *c* unto the land of Seir, *d* the ² country of Edom.

4 And he commanded them, saying, *e* Thus shall ye speak unto my lord Esau; Thy servant Jacob saith thus, I have sojourned with Laban, and stayed there until now:

5 And *f* I have oxen, and asses, flocks, and men-servants, and women-servants: and I have sent to tell my lord, that *g* I may find grace in thy sight.

6 ¶ And the messengers returned to Jacob, saying, We came to thy brother Esau, and also *h* he cometh to meet thee, and four hundred men with him.

7 Then Jacob was greatly afraid and *i* distressed: and he *j* divided the people that was with him, and the flocks, and herds, and the camels, into two bands;

8 And said, If Esau come to the one company, and smite it, then the other company which is left shall escape.

9 ¶ *k* And Jacob said, *l* O God of my father Abraham, and God of my father Isaac, the LORD *m* which saidst unto me, Return unto thy country, and to thy kindred, and I will deal well with thee:

10 ³ I am not *n* worthy of the least of all the *o* mercies, and of all the truth, which thou hast showed unto thy servant; for with my *p* staff I passed over this Jordan, and now I am become two bands.

11 *q* Deliver me, I pray thee, from the hand of my brother, from the hand of Esau: for I fear him, lest he will come and smite me, and *r* the mother ⁴ with the children.

12 And *s* thou saidst, I will surely do thee good, and make thy seed as the sand of the sea, which cannot be numbered for multitude.

13 ¶ And he lodged there that same night; and took of that which came to his hand a *t* present for Esau his brother:

14 Two hundred she-goats, and twenty he-goats, two hundred ewes, and twenty rams,

15 Thirty milch camels with their colts, forty kine, and ten bulls, twenty she-asses, and ten foals.

16 And he delivered *them* into the hand of his servants, every drove by themselves; and said unto his servants, Pass over before me, and put a space betwixt drove and drove.

17 And he commanded the foremost, saying, When Esau my brother meeteth thee, and asketh thee, saying, Whose *art* thou? and whither goest thou? and whose *are* these before thee?

18 Then thou shalt say, *They be* thy servant Jacob's; it *is* a present sent unto my lord Esau: and, behold, also he *is* behind us.

19 And so commanded he the second, and the third, and all that followed the droves, saying, On this manner shall ye speak unto Esau, when ye find him.

20 And say ye moreover, Behold, thy servant Jacob *is* behind us. For he said, I will *u* appease him with the present that goeth before me, and afterward I will see his face; peradventure he will accept ⁵ of me.

21 So went the present over before him: and himself lodged that night in the company.

22 And he rose up that night, and took his

B. C. 1739.

CHAP. 32.
b Josh. 5. 14.
2 Ki. 6. 16.
Ps. 103. 21.
Ps. 148. 2.
Luke, 2. 13.
1 That is, two hosts, or camps.
c ch.33.14.16.
d ch. 36. 6-8.
Deut. 2. 5.
Josh. 24. 4.
2 field.
e Prov. 15. 1.
f ch. 30. 43.
g ch. 33. 8, 15
h ch. 33. 1.
i ch. 35. 3.
j Ps. 112. 5.
Pr. 2. 11.
Is. 28. 26.
Mat. 10. 16.
Ro. 16. 19.
Eph. 5. 15.
k Ps. 50. 15.
l ch. 28. 13.
m ch.31.3,13
3 I am less than all, etc.
n 2 Sam. 9. 8.
Dan. 9. 9.
o ch. 24. 27.
p Job 8. 7.
q Ps. 59. 1, 2.
r Hos. 10. 14.
4 upon.
e ch. 28. 13-15.
s ch. 43. 11.
Pro. 18. 16
t Pro. 21. 14
5 my face.
v Deut. 3. 16.
6 caused to pass.
7 ascending of the morning.
w Mat. 26.41.
x Luke 24.28.
y Hos. 12. 4.
8 That is, a prince of God.
z Hos. 12. 34.
a ch. 25. 31.
ch. 27. 33.
b Jud. 13. 16.
9 That is, the face of God.
c Ex. 33. 20.
Deut. 5. 24.
Judg. 6. 22
Jud. 13. 22.
Is. 6. 5.

CHAP. 33.
a ch. 32. 6.
b ch. 18. 2.
ch. 42. 6.
ch. 43. 26.
c ch. 32. 28.
d ch. 45. 14.
1 to thee.
e ch. 48. 9.
Ps. 127. 3.
Is. 8. 18.
2 What is all this band to thee?
f ch. 32. 16.
g ch. 32. 5.
3 be that to thee that is thine.
h Mat. 18.10.

two wives, and his two women-servants, and his eleven sons, and *v* passed over the ford Jabbok.

23 And he took them, and ⁶ sent them over the brook, and sent over that he had.

24 ¶ And Jacob was left alone: and there wrestled a man with him until the ⁷ breaking of the day.

25 And when he saw that he prevailed not against him, he touched the hollow of his thigh; and the *w* hollow of Jacob's thigh was out of joint as he wrestled with him.

26 And *x* he said, Let me go, for the day breaketh. And he said, *y* I will not let thee go, except thou bless me.

27 And he said unto him, What *is* thy name? And he said, Jacob.

28 And he said, Thy name shall be called no more Jacob, but ⁸ Israel: for as a prince hast thou *z* power with God and *a* with men, and hast prevailed.

29 And Jacob asked *him*, and said, Tell me, I pray thee, thy name. And he said, *b* Wherefore *is* it *that* thou dost ask after my name? And he blessed him there.

30 And Jacob called the name of the place ⁹ Peniel: for *c* I have seen God face to face, and my life is preserved.

31 And as he passed over Penuel the sun rose upon him, and he halted upon his thigh.

32 Therefore the children of Israel eat not of the sinew which shrank, which *is* upon the hollow of the thigh, unto this day: because he touched the hollow of Jacob's thigh in the sinew that shrank.

CHAPTER XXXIII.

1 *The kindness of Jacob and Esau at their meeting.* 17 *Jacob cometh to Succoth:* 18 *He buyeth a field, and buildeth an altar.*

AND Jacob lifted up his eyes, and looked, and, behold, *a* Esau came, and with him four hundred men. And he divided the children unto Leah, and unto Rachel, and unto the two handmaids.

2 And he put the handmaids and their children foremost, and Leah and her children after, and Rachel and Joseph hindermost.

3 And he passed over before them, and *b* bowed himself to the ground seven times, until he came near to his brother.

4 *c* And Esau ran to meet him, and embraced him, *d* and fell on his neck, and kissed him: and they wept.

5 And he lifted up his eyes, and saw the women and the children; and said, Who *are* those ¹ with thee? And he said, The children *e* which God hath graciously given thy servant.

6 Then the handmaidens came near, they and their children, and they bowed themselves:

7 And Leah also with her children came near, and bowed themselves: and after came Joseph near and Rachel, and they bowed themselves.

8 And he said, ² What *meanest* thou by *f* all this drove which I met? And he said, *These are* ³ to find grace in the sight of my lord.

9 And Esau said, I have enough, my brother; ³ keep that thou hast unto thyself.

10 And Jacob said, Nay, I pray thee, if now I have found grace in thy sight, then receive my present at my hand; for therefore I *h* have seen thy face, as though I had

elder brother, was, according to the custom of the East, entitled to respectful treatment from his younger brother. His attendants would be struck by it, and, according to Eastern habits, would magnify it in the hearing of their master. **4.** Esau ran to meet him —What a sudden and surprising change! Whether the sight of the princely present and the profound homage of Jacob had produced this effect, or it proceeded from the impulsive character of Esau, the cherished enmity of twenty years in a moment disappeared; the weapons of war were laid aside, and the warmest tokens of mutual affection reciprocated between the brothers. But, doubtless, the efficient cause was the secret, subduing influence of grace (Pro. 21. 1), which converted Esau from an enemy into a friend. **5.** Who are those with thee?—It might have been enough to say, They are my children; but Jacob was a pious man, and he could not give even a common answer but in the language of piety (Ps. 137. 3; 113. 9; 107. 41.). **11.** He urged him, and he took it—In the East the acceptance of a present by a superior is a proof of friendship, and by an enemy of reconciliation. It was on both accounts Jacob was so anxious that his brother should receive the cattle; and in Esau's acceptance he had the strongest proofs of a good feeling being established that eastern notions admit of.

12-20. THE PARTING. 12. Let us take our journey—Esau proposed to accompany Jacob and his family through the country, both as a mark of friendship and as an escort to guard them. But the proposal was prudently declined. Jacob did not need any worldly state or equipage. Notwithstanding the present cordiality, the brothers were so different in spirit, character, and habits—the one so much a man of the world, and the other a man of God, that there was great risk of something occurring to disturb the harmony. Jacob having alleged a very reasonable excuse for the tardiness of his movements, the brothers parted in peace. **14.** until I come unto my lord—It seems to have been Jacob's intention, passing round the Dead Sea, to visit his brother in Seir, and thus, without crossing the Jordan, go to Beersheba to Isaac; but he changed his plan, and whether the intention was carried out then or at a future period has not been recorded. **17.** journeyed to Succoth—that is, booths, that being the first station at which Jacob halted on his arrival in Canaan. His posterity, when dwelling in houses of stone, built a city there and called it Succoth, to commemorate the fact that their ancestor, "a Syrian ready to perish," was glad to dwell in booths. **18.** Shalem—*i.e.*, peace; and the meaning may be that Jacob came into Canaan, arriving safe and sound at the city Shechem—a tribute to Him who had promised such a return (cf. 28. 15.). But most writers take Shalem as a proper name—a city of Shechem, and that the site is marked by one of the little villages about two miles to the north-east. A little further in the valley below Shechem "he bought a parcel of a field, where he spread his tent," thus being the first of the patriarchs who became a proprietor of land in Canaan. **19.** an hundred pieces of money—pieces, *lit.*, "lambs;" probably a coin with the figure of a lamb on it. **20.** erected an altar—A beautiful proof of his personal piety, a most suitable conclusion to his journey, and a lasting memorial of a distinguished favour in the name "God, the God of Israel." Wherever we pitch a tent God should have an altar.

CHAPTER XXXIV.

Ver. 1-31. THE DISHONOUR OF DINAH. **1-4.** Though freed from foreign troubles, Jacob met with a great domestic calamity in the fall of his only daughter. According to Josephus, she had been attending a festival; but it is highly probable that she had been often and freely mixing in the society of the place, and that being a simple, inexperienced, and vain young woman, had been flattered by the attentions of the ruler's son. There must have been time and opportunities of acquaintance to produce the strong attachment that Shechem had for her. **5-7.** Jacob held his peace—Jacob, as a father and a good man, must have been deeply distressed. But he could do little. In the case of a family by different wives, it is not the father, but the full brothers, on whom the protection of the daughters devolves—they are the guardians of a sister's welfare and the avengers of her wrongs. It was for this reason that Simeon and Levi, the two brothers of Dinah by Leah, appear the chief actors in this episode; and though the two fathers would have probably brought about an amicable arrangement of the affair, the hasty arrival of these enraged brothers introduced a new element into the negotiations. **6.** Hamor—*i. e.*, ass; and it is a striking proof of the very different ideas which, in the East, are associated with that animal, which there appears sprightly, well proportioned, and of great activity. This chief is called Emmor (A. 7. 16.). **7.** were grieved and very wroth—Good men in such a case could not but grieve; but it would have been well if their anger had been less, or that they had known the precept "let the sun go down upon your wrath." No injury can justify revenge; but Jacob's sons planned a scheme of revenge in the most deceitful manner (Deut. 32. 35; Ro. 12. 9.). **8.** Hamor communed with them—The prince and his son seem at first sight to have acted honestly, and our feelings are enlisted on their side. They betray no jealousy of the powerful shepherds; on the contrary, shew every desire to establish friendly intercourse. But their conduct was unjustifiable in neither expressing regret nor restoring Dinah to her family; and this great error was the true cause of the negotiations ending in so unhappy a manner. **11.** Shechem said unto her father and brethren—The consideration of the proposal for marriage belonged to Jacob, and he certainly shewed great weakness in yielding so much to the fiery impetuosity of his sons. The sequel shows the unhappy consequences of that concession. **12.** Ask me never so much dowry and gift—The gift refers to the presents made at betrothal, both to the bride elect and her relations (cf. 24. 53); the dowry to a suitable settlement upon her. **13.** The sons of Jacob answered—The honour of their family consisted in having the sign of the covenant. Circumcision was the external rite by which persons were admitted to members of the ancient Church. But that outward rite could not make the Shechemites true Israelites; and yet it does not appear that Jacob's required anything more. Nothing is said of their teaching them to worship the true God, but only of their

seen the face of God, and thou wast pleased with me.

11 Take, I pray thee, *my blessing that is brought to thee; because God hath dealt graciously with me, and because I have *enough. *And he urged him, and he took it.

12 And he said, Let us take our journey, and let us go, and I will go before thee.

13 And he said unto him, My lord knoweth that the children *are* tender, and the flocks and herds with young *are* with me; and if men should overdrive them one day, all the flock will die.

14 Let my lord, I pray thee, pass over before his servant; and I will lead on softly, according 5 as the cattle that goeth before me and the children be able to endure, until I come unto my lord *unto Seir.

15 And Esau said, Let me now 6 leave with thee *some* of the folk that *are* with me. And he said, 7 What needeth it? *let me find grace in the sight of my lord.

16 ¶ So Esau returned that day on his way unto Seir.

17 And Jacob journeyed to *m* Succoth, and built him an house, and made booths for his cattle: therefore the name of the place is called 8 Succoth.

18 ¶ And Jacob came to *n* Shalem a city of 9 Shechem, which *is* in the land of Canaan, when he came from Padan-aram; and pitched his tent before the city.

19 And *o* he bought a parcel of a field, where he had spread his tent, at the hand of the children of 10 Hamor, Shechem's father, for an hundred 11 pieces of money.

20 And he erected there an altar, and *p* called it 12 El-elohe-Israel.

CHAPTER XXXIV.

1 *Dinah defiled.* 20 *The Shechemites are circumcised.* 25 *The sons of Jacob taking advantage thereof slay them, and spoil their city.* 30 *Jacob reproveth Simeon and Levi.*

AND *a* Dinah the daughter of Leah, which she bare unto Jacob, *b* went out to see the daughters of the land.

2 And when Shechem the son of Hamor the Hivite, prince of the country, *c* saw her, he *d* took her, and lay with her, and 1 defiled her.

3 And his soul clave unto Dinah the daughter of Jacob, and he loved the damsel, and spake 2 kindly unto the damsel.

4 And Shechem *e* spake unto his father Hamor, saying, Get me this damsel to wife.

5 And Jacob heard that he had defiled Dinah his daughter: now his sons were with his cattle in the field: and Jacob held his peace until they were come.

6 ¶ And Hamor the father of Shechem went out unto Jacob to commune with him.

7 And the sons of Jacob came out of the field when they heard *it:* and the men were grieved, and they were *f* very wroth, because he had *g* wrought folly in Israel, in lying with Jacob's daughter; *h* which thing ought not to be done.

8 And Hamor communed with them, saying, The soul of my son Shechem longeth for your daughter: I pray you give her him to wife.

9 And *i* make ye marriages with us, *and* give your daughters unto us, and take our daughters unto you.

10 And ye shall dwell with us: and *f* the land shall be before you; dwell and *k* trade ye therein, and *l* get you possessions therein.

11 And Shechem said unto her father and unto her brethren, Let me find grace in your eyes, and what ye shall say unto me I will give.

12 Ask me never so much *m* dowry and gift, and I will give according as ye shall say unto me: but give me the damsel to wife.

13 And the sons of Jacob answered Shechem and Hamor his father *n* deceitfully, and said, because he had defiled Dinah their sister:

14 And they said unto them, We cannot do this thing, to give our sister to one that is uncircumcised; for *o* that *were* a reproach unto us:

15 But in this will we consent unto you: If ye will be as we *be*, that every male of you be circumcised;

16 Then will we give our daughters unto you, and we will take your daughters to us, and we will dwell with you, and we will become one people.

17 But if ye will not hearken unto us, to be circumcised; then will we take our daughter, and we will be gone.

18 And their words pleased Hamor, and Shechem, Hamor's son.

19 And the young man deferred not to do the thing, because he had delight in Jacob's daughter: and he *was p* more honourable than all the house of his father.

20 And Hamor and Shechem his son came unto the *q* gate of their city, and communed with the men of their city, saying,

21 These men *are* peaceable with us; therefore let them dwell in the land, and trade therein; for the land, behold, *it is* large enough for them; let us take their daughters to us for wives, and let us give them our daughters.

22 Only herein will the men consent unto us for to dwell with us, to be one people, if every male among us be circumcised, as they *are* circumcised.

23 *Shall* not their cattle and their substance and every beast of theirs *be* ours? only let us consent unto them, and they will dwell with us.

24 And unto Hamor, and unto Shechem his son, hearkened all that *r* went out of the gate of his city; and every male was circumcised, all that went out of the gate of his city.

25 ¶ And it came to pass on the third day, when they were sore, that two of the sons of Jacob, *s* Simeon and Levi, Dinah's brethren, took each man his sword, and came upon the city boldly, and slew all the males.

26 And they slew Hamor and Shechem his son with the 3 edge of the sword, and took Dinah out of Shechem's house, and went out.

27 The sons of Jacob came upon the slain, and spoiled the city, because they had defiled their sister.

28 They took their sheep, and their oxen, and their asses, and that which *was* in the city, and that which *was* in the field,

29 And all their wealth, and all their little ones, and their wives took they captive, and spoiled even all that *was* in the house.

30 And Jacob said to Simeon and Levi, *t* Ye have *u* troubled me *v* to make me to stink among the inhabitants of the land,

insisting on their being circumcised; and it is evident that they did not seek to convert Shechem, but only made a show of religion—a cloak to cover their diabolical design. Hypocrisy and deceit, in all cases vicious, are infinitely more so when accompanied with a shew of religion; and here the sons of Jacob, under the pretence of conscientious scruples, conceal a scheme of treachery as cruel and diabolical as was, perhaps, ever perpetrated. 20. Hamor and Shechem came unto the gate of their city—That was the place where every public communication was made; and in the ready obsequious submission of the people to this measure we see an evidence either of the extraordinary affection for the governing family, or of the abject despotism of the East, where the will of a chief is an absolute command. 30. Jacob said, Ye have troubled me—This atrocious outrage perpetrated on the defenceless citizens and their families made the cup of Jacob's affliction overflow. We may wonder that, in speaking of it to his sons, he did not represent it as a heinous sin—an atrocious violation of the laws of God and man, but dwelt solely on the present consequences. It was probably because that was the only view likely to rouse the cold-blooded apathy, the hardened consciences of those ruffian sons. Nothing but the restraining power of God saved him and his family from the united vengeance of the people (cf. 25. 5.). All his sons had not been engaged in the massacre. Joseph was a boy, Benjamin not yet born, and the other eight not concerned in it. Simeon and Levi alone, with their retainers, had been the guilty actors in the bloody tragedy. But the Canaanites would not be discriminating in their vengeance; and if *all* the Shechemites were put to death for the offence of their chief's son, what wonder if the natives should extend their hatred to all the family of Jacob; and who, probably, equalled, in number, the inhabitants of that village.

CHAPTER XXXV.

Ver. 1-15. REMOVAL TO BETHEL. God said to Jacob, Arise, &c.—This command was given as seasonably in point of time, as tenderly in respect of language. The disgraceful and perilous events that had recently taken place in the patriarch's family must have produced in him a strong desire to remove without delay from the vicinity of Shechem. Borne down by an overwhelming sense of the criminality of his two sons—of the offence they had given to God, and the dishonour they had brought on the true faith; distracted, too, with anxiety, about the probable consequences which their outrage might bring upon himself and family, should the Canaanite people combine to extirpate such a band of robbers and murderers: he must have felt this call as affording a great relief to his afflicted feelings. At the same time it conveyed a tender rebuke. go up to Bethel, &c.—Bethel was about thirty miles south of Shechem; and was an ascent from a low to a highland country. There, he would not only be released from the painful associations of the latter place, but be established on a spot, that would revive the most delightful and sublime recollections. The pleasure of revisiting it, however, was not altogether unalloyed. make an altar unto God that appeared—It too frequently happens that early impressions are effaced through lapse of time—that promises made, in seasons of distress, are forgotten; or, if remembered on the return of health and prosperity, there is not the same alacrity and sense of obligation felt to fulfil them. Jacob was lying under that charge. He had fallen into spiritual indolence. It was now eight or ten years since his return to Canaan. He had effected a comfortable settlement; and had acknowledged the divine mercies, by which that return and settlement had been signally distinguished (cf. 33. 19.). But for some unrecorded reason, his early vow at Bethel, in a great crisis of his life, remained unperformed. The Lord appeared now to remind him of his neglected duty, in terms, however, so mild, as awakened less the memory of his fault, than of the kindness of his heavenly Guardian; and how much Jacob felt the touching nature of the appeal to that memorable scene at Bethel, appears in the immediate preparations he made to *arise* and *go up* thither (Ps. 66. 13.). 2. And he said ... household put away strange gods—*Heb.* gods of the stranger—of foreign nations. Jacob had brought, in his service, a number of Mesopotamian retainers, who were addicted to superstitious practices; and there is some reason to fear that the same high testimony as to the religious superintendance of his household could not have been borne of him as was done of Abraham (18. 19.). He might have been too negligent hitherto in winking at these evils in his servants; or, perhaps it was not till his arrival in Canaan, that he had learnt, for the first time, that one nearer and dearer to him was secretly infected with the same corruption (31. 34.). Be that as it may, he resolved on an immediate and thorough reformation of his household; and in commanding them to put away the strange gods, he added, "be clean, and change your garments;" as if some defilement, from contact with idolatry, should still remain about them. In the law of Moses, many ceremonial purifications were ordained, and observed by persons who had contracted certain defilements, and without the observance of which, they were reckoned unclean and unfit to join in the social worship of God. These bodily purifications were purely figurative; and as sacrifices were offered before the law, so also were external purifications, as appears from the words of Jacob; hence it would seem that types and symbols were used from the fall of man, representing and teaching the two great doctrines of revealed truth—*viz.* the atonement of Christ, and the sanctification of our nature. 4. They gave all the strange gods and earrings—Strange gods—the Teraphim (cf. 31. 30,) as well, perhaps, as other idols got amongst the Shechemite spoil—earrings of various forms, sizes, and materials, which are universally worn in the East, and, then as now, connected with incantation and idolatry (cf. Hos. 2. 13.). The decided tone which Jacob now assumed, was the probable cause of the alacrity with which those favourite objects of superstition were surrendered. Jacob hid them under the oak—or terebinth—a towering tree, which, like all others of the kind, were striking objects in the scenery of Palestine; and beneath which at Shechem, the patriarch had pitched his tent. He hid the images and amulets, delivered to him by his Mesopotamian depend-

among the Canaanites and the Perizzites: *and I being few in number, they shall gather themselves together against me, and slay me; and I shall be destroyed, I and my house.

31 And they said, *Should he deal with our sister as with an harlot?

CHAPTER XXXV.

1 *God sendeth Jacob to Beth-el; 2 he purgeth his house of idols, 6 and buildeth an altar. 9 God blesseth him there. 16 Rachel beareth Benjamin, and dies. 23 The sons of Jacob. 28 Isaac's death.*

AND God said unto Jacob, Arise, go up to *a* Beth-el, and dwell there: and make there an altar unto God, *b* that appeared unto thee *c* when thou fleddest from the face of Esau thy brother.

2 Then Jacob said unto his *d* household, and to all that *were* with him, Put away *the strange gods that are among you, and *be clean, and change your garments:

3 And let us arise, and go up to Beth-el; and I will make there an altar unto God, *g* who answered me in the day of my distress, *h* and was with me in the way which I went.

4 And they gave unto Jacob all the strange gods which *were* in their hand, and all their *earrings which were in their ears; and Jacob hid them under *j* the oak which *was* by Shechem.

5 And they journeyed: and *k* the terror of God was upon the cities that *were* round about them, and they did not pursue after the sons of Jacob.

6 ¶ So Jacob came to *l* Luz, which *is* in the land of Canaan, that *is*, Beth-el, he, and all the people that *were* with him.

7 And he *m* built there an altar, and called the place ¹ El-beth-el; because *n* there God appeared unto him, when he fled from the face of his brother.

8 But *o* Deborah, Rebekah's nurse, died, and she was buried beneath Beth-el under an oak: and the name of it was called ² Allon-bachuth.

9 ¶ And *p* God appeared unto Jacob again, when he came out of Padan-aram, and blessed him.

10 And God said unto him, Thy name *is* Jacob: *q* thy name shall not be called any more Jacob, but *r* Israel shall be thy name: and he called his name Israel.

11 And God said unto him, *s* I *am* God Almighty; be fruitful and multiply; a *t* nation, and a company of nations, shall be of thee, and kings shall come out of thy loins;

12 And the land *u* which I gave Abraham and Isaac, to thee I will give it, and to thy seed after thee will I give the land.

13 And God *v* went up from him in the place where he talked with him.

14 And Jacob *w* set up a pillar in the place where he talked with him, *even* a pillar of stone: and he poured a drink offering thereon, and he poured oil thereon.

15 And Jacob called the name of the place where God spake with him, *x* Beth-el.

16 ¶ And they journeyed from Beth-el; and there was but ³ a little way to come to Ephrath: and Rachel travailed, and she had hard labour.

17 And it came to pass, when she was in hard labour, that the midwife said unto her, Fear not; *y* thou shalt have this son also.

18 And it came to pass, as her soul was in departing, (for she died,) that she called his

B. C. 1732.

CHAP. 34.
w Deu. 4. 27.
Ps. 105.12.
x Prov. 6. 34.

CHAP. 35.
a ch. 28. 19.
b ch. 28. 13.
c ch. 27. 43.
d ch. 18. 19.
e ch.31.19,34.
1 Sam. 7. 3.
f Ex. 19. 10.
g ch. 32, 7,24.
Ps. 107. 6.
h ch. 28. 20.
ch. 31, 3,42.
i Hos. 2. 13.
j Josh. 24,26.
k Ex. 15. 16.
Ex. 34. 24.
Deu. 11.25.
l ch. 28. 22.
m Eccl. 5. 4.
1 That is, the God of Beth-el.
n ch. 28. 13.
o ch. 24. 59.
2 That is, the oak of weeping.
p Heb. 12. 4.
q ch. 17. 5.
r ch. 32. 28.
s ch. 17. 1.
Ez. 6. 3.
t ch. 17. 5, 6.
ch. 48. 4.
u ch. 12. 7.
ch. 28. 13.
ch. 17. 22.
w ch. 28. 18.
x ch. 28. 19.
3 a little piece of ground.
y ch. 30. 24.
4 That is, the son of my sorrow.
5 That is, the son of the right hand.
z ch. 48. 7.
a Ruth 1. 2.
Mat. 2. 6.
b 1 Sa. 10. 2.
c Mic. 4. 8.
d ch. 49. 4.
1 Chr. 5. 1.
e ch. 46. 8.
Ex. 1. 2.
f ch. 13. 18.
g Jos. 14. 15.
h Ec. 12. 7.
i ch. 15. 15.
j ch. 25. 9.
ch. 49. 31.

CHAP. 36.
a ch. 25. 30.
b ch. 26. 34.
c ver. 25.
d ch. 28. 9.
e 1 Chr. 1. 35.
1 souls.
f Deut. 23. 7.
g ch. 13.6, 11.
h ch. 17. 8.
i ch. 32. 3.
j ver. 1.
2 Edom.
k 1 Chr. 1. 35, etc.
3 Or, Zephi.
l Ex. 17. 8.

name *4* Ben-oni: but his father called him *5* Benjamin.

19 And *z* Rachel died, and was buried in the way to *a* Ephrath, which *is* Beth-lehem.

20 And Jacob set a pillar upon her grave: that *is* the pillar of Rachel's grave *b* unto this day.

21 ¶ And Israel journeyed, and spread his tent beyond *c* the tower of Edar.

22 And it came to pass, when Israel dwelt in that land, that Reuben went and *d* lay with Bilhah his father's concubine: and Israel heard *it*. Now the sons of Jacob were twelve:

23 The sons of Leah; *e* Reuben, Jacob's first-born, and Simeon, and Levi, and Judah, and Issachar, and Zebulun:

24 The sons of Rachel; Joseph and Benjamin:

25 And the sons of Bilhah, Rachel's handmaid; Dan and Naphtali:

26 And the sons of Zilpah, Leah's handmaid; Gad and Asher: these *are* the sons of Jacob, which were born to him in Padan-aram.

27 ¶ And Jacob came unto Isaac his father unto *f* Mamre, unto the *g* city of Arba, which *is* Hebron, where Abraham and Isaac sojourned.

28 And the days of Isaac were an hundred and fourscore years.

29 And Isaac *h* gave up the ghost, and died, and *i* was gathered unto his people, *being* old and full of days: and *j* his sons Esau and Jacob buried him.

CHAPTER XXXVI.

2 *Esau's family in Canaan. 6 He removeth to mount Seir. 9 His sons. 15 The dukes which descended of his sons. 20 The sons and dukes of Seir. 31 The kings of Edom.*

NOW these *are* the generations of Esau, *a* who *is* Edom.

2 *b* Esau took his wives of the daughters of Canaan; Adah the daughter of Elon the Hittite, and *c* Aholibamah the daughter of Anah the daughter of Zibeon the Hivite;

3 And *d* Bashemath, Ishmael's daughter, sister of Nebajoth.

4 And *e* Adah bare to Esau Eliphaz; and Bashemath bare Reuel;

5 And Aholibamah bare Jeush, and Jaalam, and Korah: these *are* the sons of Esau, which were born unto him in the land of Canaan.

6 And Esau took his wives, and his sons, and his daughters, and all the ¹ persons of his house, and his cattle, and all his beasts, and all his substance, which he had got in the land of Canaan; and went into the country from the face of his *f* brother Jacob.

7 *g* For their riches were more than that they might dwell together; and *h* the land wherein they were strangers could not bear them because of their cattle.

8 Thus dwelt Esau in *i* mount Seir: *j* Esau *is* Edom.

9 ¶ And these *are* the generations of Esau the father of ² the Edomites in mount Seir:

10 These *are* the names of Esau's sons; *k* Eliphaz the son of Adah the wife of Esau, Reuel the son of Bashemath the wife of Esau.

11 And the sons of Eliphaz were Teman, Omar, ³ Zepho, and Gatam, and Kenaz.

12 And Timna was concubine to Eliphaz, Esau's son; and she bare to Eliphaz *l* Amalek: these *were* the sons of Adah, Esau's wife.

ents, at the root of this tree. The oak being deemed a consecrated tree, to bury them at its root was to deposit them in a place where no bold hand would venture to disturb the ground; and hence it was called from this circumstance—"the plain of Meonenim"—*i. e.*, the oak of enchantments (Jud. 9. 37); and from the great stone which Joshua set up—"the oak of the pillar" (Jud. 9. 6.). The terror of God was upon the cities—There was every reason to apprehend that a storm of indignation would burst from all quarters upon Jacob's family, and that the Canaanite tribes would have formed one united plan of revenge. But a supernatural panic seized them; and thus, for the sake of the "heir of the promise," the protecting shield of Providence was specially held over his family. 6. So Jacob came to Luz .. that is, Beth-el—It is probable that this place was unoccupied ground when Jacob first went to it; and that after that period [CAL.], the Canaanites built a town, to which they gave the name of Luz, from the profusion of almond trees that grew around. The name of Bethel, which would, of course, be confined to Jacob and his family, did not supersede the original one till long after. It is now identified with the modern Beitin, and lies on the western slope of the mountain on which Abraham built his altar (Gen. 12. 8.). 7. El-Bethel—*i. e.* the God of Bethel. 8. Deborah, Rebekah's nurse, died—this event seems to have taken place before the solemnities were commenced. Deborah—a bee—supposing her to have been fifty years, on coming to Canaan, she had attained the great age of 180. When she was removed from Isaac's household to Jacob's, is unknown. But it probably was on his return from Mesopotamia; and she would have been of invaluable service to his young family. Old nurses, like her, were not only honoured, but loved as mothers; and, accordingly, her death was the occasion of a great lamentation. She was buried under *the* oak—hence called the "terebinth of tears" (cf. 1 Kings, 13. 14.). God was pleased to make a new appearance to him after the solemn rites of devotion were over. By this manifestation of his presence, God testified his acceptance of Jacob's sacrifice, renewed the promise of the blessings guaranteed to Abraham and Isaac; and the patriarch observed the ceremony with which he had formerly consecrated the place; comprising a sacramental offering and the oil that he poured on the pillar; and reimposing the memorable name. The whole scene was in accordance with the character of the patriarchal dispensation, in which the great truths of religion were exhibited to the senses, and "the world's grey fathers" taught in a manner suited to the weakness of an infantine condition. 13. God went up from him—the presence of God was indicated in some visible form, and his acceptance of the sacrifice shewn by the miraculous descent of fire from heaven, consuming it on the altar.

16–27. BIRTH OF BENJAMIN — DEATH OF RACHEL, &c. 16. They journeyed from Beth-el—There can be no doubt that much enjoyment was experienced at Bethel, and that in the religious observances solemnized, as well as in the vivid recollections of the glorious vision seen there, the affections of the patriarch were powerfully animated, and that he left the place a better and more devoted servant of God. When the solemnities were over, Jacob, with his family, pursued a route directly southward, and they had reached Ephrath, when they were plunged into mourning by the death of Rachel, who sank in child-birth, leaving a posthumous son. A very affecting death, considering how ardently the mind of Rachel had been set on offspring (cf. 30. 1.). 18. Ben-oni—the dying mother gave this name to her child, significant of her circumstances; but Jacob changed it into Benjamin. This is thought by some to have been originally Benjamin, "a son of days"—*i.e.*, of old age. But with its present ending it means "son of the right hand"—*i.e.*, particularly dear and precious. 19. Ephrath, which is Beth-lehem—the one the old, the other the later name, signifying "house of bread." 20. set a pillar on her grave ... unto this day—The spot still marked out as the grave of Rachel exactly agrees with the Scripture record, being about a mile from Bethlehem. Anciently it was surmounted by a pyramid of stones, but the present tomb is a Mahommedan erection. 22-26. Sons of Jacob born in Padan-aram—It is a common practice of the sacred historian to say of a company or body of men that which, though true of the majority, may not be applicable to every individual. See M. 19. 28; J. 20. 24; Heb. 11. 13. Here is an example, for Benjamin was born in Canaan.

28, 29. DEATH OF ISAAC. Isaac gave up the ghost—The death of this venerable patriarch is here recorded by anticipation, for it did not take place till fifteen years after Joseph's disappearance. Feeble and blind though he was, he lived to a very advanced age; and it is a pleasing evidence of the permanent reconciliation between Esau and Jacob that they met at Mamre to perform the funeral rites of their common father.

CHAPTER XXXVI.

Ver. 1-43. POSTERITY OF ESAU. 1. These are the generations—history of the leading men and events (cf. 2. 4.). Esau, who is Edom—a name applied to him in reference to the peculiar colour of his skin at birth, rendered more significant by his inordinate craving for the *red* pottage, and also by the fierce sanguinary character of his descendants (cf. Ez. 25. 12; Ob. 10.). 2, 3. Esau took his wives—There were three, mentioned under different names; for it is evident that Bashemath is the same as Mahalath (28. 9), since they both stand in the relation of daughter to Ishmael and sister to Nebajoth; and hence it may be inferred that Adah is the same as Judith, Aholibamah, as Bathsemath (26. 34.). It was not unusual for women, in that early age, to have two names, as Sarai was also Iscah; and this is the more probable in the case of Esau's wives, who of course would have to take new names when they went from Canaan to settle in mount Seir. 6, 7. Esau went into the country from the face—*lit.*, a country, without any certain prospect of a settlement. The design of this historical sketch of Esau and his family is to shew how the promise (27. 39, 40.) was fulfilled. In temporal prosperity he far exceeds his brother; and it is remarkable that, in the overruling providence of God, the vast increase of his worldly substance was the occasion of his leaving Canaan, and thus making way for the return of Jacob. 8. Thus dwelt Esau in mount Seir—This was divinely

13 And these *are* the sons of Reuel; Nahath, and Zerah, Shammah, and Mizzah: these were the sons of Bashemath, Esau's wife.
14 And these were the sons of Aholibamah the daughter of Anah the daughter of Zibeon, Esau's wife: and she bare to Esau Jeush, and Jaalam, and Korah.
15 ¶ These *were* dukes of the sons of Esau: the sons of Eliphaz the first-born *son* of Esau; duke Teman, duke Omar, duke Zepho, duke Kenaz,
16 Duke Korah, duke Gatam, *and* duke Amalek: these *are* the dukes *that came* of Eliphaz in the land of Edom; these *were* the sons of Adah.
17 And these *are* the sons of Reuel, Esau's son; duke Nahath, duke Zerah, duke Shammah, duke Mizzah: these *are* the dukes *that came* of Reuel in the land of Edom; these *are* the sons of Bashemath, Esau's wife.
18 And these *are* the sons of Aholibamah, Esau's wife; duke Jeush, duke Jaalam, duke Korah: these *were* the dukes *that came* of Aholibamah the daughter of Anah, Esau's wife.
19 These *are* the sons of Esau, who *is* Edom, and these *are* their dukes.
20 ¶ These *are* the sons of Seir the Horite, who inhabited the land; Lotan, and Shobal, and Zibeon, and Anah,
21 And Dishon, and Ezer, and Dishan: these *are* the dukes of the Horites, the children of Seir in the land of Edom.
22 And the children of Lotan were Hori and Heman; and Lotan's sister *was* Timna.
23 And the children of Shobal *were* these; Alvan, and Manahath, and Ebal, Shepho, and Onam.
24 And these *are* the children of Zibeon; both Ajah and Anah: this *was that* Anah that found the mules in the wilderness, as he fed the asses of Zibeon his father.
25 And the children of Anah *were* these; Dishon, and Aholibamah the daughter of Anah.
26 And these *are* the children of Dishon; Hemdan, and Eshban, and Ithran, and Cheran.
27 The children of Ezer *are* these; Bilhan, and Zaavan, and Akan.
28 The children of Dishan *are* these; Uz, and Aran.
29 These *are* the dukes *that came* of the Horites; duke Lotan, duke Shobal, duke Zibeon, duke Anah,
30 Duke Dishon, duke Ezer, duke Dishan: these *are* the dukes *that came* of Hori, among their dukes in the land of Seir.
31 ¶ And these *are* the kings that reigned in the land of Edom, before there reigned any king over the children of Israel.
32 And Bela the son of Beor reigned in Edom: and the name of his city *was* Dinhabah.
33 And Bela died, and Jobab the son of Zerah of Bozrah reigned in his stead.
34 And Jobab died, and Husham of the land of Temani reigned in his stead.
35 And Husham died, and Hadad the son of Bedad, who smote Midian in the field of Moab, reigned in his stead: and the name of his city *was* Avith.
36 And Hadad died, and Samlah of Masrekah reigned in his stead.
37 And Samlah died, and Saul of Rehoboth *by* the river reigned in his stead.

38 And Saul died, and Baal-hanan the son of Achbor reigned in his stead.
39 And Baal-hanan the son of Achbor died, and Hadar reigned in his stead: and the name of his city *was* Pau; and his wife's name *was* Mehetabel, the daughter of Matred, the daughter of Mezahab.
40 ¶ And these *are* the names of the dukes *that came* of Esau, according to their families, after their places, by their names; duke Timnah, duke Alvah, duke Jetheth,
41 Duke Aholibamah, duke Elah, duke Pinon,
42 Duke Kenaz, duke Teman, duke Mibzar,
43 Duke Magdiel, duke Iram: these *be* the dukes of Edom, according to their habitations in the land of their possession: he *is* Esau the father of the Edomites.

CHAPTER XXXVII.

2 Joseph hated of his brethren: 5 his two dreams: 18 his brethren conspire his death. 23 He is cast into a pit. 26 They sell him to the Ishmeelites, 36 who sell him to Potiphar in Egypt.

AND Jacob dwelt in the land wherein his father was a stranger, in the land of Canaan.
2 These *are* the generations of Jacob. Joseph, *being* seventeen years old, was feeding the flock with his brethren; and the lad *was* with the sons of Bilhah, and with the sons of Zilpah, his father's wives: and Joseph brought unto his father their evil report.
3 Now Israel loved Joseph more than all his children, because he *was* the son of his old age: and he made him a coat of many colours.
4 And when his brethren saw that their father loved him more than all his brethren, they hated him, and could not speak peaceably unto him.
5 ¶ And Joseph dreamed a dream, and he told *it* his brethren: and they hated him yet the more.
6 And he said unto them, Hear, I pray you, this dream which I have dreamed:
7 For, behold, we *were* binding sheaves in the field, and, lo, my sheaf arose, and also stood upright; and, behold, your sheaves stood round about, and made obeisance to my sheaf.
8 And his brethren said to him, Shalt thou indeed reign over us? or shalt thou indeed have dominion over us? And they hated him yet the more for his dreams, and for his words.
9 And he dreamed yet another dream, and told it his brethren, and said, Behold, I have dreamed a dream more; and, behold, the sun, and the moon, and the eleven stars, made obeisance to me.
10 And he told *it* to his father, and to his brethren: and his father rebuked him, and said unto him, What *is* this dream that thou hast dreamed? Shall I and thy mother and thy brethren indeed come to bow down ourselves to thee to the earth?
11 And his brethren envied him; but his father observed the saying.
12 ¶ And his brethren went to feed their father's flock in Shechem.
13 And Israel said unto Joseph, Do not thy brethren feed *the flock* in Shechem? come, and I will send thee unto them. And he said to him, Here am I.
14 And he said to him, Go, I pray thee, see whether it be well with thy brethren,

assigned as his possession (Josh. 24. 4; Deu. 2. 5.). **15 19.** dukes—The Edomites, like the Israelites, were divided into tribes, which took their names from his sons. The head of each tribe was called by a term which in our version is rendered duke—not of the high rank and wealth of a British peer, but like the sheicks or emirs of the modern East, or the chieftains of our highland clans. Fourteen are mentioned who flourished contemporaneously. **20-30.** Sons of Seir, the Horite—native dukes, who were incorporated with those of the Edomite race. **31-39.** kings of Edom—The royal power was not built on the ruins of the dukedoms, but existed at the same time. **40-43.** Recapitulation of the dukes according to their residences. **44.** This is that Anah that found the mules—The word "mules" is, in several ancient versions, rendered "water springs;" and this discovery of some remarkable fountain was sufficient, among a wandering or pastoral people, to entitle him to such a distinguishing notice.

CHAPTER XXXVII.

Ver. 1–4. **PARENTAL PARTIALITY.** Jacob dwelt... father... stranger—*i. e.* sojourner; father used collectively. The patriarch was at this time at Mamre, in the valley of Hebron (cf. 35. 27); and his dwelling there was continued in the same manner, and prompted by the same motives as that of Abraham and Isaac (Heb. 12. 13.). **2.** generations—leading occurrences, in the domestic history of Jacob, as shewn in the narrative about to be commenced. Joseph was feeding—*lit.* Joseph being seventeen years old was a shepherd over the flock—he a lad, with the sons of Bilhah and Zilpah. Oversight or superintendance is evidently implied. This post of chief shepherd in the party might be assigned him either from his being the son of a principal wife, or from his own superior qualities of character; and if invested with this office, he acted not as a gossiping tell-tale, but as "a faithful steward" in reporting the scandalous conduct of his brethren. **3.** son of his old age—Benjamin being younger, was more the son of his old age, and consequently on that ground might have been expected to be the favourite. Literally rendered, it is "son of old age to him"—*Heb.* phrase, for "a wise son"—one who possessed observation and wisdom above his years—an old head on young shoulders. made him a coat of colours—formed in those early days by sewing together patches of coloured cloth, and considered a dress of distinction (Jud. 5. 30; 2 Sam. 13.18.). The passion for various colours still reigns amongst the Arabs and other people of the East, who are fond of dressing their children in this gaudy attire. But since the art of interweaving various patterns was introduced, "the coats of colours" are different now from what they seem to have been in patriarchal times, and bear a close resemblance to the varieties of tartan. **4.** could not speak peaceably to him—did not say "peace be to thee," the usual expression of good wishes amongst friends and acquaintances. It is deemed a sacred duty to give all this form of salutation; and the withholding of it is an unmistakeable sign of dislike or secret hostility. The habitual refusal of Joseph's brethren, therefore, to meet him with "the *salaam*," showed how ill-disposed they were towards him. It is very natural in parents to love the youngest, and feel partial to those who excel in talents or amiableness. But in a family constituted as Jacob's—many children by different mothers—he showed great and criminal indiscretion. **5-36. THE DREAMS OF JOSEPH.** Dreamed a dream—Dreams in ancient times were much attended to, and hence the dream of Joseph, though but a mere boy, engaged the serioud consideration of his family. But this dream was evidently symbolical. The meaning was easily discerned, and, from its being repeates under different emblems, the fulfilment was considered certain (cf. 41. 32.)—whence it was that "his brethren envied him, but his father observed the saying." **12.** his brethren went to... in Shechem—the vale of Shechem was, from the earliest mention of Canaan, blest with extraordinary abundance of water. Therefore did the sons of Jacob go from Hebron to this place, though it must have cost them near twenty hours travelling—*i. e.*, at the shepherd rate, a little more than fifty miles. But the herbage there is so rich and nutritious, that they thought it well worth the pains of so long a journey to the neglect of the grazing district of Hebron." [VANDE VELDE.] **13-17.** Israel said, Do not thy brethren, &c.—anxious to learn how his sons were doing in their distant encampment, Jacob despatched Joseph; and the youth accepting the mission with alacrity, left the vale of Hebron, sought them at Shechem—heard of them from a man in "the field,"—the wide and richly-cultivated plain of Esdraelon, and found that they had left that neighbourhood for Dothan, probably being compelled by the detestation in which, from the horrid massacre, their name was held, found them in Dothan—*Heb.* Dothaim, or "two wells," recently discovered in the modern "Dotan," situated a few hours' distance from Shechem. **18-22.** when they saw him afar off—on the level grass-field, where they were watching their cattle, they could perceive him approaching in the distance from the side of Shechem, or rather Samaria. behold this dreamer cometh—*lit.*, "master of dreams"—a bitterly ironical sneer. Dreams being considered suggestions from above, to make false pretensions to having received one was detested as a species of blasphemy, and in this light Joseph was regarded by his brethren—an artful pretender. They already began to form a plot for his assassination, from which he was rescued only by the address of Reuben, who suggested that he should rather be cast into one of the wells, which are, and probably were, completely dried up in summer. they stript... coat of colours—Imagine him advancing in all the unsuspecting openness of brotherly affection. How astonished and terrified must he have been at the cold reception, the ferocious aspect, the rough usage of his unnatural assailants. A vivid picture of his state of agony and despair was afterwards drawn by themselves (cf. 42. 21.). **25.** they sat down to eat bread—what a view does this exhibit of those hardened profligates! Their common share in this conspiracy is not the only dismal feature in the story. The rapidity, the almost instantaneous manner in which the proposal was followed by their joint resolution, and the cool indifference, or rather the fiendish satisfaction, with which they sat down to regale themselves (Amos, 6. 6.)—it is impossible that mere envy at his dreams, his gaudy

and well with the flocks; and bring me word again. So he sent him out of the vale of Hebron, and he came to Shechem.

15 And a certain man found him, and, behold, *he was* wandering in the field: and the man asked him, saying, What seekest thou?

16 And he said, I seek my brethren: tell me, I pray thee, where they feed *their flocks.*

17 And the man said, They are departed hence; for I heard them say, Let us go to Dothan. And Joseph went after his brethren, and found them in Dothan.

18 ¶ And when they saw him afar off, even before he came near unto them, they conspired against him to slay him.

19 And they said one to another, Behold, this dreamer cometh.

20 Come now therefore, and let us slay him, and cast him into some pit, and we will say, Some evil beast hath devoured him: and we shall see what will become of his dreams.

21 And Reuben heard *it,* and he delivered him out of their hands; and said, Let us not kill him.

22 And Reuben said unto them, Shed no blood, *but* cast him into this pit that *is* in the wilderness, and lay no hand upon him; that he might rid him out of their hands, to deliver him to his father again.

23 ¶ And it came to pass, when Joseph was come unto his brethren, that they stripped Joseph out of his coat, *his* coat of many colours that *was* on him;

24 And they took him, and cast him into a pit: and the pit *was* empty, *there was* no water in it.

25 And they sat down to eat bread: and they lifted up their eyes and looked, and, behold, a company of Ishmeelites came from Gilead, with their camels bearing spicery and balm and myrrh, going to carry *it* down to Egypt.

26 And Judah said unto his brethren, What profit *is it* if we slay our brother, and conceal his blood?

27 Come, and let us sell him to the Ishmeelites, and let not our hand be upon him; for he *is* our brother *and* our flesh. And his brethren were content.

28 Then there passed by Midianites, merchantmen; and they drew and lifted up Joseph out of the pit, and sold Joseph to the Ishmeelites for twenty *pieces* of silver: and they brought Joseph into Egypt.

29 ¶ And Reuben returned unto the pit; and, behold, Joseph *was* not in the pit; and he rent his clothes.

30 And he returned unto his brethren, and said, The child *is* not; and I, whither shall I go?

31 ¶ And they took Joseph's coat, and killed a kid of the goats, and dipped the coat in the blood;

32 And they sent the coat of many colours, and they brought *it* to their father; and said, This have we found: know now whether it *be* thy son's coat or no.

33 And he knew it, and said, *It is* my son's coat; an evil beast hath devoured him; Joseph is without doubt rent in pieces.

34 And Jacob rent his clothes, and put sackcloth upon his loins, and mourned for his son many days.

35 And all his sons and all his daughters rose up to comfort him; but he refused to be comforted: and he said, For I will go down into the grave unto my son mourning. Thus his father wept for him.

36 And the Midianites sold him into Egypt unto Potiphar, an officer of Pharaoh's, *and* captain of the guard.

CHAPTER XXXVIII.

1 *Judah begetteth Er, Onan, and Shelah.* 6 *Er marrieth Tamar.* 8 *The trespass of Onan.* 13 *Tamar deceiveth Judah.* 27 *She beareth twins, Pharez and Zarah.*

AND it came to pass at that time, that Judah went down from his brethren, and turned in to a certain Adullamite, whose name *was* Hirah.

2 And Judah saw there a daughter of a certain Canaanite, whose name *was* Shuah; and he took her, and went in unto her.

3 And she conceived, and bare a son; and he called his name Er.

4 And she conceived again, and bare a son; and she called his name Onan.

5 And she yet again conceived, and bare a son; and called his name Shelah: and he was at Chezib when she bare him.

6 And Judah took a wife for Er his first-born, whose name *was* Tamar.

7 And Er, Judah's first-born, was wicked in the sight of the LORD; and the LORD slew him.

8 And Judah said unto Onan, Go in unto thy brother's wife, and marry her, and raise up seed to thy brother.

9 And Onan knew that the seed should not be his: and it came to pass, when he went in unto his brother's wife, that he spilled *it* on the ground, lest that he should give seed to his brother.

10 And the thing which he did displeased the LORD: wherefore he slew him also.

11 Then said Judah to Tamar his daughter-in-law, Remain a widow at thy father's house, till Shelah my son be grown: for he said, Lest peradventure he die also, as his brethren *did.* And Tamar went and dwelt in her father's house.

12 ¶ And in process of time the daughter of Shuah, Judah's wife, died; and Judah was comforted, and went up unto his sheep-shearers to Timnath, he and his friend Hirah the Adullamite.

13 And it was told Tamar, saying, Behold, thy father-in-law goeth up to Timnath to shear his sheep.

14 And she put her widow's garments off from her, and covered her with a veil, and wrapped herself, and sat in an open place, which *is* by the way to Timnath: for she saw that Shelah was grown, and she was not given unto him to wife.

15 When Judah saw her, he thought her *to be* an harlot; because she had covered her face.

16 And he turned unto her by the way, and said, Go to, I pray thee, let me come in unto thee; (for he knew not that she *was* his daughter-in-law.) And she said, What wilt thou give me, that thou mayest come in unto me?

17 And he said, I will send thee a kid from the flock. And she said, Wilt thou give me a pledge till thou send it?

18 And he said, What pledge shall I give thee? And she said, Thy signet, and thy bracelets, and thy staff that *is* in thine hand. And he gave *it* her, and came in unto her; and she conceived by him.

dress, or the doating partiality of their common father, could have goaded them on to such a pitch of frenzied resentment, or confirmed them in such consummate wickedness. Their hatred to Joseph must have had a far deeper seat—must have been produced by dislike to his piety and other excellencies, which made his character and conduct a constant censure upon theirs, and on account of which they found that they could never be at ease till they had rid themselves of his hated presence. This was the true solution of the mystery, just as it was in the case of Cain (1 John, 3. 12.). they lifted up their eyes, and behold... Ishmaelites—they are called Midianites (v. 28.), and Medanites, *Heb.* (v. 36.), being a travelling caravan composed of a mixed association of Arabians. Those tribes of Northern Arabia had already addicted themselves to commerce, and long did they enjoy a monopoly, the carrying trade being entirely in their hands. Their approach could easily be seen. for as their road, after crossing the ford from the transjordanic district, led along the south side of the mountains of Gilboa, a party seated on the plain of Dothan could trace them and their string of camels in the distance as they proceeded through the broad and gently-sloping valley that intervenes. Trading in the produce of Arabia and India, they were in the regular course of traffic on their way to Egypt; and the chief articles of commerce in which this clan dealt, were "spicery," from India, *i. e.*, a species of resinous gum, called *storax*, "balm of Gilead," the juice of the balsam tree, a native of Arabia-Felix, and "myrrh," an Arabic gum of a strong fragrant smell. For these articles there must have been an enormous demand in Egypt, as they were constantly used in the process of embalment. 26-28. Judah said, What profit?—the sight of these travelling merchants gave a sudden turn to the views of the conspirators; for having no wish to commit a greater degree of crime than was necessary for the accomplishment of their end, they readily approved of Judah's suggestion to dispose of their obnoxious brother as a slave. The proposal, of course, was founded on their knowledge that the Arabian merchants trafficked in slaves; and there is the clearest evidence furnished by the monuments of Egypt, that the traders who were in the habit of bringing slaves from the countries through which they passed, found a ready market in the cities of the Nile. they lifted up Joseph and sold him—acting impulsively on Judah's advice, they had their poor victim ready by the time the merchants reached; and money being no part of their object, they sold him for "twenty pieces of silver." The money was probably in rings or pieces (shekels), and silver is always mentioned in the records of that early age before gold, on account of its rarity. The whole sum, if in shekel weight, did not exceed £3. they brought Joseph into Egypt—there were two routes to Egypt—the one was overland by Hebron, where Jacob dwelt, and by taking which the fate of his hapless son would likely have reached the paternal ears; the other was directly westward across the country from Dothan to the maritime coast, and in this—the safest and most expeditious way, the merchants carried Joseph to Egypt. Thus did an overruling Providence lead this murderous conclave of brothers, as well as the slave-merchants,—both following their own free courses, to be parties in an act by which He was to work out, in a marvellous manner, the great purposes of His wisdom and goodness towards his ancient Church and people. 29, 30. Reuben returned unto the pit—he seems to have designedly taken a circuitous route, with a view of secretly rescuing the poor lad from a lingering death by starvation. His intentions were excellent, and his feelings no doubt painfully lacerated, when he discovered what had been done in his absence. But the thing was of God, who had designed that Joseph's deliverance should be accomplished by other means than his. 31-35. they took Joseph's coat—the commission of one sin necessarily leads to another to conceal it; and the scheme of deception which the sons of Jacob planned and practised on their aged father was a necessary consequence of the atrocious crime they had perpetrated. What a wonder that their cruel sneer, "thy son's coat," and their forced efforts to comfort him, did not awaken suspicion. But extreme grief, like every other passion, is blind, and Jacob, great as his affliction was, did allow himself to indulge his sorrow more than became one who believed in the government of a supreme and all-wise Disposer. 34. Jacob rent his clothes... sackcloth—the common signs of Oriental mourning. A rent is made in the skirt more or less long according to the afflicted feelings of the mourner, and a coarse rough piece of black sackcloth or camel's hair cloth is wound round the waist. grave—not the earth, for Joseph was supposed to be torn in pieces, but the unknown place—the place of departed souls, where Jacob expected at death to meet his beloved son.

CHAPTER. XXXVIII.

Ver. 1-11. JUDAH AND FAMILY. 1. At that time—a formula frequently used by the sacred writers, not to describe any precise period, but an interval near about it. 2. saw the daughter of a certain Canaanite—Like Esau, this son of Jacob, casting off the restraints of religion, married into a Canaanite family; and it is not surprising that the family which sprang from such an unsuitable connexion should be infamous for bold and unblushing wickedness. 8. marry her, and raise up seed to thy brother—The first instance of a custom which was afterwards incorporated amongst the laws of Moses, that when a husband died leaving a widow, his brother next of age was to marry her, and the issue, if any, was to be served heir to the deceased (cf. Deu. 25, 5.). 12. Judah went up to his sheep-shearers—This season, which occurs in Palestine towards the end of March, was spent in more than usual hilarity, and the wealthier masters invited their friends, as well as treated their servants, to sumptuous entertainments. Accordingly, it is said, Judah was accompanied by his friend Hirah, Timnath—in the mountains of Judah. 18. signet, &c.—bracelets, including armlets, were worn by men as well as women among the Hebrews. But the *Heb.* word here rendered bracelets is everywhere else translated "lace" or "ribbon;" so that as the signet alone was probably more than an equivalent for the kid, it is not easy to conjecture why the other things were given in addition, except by supposing the perforated seal was attached by a ribbon to

19 And she arose, and went away, and *laid by her veil from her, and put on the garments of her widowhood.

20 And Judah sent the kid by the hand of his friend the Adullamite, to receive *his* pledge from the woman's hand; but he found her not.

21 Then he asked the men of that place, saying, Where *is* the harlot that *was* openly by the way-side? And they said, There was no harlot in this *place*.

22 And he returned to Judah, and said, I cannot find her; and also the men of the place said, *that* there was no harlot in this *place*.

23 And Judah said, Let her take *it* to her, lest we be shamed: behold, I sent this kid, and thou hast not found her.

24 ¶ And it came to pass, about three months after, that it was told Judah, saying, Tamar thy daughter-in-law hath played the harlot; and also, behold, she *is* with child by whoredom. And Judah said, Bring her forth, and let her be burnt.

25 When she *was* brought forth, she sent to her father-in-law, saying, By the man whose these *are am* I with child: and she said, Discern, I pray thee, whose *are* these, the signet, and bracelets, and staff.

26 And Judah acknowledged *them*, and said, She hath been more righteous than I; because that I gave her not to Shelah my son. And he knew her again no more.

27 ¶ And it came to pass, in the time of her travail, that, behold, twins *were* in her womb.

28 And it came to pass, when she travailed, that *the one* put out *his* hand: and the midwife took and bound upon his hand a scarlet thread, saying, This came out first.

29 And it came to pass, as he drew back his hand, that, behold, his brother came out; and she said, How hast thou broken forth? *this* breach *be* upon thee: therefore his name was called Pharez.

30 And afterward came out his brother, that had the scarlet thread upon his hand: and his name was called Zarah.

CHAPTER XXXIX.

1 *Joseph, advanced in Potiphar's house, resisteth his mistress's temptation:* 13 *he is falsely accused,* 20 *and imprisoned:* 21 *God is with him there.*

AND Joseph was brought down to Egypt; and Potiphar, an officer of Pharaoh, captain of the guard, an Egyptian, bought him of the hands of the Ishmeelites, which had brought him down thither.

2 And the LORD was with Joseph, and he was a prosperous man; and he was in the house of his master the Egyptian.

3 And his master saw that the LORD *was* with him, and that the LORD made all that he did to prosper in his hand.

4 And Joseph found grace in his sight, and he served him: and he made him overseer over his house, and all *that* he had he put into his hand.

5 And it came to pass, from the time *that* he had made him overseer in his house, and over all that he had, that the LORD blessed the Egyptian's house for Joseph's sake; and the blessing of the LORD was upon all that he had in the house, and in the field.

6 And he left all that he had in Joseph's hand; and he knew not ought he had, save

the bread which he did eat. And Joseph was a goodly *person*, and well-favoured.

7 ¶ And it came to pass after these things, that his master's wife cast her eyes upon Joseph; and she said, Lie with me.

8 But he refused, and said unto his master's wife, Behold, my master wotteth not what *is* with me in the house, and he hath committed all that he hath to my hand;

9 *There is* none greater in this house than I; neither hath he kept back any thing from me but thee, because thou *art* his wife: how then can I do this great wickedness, and sin against God?

10 And it came to pass, as she spake to Joseph day by day, that he hearkened not unto her, to lie by her, *or* to be with her.

11 And it came to pass about this time, that *Joseph* went into the house to do his business; and *there was* none of the men of the house there within.

12 And she caught him by his garment, saying, Lie with me: and he left his garment in her hand, and fled, and got him out.

13 And it came to pass, when she saw that he had left his garment in her hand, and was fled forth,

14 That she called unto the men of her house, and spake unto them, saying, See, he hath brought in an Hebrew unto us to mock us; he came in unto me to lie with me, and I cried with a loud voice:

15 And it came to pass, when he heard that I lifted up my voice and cried, that he left his garment with me, and fled, and got him out.

16 And she laid up his garment by her until his lord came home.

17 And she spake unto him according to these words, saying, The Hebrew servant, which thou hast brought unto us, came in unto me to mock me:

18 And it came to pass, as I lifted up my voice and cried, that he left his garment with me, and fled out.

19 And it came to pass, when his master heard the words of his wife, which she spake unto him, saying, After this manner did thy servant to me, that his wrath was kindled.

20 And Joseph's master took him, and put him into the prison, a place where the king's prisoners *were* bound: and he was there in the prison.

21 But the LORD was with Joseph, and showed him mercy, and gave him favour in the sight of the keeper of the prison.

22 And the keeper of the prison committed to Joseph's hand all the prisoners that *were* in the prison; and whatsoever they did there, he was the doer of *it*.

23 The keeper of the prison looked not to any thing *that was* under his hand; because the LORD was with him, and *that* which he did, the LORD made *it* to prosper.

CHAPTER XL.

1 *The butler and baker of Pharaoh are imprisoned;* 4 *Joseph hath charge of them;* 5 *he interpreteth their dreams.* 20 *The ingratitude of the butler.*

AND it came to pass after these things, *that* the butler of the king of Egypt and *his* baker had offended their lord the king of Egypt.

2 And Pharaoh was wroth against two *of* his officers, against the chief of the butlers, and against the chief of the bakers.

3 And he put them in ward in the house

the staff. 24. Bring her forth, and let her be burnt—In patriarchal times fathers seem to have possessed the power of life and death over the members of their families. The crime of adultery was anciently punished in many places by burning Lev. 21. 9; Jud. 15. 6; Jer. 29. 22. This chapter contains details which probably would never have obtained a place in the inspired record had it not been to exhibit the full links of the chain that connects the genealogy of the Saviour with Abraham; and in the disreputable character of the ancestry who figure in this passage we have a remarkable proof that "He made himself of no reputation."

CHAPTER XXXIX.

Ver. 1-23. JOSEPH IN POTIPHAR'S HOUSE. 1. Potiphar, a captain of the guard—This name, Potiphar, signifies one "devoted to the sun," the local deity of On or Heliopolis,—a circumstance which fixes the place of his residence in the Delta, the district of Egypt bordering on Canaan. officer—*lit.*, prince of Pharaoh—*i. e.*, in the service of government. captain of the guard—the import of the original term has been variously interpreted, some considering it means "chief cook," others "chief inspector of plantations;" but that which seems best founded is "chief of the executioners," "head of the police," the same as the captain of the watch, the *zabut* of modern Egypt, [WILK.] bought him of the Ishmaelites—The age, appearance, and intelligence of the Hebrew slave would soon make him picked up in the market. But the unseen, unfelt influence of the great Disposer drew the attention of Potiphar towards him, in order that in the house of one so closely connected with the court he might receive that previous training which was necessary for the high office he was destined to fill, and in the school of adversity learn the lessons of practical wisdom that were to be of greatest utility and importance in his future career. Thus it is, that when God has any important work to be done, He always prepares fitting agents to accomplish it. 2. he was in the house of his master—Those slaves who had been war captives were generally sent to labour in the field, and subjected to hard treatment under the "stick" of taskmasters. But those who were bought with money were employed in domestic purposes, were kindly treated, and enjoyed as much liberty as the same class does in modern Egypt. 3. His master saw that the Lord was with him—Though changed in condition, Joseph was not changed in spirit; though stripped of the gaudy coat that had adorned his person, he had not lost the moral graces that distinguished his character; though separated from his father on earth, he still lived in communion with his Father in heaven; though in the house of an idolater, he continued a worshipper of the true God. 5. The Lord blessed the Egyptian's house, &c.—It might be—it probably was that a special, a miraculous blessing was poured out on a youth, who so faithfully and zealously served God amid all the disadvantages of his place. But it may be useful to remark that such a blessing usually follows in the ordinary course of things; and the most worldly unprincipled masters always admire and respect religion in a servant when they see that profession supported by conscientious principle and a consistent life. made him overseer in his house—We do not know in what capacity Joseph entered into the service of Potiphar; but the observant eye of his master soon discovered his superior qualities, and made him his chief, his confidential servant cf. Eph. 6. 7; Col. 3. 23. . The advancement of domestic slaves is not uncommon, and it is considered a great disgrace not to raise one who has been a year or two in the family. But this extraordinary advancement of Joseph was the doing of the Lord, though on the part of Potiphar it was the consequence of observing the astonishing prosperity that attended him in all that he did. 7. his master's wife cast her eyes upon Joseph—Egyptian women were not kept in the same secluded manner as females are in most Oriental countries now. They were treated in a manner more worthy of a civilized people—in fact, enjoyed as much freedom both at home and abroad as ladies do in Britain. Hence Potiphar's wife had constant opportunity of meeting Joseph. But the ancient women of Egypt were very loose in their morals. Intrigues and intemperance were vices very prevalent amongst the sex, as the monuments too plainly attest. [WILK.] Potiphar's wife was probably not worse than many of the same rank, and her infamous advances made to Joseph arose from her superiority of station. 9. How can I do this great wickedness?—This remonstrance, when all inferior arguments had failed, embodied the true principles of moral purity—a principle always sufficient where it exists, and alone sufficient. 14. Then she called to the men—Disappointed and affronted, she vowed revenge, and accused Joseph, first to the servants of the house, and on his return to her lord. an Hebrew to mock me—an affected and blind aspersion of her husband for keeping in his house an Hebrew, the very abomination of Egyptians. 20. Joseph's master took and put him into the prison—the round-house, from the form of its construction, usually attached to the dwelling of such an officer as Potiphar. It was partly a subterranean dungeon 41. 14 , though the brick-built walls rose considerably above the surface of the ground, and were surmounted by a vaulted roof somewhat in the form of an inverted bowl. Into such a dungeon Potiphar, in the first ebullition of rage, threw Joseph, and ordered him to be subjected further to as great harshness of treatment Ps. 105. 18 as he durst; for the power of masters over their slaves was very properly restrained by law, and the murder of a slave was a capital crime. the prison, a place where the king's prisoners were bound—Though prisons seem to have been an inseparable appendage of the palaces, this was not a common jail—it was the receptacle of state criminals; and, therefore, it may be presumed that more than ordinary strictness and vigilance were exercised over the prisoners. In general, however, the Egyptian, like other Oriental prisons, were used solely for the purposes of detention. Accused persons were cast into them until the charges against them could be investigated; and though the jailor was responsible for the appearance of those placed under his custody, yet provided they were produced when called, he was never interrogated as to the way in which he had kept them. 21-23. The Lord gave him favour, &c.—It is highly probable,

of the captain of the guard, into the prison, the place where Joseph *was* bound.

4 And the captain of the guard charged Joseph with them, and he served them: and they continued a season in ward.

5 ¶ And they dreamed a dream both of them, each man his dream in one night, each man according to the interpretation of his dream, the butler and the baker of the king of Egypt, which *were* bound in the prison.

6 And Joseph came in unto them in the morning, and looked upon them, and, behold, they *were* sad.

7 And he asked Pharaoh's officers, that *were* with him in the ward of his lord's house, saying, Wherefore ¹ look ye *so* sadly to-day?

8 And they said unto him, *d* We have dreamed a dream, and *there is* no interpreter of it. And Joseph said unto them, *Do* not interpretations *belong* to God? tell me *them*, I pray you.

9 And the chief butler told his dream to Joseph, and said to him, In my dream, behold, a vine *was* before me;

10 And in the vine *were* three branches: and it *was* as though it budded, *and* her blossoms shot forth; and the clusters thereof brought forth ripe grapes:

11 And Pharaoh's cup *was* in my hand: and I took the grapes, and pressed them into Pharaoh's cup, and I gave the cup into Pharaoh's hand.

12 And Joseph said unto him, *f* This *is* the interpretation of it: The three branches *are* three days:

13 Yet within three days shall Pharaoh ² lift *g* up thine head, and restore thee unto thy place: and thou shalt deliver Pharaoh's cup into his hand, after the former manner when thou wast his butler.

14 But ³ think *h* on me when it shall be well with thee, and *i* show kindness, I pray thee, unto me, and make mention of me unto Pharaoh, and bring me out of this house:

15 For indeed I was stolen away out of the land of the Hebrews; *j* and here also have I done nothing that they should put me into the dungeon.

16 When the chief baker saw that the interpretation was good, he said unto Joseph, I also *was* in my dream, and, behold, *I had* three ⁴ white baskets on my head:

17 And in the uppermost basket *there was* of all manner of ⁵ bake-meats for Pharaoh; and the birds did eat them out of the basket upon my head.

18 And Joseph answered and said, This *is* the interpretation thereof: The three baskets *are* three days:

19 Yet within three days shall Pharaoh ⁶ lift up thy head from off thee, and shall hang thee on a tree; and the birds shall eat thy flesh from off thee.

20 ¶ And it came to pass the third day, *which was* Pharaoh's *k* birthday, that he *l* made a feast unto all his servants: and he ⁷ lifted *m* up the head of the chief butler and of the chief baker among his servants.

21 And he *n* restored the chief butler unto his butlership again; and *o* he gave the cup into Pharaoh's hand:

22 But he *p* hanged the chief baker: as Joseph had interpreted to them.

23 Yet did not the chief butler remember Joseph, but *q* forgat him.

B. C. 1718.

CHAP. 40.
1 are your faces evil?
Neh. 2. 2.
d ch. 41. 15.
e ch. 41. 16.
Dan. 2. 11, 28, 47.
f Judg. 7. 14.
Dan. 2. 36.
Dan. 4. 19.
2 Or, reckon.
g Ps. 3. 3.
Jer. 52. 31.
3 remember me with thee.
h Lu. 23. 42.
i Josh. 2. 12.
1 Sam. 20. 14. 15.
1 Kin. 2. 7.
j ch. 39. 20.
4 Or, full of holes.
5 meat of Pharaoh, the work of a baker, or, cook.
6 Or, reckon thee, and take thy office from thee.
k Mat. 14. 6.
l Mark 6. 21.
7 Or, reckoned.
m Mat.25.19.
n ver. 13.
o Neh. 2. 1.
p Esth. 7. 10.
q Job 19. 14.
Ps. 31. 12.
Prov. 3. 27.
Ec. 9. 15.
Amos 6. 6.

CHAP. 41.
1 fat.
a Dan. 4. 5.
b Ex. 7. 11.
Is. 29. 14.
Dan. 1. 20.
Dan. 2. 2.
c Mat. 2. 1.
d ch. 40. 2, 3.
e ch. 39. 20.
f ch. 40. 5.
g 2 Kin. 5. 4.
h ch. 37. 36.
i ch. 40. 12.
j ch. 41. 22.
k Ps. 105. 20.
l Dan. 2. 25.
2 made him run.
m 1 Sa. 2. 8.
Ps. 113.7.8.
n Ps. 25. 14.
Dan. 5.16.
3 Or, when thou hearest a dream thou canst interpret it.
o Dan. 2. 30.
Acts 3. 12.
2 Cor. 3. 5.
p ch. 40. 6.
Dan. 2. 22, 28, 47.
Dan. 4. 2.
4 come to the inward parts of them.

CHAPTER XLI.

1 *Pharaoh's two dreams:* 25 *Joseph interpreteth them:* 33 *he giveth Pharaoh counsel.* 38 *Joseph is advanced:* 50 *he begetteth Manasseh and Ephraim.* 53 *The famine beginneth.*

AND it came to pass at the end of two full years, that Pharaoh dreamed: and, behold, he stood by the river.

2 And, behold, there came up out of the river seven well-favoured kine and fat-fleshed; and they fed in a meadow.

3 And, behold, seven other kine came up after them out of the river, ill-favoured and lean-fleshed; and stood by the *other* kine upon the brink of the river.

4 And the ill-favoured and lean-fleshed kine did eat up the seven well-favoured and fat kine. So Pharaoh awoke.

5 And he slept and dreamed the second time: and, behold, seven ears of corn came up upon one stalk, ¹ rank and good.

6 And, behold, seven thin ears and blasted with the east wind sprung up after them.

7 And the seven thin ears devoured the seven rank and full ears. And Pharaoh awoke, and, behold, it *was* a dream.

8 And it came to pass in the morning, *a* that his spirit was troubled; and he sent and called for all *b* the magicians of Egypt, and all the *c* wise men thereof: and Pharaoh told them his dreams; but *there was* none that could interpret them unto Pharaoh.

9 ¶ Then spake the chief butler unto Pharaoh, saying, I do remember my faults this day:

10 Pharaoh was *d* wroth with his servants, *e* and put me in ward in the captain of the guard's house, *both* me and the chief baker:

11 And *f* we dreamed a dream in one night, I and he; we dreamed each man according to the interpretation of his dream.

12 And *g* there was there with us a young man, an Hebrew, *h* servant to the captain of the guard; and we told him, and he *i* interpreted to us our dreams; to each man according to his dream he did interpret.

13 And it came to pass, *j* as he interpreted to us, so it was; me he restored unto mine office, and him he hanged.

14 ¶ *k* Then Pharaoh sent and called Joseph, and ² they brought him hastily *m* out of the dungeon: and he shaved himself, and changed his raiment, and came in unto Pharaoh.

15 And Pharaoh said unto Joseph, I have dreamed a dream, and *there is* none that can interpret it: *n* and I have heard say of thee, that ³ thou canst understand a dream to interpret it.

16 And Joseph answered Pharaoh, saying, *o* *It is* not in me: *p* God shall give Pharaoh an answer of peace.

17 And Pharaoh said unto Joseph, In my dream, behold, I stood upon the bank of the river:

18 And, behold, there came up out of the river seven kine, fat-fleshed and well-favoured; and they fed in a meadow:

19 And, behold, seven other kine came up after them, poor and very ill-favoured and lean-fleshed, such as I never saw in all the land of Egypt for badness:

20 And the lean and the ill-favoured kine did eat up the first seven fat kine:

21 And when they had ⁴ eaten them up, it could not be known that they had eaten

from the situation of this prison 40. 3), that the keeper might have been previously acquainted with Joseph, and have had access to know his innocence of the crime laid to his charge as with all the high integrity of his character. That may partly account for his shewing so much kindness and confidence to his prisoner. But there was a higher influence at work; for "the Lord was with Joseph, and that which he did, the Lord made it to prosper."

CHAPTER XL.

Ver. 1-8. TWO STATE PRISONERS. The butler—not only the cup-bearer; but overseer of the royal vineyards, as well as the cellars; having, probably, some hundreds of people under him. the baker—or cook, had the superintendence of everything relating to the providing and preparing of meats for the royal table. Both officers, especially the former, were, in ancient Egypt, always persons of great rank and importance; and from the confidential nature of their employment, as well as their access to the royal presence, —they were, generally, the highest nobles or princes of the blood. 2. Pharaoh put them in ward, &c.—Whatever was their crime, they were committed—until their case could be investigated—to the custody of the captain of the guard, *i. e.* Potiphar, in an outer part of whose house the royal prison was situated. The captain of the guard charged Joseph with them—not the keeper, though he was most favourably disposed; but Potiphar himself, who, it would seem, was by this time satisfied of the perfect innocence of the young Hebrew, though, probably, to prevent the exposure of his family, he deemed it prudent to detain him in confinement (see Ps. 37. 5.). They continued a season in ward—*lit.* days — how long, is uncertain; but as they were called to account on the king's birth-day, it has been supposed that their offence had been committed on the preceding anniversary. [CAL] 5-8. they dreamed a dream — Joseph, influenced by the spirit of true religion, could feel for others Eccl. 4. 1; Ro. 12. 15; Phil. 2. 4.). Observing them one day extremely depressed, he enquired the cause of their melancholy; and being informed it was owing to a dream they had respectively dreamed during the previous night, after piously directing them to God (Dan. 11. 30; Is. 26. 10.) he volunteered to aid them, through the divine help, in discovering the import of their vision. The influence of Providence must be seen in the remarkable fact of both officers dreaming such dreams in one night. He moveth the spirits of men.
9-15. THE BUTLER'S DREAM. 9. Behold a vine was before me—The visionary scene described, seems to represent the king as abroad, taking exercise, and attended by his butler who gave him a cooling draught. On all occasions, the kings of ancient Egypt were required to practice temperance in the use of wine [WILK.]; but in this scene, it is a prepared beverage he is drinking, probably the sherbet of the present day. Everything was done in the king's presence—the cup was washed, the juice of the grapes pressed into it; and it was then handed to him—not grasped; but lightly resting on the tips of the fingers. 11-15. Joseph said, This is the interpretation—speaking as an inspired interpreter, he told the butler that within three days he would be restored to all the honours and privileges of his office; and while making that joyful announcement, earnestly bespoke the officer's influence for his own liberation. Nothing has hitherto met us in the record indicative of Joseph's feelings; but this earnest appeal reveals a sadness and impatient longing for release, which not all his piety and faith in God could dispel. 16-23. THE BAKER'S DREAM. I had three white baskets—The circumstances mentioned exactly describe his duties, which, notwithstanding numerous assistants, he performed with his own hands. white—*lit.* full of holes —*i. e.*, wicker baskets. The meats were carried to table upon the head in three baskets, one piled upon the other; and in the uppermost, the bakemeats. And in crossing the open courts, from the kitchen to the dining-rooms, the abstraction of the viands by a vulture, eagle, ibis, or other rapacious bird was a frequent occurrence in the palaces of Egypt, as it is an every-day incident in the hot countries of the East still. The risk from these carnivorous birds was the greater in the cities of Egypt— that being held sacred, it was unlawful to destroy them; and they swarmed in such numbers, as to be a great annoyance to the people. 18, 19. Joseph answered, This is the interpretation—The purport was that, in three days, his execution should be ordered. The language of Joseph describes minutely one form of capital punishment that prevailed in Egypt—viz., that the criminal was decapitated, and then his headless body gibbeted on a tree by the high-way, till it was gradually devoured by the ravenous birds. 20-22. the third day.. Pharaoh's birthday—This was a holiday season, celebrated at court with great magnificence and honoured by a free pardon to prisoners. Accordingly, the issue happened to the butler and baker, as Joseph had foretold. Doubtless, he felt it painful to communicate such dismal tidings to the baker; but he could not help announcing what God had revealed to him; and it was for the honour of the true God that he should speak plainly. 23. yet did not the chief butler, &c.—This was human nature. How prone are men to forget and neglect in prosperity, those who have been their companions in adversity (Amos 6. 6.). But although reflecting no credit on the butler, it was wisely ordered in the providence of God that he should forget him. The divine purposes required that Joseph should obtain his deliverance in another way, and by other means.

CHAPTER XLI.

Ver. 1-24. PHARAOH'S DREAM. at the end of two full years—It is not certain whether these years are reckoned from the beginning of Joseph's imprisonment, or from the events described in preceding chapter—most likely the latter. What a long time for Joseph to experience the sickness of hope deferred. But the time of his enlargement was come when he had sufficiently learned the lessons God designed for him; and the plans of Providence were matured. Pharaoh dreamed— Pharaoh, from an Egyptian word Phre, signifying the "sun," was the official title of the kings of that country. The prince, who occupied the throne of Egypt, was Aphophis, one of the Memphite kings, whose capital was On or Heliopolis; and who is universally

them; but they *were* still ill-favoured, as at the beginning. So I awoke.

22 And I saw in my dream, and, behold, seven ears came up in one stalk, full and good:

23 And, behold, seven ears, ⁵ withered, thin, *and* blasted with the east wind, sprung up after them;

24 And the thin ears devoured the seven good ears. And ⁹ I told *this* unto the magicians; but *there was* none that could declare *it* to me.

25 ¶ And Joseph said unto Pharaoh, The dream of Pharaoh *is* one: ⁷ God hath showed Pharaoh what he *is* about to do.

26 The seven good kine *are* seven years; and the seven good ears *are* seven years: the dream *is* one.

27 And the seven thin and ill-favoured kine that came up after them *are* seven years; and the seven empty ears, blasted with the east wind, shall be ⁸ seven years of famine.

28 This *is* the thing which I have spoken unto Pharaoh: What God *is* about to do he showeth unto Pharaoh.

29 Behold, there come seven years of great plenty throughout all the land of Egypt:

30 And there shall arise after them seven years of famine; and all the plenty shall be forgotten in the land of Egypt; and the famine ᵗ shall consume the land;

31 And the plenty shall not be known in the land by reason of that famine following; for it *shall be* very ⁶ grievous.

32 And for that the dream was doubled unto Pharaoh twice; *it is* because the thing *is* ⁷established by God, and God will shortly bring it to pass.

33 Now therefore let Pharaoh look out a man discreet and wise, and set him over the land of Egypt.

34 Let Pharaoh do *this*, and let him appoint ⁸ officers over the land, and take up the fifth part of the land of Egypt in the seven plenteous years.

35 And let them gather all the food of those good years that come, and lay up corn under the hand of Pharaoh, and let them keep food in the cities.

36 And that food shall be for store to the land against the seven years of famine, which shall be in the land of Egypt; that the land ⁹ perish not through the famine.

37 ¶ And the thing was good in the eyes of Pharaoh, and in the eyes of all his servants.

38 And Pharaoh said unto his servants, Can we find *such a one* as this *is*, a man ᵘ in whom the Spirit of God *is?*

39 And Pharaoh said unto Joseph, Forasmuch as God hath showed thee all this, *there is* none so discreet and wise as thou *art:*

40 Thou shalt be over my house, and according unto thy word shall all my people ¹⁰ be ruled: only in the throne will I be greater than thou.

41 And Pharaoh said unto Joseph, See, I ˣ have set thee over all the land of Egypt.

42 And Pharaoh ʷ took off his ring from his hand, and put it upon Joseph's hand, and arrayed him in vestures of ¹¹ fine linen, ˣ and put a gold chain about his neck;

43 And he made him to ride in the second chariot which he had; and they cried before him, ¹² Bow the knee: and he made him *ruler* over all the land of Egypt.

B. C. 1715.
—
CHAP. 41.
5 Or, small.
q Dan. 4. 7.
r Dan. 2. 28.
29, 45.
Rev. 4. 1.
s 2 Kin. 8. 1.
t ch. 47. 13.
Ps. 105. 16.
1 Kin. 17. 1.
6 heavy.
7 Or, prepared of God.
8 Or, overseers.
9 be not cut off.
u Num. 27. 18.
Job 32. 8.
Dan. 4. 8.
10 be armed, or, kiss.
v Dan. 6. 3.
Ec. 4. 13, 14.
Prov. 14. 35.
w Est. 8. 2.
11 Or, silk.
x Dan. 5. 29.
12 Abrech, or, tender father.
13 Which in the Coptic signifies, A revealer of secrets, or, The man to whom secrets are revealed.
14 Or, prince.
Ex. 2. 16.
2 Sam. 8. 18.
2 Sam. 20. 26.
y 1 Sam. 16. 21.
1 Kin. 12. 6, 8.
Dan. 1. 19.
z ch. 22. 17.
Judg. 7. 12.
1 Sa. 13. 5.
Ps. 78. 27.
a ch. 46. 20.
ch. 48. 5.
15 Or, prince.
16 That is, forgetting.
17 That is, fruitful.
b Ps. 105. 16.
Acts 7. 11.
18 all where-in was.
c ch. 42. 6.
ch. 47. 14, 24.
Pro. 11. 26.
d Deu. 9. 28.
—
CHAP. 42.
a Acts 7. 12.
b ch. 43. 8.
Ps. 118. 17.
Is. 38. 1.
ᵛ ver. 38.
d ch. 12. 10.
ch. 26. 1.
Acts 7. 11.
e ch. 41. 41.

44 And Pharaoh said unto Joseph, I *am* Pharaoh, and without thee shall no man lift up his hand or foot in all the land of Egypt.

45 And Pharaoh called Joseph's name 13 Zaphnath-paaneah; and he gave him to wife Asenath the daughter of Poti-pherah 14 priest of On. And Joseph went out over *all* the land of Egypt.

46 And Joseph *was* thirty years old when he ʸ stood before Pharaoh king of Egypt. And Joseph went out from the presence of Pharaoh, and went throughout all the land of Egypt.

47 And in the seven plenteous years the earth brought forth by handfuls.

48 And he gathered up all the food of the seven years, which were in the land of Egypt, and laid up the food in the cities: the food of the field, which *was* round about every city, laid he up in the same.

49 And Joseph gathered corn ᶻ as the sand of the sea, very much, until he left numbering; for *it was* without number.

50 ᵃ And unto Joseph were born two sons before the years of famine came, which Asenath the daughter of Poti-pherah 15 priest of On bare unto him.

51 And Joseph called the name of the first-born 16 Manasseh: For God, *said he,* hath made me forget all my toil, and all my father's house.

52 And the name of the second called he 17 Ephraim: For God hath caused me to be fruitful in the land of my affliction.

53 ¶ And the seven years of plenteousness that was in the land of Egypt were ended.

54 ᵇ And the seven years of dearth began to come, according as Joseph had said: and the dearth was in all lands; but in all the land of Egypt there was bread.

55 And when all the land of Egypt was famished, the people cried to Pharaoh for bread: and Pharaoh said unto all the Egyptians, Go unto Joseph; what he saith to you, do.

56 And the famine was over all the face of the earth. And Joseph opened ¹⁸ all the storehouses, and ᶜ sold unto the Egyptians; and the famine waxed sore in the land of Egypt.

57 And ᵈ all countries came into Egypt to Joseph for to buy *corn*; because that the famine was *so* sore in all lands.

CHAPTER XLII.

1 *Jacob sendeth his ten sons to buy corn in Egypt:* 17 *they are imprisoned by Joseph for spies:* 21 *their remorse for Joseph:* 25 *their return:* 29 *their relation to Jacob, etc.*

NOW when ᵃ Jacob saw that there was corn in Egypt, Jacob said unto his sons, Why do ye look one upon another?

2 And he said, Behold, I have heard that there is corn in Egypt: get you down thither, and buy for us from thence; that we may ᵇ live, and not die.

3 ¶ And Joseph's ten brethren went down to buy corn in Egypt.

4 But Benjamin, Joseph's brother, Jacob sent not with his brethren: for he said, ᶜ Lest peradventure mischief befall him.

5 And the sons of Israel came to buy *corn* among those that came: for the famine was ᵈ in the land of Canaan.

6 And Joseph *was* the governor ᵉ over the land, *and* he *it was* that sold to all the people of the land: and Joseph's brethren

acknowledged to have been a patriot king. Between the arrival of Abraham and the appearance of Joseph in that country, somewhat more than two centuries had elapsed. Kings sleep and dream, as well as their subjects. And this Pharaoh had two dreams in one night so singular, and so similar, so distinct and so apparently significant, so coherent and vividly impressed on his memory, that his spirit was troubled. **8. he called for all the magicians**—It is not possible to define the exact distinction between "magicians" and "wise men:" but they formed different branches of a numerous body, who laid claim to supernatural skill in occult arts and sciences; in revealing mysteries, explaining portents; and, above all, interpreting dreams. Long practice had rendered them expert in devising a plausible way of getting out of every difficulty, and framing an answer suitable to the occasion. But the dreams of Pharaoh baffled their united skill. Unlike their Assyrian brethren Dan. 2. 4, they did not pretend to know the meaning of the symbols contained in them, and the providence of God had determined that they should all be non-plussed in the exercise of their boasted powers, in order that the inspired wisdom of Joseph might the more remarkably appear. **9–13. chief butler ... I remember my faults**—This public acknowledgment of the merits of the young Hebrew would, tardy though it was, have reflected credit on the butler—had it not been obviously made to ingratiate himself with his royal master. It is right to confess our faults against God, and against our fellow-men, when that confession is made in the spirit of godly sorrow and penitence. But this man was not much impressed with a sense of the fault he had committed against Joseph; he never thought of God, to whose goodness he was indebted for the prophetic announcement of his release and in acknowledging his former fault against the king, he was practising the courtly art of pleasing his master. **14. Then Pharaoh sent and called Joseph**—Now that God's set time had come Ps. 105. 19,) no human power nor policy could detain Joseph in prison. During his protracted confinement, he might have often been distressed with perplexing doubts; but the mystery of Providence was about to be cleared up, and all his sorrows forgotten in the course of honour and public usefulness in which his services were to be employed. **shaved himself** —The Egyptians were the only Oriental nation that liked a smooth chin. All slaves and foreigners who were reduced to that condition, were obliged, on their arrival in that country, to conform to the cleanly habits of the natives, by shaving their beards and heads, the latter of which were covered with a close cap. Thus prepared, Joseph was conducted to the palace, where the king seemed to have been anxiously waiting his arrival. **15, 16. Pharaoh said, I have dreamed a dream**—The king's brief statement of the service required, brought out the genuine piety of Joseph; disclaiming all merit—he ascribed, whatever gifts or sagacity he possessed to the divine source of all wisdom—declared his own inability, to penetrate futurity; but, at the same time, his confident persuasion—that God would reveal what was necessary to be known.

17. Pharaoh said, In my dream I stood—The dreams were purely Egyptian—founded on the productions of that country, and the experience of a native. The fertility of Egypt being wholly dependent on the Nile —the scene is laid on the banks of that river; and oxen being in the ancient hieroglyphics symbolical of the earth and of food, animals of that species were introduced in the first dream. **there came up out of the river** —cows now, of the buffalo kind, are seen daily plunging into the Nile; when their huge form is gradually emerging, they seem as if rising "out of the river." **fed in a meadow** —Nile grass, the aquatic plants that grow on the marshy banks of that river, particularly the lotus kind; on which cattle were usually fattened. **19. behold, seven other kine, poor and ill-favoured**—The cow being the emblem of fruitfulness—the different years of plenty and of famine were aptly represented by the different condition of those kine;—the plenty, by the cattle feeding on the richest fodder; and the dearth, by the lean and famishing kine, which the pangs of hunger drove to act contrary to their nature. **22. Behold I saw in my dream seven ears**—that is, of Egyptian wheat, which, when "full and good," is remarkable in size—a single seed sprouting into seven, ten, or fourteen stalks—and each stalk bearing an ear. **blasted by the east wind**—destructive everywhere to grain, but particularly so in Egypt; where, sweeping over the sandy deserts of Arabia, it comes in the character of a hot, blighting wind, that quickly withers all vegetation (cf. Ez. 19. 12; Hos. 13. 15.). **24. devoured, the seven rank and full ears** —*devoured* is a different word from that used (v. 4,) and conveys the idea of destroying, by absorbing to themselves all the nutritious virtue of the soil around them.

25–36. JOSEPH INTERPRETS PHARAOH'S DREAMS. 25. Joseph said, The dream is one— They both pointed to the same event—a remarkable dispensation of seven years of unexampled abundance, to be followed by a similar period of unparalleled dearth. The repetition of the dream in two different forms was designed to shew the absolute certainty and speedy arrival of this public crisis; the interpretation was accompanied by several suggestions of practical wisdom for meeting so great an emergency as was impending. **33. Now, therefore, let Pharaoh look out a man**—The explanation given, when the key to the dreams was supplied, appears to have been satisfactory to the king and his courtiers; and we may suppose that much and anxious conversation would arise, in the course of which Joseph might have been asked whether he had anything further to say. No doubt the providence of God provided the opportunity of his suggesting what was necessary. **34. appoint officers over all the land**—overseers, equivalent to the beys of modern Egypt. **take up a fifth part of the land**—*i.e.*, of the land produce to be purchased and stored by government, instead of being sold to foreign corn merchants.

37–57. JOSEPH MADE RULER OF EGYPT. 38. Pharaoh said unto his servants—The kings of ancient Egypt were assisted in the management of state affairs by the advice of the most distinguished members of the priestly order; and, accordingly, before admitting Joseph to the new and extraordinary office

came, and *f* bowed down themselves before him *with* their faces to the earth.

7 And Joseph saw his brethren, and he knew them, but made himself strange unto them, and spake [1] roughly unto them; and he said unto them, Whence come ye? And they said, From the land of Canaan to buy food.

8 And Joseph knew his brethren, but they knew not him.

9 And Joseph *g* remembered the dreams which he dreamed of them, and said unto them, Ye *are* spies; to see the nakedness of the land ye are come.

10 And they said unto him, Nay, my lord, but to buy food are thy servants come.

11 We *are* all one man's sons: we *are* true *men*, thy servants are no spies.

12 And he said unto them, Nay, but to see the nakedness of the land ye are come.

13 And they said, Thy servants *are* twelve brethren, the sons of one man in the land of Canaan; and, behold, the youngest *is* this day with our father, and one *h is* not.

14 And Joseph said unto them, That *is* it that I spake unto you, saying, Ye *are* spies:

15 Hereby ye shall be proved: *i* By the life of Pharaoh ye shall not go forth hence, except your youngest brother come hither.

16 Send one of you, and let him fetch your brother, and ye shall be [2] kept in prison, that your words may be proved, whether *there be any* truth in you: or else, by the life of Pharaoh surely ye *are* spies.

17 And he [3] put them all together into ward three days.

18 And Joseph said unto them the third day, This do, and live; *j for* I fear God:

19 If ye *be* true *men*, let one of your brethren be bound in the house of your prison: go ye, carry corn for the famine of your houses:

20 But *k* bring your youngest brother unto me; so shall your words be verified, and ye shall not die. And they did so.

21 ¶ And they said one to another, *l* We *are* verily guilty concerning our brother, in that we saw the anguish of his soul, when he besought us, and we would not hear; *m* therefore is this distress come upon us.

22 And Reuben answered them, saying, *n* Spake I not unto you, saying, Do not sin against the child; and ye would not hear? therefore, behold, also his blood is *o* required.

23 And they knew not that Joseph understood *them;* for [4] he spake unto them by an interpreter.

24 And he turned himself about from them, and wept; and returned to them again, and communed with them, and took from them Simeon, and bound him before their eyes.

25 ¶ Then Joseph commanded to fill their sacks with corn, and to restore every man's money into his sack, and to give them provision for the way: and *p* thus did he unto them.

26 And they laded their asses with the corn, and departed thence.

27 And as *q* one of them opened his sack, to give his ass provender in the inn, he espied his money; for, behold, it *was* in his sack's mouth.

28 And he said unto his brethren, My money is restored; and, lo, *it is* even in my sack: and their heart [5] failed *them*, and they were afraid, saying one to another,

B. C. 1707.

CHAP. 42
f ch. 27. 29.
ch. 33. 6.
ch. 37. 7.
Ruth 2. 10.
1 Kin. 1. 16.
Isa. 60. 14.
1 hard things with them.
g ch. 37. 5, 9.
h ch. 37. 30.
ch. 44. 20.
Lam. 5. 7.
i 1 Sa. 1. 26.
1 Sam. 17. 55.
2 bound.
3 gathered.
j Lev. 25. 43.
Neh. 5. 15.
k ver. 34.
ch. 43. 5.
ch. 44. 23.
l Job 36, 8, 9.
Hos. 5. 15.
m Ps. 107. 17.
Pro. 5. 22.
Prov. 11. 21.
Prov. 21. 13.
Mat. 7. 2.
n ch. 37. 21.
o ch. 9. 5.
1 Kin. 2. 32.
2 Chr. 24, 22.
Ps. 9. 12.
Luke 11. 50, 51.
4 an interpreter was between them.
p Mat. 5. 44.
Rom. 12. 17, 20, 21.
1 Pet. 3. 9.
q ch. 43. 21.
5 went forth.
r ver. 7.
6 with us hard things.
s ver. 15. 19, 20.
t ch. 34. 10.
u ch. 43. 21.
v ch. 43. 14.
w ver. 13.
ch. 37. 33.
ch. 44. 28.
x ver. 4.
ch. 44. 29.
y ch. 37. 35.
ch. 44. 31.

CHAP. 43.
a 1 Ki. 18. 2.
Jer. 52 6.
Lam. 5. 10.
1 protesting protested.
b ch. 42. 20.
ch. 44. 23.
2 asking asked us.
3 mouth.
4 knowing could we know.
c ch. 44. 32.
Philem 18. 19.

What *is* this *that* God hath done unto us?

29 ¶ And they came unto Jacob their father unto the land of Canaan, and told him all that befell them; saying,

30 The man, *who is* the lord of the land, *r* spake [6] roughly to us, and took us for spies of the country.

31 And we said unto him, We *are* true *men;* we are no spies:

32 We *be* twelve brethren, sons of our father: one *is* not, and the youngest *is* this day with our father in the land of Canaan.

33 And the man, the lord of the country, said unto us, *s* Hereby shall I know that ye *are* true *men;* leave one of your brethren here with me, and take *food for* the famine of your households, and be gone;

34 And bring your youngest brother unto me: then shall I know that ye *are* no spies, but *that* ye are true *men:* so will I deliver you your brother, and ye shall *t* traffic in the land.

35 And it came to pass as they emptied their sacks, that, behold, *u* every man's bundle of money *was* in his sack: and when *both* they and their father saw the bundles of money, they were afraid.

36 And Jacob their father said unto them, Me have ye *v* bereaved *of my children:* Joseph *is* not, and Simeon *is* not, and ye will take Benjamin *away:* all these things are against me.

37 And Reuben spake unto his father, saying, Slay my two sons, if I bring him not to thee: deliver him into my hand, and I will bring him to thee again.

38 And he said, My son shall not go down with you; for his *w* brother is dead, and he is left alone: *x* if mischief befall him by the way in the which ye go, then shall ye *y* bring down my grey hairs with sorrow to the grave.

CHAPTER XLIII.

1 *Jacob is hardly persuaded to send Benjamin.* 15 *Joseph entertaineth his brethren;* 10 *their fears;* 31 *he maketh them a feast.*

AND the famine *was a* sore in the land.

2 And it came to pass, when they had eaten up the corn which they had brought out of Egypt, their father said unto them, Go again, buy us a little food.

3 And Judah spake unto him, saying, The man [1] did solemnly protest unto us, saying, Ye shall not see my face, except your *b* brother *be* with you.

4 If thou wilt send our brother with us, we will go down and buy thee food:

5 But if thou wilt not send *him*, we will not go down: for the man said unto us, Ye shall not see my face, except your brother be with you.

6 And Israel said, Wherefore dealt ye so ill with me, *as* to tell the man whether ye had yet a brother?

7 And they said, The man [2] asked us straitly of our state, and of our kindred, saying, *Is* your father yet alive? have ye *another* brother? and we told him according to the [3] tenor of these words: [4] could we certainly know that he would say, Bring your brother down?

8 And Judah said unto Israel his father, Send the lad with me, and we will arise and go; that we may live, and not die, both we, and thou *and* also our little ones.

9 I will be surety for him; of my hand shalt thou require him: *c* if I bring him not unto

that was to be created, those ministers were consulted as to the expediency and propriety of the appointment. **a man in whom the Spirit of God is**—An acknowledgment of the being and power of the true God, though faint and feeble, continued to linger amongst the higher classes long after idolatry had come to prevail. **39-44. Thou shalt be over my house**—This sudden change in the condition of a man who had just been taken out of prison, could take place nowhere, except in Egypt. In ancient as well as modern times, slaves have often risen to be its rulers. But the special providence of God had determined to make Joseph governor of Egypt; and the way was paved for it by the deep and universal conviction produced in the minds both of the king and his councillors, that a divine spirit animated his mind, and had given him such extraordinary knowledge. **40. according to thy word shall my people be ruled**—*lit.* kiss. This refers to the edict granting official power to Joseph, to be issued in the form of a firman, as in all Oriental countries; and all who should receive that order would kiss it, according to the usual Eastern mode of acknowledging obedience and respect for the sovereign. [WILK.] **41. Pharaoh said, See, I have set thee**—These words were preliminary to investiture with the insignia of office, which were these — the signet ring, used for signing public documents, and its impression was more valid than the sign-manual of the king; the khelaat or dress of honour, a coat of finely wrought linen, or rather cotton, worn only by the highest personages; the gold necklace, a badge of rank—the plain or ornamental *form* of it indicating the degree of rank and dignity; the privilege of riding in a state carriage, the second chariot; and lastly, —**they cried ... bow the knee** — *abrech*, an Egyptian term; not referring to prostration, but signifying, according to some, "father" (cf. 45. 8 ; according to others, " native prince"—*i.e.*, proclaimed him naturalized, in order to remove all popular dislike to him as a foreigner. **44.** These ceremonies of investiture were closed in usual form by the king in council solemnly ratifying the appointment. **I am Pharaoh, and without thee, &c.**—a proverbial mode of expression for great power. **45. Zaphnath-paaneah**—variously interpreted, "revealer of secrets;" "saviour of the land;" and from the hieroglyphics "a wise man fleeing from pollution" — *i. e.*, adultery. **gave him to wife** — his naturalization was completed by this alliance with a family of high distinction. On being founded by an Arab colony, Poti-pherah, like Jethro, priest of Midian, might be a worshipper of the true God; and thus Joseph, a pious man, will be freed from the charge of marrying an idolatress for worldly ends. **On**—called Aven (Ez. 30. 17), and also Beth-shemesh Jer. 43. 13.. In looking at this profusion of honours heaped suddenly upon Joseph, it cannot be doubted that he would humbly yet thankfully acknowledge the hand of a special Providence in conducting him through all his chequered course to almost royal power; and we, who know more than Joseph did, can not only see that his advancement was subservient to the most important purposes relative to the Church of God, but learn the great lesson that a Providence directs the minutest events of human life. **46.** thirty years—seventeen when brought into Egypt, probably three in prison, and thirteen in the service of Potiphar. **went out over all the land**—made an immediate survey, to determine the site and size of the store-houses required for the different quarters of the country. **47. brought forth by handfuls**—a singular expression, alluding not only to the luxuriance of the crop, but the practice of the reapers grasping the ears, which alone were cut. **48. gathered up all the food**—It gives a striking idea of the exuberant fertility of this land, that, from the superabundance of the seven plenteous years, corn enough was laid up for the subsistence, not only of its home population, but of the neighbouring countries, during the seven years of dearth. **50-52. unto Joseph were born two sons**—These domestic events, which increased his temporal happiness, develop the piety of his character in the names conferred upon his children. **53-56. The seven years of plenteousness ended**—Over and above the proportion purchased for the government during the years of plenty, the people could still have husbanded much for future use. But improvident as men commonly are in the time of prosperity, they found themselves in want, and must have starved in thousands had not Joseph anticipated and provided for the protracted calamity. **57. The famine was sore in all lands**—*i.e.*, the lands contiguous to Egypt—Canaan, Syria, and Arabia.

CHAPTER XLII.

Ver. 1-38. JOURNEY INTO EGYPT. **1. Now when Jacob saw**—learned from common rumour. It is evident, from Jacob's language, that his own and his sons' families had suffered greatly from the scarcity; and through the increasing severity of the scourge, those men, who had formerly shown both activity and spirit, were sinking into despondency, God would not interpose miraculously, when natural means of preservation were within reach. **5. the famine was sore in the land of Canaan**—The tropical rains, which annually falling swell the Nile, are those of Palestine also; and their failure would produce the same disastrous effects in Canaan as in Egypt. Numerous caravans of its people, therefore, poured over the sandy desert of Suez, with their beasts of burden, for the purchase of corn; and amongst others, " the sons of Israel " were compelled to undertake a journey from which painful associations made them strongly averse. **6. Joseph was governor**—in the zenith of his power and influence. **he it was that sold**—*i. e.*, directed the sales; for it is impossible that he could give attendance in every place. It is probable, however, that he may have personally superintended the storehouses near the border of Canaan, both because that was the most exposed part of the country, and because he must have anticipated the arrival of some messengers from his father's house. **bowed down themselves before him**—His prophetic dreams were in the course of being fulfilled, and the atrocious barbarity of his brethren had been the means of bringing about the very issue they had planned to prevent (Is. 60. 14; Rev. 3. 9, last clause.). **7, 8.** Joseph saw his brethren ... they knew not him—this is not wonderful. They were full-grown men—he was but a lad at parting. They were in their usual garb—he was in his

thee, and set him before thee, then let me bear the blame for ever:

10 For except we had lingered, surely now we had returned ⁵ this second time.

11 And their father Israel said unto them, If *it must be* so now, do this; take of the best fruits in the land in your vessels, and ᵈ carry down the man a present, a little ᵉ balm, and a little honey, spices, and myrrh, nuts, and almonds.

12 And take double money in your hand; and the money ᶠ that was brought again in the mouth of your sacks, carry *it* again in your hand; peradventure it *was* an oversight;

13 Take also your brother, and arise, go again unto the man:

14 And God Almighty give you mercy before the man, that he may send away your other brother, and Benjamin. 6 If ᵍ I be bereaved *of my children*, I am bereaved.

15 ¶ And the men took that present, and they took double money in their hand, and Benjamin; and rose up, and went down to Egypt, and stood before Joseph.

16 And when Joseph saw Benjamin with them, he said to the ʰ ruler of his house, Bring *these* men home, and ⁷ slay, and make ready; for *these* men shall ⁸ dine with me at noon.

17 And the man did as Joseph bade; and the man brought the men into Joseph's house.

18 And the men were afraid, because they were brought into Joseph's house; and they said, Because of the money that was returned in our sacks at the first time are we brought in; that he may ⁹ seek occasion against us, and fall upon us, and take us for bondmen, and our asses.

19 And they came near to the steward of Joseph's house, and they communed with him at the door of the house,

20 And said, O sir, ¹⁰ we came indeed down at the first time to buy food:

21 And ⁱ it came to pass, when we came to the inn, that we opened our sacks, and, behold, every man's money *was* in the mouth of his sack, our money in full weight: and we have brought it again in our hand.

22 And other money have we brought down in our hands to buy food: we cannot tell who put our money in our sacks.

23 And he said, Peace *be* to you, fear not: your God, and the God of your father, hath given you treasure in your sacks: ¹¹ I had your money. And he brought Simeon out unto them.

24 And the man brought the men into Joseph's house, and ʲ gave *them* water, and they washed their feet; and he gave their asses provender.

25 And they made ready the present against Joseph came at noon: for they heard that they should eat bread there.

26 And when Joseph came home, they brought him the present which *was* in their hand into the house, and ᵏ bowed themselves to him to the earth.

27 And he asked them of *their* ¹² welfare, and said, ¹³ *Is* your father well, the old man ˡ of whom ye spake? *is* he yet alive?

28 And they answered, Thy servant our father *is* in good health, he *is* yet alive. ᵐ And they bowed down their heads, and made obeisance.

29 And he lifted up his eyes, and saw his brother Benjamin, ⁿ his mother's son, and

B. C. 1707.

CHAP. 43.

5 Or, twice by this.
d ch. 32. 20. Prov. 18. 16.
e ch. 37. 25. Jer. 8. 22.
f ch. 42. 25, 35.
6 Or, and I, as I have been, etc.
g Esth. 4. 16.
h ch. 24. 2. ch. 44. 1.
7 Kill a killing.
1 Sam. 25. 11.
8 eat.
9 roll himself upon us. Job 30. 14.
10 coming down we came down.
ch. 42. 3, 10.
i ch. 42. 27, 35.
11 your money came to me.
j ch. 18. 4. ch. 24. 32. Luke 7. 44. John 13. 5. 1 Tim. 5. 10.
k ch. 27. 29. ch. 33. 6. ch. 37. 7, 10. Ruth 2. 10.
12 peace.
13 Is there peace to your father?
l ch. 42. 11, 13.
m ch. 37. 7, 10. Prov. 14. 19.
n ch. 35. 17, 18.
o ch. 42. 13.
p 1 Ki. 3. 26.
q ch. 42. 24. 2 Sa. 18. 33.
r ver. 25.
s ch. 46. 34. Ex. 8. 26.
t ch. 45. 22.
14 drank largely. Hag. 1. 6. John 2. 10.

CHAP. 44.
1 him that was over his house.
2 Or, maketh trial.
a ch. 43. 21.
b ch. 31. 32.
c ch. 37. 29, 34. Num. 14. 6. 2 Sam. 1. 11.
d ch. 37. 7.

said, *Is* this your younger brother, ᵒ of whom ye spake unto me? And he said, God be gracious unto thee, my son.

30 And Joseph made haste; for ᵖ his bowels did yearn upon his brother: and he sought *where* to weep; and he entered into *his* chamber, and ᵠ wept there.

31 And he washed his face, and went out, and refrained himself, and said, Set on ʳ bread.

32 And they set on for him by himself, and for them by themselves, and for the Egyptians which did eat with him by themselves: because the Egyptians might not eat bread with the Hebrews; for that *is* ˢ an abomination unto the Egyptians.

33 And they sat before him, the firstborn according to his birthright, and the youngest according to his youth: and the men marvelled one at another.

34 And he took *and sent* messes unto them from before him: but Benjamin's mess was ᵗ five times so much as any of theirs. And they drank, and ¹⁴ were merry with him.

CHAPTER XLIV.

1 *Joseph's policy to stay Benjamin.* 14 *Judah's humble supplication to Joseph.*

AND he commanded ¹ the steward of his house, saying, Fill the men's sacks *with* food, as much as they can carry, and put every man's money in his sack's mouth.

2 And put my cup, the silver cup, in the sack's mouth of the youngest, and his corn money. And he did according to the word that Joseph had spoken.

3 As soon as the morning was light, the men were sent away, they and their asses.

4 *And* when they were gone out of the city, *and* not *yet* far off, Joseph said unto his steward, Up, follow after the men; and when thou dost overtake them, say unto them, Wherefore have ye rewarded evil for good?

5 *Is* not this *it* in which my lord drinketh, and whereby indeed he ² divineth? Ye have done evil in so doing.

6 And he overtook them, and he spake unto them these same words.

7 And they said unto him, Wherefore saith my lord these words? God forbid that thy servants should do according to this thing.

8 Behold, ᵃ the money which we found in our sacks' mouths we brought again unto thee out of the land of Canaan: how then should we steal out of thy lord's house silver or gold?

9 With whomsoever of thy servants it be found, ᵇ both let him die, and we also will be my lord's bondmen.

10 And he said, Now also *let* it be according unto your words: he with whom it is found shall be my servant; and ye shall be blameless.

11 Then they speedily took down every man his sack to the ground, and opened every man his sack.

12 And he searched, *and* began at the eldest, and left at the youngest: and the cup was found in Benjamin's sack.

13 Then they ᶜ rent their clothes, and laded every man his ass, and returned to the city.

14 And Judah and his brethren came to Joseph's house; for he *was* yet there: and they ᵈ fell before him on the ground.

15 And Joseph said unto them, What deed

official robes. They never dreamt of him as governor of Egypt, while he had been expecting them. They had but one face—he had ten persons to judge by. **7. made himself strange... spake roughly**—it would be an injustice to Joseph's character, to suppose that this stern manner was prompted by any vindictive feelings—he never indulged any resentment against others who had injured him. But he spoke in the authoritative tone of the governor, in order to elicit some much-longed for intelligence respecting the state of his father's family, as well as to bring his brethren, by their own humiliation and distress, to a sense of the evils they had done to him. **9-12. ye are spies**—this is a suspicion entertained regarding strangers in all Eastern countries down to the present day. Joseph, however, who was well aware that his brethren were not spies, has been charged with cruel dissimulation, with a deliberate violation of what he knew to be the truth, in imputing to them such a character. But it must be remembered that he was sustaining the part of a ruler; and, in fact, acting on the very principle sanctioned by many of the sacred writers, and our Lord himself, who spoke parables (fictitious stories) to promote a good end. **by the life of Pharaoh**—it is a very common practice in Western Asia to swear by the life of the king. Joseph spoke in the style of an Egyptian, and perhaps did not think there was any evil in it. But we are taught to regard all such expressions in the light of an oath (Matt. 5. 34; Ja. 5. 12.). **17-24. put them into ward three days**—Their confinement had been designed to bring them to salutary reflection. And this object was attained, for they looked upon the retributive justice of God as now pursuing them in that foreign land. The drift of their conversation is one of the most striking instances of the power of conscience on record. **24. took Simeon and bound him**—he had probably been the chief instigator—the most violent actor in the outrage upon Joseph; and if so, his selection to be the imprisoned and fettered hostage for their return would, in the present course of their reflections, have a painful significance. **25-28. commanded... fill sacks, and restore money**—This private generosity was not an infringement of his duty—a defrauding of the revenue. He would have a discretionary power—he was daily enriching the king's exchequer—and he might have paid the sum from his own purse. **27. inn**—a mere station for baiting beasts of burden. **espied his money**—the discovery threw them into greater perplexity than ever. If they had been congratulating themselves on escaping from the ruthless governor, they perceived that now he would have a handle against them; and it is observable, that they looked upon this as a judgment of heaven. Thus one leading design of Joseph was gained in their consciences being roused to a sense of guilt. **35. as they emptied their sacks**—it appears that they had been silent about the money discovery at the resting-place, as their father might have blamed them for not instantly returning. However innocent they knew themselves to be, it was universally felt to be an unhappy circumstance, which might bring them into new and greater perils. **36. Me have ye bereaved**—this exclamation indicates a painfully excited state of feeling, and it shows how difficult it is for even a good man to yield implicit submission to the course of Providence. The language does not imply that his missing sons had got foul play from the hands of the rest, but he looks upon Simeon as lost, as well as Joseph, and he insinuates it was by some imprudent statements of theirs that he was exposed to the risk of losing Benjamin also. **37. Reuben said, Slay my two sons**—this was a thoughtless and unwarrantable condition—one that he never seriously expected his father would accept. It was designed only to give assurance of the greatest care being taken of Benjamin. But unforeseen circumstances might arise to render it impossible for all of them to preserve that young lad (Ja. 4. 13.), and Jacob was much pained by the prospect. Little did he know that God was dealing with him severely, but in kindness (Heb. 12. 7, 8.), and that all those things he thought against him were working together for his good.

CHAPTER XLIII.

Ver. 1-14. PREPARATIONS FOR A SECOND JOURNEY TO EGYPT. **2. Father said, Go again, buy us corn**—it was no easy matter to bring Jacob to agree to the only conditions on which his sons could return to Egypt (42. 15.). The necessity of immediately procuring fresh supplies for the maintenance of themselves and their families overcame every other consideration; and extorted his consent to Benjamin joining in a journey, which his sons entered on with mingled feelings of hope and anxiety—of hope, because having now complied with the governor's demand to bring down their youngest brother, they flattered themselves that the alleged ground of suspecting them would be removed; and of apprehension, that some ill designs were meditated against them. **11. take of the best fruits a present**—it is an Oriental practice never to approach a man of power without a present, and Jacob might remember how he pacified his brother (Pro. 21. 14.)—**balm, spices, and myrrh** (37. 25.), **honey**, which some think was *dibs*, a syrup made from ripe dates [Bo.]; but others, the honey of Hebron, which is still valued as far superior to that of Egypt; **nuts, pistachio nuts**, of which Syria grows the best in the world; **almonds**, which were most abundant in Palestine. **12. take double money**—the first sum to be returned, and another sum for a new supply. The restored money in the sack's mouth was a perplexing circumstance. But it might have been done inadvertently by one of the servants—so Jacob persuaded himself—and happy it was for his own peace and the encouragement of the travellers that he took this view. Besides the duty of restoring it, honesty in their case was clearly the best—the safest policy. **14. God Almighty give you mercy**—Jacob is here committing them all to the care of God, and, resigned to what appears a heavy trial, prays that it may be overruled for good.

15, 16. ARRIVAL IN EGYPT. **15. stood before Joseph**—We may easily imagine the delight with which, amid the crowd of other applicants, the eye of Joseph would fix on his brethren and Benjamin. But occupied with his public duties, he consigned them to the care of a confidential servant till he should have finished the business of the day. **ruler of his house**—in the houses of wealthy Egyptians one

is this that ye have done? wot ye not that such a man as I can certainly ³divine?

16 And Judah said, ᵉ What shall we say unto my lord? what shall we speak? or how shall we clear ourselves? God hath found out the iniquity of thy servants: behold, ᶠ we *are* my lord's servants, both we, and *he* also with whom the cup is found.

17 And he said, ᵍ God forbid that I should do so: *but* the man in whose hand the cup is found, he shall be my servant; and as for you, get you up in peace unto your father.

18 ¶ Then Judah came near unto him, and said, Oh my lord, let thy servant, I pray thee, speak a word in my lord's ears, and ʰ let not thine anger burn against thy servant: for thou ⁱ art even as Pharaoh.

19 My lord asked his servants, saying, Have ye a father, or a brother?

20 And we said unto my lord, We have a father, an old man, and ʲ a child of his old age, a little one; and his brother is dead, and he alone is left of his mother, and his father loveth him.

21 And thou saidst unto thy servants, ᵏ Bring him down unto me, that I may set mine eyes upon him.

22 And we said unto my lord, The lad cannot leave his father: for if he should leave his father, *his father* would die.

23 And thou saidst unto thy servants, ˡ Except your youngest brother come down with you, ye shall see my face no more.

24 And it came to pass, when we came up unto thy servant my father, we told him the words of my lord.

25 And ᵐ our father said, Go again, *and* buy us a little food.

26 And we said, We cannot go down: if our youngest brother be with us, then will we go down: for we may not see the man's face, except our youngest brother *be* with us.

27 And thy servant my father said unto us, Ye know that ⁿ my wife bare me two *sons:*

28 And the one went out from me, and I said, ᵒ Surely he is torn in pieces; and I saw him not since:

29 And if ye ᵖ take this also from me, and mischief befall him, ye shall bring down my grey hairs with sorrow to the grave.

30 Now therefore, when I come to thy servant my father, and the lad *be* not with us; seeing that ᵠ his life is bound up in the lad's life;

31 It shall come to pass, when he seeth that the lad *is* not *with us,* that he will die: and thy servants shall bring down the grey hairs of thy servant our father with sorrow to the grave.

32 For thy servant became surety for the lad unto my father, saying, ʳ If I bring him not unto thee, then I shall bear the blame to my father for ever.

33 Now therefore, I pray thee, ˢ let thy servant abide instead of the lad a bondman to my lord; and let the lad go up with his brethren.

34 For how shall I go up to my father, and the lad *be* not with me? lest peradventure I see the evil that ᵗ come on my father.

CHAPTER XLV.

1 *Joseph maketh himself known to his brethren, and comforteth them in God's providence.* 9 *He sendeth for his father.* 27 *The spirit of Jacob is revived.*

THEN Joseph could not refrain himself before all them that stood by him; and

B. C. 1707.

CHAP. 44.
3 Or, make trial.
ver. 5.
ᵉ Job 40. 4.
ᶠ ver. 9.
ᵍ Prov. 17, 15.
ʰ ch. 18. 30, 32.
Ex. 32. 22.
ⁱ Prov. 19, 12.
ch. 41. 40.
ʲ ch. 37. 3.
ᵏ ch. 42. 15. 20.
ˡ ch. 43. 3, 5.
ᵐ ch. 43. 2.
ⁿ ch. 46. 19.
ᵒ ch. 37. 33.
ᵖ ch. 42. 36, 38.
ᵠ 1 Sam. 18. 1.
ʳ ch. 43. 9.
ˢ Ex. 32. 32.
4 find my father.
Ex. 18. 8.
Job 31. 29.
Ps. 116, 3.
Ps. 119, 143.

CHAP. 45.
1 gave forth his voice in weeping.
Nu. 14. 1.
ᵃ Acts 7. 13.
2 Or, terrified.
Job 4. 5.
Job 22. 15.
Zech. 12. 10.
Ps. 77. 4.
Mat. 14. 26.
Mark 6. 50.
ᵇ ch. 37. 28.
ᶜ Is. 40. 2.
2 Cor. 2. 7.
3 neither let there be anger in your eyes.
ᵈ ch. 50. 20.
Ps. 105.16, 17.
2 Sam. 16. 10, 11.
Acts 4. 24.
4 to put for you a remnant.
ᵉ ch. 41. 43.
Judg. 17. 10.
Job 29. 16.
ᶠ ch. 47. 1.
ᵍ 1 Tim. 5. 4.
ʰ ch. 42. 23.
ⁱ Acts 7. 14.
5 was good in the eyes of Pharaoh.
ᵏ ch. 41. 37.
ˡ ch. 27. 28.
6 let not your eye spare, etc.
7 mouth.

he cried, Cause every man to go out from me. And there stood no man with him while Joseph made himself known unto his brethren.

2 And he ¹wept aloud: and the Egyptians and the house of Pharaoh heard.

3 And Joseph said unto his brethren, ᵃ I am Joseph: doth my father yet live? And his brethren could not answer him; for they were ²troubled at his presence.

4 And Joseph said unto his brethren, Come near to me, I pray you. And they came near. And he said, I am Joseph your brother, ᵇ whom ye sold into Egypt.

5 Now therefore ᶜ be not grieved ³ nor angry with yourselves that ye sold me hither; for ᵈ God did send me before you to preserve life.

6 For these two years *hath* the famine *been* in the land: and yet *there are* five years, in the which *there shall* neither be earing nor harvest.

7 And God sent me before you ⁴ to preserve you a posterity in the earth, and to save your lives by a great deliverance.

8 So now, *it was* not you *that* sent me hither, but God: and he hath made me ᵉ a father to Pharaoh, and lord of all his house, and a ruler throughout all the land of Egypt.

9 Haste ye, and go up to my father, and say unto him, Thus saith thy son Joseph, God hath made me lord of all Egypt: come down unto me, tarry not:

10 And ᶠ thou shalt dwell in the land of Goshen, and thou shalt be near unto me, thou, and thy children, and thy children's children, and thy flocks, and thy herds, and all that thou hast:

11 And there will I nourish thee; for ᵍ yet *there are* five years of famine; lest thou, and thy household, and all that thou hast, come to poverty.

12 And, behold, your eyes see, and the eyes of my brother Benjamin, that *it is* ʰ my mouth that speaketh unto you.

13 And ye shall tell my father of all my glory in Egypt, and of all that ye have seen; and ye shall haste and ⁱ bring down my father hither.

14 And he fell upon his brother Benjamin's neck, and wept; and Benjamin wept upon his neck.

15 Moreover, he kissed all his brethren, and wept upon them: and after that his brethren talked with him.

16 ¶ And the fame thereof was heard in Pharaoh's house, saying, Joseph's brethren are come: and it ⁵ pleased Pharaoh well, and his servants.

17 And Pharaoh said unto Joseph, Say unto thy brethren, This do ye; lade your beasts, and go, get you unto the land of Canaan;

18 And take your father, and your households, and come unto me: and I will give you the good of the land of Egypt, and ye shall eat ʲ the fat of the land.

19 Now thou art commanded, this do ye; take you wagons out of the land of Egypt for your little ones, and for your wives, and bring your father, and come.

20 Also ⁶ regard not your stuff; for the good of all the land of Egypt *is* yours.

21 And the children of Israel did so: and Joseph gave them wagons, according to the ⁷ commandment of Pharaoh, and gave them provision for the way.

upper man-servant was intrusted with the management of the house (cf. 30. 5.). slay and make ready—*Heb.* "kill a killing"—implying preparations for a grand entertainment (cf. 31. 54; 1 Sam. 25. 11; Pro. 9. 2; Matt. 22. 4.). The animals have to be killed as well as prepared at home. The heat of the climate requires that the cook should take the joints directly from the hands of the flesher, and the Oriental taste is, from habit, fond of newly-killed meat. A great profusion of viands, with an inexhaustible supply of vegetables, was provided for the repasts, to which strangers were invited, the pride of Egyptian nations consisting rather in the quantity and variety than in the choice or delicacy of the dishes at their table. dine at noon—the hour of dinner was at midday. 18. the men were afraid—Their feelings of awe on entering the stately mansion, unaccustomed as they were to houses at all—their anxiety at the reasons of their being taken there—their solicitude about the restored money—their honest simplicity in communicating their distress to the steward, and his assurance of having received their money in "full weight"—the offering of their fruit present, which would, as usual, be done with some parade, and the Oriental salutations that passed between their host and them,—are all described in a graphic and animated manner.

31-34. THE DINNER. Joseph said, Set on bread—equivalent to having dinner served, bread being a term inclusive of all victuals. The table was a small stool, most probably the usual round form, "since persons might even then be seated according to their rank or seniority, and the modern Egyptian table is not without its post of honour and a fixed gradation of place." [WILK.] Two or at most three persons were seated at one table. But the host being the highest in rank of the company, had a table to himself; whilst it was so arranged that an Egyptian was not placed nor obliged to eat from the same dish as an Hebrew, for that is an abomination—the prejudice probably arose from the detestation in which, from the oppressions of the shepherd-kings, the nation held all of that occupation. 34. took mess ... Benjamin's five times—in Egypt, as in other Oriental countries, there were, and are, two modes of paying attention to a guest whom the host wishes to honour—either by giving a choice piece from his own hand, or ordering it to be taken to the stranger. The degree of respect shown consists in the quantity, and while the ordinary rule of distinction is a double mess, it must have appeared a very distinguished mark of favour bestowed on Benjamin to have no less than five times any of his brethren. drank and were merry—*Heb.* "drank freely," same as Sol. Song, 5. 1; Jo. 11. 10. In all these cases the idea of intemperance is excluded. The painful anxieties and cares of Joseph's brethren were dispelled, and they were at ease.

CHAPTER XLIV.

1-34. POLICY TO STAY HIS BRETHREN. And Joseph commanded his steward—The design of putting the cup into the sack of Benjamin was obviously to bring that young man into a situation of difficulty or danger, in order thereby to discover how far the brotherly feelings of the rest would be roused to sympathise with his distress, and stimulate their exertions in procuring his deliverance. But for what purpose was the money restored? It was done, in the first instance, from kindly feelings to his father; but another and further design seems to have been, the prevention of any injurious impressions as to the character of Benjamin. The discovery of the cup in *his* possession, if there had been nothing else to judge by, might have fastened a painful suspicion of guilt on the youngest brother; but the sight of the money in each man's sack would lead all to the same conclusion, that Benjamin was just as innocent as themselves, although the additional circumstance of the cup being found in his sack would bring him into greater trouble and danger. 2. my cup, the silver cup—it was a large goblet, as the original denotes, highly valued by its owner, on account of its costly material, or its elegant finish, and which had probably graced his table at the sumptuous entertainment of the previous day. 3. as soon as the morning... the men were sent away — they commenced their homeward journey at early dawn (see on 18. 2,); and it may be readily supposed in high spirits, after so happy an issue from all their troubles and anxieties. 4. when gone out of the city ... Joseph sent his steward—they were brought to a sudden halt by the stunning intelligence that an article of rare value was a-missing from the governor's house. It was a silver cup; so strong suspicions were entertained against them, that a special messenger was despatched to search them. 5. is not this it—not only kept for the governor's personal use, but whereby he divineth. Divination by cups, to ascertain the course of futurity, was one of the prevalent superstitions of ancient Egypt, as it is of Eastern countries still. It is not likely that Joseph, a pious believer in the true God, would have addicted himself to this superstitious practice. But he might have availed himself of that popular notion to carry out the successful execution of his stratagem for the last decisive trial of his brethren. 6, 7. he overtook them, and spake these words — the intelligence must have come upon them like a thunderbolt, and one of their most predominant feelings must have been the humiliating and galling sense of being made so often objects of suspicion. Protesting their innocence, they invited a search. The challenge was accepted. Beginning with the eldest, every sack was examined, and the cup being found in Benjamin's, they all returned in an indescribable agony of mind to the house of the governor, throwing themselves at his feet, with the remarkable confession, "God hath found out the iniquity of thy servants." 16-34. Judah ... what shall we say?—this address needs no comment—consisting at first of short, broken sentences, as if, under the overwhelming force of the speaker's emotions, his utterance were choked. it becomes more free and copious by the effort of speaking, as he proceeds. Every word finds its way to the heart; and it may well be imagined that Benjamin, who stood there speechless, like a victim about to be laid on the altar, when he heard the magnanimous offer of Judah to submit to slavery for his ransom: would be bound by a lifelong gratitude to his generous brother—a tie that seems to have become hereditary in his tribe. Joseph's behaviour must not be viewed from any single point, or in separate

Jacob goeth into Egypt.   GENESIS, XLVI, XLVII.   *Joseph meeteth him.*

22 To all of them he gave each man changes of raiment; but to Benjamin he gave three hundred *pieces* of silver, and five changes of raiment.

23 And to his father he sent after this *manner;* ten asses laden with the good things of Egypt, and ten she-asses laden with corn and bread and meat for his father by the way.

24 So he sent his brethren away, and they departed; and he said unto them, See that ye fall not out by the way.

25 And they went up out of Egypt, and came into the land of Canaan unto Jacob their father,

26 And told him, saying, Joseph *is* yet alive, and he *is* governor over all the land of Egypt. And Jacob's heart fainted, for he believed them not.

27 And they told him all the words of Joseph, which he had said unto them: and when he saw the wagons which Joseph had sent to carry him, the spirit of Jacob their father revived:

28 And Israel said, *It is* enough; Joseph my son *is* yet alive: I will go and see him before I die.

CHAPTER XLVI.

1 Jacob is comforted by God at Beer-sheba: 5 he goeth into Egypt: 8 the number of his family: 28 Joseph meeteth him.

AND Israel took his journey with all that he had, and came to Beer-sheba, and offered sacrifices unto the God of his father Isaac.

2 And God spake unto Israel in the visions of the night, and said, Jacob, Jacob. And he said, Here *am* I.

3 And he said, I *am* God, the God of thy father: fear not to go down into Egypt; for I will there make of thee a great nation.

4 I will go down with thee into Egypt; and I will also surely bring thee up *again:* and Joseph shall put his hand upon thine eyes.

5 And Jacob rose up from Beer-sheba: and the sons of Israel carried Jacob their father, and their little ones, and their wives, in the wagons which Pharaoh had sent to carry him.

6 And they took their cattle, and their goods, which they had gotten in the land of Canaan, and came into Egypt, Jacob, and all his seed with him:

7 His sons, and his sons' sons with him, his daughters, and his sons' daughters, and all his seed, brought he with him into Egypt.

8 ¶ And these *are* the names of the children of Israel which came into Egypt, Jacob and his sons: Reuben, Jacob's first-born.

9 And the sons of Reuben; Hanoch, and Phallu, and Hezron, and Carmi.

10 And the sons of Simeon; Jemuel, and Jamin, and Ohad, and Jachin, and Zohar, and Shaul the son of a Canaanitish woman.

11 And the sons of Levi; Gershon, Kohath, and Merari.

12 And the sons of Judah; Er, and Onan, and Shelah, and Pharez, and Zarah: but Er and Onan died in the land of Canaan. And the sons of Pharez were Hezron and Hamul.

13 And the sons of Issachar; Tola, and Phuvah, and Job, and Shimron.

14 And the sons of Zebulun; Sered, and Elon, and Jahleel.

15 These *be* the sons of Leah, which she bare unto Jacob in Padan-aram, with his daughter Dinah: all the souls of his sons and his daughters *were* thirty and three.

16 And the sons of Gad; Ziphion, and Haggi, Shuni, and Ezbon, Eri, and Arodi, and Areli.

17 And the sons of Asher; Jimnah, and Ishuah, and Isui, and Beriah, and Serah their sister: and the sons of Beriah; Heber, and Malchiel.

18 These *are* the sons of Zilpah, whom Laban gave to Leah his daughter; and these she bare unto Jacob, *even* sixteen souls.

19 The sons of Rachel, Jacob's wife; Joseph, and Benjamin.

20 And unto Joseph in the land of Egypt were born Manasseh and Ephraim, which Asenath the daughter of Poti-pherah priest of On bare unto him.

21 And the sons of Benjamin *were* Belah, and Becher, and Ashbel, Gera, and Naaman, Ehi, and Rosh, Muppim, and Huppim, and Ard.

22 These *are* the sons of Rachel, which were born to Jacob: all the souls *were* fourteen.

23 And the sons of Dan; Hushim.

24 And the sons of Naphtali; Jahzeel, and Guni, and Jezer, and Shillem.

25 These *are* the sons of Bilhah, which Laban gave unto Rachel his daughter; and she bare these unto Jacob: all the souls *were* seven.

26 All the souls that came with Jacob into Egypt, which came out of his loins, besides Jacob's sons' wives, all the souls *were* threescore and six.

27 And the sons of Joseph, which were born him in Egypt, *were* two souls: all the souls of the house of Jacob, which came into Egypt, *were* threescore and ten.

28 ¶ And he sent Judah before him unto Joseph, to direct his face unto Goshen; and they came into the land of Goshen.

29 And Joseph made ready his chariot, and went up to meet Israel his father, to Goshen, and presented himself unto him; and he fell on his neck, and wept on his neck a good while.

30 And Israel said unto Joseph, Now let me die, since I have seen thy face, because thou *art* yet alive.

31 And Joseph said unto his brethren, and unto his father's house, I will go up, and show Pharaoh, and say unto him, My brethren, and my father's house, which *were* in the land of Canaan, are come unto me;

32 And the men *are* shepherds, for their trade hath been to feed cattle; and they have brought their flocks, and their herds, and all that they have.

33 And it shall come to pass, when Pharaoh shall call you, and shall say, What *is* your occupation?

34 That ye shall say, Thy servants' trade hath been about cattle from our youth even until now, both we *and* also our fathers: that ye may dwell in the land of Goshen: for every shepherd *is* an abomination unto the Egyptians.

CHAPTER XLVII.

1 Joseph presenteth five of his brethren, 7 and his father, before Pharaoh: 11 he giveth them habitation and maintenance. 13 He getteth all the Egyptians' property to Pharaoh. 22 The priests' land not bought, etc.

THEN Joseph came and told Pharaoh, and said, My father and my brethren,

parts, but as a whole—a well-thought, deep-laid, closely-connected plan; and though some features of it do certainly exhibit an appearance of harshness, yet the pervading principle of his conduct was real, genuine brotherly kindness. Read in this light, the narrative of the proceedings describes the continuous, though secret pursuit of one end; and Joseph discovers, in his management of the scheme, a very high order of intellect—a warm and susceptible heart, united to a judgment that exerted a complete control over his feelings—a happy invention in devising means towards the attainment of his ends, and an inflexible adherence to the course however painful which prudence required.

CHAPTER XLV.

Ver. 1-28. JOSEPH MAKING HIMSELF KNOWN. 1. Then Joseph could not refrain— The severity of the inflexible magistrate here gives way to the natural feelings of the man and the brother. However well he had disciplined his mind, he felt it impossible to resist the artless eloquence of Judah. He saw a satisfactory proof, in the return of *all* his brethren on such an occasion, that they were affectionately united to one another; he had heard enough to convince him, that time, reflection, or grace had made a happy improvement on their character; and he would, probably, have proceeded in a calm and leisurely manner, to reveal himself as prudence might have dictated. But when he heard the heroic self-sacrifice of Judah, and realised all the affection of that proposal—a proposal for which he was totally unprepared—he was completely unmanned; he felt himself forced to bring this painful trial to an end. he cried, Cause every man to go out—In ordering the departure of witnesses, of this last scene, he acted as a warm-hearted and real friend to his brothers—his conduct was dictated by motives of the highest prudence—that of preventing their early iniquities from becoming known either to the members of his household, or amongst the people of Egypt. 2. he wept aloud—No doubt, from the fulness of highly excited feelings; but to indulge in vehement and long-continued transports of sobbing, is the usual way in which the Orientals express their grief. 3–12. I am Joseph—The emotions that now rose in the breast of himself as well as his brethren—and chased each other in rapid succession—were many and violent. He was agitated by sympathy and joy; they were astonished, confounded, terrified; and betrayed their terror, by shrinking as far as they could from his presence. So "troubled" were they, that he had to repeat his announcement of himself; and what kind, affectionate terms did he use. He spoke of their having sold him—not to wound their feelings; but to convince them of his identity; and then, to re-assure their minds, he traced the agency of an overruling Providence, in his exile and present honour. Not that he wished them to roll the responsibility of their crime on God; no, his only object was to encourage their confidence, and induce them to trust in the plans he had formed for the future comfort of their father and themselves. 6. for yet five years... neither earing nor harvest—Ear is an *old* English word, meaning to plough (cf. 1 Sam. 8. 12; Is. 30. 24.). This seems to confirm the view given (41. 57,) that the famine was caused by an extraordinary drought, which prevented the annual overflowing of the Nile; and of course made the land unfit to receive the seed of Egypt. 14, 15. and he fell upon the neck of Benjamin— The sudden transition from a condemned criminal to a fondled brother, might have occasioned fainting or even death, had not his tumultuous feelings been relieved by a torrent of tears. But Joseph's attentions were not confined to Benjamin. He affectionately embraced every one of his brothers in succession; and by those actions, his forgiveness was demonstrated more fully than it could be by words. 17–20. Pharaoh said unto Joseph, Say unto your brethren— As Joseph might have been prevented by delicacy—the king himself invited the patriarch and all his family to migrate into Egypt; and made most liberal arrangements for their removal and their subsequent settlement. It displays the character of this Pharaoh to advantage, that he was so kind to the relatives of Joseph, but indeed the greatest liberality he could shew, could never recompense the services of so great a benefactor of his kingdom. 21. Joseph gave them wagons—which must have been novelties in Palestine; for wheeled carriages were and are almost unknown there. 22. changes of raiment—It was and is customary with great men, to bestow on their friends dresses of distinction, and in places, where they are of the same description and quality, the value of these presents consists in their number. The great number given to Benjamin, bespoke the warmth of his brother's attachment to him; and Joseph felt, from the amiable temper they now all displayed —he might, with perfect safety, indulge this fond partiality for a mother's son. 23. to his father he sent—a supply of every thing that could contribute to his support and comfort—the large and liberal scale on which that supply was given being intended —like the five messes of Benjamin—as a token of his filial love. 24. so he sent his brethren away—In dismissing them on their homeward journey, he gave them this parting admonition: "See that ye fall not out by the way"—a caution that would be greatly needed; for not only during the journey would they be occupied in recalling the parts they had respectively acted in the events that led to Joseph's being sold into Egypt; but their wickedness would soon have to come to the knowledge of their venerable father.

CHAPTER XLVI.

Ver. 1-4. SACRIFICE AT BEER-SHEBA. 1. Israel took his journey with all that he had— that is, his household: for in compliance with Pharaoh's recommendation, he left his heavy furniture behind. In contemplating a step so important as that of leaving Canaan, which at his time of life he might never revisit, so pious a patriarch would ask the guidance and counsel of God. With all his anxiety to see Joseph, he would rather have died in Canaan without that highest of earthly gratifications, than leave it without the consciousness of carrying the divine blessing along with him. came to Beer-sheba—That place, which was in his direct route to Egypt, had been a favourite encampment of Abraham (21. 33.) and

and their flocks, and their herds, and all that they have, are come out of the land of Canaan; and, behold, they *are* in ^b the land of Goshen.

2 And he took some of his brethren, *even* five men, and ² presented them unto Pharaoh.

3 And Pharaoh said unto his brethren, ^d What *is* your occupation? And they said unto Pharaoh, ^e Thy servants *are* shepherds, both we, *and* also our fathers.

4 They said, moreover, unto Pharaoh, ^f For to sojourn in the land are we come; for thy servants have no pasture for their flocks; ^g for the famine *is* sore in the land of Canaan: now therefore, we pray thee, let thy servants ^h dwell in the land of Goshen.

5 And Pharaoh spake unto Joseph, saying, Thy father and thy brethren are come unto thee:

6 ⁱ The land of Egypt *is* before thee: in the best of the land make thy father and brethren to dwell; ^j in the land of Goshen let them dwell: and if thou knowest any men of activity among them, then make them ^k rulers over my cattle.

7 And Joseph brought in Jacob his father, and set him before Pharaoh: and Jacob blessed Pharaoh.

8 And Pharaoh said unto Jacob, ¹ How old *art* thou?

9 And Jacob said unto Pharaoh, ^l The days of the years of my pilgrimage *are* an hundred and thirty years: ^m few and evil have the days of the years of my life been, and ⁿ have not attained unto the days of the years of the life of my fathers in the days of their pilgrimage.

10 And Jacob ^o blessed Pharaoh, and went out from before Pharaoh.

11 ¶ And Joseph placed his father and his brethren, and gave them a possession in the land of Egypt, in the best of the land, in the land of ^p Rameses, ^q as Pharaoh had commanded.

12 And Joseph nourished his ^r father, and his brethren, and all his father's household, with bread, ² according to *their* families.

13 ¶ And *there was* no bread in all the land; for the famine *was* very sore, ^s so that the land of Egypt, and *all* the land of Canaan, fainted by reason of the famine.

14 ^t And Joseph gathered up all the money that was found in the land of Egypt, and in the land of Canaan, for the corn which they bought: and Joseph brought the money into Pharaoh's house.

15 And when money failed in the land of Egypt, and in the land of Canaan, all the Egyptians came unto Joseph, and said, Give us bread: for ^u why should we die in thy presence? for the money faileth.

16 And Joseph said, Give your cattle; and I will give you for your cattle, if money fail.

17 And they brought their cattle unto Joseph: and Joseph gave them bread *in exchange* for horses, and for the flocks, and for the cattle of the herds, and for the asses; and he ⁴ fed them with bread for all their cattle for that year.

18 When that year was ended, they came unto him the second year, and said unto him, We will not hide *it* from my lord, how that our money is spent; my lord also hath our herds of cattle: there is not ought

B.C. 1706.

CHAP. 47.
^b ch. 45. 10.
ch. 46. 28.
^c Acts 7. 13.
^d ch. 46. 33.
^e ch. 46. 34.
^f ch. 15. 13.
Deut. 26. 5.
Ps. 105. 23.
Is. 52. 4.
^g ch. 43. 1.
Acts 7. 11.
^h ch. 46. 34.
ⁱ ch. 20. 15.
^j ver. 4.
^k 1 Kings 11. 28.
Prov. 22. 29.
Prov. 12. 24.
1 How many are the days of the years of thy life?
^l Heb. 11. 9, 13.
Ps. 39. 12.
^m Job 14. 1.
Ec. 2. 23.
ⁿ ch. 25. 7.
ch. 35. 28.
^o ver. 7.
^p Ex. 1. 11.
Ex. 12. 37.
^q ver. 6.
^r Prov. 10. 1.
Ex. 20. 12.
2 Or, as a little child is nourished, according to the little ones.
ch. 50. 21.
^s ch. 41. 30.
Acts 7. 11.
^t ch. 41. 56.
^u ver. 19.
4 led them.
^v Ezra 7. 24.
5 Or, princes.
ch. 41. 45.
2 Sam. 8. 18.
^w ch. 33. 15.
^x ver. 29.
6 Or, princes.
^y ver. 11.
^z ch. 46. 3.
7 the days of the years of his life.
^a Deut. 31. 14.
1 Kin. 2. 1.
^b ch. 24. 2.
^c ch. 24. 49.
^d ch. 50. 25.
^e 2 Sam. 19. 37.
^f ch. 49. 29.
ch. 50. 5, 13.
^g ch. 48. 2.
1 Kin. 1. 47.
Heb. 11. 21.

CHAP. 48.
^a ch. 25. 13, 19.
ch. 35. 6, 9, etc.

left in the sight of my lord, but our bodies and our lands:

19 Wherefore shall we die before thine eyes, both we and our land? buy us and our land for bread, and we and our land will be servants unto Pharaoh; and give *us* seed, that we may live, and not die, that the land be not desolate.

20 And Joseph bought all the land of Egypt for Pharaoh; for the Egyptians sold every man his field, because the famine prevailed over them: so the land became Pharaoh's.

21 And as for the people, he removed them to cities from *one* end of the borders of Egypt even to the *other* end thereof.

22 ¶ Only the land of the ⁵ priests bought he not: for the priests had a portion *assigned them* of Pharaoh, and did eat their portion which Pharaoh gave them; wherefore they sold not their lands.

23 Then Joseph said unto the people, Behold, I have bought you this day and your land for Pharaoh: lo, *here* is seed for you, and ye shall sow the land.

24 And it shall come to pass in the increase, that ye shall give the fifth *part* unto Pharaoh; and four parts shall be your own, for seed of the field, and for your food, and for them of your households, and for food for your little ones.

25 And they said, Thou hast saved our lives: ^w let us find grace in the sight of my lord, and we will be Pharaoh's servants.

26 And Joseph made it a law over the land of Egypt unto this day, *that* Pharaoh should have the fifth *part*; ^x except the land of the ⁶ priests only, *which* became not Pharaoh's.

27 ¶ And Israel ^y dwelt in the land of Egypt, in the country of Goshen; and they had possessions therein, and ^z grew, and multiplied exceedingly.

28 And Jacob lived in the land of Egypt seventeen years: so ⁷ the whole age of Jacob was an hundred forty and seven years.

29 And the time ^a drew nigh that Israel must die: and he called his son Joseph, and said unto him, If now I have found grace in thy sight, ^b put, I pray thee, thy hand under my thigh, and ^c deal kindly and truly with me: ^d bury me not, I pray thee, in Egypt:

30 But ^e I will lie with my fathers: and thou shalt carry me out of Egypt, and ^f bury me in their burying-place. And he said, I will do as thou hast said.

31 And he said, Swear unto me. And he sware unto him. And ^g Israel bowed himself upon the bed's head.

CHAPTER XLVIII.

1 *Joseph with his sons visiteth his sick father.* 3 *Jacob repeateth God's promise, and taketh Ephraim and Manasseh as his own; he blesseth Joseph's two sons with their father, and preferreth the younger before the elder;* 21 *He prophesieth their return to Canaan.*

AND it came to pass after these things, that *one* told Joseph, Behold, thy father *is* sick: and he took with him his two sons, Manasseh and Ephraim.

2 And *one* told Jacob, and said, Behold, thy son Joseph cometh unto thee: and Israel strengthened himself, and sat upon the bed.

3 And Jacob said unto Joseph, God Almighty appeared unto me at ^a Luz in the land of Canaan, and blessed me,

Isaac (26. 25), and was memorable for their experience of the divine goodness; and Jacob seems to have deferred his public devotions till he had reached a spot so consecrated by covenant to his own God and the God of his fathers. 2–4. God spake unto Israel—Here is a virtual renewal of the covenant and an assurance of its blessings. Moreover, here is an answer on the chief subject of Jacob's prayer, and a removal of any doubt as to the course he was meditating. At first the prospect of paying a personal visit to Joseph had been viewed with unmingled joy. But, on calmer consideration, many difficulties appeared to lie in the way. He might remember the prophecy to Abraham that h s posterity was to be afflicted in Egypt, and also that his father had been expressly told *not* to go; he might fear the contamination of idolatry to his family and their forgetfulness of the land of promise. These doubts were removed by the answer of the oracle, and an assurance given him of great and increasing prosperity. I will make of thee a great nation —How truly this promise was fulfilled, appears in the fact, that the seventy souls who went down into Egypt increased, in the space of 215 years, to 180,000. I will surely bring thee up again—As Jacob could not expect to live till the former promise was realized, he must have seen that the latter was to be accomplished only to his posterity. To himself it was literally verified in the removal of his remains to Canaan; but, in the large and liberal sense of the words, it was made good only on the establishment of Israel in the land of promise. Joseph shall put his hand on thine eyes—shall perform the last office of filial piety; and this implied that he should henceforth enjoy, without interruption, the society of that favourite son.

5-27. IMMIGRATION TO EGYPT. 5. Jacob rose up from Beer-sheba—to cross the border, and settle in Egypt. However refreshed and invigorated in spirit by the religious services at Beer-sheba, he was now borne down by the infirmities of advanced age; and, therefore, his sons undertook all the trouble and toil of the arrangements, while the enfeebled old patriarch, with the wives and children, was conveyed, by slow and leisurely stages, in the Egyptian vehicles sent for their accommodation. 6. goods which they had gotten—not furniture, but substance—precious things. 7. daughters—As Dinah was his only daughter, this must mean daughters-in-law. all his seed brought he with him—Though disabled by age from active superintendance, yet, as the venerable shieck of the tribe, he was looked upon as their common head, and consulted in every step. 8-27. all the souls .. which came into Egypt... threescore and ten—Strictly speaking, there were only sixty-six went to Egypt; but to these add Joseph and his two sons, and Jacob the head of the clan, and the whole number amounts to seventy. In the speech of Stephen (A. 7. 14.) the number is stated to be seventy-five; but as that estimate includes five sons of Ephraim and Manasseh (1 Chron. 7, 14-20), born in Egypt, the two accounts coincide.

28-34. ARRIVAL IN EGYPT. 28. sent Judah before him unto Joseph—This precautionary measure was obviously proper for apprizing the king of the entrance of so large a company within his territories; moreover, it was necessary in order to receive instruction from Joseph as to the *locale* of their future settlement. 29, 30. Joseph made ready his chariot—The difference between chariot and waggon was not only in the lighter and more elegant construction of the former, but in the one being drawn by horses and the other by oxen. Being a public man in Egypt, Joseph was required to appear everywhere in an equipage suitable to his dignity; and, therefore, it was not owing either to pride or ostentatious parade that he drove his carriage, while his father's family were accommodated only in rude and humble waggons. presented himself—in an attitude of filial reverence (cf Ex. 22. 17.). The interview was a most affecting one—the happiness of the delighted father was now at its height; and life having no higher charms, he could, in the very spirit of the aged Simeon, have departed in peace. 31-34. Joseph said, I will go up and shew Pharaoh—It was a tribute of respect due to the king to apprize him of their arrival. And the instructions which he gave them were worthy of his character alike as an affectionate brother and a religious man.

CHAPTER XLVII.

Ver. 1-31. PRESENTATION AT COURT. 1. Joseph told Pharaoh, My father and brethren—Joseph furnishes a beautiful example of a man who could bear equally well the extremes of prosperity and adversity. High as he was, he did not forget that he had a superior. Dearly as he loved his father, and anxiously as he desired to provide for the whole family, he would not go into the arrangements he had planned for their stay in Goshen, until he had obtained the sanction of his royal master. 2. took some of his brethren—probably the five eldest brothers' seniority being the least invidious principle of selection. 4. for to sojourn are we come—the royal conversation took the course which Joseph had anticipated (46. 33.), and they answered according to previous instructions—manifesting, however, in their determination to return to Canaan, a faith and piety which affords a hopeful symptom of their having become all, or most of them, religious men. 7. Joseph brought in, &c.—there is a pathetic and most affecting interest attending this interview with royalty; and when, with all the simplicity and dignified solemnity of a man of God, Joseph signalized his entrance by imploring the Divine blessing on the royal head, it may easily be imagined what a striking impression the scene would produce (cf. Heb. 7. 7.). 8. Pharaoh said unto Jacob, &c.—the question was put from the deep and impressive interest which the appearance of the old patriarch had created in the minds of Pharaoh and his court. In the low-lying land of Egypt, and from the artificial habits of its society, the age of man was far shorter amongst the inhabitants of that country than it had yet become in the pure bracing climate and among the simple mountaineers of Canaan. The Hebrews, at least, still attained a protracted longevity. 9. the days, &c.—Though 130 years, he reckons by days (cf. Ps. 90. 12.), which he calls *few*, as they appeared in the retrospect, and *evil*, because his life had been one almost unbroken series of trouble. The answer is remarkable, considering the comparative darkness of the patriarchal age (cf. 2 Tim. 1. 10.). 11. Joseph placed ... in the

4 And said unto me, Behold, I will make thee fruitful, and multiply thee, and I will make of thee a multitude of people; and will give this land to thy seed after thee *b* for an everlasting possession.

5 And now thy *c* two sons, Ephraim and Manasseh, which were born unto thee in the land of Egypt before I came unto thee into Egypt, *are* mine: as Reuben and Simeon, they shall be mine.

6 And thy issue, which thou begettest after them, shall be thine, *and* shall be called after the name of their brethren in their inheritance.

7 And as for me, when I came from Padan, *d* Rachel died by me in the land of Canaan in the way, when yet *there was* but a little way to come unto Ephrath: and I buried her there in the way of Ephrath; the same *is* Beth-lehem.

8 And Israel beheld Joseph's sons, and said, Who *are* these?

9 And Joseph said unto his father, *e* They *are* my sons, whom God hath given me in this *place*. And he said, Bring them, I pray thee, unto me, and *f* I will bless them.

10 Now *g* the eyes of Israel were ¹dim for age, *so that* he could not see. And he brought them near unto him; and *h* he kissed them, and embraced them.

11 And Israel said unto Joseph, *i* I had not thought to see thy face: and, lo, God hath showed me also thy seed.

12 And Joseph brought them out from between his knees, and he bowed himself with his face to the earth.

13 And Joseph took them both, Ephraim in his right hand toward Israel's left hand, and Manasseh in his left hand toward Israel's right hand, and brought *them* near unto him.

14 And Israel stretched out his right hand, and laid it upon Ephraim's head, who *was* the younger, and his left hand upon Manasseh's head, guiding his hands wittingly; for Manasseh *was* the first-born.

15 ¶ And *j* he blessed Joseph, and said, God, before whom my fathers Abraham and Isaac did walk, the God which fed me all my life long unto this day,

16 The Angel *k* which redeemed me from all evil, bless the lads; and let ²my name be named on them, and the name of my fathers Abraham and Isaac; and let them ²grow into a multitude in the midst of the earth.

17 And when Joseph saw that his father *m* laid his right hand upon the head of Ephraim, it ³displeased him: and he held up his father's hand, to remove it from Ephraim's head unto Manasseh's head.

18 And Joseph said unto his father, Not so, my father; for this *is* the first-born; put thy right hand upon his head.

19 And his father refused, and said, I know *it*, my son, I know *it*: he also shall become a people, and he also shall be great; but truly *h* his younger brother shall be greater than he, and his seed shall become a ⁴multitude of nations.

20 And he blessed them that day, saying, *o* In thee shall Israel bless, saying, God make thee as Ephraim, and as Manasseh: and he set Ephraim before Manasseh.

21 And Israel said unto Joseph, Behold, I die; but *p* God shall be with you, and bring you again unto the land of your fathers.

22 Moreover *q* I have given to thee one

B. C. 1689.

CHAP. 48.
b ch. 17. 8.
c ch. 41. 50.
ch. 46. 20.
Josh. 13. 7.
Josh. 14. 4.
d ch. 35. 19.
e ch. 33. 5.
f ch. 27. 4.
g ch. 27. 1.
1 heavy.
Is. 6. 10.
h ch. 27. 27.
i ch. 45. 26.
j Heb. 11. 21.
k ch. 28. 15.
l Amos 9. 12.
Acts 15. 17.
2 as fishes do increase.
m ver. 14.
3 was evil in his eyes.
n Nu. 2. 19.
Deu. 33. 17.
4 fulness.
o Ruth 4. 11.
p ch. 50. 24.
q Jos. 24. 32.
1 Chr. 5. 2.
John 4. 5.
r ch. 34. 28.
Jos. 17. 14.

CHAP. 49.
a Deu. 33. 1.
Amos 3. 7.
b Deu. 4. 30.
Nu. 24. 14.
c Ps. 34. 11.
d Deu. 21. 17.
1 do not thou excel.
e Deu. 27. 20.
1 Chr. 5. 1.
2 or, my couch is gone.
f Prov. 18. 9.
3 Or, their swords are weapons of violence.
g ch. 34. 25.
h Pr. 1. 15. 16.
i Ps. 26. 9.
4 Or, houghed oxen.
j Josh. 21. 1.
1 Ch. 4. 24.
k Nu. 24. 9.
l Nu. 24. 17.
m Ps. 60. 7.
n 1 Chr. 5. 2.
Is. 11. 1.
Eze. 21. 27.
Dan. 9. 25.
Mat. 21. 9.
Lu. 1. 32.
o Is. 2. 2.
Is. 11. 10.
Is. 42. 1. 4.
Is. 49. 6. 23.
Is. 55. 4, 5.
Is. 60. 1-5.
Hag. 2. 7.
Lu. 2. 30.
p 2 Ki. 18. 32.
q Deu. 33. 18.
r Jud. 13. 2.
with Jud. 15. 20.
s Ju. 1. 18. 27.
5 an arrow snake.
t Ps. 119. 166.
u De. 33. 20.
6 daughters.

---

portion above thy brethren, which I took out of the hand *r* of the Amorite with my sword and with my bow.

CHAPTER XLIX.

1 *Jacob calleth his sons together: 3 he pronounceth curses on Reuben, 5 and on Simeon and Levi; 8 a blessing on Judah, etc. 28 He charges them concerning his burial: 33 his death.*

AND Jacob called unto his sons, and said, Gather yourselves together, that I may *a* tell you *that* which shall befall you *b* in the last days.

2 Gather yourselves together, and hear, ye sons of Jacob; and *c* hearken unto Israel your father.

3 ¶ Reuben, thou *art* my first-born, my might, *d* and the beginning of my strength, the excellency of dignity, and the excellency of power:

4 Unstable as water, ¹thou *e* shalt not excel; because thou wentest up to thy father's bed; then defiledst thou it: ²he went up to my couch.

5 ¶ Simeon and Levi *are* *f* brethren; ³instruments *g* of cruelty *are in* their habitations.

6 O my soul, *h* come not thou into their secret; *i* unto their assembly, mine honour, be not thou united: for in their anger they slew a man, and in their self-will they ⁴digged down a wall.

7 Cursed *be* their anger, for *it was* fierce; and their wrath, for it was cruel: *j* I will divide them in Jacob, and scatter them in Israel.

8 ¶ Judah, thou *art he* whom thy brethren shall praise: thy hand *shall be* in the neck of thine enemies; thy father's children shall bow down before thee.

9 Judah *is* a lion's whelp: from the prey, my son, thou art gone up: *k* he stooped down, he couched as a lion, and as an old lion; who shall rouse him up?

10 *l* The sceptre shall not depart from Judah, nor a *m* lawgiver from between his feet, *n* until Shiloh come; *o* and unto him *shall* the gathering of the people *be*.

11 *p* Binding his foal unto the vine, and his ass's colt unto the choice vine; he washed his garments in wine, and his clothes in the blood of grapes;

12 His eyes *shall be* red with wine, and his teeth white with milk.

13 ¶ *q* Zebulun shall dwell at the haven of the sea; and he *shall be* for an haven of ships: and his border *shall be* unto Zidon.

14 ¶ Issachar *is* a strong ass couching down between two burdens:

15 And he saw that rest *was* good, and the land that it *was* pleasant; and bowed his shoulder to bear, and became a servant unto tribute.

16 ¶ *r* Dan shall judge his people, as one of the tribes of Israel.

17 *s* Dan shall be a serpent by the way, ⁵an adder in the path, that biteth the horse heels, so that his rider shall fall backward.

18 *t* I have waited for thy salvation, O LORD.

19 ¶ *u* Gad, a troop shall overcome him: but he shall overcome at the last.

20 ¶ Out of Asher his bread *shall be* fat, and he shall yield royal dainties.

21 ¶ Naphtali *is* a hind let loose: he giveth goodly words.

22 ¶ Joseph *is* a fruitful bough, *even* a fruitful bough by a well, *whose* ⁶branches run over the wall.

best of the land—best *pasture* land in lower Egypt. Goshen, "the land of verdure," lay along the Pelusaic or eastern branch of the Nile. It included a part of the district of Heliopolis, or "On," the capital, and on the east stretched out a considerable length into the desert. The ground included within these boundaries was a rich and fertile extent of natural meadow, and admirably adapted for the purposes of the Hebrew shepherds (cf. 49. 24; Ps. 77. 72; 34. 10.). 13-22. there was no bread, &c.—this probably refers to the second year of the famine (45. 6.), when any little stores of individuals or families were exhausted, and when the people had become universally dependent on the government. At first they obtained supplies for payment. Ere long money failed. 16. and Joseph... give your cattle—"this was the wisest course that could be adopted for the preservation both of the people and the cattle, which, being bought by Joseph, was supported at the royal expense, and very likely returned to the people at the end of the famine, to enable them to resume their agricultural labours." 21. as for the people, &c.—obviously for the convenience of the country people, who were doing nothing, to the cities where the corn stores were situated. 22. only the land of the priests, &c.— these lands were inalienable, being endowments by which the temples were supported. The priests for themselves received an annual allowance of provision from the state, and it would evidently have been the height of cruelty to withhold that allowance when their lands were incapable of being tilled. 23-28. Joseph said, Behold, &c.—the land being sold to the government (v. 19, 20,) seed would be distributed for the first crop after the famine; and the people occupy them as tenants-at-will on the payment of a produce rent, almost the same rule as obtains in Egypt in the present day. 29-31. the time drew near, &c.—one only of his dying arrangements is recorded; but that one reveals his whole character. It was the disposal of his remains, which were to be carried to Canaan, not from a mere romantic attachment to his native soil, nor, like his modern descendants, from a superstitious feeling for the soil of the Holy Land, but from faith in the promises. His address to Joseph—"if I have found grace in thy sight," *i. e.,* as the vizier of Egypt—his exacting a solemn oath that his wishes would be fulfilled, and the peculiar form of that oath, all pointed significantly to the promise, and showed the intensity of his desire to enjoy its blessings (cf. Num. 10. 29.). Israel bowed himself, &c.—Oriental beds are mere mats, having no head, and the translation should be "the top of his staff," as the Apostle renders it (Heb. 11. 21.).

CHAPTER XLVIII.

Ver. 1-22. JOSEPH'S VISIT TO HIS SICK FATHER. Thy father is sick—Joseph was hastily sent for, and on this occasion he took with him his two sons. 2. Israel strengthened himself, and sat upon the bed—in the chamber where a good man lies, edifying and spiritual discourse may be expected. 3, 4. God Almighty appeared to me at Luz—the object of Jacob, in thus reverting to the memorable vision at Bethel—one of the great landmarks in his history—was to point out the splendid promises in reserve for his posterity — to engage Joseph's interest and preserve his continued connection with the people of God, rather than with the Egyptians. Behold, I will make thee fruitful—this is a repetition of the covenant (28. 13--15; 35. 12.). Whether these words are to be viewed in a limited sense, as pointing to the many centuries during which the Jews were occupiers of the Holy Land, or whether the words bear a wider meaning, and intimate that the scattered tribes of Israel are to be reinstated in the land of promise, as their "everlasting possession" are points that have not yet been satisfactorily determined. 5. thy two sons, Ephraim and Manasseh—It was the intention of the aged patriarch to adopt Joseph's sons as his own, thus giving him a double portion. The reasons of this procedure are stated (1 Chron. 5. 1, 2.). thy sons are mine — though their connections might have attached them to Egypt, and opened to them brilliant prospects in the land of their nativity, they willingly accepted the adoption, (Heb. 11. 25.). 9. bring them unto me, &c.—the Apostle (Heb. 11. 21.) selected the blessing of Joseph's sons as the chief because the most comprehensive, instance of the patriarch's faith which his whole history furnishes. 13. Joseph took them both—the very act of pronouncing the blessing was remarkable, showing that Jacob's bosom was animated by the spirit of prophecy. 21. behold, I die—the patriarch could speak of death with composure, but he wished to prepare Joseph and the rest of the family for the shock. but God shall, &c. —Jacob, in all probability, was not authorized to speak of their bondage—he dwelt only on the certainty of their restoration to Canaan. 22. moreover, I have, &c.—this was near Shechem (33. 18; Jo. 4. 5; also Josh. 16. 1; 20. 7.). And it is probable that the Amorites, having seized upon it during one of his frequent absences, the patriarch, with the united forces of his tribe, recovered it from them by his sword and his bow.

CHAPTER XLIX.

Ver. 1-33. PATRIARCHAL BLESSING. 1 Jacob called unto his sons—It is not to the sayings of the dying saint, so much as of the inspired prophet, that attention is called in this chapter. Under the immediate influence of the Holy Spirit he pronounced his prophetic benediction, and described the condition of their respective descendants in the last days, or future times.

REUBEN.—Forfeited by his crime the rights and honours of primogeniture. His posterity never made any figure,—no judge, prophet, nor ruler, sprang from this tribe.

SIMEON AND LEVI were associates in wickedness, and the same prediction would be equally applicable to both their tribes. Levi had cities allotted to them Josh. 21., in every tribe. On account of their zeal against idolatry, they were honourably "divided in Jacob;" whereas the tribe of Simeon, which was guilty of the grossest idolatry, and the vices inseparable from it, were ignominiously "scattered."

JUDAH.—A high pre-eminence is destined to this tribe (Num. 10. 14; Jud. 1. 2.). Besides the honour of giving name to the Promised land — David, and a greater than David —the Messiah sprang from it. Chief amongst the tribes, "it grew up from a lion's whelp" *i. e.,* a little power, till it became "an old lion"—*i. e.,* calm and quiet, yet still formid-

23 The archers have ᵛsorely grieved him, and shot *at him*, and hated him:

24 But his ʷbow abode in strength, and the arms of his hands were made strong by the hands of the mighty *God of Jacob*; (from thence ˣ*is* the Shepherd, ʸthe stone of Israel:)

25 *Even* by the God of thy father, who shall help thee; and by the Almighty, ᵃwho shall bless thee with blessings of heaven above, blessings of the deep that lieth under, blessings of the breasts and of the womb:

26 The blessings of thy father have prevailed above the blessings of my progenitors unto the utmost bound of the everlasting hills: they shall be on the head of Joseph, and on the crown of the head of him that was separate from his brethren.

27 ¶ Benjamin shall ᵃravin *as* a wolf: in the morning he shall devour the prey, ᵇand at night he shall divide the spoil.

28 ¶ All these *are* the twelve tribes of Israel: and this *is it* that their father spake unto them, and blessed them; every one according to his blessing he blessed them.

29 And he charged them, and said unto them, I ᶜam to be gathered unto my people: ᵈbury me with my fathers ᵉin the cave that *is* in the field of Ephron the Hittite,

30 In the cave that *is* in the field of Machpelah, which *is* before Mamre, in the land of Canaan, ᶠwhich Abraham bought with the field of Ephron the Hittite for a possession of a burying-place.

31 ᵍThere they buried Abraham and Sarah his wife; ʰthere they buried Isaac and Rebekah his wife; and there I buried Leah.

32 The purchase of the field and of the cave that *is* therein *was* from the children of Heth.

33 And when Jacob had made an end of commanding his sons, he gathered up his feet into the bed, and yielded up the ghost, and was gathered unto his people.

CHAPTER L.

1 *The mourning for Jacob;* 7 *his funeral.* 24 *Joseph prophesieth to his brethren their return to Canaan:* 24 *his age,* 26 *and death.*

AND Joseph ᵃfell upon his father's face, and ᵇwept upon him, and kissed him.

2 And Joseph commanded his servants the physicians to ᶜembalm his father: and the physicians embalmed Israel.

3 And forty days were fulfilled for him; for so are fulfilled the days of those which are embalmed: and the Egyptians ¹mourned ᵈfor him threescore and ten days.

4 And when the days of his mourning were past, Joseph spake unto ᵉthe house of Pharaoh, saying, If now I have found grace in your eyes, speak, I pray you, in the ears of Pharaoh, saying,

5 My father made me swear, saying, Lo, I die: in my grave ᶠwhich I have digged for me in the land of Canaan, there shalt thou bury me. Now therefore let me go up, I pray thee, and bury my father, and I will come again.

6 And Pharaoh said, Go up and bury thy father, according as he made thee swear.

7 ¶ And Joseph went up to bury his father: and with him went up all the servants of Pharaoh, the elders of his house, and all the elders of the land of Egypt,

8 And all the house of Joseph, and his brethren, and his father's house: only their little ones, and their flocks, and their herds, they left in the land of Goshen.

9 And there went up with him both chariots and horsemen: and it was a very great company.

10 And they came to the threshing-floor of Atad, which *is* beyond Jordan, and there they ᵍmourned with a great and very sore lamentation: ʰand he made a mourning for his father seven days.

11 And when the inhabitants of the land, the Canaanites, saw the mourning in the floor of Atad, they said, This *is* a grievous mourning to the Egyptians: wherefore the name of it was called ²Abel-mizraim, which *is* beyond Jordan.

12 And his sons did unto him according as he commanded them:

13 For ⁱhis sons carried him into the land of Canaan, and buried him in the cave of the field of Machpelah, which Abraham bought with the field for a possession of a burying-place of Ephron the Hittite, before Mamre.

14 And Joseph returned into Egypt, he, and his brethren, and all that went up with him to bury his father, after he had buried his father.

15 ¶ And when Joseph's brethren saw that their father was dead, ʲthey said, Joseph will peradventure hate us, and will certainly requite us all the evil which we did unto him.

16 And they ³sent a messenger unto Joseph, saying, Thy father did command before he died, saying,

17 So shall ye say unto Joseph, Forgive, I pray thee now, the trespass of thy brethren, and their sin; ᵏfor they did unto thee evil: and now, we pray thee, forgive the trespass of the servants of ˡthe God of thy father. And Joseph wept when they spake unto him.

18 And his brethren also went and ᵐfell down before his face; and they said, Behold, we *be* thy servants.

19 And Joseph said unto them, Fear not; ⁿfor *am* I in the place of God?

20 But as for you, ye thought evil against me; but ᵖGod meant it unto good, to bring to pass, as *it is* this day, to save much people alive.

21 Now therefore fear ye not; ᑫI will nourish you, and your little ones. And he comforted them, and spake ᑫkindly unto them.

22 ¶ And Joseph dwelt in Egypt, he and his father's house: and Joseph lived an hundred and ten years.

23 And Joseph saw Ephraim's children ʳof the third *generation:* the children also of Machir the son of Manasseh ˢwere ⁵brought up upon Joseph's knees.

24 And Joseph said unto his brethren, I die: and ᵗGod will surely visit you, and bring you out of this ᵘland unto the land which he sware to Abraham, to Isaac, and to Jacob.

25 And ᵛJoseph took an oath of the children of Israel, saying, God will surely visit you, and ye shall carry up my bones from hence.

26 So Joseph died, *being* an hundred and ten years old: and they embalmed him, and he was put in a coffin in Egypt.

able. until Shiloh come — until "*Shiloh come*" — a word variously interpreted to mean "the sent" (Jo. 17. 3), "the seed" (Is. 11. 1), the "peaceable or prosperous one" (Eph. 2. 14 —*i.e.*, the Messiah Is. 11. 10; Ro. 15. 12); and when He should come, 'the tribe of Judah should no longer boast either an independent king or a judge of their own.' [CAL.] The Jews have been for eighteen centuries without a ruler and without a judge since Shiloh came, and "to Him the gathering of the people has been."

ZEBULUN was to have its lot on the sea coast, close to Zidon, and to engage, like that state, in maritime pursuits and commerce.

ISSACHAR.—A strong ass couching down between two burdens— *i.e.*, it was to be active, patient, given to agricultural labours. It was established in lower Galilee—a "good land," settling down in the midst of the Canaanites, where, for the sake of quiet, they "bowed their shoulder to bear, and became a servant unto tribute."

DAN.—Though the son of a secondary wife, was to be "as one of the tribes of Israel." Dan —"a judge," a serpent, an adder—a serpent, an adder, implies subtlety and stratagem; such was pre-eminently the character of Samson the most illustrious of its judges.

GAD.—This tribe should be often attacked and wasted by hostile powers on their borders. (Jud. 10. 8; Jer. 49. 1.) But they were generally victorious in the close of their wars.

ASHER.—"Blessed"—Its allotment was the sea coast between Tyre and Carmel, a district fertile in the production of the finest corn and oil in all Palestine.

NAPHTALI.—The best rendering we know is this, "Naphtali is a deer roaming at liberty; he shooteth forth goodly branches, or majestic antlers, [Taylor's Scrip. Illust.] and the meaning of the prophecy seems to be that the tribe of Naphtali would be located in a territory so fertile and peaceable, that feeding on the richest pasture he would spread out, like a deer, its branching antlers.

JOSEPH.—"A fruitful bough, &c.—denotes the extraordinary increase of that tribe (cf. Num. 1. 33-35; Josh. 16; 17; Deu. 33, 17.). The patriarch describes him as attacked by envy, revenge, temptation, ingratitude, yet still, by the grace of God, he triumphed over all opposition, so that he became the *sustainer* of Israel; and then he proceeds to shower blessings of every kind upon the head of this favourite son. The history of the tribes of Ephraim and Manasseh, shows how fully these blessings were realized.

BENJAMIN shall ravin like a wolf.—This tribe in its early history spent its energies in petty or inglorious warfare, and especially in the violent and unjust contest (Judg. 19; 20.), in which it engaged with the other tribes, when, notwithstanding two victories, it was almost exterminated. 28. all these are the twelve tribes of Israel—or ancestors. Jacob's prophetic words obviously refer not so much to the sons as to the tribes of Israel. 29. he charged them—the charge had already been given, and solemnly undertaken (47. 31.). But in mentioning his wishes now, and rehearsing all the circumstances connected with the purchase of Machpelah, he wished to declare, with his latest breath, before all his family, that he died in the same faith as Abraham. 33. when Jacob had made an end—It is probable that he was supernaturally strengthened for this last momentous office of the patriarch, and that when the divine afflatus ceased, his exhausted powers giving way, he yielded up the ghost, and was gathered unto his people.

CHAPTER L.

Ver. 1-16. MOURNING FOR JACOB. Joseph fell, &c.—On him, as the principal member of the family, devolved the duty of closing the eyes of his venerable parent (cf. 46. 4.), and in printing the farewell kiss. 2. Joseph commanded, &c.—in ancient Egypt the embalmers were a class by themselves. The process of embalment consisted in infusing a great quantity of resinous substances into the cavities of the body, after the intestines had been removed, and then a regulated degree of heat was applied to dry up the humours as well as decompose the tarry materials which had been previously introduced. Thirty days were allotted for the completion of this process; forty more were spent in anointing it with spices: the body, tanned from this operation, being then washed, was wrapped in numerous folds of linen cloth—the joinings of which were fastened with gum, and then deposited in a wooden chest, made in the form of a human figure. 3. the Egyptians, &c.—it was made a period of public mourning, as on the death of a royal personage. Joseph spake, &c. — Care was taken to let it be known that the family sepulchre was provided before leaving Canaan, and that an oath bound his family to convey the remains thither. Besides, Joseph deemed it right to apply for a special leave of absence; and being unfit, as a mourner, to appear in the royal presence, he made the request through the medium of others. 7-26. went up to bury his father—a journey of 300 miles. The funeral cavalcade, composed of the nobility and military, with their equipages, would exhibit an imposing appearance. 10. they came, &c. — "atad" may be taken as a common noun, signifying " the plain of the thorn-bushes." It was on the border between Egypt and Canaan; and as the last opportunity of indulging grief was always the most violent, the Egyptians made a prolonged halt at this spot, while the family of Jacob probably proceeded by themselves to the place of sepulture. 15--21. When Joseph's brethren saw, &c.— Joseph was deeply affected by this communication. He gave them the strongest assurances of his forgiveness, and thereby gave both a beautiful trait of his own pious character, as well as appeared an eminent type of the Saviour. 22--25. Joseph dwelt in Egypt—He lived eighty years after his elevation to the chief power, witnessing a great increase in the prosperity of the kingdom, and also of his own family and kindred — the infant church of God. 24. said unto his brethren, I am dying—The national feelings of the Egyptians would have been opposed to his burial in Canaan; but he gave the strongest proof of the strength of his faith and full assurance of the promises, by "the commandment concerning his bones." 26. They embalmed him—His funeral would be conducted in the highest style of Egyptian magnificence, and his mummied corpse carefully preserved till the Exodus.

THE SECOND BOOK OF MOSES, CALLED

EXODUS

CHAPTER I.

The children of Israel multiply: 8 they are oppressed by a new king. 15 The piety of the midwives. 22 The male-children destroyed.

NOW *a* these *are* the names of the children of Israel, which came into Egypt; every man and his household came with Jacob.

2 Reuben, Simeon, Levi, and Judah,
3 Issachar, Zebulun, and Benjamin,
4 Dan, and Naphtali, Gad, and Asher.
5 And all the souls that came out of the ¹loins of Jacob were *b* seventy souls: for Joseph was in Egypt *already*.
6 And *c* Joseph died, and all his brethren, and *d* all that generation.
7 *e* And the children of Israel were fruitful, and increased abundantly, and multiplied, and waxed exceeding mighty; and the land was filled with them.
8 ¶ Now there arose up a new king over Egypt, which knew not Joseph.
9 And he said unto his people, Behold, *f* the people of the children of Israel *are* more and mightier than we:
10 *g* Come on, let us *h* deal wisely with them; lest they multiply, and it come to pass, that, when there falleth out any war, they join also unto our enemies, and fight against us, and *so* get them up out of the land.
11 Therefore they did set over them taskmasters *i* to afflict them with their *j* burdens. And they built for Pharaoh treasure cities, Pithom *k* and Raamses.
12 ² But the more they afflicted them, the more they multiplied and grew. And they were grieved because of the children of Israel.
13 And the Egyptians made the children of Israel to serve with rigour:
14 And they *l* made their lives bitter with hard bondage, *m* in mortar, and in brick, and in all manner of service in the field: all their service, wherein they made them serve, *was* with rigour.
15 ¶ And the king of Egypt spake to the Hebrew midwives; of which the name of the one *was* Shiphrah, and the name of the other Puah;
16 And he said, When ye do the office of a midwife to the Hebrew women, and see *them* upon the stools, if it *be* a son, then ye shall kill him; but if it *be* a daughter, then she shall live.
17 But the midwives *n* feared God, and did not *o* as the king of Egypt commanded them, but saved the men-children alive.
18 And the king of Egypt called for the midwives, and said unto them, Why have ye done this thing, and have saved the men-children alive?
19 And *p* the midwives said unto Pharaoh, Because the Hebrew women *are* not as the Egyptian women; for they *are* lively, and are delivered ere the midwives come in unto them.
20 ¶ Therefore God dealt well with the midwives: and the people multiplied, and waxed very mighty.
21 And it came to pass, because the midwives feared God, *r* that he made them houses.
22 And Pharaoh charged all his people,

B. C. 1706.

CHAP. 1.
a Gen. 46. 8. ch. 6. 14.
1 thigh.
b Gen. 46. 26, 27.
Deut. 10. 22.
c Gen. 50. 26. Acts 7. 15.
d Ec. 1. 4.
e Gen. 46. 3. Deu. 26. 5. Ps. 105. 24. Acts 7. 17.
f Ps. 105. 24.
g Ps. 10. 2. Ps. 83. 3, 4. *h* Job 5. 13. Prov. 23. 16.
Acts 7. 19.
i Gen. 15. 13. ch. 3. 7.
Deu. 26. 6.
j ch. 5. 4. 5. Ps. 81. 6.
k Gen. 47. 11.
2 And as they afflicted them, so they multiplied, etc.
l ch. 2. 23. Num. 20. 15.
Pro. 14. 31. Ec. 5. 8.
m Ps. 81. 6. *n* Pro. 16. 6. *o* Dan. 3. 16, 18.
Dan. 6. 13. Acts 5. 29.
p Jos. 2. 4. 2 Sa. 17.19, 20.
q Prov. 11. 18.
Ec. 8. 12.
Is. 3. 10.
Heb. 6. 10.
r 2 Sam. 7. 11, 13, 27, 29.
1 Ki. 2. 24. 1 Kin. 11. 38.

CHAP. 2.
a ch. 6. 20. Nu. 26. 59.
b Heb. 11. 23.
c ch. 15. 20. Nu. 26. 59.
d Acts 7. 21.
1 That is, drawn out.
e Heb. 11. 24-26.
2 a man, a prince.
Gen. 13. 8.
f Gen. 24.11. Gen. 29. 2.
g ch. 3. 1.
³ Or, prince, as
Gen. 41. 45.
h Ge. 29. 10. 1 Sam. 9. 11.

saying, Every son that is born ye shall cast into the river, and every daughter ye shall save alive.

CHAPTER II.

1 Moses is born, and laid among the flags: 6 he is found, and brought up by Pharaoh's daughter: 12 he slayeth an Egyptian, and fleeth into Midian. 21 He marrieth Zipporah. 22 She beareth Gershom.

AND *a* there went a man of the house of Levi, and took *to wife* a daughter of Levi.

2 And the woman conceived, and bare a son: and *b* when she saw him that he *was* a goodly *child*, she hid him three months.
3 And when she could not longer hide him, she took for him an ark of bulrushes, and daubed it with slime and with pitch, and put the child therein; and she laid *it* in the flags by the river's brink.
4 *c* And his sister stood afar off, to wit what would be done to him.
5 ¶ And the *d* daughter of Pharaoh came down to wash *herself* at the river; and her maidens walked along by the river's side; and when she saw the ark among the flags, she sent her maid to fetch it.
6 And when she had opened *it*, she saw the child: and, behold, the babe wept. And she had compassion on him, and said, This *is* one of the Hebrews' children.
7 Then said his sister to Pharaoh's daughter, Shall I go and call to thee a nurse of the Hebrew women, that she may nurse the child for thee?
8 And Pharaoh's daughter said to her, Go. And the maid went and called the child's mother.
9 And Pharaoh's daughter said unto her, Take this child away, and nurse it for me, and I will give *thee* thy wages. And the woman took the child, and nursed it.
10 And the child grew, and she brought him unto Pharaoh's daughter, and he became her son. And she called his name ¹Moses: and she said, Because I drew him out of the water.
11 ¶ *e* And it came to pass in those days, when Moses was grown, that he went out unto his brethren, and looked on their burdens: and he spied an Egyptian smiting an Hebrew, one of his brethren.
12 And he looked this way and that way, and when he saw that *there was* no man, he slew the Egyptian, and hid him in the sand.
13 And when he went out the second day, behold, two men of the Hebrews strove together: and he said to him that did the wrong, Wherefore smitest thou thy fellow?
14 And he said, Who made thee ²a prince and a judge over us? Intendest thou to kill me, as thou killedst the Egyptian? And Moses feared, and said, Surely this thing is known.
15 Now when Pharaoh heard this thing, he sought to slay Moses. But Moses fled from the face of Pharaoh, and dwelt in the land of Midian: and he sat down by *f* a well.
16 *g* Now the ³priest of Midian had seven daughters: *h* and they came and drew water, and filled the troughs to water their father's flock.

THE SECOND BOOK OF MOSES, CALLED

EXODUS.

CHAPTER I.

Ver. 1-7 INCREASE OF THE ISRAELITES. Now these are the names—(See on 46. 8-20..., 7. children of Israel were fruitful—They were living in a land where, according to the testimony of an ancient author, mothers produced three and four sometimes at a birth; and a modern writer declares that "the females in Egypt, as well among the human race as among animals, surpass all others in fruitfulness. To this natural circumstance must be added the fulfilment of the promise made to Abraham. **8.** Now there arose up a new king—About sixty years after the death of Joseph a revolution took place—by which the old dynasty was overthrown; and upper and lower Egypt were united into one kingdom. Assuming that he had formerly reigned in Thebes, it is probable that he would know nothing about the Hebrews; and that, as foreigners and shepherds, the new government would, from the first, regard them with dislike and scorn. **9.** He said, Behold, children of Israel are greater and mightier than we—They had risen to great prosperity—as during the life-time of Joseph and his royal patron, they had, probably, enjoyed a free grant of the land. Their increase and prosperity were viewed with jealousy by the new government; and as Goshen lay between Egypt and Canaan, on the border of which latter country were a number of warlike tribes—it was perfectly conformable to the suggestions of worldly policy that they should enslave and maltreat them, through apprehension of their joining in any invasion by those foreign rovers. The new king, who neither knew the name nor cared for the services of Joseph, was either *Amosis*, or one of his immediate successors. [OSBURN.] **11.** therefore they did set over them taskmasters—Having first obliged them, it is thought, to pay a ruinous rent, and involved them in difficulties—that new government, in pursuance of its oppressive policy, degraded them to the condition of serfs—employing them exactly as the labouring-people are in the present day, driven in companies, or bands, in rearing the public works, with taskmasters, who anciently had sticks—now whips—to punish the indolent, or spur on the too languid. All public or royal buildings, in ancient Egypt, were built by captives; and on some of them was placed an inscription—that no free citizen had been engaged in this servile employment. They built for Pharaoh treasure cities—These two store places were in the land of Goshen; and being situated near a border liable to invasion, they were fortified cities cf. 2 Chron. 11. 12.). Pithon [*Gr.*], Patumos, lay on the eastern Pelusaic branch of the Nile, about twelve Roman miles from Heliopolis; and Raamses, called by the LXX. Heroopolis, lay between the same branch of the Nile and the Bitter Lakes. These two fortified cities were situated, therefore, in the same valley; and the fortifications, which Pharaoh commanded to be built around both, had probably the same common object, of obstructing the entrance into Egypt, which this valley furnished the enemy into Asia [HENG.]. **13, 14.** The Egyptians made their lives bitter in hard bondage, in mortar and in brick—Ruins of great brick buildings are found in all parts of Egypt. The use of crude brick, baked in the sun, was universal in upper and lower Egypt, both for public and private buildings; *all* but the temples themselves, were of crude brick. It is worthy of remark, that more bricks bearing the name of Thothmes III, who is supposed to have been the king of Egypt, at the time of the Exodus, have been discovered than of any other period [WILK.] Parties of these brick-makers are seen depicted on the ancient monuments with "taskmasters"—some standing, others in a sitting posture beside the labourers, with their uplifted sticks in their hands. **15-22.** The king of Egypt spake unto the Hebrew midwives—Two only were spoken to—either they were the heads of a large corporation, [LA.] or, by tampering with these two, the king designed to terrify the rest into secret compliance with his wishes. [CAL.] **16.** if it be a son, kill him—opinions are divided, however, what was the method of destruction which the king did recommend. Some think that the "stools" were low seats on which these obstetric practitioners sat by the bedside of the Hebrew women; and that, as they might easily discover the sex, so, whenever a boy appeared, they were to strangle it, unknown to its parents; while others are of opinion that the "stools" were stone troughs, by the river side — into which, when the infants were washed—they were to be, as it were, accidentally dropped. **17.** fear God—their faith inspired them with such courage as to risk their lives, by disobeying the mandate of a cruel tyrant; but it was blended with weakness, which made them shrink from speaking the truth, the whole truth, and nothing but the truth. **20.** God dealt well—this represents God as rewarding them for telling a lie. This difficulty is wholly removed by a more correct translation. To make or build up a house in *Heb.* idiom, means to have a numerous progeny. The passage then should be rendered thus: God protected the midwives, and the people waxed very mighty; and because the midwives feared, the Hebrews grew and prospered.

CHAPTER II.

Ver. 1.-10. BIRTH AND PRESERVATION OF MOSES. There went a man, &c.—Amram was the husband, and Jochebed the wife cf. 6. 2; Num. 26. 59.). The marriage took place, and two children, Miriam and Aaron, were born some years before the infanticidal edict. **2.** the woman bare a son, &c.—some extraordinary appearance or remarkable comeliness led his parents to augur his future greatness. Beauty was regarded by the ancients as a mark of the Divine favour. hid him three months—the parents were a pious couple, and the measures they took were prompted not only by parental attachment, but by a strong faith in the blessing of God prospering their endeavours to save the infant. **3.** made an ark of bulrushes—papyrus, a thick, strong, and tough reed. slime—the mud of the Nile, which, when hardened, is very tenacious. pitch—mineral tar. Boats of this description are seen daily floating on the surface of the river, with no other caulking than Nile mud.

17 And the shepherds came and drove them away: but Moses stood up and helped them, and watered their flock.

18 And when they came to ⁴Reuel their father, he said, How *is it that* ye are come so soon to-day?

19 And they said, An Egyptian delivered us out of the hand of the shepherds, and also drew *water* enough for us, and watered the flock.

20 And he said unto his daughters, And where *is* he? why *is it that* ye have left the man? call him, that he may ʲeat bread.

21 And Moses was content to dwell with the man: and he gave Moses Zipporah his daughter.

22 And she bare *him* a son, and he called his name ⁴Gershom: ᵏfor he said, I have been ᶦa stranger in a strange land.

23 ¶ And it came to pass ᵐin process of time, that the king of Egypt died: and the children of Israel ⁿsighed by reason of the bondage, and they cried; and ᵒtheir cry came up unto God by reason of the bondage.

24 And God ᵖheard their groaning, and God ᵠremembered his ʳcovenant with Abraham, with Isaac, and with Jacob.

25 And God ˢlooked upon the children of Israel, and God ⁵had respect unto *them*.

CHAPTER III.

1 *Moses keepeth Jethro's flock; God appeareth unto him in a burning bush,* 7 *and sendeth him to deliver Israel.* 19 *Pharaoh's obstinacy.*

NOW Moses kept the flock of Jethro his father-in-law, the priest of Midian: and he led the flock to the back side of the desert, and came to ᵈthe mountain of God, even to Horeb.

2 And ᵇthe Angel of the LORD appeared unto him in a flame of fire out of the midst of a bush; and he looked, and, behold, the bush burned with fire, and the bush *was* not consumed.

3 And Moses said, I will now turn aside, and see this ᵉgreat sight, why the bush is not burnt.

4 And when the LORD saw that he turned aside to see, God called ᵈunto him out of the midst of the bush, and said, Moses, Moses. And he said, Here *am* I.

5 And he said, Draw not nigh hither: ᵉput off thy shoes from off thy feet, for the place whereon thou standest *is* holy ground.

6 Moreover he said, ᶠI *am* the God of thy father, the God of Abraham, the God of Isaac, and the God of Jacob. And Moses hid his face; for ᵍhe was afraid to look upon God.

7 ¶ And the LORD said, I have surely seen the affliction of my people which *are* in Egypt, and have heard their cry by reason of their taskmasters; for ʰI know their sorrows;

8 And ᶦI am come down to ʲdeliver them out of the hand of the Egyptians, and to bring them up out of that land ᵏ unto a good land and a large, unto a land ᶦ flowing with milk and honey; unto the place of the ᵐ Canaanites, and the Hittites, and the Amorites, and the Perizzites, and the Hivites, and the Jebusites.

9 Now therefore, behold, the cry of the children of Israel is come unto me: and I have also seen the ⁿ oppression wherewith the Egyptians oppress them.

10 ᵒ Come now therefore, and I will send thee unto Pharaoh, that thou mayest bring

44

B. C. 1531.

CHAP. 2.
ⁱ Nu. 10. 29.
Called also Jethro, or Jether.
ʲ Gen. 31. 54.
⁴ That is, a stranger here.
ᵏ ch. 18. 3.
ᶦ Heb. 11. 13.
ᵐ ch. 7. 7.
ⁿ Ps. 12. 5.
ᵒ Gen. 18. 20.
Deu. 24. 15.
Jam. 5. 4.
ᵖ ch. 6. 5.
ᵠ Ps. 105. 8.
ʳ Ge. 15. 14.
ˢ 2 Sa. 16. 12.
Luke 1. 25.
5 knew.

CHAP. 3.
ᵃ 1 Ki. 19. 8.
ᵇ Deu. 33. 16.
Is. 63. 9.
Acts 7. 30.
ᶜ Ps. 111. 2.
ᵈ Deu. 33. 16.
ᵉ Josh. 5. 15.
ᶠ Gen. 28. 13.
Mark 12. 26.
ᵍ Is. 6. 1, 5.
Rev. 1. 17.
ʰ Ge. 18. 21.
ⁱ Gen. 11. 5.
ʲ ch. 12. 51.
ᵏ Deu. 1. 25.
ᶦ Nu. 13. 27.
ᵐ Ge. 15. 18.
ⁿ ch. 1. 11.
ᵒ Ps. 105. 26.
Mic. 6. 4.
ᵖ 1 Sam. 18. 18.
1 Kings 3. 7-9.
Is. 6. 5, 8.
Jer. 1. 6.
ᵠ Gen. 31. 3.
De. 31. 23.
Josh. 1. 5.
Is. 43. 2.
Ro. 8. 31.
ʳ Gen. 32. 29.
ˢ ch. 6. 3.
John 8. 58.
Heb. 13. 8.
Rev. 1. 4.
ᵗ Ps. 135. 13.
Hos. 12. 5.
ᵘ Gen. 48. 15.
ᵛ Gen. 50. 24.
Lu. 1. 68.
ʷ Gen. 15. 14.
ˣ Nu. 23. 3.
1 Or, but by strong hand.
ʸ ch. 7. 3.
Deu. 6. 22.
Neh. 9. 10.
Ps. 135. 9.
Jer. 32. 20.
ᶻ ch. 12. 31.
ᵃ ch. 11. 3.
Ps. 106. 46.
Pro. 16. 7.
ᵇ Gen. 15. 14.
ch. 11. 2.
ᶜ Job 27. 17.
Prov. 13. 22.
Ezek. 39. 10.
2 Or, Egypt.

forth my people the children of Israel out of Egypt.

11 ¶ And Moses said unto God, ᵖ Who *am* I, that I should go unto Pharaoh, and that I should bring forth the children of Israel out of Egypt?

12 And he said, ᵠ Certainly I will be with thee; and this *shall be* a token unto thee that I have sent thee: When thou hast brought forth the people out of Egypt, ye shall serve God upon this mountain.

13 And Moses said unto God, Behold, *when* I come unto the children of Israel, and shall say unto them, The God of your fathers hath sent me unto you; and they shall say to me, ʳ What *is his* name? what shall I say unto them?

14 And God said unto Moses, I AM THAT I AM: and he said, Thus shalt thou say unto the children of Israel, ˢI AM hath sent me unto you.

15 And God said moreover unto Moses, Thus shalt thou say unto the children of Israel, The LORD God of your fathers, the God of Abraham, the God of Isaac, and the God of Jacob, hath sent me unto you: this *is* ᵗ my name for ever, and this *is* my memorial unto all generations.

16 Go, and gather the elders of Israel together, and say unto them, The ᵘ LORD God of your fathers, the God of Abraham, of Isaac, and of Jacob, appeared unto me, saying, ᵛ I have surely visited you, and *seen* that which is done to you in Egypt:

17 And I have said, ʷ I will bring you up out of the affliction of Egypt unto the land of the Canaanites, and the Hittites, and the Amorites, and the Perizzites, and the Hivites, and the Jebusites, unto a land flowing with milk and honey.

18 And they shall hearken to thy voice: and thou shalt come, thou and the elders of Israel, unto the king of Egypt, and ye shall say unto him, The LORD God of the Hebrews hath ˣ met with us: and now let us go, we beseech thee, three days' journey into the wilderness, that we may sacrifice to the LORD our God.

19 And I am sure that the king of Egypt will not let you go, ¹ no, not by a mighty hand.

20 And I will stretch out my hand, and smite Egypt with ʸ all my wonders which I will do in the midst thereof: and ᶻ after that he will let you go.

21 And ᵃ I will give this people favour in the sight of the Egyptians: and it shall come to pass, that, when ye go, ye shall not go empty:

22 ᵇ But every woman shall borrow of her neighbour, and of her that sojourneth in her house, jewels of silver, and jewels of gold, and raiment: and ye shall put *them* upon your sons, and upon your daughters; and ᶜ ye shall spoil ² the Egyptians.

CHAPTER IV.

1 *Moses' rod is turned into a serpent;* 6 *his hand is leprous.* 18 *He departs from Jethro.* 21 *God's message to Pharaoh.* 27 *Aaron is sent to meet Moses.*

AND Moses answered and said, But, behold, they will not believe me, nor hearken unto my voice: for they will say, The LORD hath not appeared unto thee.

2 And the LORD said unto him, What *is* that in thine hand? And he said, A rod.

3 And he said, Cast it on the ground. And he cast it on the ground, and it

(cf. Is. 18. 2,) and they are perfectly water-tight, unless the coating is forced off by stormy weather, flags—a general term for sea or river-weed. The chest was not, as is often represented, committed to the bosom of the water, but laid on the bank, where it would naturally appear to have been drifted by the current and arrested by the reedy thicket. The spot is traditionally said to be the Isle of Rodah, near Old Cairo. 4. his sister—Miriam, would probably be a girl of ten or twelve years of age at the time. 5. Daughter of Pharaoh...wash—The occasion is thought to have been a religious solemnity which the royal family opened by bathing in the sacred stream. Peculiar sacredness was attached to those portions of the Nile which flowed near the temples. The water was there fenced off as a protection from the crocodiles; and doubtless the princess had an enclosure reserved for her own use, the road to which seems to have been well known to Jochebed. walked along—in procession or in file. sent her maid—her immediate attendant. The term is different from that rendered "maidens." 6-10. when she had opened it—The narrative is picturesque. No tale of romance ever described a plot more skilfully laid, or more full of interest in the development. The expedient of the ark, the slime and pitch—the choice of the time and place—the appeal to the sensibilities of the female breast—the stationing of the sister as a watch of the proceedings—her timely suggestion of a nurse—and the engagement of the mother herself—all bespeak a more than ordinary measure of ingenuity as well as intense solicitude on the part of the parents. But the origin of the scheme was most probably owing to a divine suggestion, as its success was due to an overruling Providence, who not only preserved the child's life, but provided for his being trained in the nurture and admonition of the Lord. Hence it is said to have been done by faith, (Heb. 11. 23,) either in the general promise of deliverance, or some special revelation made to Amram and Jochebed—and in this view, the pious couple gave a beautiful example of a firm reliance on the word of God, united with an active use of the most suitable means. 10. She brought him unto Pharaoh's daughter—Though it must have been nearly as severe a trial for Jochebed to part with him the second time as the first, she was doubtless reconciled to it by her belief in his high destination as the future deliverer of Israel. His age when removed to the palace is not stated; but he was old enough to be well instructed in the principles of the true religion; and those early impressions, deepened by the power of divine grace, were never forgotten or effaced. he became her son—by adoption, and his high rank afforded him advantages in education, which in the providence of God were made subservient to far different purposes from what his royal patroness intended. called his name Moses—His parents might, as usual, at the time of his circumcision, have given him a name, which is traditionally said to have been Joachim. But the name chosen by the Princess, whether of Egyptian or Hebrew origin, is the only one by which he has ever been known to the church; and it is a permanent memorial of the painful incidents of his birth and infancy.

11-25. HIS SYMPATHY WITH THE HEBREWS. In those days when Moses was grown—not in age and stature only, but in power as well as in renown for accomplishments and military prowess. (A. 7. 23.) There is a gap here in the sacred history which, however, is supplied by the inspired commentary of Paul, who has fully detailed the reasons as well as extent of the change that took place in his worldly condition; and whether, as some say, his royal mother had proposed to make him co-regent and successor to the crown, or some other circumstances led to a declaration of his mind, he determined to renounce the palace and identify himself with the suffering people of God. (He. 11. 24-26.) The descent of some great sovereigns like Diocletian and Charles V. from a throne into private life, is nothing to the sacrifice which Moses made through the power of faith. went out unto his brethren—to make a full and systematic inspection of their condition in the various parts of the country where they were dispersed (A. 7. 23.), and he adopted this proceeding in pursuance of the patriotic purpose that the faith, which of the operation of God, was even then forming in his heart. spied an Egyptian—one of the taskmasters scourging a Hebrew slave without any just cause, (A. 7. 24,) and in so cruel a manner, that he seems to have died under the barbarous treatment—for the conditions of the sacred story imply such a fatal issue. The sight was new and strange to him, and though pre-eminent for meekness (Nu. 12. 3,) he was fired with indignation. slew the Egyptian—This act of Moses may seem, and indeed by some has been condemned as rash and unjustifiable—in plain terms as a deed of assassination. But we must not judge of his action in such a country and age by the standard of law and the notions of right which prevail in our Christian land: and besides, not only is it not spoken of as a crime in scripture or as distressing the perpetrator with remorse, but according to existing customs among nomadic tribes, he was bound to avenge the blood of a brother. The person he slew, however, being a government officer, he had rendered himself amenable to the laws of Egypt, and therefore he endeavoured to screen himself from the consequences by concealment of the corpse. 13, 14. two men of the Hebrews strove—His benevolent mediation in this strife—though made in the kindest and mildest manner was resented, and the taunt of the aggressor shewing that Moses' conduct on the preceding day had become generally known, he determined to consult his safety by immediate flight. (He. 11. 27.) These two incidents prove that neither were the Israelites yet ready to go out of Egypt, nor Moses prepared to be their leader. (Ja. 1. 20.) It was by the staff and not the sword,—by the meekness, and not the wrath of Moses that God was to accomplish that great work of deliverance. Both he and the people of Israel were for forty years longer cast into the furnace of affliction, yet it was therein that He had chosen them. (Is. 48. 10.) 15. Moses fled—his flight took place in the second year of Thothmes I. dwelt in the land of Midian—situated on the shore of the Eastern gulf of the Red Sea, and occupied by the posterity of Midian the son of Cush. The territory extended northward to the top of the gulf, and westward far across the

became a serpent; and Moses fled from before it.

4 And the LORD said unto Moses, Put forth thine hand, and take it by the tail. And he put forth his hand, and caught it, and it became a rod in his hand:

5 That they may *a* believe that the LORD God of their fathers, the God of Abraham, the God of Isaac, and the God of Jacob, hath appeared unto thee.

6 ¶ And the LORD said furthermore unto him, Put now thine hand into thy bosom. And he put his hand into his bosom: and when he took it out, behold, his hand *was* leprous *b* as snow.

7 And he said, Put thine hand into thy bosom again. And he put his hand into his bosom again; and plucked it out of his bosom, and, behold, *c* it was turned again as his *other* flesh.

8 And it shall come to pass, if they will not believe thee, neither hearken to the voice of the first sign, that they will believe the voice of the latter sign.

9 And it shall come to pass, if they will not believe also these two signs, neither hearken unto thy voice, that thou shalt take of the water of the river, and pour *it* upon the dry *land*: and *d* the water, which thou takest out of the river *1* shall become blood upon the dry land.

10 ¶ And Moses said unto the LORD, O my Lord, I am not *2* eloquent, neither *3* heretofore, nor since thou hast spoken unto thy servant; but *e* I am slow of speech, and of a slow tongue.

11 And the LORD said unto him, *f* Who hath made man's mouth? or who maketh the dumb, or deaf, or the seeing, or the blind? have not I the LORD?

12 Now therefore go, and I will be *g* with thy mouth, and teach thee what thou shalt say.

13 And he said, O my Lord, *h* send, I pray thee, by the hand *of him whom* thou *4* wilt send.

14 And the anger of the LORD was kindled against Moses, and he said, *Is* not Aaron the Levite thy brother? I know that he can speak well. And also, behold, he cometh forth to meet thee: and when he seeth thee, he will be glad in his heart.

15 And thou shalt speak unto him, and *i* put words in his mouth: and I will be with thy mouth, and with his mouth, and *j* will teach you what ye shall do.

16 And he shall be thy spokesman unto the people; and he shall be, *even* he shall be to thee instead of a mouth, and *k* thou shalt be to him instead of God.

17 And thou shalt take this rod in thine hand, wherewith thou shalt do signs.

18 ¶ And Moses went and returned to *5* Jethro his father-in-law, and said unto him, Let me go, I pray thee, and return unto my brethren which *are* in Egypt, and see whether they be yet alive. And Jethro said to Moses, Go in peace.

19 And the LORD said unto Moses in Midian, Go, return into Egypt: for *l* all the men are dead which sought thy life.

20 And Moses took his wife and his sons, and set them upon an ass, and he returned to the land of Egypt: and Moses took the *m* rod of God in his hand.

21 And the LORD said unto Moses, When thou goest to return into Egypt, see that thou do all those wonders before Pharaoh

B. C. 1491.

CHAP. 4.
a ch. 19. 9.
b Nu. 12. 10.
c Deu. 32.39.
d ch. 7. 19.
1 shall be and shall be.
2 a man of words.
3 since yesterday, nor since the third day.
e Jer. 1. 6.
f Ps. 94. 9.
g Is. 50. 4. Jer. 1. 9. Mark 13. 11.
Lu. 21. 14.
h Jonah 1. 3.
4 Or, shouldest.
i Num. 23. 12.
Deu. 18. 18. Is. 51. 16. Jer. 1. 9.
j Deu. 5. 31.
k ch. 7. 1. ch. 18. 19.
5 Jether.
l ch. 2. 15, 23.
Mat. 2. 20.
m ch. 17. 9. Num. 20. 8, 9.
n Jos. 11. 20. 1 Sa. 6. 6. Dan. 5. 20. Rom. 9. 14-23. James 1. 13-17.
o Hos. 11. 1. Rom. 9. 4. 2 Cor. 6. 18.
p Jer. 31. 9. Jam. 1. 18.
q ch. 11. 5. ch. 12. 29.
r Nu. 22. 22.
s Gen. 17. 14. *t* Jos. 5. 2, 3.
6 Or, knife.
7 made it touch.
u ch. 3. 1.
v ch. 3. 16.
w ch. 3. 18.
x ch. 3. 16.
y ch. 2. 25. ch. 3. 7.
z Gen. 24 26. ch. 12. 27. 1 Chr. 29.20.

CHAP. 5.
a ch. 10. 9.
b 2 Ki. 18. 35. Job 21. 15. Ps. 12. 3-5. 2 Chron. 32. 14.
c ch. 3. 19.
d ch. 3. 18.
e Pro. 23. 15.
f ch. 1. 11.
g ch. 1. 7. 9.
h ch. 1. 11.
1 Let the work be heavy upon the men.

which I have put in thine hand: but *n* I will harden his heart, that he shall not let the people go.

22 And thou shalt say unto Pharaoh, Thus saith the LORD, *o* Israel *is* my son, *p* even my first-born:

23 And I say unto thee, Let my son go, that he may serve me: and if thou refuse to let him go, behold, *q* I will slay thy son, even thy first-born.

24 ¶ And it came to pass by the way in the inn, that the LORD *r* met him, and sought to *s* kill him.

25 Then Zipporah took *t* a sharp *6* stone, and cut off the foreskin of her son, and *7* cast it at his feet, and said, Surely a bloody husband *art* thou to me.

26 So he let him go: then she said, A bloody husband *thou art*, because of the circumcision.

27 ¶ And the LORD said to Aaron, Go into the wilderness to meet Moses. And he went, and met him in *u* the mount of God, and kissed him.

28 And Moses told Aaron all the words of the LORD who had sent him, and all the signs which he had commanded him.

29 ¶ And Moses and Aaron *v* went and gathered together all the elders of the children of Israel:

30 And Aaron spake all the words which the LORD had spoken unto Moses, and did the signs in the sight of the people.

31 And the people *w* believed: and when they heard that the LORD had *x* visited the children of Israel, and that he *y* had looked upon their affliction, then *z* they bowed their heads and worshipped.

CHAPTER V.

1 *Pharaoh chideth Moses and Aaron; 6 he increaseth the Israelites' task; 10 the people have no straw. 15 Pharaoh checketh their complaints; 20 they cry out upon Moses and Aaron. 22 Moses complaineth to God.*

AND afterward Moses and Aaron went in, and told Pharaoh, Thus saith the LORD God of Israel, Let my people go, that they may hold *a* a feast unto me in the wilderness.

2 And Pharaoh said, *b* Who *is* the LORD, that I should obey his voice to let Israel go? I know not the LORD, *c* neither will I let Israel go.

3 And they said, *d* The God of the Hebrews hath met with us: let us go, we pray thee, three days' journey into the desert, and sacrifice unto the LORD our God; lest he fall upon us with pestilence, or with the sword.

4 And the king of Egypt said unto them, *e* Wherefore do ye, Moses and Aaron, let the people from their works? get you unto your *f* burdens.

5 And Pharaoh said, Behold, the people of the land now *are g* many, and ye make them rest from their burdens.

6 And Pharaoh commanded the same day the *h* taskmasters of the people, and their officers, saying,

7 Ye shall no more give the people straw to make brick, as heretofore: let them go and gather straw for themselves.

8 And the tale of the bricks, which they did make heretofore, ye shall lay upon them; ye shall not diminish *ought* thereof: for they *be* idle; therefore they cry, saying, Let us go *and* sacrifice to our God.

9 *1* Let there more work be laid upon the

desert of Sinai. And from their position near the sea, they early combined trading with pastoral pursuits. (Ge. 37. 28.) The head-quarters of Jethro are supposed to have been where Dahab-Madian now stands; and from Moses coming direct to that place, he may have travelled with a caravan of merchants. But another place is fixed by tradition in Wady Shuweib, or Jethro's valley on the east of the mountain of Moses. sat by a well—See on Ge. 29. 5. 16-22. The priest of Midian—as the offices were usually conjoined, he was the ruler also of the people called Cushites or Ethiopians, and like many other chiefs of pastoral people in that early age, he still retained the faith and worship of the true God. seven daughters—were shepherdesses to whom Moses was favourably introduced, by an act of courtesy and courage in protecting them from the rude shepherds of some neighbouring tribe at a well. He afterwards formed a close and permanent alliance with this family, by marrying one of the daughters, Zipporah (a little bird), called a Cushite or Ethiopian, (Num. 12. 1.) and whom he doubtless obtained in the manner of Jacob by service. He had by her two sons, whose names were according to common practice commemorative of incidents in the family history. 23. The king of Egypt died, and the children of Israel sighed—The language seems to imply that the Israelites had experienced a partial relaxation, probably through the influence of Moses' royal patroness: but in the reign of her father's successor the persecution was renewed with increased severity.

CHAPTER III.

Ver. 1-22. DIVINE APPEARANCE AND COMMISSION TO MOSES. 1. Now Moses kept the flock—This employment he had entered on in furtherance of his matrimonial views, (see on ch. 2. 21,) but it is probable he was continuing his services now on other terms like Jacob during the latter years of his stay with Laban. (Ge. 30. 28.) led the flock to the back side of the desert—*i.e.*, on the west of the desert [GESENIUS], and assuming Jethro's head-quarters to have been at Dahab—the route by which Moses led his flock must have been west through the wide valley called by the Arabs, Wady-es-Zugherah [ROBINSON], which conducted into the interior of the wilderness. Mountain of God—so named either according to Heb. idiom from its great height, as "great mountains." *Heb.* "mountains of God," (Ps. 36. 6.) "Goodly cedars." *Heb.* "cedars of God," (Ps. 80. 10,) or as some think from its being the old abode of "the glory:"—or finally from its being the theatre of transactions most memorable in the history of the true religion. to Horeb, rather Horeb-ward—Horeb, *i.e.*, dry, desert, was the general name for the mountainous district in which Sinai is situated, and of which it is a part. (See on ch. 19.) It was used to designate the region comprehending that immense range of lofty, desolate, and barren hills, at the base of which, however, there are not only many patches of verdure to be seen, but almost all the valleys, or *wadys*, as they are called, shew a thin coating of vegetation —which towards the south, becomes more luxuriant. The Arab shepherds seldom take their flocks to a greater distance than one day's journey from their camp. Moses must have gone at least two days' journey, and although he seems to have been only following his pastoral course, that region from its numerous springs in the clefts of the rocks being the chief resort of the tribes during the summer heats, the Providence of God led him thither for an important purpose. 2, 3. The angel of the Lord appeared—It is common in the Scriptures to represent the elements and operations of nature, as winds, fires, earthquakes, pestilence, every thing enlisted in executing the divine will, as the "angels" or messengers of God. But in such cases God himself is considered as really, though invisibly present. Here the preternatural fire may be primarily meant by the expression "angel of the Lord;" but it is clear that under this symbol, the divine Being was present, whose name is given (v. 4, 6,) and elsewhere called the angel of the covenant, Jehovah-Jesus. in the midst of a bush—The wild acacia, or thorn with which that desert abounds, and which is generally dry and brittle, so much so, that at certain seasons, a spark might kindle a district far and wide into a blaze. A fire, therefore, being in the midst of such a desert bush was "a great sight." It is generally supposed to have been emblematical of the Israelites' condition in Egypt—oppressed by a grinding servitude and a bloody prosecution, and yet in spite of the cruel policy that was bent on annihilating them, they continued as numerous and thriving as ever. The reason was "God was in the midst of them." The symbol may also represent the present state of the Jews, as well as of the Church generally in the world. 4. When the Lord saw that he turned—The manifestations which God anciently made of himself were always accompanied by clear, unmistakeable signs that the communications were really from heaven. This certain evidence was given to Moses. He saw a fire, but no human agent to kindle it; he heard a voice, but no human lips from which it came; he saw no living Being, but One was in the bush, in the heat of the flames who knew him and addressed him by name. Who could this be but a Divine Being? 5. Put off thy shoes—The direction was in conformity with a usage which was well known to Moses—for the Egyptian priests observed it in their temples, and which is observed in all eastern countries—where the people take off their shoes or sandals, as we do our hats. But the Eastern idea is not precisely the same as the Western. With us, the removal of the hat is an expression of reverence for the place we enter, or rather of Him who is worshipped there. With them the removal of the shoes is a confession of personal defilement, and conscious unworthiness to stand in the presence of unspotted holiness. I am the God . . . come to deliver—The reverential awe of Moses must have been relieved by the Divine Speaker, (see on M. 22. 32,) announcing himself in his covenant character, and by the welcome intelligence communicated. Moreover, the time as well as all the circumstances of this miraculous appearance were such as to give him an illustrious display of God's faithfulness to his promises. The period of Israel's journey and affliction in Egypt had been predicted, (Ge. 15. 13,) and it was during the last year of the term which had still to run that the Lord appeared in the burning bush. 10-22. Come, now, therefore, and I will

men, that they may labour therein; and let them not regard vain words.

10 ¶ And the taskmasters of the people went out, and their officers, and they spake to the people, saying, Thus saith Pharaoh, I will not give you straw.

11 Go ye, get you straw where ye can find it: yet not ought of your work shall be diminished.

12 So the people were scattered abroad throughout all the land of Egypt to gather stubble instead of straw.

13 And the taskmasters hasted *them*, saying, Fulfil your works, *your* ² daily tasks, as when there was straw.

14 ¶ And the officers of the children of Israel, which Pharaoh's taskmasters had set over them, were beaten, *and* demanded, Wherefore have ye not fulfilled your task in making brick both yesterday and to-day, as heretofore?

15 ¶ Then the officers of the children of Israel came and cried unto Pharaoh, saying, Wherefore dealest thou thus with thy servants?

16 There is no straw given unto thy servants, and they say to us, Make brick: and, behold, thy servants *are* beaten; but the fault *is* in thine own people.

17 But he said, Ye *are* idle, *ye are* idle: therefore ye say, Let us go *and* do sacrifice to the LORD.

18 Go therefore now *and* work: for there shall no straw be given you, yet shall ye deliver the tale of bricks.

19 And the officers of the children of Israel did see *that* they *were* in evil *case*, after it was said, Ye shall not minish ought from your bricks of your daily task.

20 ¶ And they met Moses and Aaron, who stood in the way, as they came forth from Pharaoh:

21 * And they said unto them, The LORD look upon you, and judge; because ye have made our savour ³ to be abhorred in the eyes of Pharaoh, and in the eyes of his servants, to put a sword in their hand to slay us.

22 And Moses * returned unto the LORD, and said, Lord, wherefore hast thou so evil entreated this people? why *is* it *that* thou hast sent me?

23 For since I came to Pharaoh to speak in thy name, he hath done evil to this people; * neither * hast thou delivered thy people at all.

CHAPTER VI.

1 *God reneweth his promise by his name JEHOVAH:* 10 *he sendeth Moses to Pharaoh.* 14 *The generations of Reuben,* 15 *of Simeon,* 16 *of Levi.*

THEN the LORD said unto Moses, Now shalt thou see what I will do to Pharaoh: for with a strong hand shall he let them go, and with a strong hand ª shall he drive them out of his land.

2 And God spake unto Moses, and said unto him, I am ¹ the LORD:

3 And I appeared unto Abraham, unto Isaac, and unto Jacob, by *the name of* ᵇ God Almighty; but by my name ᶜ JEHOVAH was I not known to them.

4 ᵈ And I have also established my covenant with them, ᵉ to give them the land of Canaan, the land of their pilgrimage, wherein they were strangers.

5 And ᶠ I have also heard the groaning of the children of Israel, whom the Egyptians

B. C. 1491.

CHAP. 5.
i ch. 1. 11.
Pro. 29. 12.
2 a matter of a day in his day.
j Gen. 15. 13.
k ch. 6. 9.
3 to stink.
Gen. 34. 30.
1 Sa. 13. 4.
2 Sa. 10. 6.
1 Ch. 19. 6.
l Nu. 11. 11.
1 Sa. 30. 6.
4 delivering thou hast not delivered.
m Mat. 14. 31.
Heb. 10. 23.

CHAP. 6.
ª ch. 11. 1.
ch. 12. 31.
1 Or, JEHOVAH.
ᵇ Gen. 17. 1.
Gen. 35. 11.
Gen. 48. 3.
ᶜ ch. 3. 14.
Ps. 68. 4.
John 8 58.
Rev. 1. 4.
ᵈ Gen. 15. 18.
Gen. 17. 4, 7.
ᵉ Gen. 17. 8.
ᶠ ch. 2. 24.
ᵍ ch. 3. 17.
ch. 7. 4.
Deu. 26. 8.
Ps. 81. 6.
Ps. 136. 11, 12.
ʰ ch. 15. 13.
Deut. 7. 8.
1 Chr. 17. 21.
Neh. 1. 10.
ⁱ Deut. 7. 6.
2 Sa. 7. 24.
ʲ Gen. 17. 7, 8.
ch. 29. 45, 46.
Deu. 29. 13.
Rev. 21 7.
ᵏ Ps. 81. 6.
2 lift up my hand.
Gen. 14. 22.
ˡ Gen. 15. 18.
Gen. 26. 3.
3 shortness, or, straitness.
ᵐ Jer. 1. 6.
ⁿ Gen. 49. 9.
1 Chr. 5. 3.
ᵒ Gen. 46. 10.
1 Ch. 4. 24.
ᵖ Gen. 46. 11.
Num. 3. 17.
1 Chr. 6. 1.
ᑫ Nu. 26. 57.
ch. 2. 1, 2.
Nu. 26. 59.
ʳ Nu. 16. 1.
ˢ Lev. 10. 4.
Nu. 3. 30.
ᵗ Mat. 1. 4.
ᵘ Lev. 10. 1.
Num. 3. 2.
ʷ Nu. 26. 11.
ˣ Jos. 24. 33.

keep in bondage; and I have remembered my covenant.

6 Wherefore say unto the children of Israel, I *am* the LORD, and ᵍ I will bring you out from under the burdens of the Egyptians, and I will rid you out of their bondage, and I will ʰ redeem you with a stretched-out arm, and with great judgments:

7 And I will ⁱ take you to me for a people, and ʲ I will be to you a God: and ye shall know that I *am* the LORD your God, which bringeth you out ᵏ from under the burdens of the Egyptians.

8 And I will bring you in unto the land, concerning the which I did ² swear ˡ to give it to Abraham, to Isaac, and to Jacob: and I will give it you for an heritage: I *am* the LORD.

9 ¶ And Moses spake so unto the children of Israel: but they hearkened not unto Moses for ³ anguish of spirit, and for cruel bondage.

10 And the LORD spake unto Moses, saying,

11 Go in, speak unto Pharaoh king of Egypt, that he let the children of Israel go out of his land.

12 And Moses spake before the LORD, saying, Behold, the children of Israel have not hearkened unto me; how then shall Pharaoh hear me, ᵐ who *am* of uncircumcised lips?

13 And the LORD spake unto Moses and unto Aaron, and gave them a charge unto the children of Israel, and unto Pharaoh king of Egypt, to bring the children of Israel out of the land of Egypt.

14 ¶ These *be* the heads of their fathers' houses: ⁿ The sons of Reuben the first-born of Israel; Hanoch, and Pallu, Hezron, and Carmi: these *be* the families of Reuben.

15 ᵒ And the sons of Simeon; Jemuel, and Jamin, and Ohad, and Jachin, and Zohar, and Shaul the son of a Canaanitish woman: these *are* the families of Simeon.

16 And these *are* the names of ᵖ the sons of Levi according to their generations; Gershon, and Kohath, and Merari: and the years of the life of Levi *were* an hundred thirty and seven years.

17 The sons of Gershon; Libni and Shimi, according to their families.

18 And ᑫ the sons of Kohath; Amram, and Izhar, and Hebron, and Uzziel. And the years of the life of Kohath *were* an hundred thirty and three years.

19 And the sons of Merari; Mahli and Mushi: these *are* the families of Levi according to their generations.

20 And ʳ Amram took him Jochebed his father's sister to wife; and she bare him Aaron and Moses: and the years of the life of Amram *were* an hundred and thirty and seven years.

21 And ˢ the sons of Izhar; Korah, and Nepheg, and Zichri.

22 And ᵗ the sons of Uzziel; Mishael, and Elzaphan, and Zithri.

23 And Aaron took him Elisheba, daughter of ᵘ Amminadab, sister of Naashon, to wife; and she bare him ᵛ Nadab, and Abihu, Eleazar, and Ithamar.

24 And the ʷ sons of Korah; Assir, and Elkanah, and Abiasaph: these *are* the families of the Korhites.

25 And Eleazar, Aaron's son, took him one of the daughters of Putiel to wife; and ˣ she bare him Phinehas: these *are* the

send thee—Considering the patriotic views that had formerly animated the breast of Moses, we might have anticipated that no mission could have been more welcome to his heart than to be employed in the national emancipation of Israel. But he evinced great reluctance to it and stated a variety of objections, all of which were successively met and removed—and the happy issue of his labours was minutely described.

CHAPTER IV.

Ver. 1-31. MIRACULOUS CHANGE OF THE ROD, &c. 1. But behold—*Heb.* "if," "perhaps," "they will not believe me."—What evidence can I produce of my divine mission? There was still a want of full confidence, not in the character and divine power of his employer, but in His presence and power always accompanying him. He insinuated that his communication might be rejected and himself treated as an impostor. 2. what is that in thine hand?—The question was put not to elicit information which God required, but to draw the particular attention of Moses. a rod — probably the shepherd's crook—among the Arabs, a long staff, with a curved head, varying from three to six feet in length. 6. put...hand into thy bosom—the open part of his outer robe, worn about the girdle. 9. take water out of the river—Nile. Those miracles, two of which were wrought then, and the third to be performed on his arrival in Goshen, were at first designed to encourage himself as satisfactory proofs of his divine mission, and to be repeated for the special confirmation of his embassy before the Israelites. 10-17. I am not eloquent—It is supposed that Moses laboured under a natural defect of utterance, or had a difficulty in the free and fluent expression of his ideas in the Egyptian language, which he had long disused. This new objection was also overruled, but still Moses who foresaw the manifold difficulties of the undertaking, was anxious to be freed from the responsibility. 14. The anger of the Lord was kindled—The Divine Being is not subject to ebullitions of passion; but his displeasure was manifested by transferring the honour of the priesthood, which would otherwise have been bestowed on Moses to Aaron, who was from this time destined to be the head of the house of Levi, (1 Ch. 23. 13.) Marvellous had been his condescension and patience in dealing with Moses; and now every remaining scruple was removed by the unexpected and welcome intelligence that his brother Aaron was to be his colleague. God knew from the beginning what Moses would do, but he reserves this motive to the last as the strongest to rouse his languid heart, and Moses now fully and cordially complied with the call. If we are surprised at his backwardness amidst all the signs and promises that were given him, we must admire his candour and honesty in recording it. 18. Moses returned to Jethro—Being in his service, it was right to obtain his consent, but Moses evinced piety, humility, and prudence, in not divulging the special object of his journey. 19. all the men are dead—The death of the Egyptian monarch took place in the four hundred and twenty-ninth year of the Hebrew sojourn in that land, and that event, according to the law of Egypt, took off his proscription of Moses, if it had been publicly issued. 20. took wife, and sons, and set them on an ass—Sept. "asses." Those animals are not now used in the desert of Sinai, except by the Arabs for short distances. Returned—entered on his journey towards Egypt. rod of God—so called from its being to be appropriated to His service, and because whatever miracles it might be employed in performing would be wrought not by its inherent properties, but by a divine power following on its use. cf. A. 3. 12.) 24. inn—*Heb.* a halting place for the night. sought to kill him—*i.e.* he was either overwhelmed with mental distress or overtaken by a sudden and dangerous malady. The narrative is obscure, but the meaning seems to be, that, led during his illness to a strict self-examination, he was deeply pained and grieved at the thought of having, to please his wife, postponed or neglected the circumcision of one of his sons, probably the younger. To dishonour that sign and seal of the covenant was criminal in any Hebrew, peculiarly so in one destined to be the leader and deliverer of the Hebrews; and he seems to have felt his sickness as a merited chastisement for his sinful omission. Concerned for her husband's safety, Zipporah overcomes her maternal feelings of aversion to the painful rite, performs herself, by means of one of the sharp flints with which part of the desert abounds, an operation, which her husband, on whom the duty devolved, was unable to do, and having brought the bloody evidence, exclaimed in the painful excitement of her feelings that from love to him she had risked the life of her child. [CAL., BULL., ROS.] 26. So he let him go—Moses recovered; but the remembrance of this critical period in his life would stimulate the Hebrew legislator to enforce a faithful attention to the rite of circumcision, when it was established as a Divine ordinance in Israel, and made their peculiar distinction as a people. 27. Aaron met...and kissed him—After a separation of 40 years, their meeting would be mutually happy. Similar are the salutations of Arab friends when they meet in the desert still; conspicuous is the kiss on each side of the head. 29. Moses and Aaron went—towards Egypt, Zipporah and her sons having been sent back. (cf. ch. 18. 2.) gathered all the elders—Aaron was spokesman, and Moses performed the appointed miracles—through which "the people," *i. e.* the elders, believed (1 Ki. 17. 24; Jo. 3. 2.), and received the joyful tidings of the errand on which Moses had come with devout thanksgiving. Formerly they had slighted the message and rejected the messenger. Formerly Moses had gone in his own strength; now he goes leaning on God, and strong only through faith in Him who had sent him. Israel also had been taught a useful lesson, and it was good for both that they had been afflicted.

CHAPTER V.

Ver. 1-23. FIRST INTERVIEW WITH PHARAOH. 1. Moses and Aaron went — As representatives of the Hebrews, they were entitled to ask an audience of the king, and their thorough Egyptian training taught them how and when to seek it. they told him—when introduced, they delivered a message in the name of the God of Israel. This is the first time He is mentioned by that national appellation in Scripture. It seems to have been used by divine direction ch. 4. 22.), and designed to put honour on the

heads of the fathers of the Levites, according to their families.

26 These *are* that Aaron and Moses, to whom the LORD said, Bring out the children of Israel from the land of Egypt, according to their armies.

27 These *are* they which spake to Pharaoh king of Egypt, to bring out the children of Israel from Egypt: these *are* that Moses and Aaron.

28 ¶ And it came to pass, on the day when the LORD spake unto Moses in the land of Egypt,

29 That the LORD spake unto Moses, saying, I *am* the LORD: speak thou unto Pharaoh king of Egypt all that I say unto thee.

30 And Moses said before the LORD, Behold, I *am* of uncircumcised lips, and how shall Pharaoh hearken unto me?

CHAPTER VII.

1 Moses is encouraged to go to Pharaoh: 10 his rod turned into a serpent; 11 the sorcerers do the like. 13 Pharaoh's heart is hardened. 19 The river is turned into blood.

AND the LORD said unto Moses, See, I have made thee a god to Pharaoh; and Aaron thy brother shall be thy prophet.

2 Thou shalt speak all that I command thee; and Aaron thy brother shall speak unto Pharaoh, that he send the children of Israel out of his land.

3 And I will harden Pharaoh's heart, and multiply my signs and my wonders in the land of Egypt.

4 But Pharaoh shall not hearken unto you, that I may lay my hand upon Egypt, and bring forth mine armies, *and* my people the children of Israel, out of the land of Egypt by great judgments.

5 And the Egyptians shall know that I *am* the LORD, when I stretch forth mine hand upon Egypt, and bring out the children of Israel from among them.

6 And Moses and Aaron did as the LORD commanded them, so did they.

7 And Moses *was* fourscore years old, and Aaron fourscore and three years old, when they spake unto Pharaoh.

8 ¶ And the LORD spake unto Moses and unto Aaron, saying,

9 When Pharaoh shall speak unto you, saying, Show a miracle for you: then thou shalt say unto Aaron, Take thy rod, and cast *it* before Pharaoh, *and* it shall become a serpent.

10 ¶ And Moses and Aaron went in unto Pharaoh, and they did so as the LORD had commanded: and Aaron cast down his rod before Pharaoh, and before his servants, and it became a serpent.

11 Then Pharaoh also called the wise men and the sorcerers: now the magicians of Egypt, they also did in like manner with their enchantments.

12 For they cast down every man his rod, and they became serpents: but Aaron's rod swallowed up their rods.

13 And he hardened Pharaoh's heart, that he hearkened not unto them; as the LORD had said.

14 ¶ And the LORD said unto Moses, Pharaoh's heart *is* hardened, he refuseth to let the people go.

15 Get thee unto Pharaoh in the morning; lo, he goeth out unto the water; and thou shalt stand by the river's brink against he come; and the rod which was turned to a serpent shalt thou take in thine hand.

16 And thou shalt say unto him, The LORD God of the Hebrews hath sent me unto thee, saying, Let my people go, that they may serve me in the wilderness: and, behold, hitherto thou wouldest not hear.

17 Thus saith the LORD, In this thou shalt know that I *am* the LORD: behold, I will smite with the rod that *is* in mine hand upon the waters which *are* in the river, and they shall be turned to blood.

18 And the fish that *is* in the river shall die, and the river shall stink; and the Egyptians shall loathe to drink of the water of the river.

19 ¶ And the LORD spake unto Moses, Say unto Aaron, Take thy rod, and stretch out thine hand upon the waters of Egypt, upon their streams, upon their rivers, and upon their ponds, and upon all their pools of water, that they may become blood; and *that* there may be blood throughout all the land of Egypt, both in *vessels of* wood, and in *vessels of* stone.

20 And Moses and Aaron did so, as the LORD commanded; and he lifted up the rod, and smote the waters that *were* in the river, in the sight of Pharaoh, and in the sight of his servants; and all the waters that *were* in the river were turned to blood.

21 And the fish that *was* in the river died; and the river stank, and the Egyptians could not drink of the water of the river: and there was blood throughout all the land of Egypt.

22 And the magicians of Egypt did so with their enchantments: and Pharaoh's heart was hardened, neither did he hearken unto them; as the LORD had said.

23 And Pharaoh turned and went into his house, neither did he set his heart to this also.

24 And all the Egyptians digged round about the river for water to drink; for they could not drink of the water of the river.

25 And seven days were fulfilled, after that the LORD had smitten the river.

CHAPTER VIII.

1 Frogs are threatened, 5 and sent. 16 The dust is turned into lice, which the magicians could not do. 20 The plague of flies. 32 Pharaoh is still hardened.

AND the LORD spake unto Moses, Go unto Pharaoh, and say unto him, Thus saith the LORD, Let my people go, that they may serve me.

2 And if thou refuse to let *them* go, behold, I will smite all thy borders with frogs:

3 And the river shall bring forth frogs abundantly, which shall go up and come into thine house, and into thy bed-chamber, and upon thy bed, and into the house of thy servants, and upon thy people, and into thine ovens, and into thy kneading troughs:

4 And the frogs shall come up both on thee, and upon thy people, and upon all thy servants.

5 ¶ And the LORD spake unto Moses, Say unto Aaron, Stretch forth thine hand with thy rod over the streams, over the rivers, and over the ponds, and cause frogs to come up upon the land of Egypt.

6 And Aaron stretched out his hand over the waters of Egypt; and the frogs came up, and covered the land of Egypt.

7 And the magicians did so with their

Hebrews in their depressed condition. (Heb. 11. 16. 2. Pharaoh said, Who is the Lord— rather "Jehovah." Lord was a common name applied to objects of worship; but Jehovah was a name he had never heard of; he estimated the character and power of this God by the abject and miserable condition of the worshippers, and concluded that He held as low a rank among the gods as his people did in the nation. To demonstrate the supremacy of the true God over all the gods of Egypt, was the design of the plagues. Will not let Israel go—As his honour and interest were both involved, he determined to crush this attempt, and in a tone of insolence, or perhaps profanity, rejected the request for the release of the Hebrew slaves. 3. The God of the Hebrews hath met us—Instead of being provoked into reproaches or threats, they mildly assured him that it was not a proposal originating among themselves, but a duty enjoined on them by their God. They had for a long series of years been debarred from the privilege of religious worship, and as there was reason to fear that a continued neglect of divine ordinances would draw down upon them the judgments of offended heaven, they begged permission to go three days' journey into the desert—a place of seclusion—where their sacrificial observances would neither suffer interruption nor give umbrage to the Egyptians. In saying this, they concealed their ultimate design of abandoning the kingdom, and by making this partial request at first, they probably wished to try the king's temper before they disclosed their intentions any farther. But they said only what God had put in their mouths (ch. 3. 12, 18.), and 'this legalizes the specific act, while it gives no sanction to the general habit of dissimulation.' [CHALMERS.] 4. Wherefore do ye, Moses and Aaron, let the people, &c.—Without taking any notice of what they had said, he treated them as ambitious demagogues, who were appealing to the superstitious feelings of the people, to stir up sedition, and diffuse a spirit of discontent, which spreading through so vast a body of slaves, might endanger the peace of the country. 6. Pharaoh commanded —It was a natural consequence of the high displeasure created by this interview, that he should put additional burdens on the oppressed Israelites. taskmasters— Egyptian overseers, appointed to exact labour of the Israelites. officers—Hebrews placed over their brethren, under the taskmasters, precisely analogous to the Arab officers set over the Arab Fellahs, the poor labourers in modern Egypt. 7. ye shall no more give the people straw—The making of bricks appears to have been a government monopoly, as the ancient bricks are nearly all stamped with the name of a king, and they were formed, as they are still in Lower Egypt, of clay mixed with chopped straw, and dried or hardened in the sun. The Israelites were employed in this drudgery; and though they still dwelt in Goshen, and held property in flocks and herds, they were compelled in rotation to serve in the brick-quarries, pressed in alternating groups, just as the *fellaheen* or peasants are marched by press-gangs in the same country still. go...gather straw, &c.— the enraged despot did not issue orders to do an impracticable thing. The Egyptian reapers in the corn-harvest were accustomed merely to cut off the ears and leave the stalk standing. 8. tale—an appointed number of bricks. The materials of their labour were to be no longer supplied, and yet, as the same amount of produce was exacted daily, it is impossible to imagine more aggravated cruelty—a more perfect specimen of Oriental despotism. 12. So the people were scattered—It was an immense grievance to the labourers individually, but there would be no hindrance from the husbandmen whose fields they entered, as almost all the lands of Egypt were in the possession of the crown. (Ge. 47. 20.). 13-19. taskmasters hasted... officers beaten—As the nearest fields were bared, and the people had to go farther for stubble, it was impossible for them to meet the demand by the usual tale of bricks. 'The beating of the officers is just what might have been expected from an Eastern tyrant, especially in the valley of the Nile, as it appears from the monuments, that ancient Egypt, like modern China, was principally governed by the stick. [TAYLOR.] The mode of beating was by the offender being laid flat on the ground, and generally held by the hands and feet while the chastisement was administered.' [WILK.] (Deut. 25. 2.). A picture representing the Hebrews in a brick-field, exactly as described in this chapter was found in an Egyptian tomb at Thebes. 20, 21. They met Moses...the Lord... judge—Thus the deliverer of Israel found that this patriotic interference did, in the first instance, only aggravate the evil he wished to remove, and that instead of receiving the gratitude, he was loaded with the reproaches of his countrymen. But as the greatest darkness is immediately before the dawn, so the people of God are often plunged into the deepest affliction when on the eve of their deliverance, and so it was in this case.

CHAPTER VI.

Ver. 1-13. RENEWAL OF THE PROMISE. Lord said unto Moses—The Lord, who is long-suffering and indulgent to the errors and infirmities of his people, made allowance for the mortification of Moses as the result of this first interview, and cheered him with the assurance of a speedy and successful termination to his embassy. 2. And God spake unto Moses—For his further encouragement, there was made to him an emphatic repetition of the promise. (ch. 3. 20.) 3. I am God Almighty—All enemies must fall, all difficulties must vanish before my Omnipotent power, and the patriarchs had abundant proofs of this. but by my name, &c.—rather, interrogatively, by my name Jehovah was I not known to them? Am not I, the Almighty God who pledged my honour for the fulfilment of the covenant, also the self-existent God who lives to accomplish it. Rest assured, therefore, that I shall bring it to pass. This passage has occasioned much discussion; and it has been thought by many to intimate that as the name Jehovah was not known to the patriarchs, at least in the full bearing or practical experience of it, the honour of the disclosure was reserved to Moses, who was the first sent with a message in the name of Jehovah, and enabled to attest it by a series of public miracles. 9-13. Moses spake—The increased severities inflicted on the Israelites seem to have so entirely crushed their spirits as well as irritated them, that they refused

enchantments, and brought up frogs upon the land of Egypt.

8 ¶ Then Pharaoh called for Moses and Aaron, and said, ʰ Entreat the Lord, that he may take away the frogs from me, and from my people; and I will let the people go, that they may do sacrifice unto the Lord.

9 And Moses said unto Pharaoh, ² Glory over me: ³ when shall I entreat for thee, and for thy servants, and for thy people, ⁴ to destroy the frogs from thee and thy houses, *that* they may remain in the river only?

10 And he said, ⁵ To-morrow. And he said, *Be* it according to thy word; that thou mayest know that ⁱ *there is* none like unto the Lord our God.

11 And the frogs shall depart from thee, and from thy houses, and from thy servants, and from thy people; they shall remain in the river only.

12 And Moses and Aaron went out from Pharaoh: and Moses ʲ cried unto the Lord because of the frogs which he had brought against Pharaoh.

13 And the Lord did according to the word of Moses; and the frogs died out of the houses, out of the villages, and out of the fields.

14 And they gathered them together upon heaps; and the land stank.

15 But when Pharaoh saw that there was ᵏ respite, ˡ he hardened his heart, and hearkened not unto them; as the Lord had said.

16 ¶ And the Lord said unto Moses, Say unto Aaron, Stretch out thy rod, and smite the dust of the earth, that it may become lice throughout all the land of Egypt.

17 And they did so; for Aaron stretched out his hand with his rod, and smote the dust of the earth, and ᵐ it became lice in man and in beast; all the dust of the land became lice throughout all the land of Egypt.

18 And ⁿ the magicians did so with their enchantments to bring forth lice, but they ᵒ could not: so there were lice upon man and upon beast.

19 Then the magicians said unto Pharaoh, This *is* ᵖ the finger of God: and Pharaoh's heart was hardened, and he hearkened not unto them; as the Lord had said.

20 ¶ And the Lord said unto Moses, ᵠ Rise up early in the morning, and stand before Pharaoh; lo, he cometh forth to the water; and say unto him, Thus saith the Lord, Let my people go, that they may serve me:

21 Else, if thou wilt not let my people go, behold, I will send ⁶ swarms *of flies* upon thee, and upon thy servants, and upon thy people, and unto thy houses: and the houses of the Egyptians shall be full of swarms *of flies,* and also the ground whereon they *are.*

22 And ʳ I will sever in that day the land of Goshen, in which my people dwell, that no swarms *of flies* shall be there; to the end thou mayest know that I *am* the Lord in the midst of the earth.

23 And I will put ⁷ a division between my people and thy people: ⁸ to-morrow shall this sign be.

24 And the Lord did so: and ˢ there came a grievous swarm *of flies* into the house of Pharaoh, and *into* his servants' houses, and into all the land of Egypt: the land was ⁹ corrupted by reason of the swarm *of flies.*

25 ¶ And Pharaoh called for Moses and for Aaron, and said, Go ye, sacrifice to your God in the land.

26 And Moses said, It is not meet so to do; for we shall sacrifice the ᵗ abomination of the Egyptians to the Lord our God: lo, shall we sacrifice the abomination of the Egyptians before their eyes, and will they not stone us?

27 We will go ᵘ three days' journey into the wilderness, and sacrifice to the Lord our God, as ᵛ he shall command us.

28 And Pharaoh said, I will let you go, that ye may sacrifice to the Lord your God in the wilderness; only ye shall not go very far away: ʷ entreat for me.

29 And Moses said, Behold, I go out from thee, and I will entreat the Lord that the swarms *of flies* may depart from Pharaoh, from his servants, and from his people, to-morrow: but let not Pharaoh deal deceitfully any more in not letting the people go to sacrifice to the Lord.

30 And Moses went out from Pharaoh, and entreated the Lord.

31 And ˣ the Lord did according to the word of Moses; and he removed the swarms *of flies* from Pharaoh, from his servants, and from his people: there remained not one.

32 And Pharaoh ʸ hardened his heart at this time also, neither would he let the people go.

CHAPTER IX.

1 *The murrain of beasts.* 8 *The plague of boils and blains,* 22 *of hail.* 27 *Pharaoh sueth to Moses,* 35 *but yet is hardened.*

THEN the Lord said unto Moses, ᵃ Go in unto Pharaoh, and tell him, Thus saith the Lord God of the Hebrews, Let my people go, that they may serve me.

2 For if thou ᵇ refuse to let *them* go, and wilt hold them still,

3 Behold, the ᶜ hand of the Lord is upon thy cattle which *is* in the field, upon the horses, upon the asses, upon the camels, upon the oxen, and upon the sheep: *there shall be* a very grievous murrain.

4 And ᵈ the Lord shall sever between the cattle of Israel and the cattle of Egypt: and there shall nothing die of all *that is* the children's of Israel.

5 And the Lord appointed a set time, saying, To-morrow the Lord shall do this thing in the land.

6 And the Lord did that thing on the morrow, and ᵉ all the cattle of Egypt died: but of the cattle of the children of Israel died not one.

7 And Pharaoh sent, and, behold, there was not one of the cattle of the Israelites dead. And ᶠ the heart of Pharaoh was hardened, and he did not let the people go.

8 ¶ And the Lord said unto Moses and unto Aaron, Take to you handfuls of ashes of the furnace, and let Moses sprinkle it toward the heaven in the sight of Pharaoh.

9 And it shall become small dust in all the land of Egypt, and shall be ᵍ a boil breaking forth *with* blains upon man, and upon beast, throughout all the land of Egypt.

10 And they took ashes of the furnace, and stood before Pharaoh; and Moses sprinkled it up toward heaven; and it became ʰ a boil breaking forth *with* blains upon man and upon beast.

11 And the ⁱ magicians could not stand

to listen to any more communications. (Ex. 14. 12.) Even the faith of Moses himself was faltering; and he would have abandoned the enterprise in despair had he not received a positive command from God to revisit the people without delay, and at the same time renew their demand on the king in a more decisive and peremptory tone. 12. how shall I speak ... uncircumcised lips?—A metaphorical expression among the Hebrews, who, taught to look on the circumcision of any part as denoting perfection, signified its deficiency or unsuitableness by uncircumcision. The words here express how painfully Moses felt his want of utterance or persuasive oratory. He seems to have fallen into the same deep despondency as his brethren, and to be shrinking with nervous timidity from a difficult, if not desperate cause. If he had succeeded so ill with the people, whose dearest interests were involved, what better hope could he entertain of his making more impression on the heart of a king elated with pride and strong in the possession of absolute power? How strikingly was the indulgent forbearance of God displayed towards his people amid all their backwardness to hail his announcement of approaching deliverance! No perverse complaints or careless indifference on their part retarded the development of His gracious purposes. On the contrary, here, as generally, the course of his Providence is slow in the infliction of judgments, while it moves more quickly, as it were, when misery is to be relieved or benefits conferred.

14-27. THE GENEALOGY OF MOSES. 14. These be the heads—Chiefs or governors of their houses. The insertion of this genealogical table in this part of the narrative was intended to authenticate the descent of Moses and Aaron. Both of them were commissioned to act so important a part in the events transacted in the court of Egypt, and afterwards elevated to so high offices in the government and Church of God, that it was of the utmost importance that their lineage should be accurately traced. Reuben and Simeon being the eldest of Jacob's sons, a passing notice is taken of them, and then the historian advances to the enumeration of the principal persons in the house of Levi. 20. Jochebed ... father's sister—The Septuagint and Syriac versions render it his cousin. 23. Elisheba—*i.e.*, Elisabethan. These minute particulars recorded of the family of Aaron, while he has passed over his own, indicate the real modesty of Moses. An ambitious man or an impostor would have acted in a different manner.

CHAPTER VII.

Ver. 1-25. SECOND INTERVIEW WITH PHARAOH. 1. The Lord said unto Moses— He is here encouraged to wait again on the king—not, however, as formerly in the attitude of a humble suppliant, but now armed with credentials as God's ambassador, and to make his demand in a tone and manner which no earthly monarch or court ever witnessed. I have made thee a god—made, *i.e.*, set, appointed; "a god," *i. e.*, he was to act in this business as God's representative, to act and speak in his name, and to perform things beyond the ordinary course of nature. The Orientals familiarly say of a man who is eminently great or wise "he is a god" among men. Aaron thy brother, &c.,—*i.e.*, interpreter or spokesman. The one was to be the vicegerent of God, and the other must be considered the speaker throughout all the ensuing scenes, even though his name is not expressly mentioned. 3. I will harden Pharaoh's heart— This would be the *result*. But the Divine message would be the *occasion*, not the *cause* of the king's impenitent obduracy. 4, 5. I will lay mine hand, &c.—The succession of terrible judgments with which the country was about to be scourged would fully demonstrate the supremacy of Israel's God. 7. Moses was fourscore years—This advanced age was a pledge that they had not been readily betrayed into a rash or hazardous enterprise, and that under its attendant infirmities they could not have carried through the work on which they were entering had they not been supported by a Divine hand. 8, 9. When Pharaoh shall speak, &c.—The king would naturally demand some evidence of their having been sent from God; and as he would expect the ministers of his own gods to do the same works, the contest, in the nature of the case, would be one of miracles. 9-13. Notice has already been taken of the rod of Moses, (ch. 4. 2.) but rods were carried also by all nobles and official persons in the court of Pharaoh. It was an Egyptian custom, and the rods were symbols of authority or rank. Hence God commanded his servants to use a rod. 10. Aaron cast down his rod, &c.—It is to be presumed that Pharaoh had demanded a proof of their Divine mission. 11. then Pharaoh called, &c.—His object in calling them was to ascertain whether this doing of Aaron's was really a work of Divine power or merely a feat of magical art. The magicians of Egypt in modern times have been long celebrated adepts in charming serpents, and particularly by pressing the nape of the neck, they throw them into a kind of catalepsy, which renders them stiff and immoveable—thus seeming to change them into a rod. They conceal the serpent about their persons, and by acts of legerdemain produce it from their dress, stiff and straight as a rod. Just the same trick was played off by their ancient predecessors, the most renowned of whom, Jannes and Jambres (2 Tim. 3. 8.), were called in on this occasion. They had time after the summons to make suitable preparations—and so it appears they succeeded by their "enchantments" in practising an illusion on the senses. 12. but Aaron's rod, &c.—This was what they could not be prepared for, and the discomfiture appeared in the loss of their rods, which were probably real serpents. 13, 14. Pharaoh's heart was hardened—Whatever might have been his first impressions, they were soon dispelled; and when he found his magicians making similar attempts, he concluded that Aaron's affair was a magical deception, the secret of which was not known to his wise men. 15. Get thee unto Pharaoh— Now therefore began those appalling miracles of judgment by which the God of Israel, through his ambassadors, proved his sole and unchallengeable supremacy over all the gods of Egypt, and which were the natural phenomena of Egypt, at an unusual season, and in a miraculous degree of intensity. The court of Egypt, whether held in Rameses, or Memphis, or Tanis in the field of Zoan Ps. 78. 12.), was the scene of those extraordinary transactions, and Mose

before Moses because of the boils; for the boil was upon the magicians, and upon all the Egyptians.

12 And ʲ the LORD hardened the heart of Pharaoh, and he hearkened not unto them; as ᵏ the LORD had spoken unto Moses.

13 ¶ And the LORD said unto Moses, ˡ Rise up early in the morning, and stand before Pharaoh, and say unto him, Thus saith the LORD God of the Hebrews, Let my people go, that they may serve me.

14 For I will at this time send all my plagues upon thine heart, and upon thy servants, and upon thy people; ᵐ that thou mayest know that *there is* none like me in all the earth.

15 For now I will ⁿ stretch out my hand, that I may smite thee and thy people with pestilence; and thou shalt be cut off from the earth.

16 And in very deed for ᵒ this *cause* have I ¹ raised thee up, for to show in thee my power; and that my name may be declared throughout all the earth.

17 As yet exaltest thou thyself against my people, that thou wilt not let them go?

18 Behold, to-morrow about this time I will cause it to rain a very grievous hail, such as hath not been in Egypt since the foundation thereof even until now.

19 Send therefore now, *and* gather thy cattle, and all that thou hast in the field; for upon every man and beast which shall be found in the field, and shall not be brought home, the hail shall come down upon them, and they shall die.

20 He that feared the word of the LORD among the servants of Pharaoh made his servants and his cattle flee into the houses:

21 And he that ² regarded not the word of the LORD left his servants and his cattle in the field.

22 ¶ And the LORD said unto Moses, Stretch forth thine hand toward heaven, that there may be ᵖ hail in all the land of Egypt, upon man, and upon beast, and upon every herb of the field, throughout the land of Egypt.

23 And Moses stretched forth his rod toward heaven; and ᑫ the LORD sent thunder and hail, and the fire ran along upon the ground; and the LORD rained hail upon the land of Egypt.

24 So there was hail, and fire mingled with the hail, very grievous, such as there was none like it in all the land of Egypt since it became a nation.

25 And the hail smote throughout all the land of Egypt all that *was* in the field, both man and beast; and the hail ʳ smote every herb of the field, and brake every tree of the field.

26 Only ˢ in the land of Goshen, where the children of Israel *were*, was there no hail.

27 ¶ And Pharaoh sent, and called for Moses and Aaron, and said unto them, ᵗ I have sinned this time: ᵘ the LORD *is* righteous, and I and my people are wicked.

28 Entreat ᵛ the LORD (for *it is* enough) that there be no *more* ³ mighty thunderings and hail; and I will let you go, and ye shall stay no longer.

29 And Moses said unto him, As soon as I am gone out of the city, I will ʷ spread abroad my hands unto the LORD; *and* the thunder shall cease, neither shall there be any more hail; that thou mayest know how that ᵗʰᵉ ˣ earth *is* the LORD'S.

49

B. C. 1491.

CHAP. 9.
ʲ ch. 8. 32.
ᵏ ch. 4. 21.
ˡ ch. 8. 20.
ᵐ De. 3. 24.
De. 33. 26.
2 Sa. 7. 22.
1 Ch. 17. 20.
Ps. 71. 19.
Ps. 86. 8.
Isa. 46. 9.
Isa. 45. 5–23.
Jer. 10. 6, 7.
ⁿ ch. 3. 20.
ᵒ Prov. 16. 4.
Rom. 9. 17.
1 Pet. 2. 9.
1 made thee stand.
2 set not his heart unto.
ᵖ Rev. 16. 21.
ᑫ Jos. 10. 11.
Ps. 18. 13.
Ps. 78. 47.
Ps. 105. 32.
Ps. 148. 8.
Is. 30. 30.
Ez. 38. 22.
Rev. 8. 7.
ʳ Ps. 105. 33.
ˢ ch. 9. 4, 6.
ch. 11. 7.
Is. 32. 18, 19.
ᵗ ch. 10. 16.
ᵘ 2 Chr. 12. 6.
Ps. 129. 4.
Ps. 145. 17.
Lam. 1. 18.
Dan. 9. 14.
ᵛ ch. 8. 8, 28.
ch. 10. 17.
Acts 8. 24.
3 voices of God.
Ps. 29. 3, 4.
ʷ 1 Ki. 8. 22, 38.
Ps. 143. 6.
Is. 1. 15.
ˣ Ps. 24. 1.
1 Co. 10. 26.
ʸ Is. 26. 10.
ᶻ Ruth 1. 22.
Ruth 2. 23.
4 hidden, or, dark.
ᵃ ch. 8. 12.
5 by the hand of Moses.
ch. 4. 13.

CHAP. 10.
ᵃ ch. 7. 14.
ᵇ ch. 7. 4.
ᶜ Deu. 4. 9.
Ps. 44. 1.
Ps. 71. 18.
Joel 1. 3.
ᵈ 1 Ki. 21. 29.
2 Ch. 34. 27.
Jam. 4. 10.
1 Pet. 5. 6.
ᵉ Pro. 30. 27.
Rev. 9. 3.
1 eye.
ᶠ Joel 2. 25.
ᵍ ch. 8. 3, 21.
ʰ ch. 23. 33.
Jos. 23. 13.
1 Sa. 18. 21.
Ec. 7. 26.
1 Cor. 7. 35.
2 who, and who, etc.
ⁱ Prov. 3. 9.
ʲ ch. 9. 1.

30 But as for thee and thy servants, ʸ I know that ye will not yet fear the LORD God.

31 And the flax and the barley was smitten; ᶻ for the barley *was* in the ear, and the flax *was* bolled.

32 But the wheat and the rye were not smitten; for they *were* ⁴ not grown up.

33 And Moses went out of the city from Pharaoh, and ᵃ spread abroad his hands unto the LORD; and the thunders and hail ceased, and the rain was not poured upon the earth.

34 And when Pharaoh saw that the rain and the hail and the thunders were ceased, he sinned yet more, and hardened his heart, he and his servants.

35 And the heart of Pharaoh was hardened, neither would he let the children of Israel go; as the LORD had spoken ⁵ by Moses.

CHAPTER X.

4 *God threateneth to send locusts.* 7 *Pharaoh moved by his servants, inclineth to let the Israelites go.* 12 *The plague of locusts,* 21 *of darkness.* 24 *Pharaoh sueth to Moses:* 27 *his heart is yet hardened.*

AND the LORD said unto Moses, Go in unto Pharaoh: ᵃ for I have hardened his heart, and the heart of his servants, that ᵇ I might show these my signs before him:

2 And that ᶜ thou mayest tell in the ears of thy son, and of thy son's son, what things I have wrought in Egypt, and my signs which I have done among them; that ye may know how that I *am* the LORD.

3 And Moses and Aaron came in unto Pharaoh, and said unto him, Thus saith the LORD God of the Hebrews, How long wilt thou refuse to ᵈ humble thyself before me? let my people go, that they may serve me:

4 Else, if thou refuse to let my people go, behold, to-morrow will I bring the ᵉ locusts into thy coast:

5 And they shall cover the ¹ face of the earth, that one cannot be able to see the earth: and ᶠ they shall eat the residue of that which is escaped, which remaineth unto you from the hail, and shall eat every tree which groweth for you out of the field:

6 And they ᵍ shall fill thy houses, and the houses of all thy servants, and the houses of all the Egyptians; which neither thy fathers, nor thy fathers' fathers have seen, since the day that they were upon the earth unto this day. And he turned himself, and went out from Pharaoh.

7 And Pharaoh's servants said unto him, How long shall this man be ʰ a snare unto us? let the men go, that they may serve the LORD their God: knowest thou not yet that Egypt is destroyed?

8 And Moses and Aaron were brought again unto Pharaoh: and he said unto them, Go, serve the LORD your God: ² but who *are* they that shall go?

9 And Moses said, ⁱ We will go with our young and with our old, with our sons and with our daughters, with our flocks and with our herds will we go: for ʲ we *must hold* a feast unto the LORD.

10 And he said unto them, Let the LORD be so with you, as I will let you go, and your little ones; look to *it*; for evil *is* before you.

D

must have resided during that terrible period in the immediate neighbourhood. in the morning, &c.—for the purpose of ablutions or devotions, perhaps, for the Nile was an object of superstitious reverence, the patron deity of the country. It might be that Moses had been denied admission into the palace; but be that as it may, the river was to be the subject of the first plague, and therefore he was ordered to repair to its banks with the miracle-working rod, now to be raised not in demonstration, but in judgment, if the refractory spirit of the king should still refuse consent to Israel's departure for their sacred rites. 17-21. Aaron lifted up his rod, &c.—Whether the water was changed into real blood, or only the appearance of it, (and Omnipotence could effect the one as easily as the other), this was a severe calamity. How great must have been the disappointment and disgust throughout the land when the river became of a blood-red colour, of which they had a national abhorrence; their favourite beverage became a nauseous draught, and when the fish, which formed so large an article of food, were destroyed. The immense scale on which the plague was inflicted is seen by its extending to "the streams," or branches of the Nile—to the "rivers"—the canals—the "ponds" and "pools," that which is left after an overflow—the reservoirs, and the many domestic vessels in which the Nile water was kept to filter. And accordingly the sufferings of the people from thirst must have been severe. Nothing could more humble the pride of Egypt than this dishonour brought on their national god. 22. The magicians did so, &c.—Little or no pure water could be procured, and therefore their imitation must have been on a small scale—the only drinkable water to be got being dug among the sands. It must have been on a sample or specimen of water dyed red with some colouring matter. But it was sufficient to serve as a pretext or command for the king to turn unmoved and go to his house.

CHAPTER VIII.

Ver. 1-15. PLAGUE OF FROGS. 1. The Lord spake...go unto Pharaoh—The duration of the first plague for a whole week must have satisfied all that it was produced not by any accidental causes, but by the agency of Omnipotent power. As a judgment of God, however, it produced no good effect, and Moses was commanded to wait on the king and threaten him in the event of his continued obstinacy with the infliction of a new and different plague. As Pharaoh's answer is not given, it may be inferred to have been unfavourable, for the rod was again raised. 2. I will smite, &c.—Those animals, though the natural spawn of the river, and therefore objects familiar to the people were on this occasion miraculously multiplied to an amazing extent, and it is probable that the ova of the frogs, which had been previously deposited in the mire and marshes were miraculously brought to perfection at once. 3. bed-chambers, bed—mats strewed on the floor as well as more sumptuous divans of the rich. ovens—holes made in the ground and the sides of which are plastered with mortar. kneading troughs—those used in Egypt were bowls of wicker or rush-work. What must have been the state of the people when they could find no means of escape from the cold, damp touch and unsightly presence of the frogs, as they alighted on every article and vessel of food. 5, 6. stretch forth, &c.—The miracle consisted in the reptiles leaving their marshes at the very time he commanded them. 7. The magicians did so with their enchantments—required great art to make the offensive reptiles appear on any small spot of ground. What they undertook to do already existed in abundance all around. They would better have shewn their power by removing the frogs. 8. Pharaoh called, entreat the Lord—The frog which was now used as an instrument of affliction whether from reverence or abhorrence, was an object of national superstition with the Egyptians; the god Ptha being represented with a frog's head. But the vast numbers, together with their stench, made them an intolerable nuisance, so that the king was so far humbled as to promise that if Moses would intercede for their removal he would consent to the departure of Israel, and in compliance with this appeal, they were withdrawn at the very hour named by the monarch himself. But many, while suffering the consequences of their sins, make promises of amendment and obedience which they afterwards forget, and so Pharaoh when he saw there was a respite, was again hardened. 16-19. PLAGUE OF LICE. 16. smite the dust of the land, &c.—Aaron's rod, by the direction of Moses who was commanded by God, was again raised, and the land was filled with gnats, mosquitoes,—that is the proper meaning of the original term. In ordinary circumstances they embitter life in Eastern countries, and therefore the terrible nature of this infliction on Egypt may be judged of when no precautions could preserve from their painful sting. The very smallness and insignificance of these fierce insects made them a dreadful scourge. The magicians never attempted any imitation, and what neither the blood of the river nor the nuisance of the frogs had done, the visitation of this tiny enemy constrained them to acknowledge " this is the finger of God," properly " gods," for they spoke as heathens. 20-32. PLAGUE OF FLIES. 20. Rise up early ...Pharaoh cometh, &c.—Pharaoh still appearing obdurate, Moses was ordered to meet him while walking on the banks of the Nile, and repeat his request for the liberation of Israel, threatening in case of continued refusal to cover every house from the palace to the cottage with swarms of flies—while, as a proof of the power that accomplished this judgment, the land of Goshen should be exempted from the calamity. The appeal was equally vain as before, and the predicted evil overtook the country in the form of what was not "flies" such as we are accustomed to, but divers sorts of flies, (Ps. 78, 45, the gad-fly, the dog-fly, the cock roach, the Egyptian beetle, for all these are mentioned by different writers. They are very destructive, some of them inflicting severe bites on animals, others destroying clothes, books, plants, every thing;—the worship of flies, particularly of the beetle, was a prominent part of the religion of the ancient Egyptians. The employment of these winged deities to chastise them must have been painful and humiliating to the Egyptians, while it must at the same time have strengthened the faith

11 Not so: go now ye *that are* men, and serve the Lord; for that ye did desire. And they were driven out from Pharaoh's presence.

12 ¶ And the Lord said unto Moses, Stretch out thine hand over the land of Egypt for the locusts, that they may come up upon the land of Egypt, and eat every herb of the land, *even* all that the hail hath left.

13 And Moses stretched forth his rod over the land of Egypt, and the Lord brought an east wind upon the land all that day, and all *that* night; *and* when it was morning, the east wind brought the locusts.

14 And the locusts went up over all the land of Egypt, and rested in all the coasts of Egypt: very grievous *were they;* before them there were no such locusts as they, neither after them shall be such.

15 For they covered the face of the whole earth, so that the land was darkened; and they did eat every herb of the land, and all the fruit of the trees which the hail had left: and there remained not any green thing in the trees, or in the herbs of the field, through all the land of Egypt.

16 ¶ Then Pharaoh called for Moses and Aaron in haste; and he said, I have sinned against the Lord your God, and against you.

17 Now therefore forgive, I pray thee, my sin only this once, and entreat the Lord your God, that he may take away from me this death only.

18 And he went out from Pharaoh, and entreated the Lord.

19 And the Lord turned a mighty strong west wind, which took away the locusts, and cast them into the Red sea; there remained not one locust in all the coasts of Egypt.

20 But the Lord hardened Pharaoh's heart, so that he would not let the children of Israel go.

21 ¶ And the Lord said unto Moses, Stretch out thine hand toward heaven, that there may be darkness over the land of Egypt, even darkness *which* may be felt.

22 And Moses stretched forth his hand toward heaven; and there was a thick darkness in all the land of Egypt three days:

23 They saw not one another, neither rose any from his place for three days: but all the children of Israel had light in their dwellings.

24 ¶ And Pharaoh called unto Moses, and said, Go ye, serve the Lord; only let your flocks and your herds be stayed: let your little ones also go with you.

25 And Moses said, Thou must give us also sacrifices and burnt offerings, that we may sacrifice unto the Lord our God.

26 Our cattle also shall go with us; there shall not an hoof be left behind: for thereof must we take to serve the Lord our God; and we know not with what we must serve the Lord until we come thither.

27 ¶ But the Lord hardened Pharaoh's heart, and he would not let them go.

28 And Pharaoh said unto him, Get thee from me, take heed to thyself, see my face no more: for in *that* day thou seest my face thou shalt die.

29 And Moses said, Thou hast spoken well, I will see thy face again no more.

CHAPTER XI.

1 *God's message to the Israelites to borrow jewels of their neighbours.* 4 *The death of the firstborn of Egypt threatened, etc.*

AND the Lord said unto Moses, Yet will I bring one plague *more* upon Pharaoh, and upon Egypt; afterwards he will let you go hence: when he shall let you go, he shall surely thrust you out hence altogether.

2 Speak now in the ears of the people, and let every man borrow of his neighbour, and every woman of her neighbour, jewels of silver, and jewels of gold.

3 And the Lord gave the people favour in the sight of the Egyptians. Moreover the man Moses *was* very great in the land of Egypt, in the sight of Pharaoh's servants, and in the sight of the people.

4 ¶ And Moses said, Thus saith the Lord, About midnight will I go out into the midst of Egypt:

5 And all the first-born in the land of Egypt shall die, from the first-born of Pharaoh that sitteth upon his throne, even unto the first-born of the maid-servant that *is* behind the mill; and all the first-born of beasts.

6 And there shall be a great cry throughout all the land of Egypt, such as there was none like it, nor shall be like it any more.

7 But against any of the children of Israel shall not a dog move his tongue, against man or beast; that ye may know how that the Lord doth put a difference between the Egyptians and Israel.

8 And all these thy servants shall come down unto me, and bow down themselves unto me, saying, Get thee out, and all the people that follow thee: and after that I will go out. And he went out from Pharaoh in a great anger.

9 And the Lord said unto Moses, Pharaoh shall not hearken unto you; that my wonders may be multiplied in the land of Egypt.

10 And Moses and Aaron did all these wonders before Pharaoh: and the Lord hardened Pharaoh's heart, so that he would not let the children of Israel go out of his land.

CHAPTER XII.

1 *The beginning of the year changed.* 3 *The passover instituted.* 11 *The rite of the passover.* 15 *Unleavened bread.* 29 *The first-born of Egypt are slain.* 31 *The Israelites are driven out of the land.* 43 *Ordinance of the passover.*

AND the Lord spake unto Moses and Aaron in the land of Egypt, saying,

2 This month *shall* be unto you the beginning of months: it *shall* be the first month of the year to you.

3 ¶ Speak ye unto all the congregation of Israel, saying, In the tenth *day* of this month they shall take to them every man a lamb, according to the house of *their* fathers, a lamb for an house.

4 And if the household be too little for the lamb, let him and his neighbour next unto his house take *it* according to the number of the souls: every man according to his eating shall make your count for the lamb.

5 Your lamb shall be without blemish, a male of the first year: ye shall take *it* out from the sheep, or from the goats:

6 And ye shall keep it up until the four-

of the Israelites in the God of their fathers as the only object of worship, 25-32. Pharaoh called for Moses...go, sacrifice, &c.—Between impatient anxiety to be freed from this scourge, and a reluctance to part with the Hebrew bondsmen, the king followed the course of expediency: he proposed to let them free to engage in their religious rites within any part of the kingdom. But true to his instructions, Moses would accede to no such arrangement, he stated a most valid reason to shew the danger of it; and the king having yielded so far as to allow them a brief holiday *across the border*, annexed to this concession a request that Moses would entreat with Jehovah for the removal of the plague. He promised to do so, and it was removed the following day. But no sooner was the pressure over than the spirit of Pharaoh, like a bent bow, sprang back to its wonted obduracy, and regardless of his promise, he refused to let the people depart.

CHAPTER IX.

Ver. 1-7. MURRAIN OF BEASTS. 3. Behold the hand of the Lord is on thy cattle—A fifth application was made to Pharaoh in behalf of the Israelites by Moses, who was instructed to tell him that, if he persisted in opposing their departure, a pestilence would be sent amongst all the flocks and herds of the Egyptians, while those of the Israelites would be spared. As he showed no intention of keeping his promise, he was still a mark for the arrows from the Almighty's quiver, and the threatened plague of which he was forewarned was executed. But it is observable, that in this instance it was not inflicted through the instrumentality or waving of Aaron's rod, but directly by the hand of the Lord, and the fixing of the precise time tended still further to determine the true character of the calamity. (Jer. 12. 4.) 6. all the cattle of Egypt died—not absolutely every beast, for we find (*v.* 19, 21.) that there were still some; but a great many died of each herd—the mortality was frequent and wide-spread. The adaptation of this judgment consisted in the Egyptians venerating the more useful animals, such as the ox, the cow, and the ram; in all parts of the country temples were reared and divine honours paid to these domesticated beasts, and thus while the pestilence caused a great loss in money, it struck a heavy blow at their superstition. 7. Pharaoh sent... there was not one, &c.—The despatch of confidential messengers indicates that he would not give credit to vague reports, and we may conclude that some impression had been made on his mind by that extraordinary exemption, but it was neither a good nor a permanent impression. His pride and obstinacy were in no degree subdued.

8-17. PLAGUE OF BOILS. 8. Take to you handfuls, &c.—The next plague assailed the persons of the Egyptians, and it appeared in the form of ulcerous eruptions upon the skin and flesh. (Le. 13. 20; Job, 2. 7; 2 Ki. 20. 7.) That this epidemic did not arise from natural causes was evident from its taking effect from the particular action of Moses done in the sight of Pharaoh. The attitude he assumed was similar to that of Eastern magicians, who, when they pronounce an imprecation on an individual, a village, or a country, take the ashes of cows' dung (that is, from a common fire) and *throw them in the air*, saying to the objects of their displeasure, such a sickness or such a curse shall come upon you," [ROBERTS.] Moses took ashes from the furnace — *Heb.*, brickkiln. The magicians being sufferers in their own persons, could do nothing, though they had been called; and as the brickkiln was one of the principal instruments of oppression to the Israelites, it was now converted into a means of chastisement to the Egyptians, who were made to read their sin in their punishment.

18-35. PLAGUE OF HAIL. 18. I will cause it to rain, &c.—The seventh plague which Pharaoh's hardened heart provoked was that of hail, a phenomenon which must have produced the greatest astonishment and consternation in Egypt, as rain and hailstones, accompanied by thunder and lightning, were very rare occurrences. such as hath not been in Egypt—In the Delta, or lower Egypt, where the scene is laid, rain occasionally falls between January and March — hail is not unknown, and thunder sometimes heard. But a storm, not only exhibiting all these elements, but so terrific, that hailstones fell of immense size, thunder pealed in awful volleys, and lightning swept the ground like fire, was an unexampled calamity. 20, 21. He that feared ... regarded not, &c.—Due premonition, it appears, had been publicly given of the impending tempest—the cattle seem to have been sent out to graze, which is from January to April, when alone pasturage can be obtained, and accordingly the cattle were in the fields. This storm occurring at that season, not only struck universal terror into the minds of the people, but occasioned the destruction of all—people and cattle, which, in neglect of the warning, had been left in the fields, as well as of all vegetation. It was the more appalling that hailstones in Egypt are small and of little force—lightning also is scarcely ever known to produce fatal effects, and to enhance the wonder, not a trace of any storm was found in Goshen. 31, 32. The flax and barley was smitten, &c.— The peculiarities that are mentioned in these cereal products arise from the climate and physical constitution of Egypt. In that country flax and barley are almost ripe when wheat and rye (spelt) are green. And hence the flax must have been "bolled"—*i.e.*, risen in stalk or podded in February, thus fixing the particular month when the event took place. Barley ripens about a month earlier than wheat. Flax and barley are generally ripe in March, wheat and rye (properly spelt) in April. 27-35. Pharaoh .. I have sinned—this awful display of Divine displeasure did seriously impress the mind of Pharaoh, and, under the weight of his convictions, he humbles himself to confess he has done wrong in opposing the Divine will. At the same time he calls for Moses to intercede for cessation of the calamity. Moses accedes to his earnest wishes, and this most awful visitation ended. But his repentance proved a transient feeling, and his obduracy soon became as great as before.

CHAPTER X.

Ver. 1-20. PLAGUE OF LOCUSTS. 1. shew these my signs, &c.—Sinners even of the worst description are to be admonished, even though there may be little hope of amendment, and hence those striking miracles that carried so clear and conclusive

The rite of the passover.   EXODUS, XII.   *The first-born of Egypt slain.*

teenth day of the same month: and the whole assembly of the congregation of Israel shall kill it ³ in the evening.

7 And they shall take of the blood, and strike it on the two side posts and on the upper door post of the houses, wherein they shall eat it.

8 And they shall eat the flesh in that night, roast with fire, and ᵈ unleavened bread; *and* with bitter *herbs* they shall eat it.

9 Eat not of it raw, nor sodden at all with water, but roast *with* fire; his head with his legs, and with the purtenance thereof.

10 And ᵉ ye shall let nothing of it remain until the morning; and that which remaineth of it until the morning ye shall burn with fire.

11 And thus shall ye eat it; *with* your loins girded, your shoes on your feet, and your staff in your hand; and ye shall eat it in haste: ᶠ it *is* the Lord's passover.

12 For I ᵍ will pass through the land of Egypt this night, and will smite all the first-born in the land of Egypt, both man and beast; and ʰ against all the ⁴ gods of Egypt I will execute judgment: I *am* the Lord.

13 And ⁱ the blood shall be to you for a token upon the houses where ye *are:* and when I see the blood, I will pass over you, and the plague shall not be upon you ᵇ to destroy *you*, when I smite the land of Egypt.

14 And this day shall be unto you for a memorial; and ye shall keep it a ʲ feast to the Lord throughout your generations; ye shall keep it a feast by an ordinance for ever.

15 ¶ Seven ᵏ days shall ye eat unleavened bread; even the first day ye shall put away leaven out of your houses: for whosoever eateth leavened bread from the first day until the seventh day, ˡ that soul shall be cut off from Israel.

16 And in the first day *there shall be* an holy convocation, and in the seventh day there shall be an holy convocation to you; no manner of work shall be done in them, save *that* which every ⁶ man must eat, that only may be done of you.

17 And ye shall observe *the feast of* unleavened bread; for ᵐ in this self-same day have I brought your armies out of the land of Egypt: therefore shall ye observe this day in your generations by an ordinance for ever.

18 In ⁿ the first *month*, on the fourteenth day of the month at even, ye shall eat unleavened bread, until the one and twentieth day of the month at even.

19 Seven ᵒ days shall there be no leaven found in your houses: for whosoever eateth that which is leavened, ᵖ even that soul shall be cut off from the congregation of Israel, whether he be a stranger, or born in the land.

20 Ye shall eat nothing leavened; in all your habitations shall ye eat unleavened bread.

21 ¶ Then Moses called for all the elders of Israel, and said unto them, ᵠ Draw out and take you a ⁷ lamb according to your families, and kill the passover.

22 And ye shall take a bunch of hyssop, and dip *it* in the blood that *is* in the basin, and strike the lintel and the two side posts with the blood that *is* in the basin; and

B. C. 1491.

CHAP. 12.
3 between the two evenings.
ch. 16. 12.
ᵈ Nu. 9. 11.
1 Cor. 5. 8.
ᵉ ch. 23. 18.
ᶠ Deu. 16. 5.
ᵍ ch. 11. 4, 5.
Amos 5.17.
ʰ Nu. 33. 4.
⁴ Or, princes.
ch. 22, 28.
Ps. 82. 1, 6.
John 10.34.
ⁱ Heb. 11. 28.
5 for a destruction.
ʲ Le. 23. 4. 5.
2 Ki. 23. 21.
ᵏ Nu. 28. 17.
De. 16. 3, 8.
1 Cor. 5. 7.
ˡ Gen. 17. 14.
Nu. 9. 13.
6 soul.
ᵐ ch. 13. 3.
ⁿ Lev. 23. 5.
ᵒ ch. 23. 15.
ch. 34. 18.
ᵖ Nu. 9. 13.
ᵠ Nu. 9. 4.
Josh. 5. 10.
Ezra 6. 20.
Lu. 22. 7.
⁷ Or, kid.
ʳ Ezek. 9. 6.
Rev. 7. 3.
Rev. 9. 4.
ˢ 2 Sa. 24. 10.
1 Cor. 10.10.
ᵗ Deu. 32. 7.
Josh. 4. 6.
Ps. 78. 6.
ᵘ Nu. 8. 17.
Nu. 33. 4.
Ps. 135. 8.
Ps. 136. 10.
Is. 37. 36.
8 house of the pit.
ᵛ ch. 11. 6.
Pro. 21. 13.
Ezek. 7. 27.
Jam. 2. 13.
ʷ ch. 10. 9.
ˣ Gen. 27. 34.
ʸ ch. 11. 8.
Ps. 105. 38.
ᶻ Gen. 20. 3.
9 Or, dough.
ch. 8. 3.
10 Or, demanded.
ᵃ ch. 3. 22.
ch. 11. 2.
ᵇ Gen. 15. 14.
ch. 3. 22.
ᶜ Gen. 33. 3, 5.
ᵈ Gen. 47. 11.
ᵉ Gen. 12. 2.
Gen. 46. 3.
ch. 38. 26.
Num. 1. 46.
Num. 11. 21.
11 a great mixture.
Nu. 11. 4.
ᶠ ch. 6. 1.
ch. 11. 1.
ᵍ Ge. 15. 13.
Acts 7. 6.
Gal. 3. 17.

none of you shall go out at the door of his house until the morning.

23 For the Lord will pass through to smite the Egyptians; and when he seeth the blood upon the lintel, and on the two side posts, the Lord will pass over the door, and ʳ will not suffer ᵉ the destroyer to come in unto your houses to smite *you*.

24 And ye shall observe this thing for an ordinance to thee and to thy sons for ever.

25 And it shall come to pass, when ye be come to the land which the Lord will give you, according as he hath promised, that ye shall keep this service.

26 And ᵗ it shall come to pass, when your children shall say unto you, What mean ye by this service?

27 That ye shall say, It *is* the sacrifice of the Lord's passover, who passed over the houses of the children of Israel in Egypt, when he smote the Egyptians, and delivered our houses. And the people bowed the head and worshipped.

28 And the children of Israel went away, and did as the Lord had commanded Moses and Aaron, so did they.

29 ¶ And it came to pass, that at midnight the ᵘ Lord smote all the first-born in the land of Egypt, from the first-born of Pharaoh that sat on his throne unto the first-born of the captive that *was* in the ⁸ dungeon; and all the first-born of cattle.

30 And Pharaoh rose up in the night, he, and all his servants, and all the Egyptians; and there was a ᵛ great cry in Egypt; for *there was* not a house where *there was* not one dead.

31 ¶ And he called for Moses and Aaron by night, and said, Rise up, *and* get you forth from among my people, ʷ both ye and the children of Israel; and go, serve the Lord, as ye have said.

32 Also take your flocks and your herds, as ye have said, and be gone; and ˣ bless me also.

33 And ʸ the Egyptians were urgent upon the people, that they might send them out of the land in haste; for they said, ᶻ We *be* all dead *men*.

34 And the people took their dough before it was leavened, their ⁹ kneading troughs being bound up in their clothes upon their shoulders.

35 And the children of Israel did according to the word of Moses; and they ¹⁰ borrowed of the Egyptians ᵃ jewels of silver, and jewels of gold, and raiment.

36 And the Lord gave the people favour in the sight of the Egyptians, so that they lent unto them *such things as they required:* and ᵇ they spoiled the Egyptians.

37 ¶ And ᶜ the children of Israel journeyed from ᵈ Rameses to Succoth, about ᵉ six hundred thousand on foot *that were* men, besides children.

38 And ¹¹ a mixed multitude went up also with them; and flocks and herds, *even* very much cattle.

39 And they baked unleavened cakes of the dough which they brought forth out of Egypt, for it was not leavened; because they ᶠ were thrust out of Egypt, and could not tarry, neither had they prepared for themselves any victual.

40 ¶ Now the sojourning of the children of Israel, who dwelt in Egypt, *was* ᵍ four hundred and thirty years.

41 And it came to pass at the end of the

demonstration of the being and character of the true God were performed in lengthened series before Pharaoh to leave him without excuse, when judgment should be finally executed. 2. and that thou mayest tell, &c.—There was a further and higher reason for the infliction of those awful judgments, viz., that the knowledge of them there, and the permanent record of them still might furnish a salutary and impressive lesson to the Church down to the latest ages. Worldly historians might have described them as extraordinary occurrences that marked this era of Moses in ancient Egypt. But we are taught to trace them to their cause; the judgments of divine wrath on a grossly idolatrous king and nation. 4. to-morrow, I will bring locusts—Moses was commissioned to renew the request so often made and denied, with an assurance that an unfavourable answer would be followed on the morrow by an invasion of locusts. This species of insect resembles a large, spotted, red and black, double-winged grasshopper, about three inches or less in length, with the two hind legs working like hinged springs of immense strength and elasticity. Perhaps no more terrible scourge was ever brought on a land than those voracious insects, which fly in such countless numbers as to darken the land which they infest, and on whatever place they alight, they convert it into a waste and barren desert, stripping the ground of its verdure, the trees of their leaves and bark, and producing in a few hours a degree of desolation, which it requires the lapse of years to repair. 7-11. Pharaoh's servants said—Many of his courtiers must have suffered serious losses from the late visitations, and the prospect of such a calamity, as that which was threatened and the magnitude of which former experience enabled them to realise, led them to make a strong remonstrance with the king. Finding himself not seconded by his counsellors in his continued resistance, he recalled Moses and Aaron, and having expressed his consent to their departure, inquired who were to go? The prompt and decisive reply, "all;" neither man nor beast shall remain, raised a storm of indignant fury in the breast of the proud king; he would permit the grown up men to go away. But no other terms would be listened to. they were driven out, &c.—In the East, when a person of authority and rank feels annoyed by a petition which he is unwilling to grant, he makes a signal to his attendants who rush forward, and seizing the obnoxious suppliant by the neck, drag him out of the chamber with violent haste. Of such a character was the impassioned scene in the court of Egypt, when the king had wrought himself into such a fit of uncontrollable fury as to treat ignominiously the two venerable representatives of the Hebrew people. 13. The Lord brought an east wind—The rod of Moses was again raised, and the locusts came. They are natives of the desert, and are only brought by an East wind into Egypt, where they sometimes come in sun-obscuring clouds, destroying in a few days every green blade in the track they traverse. Man, with all his contrivances, can do nothing to protect himself from the overwhelming invasion. Egypt has often suffered from locusts. But the one that followed the wave of the miraculous rod was altogether unexampled. Pharaoh fearing irretrievable ruin to his country, sent in haste for Moses, and confessing his sin, implored the intercession of Moses, who entreated the Lord, and a "mighty strong west wind took away the locusts."

21-23. PLAGUE OF DARKNESS. 21. Stretch out thine hand...darkness—Whatever secondary means were employed in producing it, whether thick clammy fogs and vapours, according to some, a sand-storm, or the chamsin, according to others; it was such that it could be almost perceived by the organs of touch, and so protracted as to continue for three days, which the chamsin does. [HENG.] The appalling character of this calamity consisted in this that the sun was an object of Egyptian idolatry; that their pure and serene sky of that country was never marred by the appearance of a cloud. And here, too, the Lord made a marked difference between Goshen and the rest of Egypt. 24-26. Pharaoh called unto Moses—Terrified by the preternatural darkness, the stubborn king relents, and proposes another compromise—the flocks and herds to be left, as hostages for their return. But the crisis is approaching, and Moses insists on all he had asked for. The cattle would be needed for sacrifice—how many or how few, could not be known till their arrival at the scene of religious observance. But the emancipation of Israel from Egyptian bondage was to be complete. 28. Pharaoh said, Get thee from me—The calm firmness of Moses provoked the tyrant. Frantic with disappointment and rage, with offended and desperate malice, he ordered him from his presence, and forbade him ever to return. 29. Moses said, Thou hast spoken well.

CHAPTER XI.

Ver. 1-8. 1. DEATH OF THE FIRST-BORN THREATENED. 1. The Lord said—rather HAD said unto Moses. It may be inferred, therefore, that he had been apprized that the crisis was now arrived, that the next plague would so effectually humble and alarm the mind of Pharaoh, that he would "*thrust* them out thence altogether;" and thus the word of Moses (ch. 10. 29.), must be regarded as a prediction. 2, 3. Speak now in the ears of the people—These verses, describing the communication which had been made in private to Moses, are inserted here as a parenthesis, and will be considered (ch. 12. 35.). 4. Thus saith the Lord, About midnight—Here is recorded the announcement of the last plague made in the most solemn manner to the king, on whose hardened heart all his painful experience had hitherto produced no softening, at least no permanently good effect. will I go out—Language used after the manner of men. 5. all the first-born in the land shall die—the time, the suddenness, the dreadful severity of this coming calamity, and the peculiar description of victims, both amongst men and beasts, on whom it was to fall, would all contribute to aggravate its character. maid-servant... behind the mill—The grinding of the meal for daily use in every household is commonly done by female slaves, and is considered the lowest employment. Two portable millstones are used for the purpose, of which the uppermost is turned by a small wooden handle, and during the operation the maid sits behind the mill. 6. shall be a great cry—In the case of a death,

four hundred and thirty years, even the self-same day it came to pass, that all ʰ the hosts of the LORD went out from the land of Egypt.

42 It is ¹² a night to be much observed unto the LORD for bringing them out from the land of Egypt: this is that night of the LORD to be observed of all the children of Israel in their generations.

43 ¶ And the LORD said unto Moses and Aaron, This is ⁱ the ordinance of the passover: There shall no stranger eat thereof:

44 But every man's servant that is bought for money, when thou hast ʲ circumcised him, then shall he eat thereof.

45 A ᵏ foreigner and an hired servant shall not eat thereof.

46 In one house shall it be eaten: thou shalt not carry forth ought of the flesh abroad out of the house; ˡ neither shall ye break a bone thereof.

47 All the congregation of Israel shall ¹³ keep it.

48 And ᵐ when a stranger shall sojourn with thee, and will keep the passover to the LORD, let all his males be circumcised, and then let him come near and keep it; and he shall be as one that is born in the land: for no uncircumcised person shall eat thereof.

49 One ⁿ law shall be to him that is homeborn, and unto the stranger that sojourneth among you.

50 Thus did all the children of Israel; as the LORD commanded Moses and Aaron, so did they.

51 And it came to pass the self-same day, that the LORD did bring the children of Israel out of the land of Egypt by ᵒ their armies.

CHAPTER XIII.

1 *The first-born sanctified to God.* 3 *The memorial of the passover is commanded to be observed yearly.* 11 *The firstlings of beasts are set apart.* 17 *The Israelites go out of Egypt, and carry Joseph's bones with them.* 20 *they come to Etham:* 21 *God guideth them by a pillar of a cloud and a pillar of fire.*

AND the LORD spake unto Moses, saying, 2 Sanctify ᵃ unto me all the first-born, whatsoever openeth the womb among the children of Israel, both of man and of beast: it is mine.

3 ¶ And Moses said unto the people, ᵇ Remember this day, in which ye came out from Egypt, out of the house of ¹ bondage; for by ᶜ strength of hand the LORD brought you out from this place: there shall no leavened bread be eaten.

4 This ᵈ day came ye out, in the month Abib.

5 And it shall be, when the LORD shall bring thee into the land of the Canaanites, and the Hittites, and the Amorites, and the Hivites, and the Jebusites, which he sware unto thy fathers to give thee, a land flowing with milk and honey, that thou shalt keep this service in this month.

6 Seven ᵉ days thou shalt eat unleavened bread, and in the seventh day shall be a feast to the LORD.

7 Unleavened bread shall be eaten seven days; and there shall no leavened bread be seen with thee, neither shall there be leaven seen with thee in all thy quarters.

8 And thou shalt ᶠ show thy son in that day, saying, This is done because of that which the LORD did unto me when I came forth out of Egypt.

9 And it shall be for a ᵍ sign unto thee upon thine hand, and for a memorial between thine eyes, that the LORD's law may be in thy mouth: for with a strong hand hath the LORD brought thee out of Egypt.

10 Thou shalt therefore keep this ordinance in his season from year to year.

11 ¶ And it shall be, when the LORD shall bring thee into the land of the Canaanites, as he ʰ sware unto thee and to thy fathers, and shall give it thee,

12 That ⁱ thou shalt ² set apart unto the LORD all that openeth the matrix, and every firstling that cometh of a beast which thou hast; the males shall be the LORD's.

13 And every firstling of an ass thou shalt redeem with a ³ lamb; and if thou wilt not redeem it, then thou shalt break his neck: and all the first-born of man among thy children ʲ shalt thou redeem.

14 ¶ And ᵏ it shall be when thy son asketh thee ⁴ in time to come, saying, What is this? that thou shalt say unto him, By strength of hand the LORD brought us out from Egypt, from the house of bondage:

15 And it came to pass, when Pharaoh would hardly let us go, that the LORD slew all the first-born in the land of Egypt, both the first-born of man, and the first-born of beast: therefore I sacrifice to the LORD all that openeth the matrix, being males; but all the first-born of my children I redeem.

16 And it shall be for ⁴ a token upon thine hand, and for frontlets between thine eyes: for by strength of hand the LORD brought us forth out of Egypt.

17 ¶ And it came to pass, when Pharaoh had let the people go, that God led them not through the way of the land of the Philistines, although that was near; for God said, Lest peradventure the people repent ᵐ when they see war, and ⁿ they return to Egypt:

18 But God ᵒ led the people about, through the way of the wilderness of the Red sea. And the children of Israel went up ⁵ harnessed out of the land of Egypt.

19 And Moses took the bones of Joseph with him: for he had straitly sworn the children of Israel, saying, ᵖ God will surely visit you; and ye shall carry up my bones away hence with you.

20 ¶ And ᑫ they took their journey from Succoth, and encamped in Etham, in the edge of the wilderness.

21 And ʳ the LORD went before them by day in a pillar of a cloud, to lead them the way; and by night in a pillar of fire, to give them light; to go by day and night:

22 He ˢ took not away the pillar of the cloud by day, nor the pillar of fire by night, from before the people.

CHAPTER XIV.

1 *God instructeth the Israelites in their journey.* 5 *Pharaoh pursueth.* 10 *The Israelites murmur;* 13 *Moses comforteth them.* 15 *God instructeth Moses.* 19 *The cloud removeth behind the camp.* 21 *They pass through the Red sea.* 26 *The Egyptians drowned.*

AND the LORD spake unto Moses, saying, 2 Speak unto the children of Israel, that they turn and encamp before ᵃ Pihahiroth, between ᵇ Migdol and the sea, over against Baal-zephon: before it shall ye encamp by the sea.

3 For Pharaoh will say of the children of Israel, ᶜ They are entangled in the land, the wilderness hath shut them in.

people in the East set up loud wailings, and imagination may conceive what "a great cry" would be raised when death would invade every family in the kingdom. **7.** not a dog— No town or village in Egypt or in the East generally is free from the nuisance of dogs, who prowl about the streets and make the most hideous noise at any passengers at night. What an emphatic significance does the knowledge of this circumstance give to the fact in the sacred record, that on the awful night that was coming, when the air should be rent with the piercing shrieks of mourners, so great and universal would be the panic inspired by the hand of God, that not a dog would move his tongue against the children of Israel. **8.** all these thy servants shall bow themselves unto me—This should be the effect of the universal terror; the hearts of the proudest would be humbled and do reverential homage to God, in the person of His representative. went out in great anger —holy and righteous indignation at the duplicity, repeated falsehood, and hardened impenitence of the king; and this strong emotion was stirred in the bosom of Moses, not at the ill reception given to himself, but the dishonour done to God. (M. 19. 8; Eph. 4. 26.)

CHAPTER XII.

Ver. 1-10. THE PASSOVER INSTITUTED. **1.** The Lord spake—rather *had* spoken unto Moses and Aaron, for it is evident that the communication here described must have been made to them on or before the tenth of the month. **2.** This month....the beginning of months—The first not only in order, but in estimation. It had formerly been the seventh according to the reckoning of the civil year, which began in September, and continued unchanged, but it was thenceforth to stand first in the national religious year which began in March, April. **3.** Speak ye unto all the congregation—The recent events had prepared the Israelitish people for a crisis in their affairs, and they seem to have yielded implicit obedience at this time to Moses. It is observable that, amid all the hurry and bustle of such a departure, their serious attention was to be given to a solemn act of religion. a lamb for a house—a kid might be taken *v*. 5.) The service was to be a domestic one, for the deliverance was to be from an evil threatened to every house in Egypt. **4.** If the household, &c.—It appears from Josephus that ten persons were required to make up the proper paschal communion. every man according to his eating—It is said that the quantity eaten of the paschal lamb, by each individual, was about the size of an olive. **5.** lamb without blemish—The smallest deformity or defect made a lamb unfit for sacrifice—a type of Christ. (He. 7. 26; 1 Pe. 1. 19.) male of the first year—Christ in the prime of life. **6.** keep it, &c.—being selected from the rest of the flock it was to be separated four days before sacrifice; and for the same length of time was Christ under examination and his spotless innocence declared before the world. kill it in the evening—*i.e.*, the interval between the sun's beginning to decline, and sunset, corresponding to our three o'clock in the afternoon. **7.** Strike it, &c.—as a sign of safety to those within. The posts must be considered of tents, in which the Israelites generally lived, though some might be in houses. Though the Israelites were sinners as well as the Egyptians, God was pleased to accept the substitution of a lamb—the blood of which being seen *sprinkled* on the door-posts, procured them mercy. It was to be on the sideposts and upper door-posts, where it might be *looked to*, not on the threshold, where it might be trodden under foot. This was an emblem of the blood of sprinkling. (He. 12, 24, 29.) **8.** Roast with fire—for the sake of expedition; and this difference was always observed between the cooking of the paschal lamb and the other offerings. (2 Ch. 35. 13.) unleavened bread — also for the sake of despatch (Deut. 16. 3,) but as leaven is corruption (Lu. 12. 1,) there seems to have been a typical meaning under it. (1 Co. 5. 8,) bitter herbs—*lit.* bitters—to remind the Israelites of their affliction in Egypt, and morally of the trials to which God's people are subject on account of sin. **9.** Eat not of it raw—*i. e.*, with any blood remaining—a caveat against conformity to idolatrous practices. It was to be roasted whole, not a bone to be broken, and this pointed to Christ. (J. 19. 36.) **10.** let nothing remain— which might be applied in a superstitious manner, or allowed to putrefy, which in a hot climate would speedily have ensued; and which was not becoming in what had been offered to God.

11-14. THE RITE OF THE PASSOVER. **11.** loins girded...shoes on feet—as prepared for a journey. The first was done by the skirts of the loose outer cloth being drawn up and fastened in the girdle, so as to leave the leg and knee free for motion. As to the other the Orientals never wear shoes in-doors, and the ancient Egyptians, as appears from the monuments, did not usually wear either shoes or sandals. These injunctions seem to have applied chiefly to the first celebration of the rite. It is the Lord's passover— called by this name from the blood-marked dwellings of the Israelites being *passed* over figuratively by the destroying angel. **12.** smite...gods of Egypt—perhaps used here for princes and grandees. But, according to Jewish tradition, the idols of Egypt were all on that night broken in pieces. (See Nu. 33. 4; Is. 19. 1.) **13, 14.** for a memorial, &c.—The close analogy traceable in all points between the Jewish and Christian passovers is seen also in the circumstance that both festivals were instituted before the events they were to commemorate had transpired.

15-51. UNLEAVENED BREAD. **15.** Seven days ...Eat, &c.—This was to commemorate another circumstance in the departure of the Israelites, who were urged to leave so hurriedly that their dough was unleavened (*v*. 39), and they had to eat unleavened cakes. (Deut. 16. 3.) The greatest care was always taken by the Jews to free their houses from leaven—the owner searching every corner of his dwelling with a lighted candle. A figurative allusion to this is made (1 Co. 5. 7.) The exclusion of leaven for seven days would not be attended with inconvenience in the East, where the usual leaven is dough, kept till it becomes sour, and it is kept from one day to another for the purpose of preserving leaven in readiness. Thus even were there none in all the country, it could be got within twenty-four hours. [HARMER.] cut off — Excommunicated from the community and privileges of the chosen people. **16.** holy

4 And ᵈ I will harden Pharaoh's heart, that he shall follow after them; and I ᵉ will be honoured upon Pharaoh, and upon all his host; that the Egyptians may know that I am the Lord. And they did so.

5 ¶ And it was told the king of Egypt that the people fled: and the heart of Pharaoh and of his servants was turned against the people, and they said, Why have we done this, that we have let Israel go from serving us?

6 And he made ready his chariot, and took his people with him:

7 And he took six hundred chosen chariots, and all the chariots of Egypt, and captains over every one of them.

8 And the Lord hardened the heart of Pharaoh king of Egypt, and he pursued after the children of Israel: and ᶠ the children of Israel went out with an high hand.

9 But the ᵍ Egyptians pursued after them, all the horses and chariots of Pharaoh, and his horsemen, and his army, and overtook them encamping by the sea, beside Pi-hahiroth, before Baal-zephon.

10 ¶ And when Pharaoh drew nigh, the children of Israel lifted up their eyes, and, behold, the Egyptians marched after them; and they were sore afraid: and the children of Israel cried out unto the Lord.

11 And ⁱ they said unto Moses, Because there were no graves in Egypt, hast thou taken us away to die in the wilderness? wherefore hast thou dealt thus with us, to carry us forth out of Egypt?

12 Is ʲ not this the word that we did tell thee in Egypt, saying, Let us alone, that we may serve the Egyptians? For it had been better for us to serve the Egyptians, than that we should die in the wilderness.

13 ¶ And Moses said unto the people, Fear ᵏ ye not, stand still, and see the salvation of the Lord, which he will show to you to-day: ˡ for the Egyptians whom ye have seen to-day, ye shall see them again no more for ever.

14 The ˡ Lord shall fight for you, and ye shall ᵐ hold your peace.

15 ¶ And the Lord said unto Moses, Wherefore criest thou unto me? speak unto the children of Israel, that they go forward:

16 But ⁿ lift thou up thy rod, and stretch out thine hand over the sea, and divide it; and the children of Israel shall go on dry ground through the midst of the sea.

17 And I, behold, I will ᵒ harden the hearts of the Egyptians, and they shall follow them: and I will get me honour upon Pharaoh, and upon all his host, upon his chariots, and upon his horsemen.

18 And the Egyptians shall know that I am the Lord, when I have gotten me honour upon Pharaoh, upon his chariots, and upon his horsemen.

19 ¶ And ᵖ the angel of God, which went before the camp of Israel, removed and went behind them; and the pillar of the cloud went from before their face, and stood behind them:

20 And it came between the camp of the Egyptians and the camp of Israel; and ᵠ it was a cloud and darkness to them, but it gave light by night to these: so that the one came not near the other all the night.

21 And Moses stretched out his hand over the sea; and the Lord caused the sea to go back by a strong east wind all that night,

and made the sea dry land, and the waters were ʳ divided.

22 And ˢ the children of Israel went into the midst of the sea upon the dry ground: and the waters were ᵗ a wall unto them on their right hand, and on their left.

23 ¶ And the Egyptians pursued, and went in after them to the midst of the sea, even all Pharaoh's horses, his chariots, and his horsemen.

24 And it came to pass, that in the morning watch the Lord looked unto the host of the Egyptians through the pillar of fire and of the cloud, and troubled the host of the Egyptians,

25 And took off their chariot wheels, ᵘ that they drave them heavily: so that the Egyptians said, Let us flee from the face of Israel; for the Lord fighteth for them against the Egyptians.

26 And the Lord said unto Moses, Stretch out thine hand over the sea, that the waters may come again upon the Egyptians, upon their chariots, and upon their horsemen.

27 And Moses stretched forth his hand over the sea, and the sea ᵛ returned to his strength when the morning appeared; and the Egyptians fled against it; and the Lord ʷ overthrew the Egyptians in the midst of the sea.

28 And ˣ the waters returned, and covered the chariots, and the horsemen, and all the host of Pharaoh that came into the sea after them; there remained not so much as one of them.

29 But ʸ the children of Israel walked upon dry land in the midst of the sea: and the waters were a wall unto them on their right hand, and on their left.

30 Thus the Lord ᶻ saved Israel that day out of the hand of the Egyptians: and Israel saw ᵃ the Egyptians dead upon the seashore.

31 And Israel saw that great ᵇ work which the Lord did upon the Egyptians: and the people feared the Lord, and ᶜ believed the Lord, and his servant Moses.

CHAPTER XV.

1 Moses' song. 23 The people want water. 23 The bitter waters at Marah are sweetened. 27 They remove to Elim.

THEN sang ᵃ Moses and the children of Israel this song unto the Lord, and spake, saying, I will sing unto the Lord, for he hath triumphed gloriously: the horse and his rider hath he thrown into the sea.

2 The Lord is my strength and ᵇ song, and he is become my salvation: he is my God, and I will prepare him an habitation; my father's God, and I ᶜ will exalt him.

3 The Lord is a man of ᵈ war: the Lord is his ᵉ name.

4 Pharaoh's chariots and his host hath he cast into the sea: his chosen captains also are drowned in the Red sea.

5 The depths have covered them: they sank into the bottom as a stone.

6 ᶠ Thy right hand, O Lord, is become glorious in power: thy right hand, O Lord, hath dashed in pieces the enemy.

7 And in the greatness of thine excellency thou hast overthrown them that rose up against thee: thou sentest forth thy wrath, which consumed them ʰ as stubble.

8 And ⁱ with the blast of thy nostrils the waters were gathered together, ʲ the floods stood upright as an heap, and the depths were congealed in the heart of the sea.

convocation—*lit. calling* of the people, which was done by sound of trumpet, (Nu. 10. 2,) a sacred assembly—for these days were to be regarded as Sabbaths—excepting only that meat might be cooked on them (ch. 6. 23.) **16. Ye shall observe,&c.**—The seven days of this feast were to commence the day after the passover. It was a distinct festival following that feast; but although this feast was instituted like the passover *before* the departure, the observance of it did not take place till *after*. **19. Stranger**—No foreigner could partake of the passover, unless circumcised—The "stranger" specified as admissible to the privilege must, therefore, be considered a gentile *proselyte*. **21-25. Then Moses called, &c.**—Here are given special directions for the observance. **hyssop**—a small red moss, [HASSELQUIST.] The caper-plant, [ROYLE.] It was used in the sprinkling, being well adapted for such purposes, as it grows in bushes—putting out plenty of suckers from a single root. And it is remarkable that it was ordained in the arrangements of an all-wise Providence that the Roman soldiers should undesignedly, on their part, make use of this symbolical plant to Christ when, as our passover, he was sacrificed for us. **None shall go out, &c.**—this regulation was peculiar to the first celebration, and intended, as some think, to prevent any suspicion attaching to them of being agents in the impending destruction of the Egyptians; there is an allusion to it, (Is. 26. 20.). **26. When your children shall say**—independently of some observances which were not afterwards repeated, the usages practised at this yearly commemorative feast were so peculiar that the curiosity of the young would be stimulated, and thus parents have an excellent opportunity which they were enjoined to embrace for instructing each rising generation in the origin and leading facts of the national faith. **27, 28. people bowed the head**—All the preceding directions were communicated through the elders, and the Israelites being deeply solemnized by the influence of past and prospective events, gave prompt and faithful obedience. **29. at midnight the Lord smote**—At the moment when the Israelites were observing the newly instituted feast in the singular manner described, the threatened calamity overtook the Egyptians. It is more easy to imagine than describe the confusion and terror of that people suddenly roused from sleep and enveloped in darkness—none could assist their neighbours, when the groans of the dying and the wild shrieks of mourners were heard every where around. The hope of every family was destroyed at a stroke. This judgment, terrible though it was, evinces the equity of divine retribution. For eighty years the Egyptians had caused the male children of the Israelites to be cast into the river, and now all their own first-born fell under the stroke of the destroying angel. They were made, in the justice of God, to feel something of what they had made His people feel. Many a time have the hands of sinners made the snares in which they have themselves been entangled, and fallen into the pit which they have dug for the righteous. "Verily there is a God that judgeth in the earth." **30. not a house where ... not one dead**—Perhaps this statement is not to be taken absolutely. The Scriptures frequently use the word "all," "none," in a comparative sense—and so in this case. There would be many a house in which there would be no child, and many in which the first-born might be already dead. What is to be understood is, that almost every house in Egypt had a death in it. **31. called for Moses and Aaron**—a striking fulfilment of the words of Moses (ch. 11. 8.), and showing that they were spoken under divine suggestion. **32. also take your flocks, &c.**—all the terms the king had formerly insisted on were now departed from, his pride had been effectually humbled. Appalling judgments in such rapid succession showed plainly that the hand of God was against him. His own family bereavement had so crushed him to the earth that he not only showed impatience to rid his kingdom of such formidable neighbours, but even begged an interest in their prayers. **34. people took ... kneading troughs**—Having lived so long in Egypt, they must have been in the habit of using the utensils common in that country. The Egyptian kneading trough was a bowl of wicker or rush work, and it admitted of being hastily wrapped up with the dough in it and slung over the shoulder in their *hykes* or loose upper garments. **35. Children of Israel borrowed**—When the Orientals go to their sacred festivals, they always put on their *best jewels*. The Israelites themselves thought they were only going 3 days' journey to hold a feast unto the Lord, and in these circumstances it would be easy for them to *borrow* what was necessary for a sacred festival. But "borrow" conveys a wrong meaning. The word rendered *borrow* signifies properly to *ask, demand, require*. The Israelites had been kept in great poverty, having received little or no wages. They now insisted on full remuneration for all their labour, and it was paid in light and valuable articles adapted for convenient carriage. **36. The Lord gave the people favour**—Such a dread of them was inspired into the universal minds of the Egyptians, that whatever they asked was readily given. **spoiled the Egyptians**—the accumulated earnings of many years being paid them at this moment, the Israelites were suddenly enriched, according to the promise made to Abraham, (Ge. 15. 14.) and they left the country like a victorious army laden with spoil. (Ps. 105. 37; Ez. 39. 10.) **37. Journeyed from Rameses**—now generally identified with the ancient Heroopolis, and fixed at the modern *Abu*-Keisheid. This position agrees with the statement that the scene of the miraculous judgments against Pharaoh was "in the field of Zoan." And it is probable that, in expectation of their departure, which the king on one pretext or another delayed, the Israelites had been assembled there as a general rendezvous. In journeying from Rameses to Palestine, there was a choice of two routes—the one along the shores of the Mediterranean to El-Arish, the other more circuitous round the head of the Red Sea and the desert of Sinai. The latter Moses was directed to take. (ch. 13. 17.) to **Succoth**—*i.e.*, booths, probably nothing more than a place of temporary encampment. The Hebrew word signifies a covering or shelter, formed by the boughs of trees; and hence, in memory of this lodgement, the Israelites kept the feast of tabernacles yearly in this manner. **six hundred thousand men**—It appears from Num. 1. that the enu-

9 The enemy said, I will pursue, I will overtake, I will *k* divide the spoil; my lust shall be satisfied upon them; I will draw my sword, my hand shall *l* destroy them.
10 Thou didst blow with thy wind, the sea covered them: they sank as lead in the mighty waters.
11 Who *is* like unto thee, O LORD, among the *2* gods! who *is* like thee, glorious in holiness, fearful *in* praises, doing wonders!
12 Thou stretchedst out thy right hand, the earth swallowed them.
13 Thou in thy mercy hast led forth the people *which* thou hast redeemed: thou hast guided *them* in thy strength unto *m* thy holy habitation.
14 The *n* people shall hear, *and* be afraid: sorrow *o* shall take hold on the inhabitants of Palestina.
15 Then the dukes of Edom shall be amazed; *p* the mighty men of Moab, trembling shall take hold upon them; all the inhabitants of Canaan shall melt away.
16 Fear *q* and dread shall fall upon them; by the greatness of thine arm they shall be *as* still *as* a stone; till thy people pass over, O LORD, till the people pass over, *which r* thou hast purchased.
17 Thou shalt bring them in, and *s* plant them in the mountain of thine inheritance, in the place, O LORD, *which* thou hast made for thee to dwell in; *in* the Sanctuary, O LORD, *which* thy hands have established.
18 The LORD shall reign for ever and ever.
19 For the horse of Pharaoh went in with his chariots and with his horsemen into the sea, and the LORD brought again the waters of the sea upon them; but the children of Israel went on dry *land* in the midst of the sea.
20 ¶ And Miriam the prophetess, the sister of Aaron, *u* took a timbrel in her hand; and all the women went out after her with timbrels and with dances.
21 And Miriam answered them, Sing ye to the LORD, for he hath triumphed gloriously; the horse and his rider hath he thrown into the sea.
22 ¶ So Moses brought Israel from the Red sea; and they went out into the wilderness of Shur; and they went three days in the wilderness, and found no water.
23 ¶ And when they came to *v* Marah, they could not drink of the waters of Marah, for they *were* bitter: therefore the name of it was called *x* Marah.
24 And the people murmured against Moses, saying, What shall we drink?
25 And he *w* cried unto the LORD; and the LORD showed him a tree, *x which* when he had cast into the waters, the waters were made sweet: there he *y* made for them a statute and an ordinance, and there *z* he proved them,
26 And said, *a* If thou wilt diligently hearken to the voice of the LORD thy God, and wilt do that which is right in his sight, and will give ear to his commandments, and keep all his statutes, I will put none of these *b* diseases upon thee, which I have brought upon the Egyptians: for I *am* the LORD *c* that healeth thee.
27 ¶ And *d* they came to Elim, where *were* twelve wells of water, and threescore and ten palm trees: and they encamped there by the waters.

54

B. C. 1491.

CHAP. 15.
k Is. 53. 12.
Lu. 11. 22.
1 Or. repossess.
l 2 Sa. 7. 23.
1 Ki. 8. 23.
Ps. 86. 8.
Jer. 49. 19.
2 Or, mighty ones.
m Ps. 78. 54.
l Josh. 2. 9.
o Ps. 48. 6.
p Hab. 3. 7.
q Deu. 2. 25.
l 1 Sa. 25. 37.
s Deu. 32. 9.
Is. 43. 1.
Jer. 31. 11.
Ti. 2. 14.
1 Pet. 2. 9.
2 Pet. 2. 1.
u Ps. 44. 2.
v 1 Sa. 18. 6.
r Nu. 33. 8.
3 That is, bitterness.
Ruth 1. 20.
w Ps. 50. 15.
x 2 Ki. 2. 21.
y Josh. 24. 25.
z De. 8. 2. 16.
Ju. 3. 1. 4.
Ps. 81. 7.
a Deu. 7. 12.
b Deu. 28. 27.
c Ps. 41. 3. 4.
Ps. 103. 3.
Ps. 147. 3.
d Nu. 33. 9.

CHAP. 16.
b Ex. 30. 15.
b Ps. 106. 25.
1 Cor. 10. 10.
c Num. 11. 4.
d John 6. 31.
1 Cor. 10. 3.
1 the portion of a day in his day.
Pro. 30. 8.
Mat. 6. 11.
e De. 8. 2. 16.
f Lev. 25. 21.
g Nu. 16. 22.
h Is. 35. 2.
John 11. 4, 40.
i 1 Sam. 8. 7.
Lu. 10. 16.
Rom. 13. 2.
1 Thess. 4. 8.
j 1 Ki. 8. 10.
k Nu. 14. 27.
l ver. 6.
m ver. 7.
n ch. 6. 7.
1 Ki. 20. 28.
Joel 3. 17.
o Nu. 11. 31.
Ps. 105. 40.
p Nu. 11. 9.
q Nu. 11. 7.
Deut. 8. 3.
Neh. 9. 15.
Ps. 78. 24.
Ps. 105. 40.
2 Or, What is this? or, it is a portion.
r Is. 25. 6.
John 6. 31, 49. &c.
1 Cor. 10. 3.

CHAPTER XVI.

1 *The Israelites come to Sin.* 2 *They murmur for want of bread.* 11 *Quails and manna are sent.* 25 *The manna was not to be found on the sabbath.* 32 *An omer of it preserved.*

AND they took their journey from Elim, and all the congregation of the children of Israel came unto the wilderness of *a* Sin, which *is* between Elim and Sinai, on the fifteenth day of the second month after their departing out of the land of Egypt.
2 And the whole congregation of the children of Israel *b* murmured against Moses and Aaron in the wilderness:
3 And the children of Israel said unto them, Would to God we had died by the hand of the LORD in the land of Egypt, when *c* we sat by the flesh pots, *and* when we did eat bread to the full: for ye have brought us forth into this wilderness, to kill this whole assembly with hunger.
4 ¶ Then said the LORD unto Moses, Behold, I will rain *d* bread from heaven for you; and the people shall go out and gather *1* a certain rate every day, that I *e* may prove them, whether they will walk in my law, or no.
5 And it shall come to pass, that on the sixth day they shall prepare *that* which they bring in; and *f it* shall be twice as much as they gather daily.
6 And Moses and Aaron said unto all the children of Israel, *g* At even, then ye shall know that the LORD hath brought you out from the land of Egypt:
7 And in the morning, then ye shall see the *h* glory of the LORD: for that he heareth your murmurings against the LORD: and what *are* we, that ye murmur against us?
8 And Moses said, *This shall be*, when the LORD shall give you in the evening flesh to eat, and in the morning bread to the full; for that the LORD heareth your murmurings which ye murmur against him: and what *are* we? your murmurings *are* not against us, but *i* against the LORD.
9 And Moses spake unto Aaron, Say unto all the congregation of the children of Israel, Come near before the LORD: for he hath heard your murmurings.
10 ¶ And it came to pass, as Aaron spake unto the whole congregation of the children of Israel, that they looked toward the wilderness, and, behold, the glory of the LORD appeared *j* in the cloud.
11 And the LORD spake unto Moses, saying,
12 I *k* have heard the murmurings of the children of Israel: speak unto them, saying, *l* At even ye shall eat flesh, and *m* in the morning ye shall be filled with bread; and *n* ye shall know that I *am* the LORD your God.
13 And it came to pass, that at even *o* the quails came up, and covered the camp; and in the morning *p* the dew lay round about the host.
14 And when the dew that lay was gone up, behold, upon the face of the wilderness *there lay q* a small round thing, *as* small as the hoar frost on the ground.
15 And when the children of Israel saw *it*, they said one to another, *2* It *is* manna: for they wist not what it *was*. And Moses said unto them, *r* This *is* the bread which the LORD hath given you to eat.
16 This *is* the thing which the LORD hath

meration is of men above 20 years of age. Assuming, what is now ascertained by statistical tables, that the numbers of males above that age is as nearly as possible the half of the total number of males, the whole male population of Israel, on this computation, would amount to 1,200,000; and adding an equal number for women and children, the aggregate number of Israelites who left Egypt would be 2,400,000. 38. a mixed multitude—*lit.*, a great rabble, (see also Num. 11. 4; Deu. 29. 11.) slaves, persons in the lowest grades of society, partly natives and partly foreigners, bound close to them as companions in misery, and gladly availing themselves of the opportunity to escape in the crowd. (cf. Zech. 8. 23.) 40. the sojourning of the children of Israel—The Septuagint renders it thus: "The sojourning of the children and of their fathers, which they sojourned in the land of Canaan and in the land of Egypt." These additions are important, for the period of sojourn in Egypt did not exceed 215 years; but if we reckon from the time that Abraham entered Canaan and the promise was made in which the sojourn of his posterity in Egypt was announced, this makes up the time to 430 years. 41. even the self-same day—implying an exact and literal fulfilment of the predicted period. 49. One law—This regulation displays the liberal spirit of the Hebrew institutions. Any foreigner might obtain admission to the privileges of the nation on complying with their sacred ordinances. In the Mosaic equally as the Christian dispensation privilege and duty were inseparably conjoined.

CHAPTER XIII.

Ver. 1, 2. THE FIRST-BORN SANCTIFIED. Sanctify unto me all the first-born—To sanctify means to consecrate, to set apart from a common to a sacred use. The foundation of this duty rested on the fact, that the Israelites having had their first born preserved by a distinguishing act of grace from the general destruction that overtook the families of the Egyptians, were bound in token of gratitude to consider them as the Lord's peculiar property. (cf. He. 12. 23.)
3-10. MEMORIAL OF THE PASSOVER. 3. Moses said ... Remember this day—The day that gave them a national existence and introduced them into the privileges of independence and freedom, deserved to live in the memories of the Hebrews and their posterity; and, considering the signal interposition of God displayed in it, to be held not only in perpetual, but devout remembrance. house of bondage—*lit.* house of slaves—*i.e.*, a servile and degrading condition. by strength of hand—the emancipation of Israel would never have been obtained except it had been wrung from the Egyptian tyrant by the appalling judgments of God, as had been at the outset of his mission announced to Moses. (ch. 3. 19.) There shall no leavened bread, &c.—the words are elliptical, and the meaning of the clause may be paraphrased thus:—" For by strength of hand the Lord brought you out from this place, in such haste, that there could or should be no leavened bread eaten." 4. month Abib—*lit.* a green ear, and hence the month Abib is the month of green ears, corresponding to the middle of our March. It was the best season for undertaking a journey to the desert-region of Sinai, especially with flocks and herds: for then the winter torrents have subsided, and the wadys are covered with an early and luxuriant verdure. 5-7. When the Lord shall bring thee—The passover is here instituted as a permanent festival of the Israelites. It was, however, only a prospective observance: we read of only one celebration of the passover during the protracted sojourn in the wilderness; but on their settlement in the promised land, the season was hallowed as a sacred anniversary, in conformity with the directions here given. 8-10. thou shalt shew thy son—The establishment of this and the other sacred festivals presented the best opportunities of instructing the young in a knowledge of His gracious doings to their ancestors in Egypt. 9. It shall be for a sign, &c.—There is no reason to believe that the Oriental tatooing—the custom of staining the hands with the power of Hennah, as Eastern females now do—is here referred to. Nor is it probable that either this practice or the phylactories of the Pharisees—parchment scrolls, which were worn on their wrists and foreheads—had so early an existence. The words are to be considered only as a figurative mode of expression. that the Lord's law, &c.—*i.e.*, that it may be the subject of frequent conversation and familiar knowledge among the people.
11--16. FIRSTLINGS OF BEASTS. 15. every firstling, &c.—The injunction respecting the consecration of the first-born, as here repeated, with some additional circumstances. The firstlings of clean beasts, such as lambs, kids, and calves, if males, were to be devoted to God and employed in sacrifice. Those unclean beasts as the ass's colt, being unfit for sacrifice, were to be redeemed. (Num. 18. 15.)
17-21. JOURNEY FROM EGYPT. 17. God led them, &c.—The shortest and most direct route from Egypt to Palestine was the usual caravan road that leads by Belbeis, El-Arish, to Ascalon and Gaza. The Philistines, who then possessed the latter, would have been sure to dispute their passage, for between them and the Israelites there was a hereditary feud; (1 Chr. 7.21,22:) and so early a commencement of hostilities would have discouraged or dismayed the unwarlike band which Moses led. Their faith was to be exercised and strengthened, and from the commencement of their travels we observe the same careful proportion of burdens and trials to their character and state, as the gracious Lord shows to his people still in that spiritual journey of which the former was typical. 18. led them about, &c.—This wondrous expanse of water is a gulf of the Indian ocean. It was called in Hebrew "the weedy sea," from the forest of marine plants with which it abounds. But the name of the Red Sea is not so easily traced. Some think it was given from its contiguity to the countries of Edom (red), others derive it from its coral rocks, while a third class ascribe the origin of the name to an extremely red appearance of the water in some parts, caused by a numberless multitude of very small mollusca. This sea, at its northern extremity, separates into two smaller inlets—the eastern called anciently the Elanitic gulf, now the gulf of Akaba; and the western the Heroopolite gulf, now the gulf of Suez, which there can be no doubt extended much more to the

commanded. Gather of it every man according to his eating, *an omer ³ for every man, *according to* the number of your ⁴ persons; take ye every man for *them* which *are* in his tents.

17 And the children of Israel did so, and gathered, some more, some less.

18 And when they did mete it with an omer, ⁿ he that gathered much had nothing over, and he that gathered little had no lack: they gathered every man according to his eating.

19 And Moses said, Let no man leave of it till the morning.

20 Notwithstanding they hearkened not unto Moses; but some of them left of it until the morning, and it bred worms, and stank: and Moses was wroth with them.

21 And they gathered it every morning, every man according to his eating: and when the sun waxed hot, it melted.

22 ¶ And it came to pass, that on the sixth day they gathered twice as much bread, two omers for one *man:* and all the rulers of the congregation came and told Moses.

23 And he said unto them, This *is that* which the LORD hath said, To-morrow *is* ᵘ the rest of the holy sabbath unto the LORD: bake *that* which ye will bake to-day, and seethe that ye will seethe; and that which remaineth over lay up for you to be kept until the morning.

24 And they laid it up till the morning, as Moses bade: and it did not ᵛ stink, neither was there any worm therein.

25 And Moses said, Eat that to-day; for to-day ʷ *is* a sabbath unto the LORD: to-day ye shall not find it in the field.

26 Six ˣ days ye shall gather it; but on the seventh day, *which is* the sabbath, in it there shall be none.

27 ¶ And it came to pass, *that* there went out *some* of the people on the seventh day for to gather, and they found none.

28 And the LORD said unto Moses, How long ʸ refuse ye to keep my commandments and my laws?

29 See, for that the LORD hath given you the sabbath, therefore he giveth you on the sixth day the bread of two days: abide ye every man in his place; let no man go out of his place on the seventh day.

30 So the people rested on the seventh day.

31 And the house of Israel called the name thereof Manna: and ᶻ it *was* like coriander seed, white; and the taste of it *was* like wafers *made* with honey.

32 ¶ And Moses said, This *is* the thing which the LORD commandeth, Fill an omer of it to be kept for your generations; that they may see the bread wherewith I have fed you in the wilderness, when I brought you forth from the land of Egypt.

33 And Moses said unto Aaron, ᵃ Take a pot, and put an omer full of manna therein, and lay it up before the LORD, to be kept for your generations.

34 As the LORD commanded Moses, so Aaron laid it up ᵇ before the Testimony, to be kept.

35 And the children of Israel did eat manna ᶜ forty years, ᵈ until they came to a land inhabited; they did eat manna until they came unto the borders of the land of Canaan.

36 Now an omer *is* the tenth *part* of an ephah.

CHAPTER XVII.

1 *The people murmur for water at Rephidim, and are sent to the rock in Horeb.* 13 *Amalek overcome.* 14 *God's vengeance against them.* 15 *Moses buildeth an altar.*

AND ᵃ all the congregation of the children of Israel journeyed from the wilderness of Sin, after their journeys, according to the commandment of the LORD, and pitched in Rephidim: and *there was* no water for the people to drink.

2 Wherefore ᵇ the people did chide with Moses, and said, Give us water that we may drink. And Moses said unto them, Why chide ye with me? wherefore do ye ᶜ tempt the LORD?

3 And the people thirsted there for water; and the people ᵈ murmured against Moses, and said, Wherefore *is* this *that* thou hast brought us up out of Egypt, to kill us and our children and our cattle with thirst?

4 And Moses cried unto the LORD, saying, What shall I do unto this people? they be almost ready to ᵉ stone me.

5 And the LORD said unto Moses, ᶠ Go on before the people, and take with thee of the elders of Israel; and thy rod, wherewith thou ᵍ smotest the river, take in thine hand, and go.

6 Behold, ʰ I will stand before thee there upon the rock in Horeb; and thou shalt smite the rock, and there shall come water out of it, that the people may drink. And Moses did so in the sight of the elders of Israel.

7 And he called the name of the place ¹ Massah, and ² Meribah, because of the chiding of the children of Israel, and because they tempted the LORD, saying, Is the LORD among us, or not?

8 ¶ Then ⁱ came Amalek, and fought with Israel in Rephidim.

9 And Moses said unto ʲ Joshua, Choose us out men, and go out, fight with Amalek: to-morrow I will stand on the top of the hill with the rod of God in mine hand.

10 So Joshua did as Moses had said to him, and fought with Amalek: and Moses, Aaron, and Hur, went up to the top of the hill.

11 And it came to pass, when Moses ᵏ held up his hand, that Israel prevailed; and when he let down his hand, Amalek prevailed.

12 But Moses' hands *were* heavy; and they took a stone, and put *it* under him, and he sat thereon; and Aaron and Hur stayed up his hands, the one on the one side, and the other on the other side; and his hands were steady until the going down of the sun.

13 And Joshua discomfited Amalek and his people with the edge of the sword.

14 And the LORD said unto Moses, ˡ Write this *for* a memorial in a book, and rehearse *it* in the ears of Joshua: for ᵐ I will utterly put out the remembrance of Amalek from under heaven.

15 And Moses built an altar, and called the name of it ³ JEHOVAH-nissi:

16 For he said, ⁴ Because ⁵ the LORD hath sworn *that* the LORD *will have* war with Amalek from generation to generation.

north anciently than it does now. It was toward the latter the Israelites marched. went up harnessed—*i. e.*, girded, equipped for a long journey. (See Ps. 105. 37.) The margin renders it "five in a rank," meaning obviously five large divisions, under five presiding officers, according to the usages of all caravans; and a spectacle of such a mighty and motley multitude must have presented an imposing appearance, and its orderly progress could have been effected only by the superintending influence of God. 19. took the bones of Joseph—in fulfilment of the oath he exacted from his brethren. (Ge. 50. 25, 26.) The remains of the other patriarchs—not noticed from their obscurity—were also carried out of Egypt; (A. 7. 16,) and there would be no difficulty as to the means of conveyance—a few camels bearing these precious relics would give a true picture of Oriental customs, such as is still to be seen in the immense pilgrimages to Mecca. 20. encamped in Etham—This place is supposed by the most intelligent travellers to be the modern Ajrud, where is a watering place, and which is the third stage of the pilgrim caravans to Mecca. "It is remarkable that either of the different routes eastward from Heliopolis, or southward from Heroopolis, equally admit [of Ajrud being Etham. It is 12 miles north-west from Suez, and is literally on the edge of the desert." [PICT. BIB.] 21, 22. the Lord went before them—by a visible token of his presence the Shecinah, in a majestic cloud, (Ps. 78. 14; Ne. 9. 12; 1 Co. 10. 1,) called the angel of God. (ch. 14. 19; 23. 20-23; Ps. 99. 6, 7; Is. 63. 8, 9.)

CHAPTER XIV.

Ver. 1-4. GOD INSTRUCTETH THE ISRAELITES AS TO THEIR JOURNEY. Speak...that they turn and encamp—The Israelites had now completed their three days' journey, and at Etham the decisive step would have to be taken, whether they would celebrate their intended feast and return, or march onwards by the head of the Red Sea into the desert, with a view to a final departure. They were already on the borders of the desert, and a short march would have placed them beyond the reach of pursuit, as the chariots of Egypt could have made little progress over dry and yielding sand. But, at Etham, instead of pursuing their journey eastward with the sea on their right, they were suddenly commanded to diverge to the south, keeping the gulf on their left; a route, which not only detained them lingering on the confines of Egypt, but in adopting it, they actually turned their backs on the land of which, they had set out to obtain the possession. A movement so unexpected, and of which the ultimate design was carefully concealed, could not but excite the astonishment of all, even of Moses himself, although from his implicit faith in the wisdom and power of his Heavenly Guide, he obeyed. The object was to entice Pharaoh to pursue, in order that the moral effect which the judgments on Egypt had produced in releasing God's people from bondage, might be still further extended over the nations by the awful events transacted at the Red Sea. Pi-hahiroth—the mouth of the defile, or pass—a description well suited to that of Bedea, which extended from the Nile, and opens on the shore of the Red Sea. Migdol—a fortress or citadel. Baal-zephon—some marked site on the opposite or Eastern coast. the wilderness hath shut them in—Pharaoh, who would eagerly watch their movements, was now satisfied that they were meditating flight, and he naturally thought from the error into which they appeared to have fallen by entering that defile, he could intercept them. He believed them now entirely in his power, the mountain chain being on one side, the sea on the other, so that, if he pursued them in the rear, escape seemed impossible. 5-9. The heart of Pharaoh, &c.—Alas, how soon the obduracy of this reprobate king re-appears. He had been convinced, but not converted—overawed, but not sanctified by the appalling judgments of heaven. He bitterly repented of what he now thought a hasty concession. Pride and revenge, the honour of his kingdom, and the interests of his subjects, all prompted him to recall his permission to reclaim those runaway slaves, and force them to their wonted labour. Strange that he should yet allow such considerations to obliterate or outweigh all his painful experience of the danger of oppressing that people. But those whom the Lord has doomed to destruction are first infatuated by sin. 6. he made ready his chariot—His preparations for an immediate and hot pursuit are here described: a difference is made between "the chosen chariots, and the chariots of Egypt." The first evidently composed the king's guard, amounting to six hundred, and they are called "chosen," *lit.* "third men;" three men being allotted to each chariot, the charioteer and two warriors. As to "the chariots of Egypt, the common cars contained only two persons, one for driving and the other for fighting;" sometimes only one person was in the chariot, the driver lashed the reins round his body and fought; infantry being totally unsuitable for a rapid pursuit, and the Egyptians having had no cavalry, the word "riders" is in the grammatical connection applied to war chariots employed, and these were of light construction, open behind, and hung on small wheels. When Pharaoh drew nigh—The great consternation of the Israelites is somewhat astonishing considering their vast superiority in numbers, but their deep dismay and absolute despair at the sight of this armed host receives a satisfactory explanation from the fact that the civilised state of Egyptian society required the absence of all arms, except when they were on service. If the Israelites were entirely unarmed at their departure, they could not think of making any resistance. [WILK., HENG.] 13, 14. Moses said, Fear ye not—Never, perhaps, was the fortitude of a man so severely tried as that of the Hebrew leader in this crisis, exposed as he was to various and inevitable dangers, the most formidable of which was the vengeance of a seditious and desperate multitude; but his meek, unruffled, magnanimous composure, presents one of the sublimest examples of moral courage to be found in history. And whence did his courage arise? He saw the miraculous cloud still accompanying them, and his confidence arose solely from the hope of a divine interposition, although, perhaps, he might have looked for the expected deliverance in every quarter, rather than in the direction of the sea. 15-18. The Lord said, &c.—When in answer to his prayers, he received the divine

CHAPTER XVIII.

1 *Jethro bringeth to Moses his wife and two sons:* 7 *Moses entertaineth him.* 13 *Jethro giveth Moses counsel; it is accepted.* 27 *Jethro departeth.*

WHEN Jethro, the priest of Midian, Moses' father-in-law, heard of all that God had done for Moses, and for Israel his people, *and* that the LORD had brought Israel out of Egypt;

2 Then Jethro, Moses' father-in-law, took Zipporah, Moses' wife, after he had sent her back,

3 And her two sons; of which the name of the one *was* ¹ Gershom; for he said, I have been an alien in a strange land:

4 And the name of the other *was* ² Eliezer; for the God of my father, *said he, was* mine help, and delivered me from the sword of Pharaoh.

5 And Jethro, Moses' father-in-law, came with his sons and his wife unto Moses into the wilderness, where he encamped at the mount of God:

6 And he said unto Moses, I thy father-in-law Jethro am come unto thee, and thy wife, and her two sons with her.

7 And Moses went out to meet his father-in-law, and did obeisance, and kissed him; and they asked each other of *their* ³ welfare; and they came into the tent.

8 And Moses told his father-in-law all that the LORD had done unto Pharaoh and to the Egyptians for Israel's sake, *and* all the travail that had ⁴ come upon them by the way, and *how* the LORD delivered them.

9 And Jethro rejoiced for all the goodness which the LORD had done to Israel, whom he had delivered out of the hand of the Egyptians.

10 And Jethro said, Blessed *be* the LORD, who hath delivered you out of the hand of the Egyptians, and out of the hand of Pharaoh, who hath delivered the people from under the hand of the Egyptians.

11 Now I know that the LORD *is* ᵃ greater than all gods: ᵇ for in the thing wherein they dealt ᶜ proudly *he was* above them.

12 And Jethro, Moses' father-in-law, took a burnt offering and sacrifices for God: and Aaron came, and all the elders of Israel, to eat bread with Moses' father-in-law ᵈ before God.

13 ¶ And it came to pass on the morrow, that Moses sat to judge the people: and the people stood by Moses from the morning unto the evening.

14 And when Moses' father-in-law saw all that he did to the people, he said, What *is* this thing that thou doest to the people? why sittest thou thyself alone, and all the people stand by thee from morning unto even?

15 And Moses said unto his father-in-law, Because the people come unto me to enquire of God:

16 When they have ᵉ a matter, they come unto me; and I judge between ⁵ one and another, and I do ᶠ make *them* know the statutes of God, and his laws.

17 And Moses' father-in-law said unto him, The thing that thou doest *is* not good.

18 ⁶ Thou wilt surely wear away, both thou and this people that *is* with thee: for this thing *is* too heavy for thee; ᵍ thou art not able to perform it thyself alone.

19 Hearken now unto my voice, I will give thee counsel, and God shall be with thee: Be thou ʰ for the people to God-ward, that thou mayest ⁱ bring the causes unto God:

20 And thou shalt ʲ teach them ordinances and laws, and shalt show them ᵏ the way wherein they must walk, and ˡ the work that they must do.

21 Moreover thou shalt provide out of all the people ᵐ able men, such as ⁿ fear God, ᵒ men of truth, hating covetousness; and place such over them, *to be* rulers of thousands, *and* rulers of hundreds, rulers of fifties, and rulers of tens:

22 And let them judge the people at all seasons: ᵖ and it shall be, *that* every great matter they shall bring unto thee, but every small matter they shall judge: so shall it be easier for thyself, and they shall bear *the burden* with thee.

23 If thou shalt do this thing, and God command thee so, then thou shalt be able to endure, and all this people shall also go to their place in peace.

24 So Moses hearkened to the voice of his father-in-law, and did all that he had said.

25 And ᵠ Moses chose able men out of all Israel, and made them heads over the people, rulers of thousands, rulers of hundreds, rulers of fifties, and rulers of tens.

26 And they judged the people at all seasons: the ʳ hard causes they brought unto Moses, but every small matter they judged themselves.

27 ¶ And Moses let his father-in-law depart; and ˢ he went his way into his own land.

CHAPTER XIX.

1 *The people come to Sinai.* 3 *God's message to them.* 8 *Their answer.* 10 *They are prepared against the third day;* 12 *the mountain must not be touched.* 16 *The fearful presence of God upon the mount.*

IN the third month, when the children of Israel were gone forth out of the land of Egypt, the same day came they *into* the wilderness of Sinai.

2 For they were departed from Rephidim, and were come *to* the desert of Sinai, and had pitched in the wilderness: and there Israel camped before the mount.

3 And ᵃ Moses went up unto God, and the LORD called unto him out of the mountain, saying, Thus shalt thou say to the house of Jacob, and tell the children of Israel;

4 Ye have seen what I did unto the Egyptians, and *how* ᵇ I bare you on eagles' wings, and brought you unto myself.

5 Now therefore, if ye will obey my voice indeed, and keep my covenant, then ᶜ ye shall be a peculiar treasure unto me above all people: for ᵈ all the earth *is* mine.

6 And ye shall be unto me a ᵉ kingdom of priests, and an ᶠ holy nation. These *are* the words which thou shalt speak unto the children of Israel.

7 ¶ And Moses came and called for the elders of the people, and laid before their faces all these words which the LORD commanded him.

8 And ᵍ all the people answered together, and said, All that the LORD hath spoken we will do. And Moses returned the words of the people unto the LORD.

9 And the LORD said unto Moses, Lo, I come unto thee ʰ in a thick cloud, ⁱ that the people may hear when I speak with thee, and believe thee for ever. And Moses told the words of the people unto the LORD.

command to go forward, he no longer doubted by what kind of miracle the salvation of his mighty charge was to be effected. **19. The angel of God**—*i.e.*, the pillar of cloud. The slow and silent movement of that majestic column through the air, and occupying a position behind them must have excited the astonishment of the Israelites. (Is. 58. 8.) It was an effectual barrier between them and their pursuers, not only protecting them, but concealing their movements. Thus, the same cloud produced light (a symbol of favour) to the people of God, and darkness (a symbol of wrath) to their enemies. (cf. 2 Co. 2. 16.) **21. Moses stretched out his hand, &c.**—The waving of the rod was of great importance on this occasion to give public attestation in the presence of the assembled Israelites, both to the character of Moses and the divine mission with which he was charged. **The Lord caused...a strong East wind** all that night—Suppose a mere ebb-tide caused by the wind, raising the water to a great height on *one side*, still as there was not only "dry land," but according to the tenor of the sacred narrative, a wall on the right hand and on the left, it would be impossible on the hypothesis of a natural cause to rear the wall on the *other*. The idea of divine interposition, therefore, is imperative; and assuming the passage to have been made at Mount Attakah, or at the mouth of Wady-Tawarik, *an east* wind would cut the sea in that line. The Hebrew word *kedem*, however, rendered in our translation, *East*, means, in its primary signification *previous*; so that this verse might, perhaps, be rendered, "the Lord caused the sea to go back by a strong *previous* wind all that night," a rendering, which would remove the difficulty of supposing the host of Israel marched over on the sand in the teeth of a rushing column of wind strong enough to heap up the waters as a wall on each side of a dry path, and give the intelligible narrative of Divine interference. **22. The children of Israel, &c.**—It is highly probable that Moses, along with Aaron, first planted his footsteps on the untrodden sand, encouraging the people to follow him without fear of the treacherous walls; and when we take into account the multitudes that followed him, the immense number who through infancy and old age were incapable of hastening their movements, together with all the appurtenances of the camp, the strong and steadfast character of the leaders' faith was strikingly manifested. (Jos. 2. 10; 4. 23; Ps. 66. 6; 74. 13; 106. 9; 136. 13; Is. 63. 11-13; 1 Cor. 10. 1; He. 11. 29.) **23-30. The Egyptians pursued**—From the darkness caused by the intercepting cloud, it is probable that they were not aware what ground they were driving: they heard the sound of the fugitives before them, and they pushed on with the fury of the avengers of blood, without dreaming that they were on the bared bed of the sea. **24. Lord looked through the cloud and troubled them**—We suppose the fact to have been that the side of the pillar of cloud toward the Egyptians was suddenly, and for a few moments illuminated with a blaze of light, which, coming as it were in a refulgent flash upon the dense darkness which had preceded, so frightened the horses of the pursuers that they rushed confusedly together and became unmanageable. "Let us flee," was the cry that resounded through the broken and trembling ranks, but it was too late, all attempts at flight were vain. [BUSH.] **27. Moses stretched forth his hand, &c.**—What circumstances could more clearly demonstrate the miraculous character of this transaction than that at the waving of Moses' rod, the dividing waters left the channel dry, and on his making the same motion on the opposite side, they returned, commingling with instantaneous fury. Is such the character of any ebb-tide? **28. there remained not so much as one of them**—It is surprising that, with such a declaration, some intelligent writers can maintain there is no evidence of the destruction of Pharaoh himself, Ps. 105. 11. **30. Israel saw the Egyptians, &c.**—The tide threw them up and left multitudes of corpses on the beach; a result that brought greater infamy on the Egyptians, that tended on the other hand to enhance the triumph of the Israelites, and doubtless enriched them with arms, which they had not before. The locality of this famous passage has not yet been, and probably never will be satisfactorily fixed. Some place it in the immediate neighbourhood of Suez; where, they say, the part of the sea is most likely to be affected by "a strong East wind;" where the road from the defile of Migdol (now Muktala), leads directly to this point; and where the sea, not above two miles broad, could be crossed in a short time. The vast majority, however, who have examined the spot, reject this opinion, and fix the passage, as does local tradition, about ten or twelve miles farther down the shore at Wady-Tawarik. "The time of the miracle was the whole night, at the season of the year, too, when the night would be about its average length. The sea at that point extends from six-and-a-half to eight miles in breadth. There was thus ample time for the passage of the Israelites from any part of the valley, especially considering their excitement and animation by the gracious and wonderful interposition of Providence in their behalf. [WILSON.]

CHAPTER XV.

Ver. 1-27. SONG OF MOSES. **1. Then sang Moses and the children of Israel**—The scene of this thanksgiving song is supposed to have been at the landing place on the eastern shore of the Red Sea, at Ayoun Musa, the fountains of Moses. They are situated somewhat farther northward along the shore than the opposite point from which the Israelites set out. But the line of the people would be extended during the passage, and one extremity of it would reach as far north as these fountains, which would supply them with water on landing. The time when it was sung is supposed to have been the morning after the passage. This song is by some hundred years the oldest poem in the world. There is a sublimity and beauty in the language that is unexampled. But its unrivalled superiority arises not solely from the splendour of the diction. Its poetical excellencies have often drawn forth the admiration of the best judges, while the character of the event commemorated, and its being prompted by Divine inspiration, contribute to give it an interest and sublimity peculiar to itself. **I will sing unto the Lord**—Considering the state of servitude in which they had been born

10 ¶ And the Lord said unto Moses, Go unto the people, and ʲ sanctify them to-day and to-morrow, and let them ᵏ wash their clothes,

11 And be ready against the third day: for the third day the Lord ˡ will come down in the sight of all the people upon mount Sinai.

12 And thou shalt set bounds unto the people round about, saying, Take heed to yourselves *that ye go not* up into the mount, or touch the border of it: ᵐ whosoever toucheth the mount shall be surely put to death:

13 There shall not an hand touch it, but he shall surely be stoned, or shot through; whether *it be* beast or man, it shall not live: when the ¹ trumpet soundeth long, they shall come up to the mount.

14 ¶ And Moses went down from the mount unto the people, and sanctified the people; and they washed their clothes.

15 And he said unto the people, Be ready against the third day: ⁿ come not at *your* wives.

16 ¶ And it came to pass on the third day, in the morning, that there were thunders and lightnings, and a thick cloud upon the mount, and the voice of the trumpet exceeding loud; so that all the people that *was* in the camp trembled.

17 And ᵒ Moses brought forth the people out of the camp to meet with God; and they stood at the nether part of the mount.

18 And ᵖ mount Sinai was altogether on a smoke, because the Lord descended upon it ᵠ in fire: ʳ and the smoke thereof ascended as the smoke of a furnace, and the ˢ whole mount quaked greatly.

19 And when the voice of the trumpet sounded long, and waxed louder and louder, Moses spake, and ᵗ God answered him by a voice.

20 And the Lord came down upon mount Sinai, on the top of the mount: and the Lord called Moses *up* to the top of the mount; and Moses went up.

21 And the Lord said unto Moses, Go down, ² charge the people, lest they break through unto the Lord ᵘ to gaze, and many of them perish.

22 And let the priests also, which come near to the Lord, ᵛ sanctify themselves, lest the Lord ʷ break forth upon them.

23 And Moses said unto the Lord, The people cannot come up to mount Sinai: for thou chargedst us, saying, ˣ Set bounds about the mount, and sanctify it.

24 And the Lord said unto him, Away, get thee down, and thou shalt come up, thou, and Aaron with thee: but let not the priests and the people break through to come up unto the Lord, lest he break forth upon them.

25 So Moses went down unto the people, and spake unto them.

CHAPTER XX.

1 The ten commandments. 22 Idolatry forbidden. 24 Directions concerning the altar.

AND God spake ᵃ all these words, saying,
2 ᵇ I am the Lord thy God, which have brought thee out of the land of Egypt, ᶜ out of the house of ¹ bondage.

3 Thou ᵈ shalt have no other gods before me.

4 Thou ᵉ shalt not make unto thee any graven image, or any likeness *of any thing that is* in heaven above, or that *is* in the earth beneath, or that *is* in the water under the earth:

5 Thou ᶠ shalt not bow down thyself to them, nor serve them: for I the Lord thy God *am* ᵍ a jealous God, ʰ visiting the iniquity of the fathers upon the children unto the third and fourth *generation* of them that hate me;

6 And ⁱ showing mercy unto thousands of them that love me, and keep my commandments.

7 Thou ʲ shalt not take the name of the Lord thy God in vain: for the Lord ᵏ will not hold him guiltless that taketh his name in vain.

8 Remember ˡ the sabbath day, to keep it holy.

9 Six ᵐ days shalt thou labour and do all thy work:

10 But the ⁿ seventh day *is* the sabbath of the Lord thy God: *in it* thou shalt not do any work, thou, nor thy son, nor thy daughter, thy man-servant, nor thy maid-servant, nor thy cattle, ᵒ nor thy stranger that *is* within thy gates:

11 For *in* six days the Lord made heaven and earth, the sea, and all that in them *is*, and rested the seventh day: wherefore the Lord blessed the sabbath day, and hallowed it.

12 ¶ Honour ᵖ thy father and thy mother, that thy days may be long upon the land which the Lord thy God giveth thee.

13 Thou ᵠ shalt not kill.

14 Thou ʳ shalt not commit adultery.

15 Thou ˢ shalt not steal.

16 Thou shalt not bear false witness against thy neighbour.

17 Thou ᵗ shalt not covet thy neighbour's house, thou ᵘ shalt not covet thy neighbour's wife, nor his man-servant, nor his maid-servant, nor his ox, nor his ass, nor any thing that *is* thy neighbour's.

18 ¶ And ᵛ all the people saw the thunderings, and the lightnings, and the noise of the trumpet, and the mountain smoking: and when the people saw *it*, they removed, and stood afar off.

19 And they said unto Moses, ʷ Speak thou with us, and we will hear: but let not God speak with us, lest we die.

20 And Moses said unto the people, Fear not: ˣ for God is come to prove you, and ʸ that his fear may be before your faces, that ye sin not.

21 And the people stood afar off: and Moses drew near unto the thick darkness where God *was*.

22 ¶ And the Lord said unto Moses, Thus thou shalt say unto the children of Israel, Ye have seen that I have talked with you from heaven.

23 Ye shall not make with me gods of silver, neither shall ye make unto you gods of gold.

24 An altar of earth thou shalt make unto me, and shalt sacrifice thereon thy burnt offerings, and thy peace offerings, thy sheep, and thine oxen. In all ᶻ places where I record my name I will come unto thee, and I will ᵃ bless thee.

25 And ᵇ if thou wilt make me an altar of stone, thou shalt not ² build it of hewn stone: for if thou lift up thy tool upon it, thou hast polluted it.

26 Neither shalt thou go up by steps unto mine altar, that thy nakedness be not discovered thereon.

and bred, and the rude features of character which their subsequent history often displays, it cannot be supposed that the children of Israel generally were qualified to commit to memory or to appreciate the beauties of this inimitable song. But they might perfectly understand its pervading strain of sentiment; and, with the view of suitably improving the occasion, it was thought necessary that all, old and young, should join their united voices in the rehearsal of its words. As every individual had cause, so every individual gave utterance, to his feelings of gratitude. **20, 21. Miriam the prophetess** — so called from her receiving Divine revelations, (Nu. 12. 1; Mi. 6. 4,) but in this instance principally from her being eminently skilled in music, and in this sense the word "prophesy" is sometimes used in Scripture. (1 Chro. 25. 1; 1 Co. 11. 5.) **took a timbrel—or tabret**—a musical instrument in the form of a hoop, edged round with rings or pieces of brass to make a jingling noise, and covered over with tightened parchment like a drum. It was beat with the fingers, and corresponds to our tambourine. **all the women, &c.**—we shall understand this by attending to the modern customs of the East, where the dance—a slow, grave, and solemn gesture, generally accompanied with singing and the sound of the timbrel—is still led by the principal female of the company, the rest imitating her movements, and repeating the words of the song as they drop from her lips. **answered them**—"them" in the Hebrew is masculine, so that Moses probably led the men and Miriam the women—the two bands responding alternately, and singing the first verse as a chorus. **22. wilderness of Shur**—comprehending all the western part of Arabia-Petræa. The desert of Etham was a part of it, extending round the northern portion of the Red Sea, and a considerable distance along its eastern shore; whereas the "wilderness of Shur" (now Sudhr; was the designation of all the desert region of Arabia-Petræa, that lay next to Palestine. **23. came to Marah**—Following the general route of all travellers southward, between the sea and the table-land of the Tih, (valley of wandering,) Marah is almost universally believed to be what is now called Howârah, in Wady Amarah, about 30 miles from the place where the Israelites landed on the eastern shore of the Red Sea—a distance quite sufficient for their march of 3 days. There is no other perennial spring in the intermediate space. The water still retains its ancient character, and has a bad name among the Arabs, who seldom allow their camels to partake of it. **25. the Lord showed him a tree**—Some travellers have pronounced this to be the Elvah of the Arabs—a shrub in form and flower resembling our hawthorn; others, the berries of the Ghûrkhûd—a bush found growing around all brackish fountains. But neither of these shrubs are known by the natives to possess such natural virtues. It is far more likely that God miraculously endowed some tree with the property of purifying the bitter water—a tree employed as the medium, but the sweetening was not dependent upon the nature or quality of the tree, but the power of God. (cf. J. 9. 6.) And hence the "statute and ordinance" that followed, which would have been singularly inopportune if there had no miracle been wrought, proved them—God now brought the Israelites into circumstances which would put their faith and obedience to the test. (cf. Ge. 22. 1.) **27. came to Elim**—supposed to be what is now called Wady Ghurandel, the most extensive water course in the western desert—an oasis, adorned with a great variety of trees, among which the palm is still conspicuous, and fertilized by a copious stream. It is estimated to be a mile in breadth, but stretching out far to the north-east. After the weary travel through the desert, this must have appeared a most delightful encampment from its shade and verdure, as well as from its abundant supply of sweet water for the thirsty multitude. The palm is called "the tree" of the desert, as its presence is always a sign of water. The palms in this spot are greatly increased in number, but the wells are diminished.

CHAPTER XVI.

Ver. 1–36. MURMURS FOR WANT OF BREAD. 1. Took their journey from Elim—where they had remained several days. **came into the wilderness of Sin**—It appears from Num. 32. that several stations are omitted in this historical notice of the journey. This passage represents the Israelites as advanced into the great plain, which, beginning near el-Murkah, extends with a greater or less breadth to almost the extremity of the peninsula. In its broadest part northward of Tûr it is called el-Kaa, which is probably the desert of Sin. [ROBINSON.] **2. Congregation murmured**—Modern travellers through the desert of Sinai are accustomed to take as much as is sufficient for the sustenance of men and beasts during 40 days. The Israelites having been rather more than a month on their journey, their store of corn or other provisions was altogether or nearly exhausted; and there being no prospect of procuring any means of subsistence in the desert, except some wild olives and wild honey, (Deu. 32. 13,) loud complaints were made against the leaders. **3. would to God we had died**—How unreasonable and absurd the charge against Moses and Aaron! how ungrateful and impious against God! After all their experieuce of the Divine wisdom, goodness, and power, we pause and wonder over the sacred narrative of their hardness and unbelief. But the expression of feeling is contagious in so vast a multitude, and there is a feeling of solitude and despondency in the desert which numbers cannot dispel; and besides, we must remember that they were men, engrossed with the *present*—that the Comforter was not then given, and that they were destitute of all visible means of sustenance, and cut off from every visible comfort, with only the promises of an *unseen* God to look to as the ground of their hope. And though we may lament they should tempt God in the wilderness, and freely admit their sin in so doing, we can be at no loss for a reason why those who had all their lives been accustomed to walk by *sight* should, in circumstances of unparalleled difficulty and perplexity, find it hard to walk by *faith*. Do not even *we* find it difficult to walk by faith through the wilderness of this world, though in the light of a clearer revelation, and under a nobler leader than Moses? [FISK.] (See 1 Co. 10. 11, 12.) **4. then said the Lord unto Moses**—Though the out-

CHAPTER XXI.

1 Laws for men-servants, 7 for women-servants, 12 for murder and man-slaughter, 16 for men-stealers, 17 for cursers of parents, 18 for smiters, etc.

NOW these *are* the judgments which thou shalt ᵃ set before them.

2 If ᵇ thou buy an Hebrew servant, six years he shall serve; and in the seventh he shall go out free for nothing.

3 If he came in ¹ by himself, he shall go out by himself: if he were married, then his wife shall go out with him.

4 If his master have given him ᶜ a wife, and she have born him sons or daughters; the wife and her children shall be her master's, and he shall go out by himself.

5 And ᵈ if the servant ² shall plainly say, I love my master, my wife, and my children; I will not go out free:

6 Then his master shall bring him unto the ᵉ judges; he shall also bring him to the door, or unto the door post; and his master shall ᶠ bore his ear through with an awl; and he shall serve him for ever.

7 ¶ And if a man ᵍ sell his daughter to be a maid-servant, she shall not go out as the men-servants do.

8 If she ³ please not her master, who hath betrothed her to himself, then shall he let her be redeemed: to sell her unto a strange nation he shall have no power, seeing he hath dealt deceitfully with her.

9 And if he hath betrothed her unto his son, he shall deal with her after the manner of daughters.

10 If he take him another *wife*; her food, her raiment, ʰ and her duty of marriage, shall he not diminish.

11 And if he do not these three unto her, then shall she go out free without money.

12 ¶ He ⁱ that smiteth a man so that he die, shall be surely put to death.

13 And ʲ if a man lie not in wait, but God ᵏ deliver *him* into his hand; then ˡ I will appoint thee a place whither he shall flee.

14 But if a man come ᵐ presumptuously upon his neighbour, to slay him with guile; thou ⁿ shalt take him from mine altar, that he may die.

15 And he that smiteth his father or his mother shall be surely put to death.

16 ¶ And ᵒ he that stealeth a man, and selleth ᵖ him, or if he be ᑫ found in his hand, he shall surely be put to death.

17 ¶ And ʳ he that ⁴ curseth his father or his mother shall surely be put to death.

18 ¶ And if men strive together, and one smite ⁵ another with a stone, or with *his* fist, and he die not, but keepeth *his* bed;

19 If he rise again, and walk abroad ᵉ upon his staff, then shall he that smote *him* be quit: only he shall pay *for* ⁶ the loss of his time, and shall cause *him* to be thoroughly healed.

20 ¶ And if a man smite his servant, or his maid, with a rod, and he die under his hand; he shall be surely ⁷ punished.

21 Notwithstanding, if he continue a day or two, he shall not be punished: for ᵗ he *is* his money.

22 ¶ If men strive, and hurt a woman with child, so that her fruit depart *from her*, and yet no mischief follow: he shall be surely punished, according as the woman's husband will lay upon him; and he shall ᵘ pay as the judges *determine*.

23 And if *any* mischief follow, then thou shalt give ᵛ life for life.

24 Eye ʷ for eye, tooth for tooth, hand for hand, foot for foot,

25 Burning for burning, wound for wound, stripe for stripe.

26 ¶ And ˣ if a man smite the eye of his servant, or the eye of his maid, that it perish; he shall let him go free for his eye's sake.

27 And if he smite out his man-servant's tooth, or his maid-servant's tooth; he shall let him go free for his tooth's sake.

28 ¶ If an ox gore a man or a woman, that they die: then ʸ the ox shall be surely stoned, and his flesh shall not be eaten; but the owner of the ox *shall be* quit.

29 But if the ox were wont to push with his horn in time past, and it hath been testified to his owner, and he hath not kept him in, but that he hath killed a man or a woman; the ox shall be stoned, and his owner also shall be put to death.

30 If there be laid on him a sum of money, then he shall give for ᶻ the ransom of his life whatsoever is laid upon him.

31 Whether he have gored a son, or have gored a daughter, according to this judgment shall it be done unto him.

32 If the ox shall push a man-servant or maid-servant; he shall give unto their master ᵃ thirty shekels of silver, and the ox shall be stoned.

33 ¶ And if a man shall open a pit, or if a man shall dig a pit, and not cover it, and an ox or an ass fall therein;

34 The owner of the pit shall make *it* good, *and* give money unto the owner of them; and the dead *beast* shall be his.

35 ¶ And if one man's ox hurt another's, that he die; then they shall sell the live ox, and divide the money of it; and the dead ox also they shall divide.

36 Or if it be known that the ox hath used to push in time past, and his owner hath not kept him in; he shall surely pay ox for ox; and the dead shall be his own.

CHAPTER XXII.

1 Laws concerning theft; 5 damage; 7 trusts and trespasses; 14 borrowing; 16 fornication; 18 witchcraft; 19 bestiality; 20 idolatry; 21 strangers, widows, etc.

IF a man shall steal an ox, or a ¹ sheep, and kill it, or sell it; he shall restore five oxen for an ox, and ᵃ four sheep for a sheep.

2 If a thief be found ᵇ breaking up, and be smitten that he die, *there shall* ᶜ no blood *be* shed for him.

3 If the sun be risen upon him, *there shall* be blood shed for him; *for* he should make full restitution: if he have nothing, then he shall be ᵈ sold for his theft.

4 If the ² theft be certainly ᵉ found in his hand alive, whether it be ox, or ass, or sheep, he shall ᶠ restore double.

5 ¶ If a man shall cause a field or vineyard to be eaten, and shall put in his beast, and shall feed in another man's field; of the best of his own field, and of the best of his own vineyard, shall he make restitution.

6 ¶ If fire break out, and catch in thorns, so that the stacks of corn, or the standing corn, or the field, be consumed *therewith*; he that kindled the fire shall surely make restitution.

7 ¶ If a man shall deliver unto his neighbour money or stuff to keep, and it be stolen

break was immediately against the human leaders, it was indirectly against God; yet mark his patience, and how graciously he promised to redress the grievance. I will rain bread from heaven—Israel, a type of the Church which is from above, and being under the conduct, government, and laws of heaven, received their food from heaven also. (Ps. 78. 24.) that I may prove them—The grand object of their being led into the wilderness was that they might receive a religious training directly under the eye of God; and the first lesson taught them was a constant dependence on God for their daily nourishment. 13. At even the quails came up—This bird is of the gallinaceous kind, resembling the red partridge, but not larger than the turtle dove. They are found in certain seasons in the places through which the Israelites passed, being migratory birds, and they were probably brought to the camp by "a wind from the Lord" as on another occasion. (Nu. 11. 31.) 15-31. And in the morning ... a small round thing, manna—There is a gum of the same name distilled in this desert region from the tamarisk, which is much prized by the natives, and preserved carefully by those who gather it. It is collected early in the morning, melts under the heat of the sun, and is congealed by the cold of night. In taste it is as sweet as honey, and has been supposed by distinguished travellers, from its whitish colour, time and place of its appearance, to be the manna on which the Israelites were fed; so that, according to the views of some, it was a production indigenous to the desert; according to others, there was a miracle, which consisted, however, only in the preternatural arrangements regarding its supply. But more recent and accurate examination has proved this gum of the tarfa-tree to be wanting in all the principal characteristics of the Scripture manna. It exudes only in small quantities, and not every year; it does not admit of being baked (Nu. 11. 8.) or boiled (v. 23.). Though it may be exhaled by the heat and afterwards fall with the dew, it is a medicine, not food—it is well known to the natives of the desert, while the Israelites were strangers to theirs; and in taste as well as in the appearance of double quantity on Friday, none on Sabbath, and in not breeding worms, it is essentially different from the manna furnished to the Israelites. 32-36. Fill the pot ... to be kept for your generations—The mere fact of such a multitude being fed for 40 years in the wilderness, where no food of any kind is to be obtained, will show the utter impossibility of their subsisting on a natural production of the kind and quantity as this tarfa-gum; and as if for the purpose of removing all such groundless speculations, Aaron was commanded to put a sample of it in a pot—a golden pot—(He. 9. 4.) to be laid before the Testimony—to be kept for future generations, that they might see the bread on which the Lord fed their fathers in the wilderness. But we have the bread of which that was merely typical. (1 Co. 10. 3; J. 6. 32.)

CHAPTER XVII.

Ver. 1-7. THE PEOPLE MURMUR FOR WATER. 1. Journeyed from the wilderness of Sin—In the succinct annals of this book, those places only are selected for particular notice by the inspired historian, which were scenes memorable for their happy or painful interest in the history of the Israelites. A more detailed itinerary is given in the later books of Moses, and we find that here, two stations are omitted. (Nu. 33.) according to the commandment, &c.—not given in oracular response, nor a vision of the night, but indicated by the movement of the cloudy pillar. The same phraseology occurs elsewhere. (Nu. 9. 18, 19.) pitched in Rephidim—now believed, on good grounds, to be Wady Feiran, which is exactly a day's march from Mount Sinai, and at the entrance of the Horeb district. It is a long circuitous defile about forty feet in breadth, with perpendicular granite rocks on both sides. The wilderness of Sin through which they approached to this valley is very barren, has an extremely dry and thirsty aspect, little or no water, scarcely even a dwarfish shrub to be seen, and the only shelter to the panting pilgrims is under the shadow of the great overhanging cliffs. 2, 3. People did chide with Moses—The want of water was a privation, the severity of which we cannot estimate, and it was a great trial to the Israelites, but their conduct on this new occasion was outrageous: it amounted even to "a tempting of the Lord." It was an opposition to his minister, a distrust of his care, an indifference to his kindness, an unbelief in his providence, a trying of his patience and fatherly forbearance. 4-6. Moses cried unto the Lord—His language, instead of betraying any signs of resentment or vindictive imprecation on a people who had given him a cruel and unmerited treatment, was the expression of an anxious wish to know what was the best to be done in the circumstances. (cf. M. 5. 44; Ro. 12. 21.) 5. The Lord said, &c.—not to smite the rebels, but the rock; not to bring a stream of blood from the breast of the offenders, but a stream of water from the granite cliffs. The cloud rested on a particular rock, just as the star rested on the house where the Infant Saviour was lodged. And from the rod-smitten rock there forthwith gushed a current of pure and refreshing water. It was perhaps the greatest miracle performed by Moses, and in many respects bore a resemblance to the greatest of Christ's: being done without ostentation, and in the presence of a few chosen witnesses. (1 Cor. 10. 4.) 7. called the name of the place—Massah ;temptation; Meribah—chiding,—strife; the same word which is rendered "provocation." (He. 3. 8.)

8-16. ATTACK OF AMALEK. 8. Then came Amalek—Some time probably elapsed before they were exposed to this new evil: and the presumption of there being such an interval affords the only ground on which we can satisfactorily account for the altered—the better and firmer spirit that animated the people in this sudden contest. The miracles of the manna and the water from the rock had produced a deep impression and permanent conviction that God was indeed among them; and with feelings elevated by the conscious experience of the divine Presence and aid, they remained calm, resolute, and courageous, under the attack of their unexpected foe. fought with Israel—The language implies that no occasion had been furnished for this attack; but, as descendants of Esau, the Amalekites enter-

out of the man's house; if the thief be found, let him pay double.

8 If the thief be not found, then the master of the house shall be brought unto the judges, *to see* whether he have put his hand unto his neighbour's goods.

9 For all manner of trespass, *whether it* be for ox, for ass, for sheep, for raiment, *or* for any manner of lost thing, which another challengeth to be his, the *g* cause of both parties shall come before the judges; *and* whom the judges shall condemn, he shall pay double unto his neighbour.

10 If a man deliver unto his neighbour an ass, or an ox, or a sheep, or any beast, to keep; and it die, or be hurt, or driven away, no man seeing *it:*

11 *Then* shall an *h* oath of the LORD be between them both, that he hath not put his hand unto his neighbour's goods; and the owner of it shall accept *thereof*, and he shall not make *it* good.

12 And *i* if it be stolen from him, he shall make restitution unto the owner thereof.

13 If it be torn in pieces, *then* let him bring it *for* witness, *and* he shall not make good that which was torn.

14 ¶ And if a man borrow *ought* of his neighbour, and it be hurt, or die, the owner thereof *being* not with it; he shall surely make *it* good.

15 *But* if the owner thereof *be* with it, he shall not make *it* good: if *it be* an hired thing, it came for his hire.

16 ¶ And *j* if a man entice a maid that is not betrothed, and lie with her; he shall surely endow her to be his wife.

17 If her father utterly refuse to give her unto him, he shall *g* pay money according to the *k* dowry of virgins.

18 ¶ Thou *l* shalt not suffer a witch to live.

19 ¶ Whosoever lieth with a beast shall surely be put to death.

20 ¶ He *m* that sacrificeth unto any god, save unto the LORD only, he shall be utterly destroyed.

21 ¶ Thou *n* shalt neither vex a stranger, nor oppress him: for ye were strangers in the land of Egypt.

22 Ye *o* shall not afflict any widow, or fatherless child.

23 If thou afflict them in any wise, and they *p* cry at all unto me, I will surely hear *q* their cry;

24 And my *r* wrath shall wax hot, and I will kill you with the sword; and *s* your wives shall be widows, and your children fatherless.

25 ¶ If *t* thou lend money to any *of* my people *that is* poor by thee, thou shalt not be to him as an usurer, neither shalt thou lay upon him usury.

26 If *u* thou at all take thy neighbour's raiment to pledge, thou shalt deliver it unto him by that the sun goeth down:

27 For that *is* his covering only, it *is* his raiment for his skin: wherein shall he sleep? and it shall come to pass, when he crieth unto me, that I will hear; for I *am* gracious.

28 ¶ Thou *v* shalt not revile the *5* gods, nor curse the ruler of thy people.

29 ¶ Thou shalt not delay *to offer* *5* the first *w* of thy ripe fruits, and of thy *6* liquors: the first-born of thy sons shalt thou give unto me.

30 Likewise *x* shalt thou do with thine

B. C. 1491.

CHAP. 22.
g 2Chr.19.10.
h Heb. 6.16.
i Ge. 31. 39.
j Deu. 22.28.
3 weigh.
k 1 Sa. 18.25.
l Deu. 18.10.
m Nu. 25, 2.
Hos. 8. 14.
1 Ki.18.40.
1 Ki.10.25.
n Zech. 7.10.
o Deu. 10.18.
Is. 1. 17.
Ezek. 22. 7.
p Deu. 15. 9.
Job 35. 9.
q Job 34. 28.
Jam. 5. 4.
r Job 31. 23.
s Ps. 109. 9.
t Lev. 25.35.
Neh. 5. 7.
Ezek. 18. 8.
u Job 24. 3.
Pro. 20.16.
Amos 2. 8.
v Ec. 10. 20.
2 Pet. 2.10.
4 Or, judges.
Ps. 82. 6.
5 thy fulness.
w Pro. 3. 9.
6 tear.
x Deu. 15.19.
y Lev. 22. 27.
z Lev. 19. 2.
a Ezek. 4.14.

CHAP. 23.
a Pro. 10. 18.
1 Or, receive.
b 1 Kin. 21. 10.
Pro. 19. 5.
Acts 6. 11.
c 1 Ki. 19. 10.
Job 31. 34.
Luke 23. 23.
d Ps. 72. 2.
e Lev. 19. 15.
2 answer.
f Pro. 25. 21.
1 Thes. 5. 15.
3 Or, wilt thou cease to help him? or, and wouldest cease to leave thy business for him: thou shalt surely leave it to join with him.
g Job 31. 13.
h Eph. 4. 25.
i Ro. 1. 18.
j Pro. 17. 8.
4 the seeing.
k Ps. 94. 6.
5 soul.
l Lev. 25. 8.
6 Or, olive trees.
m Lu. 13. 14.
n Hos. 2. 17.
o Deu. 16.16.
p Lev. 23.10.
7 Or, feast.
q Neh. 10.35.
Pro. 3. 9.

oxen, *and* with thy sheep: *y* seven days it shall be with his dam; on the eighth day thou shalt give it me.

31 ¶ And ye shall be *z* holy men unto me: neither *a* shall ye eat *any* flesh *that is* torn of beasts in the field; ye shall cast it to the dogs.

CHAPTER XXIII.

1 *Laws concerning slander and false witness;* 4 *charitableness;* 3, 6 *justice;* 10 *the year of rest;* 12 *the sabbath;* 13 *idolatry;* 14 *the three feasts.* 20 *An Angel promised, with a blessing, if they obey him.*

THOU *a* shalt not *1* raise a false report: put not thine hand with the wicked to be an *b* unrighteous witness.

2 Thou *c* shalt not follow a multitude to do evil; *d* neither shalt thou *2* speak in a cause to decline after many to wrest *judgment:*

3 Neither shalt thou *e* countenance a poor man in his cause.

4 ¶ If *f* thou meet thine enemy's ox or his ass going astray, thou shalt surely bring it back to him again.

5 If thou see the ass of him that hateth thee lying under his burden, *3* and wouldest forbear to help him; thou shalt surely help with him.

6 ¶ Thou *g* shalt not wrest the judgment of thy poor in his cause.

7 Keep *h* thee far from a false matter; and the innocent and righteous slay thou not: for *i* I will not justify the wicked.

8 ¶ And *j* thou shalt take no gift: for the gift blindeth *4* the wise, and perverteth the words of the righteous.

9 ¶ Also *k* thou shalt not oppress a stranger: for ye know the *5* heart of a stranger, seeing ye were strangers in the land of Egypt.

10 And *l* six years thou shalt sow thy land, and shalt gather in the fruits thereof:

11 But the seventh *year* thou shalt let it rest and lie still; that the poor of thy people may eat: and what they leave the beasts of the field shall eat. In like manner thou shalt deal with thy vineyard, *and* with thy *6* oliveyard.

12 Six *m* days thou shalt do thy work, and on the seventh day thou shalt rest; that thine ox and thine ass may rest, and the son of thy handmaid and the stranger may be refreshed.

13 And in all *things* that I have said unto you be circumspect: and *n* make no mention of the name of other gods, neither let it be heard out of thy mouth.

14 ¶ Three *o* times thou shalt keep a feast unto me in the year.

15 Thou shalt keep the feast of unleavened bread: (thou shalt eat unleavened bread seven days, as I commanded thee, in the time appointed of the month Abib; for in it thou camest out from Egypt; and none shall appear before me empty:)

16 And *p* the feast of harvest, the first-fruits of thy labours, which thou hast sown in thy field: and the feast of ingathering, *which is* in the end of the year, when thou hast gathered in thy labours out of the field.

17 Three times in the year all thy males shall appear before the Lord GOD.

18 Thou shalt not offer the blood of my sacrifice with leavened bread; neither shall the fat of my *7* sacrifice remain until the morning.

19 The *q* first of the first-fruits of thy land thou shalt bring into the house of the

tained a deep-seated grudge against them, especially as the rapid prosperity and marvellous experience of Israel showed that the blessing contained in the birth-right was taking effect. It seems to have been a mean, dastardly, insidious surprise on the rear, (Nu. 24. 20; Deut. 25. 17,) and an impious defiance of God. 9-13. Moses said unto Joshua—or Jesus (A. 7. 45; He. 4. 8,), and this is the earliest notice of a young warrior destined to act a prominent part in the history of Israel. He went with a number of picked men. There is not here a wide open plain on which the battle took place, as according to the rules of modern warfare. The Amalekites were a nomadic tribe, making an irregular attack on a multitude probably not better trained than themselves, and for such a conflict the low hills and open country around this Wady would afford ample space." [ROBINSON.] 10-12. Moses went up the hill...held up his hand—with the wonder-working rod; he acted as the standard-bearer of Israel, and also their intercessor, praying for success and victory to crown their arms,—the earnest of his friend being conspicuously evinced amid the feebleness of nature. 13. Joshua discomfited—Victory at length decided in favour of Israel, and the glory of the victory, by an act of national piety ascribed to God. (cf. 1 J. 5. 4.) 14-16. write this for a memorial—If the bloody character of this statute seems to be at variance with the mild and merciful character of God, the reasons are to be sought for in the deep and implacable vengeance they meditated against Israel, (Ps. 83. 4.)

CHAPTER XVIII.

Ver. 1-27. VISIT OF JETHRO. 1-5. Jethro...came unto Moses, &c.—It is thought by many eminent commentators that this episode is inserted out of its chronological order, for it is described as occurring when the Israelites were " encamped at the mount of God." And yet they did not reach it till the third month after their departure from Egypt. (ch. 19. 1, 2; cf. Deu. 1. 6, 9-15.) 6. thy wife and her two sons—See on ch. 4. 20. 7. Moses went out, &c.—Their salutations would be marked by all the warm and social greeting of Oriental friends—(see on ch. 4. 27.)—the one going out to "meet" the other, the "obeisance," the "kiss" on each side of the head, the silent entrance into the tent for consultation, and their conversation ran in the strain that might have been expected of two pious men, rehearsing and listening to a narrative of the wonderful works and providence of God. 12. Jethro took a burnt offering —This friendly interview was terminated by a solemn religious service—the *burnt offerings* were consumed on the altar, and the *sacrifices* were *peace* offerings, used in a feast of joy and gratitude at which Jethro, as priest of the true God, seems to have presided, and to which the chiefs of Israel were invited. This incident is in beautiful keeping with the character of the parties, and is well worthy of the imitation of Christian friends when they meet in the present day. 13-26. On the morrow Moses, &c.—We are here presented with a specimen of his daily morning occupations; and amongst the multifarious duties his Divine legation imposed, it must be considered only a small portion of his official employments. He appears in this attitude as a type of Christ in his legislative and judicial characters. people stood, &c.—governors in the East seat themselves at the most public gate of their palace or the city, and there, amid a crowd of applicants, hear causes, receive petitions, redress grievances, and adjust the claims of contending parties. 17. Moses' father-in-law ... The thing is not good—not good either for Moses himself, for the maintenance of justice, or for the satisfaction and interests of the people. Jethro gave a prudent counsel as to the division of labour, and universal experience in the Church and State has attested the soundness and advantages of the principle. 23. If thou shalt, &c.—Jethro's counsel was given merely in the form of a suggestion—it was not to be adopted without the express sanction and approval of a better and higher Counsellor; and although we are not informed of it, there can be no doubt that Moses, before appointing subordinate magistrates, would ask the mind of God, as it is the duty and privilege of every Christian in like manner to supplicate the Divine direction in all his ways.

CHAPTER XIX.

Ver. 1-25. ARRIVAL AT SINAI. 1. In the third month—according to Jewish usage the *first* day of that month—"same day,"—it is added, to mark the time more explicitly, *i.e.*, forty-five days after leaving Egypt—one day spent on the mount (v. 3.) one returning peoples' answers (v. 7, 8,); three days of preparation, making the whole time fifty days from the first passover to the promulgation of the law. Hence the feast of Pentecost, *i.e.*, the fiftieth day was the inauguration of the O. T. church, and the divine wisdom is apparent in the selection of the same season for the institution of the N. T. church. (J. 1. 17; A. 2. 1.) 2. were come to the desert of Sinai—The desert has its provinces, or divisions, distinguished by a variety of names; and the "desert of Sinai" is that wild and desolate region which occupies the very centre of the Peninsula, comprising the lofty range to which the Mount of God belongs. It is a wilderness of shaggy rocks of porphyry and red granite, and of valleys for the most part bare of verdure. camped before the Mount—Sinai, so called from Seneh, or acacia bush. It is now called Jebel Musa. Their way into the interior of the gigantic cluster was by Wady Feiran, which would lead the bulk of the host with their flocks and herds into the high valleys of Jebel Musa, with their abundant springs, especially into the great thoroughfare of the desert,—the longest, widest, and most continuous of all the valleys, the Wady-es-Sheykh, whilst many would be scattered among the adjacent valleys; so that thus secluded from the world in a wild and sublime amphitheatre of rocks, they "camped before the mount." "In this valley—a long flat valley—about a quarter of a mile in breadth, winding northwards, Israel would find ample room for their encampment. Of all the Wadys in that region, it seems the most suitable for a prolonged sojourn. The "goodly tents" of Israel could spread themselves without limit. [BONAR.] 3-6. Moses went up unto God—the Shechinah—within the cloud. (ch. 33. 20; J. 1. 18.) Thus shalt thou say, &c.—The object for which Moses went up was to receive and convey to the people the message contained in these verses,

LORD thy God. Thou shalt not seethe a kid in his mother's milk.

20 ¶ Behold, I send an Angel before thee, to keep thee in the way, and to bring thee into the place which I have prepared.

21 Beware of him, and obey his voice, provoke ʳ him not; for he will ˢ not pardon your transgressions: for ᵗ my name is in him.

22 But if thou shalt indeed obey his voice, and do all that I speak; then ᵘ I will be an enemy unto thine enemies, and an ˣ adversary unto thine adversaries.

23 For mine Angel shall go before thee, and ʷ bring thee in unto the Amorites, and the Hittites, and the Perizzites, and the Canaanites, the Hivites, and the Jebusites; and I will cut them off.

24 Thou shalt not ˣ bow down to their gods, nor serve them, nor do after their works; but thou shalt utterly overthrow them, and quite break down their images.

25 And ye shall ᶻ serve the LORD your God, and he ʸ shall bless thy bread, and thy water; and ᶻ I will take sickness away from the midst of thee.

26 ¶ There ᵃ shall nothing cast their young, nor be barren, in thy land: the number of thy days I will ᵇ fulfil.

27 I will send ᶜ my fear before thee, and will destroy all the people to whom thou shalt come; and I will make all thine enemies turn their backs unto thee.

28 And ᵈ I will send hornets before thee, which shall drive out the Hivite, the Canaanite, and the Hittite, from before thee.

29 I ᵉ will not drive them out from before thee in one year; lest the land become desolate, and the beast of the field multiply against thee.

30 By little and little I will drive them out from before thee, until thou be increased, and inherit the land.

31 And ᶠ I will set thy bounds from the Red sea even unto the sea of the Philistines, and from the desert unto the river: for I will ᵍ deliver the inhabitants of the land into your hand; and thou shalt drive them out before thee.

32 Thou ʰ shalt make no covenant with them, nor with their gods.

33 They shall not dwell in thy land, lest they make thee sin against me: for if thou serve their gods, ⁱ it will surely be a snare unto thee.

CHAPTER XXIV.

1 Moses is called up into the mountain, 3 The people promise obedience. 4 He builds an altar. 9 The glory of God appears. 14 Aaron and Hur have charge of the people, etc.

AND he said unto Moses, Come up unto the LORD, thou, and Aaron, ᵃ Nadab, and Abihu, ᵇ and seventy of the elders of Israel; and worship ye afar off.

2 And Moses alone shall come near the LORD; but they shall not come nigh, neither shall the people go up with him.

3 ¶ And Moses came and told the people all the words of the LORD, and all the judgments: and all the people answered with one voice, and said, All the words which the LORD hath said will we do.

4 And Moses ᶜ wrote all the words of the LORD, and rose up early in the morning, and builded an altar under the hill, and twelve ᵈ pillars, according to the twelve tribes of Israel.

5 And he sent young men of the children of Israel, which offered burnt offerings, and sacrificed peace offerings of oxen unto the LORD.

6 And Moses ᵉ took half of the blood, and put it in basins; and half of the blood he sprinkled on the altar.

7 And he took the book of the covenant, and read in the audience of the people: and they said, All that the LORD hath said will we do, and be obedient.

8 And Moses took the blood, and sprinkled it on the people, and said, Behold ᶠ the blood of the covenant, which the LORD hath made with you concerning all these words.

9 ¶ Then went up Moses, and Aaron, Nadab, and Abihu, and seventy of the elders of Israel;

10 And they ᵍ saw the God of Israel: and there was under his feet as it were a paved work of a ʰ sapphire stone, and as it were the ⁱ body of heaven in his clearness.

11 And upon the nobles of the children of Israel he ʲ laid not his hand: also ᵏ they saw God, and did ˡ eat and drink.

12 ¶ And the LORD said unto Moses, Come up to me into the mount, and be there: and I will give thee ᵐ tables of stone, and a law, and commandments which I have written; that thou mayest teach them.

13 And Moses rose up, and ⁿ his minister Joshua: and Moses went up into the mount of God.

14 And he said unto the elders, Tarry ye here for us, until we come again unto you: and, behold, Aaron and Hur are with you: if any man have any matters to do, let him come unto them.

15 ¶ And Moses went up into the mount, and ᵒ a cloud covered the mount.

16 And ᵖ the glory of the LORD abode upon mount Sinai, and the cloud covered it six days: and the seventh day he called unto Moses out of the midst of the cloud.

17 And the sight of the glory of the LORD was like ᵠ devouring fire on the top of the mount in the eyes of the children of Israel.

18 And Moses went into the midst of the cloud, and gat him up into the mount: and Moses ʳ was in the mount forty days and forty nights.

CHAPTER XXV.

1 What the Israelites must offer for the making of the tabernacle. 10 The form of the ark, etc.

AND the LORD spake unto Moses, saying, 2 Speak unto the children of Israel, that they ¹ bring me an ² offering: ᵃ of every man that giveth it willingly with his heart ye shall take my offering.

3 And this is the offering which ye shall take of them; gold, and silver, and brass,

4 And blue, and purple, and scarlet, and fine linen, and goats' hair,

5 And rams' skins dyed red, and badgers' skins, and shittim wood,

6 Oil for the light, spices for anointing oil, and for sweet incense,

7 Onyx stones, and stones to be set in the ephod, and in the ᵇ breastplate.

8 And let them make me a ᶜ sanctuary; that ᵈ I may dwell among them.

9 According to all that I show thee, after the pattern of the tabernacle, and the pattern of all the instruments thereof, even so shall ye make it.

10 ¶ And ᵉ they shall make an ark of shittim wood: two cubits and a half shall be the length thereof, and a cubit and a

and the purport of which was a general announcement of the terms on which God was to take the Israelites into a close and peculiar relation to himself. In thus negotiating between God and his people, the highest post of duty which any mortal man was ever called to occupy. Moses was still but a servant. The only Mediator is Jesus Christ. kingdom of priests—as the priestly order was set apart from the common mass, so the Israelites, compared with other people, were to sustain the same near relation to God:—a community of spiritual sovereigns, a holy nation—set apart to preserve the knowledge and worship of God. 7, 8. Moses came and called the elders—The message was conveyed to the mighty multitude through their elders, who, doubtless, instructed them in the conditions required. Their unanimous acceptance was conveyed through the same channel to Moses, and by him reported to the Lord. Ah! how much self-confidence did their language betray!—how little did they know what spirit they were of! 9-15. Lo, I come in a thick cloud, &c.—The deepest impressions are made on the mind through the medium of the senses; and so He who knew what was in man signalised His descent at the inauguration of the ancient church, by all the sensible tokens of august Majesty that were fitted to produce the conviction that He is the great and terrible God. The whole multitude must have anticipated the event with feelings of intense solemnity and awe. The extraordinary preparations enjoined, the ablutions and rigid abstinence they were required to observe, the barriers erected all round the base of the mount, and the stern penalties annexed to the breach of any of the conditions, all tended to create an earnest and solemn expectation which increased as the appointed day drew near. 16. On the third day, &c.—The descent of God was signalised by every object imagination can conceive connected with the ideas of grandeur and of awe. But all was in keeping with the character of the law about to be proclaimed. As the mountain burned with fire, God was exhibited a consuming fire to the transgressors of His law. The thunder and lightning, more awful amid the deep stillness of the region, and reverberating with terrific peals among the mountains, would rouse the universal attention: a thick cloud was an apt emblem of the dark and shadowy dispensation, (cf. M. 17. 5.) The voice as of a trumpet—this gave the scene the character of a miraculous transaction, in which other elements than those of nature were at work, and some other than material trumpet was blown by other means than human breath. 17. Moses brought forth the people—Wady-er-Raheh, where they stood as a spacious sandy plain, immediately in front of Es-Suksâfeh, considered by Robinson to be the mount from which the law was given, "We measured it, and estimate the whole plains at two geographical miles long, and ranging in breadth from one-third to two-thirds of a mile, or as equivalent to a surface of one square mile. This space is nearly doubled by the recess on the west, and by the broad and level area of Wady-es-Sheikh on the east, which issues at right angles to the plain, and is equally in view of the front and summit of the mount. The examination convinced us that here was space enough to satisfy all the requisitions of the scripture narrative, so far as it relates to the assembling of the congregation to receive the law. Here, too, one can see the fitness of the injunction to set bounds around the mount, that neither man nor beast might approach too near, for it rises like a perpendicular wall." But Jebel Musa, the old traditional Sinai, and the highest peak has also a spacious valley, Wady Seba'iyeh, capable of holding the people. It is not certain on which of these two they stood. 21. Lord said unto Moses, Go down—No sooner had Moses proceeded a little up the Mount, than he was suddenly ordered to return, in order to keep the people from breaking through to gaze—a course adopted to heighten the impressive solemnity of the scene. The strict injunctions renewed to all, whatever their condition, at a time and in circumstances when the whole multitude of Israel were standing at the base of the mount, was calculated in the highest degree to solemnise and awe every heart.

CHAPTER XX.

Ver. 1-26. THE TEN COMMANDMENTS. 1. God spake all these words—The Divine Being himself was the speaker, (Deu. 5. 12, 13, 32,) in tones so loud as to be heard—so distinct as to be intelligible by the whole multitude standing in the valleys below, amid the most appalling phenomena of agitated nature. Had He been simply addressing rational and intelligent creatures, He would have spoken with the still small voice of persuasion and love. But He was speaking to those who were at the same time fallen and sinful creatures, and a corresponding change was required in the manner of God's procedure, in order to give a suitable impression of the character and sanctions of the law revealed from heaven. (Ro. 2. 5-9.) 2. I am the Lord thy God—This is a preface to the ten commandments—the latter clause being specially applicable to the case of the Israelites, while the former brings it home to all mankind; showing that the reasonableness of the law is founded in their eternal relation as creatures to their Creator, and their mutual relations to each other. 3. before me—in my presence, beside, or except me. 4, 5. make any graven image... thou shalt not bow—i. e., "make in order to bow." Under the auspices of Moses himself, figures of cherubim, brazen serpents, oxen, and many other things in the earth beneath, were made, and never condemned. The mere making was no sin—it was the making with the intent to give idolatrous worship. 8. Remember the Sabbath-day—implying it was already known, and recognized as a season of sacred rest. The first four commandments comprise our duties to God—the other six our duties to our fellow-men; and as interpreted by Christ, they reach to the government of the heart as well as the lip. (M. 5. 17.) "If a man do them he shall live in them!" But, ah! what an *if* for frail and fallen man. Whoever rests his hope upon the law stands debtor to do it all; and in this view every one would be without hope, were not " the LORD OUR RIGHTEOUSNESS." J. 1. 17.) 18-21. All the people saw—They were eye and ear witnesses of the awful emblems of the Deity's descent. But they perceived not the Deity himself. 19. Let not God speak, &c.—

half the breadth thereof, and a cubit and a half the height thereof.

11 And thou shalt overlay it with pure gold, within and without shalt thou overlay it; and shalt make upon it a crown of gold round about.

12 And thou shalt cast four rings of gold for it, and put *them* in the four corners thereof; and two rings *shall be* in the one side of it, and two rings in the other side of it.

13 And thou shalt make staves *of* shittim wood, and overlay them with gold.

14 And thou shalt put the staves into the rings by the sides of the ark, that the ark may be borne with them.

15 The staves shall be in the rings of the ark; they shall not be taken from it.

16 And thou shalt put into the ark the testimony which I shall give thee.

17 ¶ And thou shalt make a mercyseat *of* pure gold: two cubits and a half *shall be* the length thereof, and a cubit and a half the breadth thereof.

18 And thou shalt make two cherubim *of* gold, *of* beaten work shalt thou make them, in the two ends of the mercyseat.

19 And make one cherub on the one end, and the other cherub on the other end; even 1 of the mercyseat shall ye make the cherubim on the two ends thereof.

20 And the cherubim shall stretch forth *their* wings on high, covering the mercyseat with their wings, and their faces *shall* look one to another; toward the mercyseat shall the faces of the cherubim be.

21 And thou shalt put the mercyseat above upon the ark; and in the ark thou shalt put the testimony that I shall give thee.

22 And there I will meet with thee, and I will commune with thee from above the mercyseat, from between the two cherubim which are upon the ark of the testimony, of all *things* which I will give thee in commandment unto the children of Israel.

23 ¶ Thou shalt also make a table *of* shittim wood: two cubits *shall be* the length thereof, and a cubit the breadth thereof, and a cubit and a half the height thereof.

24 And thou shalt overlay it with pure gold, and make thereto a crown of gold round about.

25 And thou shalt make unto it a border of an hand-breadth round about, and thou shalt make a golden crown to the border thereof round about.

26 And thou shalt make for it four rings of gold, and put the rings in the four corners that *are* on the four feet thereof.

27 Over against the border shall the rings be for places of the staves to bear the table.

28 And thou shalt make the staves *of* shittim wood, and overlay them with gold, that the table may be borne with them.

29 And thou shalt make the dishes thereof, and spoons thereof, and covers thereof, and bowls thereof, 2 to cover withal: *of* pure gold shalt thou make them.

30 And thou shalt set upon the table showbread before me alway.

31 ¶ And thou shalt make a candlestick *of* pure gold: *of* beaten work shall the candlestick be made: his shaft, and his branches, his bowls, his knops, and his flowers, shall be of the same.

32 And six branches shall come out of the sides of it; three branches of the candlestick out of the one side, and three branches of the candlestick out of the other side:

33 Three bowls made like unto almonds, *with* a knop and a flower in one branch; and three bowls made like almonds in the other branch, *with* a knop and a flower: so in the six branches that come out of the candlestick.

34 And in the candlestick *shall be* four bowls made like unto almonds, *with* their knops and their flowers.

35 And *there shall be* a knop under two branches of the same, and a knop under two branches of the same, and a knop under two branches of the same, according to the six branches that proceed out of the candlestick.

36 Their knops and their branches shall be of the same: all of it *shall be* one beaten work *of* pure gold.

37 And thou shalt make the seven lamps thereof: and they shall 3 light the lamps thereof, that they may give light over against 4 it.

38 And the tongs thereof, and the snuffdishes thereof, *shall be of* pure gold.

39 *Of* a talent of pure gold shall he make it, with all these vessels.

40 And look that thou make *them* after their pattern, 5 which was showed thee in the mount.

CHAPTER XXVI.

1 *The ten curtains of the tabernacle.* 7 *The eleven curtains of goats' hair.* 31 *The veil for the ark.* 36 *The hanging for the door.*

MOREOVER thou shalt make the tabernacle *with* ten curtains *of* fine twined linen, and blue, and purple, and scarlet: *with* cherubim of 1 cunning work shalt thou make them.

2 The length of one curtain *shall be* eight and twenty cubits, and the breadth of one curtain four cubits: and every one of the curtains shall have one measure.

3 The five curtains shall be coupled together one to another; and *other* five curtains *shall be* coupled one to another.

4 And thou shalt make loops of blue upon the edge of the one curtain, from the selvage in the coupling; and likewise shalt thou make in the uttermost edge of *another* curtain, in the coupling of the second.

5 Fifty loops shalt thou make in the one curtain, and fifty loops shalt thou make in the edge of the curtain that is in the coupling of the second, that the loops may take hold one of another.

6 And thou shalt make fifty taches of gold, and couple the curtains together with the taches; and it shall be one tabernacle.

7 ¶ And thou shalt make curtains *of* goats' hair to be a covering upon the tabernacle; eleven curtains shalt thou make.

8 The length of one curtain *shall be* thirty cubits, and the breadth of one curtain four cubits: and the eleven curtains *shall be all* of one measure.

9 And thou shalt couple five curtains by themselves, and six curtains by themselves, and shalt double the sixth curtain in the fore front of the tabernacle.

10 And thou shalt make fifty loops on the edge of the one curtain *that is* outmost in the coupling, and fifty loops in the edge of the curtain which coupleth the second.

11 And thou shalt make fifty taches of

The phenomena of thunder and lightning had been one of the plagues so fatal to Egypt, and as they heard God speaking to them now, they were apprehensive of instant death also. Even Moses himself, the mediator of the old covenant, did "exceedingly quake and fear." (He. 12. 21.) But doubtless God spake what gave *him* relief—restored him to a frame of mind fit for the ministrations committed to him; and hence immediately after he was enabled to relieve and comfort them with the relief and comfort which he himself had received from God. (2 Co. 1. 4.) 22, 23. The Lord said unto Moses—It appears from Deu. 4. 14-16, that this injunction was a conclusion drawn from the scene on Sinai—that as no similitude of God was displayed then, they should not attempt to make any visible figure or form of Him. 24. an altar of earth—a regulation applicable to special or temporary occasions. 25. not build, &c.—*i.e.*, carved with figures and ornaments that might lead to superstition. 26. by steps—a precaution taken for the sake of decency, in consequence of the loose, wide, flowing garments of the priests.

CHAPTER XXI.

Ver. 1-6. LAWS FOR MEN SERVANTS. 1. Judgments — Rules for regulating the procedure of judges and magistrates in the decision of causes and the trial of criminals. The government of the Israelites being a Theocracy, those public authorities were the servants of the Divine Sovereign, and subject to His direction. Most of these laws here noticed were primitive usages, founded on principles of natural equity, and incorporated with modifications and improvements; in the Mosaic code. 2-6. If thou buy an Hebrew—Every Israelite was freeborn; but slavery was permitted under certain restrictions. An Hebrew might be made a slave through poverty, debt, or crime; but at the end of six years he was entitled to freedom, and his wife, if she had voluntarily shared his state of bondage, also obtained release. Should he, however, have married a female slave, she and the children, after the husband's liberation, remained the master's property; and if, through attachment to his family, the Hebrew chose to forfeit his privilege and abide as he was, a formal process was gone through in a public court, and a brand of servitude stamped on his ear (Ps. 40. 6.) for life, or at least till the Jubilee. (Deu. 15. 17.)

7-36. LAWS FOR MAID SERVANTS. 7. If a man sell his daughter—Hebrew girls might be redeemed for a reasonable sum. But in the event of her parents or friends being unable to pay the redemption money, her owner was not at liberty to sell her elsewhere. Should she have been betrothed to him or his son, and either change their minds, a maintenance must be provided for her suitable to her condition as his intended wife, or her freedom instantly granted. 23-25. an eye for an eye—The law which authorized retaliation—a principle acted upon by all primitive people—was a civil one. It was given to regulate the procedure of the public magistrate in determining the amount of compensation in every case of injury, but did not encourage feelings of private revenge. The later Jews, however, mistook it for a *moral* precept, and were corrected by our Lord. (M. 5. 38-42.) 28-36. If an ox gore a man—For the purpose of sanctifying human blood, and representing all injuries affecting life in a serious light, an animal that occasioned death was to be killed or suffer punishment proportioned to the degree of damage it had caused. Punishments are still inflicted on this principle in Persia and other countries of the East; and among a rude people greater effect is produced in inspiring caution, and making them keep noxious animals under restraint, than a penalty imposed on the owners. 30. If there be laid, &c.—Blood fines are common among the Arabs as they were once general throughout the East. This is the only case where a money compensation, instead of capital punishment, was expressly allowed in the Mosaic law.

CHAPTER XXII.

Ver. 1–31. LAWS CONCERNING THEFT. 1. If a man shall steal—The law respects the theft of cattle which constituted the chief part of their property. The penalty for the theft of a sheep which was slain or sold, was fourfold; for an ox fivefold, because of its greater utility in labour: but, should the stolen animal have been recovered alive, a *double* compensation was all that was required, because it was presumable he (the thief) was not a practised adept in dishonesty. A robber breaking into a house at *midnight* might, in self-defence, be slain with impunity; but if he was slain after *sun-rise*, it would be considered murder, for it was not thought likely an assault would then be made upon the lives of the inmates. In every case where a thief could not make restitution, he was sold as a slave for the usual term. 6. If a fire break out—This refers to the common practice in the East of setting fire to the dry grass before the fall of the autumnal rains, which prevents the ravages of vermin, and is considered a good preparation of the ground for the next crop. The very parched state of the herbage and the long droughts of summer, make the kindling of a fire an operation often dangerous, and always requiring caution from its liability to spread rapidly. stack—or as it is rendered "shock" (Ju. 15, 5; Job,15. 26.), means simply a bundle of loose sheaves. 26, 27. If thou at all, &c.— From the nature of the case, this is the description of a poor man. No Orientals undress, but merely throwing off their turbans, and some of their heavy outer garments, they sleep in the clothes which they wear during the day. The bed of the poor is usually nothing else than a mat; and, in winter, they cover themselves with a cloak— a practice which forms the ground or reason of the humane and merciful law respecting the pawned coat. 28. gods—a word which is several times in this chapter rendered "judges" or magistrates. the ruler of thy people—and the chief magistrate who was also the High priest, at least in the time of Paul. (A. 23. 1-5.)

CHAPTER XXIII.

Ver. 1-33. LAWS CONCERNING SLANDER, &c. 1. put not thine hands—join not hands 2. decline—depart, deviate from the straight path of rectitude. 3. countenance—adorn, embellish—thou shalt not varnish the cause even of a poor man to give it a better colouring than it merits. 10, 11. six years thou shalt sow—intermitting the cultivation of the land every seventh year. But it appears that even then there was a spontaneous

brass, and put the taches into the loops, and couple the *tent* together, that it may be one.

12 And the remnant that remaineth of the curtains of the tent, the half-curtain that remaineth shall hang over the back side of the tabernacle.

13 And a cubit on the one side, and a cubit on the other side, *of* that which remaineth in the length of the curtains of the tent, it shall hang over the sides of the tabernacle on this side and on that side, to cover it.

14 And *f* thou shalt make a covering for the tent of rams' skins dyed red, and a covering above *of* badgers' skins.

15 ¶ And thou shalt make boards for the tabernacle *of* shittim wood standing up.

16 Ten cubits *shall be* the length of a board, and a cubit and a half *shall be* the breadth of one board.

17 Two *tenons shall there be* in one board, set in order one against another: thus shalt thou make for all the boards of the tabernacle.

18 And thou shalt make the boards for the tabernacle, twenty boards on the south side southward.

19 And thou shalt make forty *g* sockets of silver under the twenty boards; two sockets under one board for his two tenons, and two sockets under another board for his two tenons.

20 And for the second side of the tabernacle, on the north side, *there shall be* twenty boards,

21 And their forty sockets *of* silver; two sockets under one board, and two sockets under another board.

22 And for the sides of the tabernacle *h* westward thou shalt make six boards.

23 And two boards shalt thou make for the corners of the tabernacle in the two sides.

24 And they shall be coupled together beneath, and they shall be coupled together above the head of it unto one ring: thus shall it be for them both; they shall be for the two corners.

25 And they shall be eight boards, and their sockets *of* silver, sixteen sockets; two sockets under one board, and two sockets under another board.

26 ¶ And thou shalt make *i* bars *of* shittim wood; five for the boards of the one side of the tabernacle,

27 And five bars for the boards of the other side of the tabernacle, and five bars for the boards of the side of the tabernacle for the two sides westward.

28 And the middle bar in the midst of the boards shall reach from end to end.

29 And thou shalt overlay the boards with gold, and make their rings *of* gold *for* places for the bars: and thou shalt overlay the bars with gold.

30 And thou shalt rear up the tabernacle according *j* to the fashion thereof which was showed thee in the mount.

31 ¶ And *k* thou shalt make a veil *of* blue, and purple, and scarlet, and fine twined linen, of cunning work: with cherubim shall it be made:

32 And thou shalt hang it upon four pillars of shittim *wood* overlaid with gold: their hooks *shall be of* gold, upon the four sockets of silver.

33 And thou shalt hang up the veil under the taches, that thou mayest bring in thi-

B. C. 1491.

CHAP. 26.
2 Or, covering.
3 in the remainder, or surplusage.
f ch. 36. 19.
Nu. 24. 5.
4 bands.
g ch. 38. 27.
h sea-ward.
Gen. 12. 8.
5 twined.
Ps. 133. 1.
1 Cor. 1. 10.
Col. 3. 2, 19.
i ch. 36. 31.
Nu. 3. 36.
Rom. 15. 1.
1 Cor. 9. 19.
2 Cor. 13. 11.
Gal. 6. 2.
j ch. 25. 9, 40.
ch. 27. 8.
Acts 7. 44.
Heb. 8. 5.
k ch. 36. 35.
Lev. 16. 2.
2 Chr. 3. 14.
Mat. 27. 51.
Mark 15. 38.
Luke 23. 45.
Heb. 9. 3.
l ch. 25. 16.
ch. 40. 21.
1 Ki. 8. 6.
m 2 Chro. 3. 14.
n Lev. 16. 2.
Mat. 24. 15.
Heb. 9. 2, 3.
o ch. 25. 21.
ch. 40. 20.
Lev. 16. 2.
Heb. 9. 5.
p ch. 40. 22.
Heb. 9. 2.
q ch. 40. 24.
r ch. 36. 37.
s ch. 36. 38.

CHAP. 27.
a ch. 38. 1.
Ezek. 43. 13.
b 1 Kin. 1. 50.
1 Kin. 2. 28.
Ps. 128. 27.
c Num. 16. 38.
1 Or, sieve.
Amos 9. 9.
d 1 Sam. 2. 12-14.
e Nu. 4. 15.
Is. 52. 11.
f ch. 25. 40.
ch. 26. 30.
Heb. 8. 5.
Acts 7. 44.
2 he showed.
g ch. 38. 9.
Ps. 100. 4.
h Jer. 1. 18.

ther within the veil *l* the ark of the testimony: and *m* the veil shall divide unto you between *n* the holy *place* and the most holy.

34 And *o* thou shalt put the mercyseat upon the ark of the testimony in the most holy *place*.

35 And *p* thou shalt set the table without the veil, and the *q* candlestick over against the table on the side of the tabernacle toward the south: and thou shalt put the table on the north side.

36 ¶ And *r* thou shalt make an hanging for the door of the tent, *of* blue, and purple, and scarlet, and fine twined linen, wrought with needle-work.

37 And thou shalt make for the hanging five *s* pillars *of* shittim *wood*, and overlay them with gold, *and* their hooks *shall be of* gold; and thou shalt cast five sockets of brass for them.

CHAPTER XXVII.

1 *The altar of burnt offering, with the vessels.* 9 *The court of the tabernacle, with its hangings and pillars.* 18 *The measure of the court.* 20 *The oil for the lamp.*

AND thou shalt make *a* an altar *of* shittim wood, five cubits long, and five cubits broad: the altar shall be foursquare: and the height thereof *shall be* three cubits.

2 And thou shalt make the *b* horns of it upon the four corners thereof: his horns shall be of the same: and *c* thou shalt overlay it with brass.

3 And thou shalt make his pans to receive his ashes, and his ¹ shovels, and his basins, and his flesh-hooks, and his fire-pans: all the vessels thereof thou shalt make *of* brass.

4 And thou shalt make for it a *d* grate of network *of* brass; and upon the net shalt thou make four brasen rings in the four corners thereof.

5 And thou shalt put it under the compass of the altar beneath, that the net may be even to the midst of the altar.

6 And thou shalt make staves for the altar, staves *of* shittim wood, and overlay them with brass.

7 And the staves shall be put into the rings, and the staves shall be upon the two sides of the altar, to *e* bear it.

8 Hollow with boards shalt thou make it: *f as* ² it was showed thee in the mount, so shall they make *it*.

9 ¶ And *g* thou shalt make the court of the tabernacle: for the south side southward *there shall be* hangings for the court *of* fine twined linen, of an hundred cubits long for one side.

10 And the twenty *h* pillars thereof, and their twenty sockets, *shall be of* brass; the hooks of the pillars and their fillets *shall be of* silver.

11 And likewise for the north side in length *there shall be* hangings of an hundred cubits long, and his twenty pillars and their twenty sockets *of* brass; the hooks of the pillars and their fillets *of* silver.

12 And *for* the breadth of the court on the west side *shall be* hangings of fifty cubits: their pillars ten, and their sockets ten.

13 And the breadth of the court on the east side eastward *shall be* fifty cubits.

14 The hangings of one side *of the gate shall be* fifteen cubits: their pillars three, and their sockets three.

15 And on the other side *shall be* hangings

produce which the poor were permitted freely to gather for their use, and the beasts driven out fed on the remainder, the owners of fields not being allowed to reap or collect the fruits of the vineyard or oliveyard during the course of this Sabbatical year. This was a regulation subservient to many excellent purposes: for, besides inculcating the general lesson of dependence on Providence, and of confidence in his faithfulness to his promise respecting the triple increase on the sixth year, (Lev. 25. 20, 21,) it gave the Israelites a practical proof that they held their properties of the Lord as his tenants, and must conform to his rules on pain of forfeiting the lease of them. 12. Six days shalt thou do thy work—This law is repeated lest any might suppose there was a relaxation of its observance during the Sabbatical year. 13. make no mention, &c.— *i.e.*, in common conversation, for a familiar use of them would tend to lessen horror of idolatry. 14-18. Three times keep a feast in a year—This was the institution of the great religious festivals—"The feast of unleavened bread" or the Passover—"The feast of harvest" or Pentecost—"The feast of in-gathering" or the feast of Tabernacles, which was a memorial of the dwelling in booths in the wilderness, and which was observed "in the end of the year," or the seventh month, ch. 12, 2.) All the males were enjoined to repair to the Tabernacle and afterwards the temple, and the women frequently went. The institution of this national custom was of the greatest importance in many ways—by keeping up a national sense of religion and a public uniformity in worship, by creating a bond of unity, and also promoting internal commerce amongst the people. Though the absence of all the males at these three festivals left the country defenceless, a special promise was given of divine protection, and no incursion of enemies was ever permitted to happen on those occasions. 19. Thou shalt not seethe a kid—a prohibition against imitating the superstitious rites of the idolaters in Egypt, who, at the end of their harvest, seethed a kid in its mother's milk and sprinkled the broth as a magical charm on their gardens and fields, to render them more productive the following season. 20-25. Behold I send an angel before thee—The communication of these laws made to Moses and by him rehearsed to the people, was concluded by the addition of many animating promises, intermingled with several solemn warnings, that lapses into sin and idolatry would not be tolerated or passed with impunity. my Name is in him—This angel is frequently called Jehovah and Elohim, *i.e.*, God. 28. I will send hornets, &c.—(Jos. 24. 12.) Some instrument of divine judgment, but variously interpreted, as hornets in a literal sense, [BO.] As a pestilential disease, [ROS.] As a terror of the Lord—an extraordinary dejection, [JUN.] 29, 30. I will not drive out in one year—Many reasons recommended a gradual extirpation of the former inhabitants of Canaan.. But only one is here specified—the danger lest in the unoccupied grounds, wild beasts should inconveniently multiply; a clear proof that the promised land was more than sufficient to contain the actual population of the Israelites.

CHAPTER XXIV.
Ver. 1-18. DELIVERY OF THE LAW AND COVENANT. 3. Moses came and told the people—The rehearsal of the foregoing laws and the ten commandments, together with the promises of special blessings in the event of their obedience, having drawn forth from the people a unanimous declaration of their consent, it was forthwith recorded as the conditions of the *national* covenant. The next day preparations were made for having it solemnly ratified, by building an altar and twelve pillars; the altar representing God, and the pillars the tribes of Israel—the two parties in this solemn compact—while Moses acted as typical mediator. 5. young men—priests (ch. 19. 22,), probably the eldest sons of particular families, who acted under the direction of Moses. oxen—other animals, though not mentioned, were offered in sacrifice (Heb. 9. 18-20.). 6. half of the blood ... sprinkled—Preliminary to this, was the public reading of the law, and the renewed acceptance of the terms by the people; then the sprinkling of the blood was the sign of solemn ratification—half on each party in the transaction. 8. sprinkled it on the people—probably on the twelve pillars, as representing the people (also the book, Heb. 9. 19,), and the act was accompanied by a public proclamation of its import. It was setting their seal to the covenant. (cf. 1 Cor. 11. 25.) It must have been a deeply impressive, as well as instructive scene, for it taught the Israelites that the covenant was made with them only through the sprinkling of blood—that the Divine acceptance of themselves and services, was only by virtue of an atoning sacrifice, and that even the blessings of the *national* covenant were promised and secured to them only through grace. The ceremonial, however, had a further and higher significance, as is shown by the apostle (see as above). 9. Then went up Moses and Aaron, &c.—In obedience to a command given (v. 1, 2; also ch. 19. 24,), previous to the religious engagement of the people, now described. Nadab and Abihu—the two eldest sons of Aaron. seventy of the elders—a select number; what was the principle of selection is not said; but they were the chief representatives, the most conspicuous for official rank and station, as well as for their probity and weight of character in their respective tribes. 10. saw the God of Israel—That there was no visible form or representation of the divine nature, we have express intimation (Deu. 4. 15.). But a symbol or emblem of His glory was distinctly, and at a distance, displayed before those chosen witnesses. Many think, however, that in this private scene, was discovered amid the luminous blaze, the faint adumbrated form of the humanity of Christ (Ez. 1. 26. cf. Gal. 3. 24.). sapphire—one of the most valuable and lustrous of the precious gems—of a sky-blue or light azure colour, and frequently chosen to describe the throne of God (see Ez. 1. 26; 10. 1.). 11. laid not his hand—The "nobles," *i.e.* the elders, after the sprinkling of the blood, were not inspired with terror in presence of the calm, benign, radiant symbol of the divine majesty; so different from the terrific exhibitions at the giving of the law. The report of so many competent witnesses would tend to confirm the peoples' faith in the divine mission of Moses. eat and drink—feasted on the peaceoffering—on the remnants of the late sacrifices and libations. This feast had a prophetic

EXODUS, XXVIII.

fifteen *cubits:* their pillars three, and their sockets three.

16 And for the gate of the court *shall be* an hanging of twenty cubits, *of* blue, and purple, and scarlet, and fine twined linen, wrought with needle-work: *and* their pillars *shall be* four, and their sockets four.

17 All the pillars round about the court *shall be* filleted with silver; their hooks *shall be of* silver, and their sockets *of* brass.

18 The length of the court *shall be* an hundred cubits, and the breadth ³ fifty every where, and the height five cubits *of* fine twined linen, and their sockets *of* brass.

19 All the vessels of the tabernacle in all the service thereof, and all the pins thereof, and all the ⁴ pins of the court, *shall be of* brass.

20 ¶ And ⁱ thou shalt command the children of Israel, that they bring thee pure oil olive beaten for the light, to cause the lamp ⁵ to burn always.

21 In the tabernacle of the congregation without, which *is* before the testimony, ᵏ Aaron and his sons shall order it from evening to morning before the LORD. *It* ˡ *shall be* a statute for ever unto their generations on the behalf of the children of Israel.

CHAPTER XXVIII.

1 *Aaron and his sons separated for the priest's office.* 6 *The ephod.* 30 *The Urim and Thummim.* 36 *The plate of the mitre, etc.*

AND take thou unto thee ᵃ Aaron thy brother, and his sons with him, from among the children of Israel, that he may minister unto me in the priest's office, *even* Aaron, Nadab and Abihu, Eleazar and Ithamar, Aaron's sons.

2 And ᵇ thou shalt make holy garments for Aaron thy brother for glory and for beauty.

3 And ᶜ thou shalt speak unto all *that are* wise-hearted, ᵈ whom I have filled with the spirit of wisdom, that they may make Aaron's garments to consecrate him, that he may minister unto me in the priest's office.

4 And these *are* the garments which they shall make; a breastplate, and an ephod, and a robe, and a broidered coat, a mitre, and a girdle; and they shall make holy garments for Aaron thy brother, and his sons, that he may minister unto me in the priest's office.

5 And they shall take gold, and blue, and purple, and scarlet, and fine linen.

6 ¶ And ᵉ they shall make the ephod *of* gold, *of* blue, and *of* purple, *of* scarlet, and fine twined linen, with cunning work.

7 It shall have the two shoulder-pieces thereof joined at the two edges thereof; and so it shall be joined together.

8 And the ¹ curious girdle of the ephod, which *is* upon it, shall be of the same, according to the work thereof; *even of* gold, *of* blue, and purple, and scarlet, and fine twined linen.

9 And thou shalt take two onyx stones, and grave on them the names of the children of Israel:

10 Six of their names on one stone, and the other six names of the rest on the other stone, according to their birth.

11 With the work of an engraver in stone, *like* the engravings of a signet, shalt thou engrave the two stones with the names of the children of Israel: thou shalt make them to be set in ouches of gold.

12 And thou shalt put the two stones upon the shoulders of the ephod *for* stones of memorial unto the children of Israel: and ᶠ Aaron shall bear their names before the LORD upon his two shoulders ᵍ for a memorial.

13 And thou shalt make ouches *of* gold;

14 And two chains *of* pure gold at the ends; *of* wreathen work shalt thou make them, and fasten the wreathen chains to the ouches.

15 ¶ And ʰ thou shalt make the breastplate of judgment with cunning work; after the work of the ephod thou shalt make it; *of* gold, *of* blue, and *of* purple, and *of* scarlet, and *of* fine twined linen, shalt thou make it.

16 Foursquare it shall be, *being* doubled; a span *shall be* the length thereof, and a span *shall be* the breadth thereof.

17 And ⁱ thou shalt ² set in it settings of stones, *even* four rows of stones: *the first* row *shall be* a ³ sardius, a topaz, and a carbuncle: *this shall be* the first row.

18 And the second row *shall be* an emerald, a sapphire, and a diamond.

19 And the third row a ligure, an agate, and an amethyst.

20 And the fourth row a beryl, and an onyx, and a jasper; they shall be set in gold in their ⁴ inclosings.

21 And the stones shall be with the names of the children of Israel, twelve, according to their names, *like* the engravings of a signet; every one with his name shall they be *j* according to the twelve tribes.

22 And thou shalt make upon the breastplate chains at the ends *of* wreathen work *of* pure gold.

23 And thou shalt make upon the breastplate two rings of gold, and shalt put the two rings on the two ends of the breastplate.

24 And thou shalt put the two wreathen chains of gold in the two rings *which are* on the ends of the breastplate.

25 And *the other* two ends of the two wreathen chains thou shalt fasten in the two ouches, and put *them* on the shoulder-pieces of the ephod before it.

26 And thou shalt make two rings of gold, and thou shalt put them upon the two ends of the breastplate, in the border thereof, which *is* in the side of the ephod inward.

27 And two *other* rings of gold thou shalt make, and shalt put them on the two sides of the ephod underneath, toward the fore part thereof, over against the *other* coupling thereof, above the curious girdle of the ephod.

28 And they shall bind the breastplate by the rings thereof unto the rings of the ephod with a lace of blue, that *it* may be above the curious girdle of the ephod, and that the breastplate be not loosed from the ephod.

29 And Aaron shall ᵏ bear the names of the children of Israel in the breastplate of judgment upon his heart, when he goeth in unto the holy *place*, ˡ for a memorial before the LORD continually.

30 ¶ And ᵐ thou shalt put in the breastplate of judgment the Urim and the Thummim; and they shall be upon Aaron's heart when he goeth in before the LORD: and Aaron shall bear the judgment of the

bearing, intimating God's dwelling with men. 12. I will give thee the tables of stone—The ten commandments, which had already been spoken, were to be given in a permanent form. Inscribed on stone, for greater durability, by the hand of God himself, they were thus authenticated and honoured above the judicial or ceremonial parts of the law. 13. Moses went up into the mount— He was called to receive the divine transcript. Joshua was taken a little higher, and it would be a great comfort to the leader to have his company during the six days he was in patient waiting for the call on the seventh or sabbath-day. 14. elders... tarry here—There is a circular valley or hollow a good way up on the brow of Jebel Musa, which was their halting place, while he alone was privileged to ascend the highest peak. The people stood below, as in the "outer court," the elders in the "holy place," Moses, as a type of Christ, in "the holy of holies." 18. Moses went into the midst of the cloud—the visible token of God's presence. Divine grace animated and supported him to enter with holy boldness. forty days and forty nights—the six days spent in waiting are not included. During that protracted period he was miraculously supported (Deu. 9. 9.), on a peak scarcely thirty paces in compass.

CHAPTER XXV.

Ver. 1-40. CONCERNING AN OFFERING. 1. The Lord spake, &c.—The business that chiefly occupied Moses on the Mount, whatever other disclosures were made to him there, was in receiving directions about the tabernacle, and they are here recorded as given to him. 2. bring me an offering—Having declared allegiance to God as their sovereign, they were expected to contribute to his state, as other subjects to their kings; and the "offering" required of them was not to be imposed as a tax, but to come from their own loyal and liberal feelings. 3. this is the offering—The articles of which the offering should consist. brass—rather copper, brass being a composite metal. goat's hair—or leather of goat's skin. 5. badgers' skin—The badger was an unclean animal, and is not a native of the East—rather some kind of fish, of the leather of which sandals are made in the East. Shittimwood—or Shittah, (Is. 41. 19.) the acacia, a shrub which grows plentifully in the deserts of Arabia, yielding a light, strong, and beautiful wood, in long planks. 7. Ephod—a square cloak, hanging down from the shoulders, and worn by priests. 8. A sanctuary, &c.—In one sense the tabernacle was to be a palace, the royal residence of the king of Israel, in which he was to dwell amongst his people, receive their petitions, and issue his responses. But it was also to be a place of worship, in which God was to record His name and to enshrine the mystic symbols of His presence. 9. according to all that I shall show thee... pattern—The proposed erection could be in the circumstances of the Israelites, not of a fixed and stable, but of a temporary and moveable description, capable of being carried about with them in their various sojournings. It was made after "the pattern" shown to Moses, by which is now generally understood; not that it was an unheard of novelty, or an entirely original structure, for it is ascertained to have borne resemblance in form and arrangements to the style of an Egyptian temple, but that it was so altered, modified, and purified from all idolatrous associations, as to be appropriated to right objects, and suggestive of ideas connected with the true God and His worship. 10. an ark—a coffer or chest, overlaid with gold, the dimensions of which, taking the cubit at 18 inches, are computed to be 3 feet 9 inches in length, 2 feet 3 inches in breadth. 11. a crown—a rim or cornice. 12. rings—staples for the poles, with which it was to be carried from place to place. 15. staves shall be—*i.e.* always remain in the rings, whether the ark be at rest or in motion. 16. the testimony —that is, the two tables of stone, containing the ten commandments, and called "the Testimony," because by it God did testify His sovereign authority over Israel as His people, His selection of them as the guardians of His will and worship, and His displeasure in the event of their transgressing His laws; while on their part, by receiving and depositing this law in its appointed place, they testified their acknowledgment of God's right to rule over them, and their submission to the authority of His law. The superb and elaborate style of the ark that contained "the Testimony" was emblematical of the great treasure it held; in other words, the incomparable value and excellence of the Word of God, while its being placed in this chest further showed the great care which God has ever taken for preserving it. 17. mercyseat—to serve as a lid, covering it exactly. It was the propitiatory cover, as the term may be rendered, denoting that Christ, our great propitiation, has fully answered all the demands of the law, covers our transgressions, and comes between us and the curse of a violated law. 18. two cherubims—The real meaning of these figures as well as the shape or form of them is not known with certainty—probably similar to what was afterwards introduced into the temple, and described (Ez. 10,). They stretched out their wings, and their faces were turned towards the mercyseat, probably in a bowing attitude. The prevailing opinion now is, that those splendid figures were symbolical not of angelic but of earthly and human beings—the members of the church of God interested in the dispensation of grace, the redeemed in every age, and that these hieroglyphic forms symbolised the qualities of the true people of God—courage, patience, intelligence, and activity. 22. there will I meet with thee—The Shechinah or symbol of the Divine presence rested on the mercyseat, and was indicated by a cloud from the midst of which responses were audibly given when God was consulted on behalf of His people. Hence God is described as "dwelling" or "sitting" between the cherubims. 23. table of shittim wood—of the same material and decorations as the ark, and like it too, furnished with rings for the poles on which it was carried. The staves, however, were taken out of it when stationary, in order not to encumber the priests while engaged in their services at the table. It was half a cubit less than the ark, but of the same height. 24. crown—the moulding or ornamental rim, which is thought to have been raised above the level of the table, to prevent anything from falling off. 29. dishes—broad platters. spoons—cups or concave vessels, used for

children of Israel upon his heart before the LORD continually.

31 ¶ And ⁿ thou shalt make the robe of the ephod all *of* blue.

32 And there shall be an hole in the top of it, in the midst thereof: it shall have a binding of woven work round about the hole of it, as it were the hole of an habergeon, that it be not rent.

33 And *beneath* upon the ⁵ hem of it, thou shalt make pomegranates of blue, and of purple, and *of* scarlet, round about the hem thereof; and bells of gold between them round about:

34 A golden bell and a pomegranate, a golden bell and a pomegranate, upon the hem of the robe round about.

35 And it shall be upon Aaron to minister: and his sound shall be heard when he goeth in unto the holy *place* before the LORD, and when he cometh out, that he die not.

36 ¶ And ᵒ thou shalt make a plate of pure gold, and grave upon it, *like* the engravings of a signet, HOLINESS TO THE LORD.

37 And thou shalt put it on a blue lace, that it may be upon the mitre; upon the fore front of the mitre it shall be.

38 And it shall be upon Aaron's forehead, that Aaron may ᵖ bear the iniquity of the holy things, which the children of Israel shall hallow in all their holy gifts; and it shall be always upon his forehead, that they may be ᵍ accepted before the LORD.

39 ¶ And thou shalt embroider the coat of fine linen, and thou shalt make the mitre *of* fine linen, and thou shalt make the girdle *of* needle-work.

40 ¶ And ʳ for Aaron's sons thou shalt make coats, and thou shalt make for them girdles, and bonnets shalt thou make for them, for glory and for beauty.

41 And thou shalt put them upon Aaron thy brother, and his sons with him ; and shalt ˢ anoint them, and ² consecrate them, and sanctify them, that they may minister unto me in the priest's office.

42 And thou shalt make them ᵗ linen breeches to cover ⁷ their nakedness; from the loins even unto the thighs they shall ⁸ reach.

43 And they shall be upon Aaron, and upon his sons, when they come in unto the tabernacle of the congregation, or when they come near ᵘ unto the altar to minister in the holy *place*; that they ᵛ bear not iniquity, and die. ʷ *It shall be* a statute for ever unto him and his seed after him.

CHAPTER XXIX.

1 *The sacrifices and ceremonies of consecrating the priests.* 38 *The continual burnt offering.* 43 *God's promise to dwell among the children of Israel.*

AND this *is* the thing that thou shalt do unto them to hallow them, to minister unto me in the priest's office: ᵃ Take one young bullock, and two rams without blemish,

2 And ᵇ unleavened bread, and cakes unleavened tempered with oil, and wafers unleavened anointed with oil: *of* wheaten flour shalt thou make them.

3 And thou shalt put them into one basket, and bring them in the basket, with the bullock and the two rams.

4 And Aaron and his sons thou shalt bring unto the door of the tabernacle of the congregation, and ᵉ shalt wash them with water.

5 And ᵈ thou shalt take the garments, and put upon Aaron the coat, and the robe of the ephod, and the ephod, and the breastplate, and gird him with ᵉ the curious girdle of the ephod:

6 And thou shalt put the mitre upon his head, and put the holy crown upon the mitre.

7 Then shalt thou take the anointing ᶠ oil, and pour *it* upon his head, and anoint him.

8 And thou shalt bring his sons, and put coats upon them.

9 And thou shalt gird them with girdles, Aaron and his sons, and ¹ put the bonnets on them: and ᵍ the priest's office shall be theirs for a perpetual statute: and thou shalt ² consecrate Aaron and his sons.

10 And thou shalt cause a bullock to be brought before the tabernacle of the congregation: and ʰ Aaron and his sons shall put their hands upon the head of the bullock.

11 And thou shalt kill the bullock before the LORD, *by* the door of the tabernacle of the congregation.

12 And thou ⁱ shalt take of the blood of the bullock, and put *it* upon ʲ the horns of the altar with thy finger, and pour all the blood beside the bottom of the altar.

13 And ᵏ thou shalt take all the fat that covereth the inwards, and ³ the caul *that is* above the liver, and the two kidneys, and the fat that *is* upon them, and burn *them* upon the altar.

14 But ˡ the flesh of the bullock, and his skin, and his dung, shalt thou burn with fire without the camp: it *is* a sin offering.

15 ¶ Thou ᵐ shalt also take one ram; and Aaron and his sons shall ⁿ put their hands upon the head of the ram.

16 And thou shalt slay the ram, and thou shalt take his blood, and sprinkle *it* round about upon the altar.

17 And thou shalt cut the ram in pieces, and wash the inwards of him, and his legs, and put *them* unto his pieces, and ⁴ unto his head.

18 And thou shalt burn the whole ram upon the altar: it *is* a burnt offering unto the LORD: it *is* a ᵒ sweet savour, an offering made by fire unto the LORD.

19 And ᵖ thou shalt take the other ram; and Aaron and his sons shall put their hands upon the head of the ram.

20 Then shalt thou kill the ram, and take of his blood, and put *it* upon the tip of the right ear of Aaron, and upon the tip of the right ear of his sons, and upon the thumb of their right hand, and upon the great toe of their right foot, and sprinkle the blood upon the altar round about.

21 And thou shalt take of the blood that *is* upon the altar, and of ᵍ the anointing oil, and sprinkle *it* upon Aaron, and upon his garments, and upon his sons, and upon the garments of his sons with him: and ʳ he shall be hallowed, and his garments, and his sons, and his sons' garments with him.

22 Also thou shalt take of the ram the fat, and the rump, and the fat that covereth the inwards, and the caul *above* the liver, and the two kidneys, and the fat that *is* upon them, and the right shoulder; for it *is* a ram of consecration:

23 And ˢ one loaf of bread, and one cake of

holding incense. covers—both for bread and incense. bowls—cups, for though no mention is made of wine, libations were undoubtedly made to God, according to Josephus and the rabbins, once a week, when the bread was changed. To cover withal—rather to pour out withal. 30. shewbread—*lit.* *presence bread,* so called because it was constantly exhibited before the Lord, or because the bread of His presence, like the angel of His presence, pointed symbolically to Christ. It consisted of twelve unleavened loaves, said traditionally to have been laid in piles of six each. This bread was designed to be a symbol of the full and never-failing provision which is made in the church for the spiritual sustenance and refreshment of God's people. 31. candlestick—*lit.* a lampbearer. It was so constructed as to be capable of being taken to pieces for facility in removal. The shaft or stock rested on a pedestal. It had seven branches, shaped like reeds or canes—three on each side, with one in the centre—and worked out into knobs, flowers, and bowls, placed alternately. The figure represented on the arch of Titus gives the best idea of this candlestick. 33. knops—old spelling for knobs—bosses. 37. light the lamps . . . that they may give light—the light was derived from pure olive-oil, and probably kept continually burning. (cf. ch. 30. 7; Lev. 24. 2.) 38. tongs—snuffers. 39. a talent of pure gold—in weight, equivalent to 125 lbs. troy. 40. look that thou make them after their pattern—This caution, which is repeated with no small frequency in other parts of the narrative, is an evidence of the deep interest taken by the Divine King in the erection of His palace or sanctuary; and it is impossible to account for the circumstance of God's condescending to such minute details, except on the assumption that this tabernacle was to be of a typical character, and eminently subservient to the religious instruction and benefit of mankind, by shadowing forth in its leading features, the grand truths of the Christian church.

CHAPTER XXVI.

Ver. 1-37. TEN CURTAINS. 1. cunning work—*i.e.,* of elegant texture, richly embroidered—The word "cunning," in old English, is synonomous with skilful. 2. length—Each curtain was to be fifteen yards in length and a little exceeding two in breadth. 3. The five curtains, &c.—so as to form two grand divisions, each eleven yards wide. 6. taches—clasps—supposed in shape, as well as in use, to be the same as hooks-and-eyes. 7-14. curtains of goats' hair—These coarse curtains were to be one more in number than the others, and to extend a yard lower on each side, the use of them being to protect and conceal the richer curtains. 14. a covering of rams' skins dyed red—*i. e.,* of Turkey red leather. 15-30. Thou shalt make boards, ... rear the tabernacle—The tabernacle, from its name, as well as from its general appearance and arrangements, was a tent; but from the description given in these verses, the boards that formed its walls, the five (cross) bars that strengthen them, and the middle bar that "reached from end to end," and gave it solidity and compactness, it was evidently a more substantial fabric than the light and fragile tent, probably on account of the weight of its various coverings as well as for the protection of its precious furniture. 36. an hanging for the door of the tent—curtains of rich and elaborate embroidery made by the female inmates, are suspended over the doors or entrances of the tents occupied by Eastern chiefs and princes. In a similar style of elegance was the hanging finished which was to cover the door of this tabernacle—the chosen habitation of the God and King of Israel. It appears from verses 12, 22, 23, that the ark and mercy-seat were placed in the west end of the tabernacle, and consequently the door or entrance fronted the East, so that the Israelites in worshipping Jehovah, turned their faces toward the west, that they might be thus figuratively taught to turn from the worship of that luminary which was the great idol of the nations and to adore the God who made it and them. [HEWLETT.]

CHAPTER XXVII.

Ver. 1-21. ALTAR FOR BURNT OFFERING. 1. altar of Shittim wood—The dimensions of this altar which was placed at the entrance of the sanctuary were nearly three yards square, and a yard and a half in height, Under the wooden frame of this chest-like altar, the inside was hollow, and each corner was to be terminated by "horns"—angular projections, perpendicular or oblique, in the form of horns. The animals to be sacrificed were bound to these, (Ps. 118. 27,) and part of the blood was applied to them. 3. shovels—fire shovels for scraping together any of the scattered ashes. basons—for receiving the blood of the sacrifice to be sprinkled on the people. flesh-hooks—curved, three-pronged forks, (1 Sam. 2. 13, 14.) fire-pans—A large sort of vessel, wherein the sacred fire which came down from heaven (Lev. 9. 24,) was kept burning, while they cleaned the altar and the grate from the coals and ashes, and while the altar was carried from one place to another in the wilderness. [PATRICK, SPENCER, LE CLERC.] 4. a grate of net-work of brass—sunk lattice work to support the fire. 5. put it—*i.e.,* the grating in which they were carried to a clean place, (Lev. 4. 12.) 4. four brazen rings—by which the grating might be lifted and taken away as occasion required from the body of the altar. 6, 7. rings...staves—those rings were placed at the side through which the poles were inserted on occasions of removal. 9. The court of the tabernacle—The inclosure in which the edifice stood was a rectangular court, extending rather more than fifty yards in length, and half that space in breadth, and the enclosing parapet was about three yards or half the height of the tabernacle. That parapet consisted of a connected series of curtains, made of fine twined linen yarn, woven into a kind of net work, so that the people could see through; but that large curtain which overhung the entrance was of a different texture, being embroidered and dyed with variegated colours, and it was furnished with cords for pulling it up or drawing it aside when the priests had occasion to enter. The curtains of this enclosure were supported on sixty brazen pillars which stood on pedestals of the same metal, but their capitals and fillets were of silver, and the hooks on which they were suspended were of silver also. pins—were designed to hold down the curtains at the bottom, lest the wind should waft them aside. 20. pure

oiled bread, and one wafer out of the basket of the unleavened bread that *is* before the LORD:

24 And thou shalt put all in the hands of Aaron, and in the hands of his sons; and shalt *b* wave them *for* a wave offering before the LORD.

25 And *t* thou shalt receive them of their hands, and burn *them* upon the altar for a burnt offering, for a sweet savour before the LORD: it *is* an offering made by fire unto the LORD.

26 And thou shalt take *u* the breast of the ram of Aaron's consecration, and wave it *for* a wave offering before the LORD: and it *v* shall be thy part.

27 And thou shalt sanctify *w* the breast of the wave offering, and the shoulder of the heave offering, which is waved, and which is heaved up, of the ram of the consecration, *even of* that which *is* for Aaron, and of *that* which *is* for his sons:

28 And it shall be Aaron's and his sons' by *x* a statute for ever from the children of Israel; for it *is* an heave offering: and *y* it shall be an heave offering from the children of Israel of the sacrifice of their peace offerings, *even* their heave offering unto the LORD.

29 ¶ And the holy garments of Aaron shall *z* be his sons' after him, *a* to be anointed therein, and to be consecrated in them.

30 *And* *c* that son that is priest in his stead shall put them on *b* seven days, when he cometh into the tabernacle of the congregation to minister in the holy *place*.

31 ¶ And thou shalt take the ram of the consecration, and *e* seethe his flesh in the holy place.

32 And Aaron and his sons shall eat the flesh of the ram, and the *d* bread that *is* in the basket, *by* the door of the tabernacle of the congregation.

33 And *e* they shall eat those things wherewith the atonement was made, to consecrate *and* to sanctify them: but *f* a stranger shall not eat *thereof*, because they *are* holy.

34 And if ought of the flesh of the consecrations, or of the bread, remain unto the morning, then thou shalt burn the remainder with fire: it shall not be eaten, because it *is* holy.

35 And thus shalt thou do unto Aaron, and to his sons, according to all *things* which I have commanded thee: *f* seven days shalt thou consecrate them.

36 And thou shalt *g* offer every day a bullock *for* a sin offering for atonement: and thou shalt cleanse the altar, when thou hast made an atonement for it, *h* and thou shalt anoint it, to sanctify it.

37 Seven days thou shalt make an atonement for the altar, and sanctify it; *i* and it shall be an altar most holy: *j* whatsoever toucheth the altar shall be holy.

38 ¶ Now this *is that* which thou shalt offer upon the altar; *k* two lambs of the first year day *l* by day continually.

39 The one lamb thou shalt offer *m* in the morning, and the other lamb thou shalt offer at even:

40 And with the one lamb a tenth deal of flour mingled with the fourth part of an hin of beaten oil; and the fourth part of an hin of wine *for* a drink offering.

41 And the other lamb thou shalt *n* offer at even, and shalt do thereto according to the meat offering of the morning, and according to the drink offering thereof, for a sweet savour, an offering made by fire unto the LORD.

42 *This shall be* *o* a continual burnt offering throughout your generations, *at* the door of the tabernacle of the congregation, before the LORD; *p* where I will meet you, to speak there unto thee.

43 And there I will meet with the children of Israel, and *q* the *tabernacle* *r* shall be sanctified by my glory.

44 And I will sanctify the tabernacle of the congregation, and the altar: I will *r* sanctify also both Aaron and his sons, to minister to me in the priest's office.

45 And *s* I will dwell among the children of Israel, and will be their God.

46 And they shall know that I *am* the LORD their God, that brought them forth out of the land of Egypt, that I may dwell among them: I *am* the LORD their God.

CHAPTER XXX.

1 *The altar of incense.* 11 *The ransom of souls.* 17 *The brazen laver.* 22 *The holy anointing oil.* 34 *The composition of the perfume.*

AND thou shalt make *a* an altar *b* to burn incense upon: *of* shittim wood shalt thou make it.

2 A cubit *shall be* the length thereof, and a cubit the breadth thereof; foursquare shall it be; and two cubits *shall be* the height thereof: the horns thereof *shall be* of the same.

3 And thou shalt overlay it with pure gold, the [1] top thereof, and the [2] sides thereof round about, and the horns thereof: and thou shalt make unto it a crown of gold round about.

4 And two golden rings shalt thou make to it under the crown of it, by the two [3] corners thereof, upon the two sides of it shalt thou make *it*; and they shall be for places for the staves to bear it withal.

5 And thou shalt make the staves of shittim wood, and overlay them with gold.

6 And thou shalt put it before the veil that *is* by the ark of the testimony, before the mercyseat that *is* over the testimony, where I will meet with thee.

7 And Aaron shall burn thereon [4] sweet incense every morning: when he dresseth the lamps, he shall burn incense upon it.

8 And when Aaron [5] lighteth the lamps [6] at even, he shall burn incense upon it; a perpetual incense before the LORD throughout your generations.

9 Ye shall offer no *c* strange incense thereon, nor burnt sacrifice, nor meat offering; neither shall ye pour drink offering thereon.

10 And *d* Aaron shall make an atonement upon the horns of it once in a year with the blood of the sin offering of atonements: once in the year shall he make atonement upon it throughout your generations: it *is* most holy unto the LORD.

11 ¶ And the LORD spake unto Moses, saying,

12 When *e* thou takest the sum of the children of Israel after [7] their number, then shall they give every man *f* a ransom for his soul unto the LORD, when thou numberest them; that there be no *g* plague among them, when *thou* numberest them.

13 This *h* they shall give, every one that passeth among them that are numbered

oil olive beaten—*i.e.*, such as runs from the olives when bruised and without the application of fire. 21. Aaron and his sons—were to take charge of lighting it in all time coming—shall order it from evening to morning—The tabernacle having no windows, the lamps required to be lighted during the day. Josephus says that in his time only three were lighted; but his were degenerate times, and there is no scripture authority for this limitation. But although the priests were obliged from necessity to light them by day, they might have let them go out at night had it not been for this express ordinance.

CHAPTER XXVIII.

Ver. 1-43. APPOINTMENT TO THE PRIESTHOOD. 1. take thou... Aaron thy brother—Moses had hitherto discharged the priestly functions (Ps. 99. 6,), and he evinced the piety as well as humility of his character, in readily complying with the command to invest his brother with the sacred office, though it involved the perpetual exclusion of his own family. The appointment was a special act of God's sovereignty, so that there could be no ground for popular umbrage by the selection of Aaron's family, with whom the office was inalienably established and continued in unbroken succession till the introduction of the Christian era. 2-5. holy garments—No inherent holiness belonged either to the material or the workmanship. But they are called "holy" simply because they were not worn on ordinary occasions, but assumed in the discharge of the sacred functions. (Ez. 44. 19. for glory and beauty—It was a grand and sumptuous attire. In material, elaborate embroidery, and colour, it had an imposing splendour. The tabernacle being adapted to the infantine age of the church, it was right and necessary that the priest's garments should be of such superb and dazzling appearance, that the people might be inspired with a due respect for the ministers as well as the rites of religion. But they had also a further meaning; for being all made of linen, they were symbolical of the truth, purity, and other qualities in Christ that rendered Him such a high priest as became us. 6-14. ephod—It was a very gorgeous robe, made of byssus, curiously embroidered, and dyed with variegated colours, and further enriched with golden tissue, the threads of gold being either originally interwoven or afterwards inserted by the embroiderer. It was short—reaching from the breast to a little below the loins—and though destitute of sleeves, retained its position by the support of straps thrown over each shoulder. These straps or braces, connecting the one with the back, the other with the front piece of which the tunic was composed, were united on the shoulder by two onyx stones, serving as buttons, and on which the names of the twelve tribes were engraved, and set in golden encasements. The symbolical design of this was, that the high priest, who bore the names along with him in all his ministrations before the Lord, might be kept in remembrance of his duty to plead their cause, and supplicate the accomplishment of the divine promises in their favour. The ephod was fastened by a girdle of the same costly materials, *i.e.*, dyed, embroidered, and wrought with threads of gold. It was about a hand-breadth wide, and wound twice round the upper part of the waist; it fastened in front, the ends hanging down at great length. (Rev. 1. 13.) 15-30. breastplate of judgment—a very splendid and richly embroidered piece of brocade, a span square, and doubled, to enable it the better to bear the weight of the precious stones in it. There were twelve different stones, containing each the name of a tribe, and arranged in four rows, three in each. The Israelites had acquired a knowledge of the lapidary's art in Egypt, and the amount of their skill in cutting, polishing, and setting precious stones may be judged of by the *diamond* forming one of the engraved ornaments on this breastplate. A ring was attached to each corner, through which the golden chains were passed to fasten this brilliant piece of jewellery at the top and bottom tightly on the breast of the ephod. 30. Urim and Thummim—The words signify 'lights' and 'perfections,' and nothing more is meant than the precious stones of the breastplate already described. (cf. ch. 39. 8-21, Lev. 8. 8.) They received the name because the bearing of them qualified the high priest to consult the divine oracle on all public or national emergencies, by going into the holy place—standing close before the veil and putting his hand upon the Urim and Thummim, conveyed a petition from the people and asked counsel of God, who, as the Sovereign of Israel, gave response from the midst of His glory. Little, however, is known about them. But it may be remarked that Egyptian judges wore on the breast of their official robes a representation of Justice, and the High Priest in Israel long officiated also as a Judge; so that some think the Urim and Thummim had a reference to his judicial functions. 31. the robe of the ephod—it was the middle garment, under the ephod and above the coat. It had a hole through which the head was thrust, and was formed carefully of one piece, such as was the coat of Christ (J. 19. 23.). The high priest's was of a sky-blue colour. The binding at the neck was strongly woven, and it terminated below in a fringe, made of blue, purple, and scarlet tassels, in the form of a pomegranate, interspersed with small bells of gold, which tinkled as the wearer was in motion. 34. a golden bell and a pomegranate—The bells were hung between the pomegranates, which are said to have amounted to 72, and the use of them seems to have been to announce to the people when the high priest entered the most holy place, that they might accompany him with their prayers, and also to remind himself to be attired in his official dress, to minister without which was death. 36-39. mitre—crown-like cap for the head, not covering the entire head, but adhering closely to it, composed of fine linen. The Scripture has not described its form, but from Josephus we may gather that it was conical in shape, as he distinguishes the mitres of the common priests by saying that they were *not* conical—that it was encircled with swathes of blue embroidered, and that it was covered by one piece of fine linen to hide the seams. plate—*lit.* petal of a flower, which seems to have been the figure of this golden plate, which was tied with a ribbon of blue on the front of the mitre, so that every one facing him could read the inscription. 39. coat of fine linen—a garment fastened at

half a shekel after the shekel of the sanctuary: (a *shekel is* twenty gerahs:) an half shekel shall be the offering of the LORD.

14 Every one that passeth among them that are numbered, from twenty years old and above, shall give an offering unto the LORD.

15 The rich shall not give more, and the poor shall not give less, than half a shekel, when they give an offering unto the LORD, to make an atonement for your souls.

16 And thou shalt take the atonement money of the children of Israel, and shalt appoint it for the service of the tabernacle of the congregation; that it may be a memorial unto the children of Israel before the LORD, to make an atonement for your souls.

17 ¶ And the LORD spake unto Moses, saying,

18 Thou shalt also make a laver of brass, and his foot also of brass, to wash *withal*: and thou shalt put it between the tabernacle of the congregation and the altar, and thou shalt put water therein.

19 For Aaron and his sons shall wash their hands and their feet thereat.

20 When they go into the tabernacle of the congregation, they shall wash with water, that they die not; or when they come near to the altar to minister, to burn offering made by fire unto the LORD;

21 So they shall wash their hands and their feet, that they die not: and it shall be a statute for ever to them, *even* to him and to his seed throughout their generations.

22 ¶ Moreover the LORD spake unto Moses, saying,

23 Take thou also unto thee principal spices, of pure myrrh five hundred *shekels*, and of sweet cinnamon half so much, *even* two hundred and fifty *shekels*, and of sweet calamus two hundred and fifty *shekels*,

24 And of cassia five hundred *shekels*, after the shekel of the sanctuary, and of oil olive an hin:

25 And thou shalt make it an oil of holy ointment, an ointment compound after the art of the apothecary: it shall be an holy anointing oil.

26 And thou shalt anoint the tabernacle of the congregation therewith, and the ark of the testimony,

27 And the table and all his vessels, and the candlestick and his vessels, and the altar of incense,

28 And the altar of burnt offering with all his vessels, and the laver and his foot.

29 And thou shalt sanctify them, that they may be most holy: whatsoever toucheth them shall be holy.

30 And thou shalt anoint Aaron and his sons, and consecrate them, that *they* may minister unto me in the priest's office.

31 And thou shalt speak unto the children of Israel, saying, This shall be an holy anointing oil unto me throughout your generations.

32 Upon man's flesh shall it not be poured; neither shall ye make *any other* like it, after the composition of it: it *is* holy, *and* it shall be holy unto you.

33 Whosoever compoundeth *any* like it, or whosoever putteth *any* of it upon a stranger, shall even be cut off from his people.

34 ¶ And the LORD said unto Moses, Take unto thee sweet spices, stacte, and onycha, and galbanum; *these* sweet spices with pure frankincense: of each shall there be a like *weight*,

35 And thou shalt make it a perfume, a confection after the art of the apothecary, tempered together, pure *and* holy.

36 And thou shalt beat *some* of it very small, and put of it before the testimony in the tabernacle of the congregation, where I will meet with thee; it shall be unto you most holy.

37 And *as for* the perfume which thou shalt make, ye shall not make to yourselves according to the composition thereof: it shall be unto thee holy for the LORD.

38 Whosoever shall make like unto that, to smell thereto, shall even be cut off from his people.

CHAPTER XXXI.

1 *Bezaleel and Aholiab are called and qualified for the work of the tabernacle.* 12 *Of the Sabbath.* 18 *Moses receiveth the two tables.*

AND the LORD spake unto Moses, saying,

2 See, I have called by name Bezaleel the son of Uri, the son of Hur, of the tribe of Judah:

3 And I have filled him with the spirit of God, in wisdom, and in understanding, and in knowledge, and in all manner of workmanship,

4 To devise cunning works, to work in gold, and in silver, and in brass,

5 And in cutting of stones, to set *them*, and in carving of timber, to work in all manner of workmanship.

6 And I, behold, I have given with him Aholiab the son of Ahisamach, of the tribe of Dan: and in the hearts of all that are wise-hearted I have put wisdom, that they may make all that I have commanded thee:

7 The tabernacle of the congregation, and the ark of the testimony, and the mercyseat that *is* thereupon, and all the furniture of the tabernacle,

8 And the table and his furniture, and the pure candlestick with all his furniture, and the altar of incense,

9 And the altar of burnt offering with all his furniture, and the laver and his foot,

10 And the cloths of service, and the holy garments for Aaron the priest, and the garments of his sons, to minister in the priest's office,

11 And the anointing oil, and sweet incense for the holy *place*: according to all that I have commanded thee shall they do.

12 ¶ And the LORD spake unto Moses, saying,

13 Speak thou also unto the children of Israel, saying, Verily my sabbaths ye shall keep: for it *is* a sign between me and you throughout your generations; that *ye* may know that I *am* the LORD that doth sanctify you.

14 Ye shall keep the sabbath therefore; for it *is* holy unto you: every one that defileth it shall surely be put to death: for whosoever doeth *any* work therein, that soul shall be cut off from among his people.

15 Six days may work be done; but in the seventh *is* the sabbath of rest, holy to the LORD: whosoever doeth *any* work in the sabbath day, he shall surely be put to death.

16 Wherefore the children of Israel shall

the neck, and reaching far down the person, with the sleeves terminating at the elbow. girdle of needle-work—a piece of fine twined linen, richly embroidered, and variously dyed. It is said to have been very long, and being many times wound round the body, it was fastened in front, and the ends hung down, which, being an impediment to a priest in active duty, were usually thrown across the shoulders. This was the outer garment of the common priests. 40. bonnets—turbans. 42. linen breeches—drawers, which encompassed the loins and reached half way down the thighs. They are seen very frequently represented in Egyptian figures.

CHAPTER XXIX.

Ver. 1-35. CONSECRATING THE PRIESTS AND THE ALTAR. 1. hallow them—The act of inaugurating the priests was accompanied by ceremonial solemnities well calculated not only to lead the people to entertain exalted views of the office, but to impress those functionaries themselves with a profound sense of its magnitude and importance. In short, they were taught to know that the service was for them as well as for the people; and every time they engaged in a new performance of their duties, they were reminded of their personal interest in the worship, by being obliged to offer for themselves, before they were qualified to offer as the representatives of the people. this is the thing thou shalt do—Steps are taken at the beginning of a society, which would not be repeated, when the social machine was in full motion; and Moses, at the opening of the tabernacle, was employed to discharge functions, which in later periods would have been regarded as sacrilege, laying an unhallowed hand on the ark, and punished with instant death. But he acted under the special directions of God. 4. door of the tabernacle—As occupying the intermediate space between the court where the people stood, and the dwelling-place of Israel's king, and therefore the fittest spot for the priests being duly prepared for entrance, and the people witnessing the ceremony of inauguration. 4-10. wash them with water, and take the garments—The manner in which these parts of the ceremonial was performed is minutely described, and in discovering their symbolical import, which, indeed, is sufficiently plain and obvious, we have inspired authority to guide us. It signified the necessity and importance of moral purity or holiness. (Is. 52. 11; Jo. 13. 10; 2 Cor. 7. 1; 1 Pet. 3, 21.) In like manner, the investiture with the holy garments signified their being clothed with righteousness, (Rev. 19. 8,) and equipped as men active and well prepared for the service of God; the anointing the high priest with oil, denoted that he was to be filled with the influences of the Spirit, for the edification and delight of the church. (Lev. 10. 7; Ps. 45. 7; Is. 61. 1; 1 J. 2. 27.), and as he was officially a type of Christ. (Heb. 7. 26; J. 3. 34; also Matt. 3. 16; 11. 29.) Thou shalt cause a bullock—This part of the ceremonial consisted of three sacrifices—(1.) The sacrifice of a bullock, as a sin offering; and in rendering it, the priest was directed to put his hand upon the head of his sacrifice, expressing by that act a consciousness of personal guilt, and a wish that it might be accepted as a vicarious satisfaction. (2.) The sacrifice of a ram as a burnt offering—(v. 15-18)—the ram was to be wholly burnt, in token of the priest's dedication of himself to God and his service. The sin offering was *first* to be presented, and *then* the burnt-offering; for until guilt be removed, no acceptable service can be performed. (3.) There was to be a peace offering, called the ram of consecration. (v. 19-22.) And there was a marked peculiarity in the manner in which this other ram was to be disposed of. The former was for the glory of God—this was for the comfort of the priest himself; and as a sign of a mutual covenant being ratified, the blood of the sacrifice was divided,—part sprinkled on the altar round about, and part upon the persons and garments of the priests. Nay, the blood was, by a singular act, directed to be put upon the extremities of the body, thereby signifying that the benefits of the atonement would be applied to the whole nature of man. Moreover, the flesh of this sacrifice was to be divided, as it were, between God and the priest,—part of it to be put into his hand to be waived up and down, in token of its being offered to God, and then it was to be burnt upon the altar; the other part was to be eaten by the priests at the door of the tabernacle—that feast being a symbol of communion or fellowship with God. These ceremonies, performed in the order described, shewed the qualifications necessary for the priests. (See He. 7, 26, 27; 10. 14.) 35. seven days—The renewal of these ceremonies on the return of every day in the seven, with the intervention of a Sabbath, was a wise preparatory arrangement, in order to afford a sufficient interval for calm and devout reflection. (He. 9. 1; 10. 1.)

36, 37. CONSECRATION OF THE ALTAR. 36. thou shalt cleanse the altar—The phrase "when thou hast made an atonement for it," should be, *upon* it; and the purport of the direction is, that during all the time they were engaged as above from day to day, in offering the appointed sacrifices, the greatest care was to be taken to keep the altar properly cleansed,—to remove the ashes, and sprinkle it with the prescribed unction, that at the conclusion of the whole ceremonial, the altar itself should be consecrated as much as the ministers who were to officiate at it. (Matt. 23. 19.) It was thenceforth associated with the services of religion.

38-46. INSTITUTION OF DAILY SERVICE. 38. two lambs—The sacred preliminaries being completed, Moses was instructed in the end or design to which these preparations were subservient, *viz.*—the worship of God; and hence the institution of the morning and evening sacrifice. The institution was so imperative, that in no circumstances was this daily oblation to be dispensed with; and the due observance of it would secure the oft promised grace and blessing of their heavenly King.

CHAPTER XXX.

Ver. 1-10. THE ALTAR OF INCENSE. 1. Thou shalt make an altar, &c.—Its material was to be like that of the ark of the testimony, but its dimensions very small. four square—the meaning of which is not that it was to be entirely of a cubical form, but that upon its upper and under surface, it showed four equal sides. It was twice as high as it was broad, being 21 inches broad and 3 feet 6 inches high. It had "horns;" its top or flat surface was surmounted by an ornamental ledge or rim, called a crown, and it was

keep the sabbath, to observe the sabbath throughout their generations, *for* a perpetual covenant.

17 It *is* ᵏa sign between me and the children of Israel for ever: for ᶫin six days the LORD made heaven and earth, and on the seventh day he rested, and was refreshed.

18 ¶ And he gave unto Moses, when he had made an end of communing with him upon mount Sinai, ᵐtwo tables of testimony, tables of stone, written with the finger of God.

CHAPTER XXXII.

1 *The people in Moses' absence cause Aaron to make a calf.* 19 *Moses breaketh the tables.* 25 *The idolaters slain.* 30 *Moses prayeth for the people.*

AND when the people saw that Moses ᵃdelayed to come down out of the mount, the people gathered themselves together unto Aaron, and said unto him, Up, ᵇmake us gods, which shall go before us; for *as for* this Moses, the man that brought us up out of the land of Egypt, we wot not what is become of him.

2 And Aaron said unto them, Break off the ᶜgolden earrings which *are* in the ears of your wives, of your sons, and of your daughters, and bring *them* unto me.

3 And all the people brake off the golden earrings which *were* in their ears, and brought *them* unto Aaron.

4 And ᵈhe received *them* at their hand, and fashioned it with a graving tool, after he had made it a molten calf: and they said, These *be* thy gods, O Israel, which brought thee up out of the land of Egypt.

5 And when Aaron saw *it*, he built an altar before it; and Aaron made ᵉproclamation, and said, To-morrow *is* a feast to the LORD.

6 And they rose up early on the morrow, and offered burnt offerings, and brought peace offerings; and the ᶠpeople sat down to eat and to drink, and rose up to play.

7 ¶ And the LORD said unto Moses, ᵍGo, get thee down; for thy people, which thou broughtest out of the land of Egypt, ʰhave corrupted *themselves*:

8 They have turned aside quickly out of the way which I ⁱcommanded them: they have made them a molten calf, and have worshipped it, and have sacrificed thereunto, and said, ʲThese *be* thy gods, O Israel, which have brought thee up out of the land of Egypt.

9 And the LORD said unto Moses, ᵏI have seen this people, and, behold, it *is* a stiffnecked people:

10 Now therefore ᶫlet me alone, that my wrath may wax hot against them, and that I may consume them, and ᵐI will make of thee a great nation.

11 And ⁿMoses besought the ¹LORD his God, and said, LORD, why doth thy wrath wax hot against thy people, which thou hast brought forth out of the land of Egypt with great power, and with a mighty hand?

12 Wherefore should the Egyptians speak, and say, For mischief did he bring them out, to slay them in the mountains, and to consume them from the face of the earth? Turn from thy fierce wrath, and repent of this evil against thy people.

13 Remember Abraham, Isaac, and Israel, thy servants, to whom thou ᵒswarest by thine own self, and saidst unto them, ᵖI will multiply your seed as the stars of heaven, and all this land that I have spoken of will I give unto your seed, and they shall inherit *it* for ever.

14 And the LORD ᑫrepented of the evil which he thought to do unto his people.

15 ¶ And ʳMoses turned, and went down from the mount, and the two tables of the testimony *were* in his hand: the tables *were* written on both their sides; on the one side and on the other *were* they written.

16 And the ˢtables *were* the work of God, and the writing *was* the writing of God, graven upon the tables.

17 And when Joshua heard the noise of the people as they shouted, he said unto Moses, *There is* a noise of war in the camp.

18 And he said, *It is* not the voice of *them that* shout for mastery, neither *is it* the voice of *them that* cry for ²being overcome; *but* the noise of *them that* sing do I hear.

19 ¶ And it came to pass, as soon as he came nigh unto the camp, that he saw the calf, and the dancing: and Moses' anger waxed hot, and he cast the tables out of his hands, and brake them beneath the mount.

20 And he took the calf which they had made, and burnt *it* in the fire, and ground *it* to powder, and strawed *it* upon the water, and made the children of Israel drink of it.

21 And Moses said unto Aaron, ᵗWhat did this people unto thee, that thou hast brought so great a sin upon them?

22 And Aaron said, Let not the anger of my lord wax hot: ᵘthou knowest the people, that they *are* set on mischief.

23 For they said unto me, Make us gods which shall go before us: for *as for* this Moses, the man that brought us up out of the land of Egypt, we wot not what is become of him.

24 And I said unto them, Whosoever hath any gold, let them break it off. So they gave *it* me: then I cast it into the fire, and there came out this calf.

25 ¶ And when Moses saw that the people *were* ᵛnaked, (for Aaron ʷhad made them naked unto *their* shame among ³their enemies,)

26 Then Moses stood in the gate of the camp, and said, Who *is* on the LORD'S side? *let him come* unto me. And all the sons of Levi gathered themselves together unto him.

27 And he said unto them, Thus saith the LORD God of Israel, Put every man his sword by his side, *and* go in and out from gate to gate throughout the camp, and ˣslay every man his brother, and every man his companion, and every man his neighbour.

28 And the children of Levi did according to the word of Moses: and there fell of the people that day about three thousand men.

29 ⁴For Moses had said, ⁵Consecrate yourselves to-day to the LORD, even every man upon his son, and upon his brother; that he may bestow upon you a blessing this day.

30 ¶ And it came to pass on the morrow, that Moses said unto the people, ʸYe have sinned a great sin: and now I will go up unto the LORD; ᶻperadventure I shall make an atonement for your sin.

furnished at the sides with rings for carriage. Its only accompanying piece of furniture was a golden censer or pan, in which the incense was set fire to upon the altar. Hence it was called the altar of incense, or the "golden altar," from the profuse degree in which it was gilded or overlaid with the precious metal. This splendour was adapted to the early age of the church, but in later times when the worship was to be more spiritual, the altar of incense is prophetically described as not of gold but of wood, and double the size of that in the tabernacle, because the church should be vastly extended, (Mal. 1. 11.) **6. Thou shalt put it before the veil**—which separated the holy from the most holy place. The tabernacle was in the middle, between the table of show-bread and the candlestick next the holy of holies, at equal distances from the north and south walls; in other words, it occupied a spot on the outside of the great partition veil, but directly in front of the mercyseat, which was within that sacred enclosure so that although the priest who ministered at this altar could not behold the mercyseat, he was to look towards it, and present his incense in that direction. This was a special arrangement, and it was designed to teach the important lesson—that though we cannot with the eye of sense, see the throne of grace, we must "direct our prayer to it and look up." (cf. 2 Cor. 3. 14; Re. 4. 1; He. 10. 20.) **7. sweet incense**—*lit.* incense of spices—strong aromatic substances were burnt upon this altar to counteract by their odoriferous fragrance the offensive fumes of the sacrifices: or the incense was employed in an offering of tributary homage which the Orientals used to make as a mark of honour to kings; and as God was Theocratic Ruler of Israel, *His* palace was not to be wanting in a usage of such significancy. Both these ends were served by this altar,—that of fumigating the apartments of the sacred edifice, while the pure lambent flame, according to Oriental notions, was an honorary tribute to the majesty of Israel's King. But there was a far higher meaning in it still: for as the tabernacle was not only a palace for Israel's King, but a place of worship for Israel's God, this altar was immediately connected with a religious purpose. In the style of the sacred writers, incense was a symbol or emblem of prayer, (Ps. 141. 2; Re. 5. 8; 8. 3.) From the uniform combination of the two services, it is evident that the incense was an emblem of the prayers of sincere worshippers ascending to heaven in the cloud of perfume; and accordingly the priest who officiated at this altar typified the intercessory office of Christ. (Lu. 1. 10; He. 7. 25.) **8. Aaron shall burn incense**—seemingly limiting the privilege of officiating at the altar of incense to the High Priest alone, and there is no doubt that he and his successors exclusively attended this altar on the great religious festivals. But "Aaron" is frequently used for the whole priestly order; and in later times, any of the priests might have officiated at this altar in rotation. (Lu. 1. 9.) **Every morning...at even**—In every period of the national history, this daily worship was scrupulously observed. **9. Ye shall offer no strange incense**—*i.e.*, of a different composition from that of which the ingredients are described so minutely. **11-16. When thou takest, &c.**—Moses did so twice, and doubtless observed the law here prescribed. The tax was not levied from women, minors, old men (Nu. 1. 42, 45,) and the Levites, (Nu. 1. 47,) they being not numbered. Assuming the shekel of the sanctuary to be about half-an-ounce troy, though nothing certain is known about it, the sum payable by each individual was two-and-fourpence. This was not a voluntary contribution, but a ransom for the soul, or lives of the people. It was required from all classes alike, and a refusal to pay implied a wilful exclusion from the privileges of the sanctuary, as well as exposure to divine judgments. It was probably the same impost that was exacted from our Lord, (Mat. 17. 24-27,) and it was usually devoted to repairs and other purposes connected with the services of the sanctuary. **17-21. Thou shalt make a laver of brass**—Though not actually forming a component part of the furniture of the tabernacle, this vase was closely connected with it; and though from standing at the entrance it would be a familiar object, it possessed great interest and importance from the baptismal purposes to which it was applied. No data are given by which its form and size can be ascertained; but it was probably a miniature pattern of Solomon's—a circular basin. **18. his foot**—supposed not to be the pedestal on which it rested, but a trough or shallow receptacle below, into which the water, let out from a cock or spout, flowed; for the way in which all eastern people wash their hands or feet is by pouring upon them the water which falls into a bason. This laver was provided for the priests alone. But in the Christian dispensation, all believers are priests, and hence the apostle exhorts them how to draw near to God. (He. 10. 22; Jo. 13. 10.) **22, 33. Take thou also, &c.**—Oil is frequently mentioned in scripture as an emblem of sanctification, and anointing with it a means of designating objects as well as persons to the service of God. Here it is prescribed by divine authority, and the various ingredients in their several proportions described which were to compose the oil used in consecrating the furniture of the tabernacle. **myrrh**—a fragrant and medicinal gum from a little known tree in Arabia. **sweet cinnamon**—produced from a species of laurel or sweet bay, found chiefly in Ceylon, growing to a height of twenty feet: this spice is extracted from the inner bark, but it is not certain whether that mentioned by Moses is the same as that with which we are familiar. **sweet calamus**—or sweet cane, a product of Arabia and India, of a tawny colour in appearance; it is like the common cane, and strongly odoriferous. **cassia**—from the same species of tree as the cinnamon—some think the outer bark of that tree. All these together would amount to 120 lbs. troy weight. **Hin**—a word of Egyptian origin, equal to ten pints. Being mixed with the oil olive—no doubt of the purest kind—this composition probably remained always in a liquid state, and the strictest prohibition issued against using it for any other purpose than anointing the tabernacle and its furniture. **34-38. Take unto thee sweet spices**—These were: stacte, the finest myrrh; onycha, supposed to be an odoriferous shell; galbanum, a gum-resin from an umbelliferous plant. frankincense—

31 And Moses returned unto the LORD, and said, Oh, this people have sinned a great sin, and have made them gods of gold!
32 Yet now, if thou wilt forgive their sin—; and if not, *d* blot me, I pray thee, *b* out of thy book which thou hast written.
33 And the LORD said unto Moses, *c* Whosoever hath sinned against me, him will I blot out of my book.
34 Therefore now go, lead the people unto *the place* of which I have spoken unto thee: behold, *d* mine Angel shall go before thee: nevertheless *e* in the day when I visit I will visit their sin upon them.
35 And the LORD plagued the people, because *f* they made the calf which Aaron made.

CHAPTER XXXIII.

1 *The Lord refuseth to go with the people.* 7 *The tabernacle removed out of the camp.* 9 *He talketh with Moses.* 12 *Moses prayeth for God's presence:* 18 *desireth to see his glory.*

AND the LORD said unto Moses, Depart, *and* go up hence, thou and the people which thou hast brought up out of the land of Egypt, unto the land which I sware unto Abraham, to Isaac, and to Jacob, saying, Unto *a* thy seed will I give it:
2 And I will send an Angel before thee; and *b* I will drive out the Canaanite, the Amorite, and the Hittite, and the Perizzite, the Hivite, and the Jebusite:
3 Unto a land flowing with milk and honey: for I will not go up in the midst of thee; for thou *art* a *c* stiff-necked people; lest I consume thee in the way.
4 ¶ And when the people heard these evil tidings, they mourned: *d* and no man did put on him his ornaments.
5 For the LORD had said unto Moses, Say unto the children of Israel, Ye *are* a stiffnecked people: I will come up into the midst of thee in a moment, and consume thee: therefore now put off thy ornaments from thee, that I may *e* know what to do unto thee.
6 And the children of Israel stripped themselves of their ornaments by the mount Horeb.
7 And Moses took the tabernacle, and pitched it without the camp, afar off from the camp, and called it The Tabernacle of the Congregation. And it came to pass, *that* every one which *f* sought the LORD went out unto the tabernacle of the congregation, which *was* without the camp.
8 And it came to pass, when Moses went out unto the tabernacle, *that* all the people rose up, and stood every man *g* at his tent door, and looked after Moses, until he was gone into the tabernacle.
9 And it came to pass, as Moses entered into the tabernacle, the cloudy pillar descended, and stood *at* the door of the tabernacle, and *the LORD h* talked with Moses.
10 And all the people saw the cloudy pillar stand *at* the tabernacle door: and all the people rose up and worshipped, every man *in* his tent door.
11 And *i* the LORD spake unto Moses face to face, as a man speaketh unto his friend. And he turned again into the camp: but *j* his servant Joshua, the son of Nun, a young man, departed not out of the tabernacle.
12 ¶ And Moses said unto the LORD, See,

thou sayest unto me, Bring up this people: and thou hast not let me know whom thou wilt send with me: yet thou hast said, *k* I know thee by name, and thou hast also found grace in my sight.
13 Now therefore, I pray thee, *l* if I have found grace in thy sight, *m* show me now thy way, that I may know thee, that I may find grace in thy sight; and consider that this nation *is n* thy people.
14 And he said, *o* My presence shall go *with thee*, and I will give thee *p* rest.
15 And he said unto him, *q* If thy presence go not *with me*, carry us not up hence.
16 For wherein shall it be known here that I and thy people have found grace in thy sight? *r Is it* not in that thou goest with us? so *s* shall we be separated, I and thy people, from all the people that *are* upon the face of the earth.
17 And the LORD said unto Moses, *t* I will do this thing also that thou hast spoken: for thou hast found grace in my sight, and I know thee by name.
18 And he said, I beseech thee, show me thy *u* glory.
19 And he said, *v* I will make all my goodness pass before thee, and I will proclaim the name of the LORD before thee; *w* and will be *x* gracious to whom I will be gracious, and will show mercy on whom I will show mercy.
20 And he said, Thou canst not see my face: for *y* there shall no man see me, and live.
21 And the LORD said, Behold, *there is* a place by me, and thou shalt stand upon a rock:
22 And it shall come to pass, while my glory passeth by, that I will put thee *z* in a clift of the rock, and will *a* cover thee with my hand while I pass by:
23 And I will take away mine hand, and thou shalt see my back parts; but my face shall *b* not be seen.

CHAPTER XXXIV.

1 *The tables are renewed.* 5 *The name of the LORD proclaimed.* 10 *God maketh a covenant with the people.* 29 *Moses' face shineth.*

AND the LORD said unto Moses, *a* Hew thee two tables of stone like unto the first; and *b* I will write upon *these* tables the words that were in the first tables, which thou brakest.
2 And be ready in the morning, and come up in the morning unto mount Sinai, and present thyself there to me in the top of the mount.
3 And no man shall come up with thee, neither let any man be seen throughout all the mount; neither let the flocks nor herds feed before that mount.
4 ¶ And he hewed two tables of stone like unto the first: and Moses rose up early in the morning, and went up unto mount Sinai, as the LORD had commanded him, and took in his hand the two tables of stone.
5 And the LORD descended in the cloud, and stood with him there, and proclaimed the name of the LORD.
6 And the LORD passed by before him, and proclaimed, The LORD, The LORD *c* God, merciful and gracious, long-suffering, and abundant in *d* goodness and *e* truth,
7 Keeping *f* mercy for thousands, *g* forgiving iniquity and transgression and sin and that *h* will by no means clear the *guilty*;

a dry, resinous, aromatic gum, of a yellow colour, which comes from a tree in Arabia, and is obtained by incision of the bark. This incense was placed within the sanctuary, to be at hand when the priest required to burn on the altar. The art of compounding unguents and perfumes was well-known in Egypt, where sweet scented spices were extensively used not only in common life, but in the ritual of the temples. Most of the ingredients here mentioned have been found on minute examination of mummies and other Egyptian relics; and the Israelites, therefore, would have the best opportunities of acquiring in that country the skill in pounding and mixing them which they were called to exercise in the service of the tabernacle. But the receipe for the incense as well as for the oil in the tabernacle, though it receives illustration from the customs of Egypt, was peculiar, and being prescribed by divine authority, was to be applied to no common or inferior purpose.

CHAPTER XXXI.

Ver. 1-18. BEZALEEL AND AHOLIAB. 2. See I have called—Though the instructions about the tabernacle were privately communicated to Moses, it was plainly impossible that he could superintend the work in person, amid the multiplicity of his other duties. A head director or builder was selected by God himself; and the nomination by such high authority removed all ground of jealousy or discontent on the part of any who might have thought their merits overlooked. (cf. Matt. 13. 1.) by name Bezaleel—Signifying "in the shadow or protection of God;" and, as called to discharge a duty of great magnitude—to execute a confidential trust in the ancient church of God, has his family and lineage recorded with marked distinction. He belonged to the tribe of Judah, which, doubtless for wise and weighty reasons, God all along delighted to honour; and he was the grandson of Hur, a pious patriot, (17. 12,) who was associated, by a special commission, with Aaron in the government of the people during the absence of Moses. Moreover, it may be noticed that a Jewish tradition affirms Hur to be the husband of Miriam; and if this tradition may be relied on, it affords an additional reason for the appointment of Bezaleel emanating from the direct authority of God. **3-5.** I have filled him with the spirit of God—It is probable that he was naturally endowed with a mechanical genius, and had acquired in Egypt great knowledge and skill in the useful, as well as literal arts, so as to be a first-class artisan, competent to take charge of both the plain and ornamental work, which the building of the sacred edifice required. When God has any special work to be accomplished, He always raises up instruments capable of doing it; and it is likely that He had given to the son of Uri that strong natural aptitude, and those opportunities of gaining mechanical skill, with an ultimate view to this responsible office. Notwithstanding his grand duty was to conform with scrupulous fidelity to the pattern furnished, there was still plenty of room for inventive talent, and tasteful exactness in the execution; and his natural and acquired gifts were enlarged and invigorated for the important work. **6.** I have given with him Aholiab—He belonged to the tribe of Dan, one of the least influential and honourable in Israel; and here, too, we can trace the evidence of wise and paternal design, in choosing the colleague or assistant of Bezaleel from an inferior tribe. (cf. 1 Cor. 12. 14-25: also Mk. 6. 7.) all that are wise-hearted—At that period, when one spirit pervaded all Israel, it was not the man full of heavenly genius who presided over the work, but all who contributed their skill, experience, and labour, in rendering the smallest assistance, that showed their piety and devotedness to the divine service. In like manner, it was at the commencement of the Christian church. (A. 6. 5; 18. 2.) **12-17.** Verily my sabbaths ye shall keep—The reason for the fresh inculcation of the fourth commandment at this particular period was, that the great ardour and eagerness with which all classes betook themselves to the construction of the tabernacle, exposed them to the temptation of encroaching on the sanctity of the appointed day of rest. They might suppose that the erection of the tabernacle was a sacred work, and that it would be a high merit, an acceptable tribute, to prosecute the undertaking without the interruption of a day's repose; and therefore the caution here given, at the commencement of the undertaking, was a seasonable admonition. **18.** tables of stone—Containing the ten commandments, (ch. 24. 12,) called "tables of testimony," because God testified His will in them.

CHAPTER XXXII.

Ver. 1-35. THE GOLDEN CALF. 1. when the ... saw that Moses delayed—they supposed that he had lost his way in the darkness or perished in the fire. they gathered themselves together unto—rather 'against' Aaron in a tumultuous manner, to compel him to do what they wished. The incidents related in this chapter disclose a state of popular sentiment and feeling among the Israelites that stands in singular contrast to the tone of profound and humble reverence they displayed at the giving of the law. Within a space of little more than thirty days, their impressions were dissipated; and although they were still encamped upon ground, which they had every reason to regard as holy; although the cloud of glory that capped the summit of Sinai was still before their eyes, affording a visible demonstration of their being in close contact, or rather in the immediate presence, of God, they acted as if they had entirely forgotten the impressive scenes of which they had been so recently the witnesses. they said unto him, Up, make us gods—The Hebrew word rendered gods is simply the name of God in its plural form. The image made was single, and therefore it would be imputing to the Israelites a greater sin than they were guilty of, to charge them with renouncing the worship of the true God for idols. The fact is, that they required, like children, to have something to strike their senses, and as the Shechinah, "the glory of God," of which they had hitherto enjoyed the sight, was now veiled, they wished for some visible material object as the symbol of the divine presence, which should go before them as the pillar of fire had done. **2.** Aaron said, Break off your earrings—It was not an Egyptian custom for young men to wear earrings, and the circumstance, therefore, seems to point out 'the mixed rabble,' who were chiefly *foreign* slaves, as the ringleaders in this insurrection. In giving direction to break their ear-

visiting the iniquity of the fathers upon the children, and upon the children's children, unto the third and to the fourth *generation*.

8 And Moses made haste, and bowed his head toward the earth, and worshipped.

9 And he said, If now I have found grace in thy sight, O Lord, let my Lord, I pray thee, go among us; for it *is* a stiff-necked people; and pardon our iniquity and our sin, and take us for *thine inheritance.

10 ¶ And he said, Behold, I make a covenant: before all thy people I will do marvels, such as have not been done in all the earth, nor in any nation: and all the people among which thou *art* shall see the work of the Lord: for it *is* a terrible thing that I will do with thee.

11 Observe thou that which I command thee this day: behold, I drive out before thee the Amorite, and the Canaanite, and the Hittite, and the Perizzite, and the Hivite, and the Jebusite.

12 Take heed to thyself, lest thou make a covenant with the inhabitants of the land whither thou goest, lest it be for a snare in the midst of thee:

13 But ye shall destroy their altars, break their images, and cut down their groves:

14 For thou shalt worship no other god: for the Lord, whose name *is* Jealous, *is* a jealous God:

15 Lest thou make a covenant with the inhabitants of the land, and they go a-whoring after their gods, and do sacrifice unto their gods, and *one* call thee, and thou eat of his sacrifice;

16 And thou take of their daughters unto thy sons, and their daughters go a whoring after their gods, and make thy sons go a whoring after their gods.

17 Thou shalt make thee no molten gods.

18 ¶ The feast of unleavened bread shalt thou keep. Seven days thou shalt eat unleavened bread, as I commanded thee, in the time of the month Abib: for in the month Abib thou camest out from Egypt.

19 All that openeth the matrix *is* mine; and every firstling among thy cattle, *whether* ox or sheep, *that is* male.

20 But the firstling of an ass thou shalt redeem with a lamb: and if thou redeem *him* not, then shalt thou break his neck. All the first-born of thy sons thou shalt redeem. And none shall appear before me empty.

21 ¶ Six days thou shalt work; but on the seventh day thou shalt rest: in earing time and in harvest thou shalt rest.

22 ¶ And thou shalt observe the feast of weeks, of the first-fruits of wheat harvest, and the feast of ingathering at the year's end.

23 ¶ Thrice in the year shall all your men-children appear before the Lord God, the God of Israel.

24 For I will cast out the nations before thee, and enlarge thy borders: neither shall any man desire thy land, when thou shalt go up to appear before the Lord thy God thrice in the year.

25 Thou shalt not offer the blood of my sacrifice with leaven; neither shall the sacrifice of the feast of the passover be left unto the morning.

26 The first of the first-fruits of thy land thou shalt bring unto the house of the Lord thy God. Thou shalt not seethe a kid in his mother's milk.

27 And the Lord said unto Moses, Write thou these words: for after the tenor of these words I have made a covenant with thee and with Israel.

28 And he was there with the Lord forty days and forty nights; he did neither eat bread, nor drink water. And he wrote upon the tables the words of the covenant, the ten commandments.

29 ¶ And it came to pass, when Moses came down from mount Sinai with the two tables of testimony in Moses' hand, when he came down from the mount, that Moses wist not that the skin of his face shone while he talked with him.

30 And when Aaron and all the children of Israel saw Moses, behold, the skin of his face shone; and they were afraid to come nigh him.

31 And Moses called unto them; and Aaron and all the rulers of the congregation returned unto him: and Moses talked with them.

32 And afterward all the children of Israel came nigh: and he gave them in commandment all that the Lord had spoken with him in mount Sinai.

33 And *till* Moses had done speaking with them, he put a veil on his face.

34 But when Moses went in before the Lord to speak with him, he took the veil off, until he came out. And he came out, and spake unto the children of Israel that which he was commanded.

35 And the children of Israel saw the face of Moses, that the skin of Moses' face shone: and Moses put the veil upon his face again, until he went in to speak with him.

CHAPTER XXXV.

2 The sabbath. 4 The free gifts for the tabernacle. 20 The readiness of the people to offer. 30 Bezaleel and Aholiab called to the work.

AND Moses gathered all the congregation of the children of Israel together, and said unto them, These *are* the words which the Lord hath commanded, that ye should do them.

2 Six days shall work be done, but on the seventh day there shall be to you an holy day, a sabbath of rest to the Lord: whosoever doeth work therein shall be put to death.

3 Ye shall kindle no fire throughout your habitations upon the sabbath day.

4 ¶ And Moses spake unto all the congregation of the children of Israel, saying, This *is* the thing which the Lord commanded, saying,

5 Take ye from among you an offering unto the Lord: whosoever *is* of a willing heart, let him bring it, an offering of the Lord; gold, and silver, and brass,

6 And blue, and purple, and scarlet, and fine linen, and goats' *hair*,

7 And rams' skins dyed red, and badgers' skins, and shittim wood,

8 And oil for the light, and spices for anointing oil, and for the sweet incense,

9 And onyx stones, and stones to be set for the ephod, and for the breastplate.

10 And every wise-hearted among you shall come, and make all that the Lord hath commanded;

11 The tabernacle, his tent, and his covering, his taches, and his boards, his bars, his pillars, and his sockets,

rings, Aaron probably calculated on gaining time or, perhaps, on their covetousness and love of finery proving stronger than their idolatrous propensity. If such were his expectations, they were doomed to signal disappointment. Better to have calmly and earnestly remonstrated with them, or to have preferred duty to expediency, leaving the issue in the hands of Providence. 3. all the people brake off their golden earrings—The Egyptian rings, as seen on the monuments, were round massy plates of metal; and as it was rings of this sort the Israelites wore, their size and number must, in the general collection, have produced a large store of the precious material. 4. he fashioned ... after he made it a molten calf—the words are transposed, and the rendering should be, 'he framed with a graving tool the image to be made, and having poured the liquid gold into the mould, he made it a molten calf.' It is not said whether it was of life size, whether it was of solid gold or merely a wooden frame covered with plates of gold. This idol seems to have been the god Apis, the chief deity of the Egyptians, worshipped at Memphis under the form of a live ox, three years old. It was distinguished by a triangular white spot on its forehead and other peculiar marks. Images of it in the form of a whole ox, or of a calf's head on the end of a pole were very common; and it makes a great figure on the monuments, where it is represented in the van of all processions, as borne aloft on men's shoulders. they said, These be thy Gods, O Israel—It is inconceivable, that they who but a few weeks before had witnessed such amazing demonstrations of the true God, could have suddenly sunk to such a pitch of infatuation and brutish stupidity, as to imagine that human art or hands could make a god that should go before them. But it must be borne in mind, that though by election and in name they were the people of God, they were as yet, in feelings and associations, in habits and taste, little, if at all different, from Egyptians. They meant the calf to be an image, a visible sign or symbol of Jehovah, so that their sin consisted not in a breach of the FIRST but of the SECOND commandment. 5, 6. Aaron made proclamation... To-morrow is a feast to the Lord —a remarkable circumstance, strongly confirmatory of the view that they had not renounced the worship of Jehovah, but in accordance with Egyptian notions, had formed an image with which they had been familiar, to be the visible symbol of the Divine presence. But there seems to have been much of the revelry that marked the feasts of the heathen. 7-14. Go, get thee down—Intelligence of the idolatrous scene enacted at the foot of the mount was communicated to Moses in language borrowed from human passions and feelings, and the judgment of a justly offended God pronounced in terms of just indignation against the gross violation of the so recently promulgated laws. make of thee a great nation—care must be taken not to suppose this language as betokening any change or vacillation in the Divine purpose. The covenant made with the patriarchs had been ratified in the most solemn manner; it *could* not and never was intended that it *should* be broken. But the manner in which God spoke to Moses served two important purposes—it tended to develope the faith and intercessory patriotism of the Hebrew leader, and to excite the serious alarm of the people, that God would reject them and deprive them of the privileges they had fondly fancied were so secure. 15-18. Moses turned and went down from the mount—The plain, Er-Raheh, is not visible from the top of Jebel Musa, nor can the mount be descended on the side towards that valley; hence Moses and his companion who on duty had patiently waited his return in the hollow of the mountain's brow, heard the shouting sometime before they actually saw the camp. 19-24. Moses' anger waxed hot—The arrival of the leader like the appearance of a spectre arrested the revellers in the midst of their carnival, and his act of righteous indignation, when he dashed on the ground the tables of the law, in token that as they had so soon departed from their covenant relation, God would withdraw the peculiar privileges that He had promised them—that act together with the rigorous measures that followed, forms one of the most striking scenes recorded in sacred history. 20. he took the calf, &c.—It has been supposed that the gold was dissolved by *natron*, or some chemical substance. But there is no mention of solubility here (or in Deut. 9. 21,) it was "burned in the fire," to cast it into ingots of suitable size for the operations which follow—"grounded to powder:" the powder of malleable metals can be ground so fine as to resemble dust from the wings of a moth or butterfly; and these dust particles will float in water for hours, and in a running stream for days. These operations of grinding were intended to show contempt for such worthless gods, and the Israelites would be made to remember the humiliating lesson by the state of the water they had drank for a time. [NAPIER.] Others think that as the idolatrous festivals were usually ended with great use of sweet wine, the nauseous draught of the gold dust would be a severe punishment. (cf. 2 Ki. 23. 6, 15; 2 Chr. 15. 16; 34. 7.) 22. Let not the anger of my lord wax hot—Aaron cuts a poor figure, making a shuffling excuse and betraying more dread of the anger of Moses than of the Lord. (cf. Deut. 9. 20.) 25. naked—Either unarmed and defenceless, or ashamed from a sense of guilt. Some think they were literally naked, as the Egyptians performed some of their rites in that indecent manner. 26-28. Moses stood in the gate—the camp is supposed to have been protected by a rampart after the attack of the Amalekites. who is on the Lord's side?—The zeal and courage of Moses were astonishing, considering he opposed himself to an intoxicated mob. The people were separated into two divisions, and those who were the boldest and most obstinate in vindicating their idolatry were put to death, whilst the rest, who withdrew in shame or sorrow, was spared. 29. consecrate—or ye have consecrated yourselves to-day. The Levites, notwithstanding the dejection of Aaron, distinguished themselves by their zeal for the honour of God and their conduct in doing the office of executioners on this occasion; and this was one reason of their being appointed to a high and honourable office in the service of the sanctuary. 30-33. said unto the people, Ye have sinned—Moses laboured to show the people the heinous nature of their sin, and bring

12 The ^{h} ark, and the staves thereof, *with* the mercyseat, and the veil of the covering,

13 The ^{i} table, and his staves, and all his vessels, and the ^{j} showbread,

14 The ^{k} candlestick also for the light, and his furniture, and his lamps, with the oil for the light,

15 And ^{l} the incense altar, and his staves, and ^{m} the anointing oil, and ^{n} the sweet incense, and the hanging for the door at the entering in of the tabernacle,

16 The ^{o} altar of burnt offering, with his brasen grate, his staves, and all his vessels, the laver and his foot,

17 The ^{p} hangings of the court, his pillars, and their sockets, and the hanging for the door of the court,

18 The pins of the tabernacle, and the pins of the court, and their cords,

19 The ^{q} cloths of service, to do service in the holy *place*, the holy garments for Aaron the priest, and the garments of his sons, to minister in the priest's office.

20 ¶ And all the congregation of the children of Israel departed from the presence of Moses.

21 And they came, every one ^{r} whose heart stirred him up, and every one whom his spirit made willing, *and* they brought the LORD's offering to the work of the tabernacle of the congregation, and for all his service, and for the holy garments.

22 And they came, both men and women, as many as were willing-hearted, *and* brought bracelets, and earrings, and rings, and tablets, all jewels of gold: and every man that offered *offered* an offering of gold unto the LORD.

23 And ^{s} every man with whom was found blue, and purple, and scarlet, and fine linen, and goats' hair, and red skins of rams, and badgers' skins, brought *them.*

24 Every one that did offer an offering of silver and brass brought the LORD's offering: and every man with whom was found shittim wood, for any work of the service, brought *it.*

25 And all the women that were ^{t} wise-hearted did spin with their hands, and brought that which they had spun, *both* of blue, and of purple, *and* of scarlet, and of fine linen.

26 And all the women whose heart stirred them up in wisdom spun goats' *hair.*

27 And ^{u} the rulers brought onyx stones, and stones to be set, for the ephod, and for the breastplate;

28 And ^{v} spice, and oil for the light, and for the anointing oil, and for the sweet incense.

29 The children of Israel brought a ^{w} willing offering unto the LORD, every man and woman, whose heart made them willing to bring, for all manner of work which the LORD had commanded to be made by the hand of Moses.

30 ¶ And Moses said unto the children of Israel, See, ^{x} the LORD hath called by name Bezaleel the son of Uri, the son of Hur, of the tribe of Judah:

31 And he hath filled him with ^{y} the spirit of God, in wisdom, in understanding, and in knowledge, and in all manner of workmanship;

32 And to devise curious works, to work in gold, and in silver, and in brass,

33 And in the cutting of stones, to set

B. C. 1491.
———
CHAP. 35.
^{h} ch. 25. 10.
^{i} ch. 25. 23.
^{j} ch. 25. 30.
Lev. 24. 5, 6.
^{k} ch. 25. 31.
^{l} ch. 30. 1.
^{m} ch. 30. 23.
^{n} ch. 30. 34.
^{o} ch. 27. 1.
^{p} ch. 27. 9.
^{q} ch. 31. 10.
ch. 39. 1, 41.
Num. 4. 5, 6.
^{r} ch. 25. 2.
ch. 36. 2.
1 Chr. 28. 2, 9.
1Chr. 29. 9.
Ezra 7. 27.
2 Cor. 8. 12.
2 Cor. 9. 7.
^{s} 1 Chr. 29.8.
^{t} ch. 28. 3.
ch. 31. 6.
ch. 36. 1.
2 Kin. 23.7.
Prov. 31. 19, 22, 24.
^{u} 1 Chr.29.6.
Ezra 2. 68.
^{v} ch. 30. 23.
^{w} 1 Chr. 29. 9.
^{x} ch. 31. 2.
^{y} Gen. 41. 38.
Job 32. 8.
Prov. 2. 6.
^{z} ch. 31. 6.
^{a} ver. 31.
ch. 31. 3, 6.
ch. 36. 1, 2.
1 Kin. 7. 14.
2 Chr. 2. 14.
Is. 28. 26.
James 1. 5.
———
CHAP. 36.
^{a} ch. 28. 3.
ch. 31. 6.
ch. 35. 10, 35.
Job 32. 8.
Is. 28. 26.
Prov. 2. 6.
^{b} ch. 25. 8.
^{c} ch. 35. 2, 26.
1 Chr. 29.5.
^{d} ch. 35. 27.
^{e} 2 Cor. 8. 2, 3.
^{f} ch. 26. 1.
Job 32. 8.
^{g} Gen. 3. 24.
1 Kin. 6. 23.
2 Chr. 3. 10.
Ezek. 1. 5-28.
Eze. 10. 1.
^{h} ch. 26. 5.
^{i} ch. 26. 7.

them, and in carving of wood, to make any manner of cunning work.

34 And he hath put in his heart that he may teach, *both* he, and ^{z} Aholiab the son of Ahisamach, of the tribe of Dan.

35 Them hath he ^{a} filled with wisdom of heart, to work all manner of work of the engraver, and of the cunning workman, and of the embroiderer, in blue, and in purple, in scarlet, and in fine linen, and of the weaver, *even* of them that do any work, and of those that devise cunning work.

CHAPTER XXXVI.

1 *The offerings delivered to the workmen.* 4 *The liberality of the people restrained.* 8 *The curtains.* 19 *The covering.* 35 *The veil, etc.*

THEN wrought Bezaleel and Aholiab, and every ^{a} wise-hearted man, in whom the LORD put wisdom and understanding to know how to work all manner of work for the service of the ^{b} sanctuary, according to all that the LORD had commanded.

2 And Moses called Bezaleel and Aholiab, and every wise-hearted man, in whose heart the LORD had put wisdom, *even* every one whose ^{c} heart stirred him up to come unto the work to do it:

3 And they received of Moses all the offering which the children of Israel ^{d} had brought for the work of the service of the sanctuary, to make it withal. And they brought yet unto him free offerings every morning.

4 ¶ And all the wise men, that wrought all the work of the sanctuary, came every man from his work which they made;

5 And they spake unto Moses, saying, ^{e} The people bring much more than enough for the service of the work which the LORD commanded to make.

6 And Moses gave commandment, and they caused it to be proclaimed throughout the camp, saying, Let neither man nor woman make any more work for the offering of the sanctuary. So the people were restrained from bringing.

7 For the stuff they had was sufficient for all the work to make it, and too much.

8 ¶ And ^{f} every wise-hearted man among them that wrought the work of the tabernacle made ten curtains *of* fine twined linen, and blue, and purple, and scarlet: with cherubim ^{g} of cunning work made he them.

9 The length of one curtain *was* twenty and eight cubits, and the breadth of one curtain four cubits: the curtains *were* all of one size.

10 And he coupled the five curtains one unto another; and *the other* five curtains he coupled one unto another.

11 And he made loops of blue on the edge of one curtain from the selvage in the coupling: likewise he made in the uttermost side of *another* curtain, in the coupling of the second.

12 Fifty ^{h} loops made he in one curtain, and fifty loops made he in the edge of the curtain which *was* in the coupling of the second: the loops held one *curtain* to another.

13 And he made fifty taches of gold, and coupled the curtains one unto another with the taches: so it became one tabernacle.

14 ¶ And ^{i} he made curtains of goats' *hair* for the tent over the tabernacle: eleven curtains he made them.

15 The length of one curtain *was* thirty

them to repentance. But not content with that he hastened more earnestly to intercede for them. 32. Blot me out of thy book—an allusion to the registering of the living, and erasing the names of those who die. What warmth of affection did he evince for his brethren; how fully was he animated with the true spirit of a patriot, when he professed his *willingness* to die for them. But Christ actually died for his people, (Ro. 5. 8.) 35. The Lord plagued the people—No immediate judgments were inflicted, but this early lapse into idolatry was always mentioned as an aggravation of their subsequent apostacies.

CHAPTER XXXIII.

Ver. 1-3. THE LORD REFUSETH TO GO WITH THE PEOPLE. 1. The Lord said—Rather "had" said unto Moses. The conference detailed in this chapter must be considered as having occurred prior to the pathetic intercession of Moses, recorded at the close of the preceding chapter; and the historian, having mentioned the fact of his earnest and painful anxiety, under the overwhelming pressure of which he poured forth that intercessory prayer for his apostate countrymen, now enters on a detailed account of the circumstances. 3. I will not go up, lest I consume thee—Here the Lord is represented as determined to do what he afterwards did not. (See on ch. 32. 10.) 4. When the people heard these evil tidings—From Moses on his descent from the mount. 5. put off thy ornaments—In seasons of mourning, it is customary with Eastern people to lay aside all gewgaws, and divest themselves of their jewels, their gold, and everything rich and splendid in their dress. This token of sorrow, the Lord required of his offending people, that I may know what to do unto thee—The language is accommodated to the feeble apprehensions of men. God judges the state of the heart by the tenor of the conduct. In the case of the Israelites, he cherished a design of mercy; and the moment he discerned the first symptoms of contrition, by their stripping off their ornaments, as penitents conscious of their error, and sincerely sorrowful, this fact added its weight to the fervency of Moses' prayers, and gave them prevalence with God in behalf of the people. 7. Moses took the tabernacle—Not the tabernacle, of which a pattern had been given him, for it was not yet erected, but his own tent—conspicuous as that of the leader—in a part of which he heard causes, and communed with God about the people's interests; hence called "the tabernacle of the congregation," and the withdrawal of which, in abhorrence from a polluted camp, was regarded as the first step in the total abandonment with which God had threatened them. 8. all the people rose up and stood—Its removal produced deep and universal consternation; and it is easy to conceive how anxiously all eyes would be directed towards it; how rapidly the happy intelligence would spread, when a phenomenon was witnessed from which an encouraging hope could be founded. 9-11. The cloudy pillar descended—How would the downcast hearts of the people revive—how would the tide of joy swell in every bosom, when the symbolic cloud was seen slowly and majestically to descend, and stand at the entrance of the tabernacle, as Moses entered—It was when he appeared as their mediator—when he repaired from day to day to intercede for them, that welcome token of assurance was given that his advocacy prevailed, that Israel's sin was forgiven, and that God would again be gracious. 18-23. I beseech thee shew me thy glory—This is one of the most mysterious scenes described in the Bible, he had, for his comfort and encouragement, a splendid and full display of the divine majesty, not in its unveiled effulgence, but as far as the weakness of humanity would admit. The face, hand, back parts, are to be understood figuratively.

CHAPTER XXXIV.

Ver. 1-35. THE TABLES ARE RENEWED. 1. Hew thee two tables of stone—God having been reconciled to repentant Israel, through the earnest intercession, the successful mediation of Moses, means were to be taken for the restoration of the broken covenant. Intimation was given, however, in a most intelligible and expressive manner, that the favour was to be restored with some memento of the rupture: for at the former time God himself had provided the materials, as well as written upon them. Now, Moses was to prepare the stone tables, and God was only to retrace the characters originally inscribed for the use and guidance of the people. 2. in the top of the mount—Not absolutely the highest peak; for as the cloud of the Shechinah usually abode on the summit, and yet (v. 5 it "descended;" the plain inference is, that Moses was to station himself at a point not far distant, but still below the loftiest pinnacle. 3. no man, neither flocks nor herds—All these enactments were made in order that the law might be a second time renewed with the solemnity and sanctity that marked its first delivery. The whole transaction was ordered so as to impress the people with an awful sense of the holiness of God; and that it was a matter of no trifling moment to have subjected him, so to speak, to the necessity of redelivering the law of the ten commandments. 4. Moses took in his hands the two tables of stone—As he had no attendant to divide the labour of carrying them, it is evident that they must have been light, and of no great dimensions,—probably flat slabs of shale or slate, such as abound in the mountainous region of Horeb. An additional proof of their comparatively small size appears in the circumstance of their being deposited in the ark of the most holy place, (ch. 25. 10.) 5. The Lord descended in a cloud—After graciously hovering over the tabernacle, it seems to have resumed its usual position on the summit of the mount. It was the shadow of God manifest to the outward senses; and, at the same time, of God manifest in the flesh. The emblem of a cloud seems to have been chosen to signify that, although He was pleased to make known much about himself, there was more veiled from mortal view. It was to check presumption, and engender awe, and give a humble sense of human attainments in divine knowledge, as now man sees —but darkly. 6. The Lord passed by—In this remarkable scene, God performed what He had promised to Moses the day before. proclaimed the Lord, merciful and gracious—At an earlier period He had announced himself to Moses, in the glory of His self-existent and eternal majesty, as "I am;" now He makes himself known in the glory of His grace and goodness,—attributes that were to be illustriously displayed in the future history and

cubits, and four cubits *was* the breadth of one curtain: the eleven curtains *were* of one size.

16 And he coupled five curtains by themselves, and six curtains by themselves.

17 And he made fifty loops upon the uttermost edge of the curtain in the coupling, and fifty loops made he upon the edge of the curtain which coupleth the second.

18 And he made fifty taches of brass to couple the tent together, that it might be one.

19 ¶ And *j* he made a covering for the tent of rams' skins dyed red, and a covering of badgers' skins above *that*.

20 ¶ And *k* he made boards for the tabernacle of *l* shittim wood, standing up.

21 The length of a board *was* ten cubits, and the breadth of a board one cubit and a half.

22 One board had two ¹ tenons, equally distant one from another: thus did he make for all the boards of the tabernacle.

23 And he made boards for the tabernacle; twenty boards for the south side southward.

24 And forty sockets of silver he made under the twenty boards; two sockets under one board for his two tenons, and two sockets under another board for his two tenons.

25 And for the other side of the tabernacle, which is toward the north corner, he made twenty boards,

26 And their forty sockets of silver; two sockets under one board, and two sockets under another board.

27 And for the sides of the tabernacle ² westward he made six boards.

28 And two boards made he for the corners of the tabernacle in the two sides.

29 And they were ³ coupled beneath, and coupled together at the head thereof, to one ring: thus he did to both of them in both the corners.

30 And there were eight boards; and their sockets *were* sixteen sockets of silver, ⁴ under every board two sockets.

31 ¶ And he made *m* bars of shittim wood; five for the boards of the one side of the tabernacle,

32 And five bars for the boards of the other side of the tabernacle, and five bars for the boards of the tabernacle for the sides westward.

33 And he made the middle bar to shoot through the boards from the one end to the other.

34 And he overlaid the boards with gold, and made their rings of gold to be places for the bars, and overlaid the bars with gold.

35 ¶ And he made *n* a veil of blue, and purple, and scarlet, and fine twined linen: *with* cherubim made he it of cunning work.

36 And he made thereunto four pillars of shittim *wood*, and overlaid them with gold: their hooks *were* of gold; and he cast for them four sockets of silver.

37 ¶ And he made an *o* hanging for the tabernacle door of blue, and purple, and scarlet, and fine twined linen, ⁵ of needlework;

38 And the five pillars of it with their hooks: and he overlaid their *p* chapiters and their fillets with gold: but their five sockets were of brass.

B. C. 1491.

CHAP. 36.
j ch. 26. 14.
k ch. 26. 15.
l ch. 25. 5, 10.
Nu. 25. 1.
Deu. 10. 3.
Josh. 2. 1.
1 hands.
2 sea-ward.
ch. 26. 22.
3 twined.
ch. 26. 24.
2 Sa. 5. 6.
Ps. 133. 1.
Acts 2. 46.
1 Cor. 1.10.
4 two sockets, two sockets under one board.
m ch. 26. 26.
n ch. 26. 31.
Mat. 27.51.
Heb. 6. 19.
Heb. 10.20.
o ch. 26. 36.
5 the work of a needleworker, or, embroiderer.
p 1 Ki. 7. 16.
2 Chr. 4. 12.
Jer. 52. 22.

CHAP. 37.
a ch. 35. 30.
b ch. 25. 10.
c Nu. 4. 6.
d Nu. 1. 50.
2 Sa. 6. 3.
e ch. 25. 17.
1 Or, out of, etc.
2 Or, out of, etc.
f Gen. 3. 24.
ch. 25. 22.
1 Kings 6. 23.
2 Chr. 3.10.
Ps. 80. 1.
Ezek. 1. 5-23.
Ezek. 10. 1.
John 1. 51.
Phil. 2. 10.
1 Tim. 3. 16.
Heb. 1. 14.
1 Pet. 1. 12.
g ch. 25. 23.
Mal. 1. 7, 12.
h ch. 25. 29.
3 Or, to pour out withal.
i ch. 25. 31.
Lev. 24. 4.
1 Chr. 28. 15.
Zech. 4. 2.
Mat. 5. 15, 16.
John 5. 35.
Philip. 2. 15.
1 Peter 2. 9.
Rev. 1. 20.

CHAPTER XXXVII.

1 *The ark.* 6 *The mercyseat with cherubim.* 10 *The table.* 17 *The candlestick.* 25 *The altar of incense.* 29 *The anointing oil and sweet incense.*

AND *a* Bezaleel made *b* the ark of shittim wood: two cubits and a half *was* the length of it, and a cubit and a half the breadth of it, and a cubit and a half the height of it:

2 And he overlaid it with pure gold within and without, and made a crown of gold to it round about.

3 And he cast for it four rings of gold, *to be set* by the four corners of it; even two rings upon the one side of it, and two rings upon the other side of it.

4 And he made *c* staves of shittim wood, and overlaid them with gold.

5 And he *d* put the staves into the rings by the sides of the ark, to bear the ark.

6 ¶ And he made the *e* mercyseat of pure gold: two cubits and a half *was* the length thereof, and one cubit and a half the breadth thereof.

7 And he made two cherubim of gold, beaten out of one piece made he them, on the two ends of the mercyseat;

8 One cherub ¹ on the end on this side, and another cherub ² on the *other* end on that side: out of the mercyseat made he the cherubim on the two ends thereof.

9 And the *f* cherubim spread out *their* wings on high, *and* covered with their wings over the mercyseat, with their faces one to another; *even* to the mercyseat-ward were the faces of the cherubim.

10 ¶ And he made *g* the table of shittim wood: two cubits *was* the length thereof, and a cubit the breadth thereof, and a cubit and a half the height thereof:

11 And he overlaid it with pure gold, and made thereunto a crown of gold round about.

12 Also he made thereunto a border of an handbreadth round about; and made a crown of gold for the border thereof round about.

13 And he cast for it four rings of gold, and put the rings upon the four corners that *were* in the four feet thereof.

14 Over against the border were the rings, the places for the staves to bear the table.

15 And he made the staves of shittim wood, and overlaid them with gold, to bear the table.

16 And he made the vessels which *were* upon the table, his *h* dishes, and his spoons, and his bowls, and his covers ³ to cover withal, of pure gold.

17 ¶ And he made the *i* candlestick of pure gold: of beaten work made he the candlestick; his shaft, and his branch, his bowls, his knops, and his flowers, were of the same.

18 And six branches going out of the sides thereof; three branches of the candlestick out of the one side thereof, and three branches of the candlestick out of the other side thereof:

19 Three bowls made after the fashion of almonds in one branch, a knop and a flower; and three bowls made like almonds in another branch, a knop and a flower: so throughout the six branches going out of the candlestick.

20 And in the candlestick *were* four bowls

experience of the church. Being about to republish His law,—the sin of the Israelites being forgiven, and the deed of pardon about to be signed and sealed, by renewing the terms of the former covenant,—it was the most fitting time to proclaim the extent of the divine mercy which was to be displayed, not in the case of Israel only, but of all who offend. **8-26.** Moses bowed and worshipped—In the East, people bow the head to royalty, and are silent, when it passes by, while in the west, they take off their hats and shout. **9.** Moses said, If now I have found grace—On this proclamation, he, in the overflowing benevolence of his heart, founded an earnest petition for the divine presence being continued with the people; and God was pleased to give His favourable answer to his intercession by a renewal of His promise under the form of a covenant, repeating the leading points that formed the conditions of the former national compact. **27, 28.** Write thou these words—*i.e.*, the ceremonial and judicial injunctions comprehended above, (*v.* 11-26;) while the re-writing of the ten commandments on the newly prepared slabs was done by God himself. (cf. Deu. 10. 1-4.) was with the Lord—As long as formerly, being sustained for the execution of his special duties by the miraculous power of God. A special cause is assigned for his protracted fast on this second occasion, (Deu. 9. 18.,) **29-35.** Moses wist not that the skin of his face shone—It was an intimation of the exalted presence into which he had been admitted, and of the glory he had witnessed, (2 Cor. 3. 18;) and in that view, it was a badge of his high office as the ambassador of God. No testimonial needed to be produced. He bore his credentials on his very face; and whether this extraordinary effulgence was a permanent or merely temporary distinction, it cannot be doubted that this reflected glory, was given him as an honour before all the people. **30.** afraid to come nigh him—Their fear arose from a sense of guilt,—the beaming radiance of his countenance made him appear to their awe-struck consciences a flaming minister of heaven. **33.** put a veil upon his face—That veil was with the greatest propriety removed when speaking with the Lord, for every one appears unveiled to the eye of omniscience; but it was removed on returning to the people,—and this was emblematic of the dark and shadowy character of that dispensation, (2 Cor. 3. 13, 14.)

CHAPTER XXXV.

Ver. 1-35. CONTRIBUTIONS TO THE TABERNACLE. **1.** Moses gathered, &c.—On the occasion referred to in the opening of this chapter, the Israelites were specially reminded of the design to erect a magnificent tabernacle for the regular worship of God, as well as of the leading articles that were required to furnish that sacred edifice. (See on chaps. 25. 27. 30. 31.) **20, 21.** All the congregation of Israel, &c.—No exciting harangues were made, nor had the people bibles at home in which they could compare the requirements of their leader and see if these things were so. But they had no doubt as to his bearing to them the will of God, and they were impressed with so strong a sense of its being their duty, that they made a spontaneous offer of the best and most valuable treasures they possessed. every one whose heart stirred him—One powerful element doubtless of this extraordinary open-hearted liberality, was the remembrance of their recent transgression, which made them "zealous of good works." (cf. 2 Cor. 7. 11.) But along with this motive, there were others of a higher and nobler kind—a principle of love to God and devotedness to His service, an anxious desire to secure the benefit of His presence, and gratitude for the tokens of His divine favour,—it was under the combined influence of these considerations that the people were so willing and ready to pour their contributions into that exchequer of the sanctuary. every one whom his spirit made willing—Human nature is always the same, and it is implied that while an extraordinary spirit of pious liberality reigned in the bosoms of the people at large, there were exceptions—some who were too fond of the world, who loved their possessions more than their God, and who could not part with these; no, not for the service of the tabernacle. **22.** They came, &c.—*lit.* "the men over and above the women:" a phraseology which implies that the women acted a prominent part, presented their offerings *first*, and then were followed by as many of their male companions as were similarly disposed. brought bracelets, &c.—Money in the form of coins or bullion there was none in that early age. What money passed current with the merchant consisted of rings which were weighed, and principally of ornaments for personal decoration. Astonishment at the abundance of their ornaments is at an end when we learn that costly and elegant ornaments abounded in proportion as clothing was simple and scarce among the Egyptians, and some, entirely divested of clothing, yet wore rich necklaces. [HENG.] Amongst people with Oriental sentiments and tastes, scarcely any stronger proof could have been given of the power of religion than their willingness not only to lay aside, but to devote those muchvalued trinkets to the house of God: and thus all, like the Eastern sages, laid the best they had at the service of God. **30.** See the Lord hath, &c.—Moses had made this communication before. But now that the collection had been made, the materials were contributed, and the operations of building about to be commenced, it was with the greatest propriety he reminded the people that the individuals entrusted with the application of their gold and silver had been nominated to the work by authority to which all would bow. **35.** Them hath He filled—A statement which not only testifies that skill in art and science is a direct gift from God, but that weaving was especially the business of men in Egypt, (see ch. 38. 22; 39. 22, 27,) and in perfect harmony with the testimony of the monuments is the account given by Moses to the artists who were divinely taught the arts necessary for the embellishment of the tabernacle. Others, whose limited means did not admit of these expensive contributions, offered their gratuitous services in fabricating such articles of tapestry as were needed; arts which the Israelitish females learned as bondswomen, in the houses of Egyptian princes.

CHAPTER XXXVI.

Ver. 1-4. OFFERINGS DELIVERED TO THE WORKMEN. **1.** Then wrought Bezaleel, &c.—Here is an illustrious example of zeal and activity in the work of the Lord. No un-

made like *almonds*, his knops and his flowers:

21 And a knop under two branches of the same, and a knop under two branches of the same, and a knop under two branches of the same, according to the six branches going out of it.

22 Their knops and their branches were of the same: all of it was one beaten work of pure gold.

23 And he made his *k* seven lamps, and his snuffers, and his snuff-dishes, of pure gold.

24 Of a talent of pure gold made he it, and all the vessels thereof.

25 ¶ And *l* he made the incense altar of shittim wood: the length of it was a cubit, and the breadth of it a cubit; it was foursquare; and two cubits was the height of it; the horns thereof were of the same.

26 And he overlaid it with pure gold, both the top of it, and the sides thereof round about, and the horns of it: also he made unto it a crown of gold round about.

27 And he made two rings of gold for it under the crown thereof, by the two corners of it, upon the two sides thereof, to be places for the staves to bear it withal.

28 And he made the staves of shittim wood, and overlaid them with gold.

29 ¶ And he made *m* the holy anointing oil, and the pure *m* incense of sweet spices, according to the work of the apothecary.

CHAPTER XXXVIII.

1 *The altar of burnt offering.* 8 *The laver of brass.* 9 *The court.* 21 *The sum of that which the people offered.*

AND *a* he made the altar of burnt offering of shittim wood: five cubits was the length thereof, and five cubits the breadth thereof; it was foursquare; and three cubits the height thereof.

2 And he made the horns thereof on the four corners of it; the horns thereof were of the same: and he overlaid it with brass.

3 And he made all the vessels of the altar, the pots, and the shovels, and the basins, and the flesh-hooks, and the fire-pans: all the vessels thereof made he of *b* brass.

4 And he made for the altar a brasen grate of network under the compass thereof beneath unto the midst of it.

5 And he cast four rings for the four ends of the grate of brass, to be places for the staves.

6 And he made the staves of shittim wood, and overlaid them with brass.

7 And he put the staves into the rings on the sides of the altar, to bear it withal; he made the altar hollow with boards.

8 ¶ And he made *c* the laver of brass, and the foot of it of brass, of the ¹ lookingglasses of the women ² assembling, which assembled at the door of the tabernacle of the congregation.

9 ¶ And he made *d* the court: on the south side southward the hangings of the court were of fine twined linen, an hundred cubits:

10 Their pillars were twenty, and their brasen sockets twenty: the hooks of the pillars and their fillets were of silver.

11 And for the north side the hangings were an hundred cubits, their pillars were twenty, and their sockets of brass twenty; the hooks of the pillars and their fillets of silver.

12 And for the west side were hangings of fifty cubits, their pillars ten, and their sockets ten; the hooks of the pillars and their fillets of silver.

13 And for the east side eastward fifty cubits.

14 The hangings of the one side of the gate were fifteen cubits; their pillars three, and their sockets three.

15 And for the other side of the court gate, on this hand and that hand, were hangings of fifteen cubits; their pillars three, and their sockets three.

16 All the hangings of the court round about were of fine twined linen.

17 And the sockets for the pillars were of brass; the hooks of the pillars and their fillets of silver; and the overlaying of their chapiters of silver; and all the pillars of the court were filleted with silver.

18 And the hanging for the gate of the court was needlework, of *e* blue, and purple, and scarlet, and fine twined linen: and twenty cubits was the length, and the height in the breadth was five cubits, answerable to the hangings of the court.

19 And their pillars were four, and their sockets of brass four; their hooks of silver, and the overlaying of their chapiters and their fillets of silver.

20 And all the *f* pins of the tabernacle, and of the court round about, were of brass.

21 ¶ This is the sum of the tabernacle, even of *g* the tabernacle of testimony, as it was counted, according to the commandment of Moses, for the service of the Levites, *h* by the hand of Ithamar, son to Aaron the priest.

22 And *i* Bezaleel the son of Uri, the son of Hur, of the tribe of Judah, made all that the LORD commanded Moses.

23 And with him was Aholiab, son of Ahisamach, of the tribe of Dan, an engraver, and a cunning workman, and an embroiderer in blue, and in purple, and in scarlet, and fine linen.

24 All the gold that was occupied for the work in all the work of the holy place, even the gold of the offering, was twenty and nine talents, and seven hundred and thirty shekels, after *j* the shekel of the sanctuary.

25 And the silver of them that were numbered of the congregation was an hundred talents, and a thousand seven hundred and threescore and fifteen shekels, after the shekel of the sanctuary:

26 A *k* bekah for ³ every man, that is, half a shekel, after the shekel of the sanctuary, for every one that went to be numbered, from twenty years old and upward, for *l* six hundred thousand and three thousand and five hundred and fifty men.

27 And of the hundred talents of silver were cast *m* the sockets of the sanctuary, and the sockets of the veil; an hundred sockets of the hundred talents, a talent for a socket.

28 And of the thousand seven hundred seventy and five *shekels* he made hooks for the pillars, and overlaid their chapiters, and filleted them.

29 And the brass of the offering was seventy talents, and two thousand and four hundred shekels.

30 And therewith he made the sockets to the door of the tabernacle of the congregation, and the brasen altar, and the brasen grate for it, and all the vessels of the altar

necessary delay was allowed to take place: and from the moment the first pole was stuck in the ground till the final completion of the sacred edifice, he and his associates laboured with all the energies both of mind and body engaged in the work. And what was the mainspring of their arduous and untiring diligence? They could be actuated by none of the ordinary motives that give impulse to human industry, by no desire for the acquisition of gain; no ambition for honour; no view of gratifying a mere love of power in directing the labours of a large body of men. They felt the stimulus—the strong irresistible impulse of higher and holier motives—obedience to the authority, zeal for the glory and love to the service of God. **3. They brought unto Moses, &c.**—Moses, in common with other Oriental magistrates, had his morning levees for receiving the people, (see on ch. 18. 13.) and it was while he was performing his magisterial duties that the people brought unto him freewill offerings every morning." Some who had nothing but their manual labour to give would spend a great part of the night in hastening to complete their self-imposed task before the early dawn; others might find their hearts constrained by silent meditations on their bed to open their coffers and give a part of their hoarded treasure to the pious object. All whose hearts were touched by piety, penitence, or gratitude repaired with eager haste into the presence of Moses, not as heretofore, to have their controversies settled, but to lay on his tribunal their contributions to the sanctuary of God. (2 Cor. 9. 7.) They (the workmen) received of Moses, &c.—It appears that the building was begun, after the first few contributions were made; it was progressively carried, and no necessity occurred to suspend operations even for the shortest interval, from want of the requisite materials. **5. spake unto Moses, &c.**—By the calculations which the practised eyes of the workmen enabled them to make, they were unanimously of opinion that the supply already far exceeded the demand, and that no more contributions were required. Such a report reflects the highest honour on their character as men of the strictest honour and integrity, who, notwithstanding they had command of an untold amount of the most precious things, and might, without any risk of human discovery, have appropriated much to their own use, were too high principled for such acts of peculation. Forthwith; a proclamation was issued to stop further contributions. **35. made a vail**—the second or inner vail, which separated the holy from the most holy place, embroidered with cherubim and of great size and thickness. **37. made a hanging for the door**—curtains of elaborately wrought needle-work are often suspended over the entrance to tents of the great nomad sheicks, and throughout Persia, at the entrance of summer tents—mosques and palaces. They are preferred as cooler and more elegant than wooden doors. This chapter contains an instructive narrative: it is the first instance of donations made for the worship of God, given from the wages of the people's sufferings and toils. They were acceptable to God, (Phil. 4. 18,) and if the Israelites showed such liberality, how much more should those whose privilege it is to live under the Christian dispensation? (1 Cor. 6. 20; 16. 2.)

CHAPTER XXXVII.

Ver. 1-29. FURNITURE OF THE TABERNACLE. **1. Bezaleel made the ark**—The description here given of the things within the sacred edifice is almost word for word the same as that contained in ch. 25. It is not on that account to be regarded as a useless repetition of minute particulars; for by the enumeration of these details, it can be seen how exactly every thing was fashioned according to the "pattern shown on the mount," and the knowledge of this exact correspondence between the prescription and the execution was essential to the purposes of the fabric. **6-10. made the mercy-seat of pure gold**—To construct a figure, whether the body of a beast or a man, with two extended wings, measuring from 2 to 3 feet from tip to tip, with the hammer, out of a solid piece of gold, was what few, if any, artisans of the present day could accomplish. **17-22. he made the candlestick of pure gold**—practical readers will be apt to say, "Why do such works with the hammer, when they could have been cast so much easier—a process they were well acquainted with?" The only answer that can be given is, that it was done according to order. We have no doubt but there were reasons for so distinctive an order, something significant, which has not been revealed to us. [NAPIER.] The whole of that sacred building was arranged with a view to inculcate through every part of its apparatus, the great fundamental principles of revelation. Every object was symbolical of important truth—every piece of furniture was made the hieroglyphic of a doctrine or a duty—on the floor and along the sides of that moveable edifice was exhibitd, by emblematic signs addressed to the eye, the whole remedial scheme of the gospel. How far this spiritual instruction was received by every successive generation of the Israelites, it may not be easy to determine. But the tabernacle, like the law of which it was a part, was a schoolmaster to Christ; and just as the walls of schools are seen studded with pictorial figures, by which the children, in a manner level to their capacities and suited to arrest their volatile minds, are kept in constant and familiar remembrance of the lessons of piety and virtue, so the tabernacle was intended by its furniture and all its arrangements to serve as a "shadow of good things to come." In this view, the minute descriptions given in this chapter respecting the ark and mercy-seat, the table of shewbread, the candlestick, the altar of incense and the holy oil, were of the greatest utility and importance; and though there are a few things that were merely ornamental appendages, such as the knops and the flowers, yet, in introducing these into the tabernacle, God displayed the same wisdom and goodness as He has done by introducing real flowers into the kingdom of nature to engage and gratify the eye of man.

CHAPTER XXXVIII.

Ver. 1-20. FURNITURE OF THE TABERNACLE. **1. The altar of burnt-offering**—The repetitions are continued, in which may be traced the exact conformity of the execution to the order. **8. laver of brass ... of the looking-glasses of the women**—the word *mirrors* should have been used, as those implements usually round, inserted into a handle of

CHAPTER XXXIX.

1 The cloths of service and holy garments. 2 The ephod. 8 The breastplate. 22 The robe of the ephod. 27 The coats, mitre, etc. 32 All viewed and approved by Moses.

AND of *a* the blue, and purple, and scarlet, they made *b* cloths of service, to do service in the holy *place,* and made the holy garments for Aaron ; *c* as the LORD commanded Moses.

2 And *d* he made the ephod of gold, blue, and purple, and scarlet, and fine twined linen.

3 And they did beat the gold into thin plates, and cut *it into* wires, to work *it* in the blue, and in the purple, and in the scarlet, and in the fine linen, *with* cunning work.

4 They made shoulder-pieces for it, to couple *it* together: by the two edges was it coupled together.

5 And the *e* curious girdle of his ephod, that *was* upon it, *was* of the same, according to the work thereof; *of* gold, blue, and purple, and scarlet, and fine twined linen; as the LORD commanded Moses.

6 ¶ And *f* they wrought *g* onyx stones inclosed in ouches of gold, graven, as signets are graven, with the *h* names of the children of Israel.

7 And he put them on the shoulders of the ephod, *that they should be* stones for a *i* memorial to the children of Israel ; as the LORD commanded Moses.

8 ¶ And *j* he made the breastplate of cunning work, like the work of the ephod; *of* gold, blue, and purple, and scarlet, and fine twined linen.

9 It was foursquare; they made the breastplate double: a span *was* the length thereof, and a span the breadth thereof, *being* doubled.

10 And *k* they set in it four rows of stones: the *first* row *was* a ^{1} sardius, a ^{2} topaz, and a ^{3} carbuncle: this *was* the first row.

11 And the second row, an ^{4} emerald, a ^{5} sapphire, and a ^{6} diamond.

12 And the third row, a ^{7} ligure, an ^{8} agate, and an ^{9} amethyst.

13 And the fourth row, a ^{10} beryl, an ^{11} onyx, and a ^{12} jasper: *they were* inclosed in ouches of gold in their inclosings.

14 And the stones *were* according to the names of the children of Israel, twelve, according to their names, like the engravings of a signet, every one with his name, according to the twelve tribes.

15 And they made upon the breastplate chains at the ends, *of* wreathen work *of* pure gold.

16 And they made two ouches of gold, and two gold rings, and put the two rings in the two ends of the breastplate.

17 And they put the two wreathen chains of gold in the two rings on the ends of the breastplate.

18 And the two ends of the two wreathen chains they fastened in the two ouches, and put them on the shoulder-pieces of the ephod, before it.

19 And they made two rings of gold, and put *them* on the two ends of the breastplate, upon the border of it, which *was* on the side of the ephod inward.

20 And they made two *other* golden rings, and put them on the two sides of the ephod underneath, toward the fore part of it, over against the *other* coupling thereof, above the curious girdle of the ephod.

21 And they did bind the breastplate by his rings unto the rings of the ephod with a lace of blue, that it might be above the curious girdle of the ephod, and that the breastplate might not be loosed from the ephod ; as the LORD commanded Moses.

22 ¶ And *l* he made the robe of the ephod of woven work, all of blue.

23 And *there was* an hole in the midst of the robe, as the hole of an habergeon, *with* a band round about the hole, that it should not rend.

24 And they made upon the hems of the robe pomegranates of blue, and purple, and scarlet, *and* twined linen.

25 And they made *m* bells of pure gold, and put the bells between the pomegranates upon the hem of the robe, round about between the pomegranates;

26 A bell and a pomegranate, a bell and a pomegranate, round about the hem of the robe to minister *in;* as the LORD commanded Moses.

27 ¶ And *n* they made coats of fine linen, of woven work, for Aaron, and for his sons.

28 And *o* a mitre of fine linen, and goodly bonnets of fine linen, and *p* linen breeches of fine twined linen,

29 And a girdle of fine twined linen, and blue, and purple, and scarlet, of needlework; as the LORD commanded Moses.

30 ¶ And they made the plate of the holy crown of pure gold, and wrote upon it a writing, *like to* the engravings of a signet, *q* HOLINESS TO THE LORD.

31 And they tied unto it a lace of blue, to fasten *it* on high upon the mitre; as the LORD commanded Moses.

32 Thus was all the work of the tabernacle of the tent of the congregation finished: and the children of Israel did *r* according to all that the LORD commanded Moses, so did they.

33 ¶ And they brought *s* the tabernacle unto Moses, the tent, and all his furniture, his taches, his boards, his bars, and his pillars, and his sockets,

34 And the covering of rams' skins dyed red, and the covering of badgers' skins, and the veil of the covering,

35 The ark of the testimony, and the staves thereof, and the mercyseat,

36 The table, *and* all the vessels thereof, and the showbread,

37 The *t* pure candlestick, *with* the lamps thereof, *even with* the *u* lamps to be set in order, and all the vessels thereof, and the oil for light,

38 And the golden altar, and the anointing oil, and ^{13} the sweet incense, and the hanging for the tabernacle door,

39 The *v* brasen altar, and his grate of brass, his staves, and all his vessels, the laver and his foot,

40 The hangings of the court, his *w* pillars, and his sockets, and the hanging for the court gate, his cords, and his pins, and all the vessels of the service of the tabernacle, for the tent of the congregation,

41 The cloths of service to do service in the holy *place,* and the holy garments for

wood, stone, or metal, were made of brass, silver, or bronze, highly polished. [WILK.] It was customary for the Egyptian women to carry mirrors with them to the temples; and whether by taking the looking-glasses of the Hebrew women Moses designed to put it out of their power to follow a similar practice at the tabernacle, or whether the supply of brass from other sources in the camp was exhausted, it is interesting to learn how zealously and to a vast extent they surrendered those valued accompaniments of the female toilet. of the women assembling at the door—not priestesses, but females of pious character and influence, who frequented the courts of the sacred building, (Lev. 2. 36,) and whose parting with their mirrors, like the cutting the hair of the Nazarites, was their renouncing the world for a season. [HENG.] 9-21. the court—It occupied a space of one hundred and fifty feet by seventy-five, and it was enclosed by curtains of fine linen about eight feet high, suspended on brazen or copper pillars. Those curtains were secured by rods fastened to the top, and kept extended by being fastened to pins stuck in the ground. hooks—the hooks of the pillars in the court were for hanging up the carcases of the sacrificial beasts—those on the pillars at the entry of the tabernacle were for hanging the sacerdotal robes and other things used in the service. 11. sockets—mortices or holes in which the end of the pillars stood. 17. chapiters—or capitals of the pillars, were wooden posts which ran along their top, to which were attached the hooks for the hangings. 18. The height in the breadth—or in the measure. The sense is that the hangings of the courtgate, which was twenty cubits wide, were of the same height as the hangings all round the court. [WALL.] 21. This is the sum—Having completed his description of the component parts of the tabernacle, the inspired historian digresses into a statement respecting the gold and silver employed in it. the computation being made according to an order of Moses—by the Levites, under the direction of Ithamar, Aaron's youngest son. 24. Twenty and nine talents, seven hundred and thirty shekels—equivalent to £150,000 sterling. 25. The silver of them that were numbered—603,550 men at half a shekel each would contribute 301,775 shekels; which, at 2s. 4d. each, amount to £35,207 sterling. It may seem difficult to imagine how the Israelites should be possessed of so much wealth in the desert; but it should be remembered that they were enriched first by the spoils of the Egyptians, and afterwards by those of the Amalekites. Besides, it is highly probable that during their sojourn they traded with the neighbouring nations who bordered on the wilderness. [HEWLETT.]

CHAPTER XXXIX.

Ver. 1-31. GARMENTS OF THE PRIESTS. 1. Cloths of service—official robes. The ephod of the high priest, the robe of the ephod, the girdle of needlework and the broidered coat were all of fine linen; for on no material less delicate could such elaborate symbolical figures have been pourtrayed in embroidery, and all beautified with the same brilliant colours. (See on ch. xxviii.) 3. cut the gold into wires to work it—i.e., the metal was beaten with a hammer into thin plates—cut with scissors or some other instrument into long slips—then rounded into filaments or threads. "Cloth of golden tissue is not uncommon on the monuments, and specimens of it have been found rolled about mummies; but it is not easy to determine whether the gold thread was originally interwoven or subsequently inserted by the embroiderer. [TAYLOR.] 30. a writing, like the engravings of a signet—the seal-ring worn both by ancient and modern Egyptians on the little finger of the right hand, contained inscribed on a cornelion or other precious stone, along with the owner's name, a religious sentiment or sacred symbol, intimating that he was the servant of God, or expressive of trust in Him. And it was to this practice the inscription on the high priest alludes. (cf. Jo, 3. 33.) 34. The covering of rams' skins dyed red—(See ch. 25. 7.) It was probably red morocco leather, and "badgers' skins," rather " the skins of the tahash, supposed to be the dugong, or dolphin of the Red Sea, the skin of which is still used by the Arabs under the same appellation." [GOSS.] 43. Moses did look upon all the work—a formal inspection was made on the completion of the tabernacle. not only with a view to have the work transferred from the charge of the workmen, but to ascertain whether it corresponded with "the pattern." The result of a careful and minute survey showed that every plank, curtain, altar and vase, had been most accurately made of the form, and in the place designed by the Divine architect—and Moses, in accepting it off their hands, thanked God for them, and begged Him to bless them.

CHAPTER XL.

Ver. 1-12. THE TABERNACLE REARED AND ANOINTED. 1. On the first day of the first month—From a careful consideration of the incidents recorded to have happened after the Exodus, (ch. 12. 2; 13. 4; 19. 1; 20. 18; 34. 28, &c.,) it has been computed that the work of the tabernacle was commenced within six months after that emigration; and consequently, that other six months had been occupied in building it. So long a period spent in preparing the materials of a moveable pavilion, it would be difficult to understand, were it not for what we are told of the vast dimensions of the tabernacle, as well as the immense variety of curious and elaborate workmanship which its different articles of furniture required. 2. the tabernacle—the entire edifice; the tent—the covering that surmounted it, (v. 19.) 15. anoint his sons, as thou didst anoint their father—The sacred oil was used, but it does not appear that the ceremony was performed exactly in the same manner; for although the anointing oil was sprinkled over the garments both of Aaron and his sons, 29. 21; Lev. 8. 30, it was not poured over the heads of the latter. This distinction was reserved for the high priest. (ch. 29. 7; Lev. 8. 12; Ps. 133. 2.) 16. Thus did Moses—On his part, the same scrupulous fidelity was shewn in conforming to the "pattern" in the disposition of the furniture, as had been displayed by the workmen in the erection of the edifice. 33. So Moses finished the work—Though it is not expressly recorded in this passage, yet, from what took place on all similar occasions, there is reason to believe that on the inauguration day, the people were summoned from their tents,—were all drawn up a vast assemblage, yet in calm and orderly arrangement around the newly erected tabernacle. 34. a cloud—lit. "The" cloud,—the mystic

The tabernacle is reared,   EXODUS, XL.   *and filled with God's glory.*

Aaron the priest, and his sons' garments, to minister in the priest's office.

42 According to all that the Lord commanded Moses, so the children of Israel made *x* all the work.

43 And Moses did look upon all the work, and, behold, they had done it as the Lord had commanded, even so had they done it: and Moses *y* blessed them.

CHAPTER XL.

1 *The tabernacle is commanded to be reared and anointed.* 12 *Aaron and his sons to be sanctified.* 34 *A cloud covereth it.*

AND the Lord spake unto Moses, saying, 2 On the first day of the *a* first month shalt thou set up *b* the tabernacle of the tent of the congregation.

3 And *c* thou shalt put therein the ark of the testimony, and cover the ark with the veil.

4 And *d* thou shalt bring in the table, and set *e* in order *1* the things that are to be set in order upon it; and thou shalt bring in the candlestick, and light the lamps thereof.

5 And thou shalt set the *f* altar of gold for the incense before the ark of the testimony, and put the hanging of the door to the tabernacle.

6 And thou shalt set the altar of the burnt offering before the door of the tabernacle of the tent of the congregation.

7 And *g* thou shalt set the laver between the tent of the congregation and the altar, and shalt put water therein.

8 And thou shalt set up the court round about, and hang up the hanging at the court gate.

9 And thou shalt take *h* the anointing oil, and anoint the tabernacle, and all that is therein, and shalt hallow it, and all the vessels thereof: and it shall be holy.

10 And thou shalt anoint the altar of the burnt offering, and all his vessels, and sanctify the altar: and *i* it shall be an altar *2* most holy.

11 And thou shalt anoint the laver and his foot, and sanctify it.

12 And *j* thou shalt bring Aaron and his sons unto the door of the tabernacle of the congregation, and wash them with water.

13 And thou shalt put upon Aaron the holy garments, *k* and anoint him, and sanctify him; that he may minister unto me in the priest's office.

14 And thou shalt bring *l* his sons, and clothe them with coats:

15 And thou shalt anoint them, as thou didst anoint their father, that they may minister unto me in the priest's office: for their anointing shall surely be *m* an everlasting priesthood throughout their generations.

16 Thus did Moses: according to all that the Lord commanded him, so did he.

17 ¶ And it came to pass in the first month in the second year, on the first *day* of the month, *that n* the tabernacle was reared up.

B. C. 1491.

CHAP. 39.
x ch. 35. 10.
y Gen. 14. 19.
Lev. 9. 22.
Nu. 6. 23.
Jos. 22. 6.
2 Sam. 6. 18.
1 Ki. 8. 14.
2 Chr. 30. 27.

CHAP. 40.
a ch. 12. 2.
b ch. 26. 1, 30.
Num. 7. 1.
c Num. 4. 5.
d ch. 26. 35.
e Lev. 24. 5, 6.
1 the order thereof.
f Heb. 9. 24.
Heb. 10. 19-22.
g ch. 30. 18.
h ch. 30. 24-25.
i ch. 29. 36.
2 holiness of holinesses.
j Lev. 8. 1-13.
k ch. 28. 41.
Ps. 133. 2.
l Heb. 7. 23.
m Nu. 25. 13.
Heb. 7. 11.
Rev. 1. 6.
1 Pet. 2. 5, 9.
n Nu. 7. 1.
o tables of the law.
ch. 25. 16.
Ps. 78. 5.
Is. 8. 20.
p ch. 35. 12.
q ch. 26. 35.
r ch. 26. 35.
s ch. 25. 37.
t ch. 30. 6.
u ch. 30. 7.
v ch. 26. 36.
w ch. 29. 38.
x ch. 30. 18.
y ch. 30. 19.
z ch. 27. 9, 16.
a Lev. 16. 2.
Nu. 9. 15.
1 Ki. 8. 10.
2 Chr. 5. 13.
2 Chr. 7. 2.
Is. 6. 4.
Ezek. 43. 4.
Hag. 2. 7, 9.
Rev. 15. 8.
b 1 Ki. 8. 11.
2 Chr. 5. 14.
Ps. 78. 14.
c Nu. 10. 11.
Neh. 9. 19.
3 journeyed.
d Num 9. 19-22.
e ch. 13. 21.
Num. 9. 15.

18 And Moses reared up the tabernacle, and fastened his sockets, and set up the boards thereof, and put in the bars thereof, and reared up his pillars.

19 And he spread abroad the tent over the tabernacle, and put the covering of the tent above upon it; as the Lord commanded Moses.

20 ¶ And he took and put the *o* testimony into the ark, and set the staves on the ark, and put the mercyseat above upon the ark:

21 And he brought the ark into the tabernacle, and *p* set up the veil of the covering, and covered the ark of the testimony; as the Lord commanded Moses.

22 ¶ And *q* he put the table in the tent of the congregation, upon the side of the tabernacle northward, without the veil.

23 And he set the bread in order upon it before the Lord; as the Lord had commanded Moses.

24 ¶ And *r* he put the candlestick in the tent of the congregation, over against the table, on the side of the tabernacle southward.

25 And *s* he lighted the lamps before the Lord; as the Lord commanded Moses.

26 ¶ And *t* he put the golden altar in the tent of the congregation before the veil:

27 And *u* he burnt sweet incense thereon; as the Lord commanded Moses.

28 ¶ And *v* he set up the hanging *at* the door of the tabernacle.

29 And he put the altar of burnt offering *by* the door of the tabernacle of the tent of the congregation, and *w* offered upon it the burnt offering and the meat offering; as the Lord commanded Moses.

30 ¶ And *x* he set the laver between the tent of the congregation and the altar, and put water there, to wash *withal*.

31 And Moses and Aaron and his sons washed their hands and their feet thereat:

32 When they went into the tent of the congregation, and when they came near unto the altar, they washed; *y* as the Lord commanded Moses.

33 And *z* he reared up the court round about the tabernacle and the altar, and set up the hanging of the court gate. So Moses finished the work.

34 ¶ Then *a* a cloud covered the tent of the congregation, and the glory of the Lord filled the tabernacle.

35 And Moses *b* was not able to enter into the tent of the congregation, because the cloud abode thereon, and the glory of the Lord filled the tabernacle.

36 And *c* when the cloud was taken up from over the tabernacle, the children of Israel *3* went onward in all their journeys:

37 But *d* if the cloud were not taken up, then they journeyed not till the day that it was taken up.

38 For *e* the cloud of the Lord *was* upon the tabernacle by day, and fire was on it by night, in the sight of all the house of Israel, throughout all their journeys.

cloud which was the well-known symbol of the divine presence. After remaining at a great distance from them on the summit of the mount, it appeared to be in motion; and if many among them had a secret misgiving about the issue, how would the fainting heart revive, the interest of the moment intensely increase, and the tide of joy swell in every bosom, when that symbolic cloud was seen slowly and majestically descending towards the plain below, and covering the tabernacle. The entire and universal concealment of the tabernacle within the folds of an impervious cloud was not without a deep and instructive meaning,—it was a protection to the sacred edifice from the burning heats of the Arabian climate,—it was a token of the divine presence,—and it was also an emblem of the Mosaic dispensation, which, though it was a revelation from heaven, yet left many things hid in obscurity; for it was a dark cloud compared with the bright cloud, which betokened the clearer and fuller discoveries of the divine character and glory in the gospel. (M. 17. 5.) The glory of the Lord filled the tabernacle—*i. e.*, light and fire, a created splendour, which was the peculiar symbol of God. (1 J. 1. 5.) Whether this light was inherent in the cloud or not, it emanated from it on this occasion, and making its entry, not with the speed of a lightning flash, as if it were merely an electric spark, but in majestic splendour, it passed through the outer porch into the interior of the most holy place. (1 Ki. 8. 10; J. 1. 14.) Its miraculous character is shewn by the fact, that, though "it filled the tabernacle," not a curtain or any article of furniture was so much as singed. 35. Moses was not able to enter—How does this circumstance shew the incapacity of man, in his present state, to look upon the unveiled perfections of the Godhead. Moses could not endure the unclouded effulgence, nor the sublimest of the prophets. (Is. 6. 5.) But what neither Moses nor the most eminent of God's messengers to the ancient Church through the weakness of nature could endure, we can all now do by an exercise of faith; looking unto Jesus, who reflected with chastened radiance the brightness of the Father's glory; and who, having as the Forerunner for us, entered within the veil, has invited us to come boldly to the mercyseat. While Moses was compelled, through the influence of overwhelming awe, to stand aloof, and could not enter the tabernacle, Christ entered into the holy place not made with hands; nay, He is himself the true tabernacle, filled with the glory of God, ever with the grace and truth which the Shechinah typified. What reason have we to thank God for Jesus Christ, who, while He himself was the brightuess of the Father's glory, yet exhibited that glory in so mild and attractive a manner, as to allure us to draw near with confidence and love into the divine Presence? 36. When the cloud was taken up—In journeying through the sandy trackless deserts of the East, the use of torches, exhibiting a cloud of smoke by day and of fire by night, has been resorted to from time immemorial. The armies of Darius and Alexander were conducted on their marches in this manner. [FABER.] The Arab caravans in the present day observe the same custom; and materials for these torches are stored up among other necessary preparations for a journey. Live fuel, hoisted in chafing-dishes at the end of long poles, and being seen at a great distance, serves, by the smoke in the daytime and the light at night, as a better signal for march than the sound of a trumpet, which is not heard at the extremities of a large camp. [LABORDE.] This usage, and the miracle related by Moses, mutually illustrate each other. The usage leads us to think that the miracle was necessary, and worthy of God to perform; and, on the other hand, the miracle of the cloudy pillar, affording double benefit of shade by day and light at night, implies not only that the usage was not unknown to the Hebrews, but supplied all the wants which they felt in common with other travellers through those dreary regions. [FABER. HESS. GRAND.] But its peculiar appearance, unvarying character, and regular movements distinguished it from all the common atmospheric phenomena. It was an invaluable boon to the Israelites, and being recognised by all classes among that people as the symbol of the divine Presence, it guided their journeys, and regulated their encampments. (cf. Ps. 29. 105.) 38. The cloud of the Lord, &c.—While it had hitherto appeared sometimes in one place, sometimes in another, it was now found on the tabernacle only, so that from the moment that sanctuary was erected, and the glory of the Lord had filled the sacred edifice, the Israelites had to look to the place which God had chosen to put His name there, in order that they might enjoy the benefit of a heavenly Guide. (Nu. 9. 15-23.) In like manner, the church had divine revelation for its guide from the first:—long before the WORD of God existed in a written form; but ever since the setting up of that sacred canon, it rests on that as its tabernacle, and there only is it to be found. It accompanies us wherever we are or go, just as the cloud led the way of the Israelites. It is always accessible—can be carried in our pockets when we walk abroad; it may be engraven on the inner tablets of our memories and our hearts; and so true, faithful and complete a guide is it, that there is not a scene of duty or of trial through which we may be called to pass in the world, but it furnishes a clear, a safe and unerring direction. (Col. 3. 16.)

THE THIRD BOOK OF MOSES, CALLED
LEVITICUS.

CHAPTER I.

1 *The burnt offerings, 3 of the herd, 10 of the flocks, 14 of the fowls.*

B. C. 1490.

CHAP. I.
a Ex. 19. 3.
b Nu. 12. 4, 5.
c ch. 22. 18.
d Mal. 1. 14.
  Jno. 14. 3.
  Eph. 5. 27.
  Heb. 9. 14.
  1 Pet. 1. 19.
e Ex. 29. 10.
  Is. 53. 4.
  2 Cor. 5. 21.
  1 Pet. 2. 24.
f Is. 53. 7.
  Rom. 12. 1.
  Phil. 4. 18.
g Nu. 15. 25.
  Rom. 5. 11.
h Mic. 6. 6.
i He. 10. 11.
j Heb. 12. 24.
  1 Pet. 1. 2.
k Gen. 22. 9.
l Gen. 8. 21.
  Ezek. 20. 28.
  2 Cor. 2. 15.
  Eph. 5. 2.
  Phil. 4. 18.
m Lu. 2. 24.
1 Or, pinch off the head with the nail.
2 Or, the filth thereof.
n Gen. 15. 10.

CHAP. 2.
a ch. 6. 14.
  ch. 9. 17.
  Nu. 15. 4.
b ch. 5. 12.
  ch. 6. 15.
  ch. 21. 7.
  Is. 66. 3.
  Acts 10. 4.
c ch. 7. 9.
  ch. 10. 12, 13.
d Ex. 29. 37.
  Nu. 18. 9.
e Ex. 29. 2.
1 Or, on a flat plate, or, slice.
f Ex. 29. 18.
g Ex. 29. 18, 37.
h ch. 6. 17.
  Mat. 16. 12.
  Mark 8. 15.
  Luke 12. 1.
  1 Cor. 5. 8.
  Gal. 5. 9.
i Ex. 22. 29.
  ch. 23. 10, 11.
2 ascend.
j Mark 9. 49.
  Col. 4. 6.
k Nu. 18. 19.
l Ezek. 43. 24.
m Ex. 23. 19.
  Pro. 3. 9.
n ch. 23. 10, 14.
o 2 Ki. 4. 42.

AND the Lord *a* called unto Moses, and spake unto him *b* out of the tabernacle of the congregation, saying,

2 Speak unto the children of Israel, and say unto them, *c* If any man of you bring an offering unto the Lord, ye shall bring your offering of the cattle, *even* of the herd, and of the flock.

3 If his offering *be* a burnt sacrifice of the herd, let him offer a male *d* without blemish: he shall offer it of his own voluntary will at the door of the tabernacle of the congregation before the Lord.

4 And *e* he shall put his hand upon the head of the burnt offering; and it shall be accepted for him *g* to make atonement for him.

5 And he shall kill the *h* bullock before the Lord: *i* and the priests, Aaron's sons, shall bring the blood, *j* and sprinkle the blood round about upon the altar that *is* by the door of the tabernacle of the congregation.

6 And he shall flay the burnt offering, and cut it into his pieces.

7 And the sons of Aaron the priest shall put fire upon the altar, and *k* lay the wood in order upon the fire:

8 And the priests, Aaron's sons, shall lay the parts, the head, and the fat, in order upon the wood that *is* on the fire which *is* upon the altar:

9 But his inwards and his legs shall he wash in water: and the priest shall burn all on the altar, *to be* a burnt sacrifice, an offering made by fire, of a *l* sweet savour unto the Lord.

10 ¶ And if his offering *be* of the flocks, namely, of the sheep, or of the goats, for a burnt sacrifice, he shall bring it a male without blemish.

11 And he shall kill it on the side of the altar northward before the Lord: and the priests, Aaron's sons, shall sprinkle his blood round about upon the altar.

12 And he shall cut it into his pieces, with his head and his fat: and the priest shall lay them in order on the wood that *is* on the fire which *is* upon the altar:

13 But he shall wash the inwards and the legs with water: and the priests shall bring *it* all, and burn *it* upon the altar: it *is* a burnt sacrifice, an offering made by fire, of a sweet savour unto the Lord.

14 ¶ And if the burnt sacrifice for his offering to the Lord *be* of fowls, then he shall bring his offering of *m* turtle-doves, or of young pigeons.

15 And the priest shall bring it unto the altar, and *1* wring off his head, and burn *it* on the altar; and the blood thereof shall be wrung out at the side of the altar:

16 And he shall pluck away his crop with *2* his feathers, and cast it beside the altar on the east part, by the place of the ashes:

17 And he shall cleave it with the wings thereof, *but* *n* shall not divide *it* asunder: and the priest shall burn it upon the altar, upon the wood that *is* upon the fire: it *is* a burnt sacrifice, an offering made by fire, of a sweet savour unto the Lord.

CHAPTER II.

1 *The meat offering of flour, with oil and incense.* 12 *The oblation of first-fruits not to be burnt.* 13 *The salt of the meat offering.*

AND when any will offer *a* a meat offering unto the Lord, his offering shall be *of* fine flour; and he shall pour oil upon it, and put frankincense thereon:

2 And he shall bring it to Aaron's sons the priests: and he shall take thereout his handful of the flour thereof, and of the oil thereof, with all the frankincense thereof; and the priest shall burn *b* the memorial of it upon the altar, *to be* an offering made by fire, of a sweet savour unto the Lord:

3 And *c* the remnant of the meat offering *shall be* Aaron's and his sons': *d* it *is* a thing most holy of the offerings of the Lord made by fire.

4 ¶ And if thou bring an oblation of a meat offering baken in the oven, *it shall be* unleavened cakes of fine flour mingled with oil, or unleavened wafers *e* anointed with oil.

5 ¶ And if thy oblation *be* a meat offering baken *1* in a pan, it shall be *of* fine flour unleavened, mingled with oil.

6 Thou shalt part it in pieces, and pour oil thereon: it *is* a meat offering.

7 ¶ And if thy oblation *be* a meat offering baken in the frying-pan, it shall be made *of* fine flour with oil.

8 And thou shalt bring the meat offering that is made of these things unto *f* the Lord: and when it is presented unto the priest, he shall bring it unto the altar.

9 And the priest shall take from the meat offering a memorial thereof, and shall burn *it* upon the altar: *it is an g* offering made by fire, of a sweet savour unto the Lord.

10 And that which is left of the meat offering *shall be* Aaron's and his sons': it *is* a thing most holy of the offerings of the Lord *g* made by fire.

11 No meat offering, which ye shall bring unto the Lord, shall be made with *h* leaven: for ye shall burn no leaven, nor any honey, in any offering of the Lord made by fire.

12 ¶ As *i* for the oblation of the first-fruits, ye shall offer them unto the Lord: but they shall not *2* be burnt on the altar for a sweet savour.

13 And every oblation of thy meat offering shalt *j* thou season with salt; neither shalt thou suffer *k* the salt of the covenant of thy God to be lacking from thy meat offering: with *l* all thine offerings thou shalt offer salt.

14 And if thou offer a meat offering of thy first-fruits *m* unto the Lord, *n* thou shalt offer for the meat offering of thy first-fruits green ears of corn dried by the fire, *even* corn beaten out of *o* full ears.

15 And thou shalt put oil upon it, and lay frankincense thereon: it *is* a meat offering.

16 And the priest shall burn the memorial of it, *part* of the beaten corn thereof, and *part* of the oil thereof, with all the frankincense thereof: it *is* an offering made by fire unto the Lord.

THE THIRD BOOK OF MOSES, CALLED

LEVITICUS.

CHAPTER I.

Ver. 1-17. BURNT-OFFERINGS OF THE HERD. 1. The Lord spake out of the tabernacle—The laws that are contained in the previous record were delivered either to the people publicly from Sinai, or to Moses privately, on the summit of that mountain; but on the completion of the tabernacle, the remainder of the law was announced to the Hebrew leader by an audible voice from the divine glory, which surmounted the mercy-seat. **2. Speak unto the children of Israel**—If the subject of communication were of a temporal nature, the Levites were excluded; but if it were a spiritual matter, the whole tribes were comprehended under this name. Deu. 27. 12. **If any man, &c.**—The directions given here relate solely to voluntary or free-will-offerings—those rendered over and above such, as being of standing and universal obligation, could not be dispensed with or commuted for any other kind of offering. (Ex. 29. 38; ch. 23. 37; Nu. 28. 3; 28. 11-27, &c.) **bring your offering, &c.**—*i.e.*, those animals that were not only tame, innocent and gentle, but useful and adapted for food. This rule excluded horses, dogs, swine, camels and asses, which were used in sacrifice by some heathen nations, beasts and birds of prey, as also hares and deers. **3. a burnt-offering**—so called from its being wholly consumed on the altar; no part of it was eaten either by the priests or the offerer. It was designed to propitiate the anger of God incurred by original sin, or by particular transgressions; and its entire combustion indicated the self-dedication of the offerer—his whole nature—his body and soul—as necessary to form an sacrifice acceptable to God. (Ro. 12. 1; Phil. 1. 20.) This was the most ancient as well as the most conspicuous mode of sacrifice. **a male without blemish**—no animal was allowed to be offered that had any deformity or defect. Among the Egyptians, a minute inspection was made by the priest, and the bullock having been declared perfect, a certificate to that effect being fastened to its horns with wax, was sealed with his ring, and no other might be substituted. A similar process of examining the condition of the beasts brought as offerings, seems to have been adopted by the priests in Israel. (Jo. 6. 27.) **at the doors of the tabernacle**—where stood the altar of burnt-offering, (Ex. 40. 6,) and every other place was forbidden, under the highest penalty. (ch. 17. 4.) **4. Shall put his hand upon his head**—This was a significant act which implied not only that the offerer devoted the animal to God, but that he confessed his consciousness of sin, and prayed that his guilt and its punishment might be transferred to the victim, and it shall be—rather "that it may be an acceptable atonement." **5. and he shall kill, &c.**—meaning not the priest, for it was not his official duty in case of voluntary sacrifices, but the offerer; in later times, however, the office was generally performed by Levites, before the Lord—on the spot where the hands had been laid upon the animal's head, on the north side of the altar. **sprinkle the blood**—This was to be done by the priests. The blood being considered the life, the effusion of it was the essential part of the sacrifice, and the sprinkling of it—the application of the atonement—which made the person and services of the offerer acceptable to God. The skin having been stripped off, and the carcase cut up, the various pieces were disposed on the altar in the manner best calculated to facilitate their being consumed by the fire. **8. the fat**—that about the kidneys especially, which is called "suet." **9. But his inwards, &c.**—this part of the ceremony was symbolical of the *inward* purity, and the holy *walk*, that became acceptable worshippers. **a sweet savour unto the Lord**—is an expression of the offerers' piety, but especially as a sacrificial type of Christ. **10-13. If his offering be of the flocks**—Those who could not afford the expense of a bullock might offer a ram or a he-goat, and the same ceremonies were to be observed in the act of offering. **14-17. If the burnt sacrifice be of fowls**—The gentle nature and cleanly habits of the dove led to its selection, while all other fowls were rejected, either for the fierceness of their disposition or the grossness of their taste; and in this case, there being from the smallness of the animal no blood for waste, the priest was directed to prepare it *at* the altar and sprinkle the blood. This was the offering appointed for the poor. The fowls were always offered in pairs, and the reason why Moses ordered two turtle doves or two young pigeons, was not merely to suit the convenience of the offerer, but according as the latter was in season: for pigeons are sometimes quite hard and unfit for eating, at which time turtle doves are very good in Egypt and Palestine. The turtle doves are not restricted to any age, because they are always good, when they appear in those countries, being birds of passage; but the age of the pigeons is particularly marked, that they might not be offered to God at times when they are rejected by men. [HARMER.] It is obvious, from the varying scale of these voluntary sacrifices, that the disposition of the offerer was the thing looked to—not the costliness of his offering.

CHAPTER II.

Ver. 1-16. THE MEAT-OFFERINGS. 1. When any will offer a meat-offering—or gift—distinguishing a bloodless from a bloody sacrifice. The word "meat," however, is improper, as its meaning as now used is different from that attached at the date of our English translation. It was then applied not to "flesh," but "food," generally, and here it is applied to the flour of wheat. The meat-offerings were intended as a thankful acknowledgment for the bounty of providence; and hence, although meat-offerings accompanied some of the appointed sacrifices, those here described being voluntary oblations, were offered alone. **pour oil upon it**—oil was used as butter is with us—symbolically it meant the influences of the Spirit, of which oil was the emblem, as incense was of prayer, **2. shall burn the memorial**—"rather" for a memorial, *i.e.*, a part of it. **3. The remnant of the meat offering shall be Aaron's and

CHAPTER III.

1 *The peace offering of the herd, 6 of the flock, 7 whether a lamb, 12 or a goat.*

AND if his oblation *be* a *a* sacrifice of peace offering, if he offer *it* of the herd; whether it be a male or female, he shall offer it without blemish before the LORD.

2 And *b* he shall lay his hand upon the head of his offering, and kill it *at* the door of the tabernacle of the congregation: and Aaron's sons the priests shall sprinkle the blood upon the altar round about.

3 And he shall offer of the sacrifice of the peace offering an offering made by fire unto the LORD; the 1 fat that covereth the inwards, and all the fat that *is* upon the inwards,

4 And the two kidneys, and the fat that is on them, which *is* by the flanks, and the 2 caul above the liver, with the kidneys, it shall he take away.

5 And Aaron's sons *c* shall burn it on the altar upon the burnt sacrifice, which *is* upon the wood that *is* on the fire: *it is* an offering made by fire, of a sweet savour unto the LORD.

6 ¶ And if his offering for a sacrifice of peace offering unto the LORD be *of* the flock, male or female, he shall offer it without *d* blemish.

7 If he offer a lamb for his offering, then shall he offer it before the LORD.

8 And he shall lay his hand upon the head of his offering, and kill it before the tabernacle of the congregation: and Aaron's sons shall sprinkle the blood thereof round about upon the altar.

9 And he shall offer of the sacrifice of the peace offering an offering made by fire unto the LORD; the fat thereof, *and* the whole rump, it shall he take off hard by the back bone; and the fat that covereth the inwards, and all the fat that *is* upon the inwards,

10 And the two kidneys, and the fat that is upon them, which *is* by the flanks, and the caul above the liver, with the kidneys, it shall he take away.

11 And the priest shall burn it upon the altar: it *is* *e* the food of the offering made by fire unto the LORD.

12 ¶ And if his offering *be* a goat, then he shall offer it before the LORD.

13 And he shall lay his hand upon the head of it, and kill it before the tabernacle of the congregation: and the sons of Aaron shall sprinkle the blood thereof upon the altar round about.

14 And he shall offer thereof his offering, *even* an offering made by fire unto the LORD; the fat that covereth the inwards, and all the fat that *is* upon the inwards,

15 And the two kidneys, and the fat that is upon them, which *is* by the flanks, and the caul above the liver, with the kidneys, it shall he take away.

16 And the priest shall burn them upon the altar: *it is* the food of the offering made by fire for a sweet savour. *f* All the fat *is* the LORD's.

17 *It* shall be a *g* perpetual statute for your generations throughout all your dwellings, that ye eat neither fat nor *h* blood.

CHAPTER IV.

1 *The sin offering of ignorance for the priest,* 13 *for the congregation,* 22 *for a ruler,* 27 *for any of the people.*

AND the LORD spake unto Moses, saying,

2 Speak unto the children of Israel, saying, *a* If a soul shall sin through ignorance against any of the commandments of the LORD *concerning things* which ought not to be done, and shall do against any of them:

3 If *b* the priest that is anointed do sin according to the sin of the people; then let him bring for his sin, which he hath sinned, a *c* young bullock without blemish unto the LORD for a sin offering.

4 And he shall bring the bullock *d* unto the door of the tabernacle of the congregation before the LORD; and shall lay his hand upon the bullock's head, and kill the bullock before the LORD.

5 And the priest that is anointed *e* shall take of the bullock's blood, and bring it to the tabernacle of the congregation:

6 And the priest shall dip his finger in the blood, and sprinkle of the blood seven times before *f* the LORD, before the veil of the sanctuary.

7 And the priest shall *g* put *some* of the blood upon the horns of the altar of sweet incense before the LORD, which is in the tabernacle of the congregation; and shall pour *h* all the blood of the bullock at the bottom of the altar of the burnt offering, which *is* at the door of the tabernacle of the congregation.

8 And he shall take off from it all the fat of the bullock for the sin offering; the fat that covereth the inwards, and all the fat that *is* upon the inwards,

9 And the two kidneys, and the fat that *is* upon them, which *is* by the flanks, and the caul above the liver, with the kidneys, it shall he take away,

10 As it was taken off from the bullock of the sacrifice of peace offerings: and the priest shall burn them upon the altar of the burnt offering.

11 And *i* the skin of the bullock, and all his flesh, with his head, and with his legs, and his inwards, and his dung,

12 Even the whole bullock shall he carry forth 1 without the camp unto a clean place, *j* where the ashes are poured out, and *k* burn him on the wood with fire: 2 where the ashes are poured out shall he be burnt.

13 ¶ And *l* if the whole congregation of Israel sin through ignorance, *m* and the thing be hid from the eyes of the assembly, and they have done *somewhat against* any of the commandments of the LORD *concerning things* which should not be done, and are guilty;

14 When the sin, which they have sinned against it, is known, then the congregation shall offer a young bullock for the sin, and bring him before the tabernacle of the congregation.

15 And the elders of the congregation shall *n* lay their hands upon the head of the bullock before the LORD; and the bullock shall be killed before the LORD.

16 And *o* the priest that is anointed shall bring of the bullock's blood to the tabernacle of the congregation:

17 And the priest shall dip his finger *in some* of the blood, and sprinkle *it* seven times before the LORD, *even* before the veil.

18 And he shall put *some* of the blood upon the horns of the altar which *is* before the LORD, that *is* in the tabernacle of the congregation, and shall pour out all the

his sons'—The circumstance of a portion of it being appropriated to the use of the priests distinguishes this from a burnt offering. They alone were to partake of it within the sacred precincts, as among "the most holy things." 4. baked in the oven—generally a circular hole excavated in the floor, from one to five feet deep; the sides of which are covered with hardened plaster, on which cakes are baked of the form and thickness of pancakes. (See on Gen. 18. 6.) The shape of Eastern ovens varies considerably according to the nomadic or settled habits of the people. 5. baked in a pan—a thin plate, generally of copper or iron, placed on a slow fire, similar to what the country people in Scotland called a "girdle" for baking oat-meal cakes. 6. part it in pieces, and pour oil thereon—pouring oil on bread is a common practice among Eastern people, who are fond of broken bread dipped in oil, butter, and milk—oil only was used in the meat-offerings, and probably for a symbolic reason. It is evident that these meat-offerings were previously prepared by the offerer, and when brought, the priest was to take it from his hands and burn a portion on the altar. 11. no leaven, nor any honey—Nothing sweet or sour was to be offered. In the warm climates of the East leavened bread soon spoils, and hence it was regarded as the emblem of hypocrisy or corruption. Some, however, think that the chief reason of the prohibition was that leaven and honey were used in the idolatrous rites of the heathen. 12. the oblation of the first-fruits—voluntary offerings made by individuals out of their increase, and leaven and honey might be used with these. (ch. 23. 17; Num. 15. 20.) Though presented at the altar, they were not consumed, but assigned by God for the use of the priests. 13. every-meat-offering shalt thou season with salt—The same reasons which led to the prohibition of leaven, recommended the use of salt—if the one soon putrefies—the other possesses a strongly preservative property, and hence it became an emblem of incorruption and purity, as well as of a perpetual covenant—a perfect reconciliation and lasting friendship. No injunction in the whole law was more sacredly observed than this application of salt, for, besides other uses of it, that will be noticed elsewhere, it had a typical meaning referred to by our Lord concerning the effect of the Gospel on those who embrace it; (Mk. 9. 49, 50, as when plentifully applied, preserves meat from spoiling, so will the Gospel keep men from being corrupted by sin. And as salt was indispensable to render sacrifices acceptable to God, so the Gospel brought home to the hearts of men by the Holy Ghost, is indispensably requisite to their offering up of themselves living sacrifices.—[BROWN.] 14. a meat-offering of thy first-fruits—From the mention of green ears, this seems to have been a voluntary offering before the harvest—the ears being prepared in the favourite way of Eastern people, by parting them at the fire, and then beating them out for use. It was designed to be an early tribute of pious thankfulness for the earth's increase, and it was offered according to the usual directions.

CHAPTER III.

Ver. 1-17. THE PEACE-OFFERING OF THE HERD. 1. If his oblation, &c.—"peace" being used in Scripture to denote prosperity and happiness generally—a peace-offering was a voluntary tribute of gratitude for health or other benefits. In this view it was eucharistic, being a token of thanksgiving for benefits already received, or it was sometimes votive, presented in prayer for benefits wished for in future. of the herd —This kind of offering being of a festive character, either male or female, if without blemish, might be used, as both of them were equally good for food, and if the circumstances of the offerer allowed it, it might be a calf. 2. he shall lay his hand upon the head—Having performed this significant act, he killed it before the door of the tabernacle, and the priests sprinkled the blood round about upon the altar. 3. he shall offer of the sacrifice—The peace-offering differed from the oblations formerly mentioned in this respect: that while the burnt-offering was wholly consumed on the altar, and the freewill-offering was partly consumed and partly assigned to the priests; in this offering the fat alone was burnt, only a small part was allotted to the priests, while the rest was granted to the offerer and his friends, thus forming a sacred feast of which the Lord, his priests and people conjointly partook, and which was symbolical of the spiritual feast, the sacred communion which, through Christ, the great peace-offering, believers enjoy, (See further on chaps. 19. 22.) The fat that covereth the inwards—i.e. the web-work that presents itself first to the eye on opening the belly of a cow. the fat upon the inwards—adhering to the intestines, but easily removable from them; or, according to some, that which was next the ventricle. 4-11. the two kidneys ... of the flock ... the whole rump—There is, in Eastern countries, a species of sheep the tails of which are not less than four feet-and-a-half in length. These tails are of a substance between fat and marrow. A sheep of this kind weighs sixty or seventy English pounds weight, of which the tail usually weighs fifteen pounds and upwards. This species is by far the most numerous in Arabia, Syria, and Palestine, and, forming probably a large portion in the flocks of the Israelites, seems to have been the kind that usually bled on the Jewish altars. The extraordinary size and deliciousness of their tails give additional importance to this law. To command by an express law the tail of a British sheep to be offered in sacrifice to God, might well surprise us; but the wonder ceases—when we are told of those broad-tailed Eastern sheep, and of the extreme delicacy of that part which was so particularly specified in the statute. [PAX.] 12. if his offering be a he-goat—Whether this or any of the other two animals were chosen, the same general directions were to be followed in the ceremony of offering. 17. Ye shall eat neither fat nor blood—The details given above distinctly define the fat in animals which was not to be eaten, so that all the rest, whatever adhered to other parts, or was intermixed with them might be used. The prohibition of blood rested on a different foundation, being intended to preserve their reverence for the Messiah, who was to shed his blood as an atoning sacrifice for the sins of the world. [BROWN.]

CHAPTER IV.

Ver. 1, 2. SIN OFFERING OF IGNORANCE. if a soul shall sin through ignorance—A soul—

blood at the bottom of the altar of the burnt offering, which *is at* the door of the tabernacle of the congregation.

19 And he shall take all his fat from him, and burn *it* upon the altar.

20 And he shall do with the bullock as he did with the bullock for a sin offering, so shall he do with this: *p* and the priest shall make an atonement for them, and it shall be forgiven them.

21 And he shall carry forth the bullock without the camp, and burn him as he burned the first bullock: it *is* a sin offering for the congregation.

22 ¶ When a *q* ruler hath sinned, and done *somewhat* through ignorance *against* any of the commandments of the LORD his God *concerning things* which should not be done, and is guilty;

23 Or if his sin, wherein he hath sinned, come to his knowledge; he shall bring his offering, a kid of the goats, a male without blemish:

24 And he shall lay his hand upon the head of the goat, and kill it in the place where they kill the burnt offering before the LORD: it *is* a sin offering.

25 And the priest shall take of the blood of the sin offering with his finger, and put *it* upon the horns of the altar of burnt offering, and shall pour out his blood at the bottom of the altar of burnt offering.

26 And he shall burn all his fat upon the altar, as *r* the fat of the sacrifice of peace offerings: *s* and the priest shall make an atonement for him as concerning his sin, and it shall be forgiven him.

27 ¶ And *t* if *3* any one of the *4* common people sin through ignorance, while he doeth *somewhat against* any of the commandments of the LORD *concerning things* which ought not to be done, and be guilty;

28 Or *u* if his sin, which he hath sinned, come to his knowledge: then he shall bring his offering, a kid of the goats, a female without blemish, for his sin which he hath sinned.

29 And *v* he shall lay his hand upon the head of the sin offering, and slay the sin offering in the place of the burnt offering.

30 And the priest shall take of the blood thereof with his finger, and put *it* upon the horns of the altar of burnt offering, and shall pour out all the blood thereof at the bottom of the altar.

31 And *w* he shall take away all the fat thereof, *x* as the fat is taken away from off the sacrifice of peace offerings; and the priest shall burn *it* upon the altar for a sweet *y* savour unto the LORD; *s* and the priest shall make an atonement for him, and it shall be forgiven him.

32 And if he bring a *a* lamb for a sin offering, *b* he shall bring it a female without blemish.

33 And he shall lay his hand upon the head of the sin offering, and slay it for a sin offering in the place where they kill the burnt offering.

34 And the priest shall take of the blood of the sin offering with his finger, and put *it* upon the horns of the altar of burnt offering, and shall pour out all the blood thereof at the bottom of the altar:

35 And he shall take away all the fat thereof, as the fat of the lamb is taken away from the sacrifice of the peace offerings; and the priest shall burn them upon

---

B. C. 1490.

CHAP. 4.
p Nu. 15. 25.
Dan. 9. 24.
Rom. 5. 11.
Ho. 2. 17.
He. 10, 10, 11. 12.
1 John 1. 7.
1 John 2 2
q Ex. 18. 21.
Nu. 16. 2.
Ezr. 9. 2.
Acts 3. 17.
r ch. 3. 5.
s Nu. 15. 28.
t Nu. 15. 27.
Ec. 7. 20.
3 any soul.
4 people of the land.
u ver. 23.
v ver. 4, 24.
w ch. 3. 14.
x ch. 2. 3.
y Ex. 29. 18.
ch. 1. 9.
s ver. 26.
a Is. 53. 7.
John 1. 29.
Acts 8. 32.
1 Pet. 1.19.
Rev. 5.
6. 14.
Rev. 13. 8.
b ch. 3. 6.
d Dan. 9. 24.
Ro. 5. 11.
Heb. 9.
8-28.
1 John 1.7.
1 John 2.2

CHAP. 5.
a 1 Ki. 8. 31.
Pro. 29. 24.
Mat. 26.63.
b Ge. 17. 14.
ch. 7. 18.
ch. 17. 16.
ch. 19. 8.
ch. 20. 17.
Nu. 9. 13.
c ch. 11. 24,
28, 31, 39.
Nu. 19. 11,
13, 16.
d ch. 12. 1.
ch. 13. 1.
ch. 15. 1.
e Rashly.
1 Sa. 14. 24.
f 1 Sam. 25.
22.
Mal. 3. 5.
Acts 23.12
g Mark 6. 23.
A ch. 26. 40.
Nu. 5. 7.
Ezra 10.
11.
i ch. 14. 21.
1 his hand cannot reach to the sufficiency of a lamb.
2 Or, pinch off the head with the nail.
j ch. 1. 14.
3 Or, ordinance.
k Num. 5. 15.
l ch. 2. 25.

---

the altar, *e* according to the offerings made by fire unto the LORD: and the priest shall make an *d*atonement for his sin that he hath committed, and it shall be forgiven him.

CHAPTER V.

1 *The trespass offering of one that concealeth his knowledge in touching an unclean thing,* 4 *or in making an oath.* 14 *The trespass offering in sacrilege,* 17 *and in sins of ignorance.*

AND if a soul sin, *a* and hear the voice of swearing, and is a witness, whether he hath seen or known *of it*; if he do not utter *it*, then he shall *b* bear his iniquity.

2 Or *c* if a soul touch any unclean thing, whether *it be* a carcase of an unclean beast, or a carcase of unclean cattle, or the carcase of unclean creeping things, and if it be hidden from him; he also shall be unclean, and guilty.

3 Or if he touch the *d* uncleanness of man, whatsoever uncleanness *it be* that a man shall be defiled withal, and it be hid from him; when he knoweth *of it*, then he shall be guilty.

4 Or if a soul *e* swear, pronouncing with *his* lips *f* to do evil, or *g* to do good, whatsoever *it be* that a man shall pronounce with an oath, and it be hid from him; when he knoweth *of it*, then he shall be guilty in one of these.

5 And it shall be, when he shall be guilty in one of these *things*, that he shall *h* confess that he hath sinned in that *thing*:

6 And he shall bring his trespass offering unto the LORD for his sin which he hath sinned, a female from the flock, a lamb, or a kid of the goats, for a sin offering; and the priest shall make an atonement for him concerning his sin.

7 And *i* if 1 he be not able to bring a lamb, then he shall bring for his trespass, which he hath committed, two turtle-doves, or two young pigeons, unto the LORD: one for a sin offering, and the other for a burnt offering.

8 And he shall bring them unto the priest, who shall offer *that* which *is* for the sin offering first, and 2 wring off his head from his neck, but shall not divide *it* asunder:

9 And he shall sprinkle of the blood of the sin offering upon the side of the altar; and the rest of the blood shall be wrung out at the bottom of the altar: it *is* a sin offering.

10 And he shall offer the second *for* a burnt offering, according to *j* the 3 manner: and the priest shall make an atonement for him for his sin, which he hath sinned, and it shall be forgiven him.

11 But if he be not able to bring two turtle-doves, or two young pigeons; then he that sinned shall bring for his offering the tenth part of an ephah of fine flour for a sin offering: *k* he shall put no oil upon it, neither shall he put any frankincense thereon; for it *is* a sin offering.

12 Then shall he bring it to the priest, and the priest shall take his handful of it, *even* a memorial thereof, and burn *it* on the altar, *l* according to the offerings made by fire unto the LORD: it *is* a sin offering.

13 And the priest shall make an atonement for him as touching his sin that he hath sinned in one of these, and it shall be forgiven him: and *the remnant* shall be the priest's, as a meat offering.

an invidual. All sins may be considered, in a certain sense, as committed "through ignorance," error, or misapprehension of one's true interests. The sins, however, referred to in this law were unintentional violations of the ceremonial laws, — breaches made through haste, or inadvertency of some negative precepts, which, if done knowingly and wilfully, would have involved a capital punishment, or do against ary of them—To bring out the meaning, it is necessary to supply, "he shall bring a sin-offering."

3-35. SIN-OFFERING FOR THE PRIEST. 3. If a priest that is anointed sin—*i.e.*, the high priest, in whom, considering his character as typical mediator, and his exalted office, the people had the deepest interest; and whose transgression of any part of the divine law, therefore, whether done unconsciously or heedlessly, was a very serious offence, both as regarded himself individually, and the influence of his example. He is the person principally meant, though the common order of the priesthood was included. do sin according to the sin of the people—*i.e.*, bring guilt on the people. He was to take a young bullock, (the age and sex being expressly mentioned, and having killed it according to the form prescribed for the burnt offerings, he was to take it into the holy place, and sprinkle the atoning blood seven times before the veil, and tip with the crimson fluid the horns of the golden altar of incense, on his way to the court of the priests,—a solemn ceremonial appointed only for very grave and heinous offences, and which betokened that his sin, though done in ignorance, had vitiated all his services; nor could any official duty he engaged in be beneficial either to himself or the people, unless it were atoned for by blood. 11. the skin of the bullock and his flesh—In ordinary circumstances these were perquisites of the priests. But in the expiation necessary for a sin of the high priest's, after the fat of the sacrifice was offered on the altar, the carcase was carried without the camp, in order that the total combustion of it in the place of ashes might the more strikingly indicate the enormity of the transgression, and the horror with which he regarded it. (cf. Heb. 13, 12, 13.) 13. If the whole congregation of Israel sin through ignorance—In consequence of some culpable neglect or misapprehension of the law, the people might contract national guilt, and national expiation was necessary. The same sacrifice was to be offered as in the former case, but with this difference in the ceremonial, that the elders or heads of the tribes, as representing the people, and being the principal aggressors in misleading the congregation, laid their hands on the head of the victim. The priest then took the blood into the holy place, where, after dipping his finger in it seven times, he sprinkled the drops seven times before the veil,—this done, he returned to the court of the priests, and ascending the altar, put some portion upon its horns; then he poured it out at the foot of the altar. The fat was the only part of the animal which was offered on the altar; for the carcase, with its appurtenances and offals, was carried without the camp, into the place where the ashes were deposited, and there consumed with fire. 22-26. When a ruler hath sinned—Whatever was the form of government, the king, judge, or subordinate, was the party concerned in this law. The trespass of such a civil functionary being less serious in its character and consequences than that either of the high priest or the congregation, a sin offering of inferior value was required—"a kid of the goats;" and neither was the blood carried into the sanctuary, but applied only to the altar of burnt offering, nor was the carcase taken without the camp, it was eaten by the priests-in-waiting. 27-35. If any of the common people sin through ignorance—In this case, the expiatory offering appointed was a female kid, or a ewe-lamb without blemish; and the ceremonies were exactly the same as those observed in the case of the offending ruler. In these two latter instances, the blood of the sin offering was applied to the altar of burnt offering—the place where bloody sacrifices were appointed to be immolated. But the transgression of a high priest, or of the whole congregation, entailing a general taint on the ritual of the tabernacle, and vitiating its services, required a further expiation; and therefore, in these cases, the blood of the sin offering was applied to the altar of incense. 35. it shall be forgiven him—None of these sacrifices possessed any intrinsic value sufficient to free the conscience of the sinner from the pollution of guilt, or to obtain his pardon from God; but they gave a formal deliverance from a secular penalty, He. 9. 13, 14); and they were figurative representations of the full and perfect sin offering which was to be made by Christ.

CHAPTER V.

Ver. 1. TRESPASS OFFERINGS FOR CONCEALING KNOWLEDGE. 1. If a soul hear the voice of swearing—or, according to some, "the words of adjuration." A proclamation was issued calling any one who could give information, to come before the court and bear testimony to the guilt of a criminal, and the manner in which witnesses were interrogated in the Jewish courts of justice was not by swearing them directly, but adjuring them by reading the words of an oath: "the voice of swearing." The offence, then, for the expiation of which this law provides, was that of a person who neglected or avoided the opportunity of lodging the information which it was in his power to communicate.

2, 3. TOUCHING ANYTHING UNCLEAN. if a soul touch any unclean thing—a person who, unknown to himself at the time, came in contact with anything unclean, and either neglected the requisite ceremonies of purification, or engaged in the services of religion while under the taint of ceremonial defilement might be afterwards convinced that he had committed an offence.

4-19. FOR SWEARING. If a soul swear—a rash oath, without duly considering the nature and consequences of the oath, perhaps inconsiderately binding himself to do anything wrong, or neglected to perform a vow to do something good. In all such cases a person might have transgressed one of the divine commandments unwittingly, and have been afterwards brought to a sense of his delinquency. 5. It shall be ... shall confess—make a voluntary acknowledgment of his sin from the impulse of his own conscience, and before it come to the knowledge of the world. A previous discovery might have subjected him to some degree of punishment from which his spontaneous confession released him, but still he was considered guilty

14 ¶ And the LORD spake unto Moses, saying,
15 If a soul commit a trespass, and sin through ignorance, in the holy things of the LORD; then he shall bring for his trespass unto the LORD a ram without blemish out of the flocks, with thy estimation by shekels of silver, after the shekel of the sanctuary, for a trespass offering:
16 And he shall make amends for the harm that he hath done in the holy thing, and shall add the fifth part thereto, and give it unto the priest: and the priest shall make an atonement for him with the ram of the trespass offering, and it shall be forgiven him.
17 ¶ And if a soul sin, and commit any of these things which are forbidden to be done by the commandments of the LORD; though he wist it not, yet is he guilty, and shall bear his iniquity.
18 And he shall bring a ram without blemish out of the flock, with thy estimation, for a trespass offering, unto the priest: and the priest shall make an atonement for him concerning his ignorance wherein he erred and wist it not, and it shall be forgiven him.
19 It is a trespass offering: he hath certainly trespassed against the LORD.

CHAPTER VI.

1 The trespass offering for sins done wittingly. 8 The law of the burnt offering. 14 and meat offering. 19 The offering at the consecration of a priest. 24 The law of the sin offering.

AND the LORD spake unto Moses, saying,
2 If a soul sin, and commit a trespass against the LORD, and lie unto his neighbour in that which was delivered him to keep, or in fellowship, or in a thing taken away by violence, or hath deceived his neighbour;
3 Or have found that which was lost, and lieth concerning it, and sweareth falsely; in any of all these that a man doeth, sinning therein:
4 Then it shall be, because he hath sinned, and is guilty, that he shall restore that which he took violently away, or the thing which he hath deceitfully gotten, or that which was delivered him to keep, or the lost thing which he found,
5 Or all that about which he hath sworn falsely: he shall even restore it in the principal, and shall add the fifth part more thereto, and give it unto him to whom it appertaineth, in the day of his trespass offering.
6 And he shall bring his trespass offering unto the LORD, a ram without blemish out of the flock, with thy estimation, for a trespass offering, unto the priest:
7 And the priest shall make an atonement for him before the LORD: and it shall be forgiven him for any thing of all that he hath done in trespassing therein.
8 ¶ And the LORD spake unto Moses, saying,
9 Command Aaron and his sons, saying, This is the law of the burnt offering: It is the burnt offering, because of the burning upon the altar all night unto the morning, and the fire of the altar shall be burning in it.
10 And the priest shall put on his linen garment, and his linen breeches shall he put upon his flesh, and take up the ashes which the fire hath consumed with the burnt offering on the altar, and he shall put them beside the altar.
11 And he shall put off his garments, and put on other garments, and carry forth the ashes without the camp unto a clean place.
12 And the fire upon the altar shall be burning in it; it shall not be put out: and the priest shall burn wood on it every morning, and lay the burnt offering in order upon it; and he shall burn thereon the fat of the peace offerings.
13 The fire shall ever be burning upon the altar; it shall never go out.
14 ¶ And this is the law of the meat offering: the sons of Aaron shall offer it before the LORD, before the altar.
15 And he shall take of it his handful, of the flour of the meat offering, and of the oil thereof, and all the frankincense which is upon the meat offering, and shall burn it upon the altar for a sweet savour, even the memorial of it, unto the LORD.
16 And the remainder thereof shall Aaron and his sons eat: with unleavened bread shall it be eaten in the holy place: in the court of the tabernacle of the congregation they shall eat it.
17 It shall not be baken with leaven. I have given it unto them for their portion of my offerings made by fire: it is most holy, as is the sin offering, and as the trespass offering.
18 All the males among the children of Aaron shall eat of it. It shall be a statute for ever in your generations concerning the offerings of the LORD made by fire: every one that toucheth them shall be holy.
19 ¶ And the LORD spake unto Moses, saying,
20 This is the offering of Aaron, and of his sons, which they shall offer unto the LORD in the day when he is anointed; the tenth part of an ephah of fine flour for a meat offering perpetual, half of it in the morning, and half thereof at night.
21 In a pan it shall be made with oil; and when it is baken, thou shalt bring it in: and the baken pieces of the meat offering shalt thou offer for a sweet savour unto the LORD.
22 And the priest of his sons that is anointed in his stead shall offer it: it is a statute for ever unto the LORD; it shall be wholly burnt.
23 For every meat offering for the priest shall be wholly burnt: it shall not be eaten.
24 ¶ And the LORD spake unto Moses, saying,
25 Speak unto Aaron and to his sons, saying, This is the law of the sin offering: In the place where the burnt offering is killed shall the sin offering be killed before the LORD: it is most holy.
26 The priest that offereth it for sin shall eat it: in the holy place shall it be eaten, in the court of the tabernacle of the congregation.
27 Whatsoever shall touch the flesh thereof shall be holy: and when there is sprinkled of the blood thereof upon any garment, thou shalt wash that whereon it was sprinkled in the holy place.
28 But the earthen vessel wherein it is sodden shall be broken: and if it be sodden

of a trespass, to expiate which he was obliged by the ceremonial law to go through certain observances. **6-14.** he shall bring his trespass-offering—a trespass-offering differed from a sin-offering in the following respects, that it was appointed for persons who had either done evil unwittingly, or were in doubt as to their own criminality; or felt themselves in such a special situation as required sacrifices of that kind. [BROWN.] The trespass-offering appointed in such cases was a female lamb or kid; if unable to make such an offering he might bring a pair of turtle doves or two young pigeons,—the one to be offered for a sin-offering, the other for a burnt-offering; or if even *that* was beyond his ability, the law would be satisfied with the tenth-part of an ephah of fine flour without oil or frankincense. **15, 16.** sin through ignorance, &c.—This is a case of sacrilege committed ignorantly, either in not paying the full due of tithes—first fruits and similar tribute in eating of meats which belonged to the priests alone,—or he was required, along with the restitution in money, the amount of which was to be determined by the priest, to offer a ram for a trespass-offering, as soon as he came to the knowledge of his involuntary fraud. **17-19.** If a soul sin ... though he wist it not—This also refers to holy things, and it differs from the preceding in being one of the *doubtful* cases, *i.e.*, where conscience suspects, though the understanding be in doubt whether criminality or sin has been committed. The Jewish Rabbis give as an example, the case of a person who, knowing that "the fat of the inwards" is not to be eaten, religiously abstained from the use of it; but should a dish happen to have been at table in which he had reason to suspect some portion of that meat was intermingled, and he had, inadvertently, partaken of that unlawful viand, he was bound to bring a ram as a trespass-offering. These provisions were all designed to impress the conscience with the sense of responsibility to God, and keep alive on the hearts of the people a salutary fear of doing any secret wrong.

CHAPTER VI.

Ver. 1-7. TRESPASS-OFFERING FOR SINS DONE WITTINGLY. **1.** If a soul ... commit a trespass against the Lord—This law, the record of which should have been joined with the previous chapter, was given concerning things stolen, fraudulently gotten, or wrongfully kept. The offender was enjoined to make restitution of the articles to the rightful owner, along with a fifth part out of his own possessions. But it was not enough thus to repair the injury done to a neighbour and to society, he was required to bring a trespass-offering, as a token of sorrow and penitence for having hurt the cause of religion and of God. That trespass-offering was a ram without blemish, which was to be made on the altar of burnt-offerings, and the flesh belonged to the priests. This penalty was equivalent to a mitigated fine, but being associated with a sacred duty, the form in which the fire was inflicted served the important purpose of rousing attention to the claims and reviving a sense of responsibility to God.

8-13. THE LAW OF THE BURNT-OFFERING. command Aaron and his sons—In this passage, Moses received instructions to be delivered to the priests respecting their official duties, and first the burnt-offering. Heb.—"a sacrifice, which went up in smoke." The daily service consisted of two lambs offered in the morning at sunrise, the other in the evening, when the day began to decline. Both of them were consumed on the altar by means of a slow fire, before which the pieces of the sacrifice were so placed that they fed it all night. At all events, the observance of this daily sacrifice on the altar of burnt-offering was a daily expression of national repentance and faith. The fire that consumed these sacrifices had been kindled from heaven at the consecration of the tabernacle, and to keep it from being extinguished, and the sacrifices from being burned with common fire, strict injunctions are here given respecting not only the removal of the ashes, but the approaching near to the fire-place in garments that were not officially "holy."

14-18. THE LAW OF THE MEAT-OFFERING. This is the law of the meat-offering—Though this was a provision for the priests and their families, it was to be regarded as "most holy;" and the way in which it was prepared was, on any meat-offerings being presented, the priest carried them to the altar, and taking a handful from each of them as an oblation, salted and burnt it on the altar; the residue became the property of the priests, and was the food of those whose duty it was to attend on the service. They themselves as well as the vessels from which they ate were typically holy, and they were not at liberty to partake of the meat-offering while they laboured under any ceremonial defilement.

19-2'. THE HIGH PRIEST'S MEAT-OFFERING. This is the offering of Aaron and his sons—The daily meat-offering of the high priest; for though his sons are mentioned along with him, it was probably only those of his descendants who succeeded him in that high office that are meant. It was to be offered one-half of it in the morning, and the other half in the evening—being daily laid by the ministering priest on the altar of burnt-offering, where, being dedicated to God, it was wholly consumed. This was designed to keep him and the other attendant priests in constant remembrance, that though they were typically expiating the sins of the people, their own persons and services could meet with acceptance only through faith, which required to be daily nourished and strengthened from above.

24-30. THE LAW OF THE SIN-OFFERING. This is the law of the sin-offering—It was slain, and the fat and inwards, after being washed and salted, were burnt upon the altar. But the rest of the carcase belonged to the officiating priest. He and his family might feast upon it—only, however, within the precincts of the Tabernacle; and none else were allowed to partake of it but the members of a priestly family—and not even they, if under any ceremonial defilement. The flesh on all occasions was boiled or sodden, with the exception of the paschal lamb, which was roasted, and if an earthen vessel had been used, it being porous, and likely to imbibe some of the liquid particles, it was to be broken; if a metallic pan had been used it was to be scoured and washed with the greatest care, not because the vessels

in a brasen pot, it shall be both scoured, and rinsed in water.

29 All *a* the males among the priests shall eat thereof: it *is* most holy.

30 And *b* no sin offering, whereof any of the blood is brought into the tabernacle of the congregation to reconcile *withal* in the holy *place*, shall be eaten; it shall be burnt in the fire.

CHAPTER VII.

1 *The law of the trespass offering.* 11 *and of the peace offerings.* 22 *The fat and the blood are forbidden.* 28 *The priests' portion.*

LIKEWISE *a* this *is* the law of the trespass offering: *b* it *is* most holy.

2 In *c* the place where they kill the burnt offering shall they kill the trespass offering: and the blood thereof shall he sprinkle round about upon the altar.

3 And he shall offer of it *d* all the fat thereof; the rump, and the fat that covereth the inwards,

4 And the two kidneys, and the fat that *is* on them, which *is* by the flanks, and the caul *that is* above the liver, with the kidneys, it shall he take away:

5 And the priest shall burn them *e* upon the altar *for* an offering made by fire unto the LORD: it *is* a trespass offering.

6 Every *f* male among the priests shall eat thereof: it shall be eaten in the holy place: it *g is* most holy.

7 As the sin offering *is*, so *is h* the trespass offering; *there is* one law for them: the priest that maketh atonement therewith shall have it.

8 And the priest that offereth any man's burnt offering, *even* the priest shall have to himself the skin of the burnt offering which he hath offered.

9 And *i* all the meat offering that is baken in the oven, and all that is dressed in the frying-pan, and *l* in the pan, shall be the priest's *j* that offereth it.

10 And every meat offering mingled with oil, and dry, shall all the sons of Aaron have, one *as much* as another.

11 ¶ And *k* this *is* the law of the sacrifice of peace offerings, which he shall offer unto the LORD.

12 If he offer it for a thanksgiving, then he shall offer with the sacrifice of thanksgiving unleavened cakes mingled with oil, and unleavened wafers *l* anointed with oil, and cakes mingled with oil, of fine flour, fried.

13 Besides the cakes, he shall offer *for* his offering *m* leavened bread with the sacrifice of thanksgiving of his peace offerings.

14 And of it he shall offer one out of the whole oblation *for* an heave offering unto the LORD, *n and* it shall be the priest's that sprinkleth the blood of the peace offerings.

15 And *o* the flesh of the sacrifice of his peace offerings for thanksgiving shall be eaten the same day that it is offered; he shall not leave any of it until the morning.

16 But *p* if the sacrifice of his offering *be* a vow, or a voluntary offering, it shall be eaten the same day that he offereth his sacrifice: and on the morrow also the remainder of it shall be eaten:

17 But the remainder of the flesh of the sacrifice on the third day shall be burnt with fire.

18 And if *any* of the flesh of the sacrifice of his peace offerings be eaten at all on the third day, it shall not be accepted, neither shall it be *q* imputed unto him that offereth it: it shall be an *r* abomination, and the soul that eateth of it shall bear his iniquity.

19 And the flesh that toucheth any unclean *thing* shall not be eaten; it shall be burnt with fire: and as for the flesh, all that be clean shall eat thereof.

20 But the soul that eateth *of* the flesh of the sacrifice of peace offerings that *pertain* unto the LORD, *s* having his uncleanness upon him, even that soul *t* shall be cut off from his people.

21 Moreover the soul that shall touch any unclean *thing*, as *u* the uncleanness of man, or any *v* unclean beast, or any *w* abominable unclean *thing*, and eat of the flesh of the sacrifice of peace offerings which *pertain* unto the LORD, even that soul shall be cut off from his people.

22 ¶ And the LORD spake unto Moses, saying,

23 Speak unto the children of Israel, saying, *x* Ye shall eat no manner of fat, of ox, or of sheep, or of goat.

24 And the fat of the *y* beast that dieth of itself, and the fat of that which is torn with beasts, may be used in any other use; but ye shall in no wise eat of it.

25 For whosoever eateth the fat of the beast, of which men offer an offering made by fire unto the LORD, even the soul that eateth it shall be cut off from his people.

26 Moreover *y* ye shall eat no manner of blood, *whether it be* of fowl or of beast, in any of your dwellings.

27 Whatsoever soul *it be* that eateth any manner of blood, even that soul shall be cut off from his people.

28 ¶ And the LORD spake unto Moses, saying,

29 Speak unto the children of Israel, saying, *z* He that offereth the sacrifice of his peace offerings unto the LORD shall bring his oblation unto the LORD of the sacrifice of his peace offerings.

30 His own hands shall bring the offerings of the LORD made by fire; the fat with the breast, it shall he bring, that *a* the breast may be waved *for* a wave offering before the LORD.

31 And *b* the priest shall burn the fat upon the altar; but the breast shall be Aaron's and his sons'.

32 And *c* the right shoulder shall ye give unto the priest *for* an heave offering of the sacrifices of your peace offerings.

33 He among the sons of Aaron that offereth the blood of the peace offerings, and the fat, shall have the right shoulder for *his* part.

34 For *d* the wave breast and the heave shoulder have I taken of the children of Israel from off the sacrifices of their peace offerings, and have given them unto Aaron the priest and unto his sons by a statute for ever from among the children of Israel.

35 ¶ This *is the portion of the anointing* of Aaron, and of the anointing of his sons, out of the offerings of the LORD made by fire, in the day *when* he presented them to minister unto the LORD in the priest's office;

36 Which the LORD commanded to be given them of the children of Israel, *e* in

had been defiled, but the reverse—because the flesh of the sin-offering having been boiled in them, those vessels were now too sacred for ordinary use. The design of all these minute ceremonies was to impress the minds, both of priests and people, with a sense of the evil nature of sin, and the care they should take to prevent the least taint of its impurities clinging to them.

CHAPTER VII.

Ver. 1-9. THE LAW OF THE TRESPASS-OFFERING. 1. likewise this is the law of the trespass-offering. This chapter is a continuation of the laws that were to regulate the duty of the priests respecting the trespass-offerings. The same regulations obtained in this case as in the burnt-offerings—part was to be consumed on the altar, while the other part was a perquisite of the priests—some fell exclusively to the officiating minister, and was the fee for his services; others were the common share of all the priestly order, who lived upon them as their provision, and whose meetings at a common table would tend to promote brotherly harmony and friendship. **8.** shall have to himself the skin —All the flesh and the fat of the burnt-offerings being consumed, nothing remained to the priest but the skin. It has been thought that this was a patriarchal usage, incorporated with the Mosaic law, and that the right of the sacrificer to the skin of the victim was transmitted from the example of Adam (see on Ge. 3, 21.). **11-14.** This is the law of the sacrifice of peace-offerings—Besides the usual accompaniments of other sacrifices, leavened bread was offered with the peace-offerings, as a thanksgiving, such bread being common at feasts. **15-17.** eaten the same day that it was offered—The flesh of the sacrifices was eaten on the day of the offering or on the day following. But if any part of it remained till the third day, it was, instead of being made use of, to be burned with fire. In the East, butcher-meat is generally eaten the day it is killed, and it is rarely kept a second day, so that as a prohibition was issued against any of the flesh in the peace-offerings being used on the third day, it has been thought, not without reason, that this injunction must have been given to prevent a superstitious notion arising, that there was some virtue or holiness belonging to it. **18.** it shall not be accepted, neither imputed—the sacrifice will not be acceptable to God nor profitable to him that offers it. **20.** cut off from his people—*i.e.*, excluded from the privileges of an Israelite—lie under a sentence of excommunication. **21.** abominable unclean thing—some copies of the Bible read. "any reptile." **22-27.** ye shall eat no manner of fat —see on ch. 3. 17.

26-38. THE PRIESTS' PORTION. He that offereth the sacrifice—In order to show that the sacrifice was voluntary, the offerer was required to bring it with his own hands to the priest. The breast having been waived to and fro in a solemn manner as devoted to God, was made over to the priests; it was assigned to the use of their order generally, but the right shoulder was the perquisite of the officiating priest. **35-38.** This is the portion of the anointing of Aaron—These verses contain a general summing up of the laws which regulate the privileges and duties of the priests. The word "anointing" is often used as synonymous with "office" or "dignity." So that the "portion of the anointing of Aaron" probably means the provision made for the maintenance of the high priest, and the numerous body of functionaries which composed the sacerdotal order. in the day, &c.—*i. e.*, from the day they approached the Lord in the duties of their ministry.

CHAPTER VIII.

Ver. 1-36. MOSES CONSECRATETH AARON AND HIS SONS. 2. Take Aaron and his sons— The consecration of Aaron and his sons had been ordered long before, Ex. 29.) but it is now described with all the details of the ceremonial, as it was gone through after the tabernacle was completed, and the regulations for the various sacrifices enacted. **3-5.** Gather thou, &c.—It was manifestly expedient for the Israelitish people to be satisfied that Aaron's appointment to the high dignity of the priesthood was not a personal intrusion, nor a family arrangement between him and Moses; and nothing, therefore, could be a more prudent or necessary measure, for impressing a profound conviction of the Divine origin and authority of the priestly institution, than to summon a general assembly of the people, and in their presence perform the solemn ceremonies of inauguration, which had been prescribed by Divine authority. **6.** Moses washed them with water —At consecration they were subjected to entire ablution, though on ordinary occasions they were required, before entering on their duties, only to wash their hands and feet. This symbolical ablution was designed to teach them the necessity of inward purity, and the imperative obligation on those who bore the vessels and conducted the services of the sanctuary to be holy. **7-9.** He put upon him the coat—The splendour of the official vestments, together with the gorgeous tiara of the high priest, was intended doubtless, in the first instance, to produce in the minds of the people a high respect for the ministers of religion; and in the next, from the predominant use of linen, to inculcate upon Aaron and his sons the duty of maintaining unspotted righteousness in their characters and lives. **10-12.** took the oil, &c.—which was designed to intimate, that persons who acted as leaders in the solemn services of worship should have the unction of the Holy One both in His gifts and graces. **14-17.** Brought the bullock, &c.— A timely expression of their sense of unworthiness—a public and solemn confession of their personal sins, and a transference of their guilt to the typical victim. **18-21.** Brought the ram, &c.—as a token of their entire dedication to the service of God. **22-30.** Brought the other ram, &c.—After the sin-offering and burnt-offering had been presented on their behalf, this was their peace-offering, by which they declared the pleasure which they felt in entering upon the service of God, and being brought into close communion with him as the ministers of his sanctuary, together with their confident reliance on his grace to help them in all their sacred duties. **33.** Ye shall not, &c.— After all these preliminaries, they had still to undergo a week's probation in the court of the tabernacle before they obtained permission to enter into the interior of the sacred building. During the whole of that period the same sacrificial rites were ob-

the day that he anointed them, by a statute *f* for ever throughout their generations.

37 This *is* the law *g* of the burnt offering, of the meat offering, *h* and of the sin offering, and of the trespass offering, *i* and of the consecrations, and of the sacrifice of the peace offerings;

38 Which the LORD commanded Moses in mount Sinai, in the day that he commanded the children of Israel to offer their oblations unto the LORD, in the wilderness of Sinai.

CHAPTER VIII.

1 *Moses consecrateth Aaron and his sons:* 14 *their sin offering:* 18 *their burnt offering.* 22 *The ram of consecration.* 31 *The place and time of their consecration.*

AND the LORD spake unto Moses, saying,
2 Take *a* Aaron and his sons with him, and the garments, and *b* the anointing oil, and a bullock for the sin offering, and two rams, and a basket of unleavened bread;

3 And gather thou all the congregation together unto the door of the tabernacle of the congregation.

4 And Moses did as the LORD commanded him; and the assembly was gathered together unto the door of the tabernacle of the congregation.

5 And Moses said unto the congregation, This *is* the thing which the LORD commanded to be done.

6 And Moses brought Aaron and his sons, and *c* washed them with water.

7 And he put upon him the *d* coat, and girded him with the girdle, and clothed him with the robe, and put the ephod upon him, and he girded him with the curious girdle of the ephod, and bound *it* unto him therewith.

8 And he put the breastplate upon him: also he *e* put in the breastplate the Urim and the Thummim.

9 And *f* he put the mitre upon his head; also upon the mitre, *even* upon his forefront, did he put the golden plate, the holy crown; as the LORD *g* commanded Moses.

10 And *h* Moses took the anointing oil, and anointed the tabernacle and all that *was* therein, and sanctified them.

11 And he sprinkled thereof upon the altar seven times, and anointed the altar and all his vessels, both the laver and his foot, to sanctify them.

12 And he *i* poured of the anointing oil upon Aaron's head, and anointed him, to sanctify him.

13 And *j* Moses brought Aaron's sons, and put coats upon them, and girded them with girdles, and *l* put bonnets upon them; as the LORD commanded Moses.

14 ¶ And *k* he brought the bullock for the sin offering: and Aaron and his sons *l* laid their hands upon the head of the bullock for the sin offering.

15 And he slew *it;* *m* and Moses took the blood, and put *it* upon the horns of the altar round about with his finger, and purified the altar, and poured the blood at the bottom of the altar, and sanctified it, to make reconciliation upon it.

16 And *n* he took all the fat that *was* upon the inwards, and the caul above the liver, and the two kidneys, and their fat, and Moses burned *it* upon the altar.

17 But the bullock, and his hide, his flesh, and his dung, he burnt with fire without the camp; as the LORD *o* commanded Moses.

18 ¶ And *p* he brought the ram for the burnt offering: and Aaron and his sons laid their hands upon the head of the ram.

19 And he killed *it;* and Moses sprinkled the blood upon the altar round about.

20 And he cut the ram into pieces; and Moses burnt the head, and the pieces, and the fat.

21 And he washed the inwards and the legs in water; and Moses burnt the whole ram upon the altar: it *was* a burnt sacrifice for a sweet savour, *and* an offering made by fire unto the LORD; *q* as the LORD commanded Moses.

22 ¶ And *r* he brought the other ram, the ram of consecration: and Aaron and his sons laid their hands upon the head of the ram.

23 And he slew *it;* and Moses took of the blood of it, and put *it* upon *s* the tip of Aaron's right ear, and upon the thumb of his right hand, and upon the great toe of his right foot.

24 And he brought Aaron's sons, and Moses put of the blood upon the tip of their right ear, and upon the thumbs of their right hands, and upon the great toes of their right feet; and Moses *t* sprinkled the blood upon the altar round about.

25 And *u* he took the fat, and the rump, and all the fat that *was* upon the inwards, and the caul above the liver, and the two kidneys, and their fat, and the right shoulder:

26 And *v* out of the basket of unleavened bread that *was* before the LORD he took one unleavened cake, and a cake of oiled bread, and one wafer, and put *them* on the fat, and upon the right shoulder:

27 And he put all *w* upon Aaron's hands, and upon his sons' hands, and waved them *for* a wave offering before the LORD.

28 And *x* Moses took them from off their hands, and burnt *them* on the altar upon the burnt offering: they *were* consecrations for *y* a sweet savour: it *is* an offering made by fire unto the LORD.

29 And Moses took the breast, and waved it *for* a wave offering before the LORD: for of the ram of consecration it was *z* Moses' part; as the LORD commanded Moses.

30 And *a* Moses took of the anointing oil, and of the blood which *was* upon the altar, and sprinkled *it* upon Aaron, *and* upon his garments, and upon his sons, and upon his sons' garments with him; and sanctified Aaron, *and* his garments, and his sons, and his sons' garments with him.

31 ¶ And Moses said unto Aaron and to his sons, *b* Boil the flesh *at* the door of the tabernacle of the congregation; and there eat it with the bread that *is* in the basket of consecrations, as I commanded, saying, Aaron and his sons shall eat it.

32 And *c* that which remaineth of the flesh and of the bread shall ye burn with fire.

33 And ye shall not go out of the door of the tabernacle of the congregation *in* seven days, until the days of your consecration be at an end: for *d* seven days shall he consecrate you.

34 As *e* he hath done this day, *so* the LORD

served as on the first day, and they were expressly admonished that the smallest breach of any of the appointed observances would lead to the certain forfeiture of their lives.

CHAPTER IX.

Ver. 1-24. THE PRIESTS' ENTRY INTO OFFICE. 2. Moses called, Take thee a young calf—The directions in these sacred things were still given by Moses, the circumstances being extraordinary. But he was only the medium of communicating the divine will to the newly-made priests. The first of their official acts was the sacrifice of another sin-offering to atone for the defects of the inauguration services; and yet that sacrifice did not consist of a bullock—the sacrifice appointed for some particular transgression: but of a calf, perhaps, not without a significant reference to Aaron's sin in the golden calf. Then followed a burnt-offering, expressive of their voluntary and entire self-devotement to the divine service. The newly consecrated priests having done this on their own account, were called to offer a sin-offering and burnt-offering for the people: ending the ceremonial by a peace-offering which was a sacred feast. This injunction "to make an atonement for himself and for the people Sept., for thy family") at the commencement of his sacred functions, furnishes a striking evidence of the divine origin of the Jewish system of worship. In all false, or corrupt forms of religion, the studied policy has been to inspire the people with an idea of the sanctity of the priesthood as, in point of purity and favour with the Divinity, far above the level of other men. But among the Hebrews, the priests were required to offer for the expiation of their sins as well as the humblest of the people. This imperfection of Aaron's priesthood, however, does not extend to the Gospel dispensation; for our Great High Priest, who has entered for us into "the true tabernacle," "knew no sin." (He. 10. 10. 11.) 8. Aaron went unto the altar, &c.—Whether it had been enjoined the first time, or it was unavoidable from the divisions of the priestly labour not being as yet completely arranged, Aaron, assisted by his sons, appears to have slain the victims with his own hands, as well as gone through all the prescribed ritual at the altar. 17-21. meat-offering ... wave-offering—It is observable that there is no notice taken of these in the offerings the priests made for themselves. They could not bear their own sins; and therefore, instead of eating any part of their own sin-offering as they were at liberty to do in the case of the people's offering, they had to carry the whole carcases "*without* the camp and burn them with fire." 22. Aaron lifted his hands and blessed—The pronouncing of a benediction on the people assembled in the court was a necessary part of the high priest's duty, and the formula in which it was to be given is described, (Nu. 6. 23-27.) came down from offering—The altar was elevated above the level of the floor, and the ascent was by a gentle slope. (Ex. 20. 26.) 23. Moses and Aaron went into the tabernacle—Moses, according to the divine instructions he had received, accompanied Aaron and his sons to initiate them into their sacred duties. Their previous occupations had detained them at the altar, and they now entered in company into the sacred edifice to bear the blood of the offerings within the sanctuary. The glory of the Lord appeared, &c.—perhaps in a resplendent effulgence above the tabernacle as a fresh token of the divine acceptance of that newly established seat of his worship. 24. There came out fire from the Lord—A flame emanating from that resplendent light that filled the holy place flashed upon the brasen altar and kindled the sacrifices. This miraculous fire—for the descent of which the people had probably been prepared—and which the priests were enjoined never to let out (ch. 6. 13,) was a sign—not only of the acceptance of the offerings and of the establishment of Aaron's authority, but of God's actual residence in that chosen dwelling-place. The moment the solemn, though welcome spectacle was seen, a simultaneous shout of joy and gratitude burst from the assembled congregation, and in the attitude of profoundest reverence they worshipped "a present Deity."

CHAPTER X.

Ver. 1-20. NADAB AND ABIHU BURNT. 1. the sons of Aaron, &c.—If this incident occured at the solemn period of the consecrating and dedicating the altar, these young men assumed an office which had been committed to Moses; or if it were some time after, it was an encroachment on duties which devolved on their father alone as the high priest. But the offence was of a far more aggravated nature than such a mere informality would imply. It consisted not only in their venturing unauthorized to perform the incense service,—the highest and most solemn of the priestly offices,—not only in their engaging together in a work, which was the duty only of one, but in their presuming to intrude into the holy of holies, to which access was denied to all but the high priest alone. In this respect, "they offered strange fire before the Lord;" they were guilty of a presumptuous and unwarranted intrusion into a sacred office which did not belong to them. But their offence was more aggravated still: for instead of taking the fire which was put into their censers from the brasen altar, they seem to have been content with common fire, and thus perpetrated an act, which, considering the descent of the miraculous fire they had so recently witnessed, and the solemn obligation under which they were laid to make use of that which was specially appropriated to the service of the altars, they betrayed a carelessness, an irreverence, a want of faith, most surprising and lamentable. A precedent of such evil tendency was dangerous, and it was imperatively necessary, therefore, as well for the priests themselves as for the sacred things, that a marked expression of the divine displeasure should be given for doing that which "God commanded them not." 2. fire from the Lord ...devoured them—Rather killed them, for it appears, (*v.* 5,) that neither their bodies nor their robes were consumed. The expression "from the Lord," indicates that this fire issued from the most holy place; and in the destruction of these two young priests, by the infliction of an awful judgment, the wisdom of God observed the same course, in repressing the first instance of contempt for sacred things, as he did at the commencement of the Christian dispensation. (A. 5. 1-11.) 3. Moses said, This is it, &c.—"They that come nigh

hath commanded to do, to make an atonement for you.

35 Therefore shall ye abide *at* the door of the tabernacle of the congregation day and night seven days, and *f* keep the charge of the LORD, that ye die not: for so I am commanded.

36 So Aaron and his sons did all things which the LORD commanded by the hand of Moses.

CHAPTER IX.

1, 8 Aaron's sin offering and burnt offering for himself and the people. 23 Moses and Aaron bless the people, and fire cometh out from the Lord upon the altar.

AND *a* it came to pass on the eighth day, *that* Moses called Aaron and his sons, and the elders of Israel;

2 And he said unto Aaron, *b* Take thee a young calf for a sin offering, and *c* a ram for a burnt offering, without blemish, and offer *them* before the LORD.

3 And unto the children of Israel thou shalt speak, saying, *d* Take ye a kid of the goats for a sin offering; and a calf and a lamb, *both* of the first year, without blemish, for a burnt offering;

4 Also a bullock and a ram for peace offerings, to sacrifice before the LORD; and a *e* meat offering mingled with oil: for *f* to-day the LORD will appear unto you.

5 ¶ And they brought *that* which Moses commanded before the tabernacle of the congregation; and all the congregation drew near and stood before the LORD.

6 And Moses said, This *is* the thing which the LORD commanded that ye should do: and *g* the glory of the LORD shall appear unto you.

7 And Moses said unto Aaron, Go unto the altar, and *h* offer thy sin offering, and thy burnt offering, and make an atonement for thyself, and for the people: and *i* offer the offering of the people, and make an atonement for them; as the LORD commanded.

8 ¶ Aaron therefore went unto the altar, and slew the calf of the sin offering which *was* for himself.

9 And *j* the sons of Aaron brought the blood unto him: and he dipped his finger in the blood, and *k* put *it* upon the horns of the altar, and poured out the blood at the bottom of the altar:

10 But *l* the fat, and the kidneys, and the caul above the liver of the sin offering, he burnt upon the altar; *m* as the LORD commanded Moses.

11 And *n* the flesh and the hide he burnt with fire without the camp.

12 And he slew the burnt offering; and Aaron's sons presented unto him the blood, which he sprinkled round about upon the altar.

13 And they presented the burnt offering unto him, with the pieces thereof, and the head: and he burnt *them* upon the altar.

14 And he did wash the inwards and the legs, and burnt *them* upon the burnt offering on the altar.

15 ¶ And *o* he brought the people's offering, and took the goat, which *was* the sin offering for the people, and slew it, and offered it for sin, as the first.

16 And he brought the burnt offering, and offered it according to the *1* manner.

17 And he brought the meat offering, and *g* took an handful thereof, and burnt *it*

B. C. 1490.

CHAP. 8.
f Nu. 9. 19.
1 Ki. 2. 3.
Eze. 48. 11.

CHAP. 9.
a Eze. 43. 27.
b Ex. 29. 1.
c ch. 8. 18.
d Ezra 6. 17.
e ch. 2. 4.
f Ex. 29. 43.
g Ex. 24. 16.
h 1 Sa. 3. 14.
Heb. 5. 3.
Heb. 9. 7.
i ch. 4. 16, 20.
j ch. 8. 15.
k ch. 4. 7.
l ch. 8. 16.
m ch. 4. 8.
n ch. 8. 17.
o Is. 53. 10.
Heb. 2. 17.
1 Or, ordinance.
2 filled his hand out of it.
p Ex. 29. 38.
q Ex. 29. 24.
r Deu. 21. 5.
Lu. 24. 50.
s 2 Sa. 6. 18.
2 Chr. 6. 3.
1 Chr. 16. 2.
t Nu. 16. 19.
u Gen. 4. 4.
Gen. 15. 17.
2 Chr. 7. 1.
v Ex. 25. 22.
w 1 Ki. 18. 39.
Ezra 3. 11.

CHAP. 10.
a Nu. 26. 61.
b Ex. 30. 9.
c Nu. 16. 35.
2 Sa. 6. 7.
d Ex. 19. 22.
Is. 52. 11.
Eze. 20. 41.
e Is. 49. 3.
Eze. 28. 22.
John 13. 31.
2 Thess. 1. 10.
f Ex. 6. 18.
Nu. 3. 19.
g Acts 5. 6.
h Nu. 6. 6, 7.
Deu. 33. 9.
i 2 Sa. 24. 1.
j ch. 21. 12.
k Ex. 28. 41.
l Pro. 31. 5.
Pro. 20. 1.
Is. 28. 7.
Isaiah 56, 10-12.
Ezek. 44. 21.
Hosea 4. 11.
Luke 1. 15.
Eph. 5. 18.
1 Tim. 3. 3.
Tit. 1. 7.
m Jer. 15. 19.
Ezek. 22. 26.
Ezek. 44. 23.
n Deu. 24. 8.
Neh. 8. 2, 13.
Jer. 18. 18.
Mal. 2. 7.

upon the altar, *p* beside the burnt sacrifice of the morning.

18 He slew also the bullock and the ram for a sacrifice of peace offerings which *was* for the people: and Aaron's sons presented unto him the blood, which he sprinkled upon the altar round about.

19 And the fat of the bullock and of the ram, the rump, and that which covereth *the inwards*, and the kidneys, and the caul above the liver:

20 And they put the fat upon the breasts, and he burnt the fat upon the altar:

21 And the breasts and the right shoulder Aaron waved *q* for a wave offering before the LORD; as Moses commanded.

22 And Aaron lifted up his hand toward the people, and *r* blessed them, and came down from offering of the sin offering, and the burnt offering, and peace offerings.

23 And Moses and Aaron went into the tabernacle of the congregation, and came out, and *s* blessed the people: *t* and the glory of the LORD appeared unto all the people.

24 And *u* there came a fire out *v* from before the LORD, and consumed upon the altar the burnt offering and the fat: *which* when all the people saw, *w* they shouted, and fell on their faces.

CHAPTER X.

1 Nadab and Abihu burnt. 8 The priests forbidden wine when they enter the tabernacle. 12 The law of eating the holy things.

AND *a* Nadab and Abihu, the sons of Aaron, took either of them his censer, and put fire therein, and put incense thereon, and offered *b* strange fire before the LORD, which he commanded them not.

2 And there *c* went out fire from the LORD, and devoured them; and they died before the LORD.

3 Then Moses said unto Aaron, This *is it* that the LORD spake, saying, I will be sanctified in them *d* that come nigh me, and before all the people I will be *e* glorified. And Aaron held his peace.

4 And Moses called Mishael and Elzaphan, the sons of *f* Uzziel the uncle of Aaron, and said unto them, Come near, *g* carry your brethren from before the sanctuary out of the camp.

5 So they went near, and carried them in their coats out of the camp; as Moses had said.

6 And Moses said unto Aaron, and unto Eleazar and unto Ithamar, his sons, *h* Uncover not your heads, neither rend your clothes, lest ye die, and lest *i* wrath come upon all the people: but let your brethren, the whole house of Israel, bewail the burning which the LORD hath kindled.

7 And *j* ye shall not go out from the door of the tabernacle of the congregation, lest ye die: *k* for the anointing oil of the LORD *is* upon you. And they did according to the word of Moses.

8 ¶ And the LORD spake unto Aaron, saying,

9 Do *l* not drink wine nor strong drink, thou, nor thy sons with thee, when ye go into the tabernacle of the congregation, lest ye die: *it shall be* a statute for ever throughout your generations;

10 And that ye may *m* put difference between holy and unholy, and between unclean and clean;

11 And *n* that ye may teach the children

me" points, in this passage, directly to the priests; and they had received repeated and solemn warnings as to the cautious and reverent manner of their approach into the divine presence. (Ex. 19. 22; 29. 44. ch. 6. 35.) Aaron held his peace—The loss of two sons in so sudden and awful a manner was a calamity overwhelming to parental feelings. But the pious priest indulged in no vehement ebullition of complaint, and gave vent to no murmur of discontent, but submitted in silent resignation to what he saw was "the righteous judgment of God." 4-5. Moses called, &c.—The removal of the two corpses for burial without the camp, would spread the painful intelligence amongst all the congregation. The interment of the priestly vestments along with them, was a sign of their being polluted by the sin of their irreligious wearers; and the remembrance of so appalling a judgment could not fail to strike a salutary fear into the hearts both of priests and people. 6. uncover not your heads They who were ordered to carry out the two bodies, being engaged in their sacred duties, were forbidden to remove their turbans, in conformity with the usual customs of mourning; and the prohibition, "neither rend your garments," was in all probability, confined also to their official costume. For at other times, the priests wore the ordinary dress of their countrymen, and, in common with their families, might indulge their private feelings by the usual signs or expressions of grief. 8-11. Do not drink wine, &c.—This prohibition, and the accompanying admonitions, following immediately the occurrence of so fatal a catastrophe, has given rise to an opinion entertained by many, that the two unhappy priests were under the influence of intoxication when they committed the offence which was expiated only by their lives. But such an idea, though the presumption is in its favour, is nothing more than conjecture. 12-15. Moses spake unto Aaron, &c.—This was a timely and considerate rehearsal of the laws that regulated the conduct of the priests. Amid the distractions of their family bereavement, Aaron and his surviving sons might have forgotten or overlooked some of their duties. 16-20. Moses diligently sought, &c.— In a sacrifice presented, as that had been, on behalf of the people, it was the duty of the priests, as typically representing them, and bearing their sins, to have eaten the flesh, after the blood had been sprinkled upon the altar. Instead of using it, however, for a sacred feast, they had burnt it without the camp; and Moses, who discovered this departure from the prescribed ritual, probably from a dread of some farther chastisements challenged—not Aaron, whose heart was too much lacerated to bear a new cause of distress—but his two surviving sons in the priesthood for the great irregularity. Their father, however, who heard the charge, and by whose directions the error had been committed, hastened to give the explanation: The import of his apology is, that all the duty pertaining to the presentation of the offering had been duly and sacredly performed, except the festive part of the observance, which privately devolved upon the priest and his family; and that this had been omitted, either because his heart was too dejected to join in the celebration of a cheerful feast, or that he supposed, from the appalling judgments that had been inflicted, the whole services of that occasion were so vitiated, that he did not complete them. Aaron was decidedly in the wrong. By the express command of God, the sin offering was to be eaten in the holy place; and no fanciful view of expediency or propriety ought to have led him to dispense at discretion with a positive statute. The law of God was clear, and where that is the case, it is sin to deviate a hair's breadth from the path of duty. But Moses sympathized with his deeply afflicted brother; and having pointed out the error, said no more.

CHAPTER XI.

Ver. 1-47. BEASTS THAT MAY AND MAY NOT BE EATEN. 1. The Lord spake unto Moses—These laws being addressed to both the civil and ecclesiastical rulers in Israel, may serve to indicate the two-fold view that is to be taken of them. Undoubtedly the first and strongest reason for instituting a distinction among meats, was to discourage the Israelites from spreading into other countries, and from general intercourse with the world—to prevent them acquiring familiarity with the inhabitants of the countries bordering on Canaan, so as to fall into their idolatries, or be contaminated with their vices; in short, to keep them a distinct and peculiar people. To this purpose, no difference of creed, no system of polity, no diversity of language or manners was so subservient as a distinction of meats founded on religion; and hence the Jews who were taught by education to abhor many articles of food, freely partaken of by other people, never even at periods of great degeneracy, could amalgamate with the nations amongst which they were dispersed. But although this was the principal foundation of these laws, dietetic reasons also had weight; for there is no doubt that the flesh of many of the animals here ranked as unclean, is everywhere, but especially in warm climates, less wholesome and adapted for food than those which are allowed to be eaten. These laws, therefore, being subservient to sanatory as well as religious ends, were addressed both to Moses and Aaron. 3-7. whatsoever parteth the hoof, and is cloven-footed, and cheweth the cud—'Ruminating animals by the peculiar structure of their stomachs digest their food more fully than others. It is found that in the act of chewing the cud, a large portion of the poisonous properties of noxious plants eaten by them, passes off by the salivary glands. This power of secreting the poisonous effects of vegetables, is said to be particularly remarkable in cows and goats, whose mouths are often sore, and sometimes bleed, in consequence. Their flesh is therefore in a better state for food, as it contains more of the nutritious juices, and is more easily digested in the human stomach, and is consequently more easily assimilated. Animals which do not chew the cud, convert their food less perfectly; their flesh is therefore unwholesome, from the gross animal juices with which they abound, and is apt to produce scorbutic and scrofulous disorders. But the animals that may be eaten are those which "part the hoof as well as chew the cud," and this is another means of freeing the flesh of the animal from noxious substances. "In the case of ant

of Israel all the statutes which the LORD hath spoken unto them by the hand of Moses.

12 ¶ And Moses spake unto Aaron, and unto Eleazar and unto Ithamar, his sons that were left, Take *the meat offering that remaineth of the offerings of the LORD made by fire, and eat it without leaven beside the altar: for *p* it *is* most holy:

13 And ye shall eat it in the holy place, because it *is* thy due, and thy sons' due, of the sacrifices of the LORD made by fire: for so I am commanded.

14 And *q* the wave breast and heave shoulder shall ye eat in a clean place; thou, and thy sons and thy daughters with thee: for *they be* thy due, and thy sons' due, *which* are given out of the sacrifices of peace offerings of the children of Israel.

15 The heave shoulder and the wave breast shall they bring with the offerings made by fire of the fat, to wave *it for* a wave offering before the LORD; and it shall be thine, and thy sons' with thee, by a statute for ever; as the LORD hath commanded.

16 ¶ And Moses diligently sought *r* the goat of the sin offering, and, behold, it was burnt: and he was angry with Eleazar and Ithamar, the sons of Aaron *which were* left alive, saying,

17 Wherefore *s* have ye not eaten the sin offering in the holy place, seeing it *is* most holy, and *God* hath given it you to bear the iniquity of the congregation, to make atonement for them before the LORD?

18 Behold, the blood of it was not brought in within the holy *place:* ye should indeed have eaten it in the holy *place, t* as I commanded.

19 And Aaron said unto Moses, Behold, this *u* day have they offered their sin offering and their burnt offering before the LORD; and such things have befallen me: and *if* I had eaten the sin offering to-day, should *v* it have been accepted in the sight of the LORD?

20 And when Moses heard *that,* he was content.

CHAPTER XI.

What beasts may and what may not be eaten, etc.

AND the LORD spake unto Moses and to Aaron, saying unto them,

2 Speak unto the children of Israel, saying, *a* These *are* the beasts which ye shall eat among all the beasts that *are* on the earth.

3 Whatsoever parteth the hoof, and is cloven-footed, *and* cheweth the cud, among the beasts, that shall ye eat.

4 Nevertheless these shall ye not eat of them that chew the cud, or of them that divide the hoof: *as* the camel, because he cheweth the cud, but divideth not the hoof; he *is* unclean unto you.

5 And the coney, because he cheweth the cud, but divideth not the hoof; he *is* unclean unto you.

6 And the hare, because he cheweth the cud, but divideth not the hoof; he *is b* unclean unto you.

7 And the swine, though he divide the hoof, and be cloven-footed, yet he cheweth not the cud; *c* he *is* unclean to you.

8 Of their flesh shall ye not eat, and their carcase shall ye not touch; *d* they *are* unclean to you.

9 ¶ These *e* shall ye eat of all that *are* in the waters: whatsoever hath fins and scales in the waters, in the seas, and in the rivers, them shall ye eat.

10 And all that have not fins and scales in the seas, and in the rivers, of all that move in the waters, and of any living thing which *is* in the waters, they *shall be* an *f* abomination unto you:

11 They shall be even an abomination unto you; ye shall not eat of their flesh, but ye shall have their carcases in abomination.

12 Whatsoever hath no fins nor scales in the waters, that *shall be* an abomination unto you.

13 ¶ And *g* these *are they which* ye shall have in abomination among the fowls; they shall not be eaten, they *are* an abomination: the eagle, and the ¹ ossifrage, and the ² ospray,

14 And the vulture, and the kite after his kind;

15 Every raven after his kind;

16 And the owl, and the night hawk, and the cuckoo, and the hawk after his kind,

17 And the little owl, and the cormorant, and the great owl,

18 And the swan, and the *h* pelican, and the ³ gier eagle,

19 And the stork, the heron after her kind, and the lapwing, and the bat.

20 All ⁴ fowls that creep, going upon *all* four, *shall be* an abomination unto you.

21 Yet these may ye eat of every flying creeping thing that goeth upon *all* four, which have legs above their feet, to leap withal upon the earth;

22 *Even* these of them ye may eat; *i* the locust after his kind, and the bald locust after his kind, and the beetle after his kind, and the *j* grasshopper after his kind.

23 But all *other* flying creeping things, which have four feet, *shall be* an abomination unto you.

24 And for these ye shall be unclean: whosoever toucheth the carcase of them shall be unclean until the even.

25 And whosoever beareth *ought* of the carcase of them *k* shall wash his clothes, and be unclean until the even.

26 *The carcases* of every beast which divideth the hoof, and is not cloven-footed, nor cheweth the cud, *are* unclean unto you: every one that toucheth them shall be unclean.

27 And ⁵ whatsoever goeth upon his paws, among all manner of beasts that go on *all* four, those *are* unclean unto you: whoso toucheth their carcase shall be unclean until the even.

28 And he that beareth the carcase of them shall wash his clothes, and be unclean until the even: they *are* unclean unto you.

29 ¶ These also *shall be l* unclean unto you among the creeping things that creep upon the earth; the weasel, and *m* the mouse, and the ⁶ tortoise after his kind,

30 And the ferret, and the chameleon, and the lizard, and the *n* snail, and the *o* mole.

31 These *are* unclean to you among all that creep: whosoever doth touch them, when they be dead, shall be unclean until the even.

32 And upon whatsoever *any* of them, when they are dead, doth fall, it shall be unclean; whether *it be* any vessel of wood, or raiment, or skin, or sack, whatsoever vessel *it be,* wherein *any* work is done, *p* it

mals with parted hoofs, when feeding in unfavourable situations, a prodigious amount of fœtid matter is discharged and passes off between the toes; while animals with undivided hoofs, feeding on the same ground, become severely affected in the legs, from the poisonous plants among the pasture." [WHITLAW'S CODE OF HEALTH.] All experience attests this, and accordingly the use of ruminating animals, that is, which both chew the cud, and part the hoof, has always obtained in most countries, though it was observed most carefully by the people who were favoured with the promulgation of God's law. 4. the camel—It does to a certain extent divide the hoof, for the foot consists of two large parts, but the division is not complete, the toes rest upon an elastic pad on which the animal goes; as a beast of burden its flesh is tough, and an additional reason for its prohibition might be to keep the Israelites apart from the descendants of Ishmael. 5. the coney—not the rabbit, for it is not found in Palestine or Arabia, but the Hyrax, a little animal of the size and general shape of the rabbit, but differing from it in several essential features; it has no tail, singular long hairs bristling, like thorns, amongst the fur on its back; its feet are bare, its nails flat and round, except those on each inner toe of the hind feet which are sharp and project like an awl. It does not burrow in the ground, but frequents the clefts of rocks. 6. the hare—two species of hare must have been pointed at, the Sinai hare—the hare of the desert, small and generally brown; the other, the hare of Palestine and Syria, about the size and appearance of that known in our own country. Neither the hare nor the coney are really ruminating. They only *appear* to be so from working the jaws on the grasses they live on. They are not cloven footed, and besides it is said that from the great quantity of down upon them, they are very much subject to vermin, that in order to expel these, they eat poisonous plants, and if used as food while in that state, they are most deleterious. [WHIT.] 7. the swine—It is a filthy, foul feeding animal, and it wants one of the natural provisions for purifying the system, " it cheweth not the cud;" in hot climates indulgence in swines' flesh is particularly liable to produce leprosy, scurvy, and various cutaneous eruptions. It was therefore strictly avoided by the Israelites, and its prohibition was further necessary to prevent their adopting many of the grossest idolatries practised by neighbouring nations. 9. These shall ye eat, whatsoever hath fins and scales—" The fins and scales are the means by which the excrescences of fish are carried off, the same as in animals by perspiration. I have never known an instance of disease produced by eating such fish; but those that have no fins and scales cause, in hot climates, the most malignant disorders when eaten; in many cases they prove a mortal poison." [WHITLAW.] 12. Whatsoever hath no fins nor scales, &c.—Under this classification, frogs, eels, shell-fish of all descriptions were included as unclean, " many of the latter (shell-fish) enjoy a reputation they do not deserve, and have, when plentifully partaken of, produced effects which have led to a suspicion of their containing something of a poisonous nature. 13-19. These are they....abomination among fowls—All birds of prey are particularly ranked in the class unclean. all those which feed on flesh and carrion, no less than twenty species of birds, all probably then known, are mentioned under this category, and the inference follows that all which are not mentioned were allowed, that is fowls which subsist on vegetable substances. From our imperfect knowledge of the natural history of Palestine, Arabia, and the contiguous countries, it is not easy to determine exactly what some of the prohibited birds are; although they must have been all well known among the people to whom these laws were given. the ossifrage—*Heb.*, bone-breaker, rendered in the Septuagint *griffon*, supposed to be the Gypœtos barbatus, the Lammer Geyer of the Swiss—a bird of the eagle or vulture species, inhabiting the highest mountain-ranges in Western Asia as well as Europe, and pursues as its prey the chamois, ibex, or marmot, among rugged cliffs, till it drives them over a precipice — thus obtaining the name of " bone-breaker." the osprey—the black eagle, among the smallest, but swiftest and strongest of its kind. the vulture—the word so rendered in our version means more probably " the kite" or " glede," and describes a varying but majestic flight, exactly that of the kite, which now darts forward with the rapidity of an arrow, now rests motionless on its expanded wings in the air—it feeds on small birds, insects, and fish. the kite—the vulture. In Egypt, and perhaps in the adjoining countries also, the kite and vulture are often seen together flying in company, or busily pursuing their foul but important office of devouring the carrion and relics of putrefying flesh, which might otherwise pollute the atmosphere. after his kind—*i.e.*, the prohibition against eating it extended to the whole species. the raven—including the crow, the pie. the owl—it is generally supposed the ostrich is denoted by the original word. the night hawk—a very small bird, with which, from its nocturnal habits, many superstitious ideas were associated. the cuckoo—evidently some other bird is meant by the original term, from its being ranged among rapacious birds. Dr. Shaw thinks it is the saf-saf; but that being a gramanivorous and gregarious bird, is equally objectionable. Others think that the term the sea-mew, or some of the small sea-fowl, are intended. the hawk—the Hebrew word includes every variety of the falcon family—as the goshawk, the jer-hawk, the sparrow-hawk, &c. Several species of hawks are found in Western Asia and Egypt, where they find inexhaustible prey in the immense numbers of pigeons and turtle-doves that abound in those quarters. The hawk was held pre-eminently sacred among the Egyptians; and this, besides its rapacious disposition and gross habits, might have been a strong reason for its prohibition as an article of food to the Israelites. the little owl—or horned owl, as some render it. The common barn owl, which is well known in the East. It is the only bird of the kind here referred to, although the word is thrice mentioned in our version. cormorant—supposed to be the gull. the great owl—according to some, the Ibis of the Egyptians. It was well known to the Israelites, and so rendered by the Septuagint, (Deu. 14. 16 ; Is. 34. 11.) according to Parkhurst, the bittern, but not deter-

must be put into water, and it shall be unclean until the even; so it shall be cleansed.

33 And every earthen vessel whereinto *any* of them falleth, whatsoever *is* in it shall be unclean; and *q* ye shall break it.

34 Of all meat which may be eaten, *that* on which *such* water cometh shall be unclean: and all drink that may be drunk in every *such* vessel shall be unclean.

35 And every thing whereupon *any part* of their carcase falleth shall be unclean; *whether it be* oven, or ranges for pots, they shall be broken down: *for* they *are* unclean, and shall be unclean unto you.

36 Nevertheless a fountain or pit, ¹ *wherein there is* plenty of water, shall be clean: but that which toucheth their carcase shall be unclean.

37 And if *any part* of their carcase fall upon any sowing seed which is to be sown, it *shall be* clean.

38 But if *any* water be put upon the seed, and *any part* of their carcase fall thereon, it *shall be* unclean unto you.

39 And if any beast of which ye may eat die; he that toucheth the carcase thereof shall be unclean until the even.

40 And *r* he that eateth of the carcase of it shall wash his clothes, and be unclean until the even: he also that beareth the carcase of it shall wash his clothes, and be unclean until the even.

41 And every creeping thing that creepeth upon the earth *shall be* an abomination; it shall not be eaten.

42 Whatsoever goeth upon the belly, and whatsoever goeth upon *all* four, or whatsoever ² hath more feet among all creeping things that creep upon the earth, them ye shall not eat; for they *are* an abomination.

43 Ye *s* shall not make ³ yourselves abominable with any creeping thing that creepeth, neither shall ye make yourselves unclean with them, that ye should be defiled thereby.

44 For *t* I am the LORD your God: ye shall therefore sanctify yourselves, and *u* ye shall be holy; for I am holy: neither shall ye defile yourselves with any manner of creeping thing that creepeth upon the earth.

45 For *v* I am the LORD that bringeth you up out of the land of Egypt, to be your God: *w* ye shall therefore be holy, for I am holy.

46 This *is* the law of the beasts, and of the fowl, and of every living creature that moveth in the waters, and of every creature that creepeth upon the earth;

47 To *x* make a difference between the unclean and the clean, and between the beast that may be eaten and the beast that may not be eaten.

CHAPTER XII.

1 *The purification of a woman after childbirth,* 6 *her offerings for her purifying.*

AND the LORD spake unto Moses, saying, 2 Speak unto the children of Israel, saying, If a woman have conceived seed, and born a man-child: then *a* she shall be unclean seven days; *b* according to the days of the separation for her infirmity shall she be unclean.

3 And in the *c* eighth day the flesh of his foreskin shall be circumcised.

4 And she shall then continue in the blood of her purifying three and thirty days; she shall touch no hallowed thing, nor come

B. C. 1490.

CHAP. 11.
q ch. 6. 28.
1 a gathering together of waters.
r ch. 22. 8.
Deu. 14. 21.
Ezek. 4. 14.
Ezek. 44. 31.
2 doth multiply feet.
s ch. 20. 25.
3 your souls.
t Is. 51. 15.
Is. 43. 3.
u Ex. 19. 6.
ch. 19. 2.
1 Thes. 4. 7.
1 Pet. 1. 15.
v Gen. 35. 1, 2.
Ex. 6. 7.
Ex. 20. 2.
Ro. 14. 17.
w Ro. 12. 1.
1 Cor. 6. 11.
x ch. 10. 10.
Jer. 15. 19.
Eze. 22. 26.
Eze. 44. 23.

CHAP. 12.
a Lu. 2. 22.
b ch. 15. 19.
c Ge. 17. 12.
Luke 1. 59.
Luke 2. 21.
John 7. 22, 23.
d Lu. 2. 22.
e Isa. 53. 7.
Luke 24. 26, 27.
John 1. 29, 36.
1 Pet. 1. 18, 19.
Rev. 5. 6-8.
Rev. 7. 14.
1 a son of his year.
f Heb. 9. 9-28.
Heb. 10. 1-12.
g ch. 5. 7.
Lu. 2. 24.
2 her hand find not sufficiency of.
h ch. 4. 26.

CHAP. 13.
1 Or, swelling.
a Deut. 28. 27.
Is. 3. 17.
b Deut. 17. 8. 9.
Deu. 24. 8.
Lu. 17. 14.
c ch. 11. 25.
ch. 14. 8.
d 2 Sam. 3. 29.
e 2 Ki. 5. 3.
f Num. 12. 10, 12.
2 Kin. 5. 27.
1 Chr. 26. 20.
2 the quickening of living flesh.

into the sanctuary, until the days of her purifying be fulfilled.

5 But if she bear a maid-child, then she shall be unclean two weeks, as in her separation: and she shall continue in the blood of her purifying threescore and six days.

6 And *d* when the days of her purifying are fulfilled, for a son, or for a daughter, she shall bring *e* a lamb ¹ of the first year for a burnt offering, and a young pigeon, or a turtle-dove, for a sin offering, unto the door of the tabernacle of the congregation, unto the priest:

7 Who shall offer it before the LORD, and make *f* an atonement for her; and she shall be cleansed from the issue of her blood. This *is* the law for her that hath born a male or a female.

8 And *g* if ² she be not able to bring a lamb, then she shall bring two turtles, or two young pigeons; the one for the burnt offering, and the other for a sin offering: and *h* the priest shall make an atonement for her, and she shall be clean.

CHAPTER XIII.

The laws and tokens in discerning leprosy.

AND the LORD spake unto Moses and Aaron, saying,

2 When a man shall have in the skin of his flesh a ¹ rising, *a* a scab, or bright spot, and it be in the skin of his flesh *like* the plague of leprosy; *b* then he shall be brought unto Aaron the priest, or unto one of his sons the priests:

3 And the priest shall look on the plague in the skin of the flesh: and *when* the hair in the plague is turned white, and the plague in sight *be* deeper than the skin of his flesh, it *is* a plague of leprosy: and the priest shall look on him, and pronounce him unclean.

4 If the bright spot *be* white in the skin of his flesh, and in sight *be* not deeper than the skin, and the hair thereof be not turned white; then the priest shall shut up *him that hath* the plague seven days:

5 And the priest shall look on him the seventh day: and, behold, *if* the plague in his sight be at a stay, *and* the plague spread not in the skin; then the priest shall shut him up seven days more:

6 And the priest shall look on him again the seventh day: and, behold, *if* the plague be somewhat dark, *and* the plague spread not in the skin, the priest shall pronounce him clean; it *is but* a scab: and he *c* shall wash his clothes, and be clean.

7 But if the scab spread much abroad in the skin, after that he hath been seen of the priest for his cleansing, he shall be seen of the priest again:

8 And *if* the priest see that, behold, the scab spreadeth in the skin, then the priest shall pronounce him unclean: it *is d* a leprosy.

9 ¶ When the plague of leprosy is in a man, then he shall *e* be brought unto the priest;

10 And *f* the priest shall see *him:* and, behold, *if* the rising *be* white in the skin, and it have turned the hair white, and *there be* ² quick raw flesh in the rising,

11 It is an old leprosy in the skin of his flesh: and the priest shall pronounce him unclean, and shall not shut him up; for he *is* unclean.

mined. the swan—found in great numbers in all the countries of the Levant, and frequents marshy places—the vicinity of rivers and lakes. It was held sacred by the Egyptians, and kept tame within the precincts of heathen temples. It was probably on this account chiefly its use as food was prohibited. Michaelis considers it the goose. the pelican —remarkable for the bag or pouch under its lower jaw, which serves not only as a net to catch, but also as a receptacle of food It is solitary in its habits, and, like other large aquatic birds, often flies to a great distance from its favourite haunts. the gier-eagle — Being here associated with water fowl, it has been questioned, whether any species of eagle is referred to. Some think as the original name *racham* denotes *tenderness, affection*, the halcyon or kings' fisher is intended. [CALMET.] Others that it is the bird now called *rachami*, a kind of Egyptian vulture, abundant in the streets of Cairo, and popularly called Pharaoh's fowl. It is white in colour, in size like a raven, and feeds on carrion; it is one of the foulest and filthiest birds in the world. the stork— a bird of benevolent temper, and held in the highest estimation in all Eastern countries; it was declared unclean, probably, from its feeding on serpents and other venomous reptiles, as well as rearing its young on the same food. the heron—the word so translated only occurs in the prohibited list of food and has been variously rendered—the crane, the plover, the woodcock, the parrot. In this great diversity of opinion nothing certain can be affirmed regarding it, and as from the group with which it is classified, it must be an aquatic bird that is meant, it may as well be the heron as any other bird, the more especially as herons abound in Egypt and in the Hauran of Palestine. the lapwing — or hoopoe—found in warm regions, a very pretty but filthy species of bird, and was considered unclean, probably from its feeding on insects, worms, and snails. the bat—the great or Ternat bat, known in the East, noted for its voracity and filthiness. 20. all fowls that creep, &c.—by "fowls" here are to be understood all creatures with wings, and by "going upon all fours," not a restriction to animals which have exactly four feet, because many "creeping things" have more than that number. The prohibition is regarded generally as extending to insects, reptiles, and worms. 21. Yet these ye may eat ... legs above their feet—Nothing short of a scientific description could convey more accurately the nature "of the locust after its kind." They were allowed as lawful food to the Israelites, and they are eaten by the Arabs, who fry them in olive oil; or when sprinkled with salt, dried, smoked, and fried, they are said to taste not unlike red herrings. 26. Every beast not cloven-footed—The prohibited animals under this description include not only the beasts which have a single hoof, as horses and asses, but those also which divided the foot into paws, as lions, tigers, &c. 29. the weasel, rather the mole. the mouse— from its diminutive size is placed among the reptiles instead of the quadrupeds. the tortoise—a lizard, resembling very nearly in shape, and in the hard pointed scales of the tail, the *shake-tail.* the ferret—the Hebrew word is thought by some to signify the newt or chameleon; by others the frog. the chameleon—called by the Arabs the warral, a green lizard. the snail—a lizard, which lives in the sand, and is called by the Arabs *chulca*, of an azure colour. the mole—another species of lizard is meant, probably the chameleon. 31-35. touch them when dead—These regulations must have often caused annoyance, by suddenly requiring the exclusion of people from society, as well as the ordinances of religion. Nevertheless they were extremely useful and salutary, especially as enforcing attention to cleanliness. This is a matter of essential importance in the East, where venomous reptiles often creep into houses, and are found lurking in boxes, vessels, or holes in the wall: and the carcase of one of them, or a dead mouse, mole, lizard, or other unclean animal, might be inadvertently touched by the hand, or fall on clothes, skin-bottles, or any article of common domestic use. By connecting, therefore, the touch of such creatures with ceremonial defilement, which required immediately to be removed, an effectual means was taken to prevent the bad effects of venom and all unclean or noxious matter. 47. make a difference between the unclean and the clean—*i. e.* between animals used and not used for food. It is probable that the laws contained in this chapter were not entirely new, but only gave the sanction of divine enactment to ancient usages. Some of the prohibited animals have, on physiological grounds, been everywhere rejected by the general sense or experience of mankind, while others may have been declared unclean from their unwholesomeness in warm countries, or from some reasons, which are now imperfectly known, connected with contemporary idolatry.

CHAPTER XII.

Ver. 1-8. WOMAN'S UNCLEANNESS BY CHILD-BIRTH. 2. If a woman, &c.—The mother of a boy was ceremonially unclean for a week, at the end of which the child was circumcised, (Gen. 17. 12; Ro. 4. 11-13; the mother of a girl for two weeks—a stigma on the sex, (1 Tim. 2. 14. 15.), for sin, which was removed by Christ; every one who came near her during that time contracted a similar defilement. After these periods, visitors might approach her, though she was still excluded from the public ordinances of religion. 6-8. the days of her purification—Though the occasion was of a festive character, yet the sacrifices appointed were not a peace offering, but a burnt offering and sin offering, in order to impress the mind of the parent with recollections of the origin of sin and that the child inherited a fallen and sinful nature. The offerings were to be presented the day after the period of her separation had ended—*i.e.,* 41st for a boy, 81st for a girl. bring two turtle doves, &c.—(See on ch. 5. 7.) This was the offering made by Mary, the mother of Jesus, and it affords an incontestible proof of the poor and humble condition of the family. (Lu. 2. 22-24.)

CHAPTER XIII.

Ver. 1-59. THE LAWS AND TOKENS IN DISCERNING LEPROSY. 2. When a man shall have in the skin, &c.—The fact of the following rules for distinguishing the plague of leprosy being incorporated with the Hebrew code of laws, proves the existence of the odious disease among that people. But a short time, little more than a year, if so long a

12 And if a leprosy break out abroad in the skin, and the leprosy cover all the skin of *him that hath* the plague from his head even to his foot, wheresoever the priest looketh;
13 Then the priest shall consider: and, behold, *if* the leprosy have covered all his flesh, he shall *pronounce him* clean *that hath* the plague: it is all turned white: he *is* clean.
14 But when raw flesh appeareth in him, he shall be unclean.
15 And the priest shall see the raw flesh, and pronounce him to be unclean: *for* the raw flesh *is* unclean: it *is* a leprosy.
16 Or if the raw flesh turn again, and be changed unto white, he shall come unto the priest;
17 And the priest shall see him: and, behold, *if* the plague be turned into white; then the priest shall pronounce *him* clean *that hath* the plague: he *is* clean.
18 ¶ The flesh also, in which, *even* in the skin thereof, was a boil, and is healed,
19 And in the place of the boil there be a white rising, or a bright spot, white, and somewhat reddish, and it be showed to the priest;
20 And if, when the priest seeth it, behold, it *be* in sight lower than the skin, and the hair thereof be turned white; the priest shall pronounce him unclean: it *is* a plague of leprosy broken out of the boil.
21 But if the priest look on it, and, behold, *there be* no white hairs therein, and *if* it *be* not lower than the skin, but *be* somewhat dark; then the priest shall shut him up seven days:
22 And if it spread much abroad in the skin, then the priest shall pronounce him unclean: it *is* a plague.
23 But if the bright spot stay in his place, *and* spread not, it *is* a burning boil; and the priest shall pronounce him clean.
24 ¶ Or if there be *any* flesh, in the skin whereof *there is* a hot burning, and the quick *flesh* that burneth have a white bright spot, somewhat reddish, or white;
25 Then the priest shall look upon it: and, behold, *if* the hair in the bright spot be turned white, and it *be* in sight deeper than the skin, it *is* a leprosy broken out of the burning: wherefore the priest shall pronounce him unclean: it is the plague of leprosy.
26 But if the priest look on it, and, behold, *there be* no white hair in the bright spot, and it *be* no lower than the *other* skin, but *be* somewhat dark; then the priest shall shut him up seven days:
27 And the priest shall look upon him the seventh day: *and* if it be spread much abroad in the skin, then the priest shall pronounce him unclean: it *is* the plague of leprosy.
28 And if the bright spot stay in his place, *and* spread not in the skin, but it *be* somewhat dark; it *is* a rising of the burning, and the priest shall pronounce him clean: for it *is* an inflammation of the burning.
29 ¶ If a man or woman have a plague upon the head or the beard;
30 Then the priest shall see the plague: and, behold, if it *be* in sight deeper than the skin, and *there be* in it a yellow thin hair; then the priest shall pronounce him unclean: it *is* a dry scall, *even* a leprosy upon the head or beard.

31 And if the priest look on the plague of the scall, and, behold, it *be* not in sight deeper than the skin, and *that there is* no black hair in it; then the priest shall shut up *him that hath* the plague of the scall seven days.
32 And in the seventh day the priest shall look on the plague: and, behold, *if* the scall spread not, and there be in it no yellow hair, and the scall *be* not in sight deeper than the skin;
33 He shall be shaven, but the scall shall he not shave; and the priest shall shut up *him that hath* the scall seven days more.
34 And in the seventh day the priest shall look on the scall: and, behold, *if* the scall be not spread in the skin, nor *be* in sight deeper than the skin; then the priest shall pronounce him clean: and he shall wash his clothes, and be clean.
35 But if the scall spread much in the skin after his cleansing;
36 Then the priest shall look on him: and, behold, if the scall be spread in the skin, the priest shall not seek for yellow hair; he is unclean.
37 But if the scall be in his sight at a stay, and *that* there is black hair grown up therein; the scall is healed, he *is* clean: and the priest shall pronounce him clean.
38 ¶ If a man also or a woman have in the skin of their flesh bright spots, *even* white bright spots;
39 Then the priest shall look: and, behold, *if* the bright spots in the skin of their flesh *be* darkish white; it *is* a freckled spot that groweth in the skin; he *is* clean.
40 And the man whose hair is fallen off his head, he *is* bald; *yet is* he clean.
41 And he that hath his hair fallen off from the part of his head toward his face, he *is* forehead bald: *yet is* he clean.
42 And if there be in the bald head, or bald forehead, a white reddish sore; it *is* a leprosy sprung up in his bald head, or his bald forehead.
43 Then the priest shall look upon it: and, behold, *if* the rising of the sore *be* white reddish in his bald head, or in his bald forehead, as the leprosy appeareth in the skin of the flesh;
44 He is a leprous man, he *is* unclean: the priest shall pronounce him utterly unclean; his plague *is* in his head.
45 And the leper in whom the plague *is*, his clothes shall be rent, and his head bare, and he shall put a covering upon his upper lip, and shall cry, Unclean, unclean.
46 All the days wherein the plague *shall* be in him he shall be defiled; he *is* unclean: he shall dwell alone; without the camp *shall* his habitation *be*.
47 ¶ The garment also that the plague of leprosy is in, *whether it be* a woollen garment, or a linen garment;
48 Whether *it be* in the warp, or woof, of linen, or of woollen, whether in a skin, or in any thing made of skin;
49 And if the plague be greenish or reddish in the garment, or in the skin, either in the warp, or in the woof, or in any thing of skin; it *is* a plague of leprosy, and shall be showed unto the priest.
50 And the priest shall look upon the plague, and shut up *it that hath* the plague seven days:
51 And he shall look on the plague on the seventh day: if the plague be spread in the

period had elapsed since the Exodus, when symptoms of leprosy seem extensively to have appeared among them; and as they could not be very liable to such a cutaneous disorder amid their active journeyings, and in the dry open air of Arabia, the seeds of the disorder must have been laid in Egypt, where it has always been endemic. There is every reason to believe that this was the case;—that the leprosy was not a family complaint, hereditary among the Hebrews; but that they got it from intercourse with the Egyptians, and from the unfavourable circumstances of their condition in the house of bondage. The great excitement and irritability of the skin in the hot and sandy regions of the East, produce a far greater predisposition to leprosy of all kinds than in the cooler temperature of Europe; and cracks or blotches, inflammations, or even contusions of the skin, very often lead to these in Arabia and Palestine to some extent, but particularly in Egypt. Besides, the subjugated and distressed state of the Hebrews in the latter country, and the nature of their employment, must have rendered them very liable to this as well as to various other blemishes and misaffections of the skin; in the production of which there are no causes more active or powerful than a depressed state of body and mind, hard labour under a burning sun, the body constantly covered with the excoriating dust of brickfields, and an impoverished diet—to all of which the Israelites were exposed whilst under the Egyptian bondage. It appears that, in consequence of these hardships, there was, even after they had left Egypt, a general predisposition among the Hebrews to the contagious forms of leprosy—so that it often occurred as a consequence of various other affections of the skin. And hence all cutaneous blemishes or blains—especially such as had a tendency to terminate in leprosy—were watched with a jealous eye from the first. [GOOD'S STUDY OF MEDICINE.] A swelling, a pimple, or bright spot on the skin, created a strong ground of suspicion of a man's being attacked by the dreaded disease. *Then he shall be brought unto Aaron, &c.*—Like the Egyptian priests, the Levites united the character of physician with that of the sacred office; and on the appearance of any suspicious eruptions on the skin, the person having these was brought before the priest—not, however, to receive medical treatment, though it is not improbable that some purifying remedies might be prescribed—but to be examined with a view to those sanatory precautions which it belonged to legislation to adopt. 3-6. *The priest shall look, &c.*—The leprosy, as covering the person with a white scaly scurf, has always been accounted an offensive blemish rather than a serious malady in the East, unless when it assumed its less common and malignant forms. When a Hebrew priest, after a careful inspection, discovered under the cutaneous blemish the distinctive signs of contagious leprosy, the person was immediately pronounced unclean, and is supposed to have been sent out of the camp to a lazaretto provided for that purpose. If the symptoms appeared to be doubtful, he ordered the person to be kept in domestic confinement for seven days, when he was subjected to a second examination; and if during the previous week the eruption had subsided or appeared to be harmless, he was instantly discharged. But if the eruption continued unabated and still doubtful, he was put under surveillance for another week; at the end of which the character of the disorder never failed to manifest itself, and he was either doomed to perpetual exclusion from society, or allowed to go at large. A person who had thus been detained on suspicion, when at length set at liberty, was obliged to "wash his clothes," as having been tainted by ceremonial pollution; and the purification through which he was required to go was, in the spirit of the Mosaic dispensation, symbolical of that inward purity it was instituted to promote. 6-8. *But if the scab spread much*—Those doubtful cases, when they assumed a malignant character, appeared in one of two forms, apparently according to the particular constitution of the skin or of the habit generally. The one was "somewhat dark"—*i.e.*, the obscure or dusky leprosy, in which the natural colour of the hair, which in Egypt and Palestine is black, is not changed, as is repeatedly said in the sacred code, nor is there any depression in the dusky spot, while the patches, instead of keeping stationary to their first size, are perpetually enlarging their boundary. The patient labouring under this form was pronounced unclean by the Hebrew priest or physician, and hereby sentenced to a separation from his family and friends—a decisive proof of its being contagious. 10-17. *If the rising be white*—This BRIGHT WRITE leprosy is the most malignant and inveterate of all the varieties the disease exhibits, and it was marked by the following distinctive signs:—A glossy white and spreading scale, upon an elevated base, the elevation depressed in the middle, but without a change of colour; the black hair on the patches participating in the whiteness, and the scaly patches themselves perpetually enlarging their boundary. Several of these characters, taken separately, belong to other blemishes of the skin as well; so that none of them was to be taken alone, and it was only when the whole of them concurred that the Jewish priest, in his capacity of physician, was to pronounce the disease a malignant leprosy. If it spread over the entire frame without producing any ulceration, it lost its contagious power by degrees; or, in other words, ran through its course and exhausted itself. In that case, there being no longer any fear of further evil either to the individual himself or to the community, the patient was declared clean by the priest, while the dry scales were yet upon him, and restored to society. If, on the contrary, the patches ulcerated, and quick or fungous flesh sprung up in them, the purulent matter, of which, if brought into contact with the skin of other persons, would be taken into the constitution by means of absorbent vessels, the priest was at once to pronounce it an inveterate leprosy; a temporary confinement was declared to be totally unnecessary, and he was regarded as unclean for life." [DR. GOOD.] Other skin affections, which had a tendency to terminate in leprosy though they were not decided symptoms when alone, were 18-23. "a boil," and 24-28. "a hot burning"—*i.e.*, a fiery inflammation or carbuncle, and 29-38. "a dry scall," when

garment, either in the warp, or in the woof, or in a skin, *or* in any work that is made of skin; the plague is *a* fretting leprosy; it *is* unclean.

52 He shall therefore burn that garment, whether warp or woof, in woollen or in linen, or any thing of skin, wherein the plague is: for it *is* a fretting leprosy; it shall be burnt in the fire.

53 And if the priest shall look, and, behold, the plague be not spread in the garment, either in the warp, or in the woof, or in any thing of skin;

54 Then the priest shall command that they wash *the thing* wherein the plague *is*, and he shall shut it up seven days more:

55 And the priest shall look on the plague, after that it is washed: and, behold, *if* the plague have not changed his colour, and the plague be not spread; it *is* unclean; thou shalt burn it in the fire; it *is* fret inward, *whether* it *be* bare within or without.

56 And if the priest look, and, behold, the plague *be* somewhat dark after the washing of it; then he shall rend it out of the garment, or out of the skin, or out of the warp, or out of the woof:

57 And if it appear still in the garment, either in the warp, or in the woof, or in any thing of skin, it *is* a spreading *plague:* thou shalt burn that wherein the plague is with fire.

58 And the garment, either warp or woof, or whatsoever thing of skin *it be*, which thou shalt wash, if the plague be departed from them, then it shall be washed the second time, and shall be clean.

59 This *is* the law of the plague of leprosy in a garment of woollen or linen, either in the warp, or woof, or any thing of skins, to pronounce it clean, or to pronounce it unclean.

CHAPTER XIV.

1 *The rites and sacrifices in cleansing of the leper.* 33 *The signs of leprosy in a house;* 48 *the cleansing of that house.*

AND the LORD spake unto Moses, saying,

2 This shall be the law of the leper in the day of his cleansing: He shall be brought unto the priest:

3 And the priest shall go forth out of the camp; and the priest shall look, and, behold, *if* the plague of leprosy be healed in the leper;

4 Then shall the priest command to take for him that is to be cleansed two birds alive *and* clean, and cedar wood, and scarlet, and hyssop:

5 And the priest shall command that one of the birds be killed in an earthen vessel over running water:

6 As for the living bird, he shall take it, and the cedar wood, and the scarlet, and the hyssop, and shall dip them and the living bird in the blood of the bird *that was* killed over the running water:

7 And he shall sprinkle upon him that is to be cleansed from the leprosy seven times, and shall pronounce him clean, and shall let the living bird loose into the open field.

8 And he that is to be cleansed shall wash his clothes, and shave off all his hair, and wash himself in water, that he may be clean: and after that he shall come into the camp, and shall tarry abroad out of his tent seven days.

9 But it shall be on the seventh day, that he shall shave all his hair off his head and his beard and his eyebrows, even all his hair he shall shave off: and he shall wash his clothes, also he shall wash his flesh in water, and he shall be clean.

10 And on the eighth day he shall take two he-lambs without blemish, and one ewe lamb of the first year without blemish, and three tenth deals of fine flour *for* a meat offering, mingled with oil, and one log of oil.

11 And the priest that maketh *him* clean shall present the man that is to be made clean, and those things, before the LORD, at the door of the tabernacle of the congregation:

12 And the priest shall take one he-lamb, and offer him for a trespass offering, and the log of oil, and wave them *for* a wave offering before the LORD:

13 And he shall slay the lamb in the place where he shall kill the sin offering and the burnt offering, in the holy place: for as the sin offering *is* the priest's, *so is* the trespass offering: it *is* most holy:

14 And the priest shall take *some* of the blood of the trespass offering, and the priest shall put *it* upon the tip of the right ear of him that is to be cleansed, and upon the thumb of his right hand, and upon the great toe of his right foot:

15 And the priest shall take *some* of the log of oil, and pour *it* into the palm of his own left hand:

16 And the priest shall dip his right finger in the oil that *is* in his left hand, and shall sprinkle of the oil with his finger seven times before the LORD:

17 And of the rest of the oil that *is* in his hand shall the priest put upon the tip of the right ear of him that is to be cleansed, and upon the thumb of his right hand, and upon the great toe of his right foot, upon the blood of the trespass offering:

18 And the remnant of the oil that *is* in the priest's hand he shall pour upon the head of him that is to be cleansed: and the priest shall make an atonement for him before the LORD.

19 And the priest shall offer the sin offering, and make an atonement for him that is to be cleansed from his uncleanness; and afterward he shall kill the burnt offering:

20 And the priest shall offer the burnt offering and the meat offering upon the altar: and the priest shall make an atonement for him, and he shall be clean.

21 And if he *be* poor, and cannot get so much; then he shall take one lamb *for* a trespass offering to be waved, to make an atonement for him, and one tenth deal of fine flour mingled with oil for a meat offering, and a log of oil;

22 And two turtle-doves, or two young pigeons, such as he is able to get; and the one shall be a sin offering, and the other a burnt offering.

23 And he shall bring them on the eighth day for his cleansing unto the priest, unto the door of the tabernacle of the congregation, before the LORD.

24 And the priest shall take the lamb of the trespass offering, and the log of oil, and

the leprosy was distinguished by being in sight deeper than the skin; and the hair became thin and yellow. **38, 39. If a man or a woman have bright spots**—This modification of the leprosy is distinguished by a dull-white colour, and it is entirely a cutaneous disorder, never injuring the constitution. It is described as not penetrating below the skin of the flesh, and as not rendering necessary an exclusion from society. It is evident, then, that this common form of leprosy is not contagious, otherwise Moses would have prescribed as strict a quarantine in this as in the other cases. And hereby we see the great superiority of the Mosaic law, which so accurately distinguished the characters of the leprosy, and preserved to society the services of those who were labouring under the uncontagious forms of the disease, over the customs and regulations of Eastern countries in the present day, where all lepers are indiscriminately proscribed, and are avoided as unfit for free intercourse with their fellow-men. **40, 41. Bald ... forehead bald**—The falling off of the hair is another symptom which creates a suspicion of leprosy, when the baldness commences in the back part of the head. But it was not of itself a decisive sign unless when taken in connection with other tokens;—a "sore of a reddish white colour;" and the Hebrews as well as other Orientals were accustomed to distinguish between the forehead baldness, which might be natural, and that baldness which might be the consequence of disease. **45. Clothes rent, &c.**—The person who was declared affected with the leprosy forthwith exhibited all the tokens of suffering from a heavy calamity. Rending garments and uncovering the head were common signs of mourning. As to "the putting a covering upon the upper lip," that means either wearing a moustache, as the Hebrews used to shave the upper lip, [CALMET], or simply keeping a hand over it. All these external marks of grief were intended to proclaim, in addition to his own exclamation, "unclean!" that the person was a leper, whose company every one must shun. **46. dwell alone without the camp**—in a lazaretto by himself, or associated with other lepers. (2 Ki. 7. 3, 8.) **47-59. The garment that the leprosy is in**—It is well known that infectious diseases—such as scarlet fever, measles, the plague—are latently imbibed and carried by the clothes. But the language of this passage clearly indicates a disease to which clothes themselves were subject, and which was followed by effects on them analogous to those which malignant leprosy produces on the human body—for similar regulations were made for the rigid inspection of suspected garments by a priest, as for the examination of a leprous person. It has long been conjectured, and recently ascertained by the use of a lens, that the leprous condition of swine is produced by myriads of minute insects engendered in their skin; and regarding all leprosy as of the same nature, it is thought that this affords a sufficient reason for the injunction in the Mosaic law to destroy the clothes in which the disease, after careful observation, seemed to manifest itself. Clothes are sometimes seen contaminated by this disease in the West Indies and the southern parts of America, 'WHITLAW'S CODE OF HEALTH], and it may be presumed that as the Hebrews were living in the desert, where they had not the convenience of frequent changes and washing, the clothes they wore, and the skin mats on which they lay, would be apt to breed infectious vermin, which being settled in the stuff, would imperceptibly gnaw it, and leave stains similar to those described by Moses. It is well known that the wool of sheep dying of disease, if it had not been shorn from the animal while living, and also skins, if not thoroughly prepared by scouring, are liable to the effects described in this passage. The stains are described as of a greenish or reddish colour, according, perhaps, to the colour or nature of the ingredients used in preparing them; for acids convert blue vegetable colours into red, and alkalies change them into green. [BROWN.] It appears, then, that the leprosy, though sometimes inflicted as a miraculous judgment, (Nu. 12, 10; 2 Ki. 5. 27.), was a natural disease, which is known in Eastern countries still; while the rules prescribed by the Hebrew legislator for distinguishing the true character and varieties of the disease, and which are far superior to the method of treatment now followed in those regions, show the Divine wisdom by which he was guided. Doubtless the origin of the disease is owing to some latent causes in nature; and perhaps a more extended acquaintance with the archæology of Egypt, and the natural history of the adjacent countries, may confirm the opinion that the leprosy results from noxious insects or a putrid fermentation. But whatever the origin or cause of the disease, the laws enacted by Divine authority regarding it, while they pointed in the first instance to sanatory ends, were at the same time intended, by stimulating to carefulness against ceremonial defilement, to foster a spirit of religious fear and inward purity.

CHAPTER XIV.

Ver. 1-32. THE RITES AND SACRIFICES IN CLEANSING OF THE LEPER. **2. Law of the leper in the day of his cleansing**—Though quite convalescent, a leper was not allowed to return to society immediately and at his own will. The malignant character of his disease rendered the greatest precautions necessary to his re-admission amongst the people. One of the priests, most skilled in the diagnostics of disease [GROTIUS], being deputed to attend such outcasts, the restored leper compeared before this official, and when after examination a certificate of health was given, the ceremonies here described were forthwith observed outside the camp. **4. two birds**—*lit.* sparrows. The Septuagint, however, renders the expression "little birds;" and it is evident that it is to be taken in this generic sense from their being specified as "clean"—a condition which would have been altogether superfluous to mention in reference to sparrows. In all the offerings prescribed in the law, Moses ordered only common and accessible birds; and hence we may presume that he points here to such birds as sparrows or pigeons, as in the desert it might have been very difficult to procure wild birds alive. **Cedar wood, scarlet, and hyssop**—The cedar here meant was certainly not the famous tree of Lebanon, and it is generally supposed to have been the juniper,

the priest shall wave them *for* a wave offering before the LORD:

25 And he shall kill the lamb of the trespass offering, and the priest shall take some of the blood of the trespass offering, and put *it* upon the tip of the right ear of him that is to be cleansed, and upon the thumb of his right hand, and upon the great toe of his right foot:

26 And the priest shall pour of the oil into the palm of his own left hand:

27 And the priest shall sprinkle with his right finger *some* of the oil that *is* in his left hand seven times before the LORD:

28 And the priest shall put of the oil that *is* in his hand upon the tip of the right ear of him that is to be cleansed, and upon the thumb of his right hand, and upon the great toe of his right foot, upon the place of the blood of the trespass offering:

29 And the rest of the oil that *is* in the priest's hand he shall put upon the head of him that is to be cleansed, to make an atonement for him before the LORD.

30 And he shall offer the one of the turtle-doves, or of the young pigeons, such as he can get;

31 *Even* such as he is able to get, the one *for* a sin offering, and the other *for* a burnt offering, with the meat offering: and the priest shall make an atonement for him that is to be cleansed before the LORD.

32 This *is* the law *of him* in whom *is* the plague of leprosy, whose hand is not able to get *that which pertaineth* to his cleansing.

33 ¶ And the LORD spake unto Moses and unto Aaron, saying,

34 When ye be come into the land of Canaan, which I give to you for a possession, and I put the plague of leprosy in a house of the land of your possession;

35 And he that owneth the house shall come and tell the priest, saying, It seemeth to me there is as it were a plague in the house:

36 Then the priest shall command that they empty the house, before the priest go into it to see the plague, that all that is in the house be not made unclean: and afterward the priest shall go in to see the house.

37 And he shall look on the plague: and, behold, if the plague be in the walls of the house with hollow strakes, greenish or reddish, which in sight are lower than the wall;

38 Then the priest shall go out of the house to the door of the house, and shut up the house seven days:

39 And the priest shall come again the seventh day, and shall look: and, behold, if the plague be spread in the walls of the house;

40 Then the priest shall command that they take away the stones in which the plague is, and they shall cast them into an unclean place without the city:

41 And he shall cause the house to be scraped within round about, and they shall pour out the dust that they scrape off without the city into an unclean place:

42 And they shall take other stones, and put *them* in the place of those stones; and he shall take other mortar, and shall plaster the house.

43 And if the plague come again, and break out in the house, after that he hath taken away the stones, and after he hath scraped the house, and after it is plastered;

44 Then the priest shall come and look, and, behold, if the plague be spread in the house, it *is* a fretting leprosy in the house: it *is* unclean.

45 And he shall break down the house, the stones of it, and the timber thereof, and all the mortar of the house; and he shall carry *them* forth out of the city into an unclean place.

46 Moreover he that goeth into the house all the while that it is shut up shall be unclean until the even.

47 And he that lieth in the house shall wash his clothes; and he that eateth in the house shall wash his clothes.

48 And if the priest shall come in, and look *upon it*, and, behold, the plague hath not spread in the house, after the house was plastered; then the priest shall pronounce the house clean, because the plague is healed.

49 And he shall take to cleanse the house two birds, and cedar wood, and scarlet, and hyssop:

50 And he shall kill the one of the birds in an earthen vessel over running water:

51 And he shall take the cedar wood, and the hyssop, and the scarlet, and the living bird, and dip them in the blood of the slain bird, and in the running water, and sprinkle the house seven times:

52 And he shall cleanse the house with the blood of the bird, and with the running water, and with the living bird, and with the cedar wood, and with the hyssop, and with the scarlet:

53 But he shall let go the living bird out of the city into the open fields, and make an atonement for the house: and it shall be clean.

54 This *is* the law for all manner of plague of leprosy, and scall,

55 And for the leprosy of a garment, and of a house,

56 And for a rising, and for a scab, and for a bright spot;

57 To teach when *it is* unclean, and when *it is* clean: this *is* the law of leprosy.

CHAPTER XV.

1, 19 *The uncleanness of men and women by their issues.* 13. 28 *Their cleansing.*

AND the LORD spake unto Moses and to Aaron, saying,

2 Speak unto the children of Israel, and say unto them, "When any man hath a running issue out of his flesh, *because of* his issue he *is* unclean.

3 And this shall be his uncleanness in his issue: whether his flesh run with his issue, or his flesh be stopped from his issue, it *is* his uncleanness.

4 Every bed whereon he lieth that hath the issue is unclean; and every thing whereon he sitteth shall be unclean.

5 And whosoever toucheth his bed shal' wash his clothes, and bathe *himself* ir water, and be unclean until the even.

6 And he that sitteth on *any* thing whereon he sat that hath the issue shall wash his clothes, and bathe *himself* in water, and be unclean until the even.

7 And he that toucheth the flesh of him that hath the issue shall wash his clothes,

as several varieties of that shrub are found growing abundantly in the clefts and crevices of the Sinaitic mountains. A stick of this shrub was bound to a bunch of hyssop by a scarlet ribbon, and the living bird was to be so attached to it, that when they dipped the branches in the water, the tail of the bird might also be moistened, but not the head nor the wings, that it might not be impeded in its flight when let loose. 5. one of the birds be killed over running water—as the blood of a single bird would not have been sufficient to immerse the body of another bird, it was mingled with spring water to increase the quantity necessary for the appointed sprinklings, which were to be repeated *seven times*, denoting a complete purification. (See 2 Ki. 5. 10; Ps. 51. 2; M, 8. 4; L. 5, 14.) The living bird being then set free, in token of the leper's release from quarantine, the priest pronounced him clean; and this official declaration was made with all solemnity, in order both that the mind of the leper might be duly impressed with a sense of the Divine goodness, and that others might be satisfied they might safely hold intercourse with him. Several other purifications had to be gone through during a series of seven days, and the whole process had to be repeated on the seventh, ere he was allowed to re-enter the camp. The circumstance of a priest being employed seems to imply that instructions suitable to the newly recovered leper would be given, and that the symbolical ceremonies used in the process of cleansing leprosy would be explained. How far they were then understood we cannot tell. But we can trace some instructive analogies between the leprosy and the disease of sin, and between the rites observed in the process of cleansing leprosy and the provisions of the Gospel. The chief of these analogies are, that as it was only when a leper exhibited a certain change of state, that orders were given by the priest for a sacrifice, so a sinner must be in the exercise of faith and penitence ere the benefits of the Gospel remedy can be enjoyed by him. The slain bird and the bird let loose are supposed to typify, the one the death and the other the resurrection of Christ; while the sprinklings on him that had been leprous typified the requirements which led a believer to cleanse himself from all filthiness of the flesh and spirit, and to perfect his holiness in the fear of the Lord. 10-20. Two he-lambs and one ewe-lamb—The purification of the leper was not completed till at the end of seven days, after the ceremonial of the birds, and during which, though permitted to come into the camp, he had to tarry abroad out of his tent, from which he came daily to appear at the door of the tabernacle with the offerings required. He was presented before the Lord by the priest that made him clean. And hence it has always been reckoned amongst pious people the first duty of a patient newly restored from a long and dangerous sickness to repair to the Church to offer his thanksgiving, where his body and soul, in order to be an acceptable offering, must be presented by our great Priest, whose blood alone makes any clean. The offering was to consist of 3 lambs, 3 tenth-deals, or decimal parts of an ephah of fine flour—2 pints , and one log— ⅔ pint of oil. (ch. 2. 1.) One of the lambs was for a trespass-offering, which was necessary from the inherent sin of his nature, or from his defilement of the camp by his leprosy previous to his expulsion; and it is remarkable that the blood of the trespass-offering was applied exactly in the same particular manner to the extremities of the restored leper, as that of the ram in the consecration of the priests. The parts sprinkled with this blood were then anointed with oil—a ceremony which is supposed to have borne this spiritual import: that while the blood was a token of forgiveness, the oil was an emblem of healing—as the blood of Christ justifies, the influence of the Spirit sanctifies. Of the other two lambs—the one was to be a sin-offering, and the other a burnt-offering, which had also the character of a thank-offering for God's mercy in his restoration. And this was considered to make atonement "for him:" *i.e.*, it removed that ceremonial pollution which had excluded him from the enjoyment of religious ordinances, just as the atonement of Christ restores all who are cleansed through faith in his sacrifice to the privileges of the children of God. 21-32. If he be poor—a kind and considerate provision for an extension of the privilege to lepers of the poorer class. The blood of their smaller offering was to be applied in the same process of purification, and they were as publicly and completely cleansed as those who brought a costlier offering. (A. 10. 34. 34-48. leprosy in a house—This law was prospective, not being to come into operation till the settlement of the Israelites in Canaan. The words " I put the leprosy," has led many to think that this plague was a judicial infliction from heaven for the sins of the owner; while others do not regard it in this light, it being common in Scripture to represent God as doing that which He only permits in His providence to be done. Assuming it to have been a natural disease, a new difficulty arises as to whether we are to consider that the house had become infected by the contagion of leprous occupiers; or that the leprosy was in the house itself. It is evident that the latter was the true state of the case from the furniture being removed out of it on the first suspicion of disease on the walls. Some have supposed that the name of leprosy was analogically applied to it by the Hebrews, as we speak of cancer in trees, when they exhibit corrosive effects similar to what the disease so named produces on the human body; while others have pronounced it a mural efflorescence, or species of mil-dew on the wall, apt to be produced in very damp situations, and which was followed by effects so injurious to health as well as to the stability of a house, particularly in warm countries, as to demand the attention of a legislator. Moses enjoined the priests to follow the same course and during the same period of time for ascertaining the true character of this disease as in human leprosy, in case of being found leprous, to remove the infected parts, or if afterwards there appeared a risk of the contagion spreading, to destroy the house altogether, and remove the materials to a distance. The stones were probably rough unhewn stones, built up without cement in the manner now frequently used in fences, and plastered over, or else laid in mortar. The oldest examples of architecture are of this character. The very same thing has

and bathe *himself* in water, and be unclean until the even.

8 And if he that hath the issue spit upon him that is clean; then he shall wash his clothes, and bathe *himself* in water, and be unclean until the even.

9 And what saddle soever he rideth upon that hath the issue shall be unclean.

10 And whosoever toucheth any thing that was under him shall be unclean until the even: and he that beareth *any of* those things shall wash his clothes, and bathe *himself* in water, and be unclean until the even.

11 And whomsoever he toucheth that hath the issue, and hath not rinsed his hands in water, he shall wash his clothes, and bathe *himself* in water, and be unclean until the even.

12 And the vessel of earth that he toucheth which hath the issue shall be broken: and every vessel of wood shall be rinsed in water.

13 And when he that hath an issue is cleansed of his issue; then he shall number to himself seven days for his cleansing, and wash his clothes, and bathe his flesh in running water, and shall be clean.

14 And on the eighth day he shall take to him two turtle-doves, or two young pigeons, and come before the LORD unto the door of the tabernacle of the congregation, and give them unto the priest:

15 And the priest shall offer them, the one for a sin offering, and the other for a burnt offering; and the priest shall make an atonement for him before the LORD for his issue.

16 And if any man's seed of copulation go out from him, then he shall wash all his flesh in water, and be unclean until the even.

17 And every garment, and every skin, whereon is the seed of copulation, shall be washed with water, and be unclean until the even.

18 The woman also with whom man shall lie *with* seed of copulation, they shall both bathe *themselves* in water, and be unclean until the even.

19 ¶ And if a woman have an issue, *and* her issue in her flesh be blood, she shall be put apart seven days; and whosoever toucheth her shall be unclean until the even.

20 And every thing that she lieth upon in her separation shall be unclean: every thing also that she sitteth upon shall be unclean.

21 And whosoever toucheth her bed shall wash his clothes, and bathe *himself* in water, and be unclean until the even.

22 And whosoever toucheth any thing that she sat upon shall wash his clothes, and bathe *himself* in water, and be unclean until the even.

23 And if it *be* on *her* bed, or on any thing whereon she sitteth, when he toucheth it, he shall be unclean until the even.

24 And if any man lie with her at all, and her flowers be upon him, he shall be unclean seven days; and all the bed whereon he lieth shall be unclean.

25 And if a woman have an issue of her blood many days out of the time of her separation, or if it run beyond the time of her separation; all the days of the issue of her uncleanness shall be as the days of her separation: she *shall be* unclean.

26 Every bed whereon she lieth all the days of her issue shall be unto her as the bed of her separation: and whatsoever she sitteth upon shall be unclean, as the uncleanness of her separation.

27 And whosoever toucheth those things shall be unclean, and shall wash his clothes, and bathe *himself* in water, and be unclean until the even.

28 But if she be cleansed of her issue, then she shall number to herself seven days, and after that she shall be clean.

29 And on the eighth day she shall take unto her two turtles, or two young pigeons, and bring them unto the priest, to the door of the tabernacle of the congregation.

30 And the priest shall offer the one for a sin offering, and the other for a burnt offering; and the priest shall make an atonement for her before the LORD for the issue of her uncleanness.

31 Thus shall ye separate the children of Israel from their uncleanness; that they die not in their uncleanness, when they defile my tabernacle that *is* among them.

32 This *is* the law of him that hath an issue, and *of him* whose seed goeth from him, and is defiled therewith;

33 And of her that is sick of her flowers, and of him that hath an issue, of the man, and of the woman, and of him that lieth with her that is unclean.

CHAPTER XVI.

1 *How the high priest must enter into the holy place.* 11 *The sin offering for himself.* 15 *The sin offering for the people.* 20 *The scape-goat.* 29 *The yearly feast of the expiations.*

AND the LORD spake unto Moses, after the death of the two sons of Aaron, when they offered before the LORD, and died;

2 And the LORD said unto Moses, Speak unto Aaron thy brother, that he come not at all times into the holy *place* within the veil before the mercyseat, which *is* upon the ark, that he die not: for I will appear in the cloud upon the mercyseat.

3 Thus shall Aaron come into the holy *place:* with a young bullock for a sin offering, and a ram for a burnt offering.

4 He shall put on the holy linen coat, and he shall have the linen breeches upon his flesh, and shall be girded with a linen girdle, and with the linen mitre shall he be attired: these *are* holy garments; therefore shall he wash his flesh in water, and so put them on.

5 And he shall take of the congregation of the children of Israel two kids of the goats for a sin offering, and one ram for a burnt offering.

6 And Aaron shall offer his bullock of the sin offering which *is* for himself, and make an atonement for himself, and for his house.

7 And he shall take the two goats, and present them before the LORD at the door of the tabernacle of the congregation.

8 And Aaron shall cast lots upon the two goats; one lot for the LORD, and the other lot for the scape-goat.

9 And Aaron shall bring the goat upon which the LORD's lot fell, and offer him for a sin offering;

10 But the goat, on which the lot fell to be the scape-goat, shall be presented alive

to be done still with houses infected with mural salt. The stones covered with the nitrous incrustation must be removed, and if the infected walls is suffered to remain, it must be plastered all over anew. **48-57.** The priest shall pronounce the house clean—The precautions here described show that there is great danger in warm countries from the house leprosy, which was likely to be increased by the smallness and rude architecture of the houses in the early ages of the Israelitish history. As a house could not contract any impurity in the sight of God, the "atonement" which the priest was to make for it must either have a reference to the sins of its occupiers, or to the ceremonial process appointed for its purification the very same as that observed for a leprous person. This solemn declaration that it was "clean," as well as the offering made on the occasion, were admirably calculated to make known the fact, to remove apprehension from the public mind as well as relieve the owner from the aching suspicion of dwelling in an infected house.

CHAPTER XV.

Ver. 1-18. UNCLEANNESS OF MEN. **2.** when any man hath a running issue—This chapter describes other forms of uncleanness, the nature of which is sufficiently intelligible in the text without any explanatory comment. Being the effects of licentiousness, they properly came within the notice of the legislator, and the very stringent rules here prescribed both for the separation of the person diseased, and for avoiding contamination from anything connected with him, were well calculated not only to prevent contagion, but to discourage the excesses of licentious indulgence. **9.** saddle he rideth upon. (See on Ge. 31. 34.) **12.** the vessel of earth shall be broken—It is thought the pottery of the Israelites, like the earthenware jars in which the Egyptians kept their water was unglazed, and consequently porous, and that it was its porousness which, rendering it extremely liable to imbibe small particles of impure matter, was the reason of the vessel touched by an unclean person being ordered to be broken. **13, 14.** number to himself seven days —Like a leprous person he underwent a week's probation, whether he was completely healed, and then with the sacrifices prescribed the priest made an atonement for him, *i.e.*, offered the oblations necessary for the removal of his ceremonial defilement, as well as the typical pardon of his sins.

19-33. UNCLEANNESS OF WOMEN. If a woman have an issue—Though this, like the leprosy, might be a natural affection, it was anciently considered contagious, and entailed a ceremonial defilement which typified a moral impurity. This ceremonial defilement had to be removed by an appointed method of ceremonial expiation, and the neglect of it subjected any one to the guilt of defiling the tabernacle, and to death as the penalty of profane temerity. **31-33.** Thus shall ye separate ... from their uncleanness—The divine wisdom was manifested in inspiring the Israelites with a profound reverence for holy things; and nothing was more suited to this purpose than to debar from the tabernacle all who were polluted by any kind of uncleanness, ceremonial as well as natural, mental as well as physical. The better to mark out that people as his family, his servants and priests, dwelling in the camp as in a holy place, consecrated by his presence and his tabernacle, he required of them complete purity and did not allow them to come before him when defiled, even by involuntary or secret impurities, as a want of respect due to his majesty. And when we bear in mind that God was training up a people to live in his presence in some measure as priests devoted to his service, we shall not consider these rules for the maintenance of personal purity either too stringent or too minute. (1 Thess. 4. 4.)

CHAPTER XVI.

Ver. 1-34. HOW THE HIGH PRIEST MUST ENTER INTO THE HOLY PLACE. **1.** After the death of the two sons of Aaron—It is thought by some that this chapter has been transposed out of its right place in the sacred record, which was immediately after the narrative of the deaths of Nadab and Abihu. That appalling catastrophe must have filled Aaron with painful apprehensions, lest the guilt of those two sons might be entailed on his house, or that other members of his family might share the same fate by some irregularities or defects in the discharge of their sacred functions. And, therefore, this law was established, by the due observance of whose requirements the Aaronic order would be securely maintained and accepted in the priesthood. **2.** not come at all times, &c.—Common priests went every day to burn incense on the golden altar into the part of the sanctuary *without* the veil. But none except the high priest was allowed to enter *within* the veil, and that, only once a year with the greatest care and solemnity. This arrangement was evidently designed to inspire a reverence for the most holy place, and the precaution was necessary, at a time when the presence of God was indicated by sensible symbols, the impression of which might have been diminished or lost by daily and familiar observation. I will appear in the cloud—*i.e.*, the smoke of the incense which the high priest burnt on his yearly entrance into the most holy place; and this was the cloud which at that time covered the mercy-seat. **3, 4.** Thus shall Aaron come—As the duties of the great day of atonement led to the nearest and most solemn approach to God, the directions as to the proper course to be followed were minute and special. **with a young bullock and a ram**— These victims he brought alive, but they were not offered in sacrifice till he had gone through the ceremonies described between this and the 11th verse. He was not to attire himself on that occasion in the splendid robes that were proper to his sacred office, but in a plain dress of linen, like the common Levites,—for, as he was then to make atonement for his own sins, as well as for those of the people, he was to appear in the humble character of a suppliant. That plain dress was more in harmony with a season of humiliation, as well as lighter and more convenient for the duties which on that occasion he had singly to perform, than the gorgeous robes of the pontificate. It shewed that when all appeared as sinners, the highest and lowest were then on a level, and that there is no distinction of persons with God. **5-10. shall take of the congregation two kids of the goat**

before the LORD, to make an atonement with him, and to let him go for a scape-goat into the wilderness.

11 And Aaron shall bring the bullock of the sin offering which is for himself, and shall make an atonement for himself, and for his house, and shall kill the bullock of the sin offering which is for himself:

12 And he shall take a censer full of burning coals of fire from off the altar before the LORD, and his hands full of sweet incense beaten small, and bring it within the veil:

13 And he shall put the incense upon the fire before the LORD, that the cloud of the incense may cover the mercyseat that is upon the testimony, that he die not:

14 And he shall take of the blood of the bullock, and sprinkle it with his finger upon the mercyseat eastward; and before the mercyseat shall he sprinkle of the blood with his finger seven times.

15 Then shall he kill the goat of the sin offering, that is for the people, and bring his blood within the veil, and do with that blood as he did with the blood of the bullock, and sprinkle it upon the mercyseat, and before the mercyseat:

16 And he shall make an atonement for the holy place, because of the uncleanness of the children of Israel, and because of their transgressions in all their sins: and so shall he do for the tabernacle of the congregation, that remaineth among them in the midst of their uncleanness.

17 And there shall be no man in the tabernacle of the congregation when he goeth in to make an atonement in the holy place, until he come out, and have made an atonement for himself, and for his household, and for all the congregation of Israel.

18 And he shall go out unto the altar that is before the LORD, and make an atonement for it; and shall take of the blood of the bullock, and of the blood of the goat, and put it upon the horns of the altar round about.

19 And he shall sprinkle of the blood upon it with his finger seven times, and cleanse it, and hallow it from the uncleanness of the children of Israel.

20 ¶ And when he hath made an end of reconciling the holy place, and the tabernacle of the congregation, and the altar, he shall bring the live goat:

21 And Aaron shall lay both his hands upon the head of the live goat, and confess over him all the iniquities of the children of Israel, and all their transgressions in all their sins, putting them upon the head of the goat, and shall send him away by the hand of a fit man into the wilderness.

22 And the goat shall bear upon him all their iniquities unto a land not inhabited: and he shall let go the goat in the wilderness.

23 And Aaron shall come into the tabernacle of the congregation, and shall put off the linen garments which he put on when he went into the holy place, and shall leave them there:

24 And he shall wash his flesh with water in the holy place, and put on his garments, and come forth, and offer his burnt offering, and the burnt offering of the people, and make an atonement for himself, and for the people.

25 And the fat of the sin offering shall he burn upon the altar.

26 And he that let go the goat for the scape-goat shall wash his clothes, and bathe his flesh in water, and afterward come into the camp.

27 And the bullock for the sin offering, and the goat for the sin offering, whose blood was brought in to make atonement in the holy place, shall one carry forth without the camp; and they shall burn in the fire their skins, and their flesh, and their dung.

28 And he that burneth them shall wash his clothes, and bathe his flesh in water, and afterward he shall come into the camp.

29 ¶ And this shall be a statute for ever unto you, that in the seventh month, on the tenth day of the month, ye shall afflict your souls, and do no work at all, whether it be one of your own country, or a stranger that sojourneth among you:

30 For on that day shall the priest make an atonement for you, to cleanse you, that ye may be clean from all your sins before the LORD.

31 It shall be a sabbath of rest unto you, and ye shall afflict your souls, by a statute for ever.

32 And the priest whom he shall anoint, and whom he shall consecrate to minister in the priest's office in his father's stead, shall make the atonement, and shall put on the linen clothes, even the holy garments.

33 And he shall make an atonement for the holy sanctuary, and he shall make an atonement for the tabernacle of the congregation, and for the altar, and he shall make an atonement for the priests, and for all the people of the congregation.

34 And this shall be an everlasting statute unto you, to make an atonement for the children of Israel, for all their sins, once a year. And he did as the LORD commanded Moses.

CHAPTER XVII.

1 *Blood of beasts must be offered at the tabernacle door.* 10 *Eating of blood forbidden.*

AND the LORD spake unto Moses, saying,

2 Speak unto Aaron, and unto his sons, and unto all the children of Israel, and say unto them, This is the thing which the LORD hath commanded, saying,

3 What man soever there be of the house of Israel that killeth an ox, or lamb, or goat, in the camp, or that killeth it out of the camp,

4 And bringeth it not unto the door of the tabernacle of the congregation, to offer an offering unto the LORD before the tabernacle of the LORD, blood shall be imputed unto that man; he hath shed blood; and that man shall be cut off from among his people:

5 To the end that the children of Israel may bring their sacrifices, which they offer in the open field, even that they may bring them unto the LORD, unto the door of the tabernacle of the congregation, unto the priest, and offer them for peace offerings unto the LORD.

6 And the priest shall sprinkle the blood upon the altar of the LORD at the door of the tabernacle of the congregation, and burn the fat for a sweet savour unto the LORD.

and a ram—The sacrifices were to be offered by the high priest respectively for himself and the other priests, as well as for the people. The bullock (v. 3) and the goats were for sin offerings, and the rams for burnt offerings. The goats, though used in different ways, constituted only one offering. They were both presented before the Lord, and the disposal of them determined by lot, which Jewish writers have thus described:—The priest, placing one of the goats on his right hand, and the other on his left, took his station by the altar, and cast into an urn two pieces of gold exactly similar, inscribed, the one with the words "for the Lord," and the other for "Azazel," (the scape-goat.) After having well shaken them together, he put both his hands into the box and took up a lot in each; that in his right hand he put on the head of the goat which stood on his right, and that in his left he dropt on the other. In this manner the fate of each was decided. **11-14. Aaron shall bring the bullock, &c.**—The first part of the service was designed to solemnize his own mind, as well as the minds of the people, by offering the sacrifices for their sins. The sin offerings being slain had the sins of the offerer judicially transferred to them by the imputation of his hands on their head, (ch. 4.) and thus the young bullock, which was to make atonement for himself and the other priests, called his house, Ps. 135. 19,) was killed by the hands of the high priest. While the blood of the victim was being received into a vessel, taking a censer of live coals in his right hand, and a platter of sweet incense in his left, he, amid the solemn attention and the anxious prayers of the assembled multitude, crossed the porch and the Holy Place, opened the outer veil which led into the holy of holies, then the inner veil, and, standing before the ark, deposited the censer of coals on the floor, emptied the plate of incense into his hand, poured it on the burning coals, and the apartment was filled with fragrant smoke, intended, according to Jewish writers, to prevent any presumptuous gazer prying too curiously into the form of the mercy seat, which was the Lord's throne. The high priest having done this, perfumed the sanctuary, returned to the door, took the blood of the slain bullock, and carrying it into the Holy of Holies, sprinkled it with his finger once upon the mercy seat "eastward,"—*i.e.*, on the side next to himself; and seven times "before the mercy seat,"—*i.e.*, on the front of the ark. Leaving the coals and the incense burning, he went out a second time, to sacrifice at the altar of burnt offering the goat which had been assigned as a sin offering for the people; and carrying its blood into the Holy of Holies, made similar sprinklings as he had done before with the blood of the bullock. While the high priest was thus engaged in the most holy place, none of the ordinary priests were allowed to remain within the precincts of the tabernacle. The Sanctuary or Holy place, and the altar of burnt offering were in like manner sprinkled seven times with the blood of the bullock and the goat. The object of this solemn ceremonial was to impress the minds of the Israelites with the conviction that the whole tabernacle was stained by the sins of a guilty people, that by their sins they had forfeited the privileges of the divine presence and worship, and that an atonement had to be made as the condition of God's remaining with them. The sins and shortcomings of the past year having polluted the sacred edifice, the expiation required to be annually renewed. The exclusion of the priests indicated their unworthiness, and the impurities of their service. The mingled blood of the two victims being sprinkled on the horns of the altar indicated that the priests and the people equally needed an atonement for their sins. But the sanctuary being thus ceremonially purified, and the people of Israel reconciled by the blood of the consecrated victim, the Lord continued to dwell in the midst of them, and honour them with his gracious presence. **20-22. he shall bring the live goat**—Having already been presented before the Lord, (v. 10,) it was now brought forward to the high priest, who, placing his hands upon its head, and "having confessed over it all the iniquities of the people of Israel, and all their transgressions in all their sins," transferred them by this act to the goat as their substitute. It was then delivered into the hands of a person, who was appointed to lead him away into a distant, solitary, and desert place, where in early times he was let go, to escape for his life, but in the time of Christ, was carried to a high rock 12 miles from Jerusalem, and there, being thrust over the precipice, he was killed. Commentators have differed widely in their opinions about the character and purpose of this part of the ceremonial; some considering the word Azazel, with the Seventy; and our translators to mean "the scape goat;" others, "a lofty, precipitous rock," [BOCHART]; others, "a thing separated to God," [EWALD, THOLUCK]; while others think it designates Satan, [GESENIUS, HENG.] This last view is grounded on the idea of both goats forming one and the same sacrifice of atonement, and it is supported by Zech. 3. which presents a striking commentary on this passage. Whether there was in this peculiar ceremony any reference to an Egyptian superstition about Typhon, the spirit of evil, inhabiting the wilderness, and the design was to ridicule it by sending a cursed animal into his gloomy dominions, it is impossible to say. The subject is involved in much obscurity. But in any view there seems to be a typical reference to Christ who bore away our sins. **23-28. Aaron shall come into the tabernacle**—On the dismissal of the scape-goat, the high priest prepared for the important parts of the service which still remained; and for the performance of these he laid aside his plain linen clothes, and having bathed himself in water, he assumed his pontifical dress. Thus gorgeously attired, he went to present the burnt-offerings which were prescribed for himself and the people, consisting of the two rams which had been brought with the sin-offerings, but reserved till now. The fat was ordered to be burnt upon the altar; the rest of the carcases to be cut down and given to some priestly attendants to burn without the camp, in conformity with the general law for the sin-offerings, (ch. 4. 8-12; 8. 14-17.) The persons employed in burning them, as well as the conductor of the scape-goat, were obliged to wash their clothes and bathe their flesh in water before they were allowed to return into the camp. **29-34. This shall be a**

7 And they shall no more offer their sacrifices unto devils, after whom they have gone a whoring. This shall be a statute for ever unto them throughout their generations.

8 And thou shalt say unto them, Whatsoever man *there be* of the house of Israel, or of the strangers which sojourn among you, that offereth a burnt offering or sacrifice,

9 And bringeth it not unto the door of the tabernacle of the congregation, to offer it unto the LORD, even that man shall be cut off from among his people.

10 ¶ And whatsoever man *there be* of the house of Israel, or of the strangers that sojourn among you, that eateth any manner of blood; I will even set my face against that soul that eateth blood, and will cut him off from among his people.

11 For the life of the flesh *is* in the blood: and I have given it to you upon the altar to make an atonement for your souls: for it *is* the blood *that* maketh an atonement for the soul.

12 Therefore I said unto the children of Israel, No soul of you shall eat blood, neither shall any stranger that sojourneth among you eat blood.

13 And whatsoever man *there be* of the children of Israel, or of the strangers that sojourn among you, which hunteth and catcheth any beast or fowl that may be eaten; he shall even pour out the blood thereof, and cover it with dust.

14 For *it is* the life of all flesh; the blood of it *is* for the life thereof: therefore I said unto the children of Israel, Ye shall eat the blood of no manner of flesh: for the life of all flesh *is* the blood thereof: whosoever eateth it shall be cut off.

15 And every soul that eateth that which died *of itself*, or that which was torn *with beasts*, *whether it be* one of your own country, or a stranger, he shall both wash his clothes, and bathe *himself* in water, and be unclean until the even; then shall he be clean.

16 But if he wash *them* not, nor bathe his flesh, then he shall bear his iniquity.

CHAPTER XVIII.

6 *Unlawful marriages.* 19 *Unlawful lusts.*

AND the LORD spake unto Moses, saying,
2 Speak unto the children of Israel, and say unto them, I am the LORD your God.

3 After the doings of the land of Egypt, wherein ye dwelt, shall ye not do: and after the doings of the land of Canaan, whither I bring you, shall ye not do; neither shall ye walk in their ordinances.

4 Ye shall do my judgments, and keep mine ordinances, to walk therein: I am the LORD your God.

5 Ye shall therefore keep my statutes, and my judgments; which if a man do, he shall live in them: I am the LORD.

6 ¶ None of you shall approach to any that is near of kin to him, to uncover *their* nakedness: I am the LORD.

7 The nakedness of thy father, or the nakedness of thy mother, shalt thou not uncover: she *is* thy mother; thou shalt not uncover her nakedness.

8 The nakedness of thy father's wife shalt thou not uncover: it *is* thy father's nakedness.

9 The nakedness of thy sister, the daughter of thy father, or daughter of thy mother, whether *she be* born at home, or born abroad, *even* their nakedness thou shalt not uncover.

10 The nakedness of thy son's daughter, or of thy daughter's daughter, *even* their nakedness thou shalt not uncover: for theirs is thine own nakedness.

11 The nakedness of thy father's wife's daughter, begotten of thy father, (she *is* thy sister,) thou shalt not uncover her nakedness.

12 Thou shalt not uncover the nakedness of thy father's sister: she *is* thy father's near kinswoman.

13 Thou shalt not uncover the nakedness of thy mother's sister: for she *is* thy mother's near kinswoman.

14 Thou shalt not uncover the nakedness of thy father's brother, thou shalt not approach to his wife: she *is* thine aunt.

15 Thou shalt not uncover the nakedness of thy daughter-in-law: she *is* thy son's wife; thou shalt not uncover her nakedness.

16 Thou shalt not uncover the nakedness of thy brother's wife: it *is* thy brother's nakedness.

17 Thou shalt not uncover the nakedness of a woman and her daughter, neither shalt thou take her son's daughter, or her daughter's daughter, to uncover her nakedness; *for* they *are* her near kinswomen: it *is* wickedness.

18 Neither shalt thou take a wife to her sister, to vex her, to uncover her nakedness, besides the other in her life-*time*.

19 Also thou shalt not approach unto a woman to uncover her nakedness as long as she is put apart for her uncleanness.

20 Moreover thou shalt not lie carnally with thy neighbour's wife, to defile thyself with her.

21 And thou shalt not let any of thy seed pass through *the fire* to Molech, neither shalt thou profane the name of thy God: I am the LORD.

22 Thou shalt not lie with mankind as with womankind: it *is* abomination.

23 Neither shalt thou lie with any beast to defile thyself therewith; neither shall any woman stand before a beast to lie down thereto: it *is* confusion.

24 Defile not ye yourselves in any of these things: for in all these the nations are defiled which I cast out before you:

25 And the land is defiled: therefore I do visit the iniquity thereof upon it, and the land itself vomiteth out her inhabitants.

26 Ye shall therefore keep my statutes and my judgments, and shall not commit *any* of these abominations; neither any of your own nation, nor any stranger that sojourneth among you;

27 (For all these abominations have the men of the land done which *were* before you, and the land is defiled:)

28 That the land spue not you out also, when ye defile it, as it spued out the nations that *were* before you.

29 For whosoever shall commit any of these abominations, even the souls that commit *them* shall be cut off from among their people.

30 Therefore shall ye keep mine ordinance, that ye commit not *any* one of these abominable customs, which were committed before you, and that ye defile not yourselves therein: I am the LORD your God.

statute for ever unto you—This day of annual expiation for all the sins, irreverences and impurities of all classes in Israel during the previous year, was to be observed as a solemn fast, in which "they were to afflict their souls;" it was reckoned a Sabbath—kept as a season of "holy convocation," or assembling for religious purposes, and the persons who performed any labour were subject to the penalty of death. It took place on the tenth day of the seventh month, corresponding to our 3rd of October, and this chapter, together with ch. 23. 27-32, as containing special allusion to the observances of the day were publicly read. The rehearsal of these passages appointing the solemn ceremonial was very appropriate, and the details of the successive parts of it—above all the spectacle of the public departure of the scape-goat under the care of its leader, must have produced salutary impressions both of sin and of duty that would not be soon effaced.

CHAPTER XVII.

Ver. 1-16. BLOOD OF BEASTS MUST BE OFFERED AT THE TABERNACLE DOOR. 3. What man killeth an ox?—The Israelites, like other people, living in the desert, would not make much use of animal food, and when they did kill a lamb or a kid for food, it would almost always be as in Abraham's entertainment of the angels, on occasion of a feast, to be eaten in company. This was what was done with the peace-offerings, and accordingly it is here enacted, that the same course shall be followed in slaughtering the animals as in the case of those offerings, viz., that they should be killed publicly, and after being devoted to God, partaken of by the officers. This law, it is obvious, could only be observable in the wilderness, while the people were encamped within an accessible distance from the tabernacle. The reason of it is to be found in the strong addictedness of the Israelites to idolatry at the time of their departure from Egypt; and as it would have been easy for any by killing an animal, to sacrifice privately to a favourite object of worship, a strict prohibition was made against their slaughtering at home. (See on Deut. 12. 13.) 5. they offer in the open field—"they" is supposed by some commentators, to refer to the Egyptians, so that the verse will stand thus: "the children of Israel may bring their sacrifices which they (the Egyptians) offer in the open field." The law is thought to have been directed against numbers whose Egyptian habits led them to imitate this idolatrous practice. 7. devils—*lit.* "goats." The prohibition evidently alludes to the worship of the hirei-footed kind such as Pan, Faunus, and Saturn, whose recognised symbol was a goat. This was a form of idolatry enthusiastically practised by the Egyptians, particularly in the nome or province of Mendes. Pan was supposed especially to preside over mountainous and desert regions, and it was while they were in the wilderness the Israelites seem to have been powerfully influenced by a feeling to propitiate this idol. Moreover, the ceremonies observed in this idolatrous worship, were extremely licentious and obscene, and the gross impurity of the rites gives great point and significance to the expression of Moses, "they have gone a whoring." 8, 9. Whatsoever man offereth, and bringeth it not unto the door—Before the promulgation of the law, men worshipped wherever they pleased or pitched their tents. But after that event the rites of religion could be acceptably performed only at the appointed place of worship. This restriction with respect to place was necessary as a preventive of idolatry; for it prohibited the Israelites, when at a distance from repairing to the altars of the heathen, which were commonly in groves or fields. 10. I will set my face against that soul that eateth blood—The face of God is often used in scripture to denote his anger, (Ps. 34. 16; Rev. 6. 16; Ez. 38. 18,) and the manner in which God's face would be set against such an offender, was, that if the crime were public and known, he was condemned to death; if it were secret, vengeance would overtake him. (See on Gen. 9. 4.) But the practice against which the law is here pointed was an idolatrous rite. The Zabians, or worshippers of the heavenly host, were accustomed, in sacrificing animals, to pour out the blood, and eat a part of the flesh at *the place* where the blood was poured out, and sometimes the blood itself, believing that by means of it, friendship, brotherhood and familiarity were contracted between the worshippers and the deities. They, moreover, supposed that the blood was very beneficial in obtaining for them a vision of the demon during their sleep, and a revelation of future events. The prohibition against eating blood, viewed in the light of this historic commentary, and unconnected with the peculiar terms in which it is expressed, seems to have been levelled against idolatrous practices, as is still farther evident from (Ez. 33. 25, 26; 1 Cor. 10. 20, 21.) 11. I have given it to you upon the altar—God, as the sovereign author and proprietor of nature, reserved the blood to himself, and allowed men only one use of it—in the way of sacrifices. 13, 14. whatsoever man hunteth—It was customary with heathen sportsmen, when they killed any game or venison, to pour out the blood as a libation to the god of the chase. The Israelites, on the contrary, were enjoined, instead of leaving it exposed, to cover it with dust, and, by this means, were effectually debarred from all the superstitious uses to which the heathen applied it. 15, 16. Every soul that eateth that which died of itself—Ex. 22. 31; ch. 11. 39; Acts, 15. 20. shall be unclean until the even—*i.e.*, from the moment of his discovering his fault, until the evening. This law, however, was binding only on an Israelite. (See Deu. 14. 21.)

CHAPTER XVIII.

Ver. 1-30. UNLAWFUL MARRIAGES. 2-4. I am the Lord your God—This renewed mention of the divine sovereignty over the Israelites was intended to bear particularly on some laws that were widely different from the social customs, that obtained both in Egypt and Canaan; for the enormities which the laws enumerated in this chapter were intended to put down, were freely practised or publicly sanctioned in both of those countries; and, indeed, the extermination of the ancient Canaanites is described as owing to the abominations with which they had polluted the land. 5. which if a man do, he shall live in them—A special blessing was promised to the Israelites on condition of their obedience to the divine law; and this promise was remarkably verified at particular eras of their history, when pure and undefiled religion

CHAPTER XIX.
A repetition of sundry laws.

AND the LORD spake unto Moses, saying,
2 Speak unto all the congregation of the children of Israel, and say unto them, Ye *a* shall be holy: for I the LORD your God *am* holy.
3 ¶ Ye shall fear every man his mother and his father, and *b* keep my sabbaths: I *am* the LORD your God.
4 ¶ Turn *c* ye not unto idols, nor make to yourselves molten gods: I *am* the LORD your God.
5 ¶ And if ye offer a sacrifice of peace offerings unto the LORD, ye shall offer it at your own will.
6 It shall be eaten the same day ye offer it, and on the morrow: and if ought remain until the third day, it shall be burnt in the fire.
7 And if it be eaten at all on the third day, it *is* abominable; it shall not be accepted.
8 Therefore every one that eateth it shall bear his iniquity, because he hath profaned the hallowed thing of the LORD: and that soul shall be cut off from among his people.
9 ¶ And *d* when ye reap the harvest of your land, thou shalt not wholly reap the corners of thy field, neither shalt thou gather the gleanings of thy harvest.
10 And thou shalt not glean thy vineyard, neither shalt thou gather *every* grape of thy vineyard; thou shalt leave them *e* for the poor and stranger: I *am* the LORD your God.
11 ¶ Ye shall not steal, neither deal falsely, neither *f* lie one to another.
12 ¶ And ye shall not swear by my name falsely, neither shalt thou profane the name of thy God: I *am* the LORD.
13 ¶ Thou shalt not defraud thy neighbour, neither rob *him*: *g* the wages of him that is hired shall not abide with thee all night until the morning.
14 ¶ Thou shalt not curse the deaf, *h* nor put a stumblingblock before the blind, but shalt *i* fear thy God: I *am* the LORD.
15 ¶ Ye *j* shall do no unrighteousness in judgment: thou shalt not respect the person of the poor, nor honour the person of the mighty: *but* in righteousness shalt thou judge thy neighbour.
16 ¶ Thou shalt not go up and down *as a* tale-bearer among thy people; neither shalt thou *k* stand against the blood of thy neighbour: I *am* the LORD.
17 ¶ Thou *l* shalt not hate thy brother in thine heart: *m* thou shalt in any wise rebuke thy neighbour, *1* and not suffer sin upon him.
18 ¶ Thou *n* shalt not avenge, nor bear any grudge against the children of thy people; *o* but thou shalt love thy neighbour as thyself: I *am* the LORD.
19 ¶ Ye shall keep my statutes. Thou shalt not let thy cattle gender with a diverse kind: thou shalt not sow thy field with mingled seed: neither shall a garment mingled of linen and woollen come upon thee.
20 ¶ And whosoever lieth carnally with a woman that *is* a bondmaid, *2* betrothed to an husband, and not at all redeemed, nor freedom given her; *3* she shall be scourged; they shall not be put to death, because she was not free.
21 And he shall bring his trespass offering unto the LORD, unto the door of the tabernacle of the congregation, *even* a ram for a trespass offering.
22 And the priest shall make an atonement for him with the ram of the trespass offering before the LORD for his sin which he hath done: and the sin which he hath done shall be forgiven him.
23 ¶ And when ye shall come into the land, and shall have planted all manner of trees for food, then ye shall count the fruit thereof as uncircumcised: three years shall it be as uncircumcised unto you: it shall not be eaten of.
24 But in the fourth year all the fruit thereof shall be *4* holy, *p* to praise the LORD withal.
25 And in the fifth year shall ye eat of the fruit thereof, that it may yield unto you the increase thereof: I *am* the LORD your God.
26 ¶ Ye shall not eat *any thing* with the blood: *q* neither shall ye use enchantment, nor observe times.
27 ¶ Ye *r* shall not round the corners of your heads, neither shalt thou mar the corners of thy beard.
28 ¶ Ye shall not *s* make any cuttings in your flesh for the dead, nor print any marks upon you: I *am* the LORD.
29 ¶ Do *t* not *5* prostitute thy daughter, to cause her to be a whore; lest the land fall to whoredom, and the land become full of wickedness.
30 ¶ Ye *u* shall keep my sabbaths, and reverence *1* my sanctuary: I *am* the LORD.
31 ¶ Regard *w* not them that have familiar spirits, neither seek after wizards, to be defiled by them: I *am* the LORD your God.
32 ¶ Thou *x* shalt rise up before the hoary head, and honour the face of the old man, and fear thy God: I *am* the LORD.
33 ¶ And *y* if a stranger sojourn with thee in your land, ye shall not *6* vex him.
34 *But 5* the stranger that dwelleth with you shall be unto you as one born among you, and *a* thou shalt love him as thyself; for ye were strangers in the land of Egypt: I *am* the LORD your God.
35 ¶ Ye shall do no unrighteousness in judgment, in mete-yard, in weight, or in measure.
36 Just *b* balances, just *7* weights, a just ephah, and a just hin, shall ye have: I *am* the LORD your God, which brought you out of the land of Egypt.
37 Therefore *c* shall ye observe all my statutes, and all my judgments, and do them: I *am* the LORD.

CHAPTER XX.

1 *Of him that giveth of his seed unto Molech:* 4 *of him that favoureth such an one:* 6 *of going to wizards:* 7 *of sanctification:* 9 *of him that curseth his parents:* 10 *of adultery:* 11, 14, 17, 19 *of incest:* 13 *of sodomy, etc.*

AND the LORD spake unto Moses, saying, 2 Again, thou shalt say to the children of Israel, *a* Whosoever *he be* of the children of Israel, or of the strangers that sojourn in Israel, that giveth *any* of his seed unto Molech, he shall surely be put to death: the people of the land shall stone him with stones.
3 And I will set my face against that man, and will cut him off from among his people; because he hath given of his seed unto Molech, to *b* defile my sanctuary, and to profane my holy name.

prevailed among them, in the public prosperity and domestic happiness enjoyed by them as a people. Obedience to the divine law always, indeed, ensures temporal advantages; and this, doubtless, was the primary meaning of the words, "which if a man do, he shall live in them." But that they had a higher reference to spiritual life is evident from the application made of them by our Lord, (L. 10, 28, and the apostle, (Ro. 10. 5.) 6. None of you shall approach any that is near of kin—Very great laxity prevailed amongst the Egyptians in their sentiments and practice about the conjugal relation, as they not only openly sanctioned marriages between brothers and sisters, but even between parents and children. Such incestuous alliances Moses wisely prohibited, and his laws form the basis on which the marriage regulations of this and other Christian nations are chiefly founded. 21. Thou shalt not let any of thy seed pass, &c.—Molech, or Moloch, which signifies "king," was the idol of the Ammonites. His statue was of brass, and rested on a pedestal or throne of the same metal. His head, resembling that of a calf, was adorned with a crown, and his arms were extended in the attitude of embracing those who approached him. His devotees dedicated their children to him, and when this was to be done, they heated the statue to a high pitch of intensity by a fire within; and then the infants were either shaken over the flames, or passed through the ignited arms, by way of lustration to ensure the favour of the pretended deity. The fire-worshippers asserted, that all children who did not undergo this purifying process would die in infancy; and the influence of this Zabian superstition was still so extensively prevalent in the days of Moses, that the divine law-giver judged it necessary to prohibit it by an express statute. neither shalt thou profane the name of thy God—by giving it to false or pretended divinities; or, perhaps, from this precept standing in close connection with the worship of Molech, the meaning rather is—do not, by devoting your children to him, give foreigners occasion to blaspheme the name of your God as a cruel and sanguinary deity, who demands the sacrifice of human victims, and who encourages cruelty in his votaries. 24-30. In all these the nations are defiled, &c.—Ancient history gives many appalling proofs that the enormous vices described in this chapter were very prevalent, nay, were regularly practised from religious motives in the temples of Egypt and the groves of Canaan, and it was these gigantic social disorders that occasioned the expulsion, of which the Israelites were, in the hands of a righteous and retributive providence, the appointed instruments. (Gen. 15. 16.) The strongly figurative language of "the land itself vomiting out her inhabitants," shows the hopeless depth of their moral corruption. 30. Therefore ye shall keep mine ordinances—In giving the Israelites these particular institutions, God was only re-delivering the law imprinted on the natural heart of man; for there is every reason to believe that the incestuous alliances and unnatural crimes prohibited in this chapter were forbidden to all men by a law expressed or understood, from the beginning of the world, or at least from the era of the flood; since God threatens to condemn and punish in a manner so sternly severe, these atrocities in the practice of the Canaanites and their neighbours, who were not subject to the laws of the Hebrew nation.

CHAPTER XIX.

Ver. 1-37. A REPETITION OF SUNDRY LAWS. 2. Speak unto all the congregation—Many of the laws enumerated in this chapter had been previously announced. As they were, however, of a general application, not suited to particular classes, but to the nation at large, so Moses seems, according to divine instructions, to have rehearsed them, perhaps on different occasions, and to successive divisions of the people, till "all the congregation of the children of Israel" were taught to know them. The will of God in the Old as well as the New Testament Church was not locked up in the repositories of an unknown tongue, but communicated plainly and openly to the people. ye shall be holy: for I am holy—Separated from the world, the people of God required to be holy, for his character, his laws and service were holy. (See 1 Pe. 1. 15.) 3. ye shall fear every man—The duty of obedience to parents is placed in connection with the proper observance of the sabbaths, as both of them lying at the foundation of practical religion. 5-8. If ye offer a sacrifice of peace offerings—Those which included thank offerings, or offerings made for vows, were always free-will offerings. Except the portions which, being waved and heaved, became the property of the priests, (see ch. 3.) the rest of the victim was eaten by the offerer and his friend, under the following regulations, however, that, if thank offerings, they were to be eaten on the day of their presentation; and if a free-will offering, although it might be eaten on the second day, yet if any remains of it were left till the third day, it was to be burnt, or deep criminality was incurred by the person who then ventured to partake of it. The reason of this strict prohibition seems to have been to prevent any mysterious virtue being superstitiously attached to meat offered on the altar. 9, 10. When ye reap the harvest of your land—The right of the poor in Israel to glean after reapers, as well as to the unreaped corners of the field, was secured by a positive statute, and this, in addition to other enactments connected with the ceremonial law, formed a beneficial provision for their support. At the same time, proprietors were not obliged to admit them into the field until the grain had been carried off the field; and they seem also to have been left at liberty to choose the poor whom they deemed the most deserving or needful. (Ruth, 2. 2, 8.) This was the earliest poor-law that we read of in the code of any people; and it combined in admirable union the obligation of a public duty with the exercise of private and voluntary benevolence at a time when the hearts of the rich would be strongly inclined to liberality. 11-16. Ye shall not steal—A variety of social duties are inculcated in this passage, chiefly in reference to common and little-thought-of vices to which mankind are exceedingly prone; such as committing petty frauds; or not scrupling to violate truth in transactions of business; ridiculing bodily infirmities; or circulating stories to the prejudice of others. In opposition to these bad habits, a spirit of humanity and brotherly kindness is strongly enforced. 17. Thou shalt in any wise rebuke thy neighbour—Instead of

4 And if the people of the land do any ways hide their eyes from the man, when he giveth of his seed unto Molech, and kill him not;

5 Then I will set my face against that man, and ᵉ against his family, and will cut him off, and all that ᵈ go awhoring after him, to commit whoredom with Molech, from among their people.

6 ¶ And ᵉ the soul that turneth after such as have familiar spirits, and after wizards, to go awhoring after them, I will even set my face against that soul, and will cut him off from among his people.

7 Sanctify ᶠ yourselves therefore, and be ye holy: for I am the Lord your God.

8 And ye shall keep my statutes, and do them: ᵍ I am the Lord which sanctify you.

9 ¶ For ʰ every one that curseth his father or his mother shall be surely put to death: he hath cursed his father or his mother; his ⁱ blood shall be upon him.

10 ¶ And ʲ the man that committeth adultery with another man's wife, even he that committeth adultery with his neighbour's wife, the adulterer and the adulteress shall surely be put to death

11 And ᵏ the man that lieth with his father's wife hath uncovered his father's nakedness: both of them shall surely be put to death; their blood shall be upon them.

12 And if a man lie with his daughter-in-law, both of them shall surely be put to death: they have wrought confusion; their blood shall be upon them.

13 ¶ If ˡ a man also lie with mankind, as he lieth with a woman, both of them have committed an abomination: they shall surely be put to death; their blood shall be upon them.

14 And ᵐ if a man take a wife and her mother, it is wickedness: they shall be burnt with fire, both he and they; that there be no wickedness among you.

15 And ⁿ if a man lie with a beast, he shall surely be put to death: and ye shall slay the beast.

16 And if a woman approach unto any beast, and lie down thereto, thou shalt kill the woman and the beast: they shall surely be put to death; their blood shall be upon them.

17 And ᵒ if a man shall take his sister, his father's daughter, or his mother's daughter, and see her nakedness, and she see his nakedness; it is a wicked thing; and they shall be cut off in the sight of their people: he hath uncovered his sister's nakedness; he shall bear his iniquity.

18 And ᵖ if a man shall lie with a woman having her sickness, and shall uncover her nakedness, he hath ¹ discovered the fountain, and she hath uncovered the fountain of her blood: and both of them shall be cut off from among their people.

19 And ᵠ thou shalt not uncover the nakedness of thy mother's sister, nor of thy father's sister; for he uncovereth his near kin: they shall bear their iniquity.

20 And if a man shall lie with his uncle's wife, he hath uncovered his uncle's nakedness: they shall bear their sin; they shall die childless.

21 And ʳ if a man shall take his brother's wife, it is ² an unclean thing: he hath uncovered his brother's nakedness: they shall be childless.

B. C. 1490.

CHAP. 20.
ᶜ Ex. 20. 5.
ᵈ ch. 17. 7.
ᵉ ch. 19. 31.
2 Ki. 21.24.
ᶠ Ex. 22. 31.
Mat. 5. 48.
Eph. 1. 4.
Col. 3. 12.
1 Thess. 5. 23.
1 Pet. 1.16.
ᵍ Ex. 31. 13.
Eze. 37.28.
ʰ Ex. 21. 17.
Deu. 27.16.
Pro. 20. 20.
Mat. 15. 4.
ⁱ 2 Sa. 1. 16.
ʲ ch. 22. 22.
Jer. 29. 23.
John 8. 4, 5.
1 Cor. 6. 9.
Heb. 13. 4.
ᵏ ch. 18. 8.
Deu. 27.23.
ˡ ch. 18. 22.
Gen. 19. 5.
Deu. 23.17.
Jud. 19. 22.
Rom. 1. 25, 32.
ᵐ ch. 18. 17.
ⁿ Deut. 27. 21.
ᵒ Gen. 20.12.
ᵖ ch. 15. 24.
¹ made naked.
ᵠ ch. 18. 12.
ʳ ch. 18. 16.
² a separation.
ˢ ch. 19. 37.
ᵗ Deut. 9. 5.
ᵘ Ex. 3. 17.
ᵛ ch. 11. 19, 47.
Deut. 7. 6.
Deu. 14. 2.
1 Ki. 8. 53.
Ps. 135. 4.
1 Pet. 2. 9.
ʷ Deu. 14. 4.
³ Or, moveth.
ˣ 1 Pet. 1.16.
ʸ Tit. 2. 14.
ᶻ Ex. 22. 18.
Deu. 13.10.
1 Sa. 28. 7.

CHAP. 21.
ᵃ Ezek.44.25.
¹ Or, being an husband among his people, he shall not defile himself for his wife, etc.
Ezek.24.16.
ᵇ Deu. 14. 1.
Ezek.44.20.
ᶜ ch. 19. 21.
ᵈ ch. 3. 11.
ᵉ Ezek.44.22.
ᶠ Deu. 24.1.2.
ᵍ ch. 20. 7, 8.
Is. 43. 15.
ʰ Gen. 38.24.
ⁱ Ex. 29. 29.
Nu. 35. 25.
ʲ Ex. 28. 2.
ᵏ ch. 10. 6.
ˡ Nu. 19. 14.
ᵐ ch. 10. 7.

22 ¶ Ye shall therefore keep all my ˢ statutes, and all my judgments, and do them; that the land, whither I bring you to dwell therein, spue you not out.

23 And ye shall not walk in the manners of the nations which I cast out before you: for they committed all these things, and therefore ᵗ I abhorred them.

24 But ᵘ I have said unto you, Ye shall inherit their land, and I will give it unto you to possess it, a land that floweth with milk and honey: I am the Lord your God, which ᵛ have separated you from other people.

25 Ye ʷ shall therefore put difference between clean beasts and unclean, and between unclean fowls and clean: and ye shall not make your souls abominable by beast, or by fowl, or by any manner of living thing that ³ creepeth on the ground, which I have separated from you as unclean.

26 And ye shall be holy unto me: ˣ for I the Lord am holy, and ʸ have severed you from other people, that ye should be mine.

27 ¶ A ᶻ man also or woman that hath a familiar spirit, or that is a wizard, shall surely be put to death: they shall stone them with stones; their blood shall be upon them.

CHAPTER XXI.

1 Of the priests' mourning, 6 of their holiness; 7, 13 of their marriages. 16 The priests that have blemishes must not minister in the sanctuary.

AND the Lord said unto Moses, Speak unto the priests the sons of Aaron, and say unto them, ᵃ There shall none be defiled for the dead among his people:

2 But for his kin that is near unto him, that is, for his mother, and for his father, and for his son, and for his daughter, and for his brother,

3 And for his sister a virgin, that is nigh unto him, which hath had no husband; for her may he be defiled.

4 But ¹ he shall not defile himself, being a chief man among his people, to profane himself.

5 They ᵇ shall not make baldness upon their head, neither shall they shave off the corner of their beard, nor make any cuttings in their flesh.

6 They shall be holy unto their God, and not ᶜ profane the name of their God: for the offerings of the Lord made by fire, and the ᵈ bread of their God, they do offer: therefore they shall be holy.

7 They ᵉ shall not take a wife that is a whore, or profane; neither shall they take a woman ᶠ put away from her husband: for he is holy unto his God.

8 Thou shalt sanctify him therefore; for he offereth the bread of thy God: he shall be holy unto thee: ᵍ for I the Lord, which sanctify you, am holy.

9 And ʰ the daughter of any priest, if she profane herself by playing the whore, she profaneth her father: she shall be burnt with fire.

10 ¶ And ⁱ he that is the high priest among his brethren, upon whose head the anointing oil was poured, and ʲ that is consecrated to put on the garments, ᵏ shall not uncover his head, nor rend his clothes;

11 Neither shall he ˡ go in to any dead body, nor defile himself for his father, or for his mother;

12 Neither ᵐ shall he go out of the sanctuary, nor profane the sanctuary of his

cherishing latent feelings of malice, or meditating purposes of revenge against a person who has committed an insult or injury against them, God's people were taught to remonstrate with the offender, and endeavour, by calm and kindly reason, to bring him to a sense of his fault, not suffer sin upon him—*lit.* that ye may not participate in his sin. 18. thou shalt love thy neighbour as thyself—The word "neighbour" is used as synonymous with fellow creature. The Israelites in a later age restricted its meaning as applicable only to their own countrymen. This narrow interpretation was refuted by our Lord in a beautiful parable, (L. 10. 30.) 19. thou shalt not let thy cattle gender with a diverse kind—This prohibition was probably intended to discourage a practice which seemed to infringe upon the economy which God has established in the animal kingdom. thou shalt not sow thy field with mingled seed—This also was directed against an idolatrous pract'ce, viz., that of the ancient Zabians, or fire-worshippers, who sowed different seeds, accompanying the act with magical rites and invocations; and commentators have generally thought the design of this and the preceding law was to put an end to the unnatural lusts and foolish superstitions which were prevalent amongst the heathen. But the reason of the prohibition was probably deeper; for those who have studied the diseases of land and vegetables tell us, that the practice of mingling seeds is injurious both to flowers and to grains. "If the various genera of the natural order Gramineæ, which includes the grains and the grasses, should be sown in the same field, and flower at the same time, so that the pollen of the two flowers mix, a spurious seed will be the consequence, called by the farmers *chess*, and is always inferior, and unlike either of the two grains that produced it, in size, flavour, and nutritious principles. Independently of contributing to disease the soil, they never fail to produce the same in animals, and men that feed on them." [WHITLAW.] neither shall a garment of linen and woollen come upon thee—although this precept, like the other two with which it is associated, was in all probability designed to root out some superstition, it seems to have had a farther meaning. The law, it is to be observed, did not prohibit the Israelites wearing many different kinds of cloths together, but only the two specified; and the observations and researches of modern science have proved that "wool, when combined with linen, increases its power of passing off the electricity from the body; in hot climates, it brings on malignant fevers, and exhausts the strength, and when passing off from the body, it meets with the heated air, inflames and excoriates like a blister." [WHITLAW.] (see Ez. 44. 17, 18.) 23-25. fruit; three years it shall not be eaten—"The wisdom of this law is very striking. Every gardener will teach us not to let fruit trees bear in their earliest years, but to pluck off the blossoms: and for this reason, that they will thus thrive the better, and bear more abundantly afterwards. The very expression, "to regard them as uncircumcised," suggests the propriety of pinching them off; I do not say *cutting* them off, because it is generally the hand, and not a knife, that is employed in this operation." [MICHAELIS.] 26. Ye shall not eat any thing with the blood— (See on ch. 17. 10.) neither use enchantments, nor observe times—The former refers to divination by serpents—one of the earliest forms of enchantment, and the other means the observation *lit.* of *clouds*, as a study of the appearance and motion of clouds was a common way of foretelling good or bad fortune. Such absurd but deep-rooted superstitions often put a stop to the prosecution of serious and important transactions, but they were forbidden especially as implying a want of faith in the being, or of reliance on the providence of God. 27. Ye shall not round, &c.—It seems probable that this fashion had been learned by the Israelites in Egypt, for the ancient Egyptians had their dark locks cropped short or shaved with great nicety, so that what remained on the crown appeared in the form of a circle surrounding the head, whilst the beard was dressed into a square form. This kind of coiffure had a highly idolatrous meaning; and it was adopted, with some slight variations, by almost all idolaters in ancient times. (Jer. 9. 25, 26; 25. 23, where "in the utmost corners" means having the corners of their hair cut.) Frequently a lock or tuft of hair was left on the hinder part of the head, the rest being cut round in the form of a ring, as the Turks, Chinese, and Hindoos do at the present day. neither shalt thou mar, &c.—The Egyptians used to cut or shave off their whiskers, as may be seen in the coffins of mummies, and the representations of divinities on the monuments. But the Hebrews, in order to separate them from the neighbouring nations, or perhaps to put a stop to some existing superstition, were forbidden to imitate this practice. It may appear surprising that Moses should condescend to such minutiæ as that of regulating the fashion of the hair and the beard—matters which do not usually occupy the attention of a legislator—and which appear widely remote from the province either of government or of a religion. A strong presumption, therefore, arises that he had it in view by these regulations to combat some superstitious practices of the Egyptians. 28. Ye shall not make any cuttings, &c.— The practice of making deep gashes on the face and arms and legs, in time of bereavement, was universal among the heathen, and it was deemed a becoming mark of respect for the dead as well as a sort of propitiatory offering to the deities who presided over death and the grave. The Jews learned this custom in Egypt, and though weaned from it, relapsed in a later and degenerate age into this old superstition. (Is. 15. 2; Jer. 16. 6; 41. 5.) nor print any marks upon you— by *tatooing*—imprinting figures of flowers, leaves, stars, and other fanciful devices on various parts of their person—the impression was made sometimes by means of a hot iron, sometimes by ink or paint, as is done by the Arab females of the present day and the different castes of the Hindoos. It is probable that a strong propensity to adopt such marks in honour of some idol gave occasion to the prohibition in this verse; and they were wisely forbidden, for they were signs of apostacy, and, when once made, were insu perable obstacles to a return. (See allusion,

God; for the crown of the anointing oil of his God is upon him: I am the LORD.

13 And he shall take a wife in her virginity.

14 A widow, or a divorced woman, or profane, or an harlot, these shall he not take; but he shall take a virgin of his own people to wife.

15 Neither shall he profane his seed among his people: for I the LORD do sanctify him.

16 ¶ And the LORD spake unto Moses, saying,

17 Speak unto Aaron, saying, Whosoever he be of thy seed in their generations that hath any blemish, let him not approach to offer the bread of his God:

18 For whatsoever man he be that hath a blemish, he shall not approach; a blind man, or a lame, or he that hath a flat nose, or any thing superfluous,

19 Or a man that is broken-footed, or broken-handed,

20 Or crook-backt, or a dwarf, or that hath a blemish in his eye, or be scurvy, or scabbed, or hath his stones broken;

21 No man that hath a blemish of the seed of Aaron the priest shall come nigh to offer the offerings of the LORD made by fire: he hath a blemish; he shall not come nigh to offer the bread of his God.

22 He shall eat the bread of his God, both of the most holy, and of the holy;

23 Only he shall not go in unto the veil, nor come nigh unto the altar, because he hath a blemish; that he profane not my sanctuaries: for I the LORD do sanctify them.

24 And Moses told it unto Aaron, and to his sons, and unto all the children of Israel.

CHAPTER XXII.

1 The priests in their uncleanness must abstain from holy things. 10 Who of the priest's house may eat of them. 17 The sacrifices must be without blemish. 26 The age of the sacrifice.

AND the LORD spake unto Moses, saying,

2 Speak unto Aaron and to his sons, that they separate themselves from the holy things of the children of Israel, and that they profane not my holy name in those things which they hallow unto me: I am the LORD.

3 Say unto them, Whosoever he be of all your seed among your generations, that goeth unto the holy things, which the children of Israel hallow unto the LORD, having his uncleanness upon him, that soul shall be cut off from my presence: I am the LORD.

4 What man soever of the seed of Aaron is a leper, or hath a running issue, he shall not eat of the holy things, until he be clean. And whoso toucheth any thing that is unclean by the dead, or a man whose seed goeth from him;

5 Or whosoever toucheth any creeping thing, whereby he may be made unclean, or a man of whom he may take uncleanness, whatsoever uncleanness he hath;

6 The soul which hath touched any such shall be unclean until even, and shall not eat of the holy things, unless he wash his flesh with water.

7 And when the sun is down, he shall be clean, and shall afterward eat of the holy things, because it is his food.

8 That which dieth of itself, or is torn with beasts, he shall not eat to defile himself therewith: I am the LORD.

9 They shall therefore keep mine ordinance, lest they bear sin for it, and die therefore, if they profane it: I the LORD do sanctify them.

10 There shall no stranger eat of the holy thing: a sojourner of the priest, or an hired servant, shall not eat of the holy thing.

11 But if the priest buy any soul with his money, he shall eat of it, and he that is born in his house: they shall eat of his meat.

12 If the priest's daughter also be married unto a stranger, she may not eat of an offering of the holy things.

13 But if the priest's daughter be a widow, or divorced, and have no child, and is returned unto her father's house, as in her youth, she shall eat of her father's meat; but there shall no stranger eat thereof.

14 And if a man eat of the holy thing unwittingly, then he shall put the fifth part thereof unto it, and shall give it unto the priest with the holy thing.

15 And they shall not profane the holy things of the children of Israel, which they offer unto the LORD;

16 Or suffer them to bear the iniquity of trespass when they eat their holy things: for I the LORD do sanctify them.

17 ¶ And the LORD spake unto Moses, saying,

18 Speak unto Aaron, and to his sons, and unto all the children of Israel, and say unto them, Whatsoever he be of the house of Israel, or of the strangers in Israel, that will offer his oblation for all his vows, and for all his free-will offerings, which they will offer unto the LORD for a burnt offering;

19 Ye shall offer at your own will a male without blemish, of the beeves, of the sheep, or of the goats.

20 But whatsoever hath a blemish, that shall ye not offer; for it shall not be acceptable for you.

21 And whosoever offereth a sacrifice of peace offerings unto the LORD to accomplish his vow, or a free-will offering in beeves or sheep, it shall be perfect to be accepted; there shall be no blemish therein.

22 Blind, or broken, or maimed, or having a wen, or scurvy, or scabbed, ye shall not offer these unto the LORD, nor make an offering by fire of them upon the altar unto the LORD.

23 Either a bullock or a lamb that hath any thing superfluous or lacking in his parts, that mayest thou offer for a free-will offering; but for a vow it shall not be accepted.

24 Ye shall not offer unto the LORD that which is bruised, or crushed, or broken, or cut; neither shall ye make any offering thereof in your land.

25 Neither from a stranger's hand shall ye offer the bread of your God of any of these; because their corruption is in them, and blemishes be in them: they shall not be accepted for you.

26 ¶ And the LORD spake unto Moses, saying,

27 When a bullock, or a sheep, or a goat, is brought forth, then it shall be seven days under the dam; and from the eighth

to the practice Is. 44. 5; Re. 13, 17; 14. 1.) 30. Keep my sabbaths and reverence my sanctuary—This precept is frequently repeated along with the prohibition of idolatrous practices, and here it stands closely connected with the superstitions forbidden in the previous verses. 31. Regard not them that have familiar spirits—The *Heb.* word, rendered "familiar spirit," signifies the belly, and sometimes a leathern bottle, from its similarity to the belly. It was applied in the sense of this passage to ventriloquists, who pretended to have communication with the invisible world; and the Hebrews were strictly forbidden to consult them; as the vain but high pretensions of those impostors were derogatory to the honour of God, and subversive of their covenant relations with him as his people. neither seek after wizards—fortune-tellers, who pretended, as the *Heb.* word indicates, to prognosticate by palmistry, or an inspection of the l'nes of the hand, the future fate of those who applied to them. 33, 34. If a stranger sojourn with you—The Israelites were to hold out encouragement to strangers to settle among them, that they might be brought to the knowledge and worship of the true God; and with this view, they were enjoined to treat them not as aliens, but as friends, on the ground that they themselves, who were strangers in Egypt, were at first kindly and hospitably received in that country. 37. I am the Lord—This solemn admonition, by which these various precepts are repeatedly sanctioned, is equivalent to "I, your Creator —your Deliverer from bondage, and your Sovereign, who have wisdom to establish laws, have power also to punish the violation of them." It was well fitted to impress the minds of the Israelites with a sense of their duty, and God's claims to obedience.

CHAPTER XX.

Ver. 1-24. GIVING ONE'S SEED TO MOLECH. 2. Whosoever ... giveth ... to Molech—See on ch. 18. 21. The people of the land shall stone, &c.—Criminals who were condemned to be stoned were led, with their hands bound, without the gates to a small eminence, where was a large stone placed at the bottom. When they had approached within 10 cubits of the spot, they were exhorted to confess, that, by faith and repentance, their souls might be saved. When led forward to within 4 cubits, they were stripped almost naked, and received some stupefying draught, during which the witnesses prepared, by laying aside their outer garments, to carry into execution the capital sentence which the law bound them to do. The criminal, being placed on the edge of the precipice, was then pushed backwards, so that he fell down the perpendicular height on the stone lying below: if not killed by the fall, the second witness dashed a large stone down upon his breast, and then the "people of the land," who were bystanders, rushed forward, and with stones completed the work of death. (M. 21, 44; A. 7, 58.) 4. If the people of the land, &c.—*i. e.*, connive at their countrymen practising the horrid rites of Molech. Awful was it that any Hebrew parents could so violate their national covenant; and no wonder that God denounced the severest penalties against them and their families. 7-20. Sanctify yourselves, and be ye holy—The minute specification of the incestuous and unnatural crimes here enumerated shows their sad prevalence amongst the idolatrous nations around, and the extreme proneness of the Israelites to follow the customs of their neighbours. It is to be understood, that, whenever mention is made that the offender was "to be put to death" without describing the mode, stoning is meant. The only instance of another form of capital punishment occurs in *v.* 14, that of being burnt with fire: and yet it is probable that even here death was first inflicted by stoning, and the body of the criminal afterwards consumed by fire. (Josh. 7. 15.) 20. They shall die childless—Either by the judgment of God they shall have no children, or their spurious offspring shall be denied by human authority the ordinary privileges of children in Israel. 24. I ... have separated you—Their selection from the rest of the nations was for the all-important end of preserving the knowledge and worship of the true God amidst the universal apostacy; and as the distinction of meats was one great means of completing that separation, the law about making a difference between clean and unclean beasts is here repeated with emphatic solemnity.

CHAPTER XXI.

Ver. 1-24. OF THE PRIESTS' MOURNING. 1. There shall none be defiled for the dead—The obvious design of the regulations contained in this chapter was to keep inviolate the purity and dignity of the sacred office. Contact with a corpse, or even contiguity to the place where it lay, entailing ceremonial defilement, (Nu. 19. 14,) all mourners were debarred from the tabernacle for a week; and as the exclusion of a priest during that period would have been attended with great inconvenience, the whole order were enjoined to abstain from all approaches to the dead, except at the funerals of relatives, to whom affection or necessity might call them to perform the last offices. Those exceptional cases, which are specified, were strictly confined to the members of their own family, within the nearest degrees of kindred. 4. But he shall not defile himself— "for any other," as the sense may be fully expressed. The priest, in discharging his sacred functions, might well be regarded as a chief man among his people, and by these defilements might be said to profane himself. [BISHOP PATRICK.] The word rendered "chief man" signifies also "a husband;" and the sense according to others is, "But he being a husband, shall not defile himself by the obsequies of a wife." Ez. (44. 25.) 5. They shall not make baldness ... nor cuttings in their flesh—The superstitious marks of sorrow, as well as the violent excesses in which the heathen indulged at the death of their friends, were forbidden by a general law to the Hebrew people. (ch. 19. 28.) But the priests were to be laid under a special injunction, not only that they might exhibit examples of piety in the moderation of their grief, but also by the restraint of their passions, be the better qualified to administer the consolations of religion to others, and show, by their faith in a blessed resurrection, the reasons for sorrowing not as those who have no hope. 7-9. They shall not take a wife—Private individuals might form several connections, which were forbidden as inexpedient or improper in priests. The

day and thenceforth it shall be accepted for an offering made by fire unto the LORD.
28 And *whether it be* cow or ewe, ye shall not kill it *and* her young both in one day.
29 ¶ And when ye will offer a sacrifice of thanksgiving unto the LORD, offer *it* at your own will.
30 On the same day it shall be eaten up; ye shall leave none of it until the morrow: I *am* the LORD.
31 Therefore shall ye keep my commandments, and do them: I *am* the LORD.
32 Neither shall ye profane my holy name; but I will be hallowed among the children of Israel: I *am* the LORD which hallow you,
33 That brought you out of the land of Egypt, to be your God: I *am* the LORD.

CHAPTER XXIII.

1 *Of sundry feasts.* 3 *The sabbath.* 4 *The passover.* 26 *The day of atonement, etc.*

AND the LORD spake unto Moses, saying,
2 Speak unto the children of Israel, and say unto them, Concerning the feasts of the LORD, which ye shall proclaim *to be* holy convocations, *even* these *are* my feasts.
3 Six days shall work be done: but the seventh day *is* the sabbath of rest, an holy convocation; ye shall do no work *therein:* it *is* the sabbath of the LORD in all your dwellings.
4 ¶ These *are* the feasts of the LORD, *even* holy convocations, which ye shall proclaim in their seasons.
5 In the fourteenth *day* of the first month at even *is* the LORD's passover.
6 And on the fifteenth day of the same month *is* the feast of unleavened bread unto the LORD: seven days ye must eat unleavened bread.
7 In the first day ye shall have an holy convocation; ye shall do no servile work therein.
8 But ye shall offer an offering made by fire unto the LORD seven days: in the seventh day *is* an holy convocation: ye shall do no servile work *therein.*
9 ¶ And the LORD spake unto Moses, saying,
10 Speak unto the children of Israel, and say unto them, When ye be come into the land which I give unto you, and shall reap the harvest thereof, then ye shall bring a sheaf of the first-fruits of your harvest unto the priest:
11 And he shall wave the sheaf before the LORD, to be accepted for you: on the morrow after the sabbath the priest shall wave it.
12 And ye shall offer that day when ye wave the sheaf an he-lamb without blemish of the first year for a burnt offering unto the LORD.
13 And the meat offering thereof *shall be* two tenth deals of fine flour mingled with oil, an offering made by fire unto the LORD *for* a sweet savour: and the drink offering thereof *shall be* of wine, the fourth *part* of an hin.
14 And ye shall eat neither bread, nor parched corn, nor green ears, until the selfsame day that ye have brought an offering unto your God: *it shall be* a statute for ever throughout your generations in all your dwellings.
15 ¶ And ye shall count unto you from the morrow after the sabbath, from the day that ye brought the sheaf of the wave offering; seven sabbaths shall be complete:
16 Even unto the morrow after the seventh sabbath shall ye number fifty days; and ye shall offer a new meat offering unto the LORD.
17 Ye shall bring out of your habitations two wave loaves of two tenth deals: they shall be of fine flour; they shall be baken with leaven; *they are* the first-fruits unto the LORD.
18 And ye shall offer with the bread seven lambs without blemish of the first year, and one young bullock, and two rams: they shall be *for* a burnt offering unto the LORD, with their meat offering and their drink offerings, *even* an offering made by fire, of sweet savour unto the LORD.
19 Then ye shall sacrifice one kid of the goats for a sin offering, and two lambs of the first year for a sacrifice of peace offerings.
20 And the priest shall wave them with the bread of the first-fruits, *for* a wave offering before the LORD, with the two lambs: they shall be holy to the LORD for the priest.
21 And ye shall proclaim on the selfsame day, *that* it may be an holy convocation unto you: ye shall do no servile work *therein:* *it shall be* a statute for ever in all your dwellings throughout your generations.
22 ¶ And when ye reap the harvest of your land, thou shalt not make clean riddance of the corners of thy field when thou reapest, neither shalt thou gather any gleaning of thy harvest; thou shalt leave them unto the poor, and to the stranger: I *am* the LORD your God.
23 ¶ And the LORD spake unto Moses, saying,
24 Speak unto the children of Israel, saying, In the seventh month, in the first *day* of the month, shall ye have a sabbath, a memorial of blowing of trumpets, an holy convocation.
25 Ye shall do no servile work *therein;* but ye shall offer an offering made by fire unto the LORD.
26 ¶ And the LORD spake unto Moses, saying,
27 Also on the tenth *day* of this seventh month *there shall be* a day of atonement: it shall be an holy convocation unto you; and ye shall afflict your souls, and offer an offering made by fire unto the LORD.
28 And ye shall do no work in that same day; for it *is* a day of atonement, to make an atonement for you before the LORD your God.
29 For whatsoever soul *it be* that shall not be afflicted in that same day, he shall be cut off from among his people.
30 And whatsoever soul *it be* that doeth any work in that same day, the same soul will I destroy from among his people.
31 Ye shall do no manner of work: *it shall be* a statute for ever throughout your generations in all your dwellings.
32 *It shall be* unto you a sabbath of rest, and ye shall afflict your souls: in the ninth day of the month at even, from even unto even, shall ye celebrate your sabbath.
33 ¶ And the LORD spake unto Moses, saying,
34 Speak unto the children of Israel,

respectability of their office, and the honour of religion, required unblemished sanctity in their families as well as themselves, and departures from it in their case were visited with severer punishment than in that of others. **10-15. He that is the high priest**—The indulgence in the excepted cases of family bereavement, mentioned above, which was granted to the common priests, was denied to him; for his absence from the sanctuary for the removal of any contracted defilement could not have been dispensed with, neither could he have acted as intercessor for the people, unless ceremonially clean. Moreover, the high dignity of his office demanded a corresponding superiority in personal holiness, and stringent rules were prescribed for the purpose of upholding the suitable dignity of his station and family. The same rules are extended to the families of Christian ministers. (1 Tim. 3. 2; Tit. 1. 6.) **16-24. Any blemish**—As visible things exert a strong influence on the minds of men, any physical infirmity or mal-formation of body in the ministers of religion, which disturbs the associations or excites ridicule, tends to detract from the weight and authority of the sacred office. Priests labouring under any personal defect were not allowed to officiate in the public service; they might be employed in some inferior duties about the sanctuary, but could not perform any sacred office. In all these regulations for preserving the unsullied purity of the sacred character and office, there was a typical reference to the priesthood of Christ. (He. 7, 26.)

CHAPTER XXII.

Ver. 1-9. **The Priests in their Uncleanness. 2. Separate themselves from the holy things**—"To separate" means, in the language of the Mosaic ritual, "to abstain;" and therefore the import of this injunction is, that the priests should abstain from eating that part of the sacrifices which, though belonging to their order, was to be partaken of only by such of them as were free from legal impurities, **that they profane not my holy name,** &c.—i. e., let them not, by their want of due reverence, give occasion to profane my holy name. A careless or irreverent use of things consecrated to God, tends to dishonour the name and bring disrespect on the worship of God. **3. Whosoever he be ... that goeth unto the holy things**—The multitude of minute restrictions to which the priests, from accidental defilement, were subjected, by keeping them constantly on their guard, lest they should be unfit for the sacred service, tended to preserve in full exercise the feeling of awe and submission to the authority of God. The ideas of sin and duty were awakened in their breasts by every case to which either an interdict or an injunction was applied. But why enact an express statute for priests disqualified by the leprosy or polluting touch of a carcase, when a general law was already in force which excluded from society all persons in that condition? Because priests might be apt, from familiarity to trifle with religion, and in committing irregularities or sins, to shelter themselves under the cloak of the sacred office. This law, therefore, was passed, specifying the chief forms of temporary defilement which excluded from the sanctuary, that priests might not deem themselves entitled to greater license than the rest of the people; and that so far from being in any degree exempted from the sanctions of the law, they were under greater obligations, by their priestly station, to observe it in its strict letter and its smallest enactments.

10-16. Who of the Priests' House may Eat of Them. 10. There shall no stranger eat the holy thing—The portion of the sacrifices assigned for the support of the officiating priests was restricted to the exclusive use of his own family. A temporary guest or a hired servant was not at liberty to eat of them; but an exception was made in favour of a bought or home-born slave, because such was a stated member of his household. On the same principle, his own daughter, who married a husband not a priest, could not eat of them: though, if a widow and childless, she was reinstated in the privileges of her father's house as before her marriage. But if she had become a mother, as her children had no right to the privileges of the priesthood, she was under a necessity of finding support for them elsewhere than under her father's roof. **13. There shall no stranger eat thereof**—The interdict recorded (v. 10) is repeated to show its stringency. All the Hebrews, even the nearest neighbours of the priest, the members of his family excepted, were considered strangers in this respect that they had no right to eat of things offered at the altar. **14. Eat of the holy things unwittingly**—A common Israelite might unconsciously partake of what had been offered as tithes, first-fruits, &c., and on discovering his unintentional error, he was not only to restore as much as he had used, but be fined in a fifth part more for the priest to carry into the sanctuary. **15, 16. They shall not profane**—There is some difficulty felt in determining to whom "they" refers. The subject of the preceding context being occupied about the priests, it is supposed by some that this relates to them also; and the meaning is, that the whole people would incur guilt through the fault of the priests, if they should defile the sacred offerings, which they would have done had they presented them while under any defilement. [CALVIN.] According to others, "the children of Israel" is the nominative in the sentence; which thus signifies, the children of Israel shall not profane or defile their offerings, by touching them or reserving any part of them, lest they incur the guilt of eating what is divinely appointed to the priests alone. [CALMET.]

19-33. The Sacrifices must be without Blemish. 19. Ye shall offer at your own will—rather, to your being accepted. **a male without blemish**—This law (ch. 1. 3,) is founded on a sense of natural propriety, and hence the reasonableness of God's strong remonstrance with the worldly-minded Jews, (Mal. 1. 8.) **23. that mayest thou offer,** &c.—The passage should be rendered thus: if thou offer it either for a free-will offering, or for a vow, it shall not be accepted. This sacrifice being required to be "without blemish," symbolically implied that the people of God were to dedicate themselves wholly with sincere purpose of heart, and its being required to be "perfect to be accepted," led them typically to Him, without whom no sacrifice could be offered acceptable to God. **27-28. it shall be seven days under the dam**—Animals were not considered perfect nor good for food till the eighth day. As sacrifices are called the bread

saying, "The fifteenth day of this seventh month shall be the feast of tabernacles for seven days unto the Lord.

35 On the first day shall be an holy convocation: ye shall do no servile work therein.

36 Seven days ye shall offer an offering made by fire unto the Lord: on the eighth day shall be an holy convocation unto you; and ye shall offer an offering made by fire unto the Lord: it is a solemn assembly; and ye shall do no servile work therein.

37 These are the feasts of the Lord, which ye shall proclaim to be holy convocations, to offer an offering made by fire unto the Lord, a burnt offering, and a meat offering, a sacrifice, and drink offerings, every thing upon his day:

38 Beside the sabbaths of the Lord, and beside your gifts, and beside all your vows, and beside all your free-will offerings, which ye give unto the Lord.

39 Also in the fifteenth day of the seventh month, when ye have gathered in the fruit of the land, ye shall keep a feast unto the Lord seven days: on the first day shall be a sabbath, and on the eighth day shall be a sabbath.

40 And ye shall take you on the first day the boughs of goodly trees, branches of palm trees, and the boughs of thick trees, and willows of the brook; and ye shall rejoice before the Lord your God seven days.

41 And ye shall keep it a feast unto the Lord seven days in the year. It shall be a statute for ever in your generations: ye shall celebrate it in the seventh month.

42 Ye shall dwell in booths seven days; all that are Israelites born shall dwell in booths:

43 That your generations may know that I made the children of Israel to dwell in booths, when I brought them out of the land of Egypt: I am the Lord your God.

44 And Moses declared unto the children of Israel the feasts of the Lord.

CHAPTER XXIV.

1 *The oil for the lamps.* 5 *The showbread.* 10 *Shelomith's son blasphemeth.* 17 *Of murder:* 18 *of damage.* 23 *The blasphemer stoned.*

AND the Lord spake unto Moses, saying,
2 Command the children of Israel, that they bring unto thee pure oil olive beaten for the light, to cause the lamps to burn continually.

3 Without the veil of the testimony, in the tabernacle of the congregation, shall Aaron order it from the evening unto the morning before the Lord continually: it shall be a statute for ever in your generations.

4 He shall order the lamps upon the pure candlestick before the Lord continually.

5 ¶ And thou shalt take fine flour, and bake twelve cakes thereof: two tenth deals shall be in one cake.

6 And thou shalt set them in two rows, six on a row, upon the pure table before the Lord.

7 And thou shalt put pure frankincense upon each row, that it may be on the bread for a memorial, even an offering made by fire unto the Lord.

8 Every sabbath he shall set it in order before the Lord continually, being taken from the children of Israel by an everlasting covenant.

9 And it shall be Aaron's and his sons'; and they shall eat it in the holy place: for it is most holy unto him of the offerings of the Lord made by fire by a perpetual statute.

10 ¶ And the son of an Israelitish woman, whose father was an Egyptian, went out among the children of Israel: and this son of the Israelitish woman and a man of Israel strove together in the camp;

11 And the Israelitish woman's son blasphemed the name of the LORD, and cursed. And they brought him unto Moses: (and his mother's name was Shelomith, the daughter of Dibri, of the tribe of Dan:)

12 And they put him in ward, that the mind of the Lord might be showed them.

13 And the Lord spake unto Moses, saying,

14 Bring forth him that hath cursed without the camp; and let all that heard him lay their hands upon his head, and let all the congregation stone him.

15 And thou shalt speak unto the children of Israel, saying, Whosoever curseth his God shall bear his sin.

16 And he that blasphemeth the name of the Lord, he shall surely be put to death, and all the congregation shall certainly stone him: as well the stranger, as he that is born in the land, when he blasphemeth the name of the LORD, shall be put to death.

17 And he that killeth any man shall surely be put to death.

18 And he that killeth a beast shall make it good; beast for beast.

19 And if a man cause a blemish in his neighbour; as he hath done, so shall it be done to him;

20 Breach for breach, eye for eye, tooth for tooth: as he hath caused a blemish in a man, so shall it be done to him again.

21 And he that killeth a beast, he shall restore it: and he that killeth a man, he shall be put to death.

22 Ye shall have one manner of law, as well for the stranger, as for one of your own country: for I am the Lord your God.

23 ¶ And Moses spake unto the children of Israel, that they should bring forth him that had cursed out of the camp, and stone him with stones. And the children of Israel did as the Lord commanded Moses.

CHAPTER XXV.

1 *Sabbath of the seventh year.* 8 *The jubilee.* 14 *Of oppression.* 18 *A blessing of obedience.* 35 *Of compassion:* 47 *of redeeming servants.*

AND the Lord spake unto Moses in mount Sinai, saying,
2 Speak unto the children of Israel, and say unto them, When ye come into the land which I give you, then shall the land keep a sabbath unto the Lord.

3 Six years thou shalt sow thy field, and six years thou shalt prune thy vineyard, and gather in the fruit thereof;

4 But in the seventh year shall be a sabbath of rest unto the land, a sabbath for the Lord: thou shalt neither sow thy field, nor prune thy vineyard.

5 That which groweth of its own accord of thy harvest thou shalt not reap, neither gather the grapes of thy vine undressed: for it is a year of rest unto the land.

6 And the sabbath of the land shall be meat for you; for thee, and for thy servant,

or food of God, *v.* 25,) to offer them immediately after birth, when they were unfit to be eaten, would have indicated a contempt of religion; and besides, this prohibition, as well as that contained in the following verse, inculcated a lesson of humanity or tenderness to the dam, as well as secured the sacrifices from all appearance of unfeeling cruelty.

CHAPTER XXIII.

Ver. 1-4. OF SUNDRY FEASTS. 2. Speak unto the children of Israel concerning the feasts —*lit.*, "the times of assembling, or solemnities, (Is. 33. 20 ; and this is a preferable rendering, applicable to all sacred seasons mentioned in this chapter, even the day of atonement, which was observed as a fast. They were appointed by the direct authority of God, and announced by a public proclamation, which is called " the joyful sound." (Ps. 89. 15.) Those "holy convocations," were evidences of Divine wisdom, and eminently subservient to the maintenance and diffusion of religious knowledge and piety. 3. seventh day is the sabbath—(See on Ex. 20. 8, 9.) The Sabbath has the precedence given to it, and it was to be "a holy convocation," observed by families " in their dwellings;" where practicable, by the people repairing to the door of the tabernacle; at later periods, by meeting in the schools of the prophets, and in synagogues. 4. Feasts of the Lord in their seasons—Their observance took place in the parts of the year corresponding to our March, May, and September. Divine wisdom was manifested in fixing them at those periods; in winter, when the days were short, and the roads broken up, a long journey was impracticable; while in summer, the harvest and vintage gave busy employment in the fields. Besides, another reason for the choice of those seasons probably was to counteract the influence of Egyptian associations and habits. And God appointed more sacred festivals for the Israelites on the month of September than the people of Egypt had in honour of their idols. These institutions, however, were for the most part prospective, the observance being not binding on the Israelites during their wanderings in the wilderness, while the regular celebration was not to commence till their settlement in Canaan.

5-8. THE PASSOVER. the Lord's passover—(See Ex. 12. 2, 14, 18.) The institution of the Passover was intended to be a perpetual memorial of the circumstances attending the redemption of the Israelites, while it had a typical reference to a greater redemption to be effected for God's spiritual people. On the first and last days of this feast, the people were forbidden to work; but while on the Sabbath they were not to do *any* work, on feast days they were permitted to dress meat—and hence the prohibition is restricted to " no servile work." At the same time, those two days were devoted to " holy convocation"—special seasons of social devotion. In addition to the ordinary sacrifices of every day, there were to be "offerings by fire" on the altar, (see on Nu. 28. 19,) while unleavened bread was to be eaten in families all the seven days. (See I Cor. 5. 8.)

9-14. THE SHEAF OF FIRST-FRUITS. 10. A sheaf of the first-fruits—A sheaf, *lit.* an omer, of the first-fruits of the barley harvest. The barley being sooner ripe than the other grains, the reaping of it formed the commencement of the general harvest season. The offering described in this passage was made on the 16th of the first month, and the day following the first Passover Sabbath, which was on the 15th, (corresponding to the beginning of our April); but it was reaped after sunset on the previous evening by persons deputed to go with sickles, and obtain samples from different fields. These being laid together in a sheaf or loose bundle, were brought to the court of the temple, where the grain was winnowed, parched, and bruised in a mortar. Then, after some incense had been sprinkled on it, the priest waved it aloft before the Lord towards the four different points of the compass, took a part of it and threw it into the fire of the altar—all the rest being reserved to himself. It was a proper and beautiful act, expressive of dependence on the God of nature and providence—common amongst all people, but more especially becoming the Israelites, who owed their land itself as well as all it produced to the Divine bounty. The offering of the wave-sheaf sanctified the whole harvest. (Ro. 11. 16.) At the same time, this feast had a typical character, and pre-intimated the resurrection of Christ, 1 Cor. 15. 20.) who rose from the dead on the very day the first-fruits were offered.

15-22. FEAST OF PENTECOST. Ye shall count from the morrow after the Sabbath—*i. e.*, after the first day of the passover week, which was observed as a Sabbath. 16. Number fifty days—The 49th day after the presentation of the first-fruits, or the 50th, including it, was the feast of Pentecost. (See also Ex. 23. 16; Deu. 16. 9.) 17. Ye shall bring out of your habitations, &c.—These loaves were made of "fine" or wheaten flour, the quantity contained in them being somewhat more than 10 lbs. weight. As the wave-sheaf gave the signal for the commencement, the two loaves solemnized the termination of the harvest season. They were the first-fruits of that season, being offered unto the Lord by the priest in name of the whole nation. (See on Ex. 34. 22.) The loaves used at the Passover were unleavened; those presented at Pentecost were leavened—a difference which is thus accounted for, that the one was a memorial of the bread hastily prepared at their departure, while the other was a tribute of gratitude to God for their daily food, which was leavened. 21. Ye shall proclaim on the selfsame day . . . an holy convocation—Though it extended over a week, the first day only was held as a Sabbath, both for the national offering of first-fruits, and a memorial of the giving of the law. 22. Thou shalt not make clean riddance, &c.—See on ch. 19. 9. The repetition of this law here probably arose from the priests reminding the people, at the presentation of the first-fruits, to unite piety to God with charity to the poor.

23-25. FEAST OF TRUMPETS. In the seventh month, the first day of the month—That was the first day of the ancient civil year. a memorial of blowing of trumpets—Jewish writers say that the trumpets were sounded 30 successive times, and the reason for the institution was for the double purpose of announcing the commencement of the new year, which was (*v.* 25 to be religiously observed, (see Nu. 29. 3,) and of preparing

and for thy maid, and for thy hired servant, and for thy stranger that sojourneth with thee,

7 And for thy cattle, and for the beast that *are* in thy land, shall all the increase thereof be meat.

8 ¶ And thou shalt number seven sabbaths of years unto thee, seven times seven years; and the space of the seven sabbaths of years shall be unto thee forty and nine years.

9 Then shalt thou cause the trumpet of the jubilee to sound on the tenth *day* of the seventh month; in the day of atonement shall ye make the trumpet sound throughout all your land.

10 And ye shall hallow the fiftieth year, and proclaim liberty throughout all the land unto all the inhabitants thereof: it shall be a jubilee unto you; and ye shall return every man unto his possession, and ye shall return every man unto his family.

11 A jubilee shall that fiftieth year be unto you: ye shall not sow, neither reap that which groweth of itself in it, nor gather *the grapes* in it of thy vine undressed.

12 For it *is* the jubilee; it shall be holy unto you: ye shall eat the increase thereof out of the field.

13 In the year of this jubilee ye shall return every man unto his possession.

14 And if thou sell ought unto thy neighbour, or buyest *ought* of thy neighbour's hand, ye shall not oppress one another:

15 According to the number of years after the jubilee thou shalt buy of thy neighbour, *and* according unto the number of years of the fruits he shall sell unto thee:

16 According to the multitude of years thou shalt increase the price thereof, and according to the fewness of years thou shalt diminish the price of it: for *according* to the number *of the years* of the fruits doth he sell unto thee.

17 Ye shall not therefore oppress one another; but thou shalt fear thy God: for I *am* the LORD your God.

18 ¶ Wherefore ye shall do my statutes, and keep my judgments, and do them; and ye shall dwell in the land in safety.

19 And the land shall yield her fruit, and ye shall eat your fill, and dwell therein in safety.

20 And if ye shall say, What shall we eat the seventh year? behold, we shall not sow, nor gather in our increase:

21 Then I will command my blessing upon you in the sixth year, and it shall bring forth fruit for three years.

22 And ye shall sow the eighth year, and eat *yet* of old fruit until the ninth year; until her fruits come in ye shall eat *of* the old *store*.

23 ¶ The land shall not be sold for ever: for the land *is* mine; for ye *are* strangers and sojourners with me.

24 And in all the land of your possession ye shall grant a redemption for the land.

25 ¶ If thy brother be waxen poor, and hath sold away *some* of his possession, and if any of his kin come to redeem it, then shall he redeem that which his brother sold.

26 And if the man have none to redeem it, and himself be able to redeem it;

27 Then let him count the years of the sale thereof, and restore the overplus unto the man to whom he sold it, that he may return unto his possession.

28 But if he be not able to restore *it* to him, then that which is sold shall remain in the hand of him that hath bought it until the year of jubilee: and in the jubilee it shall go out, and he shall return unto his possession.

29 And if a man sell a dwelling house in a walled city, then he may redeem it within a whole year after it is sold; *within* a full year may he redeem it.

30 And if it be not redeemed within the space of a full year, then the house that *is* in the walled city shall be established for ever to him that bought it, throughout his generations: it shall not go out in the jubilee.

31 But the houses of the villages which have no wall round about them shall be counted as the fields of the country: they may be redeemed, and they shall go out in the jubilee.

32 Notwithstanding the cities of the Levites, *and* the houses of the cities of their possession, may the Levites redeem at any time.

33 And if a man purchase of the Levites, then the house that was sold, and the city of his possession, shall go out in *the year of* jubilee: for the houses of the cities of the Levites *are* their possession among the children of Israel.

34 But the field of the suburbs of their cities may not be sold; for it *is* their perpetual possession.

35 ¶ And if thy brother be waxen poor, and fallen in decay with thee, then thou shalt relieve him; *yea, though he be* a stranger, or a sojourner; that he may live with thee.

36 Take thou no usury of him, or increase: but fear thy God; that thy brother may live with thee.

37 Thou shalt not give him thy money upon usury, nor lend him thy victuals for increase.

38 I *am* the LORD your God, which brought you forth out of the land of Egypt, to give you the land of Canaan, *and* to be your God.

39 ¶ And if thy brother *that dwelleth* by thee be waxen poor, and be sold unto thee; thou shalt not compel him to serve as a bond-servant:

40 *But* as an hired servant, *and* as a sojourner, he shall be with thee, *and* shall serve thee unto the year of jubilee.

41 And *then* shall he depart from thee, *both* he and his children with him, and shall return unto his own family, and unto the possession of his fathers shall he return.

42 For they *are* my servants, which I brought forth out of the land of Egypt: they shall not be sold as bondmen.

43 Thou shalt not rule over him with rigour, but shalt fear thy God.

44 Both thy bondmen and thy bondmaids, which thou shalt have, *shall be* of the heathen that are round about you; of them shall ye buy bondmen and bondmaids.

45 Moreover of the children of the strangers that do sojourn among you, of them shall ye buy, and of their families that *are* with you, which they begat in your land: and they shall be your possession.

the people for the approaching solemn fast. 27-32. A day of atonement—An annual festival, at which the sins of the whole year were expiated. (See ch. 16. 29-34.) It is here only stated that the severest penalty was incurred by the violation of this day. 33-44. The feast of tabernacles—This festival, which was instituted in grateful commemoration of the Israelites having securely dwelt in booths or tabernacles in the wilderness, was the third of the three great annual festivals, and, like the other two, it lasted a week. It began on the 15th day of the month, corresponding to the end of our September and beginning of October, which was observed as a Sabbath; and it could be celebrated only at the place of the sanctuary, offerings being made on the altar every day of its continuance. The Jews were commanded during the whole period of the festival to dwell in booths, which were erected on the flat roofs of houses, in the streets or fields; and the trees made use of are by some stated to be the citron, the palm, the myrtle, and the willow, while others maintain the people were allowed to take any trees they could obtain that were distinguished for verdure and fragrance. While the solid branches were reserved for the construction of the booths, the lighter branches were carried by men, who marched in triumphal procession, singing psalms, and crying "Hosanna!" which signifies, "Save, we beseech thee!" (Ps. 118. 15, 25, 26.) It was a season of great rejoicing. But the ceremony of drawing water from the pool, which was done on the last day, seems to have been the introduction of a later period. (J. 7. 37.) That last day was the eighth, and, on account of the scene at Siloam, was called "the great day of the feast." The feast of ingathering, when the vintage was over, was celebrated also on that day, and as the conclusion of one of the great festivals, it was kept as a Sabbath.

CHAPTER XXIV.
Ver. 1-23. OIL FOR THE LAMPS. 2. Command the children of Israel—This is the repetition of a law given. (Ex. 27. 20, 21.) pure oil olive beaten—or cold-drawn, which is always of great purity. 3, 4. Aaron shall order it from the evening unto the morning—The daily presence of the priests was necessary to superintend the cleaning and trimming. of the pure candlestick—so called because of pure gold. This was symbolical of the light which ministers are to diffuse through the Church. 5-9. Take fine flour and bake twelve cakes—for the show bread, as previously appointed. (Ex. 25. 30.) Those cakes were baked by the Levites, the flour being furnished by the people, (1 Chr. 9. 32; 23. 29,) oil, wine, and salt being the other ingredients. (ch. 2. 13.) two tenth deals—*i.e.*, of an ephah—12⅘ lbs. weight each; and on each row or pile of cakes some frankincense was strewed, which, being burnt, led to the show bread being called " an offering made by fire." Every Sabbath a fresh supply was furnished: hot loaves were placed on the altar instead of the stale ones which, having lain a week, were removed, and eaten only by the priests, except in cases of necessity. (1 Sa. 21. 3-6; also L. 6. 3, 4.) 10. The son of an Israelitish woman, &c.—This passage narrates the enactment of a new law, with a detail of the circumstances which gave rise to it. The "mixed multitude" that accompanied the Israelites in their Exodus from Egypt, creates a presumption that marriage connections of the kind described were not infrequent. And it was most natural, in the relative circumstances of the two people, that the father should be an Egyptian, and the mother an Israelite. 11. Blasphemed the name of the Lord—A youth of this half-blood, having quarrelled with a native Israelite, vented his rage in some horrid form of impiety. It was a common practice among the Egyptians to curse their idols, when disappointed in obtaining the object of their petitions. The Egyptian mind of this youth thought the greatest insult to his opponent was to blaspheme the object of his religious reverence. He spoke disrespectfully of one who sustained the double character of the king as well as the God of the Hebrew people; and as the offence was a new one, he was put in ward till the mind of the Lord was ascertained as to his disposal. 14. Bring forth him without the camp—All executions took place without the camp; and this arrangement probably originated in the idea, that, as the Israelites were to be "a holy people," all flagrant offenders should be thrust out of their society. let all that heard him lay, &c.—The imposition of hands formed a public and solemn testimony against the crime, and at the same time made the punishment legal. 16. As well the stranger as he that is born in the land—Although strangers were not obliged to be circumcised, yet by joining the Israelitish camp they became amenable to the law, especially that which related to blasphemy. 17 22. He that killeth any man—These verses contain a repetition of some other laws, relating to offences of a social nature, the penalties for which were to be inflicted not by the hand of private parties, but through the medium of the judges before whom the cause was brought. 23. The children of Israel did as the Lord commanded—The chapter closes with the execution of Shelomith's son—and stoning having afterwards became the established punishment in all cases of blasphemy, illustrates the fate of Stephen, who suffered under a false imputation of that crime.

CHAPTER XXV.
Ver. 1--7. SABBATH OF THE SEVENTH YEAR. 2-4. When ye come to the land which I give unto you—It has been questioned on what year, after the occupation of Canaan, the Sabbatic year began to be observed. Some think it was the seventh year after their entrance. But others, considering that as the first six years were spent in the conquest and division of the land, (Josh. 5. 12,) and that the Sabbatical year was to be observed after six years of agriculture, maintain that the observance did not commence till the 14th year. the land keep a Sabbath unto the Lord—This was a very peculiar arrangement. Not only all agricultural processes were to be intermitted every seventh year, but the cultivators had no right to the soil. It lay entirely fallow, and its spontaneous produce was the common property of the poor and the stranger, the cattle and game. This year of rest was to invigorate the productive powers of the land, as the weekly Sabbath was a refreshment to men and cattle. It commenced immediately after the feast of ingathering; and it was calculated to teach the people, in a remarkable manner, the reality of the presence and providential power of God.

8-23. THE JUBILEE. Thou shalt number

46 And ye shall take them as an inheritance for your children after you, to inherit *them for* a possession; [12] they shall be your bondmen for ever: but over your brethren the children of Israel ye shall not rule one over another with rigour.

47 ¶ And if a sojourner or stranger [13] wax rich by thee, and thy brother *that dwelleth* by him wax poor, and sell himself unto the stranger *or* sojourner by thee, or to the stock of the stranger's family:

48 After that he is sold he may be redeemed again; one of his brethren may redeem him:

49 Either his uncle, or his uncle's son, may redeem him, or *any* that is nigh of kin unto him of his family may redeem him; or, if he be able, he may redeem himself.

50 And he shall reckon with him that bought him from the year that he was sold to him unto the year of jubilee: and the price of his sale shall be according unto the number of years, according to the time of an hired servant shall it be with him.

51 If *there be* yet many years *behind*, according unto them he shall give again the price of his redemption out of the money that he was bought for.

52 And if there remain but few years unto the year of jubilee, then he shall count with him, *and* according unto his years shall he give him again the price of his redemption.

53 *And* as a yearly hired servant shall he be with him: *and the other* shall not rule with rigour over him in thy sight.

54 And if he be not redeemed [14] in these *years*, then he shall go out in the year of jubilee, *both* he, and his children with him.

55 For unto me the children of Israel *are* servants; they *are* my servants whom I brought forth out of the land of Egypt: I am the LORD your God.

CHAPTER XXVI.

1 *Of idolatry.* 2 *Of religiousness.* 3 *A blessing to the obedient* 14 *A curse to the disobedient.* 40 *A promise to the penitent.*

YE shall make you *a* no idols nor graven image, neither rear you up a [1] standing image, neither shall ye set up *any* [2] image of stone in your land, to bow down unto it: for I *am* the LORD your God.

2 Ye shall keep my sabbaths, and reverence my sanctuary: I *am* the LORD.

3 ¶ If ye walk in my statutes, and keep my commandments, and do them;

4 Then *b* I will give you rain in due season, and the land shall yield her increase, and the trees of the field shall yield their fruit.

5 And your threshing shall reach unto the vintage, and the vintage shall reach unto the sowing time; and *c* ye shall eat your bread to the full, and *d* dwell in your land safely.

6 And *e* I will give peace in the land, and ye *f* shall lie down, and none shall make you afraid: and I will *g* rid *h* evil beasts out of the land, neither shall *h* the sword go through your land.

7 And ye shall chase your enemies, and they shall fall before you by the sword.

8 And five of you shall chase an hundred, and an hundred of you shall put ten thousand to flight: and your enemies shall fall before you by the sword.

B. C. 1490.

CHAP. 25.
12 ye shall serve yourselves with them.
13 his hand obtain, etc.
14 Or, by these means.

CHAP. 26.
a Ex. 20. 4, 5. Ps. 97. 7.
1 Or, pillar.
2 a stone of picture, or, figured stone.
b Is. 30. 23.
c Deu. 11. 15. Joel 2. 19, 26.
d Job 11. 18. Ezek. 34. 25.
e 1 Chr. 22. 9. Is. 45. 7.
f Ps. 3. 5. Jer. 30. 10.
3 cause to cease.
g 2 Kin. 17. 25. Ezek. 5. 17. Ezek. 14. 15.
h Josh. 23. 10. Ezek. 14 17.
i Ex. 2. 25. 2 Kings 13. 23.
j Ge. 17. 6, 7.
k Ezek. 37. 26.
l Deu. 32. 19.
m 2 Cor. 6. 16. Eph. 2. 21. Heb. 3. 6.
n Ezek. 11. 20.
o Ezek. 34. 27.
p Deu. 28. 15.
q 2 Kin. 17. 15.
4 upon you.
r Deu. 28. 22.
s 1 Sa. 2. 33.
t Job 31. 8.
u Judg. 2. 14.
v Ps. 106. 41.
w Ps. 53. 5.
x 1 Sa. 2. 5.
y 1 Sa. 4. 10. Is. 25. 11.
z Ps. 127. 1. Is. 49. 4.
a Deu. 28. 18. Hag. 1. 10.
5 Or, at all adventures with me.
b 2 Ki. 17. 25.
c Judg. 5. 6. 2 Chr. 15. 5. Zech. 7. 14.
d Jer. 5. 3.
e 2 Sam. 22. 27.
f Ezek. 5. 3.
g Amos 4. 10.
h Is. 3. 1.
i Mic. 6. 14.
j Is. 59. 19.
k 2 Ki. 6. 29.

9 For I will *i* have respect unto you, and make *j* you fruitful, and multiply you, and establish my covenant with you.

10 And ye shall eat old store, and bring forth the old because of the new.

11 And *k* I will set my tabernacle among you, and my soul shall not *l* abhor you.

12 And *m* I will walk among you, and will *n* be your God, and ye shall be my people.

13 I *am* the LORD your God, which brought you forth out of the land of Egypt, that *e* should not be their bondmen; *o* and I have broken the bands of your yoke, and made you go upright.

14 ¶ But *p* if ye will not hearken unto me, and will not do all these commandments;

15 And if ye shall *q* despise my statutes, or if your soul abhor my judgments, so that ye will not do all my commandments, *but* that ye break my covenant;

16 I also will do this unto you; I will even appoint [4] over you terror, *r* consumption, and the burning ague, that shall *s* consume the eyes, and cause sorrow of heart: and ye *t* shall sow your seed in vain, for your enemies shall eat it.

17 And I will set my face against you, and ye *u* shall be slain before your enemies: they *v* that hate you shall reign over you; and *w* ye shall flee when none pursueth you.

18 And if ye will not yet for all this hearken unto me, then I will punish you *x* seven times more for your sins.

19 And I will *y* break the pride of your power; and I will make your heaven as iron, and your earth as brass:

20 And your *z* strength shall be spent in vain: for *a* your land shall not yield her increase, neither shall the trees of the land yield their fruits.

21 And if ye walk [5] contrary unto me, and will not hearken unto me; I will bring seven times more plagues upon you, according to your sins.

22 I *b* will also send wild beasts among you, which shall rob you of your children, and destroy your cattle, and make you few in number; and *c* your *high* ways shall be desolate.

23 And if ye *d* will not be reformed by me by these things, but will walk contrary unto me;

24 Then *e* will I also walk contrary unto you, and will punish you yet seven times for your sins.

25 And *f* I will bring a sword upon you, that shall avenge the quarrel of *my* covenant: and when ye are gathered together within your cities, I *g* will send the pestilence among you; and ye shall be delivered into the hand of the enemy.

26 *And* *h* when I have broken the staff of your bread, ten women shall bake your bread in one oven, and they shall deliver *you* your bread again by weight; and *i* ye shall eat, and not be satisfied.

27 And if ye will not for all this hearken unto me, but walk contrary unto me;

28 Then I will walk contrary unto you also *j* in fury; and I, even I, will chastise you seven times for your sins.

29 And *k* ye shall eat the flesh of your sons, and the flesh of your daughters shall ye eat.

seven Sabbaths of years—This most extraordinary of all civil institutions, which received the name of "Jubilee" from a *Heb.* word signifying a musical instrument, a horn or trumpet, began on the 10th day of the seventh month, or the great day of atonement, when, by order of the public authorities, the sound of trumpets proclaimed the beginning of the universal redemption All prisoners and captives obtained their liberties, slaves were declared free, and debtors were absolved. The land, as on the Sabbatic year, was neither sowed nor reaped, but allowed to enjoy with its inhabitants a Sabbath of repose; and its natural produce was the common property of all. Moreover, every inheritance throughout the land of Judea was restored to its ancient owner. hallow the fiftieth year—Much difference of opinion exists as to whether the jubilee was observed on the 49th, or in round numbers, it is called the 50th. The prevailing opinion, both in ancient and modern times, has been in favour of the latter. 12. Ye shall eat the increase thereof, &c.—All that the ground yielded spontaneously during that period might be eaten for their necessary subsistence, but no persons were at liberty to hoard or form a private stock in reserve. 13. Ye shall return, &c.—Inheritances, from whatever cause, and how frequently soever they had been alienated, came back into the hands of the original proprietors. This law of entail, by which the right heir could never be excluded, was a provision of great wisdom for preserving families and tribes perfectly distinct, and their genealogies faithfully recorded, in order that all might have evidence to establish their right to the ancestral property. Hence the tribe and family of Christ were readily discovered at his birth. 17. Ye shall not oppress one another —This, which is the same as *v.* 14, related to the sale or purchase of possessions, and the duty of paying an honest and equitable regard, on both sides, to the limited period during which the bargain could stand. The object of the legislator was, as far as possible, to maintain the original order of families, and an equality of condition among the people. 21, 22. I will command my blessing, &c.—A provision was made, by the special interposition of God, to supply the deficiency of food which would otherwise have resulted from the suspension of all labour during the Sabbatic year. The sixth year was to yield a miraculous supply for three continuous years. And the remark is applicable to the year of Jubilee as well as the Sabbatic year. (See allusions to this extraordinary provision in 2 Ki. 19. 29; Is. 37. 30.) None but a legislator who was conscious of acting under Divine authority would have staked his character on so singular an enactment as that of the Sabbatical year; and none but a people who had witnessed the fulfilment of the Divine promise would have been induced to suspend their agricultural preparations on a recurrence of a periodical Jubilee. 23-28. The land shall not be sold for ever—or, "be quite cut off," as the margin better renders it. The land was God's, and, in prosecution of an important design, he gave it to the people of his choice, dividing it amongst their tribes and families—who, however, held it of Him merely as tenants at will, and had no right or power of disposing of it to strangers. In necessitous circumstances, individuals might effect a temporary sale. But they possessed the right of redeeming it, at *any time,* on payment of an adequate compensation to the present holder; and by the enactments of the Jubilee they recovered it free—so that the land was rendered inalienable. (See an exception to this law, ch. 27. 20. 29-31. If a man sell a dwelling-house—All sales of houses were subject to the same condition. But there was a difference between the houses of villages, which, being connected with agriculture, were treated as parts of the land; and houses possessed by trading people or foreigners in walled towns, which could only be redeemed within the year after the sale; if not then redeemed, these did not revert to the former owner at the Jubilee. 32-34. Notwithstanding the cities, &c.—The Levites, having no possessions but their towns and their houses, the law conferred on them the same privileges that were granted to the lands of the other Israelites. A certain portion of the lands surrounding the Levitical cities was appropriated to them for the pasturage of their cattle and flocks. (Nu. 35. 4, 5.) This was a permanent endowment for the support of the ministry, and could not be alienated for any time. The Levites, however, were at liberty to make exchanges amongst themselves; and a priest might sell his house, garden, and right of pasture to another priest, but not to an Israelite of another tribe. (Jer. 31. 7-9.) 35-38. If thy brother be waxen poor, relieve him—This was a most benevolent provision for the poor and unfortunate, designed to aid them or alleviate the evils of their condition. Whether a native Israelite or a mere sojourner, his richer neighbour was required to give him food, lodging, and a supply of money without usury. The latter was severely condemned. Ps. 15. 5; Ez. 18. 8, 17.) but the prohibition cannot be considered as applicable to the modern practice of men in business borrowing and lending at legal rates of interest. 39-46. If thy brother be waxen poor, and be sold unto thee—An Israelite might be compelled, through misfortune, not only to mortgage his inheritance, but himself. In the event of his being reduced to this distress, he was to be treated not as a slave, but a hired servant, whose engagement was temporary, and who might, through the friendly aid of a relative, be redeemed at any time before the Jubilee. The ransom money was determined on a most equitable principle. Taking account of the number of years from the proposal to redeem and the Jubilee—of the current wages of labour for that time, and multiplying the remaining years by that sum, the amount was to be paid to the master for his redemption. But if no such friendly interposition was made for a Hebrew slave, he continued in servitude till the year of Jubilee, when, as a matter of course, he regained his liberty, as well as his inheritance. Viewed in the various aspects in which it is presented in this chapter, the Jubilee was an admirable institution, and subservient in an eminent degree to uphold the interests of religion, social order, and freedom amongst the Israelites.

CHAPTER XXVI.

Ver. 1, 2. OF IDOLATRY. 1. Ye shall make

30 And I will destroy your high places, and cut down your images, and cast your carcases upon the carcases of your idols, and my soul shall abhor you.

31 And I will make your cities waste, and bring your sanctuaries unto desolation, and I will not smell the savour of your sweet odours.

32 And I will bring the land into desolation: and your enemies which dwell therein shall be astonished at it.

33 And I will scatter you among the heathen, and will draw out a sword after you: and your land shall be desolate, and your cities waste.

34 Then shall the land enjoy her sabbaths, as long as it lieth desolate, and ye be in your enemies' land; even then shall the land rest, and enjoy her sabbaths.

35 As long as it lieth desolate it shall rest; because it did not rest in your sabbaths, when ye dwelt upon it.

36 And upon them that are left *alive* of you I will send a faintness into their hearts in the lands of their enemies; and the sound of a shaken leaf shall chase them; and they shall flee, as fleeing from a sword; and they shall fall when none pursueth.

37 And they shall fall one upon another, as it were before a sword, when none pursueth: and ye shall have no power to stand before your enemies.

38 And ye shall perish among the heathen, and the land of your enemies shall eat you up.

39 And they that are left of you shall pine away in their iniquity in your enemies' lands; and also in the iniquities of their fathers shall they pine away with them.

40 If they shall confess their iniquity, and the iniquity of their fathers, with their trespass which they trespassed against me, and that also they have walked contrary unto me;

41 And *that* I also have walked contrary unto them, and have brought them into the land of their enemies; if then their uncircumcised hearts be humbled, and they then accept of the punishment of their iniquity;

42 Then will I remember my covenant with Jacob, and also my covenant with Isaac, and also my covenant with Abraham will I remember; and I will remember the land.

43 The land also shall be left of them, and shall enjoy her sabbaths, while she lieth desolate without them: and they shall accept of the punishment of their iniquity: because, even because they despised my judgments, and because their soul abhorred my statutes.

44 And yet for all that, when they be in the land of their enemies, I will not cast them away, neither will I abhor them, to destroy them utterly, and to break my covenant with them: for I *am* the LORD their God.

45 But I will for their sakes remember the covenant of their ancestors, whom I brought forth out of the land of Egypt in the sight of the heathen, that I might be their God: I *am* the LORD.

46 These *are* the statutes and judgments and laws which the LORD made between him and the children of Israel in mount Sinai by the hand of Moses.

CHAPTER XXVII.

1 *Concerning vows.* 28 *Of the Lord's firstlings.* 28 *No devoted thing may be redeemed.* 30 *The tithe may not be changed.*

AND the LORD spake unto Moses, saying,

2 Speak unto the children of Israel, and say unto them, When a man shall make a singular vow, the person *shall be* for the LORD by thy estimation.

3 And thy estimation shall be of the male from twenty years old even unto sixty years old, even thy estimation shall be fifty shekels of silver, after the shekel of the sanctuary.

4 And if it be a female, then thy estimation shall be thirty shekels.

5 And if *it be* from five years old even unto twenty years old, then thy estimation shall be of the male twenty shekels, and for the female ten shekels.

6 And if *it be* from a month old even unto five years old, then thy estimation shall be of the male five shekels of silver, and for the female thy estimation *shall be* three shekels of silver.

7 And if *it be* from sixty years old and above; if *it be* a male, then thy estimation shall be fifteen shekels, and for the female ten shekels.

8 But if he be poorer than thy estimation, then he shall present himself before the priest, and the priest shall value him; according to his ability that vowed shall the priest value him.

9 And if *it be* a beast, whereof men bring an offering unto the LORD, all that any man giveth of such unto the LORD shall be holy.

10 He shall not alter it, nor change it, a good for a bad, or a bad for a good: and if he shall at all change beast for beast, then it and the exchange thereof shall be holy.

11 And if *it be* any unclean beast, of which they do not offer a sacrifice unto the LORD, then he shall present the beast before the priest:

12 And the priest shall value it, whether it be good or bad: as thou valuest it, *who* art the priest, so shall it be.

13 But if he will at all redeem it, then he shall add a fifth *part* thereof unto thy estimation.

14 ¶ And when a man shall sanctify his house *to be* holy unto the LORD, then the priest shall estimate it, whether it be good or bad: as the priest shall estimate it, so shall it stand.

15 And if he that sanctified it will redeem his house, then he shall add the fifth *part* of the money of thy estimation unto it, and it shall be his.

16 And if a man shall sanctify unto the LORD *some part* of a field of his possession, then thy estimation shall be according to the seed thereof: an homer of barley seed *shall be valued* at fifty shekels of silver.

17 If he sanctify his field from the year of jubilee, according to thy estimation it shall stand.

18 But if he sanctify his field after the jubilee, then the priest shall reckon unto him the money according to the years that remain, even unto the year of the jubilee, and it shall be abated from thy estimation.

19 And if he that sanctified the field will in any wise redeem it, then he shall add

A Blessing to the Obedient.   LEVITICUS, XXVI.   *A Curse to the Disobedient.*

you no idols—Idolatry had been previously forbidden, (Ex. 20. 4, 5,) but the law was repeated here with reference to some particular forms of it that were very prevalent among the neighbouring nations. a standing image—*i.e.*, upright pillar. the image of stone—*i.e.*, an obelisk, inscribed with hieroglyphical and superstitious characters. The former denoting the common and smaller pillars of the Syrians or Canaanites; the latter, pointing to the large and elaborate obelisks which the Egyptians worshipped as guardian divinities, or used as stones of adoration to stimulate religious worship. The Israelites were enjoined to beware of them. 2. Ye shall keep my Sabbaths—Very frequently, in this book of the law, the Sabbath and the sanctuary are mentioned as antidotes to idolatry.

3-13. A BLESSING TO THE OBEDIENT. 3. If ye walk in my statutes—In that covenant into which God graciously entered with the people of Israel, He promised to bestow upon them a variety of blessings, so long as they continued obedient to Him as their Almighty Ruler; and in their subsequent history that people found every promise amply fulfilled, in the enjoyment of plenty, peace, a populous country, and victory over all enemies. 4. I will give you rain in due season —Rain seldom fell in Judea except at two seasons—the former rain at the end of autumn—the seed time; and the latter rain in spring, before the beginning of harvest. (Jer. 5. 24.) 5. Your threshing shall reach, &c.—The barley harvest in Judea was about the middle of April; the wheat harvest about six weeks after, or in the beginning of June. After the harvest comes the vintage, and fruit-gathering towards the latter end of July. Moses led the Hebrews to believe, that, provided they were faithful to God, there would be no idle time between the harvest and vintage, so great would be the increase. (See Amos, 9. 13.) This promise would be very animating to a people who had come from a country where, for three months, they were pent up without being able to walk abroad, from the fields being under water. 10. Ye shall eat old store—Their stock of old corn would be still unexhausted and large when the next harvest brought a new supply. 13. I have broken the bands of your yoke—a metaphorical expression to denote their emancipation from Egyptian slavery.

14-39. A CURSE TO THE DISOBEDIENT. But if ye will not, &c.—In proportion to the great and manifold privileges bestowed upon the Israelites, would be the extent of their national criminality and the severity of their national punishments if they disobeyed. 16. Terror—the falling sickness. [PATRICK.] consumption and the burning ague—Some consider these as symptoms of the same disease; consumption followed by the shivering, burning, and sweating fits that are the usual concomitants of that malady. According to the Septuagint, ague is "the jaundice," which disorders the eyes and produces great depression of spirits. Others, however, consider the word as referring to a scorching wind;—no certain explanation can be given. 18. Punish you seven times more—*i.e.*, with far more severe and protracted calamities. 19. Will make your heaven as iron—No figures could have been employed to convey a better idea of severe and long-continued famine. 22. I will send wild beasts—This was one of the four judgments threatened. (Ez. 14. 21; see also 2 Ki. 2. 24.) your highways, &c.—Trade and commerce will be destroyed—freedom and safety will be gone —neither stranger nor native will be found on the roads. (Is. 33. 8.) This is an exact picture of the present state of the Holy Land, which has long lain in a state of desolation, brought on by the sins of the ancient Jews. 26. Ten women shall bake, &c.—The bread used in families is usually baked by women, and at home. But, sometimes also, in times of scarcity, it is baked in public ovens for want of fuel; and the scarcity predicted here would be so great, that one oven would be sufficient to bake as much as ten women used in ordinary occasions to provide for family use; and even this scanty portion of bread would be distributed by weight. (Ez. 4. 16.) 29. Ye shall eat the flesh of your sons—The revolting picture was actually exhibited at the siege of Samaria, at the siege of Jerusalem by Nebuchadnezzar, (Lam. 4. 10,) and at the destruction of that city by the Romans. (See on Deu. 28.) 30. I will destroy your high places—Consecrated enclosures on the tops of mountains, or on little hillocks, raised for practising the rites of idolatry. Cut down your images—According to some, those images were made in the form of chariots, (2 Ki. 23, 11;) according to others, they were of a conical form, like small pyramids. Reared in honour of the sun, they were usually placed on a very high situation, to enable the worshippers to have a better view of the rising sun. They were forbidden to the Israelites, and when set up, ordered to be destroyed. Cast your carcases, &c.—Like the statues of idols, which, when broken, lie neglected and contemned, the Jews during the sieges and subsequent captivity often wanted the rites of sepulture. 31. I will make your cities waste—This destruction of its numerous and flourishing cities which was brought upon Judea, through the sins of Israel, took place by the forced removal of the people during, and long after, the captivity. But it is realized to a far greater extent now. Bring your sanctuaries, &c.—The tabernacle and temple, as is evident from the tenor of the subsequent clause, in which God announces that He will not accept or regard their sacrifices. 33. I will scatter, &c.—as was done when the elite of the nation were removed into Assyria, and placed in various parts of that kingdom. 34. Then shall the land, &c.—A long arrear of Sabbatic years had accumulated through the avarice and apostacy of the Israelites, who had deprived their land of its appointed season of rest. The number of those Sabbatic years seems to have been 70, as determined by the duration of the captivity. This early prediction is very remarkable, considering that the usual policy of the Assyrian conquerors was to send colonies to cultivate and inhabit their newly acquired provinces. 38. The land of your enemies, &c.—On the removal of the ten tribes into captivity, they never returned, and all traces of them were lost. 40-45. If they shall confess, &c.—This passage holds out the gracious promise of Divine forgiveness and favour on their repentance, and their happy restoration to their own land, in memory of the covenant made with their fathers. (Ro. 2.) 46. These are the statutes—It has been thought by some that the last chapter was originally placed

the fifth *part* of the money of thy estimation unto it, and it shall be assured to him.

20 And if he will not redeem the field, or if he have sold the field to another man, it shall not be redeemed any more.

21 But the field, *f* when it goeth out in the jubilee, shall be holy unto the LORD, as a field devoted; *g* the possession thereof shall be the priest's.

22 And if *a man* sanctify unto the LORD a field which he hath bought, which *is* not of the fields of his possession;

23 Then the priest shall reckon unto him the worth of thy estimation, *even* unto the year of the jubilee: and he shall give thine estimation in that day, *as* a holy thing unto the LORD.

24 In *h* the year of the jubilee the field shall return unto him of whom it was bought, *even* to him to whom the possession of the land *did belong*.

25 And all thy estimations shall be according to the shekel of the sanctuary: twenty *i* gerahs shall be the shekel.

26 ¶ Only the *k* firstling of the beasts, which should be the LORD's firstling, no man shall sanctify it: whether *it be* ox or sheep, it *is* the LORD's.

27 And if *it be* of an unclean beast, then he shall redeem *it* according to thine estimation, and shall add a fifth *part* of it thereto: or if it be not redeemed, then it shall be sold according to thy estimation.

28 Notwithstanding *j* no devoted thing that a man shall devote unto the LORD of all that he hath, *both* of man and beast, and of the field of his possession, shall be sold or redeemed: every devoted thing *is* most holy unto the LORD.

29 ¶ None devoted, which shall be devoted of men, shall be redeemed; *but* shall surely be put to death.

30 And *k* all the tithe of the land, *whether* of the seed of the land, *or* of the fruit of the tree, *is* the LORD's: *it is* holy unto the LORD.

31 And if a man will at all redeem *ought* of his tithes, he shall add thereto the fifth *part* thereof.

32 And concerning the tithe of the herd, or of the flock, *even* of whatsoever *l* passeth under the rod, the tenth shall be holy unto the LORD.

33 He shall not search whether it be good or bad, neither shall he change it: and if he change it at all, then both it and the change thereof shall be holy; it shall not be redeemed.

34 These *are* the commandments, which the LORD commanded Moses for the children of Israel in mount Sinai.

THE FOURTH BOOK OF MOSES, CALLED

NUMBERS.

CHAPTER I.

1, 17 The men of war numbered. 47 The Levites exempted for the tabernacle service.

AND the LORD spake unto Moses *a* in the wilderness of Sinai, *b* in the tabernacle of the congregation, on the first *day* of the second month, in the second year after they were come out of the land of Egypt, saying,

2 Take *c* ye the sum of all the congregation of the children of Israel, after their families, by the house of their fathers, with the number of *their* names, every male by their polls;

3 From twenty years old and upward, all that are able to go forth to war in Israel: thou and Aaron shall number them by their armies.

4 And with you there shall be *d* a man of every tribe; every one head of the house of his fathers.

5 ¶ And these *are* the names of the men that shall stand with you: of *e the tribe of* Reuben; Elizur the son of Shedeur.

6 Of Simeon; Shelumiel the son of Zurishaddai.

7 Of Judah; *f* Nahshon the son of Amminadab.

8 Of Issachar; Nethaneel the son of Zuar.

9 Of Zebulun; Eliab the son of Helon.

10 Of the children of Joseph: of Ephraim; Elishama the son of Ammihud: of Manasseh; Gamaliel the son of Pedahzur.

11 Of Benjamin; Abidan the son of Gideoni.

12 Of Dan; Ahiezer the son of Ammishaddai.

13 Of Asher; Pagiel the son of Ocran.

14 Of Gad; Eliasaph the son of *g* Deuel.

15 Of Naphtali; Ahira the son of Enan.

16 These *h* were the renowned of the congregation, princes of the tribes of their fathers, heads *i* of thousands in Israel.

17 ¶ And Moses and Aaron took these men which are expressed by *their* names:

18 And they assembled all the congregation together on the first *day* of the second month, and they declared their *j* pedigrees after their families, by the house of their fathers, according to the number of the names, from twenty years old and upward, by their polls.

19 As *k* the LORD commanded Moses, so he numbered them in the wilderness of Sinai.

20 ¶ And the children of Reuben, Israel's eldest son, by their generations, after their families, by the house of their fathers, according to the number of the names, by their polls, every male from twenty years old and upward, all that were able to go forth to war;

21 Those that were numbered of them, *even* of the tribe of Reuben, *were* forty and six thousand and five hundred.

22 ¶ Of the children of Simeon, by their generations, after their families, by the house of their fathers, those that were numbered of them, according to the number of the names, by their polls, every male from twenty years old and upward, all that were able to go forth to war;

23 Those that were numbered of them, *even* of the tribe of Simeon, *were* fifty and nine thousand and three hundred.

24 ¶ Of the children of *m* Gad, by their generations, after their families, by the

after the 25th, [ADAM CLARKE,] while others consider that the next chapter was added as an appendix, in consequence of many people being influenced by the promises and threats of the preceding one, to resolve that they would dedicate themselves and their possessions to God. [CALMET.]

CHAPTER XXVII.

Ver. 1-19. CONCERNING VOWS. 2-8. When a man shall make, &c.—Persons have, at all times and in all places, been accustomed to present votive offerings, either from gratitude for benefits received, or in the event of deliverance from apprehended evil. And Moses was empowered, by Divine authority, to prescribe the conditions of this voluntary duty. the person shall be for the Lord, &c.—better rendered thus:—" According to thy estimation, the persons shall be for the Lord." Persons might consecrate themselves or their children to the Divine service, in some inferior or servile kind of work about the sanctuary. (1 Sam. 3. 1.) In the event of any change, the persons so devoted had the privilege in their power of redeeming themselves; and this chapter specifies the amount of the redemption money, which the priest had the discretionary power of reducing, as circumstances might seem to require. Those of mature age, between 20 and 60, being capable of the greatest service, were rated highest; young people, from 5 till 20, less, because not so serviceable; infants, though devotable by their parents before birth, (1 Sam. 1. 11,) could not be offered nor redeemed till a month after it; old people were valued below the young, but above children; and the poor—in no case freed from payment in order to prevent the rash formation of vows—were rated according to their means. 9-13. If it be a beast—a clean beast, after it had been vowed, it could neither be employed in common purposes nor exchanged for an equivalent—it must be sacrificed—or if, through some discovered blemish, it was unsuitable for the altar, it might be sold, and the money applied for the sacred service. If an unclean beast—such as an ass or camel, for instance—had been vowed, it was to be appropriated to the use of the priest at the estimated value, or it might be redeemed by the person vowing on payment of that value, and the additional fine of a fifth more. 14-16. When a man, &c.—In this case, the house having been valued by the priest and sold, the proceeds of the sale were to be dedicated to the sanctuary. But if the owner wished, on second thoughts, to redeem it, he might have it by adding a fifth part to the price. 16-24. If a man, &c.—In the case of acquired property in land, if not redeemed, it returned to the donor at the Jubilee; whereas the part of a hereditary estate, which had been vowed, did not revert to the owner, but remained attached to the sanctuary. The reason of this remarkable difference was to lay every man under an obligation to redeem the property, or stimulate his nearest kinsman to do it, in order to prevent a patrimonial inheritance going out from any family in Israel. 26, 27. Only the firstlings—These, in the case of clean beasts, being consecrated to God by a universal and standing law, (Ex. 13. 12; 34. 19,) could not be devoted; and in that of unclean beasts, were subject to the rule mentioned (v. 11, 12.). 28, 29. No devoted thing . . . shall be sold or redeemed—This relates to vows of the most solemn kind — the devotee accompanying his vow with a solemn imprecation on himself not to fail in accomplishing his declared purpose. shall surely be put to death—This announcement imported not that the person was to be sacrificed or doomed to a violent death; but only that he should remain till death unalterably in the devoted condition. The preceding regulations were evidently designed to prevent rashness in vowing, (Ec. 5. 4,) and to encourage serious and considerate reflection in all matters between God and the soul. (L. 21. 4.) 30-33. All the tithe of the land—This law gave the sanction of Divine authority to an ancient usage. (Ge. 14. 20; 28. 22.) The whole produce of the land was subjected to the tithe tribute—it was a yearly rent which the Israelites, as tenants, paid to God, the owner of the land, and a thank-offering they rendered to Him for the bounties of His providence. (See Pro. 3. 9; 1 Co. 9. 11; Gal. 6. 6.) 32. Whatsoever passeth, &c.—This alludes to the mode of taking the tithe of cattle, which were made to pass singly through a narrow gateway, where a person with a rod, tipped in ochre, stood, and counting them, marked the back of every tenth beast, whether male or female, sound or unsound. 34. These are the commandments, &c.—The laws contained in this book, for the most part ceremonial, had an important spiritual bearing, the study of which is highly instructive. (Ro. 10. 4; He. 4. 2; 12. 18.) They imposed a burdensome yoke, (A. 15. 10,) but yet in the infantine age of the Church formed the necessary discipline of "a schoolmaster to Christ."

THE FOURTH BOOK OF MOSES, CALLED

NUMBERS.

CHAPTER I.

Ver. 1-54. MOSES NUMBERING THE MEN OF WAR. 1. On the first day, &c.—Thirteen months had elapsed since the Exodus. About one month had been occupied in the journey; and the rest of the period had been passed in encampment amongst the recesses of Sinai, where the transactions took place, and the laws, religious and civil, were promulgated, which are contained in the two preceding books. As the tabernacle was erected on the first day of the first month, and the order here mentioned was given on the first day of the second, some think the laws in Leviticus were all given in one month. The Israelites having been formed into a separate nation, under the special government of God as their king, it was necessary, before re-

house of their fathers, according to the number of the names, from twenty years old and upward, all that were able to go forth to war;

25 Those that were numbered of them, even of the tribe of Gad, were forty and five thousand six hundred and fifty.

26 ¶ Of the *n* children of Judah, by their generations, after their families, by the house of their fathers, according to the number of the names, from twenty years old and upward, all that were able to go forth to war;

27 Those that were numbered of them, even of the tribe of Judah, were threescore and fourteen thousand and six hundred.

28 ¶ Of the children of Issachar, by their generations, after their families, by the house of their fathers, according to the number of the names, from twenty years old and upward, all that were able to go forth to war;

29 Those that were numbered of them, even of the tribe of Issachar, were fifty and four thousand and four hundred.

30 ¶ Of the children of Zebulun, by their generations, after their families, by the house of their fathers, according to the number of the names, from twenty years old and upward, all that were able to go forth to war;

31 Those that were numbered of them, even of the tribe of Zebulun, were fifty and seven thousand and four hundred.

32 ¶ Of the children of Joseph, *namely*, of the *o* children of Ephraim, by their generations, after their families, by the house of their fathers, according to the number of the names, from twenty years old and upward, all that were able to go forth to war;

33 Those that were numbered of them, even of the tribe of Ephraim, were forty thousand and five hundred.

34 ¶ Of the children of Manasseh, by their generations, after their families, by the house of their fathers, according to the number of the names, from twenty years old and upward, all that were able to go forth to war;

35 Those that were numbered of them, even of the tribe of Manasseh, were thirty and two thousand and two hundred.

36 ¶ Of the *p* children of Benjamin, by their generations, after their families, by the house of their fathers, according to the number of the names, from twenty years old and upward, all that were able to go forth to war;

37 Those that were numbered of them, even of the tribe of Benjamin, were thirty and five thousand and four hundred.

38 ¶ Of the *q* children of Dan, by their generations, after their families, by the house of their fathers, according to the number of the names, from twenty years old and upward, all that were able to go forth to war;

39 Those that were numbered of them, even of the tribe of Dan, were threescore and two thousand and seven hundred.

40 ¶ Of the children of Asher, by their generations, after their families, by the house of their fathers, according to the number of the names, from twenty years old and upward, all that were able to go forth to war;

41 Those that were numbered of them, even of the tribe of Asher, were forty and one thousand and five hundred.

42 ¶ Of the children of Naphtali, throughout their generations, after their families, by the house of their fathers, according to the number of the names, from twenty years old and upward, all that were able to go forth to war;

43 Those that were numbered of them, even of the tribe of Naphtali, were fifty and three thousand and four hundred.

44 ¶ These *r* are those that were numbered, which Moses and Aaron numbered, and the princes of Israel, *being* twelve men: each one was for the house of his fathers.

45 So were all those that were numbered of the children of Israel, by the house of their fathers, from twenty years old and upward, all that were able to go forth to war in Israel;

46 Even all they that were numbered, were *s* six hundred thousand and three thousand and five hundred and fifty.

47 ¶ But *t* the Levites after the tribe of their fathers were not numbered among them.

48 For the LORD had spoken unto Moses, saying,

49 Only *u* thou shalt not number the tribe of Levi, neither take the sum of them among the children of Israel:

50 But *v* thou shall appoint the Levites over the tabernacle of testimony, and over all the vessels thereof, and over all things that *belong* to it: they shall bear the tabernacle, and all the vessels thereof; and they shall minister unto it, *w* and shall encamp round about the tabernacle.

51 And *x* when the tabernacle setteth forward, the Levites shall take it down; and when the tabernacle is to be pitched, the Levites shall set it up; and *y* the stranger that cometh nigh shall be put to death.

52 And the children of Israel shall pitch their tents, *z* every man by his own camp, and every man by his own standard, throughout their hosts.

53 But the Levites shall pitch round about the tabernacle of testimony, that there be *a* no wrath upon the congregation of the children of Israel: *b* and the Levites shall keep the charge of the tabernacle of testimony.

54 And the children of Israel did according to all that the LORD commanded Moses, so did they.

CHAPTER II.
The order of the tribes in their tents, etc.

AND the LORD spake unto Moses and unto Aaron, saying,

2 Every *a* man of the children of Israel shall *b* pitch by his own standard, with the ensign of their father's house: ¹ far off about the tabernacle of the congregation shall they pitch.

3 ¶ And on the east side toward the rising of the sun shall they of the standard of the camp of Judah pitch, throughout their armies: and *c* Nahshon the son of Amminadab *shall be* captain of the children of Judah.

4 And his host, and those that were numbered of them, *were* threescore and fourteen thousand and six hundred.

5 And those that do pitch next unto him *shall be* the tribe of Issachar: *d* and

suming their march towards the promised land, to put them into good order. And accordingly Moses was commissioned, along with Aaron, to take a census of the people. This census was incidentally noticed (Ex. 38. 26,) in reference to the poll-tax for the works of the tabernacle; but it is here described in detail, in order to show the relative increase and military strength of the different tribes. The enumeration was confined to those capable of bearing arms, and it was to be made with a careful distinction of the tribe, family, and household to which every individual belonged. By this rule of summation many important advantages were secured—an exact genealogical register was formed—the relative strength of each tribe was ascertained, and the reason found for arranging the order of precedence in march as well as disposing the different tribes in camp around the tabernacle. The promise of God to Abraham was seen to be fulfilled in the extraordinary increase of his posterity, and provision made for tracing the regular descent of the Messiah. **3. By their armies—or companies.** In their departure from Egypt they were divided into five grand companies, Ex. 13. 18,) but from the sojourn in the wilderness to the passage of the Jordan they were formed into four great divisions. The latter is here referred to. **4-16. With you there shall be a man, &c.**—The social condition of the Israelites in the wilderness bore a close resemblance to that of the nomad tribes of the East in the present day. The head of the tribe was a hereditary dignity, vested in the eldest son or some other to whom the right of primogeniture was transferred, and under whom were other inferior heads, also hereditary, among the different branches of the tribe. The Israelites being divided into 12 tribes, there were 12 chiefs appointed to assist in taking the census of the people. **5. These are the names, &c.**—Each is designated by adding the name of the ancestors of his tribe, the people of which were called "Beni-Reuben, Beni-Levi," sons of Reuben, sons of Levi, according to the custom of the Arabs still, as well as other nations which are divided into clans, as the Macs of Scotland, the Aps of Wales, and the O's and Fitz's of Ireland. [CHALMERS.] **16-18. These were the renowned**—*lit.* the called of the congregation, summoned by name; and they entered upon the survey the very day the order was given. by their polls—individually, one by one. **19. As the Lord commanded, &c.**—The numbering of the people was not an act sinful in itself, as Moses did it by Divine appointment; but David incurred guilt by doing it without the authority of God. (See on 2 Sam. 24. 10.) **20-44. These are those that were numbered**—In this registration the tribe of Judah appears the most numerous; and accordingly, as the pre-eminence had been assigned to it by Jacob, it got the precedence in all the encampments of Israel. Of the two half tribes of Joseph, who is seen to be "a fruitful bough," that of Ephraim was the larger, as had been predicted. The relative increase of all, as in the two just mentioned, was owing to the special blessing of God, conformably to the prophetic declaration of the dying patriarch. But the Divine blessing is usually conveyed through the influence of secondary causes; and there is reason to believe that the relative populousness of the tribes would, under God, depend upon the productiveness of the respective localities assigned to them. **45, 46. Six hundred thousand, &c.**—What an astonishing increase from 75 persons who went down to Egypt about 215 years before, and who were subjected to the greatest privations and hardships! And yet this enumeration was restricted to men from 20 years and upwards. Including women, children, and old men, together with the Levites, the whole population of Israel, on the ordinary principles of computation, amounted to about 2,400,000. **47-54. But the Levites were not numbered**—They were obliged to keep a register of their own. They were consecrated to the priestly office, which in all countries has been exempted customarily, and in Israel by the express authority of God, from military service. The custody of the things devoted to the Divine service was assigned to them so exclusively, that "no stranger"—*i. e.*, no person, not even an Israelite of any other tribe, was allowed, under penalty of death, to approach these, and hence they encamped round the tabernacle, that there should be no manifestation of the Divine displeasure among the people. Thus the numbering of the people was subservient to the separation of the Levites from those Israelites who were fit for military service, and to the practical introduction of the law respecting the first-born, for whom the tribe of Levi became a substitute.

CHAPTER II.

Ver. 1-34. THE ORDER OF THE TRIBES IN THEIR TENTS. **2. Every man shall pitch by his own standard**—Standards were visible signs of a certain recognized form for directing the movements of large bodies of people. As the Israelites were commanded to encamp "each by his own standard, with the ensign of their father's house," the direction has been considered as implying that they possessed three varieties—(1.) the great tribal standards, which served as rallying points for the twelve large clans of the people; (2.) the standards of the subdivided portions; and, (3.) those of families or houses. The latter must have been absolutely necessary, as one ensign only for a tribe would not have been visible at the extremities of so large a body. We possess no authentic information as to their forms, material, colours, and devices. But it is probable that they might bear some resemblance to those of Egypt, only stripped of any idolatrous symbols. These were of an umbrella or a fan-like form, made of ostrich feathers, shawls, &c., lifted on the points of long poles, which were borne, either like the sacred central one, on a car, or on men's shoulders, whilst others might be like the beacon lights which are set on poles by Eastern pilgrims at night. Jewish writers say that the standards of the Hebrew tribes were symbols borrowed from the prophetic blessing of Jacob—Judah's being a lion, Benjamin's a wolf, &c.; and that the ensigns or banners were distinguished by their colours—the colours of each tribe being the same as that of the precious stone representing that tribe in the breastplate of the high priest. **far off ... about the tabernacle, &c.**—*i. e.*, over against at a reverential distance. The place of every tribe is successively and specifically described, because each had a certain part assigned both in the order of

Nethaneel the son of Zuar shall be captain of the children of Issachar.

6 And his host, and those that were numbered thereof, were *fifty and four thousand and four hundred.

7 *Then the tribe of ƒ Zebulun: and Eliab the son of Helon shall be captain of the children of Zebulun.

8 And his host, and those that were numbered thereof, were fifty and seven thousand and four hundred.

9 All that were numbered in the camp of Judah were an hundred thousand and fourscore thousand and six thousand and four hundred, throughout their armies. ƒ These shall first set forth.

10 ¶ On the south side shall be the standard of the camp of ʰ Reuben according to their armies: and the captain of the children of Reuben shall be Elizur the son of Shedeur.

11 And his host, and those that were numbered thereof, were forty and six thousand and five hundred.

12 And those which pitch by him shall be the tribe of Simeon: and the captain of the children of Simeon shall be Shelumiel the son of Zurishaddai.

13 And his host, and those that were numbered of them, were fifty and nine thousand and three hundred.

14 Then the tribe of Gad: and the captain of the sons of Gad shall be Eliasaph the son of ᶻ Reuel.

15 And his host, and those that were numbered of them, were forty and five thousand and six hundred and fifty.

16 All that were numbered in the camp of Reuben were an hundred thousand and fifty and one thousand and four hundred and fifty, throughout their armies. ⁱ And they shall set forth in the second rank.

17 ¶ Then ʲ the tabernacle of the congregation shall set forward with the camp of the Levites in the midst of the camp: as they encamp, so shall they set forward, every ᵏ man in his place by their standards.

18 ¶ On the west side shall be the standard of the camp of ˡ Ephraim according to their armies: and the captain of the sons of Ephraim shall be Elishama the son of Ammihud.

19 And his host, and those that were numbered of them, were forty thousand and five hundred.

20 And by him shall be the tribe of Manasseh: and the captain of the children of Manasseh shall be Gamaliel the son of Pedahzur.

21 And his host, and those that were numbered of them, were thirty and two thousand and two hundred.

22 Then the tribe of ᵐ Benjamin: and the captain of the sons of Benjamin shall be Abidan the son of ³ Gideoni.

23 And his host, and those that were numbered of them, were thirty and five thousand and four hundred.

24 All that were numbered of the camp of Ephraim were an hundred thousand and eight thousand and an hundred, throughout their armies. And ⁿ they shall go forward in the third rank.

25 ¶ The standard of the camp of ᵒ Dan shall be on the north side by their armies: and the captain of the children of Dan shall be Ahiezer the son of Ammishaddai.

26 And his host, and those that were numbered of them, were threescore and two thousand and seven hundred.

27 And those that encamp by him shall be the tribe of Asher: and the captain of the children of Asher shall be Pagiel the son of Ocran.

28 And his host, and those that were numbered of them, were forty and one thousand and five hundred.

29 ¶ Then the tribe of ᵖ Naphtali: and the captain of the children of Naphtali shall be Ahira the son of Enan.

30 And his host, and those that were numbered of them, were fifty and three thousand and four hundred.

31 All they that were numbered in the camp of Dan were an hundred thousand and fifty and seven thousand and six hundred. ᑫ They shall go hindmost with their standards.

32 ¶ These are those which were numbered of the children of Israel, by the house of their fathers: ʳ all those that were numbered of the camps, throughout their hosts, were six hundred thousand and three thousand and five hundred and fifty.

33 But ˢ the Levites were not numbered among the children of Israel; as the LORD commanded Moses.

34 And the children of Israel did according to all that ᵗ the LORD commanded Moses: so they ᵘ pitched by their standards, and so they set forward, every one after their families, according to the house of their fathers.

CHAPTER III.

1 *The Levites' service.* 40 *The first-born freed by the Levites.* 44 *The overplus redeemed.*

THESE also are the generations of Aaron and Moses, in the day that the LORD spake with Moses in mount Sinai.

2 And these are the names of the sons of Aaron; Nadab the ᵃ first-born, and Abihu, Eleazar, and Ithamar.

3 These are the names of the sons of Aaron, ᵇ the priests which were anointed, ᶜ whom he consecrated to minister in the priest's office.

4 And ᵉ Nadab and Abihu died before the LORD, when they offered strange fire before the LORD, in the wilderness of Sinai, and they had no children: and Eleazar and Ithamar ministered in the priest's office in the sight of Aaron their father.

5 ¶ And the LORD spake unto Moses, saying,

6 Bring ᵈ the tribe of Levi near, and present them before Aaron the priest, that they may minister unto him.

7 And they shall keep his charge, and the charge of the whole congregation before the tabernacle of the congregation, to do the ᵉ service of the tabernacle.

8 And they shall keep all the instruments of the tabernacle of the congregation, and the charge of the children of Israel, to do the service of the tabernacle.

9 And ƒ thou shalt give the Levites unto Aaron and to his sons: they are wholly given unto him out of the children of Israel.

10 And thou shalt appoint Aaron and his sons, ᵍ and they shall wait on their priest's office; ʰ and the stranger that cometh nigh shall be put to death.

11 ¶ And the LORD spake unto Moses, saying,

12 And I, behold, ⁱ I have taken the Levites

march and the disposition of the encampment. **3.** On the east side, &c.—Judah was placed at the head of a camp composed of three tribes rallying under its standard, said to have combined the united colours in the high priest's breastplate, but called by the name of Judah. They were appointed to occupy the east side, and to take the lead in the march, which, for the most part, was in an easterly direction. **5.** Those that pitch next unto him—i. e., on the one side. **7.** Then the tribe of Zebulun—on the other side. While Judah's tribe was the most numerous, those of Issachar and Zebulun were also very numerous; so that the association of those 3 tribes formed a strong and imposing van. Nahshon, or Naasson, (M. 1. 4,) shall be captain—It appears that the 12 men who were called to superintend the census were also appointed to be the captains of their respective tribes—a dignity which they owed probably to the circumstances, formerly noticed, of their holding the hereditary office of head or "prince." **10-31.** On the south side the standard of the camp of Reuben—The description given of the position of Reuben and his attendant tribes on the south, of Ephraim and his associates on the west, of Dan and his confederates on the north, with that of Judah on the east, suggests the idea of a square or quadrangle, which allowing one square cubit to each soldier whilst remaining close in the ranks, has been computed to extend over an area of somewhat more than 12 square miles. But into our calculations of the occupied space must be taken not only the fighting men, whose numbers are here given, but also the families, tents, and baggage. The tabernacle or sacred tent of their Divine King, with the camp of the Levites around it, (see on ch. 3. 38,) formed the centre, as does the chief's in the encampments of all nomad people. In marching, this order was adhered to, with some necessary variations. Judah led the way, followed, it is most probable, by Issachar and Zebulun. Reuben, Simeon, and Gad, formed the second great division. They were followed by the central company, composed of the Levites, bearing the tabernacle. Then the third and posterior squadron consisted of Ephraim, Manasseh, and Benjamin, while the hindmost place was assigned to Dan, Asher, and Naphtali. Thus Judah's, which was the most numerous, formed the van; and Dan's, which was the next in force, brought up the rear; while Reuben's and Ephraim's, with the tribes associated with them respectively, being the smallest and weakest, were placed in the centre. (See on ch. 10. 14.)

CHAPTER III.

Ver. 1-51. THE LEVITES' SERVICE. **1.** These are the generations, &c.—This chapter contains an account of their families; and although that of Moses is not detailed like his brother's, his children are included under the general designation of the Amramites, (v. 27,) a term which comprehends all the descendants of their common father Amram. The reason why the family of Moses was so undistinguished in this record is, that they were in the private ranks of the Levites, the dignity of the priesthood being conferred exclusively on the posterity of Aaron; and hence, as the sacerdotal order is the subject of this chapter, Aaron, contrary to the usual style of the sacred history, is mentioned before Moses. In the day that the Lord, &c.—This is added, because at the date of the following record the family of Aaron was unbroken. **2-4.** These are the names—All the sons of Aaron, four in number, were consecrated to minister in the priest's office. The two eldest enjoyed but a brief term of office; (Le. 10. 1, 2; ch. 26. 61;) but Eleazar and Ithamar, the other two, were dutiful, and performed the sacred service during the lifetime of their father, as his assistants, and under his superintendance. **5-10.** Bring the tribe of Levi near—The *Heb.* word "bring near" is a sacrificial term, denoting the presentation of an offering to God; and the use of the word, therefore, in connection with the Levites, signifies that they were devoted as an offering to the sanctuary, no longer to be employed in any common offices. They were subordinate to the priests, who alone enjoyed the privilege of entering the holy place; but they were employed in discharging many of the humbler duties which belonged to the sanctuary, as well as in various offices of great utility and importance to the religion and morals of the people. **9.** They are wholly given, &c.—The priests hold the place of God, and the Levites are the servants of God in the obedience they render to the priests. **11-13.** I have taken the Levites, &c.—The consecration of this tribe did not originate in the legislative wisdom of Moses, but in the special appointment of God, who chose them as substitutes for the first-born. By an appointment made in memory of the last solemn judgment on Egypt, from which the Israelitish households were miraculously exempt, all the first-born were consecrated to God, (Ex. 13. 12; 22. 29,) who thus, under peculiar circumstances, seemed to adopt the patriarchal usage of appointing the eldest to act as the priest of the family. But the privilege of redemption that was allowed the first-born opened the way for a change; and accordingly, on the full organization of the Mosaic economy, the administration of sacred things formerly committed to the first-born was transferred from them to the Levites, who received that honour partly as a tribute to Moses and Aaron, partly because this tribe had distinguished themselves by their zeal in the affair of the golden calf, (Ex. 32. 29,) and also because, being the smallest of the tribes, they could ill find suitable employment and support in the work. (See on Deu. 33. 9.) The designation of a special class for the sacred offices of religion was a wise arrangement; for, on their settlement in Canaan, the people would be so occupied that they might not be at leisure to wait on the service of the sanctuary, and sacred things might, from various causes, fall into neglect. But the appointment of an entire tribe to the Divine service insured the regular performance of the rites of religion. The subsequent portion of the chapter relates the formal substitution of this tribe. I am the Lord—i. e., I decree it to be so; and being possessed of sovereign authority, expect full obedience. **14-27.** Number the children of Levi—They were numbered as well as the other tribes; but the enumeration was made on a different principle—for while in the other tribes the amount of males was calculated from 20 years and upward, in that of Levi they were counted from a month old and upwards. The reason of the distinction

from among the children of Israel instead of all the first-born that openeth the matrix among the children of Israel: therefore the Levites shall be mine;

13 Because *j* all the first-born *are* mine: for *k* on the day that I smote all the first-born in the land of Egypt I hallowed unto me all the first-born in Israel, both man and beast; mine they shall be: I am the LORD.

14 ¶ And the LORD spake unto Moses in the wilderness of *l* Sinai, saying,

15 Number the children of Levi after the house of their fathers, by their families: every *m* male from a month old and upward shalt thou number them.

16 And Moses numbered them, according to the *n* word of the LORD, as he was commanded.

17 And *o* these were the sons of Levi by their names; Gershon, and Kohath, and Merari.

18 And these *are* the names of the sons of Gershon by their families; *o* Libni, and Shimei.

19 And the sons of Kohath by their families; Amram, and Izhar, Hebron, and Uzziel.

20 And the sons of Merari by their families; Mahli, and Mushi. These *are* the families of the Levites according to the house of their fathers.

21 ¶ Of Gershon *was* the family of the Libnites, and the family of the Shimites: these *are* the families of the Gershonites.

22 Those that were numbered of them, according to the number of all the males, from a month old and upward, even those that were numbered of them, were seven thousand and five hundred.

23 The *p* families of the Gershonites shall pitch behind the tabernacle westward.

24 And the chief of the house of the father of the Gershonites *shall be* Eliasaph the son of Lael.

25 And *q* the charge of the sons of Gershon in the tabernacle of the congregation *shall be* *r* the tabernacle, and *s* the tent, *t* the covering thereof, and *u* the hanging for the door of the tabernacle of the congregation,

26 And *v* the hangings of the court, and the *w* curtain for the door of the court, which *is* by the tabernacle, and by the altar round about, and *x* the cords of it, for all the service thereof.

27 ¶ And *y* of Kohath *was* the family of the Amramites, and the family of the Izharites, and the family of the Hebronites, and the family of the Uzzielites: these *are* the families of the Kohathites.

28 In the number of all the males, from a month old and upward, *were* eight thousand and six hundred, keeping the charge of the sanctuary.

29 The *z* families of the sons of Kohath shall pitch on the side of the tabernacle southward.

30 And the chief of the house of the father of the families of the Kohathites *shall be* Elizaphan the son of Uzziel.

31 And *a* their charge *shall be* *b* the ark, and *c* the table, and *d* the candlestick, and the *e* altars, and the vessels of the sanctuary wherewith they minister, and *f* the hanging, and all the service thereof.

32 And Eleazar the son of Aaron the priest *shall be* chief over the chief of the

B. C. 1490.

CHAP. 3.
j Ex. 13. 2.
Ex. 22. 9.
Ex. 34. 20.
Lev. 27. 26.
ch. 8. 16.
Neh. 10 36.
Ezek. 44. 30.
Luke 2. 23.
k Ex. 13. 12, 15.
l Ex. 19. 1. *m* ch. 26. 62.
2 month.
n Gen. 46. 11.
Ex. 6. 16.
ch. 26. 57.
1 Chr. 6. 1, 16.
1 Chr 23. 6.
o Ex. 6. 17.
p ch. 1. 53.
q ch. 4. 24, 25, 26.
r Ex. 25. 9.
s Ex. 26. 1.
t Ex. 26. 7.
u Ex. 26. 36.
v Ex. 27. 9.
w Ex. 27. 16.
x Ex. 35. 18.
y 1 Chr. 26. 23.
z ch. 1. 53.
a ch. 4. 15.
b Ex. 25. 10.
c Ex. 25. 23.
d Ex. 25. 31.
e Ex. 27. 1. Ex. 30. 1.
f Ex. 26. 32.
g 2 Kin. 23. 18.
3 the office of the charge.
Ex. 26. 15.
ch. 4. 31, 32.
i ch. 1. 53.
j ch. 18. 5.
k ver. 7, 8.
l Every one not a Levite.
ch. 16. 40.
1 Sam. 6. 19.
2 Sa. 6. 7.
m ch. 26. 62.
n ver. 15.
o ver. 12, 45.
p ver. 12, 41.
1 Sam. 1. 28.
q Ex. 13. 13. ch. 18. 15.
r ver. 39, 43.
s Lev. 27. 6.
ch. 18. 16.
t Ex. 30. 13.
Lev. 27. 25.
ch. 18. 16.
Ezek. 45.
u 1 Tim. 2. 6.
Titus 2. 14.
Heb. 9. 12.
1 Pet. 1. 18.
Gal. 4. 4, 5.
v ver. 46, 47.

Levites, *and have* the oversight of them that keep the charge of the sanctuary.

33 ¶ Of Merari *was* the family of the Mahlites, and the family of the Mushites: these *are* the families of Merari.

34 And those that were numbered of them, according to the number of all the males, from a month old and upward, *were* six thousand and two hundred.

35 And the chief of the house of the father of the families of Merari *was* Zuriel the son of Abihail: *h these* shall pitch on the side of the tabernacle northward.

36 And *i* under the custody and charge of the sons of Merari *shall be* the boards of the tabernacle, and the bars thereof, and the pillars thereof, and the sockets thereof, and all the vessels thereof, and all that serveth thereto,

37 And the pillars of the court round about, and their sockets, and their pins, and their cords.

38 ¶ But *j* those that encamp before the tabernacle toward the east, *even* before the tabernacle of the congregation eastward, *shall be* Moses, and Aaron and his sons, keeping *k* the charge of the sanctuary *k* for the charge of the children of Israel; and the *l* stranger that cometh nigh shall be put to death.

39 All *m* that were numbered of the Levites, which Moses and Aaron numbered at the commandment of the LORD, throughout their families, all the males, from a month old and upward, *were* twenty and two thousand.

40 ¶ And the LORD said unto Moses, Number *n* all the first-born of the males of the children of Israel from a month old and upward, and take the number of their names.

41 And *o* thou shalt take the Levites for me (I am the LORD) instead of all the first-born among the children of Israel; and the cattle of the Levites instead of all the firstlings among the cattle of the children of Israel.

42 And Moses numbered, as the LORD commanded him, all the first-born among the children of Israel.

43 And all the first-born males by the number of names, from a month old and upward, of those that were numbered of them, were twenty and two thousand two hundred and threescore and thirteen.

44 ¶ And the LORD spake unto Moses, saying,

45 Take *p* the Levites instead of all the first-born among the children of Israel, and the cattle of the Levites instead of their cattle; and the Levites shall be mine: I am the LORD.

46 And for those that are to be *q* redeemed of the two hundred and threescore and thirteen of the first-born of the children of Israel, *r* which are more than the Levites;

47 Thou shalt even take *s* five shekels apiece by the poll; after the shekel of the sanctuary shalt thou take *them:* (*t* the shekel *is* twenty gerahs:)

48 And thou shalt give the money, wherewith the odd number of them is to be redeemed, unto Aaron and to his sons.

49 And Moses took the *u* redemption money of them that were over and above them that were redeemed by the Levites:

50 Of the first-born of the children of Israel took he the money; *v* a thousand three

is obvious. In the other tribes the survey was made for purposes of war, from which the Levites were totally exempt, and were appointed to a work on which they entered as soon as they were capable of instruction. They are mentioned under the names of Gershon, Kohath, and Merari, sons of Levi, and chiefs or ancestral heads of three subdivisions into which this tribe was distributed. Their duties were to assist in the conveyance of the tabernacle when the people were removing the various encampments, and to form its guard whilst stationary—the Gershonites being stationed on the west, the Kohathites on the south, and the families of Merari on the north. The Kohathites had the principal place about the tabernacle, and charge of the most precious and sacred things—a distinction with which they were honoured, probably, from the Aaronic family belonging to this division of the Levitical tribe. The Gershonites being the oldest, had the next honourable post assigned them, while the burden of the drudgery was thrown on the division of Merari. 32. Chief—rather, chiefs of the Levites. Three persons are mentioned as chiefs of these respective divisions. And Eleazar presided over them; whence he is called "the second priest;" (2 Ki. 25. 18;) and in case of the high priest's absence from illness or other necessary occasions, he performed the duties. (1 Ki. 4. 4.) 38. Those that encamp, &c.—That being the entrance-side, was the post of honour, and consequently reserved to Moses and the priestly family. But the sons of Moses had no station there. 39. Twenty and two thousand—The result of this census, though made on conditions most advantageous to Levi, proved it to be by far the smallest in Israel. The separate numbers stated in v. 22. 28, 34, when added together, amount to 22,300. The omission of the 300 is variously accounted for—by some, because they might be firstborn who were already devoted to God, and could not be counted as substitutes; and by others, because, in Scripture style, the sum is reckoned in round numbers. The most probable conjecture is, that as *Heb.* letters are employed for figures, one letter was, in the course of transcription, taken for another of like form but smaller value. 40-51. Number all the first-born, &c.—The principle on which the enumeration of the Levites had been made was now to be applied to the other tribes. The number of their male children, from a month old and upwards, was to be reckoned, in order that a comparison might be instituted with that of the Levites, for the formal adoption of the latter as substitutes for the first-born. The Levites, amounting to 22,000, were given in exchange for an equal number of the first-born from the other tribes, leaving an excess of 273; and as there were no substitutes for these, they were redeemed at the rate of 5 shekels for each. (ch. 18. 15, 16.) Every Israelite would naturally wish that his son might be redeemed by a Levite without the payment of this tax, and yet some would have to incur the expense, for there were not Levites enough to make an equal exchange. Jewish writers say the matter was determined by lot, in this manner:—Moses put into an urn 22,600 pieces of parchment, on each of which he wrote "a son of Levi," and 273 more, containing the words, "five shekels." These being shaken, he ordered each of the first-born to put in his hand and take out a slip. If it contained the first inscription, the boy was redeemed by a Levite; if the latter, the parent had to pay. The ransom money, which, reckoning the shekel at half a crown, would amount to 12s. 6d. each, was appropriated to the use of the sanctuary. The excess of the general over the Levitical firstborn is so small, that the only way of accounting for it is, by supposing those first-born only were counted as were males remaining in their parents' household, or that those first-born only were numbered which had been born since the departure from Egypt, when God claimed all the first-born as his special property. 41. The cattle of the Levites—These, which they kept to graze on the glebes and meadows in the suburbs of their cities, and supply their families with dairy produce and animal food, were also taken as an equivalent for all the firstlings of the cattle which the Israelites at that time possessed. In consequence of this exchange the firstlings were not brought then, as afterwards, to the altar and the priests.

CHAPTER IV.

Ver. 1-49. OF THE LEVITES' SERVICE. 2, 3. Sons of Kohath, from thirty years old and upward—This age was specifically fixed on, (see on ch. 8. 24,) as the full maturity of bodily energy to perform the laborious duties assigned them in the wilderness, as well as of mental activity to assist in the management of the sacred services. And hence it was the period of life at which the Baptist and Christ entered on their respective ministries. even until fifty—The term prescribed for active duty was a period of 20 years, at the end of which they were exempted from the physical labours of the office, though still expected to attend in the tabernacle. (ch. 8, 26.) all that enter into the host — so called from their number, the order and discipline maintained through their ranks, and their special duty as guards of the tabernacle. The *Heb.* word, however, signifies also a station or office; and hence the passage may be rendered, "All that enter into the sacerdotal office." (v. 23.) 4-15. This shall be the service, &c.—They are mentioned first, from their close connection with Aaron; and the special department of duty assigned to them during the journeyings of Israel accorded with the charge they had received of the precious contents of the tabernacle. But these were to be previously covered by the common priests, who, as well as the high priest, were admitted on such necessary occasions into the holy place. This was an exception to the general rule, which prohibited the entrance of any but the high priest. But when the cloud removed from the tabernacle, the sanctuary might be entered by the common priests, as to them was reserved the exclusive privilege of packing the sacred utensils; and it was not till the holy things were thus ready for carriage, that the Kohathites were allowed to approach. 5. Covering veil—the inner veil, which separated the holy from the most holy place. (See on Ex. 36. 3.) covering of badgers' skins—See on Ex. 25. 5. The covering, however, referred to was not that of the tabernacle, but one made for the special purpose of protecting the ark. put in the staves—These golden staves were now taken out. (See on Ex. 25. 15, compared with 1 Ki.

hundred and threescore and five *shekels*, after the shekel of the sanctuary:

51 And Moses gave the money of them that were redeemed unto Aaron and to his sons, according to the word of the LORD, as the LORD commanded Moses.

CHAPTER IV.

1 *Of the Levites' service.* 17 *The office of the priests.* 34 *The number of the Kohathites,* 38 *of the Gershonites,* 42 *and of the Merarites.*

AND the LORD spake unto Moses and unto Aaron, saying,

2 Take the sum of the sons of Kohath from among the sons of Levi, after their families, by the house of their fathers;

3 From *a* thirty years old and upward even until fifty years old, all that enter into the ¹ host, to do the work in the tabernacle of the congregation.

4 ¶ This *b shall* be the service of the sons of Kohath in the tabernacle of the congregation, *about* the most holy things.

5 And when the camp setteth forward, Aaron shall come, and his sons, and they shall take down *c* the covering veil, and cover the *d* ark of testimony with it:

6 And shall put thereon the covering of badgers' skins, and shall spread over *it* a cloth wholly of blue, and shall put in *e* the staves thereof.

7 And upon the *f* table of showbread they shall spread a cloth of blue, and put thereon the dishes, and the spoons, and the bowls, and covers to ¹ cover withal: and the continual bread shall be thereon.

8 And they shall spread upon them a cloth of scarlet, and cover the same with a covering of badgers' skins, and shall put in the staves thereof.

9 And they shall take a cloth of blue, and cover the *g* candlestick of the light, *h* and his lamps, and his tongs, and his snuffdishes, and all the oil vessels thereof, wherewith they minister unto it:

10 And they shall put it and all the vessels thereof within a covering of badgers' skins, and shall put *it* upon a bar.

11 And upon *i* the golden altar they shall spread a cloth of blue, and cover it with a covering of badgers' skins, and shall put to the staves thereof:

12 And they shall take all the instruments of ministry, wherewith they minister in the sanctuary, and put *them* in a cloth of blue, and cover them with a covering of badgers' skins, and shall put *them* on a bar:

13 And they shall take away the ashes from the altar, and spread a purple cloth thereon:

14 And they shall put upon it all the vessels thereof, wherewith they minister about it, *even* the censers, the flesh-hooks, and the shovels, and the ² basins, all the vessels of the altar; and they shall spread upon it a covering of badgers' skins, and put to the staves of it.

15 And when Aaron and his sons have made an end of covering the sanctuary, and all the vessels of the sanctuary, as the camp is to set forward; after that, *j* the sons of Kohath shall come to bear it: *k* but they shall not touch *any* holy thing, lest they die. *l* These *things are* the burden of the sons of Kohath in the tabernacle of the congregation.

16 ¶ And to the office of Eleazar the son of Aaron the priest *pertaineth* ᵐ the oil for the light, and the ⁿ sweet incense, and *o* the

B. C. 1490.

CHAP. 4.
a ch. 8. 24.
1 Chr. 23. 3, 24, 27.
Ezra 3. 8.

1 Or, warfare.
2 Cor. 10.4.
1 Tim. 1. 18.
b ver. 15.
c Ex. 26. 31.
d Ex. 25. 10, 16.
e Ex. 25. 13.
f Ex. 25. 23, 29, 30.
Lev. 24. 6, 8.
1 Or, pour out withal.
g Ex. 25. 31.
h Ex. 25. 37, 38.
i Ex. 30. 1.
2 Or, bowls.
j ch. 7. 9.
ch. 10. 21.
Deu. 31. 9.
2 Sam. 6. 13.
1 Chr. 15, 2. 15.
k 2 Sam. 6. 6, 7.
1 Chr. 13. 9, 10.
l ch. 3. 31.
m Ex. 25. 6.
Lev. 24. 2.
n Ex. 30. 34.
o Ex. 29. 40.
p Ex. 30. 23.
q ver. 4.
Ex. 19. 21.
1 Sam. 6. 19.
r 1 Chr. 23. 3, 24, 27.
3 to war the war are.
Is.53.1-12.
Is. 63. 1-4.
Rom. 7. 14 24.
2Cor.10.4.
Gal. 5. 17-24.
Eph. 6. 10-19.
Col. 2. 14.
4 Or, carriage.
t Ex.26.1-14.
Ex. 36. 9.
Ex. 40. 19.
ch. 3. 25,26.
5 mouth.
u ver. 3.
6 warfare.
Ps.110.1-7.
1 Tim.6.11.
2 Tim. 2. 4.
2 Tim. 4. 7.
v ch. 3. 36, 37.
Ex. 26, 15.
Ex. 36. 10.
Ex. 39. 3.
w Ex. 25. 9.
Ex. 38. 21.
1 Chr.9.29.
x ver. 2.
y 1 Chr. 23. 24.
1 Chr. 23. 13.
Lu. 3. 23.
1 Tim. 3.6.

daily meat offering, and the *p* anointing oil, *and* the oversight of all the tabernacle, and of all that therein *is*, in the sanctuary, and in the vessels thereof.

17 ¶ And the LORD spake unto Moses and unto Aaron, saying,

18 Cut ye not off the tribe of the families of the Kohathites from among the Levites:

19 But thus do unto them, that they may live, and not die, when they approach unto the *q* most holy things: Aaron and his sons shall go in, and appoint them every one to his service, and to his burden:

20 But *r* they shall not go in to see when the holy things *are* covered, lest they die.

21 ¶ And the LORD spake unto Moses, saying,

22 Take also the sum of the sons of Gershon, throughout the houses of their fathers, by their families;

23 From *s* thirty years old and upward until fifty years old shalt thou number them; all that enter in ³ to perform the service, to do the work in the tabernacle of the congregation.

24 This *is* the service of the families of the Gershonites, to serve, and for ⁴ burdens:

25 And *t* they shall bear the curtains of the tabernacle, and the tabernacle of the congregation, his covering, and the covering of the badgers' skins that *is* above upon it, and the hanging for the door of the tabernacle of the congregation,

26 And the hangings of the court, and the hanging for the door of the gate of the court, which *is* by the tabernacle and by the altar round about, and their cords, and all the instruments of their service, and all that is made for them: so shall they serve.

27 At the ⁵ appointment of Aaron and his sons shall be all the service of the sons of the Gershonites, in all their burdens, and in all their service: and ye shall appoint unto them in charge all their burdens.

28 This *is* the service of the families of the sons of Gershon in the tabernacle of the congregation: and their charge *shall be* under the hand of Ithamar the son of Aaron the priest.

29 ¶ As for the sons of Merari, thou shalt number them after their families, by the house of their fathers;

30 From *u* thirty years old and upward even unto fifty years old shalt thou number them, every one that entereth into the ⁶ service, to do the work of the tabernacle of the congregation.

31 And *v* this *is* the charge of their burden, according to all their service in the tabernacle of the congregation; the boards of the tabernacle, and the bars thereof, and the pillars thereof, and sockets thereof,

32 And the pillars of the court round about, and their sockets, and their pins, and their cords, with all their instruments, and with all their service: and by name ye shall ʷ reckon the instruments of the charge of their burden.

33 This *is* the service of the families of the sons of Merari, according to all their service, in the tabernacle of the congregation, under the hand of Ithamar the son of Aaron the priest.

34 ¶ And *x* Moses and Aaron and the chief of the congregation numbered the sons of the Kohathites after their families, and after the house of their fathers,

35 From *y* thirty years old and upward

8. 8.) The *Heb.* word rendered "put in" signifies also "dispose," and probably refers here to their insertion through the openings in the covering made for receiving them, to preserve them from the touch of the carriers as well as from the influences of the weather. It is worthy of notice, that the coverings did not consist of canvass or coarse tarpauling, but of a kind which united beauty with decency. **7.** Continual shew bread—Though the people were in the wilderness fed upon manna, the sacred loaves were constantly made of corn, which was probably raised in small quantities from the verdant patches of the desert. **10.** A bar—or bier, formed of two poles fastened by two cross pieces, and borne by two men, after the fashion of a sedan chair. **12.** Instruments of ministry—the official dress of the priests. (Ex. 31. 10.) **13.** Shall take away the ashes, &c.—The necessity of removing ashes from the altar plainly implies that sacrifices were offered in the wilderness, (cf. Ex. 18. 12; 24. 4,) though that rebellious race seem frequently to have neglected the duty. (Am 5 25.) No mention is made of the sacred fire; but as, by Divine command, it was to be kept constantly burning, it must have been transferred to some pan or brazier under the covering, and borne by the appointed carriers. **15.** Bear it, but shall not touch—The mode of transport was upon the shoulders of the Levites, see on ch. 7. 9, although afterwards wheeled vehicles were employed. (2 Sa. 6. 3 ; 1 Chr. 15. 12.) And it was allowable to touch the covering, but not the things covered, on the penalty of death, which was more than once inflicted. (1 Sa. 6. 19; 2 Sa. 6. 6, 7.) This stern denunciation was designed to inspire a sentiment of deep and habitual reverence in the minds of those who were officially engaged about holy things. **16.** To the office of Eleazar, &c.—He was charged with the special duty of superintending the squadron who were employed in the carriage of the sacred furniture; besides, to his personal care were committed the materials requisite for the daily service, and which it was necessary he should have easily at command. (Ex. 29. 38.) **17-20.** Cut ye not off, &c.—a solemn admonition to Moses and Aaron to beware, lest, by any negligence on their part, disorder and improprieties should creep in, and to take the greatest care that all the parts of this important service be apportioned to the proper parties, lest the Kohathites should be disqualified for their high and honourable duties. The guilt of their death would be incurred by the superintending priest, if they failed to give proper directions, or allowed any irreverent familiarity with sacred things. **24-28.** This is the service, &c.—They were appointed to carry "the curtains of the tabernacle"—*i.e.*, the goats' hair covering of the tent—the ten curious curtains and embroidered hangings at the entrance, with their red morocco covering, &c. **28.** Their charge shall be, &c.—The Levites were subject to the official command of the priests generally in doing the ordinary work of the tabernacle. But during the journeyings Eleazar, who was next in succession to his father, took the special charge of the Kohathites, while his brother Ithamar had the superintendence of the Gershonites and Merarites. **29-33.** As for the sons of Merari—They carried the coarser and heavier appurtenances, which, however, were so important and necessary, that an inventory was kept of them—not only on account of their number and variety, but of the comparative commonness and smallness, which might have led to their being lost or missing through carelessness, inadvertency, or neglect. It was a useful lesson, showing that God disregards nothing pertaining to his service, and that even in the least and most trivial matters he requires the duty of faithful obedience. **34-49. Moses and Aaron,** &c.— This enumeration was made on a different principle from that which is recorded in the preceding chapter. That was confined to the males from a month old and upwards, while this was extended to all capable of service in the three classes of the Levitical tribe. In considering their relative numbers, the wisdom of Divine Providence appears in arranging that, whereas in the Kohathites and Gershonites, whose burdens were few and easier, there were but about a third part of them which were fit for service; the Merarites, whose burdens were more and heavier, had above one half of them fit for this work. [POOLE.] The small population of this tribe, so inferior to that of the other tribes, is attempted to be explained, (see on ch. 3. 39.)

CHAPTER V.

Ver. 1-4. THE UNCLEAN TO BE REMOVED OUT OF THE CAMP. **2.** put out of the camp every leper—The exclusion of leprous persons from the camp in the wilderness, as from cities and villages afterwards, was a sanatory measure taken according to prescribed rules. (Lev. chaps. 13. 14.) This exclusion of lepers from society has been acted upon ever since; and it affords almost the only instance in which any kind of attention is paid in the East to the prevention of contagion. The usage still more or less prevails in the East among people who do not think the least precaution against the plague or cholera necessary; but judging from personal observation, we think that in Asia the leprosy has now much abated in frequency and virulence. It usually appears in a comparatively mild form in Egypt, Palestine, and other countries where the disorder is, or was, endemic. Small societies of excluded lepers live miserably in paltry huts. Many of them are beggars, going out into the roads to solicit alms, which they receive in a wooden bowl; charitable people also sometimes bring different articles of food, which they leave on the ground at a short distance from the hut of the lepers, for whom it is intended. They are generally obliged to wear a distinctive badge, that people may know them at first sight and be warned to avoid them. Other means were adopted amongst the ancient Jews by putting their hand on their mouth and crying, "Unclean, unclean." But their general treatment, as to exclusion from society, was the same as now described. The association of the leper, however, in this passage, with those who were subject only to ceremonial uncleanness, shews that one important design in the temporary exile of such persons was to remove all impurities that reflected dishonour on the character and residence of Israel's king. And this vigilant care to maintain external cleanliness in the people was typically designed to teach them the practice of moral purity, or cleansing

even unto fifty years old, every one that entereth into the service, for the work in the tabernacle of the congregation:

36 And those that were numbered of them by their families were two thousand seven hundred and fifty.

37 These *were* they that were numbered of the families of the Kohathites, all that might do service in the tabernacle of the congregation, which Moses and Aaron did number, according to the commandment of the LORD by the hand of Moses.

38 ¶ And those that were numbered of the sons of Gershon, throughout their families, and by the house of their fathers,

39 From thirty years old and upward even unto fifty years old, every one that entereth into the service, for the work in the tabernacle of the congregation,

40 Even those that were numbered of them throughout their families, by the house of their fathers, were two thousand and six hundred and thirty.

41 These *are* they that were numbered of the families of the sons of Gershon, of all that might do service in the tabernacle of the congregation, whom Moses and Aaron did number according to the commandment of the LORD.

42 ¶ And those that were numbered of the families of the sons of Merari, throughout their families, by the house of their fathers,

43 From *s* thirty years old and upward even unto fifty years old, every one that entereth into the service, for the work in the tabernacle of the congregation,

44 Even those that were numbered of them after their families, were three thousand and two hundred.

45 These be those that were numbered of the families of the sons of Merari, whom Moses and Aaron numbered, according to the word of the LORD by the hand of Moses.

46 All those that were numbered of the Levites, whom Moses and Aaron and the chief of Israel numbered, after their families, and after the house of their fathers,

47 From *a* thirty years old and upward even unto fifty years old, every one that came to do the service of the ministry, and the service of the burden in the tabernacle of the congregation,

48 Even those that were numbered of them, were eight thousand and five hundred and fourscore.

49 According to the commandment of the LORD they were numbered by the hand of Moses, *b* every one according to his service, and according to his burden : thus were they numbered of him, as the LORD commanded Moses.

CHAPTER V.

1 *The unclean to be removed out of the camp.* 5 *Restitution enjoined.* 9 *Hallowed things belong to the priest.* 11 *The trial of jealousy.*

AND the LORD spake unto Moses, saying,

2 Command the children of Israel, that they put out of the camp every *a* leper, and every one that hath an *b* issue, and whosoever is defiled by the *c* dead:

3 Both male and female shall ye put out, without the camp shall ye put them; that they defile not their camps, *d* in the midst whereof I dwell.

4 And the children of Israel did so, and put them out without the camp: as the LORD spake unto Moses, so did the children of Israel.

5 ¶ And the LORD spake unto Moses, saying,

6 Speak unto the children of Israel, When *e* a man or woman shall commit any sin that men commit, to do a trespass against the LORD, and that person be guilty;

7 Then *f* they shall confess their sin which they have done: and he shall recompense his trespass *g* with the principal thereof, and add unto it the fifth *part* thereof, and give *it* unto *him* against whom he hath trespassed.

8 But if the man have no kinsman to recompense the trespass unto, let the trespass be recompensed unto the LORD, *even* to the priest, beside *h* the ram of the atonement, whereby an atonement shall be made for him.

9 And every ¹ offering of all the holy things of the children of Israel, which they bring unto the priest, shall be his.

10 And every man's hallowed things shall be his: whatsoever any man giveth the priest, it shall be *i* his.

11 ¶ And the LORD spake unto Moses, saying,

12 Speak unto the children of Israel, and say unto them, If any man's wife *j* go aside, and commit a trespass against him,

13 And a man *k* lie with her carnally, and it be hid from the eyes of her husband, and be kept close, and she be defiled, and *there be* no witness against her, neither she be taken *with the manner;*

14 And *l* the spirit of jealousy come upon him, and he be jealous of his wife, and she be defiled: or if the spirit of jealousy come upon him, and he be jealous of his wife, and she be not defiled:

15 Then shall the man bring his wife unto the priest, and he shall bring her *m* offering for her, the tenth *part* of an ephah of barley meal; he shall pour no oil upon it, nor put frankincense thereon; for it is an offering of jealousy, an offering of memorial, *n* bringing iniquity to remembrance.

16 And the priest shall bring her near, and *o* set her before the LORD:

17 And the priest shall take holy water in an earthen vessel; and of the dust that is in the floor of the tabernacle the priest shall take, and put *it* into the water:

18 And the priest shall set the woman before the LORD, and uncover the woman's head, and put the offering of memorial in her hands, which *is* the jealousy offering: and the priest shall have in his hand the bitter water that causeth the curse:

19 And the priest shall charge her by an oath, and say unto the woman, If no man have lain with thee, and if thou hast not gone aside to uncleanness ² *with another* instead of thy husband, be thou free from this bitter water that causeth the curse:

20 But if thou hast gone aside *to another* instead of thy husband, and if thou be defiled, and some man have lain with thee besides thine husband:

21 Then the priest shall *p* charge the woman with an oath of cursing, and the priest shall say unto the woman, *q* The LORD make thee a curse and an oath among thy people, when the LORD doth make thy thigh to ³ rot, and thy belly to swell;

22 And this water that causeth the curse

themselves from all filthiness of the flesh and spirit. The regulations made for ensuring cleanliness in the camp suggest the adoption of similar means for maintaining purity in the church. And although in large communities of Christians, it may be often difficult or delicate to do this, the suspension, or, in flagrant cases of sin, the total excommunication of the offender from the privileges and communion of the church is an imperative duty as necessary to the moral purity of the Christian as the exclusion of the leper from the camp was to physical health and ceremonial purity in the Jewish Church.

5-9. RESTITUTION ENJOINED. 6. **trespass against the Lord**—This is a wrong or injury done by one man to the property of another, and as it is called "a trespass against the Lord," it is implied, in the case supposed, that the offence has been aggravated by prevaricating—by a false oath, or a fraudulent lie in denying it, which is a "trespass" committed against God, who is the sole judge of what is falsely sworn or spoken. (A. 5. 3, 4.) **And that person be guilty**—i.e., from the obvious tenor of the passage, conscience-smitten, or brought to a sense and conviction of his evil conduct. (See on Lev. 6. 4.) In that case there must be, first, confession, a penitential acknowledgment of sin; secondly, restitution of the property, or the giving of an equivalent, with the additional fine of a fifth part, both as a compensation to the person defrauded, and as a penalty inflicted on the injurer, to deter others from the commission of similar trespasses. (See on Ex. 22. 1.) The difference between the law recorded in that passage and this is, that the one was enacted against flagrant and determined thieves, the other against those whose necessities might have urged them into fraud, and whose consciences were distressed by their sin. This law also supposes the injured party to be dead, in which case, the compensation due to his representatives was to be paid to the riest, who, as God's deputy, received the required satisfaction. 9, 10. **every offering shall be his**—Whatever was given in this way, or otherwise, as by free-will offerings, irrevocably belonged to the priest.

11-31. THE TRIAL OF JEALOUSY. if any **man's wife go aside**—This law was given both as a strong discouragement to conjugal infidelity on the part of a wife, and a sufficient protection of her from the consequences of a hasty and groundless suspicion on the part of the husband. His suspicions, however, were sufficient in the absence of witnesses, (Lev. 20. 10,) to warrant the trial described; and the course of proceeding to be followed was for the jealous husband to bring his wife unto the priest with an offering of barley meal, because none were allowed to approach the sanctuary empty-handed. (Ex. 23. 15.) On other occasions, there were mingled with the offering, oil which signified joy, and frankincense which denoted acceptance. (Ps. 141. 2.) But on the occasion referred to, both these ingredients were to be excluded, partly because it was a solemn appeal to God in distressing circumstances, and partly because it was a sin offering on the part of the wife, who came before God in the character of a real or suspected offender. 17. **the priest shall take holy water**—Water from the laver, which was to be mixed with dust—an emblem of vileness and misery. (Ge. 3. 14; Ps. 22. 15.) **in an earthen vessel**—This fragile ware was chosen, because after being used it was broken in pieces. (Lev. 6. 28; 11. 33.) The whole circumstances of this awful ceremony—her being placed with her face toward the ark—her uncovered head, a sign of her being deprived of the protection of her husband, (1 Cor. 11. 7)—the bitter potion being put into her hands preparatory to an appeal to God—the solemn adjuration of the priest, (v. 19-22,) all were calculated in no common degree to excite and appal the imagination of a person conscious of guilt. 21. **the Lord make thee a curse, &c.**—a usual form of imprecation. (Is. 65. 15; Jer. 29. 22.) 22. **Amen, Amen**—The Israelites were accustomed, instead of formally repeating the words of an oath, merely to say Amen, a "so be it" to the imprecations it contained. The reduplication of the word was designed as an evidence of the woman's innocence, and a willingness that God would do to her according to her desert. 23, 24. **Write these curses in a book**—The imprecations, along with her name, were inscribed in some kind of record—on parchment, or more probably on a wooden tablet. **blot them out with the bitter water**—If she were innocent, they could be easily erased, and perfectly harmless; but if guilty, she would experience the fatal effects of the water she had drunk. 29. this is the law of jealousies—Adultery discovered and proved was punished with death. But strongly suspected cases would occur, and this law made provision for the conviction of the guilty person. It was, however, not a trial conducted according to the forms of judicial process, but an ordeal through which a suspected adulteress was made to go—the ceremony being of that terrifying nature, that, on the known principles of human nature, guilt or innocence could not fail to appear. From the earliest times, the jealousy of Eastern people has established ordeals for the detection and punishment of suspected unchastity in wives. The practice was deep-rooted as well as universal. And it has been thought, that the Israelites being strongly biassed in favour of such usages, this law of jealousies "was incorporated amongst the other institutions of the Mosaic economy, in order to free it from the idolatrous rites which the heathens had blended with it." Viewed in this light, its sanction by Divine authority in a corrected and improved form exhibits a proof at once of the wisdom and condescension of God.

CHAPTER VI.

Ver. 1-21. THE LAW OF THE NAZARITE IN HIS SEPARATION. 2-6. When either man or woman...**shall vow a vow of a Nazarite**—i.e., "a separated one," from a Hebrew word, to separate. And it was used to designate a class of persons who, under the impulse of extraordinary piety, and with a view to higher degrees of religious improvement, voluntarily renounced the occupations and pleasures of the world to dedicate themselves unreservedly to the divine service. The vow might be taken by either sex, provided they had the disposal of themselves, (ch. 30. 4,) and for a limited period—usually a month (or a life-time. (Jud. 13. 5; 16. 17.) We do not know, perhaps, the whole extent of abstinence they practised. But they separated themselves from three things in

shall go ʳ into thy bowels, to make *thy* belly to swell, and *thy* thigh to rot. ˢAnd the woman shall say, Amen, amen.

23 And the priest shall write these curses in a book, and he shall blot *them* out with the bitter water:

24 And he shall cause the woman to drink the bitter water that causeth the curse: and the water that causeth the curse shall enter into her, *and become* bitter.

25 Then the priest shall take the jealousy offering out of the woman's hand, and shall wave ᵗ the offering before the LORD, and offer it upon the altar.

26 And ᵘ the priest shall take an handful of the offering, *even* the memorial thereof, and burn *it* upon the altar, and afterward shall cause the woman to drink the water.

27 And when he hath made her to drink the water, then it shall come to pass, *that*, if she be defiled, and have done trespass against her husband, that the water that causeth the curse shall enter into her, *and become* bitter, and her belly shall swell, and her thigh shall rot: and the woman shall ᵛ be a curse among her people.

28 And if the woman be not defiled, but be clean; then she shall ʷ be free, and shall conceive seed.

29 This *is* the law of jealousies, when a wife goeth aside *to another* instead of her husband, and is defiled;

30 Or when the spirit of jealousy cometh upon him, and he be jealous over his wife, and shall set the woman before the LORD, and the priest shall execute upon her all this law.

31 Then shall the man be guiltless from iniquity, and this woman ˣ shall bear her iniquity.

CHAPTER VI.

1 *The law of the Nazarite in his separation.* 22 *The form of blessing the people.*

AND the LORD spake unto Moses, saying, 2 Speak unto the children of Israel, and say unto them, When either man or woman shall ¹ separate *themselves* to vow a vow of a Nazarite, to separate *themselves* unto the LORD;

3 He ᵃ shall separate *himself* from wine and strong drink, and shall drink no vinegar of wine, or vinegar of strong drink, neither shall he drink any liquor of grapes, nor eat moist grapes, or dried.

4 All the days of his ᶻ separation shall he eat nothing that is made of the ³ vine tree, from the kernels even to the husk.

5 All the days of the vow of his separation there shall no ᵇ razor come upon his head; until the days be fulfilled, in the which he separateth *himself* unto the LORD, he shall be holy, *and* shall let the locks of the hair of his head grow.

6 All the days that he separateth *himself* unto the LORD ᶜ he shall come at no dead body.

7 He ᵈ shall not make himself unclean for his father, or for his mother, for his brother, or for his sister, when they die; because the ⁴ consecration of his God *is* upon his head.

8 All the days of his separation he *is* holy unto the LORD.

9 And if any man die very suddenly by him, and he hath defiled the head of his consecration; then he shall ᵉ shave his head in the day of his cleansing, on the seventh day shall he shave it.

10 And ᶠ on the eighth day he shall bring

two turtles, or two young pigeons, to the priest, to the door of the tabernacle of the congregation:

11 And the priest shall offer the one for a sin offering, and the other for a burnt offering, and make an atonement for him, for that he sinned by the dead, and shall hallow his head that same day.

12 And he shall consecrate unto the LORD the days of his separation, and shall bring a lamb of the first year for a trespass offering: but the days that were before shall ⁵ be lost, because his separation was defiled.

13 ¶ And this *is* the law of the Nazarite, when ᵍ the days of his separation are fulfilled: he shall be brought unto the door of the tabernacle of the congregation;

14 And he shall offer his offering unto the LORD, one he-lamb of the first year without blemish for a burnt offering, and one ewe lamb of the first year without blemish ʰ for a sin offering, and one ram without blemish for ⁶ peace offerings,

15 And a basket of unleavened bread, cakes ⁱ of fine flour mingled with oil, and wafers of unleavened bread ᵏ anointed with oil, and their meat offering, and their drink ˡ offerings.

16 And the priest shall bring *them* before the LORD, and shall offer his sin offering, and his burnt offering:

17 And he shall offer the ram *for* a sacrifice of peace offerings unto the LORD, with the basket of unleavened bread: the priest shall offer also his meat offering, and his drink offering.

18 And ᵐ the Nazarite shall shave the head of his separation *at* the door of the tabernacle of the congregation, and shall take the hair of the head of his separation, and ⁿ put *it* in the fire which *is* under the sacrifice of the peace offerings.

19 And the priest shall take the ᵒ sodden shoulder of the ram, and one unleavened cake out of the basket, and one unleavened wafer, and ᵖ shall put *them* upon the hands of the Nazarite, after the hair of his separation is shaven:

20 And the priest shall ᑫ wave them *for* a wave offering before the LORD: this *is* holy for the priest, with the wave breast and heave shoulder: and ʳ after that the Nazarite may drink wine.

21 This *is* the law of the Nazarite who hath vowed, *and of* his offering unto the LORD for his separation, besides *that* that his hand shall get: according to the vow which he vowed, so he must do after the law of his separation.

22 ¶ And the LORD spake unto Moses, saying,

23 Speak unto Aaron, and unto his sons, saying, On this wise ˢ ye shall bless the children of Israel, saying unto them,

24 The LORD ᵗ bless thee, and "keep thee;

25 The LORD ᵘ make his face shine upon thee, and ʷ be gracious unto thee;

26 The ˣ LORD lift up his countenance upon thee, and ʸ give thee peace.

27 And ᶻ they shall put my name upon the children of Israel; and ᵃ I will bless them.

CHAPTER VII.

1, 10 *The princes' offerings.* 89 *God speaketh to Moses from the mercyseat.*

AND it came to pass on the day that Moses had fully set up the tabernacle, and had anointed it, and sanctified it, and all the instruments thereof, both the altar

particular—viz., from wine, and all the varieties of vinous produce; from the application of a razor to their head, allowing their hair to grow; and from pollution by a dead body. The reasons of the self-restriction are obvious. The use of wine tended to inflame the passions, intoxicate the brain, and create a taste for luxurious indulgence. The cutting off the hair being a recognised sign of uncleanness, (Le. 14. 8, 9,) its unpolled luxuriance was a symbol of the purity he professed. Besides, its extraordinary length kept him in constant remembrance of his vow, as well as stimulated others to imitate his pious example. Moreover, contact with a dead body, disqualifying for the Divine service, the Nazarite carefully avoided such a cause of unfitness, and, like the high priest, did not assist at the funeral rites of his nearest relatives, preferring his duty to God to the indulgence of his strongest natural affections. 8-11. If any man die suddenly by him—Cases of sudden death might occur to make him contract pollution; and in such circumstances he required, after shaving his head, to make the prescribed offerings necessary for the removal of ceremonial defilement. (Le. 15. 13; ch. 19. 11.) But by the terms of this law an accidental defilement vitiated the whole of his previous observances, and he required to begin the period of his Nazaritism afresh. But even this full completion did not supersede the necessity of a sin-offering at the close. Sin mingles with our best and holiest performances, and the blood of sprinkling is necessary to procure acceptance to us and our services. 13-20. When the days of his separation, &c.—On the accomplishment of a limited vow of Nazaritism, Nazarites might cut their hair wherever they happened to be, (A. 18. 18;) but the hair was to be carefully kept and brought to the door of the sanctuary. Then after the presentation of sin-offerings and burnt-offerings, it was put under the vessel in which the peace-offerings were boiled; and the priest, taking the shoulder, (Le. 7. 32,) when boiled, and a cake and wafer of the meat-offering, put them on the hands of the Nazarites to wave before the Lord, as a token of thanksgiving, and thus released them from their vow.

23-27. THE FORM OF BLESSING THE PEOPLE. Speak unto Aaron, &c.—This passage records the solemn benediction which God appointed for dismissing the people at the close of the daily service. The repetition of the name "Lord" or "Jehovah" three times, express the great mystery of the Godhead—three persons, and yet one God. The expressions in the separate clauses correspond to the respective offices of the Father, to "bless and keep us;" of the Son, to be "gracious to us;" and of the Holy Ghost, to "give us peace." And that the benediction, though pronounced by the lips of a fellowman, derived its virtue, not from the priest, but from God, the encouraging assurance was added, "I the Lord will bless them."

CHAPTER VII.

Ver. 1-89. THE PRINCES' OFFERINGS. 1. the day that Moses had fully set up the tabernacle—Those who take the word "day" as literally pointing to the exact date of the completion of the tabernacle, are under a necessity of considering the sacred narrative as disjointed and this portion of the history from the seventh to the eleventh chapters as out of its place—the chronology requiring that it should have immediately followed the fortieth chapter of Exodus, which relates that the tabernacle was reared on the first day of the first month of the second year. But that the term "day" is used in a loose and indeterminate sense, as synonymous with time, is evident from the fact that not one day but several days were occupied with the transactions about to be described. So that this chapter stands in its proper place in the order of the history;—after the tabernacle and its instruments, the altar and its vessels, had been anointed, Lev. 8. 10,) the Levites separated to the sacred service—the numbering of the people, and the disposal of the tribes about the tabernacle, in a certain order, which was observed by the princes in the presentation of their offerings. This would fix the period of the imposing ceremonial described in this chapter about a month after the completion of the tabernacle. 2, 3. The princes of Israel...brought their offering before the Lord—The finishing of the sacred edifice would, it may well be imagined, be hailed as an auspicious occasion, diffusing great joy and thankfulness throughout the whole population of Israel. But the leading men, not content with participating in the general expression of satisfaction, distinguished themselves by a movement, which, while purely spontaneous, was at the same time so appropriate in the circumstances, and so equal in character, as indicates it to have been the result of concert and previous arrangement. It was an offer of the means of carriage, suitable to the migratory state of the nation in the wilderness, for transporting the tabernacle from place to place. In the pattern of that sacred tent exhibited on the mount, and to which its symbolic and typical character required a faithful adherence, no provision had been made for its removal in the frequent journeyings of the Israelites. That not being essential to the plan of the divine architect, was left to be accomplished by voluntary liberality; and whether we look to the judicious character of the gifts, or to the public manner in which they were presented, we have unmistakeable evidence of the pious and patriotic feelings from which they emanated, and the extensive interest the occasion produced. The offerers were "the princes of Israel, heads of the house of their fathers," and the offering consisted of six covered waggons or litter cars, and twelve oxen, two of the princes being partners in a waggon, and each furnishing an ox. 4, 5. The Lord spake..Take it of them—They exhibited a beautiful example to all who are great in dignity and in wealth, to be foremost in contributing to the support, and in promoting the interests of religion. The strictness of the injunctions Moses had received to adhere with scrupulous fidelity to the divine model of the tabernacle probably led him to doubt whether he was at liberty to act in this matter without orders. God, however, relieved him by declaring his acceptance of the free-will offerings, as well as by giving instructions as to the mode of their distribution amongst the Levites. It is probable that in doing so, He merely sanctioned the object for which they were offered, and that the practical wisdom of the offerers had previously determined that they should

CHAP. 7.

and all the vessels thereof, and had anointed them, and sanctified them,

2 That the princes of Israel, heads of the house of their fathers, who were the princes of the tribes, and were over them that were numbered, offered:

3 And they brought their offering before the LORD, six covered wagons, and twelve oxen; a wagon for two of the princes, and for each one an ox: and they brought them before the tabernacle.

4 And the LORD spake unto Moses, saying,

5 Take it of them, that they may be to do the service of the tabernacle of the congregation; and thou shalt give them unto the Levites, to every man according to his service.

6 And Moses took the wagons and the oxen, and gave them unto the Levites.

7 Two wagons and four oxen he gave unto the sons of Gershon, according to their service:

8 And four wagons and eight oxen he gave unto the sons of Merari, according unto their service, under the hand of Ithamar the son of Aaron the priest.

9 But unto the sons of Kohath he gave none; because the service of the sanctuary belonging unto them was that they should bear upon their shoulders.

10 ¶ And the princes offered for dedicating of the altar in the day that it was anointed, even the princes offered their offering before the altar.

11 And the LORD said unto Moses, They shall offer their offering, each prince on his day, for the dedicating of the altar.

12 ¶ And he that offered his offering the first day was Nahshon the son of Amminadab, of the tribe of Judah:

13 And his offering was one silver charger, the weight whereof was an hundred and thirty shekels, one silver bowl of seventy shekels, after the shekel of the sanctuary, both of them were full of fine flour mingled with oil, for a meat offering:

14 One spoon of ten shekels of gold, full of incense:

15 One young bullock, one ram, one lamb of the first year, for a burnt offering:

16 One kid of the goats for a sin offering:

17 And for a sacrifice of peace offerings, two oxen, five rams, five he-goats, five lambs of the first year: this was the offering of Nahshon the son of Amminadab.

18 ¶ On the second day Nethaneel the son of Zuar, prince of Issachar, did offer:

19 He offered for his offering one silver charger, the weight whereof was an hundred and thirty shekels, one silver bowl of seventy shekels, after the shekel of the sanctuary, both of them full of fine flour mingled with oil, for a meat offering:

20 One spoon of gold of ten shekels, full of incense:

21 One young bullock, one ram, one lamb of the first year, for a burnt offering:

22 One kid of the goats for a sin offering:

23 And for a sacrifice of peace offerings, two oxen, five rams, five he-goats, five lambs of the first year: this was the offering of Nethaneel the son of Zuar.

24 ¶ On the third day Eliab the son of Helon, prince of the children of Zebulun, did offer:

25 His offering was one silver charger, the weight whereof was an hundred and thirty shekels, one silver bowl of seventy shekels, after the shekel of the sanctuary, both of them full of fine flour mingled with oil, for a meat offering:

26 One golden spoon of ten shekels, full of incense:

27 One young bullock, one ram, one lamb of the first year, for a burnt offering:

28 One kid of the goats for a sin offering:

29 And for a sacrifice of peace offerings, two oxen, five rams, five he-goats, five lambs of the first year: this was the offering of Eliab the son of Helon.

30 ¶ On the fourth day Elizur the son of Shedeur, prince of the children of Reuben, did offer:

31 His offering was one silver charger of the weight of an hundred and thirty shekels, one silver bowl of seventy shekels, after the shekel of the sanctuary, both of them full of fine flour mingled with oil, for a meat offering:

32 One golden spoon of ten shekels, full of incense:

33 One young bullock, one ram, one lamb of the first year, for a burnt offering:

34 One kid of the goats for a sin offering:

35 And for a sacrifice of peace offerings, two oxen, five rams, five he-goats, five lambs of the first year: this was the offering of Elizur the son of Shedeur.

36 ¶ On the fifth day Shelumiel the son of Zurishaddai, prince of the children of Simeon, did offer:

37 His offering was one silver charger, the weight whereof was an hundred and thirty shekels, one silver bowl of seventy shekels, after the shekel of the sanctuary, both of them full of fine flour mingled with oil, for a meat offering:

38 One golden spoon of ten shekels, full of incense:

39 One young bullock, one ram, one lamb of the first year, for a burnt offering:

40 One kid of the goats for a sin offering:

41 And for a sacrifice of peace offerings, two oxen, five rams, five he-goats, five lambs of the first year: this was the offering of Shelumiel the son of Zurishaddai.

42 ¶ On the sixth day Eliasaph the son of Deuel, prince of the children of Gad, offered:

43 His offering was one silver charger of the weight of an hundred and thirty shekels, a silver bowl of seventy shekels, after the shekel of the sanctuary, both of them full of fine flour mingled with oil, for a meat offering:

44 One golden spoon of ten shekels, full of incense:

45 One young bullock, one ram, one lamb of the first year, for a burnt offering:

46 One kid of the goats for a sin offering:

47 And for a sacrifice of peace offerings, two oxen, five rams, five he-goats, five lambs of the first year: this was the offering of Eliasaph the son of Deuel.

48 ¶ On the seventh day Elishama the son of Ammihud, prince of the children of Ephraim, offered:

49 His offering was one silver charger, the weight whereof was an hundred and thirty shekels, one silver bowl of seventy shekels, after the shekel of the sanctuary, both of them full of fine flour mingled with oil, for a meat offering:

50 One golden spoon of ten shekels, full of incense:

be distributed "unto the Levites, to every man according to his service;" i.e., more or fewer were assigned to each of the Levitical divisions, as their department of duty seemed to require. This divine sanction it is of great importance to notice, as establishing the principle, that, while in the great matters of divine worship and church-government we are to adhere faithfully to the revealed rule of faith and duty, minor arrangements respecting them may be lawfully made, according to the means and convenience of God's people in different places. "There is a great deal left to human regulation—appendages of undoubted convenience, and which it were as absurd to resist on the ground that an express warrant cannot be produced for them, as to protest against the convening of the people to divine service, because there is no scripture for the erection and ringing of a church bell." [CHALMERS.] 6-9. Moses took the waggons and the oxen.—The *Heb.* word seems to be fairly rendered by the word "waggons." Wheel carriages of some kind are certainly intended; and as they were covered, the best idea we can form of them is, that they bore some resemblance to our tilted waggons. That wheel carriages were anciently used in Egypt, and in what is now Asiatic Turkey, is attested, not only by history, but by existing sculptures and paintings. Some of these the Israelites might have brought with them at their departure; and others, the skilful artisans, who did the mechanical work of the tabernacle, could easily have constructed, according to models with which they had been familiar. Each waggon was drawn by two oxen, and a greater number does not seem to have been employed on any of the different occasions mentioned in Scripture. Oxen seem to have been generally used for draught in ancient times among other nations as well as the Hebrews; and they continue still to be employed in dragging the few carts which are in use in some parts of Western Asia. [KITTO.] gave them unto the Levites—The principle of distribution was natural and judicious—the Merarites having twice the number of waggons and oxen appropriated to them that the Gershonites had; obviously because, while the latter had charge only of the coverings and hangings—the light but precious and richly embroidered drapery—the former were appointed to transport all the heavy and bulky materials—the boards, bars, pillars, and sockets—in short, all the larger articles of furniture. Whoever thinks only of the enormous weight of metal, the gold, silver, brass, &c., that were on the bases, chapiters, and pillars, &c., will probably come to the conclusion that four waggons and eight oxen were not nearly sufficient for the conveyance of so vast a load. Besides, the Merarites were not very numerous, as they amounted only to 3,200 men from thirty years and upwards; and, therefore, there is reason to suppose that a much greater number of waggons would afterwards be found necessary, and be furnished, than were given on this occasion. [CALMET.] Others, who consider the full number of waggons and oxen to be stated in the sacred record, suppose that the Merarites may have carried many of the smaller things in their hands—the sockets, for instance, which being each a talent weight, was one man's burden. (2 Ki. 5. 23.) The Kohathites had neither wheeled vehicles nor beasts of burden assigned them, because, being charged with the transport of the furniture belonging to the holy place, the sacred worth and character of the vessels intrusted to them (see on ch. 4. 15,) demanded a more honourable mode of conveyance. They were carried by those Levites shoulder-high. Even in this minute arrangement every reflecting reader will perceive the evidence of Divine wisdom and holiness; and a deviation from the prescribed rule of duty led, in one recorded instance, to a manifestation of holy displeasure, calculated to make a salutary and solemn impression. (2 Sa. 6. 6-13.) 10, 11. The princes offered, &c.—"Altar" is here used in the singular for the plural; for it is evident, from the kind of offerings, that the altars of burnt-offering and incense are both referred to. This was not the first or proper dedication of those altars, which had been made by Moses and Aaron some time before. But it might be considered an additional *dedication*—those offerings being the first that were made for particular persons or tribes. They shall offer, &c.—Eastern princes were accustomed anciently, as they are in Persia still on a certain yearly festival, to sit upon their thrones in great state, when the princes and nobles, from all parts of their dominions, appear before them with tributary presents, which form a large proportion of their royal revenue. And in the offering of all gifts or presents to great personages, every article is presented singly and with ostentatious display. The tabernacle being the palace of their King, as well as the sanctuary of their God, the princes of Israel may be viewed, on the occasion under notice, as presenting their tributary offerings, and in the same manner of successive detail, which accords with the immemorial usages of the East. A day was set apart for each, as much for the imposing solemnity and splendour of the ceremony, as for the prevention of disorder and hurry; and it is observable that, in the order of offering, regard was paid to priority not of birth, but of rank and dignity as they were ranged in the camp—beginning at the east, proceeding to the south, then to the west, and closing with the north, according to the course of the sun. 12-17. He that offered, &c. —Judah having had the precedence assigned to it, the prince or head of that tribe was the first admitted to offer as its representative; and his offering, as well as that of the others, is thought, from its costliness, to have been furnished not from his own private means, but from the general contributions of each tribe. Some parts of the offering, as the animals for sacrifice, were for the ritual service of the day, the peace-offerings being by much the most numerous, as the princes and some of the people joined with the priests afterwards in celebrating the occasion with festive rejoicing. Hence the feast of dedication became afterwards an anniversary festival. Other parts of the offering were intended for permanent use, as utensils necessary in the service of the sanctuary, an immense platter and bowl, (Ex. 25. 29,) which, being of silver, were to be employed at the altar of burnt-offering, or in the court, not in the holy place, all the furniture of which was of

51 One young bullock, one ram, one lamb of the first year, for a burnt offering:
52 One kid of the goats for a sin offering:
53 And for a sacrifice of peace offerings, two oxen, five rams, five he-goats, five lambs of the first year: this was the offering of Elishama the son of Ammihud.
54 ¶ On the eighth day offered Gamaliel the son of Pedahzur, prince of the children of Manasseh:
55 His offering was one silver charger of the weight of an hundred and thirty shekels, one silver bowl of seventy shekels, after the shekel of the sanctuary, both of them full of fine flour mingled with oil, for a meat offering:
56 One golden spoon of ten shekels, full of incense:
57 One young bullock, one ram, one lamb of the first year, for a burnt offering:
58 One kid of the goats for a sin offering:
59 And for a sacrifice of peace offerings, two oxen, five rams, five he-goats, five lambs of the first year: this was the offering of Gamaliel the son of Pedahzur.
60 ¶ On the ninth day Abidan the son of Gideoni, prince of the children of Benjamin, offered:
61 His offering was one silver charger, the weight whereof was an hundred and thirty shekels, one silver bowl of seventy shekels, after the shekel of the sanctuary, both of them full of fine flour mingled with oil, for a meat offering:
62 One golden spoon of ten shekels, full of incense:
63 One young bullock, one ram, one lamb of the first year, for a burnt offering:
64 One kid of the goats for a sin offering:
65 And for a sacrifice of peace offerings, two oxen, five rams, five he-goats, five lambs of the first year: this was the offering of Abidan the son of Gideoni.
66 ¶ On the tenth day Ahiezer the son of Ammishaddai, prince of the children of Dan, offered:
67 His offering was one silver charger, the weight whereof was an hundred and thirty shekels, one silver bowl of seventy shekels, after the shekel of the sanctuary, both of them full of fine flour mingled with oil, for a meat offering:
68 One golden spoon of ten shekels, full of incense:
69 One young bullock, one ram, one lamb of the first year, for a burnt offering:
70 One kid of the goats for a sin offering:
71 And for a sacrifice of peace offerings, two oxen, five rams, five he-goats, five lambs of the first year: this was the offering of Ahiezer the son of Ammishaddai.
72 ¶ On the eleventh day Pagiel the son of Ocran, prince of the children of Asher, offered:
73 His offering was one silver charger, the weight whereof was an hundred and thirty shekels, one silver bowl of seventy shekels, after the shekel of the sanctuary, both of them full of fine flour mingled with oil, for a meat offering:
74 One golden spoon of ten shekels, full of incense:
75 One young bullock, one ram, one lamb of the first year, for a burnt offering:
76 One kid of the goats for a sin offering:
77 And for a sacrifice of peace offerings, two oxen, five rams, five he-goats, five lambs of the first year: this was the offering of Pagiel the son of Ocran.
78 ¶ On the twelfth day Ahira the son of Enan, prince of the children of Naphtali, offered:
79 His offering was one silver charger, the weight whereof was an hundred and thirty shekels, one silver bowl of seventy shekels, after the shekel of the sanctuary, both of them full of fine flour mingled with oil, for a meat offering:
80 One golden spoon of ten shekels, full of incense:
81 One young bullock, one ram, one lamb of the first year, for a burnt offering:
82 One kid of the goats for a sin offering:
83 And for a sacrifice of peace offerings, two oxen, five rams, five he-goats, five lambs of the first year: this was the offering of Ahira the son of Enan.
84 This was the dedication of the altar, in the day when it was anointed, by the princes of Israel: twelve chargers of silver, twelve silver bowls, twelve spoons of gold:
85 Each charger of silver weighing an hundred and thirty shekels, each bowl seventy: all the silver vessels weighed two thousand and four hundred shekels, after the shekel of the sanctuary:
86 The golden spoons were twelve, full of incense, weighing ten shekels apiece, after the shekel of the sanctuary: all the gold of the spoons was an hundred and twenty shekels.
87 All the oxen for the burnt offering were twelve bullocks, the rams twelve, the lambs of the first year twelve, with their meat offering: and the kids of the goats for sin offering twelve.
88 And all the oxen for the sacrifice of the peace offerings, were twenty and four bullocks, the rams sixty, the he-goats sixty, the lambs of the first year sixty. This was the dedication of the altar, after that it was anointed.
89 And when Moses was gone into the tabernacle of the congregation to speak with him, then he heard the voice of one speaking unto him from off the mercy-seat that was upon the ark of testimony, from between the two cherubim: and he spake unto him.

CHAPTER VIII.

1 *How the lamps are to be lighted.* 5 *The consecration of the Levites:* 23 *the age and time of their service.*

AND the LORD spake unto Moses, saying,
2 Speak unto Aaron, and say unto him, When thou lightest the lamps, the seven lamps shall give light over against the candlestick.
3 And Aaron did so; he lighted the lamps thereof over against the candlestick, as the LORD commanded Moses.
4 And this work of the candlestick was of beaten gold, unto the shaft thereof, unto the flowers thereof, was beaten work: according unto the pattern which the LORD had showed Moses, so he made the candlestick.
5 ¶ And the LORD spake unto Moses, saying,
6 Take the Levites from among the children of Israel, and cleanse them:
7 And thus shalt thou do unto them, to cleanse them: Sprinkle water of purifying upon them, and let them shave all their

solid or plated gold; and a golden spoon, the contents of which show its destination to have been the altar of incense. The word rendered "spoon" means a hollow cup, in the shape of a hand, with which the priests on ordinary occasions might lift a quantity from the incense-box to throw on the altar-fire, or into the censers; but on the ceremonial on the day of the annual atonement no instrument was allowed but the high priest's own hands. (Le. 16. 12.) 18. On the second, Nethaneel, prince of Issachar—This tribe being stationed on the right side of Judah, offered next through its representative; then Zebulun, which was on the left side; and so on in orderly succession, every tribe making the same kind of offering and in the same amount, to show that, as each was under equal obligation, each rendered an equal tribute. Although each offering made was the same in quantity as well as quality, a separate notice is given of each, as a separate day was appointed for the presentation, that equal honour might be conferred on each, and none appear to be overlooked or slighted. And as the sacred books were frequently read in public, posterity, in each successive age, would feel a livelier interest in the national worship, from the permanent recognition of the offerings made by the ancestors of the respective tribes. But while this was done in one respect, as subjects offering tribute to their king, it was in another respect, a purely religious act. The vessels offered were for a sacrificial use—the animals brought were clean and fit for sacrifice, both symbolically denoting, that while God was to dwell amongst them as their Sovereign, they were a holy people, who by this offering dedicated themselves to God. 48. On the seventh day—Surprise has been expressed by some that this work of presentation was continued on the Sabbath. But assuming that the seventh day referred to was a Sabbath, (which is uncertain,) the work was of a directly religious character, and perfectly in accordance with the design of the sacred day. 84-88. This was the dedication of the altar—The inspired historian here sums up the separate items detailed. The preceding narrative, and the aggregate amount, is as follows:—121 silver chargers, each weighing 130 shekels = 1560; 12 silver bowls, each 70 shekels = 840: total weight. A silver charger at 130 shekels, reduced to Troy weight, makes 75 oz., 9 dwts., 16 8·31 gr.; and a silver bowl at 70 shekels amounts to 40 oz., 12 dwts., 21 21·31 gr. The total weight of the 12 chargers is therefore 905 oz., 16 dwts., 3 3·11 gr., and that of the 12 bowls 487 oz., 14 dwts., 20 4·31 gr.; making the total weight of silver vessels 1393 oz., 10 dwts., 23 7·31 gr.; which, at 5s. per oz., is equal to £383, 1s. 8¾d. The 12 golden spoons, allowing each to be 5 oz., 16 dwts., 3 3·31 gr., amount to 69 oz., 3 dwts., 13 5·31 gr., which, at £4 per oz., is equal to £320, 14s. 10½d., and added to the amount of the silver, makes a total of £703, 16s. 6¼d. Besides these, the offerings comprised 12 bullocks, 12 rams, 12 lambs, 24 goats, 60 rams, 60 he-goats, 60 lambs—amounting in all to 240. So large a collection of cattle offered for sacrifice on one occasion proves both the large flocks of the Israelites and the abundance of pastures which were then, and still are found in the valleys that lie between the Sinaitic Mountains. All travellers attest the luxuriant verdure of those extensive wadys; and that they were equally or still more rich in pasturage anciently, is confirmed by the numerous flocks of the Amalekites, as well as of Nabal, which were fed in the wilderness of Paran. (1 Sam. 15. 9.) 89. And when Moses was gone into the tabernacle of the congregation—As a king gives private audience to his minister, so special license was granted to Moses, who, though not a priest, was admitted into the sanctuary to receive instructions from his Heavenly King as occasion demanded. then he heard the voice of one speaking to him—Though standing on the outer side of the vail, he could distinctly hear it, and the mention of this circumstance is important as the fulfilment, at the dedication of the tabernacle, of a special promise made by the Lord—Christ himself, the Angel of the Covenant, commanding its erection. (Ex. 25. 22.) It was the reward of Moses' zeal and obedience; and, in like manner, to all who love Him and keep His commandments, He will manifest Himself. (J. 14. 21.)

CHAPTER VIII.

Ver. 1-4. HOW THE LAMPS ARE TO BE LIGHTED. 1. The Lord spake unto Moses—The order of this chapter suggests the idea that the following instructions were given to Moses while he was within the tabernacle of the congregation, after the princes had completed their offering. But from the tenor of the instructions, it is more likely that they were given immediately after the Levites had been given to the priests, (see on chaps. 3. 4,) and that the record of these instructions had been postponed till the narrative of other transactions in the camp had been made. [PATRICK.] Speak unto Aaron, &c.—The candlestick, which was made of one solid, massy piece of pure gold, with six lamps supported on as many branches, a seventh in the centre surmounting the shaft itself, (Ex. 25. 31; 37. 17,) and completed according to the pattern shown in the mount, was now to be lighted, when the other things in the sanctuary began to be applied to religious service. It was Aaron's personal duty, as the servant of God, to light His house, which, being without windows, required the aid of lights. (2 Pe. 1. 19.) And the course he was ordered to follow was first to light the middle lamp from the altar fire, and then the other lamps from each other—a course symbolical of all the light of heavenly truth being derived from Christ, and diffused by his ministers throughout the world. (Re. 4. 5.) over against, &c.—The candlestick stood close to the boards of the sanctuary, on the south side, in full view of the table of show bread on the north, (Ex. 26. 35,) having one set of its lamps turned towards the east, and another towards the west; so that all parts of the tabernacle were thus lighted up.

5-22. THE CONSECRATION OF THE LEVITES—Take the Levites and cleanse them—This passage describes the consecration of the Levites. Although the tribe was to be devoted to the Divine service, their hereditary descent alone was not a sufficient qualification for entering on the duties of the sacred office. They were to be set apart by a special ceremony, which, however, was much simpler than that appointed for the priests; neither washing nor anointing, nor

flesh, and let them wash their clothes, and so make themselves clean.

8 Then let them take a young bullock with ʰ his meat offering, *even* fine flour mingled with oil, and another young bullock shalt thou take for a sin offering.

9 And ⁱ thou shalt bring the Levites before the tabernacle of the congregation: ʲ and thou shalt gather the whole assembly of the children of Israel together:

10 And thou shalt bring the Levites before the LORD; and the children of Israel ᵏ shall put their hands upon the Levites:

11 And Aaron shall ² offer the Levites before the LORD for an ³ offering of the children of Israel, that ⁴ they may execute the service of the LORD.

12 And ˡ the Levites shall lay their hands upon the heads of the bullocks: and thou shalt offer the one *for* a sin offering, and the other *for* a burnt offering, unto the LORD, to make an atonement for the Levites.

13 And thou shalt set the Levites before Aaron, and before his sons, and offer them *for* an offering unto the LORD.

14 Thus shalt thou separate the Levites from among the children of Israel: and the Levites shall be ᵐ mine.

15 And after that shall the Levites go in to do the service of the tabernacle of the congregation: and thou shalt cleanse them, ⁿ and offer them *for* an offering.

16 For they *are* wholly given unto me from among the children of Israel; º instead of such as open every womb, *even instead of* the first-born of all the children of Israel, have I taken them unto me.

17 For ᵖ all the first-born of the children of Israel *are* mine, *both* man and beast: on the day that I smote every first-born in the land of Egypt I sanctified them for myself.

18 And I have taken the Levites for all the first-born of the children of Israel.

19 And ᵠ I have given the Levites *as* ⁵ a gift to Aaron and to his sons from among the children of Israel, to do the service of the children of Israel in the tabernacle of the congregation, and to make an atonement for the children of Israel; ʳ that there be no plague among the children of Israel, when the children of Israel come nigh unto the sanctuary.

20 And Moses, and Aaron, and all the congregation of the children of Israel, did to the Levites according unto all that the LORD commanded Moses concerning the Levites, so did the children of Israel unto them.

21 And the Levites were purified, and they washed their clothes; ˢ and Aaron offered them *as* an offering before the LORD; and Aaron made an atonement for them to cleanse them.

22 And ᵗ after that went the Levites in to do their service in the tabernacle of the congregation before Aaron, and before his sons: as the LORD had commanded Moses concerning the Levites, so did they unto them.

23 ¶ And the LORD spake unto Moses, saying,

24 This *is it* that *belongeth* unto the ᵘ Levites: from twenty and five years old and upward they shall go in ⁶ to wait upon the service of the tabernacle of the congregation:

25 And from the age of fifty years they shall ⁷ cease waiting upon the service thereof, and shall serve no more;

26 But shall minister with their brethren in the tabernacle of the congregation, ᵇ to keep the charge, and shall do no service. Thus shalt thou do unto the Levites touching their charge.

CHAPTER IX.

1 The passover enjoined. 9 A second passover allowed. 15 A cloud guideth the Israelites.

AND the LORD spake unto Moses in the wilderness of Sinai, in the first month of the second year after they were come out of the land of Egypt, saying,

2 Let the children of Israel also keep ᵃ the passover at his appointed season.

3 In the fourteenth day of this month, ¹ at even, ye shall keep it in his appointed season: according to all the rites of it, and according to all the ceremonies thereof, shall ye keep it.

4 And Moses spake unto the children of Israel, that they should keep the passover.

5 And ᵇ they kept the passover on the fourteenth day of the first month at even in the wilderness of Sinai: according to all that the LORD commanded Moses, so did the children of Israel.

6 ¶ And there were certain men, who were ᶜ defiled by the dead body of a man, that they could not keep the passover on that day: ᵈ and they came before Moses and before Aaron on that day:

7 And those men said unto him, We *are* defiled by the dead body of a man: wherefore are we kept back, that we may ᵉ not offer an offering of the LORD in his appointed season among the children of Israel?

8 And Moses said unto them, Stand still, and ᶠ I will hear what the LORD will command concerning you.

9 ¶ And the LORD spake unto Moses, saying,

10 Speak unto the children of Israel, saying, If any man of you or of your posterity shall be unclean by reason of a dead body, or be in a journey afar off, yet he shall keep the passover unto the LORD.

11 The ᵍ fourteenth day of the second month at even they shall keep it, *and* ʰ eat it with unleavened bread and bitter *herbs*.

12 They ⁱ shall leave none of it unto the morning, ʲ nor break any bone of it: ᵏ according to all the ordinances of the passover they shall keep it.

13 But the man that *is* clean, and is not in a journey, and forbeareth to keep the passover, even the same soul ˡ shall be cut off from among his people: because he brought not the offering of the LORD in his appointed season, that man shall ᵐ bear his sin.

14 And if a stranger shall sojourn among you, and will keep the passover unto the LORD; according to the ordinance of the passover, and according to the manner thereof, so shall he do: ⁿ ye shall have one ordinance, both for the ² stranger, and for him that was born in the land.

15 ¶ And on the day that the tabernacle was reared up, the cloud covered the tabernacle, *namely*, the tent of the testimony: and º at even there was upon the tabernacle as it were the appearance of fire, until the morning.

16 So it was alway: the ᵖ cloud covered it by day, and the appearance of fire by night.

investiture with official robes, was necessary. Their purification consisted, along with the offering of the requisite sacrifices, (Le. 1. 4; 3 2; 4. 4,) in being sprinkled by water mixed with the ashes of a red heifer, (ch. 19. 9,) and shaved all over, and their clothes washed—a combination of symbolical acts, which was intended to remind them of the mortification of carnal and worldly desires, and the maintenance of that purity in heart and life which became the servants of God. 9. The children of Israel, &c.—As it was plainly impossible that the whole multitude of the Israelites could do this, a select portion of them must be meant. This party, who laid their hands upon the Levites, are supposed by some to have been the first-born, who, by that act, transferred their peculiar privilege of acting as God's ministers to the Levitical tribe; and by others, to have been the princes, who thus blessed them. It appears, from this passage, that the imposition of hands was a ceremony used in consecrating persons to holy offices in the ancient, as, from the example of our Lord and his apostles, it has been perpetuated in the Christian Church. 11-13. Aaron shall offer the Levites—*Heb.*, as a wave offering; and it has been thought probable that the high priest, in bringing the Levites one by one to the altar, directed them to make some simple movements of their persons, analagous to what was done at the presentation of the wave offerings before the Lord. Thus were they first devoted as an offering to God, and by him surrendered to the priests to be employed in his service. The consecration ceremonial was repeated in the case of every Levite who was taken, as at a later period was done, to assist the priests in the tabernacle and temple. (See on 2 Chr. 29. 34.) 14. The Levites shall be mine—*i.e.*, exempt from all military duty or secular work—free from all pecuniary imposition, and wholly devoted to the custody and service of the sanctuary. 15. After that, the Levites shall go in —into the court, to assist the priests; and at removal into the tabernacle—*i. e.*, the door of it—to receive the covered furniture. 19. to make an atonement, &c.—to aid the priests in that expiatory work; or, as the words may be rendered, "to make redemption for," the Levites being exchanged or substituted for the first-born, for this important end, that there might be a sanctified body of men appointed to guard the sanctuary, and not allow the people to approach or presumptuously meddle with holy things, which would expose them to the angry judgments of Heaven. 23. From twenty-five years old, &c. —(cf. ch. 4. 3.) They entered on their work in their 25th year, as pupils and probationers, under the superintendance and direction of their senior brethren; and at 30 they were admitted to the full discharge of their official functions. 24. From fifty they shall cease waiting, &c.—*i. e.*, on the laborious and exhausting parts of their work. 26. But shall minister with their brethren—in the performance of easier and lighter duties—instructing and directing the young, or superintending important trusts. "They also serve who only wait." [MILTON.]

CHAPTER IX.

Ver. 1-8. THE PASSOVER ENJOINED. 2. Let the children of Israel, &c.—The date of this command to keep the passover in the wilderness was given shortly after the erection and consecration of the tabernacle, and preceded the numbering of the people by a month. (cf. *v.* 1. with ch. 1. 1, 2.) But it is narrated after that transaction, in order to introduce the notice of a particular case, for which a law was provided to meet the occasion. This was the first observance of the passover since the Exodus; and, without a positive injunction, the Israelites were under no obligation to keep it till their settlement in the land of Canaan. Ex. 12. 25.) The anniversary was kept on the exact day of the year on which they, twelve months before, had departed from Egypt; and it was marked by all the peculiar rites—the he-lamb and the unleavened bread. The materials would be easily procured—the lambs from their numerous flocks, and the meal for the unleavened bread, by the aid of Jethro, from the land of Midian, which was adjoining their camp. (Ex. 3. 1.) But their girded loins, their sandalled feet, and their staff in their hand, being mere circumstances attending a hurried departure, and not essential to the rite, were not repeated. It is supposed to have been the only observance of the feast during their 40 years' wandering; and Jewish writers say that, as none could eat the passover except they were circumcised, (Ex. 12. 43, 44, 48,) and circumcision was not practised in the wilderness, there could be no renewal of the paschal solemnity.

6-14. A SECOND PASSOVER ALLOWED. There were certain men ... defiled by the dead—To discharge the last offices to the remains of deceased relatives was imperative; and yet attendance on a funeral entailed ceremonial defilement, which led to exclusion from all society and from the camp for seven days. Some persons who were in this situation at the arrival of the first paschal anniversary, being painfully perplexed about the course of duty, because they were temporarily disqualified at the proper season, and having no opportunity of supplying their want, were liable to a total privation of all their privileges, laid their case before Moses. Jewish writers assert that these men were the persons who had carried out the dead bodies of Nadab and Abihu. 8. Stand still, &c.— A solution of the difficulty was soon obtained—it being enacted, by Divine authority, that to those who might be disqualified, by the occurrence of a death in his family circle, or unable by distance to keep the passover on the anniversary day, a special license was granted of observing it by themselves on the same day and hour of the following month, under a due attendance to all the solemn formalities. (See on 2 Chr. 30. 2.) But the observance was imperative on all who did not labour under those impediments. 14. If a stranger ... will keep the passover—Gentile converts, or proselytes, as they were afterwards called, were admitted, if circumcised, to the same privileges as native Israelites, and were liable to excommunication if they neglected the passover. But circumcision was an indispensable condition; and whoever did not submit to that rite, were prohibited, under the sternest penalties, from eating the passover.

15-23. A CLOUD GUIDETH THE ISRAELITES. The cloud covered the tabernacle—The inspired historian here enters on an entirely new subject, which might properly have

17 And when the cloud was taken up from the tabernacle, then after that the children of Israel journeyed: and in the place where the cloud abode, there the children of Israel pitched their tents.

18 At the commandment of the LORD the children of Israel journeyed, and at the commandment of the LORD they pitched: as long as the cloud abode upon the tabernacle they rested in their tents.

19 And when the cloud tarried long upon the tabernacle many days, then the children of Israel kept the charge of the LORD, and journeyed not.

20 And so it was, when the cloud was a few days upon the tabernacle; according to the commandment of the LORD they abode in their tents, and according to the commandment of the LORD they journeyed.

21 And so it was, when the cloud abode from even unto the morning, and that the cloud was taken up in the morning, then they journeyed: whether it was by day or by night that the cloud was taken up, they journeyed.

22 Or whether it were two days, or a month, or a year, that the cloud tarried upon the tabernacle, remaining thereon, the children of Israel abode in their tents, and journeyed not: but when it was taken up, they journeyed.

23 At the commandment of the LORD they rested in their tents, and at the commandment of the LORD they journeyed: they kept the charge of the LORD, at the commandment of the LORD by the hand of Moses.

CHAPTER X.

1 The use of the silver trumpets. 11 The Israelites go from Sinai to Paran. 33 Moses' blessing.

AND the LORD spake unto Moses, saying,

2 Make thee two trumpets of silver; of a whole piece shalt thou make them: that thou mayest use them for the calling of the assembly, and for the journeying of the camps.

3 And when they shall blow with them, all the assembly shall assemble themselves to thee at the door of the tabernacle of the congregation.

4 And if they blow but with one trumpet, then the princes, which are heads of the thousands of Israel, shall gather themselves unto thee.

5 When ye blow an alarm, then the camps that lie on the east parts shall go forward.

6 When ye blow an alarm the second time, then the camps that lie on the south side shall take their journey: they shall blow an alarm for their journeys.

7 But when the congregation is to be gathered together, ye shall blow, but ye shall not sound an alarm.

8 And the sons of Aaron, the priests, shall blow with the trumpets: and they shall be to you for an ordinance for ever throughout your generations.

9 And if ye go to war in your land against the enemy that oppresseth you, then ye shall blow an alarm with the trumpets; and ye shall be remembered before the LORD your God, and ye shall be saved from your enemies.

10 Also in the day of your gladness, and in your solemn days, and in the beginnings of your months, ye shall blow with the trumpets over your burnt offerings, and over the sacrifices of your peace offerings; that they may be to you for a memorial before your God: I am the LORD your God.

11 ¶ And it came to pass on the twentieth day of the second month, in the second year, that the cloud was taken up from off the tabernacle of the testimony.

12 And the children of Israel took their journeys out of the wilderness of Sinai; and the cloud rested in the wilderness of Paran.

13 And they first took their journey according to the commandment of the LORD by the hand of Moses.

14 ¶ In the first place went the standard of the camp of the children of Judah according to their armies: and over his host was Nahshon the son of Amminadab.

15 And over the host of the tribe of the children of Issachar was Nethaneel the son of Zuar.

16 And over the host of the tribe of the children of Zebulun was Eliab the son of Helon.

17 And the tabernacle was taken down; and the sons of Gershon and the sons of Merari set forward, bearing the tabernacle.

18 And the standard of the camp of Reuben set forward according to their armies: and over his host was Elizur the son of Shedeur.

19 And over the host of the tribe of the children of Simeon was Shelumiel the son of Zurishaddai.

20 And over the host of the tribe of the children of Gad was Eliasaph the son of Deuel.

21 And the Kohathites set forward, bearing the sanctuary: and the other did set up the tabernacle against they came.

22 And the standard of the camp of the children of Ephraim set forward according to their armies: and over his host was Elishama the son of Ammihud.

23 And over the host of the tribe of the children of Manasseh was Gamaliel the son of Pedahzur.

24 And over the host of the tribe of the children of Benjamin was Abidan the son of Gideoni.

25 And the standard of the camp of the children of Dan set forward, which was the rereward of all the camps throughout their hosts: and over his host was Ahiezer the son of Ammishaddai.

26 And over the host of the tribe of the children of Asher was Pagiel the son of Ocran.

27 And over the host of the tribe of the children of Naphtali was Ahira the son of Enan.

28 Thus were the journeyings of the children of Israel according to their armies, when they set forward.

29 ¶ And Moses said unto Hobab, the son of Raguel the Midianite, Moses' father-in-law, We are journeying unto the place of which the LORD said, I will give it you: come thou with us, and we will do thee good; for the LORD hath spoken good concerning Israel.

30 And he said unto him, I will not go; but I will depart to mine own land, and to my kindred.

31 And he said, Leave us not, I pray thee; forasmuch as thou knowest how we are to

formed a separate chapter, beginning at this verse and ending at v. 29 of the following chapter. [CALMET.] The cloud was a visible token of God's special presence and guardian care of the Israelites. (Ex. 14. 20; Ps. 105. 39.) It was easily distinguishable from all other clouds, by its peculiar form and its fixed position; for from the day of the completion of the tabernacle it rested by day as a dark, by night as a fiery, column, on that part of the sanctuary which contained the ark of the testimony. (Le. 16. 2.) 17. When the cloud was taken up—i. e., rose to a higher elevation, so as to be conspicuous at the remotest extremities of the camp. That was a signal for removal; and, accordingly, it is properly called, (v. 18,) "the commandment of the Lord." It was a visible token of the presence of God; and from it, as a glorious throne, He gave the order. So that its motion regulated the commencement and termination of all the journeys of the Israelites. (See on Ex. 14. 19.) 19. Israel kept the charge of the Lord—A desert life has its attractions, and constant movements create a passionate love of change. Many incidents show that the Israelites had strongly imbibed this nomad habit, and were desirous of hastening to Canaan. But still the phases of the cloud indicated the command of God; and whatsoever irksomeness they might have felt in remaining long stationary in camp, "when the cloud tarried upon the tabernacle many days, they kept the charge of the Lord, and journeyed not." Happy for them had they always exhibited this spirit of obedience! and happy for all if, through the wilderness of this world, we implicitly follow the leadings of God's providence and the directions of God's word!

CHAPTER X.

Ver. 1-36. THE USE OF THE SILVER TRUMPETS. 2. Make thee two trumpets of silver—These trumpets were of a long form, in opposition to that of the Egyptian trumpets, with which the people were convened to the worship of Osiris, and which were curved like rams' horns. Those which Moses made, as described by Josephus, and represented on the arch of Titus, were straight, a cubit or more in length, the tubes of the thickness of a flute, and both extremities bore a close resemblance to those in use amongst us. They were of solid silver—so as, from the purity of the metal, to give a shrill, distinct sound; and there were two of them, probably because there were only two sons of Aaron; but at a later period the number was greatly increased. (Josh. 6. 8; 2 Chr. 5. 12.) And although the camp comprehended 2,500,000 of people, two trumpets would be quite sufficient, for sound is conveyed easily through the pure atmosphere, and reverberated strongly amongst the valleys of the Sinaitic hills. 3. when they shall blow—There seem to have been signals made by a difference in the loudness and variety in the notes, suited for different occasions, and which experience made the Israelites easily distinguish. A simple uniform sound by both trumpets summoned a general assembly of the people; the blast of a single trumpet convoked the princes to consult on public affairs; notes of some other kind were made to sound an alarm, whether for journeying or for war. One alarm was the recognized signal for the eastern division of the camp—viz., the tribes of Judah, Issachar, and Zebulun—to march; two alarms gave the signal for the southern to move; and, though it is not in our present Heb. text, the Septuagint has, that on three alarms being sounded, those on the west; while on four blasts, those on the north decamped. Thus the greatest order and discipline were established in the Israelitish camp—no military march could be better regulated. 8. The sons of Aaron, &c.—Neither the Levites nor any in the common ranks of the people could be employed in this office of signalgiving. In order to attract greater attention and more faithful observance, it was reserved to the priests alone, as the Lord's ministers; and as anciently in Persia and other Eastern countries, the alarm trumpets were sounded from the tent of the sovereign, so were they blown from the tabernacle, the visible residence of Israel's King. 9. If ye go to war—In the land of Canaan, either when attacked by foreign invaders, or when they went to take possession according to the Divine promise, ye—i. e., the priests—shall blow an alarm. This advice was accordingly acted upon; (ch. 31. 6; 2 Chr. 13. 12;) and in the circumstances it was an act of devout confidence in God. A solemn and religious act on the eve of a battle has often animated the hearts of those who felt they were engaged in a good and just cause; and so the blowing of the trumpet, being an ordinance of God, produced that effect on the minds of the Israelites. But more is meant by the words—viz., that God would, as it were, be aroused by the trumpet to bless with His presence and aid. 10. Also in the days of your gladness—i.e., festive and thanksgiving occasions were to be ushered in with the trumpets, as all feasts afterwards were, (Ps. 81. 3; 2 Chr. 29. 27,) to intimate the joyous and delighted feelings with which they engaged in the service of God. 11. On the twentieth day, &c.—The Israelites had lain encamped in Wady-Er-Rahah and the neighbouring valleys of the Sinaitic range, for the space of 11 months 29 days. (cf. Ex. 19. 1.) Besides the religious purposes of the highest importance to which their long sojourn at Sinai was subservient, the Israelites, after the hardships and oppression of the Egyptian servitude, required an interval of repose and refreshment. They were neither physically nor morally in a condition to enter the lists with the warlike people they had to encounter before obtaining possession of Canaan. But the wondrous transactions at Sinai—the arm of Jehovah so visibly displayed in their favour—the covenant entered into, and the special blessings guaranteed, began a course of moral and religious education which moulded the character of this people—made them acquainted with their high destiny, and inspired them with those noble principles of Divine truth and righteousness, which alone make a great nation. 12. Wilderness of Paran—It stretched from the base of the Sinaitic group, or from Et-Tyh, over that extensive plateau to the south-western borders of Palestine. 13-27. The children of Israel took their journey by the hand of Moses—It is probable that Moses, on the breaking up of the encampment, stationed himself on some eminence to see the ranks defile in order through the embouchure of the mountains. The marching order is described, (ch. 2;) but as the vast horde are represented here

encamp in the wilderness, and thou mayest be to us ² instead of eyes.

32 And it shall be, if thou go with us, yea, it shall be, that what goodness the LORD shall do unto us, the same will we do unto thee.

33 ¶ And they departed from ᵃ the mount of the LORD three days' journey: and the ark of the covenant of the LORD ᵇ went before them in the three days' journey, to search out a resting place for them.

34 And ᶜ the cloud of the LORD was upon them by day, when they went out of the camp.

35 And it came to pass, when the ark set forward, that Moses said, ᵈ Rise up, LORD, and let thine enemies be scattered; and let them that hate thee flee before thee.

36 And when it rested, he said, ᵉ Return, O LORD, unto the ³ many thousands of Israel.

CHAPTER XI.

1 Manna loathed. 16 Seventy elders appointed. 31 Quails are given in wrath, etc.

AND ᵃ when the people ¹ complained, ² it displeased the LORD: and the LORD heard it; and his anger was kindled; and the ᵇ fire of the LORD burnt among them, and consumed them that were in the uttermost parts of the camp.

2 And the people cried unto Moses; and when Moses ᶜ prayed unto the LORD, the fire ³ was quenched.

3 And he called the name of the place ⁴ Taberah: because the fire of the LORD burnt among them.

4 ¶ And the ᵈ mixed multitude that was among them ⁵ fell a lusting: and the children of Israel also ⁶ wept again, and said, Who ⁶ shall give us flesh to eat?

5 We ᶠ remember the fish which we did eat in Egypt freely; the cucumbers, and the melons, and the leeks, and the onions, and the garlick:

6 But now our soul is dried away: there is nothing at all, besides this manna, before our eyes.

7 And the manna was as coriander seed, and the ⁷ colour thereof as the colour ᵍ of bdellium.

8 And the people went about, and gathered it, and ground it in mills, or beat it in a mortar, and baked it in pans, and made cakes of it: and the taste of it was as the taste of fresh oil.

9 And when the dew fell upon the camp in the night, the manna fell upon it.

10 ¶ Then Moses heard the people weep throughout their families, every man in the door of his tent: and the anger of the LORD was kindled greatly; Moses also was displeased.

11 And ʰ Moses said unto the LORD, Wherefore hast thou afflicted thy servant? and wherefore have I not found favour in thy sight, that thou layest the burden of all this people upon me?

12 Have I conceived all this people? have I begotten them, that thou shouldest say unto me, ⁱ Carry them in thy bosom, as a nursing ʲ father beareth the sucking child, unto the land which thou ᵏ swarest unto their fathers?

13 Whence ˡ should I have flesh to give unto all this people? for they weep unto me, saying, Give us flesh, that we may eat.

14 ¹ ᵐ am not able to bear all this people alone, because it is too heavy for me.

B. C. 1460.

CHAP. 10.
² Job 29. 15.
ᵃ Ex. 3. 1.
ᵇ Deu. 1. 33.
Jer. 31. 2.
ᶜ Ex. 13. 21.
Neh. 9. 12, 19.
ᵈ Ps. 68. 1, 2.
ᵉ Psalm 90. 14-17.
Ps. 132. 8.
³ ten thousand thousands.

CHAP. 11.
ᵃ Deu. 9. 22.
¹ Or, were as it were complainers.
² it was evil in the ears of, etc.
ᵇ Lev. 10. 2.
2 Ki. 1. 12.
ᶜ Jam. 5. 16.
³ sunk.
⁴ That is, a burning.
ᵈ Ex. 12. 38.
⁵ lusted a lust.
⁶ returned and wept.
ᶜ 1 Cor. 10. 6.
ᶠ Ex. 16. 3.
Phil. 3. 19.
Matth. 6. 24-34.
Rom. 8. 7.
⁷ eye of it as the eye of.
ᵍ Gen. 2. 12.
ʰ Deu. 1. 12.
ⁱ Is. 40. 11.
ʲ Is. 49. 23.
1 Thes. 2. 7.
ᵏ Gen. 50. 24.
ˡ 2 Kin. 4. 43, 44.
Mat. 15. 33.
ᵐ Ex. 18. 18.
ⁿ 1 Ki. 19. 4.
Job 6. 8-10.
Jonah 4. 3.
ᵒ Zep. 3. 15.
ᵖ Ex. 24. 1, 9.
ᵠ Gen. 11. 5.
Ex. 19. 20.
ʳ 1 Sa. 10. 6.
2 Ki. 2. 15.
Job 32. 8.
Job 33. 36.
Joel 2. 28.
ˢ Ex. 19. 10.
ᵗ Ex. 16. 7.
ᵘ Acts 7. 39.
⁸ month of days.
ᵛ 2 Kin. 7. 2.
ʷ Is. 50. 2.
ˣ Ezek. 12. 25.
Ezek. 24. 14.
ʸ ch. 12. 6.
² 2 Ki. 2. 15.
ᵃ 1 Sam. 10. 5, 6.
Joel 2. 29.
Acts 2. 17, 18.
1 Cor. 14. 1.
ᵇ 1 Sa. 20. 26.
Jer. 36. 5.
ᶜ Mar. 9. 38.
John 3. 26.
ᵈ 1 Cor. 14. 5.
ᵉ Ps. 78. 26.

---

15 And if thou deal thus with me, ⁿ kill me, I pray thee, out of hand, if I have found favour in thy sight; and let me not see ᵒ my wretchedness.

16 ¶ And the LORD said unto Moses, Gather unto me ᵖ seventy men of the elders of Israel, whom thou knowest to be the elders of the people, and officers over them; and bring them unto the tabernacle of the congregation, that they may stand there with thee.

17 And I will ᵠ come down and talk with thee there: and ʳ I will take of the spirit which is upon thee, and will put it upon them; and they shall bear the burden of the people with thee, that thou bear it not thyself alone.

18 And say thou unto the people, ˢ Sanctify yourselves against to-morrow, and ye shall eat flesh: for ye have wept ᵗ in the ears of the LORD, saying, Who shall give us flesh to eat? for ᵘ it was well with us in Egypt: therefore the LORD will give you flesh, and ye shall eat.

19 Ye shall not eat one day, nor two days, nor five days, neither ten days, nor twenty days;

20 But even a ⁸ whole month, until it come out at your nostrils, and it be loathsome unto you: because that ye have despised the LORD which is among you, and have wept before him, saying, Why came we forth out of Egypt?

21 And Moses said, The people, among whom I am, are six hundred thousand footmen; and thou hast said, I will give them flesh, that they may eat a whole month.

22 Shall ᵛ the flocks and the herds be slain for them, to suffice them? or shall all the fish of the sea be gathered together for them, to suffice them?

23 And the LORD said unto Moses, ʷ Is the LORD's hand waxed short? thou shalt see now whether ˣ my word shall come to pass unto thee or not.

24 ¶ And Moses went out, and told the people the words of the LORD, and gathered the seventy men of the elders of the people, and set them round about the tabernacle.

25 And the LORD ʸ came down in a cloud, and spake unto him, and took of the spirit that was upon him, and gave it unto the seventy elders; and it came to pass, ᶻ that, when the spirit rested upon them, ᵃ they prophesied, and did not cease.

26 But there remained two of the men in the camp, the name of the one was Eldad, and the name of the other Medad: and the spirit rested upon them; and they were of them that were written, but ᵇ went not out unto the tabernacle: and they prophesied in the camp.

27 And there ran a young man, and told Moses, and said, Eldad and Medad do prophesy in the camp.

28 And Joshua the son of Nun, the servant of Moses, one of his young men, answered and said, My lord Moses, ᶜ forbid them.

29 And Moses said unto him, Enviest thou for my sake? ᵈ Would God that all the LORD's people were prophets, and that the LORD would put his Spirit upon them!

30 And Moses gat him into the camp, he and the elders of Israel.

31 ¶ And there went forth a ᵉ wind from the LORD, and brought quails from the sea, and let them fall by the camp, as it were

in actual migration, it may be proper to notice the extraordinary care that was taken for insuring the safe conveyance of the holy things. In the rear of Judah, which, with the tribes of Issachar and Zebulun, led the van, followed the Gershonites and Merarites with the heavy and coarser materials of the tabernacle. Next in order were set in motion the flank divisions of Reuben and Ephraim; and then came the Kohathites, who occupied the centre of the moving mass, bearing the sacred utensils on their shoulders, and were so far behind the other portions of the Levitical body, that these would have time at the new encampment to rear the framework of the tabernacle ere the Kohathites arrived. Last of all, Dan, with the associated tribes, brought up the rereward of the immense caravan. Each tribe was marshalled under its prince or chief, and in all their movements rallied round its own standard. 29. Hobab, the son of Raguel the Midianite—called also Reuel, the same as Jethro. Hobab, the son of this Midianite chief, and brother-in-law to Moses, seems to have sojourned among the Israelites during the whole period of their encampment at Sinai, and now on their removal proposed returning to his own abode. Moses urged him to remain, both for his own benefit, in a religious point of view, and from the useful services his nomad habits could enable him to render. 31. Leave us not, I pray thee— The earnest importunity of Moses to secure the attendance of this man, when he enjoyed the benefit of the directing cloud, has surprised many. But it should be recollected that the guidance of the cloud, though it showed the general route to be taken through the trackless desert, would not be so special and minute as to point out the places where pasture, shade, and water were to be obtained, and which were often hid in obscure spots by the shifting sands. Besides, several detachments were sent off from the main body: the services of Hobab, not as a single Arab, but as a prince of a powerful clan, would have been exceedingly useful. 32. If thou go with us—A strong inducement is here held out; but it seems not to have changed the young man's purpose, for he departed and settled in his own district. (See on Jud. 1. 16; 1 Sa. 15. 6.) 33. They departed three days' journey—i. e., the first day's progress being very small, about 18 or 20 miles. ark of the covenant went before them—It was carried in the centre, and hence some eminent commentators think the passage should be rendered, "the ark went in their presence," the cloud above upon it being conspicuous in their eyes. But it is probable that the cloudy pillar, which, while stationary, rested upon the ark, preceded them in the march—as, when in motion at one time, (Ex. 14. 19,) it is expressly said to have shifted its place. 35. When the ark set forward, Moses said— Moses, as the organ of the people, uttered an appropriate prayer both at the commencement and the end of each journey. Thus all the journeys were sanctified by devotion; and so should our prayer be, "If thy presence go not with us, carry us not hence."

CHAPTER XI.

Ver. 1-35. MANNA LOATHED. 1. When the people complained, &c.--Unaccustomed to the fatigues of travel, and wandering into the depths of a desert, less mountainous, but far more gloomy and desolate than that of Sinai, without any near prospect of the rich country that had been promised, they fell into a state of vehement discontent, which was vented at these irksome and fruitless journeyings. The displeasure of God was manifested against the ungrateful complainers, by fire sent in an extraordinary manner. It is worthy of notice, however, that the discontent seems to have been confined to the extremities of the camp, where, in all likelihood, "the mixed multitude" had their station. At the intercession of Moses, the appalling judgment ceased, and the name given to the place, "Taberah," (a burning,) remained ever after a monument of national sin and punishment. (See on v. 34, 35.) 4. Mixed multitude fell a lusting—These consisted of Egyptians. To dream of banquets and plenty of animal food in the desert becomes a disease of the imagination; and to this excitement of the appetite no people are more liable than the natives of Egypt. But the Israelites participated in the same feelings, and expressed dissatisfaction with the manna on which they had hitherto been supported, in comparison with the vegetable luxuries with which they had been regaled in Egypt. 5. We remember the fish—See on Ex. 7. 21. The people of Egypt are accustomed to an almost exclusive diet of fish, either fresh or sun-dried, during the hot season in April and May—the very season when the Israelites were travelling in this desert. Lower Egypt, where were the brick-kilns in which they were employed, afforded great facilities for obtaining fish in the Mediterranean, the lakes and the canals of the Nile. cucumbers —The Egyptian species is smooth, of a cylindrical form, and about a foot in length. It is highly esteemed by the natives, and when in season, is liberally partaken of, being greatly mellowed by the influence of the sun. melons—The water melons are meant, which grow on the deep loamy soil after the subsidence of the Nile; and as they afford a juicy and cooling fruit, all classes make use of them for meat, drink, and medicine. leeks—by some said to be a species of grass cresses, which is much relished as a kind of seasoning. onions—the same as ours; but instead of being nauseous, and affecting the eyes, they are sweet to the taste, good for the stomach, and form to a large extent the aliment of the labouring classes. garlic —is now nearly if not altogether extinct in Egypt, although it seems to have grown anciently in great abundance. The herbs now mentioned form a diet very grateful in warm countries, where vegetables and other fruits of the season are much more used than with us. We can scarcely wonder that both the Egyptian hangers-on, and the general body of the Israelites, incited by their clamours, also complained bitterly of the want of the refreshing viands in their toilsome wanderings. But after all their experience of the bounty and care of God, their vehement longing for the luxuries of Egypt was an impeachment of the Divine arrangements; and if it was the sin that beset them in the desert, it became them more strenuously to repress a rebellious spirit, as dishonouring to God, and unbecoming their relation to Him as a chosen people. 6-9. But now there is nothing but this manna—Daily familiarity had disgusted them with the sight and taste

a day's journey on this side, and as it were a day's journey on the other side, round about the camp, and as it were two cubits *high* upon the face of the earth.

32 And the people stood up all that day, and all *that* night, and all the next day, and they gathered the quails: he that gathered least gathered ten *f* homers: and they spread *them* all abroad for themselves round about the camp.

33 And *g* while the flesh *was* yet between their teeth, ere it was chewed, the wrath of the LORD was kindled against the people; and the LORD smote the people with a very great plague.

34 And he called the name of that place ¹⁰ Kibroth-hattaavah: because there they buried the people that lusted.

35 *And* ʰ the people journeyed from Kibroth-hattaavah unto Hazeroth; and ¹¹ abode at Hazeroth.

CHAPTER XII.

1 *Miriam's and Aaron's sedition.* 10 *Her leprosy;* *Moses prayeth for her.* 14 *She is shut out of the camp seven days.*

AND Miriam and Aaron spake against Moses because of the ¹ Ethiopian woman whom he had married: for *a* he had ² married an Ethiopian woman.

2 And they said, Hath the LORD indeed spoken only by Moses? *b* hath he not spoken also by us? And the LORD *c* heard *it.*

3 (Now the man Moses *was* *d* very meek, above all the men which *were* upon the face of the earth.)

4 And *e* the LORD spake suddenly unto Moses, and unto Aaron, and unto Miriam, Come out ye three unto the tabernacle of the congregation. And they three came out.

5 And *f* the LORD came down in the pillar of the cloud, and stood *in* the door of the tabernacle, and called Aaron and Miriam: and they both came forth.

6 And he said, Hear now my words: If there be a prophet among you, *I* the LORD will make myself known unto him *g* in a vision, *and* will speak unto him *h* in a dream.

7 My *i* servant Moses *is* not so, *j* who *is* faithful in all mine house.

8 With him will I speak ᵏ mouth to mouth, even ˡ apparently, and not in dark speeches; and ᵐ the similitude of the LORD shall he behold: wherefore then ⁿ were ye not afraid to speak against my servant Moses?

9 And the anger of the LORD was kindled against them; and he departed.

10 And the cloud departed from off the tabernacle; and, *o* behold, Miriam *became* ᵖ leprous, *white* as snow: and Aaron looked upon Miriam, and, behold, *she was* leprous.

11 And Aaron said unto Moses, Alas! my lord, I beseech thee, ᵠ lay not the sin upon us, wherein we have done foolishly, and wherein we have sinned.

12 Let her not be ʳ as one dead, of whom the flesh is half consumed when he cometh out of his mother's womb.

13 And Moses *s* cried unto the LORD, saying, Heal her now, O God, I beseech thee.

14 ¶ And the LORD said unto Moses, *t* If her father had but spit in her face, should she not be ashamed seven days? let her be ᵘ shut out from the camp seven days, and after that let her be received in *again.*

B. C. 1490.

CHAP. 11.
9 the way of a day.
f Ezek. 45. 11.
g Ps. 78. 30, 31.
10 That is, the graves of lust.
Deu. 9. 22.
h ch. 33. 17.
11 they were in, etc.

CHAP. 12.
1 Or, Cushite.
a Ex. 2. 21.
2 taken.
b Ex. 15. 20.
Mic. 6. 4.
c Gen. 29. 33.
2 Ki. 19. 4.
Ps. 94. 9.
Is. 37. 4.
Ezek. 35. 12, 13.
d Mat. 21. 5.
1 Tim. 6. 11.
2 Tim. 2. 25.
1 Pet. 3. 4.
e Ps. 76. 9.
f ch. 16. 19.
g Gen. 46. 2.
Job 33. 15.
Lu. 1. 11, 22.
h Mat. 1. 20.
i Ps. 105. 26.
j Heb. 3. 2. 5.
ᵏ Ex. 33. 11.
Deu. 34. 10.
ˡ 1 Cor. 13. 12.
ᵐ Ex. 33. 19.
ⁿ 2 Pet. 2. 10.
o Deu. 24. 9.
ᵖ 2 Kin. 5. 27.
2 Chr. 26. 19.
ᵠ 2 Sam. 19. 19.
ʳ Ps. 88. 4.
ˢ Jam. 5. 16.
ᵗ Heb. 12. 9.
ᵘ Lev. 13. 46.
ᵛ Deu. 24. 9.
2 Chr. 26. 20.

CHAP. 13.
a Deu. 1. 22.
b 1 Chr. 4. 15.
c Josh. 14. 6.
d Ex. 17. 9.
e He shall save.
Acts 7. 45.
Heb. 4. 8.
f Into the south country.
Gen. 12. 9.
Josh. 15. 3.
Judg. 1. 15.
g Ju. 1. 9, 19.
h Ecc. 34. 14.
i Deu. 31. 6.
j Josh. 15. 1.
ᵏ Josh. 19. 28.
ˡ Judg. 1. 10.
ᵐ Jos. 21. 11.
ⁿ Ps. 78. 12.
o Deu. 1. 24.
1 Or, valley.
Ju. 16. 4.

15 And ᵛ Miriam was shut out from the camp seven days: and the people journeyed not till Miriam was brought in *again.*

16 And afterward the people removed from Hazeroth, and pitched in the wilderness of Paran.

CHAPTER XIII.

1 *The names of the men who were sent to search the land;* 17 *their instructions;* 21 *their acts;* 26 *and their relation.*

AND the LORD spake unto Moses, saying,
2 Send *a* thou men, that they may search the land of Canaan, which I give unto the children of Israel: of every tribe of their fathers shall ye send a man, every one a ruler among them.

3 And Moses by the commandment of the LORD sent them from the wilderness of Paran: all those men *were* heads of the children of Israel.

4 And these *were* their names: of the tribe of Reuben, Shammua the son of Zaccur.

5 Of the tribe of Simeon, Shaphat the son of Hori.

6 Of *b* the tribe of Judah, *c* Caleb the son of Jephunneh.

7 Of the tribe of Issachar, Igal the son of Joseph.

8 Of the tribe of Ephraim, Oshea the son of Nun.

9 Of the tribe of Benjamin, Palti the son of Raphu.

10 Of the tribe of Zebulun, Gaddiel the son of Sodi.

11 Of the tribe of Joseph, *namely,* of the tribe of Manasseh, Gaddi the son of Susi.

12 Of the tribe of Dan, Ammiel the son of Gemalli.

13 Of the tribe of Asher, Sethur the son of Michael.

14 Of the tribe of Naphtali, Nahbi the son of Vophsi.

15 Of the tribe of Gad, Geuel the son of Machi.

16 These *are* the names of the men which Moses sent to spy out the land. And Moses called *d* Oshea the son of Nun, *e* Jehoshua.

17 ¶ And Moses sent them to spy out the land of Canaan, and said unto them, Get you up this *way* *f* southward, and go up into *g* the mountain;

18 And see the land, what it *is;* and the people that dwelleth therein, whether they *be* strong or weak, few or many;

19 And what the land *is* that they dwell in, whether it *be* good or bad; and what cities *they be* that they dwell in, whether in tents, or in strong holds;

20 And what the land *is,* whether it *be* fat ʰ or lean, whether there be wood therein, or not: and *i* be ye of good courage, and bring of the fruit of the land. Now the time *was* the time of the first-ripe grapes.

21 So they went up, and searched *j* the land from the wilderness of Zin unto ᵏ Rehob, as men come to Hamath.

22 And they ascended by the south, and came unto Hebron; where ˡ Ahiman, Sheshai, and Talmai, the children of Anak, *were.* (Now ᵐ Hebron was built seven years ⁿ before Zoan in Egypt.)

23 And *o* they came unto the ¹ brook of Eshcol, and cut down from thence a branch with one cluster of grapes, and they bare it between two upon a staff; and they brought of the pomegranates, and of the figs.

of the monotonous food; and, ungrateful for the heavenly gift, they longed for a change of fare. It may be noticed that the resemblance of the manna to coriander seed was not in the colour, but in the size and figure; and from its comparison to bdellium, which is either a drop of white gum or a white pearl, we are enabled to form a better idea of it. Moreover, it is evident, from the process of baking into cakes, that it could not have been the natural manna of the Arabian desert, for that is too gummy or unctuous to admit of being ground into meal. In taste it is said (Ex. 16. 31,) to have been like "wafers made with honey," and here to have the taste of fresh oil. The discrepancy in these statements is only apparent; for in the former the manna is described in its raw state; in the latter, after it was ground and baked. The minute description given here of its nature and use was designed to show the great sinfulness of the people in being dissatisfied with such excellent food, furnished so plentifully and gratuitously. 10-15. Moses said unto the Lord, &c.—It is impossible not to sympathise with his feelings, although the tone and language of his remonstrances to God cannot be justified. He was in a most distressing situation—having a mighty multitude under his care, with no means of satisfying their clamorous demands. *Their* conduct shows how deeply they had been debased and demoralized by long oppression; while *his* reveals a state of mind agonized and almost overwhelmed by a sense of the undivided responsibilities of his office. 16, 17. Gather unto me seventy men of the elders—(Ex. 3. 16; 5. 6; 24. 9; 18 21, 24; Le. 4. 15.) An order of 70 was to be created, either by a selection from the existing staff of elders, or by the appointment of new ones, empowered to assist him by their collective wisdom and experience in the onerous cares of government. The Jewish writers say that this was the origin of the Sanhedrim, or supreme appellate court of their nation. But there is every reason to believe that it was only a temporary expedient, adopted to meet a trying exigency. 17. I will come down —*i. e.*, not in a visible manner, or by local descent, but by the tokens of the Divine presence and operations. And take of the spirit which is upon thee—The spirit means the gifts and influences of the Spirit, (ch. 27. 18; Joel, 2. 28; J. 7. 39; 1 Co. 14. 12,) and by "taking the spirit of Moses, and putting it upon them," is not to be understood that the qualities of the great leader were to be in any degree impaired, but that the elders would be endowed with a portion of the same gifts, especially of prophecy, (v. 25,)— *i.e.*, an extraordinary penetration in discovering hidden, and settling difficult things. 18-20. Say thou unto the people, Sanctify yourselves—*i.e.*, "prepare yourselves," by repentance and submission, to receive to-morrow the flesh you clamour for. But it is evident that the tenor of the language implied a severe rebuke, and that the blessing promised would prove a curse. 21-23. Moses said... shall the flocks and herds be slain!—The great leader, struck with a promise so astonishing as that of suddenly furnishing, in the midst of the desert, more than two millions of people with flesh for a whole month, betrayed an incredulous spirit, surprising in one who had witnessed so many stupendous miracles. But it is probable that it was only a feeling of the moment—at all events, the incredulous doubt was uttered only to himself—and not, as afterwards, publicly and to the scandal of the people. (See on ch. 20. 10.) It was, therefore, sharply reproved, but not punished. 24. Moses gathered the seventy, &c.—That place was chosen for the convocation, because, as it was there God manifested Himself, there His spirit would be directly imparted—there the minds of the elders themselves would be inspired with reverential awe, and their office invested with greater respect in the eyes of the people. 25. They prophesied, and did not cease—As those elders were constituted civil governors, their "prophesying" must be understood as meaning the performance of their civil and sacred duties, by the help of those extraordinary endowments they had received, and by their not " ceasing," either that they continued to exercise their gifts uninterruptedly the first day, (see 1 Sam. 19, 24,) or that these were permanent gifts, which qualified them in an eminent degree for discharging the duty of public magistrates. 26-29. But there remained two—They did not repair with the rest to the tabernacle, either from modesty in shrinking from the assumption of a public office, or being prevented by some ceremonial defilement. They, however, received the gifts of the Spirit as well as their brethren; and when Moses was urged to forbid their prophesying, his answer displayed a noble disinterestedness as well as zeal for the glory of God akin to that of our Lord. Mk. 9. 39.) 31-35. The wind from the Lord, &c.— These migratory birds see on Ex. 16. 13,) were on their journey from Egypt, when "the wind from the Lord," an east wind, (Ps. 78. 26,) forcing them to change their course, wafted them over the Red Sea to the camp of Israel. Let them fall a day's journey—If the journey of an individual is meant, this space might be 30 miles; if the inspired historian referred to the whole host, 10 miles would be as far as they could march in one day in the sandy desert, under a vertical sun. Assuming it to be 20 miles, this immense cloud of quails (Ps. 77. 27, covered a space of 40 miles in diameter. Others reduce it to 16. But it is doubtful whether the measurement be from the centre or the extremities of the camp. It is evident, however, that the language describes the countless number of these quails, as it were two cubits high—Some have supposed that they fell on the ground above each other to that height—a supposition which would leave a vast quantity useless as food to the Israelites, who were forbidden to eat any animal that died of itself, or from which the blood was not poured out. Others think that, being exhausted with a long flight, they could not fly more than 3 feet above the earth, and so were easily felled or caught. A more recent explanation applies the phrase, "two cubits high," not to the accumulation of the mass, but to the size of the individual birds. Flocks of large red-legged cranes, 3 feet high, measuring 7 feet from tip to tip, have been frequently seen on the western shores of the Gulf of Akaba, or eastern arm of the Red Sea. [STANLEY, SHUBERT.] 32. People stood up—*i. e.*, rose up in eager haste—some at one time, others at another—some, perhaps, through avidity both day and night. ten homers—ten ass loads; or, "homers" may be

24 The place was called the ²brook ³Eshcol, because of the cluster of grapes which the children of Israel cut down from thence.

25 And they returned from searching of the land after forty days.

26 ¶ And they went and came to Moses, and to Aaron, and to all the congregation of the children of Israel, unto the wilderness of Paran, to Kadesh; and brought back word unto them, and unto all the congregation, and showed them the fruit of the land.

27 And they told him, and said, We came unto the land whither thou sentest us, and surely it floweth with ᵖ milk and honey; and ᵍ this is the fruit of it.

28 Nevertheless ʳ the people be strong that dwell in the land, and the cities are walled, and very great: and moreover we saw the children of Anak there.

29 The ˢ Amalekites dwell in the land of the south; and the Hittites, and the Jebusites, and the Amorites, dwell in the mountains; and the Canaanites dwell by the sea, and by the coast of Jordan.

30 And ᵗ Caleb stilled the people before Moses, and said, Let us go up at once, and possess it; for we are well able to overcome it.

31 But the men that went up with him said, We be not able to go up against the people; for they are stronger than we.

32 And they ᵘ brought up an evil report of the land which they had searched unto the children of Israel, saying, The land, through which we have gone to search it, is a land that ᵛ eateth up the inhabitants thereof; and ʷ all the people that we saw in it are ⁴ men of a great stature.

33 And there we saw the giants, ˣ the sons of Anak, which come of the giants: and we were in our own sight ʸ as grasshoppers, and so we were in their sight.

CHAPTER XIV.

1 *The people murmur at the spies' report.* 11 *God threateneth them.* 13 *Moses intercedeth with God, and obtaineth pardon.*

AND all the congregation lifted up their voice, and cried; and the people wept that night.

2 And ᵃ all the children of Israel murmured against Moses and against Aaron: and the whole congregation said unto them, Would God ᵇ that we had died in the land of Egypt! or would God we had died in this wilderness!

3 And wherefore hath the LORD brought us unto this land, to fall by the sword, that our wives and our children should be a prey? Were it not better for us to return into Egypt?

4 And they said one to another, ᶜ Let us make a captain, and let us return into Egypt.

5 Then Moses and Aaron fell on their faces before all the assembly of the congregation of the children of Israel.

6 And Joshua the son of Nun, and Caleb the son of Jephunneh, which were of them that searched the land, rent their clothes:

7 And they spake unto all the company of the children of Israel, saying, The land, which we passed through to search it, is an exceeding good land.

8 If the LORD ᵈ delight in us, then he will bring us into this land, and give it us; ᵉ a land which floweth with milk and honey.

9 Only ᶠ rebel not ye against the LORD, neither ᵍ fear ye the people of the land; for they ʰ are bread for us: their ¹ defence is departed from them, ʲ and the LORD is with us: fear them not.

10 But ʲ all the congregation bade stone them with stones. And ᵏ the glory of the LORD appeared in the tabernacle of the congregation before all the children of Israel.

11 ¶ And the LORD said unto Moses, How long will this people ˡ provoke me? and how long will it be ere they ᵐ believe me, for all the signs which I have showed among them?

12 I will smite them with the pestilence, and disinherit them, and ⁿ will make of thee a greater nation and mightier than they.

13 And ᵒ Moses said unto the LORD, Then the Egyptians shall hear it, (for thou broughtest up this people in thy might from among them;)

14 And they will tell it to the inhabitants of this land; ᵖ for they have heard that thou, LORD, art among this people; that thou, LORD, art seen face to face; and that thy ᵍ cloud standeth over them; and that thou goest before them, by day time in a pillar of a cloud, and in a pillar of fire by night.

15 Now, if thou shalt kill all this people as one man, then the nations which have heard the fame of thee will speak, saying,

16 Because the LORD was not ʳ able to bring this people into the land which he sware unto them, therefore he hath slain them in the wilderness.

17 And now, I beseech thee, let the power of my Lord be great, according as thou hast spoken, saying,

18 The LORD is ˢ long-suffering, and of great mercy, forgiving iniquity and transgression, and by no means clearing the guilty; ᵗ visiting the iniquity of the fathers upon the children unto the third and fourth generation.

19 Pardon, I beseech thee, the iniquity of this people according unto the greatness of thy mercy, and as thou hast forgiven this people, from Egypt even ² until now.

20 And the LORD said, I have ᵘ pardoned, according to thy word:

21 But as truly as I live, ᵛ all the earth shall be filled with the glory of the LORD.

22 Because ʷ all those men which have seen my glory, and my miracles which I did in Egypt and in the wilderness, have tempted me now ˣ these ten times, and have not hearkened to my voice;

23 ʸ Surely ʸ they shall not see the land which I sware unto their fathers, neither shall any of them that provoked me see it:

24 But my servant Caleb, because he had another spirit with him, and hath followed me fully, him will I bring into the land whereunto he went; and ᶻ his seed shall possess it.

25 (Now the Amalekites and the Canaanites dwelt in the valley.) To-morrow turn you, and get you into the wilderness by the way of the Red sea.

26 ¶ And the LORD spake unto Moses and unto Aaron, saying,

27 How ᵃ long shall I bear with this evil congregation, which murmur against me? I ᵇ have heard the murmurings of the

used indefinitely, as in Ex. 8. 14; Jud. 15. 16; and "ten" for many: so that the phrase ten homers is equivalent to great heaps. The collectors were probably one or two from each family; and, being distrustful of God's goodness, gathered not for immediate consumption only, but for future use. In eastern and southern seas, innumerable quails are often seen, which, when weary, fall down, covering every spot on the deck and rigging of vessels; and in Egypt they come in such myriads that the people knock them down with sticks. spread them all abroad for themselves—salted and dried them for future use, by the simple process to which they had been accustomed in Egypt. 33. While the flesh ... ere it was chewed—*lit.*, cut off—*i. e.*, ere the supply of quails, which lasted a month, (*v.* 20,) was exhausted. The probability is, that their stomachs, having been long inured to manna, (a light food), were not prepared for so sudden a change of regimen—a heavy, solid diet of animal food, of which they seem to have partaken to so intemperate a degree as to produce a general surfeit, and fatal consequences. On a former occasion their murmurs for flesh were raised, (Ex. 16,) because they were in want of food. Here they proceeded, not from necessity, but wanton lustful desire; and their sin, in the righteous judgment of God, was made to carry its own punishment. 34. Called the name Kibrothhattaavah—*lit.*, the graves of lust, or those that lusted; so that the name of the place proves that the mortality was confined to those who had indulged inordinately. 35. Hazeroth—the extreme southern station of this route was a watering-place in a spacious plain, now Ain Haderah.

CHAPTER XII.

Ver. 1-9. MIRIAM AND AARON'S SEDITION. 1. An Ethiopian woman—*Heb.* A Cushite woman—Arabia was usually called in Scripture the land of Cush—its inhabitants being descendants of that son of Ham. (See on Ex. 2. 15,) and being accounted generally a vile and contemptible race. (Am. 9. 7.) The occasion of this seditious outbreak on the part of Miriam and Aaron against Moses, was the great change made in the government by the adoption of the seventy rulers—and their irritating disparagement of his wife—who, in all probability, was Zipporah, and not a second wife he had recently married, arose from jealousy of her relatives, through whose influence the innovation had been first made, (Ex. 18.) while they were overlooked or neglected. Miriam is mentioned before Aaron as being the chief instigator and leader of the sedition. 2. Hath the Lord . . . not also spoken by us—The prophetical name and character was bestowed upon Aaron, (Ex. 4. 15, 16,) and Miriam (Ex. 15. 20); and, therefore, they considered the conduct of Moses, in exercising an exclusive authority in this matter, as an encroachment on their rights. (Mi. 6. 4.) 3. The man Moses was very meek—(Ex. 14. 13; 32. 12, 13; ch. 14. 13; 21. 7; Deu. 9. 18.) This observation might have been made to account for Moses taking no notice of their angry reproaches, and for God's interposing so speedily for the vindication of His servant's cause. The circumstance of Moses recording an eulogium on a distinguishing excellence of his own character, is not without a parallel among the sacred writers, when forced to it by the insolence and contempt of opponents. (2 Cor. 11. 5; 12. 11, 12.) But it is not improbable that, as this verse appears to be a parenthesis, it may have been inserted as a gloss by Ezra or some later prophet. Others, instead of "very meek," suggest "very afflicted," as the proper rendering. 4. The Lord spake suddenly—The divine interposition was made thus openly and immediately, in order to suppress the sedition, and prevent its spreading amongst the people. 5. Stood in the door of the tabernacle—without gaining admission, as was the usual privilege of Aaron, though it was denied to all other men and women. This public exclusion was designed to be a token of the divine displeasure. 6. Hear now my words—A difference of degree is here distinctly expressed in the gifts and authority even of divinely commissioned prophets. Moses having been set over all God's house, *i.e.*, His church and people was consequently invested with supremacy over Miriam and Aaron also, and privileged beyond all others by direct and clear manifestations of the presence and will of God. 8. mouth to mouth—immediately, not by an interpreter, nor by visionary symbols presented to his fancy. apparently—plainly and surely. not in dark speeches—parables or similitudes. the similitude of the Lord shall he behold—not the face or essence of God, who is inv'si'ble (Ex. 33. 20; Col. 1. 15; Jo. 1. 18); but some unmistakeable evidence of His glorious presence. (Ex. 33. 2; 34. 5.) The latter clause should have been conjoined with the preceding one, thus: "not in dark speeches, and in a figure shall he behold the Lord." This slight change in the punctuation removes all appearance of contradiction to Deu. 4. 15.

10-16.—HER LEPROSY. 10. the cloud departed from the tabernacle—*i. e.* from the door to resume its permanent position over the mercy-seat. Miriam became leprous—This malady in its most malignant form (Ex. 4, 6, 2 Kings, 5. 27), as its colour, combined with its sudden appearance proved, was inflicted as a divine judgment; and she was made the victim, either from her extreme violence, or because the leprosy on Aaron would have interrupted or dishonoured the holy service. 11-13. On the humble and penitential submission of Aaron, Moses interceded for both the offenders, especially for Miriam, who was restored; not, however, till she had been made, by her exclusion, a public example. 14. Her father had but spit in her face—The Jews, in common with all people in the east, seem to have had an intense abhorrence of spitting, and for a parent to express his displeasure by doing so on the person of one of his children, or even on the ground in his presence, separated that child as unclean from society for seven days. 15. The people journeyed not till Miriam was brought in again —Either not to crush her by a sentence of overwhelming severity, or not to expose her, being a prophetess, to popular contempt. 16. Pitched in the wilderness of Paran—The station of encampment seems to have been Rithma. (ch. 33. 19.)

CHAPTER XIII.

Ver. 1-35. THE NAMES OF THE MEN WHO WERE SENT TO SEARCH THE LAND. 1, 2. The Lord spake unto Moses, Send thou men—(cf. Deu. 1. 22), whence it appears, that while the proposal of delegating confidential men from each tribe to explore the land of Canaan

children of Israel, which they murmur against me.

28 Say unto them, *As truly as* I live, saith the Lord, as ye have spoken in mine ears, so will I do to you:

29 Your carcases shall fall in this wilderness; and all that were numbered of you, according to your whole number, from twenty years old and upward, which have murmured against me,

30 Doubtless ye shall not come into the land *concerning* which I sware to make you dwell therein, save Caleb the son of Jephunneh, and Joshua the son of Nun.

31 But your little ones, which ye said should be a prey, them will I bring in, and they shall know the land which ye have despised.

32 But *as for* you, your carcases, they shall fall in this wilderness.

33 And your children shall wander in the wilderness forty years, and bear your whoredoms, until your carcases be wasted in the wilderness.

34 After the number of the days in which ye searched the land, *even* forty days, each day for a year, shall ye bear your iniquities, *even* forty years; and ye shall know my breach of promise.

35 I the Lord have said, I will surely do it unto all this evil congregation, that are gathered together against me: in this wilderness they shall be consumed, and there they shall die.

36 And the men which Moses sent to search the land, who returned, and made all the congregation to murmur against him, by bringing up a slander upon the land,

37 Even those men that did bring up the evil report upon the land, died by the plague before the Lord.

38 But Joshua the son of Nun, and Caleb the son of Jephunneh, *which were* of the men that went to search the land, lived still.

39 And Moses told these sayings unto all the children of Israel: and the people mourned greatly.

40 And they rose up early in the morning, and gat them up into the top of the mountain, saying, Lo, we *be here*, and will go up unto the place which the Lord hath promised: for we have sinned.

41 And Moses said, Wherefore now do ye transgress the commandment of the Lord? but it shall not prosper.

42 Go not up, for the Lord *is* not among you; that ye be not smitten before your enemies.

43 For the Amalekites and the Canaanites *are* there before you, and ye shall fall by the sword: because ye are turned away from the Lord, therefore the Lord will not be with you.

44 But they presumed to go up unto the hill-top: nevertheless the ark of the covenant of the Lord, and Moses, departed not out of the camp.

45 Then the Amalekites came down, and the Canaanites which dwelt in that hill, and smote them, and discomfited them, *even* unto Hormah.

CHAPTER XV.

1 *The law of sundry offerings.* 32 *The sabbath breaker stoned.* 37 *The law of fringes.*

AND the Lord spake unto Moses, saying,

2 Speak unto the children of Israel, and say unto them, When ye be come into the land of your habitations, which I give unto you,

3 And will make an offering by fire unto the Lord, a burnt offering, or a sacrifice in performing a vow, or in a free-will offering, or in your solemn feasts, to make a sweet savour unto the Lord, of the herd, or of the flock;

4 Then shall he that offereth his offering unto the Lord bring a meat offering of a tenth deal of flour mingled with the fourth part of an hin of oil.

5 And the fourth *part* of an hin of wine for a drink offering shalt thou prepare with the burnt offering or sacrifice, for one lamb.

6 Or for a ram, thou shalt prepare for a meat offering two tenth deals of flour mingled with the third *part* of an hin of oil.

7 And for a drink offering thou shalt offer the third *part* of an hin of wine, for a sweet savour unto the Lord.

8 And when thou preparest a bullock for a burnt offering, or for a sacrifice in performing a vow, or peace offerings unto the Lord;

9 Then shall he bring with a bullock a meat offering of three tenth deals of flour mingled with half an hin of oil.

10 And thou shalt bring for a drink offering half an hin of wine, *for* an offering made by fire, of a sweet savour unto the Lord.

11 Thus shall it be done for one bullock, or for one ram, or for a lamb, or a kid.

12 According to the number that ye shall prepare, so shall ye do to every one according to their number.

13 All that are born of the country shall do these things after this manner, in offering an offering made by fire, of a sweet savour unto the Lord.

14 And if a stranger sojourn with you, or whosoever *be* among you in your generations, and will offer an offering made by fire, of a sweet savour unto the Lord; as ye do, so he shall do.

15 One ordinance *shall be both* for you of the congregation, and also for the stranger that sojourneth *with you*, an ordinance for ever in your generations: as ye *are*, so shall the stranger be before the Lord.

16 One law and one manner shall be for you, and for the stranger that sojourneth with you.

17 ¶ And the Lord spake unto Moses, saying,

18 Speak unto the children of Israel, and say unto them, When ye come into the land whither I bring you;

19 Then it shall be, that, when ye eat of the bread of the land, ye shall offer up an heave offering unto the Lord.

20 Ye shall offer up a cake of the first of your dough *for* an heave offering: as ye do the heave offering of the threshing-floor, so shall ye heave it.

21 Of the first of your dough ye shall give unto the Lord an heave offering in your generations.

22 ¶ And if ye have erred, and not observed all these commandments which the Lord hath spoken unto Moses,

23 *Even* all that the Lord hath commanded you by the hand of Moses, from the day that the Lord commanded Moses, and henceforward among your generati...

emanated from the people who petitioned for it, the measure received the special sanction of God, who granted their request at once as a trial, and a punishment of their distrust. 3. These men were heads—Not the princes who are named (ch. 10), but chiefs, leading men, though not of the first rank. 16. Oshea—*i. e.* a desire of salvation. Jehoshua, by prefixing the name of God, means "divinely appointed." "head of salvation," "Saviour," the same as Jesus. 17. Get you up this way, and go up into the mountain—Mount Seir (Deu. 1. 2), which lay directly from Sinai across the wilderness of Paran, in a north-easterly direction into the southern parts of the promised land. 20. The time of the first-ripe grapes—This was in August, when the first clusters are gathered, the second in September, and the third in October. The spies' absence for a period of forty days, determines the grapes they brought from Eshcol to have been of the second period. 21-24. So they searched the land—Their advances from south to north, reconnoitring the whole land, the wilderness of Zin—a long level plain, or deep valley of sand —the monotony of which is relieved by a few tamarisk and rethem trees, and which, under the names of El Ghor and El Araba, forms the continuation of the Jordan valley, extending from the Dead Sea to the Gulf of Akaba. Rehob—or, Beth-rehob, was a city and district situated, according to some, eastward of Sidon; and, according to others, is the same as El Hule, an extensive and fertile champaigne country, at the foot of Antilibanus, a few leagues below Paneas. as men come unto Hamath—or, "the entering in of Hamath," (2 Ki. 14. 25,) now the valley of Balbeck, a mountain-pass or opening in the northern frontier, which formed the extreme limit in that direction of the inheritance of Israel. From the mention of these places, the route of the scouts appears to have been along the course of the Jordan in their advance, and their return was by the western border, through the territories of the Sidonians and Philistines. 22. Unto Hebron—situated in the heart of the mountains of Judah, in the southern extremity of Palestine. The town or "cities of Hebron," as it is expressed in the *Heb.*, consists of a number of sheikdoms distinct from each other, standing at the foot of one of those hills that form a bowl round and enclose it. "The children of Anak," mentioned in this verse, seem to have been also chiefs of townships; and this coincidence of polity, existing in ages so distant from each other, is remarkable. [VERE MONRO.] Hebron (Kirjath-Arba, Ge. 23, 2,) was one of the oldest cities in the world. Zoan (the Tanis of the Greeks) —was situated on one of the eastern branches of the Nile, near the lake Menzala, and the early royal residence of the Pharaohs, that boasted a higher antiquity than any other city in Egypt. Its name, which signifies flat and level, is descriptive of its situation in the low grounds of the Delta. 23. The brook of Eshcol—*i. e.*, "the torrent of the cluster." Its situation was a little to the south-west of Hebron. The valley and its sloping hills are still covered with vineyards, the character of whose fruit corresponds to its ancient celebrity. one cluster of grapes—The grapes reared in this locality are still as magnificent as formerly—they are said by one to be equal in size to prunes, and compared by another to a man's thumb. One cluster sometimes weighs 10 or 12 pounds. The mode of carrying the cluster cut down by the spies, though not necessary from its weight, was evidently adopted to preserve it entire as a specimen of the productions of the promised land; and the impression made by the sight of it would be all the greater that the Israelites were familiar only with the scanty vines and small grapes of Egypt. 26. They came to Kadesh—an important encampment of the Israelites. But its exact situation is not certainly known, nor is it determined whether it is the same or a different place from Kadesh-barnea. It is supposed to be identical with Ain-el-Weibeh, a famous spring on the eastern side of the desert, [ROBINSON,] and also with Petra, [STANLEY.] 27, 28. They told him, and said—The report was given publicly in the audience of the people, and it was artfully arranged to begin their narrative with commendations of the natural fertility of the country, in order that their subsequent slanders might the more readily receive credit. 29. The Amalekites dwell in the land of the south—Their territory lay between the Dead and Red Seas, skirting the borders of Canaan. Hittites dwell in the mountains—Their settlements were in the southern and mountainous part of Palestine, (Ge. 23, 7.) The Canaanites dwelt by the sea—The remnant of the original inhabitants, who had been dispossessed by the Philistines, were divided into two nomadic hordes—one settled eastward near the Jordan; the other westward, by the Mediterranean. 32. A land that eateth up the inhabitants—*i.e.*, an unhealthy climate and country. Jewish writers say that in the course of their travels they saw a great many funerals, vast numbers of the Canaanites being cut off at that time, in the providence of God, by a plague or the hornet. (Josh. 24. 12,) men of great stature—This was evidently a false and exaggerated report, representing, from timidity or malicious artifice, what was true of a few as descriptive of the people generally. 33. Giants, sons of Anak—The name is derived from the son of Arba—a great man among the Arabians, (Josh. 15. 14,) who probably obtained his appellation from wearing a splendid collar or chain round his neck, as the word imports. The epithet "giant" evidently refers here to stature. (See on Ge. 6. 4.) And it is probable the Anakims were a distinguished family, or perhaps a select body of warriors, chosen for their extraordinary size. in our own sight as grasshoppers—a strong Orientalism, by which the treacherous spies gave an exaggerated report of the physical strength of the people of Canaan.

CHAPTER XIV.

Ver. 1-45. THE PEOPLE MURMUR AT THE SPIES' REPORT. 1. All the congregation lifted up their voice—Not literally the whole, for there were some exceptions. 2-4. Would God that we had died—Such insolence to their generous leaders, and such base ingratitude to God, show the deep degradation of the Israelites, and the absolute necessity of the decree that debarred that generation from entering the promised land. They were punished by their wishes being granted to die in that wilderness. A leader to re-conduct them to Egypt is spoken of (Neh. 9. 17) as actually nominated. The sinfulness and insane folly of their conduct are

24 Then it shall be, *p* if *ought* be committed by ignorance *q* without the knowledge of the congregation, that all the congregation shall offer one young bullock for a burnt offering, for a sweet savour unto the Lord, with his meat offering, and his drink offering, according to the *s* manner, and one *q* kid of the goats for a sin offering.
25 And *r* the priest shall make an atonement for all the congregation of the children of Israel, and it shall be forgiven them; for it is ignorance: and they shall bring their offering, a sacrifice made by fire unto the Lord, and their sin offering before the Lord, for their ignorance:
26 And it shall be forgiven all the congregation of the children of Israel, and the stranger that sojourneth among them; seeing all the people were in ignorance.
27 ¶ And *s* if any soul sin through ignorance, then he shall bring a she-goat of the first year for a sin offering.
28 And *t* the priest shall make an atonement for the soul that sinneth ignorantly, when he sinneth by ignorance before the Lord, to make an atonement for him; and it shall be forgiven him.
29 Ye shall have one law for him that *t* sinneth through ignorance, *both for* him that is born among the children of Israel, and for the stranger that sojourneth among them.
30 ¶ But *u* the soul that doeth *ought* *b* presumptuously, *whether he be* born in the land, or a stranger, the same reproacheth the Lord; and that soul shall be cut off from among his people.
31 Because he hath *v* despised the word of the Lord, and hath broken his commandment, that soul shall utterly be cut off; his *w* iniquity *shall be* upon him.
32 ¶ And while the children of Israel were in the wilderness, *x* they found a man that gathered sticks upon the sabbath day.
33 And they that found him gathering sticks brought him unto Moses and Aaron, and unto all the congregation.
34 And they put him *y* in ward, because it was not declared what should be done to him.
35 And the Lord said unto Moses, *z* The man shall be surely put to death: all the congregation shall *a* stone him with stones without the camp.
36 And all the congregation brought him without the camp, and stoned him with stones, and he died; as the Lord commanded Moses.
37 ¶ And the Lord spake unto Moses, saying,
38 Speak unto the children of Israel, and bid *b* them that they make them fringes in the borders of their garments, throughout their generations, and that they put upon the fringe of the borders a ribband of blue:
39 And it shall be unto you for a fringe, that ye may look upon it, and remember all the commandments of the Lord, and do them; and that ye *c* seek not after your own heart and your own eyes, after which ye use *d* to go awhoring:
40 That ye may remember, and do all my commandments, and be *e* holy unto your God.
41 I am the Lord your God, which brought you out of the land of Egypt, to be your God: I am the Lord your God.

B. C. 1490.

CHAP. 15.
p Lev. 4. 13.
2 from the eyes.
3 Or, ordinance.
q Lev. 4. 23.
Ezra 8. 35.
r Lev. 4. 20.
s Lev. 4. 27, 28.
Ps. 19. 13.
Lu. 12. 48.
t Lev. 4. 35.
4 doth.
u Deu. 17.12.
Ps. 19. 13.
Ro. 10. 16.
He. 10. 26.
2 Pet. 2. 10.
5 with an high hand.
v 2 Sa. 12. 9.
Pro. 13. 13.
w Ezek. 18. 20.
x Ex. 35. 2, 3.
y Lev. 24. 12.
z Ex. 31. 14, 15.
Gal. 3. 5.
a 1 Kin. 21. 13.
Acts 7. 58.
b Deut. 22. 12.
Mat. 23. 5.
c Deut. 29. 19.
Job 31. 7.
Jer. 9. 14.
Ezek. 6. 9.
d Ps. 106. 39.
Jam. 4. 4.
e Lev. 11. 44, 45.
Mat. 5. 48.
Ro. 12. 1.
Col. 1. 22.
1 Thes. 5. 23.
1 Pet. 1. 15.

CHAP. 16.
a Jude 11.
b ch. 26. 9.
c Ps. 106. 16.
1 It is much for you.
d Ex. 19. 6.
e Ex. 29. 45.
f ch. 20. 6.
g 2 Tim. 2.19.
h Lev. 21. 6-12.
i Ex. 23. 1.
1 Sa. 2. 28.
Ps. 105. 26.
j Lev. 10. 3.
Ezek. 40.46.
k 1 Sa. 18.23.
Is. 7. 13.
l Deu. 10. 8.
m Ex. 16. 8.
1 Cor. 3. 5.
n Ex. 2. 14.
Acts 7. 27, 35.
o Ex. 3. 8.
Lev. 20.24.
2 bore out, that is, blind with fair words.
p Gen. 4. 4, 5.
q 1 Sa. 12. 3.
Ac. 20. 33.
2 Cor. 7. 2.

CHAPTER XVI.

1 *The rebellion of Korah.* 31 *The earth cleaveth asunder.* 46 *Aaron stayeth the plague.*

NOW *a* Korah, the son of Izhar, the son of Kohath, the son of Levi, and Dathan and Abiram the sons of Eliab, and On the son of Peleth, sons of Reuben, took *men:*
2 And they rose up before Moses, with certain of the children of Israel, two hundred and fifty princes of the assembly, famous *b* in the congregation, men of renown:
3 And *c* they gathered themselves together against Moses and against Aaron, and said unto them, ¹ Ye *take* too much upon you, seeing *d* all the congregation *are* holy, every one of them, *e* and the Lord *is* among them: wherefore then lift ye up yourselves above the congregation of the Lord?
4 And when Moses heard it, *f* he fell upon his face:
5 And he spake unto Korah, and unto all his company, saying, Even to-morrow the Lord will show *g* who *are* his, and *who is* *h* holy; and will cause *him* to come near unto him; even *him* whom he *i* hath chosen will he cause to *j* come near unto him.
6 This do: Take you censers, Korah, and all his company;
7 And put fire therein, and put incense in them before the Lord to-morrow; and it shall be *that* the man whom the Lord doth choose, he *shall be* holy: ye *take* too much upon you, ye sons of Levi.
8 And Moses said unto Korah, Hear, I pray you, ye sons of Levi:
9 *Seemeth it but* *k* a small thing unto you, that the God of Israel hath *l* separated you from the congregation of Israel, to bring you near to himself, to do the service of the tabernacle of the Lord, and to stand before the congregation to minister unto them?
10 And he hath brought thee near *to him,* and all thy brethren the sons of Levi with thee: and seek ye the priesthood also?
11 For which cause *both* thou and all thy company *are* gathered together against the Lord: *m* and what *is* Aaron, that ye murmur against him?
12 ¶ And Moses sent to call Dathan and Abiram, the sons of Eliab: which said, We will not come up:
13 *Is* it a small thing that thou hast brought us up out of a land that floweth with milk and honey, to kill us in the wilderness, except thou *n* make thyself altogether a prince over us?
14 Moreover thou hast not brought us into a *o* land that floweth with milk and honey, or given us inheritance of fields and vineyards: wilt thou ² put out the eyes of these men? we will not come up.
15 And Moses was very wroth, and said unto the Lord, *p* Respect not thou *q* their offering: I have not taken one ass from them, neither have I hurt one of them.
16 And Moses said unto Korah, Be thou and all thy company before the Lord, thou, and they, and Aaron, to-morrow:
17 And take every man his censer, and put incense in them, and bring ye before the Lord every man his censer, two hundred and fifty censers; thou also, and Aaron, each *of you* his censer.
18 And they took every man his censer, and put fire in them, and laid incense

almost incredible. Their conduct, however, is paralleled by too many amongst ourselves, who shrink from the smallest difficulties, and rather remain slaves to sin than resolutely try to surmount the obstacles that lie in their way to the Canaan above. **5.** Moses and Aaron fell on their faces—as humble and earnest suppliants—either to the people, entreating them to desist from so perverse a design;—or rather, to God, as the usual and only refuge from the violence of that tumultuous and stiff-necked rabble, and a hopeful means of softening and impressing their hearts. **6.** Joshua and Caleb—the two honest spies testified their grief and horror, in the strongest manner, at the mutiny against Moses and the blasphemy against God; while at the same time they endeavoured, by a truthful statement, to persuade the people of the ease with which they might obtain possession of so desirable a country, provided they did not, by their rebellion and ingratitude, provoke God to abandon them. **8.** A land flowing with milk and honey—a general expression, descriptive of a rich and fertile country; but the two articles specified were amongst the principal products of the Holy Land. **9.** Their defence is departed—*Heb.*, their shadow. The Sultan of Turkey and the Schah of Persia are called "the shadow of God," "the refuge of the world." So that the meaning of the phrase, "their defence is departed" from them, is, that the favour of God were now lost to those whose iniquities were full, (Ge. 15. 16,) and transferred to the Israelites. **10.** The glory of the Lord appeared—It was seasonably manifested on this great emergency to rescue His ambassadors from their perilous situation. **11.** The Lord said... I will smite—Not a final decree, but a threatening, suspended, as appeared from the issue, on the intercession of Moses, and the repentance of Israel. **17.** let the power of my Lord be great—be magnified. **21.** All the earth shall be filled with the glory of the Lord—This promise, in its full acceptation, remains to be verified by the eventual and universal prevalence of Christianity in the world. But the terms were used restrictively in respect of the occasion, to the report which would spread over all the land of the "terrible things in righteousness" which God would do in the infliction of the doom described, to which that rebellious race were now consigned. ten times—very frequently. **23.** my servant Caleb—Joshua was also excepted, but he is not named, because he was no longer in the ranks of the people, being a constant attendant on Moses. **24.** had another spirit—under the influence of God's Spirit, was a man of bold, generous, heroic courage, above worldly anxieties and fears. **25.** Now the Amalekites and the Canaanites dwelt in the valley—*i.e.*, on the other side of the Idumean mountain, at whose base they were then encamped. Those nomad tribes had at that time occupied it with a determination to oppose the further progress of the Hebrew people. Hence the command to seek a safe and timely retreat into the desert, to escape the pursuit of those resolute enemies, to whom, with their wives and children, they would fall a helpless prey, because they had forfeited the presence and protection of God. The 25th verse forms an important part of the narrative, and should be freed from the parenthetical form which our English translators have given it. **30.** Save Caleb and Joshua—These are specially mentioned, as honourable exceptions to the rest of the scouts, and also as the future leaders of the people. But it appears that some of the old generation did not join in the mutinous murmuring, including in that number the whole order of the priests. (Jos. 14. 1.) **34.** my breach of promise—*i.e.*, that in consequence of your violation of the covenant betwixt you and me, by breaking the terms of it, it shall be null and void on my part, as I shall withhold the blessings I promised in that covenant to confer on you on condition of your obedience. **36-38.** the men...died by the plague before the Lord—Ten of the spies were struck dead on the spot,—either by the pestilence, or some other judgment,—the great and appalling mortality occasioned, by which clearly betokened the hand of the Lord. **40-45.** They rose up early in the morning— Notwithstanding the tidings that Moses communicated, and which diffused a general feeling of melancholy and grief throughout the camp, the impression was of very brief continuance. They rushed from one extreme of rashness and perversity to another, and the obstinacy of their rebellious spirit was evinced by their active preparations to ascend the hill, notwithstanding the divine warning they had received not to undertake that enterprise. for we have sinned— *i.e.*, sensible of our sin, we now repent of it, and are eager to do as Caleb and Joshua exhorted us—or, as some render it, *though* we have sinned, we trust God will yet give us the land of promise. The entreaties of their prudent and pious leader, who represented to them that their enemies, scaling the other side of the valley, would post themselves on the top of the hill before them, were disregarded. How strangely perverse the conduct of the Israelites, who, shortly before, were afraid that, though their Almighty King was with them, they could not get possession of the land; and yet now they act still more foolishly in supposing, that though God were not with them, they could expel the inhabitants by their unaided efforts. The consequences were such as might have been anticipated. The Amalekites and Canaanites, who had been lying in ambuscade expecting their movement, rushed down upon them from the heights, and became the instruments of punishing their guilty rebellion. even unto Hormah—The name was afterwards given to that place in memory of the immense slaughter of the Israelites on this occasion.

CHAPTER XV.

Ver. 1-41. THE LAW OF SUNDRY OFFERINGS. **1, 2.** Speak unto the children of Israel—Some infer from v. 23, that the date of this communication must be fixed towards the close of the wanderings in the wilderness; and, also, that all the sacrifices prescribed in the law were to be offered only after the settlement in Canaan. **3.** a burnt-offering—It is evident that a peace-offering is referred to, because this term is frequently used in such a sense (Ex. 18. 12, Lev. 17. 5). **4.** tenth deal—*i.e.*, an omer, the tenth part of an ephah. (Ex. 16. 36.) Fourth part of an hin of oil—This element shews it to have been different from such meat-offerings as were made by themselves, and not merely accompaniments of other sacrifices. **6-12.** two tenth deals—The

thereon, and stood in the door of the tabernacle of the congregation with Moses and Aaron.

19 And Korah gathered all the congregation against them unto the door of the tabernacle of the congregation: and the glory of the LORD appeared unto all the congregation.

20 And the LORD spake unto Moses and unto Aaron, saying,

21 Separate yourselves from among this congregation, that I may consume them in a moment.

22 And they fell upon their faces, and said, O God, the God of the spirits of all flesh, shall one man sin, and wilt thou be wroth with all the congregation?

23 ¶ And the LORD spake unto Moses, saying,

24 Speak unto the congregation, saying, Get you up from about the tabernacle of Korah, Dathan, and Abiram.

25 And Moses rose up, and went unto Dathan and Abiram; and the elders of Israel followed him.

26 And he spake unto the congregation, saying, Depart, I pray you, from the tents of these wicked men, and touch nothing of theirs, lest ye be consumed in all their sins.

27 So they gat up from the tabernacle of Korah, Dathan, and Abiram, on every side: and Dathan and Abiram came out, and stood in the door of their tents, and their wives, and their sons, and their little children.

28 And Moses said, Hereby ye shall know that the LORD hath sent me to do all these works; for I have not done them of mine own mind;

29 If these men die the common death of all men, or if they be visited after the visitation of all men; then the LORD hath not sent me:

30 But if the LORD make a new thing, and the earth open her mouth, and swallow them up, with all that appertain unto them, and they go down quick into the pit; then ye shall understand that these men have provoked the LORD.

31 ¶ And it came to pass, as he had made an end of speaking all these words, that the ground clave asunder that was under them:

32 And the earth opened her mouth, and swallowed them up, and their houses, and all the men that appertained unto Korah, and all their goods.

33 They, and all that appertained to them, went down alive into the pit, and the earth closed upon them: and they perished from among the congregation.

34 And all Israel that were round about them fled at the cry of them: for they said, Lest the earth swallow us up also.

35 And there came out a fire from the LORD, and consumed the two hundred and fifty men that offered incense.

36 ¶ And the LORD spake unto Moses, saying,

37 Speak unto Eleazar the son of Aaron the priest, that he take up the censers out of the burning, and scatter thou the fire yonder; for they are hallowed.

38 The censers of these sinners against their own souls, let them make them broad plates for a covering of the altar; for they offered them before the LORD, therefore they are hallowed: and they shall be a sign unto the children of Israel.

39 And Eleazar the priest took the brasen censers, wherewith they that were burnt had offered; and they were made broad plates for a covering of the altar:

40 To be a memorial unto the children of Israel, that no stranger, which is not of the seed of Aaron, come near to offer incense before the LORD; that he be not as Korah, and as his company: as the LORD said to him by the hand of Moses.

41 ¶ But on the morrow all the congregation of the children of Israel murmured against Moses and against Aaron, saying, Ye have killed the people of the LORD.

42 And it came to pass, when the congregation was gathered against Moses and against Aaron, that they looked toward the tabernacle of the congregation; and, behold, the cloud covered it, and the glory of the LORD appeared.

43 And Moses and Aaron came before the tabernacle of the congregation.

44 And the LORD spake unto Moses, saying,

45 Get you up from among this congregation, that I may consume them as in a moment. And they fell upon their faces.

46 And Moses said unto Aaron, Take a censer, and put fire therein from off the altar, and put on incense, and go quickly unto the congregation, and make an atonement for them: for there is wrath gone out from the LORD; the plague is begun.

47 And Aaron took as Moses commanded, and ran into the midst of the congregation; and, behold, the plague was begun among the people: and he put on incense, and made an atonement for the people.

48 And he stood between the dead and the living; and the plague was stayed.

49 Now they that died in the plague were fourteen thousand and seven hundred, besides them that died about the matter of Korah.

50 And Aaron returned unto Moses unto the door of the tabernacle of the congregation: and the plague was stayed.

CHAPTER XVII.

6 *Aaron's rod only flourisheth: 10 it is laid up for a memorial against the rebels.*

AND the LORD spake unto Moses, saying,

2 Speak unto the children of Israel, and take of every one of them a rod according to the house of their fathers, of all their princes, according to the house of their fathers twelve rods: write thou every man's name upon his rod.

3 And thou shalt write Aaron's name upon the rod of Levi: for one rod shall be for the head of the house of their fathers.

4 And thou shalt lay them up in the tabernacle of the congregation before the testimony, where I will meet with you.

5 And it shall come to pass, that the man's rod, whom I shall choose, shall blossom: and I will make to cease from me the murmurings of the children of Israel, whereby they murmur against you.

6 ¶ And Moses spake unto the children of Israel, and every one of their princes gave him a rod apiece, for each prince one, according to their fathers' houses, twelve rods: and the rod of Aaron was among their rods.

7 And Moses laid up the rods before the LORD in the tabernacle of witness.

8 And it came to pass, that on the morrow

quantity of flour was increased, because the sacrifice was of superior value to the former. The accessory sacrifices were always increased in proportion to the greater worth and magnitude of its principal. 13-16. a stranger—one who had become a proselyte. There was not any of the national privileges of the Israelites, with hardly an exception, in which the Gentile stranger might not, on conforming to certain conditions, fully participate. 19. when ye eat of the bread of the land—The offering prescribed was to precede the act of eating. unto the Lord—*i.e.*, the priests of the Lord. (Ez. 44. 30.) 20. heave offering of the threshing-floor—meaning the corn on the threshing-floor—*i.e.*, after harvest, so shall ye heave it—to the priests accompanying the ceremony with the same rites. 22. if ye have erred, &c.—respecting the performance of divine worship, and the rites and ceremonies that constitute the holy service. This law relates only to any omission, and consequently is quite different from *that* laid down, (Lev. 4. 13,) which implies a transgression or positive neglect of some observances required. *This* law relates to private parties, or individual tribes; *that* to the whole congregation of Israel. 24-26. if ought be committed by ignorance—The Mosaic ritual was complicated, and the ceremonies to be gone through in the various instances of purification which are specified, would expose a worshipper, through ignorance, to the risk of omitting or neglecting some of them. This law included the stranger in the number of those for whom the sacrifice was offered for the sin of general ignorance. 27-31. if any soul sin through ignorance—Not only in common with the general body of the people, but his personal sins were to be expiated in the same manner. 30. Doeth ought presumptuously—Heb. *with a high or uplifted hand—i.e.*, knowingly, wilfully, obstinately. In this sense, the phraseology occurs. (Ex. 14. 8; Lev. 26. 21; Ps. 19. 13.) the same reproacheth the Lord—sets Him at open defiance, and dishonours His majesty. 31. his iniquity shall be upon him—*i.e.*, the punishment of his sins shall fall on himself individually; no guilt shall be incurred by the nation, unless there be a criminal carelessness in overlooking the offence. 32-34. a man that gathered sticks upon the sabbath-day—This incident is evidently narrated as an instance of presumptuous sin. The mere gathering of sticks was not a sinful act, and might be necessary for fuel to warm him, or to make ready his food. But its being done on the sabbath altered the entire character of the action. The law of the sabbath being a plain and positive commandment, this transgression of it was a known and wilful sin, and it was marked by several aggravations. For the deed was done with unblushing boldness in broad day-light, in open defiance of the divine authority—in flagrant inconsistency with his religious connection with Israel, as the covenant people of God; and it was an application to improper purposes of time, which God had consecrated to himself and the solemn duties of religion. The offender was brought before the rulers, who, on hearing the painful report, were at a loss to determine what ought to be done. That they should have felt any embarassment in such a case may seem surprising, in the face of the sabbath-law. (Ex. 31. 14.) Their difficulty probably arose from this being the first public offence of the kind which had occurred; and the appeal might be made to remove all ground of complaint—to produce a more striking effect, and that the fate of this criminal might be a beacon to warn all Israelites in future. 35, 36. The Lord said, the man... to death—The Lord was king, as well as God of Israel, and the offence being a violation of the law of the realm, the Sovereign Judge gave orders that this man should be put to death, and, moreover, required the whole congregation to unite in executing the fatal sentence. 38. bid them that they make fringes—These were narrow strips, in a wing-like form, wrapped over the shoulders, and on various parts of the attire. "Fringe," however, is the English rendering of two distinct Hebrew words—the one meaning a narrow lappet or edging, called the "hem or border," (Mat. 23. 5; Lu. 8. 44,) which, in order to make it more attractive to the eye, and consequently more serviceable to the purpose described, was covered with a riband of a blue or rather purple colour; the other term signifies strings with tassels at the end, fastened to the corners of the garment. Both of these are seen on the Egyptian and Assyrian frocks; and as the Jewish people were commanded by express and repeated ordinances to have them, the fashion was rendered subservient, in their case, to awaken high and religious associations—to keep them in habitual remembrance of the divine commandments. 41. I am the Lord your God—The import of this solemn conclusion is, that though he was displeased with them for their frequent rebellions, for which they would be doomed to forty years wandering, He would not abandon them, but continue His divine protection and care of them till they were brought into the land of promise.

CHAPTER XVI.

Ver. 1-30. THE REBELLION OF KORAH. 1, 2. Now Korah, the son of Izhar—Izhar, brother of Amram, (Ex. 6. 18,) was the second son of Kohath, and for some reason unrecorded, he had been supplanted by a descendant of the fourth son of Kohath, who was appointed prince or chief of the Kohathites. (ch. 3. 30.) Discontent with the preferment over him of a younger relative was probably the originating cause of this seditious movement on the part of Korah. Dathan, Abiram, and On—These were confederate leaders in the rebellion, but On seems to have afterwards withdrawn from the conspiracy. Took men—The latter mentioned individuals being all sons of Reuben, the eldest of Jacob's family, had been stimulated to this insurrection on the pretext that Moses had, by an arbitrary arrangement, taken away the right of primogeniture, which had vested the hereditary dignity of the priesthood in the first born of every family, with a view of transferring the hereditary exercise of the sacred functions to a particular branch of his own house; and that this gross instance of partiality to his own relations, to the permanent detriment of others, was a sufficient ground for refusing allegiance to his government. In addition to this grievance, another cause of jealousy and dissatisfaction that rankled in the breasts of the Reubenites, was the advancement of Judah to the leadership amongst the tribes. These malcontents had been incited by the artful representations of

Moses went into the tabernacle of witness; and, behold, the rod of Aaron for the house of Levi was budded, and brought forth buds, and bloomed blossoms, and yielded almonds.

9 And Moses brought out all the rods from before the LORD unto all the children of Israel: and they looked, and took every man his rod.

10 ¶ And the LORD said unto Moses, Bring Aaron's rod again before the testimony, to be kept for a token against the rebels; and thou shalt quite take away their murmurings from me, that they die not.

11 And Moses did so: as the LORD commanded him, so did he.

12 And the children of Israel spake unto Moses, saying, Behold, we die, we perish, we all perish.

13 Whosoever cometh any thing near unto the tabernacle of the LORD shall die: shall we be consumed with dying?

CHAPTER XVIII.

1 The charge of the priests and Levites. 8 The priests', 21 and the Levites' portion. 25 Of the heave offering to the priests, etc.

AND the LORD said unto Aaron, Thou, and thy sons, and thy father's house with thee, shall bear the iniquity of the sanctuary: and thou and thy sons with thee shall bear the iniquity of your priesthood.

2 And thy brethren also of the tribe of Levi, the tribe of thy father, bring thou with thee, that they may be joined unto thee, and minister unto thee: but thou and thy sons with thee *shall minister* before the tabernacle of witness.

3 And they shall keep thy charge, and the charge of all the tabernacle: only they shall not come nigh the vessels of the sanctuary and the altar, that neither they, nor ye also, die.

4 And they shall be joined unto thee, and keep the charge of the tabernacle of the congregation, for all the service of the tabernacle: and a stranger shall not come nigh unto you.

5 And ye shall keep the charge of the sanctuary, and the charge of the altar; that there be no wrath any more upon the children of Israel.

6 And I, behold, I have taken your brethren the Levites from among the children of Israel: to you *they are* given *as* a gift for the LORD, to do the service of the tabernacle of the congregation.

7 Therefore thou and thy sons with thee shall keep your priest's office for every thing of the altar, and within the veil; and ye shall serve: I have given your priest's office *unto you as* a service of gift: and the stranger that cometh nigh shall be put to death.

8 ¶ And the LORD spake unto Aaron, Behold, I also have given thee the charge of mine heave offerings of all the hallowed things of the children of Israel: unto thee have I given them, by reason of the anointing, and to thy sons, by an ordinance for ever.

9 This shall be thine of the most holy things, *reserved* from the fire: every oblation of theirs, every meat offering of theirs, and every sin offering of theirs, and every trespass offering of theirs, which they shall render unto me, *shall be* most holy for thee and for thy sons.

10 In the most holy *place* shalt thou eat it; every male shall eat it: it shall be holy unto thee.

11 And this *is* thine; the heave offering of their gift, with all the wave offerings of the children of Israel: I have given them unto thee, and to thy sons and to thy daughters with thee, by a statute for ever: every one that is clean in thy house shall eat of it.

12 All the best of the oil, and all the best of the wine, and of the wheat, the first-fruits of them which they shall offer unto the LORD, them have I given thee.

13 *And* whatsoever is first ripe in the land, which they shall bring unto the LORD, shall be thine: every one that is clean in thine house shall eat *of* it.

14 Every thing devoted in Israel shall be thine.

15 Every thing that openeth the matrix in all flesh, which they bring unto the LORD, *whether it be* of men or beasts, shall be thine: nevertheless the first-born of man shalt thou surely redeem, and the firstling of unclean beasts shalt thou redeem.

16 And those that are to be redeemed from a month old shalt thou redeem, according to thine estimation, for the money of five shekels, after the shekel of the sanctuary, which *is* twenty gerahs.

17 But the firstling of a cow, or the firstling of a sheep, or the firstling of a goat, thou shalt not redeem; they *are* holy: thou shalt sprinkle their blood upon the altar, and shalt burn their fat *for* an offering made by fire, for a sweet savour unto the LORD.

18 And the flesh of them shall be thine, as the wave breast and as the right shoulder are thine.

19 All the heave offerings of the holy things, which the children of Israel offer unto the LORD, have I given thee, and thy sons and thy daughters with thee, by a statute for ever: it *is* a covenant of salt for ever before the LORD unto thee and to thy seed with thee.

20 ¶ And the LORD spake unto Aaron, Thou shalt have no inheritance in their land, neither shalt thou have any part among them: I *am* thy part and thine inheritance among the children of Israel.

21 And, behold, I have given the children of Levi all the tenth in Israel for an inheritance, for their service which they serve, *even* the service of the tabernacle of the congregation.

22 Neither must the children of Israel henceforth come nigh the tabernacle of the congregation, lest they bear sin, and die.

23 But the Levites shall do the service of the tabernacle of the congregation, and they shall bear their iniquity. *It shall be* a statute for ever throughout your generations, that among the children of Israel they have no inheritance.

24 But the tithes of the children of Israel, which they offer *as* an heave offering unto the LORD, I have given to the Levites to inherit: therefore I have said unto them, Among the children of Israel they shall have no inheritance.

25 ¶ And the LORD spake unto Moses, saying,

26 Thus speak unto the Levites, and say unto them, When ye take of the children

Korah, (Jude, 11,) with whom the position of their camp on the south side afforded them facilities of frequent intercourse, and who, in addition to his feeling of personal wrongs, participated in their desire, if he did not originate the attempt, to recover their lost rights of primogeniture. When the conspiracy was ripe, they openly and boldly declared its object, and at the head of 250 princes, challenged Moses with an ambitious and unwarrantable usurpation of authority, especially in the appropriation of the priesthood, for they disputed the claim of Aaron also to pre-eminence. **3. They gathered themselves together**—The assemblage seems to have been composed of the whole band of conspirators; and they grounded their complaint on the fact that the whole people being separated to the divine service, (Ex. 19. 6,) were equally qualified to present offerings on the altar, and that God being graciously present amongst them, by the tabernacle and the cloud, evinced his readiness to receive sacrifices from the hand of any others as well as from theirs. **4. When Moses heard it, he fell upon his face**—This attitude of prostration indicated not only his humble and earnest desire that God would interpose to free him from the false and odious imputation, but his strong sense of the daring sin involved in this proceeding. Whatever feelings may be entertained respecting Aaron, who had formerly headed a sedition himself, it is impossible not to sympathize with Moses in this difficult emergency. But he was a devout man, and the prudential course he adopted was probably the dictate of that heavenly wisdom with which, in answer to his prayers, he was endowed. **5-11. He spake unto Korah and all his company**—They were first addressed, not only because being a party headed by his own cousin, Moses might hope to have more influence in that quarter, but because they were stationed near the tabernacle, and especially because an expostulation was the more weighty coming from him who was a Levite himself, and who was excluded along with his family from the priesthood. But to bring the matter to an issue, he proposed a test which would afford a decisive evidence of the divine appointment. **Even to-morrow**—*lit.* "in the morning," the usual time of meeting in the East for the settlement of public affairs. **him whom he hath chosen ... to come near unto him**—*i.e.*, will bear attestation to his ministry by some visible or miraculous token of his approval. **6. take you censers, Korah, &c.**—*i.e.*, since you aspire to the priesthood, then go, perform the highest function of the office—that of offering incense; and if you are accepted—well. How magnanimous the conduct of Moses, who was now as willing that God's people should be priests, as formerly that they should be prophets. (ch. 11. 29.) But he warned them that they were making a perilous experiment. **12-14. Moses sent to call Dathan and Abiram**—in a separate interview, the ground of their mutiny being different; for while Korah murmured against the exclusive appropriation of the priesthood to Aaron and his family, they were opposed to the supremacy of Moses in civil power. They refused to obey the summons; and their refusal was grounded on the plausible pretext that their stay in the desert was prolonged for some secret and selfish purposes of the leader, who was conducting them like blind men wherever it suited him. **15. Moses was very wroth**—Though the meekest of all men, he could not restrain his indignation at these unjust and groundless charges; and the highly excited state of his feelings was evinced by the utterance of a brief exclamation in the mixed form of a prayer and an impassioned assertion of his integrity. (cf. 1 Sam. 12. 3.) **Respect not their offering**—He calls it *their* offering, because, though it was to be offered by Korah and his Levitical associates, it was the united appeal of all the mutineers for deciding the contested claims of Moses and Aaron. **16-18. Korah, be thou and all thy company before the Lord**—*i.e.*, at "the door of the tabernacle," (*v.* 18,) that the assembled people might witness the experiment, and be properly impressed by the issue. two hundred and fifty censers—probably the small platters, common in Egyptian families where incense was offered to household deities, and which had been among the precious things borrowed at their departure. **20-21. The Lord spake, Separate yourselves from among this congregation**—Curiosity to witness the exciting spectacle attracted a vast concourse of the people, and it would seem that the popular mind had been incited to evil by the clamours of the mutineers against Moses and Aaron. There was something in their behaviour very offensive to God; for after His glory had appeared—as at the installation of Aaron, (Lev. 9. 23,) so now for his confirmation in the sacred office—He bade Moses and Aaron withdraw from the assembly "that He might consume them in a moment." **22. O God, the God of the spirits of all flesh**—The benevolent importunity of their prayer was the more remarkable that the intercession was made for their enemies. **24-26. Speak unto the congregation...get you up from the tabernacle**—Moses was attended in the execution of this mission by the elders. The united and urgent entreaties of so many dignified personages produced the desired effect of convincing the people of their crime, and of withdrawing them from the company of men who were doomed to destruction, lest being partakers of their sins, they should perish along with them, **27. the tabernacle of Korah, Dathan, and Abiram**—Korah being a Kohathite, his tent could not have been in the Reubenite camp, and it does not appear that he himself was on the spot where Dathan and Abiram stood with their families. Their attitude of defiance indicated their daring and impenitent character, equally regardless of God and man. **28-34. Hereby ye shall know that the Lord hath sent me**—The awful catastrophe of the earthquake which, as predicted by Moses, swallowed up those impious rebels in a living tomb, gave the divine attestation to the mission of Moses, and struck the spectators with solemn awe. there came out a fire from the Lord—*i.e.*, from the cloud—This seems to describe the destruction of Korah and those Levites who with him aspired to the functions of the priesthood. (See on ch. 26. 11, 58; 1 Chr. 6. 22, 37.) **37-39. Speak unto Eleazar**—He was selected lest the high priest might contract defilement from going among the dead carcases. the brazen censers made broad plates to be a memorial—The altar of burnt offerings, being made of wood, and covered with brass, this additional covering

of Israel the tithes which I have given you from them for your inheritance, then ye shall offer up an heave offering of it for the LORD, even a tenth *part* of the tithe.

27 And *this* your heave offering shall be reckoned unto you, as though *it were* the corn of the threshing-floor, and as the fulness of the wine-press.

28 Thus ye also shall offer an heave offering unto the LORD of all your tithes, which ye receive of the children of Israel; and ye shall give thereof the LORD's heave offering to Aaron the priest.

29 Out of all your gifts ye shall offer every heave offering of the LORD, of all the best thereof, *even* the hallowed part thereof out of it.

30 Therefore thou shalt say unto them, When ye have heaved the best thereof from it, then it shall be counted unto the Levites as the increase of the threshing-floor, and as the increase of the wine-press.

31 And ye shall eat it in every place, ye and your households: for it *is* your reward for your service in the tabernacle of the congregation.

32 And ye shall bear no sin by reason of it, when ye have heaved from it the best of it: neither shall ye pollute the holy things of the children of Israel, lest ye die.

CHAPTER XIX.

1 *The water of separation:* 11 *the use of it for purification of uncleanness.*

AND the LORD spake unto Moses and unto Aaron, saying,

2 This *is* the ordinance of the law which the LORD hath commanded, saying, Speak unto the children of Israel, that they bring thee a red heifer without spot, wherein *is* no blemish, *and* upon which never came yoke:

3 And ye shall give her unto Eleazar the priest, that he may bring her forth without the camp, and *one* shall slay her before his face.

4 And Eleazar the priest shall take of her blood with his finger, and sprinkle of her blood directly before the tabernacle of the congregation seven times:

5 And *one* shall burn the heifer in his sight; her skin, and her flesh, and her blood, with her dung, shall he burn:

6 And the priest shall take cedar wood, and hyssop, and scarlet, and cast *it* into the midst of the burning of the heifer.

7 Then the priest shall wash his clothes, and he shall bathe his flesh in water, and afterward he shall come into the camp, and the priest shall be unclean until the even.

8 And he that burneth her shall wash his clothes in water, and bathe his flesh in water, and shall be unclean until the even.

9 And a man *that is* clean shall gather up the ashes of the heifer, and lay *them* up without the camp in a clean place; and it shall be kept for the congregation of the children of Israel for a water of separation: it *is* a purification for sin.

10 And he that gathereth the ashes of the heifer shall wash his clothes, and be unclean until the even: and it shall be unto the children of Israel, and unto the stranger that sojourneth among them, for a statute for ever.

11 ¶ He that toucheth the dead body of any man shall be unclean seven days.

12 He shall purify himself with it on the third day, and on the seventh day he shall be clean: but if he purify not himself the third day, then the seventh day he shall not be clean.

13 Whosoever toucheth the dead body of any man that is dead, and purifieth not himself, defileth the tabernacle of the LORD; and that soul shall be cut off from Israel: because the water of separation was not sprinkled upon him, he shall be unclean; his uncleanness *is* yet upon him.

14 This *is* the law, when a man dieth in a tent: all that come into the tent, and all that *is* in the tent, shall be unclean seven days.

15 And every open vessel, which hath no covering bound upon it, *is* unclean.

16 And whosoever toucheth one that is slain with a sword in the open fields, or a dead body, or a bone of a man, or a grave, shall be unclean seven days.

17 And for an unclean *person* they shall take of the ashes of the burnt heifer of purification for sin, and running water shall be put thereto in a vessel:

18 And a clean person shall take hyssop, and dip *it* in the water, and sprinkle *it* upon the tent, and upon all the vessels, and upon the persons that were there, and upon him that touched a bone, or one slain, or one dead, or a grave:

19 And the clean *person* shall sprinkle upon the unclean on the third day, and on the seventh day; and on the seventh day he shall purify himself, and wash his clothes, and bathe himself in water, and shall be clean at even.

20 But the man that shall be unclean, and shall not purify himself, that soul shall be cut off from among the congregation, because he hath defiled the sanctuary of the LORD: the water of separation hath not been sprinkled upon him; he *is* unclean.

21 And it shall be a perpetual statute unto them, that he that sprinkleth the water of separation shall wash his clothes; and he that toucheth the water of separation shall be unclean until even.

22 And whatsoever the unclean *person* toucheth shall be unclean; and the soul that toucheth *it* shall be unclean until even.

CHAPTER XX.

1 *The death of Miriam.* 7 *Moses, smiting the rock, bringeth forth water.* 22 *Aaron's death; Eleazar succeedeth him.*

THEN came the children of Israel, *even* the whole congregation, into the desert of Zin in the first month: and the people abode in Kadesh; and Miriam died there, and was buried there.

2 And there was no water for the congregation: and they gathered themselves together against Moses and against Aaron.

3 And the people chode with Moses, and spake, saying, Would God that we had died when our brethren died before the LORD!

4 And why have ye brought up the congregation of the LORD into this wilderness, that we and our cattle should die there?

5 And wherefore have ye made us to come up out of Egypt, to bring us in unto this evil place? it *is* no place of seed, or of figs, or of vines, or of pomegranates; neither *is* there any water to drink.

of broad plates not only rendered it doubly secure against the fire, but served as a warning-beacon to deter all from future invasions of the priesthood. 41. Ye have killed the people of the Lord—What a strange exhibition of popular prejudice and passion—to blame the leaders for saving the rebels. Yet Moses and Aaron interceded for the people—the high priest perilling his own life in doing good to that perverse race. 48. stood between the living and the dead—The plague seems to have begun in the extremities of the camp. Aaron, in this remarkable act, was a type of Christ.

CHAPTER XVII.

Ver. 1-13. AARON'S ROD FLOURISHETH. 2. Speak unto the children of Israel—The controversy with Moses and Aaron about the priesthood was of such a nature and magnitude as required a decisive and authoritative settlement. For the removal of all doubts, and the silencing of all murmuring in future regarding the holder of the office, a miracle was wrought of a remarkable character and permanent duration, and in the manner of performing it, all the people were made to have a direct and special interest. take every one... princes... twelve rods—As the princes, being the eldest sons of the chief family, and heads of their tribes, might have advanced the best claims to the priesthood, if that sacred dignity was to be shared among all the tribes, they were therefore selected, and being twelve in number—that of Joseph being counted only one—Moses was ordered to see that the name of each was inscribed—a practice borrowed from the Egyptians—upon his rod or wand of office. The name of Aaron rather than of Levi was used, as the latter name would have opened a door of controversy among the Levites; and as there was to be one rod only for the head of each tribe, the express appointment of a rod for Aaron determined him to be the head of that tribe, as well as that branch or family of the tribe to which the priestly dignity should belong. These rods were to be laid in the tabernacle close to the ark, (cf. v. 10; and He. 9. 4,) where a divine token was promised that would for all time terminate the dispute. 6. the rod of Aaron was among their rods—either one of the twelve, or, as many suppose, a thirteenth in the midst. (He. 9. 4.) The rods were of dry sticks or wands, probably old, as transmitted from one head of the family to a succeeding. 8. Moses went into the tabernacle—being privileged to do so on this occasion by the special command of God; and he there beheld the remarkable spectacle of Aaron's rod—which, according to Josephus, was a stick of an almond tree—bearing fruit in three different stages at once—buds, blossoms, and fruit. to be kept for a token against the rebels—For if, after all admonitions and judgments, seconded by miracles, the people should still rebel, they would certainly pay the penalty by death. 12, 13. Behold we die, we perish—An exclamation of fear, both from the remembrance of former judgments, and the apprehension of future relapses into murmuring. cometh any thing near—i.e., nearer than he ought to do; an error into which many may fall. Will the stern justice of God overtake every slight offence. We shall all be destroyed. Some, however, regard this exclamation as the symptom of a new discontent, rather than the indication of a reverential and submissive spirit. Let us fear and sin not.

CHAPTER XVIII.

Ver. 1-7. THE CHARGE OF THE PRIESTS AND LEVITES. 1. The Lord said unto Aaron—Security is here given to the people from the fears expressed, ch. 17. 12,) by the responsibility of attending to all sacred things being devolved upon the priesthood, together with the penalties incurred through neglect; and thus the solemn responsibilities annexed to their high dignity, of having to answer not only for their own sins, but also for the sins of the people, were calculated in a great measure to remove all feeling of envy at the elevation of Aaron's family, when the honour was weighed in the balance with its burdens and dangers. 2-7. thy brethren of the tribe of Levi—The departments of the sacred office, to be filled respectively by the priests and Levites, are here assigned to each. To the priests were committed the charge of the sanctuary and the altar, while the Levites were to take care of everything else about the tabernacle. The Levites were to attend the priests as servants—bestowed on them as "gifts" to aid in the service of the tabernacle—while the high and dignified office of the priesthood was a "service of gift." "A stranger"—i.e., one, neither a priest nor a Levite, who should intrude into any departments of the sacred office, should incur the penalty of death.

8-20. THE PRIESTS' PORTION. 8-13. I have given thee charge of my heave-offerings—A recapitulation is made in this passage of certain perquisites specially appropriated to the maintenance of the priests. They were parts of the votive and freewill-offerings, including both meat and bread, wine and oil, and the first fruits, which formed a large and valuable item. 14. everything devoted in Israel shall be thine—provided it was adapted for food or consumable by use; for the gold and silver vessels that were dedicated as the spoils of victory were not given to the priests, but for the use and adornment of the sacred edifice. 19. it is a covenant of salt—i.e., a perpetual ordinance. This figurative form of expression was evidently founded on the conservative properties of salt, which keeps meat from corruption, and hence it became an emblem of inviolability and permanence. It is a common phrase amongst Oriental people, who consider the eating of salt a pledge of fidelity, binding them in a covenant of friendship; and hence the partaking of the altar meats, which were appropriated to the priests on condition of their services, and of which salt formed a necessary accompaniment, was naturally called a covenant of salt, (Lev. 2, 13.)

21-32. THE LEVITES' PORTION. 21, 22, I have given to the children of Levi—Neither the priests nor the Levites were to possess any allotments of land, but to depend entirely upon Him who liberally provided for them out of His own portion; and this law was subservient to many important purposes—such as that, being exempted from the cares and labours of worldly business, they might be exclusively devoted to His service; that a bond of mutual love and attachment might be formed between the people and the Levites, who, as performing religious services for the people, derived their subsistence

6 And Moses and Aaron went from the presence of the assembly unto the door of the tabernacle of the congregation, and they *h* fell upon their faces: and the glory of the Lord appeared unto them.

7 ¶ And the Lord spake unto Moses, saying,

8 Take *i* the rod, and gather thou the assembly together, thou and Aaron thy brother, and speak ye unto the rock before their eyes; and it shall give forth his water, and *j* thou shalt bring forth to them water out of the rock: so thou shalt give the congregation and their beasts drink.

9 And Moses took the rod *k* from before the Lord, as he commanded him.

10 And Moses and Aaron gathered the congregation together before the rock, and he said unto them, *l* Hear now, ye rebels; must we fetch you water out of this rock?

11 And Moses *m* lifted up his hand, and with his rod he smote the rock twice; and the *n* water came out abundantly, and the congregation drank, and their beasts *also*.

12 ¶ And the Lord spake unto Moses and Aaron, Because *o* ye believed me not, to sanctify *p* me in the eyes of the children of Israel, therefore ye shall not bring this congregation into the land which I have given them.

13 This *q* is the water of ¹ Meribah; because the children of Israel strove with the Lord, and he was sanctified in them.

14 ¶ And Moses *r* sent messengers from Kadesh unto the king of Edom, *s* Thus saith thy brother Israel, Thou knowest all the travail that hath ² befallen us;

15 How our fathers went down into Egypt, and we have dwelt in Egypt a long time; and the Egyptians vexed us and our fathers:

16 And *t* when we cried unto the Lord, he heard our voice, and *u* sent an angel, and hath brought us forth out of Egypt; and, behold, we *are* in Kadesh, a city in the uttermost of thy border:

17 Let *v* us pass, I pray thee, through thy country: we will not pass through the fields, or through the vineyards, neither will we drink *of* the water of the wells: we will go by the king's *high* way, we will not turn to the right hand nor to the left, until we have passed thy borders.

18 And Edom said unto him, Thou shalt not pass by me, lest I come out against thee with the sword.

19 And the children of Israel said unto him, We will go by the high way; and if I and my cattle drink of thy water, *w* then I will pay for it: I will only, without *doing* any thing *else*, go through on my feet.

20 And he said, *x* Thou shalt not go through. And Edom came out against him with much people, and with a strong hand.

21 Thus Edom *y* refused to give Israel passage through his border: wherefore Israel *z* turned away from him.

22 ¶ And the children of Israel, *even* the whole congregation, journeyed from *a* Kadesh, and *b* came unto mount Hor.

23 And the Lord spake unto Moses and Aaron in mount Hor, by the coast of the land of Edom, saying,

24 Aaron shall *c* be gathered unto his people: for he shall not enter into the land which I have given unto the children of Israel, because ye rebelled against my ³ word at the water of Meribah.

25 Take *d* Aaron and Eleazar his son, and bring them up unto mount Hor;

26 And strip Aaron of his garments, and put them upon Eleazar his son: and Aaron shall be gathered *unto his people*, and shall die there.

27 And Moses did as the Lord commanded: and they went up into mount Hor in the sight of all the congregation.

28 And Moses stripped Aaron of his garments, and put them upon Eleazar his son; and *e* Aaron died there in the top of the mount: and Moses and Eleazar came down from the mount.

29 And when all the congregation saw that Aaron was dead, they mourned for Aaron thirty *f* days, *even* all the house of Israel.

CHAPTER XXI.

The people murmuring are plagued with fiery serpents; 9 but healed by a brasen serpent, etc.

AND *when* *a* king Arad the Canaanite, which dwelt in the south, heard tell that Israel came by the way of the spies; then he fought against Israel, and took *some* of them prisoners.

2 And *b* Israel vowed a vow unto the Lord, and said, If thou wilt indeed deliver this people into my hand, then *c* I will utterly destroy their cities.

3 And the Lord hearkened to the voice of Israel, and delivered up the Canaanites; and they utterly destroyed them and their cities: and he called the name of the place ¹ Hormah.

4 ¶ And they journeyed from mount Hor by the way of the Red sea, to compass the land of Edom: and the soul of the people was much ² discouraged because of the way.

5 And the people *d* spake against God, and against Moses, *e* Wherefore have ye brought us up out of Egypt to die in the wilderness? for *there is* no bread, neither *is there any* water; and *f* our soul loatheth this light bread.

6 And *g* the Lord sent *h* fiery serpents among the people, and they bit the people; and much people of Israel died.

7 Therefore *i* the people came to Moses, and said, We have sinned; for we have spoken against the Lord, and against thee: pray *j* unto the Lord, that he take away the serpents from us. And Moses prayed for the people.

8 And the Lord said unto Moses, Make thee a fiery serpent, and set it upon a pole: and it shall come to pass, that every one that is bitten, when he looketh upon it, shall live.

9 And *k* Moses made a serpent of brass, and put it upon a pole; and it came to pass, that if a serpent had bitten any man, when he beheld the serpent of brass, he lived.

10 ¶ And the children of Israel set forward, and pitched in Oboth.

11 And they journeyed from Oboth, and pitched at ³ Ije-abarim, in the wilderness which *is* before Moab, toward the sunrising.

12 ¶ From thence they removed, and pitched in the valley of Zared.

13 From thence they removed, and pitched on the other side of Arnon, which *is* in the wilderness that cometh out of the coasts of the Amorites: for *l* Arnon *is* the

from them; and further, that being the more easily dispersed among the different tribes, they might be more useful in instructing and directing the people. 23. they shall bear their iniquity—They were to be responsible for the right discharge of those duties that were assigned to them, and consequently to bear the penalty that was due to negligence or carelessness in the guardianship of the holy things. 26. the Levites ... offer a tenth of the tithe—Out of their own they were to pay tithes to the priests equally as the people gave to them. The best of their tithes was to be assigned to the priests, and afterwards they enjoyed the same liberty to make use of the remainder that other Israelites had of the produce of their threshing-floors and wine-presses. 32. ye shall bear no sin, &c.—Neglect in having the best entailed sin in the use of such unhallowed food, and the holy things would be polluted by the reservation to themselves of what should be offered to God and the priests.

CHAPTER XIX.

Ver. 1-22. THE WATER OF SEPARATION. 2. This is the ordinance of the law—An institution of a peculiar nature ordained by law for the purification of sin, and provided at the public expense, because it was for the good of the whole community. red heifer, &c.—This is the only case in which the colour of the victim is specified; and it has been supposed the ordinance was designed in opposition to the superstitious notions of the Egyptians. That people never offered a vow, but they sacrificed a red bull, the greatest care being taken by their priests in examining whether it possessed the requisite characteristics, and it was an annual offering to Typhon, their evil being. By the choice, both of the sex and the colour, provision was made for eradicating from the minds of the Israelites a favourite Egyptian superstition regarding two objects of their animal worship. 3. ye shall give her unto Eleazar—He was the second or deputy high priest, and he was selected for this duty because the execution of it entailed temporary defilement, from which the acting high priest was to be preserved with the greatest care. It was led "forth without the camp," in accordance with the law regarding victims laden with the sins of the people, and thus typical of Christ (Heb. 13. 12; also Lev. 24. 14.) The priest was to sprinkle the blood "seven times" before —lit., towards or near the tabernacle, a description which seems to imply either that he carried a portion of the blood in a bason to the door of the tabernacle (Lev. 4. 17.), or that in the act of sprinkling he turned his face towards the sacred edifice, being disqualified through the defiling influence of this operation from approaching close to it. By this attitude he indicated that he was presenting an expiatory sacrifice, for the acceptance of which he hoped, in the grace of God, by looking to the mercy-seat. Every part of it was consumed by fire, except the blood used in sprinkling, and the ingredients mixed with the ashes were the same as those employed in the sprinkling of lepers (Lev. 14. 4-7.) It was a water of separation—i.e., of "sanctification" for the people of Israel. 7. the priest shall be unclean until the even—The ceremonies prescribed show the imperfection of the Levitical priesthood, while they typify the condition of Christ when expiating our sins. (2 Cor. 5. 21.) 11-22. he that toucheth the dead body of any man—This law is noticed here to show the uses to which the water of separation was applied. The case of a death is one; and as in every family which sustained a bereavement the members of the household became defiled, so in an immense population, where instances of mortality and other cases of uncleanness would be daily occurring, the water of separation must have been in constant requisition. To afford the necessary supply of the cleansing mixture, the Jewish writers say that a red heifer was sacrificed every year, and that the ashes, mingled with the sprinkling ingredients, were distributed through all the cities and towns of Israel. 12. purify himself the third day—The necessity of applying the water on the third day is inexplicable on any natural or moral ground; and, therefore, the regulation has been generally supposed to have had a typical reference to the resurrection, on that day, of Christ, by whom His people are sanctified; while the process of ceremonial purification being extended over seven days, was intended to shew that sanctification is progressive and incomplete till the arrival of the eternal Sabbath. Every one knowingly and presumptuously neglecting to have himself sprinkled with this water was guilty of an offence which was punished by excommunication. 14. when a man dieth in a tent, &c. —The instances adduced appear very minute and trivial; but important ends both of a religious and of a sanitary nature were promoted by carrying the idea of pollution from contact with dead bodies to so great an extent. While it would effectually prevent that Egyptianized race of Israelites imitating the superstitious custom of the Egyptians, who kept in their houses the mummied remains of their ancestors, it insured a speedy interment to all, thus not only keeping burial places at a distance, but removing from the habitations of the living the corpses of persons who died from infectious disorders, and from the open field the unburied remains of strangers and foreigners who fell in battle. 21. he that sprinkleth, he that toucheth the water of separation—The opposite effects ascribed to the water of separation—of cleansing one person and defiling another—are very singular, and not capable of very satisfactory explanation. One important lesson, however, was thus taught, that its purifying efficacy was not inherent in itself, but arose from the divine appointment, as in other ordinances of religion, which are effectual means of salvation, not from any virtue in them, or in him that administers them, but solely through the grace of God communicated thereby.

CHAPTER XX.

Ver. 1-29. THE DEATH OF MIRIAM. 1. Then came the children of Israel ... in the first month—i.e., of the fortieth year (cf. v. 22, 23, with ch. 33. 38.) In this history only the principal and most important incidents are recorded, those confined chiefly to the first or second and the last years of the journeyings in the wilderness, thence called Et-Tih. Between the last verse of the preceding and the first verse of this chapter there is a long and undescribed interval of thirty-seven years. abode in Kadesh—sup-

border of Moab, between Moab and the Amorites.

14 Wherefore it is said in the book of the wars of the LORD, ⁴ What he did in the Red sea, and in the brooks of Arnon,

15 And at the stream of the brooks that goeth down to the dwelling of Ar, and lieth upon the border of Moab.

16 ¶ And from thence *they went* ᵐ to Beer: that *is* the well whereof the LORD spake unto Moses, Gather the people together, and ⁿ I will give them water.

17 Then ᵒ Israel sang this song, ⁶ Spring up, O well; ⁷ sing ye unto it:

18 The princes digged the well, the nobles of the people digged it, by *the direction of* the ᵖ lawgiver, with their staves. And from the wilderness *they went* to Mattanah;

19 And from Mattanah to Nahaliel; and from Nahaliel to Bamoth;

20 And from Bamoth *in* the valley, that *is* in the ⁸ country of Moab, to the top of ⁹ Pisgah, which looketh ⁹ toward ¹⁰ Jeshimon.

21 ¶ And ʳ Israel sent messengers unto Sihon king of the Amorites, saying,

22 Let ˢ me pass through thy land: we will not turn into the fields, or into the vineyards; we will not drink *of* the waters of the well; *but* we will go along by the king's *high* way, until we be past thy borders.

23 And ᵗ Sihon would not suffer Israel to pass through his border; but Sihon gathered all his people together, and went out against Israel into the wilderness: and ᵘ he came to Jahaz, and fought against Israel.

24 And ᵛ Israel smote him with the edge of the sword, and possessed his land from Arnon unto Jabbok, even unto the children of Ammon: for the border of the children of Ammon *was* strong.

25 And Israel took all these cities: and Israel dwelt in all the cities of the Amorites, in Heshbon, and in all the ¹¹ villages thereof.

26 For Heshbon *was* the city of Sihon the king of the Amorites, who had fought against the former king of Moab, and taken all his land out of his hand, even unto Arnon.

27 Wherefore they that speak in proverbs say, Come into Heshbon, let the city of Sihon be built and prepared:

28 For there is ʷ a fire gone out of Heshbon, a flame from the city of Sihon: it hath consumed ˣ Ar of Moab, *and* the lords of the high places of Arnon.

29 Woe to thee, Moab! thou art undone, O people of ʸ Chemosh: he hath given his sons that escaped, and his daughters, into captivity unto Sihon king of the Amorites.

30 We have shot at them: Heshbon is perished even ᶻ unto Dibon, and we have laid them waste even unto Nophah, which *reacheth* unto Medeba.

31 ¶ Thus Israel dwelt in the land of the Amorites.

32 And Moses sent to spy out ᵃ Jaazer, and they took the villages thereof, and drove out the Amorites that *were* there.

33 ¶ And they turned, and went up by the way of Bashan: and Og the king of Bashan went out against them, he, and all his people, to the battle ᵇ at Edrei.

34 And the LORD said unto Moses, ᶜ Fear him not: for I have delivered him into thy

hand, and all his people, and his land; and thou ᵈ shalt do to him as thou didst unto Sihon king of the Amorites, which dwelt at Heshbon.

35 So ᵉ they smote him, and his sons, and all his people, until there was none left him alive: and they possessed his land.

CHAPTER XXII.

2 Balak's first message for Balaam refused; 15 his second obtaineth him: 22 an angel would have slain him, if his ass had not saved him.

AND ᵃ the children of Israel set forward, and pitched in the plains of Moab on this side Jordan *by* Jericho.

2 ¶ And ᵇ Balak the son of Zippor saw all that Israel had done to the Amorites.

3 And ᶜ Moab was sore afraid of the people, because they *were* many: and Moab was distressed because of the children of Israel.

4 And Moab said unto the ᵈ elders of Midian, Now shall this company lick up all *that are* round about us, as the ox licketh up the grass of the field. And Balak the son of Zippor *was* king of the Moabites at that time.

5 He ᵉ sent messengers therefore unto Balaam the son of Beor, to ᶠ Pethor, which *is* by the river of the land of the children of his people, to call him, saying, Behold, there is a people come out from Egypt: behold, they cover the ¹ face of the earth, and they abide over against me:

6 Come now therefore, I pray thee, ᵍ curse me this people; for they *are* too mighty for me: peradventure I shall prevail, *that* we may smite them, and *that* I may drive them out of the land: for I wot that he whom thou blessest *is* blessed, and he whom thou cursest is cursed.

7 And the elders of Moab and the elders of Midian departed with the ʰ rewards of divination in their hand; and they came unto Balaam, and spake unto him the words of Balak.

8 And he said unto them, Lodge here this night, and I will bring you word again, as the LORD shall speak unto me: and the princes of Moab abode with Balaam.

9 And ⁱ God came unto Balaam, and said, What men *are* these with thee?

10 And Balaam said unto God, Balak the son of Zippor, king of Moab, hath sent unto me, *saying*,

11 Behold, *there is* a people come out of Egypt, which covereth the face of the earth: come now, curse me them; peradventure ² I shall be able to overcome them, and drive them out.

12 And God said unto Balaam, Thou shalt not go with them; thou shalt not curse the people: for ʲ they *are* blessed.

13 And Balaam rose up in the morning, and said unto the princes of Balak, Get you into your land; for the LORD refuseth to give me leave to go with you.

14 And the princes of Moab rose up, and they went unto Balak, and said, Balaam refuseth to come with us.

15 ¶ And Balak sent yet again princes, more, and more honourable than they.

16 And they came to Balaam, and said to him, Thus saith Balak the son of Zippor, ³ Let nothing, I pray thee, hinder thee from coming unto me:

17 For ᵏ I will promote thee unto very great honour, and I will do whatsoever

posed to be what is now known as Ain El-Weibeh, three springs surrounded by palms. (See on ch. 13, 26.) It was their second arrival after an interval of thirty-eight years. (Deu. 11. 16.) The old generation had nearly all died, and the new one encamped in it with the view of entering the promised land, not however as formerly on the south, but by crossing the Edomite region on the east. Miriam died there—four months before Aaron. **2-13. there was no water for the congregation** — There was at Kadesh a fountain, En-Mishpat (Gen. 14. 7.), and at the first encampment of the Israelites there was no want of water. It was then either partially dried up by the heat of the season, or had been exhausted by the demands of so vast a multitude. **6. Moses and Aaron went from the presence of the assembly**—Here is a fresh ebullition of the untamed and discontented spirit of the people. The leaders fled to the precincts of the sanctuary, both as an asylum from the increasing fury of the highly-excited rabble, and as their usual refuge in seasons of perplexity and danger, to implore the direction and aid of God. **8. take the rod**—which had been deposited in the tabernacle (ch. 17. 10.), the wonder-working rod by which so many miracles had been performed, sometimes called "the rod of God" (Ex. 4. 20.), sometimes Moses, (v. 11.) or Aaron's rod, (Ex. 7. 12.) **10. Moses said, Hear now, ye rebels**—The conduct of the great leader on this occasion was hasty and passionate, (Ps. 106. 33.) He had been directed to *speak* to the rock, but he *smote it twice* in his impetuosity, thus endangering the blossoms of the rod, and instead of speaking to the *rock*, he spoke to the *people* in a fury. **the congregation drank and their beasts**—Physically the water afforded the same kind of needful refreshment to both. But in a religious point of view, this, which was only a common element to the cattle, was a sacrament to the people (1 Cor. 10. 3, 4.) —it possessed a relative sanctity imparted to it by its divine origin and use. **12. because ye believed me not, &c.**—The act of Moses in smiting twice betrayed a doubt, not of the power, but of the will of God to gratify such a rebellious people, and his exclamation seems to have emanated from a spirit of incredulity akin to Sarai's (Gen. 18. 13.) These circumstances indicate the influence of unbelief, and there might have been others unrecorded which led to so severe a chastisement. **13. this is the water of Meribah**—The word Kadesh is added to it to distinguish it from another Meribah (Ex. 17. 7.) **14-16. Moses sent messengers to the king of Edom**—The encampment at Kadesh was on the confines of the Edomite territory, through which the Israelites would have had an easy passage across the Arabah by Wady-el-Ghuweir, so that they could have continued their course around Moab, and approached Palestine by the east. [ROB.] The Edomites being the descendants of Esau, and tracing their line of descent from Abraham as their common stock, were recognized by the Israelites as brethren, and a very brotherly message sent to them. **17. We will go by the king's highway**—probably Wady-el-Ghuweir [ROB.], through which ran one of the great lines of road, constructed for commercial caravans, as well as for the progress of armies. The engineering necessary for carrying them over marshes or mountains, and the care requisite for protecting them from the shifting sands, led to their being under the special care of the state. Hence the expression, "the king's highway," which is of great antiquity. **19. If... drink of thy water... pay for it**—From the scarcity of water in the warm climates of the East, the practice of levying a tax for the use of the wells is universal; and the jealousy of the natives, in guarding the collected treasures of rain is often so great, that water cannot be procured for money. **21. Edom refused to give Israel, &c.**—a churlish refusal obliged them to take another route. (See on ch. 21. 4; Deu. 2. 4; Judg. 11. 18; see also 1 Sam. 14. 47; 2 Sam. 8. 14, which describe the retribution that was just.) **22. Came unto mount Hor**—now Gebel Haroun, the most striking and lofty elevation in the Seir range, called emphatically, (v. 28,) "the mount." It is conspicuous by its double top. **24-28. Aaron shall be gathered unto his people**—In accordance with his recent doom, he, attired in the high priest's costume, was commanded to ascend that mountain and die. But although the time of his death was hastened by the Divine displeasure as a punishment for his sins, the *manner* of his death was arranged in tenderness of love, and to do him honour at the close of his earthly service. His ascent of the mount was to afford him a last look of the camp, and a distant prospect of the promised land. The simple narrative of the solemn and impressive scene implies, though it does not describe, the pious resignation, settled faith, and inward peace of the aged pontiff. **26. Strip Aaron of his garments**—*i. e.*, his pontifical robes, in token of his resignation. (See Is. 22. 20-25.) put them on his son—as the inauguration into his high office. Having been formerly anointed with the sacred oil, that ceremony was not repeated, or, as some think, it was done on his return to the camp. **28. Aaron died on the top of the mount**—(See on Deu. 10. 6.) A tomb has been erected upon or close by the spot where he was buried. **29. When all the congregation saw**—Moses and Eleazar were the sole witnesses of his departure. According to the established law, the new high priest could not have been present at the funeral of his father without contracting ceremonial defilement. (Le. 21. 11.) But that law was dispensed with in the extraordinary circumstances; the people learnt the event not only from the recital of the two witnesses, but from their visible signs of grief and change; and this event betokened the imperfection of the Levitical priesthood. (He. 7. 12.) mourned thirty days—the usual period of public and solemn mourning. (See on Deu. 34. 8.)

CHAPTER XXI.

Ver. 1-35. ISRAEL ATTACKED BY THE CANAANITES. 1. King Arad the Canaanite—rather, the Canaanite king of Arad—an ancient town on the southernmost borders of Palestine, not far from Kadesh. A hill called Tell Arad marks the spot. **heard that Israel came by the way of the spies**—in the way or manner of spies, stealthily, or from spies sent by himself to ascertain the designs and motions of the Israelites. The Septuagint and others consider the *Heb.* word "spies" as a proper name, and render it: "Came by the way of Atharim towards Arad." [KEN-

thou sayest unto me: come therefore, I pray thee, curse me this people.

18 And Balaam answered and said unto the servants of Balak, If Balak would give me his house full of silver and gold, ᶦI cannot go beyond the word of the LORD my God, to do less or more.

19 Now therefore, I pray you, tarry ye also here this night, that I may know what the LORD will say unto me more.

20 And God came unto Balaam at night, and said unto him, If the men come to call thee, rise up, *and* go with them; but yet ᵐ the word which I shall say unto thee, that shalt thou do.

21 And Balaam rose up in the morning, and saddled his ass, and ⁿ went with the princes of Moab.

22 ¶ And God's anger was kindled because he went: ᵒ and the angel of the LORD stood in the way for an adversary against him. Now he was riding upon his ass, and his two servants *were* with him.

23 And ᵖ the ass saw the angel of the LORD standing in the way, and his sword drawn in his hand: and the ass turned aside out of the way, and went into the field: and Balaam smote the ass, to turn her into the way.

24 But the angel of the LORD stood in a path of the vineyards, a wall *being* on this side, and a wall on that side.

25 And when the ass saw the angel of the LORD, she thrust herself unto the wall, and crushed ᑫ Balaam's foot against the wall: and he smote her again.

26 And the angel of the LORD went further, and stood in a narrow place, ʳ where *was* no way to turn either to the right hand or to the left.

27 And when the ass saw the angel of the LORD, she fell down under Balaam: and Balaam's ˢ anger was kindled, and he smote the ass with a staff.

28 And the LORD ᵗ opened the mouth of the ass; and she said unto Balaam, What have I done unto thee, that thou hast smitten me these three times?

29 And Balaam said unto the ass, Because thou hast mocked me: I would there were a sword in mine hand, ᵘ for now would I kill thee.

30 And ᵛ the ass said unto Balaam, *Am* not I thine ass, ʷ upon which thou hast ridden ᵇ ever since *I was* thine unto this day? was I ever wont to do so unto thee? And he said, Nay.

31 Then the LORD ʷ opened the eyes of Balaam, and he saw the angel of the LORD standing in the way, and his sword drawn in his hand: and he ˣ bowed down his head, and ᵇ fell flat on his face.

32 And the angel of the LORD said unto him, Wherefore hast thou smitten thine ass these three times? Behold, I went out ⁷ to withstand thee, because *thy* way is ʸ perverse before me:

33 And the ass saw me, and turned from me these three times: unless she had turned from me, surely now also I had slain thee, and saved her alive.

34 And Balaam said unto the angel of the LORD, ᶻ I have sinned; for I knew not that thou stoodest in the way against me: now therefore, if it ᵍ displease thee, I will get me back again.

35 And the angel of the LORD said unto Balaam, Go with the men: but only the word that I shall speak unto thee, that thou shalt speak. So Balaam went with the princes of Balak.

36 ¶ And when Balak heard that Balaam was come, ᵃ he went out to meet him unto a city of Moab, which *is* in the border of Arnon, which *is* in the utmost coast.

37 And Balak said unto Balaam, Did I not earnestly send unto thee to call thee? wherefore camest thou not unto me? am I not able indeed to promote thee to honour?

38 And Balaam said unto Balak, Lo, I am come unto thee: have I now any power at all to say any thing? ᵇ the word that God putteth in my mouth, that shall I speak.

39 And Balaam went with Balak, and they came unto ⁹ Kirjath-huzoth.

40 And Balak offered oxen and sheep, and sent to Balaam, and to the princes that *were* with him.

41 And it came to pass on the morrow, that Balak took Balaam, and brought him up into the ᶜ high places of Baal, that thence he might see the utmost *part* of the people.

CHAPTER XXIII.

1, 14, 28 *Balak's sacrifices.* 7, 18 *Balaam's parables.*

AND Balaam said unto Balak, Build me here seven altars, and prepare me here seven oxen and seven rams.

2 And Balak did as Balaam had spoken: and Balak and Balaam offered on *every* altar a bullock and a ram.

3 And Balaam said unto Balak, Stand by thy burnt offering, and I will go: peradventure the LORD will come to meet me: and whatsoever he showeth me I will tell thee. And ¹ he went to an high place.

4 And God met Balaam: and he said unto him, I have prepared seven altars, and I have offered upon *every* altar a bullock and a ram.

5 And the LORD ᵃ put a word in Balaam's mouth, and said, Return unto Balak, and thus thou shalt speak.

6 And he returned unto him, and, lo, he stood by his burnt sacrifice, he, and all the princes of Moab.

7 And ᵇ he took up his parable, and said, Balak the king of Moab hath brought me from ᶜ Aram, out of the mountains of the east, *saying*, Come, curse me Jacob, and come, ᵈ defy Israel.

8 How shall I curse, whom God hath not cursed? or ᵉ how shall I defy, *whom* the LORD hath not defied?

9 For from the top of the rocks I see him, and from the hills I behold him: lo, ᶠ the people shall dwell alone, and ᵍ shall not be reckoned among the nations.

10 Who ʰ can count the dust of Jacob, and the number of the fourth *part* of Israel? Let ² me die ⁱ the death of the righteous, and let my last end be like his!

11 And Balak said unto Balaam, What hast thou done unto me? ʲ I took thee to curse mine enemies, and, behold, thou hast blessed *them* altogether.

12 And he answered and said, Must I not take heed to speak that which the LORD hath put in my mouth?

13 And Balak said unto him, Come, I pray thee, with me unto another place, from whence thou mayest see them: thou shalt see but the utmost part of them, and shalt not see them all; and curse me them from thence.

NICOTT.] took some of them prisoners—This discomfiture was permitted to teach them to expect the conquest of Canaan not from their own wisdom and valour, but solely from the favour and help of God. (Deu. 9. 4; Ps. 44. 3, 4.) 2, 3. Israel vowed a vow—Made to feel their own weakness, they implored the aid of Heaven, and, in anticipation of it, *devoted* the cities of this king to future destruction. The nature and consequence of such anathemas are described. (Le. 27; Deu. 13.) This vow of extermination against Arad gave name to the place Hormah, (slaughter and destruction), though it was not accomplished till after the passage of the Jordan. Others think Hormah the name of a town mentioned. (Josh. 12. 14.) 4. They journeyed from mount Hor—On being refused the passage requested, they returned through the Arabah, " the way of the Red Sea, to Elath, at the head of the eastern gulf of the Red Sea, and thence passed up through the mountains to the eastern desert, so as to make the circuit of the land of Edom. (h. 33. 41, 42.) the soul of the people, &c.—Disappointment on finding themselves so near the confines of the promised land, without entering it—vexation at the refusal of a passage through Edom, and the absence of any Divine interposition in their favour—above all, the necessity of a retrograde journey, by a long and circuitous route through the worst parts of a sandy desert, and the dread of being plunged into new and unknown difficulties—all this produced a deep depression of spirits. But it was followed, as usually, by a gross outburst of murmuring at the scarcity of water, and of expressions of disgust at the manna. 5. Our soul loatheth this light bread—*i. e.*, bread without substance or nutritious quality. The refutation of this calumny appears in the fact, that on the strength of this food they performed for 40 years so many and toilsome journeys. But they had been indulging a hope of the better and more varied fare enjoyed by a settled people; and disappointment, always the more bitter as the hope of enjoyment seems near, drove them to speak against God and against Moses. (1 Co. 10. 9.) 6. The Lord sent fiery serpents—That part of the desert where the Israelites now were—near the head of the gulf of Akaba—is greatly infested with venemous reptiles, of various kinds, particularly lizards, which raise themselves in the air and swing themselves from branches; and scorpions, which, being in the habit of lying among long grass, are particularly dangerous to the barelegged sandalled people of the East. The only known remedy consists in sucking the wound, or, in the case of cattle, in the application of ammonia. The species of serpents that caused so great mortality amongst the Israelites cannot be ascertained. They are said to have been "fiery," an epithet applied to them either from their bright, vivid colour, or the violent inflammation their bite occasioned. 7-9. we have sinned—The severity of the scourge and the appalling extent of mortality brought them to a sense of sin, and through the intercessions of Moses, which they implored, they were miraculously healed. He was directed to make the figure of a serpent in brass, to be elevated on a poll or standard, that it might be seen at the extremities of the camp, and that every bitten Israelite who looked to it might be healed. This peculiar method of cure was designed, in the first instance, to show that it was the efficacy of God's power and grace, not the effect of nature or art, and also that it might be a type of the power of faith in Christ to heal all who look to Him of their sins (Jo. 3. 14, 15; see also on 2 Kings 18. 4.) 10. the children of Israel set forward—Along the eastern frontier of the Edomites, encamping in various stations. 12. pitched in the valley—*lit.*, the brook-valley of Zared—*i.e.*, the woody (Deu. 2. 13; Is. 15. 7; Amos 6. 14.) This torrent rises among the mountains to the east of Moab, and flowing west, empties itself into the Dead Sea. Ije-Abarim is supposed to have been its ford." [CALMET.] 13. pitched on the other side of Arnon—now El-Mojib, a deep, broad, and rapid stream, dividing the dominions of the Moabites and Amorites. 14. book of the wars of the Lord—A fragment or passage is here quoted from a poem or history of the wars of the Israelites, principally with a view to decide the position of Arnon. Ar—the capital of Moab. 16. from thence they went to Beer—*i. e.*, a well. The name was probably given to it afterwards, as it is not mentioned. (ch. 33.) 17, 18. then Israel sang—this beautiful little song was in accordance with the wants and feelings of travelling caravans in the east, where water is an occasion both of prayer and thanksgiving. From the princes using their official rods only, and not spades, it seems probable that this well was concealed by the brushwood or the sand, as is the case with many wells in Idumea still. The discovery of it was seasonable, and owing to the special interposition of God. 21-23. Israel sent messengers unto Sihon—The rejection of their respectful and pacific message was resented—Sihon was discomfited in battle—and Israel obtained by right of conquest the whole of the Amorite dominions. 24. from Arnon unto the Jabbok—now the Zurka. These rivers formed the southern and northern boundaries of his usurped territory, for the border of Ammon was strong—a reason stated for Sihon not being able to push his invasion further. 25. Israel dwelt in all the cities—after exterminating the inhabitants who had been previously doomed, (Deu. 2. 34.) 26. Heshbon—(Song 7. 4.)—situated sixteen English miles north of the Arnon, and from its ruins appears to have been a large city. 27-30. wherefore they that speak in proverbs—Here is given an extract from an Amorite song exultingly anticipating an extension of their conquests to Arnon. The quotation from the poem of the Amorite bard ends at verse 28. The two following verses appear to be the strains in which the Israelites expose the impotence of the usurpers. 29. people of Chemosh—the name of the Moabite idol (1 Kings 11. 7-33; 2 Kings 23. 13; Jer. 48. 46.) he—*i. e.*, their god, hath surrendered his worshippers to the victorious arms of Sihon. 33. they went up by the way of Bashan—a name given to that district from the richness of the soil—now Batanea or El-Bottein—a hilly region east of the Jordan, lying between the mountains of Hermon on the north and those of Gilead on the south. Og—giant, an Amoritish prince, who, having opposed the progress of the Israelites, was defeated. 34. fear him not—a necessary encouragement, for his

14 ¶ And he brought him into the field of Zophim, to the top of ³ Pisgah, ᵏ and built seven altars, and offered a bullock and a ram on every altar.

15 And he said unto Balak, Stand here by thy burnt offering, while I meet the LORD yonder.

16 And the LORD met Balaam, and put a word in his mouth, and said, Go again unto Balak, and say thus.

17 And when he came to him, behold, he stood by his burnt offering, and the princes of Moab with him. And Balak said unto him, ˡ What hath the LORD spoken?

18 And he took up his parable, and said, Rise ᵐ up, Balak, and hear; hearken unto me, thou son of Zippor:

19 God ⁿ is not a man, that he should lie; neither the son of man, that he should repent: hath he said, and shall he not do it? or hath he spoken, and shall he not make it good?

20 Behold, I have received commandment to bless: and ᵒ he hath blessed; and I cannot reverse it.

21 He ᵖ hath not beheld iniquity in Jacob, neither hath he seen perverseness in Israel: the ᵍ LORD his God is with him, ʳ and the shout of a king is among them.

22 God brought them out of Egypt: he hath as it were ˢ the strength of an unicorn.

23 Surely there is no enchantment ᵗ against Jacob, neither is there any divination against Israel: according to this time it shall be said of Jacob and of Israel, ᵘ What hath God wrought!

24 Behold, the people shall rise up as a great lion, and lift up himself as a young lion: he shall not lie down until he eat of the prey, and drink the blood of the slain.

25 ¶ And Balak said unto Balaam, Neither curse them at all, nor bless them at all.

26 But Balaam answered and said unto Balak, Told not I thee, saying, All that the LORD speaketh, that I must do?

27 ¶ And Balak said unto Balaam, Come, I pray thee, I will bring thee unto another place; peradventure it will please God that thou mayest curse me them from thence.

28 And Balak brought Balaam unto the top of Peor, that looketh toward ⁵ Jeshimon.

29 And ᵘ Balaam said unto Balak, Build me here seven altars, and prepare me here seven bullocks and seven rams.

30 And Balak did as Balaam had said, and offered a bullock and a ram on every altar.

CHAPTER XXIV.

1 Balaam foretelleth Israel's happiness: 15 he prophesieth of the Star of Jacob, etc.

AND when Balaam saw that it pleased the LORD to bless Israel, he went not, as at other times, ¹ to seek for enchantments, but he set his face toward the wilderness.

2 And Balaam lifted up his eyes, and he saw Israel abiding in his tents according to their tribes; and ᵃ the Spirit of God came upon him.

3 And ᵇ he took up his parable, and said, Balaam the son of Beor hath said, and the man ² whose eyes are open hath said:

4 He hath said, which heard the words of God, which saw the vision of the Almighty, falling ᶜ into a trance, but having his eyes open:

5 How goodly are thy tents, O Jacob! and thy tabernacles, O Israel!

6 As the valleys are they spread forth, as gardens by the river's side, as the trees of lign aloes, ᵈ which the LORD hath planted, and as cedar trees beside the waters.

7 He shall pour the water out of his buckets, and his seed shall be in many waters, and his king shall be higher than ᵉ Agag, and his kingdom ᶠ shall be exalted.

8 God brought him forth out of Egypt; he hath as it were the strength of an unicorn: he shall eat up the nations his enemies, and shall break their bones, and pierce them through with his arrows.

9 He couched, he lay down as a lion, and as a great lion: who shall stir him up? Blessed ᵍ is he that blesseth thee, and cursed is he that curseth thee.

10 ¶ And Balak's anger was kindled against Balaam, and he smote his hands together: and Balak said unto Balaam, I called thee to curse mine enemies, and, behold, thou hast altogether blessed them these three times.

11 Therefore now flee thou to thy place: I thought to promote thee unto great honour; but, lo, the LORD hath kept thee back from honour.

12 And Balaam said unto Balak, Spake I not also to thy messengers which thou sentest unto me, saying,

13 If Balak would give me his house full of silver and gold, I cannot go beyond the commandment of the LORD, to do either good or bad of mine own mind; but what the LORD saith, that will I speak?

14 And now, behold, I go unto my people: come therefore, and I will advertise thee what this people shall do to thy people in the latter days.

15 And he took up his parable, and said, Balaam the son of Beor hath said, and the man whose eyes are open hath said;

16 He hath said, which heard the words of God, and knew the knowledge of the Most High, which saw the vision of the Almighty, falling into a trance, but having his eyes open:

17 I ʰ shall see him, but not now; I shall behold him, but not nigh: there shall come a ⁱ Star out of Jacob, and ʲ a Sceptre shall rise out of Israel, and shall ³ smite the corners of Moab, and destroy all the children of Sheth.

18 And ᵏ Edom shall be a possession, Seir also shall be a possession for his enemies; and Israel shall do valiantly.

19 Out of Jacob shall come he that shall have dominion, and shall destroy him that remaineth of the city.

20 And when he looked on Amalek, he took up his parable, and said, Amalek was ⁴ the first of the nations, but his latter end ⁵ shall be that he perish for ever.

21 And he looked on the Kenites, and took up his parable, and said, Strong is thy dwelling-place, and thou puttest thy nest in a rock:

22 Nevertheless ⁶ the Kenite shall be wasted, ⁷ until Asshur shall carry thee away captive.

23 And he took up his parable, and said, Alas! who shall live when God doeth this?

24 And ships shall come from the coast

CHAPTER XXII.

Ver. 1-20. BALAK'S FIRST MESSAGE FOR BALAAM REFUSED. 1. Israel pitched in the plains of Moab—So called from having formerly belonged to that people, though wrested from them by Sihon. It was a dry, sunken, desert region on the east of the Jordan valley, opposite Jericho. 2. Balak—*i.e.*, empty. Terrified (Deu. 2. 25; Ex. 15. 15.) at the approach of so vast a multitude, and not daring to encounter them in the field, he resolved to secure their destruction by other means. elders of Midian—called kings (ch. 31. 8.) and princes (Josh. 13. 21.) The Midianites, a distinct people on the southern frontier of Moab, united with them as confederates against Israel their common enemy. 5. sent messengers unto Balaam—*i.e.*, "lord" or "devourer" of people, a famous soothsayer (Josh. 13. 22.) son of Beor or, in the Chaldee form, Bosor—*i.e.*, destruction. Pethor—a city of Mesopotamia, situated on the Euphrates. 6. come, curse me this people—Among the heathen an opinion prevailed, that prayers for evil or curses, would be heard by the unseen powers as well as prayers for good, when offered by a prophet or priest, and accompanied by the use of certain rites. Many examples are found in the histories of the Greeks and Romans, of whole armies being devoted to destruction, and they occur among the natives of India and other heathen countries still. In the Burmese war, magicians were employed to curse the British troops. 7. the rewards of divination—like the fee of a fortune-teller, and being a royal present, it would be something handsome. 8-14. lodge here this night, &c.—God usually revealed His will in visions and dreams; and Balaam's birth and residence in Mesopotamia, where the remains of patriarchal religion still lingered, account for his knowledge of the true God. His real character has long been a subject of discussion. Some, judging from his language, have thought him a saint; others, looking to his conduct, have described him as an irreligious charlatan; and a third class consider him a novice in the faith, who had a fear of God, but who had not acquired power over his passions." [HENG.] 13. the Lord refuseth to give me leave—This answer has an *appearance* of being good, but it studiously concealed the reason of the divine prohibition, and it intimated his own willingness and desire to go—if permitted. Balak despatched a second mission, which held out flattering prospects both to his avarice and his ambition. (Ge. 31. 30.) 19. tarry also here this night—The divine will, as formerly declared, not being according to his desires, he hoped by a second request to bend it, as he had already bent his own conscience to his ruling passions of pride and covetousness. The permission granted to Balaam is in accordance with the ordinary procedure of providence. God often gives up men to follow the impulse of their own lusts; but there is no approval in thus leaving them to act at the prompting of their own wicked hearts. Jo. 13. 27.)

21-41. THE JOURNEY. 21. Balaam saddled his ass—Probably one of the white sprightly animals which persons of rank were accustomed to ride. The saddle, as usually in the East, would be nothing more than a pad or his outer cloak. God's anger was kindled because he went—The displeasure arose partly from his neglecting the condition on which leave was granted him—viz., to wait till the princes of Moab "came to call him," and because, through desire for "the wages of unrighteousness," he entertained the secret purpose of acting in opposition to the solemn charge of God. 24. the angel of the Lord stood in a path of the vineyards—The roads which lead through fields and vineyards are so narrow that in most parts a man could not pass a beast without care and caution. A stone or mud fence flanks each side of these roads, to prevent the soil being washed off by the rains. 28. the Lord opened the mouth of the ass—To utter, like a parrot, articulate sounds, without understanding them. That this was a visionary scene is a notion, which seems inadmissible, because of the improbability of a vision being described as an actual occurrence in the middle of a plain history. Besides, the opening of the ass's mouth must have been an external act, and that with the manifest tenor of Peter's language, strongly favours the literal view. The absence of any surprise at such a phenomenon on the part of Balaam may be accounted for by his mind being wholly engrossed with the prospect of gain, which produced "the madness of the prophet." "It was a miracle, wrought to humble his proud heart, which had to be first subjected in the school of an ass before he was brought to attend to the voice of God speaking by the angel." [CALVIN.] 34, 35. I have sinned . . . if it displease thee—Notwithstanding this confession, he evinced no spirit of penitence, as he speaks of desisting only from the outward act. The words "go with the men" was a mere withdrawal of farther restraint, but the terms in which leave was given are more absolute and peremptory than those in *v.* 20. 36, 37. Balak went out to meet him—The higher the rank of the expected guest, politeness requires a greater distance to be gone to welcome his arrival. 38. the word that God putteth in my mouth—This appears a pious answer. It was an acknowledgment that he was restrained by a superior power. 39. Kirjath-huzoth—a city of streets. 40. Balak offered oxen and sheep—made preparations for a grand entertainment to Balaam and the princes of Midian. 41. High places of Baal—eminences consecrated to the worship of Baal-peor, (ch. 25. 3,) or Chemosh.

CHAPTER XXIII.

Ver. 1-30. BALAK'S SACRIFICES. 1. Build me here seven altars—Balak, being a heathen, would naturally suppose these altars were erected in honour of Baal, the patron deity of his country. It is evident, from *v.* 4, that they were prepared for the worship of the true God, although in choosing the high places of Baal as their site, and rearing a number of altars, (2 Ki. 18. 22; Is. 17. 8; Jer. 11. 13; Hos. 8. 11; 10. 1,) instead of one only, as God had appointed, he blended his own superstitions with the divine worship. The heathen, both in ancient and modern times, attached a mysterious virtue to the number *seven;* and Balaam, in ordering the preparation of so many altars, designed to mystify and delude the king. 3. Stand by thy burnt-offering—as one in expectation of an important favour. showeth me—*i. e.*, makes known to me by word or sign. went to an high place —a part by himself, where he might practise

120

of *l* Chittim, and shall afflict Asshur, and shall afflict *m* Eber, and *n* he also shall perish for ever.

25 And Balaam rose up, and went and returned to his place: and Balak also went his way.

CHAPTER XXV.

1 The Israelites' whoredom and idolatry with Moab. 6 Zimri and Cozbi slain. 16 God commandeth to vex the Midianites.

AND Israel abode in *a* Shittim, and *b* the people began to commit whoredom with the daughters of Moab.

2 And *c* they called the people unto *d* the sacrifices of their gods: and the people did eat, and *e* bowed down to their gods.

3 And Israel joined himself unto Baal-peor: and *f* the anger of the LORD was kindled against Israel.

4 And the LORD said unto Moses, *g* Take all the heads of the people, and hang them up before the LORD against the sun, *h* that the fierce anger of the LORD may be turned away from Israel.

5 And Moses said unto the judges of Israel, Slay *i* ye every one his men that were joined unto Baal-peor.

6 ¶ And, behold, one of the children of Israel came and brought unto his brethren a Midianitish woman in the sight of Moses, and in the sight of all the congregation of the children of Israel, *j* who *were* weeping *before* the door of the tabernacle of the congregation.

7 And when Phinehas, *k* the son of Eleazar, the son of Aaron the priest, saw *it*, he rose up from among the congregation, and took ¹ a javelin in his hand;

8 And he went after the man of Israel into the tent, and thrust both of them through, the man of Israel, and the woman through her belly. So the plague was stayed from the children of Israel.

9 And *l* those that died in the plague were twenty and four thousand.

10 ¶ And the LORD spake unto Moses, saying,

11 Phinehas, *m* the son of Eleazar, the son of Aaron the priest, hath turned my wrath away from the children of Israel, while he was zealous ² for my sake among them, that I consumed not the children of Israel in my *n* jealousy.

12 Wherefore say, *o* Behold, I give unto him my covenant of peace:

13 And he shall have it, and *p* his seed after him, *even* the covenant of *q* an everlasting priesthood; because he was *r* zealous for his God, and *s* made an atonement for the children of Israel.

14 Now the name of the Israelite that was slain, *even* that was slain with the Midianitish woman, *was* Zimri, the son of Salu, a prince of a ³ chief house among the Simeonites.

15 And the name of the Midianitish woman that was slain *was* Cozbi, the daughter *t* of Zur: he *was* head over a people, *and* of a chief house in Midian.

16 ¶ And the LORD spake unto Moses, saying,

17 Vex the Midianites, and smite them:

18 For they vex you with their wiles, wherewith they have beguiled you in the matter of Peor, and in the matter of Cozbi, the daughter of a prince of Midian, their sister, which was slain in the day of the plague for Peor's sake.

B. C. 1452.

CHAP. 24.
l Gen. 10. 4.
Dan. 11. 30.
m Gen. 11. 14.
n Lev. 26. 22.
Deu. 28. 36.
Mat. 23. 37.

CHAP. 25.
a ch. 33. 49.
Mic. 6. 5.
b ch. 31. 16.
1 Cor. 10. 8.
Rev. 2. 14.
c Josh. 22. 17.
Ps. 106. 28.
Hos. 9. 10.
d Ex. 34. 15.
1 Cor. 10. 20.
e Ex. 20. 5.
f Ps. 106. 29.
g Josh. 22. 17.
h Deu. 13. 17.
i Ex. 32. 27.
Deu. 13. 6.
j Joel 2. 17.
k Ex. 6. 25.
1 a spear, or pike.
l 1 Cor. 10. 8.
m Ps. 106. 30.
2 with my zeal.
n Ex. 20. 5.
1 Kin. 14. 22.
Ezek. 16. 38.
Zeph. 1. 18.
Zeph. 3. 8.
Heb. 12. 29.
o Mal. 3. 1.
p 1 Chr. 6. 4.
q Ex. 40. 15.
r Acts 22. 3.
Ro. 10. 2.
s Heb. 2. 17.
3 house of a father.
t Josh. 13. 21.

CHAP. 26.
a Ex. 30. 12.
ch. 1. 2.
b ch. 22. 1.
ch. 31. 12.
ch. 33. 48.
ch. 35. 1.
c Gen. 46. 9.
Ex. 6. 14.
1 Chr. 5. 1.
d ch. 16. 1, 2.
Deu. 11. 6.
Is. 65. 16.
Ps. 106. 17.
e ch. 16. 32.
Ezek. 14. 8.
1 Cor. 10. 8.
2 Pet. 2. 6.
Jude 7.
f Ex. 6. 24.
1 Chr. 6. 22.
Eze. 18. 20.
g Gen. 46. 10.
Ex. 6. 15.
Jemuel.
h 1 Chr. 4. 24.
Jarib.
i Gen. 46. 10, Zohar.
j Gen. 46. 16, Ziphion.
1 Or, Esbon.
k Gen. 46. 16, Arodi.
l Gen. 38. 2.
m 1 Chr. 2. 3.

CHAPTER XXVI.

1 Israel numbered. 52 The inheritance of the land divided. 63 Of Caleb and Joshua.

AND it came to pass after the plague, that the LORD spake unto Moses and unto Eleazar the son of Aaron the priest, saying,

2 Take *a* the sum of all the congregation of the children of Israel, from twenty years old and upward, throughout their fathers' house, all that are able to go to war in Israel.

3 And Moses and Eleazar the priest spake with them *b* in the plains of Moab, by Jordan *near* Jericho, saying,

4 *Take the sum of the people*, from twenty years old and upward; as the LORD commanded Moses and the children of Israel, which went forth out of the land of Egypt.

5 *c* Reuben, the *d* eldest son of Israel: the children of Reuben; Hanoch, *of whom cometh* the family of the Hanochites: of Pallu, the family of the Palluites:

6 Of Hezron, the family of the Hezronites: of Carmi, the family of the Carmites.

7 These *are* the families of the Reubenites: and they that were numbered of them were forty and three thousand and seven hundred and thirty.

8 And the sons of Pallu; Eliab.

9 And the sons of Eliab; Nemuel, and Dathan, and Abiram. This *is that* Dathan and Abiram *which were d* famous in the congregation, who strove against Moses and against Aaron in the company of Korah, when they strove against the LORD:

10 And the earth opened her mouth, and swallowed them up together with Korah, when that company died, what time the fire devoured two hundred and fifty men: and they *e* became a sign.

11 Notwithstanding *f* the children of Korah died not.

12 ¶ The sons of Simeon after their families: of *g* Nemuel, the family of the Nemuelites: of Jamin, the family of the Jaminites: of *h* Jachin, the family of the Jachinites:

13 Of *i* Zerah, the family of the Zarhites: of Shaul, the family of the Shaulites.

14 These *are* the families of the Simeonites, twenty and two thousand and two hundred.

15 ¶ The children of Gad after their families: of *j* Zephon, the family of the Zephonites: of Haggi, the family of the Haggites: of Shuni, the family of the Shunites:

16 Of ¹ Ozni, the family of the Oznites: of Eri, the family of the Erites:

17 Of *k* Arod, the family of the Arodites: of Areli, the family of the Arelites.

18 These *are* the families of the children of Gad according to those that were numbered of them, forty thousand and five hundred.

19 ¶ The *l* sons of Judah *were* Er and Onan: and Er and Onan died in the land of Canaan.

20 And *m* the sons of Judah after their families were; of Shelah, the family of the Shelanites: of Pharez, the family of the Pharzites: of Zerah, the family of the Zarhites.

21 And the sons of Pharez were; of Hezron, the family of the Hezronites: of Hamul, the family of the Hamulites.

22 These *are* the families of Judah according to those that were numbered of

rites and ceremonies, with a view to obtain a response of the oracle, 4-6. God met Balaam—not in compliance with his incantations, but to frustrate his wicked designs, and compel him, contrary to his desires and interests, to pronounce the following benediction. 7. Took up his parable—*i. e.*, spoke under the influence of inspiration, and in the highly poetical, figurative, and oracular style of a prophet. brought me from Aram—This word, joined with "the mountains of the East," denotes the upper portion of Mesopotamia, lying on the east of Moab. The East enjoyed an infamous notoriety for magicians and soothsayers. (Is. 2. 6.) 8. How shall I curse whom God hath not cursed—A Divine blessing has been pronounced over the posterity of Jacob; and therefore, whatever prodigies can be achieved by my charms, all magical skill, all human power, is utterly impotent to counteract the decree of God. 9. From the top—*lit.*, "a bare place" on the rocks, to which Balak had taken him, for it was deemed necessary to see the people who were to be devoted to destruction. But that commanding prospect could contribute nothing to the accomplishment of the king's object, for the destiny of Israel was to be a distinct peculiar people, separated from the rest of the nations in government, religion, customs, and divine protection. (Deu. 33. 28.) So that although I might be able to gratify your wishes against other people, I can do nothing against them, (Ex. 19. 5; Le. 20. 24.) who can count the dust of Jacob?—An Oriental hyperbole for a very populous nation, as Jacob's posterity was promised to be. (Ge. 13. 16: 28. 14.) the number of the fourth part of Israel—*i. e.*, the camp consisted of four divisions; every one of these parts was formidable in numbers. 10. let me die the death of the righteous—*Heb.*, of Jeshurun; or, the Israelites. The meaning is, they are a people happy, above all others, not only in life, but at death, from their knowledge of the true God, and their hope through His grace. Balaam is a representative of a large class in the world, who express a wish for the blessedness which Christ has promised to His people, but are averse to imitate the mind that was in Him. 13-15. Come with me unto another place—Surprised and disappointed at this unexpected eulogy on Israel, Balak hoped that, if seen from a different point of observation, the prophet would give utterance to different feelings; and so having made the same solemn preparations, Balaam retired, as before, to wait the Divine afflatus. field of Zophim, top of Pisgah—a flat surface on the summit o. the mountain range, which was cultivated land. Others render it "the field of sentinels," an eminence where some of Balak's guards were posted to give signals. [CALMET.] 18. Rise up—As Balak was already standing, (v. 17,) this expression is equivalent to "now attend to me." The counsel and promises of God respecting Israel are unchangeable; and no attempt to prevail on Him to reverse them will succeed as they may with a man. 21. He hath not beheld iniquity in Jacob—Many sins were observed and punished in this people. But no such universal and hopeless apostacy had as yet appeared, to induce God to abandon or destroy them. the Lord his God is with him—has a favour for them. and the shout of a king is among them—Such joyful acclamations as of a people rejoicing in the presence of a victorious prince. 22. He hath . . . the strength—*i.e.*, Israel is not as they were at the Exodus, a horde of poor, feeble, spiritless people, but powerful and invincible as a *reem—i.e.*, a rhinoceros. (Job, 39. 9; Ps. 22. 21; 92. 10.) 23. Surely there is no enchantment—No art can ever prevail against a people who are under the shield o. Omn potence, and for whom miracles have been, and yet shall be performed, which will be a theme of admiration in succeeding ages. 26. All that the Lord speaketh, that I must do—A remarkable confession that he was divinely constrained to give utterances different from what it was his purpose and inclination to do. 28. Brought Balaam to the top of Peor—or, Beth-peor, (Deu. 3. 29,) the eminence on which a temple of Baal stood. that looketh toward Jeshimon—the desert tract in the south of Palestine, on both sides of the Dead Sea.

CHAPTER XXIV.

Ver. 1-25. BALAAM FORETELLETH ISRAEL'S HAPPINESS. 1. To seek for—*i. e.*, to use enchantments. His experience on the two former occasions had taught him that these superstitious accompaniments of his worship were useless, and therefore he now simply looked towards the camp of Israel, either with a secret design to curse them, or to await the Divine afflatus. 2. According to their tents—*i. e.*, in the orderly distribution of the camp. (ch. 2.) the Spirit of God came upon him—Before the regular ministry of the prophets was instituted, God made use of various persons as the instruments through whom He revealed His will, and Balaam was one of these. (Deu. 23. 5.) 3. The man whose eyes are open—*i. e.*, a seer, (1 Sam. 9. 9,) a prophet, to whom the visioned future was disclosed—sometimes when falling into a sleep, (Ge. 15. 15,) frequently into "a trance." 5-7. How goodly are thy tents, O Israel!—a fine burst of admiration, expressed in highly poetical strains. All travellers describe the beauty which the circular range of Bedouin tents impart to the desert. How impressive, then, must have been the view, as seen from the heights of Abarim, of the immense camp of Israel, extended over the subjacent plains. 6. As the valley—*Heb.*, brooks. the water-courses of the mountains. lign aloes—an aromatic shrub on the banks of his native Euphrates, the conical form of which suggested an apt resemblance to a tent. The redundant imagery of these verses depicts the origin, rapid progress, and prosperity of Israel. 7. Higher than Agag—The Amalekites were then the most powerful of all the desert tribes, and Agag a title common to their kings. 10-14. Balak's anger was kindled—The "smiting of the hands together" is, amongst Oriental people, an indication of the most violent rage, (see Ez. 21. 17 ; 22. 13,) and ignominious dismissal. 15. Took up his parable—or prophecy, uttered in a poetical style. 17. I shall see him—rather, "I do see" or "have seen him,"—a prophetic sight, like that of Abraham. (Jo. 8. 56.) him—*i. e.*, Israel. a star, a sceptre—This imagery, in the hieroglyphic language of the East, denotes some eminent ruler,—primarily David; but secondarily and pre-eminently, the Messiah, (See on Ge. 49. 10.) corners—border, often put for a whole country. (Ex. 8. 2; Ps. 74. 17.) children of Sheth—some prince of Moab; or, according to some, "the children of the

them, threescore and sixteen thousand and five hundred.

23 ¶ *Of* ⁿ the sons of Issachar, after their families: *of* Tola, the family of the Tolaites: of ¹ Pua, the family of the Punites:

24 Of ² Jashub, the family of the Jashubites: of Shimron, the family of the Shimronites.

25 These *are* the families of Issachar according to those that were numbered of them, threescore and four thousand and three hundred.

26 ¶ *Of* ᵒ the sons of Zebulun after their families: of Sered, the family of the Sardites: of Elon, the family of the Elonites: of Jahleel, the family of the Jahleelites.

27 These *are* the families of the Zebulunites according to those that were numbered of them, threescore thousand and five hundred.

28 ¶ The ᵖ sons of Joseph after their families *were* Manasseh and Ephraim.

29 Of the sons of Manasseh: of ᵠ Machir, the family of the Machirites: and Machir begat Gilead: of Gilead *come* the family of the Gileadites.

30 These *are* the sons of Gilead: *of* ʳ Jeezer, the family of the Jeezerites: of Helek, the family of the Helekites:

31 And *of* Asriel, the family of the Asrielites: and *of* Shechem, the family of the Shechemites:

32 And *of* Shemida, the family of the Shemidaites: and *of* Hepher, the family of the Hepherites.

33 And ˢ Zelophehad the son of Hepher had no sons, but daughters: and the names of the daughters of Zelophehad *were* Mahlah, and Noah, Hoglah, Milcah, and Tirzah.

34 These *are* the families of Manasseh, and those that were numbered of them, fifty and two thousand and seven hundred.

35 ¶ These *are* the sons of Ephraim after their families: of Shuthelah, the family of the Shuthalhites : of ᵗ Becher, the family of the Bachrites: of Tahan, the family of the Tahanites.

36 And these *are* the sons of Shuthelah: of Eran, the family of the Eranites.

37 These *are* the families of the sons of Ephraim according to those that were numbered of them, thirty and two thousand and five hundred. These *are* the sons ᵘ of Joseph after their families.

38 ¶ The ᵛ sons of Benjamin after their families: of Bela, the family of the Belaites: of Ashbel, the family of the Ashbelites: of ʷ Ahiram, the family of the Ahiramites:

39 Of ˣ Shupham, the family of the Shuphamites: of Hupham, the family of the Huphamites.

40 And the sons of Bela were ʸ Ard and Naaman: *of* Ard, the family of the Ardites: *and* of Naaman, the family of the Naamites.

41 These *are* the sons of Benjamin after their families: and they that were numbered of them *were* forty and five thousand and six hundred.

42 ¶ These ᶻ *are* the sons of Dan after their families: of ⁴ Shuham, the family of the Shuhamites. These *are* the families of Dan after their families.

43 All the families of the Shuhamites, according to those that were numbered of them, *were* threescore and four thousand and four hundred.

44 ¶ *Of* ᵃ the children of Asher after their

B. C. 1452.

CHAP. 26.
ⁿ Gen. 46.13.
1 Chr. 7.1.
² Or, Phuvah.
³ Or, Job.
ᵒ Gen. 46.14.
ᵖ Gen. 46.20.
Deu. 33. 17.
ᵠ Josh. 17. 1.
1 Chr. 7. 14, 16.
ʳ Called Abiezer, Josh. 17. 2. Judg. 6. 11, 24, 34.
ˢ ch. 27.1. ch. 36. 11. Josh. 17. 3.
ᵗ 1 Chr. 7. 20, Bered.
ᵘ Deut. 33. 13-17.
ᵛ Gen. 46. 21. 1 Chr. 7. 6.
ʷ Gen. 46. 21, Ehi. 1 Chr. 8.1, Aharah.
ˣ Gen. 46. 21, Muppim, and Huppim, 1 Chr. 8. 3, Adder.
ʸ Gen. 46. 23.
⁴ Or, Hushim.
ᵃ Gen. 46.17. 1 Chr.7.30.
ᵇ Gen. 46. 24. 1 Chr. 7.13.
ᶜ 1 Chr. 7. 13, Shallum.
ᵈ ch. 1. 46.
ᵉ Thus each man's portion would be fifteen acres. Josh.11.23. Josh. 14. 1.
ᶠ ch. 33. 54.
ᵇ multiply his inheritance.
⁶ diminish his inheritance.
ᵍ ch. 33. 54. ch. 34. 13. Josh. 11.23. Josh. 14.2.
ʰ Gen. 46.11. Ex. 6. 16. 1 Chr. 6. 1, 16.
ⁱ Ex. 2. 1, 2. Ex. 6. 20.
ʲ Lev. 10.1,2. ch. 3. 4. 1 Chr. 24.2.
ᵏ ch. 3. 39.
ˡ ch. 1. 49.
ᵐ ch. 18. 20. Deu. 10. 9. Jos. 13. 14.
ⁿ ch. 1. 1. Deu. 2. 14.
ᵒ ch. 14. 29. Psalm 90. 3-8.
Ro. 11. 22.
¹ Cor.10.5.

families: of Jimna, the family of the Jimnites: of Jesui, the family of the Jesuites: of Beriah, the family of the Berites.

45 Of the sons of Beriah: of Heber, the family of the Heberites: of Malchiel, the family of the Malchielites.

46 And the name of the daughter of Asher *was* Sarah.

47 These *are* the families of the sons of Asher according to those that were numbered of them, *who were* fifty and three thousand and four hundred.

48 ¶ *Of* ᵇ the sons of Naphtali after their families: of Jahzeel, the family of the Jahzeelites: of Guni, the family of the Gunites:

49 Of Jezer, the family of the Jezerites: of ᶜ Shillem, the family of the Shillemites.

50 These *are* the families of Naphtali according to their families: and they that were numbered of them *were* forty and five thousand and four hundred.

51 These ᵈ *were* the numbered of the children of Israel, six hundred thousand and a thousand seven hundred and thirty.

52 ¶ And the LORD spake unto Moses, saying,

53 Unto ᵉ these the land shall be divided for an inheritance, according to the number of names.

54 To ᶠ many thou shalt ⁵ give the more inheritance, and to few thou shalt ⁶ give the less inheritance: to every one shall his inheritance be given according to those that were numbered of him.

55 Notwithstanding the land shall be divided ᵍ by lot: according to the names of the tribes of their fathers they shall inherit.

56 According to the lot shall the possession thereof be divided between many and few.

57 ¶ And ʰ these *are* they that were numbered of the Levites after their families: of Gershon, the family of the Gershonites: of Kohath, the family of the Kohathites: of Merari, the family of the Merarites.

58 These *are* the families of the Levites: the family of the Libnites, the family of the Hebronites, the family of the Mahlites, the family of the Mushites, the family of the Korathites And Kohath begat Amram.

59 And the name of Amram's wife ⁱ *was* Jochebed, the daughter of Levi, whom *her* mother bare to Levi in Egypt: and she bare unto Amram Aaron and Moses, and Miriam their sister.

60 And unto Aaron was born Nadab and Abihu, Eleazar and Ithamar.

61 And ʲ Nadab and Abihu died, when they offered strange fire before the LORD.

62 And ᵏ those that were numbered of them were twenty and three thousand, all males from a month old and upward: ˡ for they were not numbered among the children of Israel, because there was ᵐ no inheritance given them among the children of Israel.

63 ¶ These *are* they that were numbered by Moses and Eleazar the priest, who numbered the children of Israel in the plains of Moab by Jordan near Jericho.

64 But ⁿ among these there was not a man of them whom Moses and Aaron the priest numbered, when they numbered the children of Israel in the wilderness of Sinai:

65 For the LORD had said of them, They shall ᵒ surely die in the wilderness. And

East." **18. Edom shall be a possession**—This prophecy was accomplished by David. (2 Sam. 8, 14.) Seir—seen in the south, and poetically used for Edom. The double conquest of Moab and Edom is alluded to. (Ps. 60, 8; 108. 9.) **19. He that shall have dominion**—David, and particularly Christ. **that remaineth of the city**—those who flee from the field to fortified places. (Ps. 60, 9.) **20. Amalek... perish for ever**—Their territory was seen at the remote extremity of the desert. (See on Ex. 17, 14; also 1 Sam. 15.) **21. Kenite.. nest in a rock**—Though securely established among the clefts in the high rocks of Engeddi towards the west, they should be gradually reduced by a succession of enemies, till the Assyrian invader carried them into captivity. (Judg. 1. 16; 4. 11, 16, 17; also 2 Ki. 15. 29; 17. 6.) **23. Who shall live**—few shall escape the desolation that shall send a Nebuchadnezzar to scourge all those regions. **24. Chittim**—the countries lying on the Mediterranean, particularly Greece and Italy. (Dan. 11. 29, 30.) The Assyrians were themselves to be overthrown—first, by the Greeks, under Alexander the Great and his successors; secondly, by the Romans. **Eber**—the posterity of the Hebrews. (Ge. 10. 24.) **he also shall perish**—*i.e.*, the conqueror of Asher and Eber, viz., the Greek and Roman empire. **25. went to his place**—Mesopotamia, to which, however, he did not return. (See on ch. 31. 8.)

CHAPTER XXV.

Ver. 1-18. THE ISRAELITES' WHOREDOM AND IDOLATRY WITH MOAB. **1. Israel abode in Shittim**—a verdant meadow, so called from a grove of acacia trees which lined the eastern side of the Jordan. (See ch. 33. 49.) **3. Israel joined himself unto Baal-Peor**—Baal was a general name for "lord," and Peor for a "mount" in Moab. The real name of the idol was Chemosh, and his rites of worship were celebrated by the grossest obscenity. In participating in this festival, then, the Israelites committed the double offence of idolatry and licentiousness. **4. Take all the heads of the people and hang them up**—Israelite criminals, who were capitally punished, were first stoned or slain, and *then* gibbeted. The persons ordered here for execution were the principal delinquents in the Baal-peor outrage—the subordinate officers, rulers of tens or hundreds. **before the Lord**—For vindicating the honour of the true God. **against the sun**—*i.e.*, as a mark of public ignominy; but they were to be removed towards sunset. (Deu. 21. 23.) **5. Judges of Israel**—the 70 elders, who were commanded not only to superintend the execution within their respective jurisdictions, but to inflict the punishment with their own hands. (See on 1 Sam. 15. 33.) **6, 7. Behold, one of the children of Israel brought**—This flagitious act most probably occurred about the time when the order was given, and before its execution. **weeping before the door**—some of the rulers and well-disposed persons were deploring the dreadful wickedness of the people, and supplicating the mercy of God to avert impending judgments. **the plague**—some sudden and wide-spread mortality. **9. Twenty and four thousand**—Only 23,000 perished (1 Co. 10. 8.) from pestilence. Moses includes those who died by the execution of the judges. **10-13. Phinehas... hath turned away my wrath**—This assurance was a signal mark of honour, that the stain of blood, instead of defiling, confirmed him in office, and that his posterity should continue as long as the national existence of Israel. **14. Zimri, a prince among the Simeonites**—The slaughter of a man of such high rank is mentioned as a proof of the undaunted zeal of Phinehas, for there might be numerous avengers of his blood. **17. Vex the Midianites**—They seem to have been the most guilty parties. (cf. ch. 22. 4; 31. 8.) **18. They vex you with their wiles**—Instead of open war, they plot insidious ways of accomplishing your ruin by idolatry and corruption. **their sister**—their countrywoman.

CHAPTER XXVI.

Ver. 1-51. ISRAEL NUMBERED. **1. After the plague**—That terrible visitation had swept away the remnant of the old generation, to whom God sware in His wrath that they should not enter Canaan (Ps. 95. 11.) **2. take the sum of the congregation**—The design of this new census, after a lapse of thirty-eight years, was primarily to establish the vast multiplication of the posterity of Abraham in spite of the severe judgments inflicted upon them; secondarily, it was to preserve the distinction of families, and to make arrangements preparatory to an entrance into the promised land, for the distribution of the country according to the relative population of the tribes. **7. these are the families**—the principal households, which were subdivided into numerous smaller families. Reuben had suffered great diminution by Korah's conspiracy and other outbreaks. **10. together with Korah**—rather, the things of Korah. (See on ch. 16. 32-35; cf. Ps. 106. 17.) **11. Notwithstanding the children of Korah died not**—Either they were not parties to their father's crime, or they withdrew from it by timely repentance. His descendants became famous in the time of David, and are often mentioned in the Psalms, also 1 Chron. 6. 22. 38. **12. the sons of Simeon**—It is supposed that this tribe had been pre-eminent in the guilt of Baal-peor, and had consequently been greatly reduced in numbers.

Tribes.	Chap. i.	Chapter xxvi.	Incr.	Decr.
Reuben,....	46,500	43,730	—	2,770
Simeon, ...	59,300	22,200	—	37,100
Gad, ...	45,650	40,500	—	5,150
Judah,......	74,600	76,500	1,900	—
Issachar,...	59,400	64,300	9,900	—
Zebulun, ...	57,400	60,500	3,100	—
Ephraim,...	40,500	32,500	—	8,000
Manasseh, ..	32,200	52,700	20,500	—
Benjamin,..	35,400	45,600	10,200	—
Dan, ...	62,700	64,400	1,700	—
Asher,......	41,500	53,400	11,900	—
Naphthali,..	53,400	45,400	—	8,000
	603,550	601,730	59,200	61,020
		Total decrease,...		1,820

Thus the justice and holiness, as well as truth and faithfulness of God, were strikingly displayed; His justice and holiness in the sweeping judgments that reduced the ranks of some tribes; while His truth and faithfulness were manifested in the extraordinary increase of others, so that the posterity of Israel continued a numerous people. **53. the land**

CHAPTER XXVII.

1 The daughters of Zelophehad sue for an inheritance. 6 The law of inheritances. 12 Moses, being told of his death, sueth for a successor: 18 Joshua appointed to succeed him.

THEN came the daughters of ᵃ Zelophehad, the son of Hepher, the son of Gilead, the son of Machir, the son of Manasseh, of the families of Manasseh the son of Joseph: and these are the names of his daughters; Mahlah, Noah, and Hoglah, and Milcah, and Tirzah.

2 And they stood before Moses, and before Eleazar the priest, and before the princes and all the congregation, by the door of the tabernacle of the congregation, saying,

3 Our father ᵇ died in the wilderness, and he was not in the company of them that gathered themselves together against the LORD ᶜ in the company of Korah; but ᵈ died in his own sin, and had no sons.

4 Why should the name of our father be ¹ done away from among his family, because he hath no son? Give unto us *therefore* a possession among the brethren of our father.

5 And Moses ᵉ brought their cause before the LORD.

6 ¶ And the LORD spake unto Moses, saying,

7 The daughters of Zelophehad speak right: thou ᶠ shalt surely give them a possession of an inheritance among their father's brethren; and thou shalt cause the inheritance of their father to pass unto them.

8 And thou shalt speak unto the children of Israel, saying, If a man die, and have no son, then ye shall cause his inheritance to pass unto his daughter.

9 And if he have no daughter, then ye shall give his inheritance unto his brethren.

10 And if he have no brethren, then ye shall give his inheritance unto his father's brethren.

11 And if his father have no brethren, then ye shall give his inheritance unto his kinsman that is next to him of his family, and he shall possess it: and it shall be unto the children of Israel ᵍ a statute of judgment; as the LORD commanded Moses.

12 ¶ And the LORD said unto Moses, ʰ Get thee up into this mount Abarim, and see the land which I have given unto the children of Israel.

13 And when thou hast seen it, thou also shalt ⁱ be gathered unto thy people, as Aaron thy brother was gathered.

14 For ye ʲ rebelled against my commandment in the desert of Zin, in the strife of the congregation, to sanctify me at the water before their eyes: that is the ᵏ water of Meribah in Kadesh in the wilderness of Zin.

15 ¶ And Moses spake unto the LORD, saying,

16 Let the LORD, the ˡ God of the spirits of all flesh, set a man over the congregation,

17 Which ᵐ may go out before them, and which may go in before them, and which may lead them out, and which may bring them in; that the congregation of the LORD be not ⁿ as sheep which have no shepherd.

18 ¶ And the LORD said unto Moses, Take thee Joshua the son of Nun, a man ᵒ in whom is the spirit, and lay thine hand upon him;

19 And set him before Eleazar the priest, and before all the congregation; and ᵖ give him a charge in their sight.

20 And ᵍ thou shalt put some of thine honour upon him, that all the congregation of the children of Israel ʳ may be obedient.

21 And ˢ he shall stand before Eleazar the priest, who shall ask *counsel* for him ᵗ after the judgment of Urim before the LORD: at his ᵘ word shall they go out, and at his word shall they come in, both he, and all the children of Israel with him, even all the congregation.

22 And Moses did as the LORD commanded him: and he took Joshua, and set him before Eleazar the priest, and before all the congregation:

23 And he laid his hands upon him, ᵛ and gave him a charge; as the LORD commanded by the hand of Moses.

CHAPTER XXVIII.

1 Offerings to be observed. 3 The continual burnt offering. 9 The sabbath offering. 11 at the new moons, 16 at the passover, 26 of first fruits.

AND the LORD spake unto Moses, saying,

2 Command the children of Israel, and say unto them, My offering, and ᵃ my bread for my sacrifices made by fire, for ¹ a sweet savour unto me, shall ye observe to offer unto me in their due season.

3 And thou shalt say unto them, ᵇ This is the offering made by fire which ye shall offer unto the LORD; two lambs of the first year without spot, ² day by day, for a continual burnt offering.

4 The one lamb shalt thou offer in the morning, and the other lamb shalt thou offer ³ at even;

5 And ᶜ a tenth part of an ephah of flour for a ᵈ meat offering, mingled with the fourth part of an ᵉ hin of beaten oil.

6 It is a continual burnt offering, which was ordained in mount Sinai for a sweet savour, a sacrifice made by fire unto the LORD.

7 And the drink offering thereof shall be the fourth part of an hin for the one lamb: in ᶠ the holy place shalt thou cause the strong wine to be poured unto the LORD for a drink offering.

8 And the other lamb shalt thou offer at even: as the meat offering of the morning, and as the drink offering thereof, thou shalt offer it, a sacrifice made by fire, of a sweet savour unto the LORD.

9 ¶ And on the sabbath day two lambs of the first year without spot, and two tenth deals of flour for a meat offering, mingled with oil, and the drink offering thereof.

10 This is ᵍ the burnt offering of every sabbath, beside the continual burnt offering, and his drink offering.

11 ¶ And ʰ in the beginnings of your months ye shall offer a burnt offering unto the LORD; two young bullocks, and one ram, seven lambs of the first year without spot;

12 And ᶦ three tenth deals of flour for a meat offering, mingled with oil, for one bullock; and two tenth deals of flour for a meat offering, mingled with oil, for one ram;

13 And a several tenth deal of flour mingled with oil for a meat offering unto

shall be divided according to the number of names—The portion of each tribe was to be greater or less, according to its populousness. **54. to many thou shalt give the more**—*i.e.*, to the more numerous tribes a larger allotment shall be granted, according to those that were numbered—*i.e.*, the number of persons twenty years old at the time of the census being made, without taking into account either the increase of those who might have attained that age, when the land should be actually distributed, or the diminution from that amount, occasioned during the war of invasion. **55. the land shall be divided by lot**—The appeal to the lot did not place the matter beyond the control of God; for it is at His disposal, (Pro. 16. 33.) and He has fixed to all the bounds of their habitation. The manner in which the lot was taken has not been recorded. But it is evident that the lot was cast for determining the quarter of the country on which each tribe should be located—not the quantity of their possessions. In other words, when the lot had decided that a particular tribe was to be settled in the north or the south, the east or the west, the extent of territory was allocated according to the rule (v. 54.). **57. Families of the Levites**—The census of this tribe was taken separately and on a different principle from the rest. See Ex. 6. 16-19.) **62. Twenty and three thousand**—So that there was an increase of a thousand. (ch. 3, 39.) **males from a month old and upward**—(See on ch. 3. 15.) **64. Among these there was not a man ... numbered in the wilderness of Sinai**—The statement in this verse must not be considered absolute. For, besides Caleb and Joshua, there were alive at this time Eleazar and Ithamar, and in all probability a considerable number of Levites, who had no participation in the popular defections in the wilderness. The tribe of Levi, having neither sent a spy into Canaan, nor being included in the enumeration at Sinai, must be regarded as not coming within the range of the fatal sentence; and therefore would exhibit a spectacle not to be witnessed in the other tribes of many in their ranks above sixty years of age.

CHAPTER XXVII.

Ver. 1-11. THE DAUGHTERS OF ZELOPHEHAD SUE FOR AN INHERITANCE. **4. Give us a possession among the brethren of our father**—Those young women, perceiving that the males only in families had been registered in the census, and that in consequence of none in their household, their family, was omitted, made known their grievance to Moses, and the authorities conjoined with him in administering justice. The case was important; and as the peculiarity of daughters being the sole members of a family would be no unfrequent or uncommon occurrence, the law of inheritance, under Divine authority, was extended not only to meet all similar cases, but other cases also—such as when there were no children left by the proprietor, and no brothers to succeed him. A distribution of the promised land was about to be made; and it is interesting to know the legal provision made in these comparatively rare cases for preserving a patrimony from being alienated to another tribe. (See on ch. 36. 6, 7.) **3. Our father died ... not in the company of Korah**—This declaration might be necessary, because his death might have occurred about the time of that rebellion; and especially because, as the children of these conspirators were involved along with themselves in the awful punishment, their plea appeared the more proper and forcible that their father did not die for any cause that doomed his family to lose their lives or their inheritance. **died in his own sin**—*i.e.*, by the common law of mortality to which men, through sin, are subject.

12-17. MOSES, BEING TOLD OF HIS DEATH, SUETH FOR A SUCCESSOR. 12. Get thee up into this mount Abarim—Although the Israelites were now on the confines of the promised land, Moses was not privileged to cross the Jordan, but died on one of the Moabite range of mountains, to which the general name of Abarim was given. (ch. 33. 47.) The privation of this great honour was owing to the unhappy conduct he had manifested in the striking of the rock at Meribah; and while the pious leader submitted with meek acquiescence to the Divine decree, he evinced the spirit of genuine patriotism in his fervent prayers for the appointment of a worthy and competent successor. **16. God of the spirits of all flesh**—The request was most suitably made to God in this character, as the Author of all the intellectual gifts and moral graces with which men are endowed, and who can raise up qualified persons for the most arduous duties and the most difficult situations. **18-23. JOSHUA APPOINTED TO SUCCEED HIM. Take Joshua ... a man in whom is the spirit**—A strong testimony is here borne to the personality of the Divine Spirit—the imposition of hands was an ancient ceremony. (See on Ge. 48. 14; Le. 1. 4; 1 Ti. 4. 14.) **20. Put some of thine honour upon him**—In the whole history of Israel there arose no prophet or ruler in all respects like unto Moses, till the Messiah appeared, whose glory eclipsed all. But Joshua was honoured and qualified in an eminent degree, through the special service of the high priest, who asked counsel for him after the judgment of Urim before the Lord.

CHAPTER XXVIII.

Ver. 1-31. OFFERINGS TO BE OBSERVED. **2. command the children of Israel, and say unto them**—The repetition of several laws formerly enacted, which is made in this chapter, was seasonable and necessary, not only on account of their importance and the frequent neglect of them, but because a new generation had sprung up since their first institution, and because the Israelites were about to be settled in the land where those ordinances were to be observed. **My offering and my bread**—used generally for the appointed offerings, and the import of the prescription is to enforce regularity and care in their observance. **9, 10. This is the burnt-offering of every Sabbath**—There is no previous mention of a Sabbath burnt-offering, which was additional to the daily sacrifices. **11-15. In the beginnings of your months**—These were held as sacred festivals; and though not possessing the character of solemn feasts, they were distinguished by the blowing of trumpets over the sacrifices, (ch. 10. 10,) by the suspension of all labour, except the domestic occupations of women, (Amos, 8. 5,) by the celebration of public worship, (2 Ki. 4. 23,) and by social or family feasts. (1 Sam. 20. 5.) These observances are not prescribed in the law, though they obtained in the practice of

one lamb, *for a burnt offering of a sweet savour, a sacrifice made by fire unto the* LORD.

14 And their drink offerings shall be half an hin of wine unto a bullock, and the third part of an hin unto a ram, and a fourth part of an hin unto a lamb: this *is* the burnt offering of every month throughout the months of the year.

15 And one kid of the goats for a sin offering unto the LORD shall be offered, beside the continual burnt offering, and his drink offering.

16 ¶ And *in* the fourteenth day of the first month *is* the passover of the LORD.

17 And *in* the fifteenth day of this month *is* the feast: seven days shall unleavened bread be eaten.

18 In the first day *shall be* an holy convocation; ye shall do no manner of servile work *therein:*

19 But ye shall offer a sacrifice made by fire *for* a burnt offering unto the LORD; two young bullocks, and one ram, and seven lambs of the first year: they shall be unto you without blemish:

20 And their meat offering *shall be of* flour mingled with oil: three tenth deals shall ye offer for a bullock, and two tenth deals for a ram;

21 A several tenth deal shalt thou offer for every lamb, throughout the seven lambs:

22 And one goat *for* a sin offering, to make an atonement for you.

23 Ye shall offer these beside the burnt offering in the morning, which *is* for a continual burnt offering.

24 After this manner ye shall offer daily, throughout the seven days, the meat of the sacrifice made by fire, of a sweet savour unto the LORD: it shall be offered beside the continual burnt offering, and his drink offering.

25 And on the seventh day ye shall have an holy convocation; ye shall do no servile work.

26 ¶ Also in the day of the first-fruits, when ye bring a new meat offering unto the LORD, after your weeks *be out,* ye shall have an holy convocation; ye shall do no servile work:

27 But ye shall offer the burnt offering for a sweet savour unto the LORD; two young bullocks, one ram, seven lambs of the first year;

28 And their meat offering of flour mingled with oil, three tenth deals unto one bullock, two tenth deals unto one ram,

29 A several tenth deal unto one lamb, throughout the seven lambs;

30 And one kid of the goats, to make an atonement for you.

31 Ye shall offer *them* beside the continual burnt offering, and his meat offering, (they shall be unto you without blemish,) and their drink offerings.

CHAPTER XXIX.

1 *The offering at the feast of trumpets.* 7 *at the day of afflicting their souls.* 13 *at the feast of tabernacles.*

AND in the seventh month, on the first day of the month, ye shall have an holy convocation; ye shall do no servile work; it is a day of blowing the trumpets unto you.

2 And ye shall offer a burnt offering for a sweet savour unto the LORD; one young bullock, one ram, *and* seven lambs of the first year, without blemish:

3 And their meat offering *shall be of* flour mingled with oil, three tenth deals for a bullock, and two tenth deals for a ram,

4 And one tenth deal for one lamb, throughout the seven lambs;

5 And one kid of the goats *for* a sin offering, to make an atonement for you:

6 Beside the burnt offering of the month, and his meat offering, and the daily burnt offering, and his meat offering, and their drink offerings, according unto their manner, for a sweet savour, a sacrifice made by fire unto the LORD.

7 ¶ And ye shall have on the tenth *day* of this seventh month an holy convocation; and ye shall afflict your souls: ye shall not do any work *therein:*

8 But ye shall offer a burnt offering unto the LORD *for* a sweet savour; one young bullock, one ram, *and* seven lambs of the first year; they shall be unto you without blemish:

9 And their meat offering *shall be of* flour mingled with oil, three tenth deals to a bullock, *and* two tenth deals to one ram,

10 A several tenth deal for one lamb, throughout the seven lambs;

11 One kid of the goats *for* a sin offering, beside the sin offering of atonement, and the continual burnt offering, and the meat offering of it, and their drink offerings.

12 ¶ And on the fifteenth day of the seventh month ye shall have an holy convocation; ye shall do no servile work, and ye shall keep a feast unto the LORD seven days:

13 And ye shall offer a burnt offering, a sacrifice made by fire, of a sweet savour unto the LORD; thirteen young bullocks, two rams, *and* fourteen lambs of the first year; they shall be without blemish:

14 And their meat offering *shall be of* flour mingled with oil, three tenth deals unto every bullock of the thirteen bullocks, two tenth deals to each ram of the two rams,

15 And a several tenth deal to each lamb of the fourteen lambs;

16 And one kid of the goats *for* a sin offering, beside the continual burnt offering, his meat offering, and his drink offering.

17 ¶ And on the second day *ye shall offer* twelve young bullocks, two rams, fourteen lambs of the first year, without spot:

18 And their meat offering, and their drink offerings, for the bullocks, for the rams, and for the lambs, *shall be* according to their number, after the manner:

19 And one kid of the goats *for* a sin offering; beside the continual burnt offering, and the meat offering thereof, and their drink offerings.

20 ¶ And on the third day eleven bullocks, two rams, fourteen lambs of the first year, without blemish:

21 And their meat offering and their drink offerings for the bullocks, for the rams, and for the lambs, *shall be* according to their number, after the manner:

22 And one goat *for* a sin offering; beside the continual burnt offering, and his meat offering, and his drink offering.

23 ¶ And on the fourth day ten bullocks, two rams, *and* fourteen lambs of the first year, without blemish:

24 Their meat offering and their drink

a later time. The beginning of the month was known, not by astronomical calculations, but, according to Jewish writers, by the testimony of messengers appointed to watch the first visible appearance of the new moon, and then the fact was announced through the whole country by signal-fires kindled on the mountain tops. The new moon festivals having been common amongst the heathen, it is probable that an important design of their institution in Israel was to give the minds of that people a better direction; and assuming this to have been one of the objects contemplated, it will account "for one of the kids being offered unto the Lord" (v. 15,) not unto the moon, as the Egyptians and Syrians did. The Sabbath and the new moon are frequently mentioned together. 16-25. In the fourteenth day of the first month is the passover—The law for that great annual festival is given (Le. 23. 5,) but some details are here introduced, as certain specified offerings are prescribed to be made on each of the seven days of unleavened bread. 26, 27. In the day of the first-fruits... offer the burnt-offering—A new sacrifice is here ordered for the celebration of this festival, in addition to the other offering, which was to accompany the first-fruits. (Le. 23. 18.)

CHAPTER XXIX.

Ver. 1-40. THE OFFERING AT THE FEAST OF TRUMPETS. 1. On the seventh month—of the ecclesiastical year, but the first month of the civil year, corresponding to our September. It was, in fact, the New Year's Day, which had been celebrated among the Hebrew and other contemporary nations with great festivity and joy, and ushered in by a flourish of trumpets. This ordinance was designed to give a religious character to the occasion by associating it with some solemn observances. (cf. Ex. 12. 2; Le. 23, 24.) it is a blowing of the trumpets unto you—This made it a solemn preparation for the sacred feasts—a greater number of which were held during this month than at any other season of the year. Although the institution of this feast was described before, there is more particularity here as to what the burnt-offering should consist of, and, in addition to it, a sin-offering is prescribed. The special offerings, appointed for certain days, were not to interfere with the offerings usually requisite on these days, for in v. 6 it is said that the daily offerings, as well as those for the first day of the month, were to take place in their ordinary course. 7-11. Ye shall have on the tenth day of the seventh month—This was the great day of atonement. Its institution, together with the observance to which that day was devoted, was described, (Le. 16, 29, 30,). But additional offerings seem to be noticed, viz., the large animal sacrifice for a general expiation, which was a sweet savour unto the Lord, and the sin-offering to atone for the sins that mingled with that day's services. The prescriptions in this passage appear supplementary to the former statement in Leviticus. 12-34. On the fifteenth day—was to be held the feast of booths or tabernacles. (See on Le. 23, 34, 35.) The feast was to last seven days, the first and last of which were to be kept as sabbaths, and a particular offering was prescribed for each day, the details of which are given with a minuteness suited to the infant state of the Church. Two things are deserving of notice —first, that this feast was distinguished by a greater amount and variety of sacrifices than any other—partly because, occurring at the end of the year, it might be intended to supply any past deficiencies—partly because, being immediately after the in-gathering of the fruits, it ought to be a liberal acknowledgment—and partly, perhaps, because God consulted the weakness of mankind, who naturally grow weary both of the charge and labour of such services when they are long continued, and made them every day less toilsome and expensive. [PATRICK.] Secondly, it will be remarked, that the sacrifices varied in a progressive ratio of decrease every day, after the manner—according to the ritual order appointed by Divine authority—that for meat-offerings (v. 3-10.), and drink-offerings, (See on ch. 28. 7, 14.) 35-40. on the eighth day—The feast of tabernacles was brought to a close on the eighth day, which was the great day. (Jo. 7. 37.) Besides the common routine sacrifices, there were special offerings appointed for that day, though these were fewer than on any of the preceding days; and there were also, as was natural on that occasion, when vast multitudes were convened for a solemn religious purpose, many spontaneous gifts and services, so that there was full scope for the exercise of a devout spirit in the people, both by their obedience to the statutory offerings, and by the presentation of those which were made by free will or in consequence of vows. 39. These things ye shall do unto the Lord in your set feasts—From the statements made in this and the preceding chapter, it appears that the yearly offerings made to the altar at the public expense, without taking into account a vast number of voluntary vow and tres-pass-offerings, were calculated at the following amount:—Goats, 15; kids, 21; rams, 72; bullocks, 132; lambs, 1,101; sum total of animals sacrificed at public cost, 1,241. This, of course, is exclusive of the prodigious addition of lambs slain at the passover, which in later times, according to Josephus, amounted in a single year to the immense number of 255,600.

CHAPTER XXX.

Ver. 1-16. VOWS ARE NOT TO BE BROKEN. 1. This is the thing which the Lord hath commanded—The subject of this chapter relates to vowing, which seems to have been an ancient usage, allowed by the law to remain; and by which some people declared their intention of offering some gift on the altar, of abstaining from particular articles of meat, or drink, of observing a private fast, or doing something to the honour, or in the service of God, over and above what was authoritatively required. In v. 39 of the preceding chapter, mention was made of "vows and free-will offerings," and it is probable, from the explanatory nature of the rules laid down in this chapter, that these were given for the removal of doubts and difficulties which conscientious persons had felt about their obligation to perform their vows in certain circumstances that had arisen. 2. If a man vow a vow—A mere secret purpose of the mind was not enough to constitute a vow; it had to be actually expressed in words; and though a purely voluntary act, yet when once the vow was made, the performance of it, like that of every other promise, became

offerings for the bullocks, for the rams, and for the lambs, *shall be* according to their number, after the manner;

25 And one kid of the goats *for* a sin offering, beside the continual burnt offering, his meat offering, and his drink offering.

26 ¶ And on the fifth day nine bullocks, two rams, *and* fourteen lambs of the first year, *m* without spot;

27 And their meat offering and their drink offerings for the bullocks, for the rams, and for the lambs, *shall be* according to their number, after the manner;

28 And one goat *for* a sin offering, beside the continual burnt offering, and his meat offering, and his drink offering.

29 ¶ And on the sixth day eight bullocks, two rams, *and* fourteen lambs of the first year, without blemish;

30 And their meat offering and their drink offerings for the bullocks, for the rams, and for the lambs, *shall be* according to their number, after the manner;

31 And one goat *for* a sin offering, beside the continual burnt offering, his meat offering, and his drink offering.

32 ¶ And on the seventh day seven bullocks, two rams, *and* fourteen lambs of the first year, without blemish:

33 And their meat offering and their drink offerings for the bullocks, for the rams, and for the lambs, *shall be* according to their number, after the manner;

34 And one goat *for* a sin offering, beside the continual burnt offering, his meat offering, and his drink offering.

35 ¶ On the eighth day ye shall have a solemn *n* assembly; ye shall do no servile work *therein*:

36 But ye shall offer a burnt offering, a sacrifice made by fire, of a sweet savour unto the LORD: one bullock, one ram, seven lambs of the first year, without blemish:

37 Their meat offering and their drink offerings for the bullock, for the ram, and for the lambs, *shall be* according to their number, after the manner;

38 And one goat *for* a sin offering, beside the continual burnt offering, and his meat offering, and his drink offering.

39 These *things* ye shall ²do unto the LORD in your *º* set feasts, beside your *ᵖ* vows, and your free-will offerings, for your burnt offerings, and for your meat offerings, and for your drink offerings, and for your peace offerings.

40 And Moses told the children of Israel according to all that the LORD commanded Moses.

CHAPTER XXX.

1 *Vows are not to be broken.* 3 *Of a maid's vow;* 9 *Of a widow's, or of her that is divorced.*

AND Moses spake unto *ª* the heads of the tribes concerning the children of Israel, saying, This *is* the thing which the LORD hath commanded.

2 If *ᵇ* a man vow a vow unto the LORD, or swear *ᶜ* an oath to bind his soul with a bond; he shall not ¹ break his word, he shall *ᵈ* do according to all that proceedeth out of his mouth.

3 If a woman also vow a vow unto the LORD, and bind *herself* by a bond, *being* in her father's house in her youth;

4 And her father hear her vow, and her bond wherewith she hath bounden her soul,

and her father shall hold his peace at her; then all her vows shall stand, and every bond wherewith she hath bound her soul shall stand.

5 But if her father disallow her in the day that he heareth; not any of her vows, or of her bonds wherewith she hath bound her soul, shall stand: and the LORD shall forgive her, because her father disallowed her.

6 And if she had at all an husband when ² she vowed, or uttered ought out of her lips, wherewith she bound her soul;

7 And her husband heard *it*, and held his peace at her in the day that he heard *it*; then her vows shall stand, and her bonds wherewith she bound her soul shall stand.

8 But if her husband *ᵉ* disallowed her on the day that he heard *it*; then he shall make her vow which she vowed, and that which she uttered with her lips, wherewith she bound her soul, of none effect: and the LORD shall forgive her.

9 But every vow of a widow, and of her that is *ᶠ* divorced, wherewith they have bound their souls, shall stand against her.

10 And if she vowed in her husband's house, or bound her soul by a bond with an oath;

11 And her husband heard *it*, and held his peace at her, *and* disallowed her not; then all her vows shall stand, and every bond wherewith she bound her soul shall stand.

12 But if her husband hath ³ utterly made them void on the day he heard *them*; then whatsoever proceeded out of her lips concerning her vows, or concerning the bond of her soul, shall not stand: her husband hath made them void; and the LORD shall forgive her.

13 Every vow, and every binding oath to afflict the soul, her husband may establish it, or her husband may make it void.

14 But if her husband altogether hold his peace at her from day to day; then he establisheth all her vows, or all her bonds, which *are* upon her: he confirmeth them, because he held his peace at her in the day that he heard *them*.

15 But if he shall any ways make them void after that he hath heard *them*; then he shall ⁴ bear her iniquity.

16 These *are* the statutes which the LORD commanded Moses, between a man and his wife, between the father and his daughter, *being yet* in her youth in her father's house.

CHAPTER XXXI.

1 *The Midianites spoiled, and Balaam slain.* 13 *Moses is wroth with the officers for saving the women alive.*

AND the LORD spake unto Moses, saying, 2 Avenge *ª* the children of Israel of the Midianites: afterward shalt thou *ᵇ* be gathered unto thy people.

3 And Moses spake unto the people, saying, Arm some of yourselves unto the war, and let them go against the Midianites, and *ᶜ* avenge the LORD of Midian.

4 ¹ Of every tribe a thousand, throughout all the tribes of Israel, shall ye send to the war.

5 So there were delivered out of the thousands of Israel, a thousand of *every* tribe, twelve thousand armed for war.

6 And Moses sent them to the war, a thousand of *every* tribe, them and Phinehas the son of Eleazar the priest, to the war, with

an indispensable duty—all the more that, referring to a sacred thing, it could not be neglected without the guilt of prevarication and unfaithfulness to God. shall not break—*lit.*, profane his word—render it vain and contemptible. (Ps. 55. 20; 89. 34.) But as it would frequently happen that parties would vow to do things, which were neither good in themselves nor in their power to perform, the law ordained that their natural superiors should have the right of judging as to the propriety of those vows, with discretionary power to sanction or interdict their fulfilment. Parents were to determine in the case of their children, and husbands in that of their wives;—being, however, allowed only a day for deliberation after the matter became known to them, and their judgment, if unfavourable, released the devotee from all obligation. 3. A woman in her father's house in her youth—Girls only are specified; but minors of the other sex, who resided under the paternal roof, were included, according to Jewish writers, who also consider the name "father" as comprehending all guardians of youth, and tell us that the age at which young people were deemed capable of vowing, was 13 for boys, and 12 for girls. The judgment of a father or guardian on the vow of any under his charge, might be given either by an expressed approval, or by silence, which was to be construed as approval. But in the case of a husband—who, after silence from day to day, should ultimately disapprove or hinder his wife's vow, the sin of non-performance was to be imputed to him and not to her. 9. Every vow of a widow—In the case of a married woman, who, in the event of a separation from her husband, or of his death, returned, as was not uncommon, to her father's house, a doubt might have been entertained whether she was not, as before, subject to paternal jurisdiction, and obliged to act with the paternal consent. The law ordained that the vow was binding, if it had been made in her husband's life-time, and he, on being made aware of it, had not interposed his veto: as, for instance, she might have vowed, when not a widow, that she would assign a proportion of her income to pious and charitable uses, of which she might repent, when actually a widow: but by this statute she was required to fulfil the obligation, provided her circumstances enabled her to redeem the pledge. The rules laid down must have been exceedingly useful for the prevention or cancelling of rash vows, as well as for giving a proper sanction to such as were legitimate in their nature, and made in a devout, reflecting spirit.

CHAPTER XXXI.

Ver. 1-54. THE MIDIANITES SPOILED AND BALAAM SLAIN. 1, 2. The Lord spake unto Moses, Avenge ... of the Midianites—a semi-nomade people, descended from Abraham and Keturah, occupying a tract of country east and south east of Moab, which lay on the eastern coast of the Dead Sea. They seem to have been the principal instigators of the infamous scheme of seduction, planned to entrap the Israelites into the double crime of idolatry and licentiousness, by which, it was hoped, the Lord would withdraw from that people the benefit of His protection and favour. Moreover, the Midianites had rendered themselves particularly obnoxious by entering into a hostile league with the Amorites. (Josh. 13. 21.) The Moabites were at this time spared in consideration of Lot, (Deu. 2. 9,) and because the measure of their iniquities was not yet full, God spoke of avenging "the children of Israel;" Moses spoke of avenging the Lord, as dishonour had been done to God, and an injury inflicted on His people. The interests were identical. God and His people have the same cause, the same friends and assailants. This, in fact, was a religious war, undertaken by the express command of God against idolaters, who had seduced the Israelites to practise their abominations. arm yourselves—This order was issued but a short time before the death of Moses. The announcement to him of that approaching event seems to have accelerated, rather than retarded, his warlike preparations. 5. There were delivered —*i. e.*, draughted, chosen, an equal amount from each tribe, to prevent the outbreak of mutual jealousy or strife. Considering the numerical force of the enemy, this was a small quota to furnish. But the design was to exercise their faith, and animate them to the approaching invasion of Canaan. 6. Moses sent .... Eleazar the priest —Although it is not expressly mentioned, it is highly probable that Joshua was the general who conducted this war. The presence of the priest, who was always with the army, (Deu. 20. 2,) was necessary to preside over the Levites, who accompanied the expedition, and to inflame the courage of the combatants by his sacred services and counsels. holy instruments—As neither the Ark nor the Urim and Thummim were carried to the battle-field till a later period in the history of Israel, the "holy instruments" must mean the "trumpets." (ch. 10. 9.) And this view is agreeable to the text, by simply changing "and" into "even," as the *Heb.* particle is frequently rendered. 7. they slew all the males—This was in accordance with a Divine order in all such cases. (Deu. 20. 13.) But the destruction appears to have been only partial—limited to those who were in the neighbourhood of the Hebrew camp, and who had been accomplices in the villanous plot of Baal-peor, while a large portion of the Midianites were absent on their pastoral wanderings, or had saved themselves by flight. (cf. Jud. 6, 1.) 8. The kings of Midian—so called, because each was possessed of absolute power within his own city or district—called also dukes or princes of Sihon, (Josh. 13. 21,) having been probably subject to that Amorite ruler, as it is not uncommon in the East to find a number of governors or pachas tributary to one great king. Zur–father of Cozbi. (ch. 25. 15.) Balaam also they slew with the sword—This unprincipled man, on his dismissal from Balak, set out for his home in Mesopotamia. (ch. 24. 25.) But, either diverging from his way to tamper with the Midianites, he remained among them, without proceeding further, to incite them against Israel, and to watch the effects of his wicked counsel; or, learning in his own country that the Israelites had fallen into the snare which he had laid, and which he doubted not would lead to their ruin, he had, under the impulse of insatiable greed, returned to demand his reward from the Midianites. He was an object of merited vengeance. In the immense slaughter of the Midianitish people—

the holy instruments, and *d* the trumpets to blow in his hand.

7 And they warred against the Midianites, as the LORD commanded Moses; and *e* they slew all the *f* males.

8 And they slew the kings of Midian, besides the rest of them that were slain; *namely*, *j* Evi, and Rekem, and Zur, and Hur, and Reba, five kings of Midian: *h* Balaam also the son of Beor they slew with the sword.

9 And the children of Israel took *all* the women of Midian captives, and their little ones, and took the spoil of all their cattle, and all their flocks, and all their goods.

10 And they burnt all their cities wherein they dwelt, and all their goodly castles, with fire.

11 And *i* they took all the spoil, and all the prey, *both* of men and of beasts.

12 And they brought the captives, and the prey, and the spoil, unto Moses, and Eleazar the priest, and unto the congregation of the children of Israel, unto the camp at the plains of Moab, which *are* by Jordan *near* Jericho.

13 ¶ And Moses, and Eleazar the priest, and all the princes of the congregation, went forth to meet them without the camp.

14 And Moses was wroth with the officers of the host, *with* the captains over thousands, and captains over hundreds, which came from the *a* battle.

15 And Moses said unto them, Have ye saved all *j* the women alive?

16 Behold, *k* these caused the children of Israel, through the *l* counsel of Balaam, to commit trespass against the LORD in the matter of Peor, and there was a plague among the congregation of the LORD.

17 Now therefore *m* kill every male among the little ones, and kill every woman that hath known man by lying with *3* him.

18 But all the women children, that have not known a man by lying with him, keep alive for yourselves.

19 And *n* do ye abide without the camp seven days: whosoever hath killed any person, and whosoever *o* hath touched any slain, purify *both* yourselves and your captives on the third day, and on the seventh day.

20 And purify all *your* raiment, and all *4* that is made of skins, and all work of goats' *hair*, and all things made of wood.

21 ¶ And Eleazar the priest said unto the men of war which went to the battle, This *is* the ordinance of the law which the LORD commanded Moses;

22 Only the gold, and the silver, the brass, the iron, the tin, and the lead,

23 Every thing that may abide the fire, ye shall make *it* go through the fire, and it shall be clean; nevertheless it shall be purified with *p* the water of separation: and all that abideth not the fire ye shall make go through the water.

24 And *q* ye shall wash your clothes on the seventh day, and ye shall be clean, and afterward ye shall come into the camp.

25 ¶ And the LORD spake unto Moses, saying,

26 Take the sum of the prey *5* that was taken, *both* of man and of beast, thou, and Eleazar the priest, and the chief fathers of the congregation;

27 And *r* divide the prey into two parts, between them that took the war upon

B. C. 1452.

CHAP. 31.
d ch. 10. 9.
e Deut. 20. 13.
Judg. 21. 11.
f Sa. 27. 9.
1 Kin. 11. 15, 16.
f Judg. 6. 1, 2, 33.
g Josh.13.21.
h Josh. 13. 22.
Ps. 9. 16.
Pro. 16. 5.
Pro. 26. 27.
Mat. 7. 22, 23.
1 Tim. 6. 9, 10.
2 Pet. 2. 14-22.
Jude 11.
Rev. 2. 14.
i Deu. 20.14.
2 host of war.
j Deu. 20.13.
1 Sa. 15. 3.
k ch. 25. 2.
l ch. 24. 14.
2 Peter 2. 15.
Rev. 2. 14.
m Judg. 21. 11.
3 a male.
n ch. 5. 2.
o ch. 19. 11.
4 instrument, or, vessel of skins.
p ch. 19. 9, 17.
q Lev. 11. 25.
ch. 19. 10. 22.
Ps. 51. 2.
Zech. 13. 1.
Eph. 5. 26.
Heb. 9. 9, 10.
Heb. 10.22.
1 John 1. 7.
5 of the captivity.
r Josh. 22. 8.
1 Sa. 30. 4.
s 2 Sam. 8. 11.
1 Chr. 26. 27.
Is. 18. 7.
Is. 23. 18.
t ch. 18. 26.
6 Or, goats.
u ch. 3. 7, 8, 25, 31, 36.
ch. 18. 3, 4.
v Pro. 3. 9.
Mat. 22.21.
Mark 12. 17.
Luke 20. 25.
w ch. 18. 8, 19.
7 hand.
x Ex. 23. 27.
Lev. 26. 7-9.
Ps. 72. 14.
Ps. 116.15.
1 Sam. 30.
8 found.
y Ex. 30. 12, 16.

them, who went out to battle, and between all the congregation:

28 And levy a *s* tribute unto the LORD of the men of war which went out to battle: one *t* soul of five hundred, *both* of the persons, and of the beeves, and of the asses, and of the sheep;

29 Take *it* of their half, and give *it* unto Eleazar the priest, *for* an heave offering of the LORD.

30 And of the children of Israel's half, thou shalt take one portion of fifty, of the persons, of the beeves, of the asses, and of the *6* flocks, of all manner of beasts, and give them unto the Levites, *u* which keep the charge of the tabernacle of the LORD.

31 And Moses and Eleazar the priest did as the LORD commanded Moses.

32 And the booty, *being* the rest of the prey which the men of war had caught, was six hundred thousand and seventy thousand and five thousand sheep,

33 And threescore and twelve thousand beeves,

34 And threescore and one thousand asses,

35 And thirty and two thousand persons in all, of women that had not known man by lying with him.

36 And the half, *which was* the portion of them that went out to war, was in number three hundred thousand and seven and thirty thousand and five hundred sheep:

37 And the LORD's *v* tribute of the sheep was six hundred and threescore and fifteen.

38 And the beeves *were* thirty and six thousand; of which the LORD's tribute *was* threescore and twelve.

39 And the asses *were* thirty thousand and five hundred; of which the LORD's tribute *was* threescore and one.

40 And the persons *were* sixteen thousand; of which the LORD's tribute *was* thirty and two persons.

41 And Moses gave the tribute, *which was* the LORD's heave offering, unto Eleazar the priest; *w* as the LORD commanded Moses.

42 And of the children of Israel's' half, which Moses divided from the men that warred,

43 (Now the half *that pertained unto* the congregation was three hundred thousand and thirty thousand *and* seven thousand and five hundred sheep,

44 And thirty and six thousand beeves,

45 And thirty thousand asses and five hundred,

46 And sixteen thousand persons;)

47 Even of the children of Israel's half, Moses took one portion of fifty, *both* of man and of beast, and gave them unto the Levites, which kept the charge of the tabernacle of the LORD; as the LORD commanded Moses.

48 ¶ And the officers which *were* over thousands of the host, the captains of thousands, and captains of hundreds, came near unto Moses:

49 And they said unto Moses, Thy servants have taken the sum of the men of war which *are* under our *7* charge, and there lacketh not one *z* man of us.

50 We have therefore brought an oblation for the LORD, what every man hath *8* gotten, of jewels of gold, chains, and bracelets, rings, earrings, and tablets, *y* to make an atonement for our souls before the LORD.

51 And Moses and Eleazar the priest took the gold of them, *even* all wrought jewels.

in the capture of their women, children, and property—and in the destruction of all their places of refuge,—the severity of a righteous God fell heavily on that base and corrupt race. But, more than all others, Balaam deserved, and got the just reward of his deeds. His conduct had been atrociously sinful, considering the knowledge he possessed, and the revelations he had received, of the will of God. For any one in his circumstances to attempt defeating the prophecies he had himself been the organ of uttering, and plotting to deprive the chosen people of the Divine favour and protection, was an act of desperate wickedness, which no language can adequately characterize. 13. went forth to meet them without the camp—partly as a token of respect and congratulation on their victory, partly to see how they had executed the Lord's commands, and partly to prevent the defilement of the camp by the entrance of warriors stained with blood. 14-18. Moses was wroth—The displeasure of the great leader, though it appears the ebullition of a fierce and sanguinary temper, arose in reality from a pious and enlightened regard to the best interests of Israel. No order had been given for the slaughter of the women, and in ancient war they were commonly reserved for slaves. By their antecedent conduct, however, the Midianitish women had for feited all claims to mild or merciful treatment; and the sacred character, the avowed object of the war, (v. 2, 3,) made their slaughter necessary without any special order. But why "kill every male among the little ones?" It was designed to be a war of extermination, such as God himself had ordered against the people of Canaan, whom the Midianites equalled in the enormity of their wickedness. 19-24. Abide without the camp seven days—Though the Israelites had taken the field in obedience to the command of God, they had become defiled by contact with the dead. A process of purification was to be undergone, as the law required, (Le. 15. 13; ch. 19. 9-12,) and this purifying ceremony was extended to dress, houses, tents, to every thing on which a dead body had lain, which had been touched by the blood-stained hands of the Israelitish warriors, or which had been the property of idolaters. This became a standing ordinance in all time coming. (Le. 6. 28; 11. 33; 15. 12.) 25-39. Take the sum of the prey—*i. e.*, of the captives and cattle, which, having been first slumped together according to ancient usage, (Ex. 15. 9; Judg. 5. 30,) were divided into two equal parts: the one to the people at large, who had sustained a common injury from the Midianites, and who were all liable to serve; and the other portion to the combatants, who, having encountered the labours and perils of war, justly received the largest share. From both parts, however, a certain deduction was taken for the sanctuary, as a thank-offering to God for preservation and for victory. The soldiers had greatly the advantage in the distribution; for a five-hundredth part only of their half went to the priest, while a fiftieth part of the congregation's half was given to the Levites. 32. the booty being the rest of the prey—Some of the captives having been killed, (v. 17,) and part of the cattle taken for the support of the army, the total amount of the booty remaining was in the following proportions:—Sheep, 675,000—half to soldiers, 337; deducted to God, 675; half to congregation, 337,500; deducted to the Levites, 6,750. Beeves, 72,000—half to soldiers, 36,000; deducted to God, 72; half to congregation, 36,000; deducted to the Levites, 720. Asses, 61,000—half to soldiers, 30,500; deducted to God, 61; half to congregation, 30,500; deducted to the Levites, 610. Persons, 32,000—half to soldiers, 16,000; deducted to God, 32; half to congregation, 16,000; deducted to the Levites, 320. 48-54. Officers said, There lacketh not one of us—A victory so signal, and the glory of which was untarnished by the loss of a single Israelitish soldier, was an astonishing miracle, and so clearly betokening the direct interposition of Heaven, might well awaken the liveliest feelings of grateful acknowledgment to God. Ps. 44. 2, 3. The oblation they brought for the Lord "was partly an atonement" or reparation for their error, (v. 14-16,) for it could not possess any expiatory virtue, and partly a tribute of gratitude for the stupendous service rendered them. It consisted of the "spoil," which, being the acquisition of individual valour, was not divided like the "prey," or live stock, each soldier retaining it in lieu of pay; it was offered by the "captains" alone, whose pious feelings were evinced by the dedication of the spoil which fell to their share. There were jewels to the amount of 16,750 shekels, equal to £87,869 16s. 5d. sterling.

CHAPTER XXXII.

Ver. 1-42. THE REUBENITES AND GADITES SUE FOR AN INHERITANCE.—The land of Jazer and the land of Gilead—A complete conquest had been made of the country east of the Jordan, comprising "the land of Jazer," which formed the southern district between the Arnon and Jabbok; "the land of Gilead," the middle region between the Jabbok and Jarmouk, or Hieromax, including Bashan, which lay on the north of that river. The whole of this region is now called the Belka. It has always been famous for its rich and extensive pastures, and it is still the favourite resort of the Bedouin shepherds, who frequently contend for securing to their immense flocks the benefit of its luxuriant vegetation. In the camp of ancient Israel, Reuben and Gad were pre-eminently pastoral; and as these two tribes, being placed under the same standard, had frequent opportunities of conversing and arranging about their common concerns, they united in preferring a request that the Transjordanic region, so well suited to the habits of a pastoral people, might be assigned to them. 6-19. shall your brethren go to war, and shall ye sit here—Their language was ambiguous—and Moses, suspicious that this proposal was an act of unbelief—a scheme of self-policy and indolence to escape the perils of warfare and live in ease and safety, addressed to them a reproachful and passionate remonstrance. Whether they had really meditated such a withdrawal from all share in the war of invasion, or the effect of their leader's expostulation, was to drive them from their original purpose, they now, in answer to his impressive appeal, declared in to be their sincere intention to co-operate with their brethren: but, if so, they ought to have been more explicit at first. 16. they came near—The narrative gives a picturesque description of this scene. The suppliants

52 And all the gold of the ⁹ offering that they offered up to the Lord, of the captains of thousands, and of the captains of hundreds, was sixteen thousand seven hundred and fifty shekels.

53 (For ᶻ the men of war had taken spoil, every man for himself.)

54 And Moses and Eleazar the priest took the gold of the captains of thousands and of hundreds, and brought it into the tabernacle of the congregation, for ᵃ a memorial for the children of Israel before the Lord.

CHAPTER XXXII.
The Reubenites and Gadites sue for their inheritance on the east side of Jordan.

NOW the children of Reuben and the children of Gad had a very great multitude of cattle: and when they saw the land ᵃ of Jazer, and the land of Gilead, that, behold, the place *was* a place for cattle;

2 The children of Gad and the children of Reuben came and spake unto Moses, and to Eleazar the priest, and unto the princes of the congregation, saying,

3 Ataroth, and Dibon, and Jazer, ᵇ and Nimrah, and Heshbon, and Elealeh, ᶜ and Shebam, and Nebo, and ᵈ Beon,

4 *Even* the country ᵉ which the Lord smote before the congregation of Israel, is a land for cattle, and thy servants have cattle:

5 Wherefore, said they, if we have found grace in thy sight, let this land be given unto thy servants for a possession, *and* bring us not over Jordan.

6 ¶ And Moses said unto the children of Gad and to the children of Reuben, Shall your brethren go to war, and shall ye sit here?

7 And wherefore ¹ discourage ye the heart of the children of Israel from going over into the land which the Lord hath given them?

8 Thus did your fathers, ᶠ when I sent them from Kadesh-barnea ᵍ to see the land.

9 For ʰ when they went up unto the valley of Eschol, and saw the land, they discouraged the heart of the children of Israel, that they should not go into the land which the Lord had given them.

10 And ⁱ the Lord's anger was kindled the same time, and he sware, saying,

11 Surely none of the men that came up out of Egypt, ʲ from twenty years old and upward, shall see the land which I sware unto Abraham, unto Isaac, and unto Jacob; because ᵏ they have not ² wholly followed me;

12 Save Caleb the son of Jephunneh the Kenezite, and Joshua the son of Nun: ˡ for they have wholly followed the Lord.

13 And the Lord's anger was kindled against Israel, and he made them ᵐ wander in the wilderness forty years, until ⁿ all the generation, that had done evil in the sight of the Lord, was consumed.

14 And, behold, ye are risen up in your fathers' stead, an increase of sinful men, to augment yet the ᵒ fierce anger of the Lord toward Israel.

15 For if ye ᵖ turn away from after him, he will yet again leave them in the wilderness; and ye shall destroy all this people.

16 ¶ And they came near unto him, and said, We will build sheep-folds here for our cattle, and cities for our little ones;

17 But ᵠ we ourselves will go ready armed before the children of Israel, until we have brought them unto their place: and our little ones shall dwell in the fenced cities because of the inhabitants of the land.

18 We ʳ will not return unto our houses, until the children of Israel have inherited every man his inheritance;

19 For we will not inherit with them on yonder side Jordan, or forward; ˢ because our inheritance is fallen to us ᵗ on this side Jordan eastward.

20 ¶ And ᵘ Moses said unto them, If ye will do this thing, if ye will go armed before the Lord to war,

21 And will go all of you armed over Jordan before the Lord, until he hath driven out his enemies from before him,

22 And ᵛ the land be subdued before the Lord; then afterward ʷ ye shall return, and be guiltless before the Lord, and before Israel; and ˣ this land shall be your possession before the Lord.

23 But if ye will not do so, behold, ye have sinned against the Lord: and be sure your ʸ sin will find you out.

24 Build ᶻ you cities for your little ones, and folds for your sheep; and do that which hath proceeded out of your mouth.

25 And the children of Gad and the children of Reuben spake unto Moses, saying, Thy servants will do as my lord commandeth.

26 Our ᵃ little ones, our wives, our flocks, and all our cattle, shall be there in the cities of Gilead;

27 But ᵇ thy servants will pass over, every man armed for war, before the Lord to battle, as my lord saith.

28 So concerning them Moses commanded Eleazar the priest, and Joshua the son of Nun, and the chief fathers of the tribes of the children of Israel:

29 And Moses said unto them, If the children of Gad and the children of Reuben will pass with you over Jordan, every man armed to battle, before the Lord, and the land shall be subdued before you; then ye shall give them the land of Gilead for a possession:

30 But if they will not pass over with you armed, they shall have possessions among you in the land of Canaan.

31 And the children of Gad and the children of Reuben answered, saying, As the Lord hath said unto thy servants, so will we do.

32 We will pass over armed before the Lord into the land of Canaan, that the possession of our inheritance on this side Jordan *may be* ours.

33 And ᶜ Moses gave unto them, *even* to the children of Gad, and to the children of Reuben, and unto half the tribe of Manasseh the son of Joseph, ᵈ the kingdom of Sihon king of the Amorites, and the kingdom of Og king of Bashan, the land, with the cities thereof in the coasts, *even* the cities of the country round about.

34 ¶ And the children of Gad built ᵉ Dibon, and Ataroth, and ᶠ Aroer,

35 And Atroth, Shophan, and ᵍ Jaazer, and Jogbehah,

36 And ʰ Beth-nimrah, and Beth-haran, fenced cities; and folds for sheep.

37 And the children of Reuben built Heshbon, and Elealeh, and Kirjathaim,

38 And ⁱ Nebo, and ʲ Baal-meon, (ᵏ their

had shrunk back, dreading from the undisguised emotions of their leader, that their request would be refused. But, perceiving, from the tenor of his discourse, that his objection was grounded only on the supposition that they would not cross the Jordan to assist their brethren, they became emboldened to approach him with assurances of their good-will. We will build... cities for our little ones—*i.e.*, rebuild, repair. It would have been impossible within two months to found new cities, or even to re-construct those which had been razed to the ground. Those of the Amorites were not absolutely demolished, and they probably consisted only of mud-built, or dry-stone walls. 17. because of the inhabitants of the land—There was good policy in leaving a sufficient force to protect the conquered region, lest the enemy should attempt reprisals; and as only 40,000 of the Reubenites and the Gadites, and a half of Manasseh, passed over the Jordan (Josh. 4. 13,) there was left for the security of the new possessions 70,580 men, besides women and children under 20 years (cf. ch. 26. 17.). We will go armed—*i.e.*, all of us in a collective body, or as many as may be deemed necessary, while the rest of our number shall remain at home to provide for the sustenance and secure the protection of our families and flocks (see on Josh. 4. 12, 13.). 20-33. if ye will do this thing —with sincerity and zeal. go before the Lord to war—The phrase was used in allusion to the order of march in which the tribes of Reuben and Gad immediately preceded the ark (see on ch. 12. 10-77), or to the passage over the Jordan, in which the ark stood in mid-channel, while all the tribes marched by in succession, (Josh. 3. 4,), of course including those of Reuben and Gad, so that, literally, they *passed over before the Lord* and before the rest of Israel (Josh. 4. 13.). Perhaps, however, the phrase is used merely in a general sense to denote their marching on an expedition, the purpose of which was blessed with the presence, and destined to promote the glory of God. The displeasure which Moses had felt on the first mention of their proposal had disappeared on the strength of their solemn assurances. But a lurking suspicion of their motives seems still to have been lingering in his mind—he continued to speak to them in an admonitory strain; and concluded by warning them that, in case of their failing to redeem their pledge, the judgments of an offended God would assuredly fall upon them. This emphatic caution against such an eventuality throws a strong doubt on the honesty of their first intentions; and yet, whether through the opposing attitude or the strong invectives of Moses, they had been brought to a better state of mind, their final reply showed that now all was right. 26-32. concerning them Moses commanded—The arrangement itself, as well as the express terms on which he assented to it, was announced by the leader to the public authorities—*i.e.*, The pastoral country the two tribes had desired was to be granted them on condition of their lending their aid to their brethren in the approaching invasion of Canaan. If they refused, or failed to perform their promise, those possessions should be forfeited, and themselves compelled to go across the Jordan, and fight for a settlement like the rest of their brethren. 33. half the tribe of Manasseh—It is no where explained in the record how they were incorporated with the two tribes, or what broke this great tribe into two parts, of which one was left to follow the fortunes of its brethren in the settled life of the western hills, while the other was allowed to wander as a nomadic tribe over the pasture lands or Gilead and Bashan. They are not mentioned as acompanying Reuben and Gad in their application to Moses, neither were they included in his first directions (ver. 25); but as they also were a people addicted to pastoral pursuits, and possessed as immense flocks as the other two, Moses invited the half of them to remain, in consequence, probably, of finding that this region was more than sufficient for the pastoral wants of the others, and gave them the preference, as some have conjectured, for their valorous conduct in the contests with the Amorites (cf. *v.* 39. with Josh. 17. 1.). 34-36. the children of Gad built—'see on *v.* 16,)—Dibon identified with Dhebon, now in ruins, an hour's distance from the Arnon, (Mojeb,) Ataroth crowns—there are several towns so-called in Scripture; but this one in the tribe of Gad has not been identified. Aroer, now Arair, standing on a precipice on the north bank of the Arnon. 35. Atroth, Shophan, or Zaphon—Josh. 13. 27.) Jaazer, near a famed fountain, Ain Hazier, the waters of which flow into Wady Schaib, about 15 miles from Hesbon. Beth-nimrah, now Nimrin; Heshbon, now Hesban; Elealeh, (the high), now Elaal; Kirjathaim (the double-city); Nebo, now Neba, near the mountain of that name; Baal-meon, now Myoun, in ruins, where was a temple of Baal Josh. 13. 17; Jer. 48. 23. ; Shibmah, or Shebam (*v.* 2.); near Heshbon, famous for vines (Is. 16, 9, 10; Jer. 4s. 32.), their names being changed—either because it was the general custom of conquerors to do so; or, rather, because from the prohibition to *mention the names of other gods* (Ex. 23. 13,), as Nebo and Baal were, it was expedient on the first settlement of the Israelites to obliterate all remembrance of those idols. (See on Josh. 13. 17-20.) 39. Gilead—now Jelúd. 41. Havoth-Jair—*i. e.*, tent-villages. Jair, who captured them, was a descendant of Manasseh on the mother's side (1 Chron. 2. 21, 22.). 42. Nobah—also a distinguished person connected with the eastern branch of this tribe.

CHAPTER XXXIII.

Ver. 1-15. TWO AND FORTY JOURNEYS OF THE ISRAELITES—FROM EGYPT TO SINAI. These are the journeys—This chapter may be said to form the winding-up of the history of the travels of the Israelites through the wilderness; for the three following chapters relate to matters connected with the occupation and division of the promised land. As several apparent discrepancies will be discovered on comparing the records here given of the journeyings from Sinai, with the detailed account of the events narrated in the book of Exodus, and the occasional notices of places that are found in that of Deuteronomy, it is probable that this itinerary comprises a list of the *most important* stations only in their journeys; those where they formed prolonged encampments, and whence they dispersed their flocks and herds to pasture on the adjacent plains till the surrounding herbage was

names being changed,) and Shibmah: and gave other names unto the cities which they builded.

39 And the children of *l* Machir the son of Manasseh went to Gilead, and took it, and dispossessed the Amorite which *was* in it.

40 And Moses gave *m* Gilead unto Machir the son of Manasseh; and he dwelt therein.

41 And *n* Jair the son of Manasseh went and took the small towns thereof, and called them *o* Havoth-jair.

42 And Nobah went and took Kenath, and the villages thereof, and called it Nobah, after *p* his own name.

CHAPTER XXXIII.

1 Two and forty journeys of the Israelites. 50 The Canaanites are to be destroyed.

THESE are the journeys of the children of Israel, which went forth out of the land of Egypt with their armies under the hand of Moses and Aaron.

2 And Moses wrote their goings out according to their journeys by the commandment of the LORD: and these *are* their journeys according to their goings out.

3 And they *a* departed from Rameses in the *b* first month, on the fifteenth day of the first month: on the morrow after the passover the children of Israel went out with *c* an high hand in the sight of all the Egyptians.

4 For the Egyptians buried all *their* firstborn, which the LORD had smitten among them: *d* upon their gods also the LORD executed judgments.

5 And *e* the children of Israel removed from Rameses, and pitched in Succoth.

6 And they departed from *f* Succoth, and pitched in Etham, which *is* in the edge of the wilderness.

7 And *g* they removed from Etham, and turned again unto Pi-hahiroth, which *is* before Baal-zephon: and they pitched before Migdol.

8 And they departed from before Pi-hahiroth, and *h* passed through the midst of the sea into the wilderness, and went three days' journey in the wilderness of Etham, and pitched in Marah.

9 And they removed from Marah, and came unto Elim: and in Elim *were* twelve fountains of water, and threescore and ten palm trees; and they pitched there.

10 And they removed from Elim, and encamped by the Red sea.

11 And they removed from the Red sea, and encamped in the *i* wilderness of Sin.

12 And they took their journey out of the wilderness of Sin, and encamped in Dophkah.

13 And they departed from Dophkah, and encamped in Alush.

14 And they removed from Alush, and encamped at *j* Rephidim, where was no water for the people to drink.

15 And they departed from Rephidim, and pitched in the *k* wilderness of Sinai.

16 And they removed from the desert of Sinai, and pitched *l* at *1* Kibroth-hattaavah.

17 And they departed from Kibroth-hattaavah, and encamped at Hazeroth.

18 And they departed from Hazeroth, and pitched in *m* Rithmah.

19 And they departed from Rithmah, and pitched at Rimmon-parez.

20 And they departed from Rimmon-parez, and pitched in *n* Libnah.

B. C. 1452.

CHAP. 32.
3 they called by names the names of the cities.
l Gen 50. 23.
m Deu. 3. 12.
Josh. 17. 1.
n Deu. 3. 14.
Josh. 13. 30.
1 Chr. 2. 21.
o Judg. 10. 4.
1 Kin. 4. 13.
p 2 Sam. 18. 18.
Ps. 49. 11.

CHAP. 33.
a Ex. 12. 37.
b Ex. 13. 4.
c Ex. 14. 8.
d Ex. 18. 11.
Is. 19. 1.
Rev. 12. 8.
e Ex. 12. 37.
f Ex. 13. 20.
g Exod. 14. 2, 9.
h Ex. 15. 22.
i Ex. 16. 1.
j Ex. 17. 1.
Ex. 19. 2.
k Ex. 16. 1.
l ch. 11. 34.
1 That is, the graves of lust.
m ch. 12. 16.
n Deu. 1. 1, Laban.
o Deu. 10. 6.
p Gen 36.27.
Deu. 10. 6.
1 Chr. 1. 42.
q Deu. 10. 7, Gudgodah.
r Deu. 2. 8.
1 Kin. 9. 26.
1 Kin. 22. 48.
s ch. 20. 1.
t ch. 21. 4.
u Deu. 10. 6.
Deut. 32. 50.
v ch. 21. 1.
2 Or, heaps of Abarim.
ch. 21. 11.
w ch. 32. 34.
x Jer. 48. 22.
Ezek. 6. 14.
y ch. 21. 20.
Deut. 32. 49.
z ch. 22. 1.
3 Mournful Shittim, or, the plains of Shittim.
ch. 25. 1.
Josh. 2. 1.
a Josh. 3. 17.
b Exod. 23. 24.
Josh. 11. 12.
Judg. 2. 2.

21 And they removed from Libnah, and pitched at Rissah.

22 And they journeyed from Rissah, and pitched in Kehelathah.

23 And they went from Kehelathah, and pitched in mount Shapher.

24 And they removed from mount Shapher, and encamped in Haradah.

25 And they removed from Haradah, and pitched in Makheloth.

26 And they removed from Makheloth, and encamped at Tahath.

27 And they departed from Tahath, and pitched at Tarah.

28 And they removed from Tarah, and pitched in Mithcah.

29 And they went from Mithcah, and pitched in Hashmonah.

30 And they departed from Hashmonah, and *o* encamped at Moseroth.

31 And they departed from Moseroth, and pitched in Bene-jaakan.

32 And they removed from *p* Bene-jaakan, and encamped at *q* Hor-hagidgad.

33 And they went from Hor-hagidgad, and pitched in Jotbathah.

34 And they removed from Jotbathah, and encamped at Ebronah.

35 And they departed from Ebronah, *r* and encamped at Ezion-gaber.

36 And they removed from Ezion-gaber, and pitched in the *s* wilderness of Zin, which *is* Kadesh.

37 And they removed from *t* Kadesh, and pitched in mount Hor, in the edge of the land of Edom.

38 And *u* Aaron the priest went up into mount Hor, at the commandment of the LORD, and died there, in the fortieth year after the children of Israel were come out of the land of Egypt, in the first *day* of the fifth month.

39 And Aaron *was* an hundred and twenty and three years old when he died in mount Hor.

40 And *v* king Arad the Canaanite, which dwelt in the south in the land of Canaan, heard of the coming of the children of Israel.

41 And they departed from mount Hor, and pitched in Zalmonah.

42 And they departed from Zalmonah, and pitched in Punon.

43 And they departed from Punon, and pitched in Oboth.

44 And they departed from Oboth, and pitched in *2* Ije-abarim, in the border of Moab.

45 And they departed from Iim, and pitched in *w* Dibon-gad.

46 And they removed from Dibon-gad, and encamped in *x* Almon-diblathaim.

47 And they removed from Almon-diblathaim, *y* and pitched in the mountains of Abarim, before Nebo.

48 And they departed from the mountains of Abarim, and *z* pitched in the plains of Moab, by Jordan *near* Jericho.

49 And they pitched by Jordan, from Beth-jesimoth even unto *3* Abel-shittim in the plains of Moab.

50 ¶ And the LORD spake unto Moses in the plains of Moab, by Jordan *near* Jericho, saying,

51 Speak unto the children of Israel, and say unto them, *a* When ye are passed over Jordan into the land of Canaan;

52 Then *b* ye shall drive out all the

exhausted. The catalogue extends from their departure out of Egypt to their arrival on the plains of Moab, went forth with their armies—*i. e.*, a vast multitude marshalled in separate companies, but regular order. 2. Moses wrote by the commandment of the Lord—The wisdom of this divine order is seen in the importance of the end to which it was subservient, viz.—partly to establish the truth of the history, partly to preserve a memorial of God's marvellous interpositions on behalf of Israel, and partly to confirm their faith in the prospect of the difficult enterprise on which they were entering, the invasion of Canaan. 3. Rameses—generally identified with Heroopolis, now the modern Abu-Keisheid (see on Ex. 12. 37,), which was probably the capital of Goshen, and, by direction of Moses, the place of general rendezvous previous to their departure. 4. upon their gods —used either according to Scripture phraseology to denote their rulers, the first-born of the king and his princes, or the idolatrous objects of Egyptian worship. 5. pitched in Succoth—*i.e.*, booths—a place of no note except as a temporary halting-place, at Birketel-Hadji (the Pilgrim's Pool), [CALMET.] 6. Etham—edge, or border of all that part of Arabia-Petræa which lay contiguous to Egypt, and was known by the general name of Shur. 7. Pi-hihiaroth, Baal-Zephon, and Migdol —see on Ex. 14. 1-4.) 8. Marah—thought to be Ain Howarah, both from its position and the time (three days) it would take them with their children and flocks to march from the water of Ayun Musa to that spot. 9. Elim—supposed to be Wady Ghurundel (see on Ex. 15. 27. . 10. Encamped by the Red sea —The road from Wady Ghurundel leads into the interior, in consequence of a high continuous ridge which excludes all view of the sea. At the mouth of Wady-et-Tayibeh, after about three days' march, it opens again on a plain along the margin of the Red Sea. The minute accuracy of the Scripture narrative, in corresponding so exactly with the geographical features of this region, is remarkably shown in describing the Israelites as proceeding by the only practicable route that could be taken. This plain, where they encamped, was the Desert of Sin (see on Ex. 16. 1.). 12-14. Dophkah, Alush, and Rephidim —these three stations, in the great valleys of El Sheikh and Feiran, would be equivalent to four days' journey for such a host. Rephidim (Ex. 17. 6,) was in Horeb, the burnt region—a generic name for a hot mountainous country. 15. Wilderness of Sinai— The Wady Er Raheh.

16-56. FROM SINAI TO KADESH AND PLAINS OF MOAB. 16-37. Kibroth-Hattaavah, (the graves of lust, see on ch. 11. 4-34.) — The route, on breaking up the encampment at Sinai, led down Wady Sheikh, then crossing Jebel-et-Tyh, which intersected the peninsula, they descended into Wady Zalaka, pitching successively at two brief, though memorable stations, (Deu. 9. 22,) and encamped at Hazeroth, unwalled villages), supposed to be at Ain-Hadera (ch. 11. 35.). Kadesh or Kadesh-barnea, is supposed to be the great valley of the Ghor, and the city Kadesh to have been situated on the border of this valley, BURCKHARDT, ROBINSON.) But as there are no less than *eighteen stations* inserted between Hazeroth and Kadesh, and only eleven days were spent in performing that journey (Deu. 1. 2,) it is evident that the intermediate stations here recorded belong to another and totally different visit to Kadesh. The first was when they left Sinai in the second month, (ch. 1. 11; ch. 13, 20,) and were in Kadesh in August (Deu. 1. 45,) and "abode many days" in it, and murmuring at the report of the spies, were commanded to return into the desert "by the way of the Red Sea." The arrival at Kadesh, mentioned in this catalogue, corresponds to the *second* sojourn at that place, being the *first* month, or April, (ch. 20. 1.) Between the two visits there intervened a period of thirty-eight years, during which they wandered hither and thither through all the region of El-Tyh, (wanderings,) often returning to the same spots as the pastoral necessities of their flocks required; and there is the strongest reason for believing that the stations named between Hazeroth, (v. 8,) and Kadesh, (v. 36,) belong to the long interval of wandering. No certainty has yet been attained in ascertaining the *locale* of many of these stations, and there must have been more than what are recorded;—for it is probable that those only are noted where they remained some time, where the tabernacle was pitched, and where Moses and the others encamped, the people being scattered for pasture in various directions. From Ezion-gaber, for instance, which stood at the head of the gulf of Akaba, to Kadesh, could not be much less than the whole length of the great valley of the Ghor, a distance of not less than 100 miles, whatever might be the exact situation of Kadesh; and, of course, there must have been several intervening stations, though none are mentioned. The incidents and stages of the rest of the journey to the plains of Moab are sufficiently explicit from the preceding chapters. Rithma—the place of the broom, a station possibly in some wady extending westward of the Ghor, (ch. 10. 40.) Rimmon-Parez, or Rimmon—a city of Judah and Simeon (Josh. 15. 32,) Libnah, so called from its white poplars (Josh. 10. 29,) or, as some think, a white hill between Kadesh and Gaza (Josh. 10. 29,) Rissah, (El-arish,) mount Shapher, (Cassius,) Moseroth, adjacent to mount Hor, in Wady Mousa. Ezion-Gaber, near Akabah, a sea-port on the western shore of the Elamitic gulf; Wilderness of Zin, on the east side of the peninsula of Sinai; Punon, in the rocky ravines of Mount Hor, and famous for the mines and quarries in its vicinity, as well as for its fruit-trees, now Taiyle, on the border of Edom; Abarim, a ridge of rugged hills, north-west of the Arnon—the part called Nebo was one of its highest peaks— opposite Jericho (See on Deut. 10. 6.). 50-53. Ye shall drive out—not, however, by expulsion, but extermination (Deu. 7. 1.), destroy all their pictures—obelisks for idolatrous worship (see on Lev. 26. 1.), molten images —by metonymy for all their groves and altars, and materials of worship on the tops of hills. 54. ye shall divide the land by lot—the particular locality of each tribe was to be determined in this manner, while a line was to be used in measuring the proportion Josh. 18, 10; P's. 16. 5, 6.). 55. but if ye will not drive— No associations were to be formed with the inhabitants; otherwise, "if let remain, they will be pricks in your eyes, and thorns in your sides"—*i.e.*, they would prove trouble-

inhabitants of the land from before you, and destroy all their pictures, and destroy all their molten images, and quite pluck down all their high places:

53 And ye shall dispossess *the inhabitants of* the land, and dwell therein: for ^c I have given you the land to possess it.

54 And ^d ye shall divide the land by lot for an inheritance among your families: *and* to the more ye shall ⁴ give the more inheritance, and to the fewer ye shall ⁵ give the less inheritance: every man's *inheritance* shall be in the place where his lot falleth; according to the tribes of your fathers ye shall inherit.

55 But if ye will not drive out the inhabitants of the land from before you; then it shall come to pass, that those which ye let remain of them *shall be* ^e pricks in your eyes, and thorns in your sides, and shall vex you in the land wherein ye dwell.

56 Moreover it shall come to pass, *that* I shall do unto you, as I thought to do unto them.

CHAPTER XXXIV.

1 The borders of the land of Canaan: 16 The names of the men which were assigned to divide it.

AND the LORD spake unto Moses, saying, 2 Command the children of Israel, and say unto them, When ye come into ^a the land of Canaan, (this *is* the land that shall fall unto you for an inheritance, *even* the land of Canaan, with the coasts thereof,)

3 Then ^b your south quarter shall be from the wilderness of Zin along by the coast of Edom, and your south border shall be the outmost coast of ^c the salt sea eastward:

4 And your border shall turn from the south to the ascent of Akrabbim, and pass on to Zin: and the going forth thereof shall be from the south ^d to Kadesh-barnea, and shall go on to Hazar-addar, and pass on to Azmon:

5 And the border shall fetch a compass from Azmon ^e unto the river of Egypt, and the goings out of it shall be at the sea.

6 And *as for* the western border, ye shall even have ^f the great sea for a border: this shall be your west border.

7 And this shall be your north border: from the great sea ye shall point out for you mount ^g Hor:

8 From mount Hor ye shall point out *your border* ^h unto the entrance of Hamath; and the goings forth of the border shall be to ⁱ Zedad:

9 And the border shall go on to Ziphron, and the goings out of it shall be at ^j Hazar-enan: this shall be your north border.

10 And ye shall point out your east border from Hazar-enan to Shepham.

11 And the coast shall go down from Shepham ^k to Riblah, on the east side of Ain; and the border shall descend, and shall reach unto the ^l side of the sea ^l of Chinnereth eastward:

12 And the border shall go down to Jordan, and the goings out of it shall be at the salt sea: this shall be your land with the coasts thereof round about.

13 And Moses commanded the children of Israel, saying, ^m This *is* the land which ye shall inherit by lot, which the LORD commanded to give unto the nine tribes, and to the half tribe:

14 For ⁿ the tribe of the children of Reuben according to the house of their

B. C. 1452.

CHAP. 33.
^c Ps. 24. 1.
Deu. 10. 14.
Job 41. 11.
Dan. 4. 35.
^d ch. 26. 53.
⁴ multiply his inheritance.
⁵ diminish his inheritance.
^e Josh. 23. 13.
Ps. 106. 34.
Ez. 28. 33.
Ezek. 28. 24.

CHAP. 34.
^a Gen. 17. 8.
Deu. 1. 7.
Ps. 78. 55.
Ps. 105. 11.
^b Josh. 15. 1.
Ezek. 47. 13.
^c Gen. 14. 3.
^d ch. 32. 8.
^e Gen. 15. 19.
1 Ki. 8. 65.
Is. 27. 12.
^f The Mediterranean.
^g Not the Mount Hor on the border of Edom, where Aaron died, but Mount Hor north of Lebanon.
^h ch. 13. 21.
2 Kin. 14. 25.
ⁱ Ezek. 47. 15.
^j Ezek. 47. 17.
^k 2 Kin. 23. 33.
Jer. 39. 5.
^l shoulder.
^l Deu. 3. 17.
Josh. 11. 2.
Josh. 19. 35.
Mat. 14. 34.
^m Josh. 14. 1, 2.
ⁿ ch. 32. 33.
Josh. 14. 2, 3.
^o Ex. 6. 23-25.
Josh. 14. 1.
Josh. 19. 51.
^p Heb. 4. 8.
^q ch. 1. 4, 16.

CHAP. 35.
^a Josh. 14. 3, 4.
Josh. 21. 2.
Ezek. 45. 1.
Ezek. 48. 8.
^b Six hundred and eight yards.
^c Deu. 4. 41.
Josh. 20. 2.
Josh. 21. 3.
¹ she *them* ye shall give.

fathers, and the tribe of the children of Gad according to the house of their fathers, have received *their inheritance;* and half the tribe of Manasseh have received their inheritance:

15 The two tribes and the half tribe have received their inheritance on this side Jordan *near* Jericho eastward, toward the sun-rising.

16 ¶ And the LORD spake unto Moses, saying,

17 These *are* the names of the men which shall divide the land unto you; ^o Eleazar the priest, and ^p Joshua the son of Nun.

18 And ye shall take one ^q prince of every tribe, to divide the land by inheritance.

19 And the names of the men *are* these: Of the tribe of Judah, Caleb the son of Jephunneh.

20 And of the tribe of the children of Simeon, Shemuel the son of Ammihud.

21 Of the tribe of Benjamin, Elidad the son of Chislon.

22 And the prince of the tribe of the children of Dan, Bukki the son of Jogli.

23 The prince of the children of Joseph, for the tribe of the children of Manasseh, Hanniel the son of Ephod.

24 And the prince of the tribe of the children of Ephraim, Kemuel the son of Shiphtan.

25 And the prince of the tribe of the children of Zebulun, Elizaphan the son of Parnach.

26 And the prince of the tribe of the children of Issachar, Paltiel the son of Azzan.

27 And the prince of the tribe of the children of Asher, Ahihud the son of Shelomi.

28 And the prince of the tribe of the children of Naphtali, Pedahel the son of Ammihud.

29 These *are they* whom the LORD commanded to divide the inheritance unto the children of Israel in the land of Canaan.

CHAPTER XXXV.

1 Eight and forty cities given to the Levites: 6 six of them to be cities of refuge. 9 The laws concerning murder and manslaughter.

AND the LORD spake unto Moses in the plains of Moab by Jordan *near* Jericho, saying,

2 Command ^a the children of Israel, that they give unto the Levites, of the inheritance of their possession, cities to dwell in; and ye shall give *also* unto the Levites suburbs for the cities round about them.

3 And the cities shall they have to dwell in; and the suburbs of them shall be for their cattle, and for their goods, and for all their beasts.

4 And the suburbs of the cities, which ye shall give unto the Levites, *shall reach* from the wall of the city and outward ^b a thousand cubits round about.

5 And ye shall measure from without the city on the east side two thousand cubits, and on the south side two thousand cubits, and on the west side two thousand cubits, and on the north side two thousand cubits; and the city *shall be* in the midst: this shall be to them the suburbs of the cities.

6 And among the cities which ye shall give unto the Levites *there shall be* ^c six cities for refuge, which ye shall appoint for the manslayer, that he may flee thither: and ¹ to them ye shall add forty and two cities.

7 So all the cities which ye shall give to

some and dangerous neighbours, enticing to idolatry, and consequently depriving you of the Divine favour and blessing. The neglect of the counsel against union with the idolatrous inhabitants became fatal to them. This earnest admonition given to the Israelites in their peculiar circumstances conveys a salutary lesson to us to allow no lurking habits of sin to remain in us. That spiritual enemy must be eradicated from our nature, otherwise it will be ruinous to our present peace and future salvation.

CHAPTER XXXIV.

Ver. 1-15. THE BORDERS OF THE LAND OF CANAAN. 2. This is the ... land of Canaan—The details given in this chapter mark the general boundary of the inheritance of Israel west of the Jordan. The Israelites never actually possessed all the territory comprised within these boundaries, even when it was most extended by the conquests of David and Solomon. 3-5. Your south quarter—The line which bounded it on the south is the most difficult to trace. According to the best Biblical geographers, the leading points here defined are as follows:—The south-west angle of the southern boundary should be where the wilderness of Zin touches the border of Edom, so that the southern boundary should extend eastward from the extremity of the Dead Sea, wind round the precipitous ridge of Akrabbim, (scorpions,) thought to be the high and difficult Pass of Safeh, which crosses the stream that flows from the south into the Jordan—*i.e.*, the great valley of the Arabah, reaching from the Dead to the Red Sea. river of Egypt—the ancient brook Sihor, the Rhinocolura of the Greeks, a little to the south of El-Arish, where this Wady gently descends towards the Mediterranean (Josh. 13. 3.). 6. The western border—There is no uncertainty about this boundary, as it is universally allowed to be the Mediterranean, which is called "the great sea" in comparison with the small inland seas or lakes known to the Hebrews. 7-9. North border—The principal difficulty in understanding the description here arises from what our translators have called Mount Hor. The Hebrew words, however, Hor-ha-Hor, properly signify "the mountain of the mountain"—"the high double mountain," which, from the situation, can mean nothing else than the mountain Amana (Song 4. 8,) a member of the great Lebanon range (Josh. 13. 5.). Entrance of Hamath—The northern plain between those mountain ranges, now the valley of Baalbeck (see on ch. 13. 21-24.). Zedad—identified as the present Sudud (Ez. 17. 15,). Ziphron (sweet odour); Hazar-Enan (village of fountains); but the places are unknown. "An imaginary line from mount Cassius, on the coast along the northern base of Lebanon to the entering into the Bekaa (Valley of Lebanon) at the Kamosa Hermel, must be regarded as the frontier that is meant. [VAN DE VELDE.] 10-12. East border—This is very clearly defined. Shepham and Riblah, which were in the valley of Lebanon, are mentioned as the boundary line, which commenced a little higher than the sources of the Jordan. Ain is supposed to be the source of that river; and thence the eastern boundary extended along the Jordan, the sea of Chinnereth (Lake of Tiberias) —the Jordan; and again terminated at the Dead Sea. The line being drawn on the east of the river and the seas, included those waters within the territory of the western tribes. 13-15. The two tribes and the half tribe have received—The conquered territories of Sihon and Og, lying between the Arnon and Mount Hermon, were allotted to them —that of Reuben in the most southerly part, Gad north of it, and the half Manasseh in the northernmost portion. 16-29. names of the men who shall divide the land—This appointment by the Lord before the passage of the Jordan tended not only to animate the Israelites' faith in the certainty of the conquest, but to prevent all subsequent dispute and discontent, which might have been dangerous in presence of the natives. The nominees were ten princes for the nine-and-a-half tribes, one of them being selected from the western section of Manasseh, and all subordinate to the great military and ecclesiastical chiefs, Joshua and Eleazar. The names are mentioned in the exact order in which the tribes obtained possession of the land, and according to *brotherly* connection.

CHAPTER XXXV.

Ver. 1-5. EIGHT AND FORTY CITIES GIVEN TO THE LEVITES. 2. Give unto the Levites ... cities to dwell in—As the Levites were to have no territorial domain allocated to them like the other tribes on the conquest of Canaan, they were to be distributed throughout the land in certain cities appropriated to their use; and these cities were to be surrounded by extensive suburbs. There is an apparent discrepancy between v. 4 and 5, with regard to the extent of these suburbs; but the statements in the two verses refer to totally different things—the one to the extent of the suburbs from the walls of the city, the other to the space of 2,000 cubits from their extremity. In point of fact, there was an extent of ground, amounting to 3,000 cubits, measured from the wall of the city. One thousand were most probably occupied with out-houses for the accommodation of shepherds and other servants, with gardens, vineyards, or oliveyards. And these which were portioned out to different families (1 Chron. 6. 60,) might be sold by one Levite to another, but not to any individual of another tribe (Jer. 32. 7.). The other two thousand cubits remained a common for the pasturing of cattle, (Le. 25. 34,) and, considering their number, that space would be fully required.

6-8. CITIES OF REFUGE. There shall be six cities ... for the man-slayer—The establishment of those privileged sanctuaries amongst the cities of the Levites is probably traceable to the idea, that they would be the most suitable and impartial judges—that their presence and counsels might calm or restrain the stormy passions of the blood-avenger—and that, from their being invested with the sacred character, they might be types of Christ, in whom sinners find a refuge from the destroyer (see Deu. 4. 43 ; Josh. 20. 8.). The cities shall be of the possession ... of Israel—The burden of furnishing those places for the residence and support of the Levitical order was to fall in equitable proportions upon the different tribes (see ch. 33. 54 ; Josh. 20. 7.).

9-15. THE BLOOD-AVENGER. Slayer may flee, which killeth any person at unawares —The practice of Goelism—*i.e.*, of the nearest relation of an individual who was killed

the Levites shall be *d* forty and eight cities: them *shall ye give* with their suburbs.

8 And the cities which ye shall give *shall be* *e* of the possession of the children of Israel: from *f* them that have many ye shall give many; but from *them that have* few ye shall give few: every one shall give of his cities unto the Levites according to his inheritance which ² he inheriteth.

9 ¶ And the LORD spake unto Moses, saying,

10 Speak unto the children of Israel, and say unto them, *g* When ye be come over Jordan into the land of Canaan,

11 Then *h* ye shall appoint you cities to be cities of refuge for you; that the slayer may flee thither, which killeth any person ³ at unawares.

12 And *i* they shall be unto you cities for refuge from the avenger; that the manslayer die not, until he stand before the congregation in judgment.

13 And of these cities which ye shall give, six cities shall ye have for refuge.

14 Ye *j* shall give three cities on this side Jordan, and three cities shall ye give in the land of Canaan, *which* shall be cities of refuge.

15 These six cities shall be a refuge, both for the children of Israel, and *k* for the stranger, and for the sojourner among them; that every one that killeth any person unawares may flee thither.

16 And *l* if he smite him with an instrument of iron, so that he die, he *is* a murderer: the murderer shall surely be put to death.

17 And if he smite him ⁴ with throwing a stone, wherewith he may die, and he die, he *is* a murderer: the murderer shall surely be put to death.

18 Or *if* he smite him with an hand-weapon of wood, wherewith he may die, and he die, he *is* a murderer: the murderer shall surely be put to death.

19 The *m* revenger of blood himself shall slay the murderer: when he meeteth him, he shall slay him.

20 But *n* if he thrust him of hatred, or hurl at him *o* by laying of wait, that he die;

21 Or in enmity smite him with his hand, that he die: he that smote *him* shall surely be put to death; *for* he *is* a murderer: the revenger of blood shall slay the murderer when he meeteth him.

22 But if he thrust him suddenly without enmity, or have cast upon him any thing without laying of wait,

23 Or with any stone, wherewith a man may die, seeing *him* not, and cast *it* upon him, that he die, and *was* not his enemy, neither sought his harm;

24 Then *p* the congregation shall judge between the slayer and the revenger of blood according to these judgments:

25 And the congregation shall deliver the slayer out of the hand of the revenger of blood, and the congregation shall restore him to the city of his refuge, whither he was fled: and he *q* shall abide in it unto the death of the high priest, *r* which was anointed with the holy oil.

26 But if the slayer shall at any time come without the border of the city of his refuge, whither he was fled;

27 And the revenger of blood find him without the borders of the city of his refuge,

130

B. C. 1451.

CHAP. 35.
d Josh. 21.41.
e Josh. 21. 3.
f ch. 26. 54.
² they
inherit.
g Deu. 19. 2.
Josh. 20. 2.
h Ex. 21. 13.
3 by error.
i Josh. 20. 3.
Deu. 4. 41.
k ch. 15. 16.
l Ex. 21, 12, 14.
Lev. 24. 17.
Deu. 19. 11, 12.
4 with a stone of the hand.
m Deu. 19. 6, 12.
He was the nearest kinsman of the person slain.
n Gen. 4. 8.
2 Sa. 3. 27.
2 Sam. 20. 10.
1 Ki. 2. 31.
o Ex. 21. 14.
Deu. 19.11.
p Josh. 20. 6.
q Eph. 1. 7.
r Ex. 29. 7.
Lev. 4. 3.
Lev. 21. 10.
5 no blood shall be to him.
Ex. 22. 2.
s ch. 27. 11.
t Deu. 17. 6.
Deu. 19. 15.
Mat. 18. 16.
2 Cor. 13. 1.
Heb. 10. 28.
6 faulty to die.
u Acts 4. 12.
Gal. 2. 21.
v Gen 4.
9-12.
Ps. 106, 38.
Mic. 4. 11.
7 there can be no expiation for the land.
w Gen. 9. 6.
x Lev. 18. 25.
Deu. 21. 23.
y Ex. 29. 45, 46.
Ps. 76. 2.
Hos. 9. 3.
2 Cor.6.16.

CHAP. 36.
a ch. 26. 29.
b ch. 26. 55.
ch. 33. 54.
Josh. 17. 3.
c ch. 27. 1, 7.
Jos. 17. 3,4.
1 unto whom they shall be.
d Lev. 25. 10.
e ch. 27. 7.
2 be wives.
f 1 Ki. 2. 3.
³ cleave to the, etc.
g 1 Ch. 23.22.

and the revenger of blood kill the slayer; ⁵ he shall not be guilty of blood:

28 Because he should have remained in the city of his refuge until the death of the high priest: but after the death of the high priest the slayer shall return into the land of his possession.

29 So these *things* shall be for *s* a statute of judgment unto you throughout your generations in all your dwellings.

30 Whoso killeth any person, the murderer shall be put to death by the *t* mouth of witnesses: but one witness shall not testify against any person *to cause him* to die.

31 Moreover ye shall take no satisfaction for the life of a murderer, which *is* ⁶ guilty of death; but he shall be surely put to death.

32 And ye shall take *u* no satisfaction for him that is fled to the city of his refuge, that he should come again to dwell in the land, until the death of the priest.

33 So ye shall not pollute the land wherein ye *are*; for blood *v* it defileth the land: and ⁷ the land cannot be cleansed of the blood that is shed therein, but *w* by the blood of him that shed it.

34 Defile *x* not therefore the land which ye shall inhabit, wherein I dwell: for *y* I the LORD dwell among the children of Israel.

CHAPTER XXXVI.

1 *The inconvenience of the inheritance of daughters,* 5 *is remedied, by marrying in their own tribes.*

AND the chief fathers of the families of the children *a* of Gilead, the son of Machir, the son of Manasseh, of the families of the sons of Joseph, came near, and spake before Moses, and before the princes, the chief fathers of the children of Israel:

2 And they said, *b* The LORD commanded my lord to give the land for an inheritance by lot to the children of Israel: and *c* my lord was commanded by the LORD to give the inheritance of Zelophehad our brother unto his daughters.

3 And if they be married to any of the sons of the *other* tribes of the children of Israel, then shall their inheritance be taken from the inheritance of our fathers, and shall be put to the inheritance of the tribe ¹ whereunto they are received: so shall it be taken from the lot of our inheritance.

4 And when *d* the jubilee of the children of Israel shall be, then shall their inheritance be put unto the inheritance of the tribe whereunto they are received: so shall their inheritance be taken away from the inheritance of the tribe of our fathers.

5 And Moses commanded the children of Israel according to the word of the LORD, saying, The tribe of the sons of Joseph hath *e* said well.

6 This *is* the thing which the LORD doth command concerning the daughters of Zelophehad, saying, Let them ² marry to whom they think best; only to the family of the tribe of their father shall they marry:

7 So shall not the *f* inheritance of the children of Israel remove from tribe to tribe; for every one of the children of Israel shall ³ keep himself to the inheritance of the tribe of his fathers.

8 And *g* every daughter, that possesseth an inheritance in any tribe of the children of Israel, shall be wife unto one of the

The Blood-Avenger. NUMBERS, XXXVI. *Of the Inheritance of Daughters.*

being bound to demand satisfaction from the author of his death, existed from a very remote antiquity (Gen. 4.14; 27.45.). It seems to have been an established usage in the age of Moses; and, although in a rude and imperfect state of society, it is a natural and intelligible principle of criminal jurisprudence, it is liable to many great abuses; the chief of the evils inseparable from it are, that the kinsman, who is bound in duty and honour to execute justice, will often be precipitate—little disposed, in the heat of passion, or under the impulse of revenge, to examine into the circumstances of the case, to discriminate between the premeditated purpose of the assassin, and the misfortune of the unintentional homicide. Moreover, it had a tendency, not only to foster a vindictive spirit, but, in case of the Goel being unsuccessful in finding his victim, to transmit animosities and feuds against his descendants from one generation to another. This is exemplified among the Arabs in the present day. Should an Arab of one tribe happen to kill one of another tribe, there is "blood" between the tribes, and the stain can only be wiped off by the death of some individual of the tribes with which the offence originated. Sometimes the penalty is commuted by the payment of a stipulated number of sheep or camels. But such an equivalent, though offered, is as often refused, and blood has to be repaid only by blood. This practice of Goelism obtained among the Hebrews to such an extent that it was not perhaps expedient to abolish it; and Moses, while sanctioning its continuance, was directed, by divine authority, to make some special regulations, which tended both to prevent the unhappy consequences of sudden and personal vengeance, and, at the same time, to afford an accused person time and means of proving his innocence. This was the humane and equitable end contemplated in the institution of cities of refuge. There were to be six of these legalized asyla, three on the east of Jordan, both because the territory there was equal in length, though not in breadth, to Canaan; and because it might be more convenient for some to take refuge across the border. They were appointed for the benefit, not of the native Israelites only, but of all resident strangers. 16-21. *If he smite him, &c.*—Various cases are here enumerated, in which the Goel or avenger was at liberty to take the life of the murderer, and every one of them proves a premeditated purpose. 22-28. *But if he thrust him suddenly without enmity, &c.*—Under the excitement of a sudden provocation, or violent passion, an injury might be inflicted issuing in death; and for a person who had thus undesignedly committed slaughter, the Levitical cities offered the benefit of full protection. Once having reached the nearest, for one or other of them was within a day's journey of all parts of the land, he was secure. But he had to "abide in it." His confinement within its walls was a wise and salutary rule, designed to shew the sanctity of human blood in God's sight, as well as to protect the manslayer himself, whose presence and intercourse in society might have provoked the passions of deceased's relatives. But the period of his release from this confinement was not until the death of the High Priest.

That was a season of public affliction, when private sorrows were sunk or overlooked under a sense of the national calamity—and when the death of so eminent a servant of God naturally led all to serious consideration about their own mortality. The moment, however, that the refugee broke through the restraints of his confinement, and ventured beyond the precincts of the asylum, he forfeited the privilege, and if he was discovered by his pursuer, might be slain with impunity. 29-34. *These things shall be for a statute of judgment*—The law of the blood-avenger, as thus established by divine authority, was a vast improvement on the ancient practice of Goelism. By the appointment of cities of refuge, the manslayer was saved, in the meantime, from the blind and impetuous fury of vindictive relatives; but he might be tried by the local court, and if proved guilty on sufficient evidence, condemned and punished as a murderer, without the possibility of deliverance by any pecuniary satisfaction. The enactment of Moses, which was in adaptation to the character and usages of the Hebrew people, secured the double advantage of promoting the ends both of humanity and of justice.

CHAPTER XXXVI.

Ver. 1-13. THE INCONVENIENCE OF THE INHERITANCE OF DAUGHTERS. 1. *The chief fathers of the families of Gilead*—Being the tribal governors in Manasseh, they consulted Moses on a case that affected the public honour and interests of their tribe. It related once more to the daughters of Zelophehad. Formerly they had applied, at their own instance, to be recognized, for want of heirs male in their family, as entitled to inherit their father's property: now the application was made on behalf of the tribe to which they belonged—that steps might be taken to prevent the alienation of their patrimony by their alliance with husbands of another tribe. The unrestricted marriages of daughters in such circumstances threatened seriously to affect the tenure of land in Israel, as their inheritance would go to the children, who, by the father's side, would belong to another tribe, and thus lead, through a complication of interests and the confusion of families, to an evil for which even the jubilee could not afford a remedy. (See on Lev. 25. 13.) 5-12. *Moses commanded . . . according to the word of the Lord*—The plea appeared just and reasonable; and accordingly, an enactment was made by which the daughters of Zelophehad, while left to the free choice of their husbands, were restricted to marry not only within their own tribe, but *within the family* of their father's tribe—*i.e.*, one of their cousins. This restriction, however, was imposed only on those who were heiresses. The law was not applicable to daughters in different circumstances (1 Chron. 23. 22.)—for they might marry into another tribe; but if they did so, they were liable to forfeit their patrimonial inheritance, which, on the death of their father or brothers, went to the nearest of the family kinsmen. Here was an instance of progressive legislation (see also Ex. 18. ch. 27.) in Israel, the enactments made being suggested by circumstances; but it is deserving of special notice that those additions to, or modifications of, the law were confined

family of the tribe of her father, that the children of Israel may enjoy every man the inheritance of his fathers.

9 Neither shall the inheritance remove from *one* tribe to another tribe; but every one of the tribes of the children of Israel shall keep himself to his own inheritance.

10 Even as the LORD commanded Moses, so did the daughters of Zelophehad:

11 For ʰ Mahlah, Tirzah, and Hoglah, and Milcah, and Noah, the daughters of Zelo-

B. C. 1451.

CHAP. 30.
ʰ ch. 27. 1.
⁴ to some that were of the families.
ⁱ ch. 26. 3.
ch. 33. 50.
ch. 22. 1.
ch. 31. 12.

phehad, were married unto their father's brothers' sons:

12 And they were married ⁴ into the families of the sons of Manasseh the son of Joseph; and their inheritance remained in the tribe of the family of their father.

13 These *are* the commandments and the judgments which the LORD commanded by the hand of Moses unto the children of Israel in ⁱ the plains of Moab by Jordan near Jericho.

THE FIFTH BOOK OF MOSES, CALLED

DEUTERONOMY.

CHAPTER I.

1 *Moses' speech at the end of the fortieth year, 6 in which he briefly rehearseth the story of God's promises to Israel, 34 and his anger for their incredulity and disobedience.*

THESE be the words which Moses spake unto all Israel ᵈ on this side Jordan in the wilderness, in the plain over against ¹ the Red sea, between Paran, and Tophel, and Laban, and Hazeroth, and Dizahab.

2 (*There are* eleven days' *journey* from Horeb by the way of mount Seir ᵇ unto Kadesh-barnea.)

3 And it came to pass ᵉ in the fortieth year, in the eleventh month, on the first day of the month, *that* Moses spake unto the children of Israel, according unto all that the LORD had given him in commandment unto them;

4 After ᵈ he had slain Sihon the king of the Amorites, which dwelt in Heshbon, and Og the king of Bashan, which dwelt at Astaroth in ᵉ Edrei:

5 On this side Jordan, in the land of Moab, began Moses to declare this law, saying,

6 The LORD our God spake unto us ᶠ in Horeb, saying, Ye have dwelt long ᵍ enough in this mount:

7 Turn you, and take your journey, and go to the mount of the Amorites, and unto ² all *the places* nigh thereunto, in the plain, in the hills, and in the vale, and in the south, and by the sea-side, to the land of the Canaanites, and unto Lebanon, unto the great river, the river Euphrates.

8 Behold, I have ³ set the land before you: go in and possess the land which the LORD sware unto your fathers, ʰ Abraham, Isaac, and Jacob, to give unto them and to their seed after them.

9 ¶ And ⁱ I spake unto you at that time, saying, I am not able to bear you myself alone:

10 The LORD your God hath multiplied you, and, behold, ʲ ye *are* this day as the stars of heaven for multitude.

11 (The LORD God of your fathers make you a thousand times so many more as ye *are*, and bless you, ᵏ as he hath promised you!)

12 How ˡ can I myself alone bear your cumbrance, and your burden, and your strife?

13 ⁴ Take you wise men, and understanding, and known among your tribes, and I will make them rulers over you.

14 And ye answered me, and said, The

B. C. 1451.

CHAP. 1.
ᵃ Josh. 9. 1.
Josh. 22. 4, 7.
¹ Or, Zuph.
ᵇ Nu. 13. 26. ch. 9. 23.
ᶜ Nu. 33. 38.
ᵈ Nu. 21. 24.
Josh. 12. 1. 2.
Noh. 9. 22.
Ps. 135. 10, 11.
ᵉ Josh. 13. 12.
ᶠ Ex. 3. 1.
ᵍ Ex. 19. 1.
Nu. 10. 11.
² all his neighbours.
³ given.
ʰ Gen. 12. 7.
Gen. 15. 18.
Gen. 26. 13.
ⁱ Ex. 18. 19.
Nu. 11. 14.
ʲ Gen. 15. 5.
ch. 10. 22.
ch. 28. 62.
ᵏ Gen. 22. 17.
Gen. 26. 4.
Ex. 32. 13.
ˡ 1 Kin. 3. 8.
2 Cor. 11. 28.
⁴ Give.
Ex. 18. 21.
Nu. 11. 16.
⁵ gave.
ᵐ John 7. 24.
ⁿ Lev. 24. 22
º 1 Sa. 16. 7.
Pro. 24. 23.
Jam. 2. 1.
⁶ acknowledge faces.
ᵖ Pro. 28. 21.
Pro. 29. 4, 25.
ᑫ 2 Chr. 19. 6.
ʳ Ex. 18. 22, 26.
ˢ Num. 10. 12.
ch. 8. 15.
Jer. 2. 6.
ᵗ Num. 13. 26.
ᵘ Josh. 1. 9.
ᵛ Nu. 13. 3.
ʷ Num. 14. 1, 2, 3, 4.
Ps. 105.24.
ˣ ch. 9. 23.

thing which thou hast spoken *is* good for us to do.

15 So I took the chief of your tribes, wise men, and known, and ⁵ made them heads over you, captains over thousands, and captains over hundreds, and captains over fifties, and captains over tens, and officers among your tribes.

16 And I charged your judges at that time, saying, Hear *the causes* between your brethren, and ᵐ judge righteously between every man and his ⁿ brother, and the stranger *that is* with him.

17 Ye º shall not ⁶ respect persons in judgment, *but* ye shall hear the small as well as the great; ye ᵖ shall not be afraid of the face of man; for the ᑫ judgment *is* God's: and the cause that is too hard for you, ʳ bring *it* unto me, and I will hear it.

18 And I commanded you at that time all the things which ye should do.

19 ¶ And when we departed from Horeb, we ˢ went through all that great and terrible wilderness, which ye saw by the way of the mountain of the Amorites, as the LORD our God commanded us; and ᵗ we came to Kadesh-barnea.

20 And I said unto you, Ye are come unto the mountain of the Amorites, which the LORD our God doth give unto us.

21 Behold, the LORD thy God hath set the land before thee: go up *and* possess *it*, as the LORD God of thy fathers hath said unto thee; fear ᵘ not, neither be discouraged.

22 ¶ And ye came near unto me every one of you, and said, We will send men before us, and they shall search us out the land, and bring us word again by what way we must go up, and into what cities we shall come.

23 And the saying pleased me well: and ᵛ I took twelve men of you, one of a tribe:

24 And they turned and went up into the mountain, and came unto the valley of Eshcol, and searched it out.

25 And they took of the fruit of the land in their hands, and brought *it* down unto us, and brought us word again, and said, It *is* a good land which the LORD our God doth give us.

26 Notwithstanding ʷ ye would not go up, but rebelled against the commandment of the LORD your God:

27 And ye murmured in your tents, and said, Because the LORD ˣ hated us, he hath brought us forth out of the land of Egypt,

to civil affairs; while the slightest change was inadmissible in the laws relating to worship, or the maintenance of religion. 13. *These commandments . . . in the plains of Moab*—The Israelitish encampment was on an extensive plateau, north of the Arnon, and which, though wrested from the Moabites by Sihon and Og, still retained the name of its original possessors. The particular site, as indicated by the words "Jordan near Jericho," is now called El Kourá—a large plain lying not far from Nebo, between the Arnon and a small tributary stream, the Wale. (BURCKHARDT.) It was a desert plain on the eastern bank, and marked only by groves of the wild thorny acacia tree.

THE FIFTH BOOK OF MOSES, CALLED
DEUTERONOMY.

CHAPTER I.

Ver. 1-46. MOSES' SPEECH AT THE END OF THE FORTIETH YEAR. 1. *These be the words which Moses spake unto all Israel*—The mental condition of the people generally in that infantine age of the church, and the greater number of them being of young or tender years, rendered it expedient to repeat the laws and counsels which God had given; and, accordingly to furnish a recapitulation of the leading branches of their faith and duty was amongst the last public services which Moses rendered to Israel. The scene of their delivery was on the plains of Moab, where the encampment was pitched "on this side Jordan," or, as the Hebrew word may be rendered, "on the bank of the Jordan." *In the wilderness, in the plain*. The Arabah, a desert plain, or steppe, extended the whole way from the Red Sea north to the Sea of Tiberias. While the high table lands of Moab were "cultivated fields," the Jordan valley, at the foot of the mountains, where Israel was encamped, was a part of the great desert plain, little more inviting than the desert of Arabia. The locale is indicated by the names of the most prominent places around it. Some of these places are unknown to us. The Hebrew word, Suph, red, (for *sea*, which our translators have inserted, is not in the original, and Moses was now farther from the Red Sea than ever), probably meant a place noted for its reeds. (Num. 21, 14.) *Tophel*—identified as Tafyle or Tafeilah, lying between Bozrah and Kerak. Hazeroth is a different place from that at which the Israelites encamped after leaving "the desert of Sinai." 2. *There are eleven days' journey from Horeb*—Distances are computed in the East still by the hours or days occupied by the journey. A day's journey on foot is about twenty miles—on camels, at the rate of three miles an hour, thirty miles—and by caravans, about twenty-five miles. But the Israelites, with children and flocks, would move at a slow rate. The length of the Ghor from Eziongaber to Kadesh is 100 miles. The days here mentioned were not necessarily successived ays, (ROBINSON,) for the journey can be made in a much shorter period. But this mention of the *time* was made to show that the great number of years spent in travelling from Horeb to the plain of Moab was not owing to the length of the way, but to a very different cause, viz., banishment for their apostasy and frequent rebellions. *Mount Seir*—the mountainous country of Edom. 3-8. *In the fortieth year, &c.*—This impressive discourse, in which Moses reviewed all that God had done for His people, was delivered about a month before his death, and after peace and tranquillity had been restored by the complete conquest of Sihon and Og. *Ashtaroth*—the royal residence of Og, so called from Astarte (the moon) the tutelary goddess of the Syrians, and he was slain at Edrei—now Edhra, the ruins of which are fourteen miles in circumference, (BURCKHARDT;) its general breadth is about two leagues.. 5. *began Moses to declare this law*—declare, i.e., explain this law. He follows the same method here that he elsewhere observes, viz., that of first enumerating the marvellous doings of God in behalf of His people, and reminding them what an unworthy requital they had made for all His kindness—then he rehearses the law and its various precepts. *Ye have dwelt long enough in this mount*—Horeb was the general name of a mountainous district—lit., "the parched or burnt region," whereas Sinai was the name appropriated to a particular peak. About a year had been spent among the recesses of that wild solitude, in laying the foundation, under the immediate direction of God, of a new and peculiar community, as to its social, political, and, above all, religious character; and when this purpose had been accomplished, they were ordered to break up their encampment in Horeb. The command given them was to march straight to Canaan, and possess it. *the land is before you*—lit., before your faces—it is accessible—there is no impediment to your occupation. The order of the journey as indicated by the places mentioned would have led to a course of invasion, the opposite of what was eventually followed, viz., from the sea-coast eastward—instead of from the Jordan westward (see on Num. 20. 1.) *the mount of the Amorites*—the hilly tract lying next to Kadesh-barnea, in the south of Canaan. *to the land of the Canaanites, and unto Lebanon*—i.e., Phœnicia, the country of Sidon, and the coast of the Mediterranean—from the Philistines to Lebanon. The name Canaanite is often used synonymously with that of Phœnician. 9-18. *I spake unto you at that time*—a little before their arrival in Horeb. Moses addresses that new generation as the representatives of their fathers, in whose sight and hearing all the transactions he recounts took place. A reference is here made to the suggestion of Jethro, (Ex. 18. 18.), and in noticing his practical adoption of a plan by which the administration of justice was committed to a select number of subordinate officers, Moses, by a beautiful allusion to the patriarchal blessing, ascribed the necessity of that memo-

to deliver us into the hand of the Amorites, to destroy us.

28 Whither shall we go up? our brethren have [7] discouraged our heart, saying, ʋ The people *is* greater and taller than we; the cities *are* great and walled up to heaven; and moreover we have seen the sons of the ² Anakims there.

29 Then I said unto you, Dread not, neither be afraid of them.

30 The *a* LORD your God, which goeth before you, he shall fight for you, according to all that he did for you in Egypt before your eyes;

31 And in the wilderness, where thou hast seen how that the LORD thy God *b* bare thee, as a man doth bear his son, in all the way that ye went, until ye came into this place.

32 Yet in this thing *c* ye did not believe the LORD your God,

33 Who *d* went in the way before you, to *e* search you out a place to pitch your tents in, in fire by night, to show you by what way ye should go, and in a cloud by day.

34 And the LORD heard the voice of your words, and was wroth, *f* and sware, saying,

35 Surely *g* there shall not one of these men of this evil generation see that good land, which I sware to give unto your fathers,

36 Save Caleb the son of Jephunneh; he shall see it, and to him will I give the land that he hath trodden upon, and to his children, because he hath *g* wholly followed the LORD.

37 Also *h* the LORD was angry with me for your sakes, saying, Thou also shalt not go in thither.

38 *But* Joshua the son of Nun, *i* which standeth before thee, he shall go in thither: encourage *j* him; for he shall cause Israel to inherit it.

39 Moreover your little ones, which ye said should be a prey, and your children, which in that day had *k* no knowledge between good and evil, they shall go in thither, and unto them will I give it, and they shall possess it.

40 But *as for* you, turn you, and take your journey into the wilderness by the way of the Red sea.

41 Then ye answered and said unto me, We have sinned against the LORD, we will go up and fight, according to all that the LORD our God commanded us. And when ye had girded on every man his weapons of war, ye were ready to go up into the hill.

42 And the LORD said unto me, Say unto them, Go not up, neither fight; for I *am* not among you; lest ye be smitten before your enemies.

43 So I spake unto you; and ye would not hear, but rebelled against the commandment of the LORD, *v* and went presumptuously up into the hill.

44 And the Amorites, which dwelt in that mountain, came out against you, and chased you, *l* as bees do, and destroyed you in Seir, *even* unto Hormah.

45 And ye returned and wept before the LORD; *m* but the LORD would not hearken to your voice, nor give ear unto you.

46 So ye abode in Kadesh many days, according unto the days that ye abode there.

B. C. 1451.

CHAP. 1.
7 melted. Josh. 2. 11.
ʋ Nu. 13. 28, 31, 32, 33. ch. 9. 1, 2.
² Nu. 13. 28
a Ex. 14. * Neh. 4. 20.
b Ex. 19. 4. ch. 32. 11. Is. 46. 3, 4. Is. 63. 9. Hos. 11. 3. Acts 13. 18.
c Ps. 106. 24. Jude 5.
d Ex. 13. 21. Ps 78. 14.
e Nu. 10. 33. Ezek. 20. 6.
f ch. 2. 14. *g* Nu. 14. 22. Ps. 95. 11.
8 fulfilled to go after.
h Nu. 27. 14. ch. 3. 26. ch. 4. 21. ch. 34. 4. Ps. 106. 32.
i Ex. 24. 13. Ex. 33. 11. 1 Sa. 16. 22.
j ch. 31. 7, 23.
k Is. 7. 15, 16. Ezek. 18. 20. Jonah 4. 11. Lu. 12. 47. Rom. 9. 11.
9 ye were presumptuous and went up.
l Ps. 118. 12.
m Job. 27. 9. Ps. 66. 18. Pro. 1. 24. Is. 1. 15. Jer. 1. 11. 7-14. Zech. 7. 11. John 9. 31.

CHAP. 2.
1 even to the treading of the sole of the foot.
a Gen. 36. 8. Josh. 24. 4.
b 1 Ki. 9. 26.
2 Or, use no hostility against Moab.
c Nu. 21. 28.
d Gen. 19. 36.
e Gen. 14. 5.
f Nu. 13. 22. ch. 9. 2.
g Gen. 36. 20.
3 inherited them.
4 Or, room.
5 Or, valley. Nu. 13. 23.
h Nu. 14. 33. Nu. 26. 64.
i ch. 1. 34, 35. Ezek. 20. 15.
j Ps. 78. 33. Ps. 106. 26.

CHAPTER II.

1 *The story is continued:* 6 *they were not to meddle with the Edomites,* 9 *nor the Moabites,* 17 *nor the Ammonites.* 24 *Sihon the Amorite to be subdued.*

THEN we turned, and took our journey into the wilderness by the way of the Red sea, as the LORD spake unto me: and we compassed mount Seir many days.

2 And the LORD spake unto me, saying,

3 Ye have compassed this mountain long enough: turn you northward.

4 And command thou the people, saying, Ye *are* to pass through the coast of your brethren the children of Esau, which dwell in Seir; and they shall be afraid of you: take ye good heed unto yourselves therefore:

5 Meddle not with them; for I will not give you of their land, 1 no, not so much as a foot breadth; *a* because I have given mount Seir unto Esau *for* a possession.

6 Ye shall buy meat of them for money, that ye may eat; and ye shall also buy water of them for money, that ye may drink.

7 For the LORD thy God hath blessed thee in all the works of thy hand: he knoweth thy walking through this great wilderness: these forty years the LORD thy God *hath been* with thee; thou hast lacked nothing.

8 And when we passed by from our brethren the children of Esau, which dwelt in Seir, through the way of the plain *b* from Elath, and from Ezion-gaber, we turned and passed by the way of the wilderness of Moab.

9 And the LORD said unto me, ² Distress not the Moabites, neither contend with them in battle: for I will not give thee of their land *for* a possession; because I have given *c* Ar unto *d* the children of Lot *for* a possession.

10 The *e* Emims dwelt therein in times past, a people great, and many, and tall, as *f* the Anakims;

11 Which also were accounted giants, as the Anakims; but the Moabites call them Emims.

12 The *g* Horims also dwelt in Seir beforetime; but the children of Esau ³ succeeded them, when they had destroyed them from before them, and dwelt in their ⁴ stead; as Israel did unto the land of his possession, which the LORD gave unto them.

13 Now rise up, *said I*, and get you over the ⁵ brook Zered: and we went over the brook Zered.

14 And the space in which we came from Kadesh-barnea, until we were come over the brook Zered, *was* thirty and eight years; until *h* all the generation of the men of war were wasted out from among the host, as *i* the LORD sware unto them.

15 For indeed the *j* hand of the LORD was against them, to destroy them from among the host, until they were consumed.

16 ¶ So it came to pass, when all the men of war were consumed and dead from among the people,

17 That the LORD spake unto me, saying,

18 Thou art to pass over through Ar, the coast of Moab, this day:

19 And *when* thou comest nigh over against the children of Ammon, distress them not, nor meddle with them: for I will not give thee of the land of the children of Ammon any possession; because I have given it

rable change in the government to the vast increase of the population. **ye are this day as the stars...for multitude**—This was neither an Oriental hyperbole, nor a mere empty boast, for Abraham was told (Gen. 15. 5, 6,) to look to the stars, and though they *appear* innumerable, yet those seen by the naked eye amount, in reality, to no more than 3010 in both hemispheres—so that the Israelites already far exceeded that number, being at the last census above 600,000. It was a seasonable memento, calculated to animate their faith in the accomplishment of other parts of the divine promise. **19–21. we went through all that great and terrible wilderness**—of Paran, which included the desert and mountainous space lying between the wilderness of Shur westward, or towards Egypt and Mount Seir, or the land of Edom eastward; between the land of Canaan northwards, and the Red Sea southwards; and thus it appears to have comprehended really the wilderness of Sin and Sinai (Fisk.) It is called by the Arabs El Tyh, "the wandering." It is a dreary waste of rock and of calcareous soil covered with black sharp flints; all travellers, from a feeling of its complete isolation from the world, describe it as a great and terrible wilderness." **22–33. ye came and said, we will send men**—The proposal to despatch spies emanated from the people through unbelief; but Moses, believing them sincere, gave his cordial assent to this measure, and God on being consulted permitted them to follow the suggestion (see on Nu. 13. 1, 2.). The issue proved disastrous to them, only through their own sin and folly. **cities are great, and walled up to heaven**—an Oriental metaphor, meaning very high. The Arab marauders roam about on horseback, and hence the walls of St. Catherine's Monastery on Sinai are so lofty that travellers are drawn up by a pulley in a basket. **Anakims**—(see on Nu. 13. 33.). The honest and uncompromising language of Moses in reminding the Israelites of their perverse conduct and outrageous rebellion at the report of the treacherous and faint-hearted scouts, affords a strong evidence of the truth of this history as well as of the divine authority of his mission. There was great reason for his dwelling on this dark passage in their history as it was their unbelief that excluded them from the privilege of entering the promised land (Heb. 3. 19.); and that unbelief was a marvellous exhibition of human perversity, considering the miracles which God had wrought in their favour, especially in the daily manifestations they had of His presence among them as their leader and protector. **34–36. The Lord was wroth**—In consequence of this aggravated offence—unbelief followed by open rebellion, the Israelites were doomed, in the righteous judgment of God, to a life of wandering in that dreary wilderness, till the whole adult generation had disappeared by death. The only exceptions mentioned are Caleb, and Joshua who was to be Moses' successor. **37. Also the Lord was angry with me for your sakes**—This statement *seems* to indicate that it was on this occasion Moses was condemned to share the fate of the people. But we know that it was several years afterwards that Moses betrayed an unhappy spirit of distrust at the waters of strife (Ps. 106. 32, 33.). This verse must be considered therefore as a parenthesis. **39. Your children...who in that day had no knowledge**—all ancient versions read "to-day" instead of "that day;" and the sense is—" your children who *now* know," or " who know not *as yet* good or evil;" as the children had not been partakers of the sinful outbreak, they were spared to obtain the privilege which their unbelieving parents had forfeited. God's ways are not as man's ways. **40–45. Turn you and take your journey into the wilderness**—This command they disregarded, and, determined in spite of the earnest remonstrances of Moses to force an onward passage, they attempted to cross the heights then occupied by the combined forces of the Amorites and Amalekites, (cf. Nu. 14. 43,) but were repulsed with great loss. People often experience distress even while in the way of duty. But how different their condition who suffer in situations where God is with them from the feelings of those who are conscious that they are in a position directly opposed to the Divine will. The Israelites were grieved when they found themselves involved in difficulties and perils; but their sorrow arose not from a sense of the guilt, so much as the sad effects of their perverse conduct; and as, "though they wept," they were not true penitents, the Lord would not hearken to their voice, nor give ear unto them." **46. So ye abode at Kadesh many days**—That place had been the site of their encampment during the absence of the spies, which lasted forty days; and it is supposed from this verse, that they prolonged their stay there after their defeat for a similar period.

CHAPTER II.

Ver. 1–37. THE STORY IS CONTINUED. **1. Then we turned and took our journey... by the way of the Red Sea.** After their unsuccessful attack upon the Canaanites, the Israelites broke up their encampment at Kadesh, and journeying southward over the west desert of Tyh, as well as through the great valley of the Ghor and Arabah, they extended their removals as far as the Gulf of Akabah. **we compassed Mount Seir many days**—In these few words Moses comprised the whole of that wandering nomadic life which they passed during 38 years, shifting from place to place, and regulating their stations by the prospect of pasturage and water. Within the interval they went northward a second time to Kadesh, but being refused a passage through Edom, and opposed by the Canaanites and Amalekites, they again had no alternative but to traverse once more the great Arabah southwards to the Red Sea, where turning to the left, and crossing the long, lofty mountain-chain to the eastward of Ezion-gaber, (Nu. 21. 4, 5.) they issued into the great and elevated plains, which are still traversed by the Syrian Pilgrims in their way to Mecca, and appear to have followed northward nearly the same route, which is now taken by the Syrian Hadj, along the western skirts of this great desert, near the mountains of Edom. [ROBINSON.] It was on entering these plains they received the command, "Ye have compassed this mountain (this hilly tract, now Jebel Shera) long enough, turn ye northward." **4. The children of Esau...shall be afraid of you**—The same

unto the *k* children of Lot *for* a possession.

20 (That also was accounted a land of giants: giants dwelt therein in old time; and the Ammonites call them *l* Zamzummims;

21 A people great, and many, and tall, as the Anakims; but the LORD destroyed them before them; and they succeeded them, and dwelt in their stead:

22 As he did to the children of Esau, which *m* dwelt in Seir, when *n* he destroyed the Horims from before them; and they succeeded them, and dwelt in their stead even unto this day:

23 And *o* the Avims which dwelt in Hazerim, *even* unto *p* Azzah, *q* the Caphtorims, which came forth out of Caphtor, destroyed them, and dwelt in their stead.)

24 ¶ Rise ye up, take your journey, and pass *r* over the river Arnon: behold, I have given into thine hand Sihon the Amorite, king of Heshbon, and his land: begin to possess *it*, and contend with him in battle.

25 This *s* day will I begin to put the dread of thee and the fear of thee upon the nations *that are* under the whole heaven, who shall hear report of thee, and shall tremble, and be in anguish because of thee.

26 ¶ And I sent messengers out of the wilderness of Kedemoth unto Sihon king of Heshbon *t* with words of peace, saying,

27 Let *u* me pass through thy land: I will go along by the high way, I will neither turn unto the right hand nor to the left.

28 Thou shalt sell me meat for money, that I may eat; and give me water for money, that I may drink: *v* only I will pass through on my feet,

29 (As *w* the children of Esau which dwell in Seir, and the Moabites which dwell in Ar, did unto me,) until I shall pass over Jordan, into the land which the LORD our God giveth us.

30 But *x* Sihon king of Heshbon would not let us pass by him: for *y* the LORD thy God hardened *z* his spirit, and made his heart obstinate, that he might deliver him into thy hand, as *appeareth* this day.

31 And the LORD said unto me, Behold, I have begun to give Sihon and his land before thee: begin to possess, that thou mayest inherit his land.

32 Then Sihon came out against us, he and all his people, to fight at Jahaz.

33 And *a* the LORD our God delivered him before us; and *b* we smote him, and his sons, and all his people.

34 And we took all his cities at that time, and *c* utterly destroyed the men, and the women, and the little ones, of every city, we left none to remain:

35 Only the cattle we took for a prey unto ourselves, and the spoil of the cities which we took.

36 From *d* Aroer, which *is* by the brink of the river Arnon, and *from* the city that is by the river, even unto Gilead, there was not one city too strong for us: *e* the LORD our God delivered all unto us:

37 Only unto the land of the children of Ammon thou camest not, *nor* unto any place of the river *f* Jabbok, nor unto the cities in the mountains, nor unto whatsoever the LORD our God forbade us.

B. C. 1451.

CHAP. 2.
k Gen. 19.38.
l Gen. 14.5, Zuzims.
m Gen. 36.8
n Job 12.23.
o Josh. 13.3.
p Jer. 25. 20.
q Gen. 10. 14.
Amos 9. 7.
r Judg.11.18.
6 begin, possess.
s Ex. 15. 14.
ch. 11. 25.
Josh. 2. 9.
t ch. 20. 10.
u Nu. 21. 21.
Judg 11.19.
v Nu. 20. 19.
w ch. 23. 3.
Judg. 11. 17.
x Nu. 21. 23.
y Josh.11.20.
z Ex. 4. 21.
Hos. 4. 17.
James 1. 13-15.
a ch. 7. 2.
ch. 29. 16.
b ch. 29. 7.
c Lev. 27. 28.
ch. 7. 2, 26.
7 every city of men, and women, and little ones.
d ch. 3. 12.
ch. 4. 48.
Josh 13.9.
e Ps. 44. 3.
f Gen. 32. 22.
Nu. 21. 24.
ch. 3. 16.

CHAP. 3.
a Nu. 21. 24.
b 1 Kings 4. 13.
c ch. 2. 24.
Ps. 135.10, 11, 12.
Ps. 136.19, 20, 21.
d Ps. 29. 6.
e 1 Chr. 5. 23.
f ch. 4. 49.
g Josh. 12. 5.
Josh.13.11.
h Amos 2. 9.
i Gen. 14. 5, Rephaim.
j 2 Sa. 12. 26.
k ch. 2. 36.
Josh. 12. 2.
l Nu. 32. 33.
m Jos. 13.29.
n 1 Chr. 2.22.
o 2 Sa. 3. 3.
2 Sa. 10. 6.
p Nu. 32. 39.
q 2 Sa. 24. 5.
r Nu. 21. 24.
s Nu. 34. 11.
Josh. 12. 3.
t Gen. 14. 3.
The sea of Sodom.
1 Or, under the springs of Pisgah, or, the hill.
2 sons of power.

CHAPTER III.

1 *Conquest of Og king of Bashan.* 21 *Moses' exhortation to Joshua.* 23 *Moses' prayer to enter into the land.* 27 *He is permitted to see it.*

THEN we turned, and went up the way to Bashan: and Og the king of Bashan came out against us, he and all his people, to battle at Edrei.

2 And the LORD said unto me, Fear him not: for I will deliver him, and all his people, and his land, into thy hand; and thou shalt do unto him as thou didst unto *a* Sihon king of the Amorites, which dwelt at Heshbon.

3 So the LORD our God delivered into our hands Og also, the king of Bashan, and all his people: and we smote him until none was left to him remaining.

4 And we took all his cities at that time, there was not a city which we took not from them, threescore cities, *b* all the region of Argob, the kingdom of Og in Bashan.

5 All these cities *were* fenced with high walls, gates, and bars; besides unwalled towns a great many.

6 And we utterly destroyed them, as we did unto Sihon king *c* of Heshbon, utterly destroying the men, women, and children, of every city.

7 But all the cattle, and the spoil of the cities, we took for a prey to ourselves.

8 And we took at that time out of the hand of the two kings of the Amorites the land that *was* on this side Jordan, from the river of Arnon unto mount Hermon;

9 (*Which d* Hermon the Sidonians call Sirion, and the Amorites call it *e* Shenir;)

10 All *f* the cities of the plain, and all Gilead, and *g* all Bashan, unto Salchah and Edrei, cities of the kingdom of Og in Bashan.

11 For *h* only Og king of Bashan remained of the remnant of *i* giants; behold, his bedstead *was* a bedstead of iron: *is it not j* in Rabbath of the children of Ammon? nine cubits *was* the length thereof, and four cubits the breadth of it, after the cubit of a man.

12 And this land, *which* we possessed at that time, *k* from Aroer, which is by the river Arnon, and half mount Gilead, and the *l* cities thereof, gave I unto the Reubenites and to the Gadites.

13 And *m* the rest of Gilead, and all Bashan, *being* the kingdom of Og, gave I unto the half tribe of Manasseh; all the region of Argob, with all Bashan, which was called the land of giants.

14 Jair *n* the son of Manasseh took all the country of Argob *o* unto the coasts of Geshuri and Maachathi, and called them after his own name, Bashan-havoth-jair, unto this day.

15 And *p* I gave Gilead unto Machir.

16 And unto the Reubenites *q* and unto the Gadites I gave from Gilead even unto the river Arnon half the valley, and the border even unto the river Jabbok, *r* which is the border of the children of Ammon;

17 The plain also, and Jordan, and the coast *thereof*, from *s* Chinnereth *t* even unto the sea of the plain, *u* even the salt sea, 1 under Ashdoth-pisgah eastward.

18 ¶ And I commanded you at that time, saying, The LORD your God hath given you this land to possess it: ye shall pass over armed before your brethren the children of Israel, all *that are* 2 meet for the war.

people who had haughtily repelled the approach of the Israelites from the western frontier, were alarmed now that they had come round up on the weak side of their country. 5. Meddle not with them—*i.e.*, "which dwell in Seir," (*v.* 4.)—for there was another branch of Esau's posterity, viz. the Amalekites, who were to be fought against and destroyed. (Gen. 36. 12; Ex. 17. 14; Deu. 25. 17.) But the people of Edom were not to be injured, either in their persons or prope:ty. And although the appoach of so vast a nomadic horde as the Israelites naturally created apprehension, they were to take no advantage of the prevailing terror to compel the Edomites to accept whatever terms they imposed. They were merely to pass "through" or along their border, and to buy meat and water of them for money (*v.*6.). The people, kinder than their king, did sell them bread, meat, fruits, and water in their passage along their border (*v.* 29.) in the same manner as the Syrian caravan of Mecca is now supplied by the people of the same mountains, who meet the pilgrims as at a fair or market on the Hadj route. [ROBINSON.] Although the Israelites still enjoyed a daily supply of the manna, there was no prohibition against their eating other food, when opportunity afforded, but only they were not to cherish an inordinate desire for it. Water is a scarce commodity, and is often paid for by travellers in those parts. It was the more incumbent on the Israelites to do so, as, by the blessing of God, they possessed plenty of means to purchase, and the long continued experience of the extraordinary goodness of God to them, should inspire such confidence in Him as would suppress the smallest thought of resorting to fraud or violence in supplying their wants. 8-18. we passed through the way of the plain—The Arabah or great valley. From Elath (trees), (the Ailah of the Greeks and Romans; the site of it is marked by extensive mounds of rubbish. Fzion-gaber, now Akabah, both were w thin the territory of Edom; and after making a circuit of its south-eastern boundary, the Israelites reached the border of Moab on the south-east of the Salt Sea. They had been forbidden by divine command to molest the Moabites in any way; and this special honour was conferred on that people not on their own account, for they were very wicked, but in virtue of their descent from Lot see on ch. 23. 3.). Their territory comprised the fine country on the south, and partly on the north of the Arnon. They had won it by their arms from the original inhabitants, the Emims, a race terrible, as their name imports, for physical power and stature (Gen. 14. 5.; in like manner as the Edomites had obtained their settlement by the overthrow of the original occupiers of Seir, the Horims (Gen. 14. 6.) who were Troglodytes, or dwellers in caves, and Moses alluded to these circumstances to encourage his countrymen to believe that God would much more enable them to expel the wicked and accursed Canaanites. At that time, however, the Moabites, having lost the greater part of their possessions through the usurpations of Sihon, were reduced to the small, but fertile region between the Zered and the Arnon. 13. Now rise up and get you over the brook Zered—The southern border of Moab, Zered (woody), now wady Absy, separates the modern district of Kerak from Jebal, and, indeed, forms a natural division of the country between the north and south. Ar, called in later times Rabbah, was the capital of Moab, and situated 25 miles south of the Arnon on the banks of a small but shady stream, the Beni-Hamed. It is here mentioned as representative of the country dependent on it,—a rich and well-cultivated country, as appears from the numerous ruins of cities, as well as from the traces of tillage still visible on the fields. 16. all the men of war are consumed and dead—The outbreak at Kadesh on the false report of the spies had been the occasion of the fatal decree by which God doomed the whole grown up population to die in the wilderness; but that outbreak only filled up the measure of their iniquities. For that generation, though not universally abandoned to heathenish and idolatrous practices, yet had all along displayed a fea:ful amount of ungodliness in the desert, which this history only hints at obscurely, but which is expressly asserted elsewhere (Ez. 20. 25, 26; Am. 5. 25, 27; Ac. 7. 42, 43.). 19-37. when thou comest nigh unto the children of Ammon—The Ammonites, being kindred to the Moabites, were, from regard to the memory of their common ancestor, to remain undisturbed by the Israelites. The territory of this people had been directly north of that of Moab, and extended as far as the Jabbok, having been taken by them from a number of small Canaanitish tribes, viz. the Zamzummins, a bullying presumptuous band of giants, as their name indicates; and the Avims, the Aborigines of the district extending from Hazerim or Hazeroth, (El Hudhera) even unto Azzah (Gaza), but of which they had been dispossessed by the Caphtorim (Philistines) who came out of Caphtor (Lower Egypt), and settled in the western coast of Palestine. The limits of the Ammonites were now compressed; but they still possessed the mountainous region beyond the Jabbok (Josh. 11. 2.). What a strange insight does this parenthesis of four verses give into the early history of Palestine. How many successive wars of conquest had swept over its early state—what changes of dynasty amongst the Canaanitish tribes had taken place long prior to the transactions recorded in this history. 24. Rise ye up and pass over the river Arnon—At its mou h, this stream is 82 feet wide, and 4 deep—it flows in a channel banked by perpendicular cliffs of sandstone. At the date of the Israelitish migration to the east of the Jordan, the whole of the fine country lying between the Arnon and the Jabbok, including the mountainous tract of Gilead, had been seized by the Amorites, who being one of the nations doomed to destruction (see ch, 7. 2; 20. 16.) were utterly exterminated, and their country fell by right of conquest into the hands of the Israelites. Moses, however, considering this doom as referring solely to the Amorite possessions west of Jordan, sent a pacific message to Sihon, requesting permission to go through his territories, which lay on the east of that river. It is always customary to send messengers before to prepare the way; but the rejection of Moses' request by Sihon, and his opposition to the advance of the Israelites (Nu. 21. 23;

19 But your wives, and your little ones, and your cattle, (for I know that ye have much cattle,) shall abide in your cities which I have given you;
20 Until the Lord have given rest unto your brethren, as well as unto you, and *until* they also possess the land which the Lord your God hath given them beyond Jordan: and *then* shall ye *v* return every man unto his possession, which I have given you.
21 ¶ And I commanded Joshua at that time, saying, Thine eyes have seen all that the Lord your God hath done unto these two kings: so shall the Lord do unto all the kingdoms whither thou passest.
22 Ye shall not fear them: for *w* the Lord your God he shall fight for you.
23 ¶ And I besought the Lord at that time, saying,
24 O Lord God, thou hast begun to show thy servant *x* thy greatness, and thy mighty hand: for *y* what God *is* there in heaven or in earth that can do according to thy works, and according to thy might?
25 I pray thee, let me go over and see the *z* good land that *is* beyond Jordan, that goodly mountain, and Lebanon.
26 But the Lord was wroth with me for your sakes, and would not hear me: and the Lord said unto me, Let it suffice thee; speak no more unto me of this matter.
27 Get thee up into the top of [3] Pisgah, and lift up thine eyes westward, and northward, and southward, and eastward, and behold *it* with thine eyes: for thou shalt not go over this Jordan.
28 But *a* charge Joshua, and encourage him, and strengthen him: for he shall go over before this people, and he shall cause them to inherit the land which thou shalt see.
29 So we abode in *b* the valley over against Beth-peor.

CHAPTER IV.

1 *An exhortation to obedience.* 14 *A particular dissuasive against idolatry.* 41 *Moses appointeth three cities of refuge on that side Jordan.*

NOW therefore hearken, O Israel, unto the *a* statutes and unto the judgments, which I teach you, for to do *them*, that ye may live, and go in and possess the land which the Lord God of your fathers giveth you.
2 Ye *b* shall not add unto the word which I command you, neither shall ye diminish *ought* from it, that ye may keep the commandments of the Lord your God which I command you.
3 Your eyes have seen what the Lord did because of Baal-peor: for all the men that followed Baal-peor, the Lord thy God hath destroyed them from among you.
4 But ye that did cleave unto the Lord your God *are* alive every one of you this day.
5 Behold, I have taught you statutes and judgments, even as the Lord my God commanded me, that ye should do so in the land whither ye go to possess it.
6 Keep therefore and do *them:* for this *is* your *c* wisdom and your understanding in the sight of the nations, which shall hear all these statutes, and say, *d* Surely this great nation *is* a wise and understanding people.
7 For *e* what nation *is there* so great, who *hath f* God so nigh unto them, as the Lord our God *is* in all *things* that we call upon him *for?*
8 And what nation *is there* so great, that hath statutes and judgments *so* righteous as all this law, which I set before you this day?
9 Only take heed to thyself, and *g* keep thy soul diligently, *h* lest thou forget the things which thine eyes have seen, and lest they depart from thy heart all the days of thy life; but *i* teach them thy sons, and thy sons' sons;
10 *Specially* the day that thou stoodest before the Lord thy God in Horeb, when the Lord said unto me, Gather me the people together, and I will make them hear my words, that they may learn to fear me all the days that they shall live upon the earth, and *that* they may teach their children.
11 And ye came near and stood under the mountain; and the mountain burned with fire unto the [1] midst of heaven, with darkness, clouds, and thick darkness.
12 And the Lord spake unto you out of the midst of the fire: ye heard the voice of the words, but saw no similitude; [2] only *ye heard* a voice.
13 And he declared unto you his covenant, which he commanded you to perform, *even* ten commandments; and he wrote them upon two tables of stone.
14 ¶ And the Lord commanded me at that time to teach you statutes and judgments, that ye might do them in the land whither ye go over to possess it.
15 Take *k* ye therefore good heed unto yourselves, (for ye saw no manner of *l* similitude on the day *that* the Lord spake unto you in Horeb out of the midst of the fire,)
16 Lest ye corrupt *yourselves*, and make you a graven image, the similitude of any figure, *m* the likeness of male or female,
17 The likeness of any beast that *is* on the earth, the likeness of any winged fowl that flieth in the air,
18 The likeness of any thing that creepeth on the ground, the likeness of any fish that *is* in the waters beneath the earth:
19 And lest thou *n* lift up thine eyes unto heaven, and when thou seest the sun, and the moon, and the stars, *even o* all the host of heaven, shouldest be driven to worship them, and serve them, which the Lord thy God hath [3] divided unto all nations under the whole heaven.
20 But the Lord hath taken you, and brought you forth out of the iron furnace, *even* out of Egypt, to be unto him a people of inheritance, as *ye are* this day.
21 Furthermore, the Lord was angry with me for your sakes, and sware that I should not go over Jordan, and that I should not go in unto that good land which the Lord thy God giveth thee *for* an inheritance:
22 But *p* I must die in this land, I must not go over Jordan: but ye shall go over, and possess that good land.
23 Take heed unto yourselves, lest ye forget the covenant of the Lord your God, which he made with you, and make you a graven image, *or* the likeness of any *thing*, which the Lord thy God hath forbidden thee.
24 For *q* the Lord thy God *is* a consuming fire, *even r* a jealous God.
25 ¶ When thou shalt beget children, and

Jud. 11. 26.), drew down on himself, and his Amorite subjects, the predicted doom in the first pitched battle-field with the Canaanites, and secured to Israel not only the possession of a fine and pastoral country, but, what was of more importance to them, a free access to the Jordan on the east.

CHAPTER III.

Ver. 1-20. CONQUEST OF OG, KING OF BASHAN. 1. we turned, and went up the way to Bashan—Bashan (fruitful or flat), now El Bottein, lay situated to the north of Gilead, and extended as far as Hermon. It was a rugged mountainous country, valuable however for its rich and luxuriant pastures. Og, King of Bashan, came out against us—Without provocation, he rushed to attack the Israelites: either disliking the presence of such dangerous neighbours, or burning to avenge the overthrow of his friends and allies. 2. The Lord said, Fear him not—His gigantic appearance, and the formidable array of forces he will bring to the field, need not discourage you; for, belonging to a doomed race, he is destined to share the fate of Sihon. 3-8. Argob was the capital of a district in Bashan of the same name, which, together with other 59 cities in the same province, were conspicuous for their lofty and fortified walls. It was a war of extermination—houses and cities were razed to the ground, all classes of people were put to the sword, and nothing was saved but the cattle, of which an immense amount fell as spoil into the hands of the conquerors. Thus, the two Amorite kings and the entire population of their dominions were extirpated, and the whole country east of the Jordan—first upland downs from the torrent of the Arnon on the south to that of the Jabbok on the north; next the high mountain tract of Gilead and Bashan from the deep ravine of Jabbok,—became the possession of the Israelites. 9. Hermon—now Jebel-Es-Shiech—the majestic hill on which the long and elevated range of anti-lebanon terminates: its summit and the ridges on its sides are almost constantly covered with snow. It is not so much one high mountain as a whole cluster of mountain peaks, the highest in Palestine. According to the survey taken by the English Government Engineers in 1840, they were about 9,376 feet above the Sea. Being a mountain chain, it is no wonder that it should have received different names at different points from the different tribes which lay a ong the base—all of them designating extraordinary height; Hermon, the lofty peak, "Sirion," or in an abbreviated form "Sion,"(ch. 4. 48.)the upraised,"Shenir," the glittering breastplate of ice, 11. only Og remained of the remnant of giants—*lit.,* of Rephaim. He was not the last giant, but the only living remnant in the Transjordanic country (Josh. 15. 14.) of a certain gigantic race, supposed to be the most ancient inhabitants of Palestine, behold his bedstead —Although beds in the east are with the common people nothing more than a simple mattress, bedsteads are not unknown; they are in use amongst the great, who prefer them of iron or other metals, not only for strength and durability, but for the prevention of the troublesome insects which in warm climates commonly infest wood. Taking the cubit at half-a-yard, the bedstead of Og would measure 13½ feet, so that as beds are usually a little larger than the persons who occupy them, the stature of the Amorite King may be estimated about 11 or 12 feet; or he might have caused his bed to be made much larger than was necessary, as Alexander the Great did for each of his foot soldiers, to impress the Indians with an idea of the extraordinary stength and stature of his men. [LECLERC.] But how did Og's bedstead come to be in Rabbath of the children of Ammon? In answer to this question it has been said, that Og had, on the eve of engagement, conveyed it to Rabbath for safety, or that Moses, after capturing it, may have sold it to the Ammonites, who had kept it as an antiquarian curiosity, till their capital was sacked in the time of David. This is a most unlikely supposition, and besides renders it necessary to consider the latter clause of this verse as an interpolation inserted long after the time of Moses. To avoid this, some eminent critics take the Hebrew word rendered "bedstead" to mean "coffin." They think that the king of Bashan having been wounded in battle, fled to Rabbath, where he died and was buried; hence the dimensions o' his"coffin"are given. [DATHE, ROS.] 12. This land which we possessed at that time—The whole territory occupied by Sihon, was parcelled out among the pastoral tribes of Reuben and Gad. It extended from the north bank of the Arnon to the south half of Mount Gilead—a small mountain ridge, now called Djelaad, about six or seven miles south of the Jabbok, and eight miles in length. The northern portion of Gilead, and the rich pasture lands of Bashan—a large province, consisting, with the exception of a few bleak and rocky spots, of strong and fertilo soil, was assigned to the half tribe of Manasseh. 14. Jair , . . took all the country of Argob—The original inhabitants of the province north of Bashan, comprising sixty cities (v. 4.), not having been extirpated along with Og, this people were afterwards brought into subjection by the energy of Jair. This chief, of the tribe of Manasseh, in accordance with the pastoral habits of his people, called these newly acquired towns by a name which signifies " Jair's: Bedouin "Villages of Tents," unto this day—This remark must evidently have been introduced by Ezra, or some of the pious men who arranged and collected the books of Moses. 15. I gave Gilead unto Machir—It was only the half of Gilead (vs. 12, 13.) which was given to the descendants of Machir, who was now dead. 16. from Gilead —*i.e.* not the mountainous region, but the town Ramoth-Gilead—even unto the river Arnon, half the valley—The word "valley" signifies a wady, either filled with water or dry, as the Arnon is in summer, and thus the proper rendering of the passage will be— "even to the half or middle of the river Arnon (cf. Josh. 12. 2.). This prudent arrangement of the boundaries was evidently made to prevent all disputes between the adjacent tribes about the exclusive right to the water. 25. that goodly mountain, and Lebanon—The natural and very earnest wish of Moses to be allowed to cross the Jordan was founded on the idea that the divine threatening might be conditional and revertible. "That goodly mountain" is supposed by Jewish writers to have pointed to the hill on which the temple was

children's children, and ye shall have remained long in the land, and shall corrupt *yourselves*, and make a graven image, or the likeness of any *thing*, and shall do evil in the sight of the LORD thy God, to provoke him to anger;

26 I call heaven and earth to witness against you this day, that ye shall soon utterly perish from off the land whereunto ye go over Jordan to possess it; ye shall not prolong *your* days upon it, but shall utterly be destroyed.

27 And the LORD shall scatter you among the nations, and ye shall be left few in number among the heathen, whither the LORD shall lead you.

28 And there ye shall serve gods, the work of men's hands, wood and stone, which neither see, nor hear, nor eat, nor smell.

29 But if from thence thou shalt seek the LORD thy God, thou shalt find *him*, if thou seek him with all thy heart and with all thy soul.

30 When thou art in tribulation, and all these things are come upon thee, *even* in the latter days, if thou turn to the LORD thy God, and shalt be obedient unto his voice;

31 (For the LORD thy God *is* a merciful God;) he will not forsake thee, neither destroy thee, nor forget the covenant of thy fathers which he sware unto them.

32 For ask now of the days that are past, which were before thee, since the day that God created man upon the earth, and *ask* from the one side of heaven unto the other, whether there hath been any such thing as this great thing *is*, or hath been heard like it?

33 Did *ever* people hear the voice of God speaking out of the midst of the fire, as thou hast heard, and live?

34 Or hath God assayed to go *and* take him a nation from the midst of *another* nation, by temptations, by signs, and by wonders, and by war, and by a mighty hand, and by a stretched-out arm, and by great terrors, according to all that the LORD your God did for you in Egypt before your eyes?

35 Unto thee it was showed, that thou mightest know that the LORD he *is* God; *there* is none else beside him.

36 Out of heaven he made thee to hear his voice, that he might instruct thee: and upon earth he showed thee his great fire; and thou heardest his words out of the midst of the fire.

37 And because he loved thy fathers, therefore he chose their seed after them, and brought thee out in his sight with his mighty power out of Egypt;

38 To drive out nations from before thee greater and mightier than thou *art*, to bring thee in, to give thee their land *for* an inheritance, as *it is* this day.

39 Know therefore this day, and consider *it* in thine heart, that the LORD he *is* God in heaven above, and upon the earth beneath: *there is* none else.

40 Thou shalt keep therefore his statutes, and his commandments, which I command thee this day, that it may go well with thee, and with thy children after thee, and that thou mayest prolong *thy* days upon the earth, which the LORD thy God giveth thee, for ever.

41 ¶ Then Moses severed three cities on this side Jordan, toward the sun-rising;

42 That the slayer might flee thither, which should kill his neighbour unawares, and hated him not in times past; and that fleeing unto one of these cities he might live:

43 *Namely*, Bezer in the wilderness, in the plain country, of the Reubenites; and Ramoth in Gilead, of the Gadites; and Golan in Bashan, of the Manassites.

44 ¶ And this *is* the law which Moses set before the children of Israel:

45 These *are* the testimonies, and the statutes, and the judgments, which Moses spake unto the children of Israel, after they came forth out of Egypt,

46 On this side Jordan, in the valley over against Beth-peor, in the land of Sihon king of the Amorites, who dwelt at Heshbon, whom Moses and the children of Israel smote, after they were come forth out of Egypt:

47 And they possessed his land, and the land of Og king of Bashan, two kings of the Amorites, which *were* on this side Jordan, toward the sun-rising;

48 From Aroer, which *is* by the bank of the river Arnon, even unto mount Sion, which *is* Hermon,

49 And all the plain on this side Jordan eastward, even unto the sea of the plain, under the springs of Pisgah.

CHAPTER V.

1 *A commemoration of the covenant in Horeb.* 6 *The ten commandments.* 22 *At the people's request Moses receiveth the law from God.*

AND Moses called all Israel, and said unto them, Hear, O Israel, the statutes and judgments which I speak in your ears this day, that ye may learn them, and keep and do them.

2 The LORD our God made a covenant with us in Horeb.

3 The LORD made not this covenant with our fathers, but with us, even us, who *are* all of us here alive this day.

4 The LORD talked with you face to face in the mount, out of the midst of the fire.

5 (I stood between the LORD and you at that time, to show you the word of the LORD: for ye were afraid by reason of the fire, and went not up into the mount;) saying,

6 ¶ I *am* the LORD thy God, which brought thee out of the land of Egypt, from the house of bondage.

7 Thou shalt have none other gods before me.

8 Thou shalt not make thee *any* graven image, *or* any likeness *of any thing* that *is* in heaven above, or that *is* in the earth beneath, or that *is* in the waters beneath the earth:

9 Thou shalt not bow down thyself unto them, nor serve them: for I the LORD thy God *am* a jealous God, visiting the iniquity of the fathers upon the children unto the third and fourth *generation* of them that hate me,

10 And showing mercy unto thousands of them that love me and keep my commandments.

11 Thou shalt not take the name of the LORD thy God in vain: for the LORD will not hold *him* guiltless that taketh his name in vain.

to be built Ex. 15. 2; Ch. 12. 5.). But Biblical scholars now, generally, render the words—" that goodly mountain even Lebanon," and consider it to be mentioned as typifying the beauty of Palestine, of which hills and mountains were so prominent a feature. 26. speak no more unto me of this matter—*i.e.*, my decree is unalterable.

CHAPTER IV.

Ver. 1-23. AN EXHORTATION TO OBEDIENCE. 1. hearken, O Israel, unto the statutes and unto the judgments—By statutes were meant all ordinances respecting religion, and the rites of divine worship; and by judgments, all enactments relative to civil matters. The two embraced the whole law of God. 2. Ye shall not add unto the word which I command you—By the introduction of any heathen superstition or forms of worship different from those which I have appointed (Nu. 15. 30; Ch. 12. 32; Matt. 15. 9.). neither shall ye diminish ought from it—by the neglect or omission of any of the observances, however trivial or irksome, which I have prescribed. The character and provisions of the ancient dispensation were adapted with divine wisdom to the instruction of that infant state of the church. But it was only a temporary economy: and although God here authorises Moses to command that all its institutions should be honoured with unfailing observance, this did not prevent Him from commissioning other prophets to alter or abrogate them when the end of that dispensation was attained. 3, 4. Your eyes have seen what the Lord did because of Baal-peor—It appears that the pestilence and the sword of justice overtook only the guilty in that affair (Nu. 25.), while the rest of the people were spared. The allusion to that recent and appalling judgment was seasonably made as a powerful dissuasive against idolatry, and the fact mentioned was calculated to make a deep impression on people who knew and felt the truth of it. 5, 6. t. is is your wisdom and your understanding in the sight of nations—Moses predicted that the faithful observance of the laws given them, would raise their national character for intelligence and wisdom: and in point of fact it did do so; for although the heathen world generally ridiculed the Hebrews for what they considered a foolish and absurd exclusiveness, some of the most eminent philosophers expressed the highest admiration of the fundamental principle in the Jewish religion—the unity of God; and their legislators borrowed some laws from the constitution of the Hebrews. 7-9. what nation is there so great—Here he represents their privileges and their duty in such significant and comprehensive terms, as were peculiarly calculated to arrest their attention and engage their interest. The former, their national advantages, are described, (vs. 7, 8,) and they were twofold:—1. God's readiness to hear and aid them at all times; and 2. the excellence of that religion in which they were instructed, set forth in the "statutes and judgments so righteous" which the law of Moses contained. Their duty corresponding to these pre-eminent advantages as a people, was also twofold:—1. their own faithful obedience to that law; and 2. their obligation to imbue the minds of the young and rising generation with similar sentiments of reverence and respect for it. 10. the day thou stoodest before the Lord in Horeb—The delivery of the law from Sinai was an era never to be forgotten in the history of Israel. Some of those whom Moses was addressing had been present, though very young; while the rest were federally represented by their parents who in their name and for their interest entered into the national covenant. 12. Ye heard the voice of the words, but saw no similitude—although articulate sounds were heard emanating from the Mount, no form or representation of the Divine Being who spoke was seen to indicate his nature or properties, according to the notions of the heathen.

14-40. A PARTICULAR DISSUASIVE AGAINST IDOLATRY. 15. Take good heed for ye saw no manner of similitude—The extreme proneness of the Israelites to idolatry, from their position in the midst of surrounding nations already abandoned to its seductions, accounts for their attention being repeatedly drawn to the fact that God did not appear on Sinai in any visible form; and an earnest caution, founded on that remarkable circumstance, is given to beware, not only of making representations of false gods, but also any fancied representation of the true God. 16-19. lest ye corrupt yourselves and make any graven images—The things are here specified of which God prohibited any image or representation to be made for the purposes of worship; and, from the variety of details entered into, an idea may be formed of the extensive prevalence of idolatry in that age. In whatever way idolatry originated, whether from an intention to worship the true God through those things which seemed to afford the strongest evidences of his power, or whether a divine principle was supposed to reside in the things themselves, there was scarcely an element or object of nature but was deified. This was particularly the case with the Canaanites and Egyptians, against whose superstitious practices the caution, no doubt, was chiefly directed. The former worshipped Baal and Astarte—the latter Osiris and Isis, under the figure of a male and a female. It was in Egypt that animal worship most prevailed, for the natives of that country deified among beasts—the ox, the heifer, the sheep, and the goat, the dog, the cat, and the ape; among birds—the ibis, the hawk and the crane; among reptiles—the crocodile, the frog and the beetle; among fishes—all the fish of the Nile; some of these as Osiris and Isis were worshipped over all Egypt, the others only in particular provinces; in addition to which they embraced the Zabian superstition, the adoration of the Egyptians, in common with that of many other people, extending to the whole starry host. The very circumstantial details here given of the Canaanitish and Egyptian idolatry were owing to the past and prospective familiarity of the Israelites with it in all these forms. 20. But the Lord hath ... brought you out of the iron furnace—*i.e.*, a furnace for smelting iron. A furnace of this kind is round, sometimes 30 feet deep, and requiring the highest intensity of heat. Such is the tremendous image chosen to represent the bondage and affliction of the Israelites. [ROSENMULLER.] to be unto him a people of inheritance—His peculiar possession from age to age; and therefore for you to abandon his worship

12 Keep ⁱ the sabbath day to sanctify it, as the LORD thy God hath commanded thee.
13 Six ᵐ days thou shalt labour, and do all thy work;
14 But the seventh day is the ⁿ sabbath of the LORD thy God: in it thou shalt not do any work, thou, nor thy son, nor thy daughter, nor thy man-servant, nor thy maid-servant, nor thine ox, nor thine ass, nor any of thy cattle, nor thy stranger that is within thy gates; that thy man-servant and thy maid-servant may rest as well as thou.
15 And remember that thou wast a servant in the land of Egypt, and that the LORD thy God brought thee out thence through a mighty hand and by a stretched-out arm: therefore the LORD thy God commanded thee to keep the sabbath day.
16 ¶ Honour ᵒ thy father and thy mother, as the LORD thy God hath commanded thee; ᵖ that thy days may be prolonged, and that it may go well with thee, in the land which the LORD thy God giveth thee.
17 Thou ᵍ shalt not kill.
18 Neither ʳ shalt thou commit adultery.
19 Neither ˢ shalt thou steal.
20 Neither ᵗ shalt thou bear false witness against thy neighbour.
21 Neither ᵘ shalt thou desire thy neighbour's wife, neither shalt thou covet thy neighbour's house, his field, or his man-servant, or his maid-servant, his ox, or his ass, or any thing that is thy neighbour's.
22 ¶ These words the LORD spake unto all your assembly in the mount, out of the midst of the fire, of the cloud, and of the thick darkness, with a great voice; and he added no more: and ᵛ he wrote them in two tables of stone, and delivered them unto me.
23 And it came to pass, when ye heard the voice out of the midst of the darkness, (for the mountain did burn with fire,) that ye came near unto me, even all the heads of your tribes, and your elders;
24 And ye said, Behold, the LORD our God hath showed us his glory, and his greatness, and we have heard his voice out of the midst of the fire: we have seen this day that God doth talk with man, and he liveth.
25 Now therefore why should we die? for this great fire will consume us: if we ³ hear the voice of the LORD our God any more, then we shall die.
26 For ʷ who is there of all flesh, that hath heard the voice of the living God speaking out of the midst of the fire, as we have, and lived?
27 Go thou near, and hear all that the LORD our God shall say; and ˣ speak thou unto us all that the LORD our God shall speak unto thee; and we will hear it, and do it.
28 And the LORD heard the voice of your words, when ye spake unto me; and the LORD said unto me, I have heard the voice of the words of this people, which they have spoken unto thee: they have well said all that they have spoken.
29 O ʸ that there were such an heart in them, that they would fear me, and ᶻ keep all my commandments always, that it might be well with them, and with their children for ever!

30 Go say to them, Get you into your tents again.
31 But as for thee, stand thou here by me, and ᵃ I will speak unto thee all the commandments, and the statutes, and the judgments, which thou shalt teach them, that they may do them in the land which I give them to possess it.
32 Ye shall observe to do therefore as the LORD your God hath commanded you: ᵇ ye shall not turn aside to the right hand or to the left.
33 Ye shall walk in ᶜ all the ways which the LORD your God hath commanded you, that ye may live, and that it may be well with you, and that ye may prolong your days in the land which ye shall possess.

CHAPTER VI.

1 *Moses exhorteth Israel to hear God, and to keep his commandments, which consists in loving him with all the heart:* 16 *they must not tempt the Lord:* 20 *they are commanded to instruct their children.*

NOW these are the commandments, the statutes, and the judgments, which the LORD your God commanded to teach you, that ye might do them in the land whither ye ¹ go to possess it:
2 That ᵈ thou mightest fear the LORD thy God, to keep all his statutes, and his commandments, which I command thee, thou, and thy son, and thy son's son, all the days of thy life; ᵇ and that thy days may be prolonged.
3 ¶ Hear therefore, O Israel, and observe to do it; that it may be well with thee, and that ye may increase mightily, as the LORD God of thy fathers hath promised thee, in the land that floweth with milk and honey.
4 Hear, O Israel: ᶜ The LORD our God is one LORD:
5 And ᵈ thou shalt love the LORD thy God with all thine heart, and with all thy soul, and with all thy might.
6 And ᵉ these words, which I command thee this day, shall be in thine heart:
7 And ᶠ thou shalt ² teach them diligently unto thy children, and shalt talk of them when thou sittest in thine house, and when thou walkest by the way, and when thou liest down, and when thou risest up.
8 And ᵍ thou shalt bind them for a sign upon thine hand, and they shall be as frontlets between thine eyes.
9 And ʰ thou shalt write them upon the posts of thy house, and on thy gates.
10 And it shall be, when the LORD thy God shall have brought thee into the land which he sware unto thy fathers, to Abraham, to Isaac, and to Jacob, to give thee great and goodly cities, ⁱ which thou buildedst not,
11 And houses full of all good things, which thou filledst not, and wells digged, which thou diggedst not, vineyards and olive trees, which thou plantedst not; when thou shalt have eaten, and be full;
12 Then beware lest thou forget the LORD, which brought thee forth out of the land of Egypt, from the house of ³ bondage.
13 Thou shalt ʲ fear the LORD thy God, and serve him, and ᵏ shalt swear by his name.
14 Ye shall not ˡ go after other gods, of the gods of the people which are round about you,
15 (For the LORD thy God is a jealous

for that of idols, especially the gross and debasing system of idolatry that prevails among the Egyptians, would be the greatest folly—the blackest ingratitude. 26. I call heaven and earth to witness against you—this solemn form of adjuration has been common in special circumstances amongst all people. It is used here figuratively, or as in other parts of Scripture where inanimate objects are called up as witnesses ch. 32. 1; Is. 1. 2.). 28. there ye shall serve gods—The compulsory measures of their tyrannical conquerors would force them into idolatry, so that their choice would become their punishment. 30. in the latter days—either towards the destined close of their captivities, when they evinced a returning spirit of repentance and faith, or in the age of Messiah, which is commonly called "the latter days," and when the scattered tribes of Israel shall be converted to the Gospel of Christ. The occurrence of this auspicious event will be the most illustrious proof of the truth of the promise made in v. 31. 41-43. Then Moses severed three cities on this side Jordan—(See on Josh. 20. 7, 8.). 44-49. This is the law which Moses set—This is a preface to the rehearsal of the law, which, with the addition of various explanatory circumstances, the following chapters contain. 46. Beth-Peor—i.e., house or temple of Peor. It is probable that a temple of this Moabite idol stood in full view of the Hebrew camp, while Moses was urging the exclusive claims of God to their worship; and this allusion would be very significant if it were the temple where so many of the Israelites had grievously offended. 49. The springs of Pisgah—more frequently Ashdoth-pisgah, (ch. 3. 17; Josh. 12. 3; 13. 20,) the roots or foot of the mountains east of the Jordan.

CHAPTER V.

Ver. 1-5. A COMMEMORATION OF THE COVENANT IN HOREB. 1. Hear, O, Israel, the statutes and judgments—Whether this rehearsal of the law was made in a solemn assembly, or as some think at a general meeting of the elders as representatives of the people, is of little moment; it was addressed either directly or indirectly to the Hebrew people as principles of their peculiar constitution as a nation; and hence, as has been well observed, "the Jewish law has no obligation upon Christians, unless so much of it as given or commanded by Jesus Christ; for whatever in this law is conformable to the laws of nature, obliges us, not as given by Moses, but by virtue of an antecedent law common to all rational beings." [BISHOP WILSON.] 3. The Lord made not this covenant with our fathers, but with us—The meaning is, "not with our fathers" only, "but with us" also, assuming it to be "a covenant" of grace; or "not with our fathers" at all, if the reference is to the peculiar establishment of the covenant at Sinai: a law was not given to them as to us, nor was the covenant ratified in the same public manner, and by the same solemn sanctions. Or, finally, "not with our fathers" who died in the wilderness, in consequence of their rebellion, and to whom God did not give the rewards promised only to the faithful; but "with us," who alone, strictly speaking, shall enjoy the benefits of this covenant by entering on the possession of the promised land. 4. The Lord talked with you face to face—not in a visible and corporeal form, of which there was no trace (ch. 4. 12, 15.), but freely, familiarly, and in such a manner that no doubt could be entertained of His presence. 5. I stood between the Lord and you—as the messenger and interpreter of thy Heavenly King, bringing near two objects, formerly removed from each other at a vast distance, viz: God and the people, (Gal. 10. 19.). In this character Moses was a type of Christ, who is the only mediator between God and men, (1 Tim. 11. 5,) the Mediator of a better covenant. (Heb. 8. 6; 9. 15; 12. 24.) to shew you the word of the Lord—not the ten commandments—for they were proclaimed directly by the Divine Speaker himself, but the statutes and judgments which are repeated in the subsequent portion of this book. 6-20. I am the Lord thy God—The word "Lord" is expressive of authority or dominion; and God, who by natural claim as well as by covenant relation, was entitled to exercise supremacy over his people Israel, had a sovereign right to establish laws for their government. The commandments which follow are, with a few slight verbal alterations, the same as formerly recorded, (Ex. 20.) and in some of them there is a distinct reference to that promulgation. 12. Keep the Sabbath day to sanctify it, as the Lord, &c. —i.e., keep it in mind as a sacred institution of former enactment and perpetual obligation. 14. that thy man-servant and thy maid-servant may rest as well as thou—This is a different reason for the observance of the Sabbath from what is assigned in Ex. 20, where that day is stated to be an appointed memorial of the creation. But the addition of another motive for the observance does not imply any necessary contrariety to the other; and it has been thought probable that, the commemorative design of the institution being well known, the other reason was specially mentioned on this repetition of the law, to secure the privilege of sabbatic rest to servants, of which, in some Hebrew families, they had been deprived. In this view, the allusion to the period of Egyptian bondage (v. 15,) when themselves were not permitted to observe the Sabbath either as a day of rest, or of public devotion, was peculiarly seasonable and significant, well fitted to come home to their business and bosoms. 16. that it may go well with thee— This clause is not in Exodus, but admitted into Eph. 6. 3. 21. neither shalt thou desire thy neighbour's wife, house, and field—an alteration is here made in the words (see Ex. 20.), but it is so slight ("wife" being put in the first clause, and house in the second) that it would not have been worth while noticing it, except that the interchange proves, contrary to the opinion of some eminent critics, that these two objects are included in one and the same commandment. 22. He added no more—(Ex. 20. 1.). The preeminence of these ten commandments was shewn in God's announcing them directly: other laws and institutions were communicated to the people through the instrumentality of Moses. 23-28. And . . . ye came near unto me—(See on Ex. 20. 19.). 29. O! that there were such an heart in them—God can bestow such a heart and has promised to give it, wherever it is asked (Jer. 32. 40.). But the wish which is here expressed on the part of God for the piety and steadfast obe-

God among you,) lest the anger of the LORD thy God be kindled against thee, and destroy thee from off the face of the earth.

16 ¶ Ye ᵐ shall not tempt the LORD your God, ⁿ as ye tempted *him* in Massah.

17 Ye shall ᵒ diligently keep the commandments of the LORD your God, and his testimonies, and his statutes, which he hath commanded thee.

18 And thou shalt do *that which is* right and good in the sight of the LORD; that it may be well with thee, and that thou mayest go in and possess the good land which the LORD sware unto thy fathers.

19 To cast out all thine enemies from before thee, as the LORD hath spoken.

20 ¶ *And* when thy son asketh thee ⁴ in time to come, saying, What *mean* the testimonies, and the statutes, and the judgments, which the LORD our God hath commanded you?

21 Then thou shalt say unto thy son, We were Pharaoh's bond-men in Egypt; and the LORD brought us out of Egypt with a mighty hand:

22 And the LORD showed signs and wonders, great and ᵇ sore, upon Egypt, upon Pharaoh, and upon all his household, before our eyes:

23 And he brought us out from thence, that he might bring us in, to give us the land which he sware unto our fathers.

24 And the LORD commanded us to do all these statutes, to fear the LORD our God, for ᵖ our good always, that ᵠ he might preserve us alive, as it *is* at this day.

25 And ʳ it shall be our righteousness, if we observe to do all these commandments before the LORD our God, as he hath commanded us.

CHAPTER VII.

1 *All communion with the nations forbidden,* 4 *for fear of idolatry,* 6 *and for the holiness of the people.* 25 *Images to be destroyed.*

WHEN the LORD thy God shall bring thee into the land whither thou goest to possess it, and hath cast out many nations before thee, the Hittites, and the Girgashites, and the Amorites, and the Canaanites, and the Perizzites, and the Hivites, and the Jebusites, seven nations greater and mightier than thou;

2 And when the LORD thy God shall deliver them before thee; thou shalt smite them, *and* ᵃ utterly destroy them; ᵇ thou shalt make no covenant with them, nor show mercy unto them:

3 Neither ᶜ shalt thou make marriages with them; thy daughter thou shalt not give unto his son, nor his daughter shalt thou take unto thy son.

4 For they will turn away thy son from following me, that they may serve other gods: so will the anger of the LORD be kindled against you, and destroy thee suddenly.

5 But thus shall ye deal with them; ye shall ᵈ destroy their altars, and break down their ¹ images, and cut down their groves, and burn their graven images with fire.

6 For ᵉ thou *art* an holy people unto the LORD thy God: ᶠ the LORD thy God hath chosen thee to be a special people unto himself, above all people that *are* upon the face of the earth.

7 The LORD did not set his love upon you, nor choose you, because ye were more in number than any people; for ye *were* the fewest of all people;

8 But because the LORD loved you, and because he would keep ᵍ the oath which he had sworn unto your fathers, ʰ hath the LORD brought you out with a mighty hand, and redeemed you out of the house of bondmen, from the hand of Pharaoh king of Egypt.

9 Know therefore that the LORD thy God, he *is* God, ⁱ the faithful God, ʲ which keepeth covenant and mercy with them that love him and keep his commandments, to a thousand generations;

10 And ᵏ repayeth them that hate him to their face, to destroy them: he will not be slack to him that hateth him, he will repay him to his face.

11 Thou shalt therefore keep the commandments, and the statutes, and the judgments, which I command thee this day, to do them.

12 Wherefore it shall come to pass, ² if ye hearken to these judgments, and keep and do them, that the LORD thy God shall keep unto thee the covenant and the mercy which he sware unto thy fathers:

13 And he will ˡ love thee, and bless thee, and multiply thee: he will also bless the fruit of thy womb, and the fruit of thy land, thy corn, and thy wine, and thine oil, the increase of thy kine, and the flocks of thy sheep, in the land which he sware unto thy fathers to give thee.

14 Thou shalt be blessed above all people: there shall not be male or female barren among you, or among your cattle.

15 And the LORD will take away from thee all sickness, and will put none of the ᵐ evil diseases of Egypt, which thou knowest, upon thee; but will lay them upon all *them* that hate thee.

16 And thou shalt consume all the people which the LORD thy God shall deliver thee; thine eye shall have no pity upon them: neither shalt thou serve their gods; for that *will be* ⁿ a snare unto thee.

17 If thou shalt say in thine heart, These nations *are* more than I; how can I ᵒ dispossess them?

18 Thou shalt not be afraid of them; *but* shalt well ᵖ remember what the LORD thy God did unto Pharaoh, and unto all Egypt:

19 The great temptations which thine eyes saw, and the signs, and the wonders, and the mighty hand, and the stretched-out arm, whereby the LORD thy God brought thee out: so shall the LORD thy God do unto all the people of whom thou art afraid.

20 Moreover ᵠ the LORD thy God will send the hornet among them, until they that are left, and hide themselves from thee, be destroyed.

21 Thou shalt not be affrighted at them: for the LORD thy God *is* ʳ among you, ˢ a mighty God and terrible.

22 And the LORD thy God will ³ put out those nations before thee by little and little: thou mayest not consume them at once, lest the beasts of the field increase upon thee.

23 But the LORD thy God shall deliver them ⁴ unto thee, and shall destroy them with a mighty destruction, until they be destroyed.

24 And ᵗ he shall deliver their kings into thine hand, and thou shalt destroy their name from under heaven; ᵘ there shall no

dience of the Israelites did not relate to them as individuals, so much as a nation, whose religious character and progress would have a mighty influence on the world at large.

CHAPTER VI.

Ver. 1-20. MOSES EXHORTETH ISRAEL TO HEAR GOD AND TO KEEP HIS COMMANDMENTS. 1. Now these are the commandments and the statutes and the judgments which the Lord commanded—The grand design of all the institutions prescribed to Israel was to form a religious people, whose national character should be distinguished by that fear of the Lord their God, which would ensure their divine observance of His worship, and their steadfast obedience to His will. The basis of their religion was an acknowledgment of the unity of God with the understanding, and the love of God in the heart (v. 4, 5.). Compared with the religious creed of all their contemporaries, how sound in principle, how elevated in character, how unlimited in the extent of its moral influence on the heart and habits of the people. Indeed, it is precisely the same basis on which rests the purer and more spiritual form of it which Christianity exhibits (Matt. 22. 37; Mk. 12. 30; Lu. 10. 27.). Moreover, to help in keeping a sense of religion in their minds, it was commanded that its great principles should be carried about with them wherever they went, as well as meet their eyes every time they entered their homes; a further provision was made for the earnest inculcation of them on the minds of the young by a system of parental training, which was designed to associate religion with all the most familiar and oft-recurring scenes of domestic life. It is probable that Moses used the phraseology in the seventh verse, merely in a figurative way, to signify assiduous, earnest, and frequent instruction; and perhaps he meant the metaphorical language in the eighth verse to be taken in the same sense also. But as the Israelites interpreted it literally, many writers suppose that a reference was made to a superstitious custom borrowed from the Egyptians, who wore jewels and ornamental trinkets on the forehead and arm, inscribed with certain words and sentences, as amulets to protect them from danger. These, it has been conjectured, Moses intended to supersede by substituting sentences of the law; and so the Hebrews understood him, for they have always considered the wearing of the *Tephilim* or frontlets a permanent obligation. The form was as follows:—Four pieces of parchment, inscribed, the first with Exodus, 13. 2-10; the second with Exodus, 13. 11-16; the third with Deuteronomy, 6. 1-8; and the fourth with Deuteronomy, 11. 18-21, were enclosed in a square case or box of tough skin, on the side of which was placed the Hebrew letter (*shin*) and bound round the forehead with a thong or ribbon. When designed for the arms. those four texts were written on one slip of parchment, which, as well as the ink, was carefully prepared for the purpose. With regard to the other usage supposed to be alluded to, the ancient Egyptians had the lintels and imposts of their doors and gates inscribed with sentences indicative of a favourable omen [WILK.]; and this is still the case, for in Egypt and other Mahommedan countries, the front doors of houses—in Cairo, for instance—are painted red, white, and green, bearing conspicuously inscribed upon them such sentences from the Koran, as "God is the Creator," "God is one, and Mahomet is his prophet." Moses designed to turn this ancient and favourite custom to a better account, and ordered that, instead of the former superstitious inscriptions, should be written the words of God, persuading and enjoining the people to hold the laws in perpetual remembrance. 20-25. When thy son asketh thee—The directions given for the instruction of their children form only an extension of the preceding counsels.

CHAPTER VII.

Ver. 1-6. ALL COMMUNION WITH THE NATIONS FORBIDDEN. 1. The Hittites—This people were descended from Heth, the second son of Canaan, (Gen. 10. 15,) and occupied the mountainous region about Hebron, in the south of Palestine. The Girgashites supposed by some to be the same as the Gergesenes, (Matt. 8. 28,) who lay to the east of Lake Gennesareth; but they are placed on the west of Jordan, (Josh. 24. 11,) and others take them for a branch of the large family of the Hivites, as they are omitted in nine out of ten places where the tribes of Canaan are enumerated; in the tenth they are mentioned, while the Hivites are not. The Amorites—descended from the fourth son of Canaan occupied, besides their conquest on the Moabite territory, extensive settlements west of the Dead Sea, in the mountains. The Canaanites—were located in Phoenicia, particularly about Tyre and Sidon, and being sprung from the eldest branch of the family of Canaan, bore his name. The Perizzites—*i.e.*, *villagers*, a tribe who were dispersed throughout the country, and lived in unwalled towns. The Hivites—who dwelt about Ebal and Gerizim, extending towards Hermon. They are supposed to be the same as the Avims. The Jebusites—resided about Jerusalem and the adjacent country. seven nations greater and mightier than thou—Ten were formerly mentioned (Gen. 15. 19-21.). But in the lapse of near 500 years, it cannot be surprising that some of them had been extinguished in the many intestine feuds that prevailed amongst those warlike tribes; and it is more than probable that some, stationed on the east of Jordan, had fallen under the victorious arms of the Israelites. 2-6. Thou shalt utterly destroy, and make no covenant with them—This relentless doom of extermination which God denounced against those tribes of Canaan cannot be reconciled with the attributes of the Divine character, except on the assumption that their gross idolatry and enormous wickedness left no reasonable hope of their repentance and amendment. If they were to be swept away like the Antediluvians, or the people of Sodom and Gomorrah, as incorrigible sinners who had filled up the measure of their iniquities, it mattered not to them in what way the judgment was inflicted; and God, as the Sovereign Disposer, had a right to employ any instruments that pleased Him for executing His judgments. Some think that they were to be exterminated as unprincipled usurpers of a country which God had assigned to the posterity of Eber, and which had been occupied ages

man be able to stand before thee, until thou have destroyed them.

25 The graven images of their gods *v* shall ye burn with fire: thou *w* shalt not desire the silver or gold *that is* on them, nor take *it* unto thee, lest thou be *x* snared therein: for it is *y* an abomination to the LORD thy God.

26 Neither shalt thou bring an abomination into thine house, lest thou be a cursed thing like it: *but* thou shalt utterly detest it, and thou shalt utterly abhor it; *z* for it *is* a cursed thing.

CHAPTER VIII.

1 *An exhortation to obedience in regard of God's mercy and goodness in his dealings with Israel.* 19 *The evil of worshipping other gods.*

ALL the commandments which I command thee this day shall ye observe to do, that ye may live, and multiply, and go in and possess the land which the LORD sware unto your fathers.

2 And thou shalt remember all the way which the LORD thy God *a* led thee these forty years in the wilderness, to humble thee, *and* to prove thee, *b* to know what *was* in thine heart, whether thou wouldest keep his commandments, or no.

3 And he humbled thee, and *c* suffered thee to hunger, and fed thee with manna, which thou knewest not, neither did thy fathers know; that he might make thee know that man doth *d* not live by bread only, but by every *word* that proceedeth out of the mouth of the LORD doth man live.

4 Thy *e* raiment waxed not old upon thee, neither did thy foot swell, these forty years.

5 Thou *f* shalt also consider in thine heart, that, as a man chasteneth his son, *so* the LORD thy God chasteneth thee.

6 Therefore thou shalt keep the commandments of the LORD thy God, to walk in his ways, and to fear him.

7 For the LORD thy God bringeth thee into a good land; a land of brooks of water, of fountains, and depths that spring out of valleys and hills;

8 A land of wheat, and barley, and vines, and fig trees, and pomegranates; a land of oil olive and honey;

9 A land wherein thou shalt eat bread without scarceness, thou shalt not lack any thing in it; a land whose stones *are* iron, and out of whose hills thou mayest dig brass.

10 When *g* thou hast eaten and art full, then thou shalt bless the LORD thy God for the good land which he hath given thee.

11 Beware that thou forget not the LORD thy God, in not keeping his commandments, and his judgments, and his statutes, which I command thee this day:

12 Lest *h when* thou hast eaten and art full, and hast built goodly houses, and dwelt *therein;*

13 And *when* thy herds and thy flocks multiply, and thy silver and thy gold is multiplied, and all that thou hast is multiplied;

14 Then *i* thine heart be lifted up, and thou *j* forget the LORD thy God, which brought thee forth out of the land of Egypt, from the house of bondage;

15 Who *k* led thee through that great and terrible wilderness, *l wherein were* fiery serpents, and scorpions, and drought, where *there was* no water; *m* who brought thee forth water out of the rock of flint;

16 Who fed thee in the wilderness *n* with manna, which thy fathers knew not, that he might humble thee, and that he might prove thee, *o* to do thee good at thy latter end;

17 And *p* thou say in thine heart, My power and the might of *mine* hand hath gotten me this wealth.

18 But thou shalt remember the LORD thy God: *q* for *it is* he that giveth thee power to get wealth, that he may establish his covenant which he sware unto thy fathers, as *it is* this day.

19 And it shall be, if thou do at all forget the LORD thy God, and walk after other gods, and serve them, and worship them, I testify against you this day, that ye shall surely perish.

20 As the nations which the LORD destroyeth before your face, *r* so shall ye perish; because ye would not be obedient unto the voice of the LORD your God.

CHAPTER IX.

1 *Moses dissuadeth them from the opinion of their own righteousness,* 7 *by rehearsing their several rebellions:* 26 *his prayer for them.*

HEAR, O Israel: Thou *art* to pass over Jordan this day, to go in to possess nations *a* greater and mightier than thyself, cities great, and *b* fenced up to heaven;

2 A people great and tall, *c* the children of the Anakims, whom thou knowest, and *of whom* thou hast heard *say,* Who can stand before the children of Anak!

3 Understand therefore this day, that the LORD thy God *is* he which *d* goeth over before thee; *as a e* consuming fire he shall destroy them, and he shall bring them down before thy face: *f* so shalt thou drive them out, and destroy them quickly, as the LORD hath said unto thee.

4 Speak *g* not thou in thine heart, after that the LORD thy God hath cast them out from before thee, saying, For my righteousness the LORD hath brought me in to possess this land; but *h* for the wickedness of these nations the LORD doth drive them out from before thee.

5 Not *i* for thy righteousness, or for the uprightness of thine heart, dost thou go to possess their land; but for the wickedness of these nations the LORD thy God doth drive them out from before thee, and that he may perform *j* the word which the LORD sware unto thy fathers, Abraham, Isaac, and Jacob.

6 Understand therefore, that the LORD thy God giveth thee not this good land to possess it for thy righteousness; for thou *art* a stiff-necked people.

7 ¶ Remember, *and* forget not, how thou provokedst the LORD thy God to wrath in the wilderness: *k* from the day that thou didst depart out of the land of Egypt, until ye came unto this place, ye have been rebellious against the LORD.

8 Also *l* in Horeb ye provoked the LORD to wrath, so that the LORD was angry with you, to have destroyed you.

9 When I was gone up into the mount to receive the tables of stone, *even* the tables of the covenant which the LORD made with you, then I *m* abode in the mount forty days and forty nights; I neither did eat bread nor drink water:

10 And the LORD delivered unto me two tables of stone, written with the finger of God: and on them *was written* according

All Communion forbidden.   DEUTERONOMY, VIII.   *Exhortation to Obedience.*

before by wandering shepherds of that race, till, on the migration of Jacob's family into Egypt through the pressure of famine, the Canaanites overspread the whole land, though they had no legitimate claim to it, and endeavoured to retain possession of it by force. In this view their expulsion was just and proper. The strict prohibition against contracting any alliances with such infamous idolators was a prudential rule, founded on the experience that "evil communications corrupt good manners," and its importance or necessity was attested by the unhappy examples of Solomon and others in the subsequent history of Israel. 5. Thus shall ye deal with them—The removal of the temples, altars, and everything that had been enlisted in the service, or might tend to perpetuate the remembrance, of Canaanite idolatry was likewise highly expedient for preserving the Israelites from all risk of contamination. It was imitated by our Scottish reformers, and although many ardent lovers of architecture and the fine arts have anathematized their proceedings as Vandalism, yet there was profound wisdom in the favourite maxim of Knox—"pull down the nests, and the rooks will disappear." 6-10. for thou art an holy people unto the Lord—*i.e.*, set apart to the service of God, or chosen to execute the important purposes of His providence. Their selection to this high destiny was neither on account of their numerical amount, for, till after the death of Joseph, they were but a handful of people; nor of their extraordinary merits, for they had often pursued a most perverse and unworthy conduct: but it was in consequence of the covenant or promise made with their pious forefathers, and the motives that led to that special act were such as tended not only to vindicate God's wisdom, but to illustrate His glory in diffusing the best and most precious blessings to all mankind. 11-26. Thou shalt therefore keep the commandments, &c.—In the covenant into which God entered with Israel, He promised to bestow upon them a variety of blessings so long as they continued obedient to Him as their heavenly King, and pledged His veracity that His infinite perfections would be exerted for this purpose as well as for delivering them from every evil to which, as a people, they would be exposed. That people accordingly were truly happy as a nation, and found every promise which the faithful God made to them amply fulfilled, so long as they adhered to that obedience which was required of them. See a beautiful illustration of this in Psalm 144. 12-15. The evil diseases of Egypt—(See Ex. 15. 26.) But besides those with which Pharaoh and his subjects were visited, Egypt has always been dreadfully scourged with diseases, and the testimony of Moses is confirmed by the reports of many modern writers, who tell us that, notwithstanding its equal temperature and sereneness, that country has some indigenous maladies which are very malignant, such as opthalmia, dysentery, small pox, and the plague. 20. God will send the hornet among them—(See on Josh. 24. 11-13.) 22. lest the beasts of the field increase upon thee— See on Ex. 23. 28-30.) The omnipotence of their Almighty Ruler could have given them possession of the promised land at once. But, the unburied corpses of the enemy, and the portions of the country that might have been left desolate for a while, would have drawn an influx of dangerous beasts. This evil would be prevented by a progressive conquest, and by the use of ordinary means which God would bless.

CHAPTER VIII.

Ver. 1-20. AN EXHORTATION TO OBEDIENCE. 1. All the commandments shall ye observe, that ye may live—Duty has been made in all the wise arrangements of our Creator inseparably connected with happiness, and the earnest enforcement of the divine law which Moses was making to the Israelites was in order to secure their being a happy, because a moral and religious people: a course of prosperity is often called life (Gen. 17. 18; Prov. 3. 2.). live and multiply— This reference to the future increase of their population proves that they were too few to occupy the land fully at first. 2. Thou shalt remember all the way which God led thee these forty years—The recapitulation of all their chequered experience during that long period was designed to awaken lively impressions of the goodness of God. First, Moses showed them the object of their protracted wanderings and varied hardships; these were trials of their obedience as well as chastisements for sin. Indeed, the discovery of their infidelity, inconstancy, and their rebellions and perverseness which this varied discipline brought to light, was of eminently practical use to the Israelites themselves, as it has been to the Church in all subsequent ages. Next, he enlarged on the goodness of God to them, while reduced to the last extremities of despair, in the miraculous provision which, without anxiety or labour, was made for their daily support (see on Ex. 16. 12.), and which, possessing no nutritious properties inherent in it, contributed to their sustenance, as indeed all food does (Matt. 4. 4.), solely through the ordinance and blessing of God. This remark is applicable to the means of spiritual as well as natural life. 4. thy raiment waxed not old, neither did thy foot swell—What a striking miracle was this. No doubt the Israelites might have brought from Egypt more clothes than they wore at their outset; they might also have obtained supplies of various articles of food and raiment in barter with the neighbouring tribes for the fleeces and skins of their sheep and goats; and in furnishing them with such opportunities the care of Providence appeared. But the strong and pointed terms which Moses here uses (see also ch. 29. 5.) indicate a special or miraculous interposition of their loving guardian in preserving them amid the tear and wear of their nomadic life in the desert. Thirdly, Moses expatiated on the goodness of the promised land. 7. For the Lord thy God bringeth thee into a good land—All accounts, ancient and modern, concur in bearing testimony to the natural beauty and fertility of Palestine, and its great capabilities if properly cultivated, a land of brooks, &c. that spring out of hills and valleys—These characteristic features are mentioned first, as they would be most striking; and all travellers describe how delightful and cheerful it is, after passing through the barren and thirsty desert, to be among running brooks and swelling hills and verdant valleys. It is observable that water is men-

138

to all the words which the LORD spake with you in the mount, out of the midst of the fire, in the day of the assembly.

11 And it came to pass, at the end of forty days and forty nights, *that* the LORD gave me the two tables of stone, *even* the tables of the covenant.

12 And the LORD said unto me, *ⁿ* Arise, get thee down quickly from hence; for thy people which thou hast brought forth out of Egypt have corrupted *themselves*; they are *ᵒ* quickly turned aside out of the way which I commanded them; they have made them a molten image.

13 Furthermore *ᵖ* the LORD spake unto me, saying, I have seen this people, and, behold, *ᵠ* it *is* a stiff-necked people:

14 Let me alone, that I may destroy them, and *ʳ* blot out their name from under heaven: and I will make of thee a nation mightier and greater than they.

15 So I turned, and came down from the mount, and the mount burned with fire: and the two tables of the covenant *were* in my two hands.

16 And I looked, and, behold, ye had sinned against the LORD your God, *and* had made you a molten calf: ye had turned aside quickly out of the way which the LORD had commanded you.

17 And *ˢ* I took the two tables, and cast them out of my two hands, and brake them before your eyes.

18 And I *ᵗ* fell down before the LORD, as at the first, forty days and forty nights: I did neither eat bread nor drink water, because of all your sins, which ye sinned, in doing wickedly in the sight of the LORD, to provoke him to anger.

19 For *ᵘ* I was afraid of the anger and hot displeasure wherewith the LORD was wroth against you to destroy you. *ᵛ* But the LORD hearkened unto me at that time also.

20 And the LORD was very angry with Aaron to have destroyed him: and I prayed for Aaron also the same time.

21 And *ʷ* I took your sin, the calf which ye had made, and burnt it with fire, and stamped it, *and* ground *it* very small, *even* until it was as small as dust: and I cast the dust thereof into the brook that descended out of the mount.

22 And at *ˣ* Taberah, and at Massah, and at *ʸ* Kibroth-hattaavah, ye provoked the LORD to wrath.

23 Likewise *ᶻ* when the LORD sent you from Kadesh-barnea, saying, Go up and possess the land which I have given you; then ye rebelled against the commandment of the LORD your God, and *ᵃ* ye believed him not, nor hearkened to his voice.

24 Ye *ᵇ* have been rebellious against the LORD from the day that I knew you.

25 Thus I fell down before the LORD forty days and forty nights, as I fell down *at the first*; because the LORD had said he would destroy you.

26 I *ᶜ* prayed therefore unto the LORD, and said, O Lord GOD, destroy not thy people and thine inheritance, which thou hast redeemed through thy greatness, which thou hast brought forth out of Egypt with a mighty hand.

27 Remember thy servants, Abraham, Isaac, and Jacob; look not unto the stubbornness of this people, nor to their wickedness, nor to their sin;

28 Lest *ᵈ* the land whence thou broughtest

B. C. 1451.

CHAP. 9.
ⁿ Ex. 32. 7.
ᵒ ch. 31. 29.
Judg. 2. 17.
ᵖ Ex. 32. 9.
ᵠ ch. 10. 16.
ch. 31. 27.
2 Kin. 17. 14.
ʳ ch. 29. 20.
Ps. 9. 5.
Ps. 109. 13.
ˢ Ps. 69. 9.
Psalm 119. 139.
ᵗ Ex. 34. 28.
Psalm 106. 23.
ᵘ Heb. 12. 29.
ᵛ Ex. 32. 14.
Ex. 33. 17.
ch. 10. 10.
Psalm 106. 23.
James 5. 15.
Amos 7. 1-6.
ʷ Is. 31. 7.
ˣ Nu. 11. 1.
ʸ Nu. 11. 4.
ᶻ Nu. 13. 3.
Nu. 14. 1.
ᵃ Psalm 106. 24.
ᵇ ch. 31. 27.
ᶜ Ex. 32. 11.
1 Sa. 7. 9.
Pro. 15. 29.
Jer. 15. 1.
ᵈ Gen. 41. 57.
1 Sam. 14. 25.
ᵉ Ex. 32. 12.
Nu. 14. 16.
ᶠ ch. 4. 20.
1 Kings 8. 51.
Neh. 1. 10.
Ps. 95. 7.

CHAP. 10.
ᵃ Ex. 34. 1, 2.
ᵇ Ex. 25. 10.
ᶜ Ex. 25. 5, 10.
Ex. 37. 1.
ᵈ Ex. 34. 28.
Jer. 31. 33.
1 words.
ᵉ Ex. 20. 1.
ᶠ Ex. 19. 17.
ch. 9. 10.
ch. 18. 16.
ᵍ Ex. 34. 29.
ʰ Ex. 40. 20.
ⁱ 1 Ki. 8. 9.
ʲ Nu. 33. 31.
ᵏ Nu. 20. 28.
Nu. 33. 38.
ˡ Lev. 9. 22.
Nu. 6. 23.
ᵐ Ezk. 44. 28.
2 Or, former days.
3 go in journey.
ⁿ Mic. 6. 8.
Jer. 7. 23.
ᵒ Mat. 22. 37.
1 Tim. 1. 5.
ᵖ 1 Kin. 8. 27.
Ps. 115. 16.
ᵠ Gen. 14. 19.
Ps. 24. 1.

us out say, *ᵉ* Because the LORD was not able to bring them into the land which he promised them, and because he hated them, he hath brought them out to slay them in the wilderness.

29 Yet *ᶠ* they *are* thy people and thine inheritance, which thou broughtest out by thy mighty power and by thy stretched-out arm.

CHAPTER X.

1 *God's mercy in restoring the two tables, 6 in continuing the priesthood, 8 in separating the tribe of Levi, 10 and hearkening to Moses' suit for the people.*

AT that time the LORD said unto me, Hew *ᵃ* thee two tables of stone like unto the first, and come up unto me into the mount, and *ᵇ* make thee an ark of wood.

2 And I will write on the tables the words that were in the first tables which thou brakest, and thou shalt put them in the ark.

3 And I made an ark of *ᶜ* shittim wood, and hewed two tables of stone like unto the first, and went up into the mount, having the two tables in mine hand.

4 And *ᵈ* he wrote on the tables, according to the first writing, the ten ¹ commandments, *ᵉ* which the LORD spake unto you in the mount, out of the midst of the fire, in *ᶠ* the day of the assembly: and the LORD gave them unto me.

5 And I turned myself, and *ᵍ* came down from the mount, and *ʰ* put the tables in the ark which I had made; *ⁱ* and there they be, as the LORD commanded me.

6 ¶ And the children of Israel took their journey from Beeroth *ʲ* of the children of Jaakan to Mosera: *ᵏ* there Aaron died, and there he was buried; and Eleazar his son ministered in the priest's office in his stead.

7 From thence they journeyed unto Gudgodah; and from Gudgodah to Jotbath, a land of rivers of waters.

8 ¶ At that time the LORD separated the tribe of Levi, to bear the ark of the covenant of the LORD, to stand before the LORD to minister unto him, and *ˡ* to bless in his name, unto this day.

9 Wherefore *ᵐ* Levi hath no part nor inheritance with his brethren; the LORD *is* his inheritance, according as the LORD thy God promised him.

10 ¶ And I stayed in the mount, according to the ² first time, forty days and forty nights; and the LORD hearkened unto me at that time also, *and* the LORD would not destroy thee.

11 And the LORD said unto me, Arise, ³ take *thy* journey before the people, that they may go in and possess the land which I sware unto their fathers to give unto them.

12 ¶ And now, Israel, *ⁿ* what doth the LORD thy God require of thee, but to fear the LORD thy God, to walk in all his ways, and *ᵒ* to love him, and to serve the LORD thy God with all thy heart and with all thy soul,

13 To keep the commandments of the LORD, and his statutes, which I command thee this day for thy good?

14 Behold, *ᵖ* the heaven, and the heaven of heavens, *is* the LORD's thy God, *ᵠ* the earth *also*, with all that therein *is*.

15 Only the LORD had a delight in thy

tioned as the chief source of its ancient fertility. **8. a land of wheat and barley**—These cereal fruits were specially promised to the Israelites in the event of their faithful allegiance to the covenant of God (Ps. 81. 16; 147. 14.). The wheat and barley were so abundant as to yield sixty and often an hundredfold (Gen. 26. 12; Matt. 13. 8.). vines, fig-trees, and pomegranates—The lime-stone rocks and abrupt valleys were entirely covered, as traces of them still were,with plantations of figs, vines, and olive trees. Though in a southern latitude, its mountainous formation tempered the excessive heat, and hence figs, pomegranates, &c., were produced in Palestine equally with wheat and barley, the produce of northern regions. Honey—the word honey is used often in a loose indeterminate sense, very frequently to signify a syrup of dates or of grapes, which under the name of *Dibs* is much used by all classes, wherever vineyards are found, as a condiment to their food. It resembles thin molasses, but is more pleasant to the taste. [ROBINSON.] This is esteemed a great delicacy in the east, and it was produced abundantly in Palestine. **9. a land whose stones are iron**—The abundance of this metal in Palestine, especially among the mountains of Lebanon, those of Kesraoun, and elsewhere, is attested not only by Josephus, but by Volney, Buckingham, and other travellers. Brass—not the alloy, brass, but the ore of copper. Although the mines may now be exhausted or neglected, they yielded plenty of those metals anciently (1 Chron. 22. 3; 29. 2-7; Is. 60. 17.). **11-20. Beware that thou forget not the Lord**—After mentioning those instances of the divine goodness, Moses founded on them an argument for their future obedience. **15. led thee through the wilderness wherein were fiery serpents and scorpions**—Large and venomous reptiles are found in great numbers there still, particularly in autumn. Travellers require to use great caution in arranging their tents and beds at night; even during the day the legs not only of men, but of the animals they ride are liable to be bitten. **who brought thee water out of the flinty rock**—(See on chap. 8. 21.).

CHAPTER IX.

Ver. 1-25. MOSES DISSUADETH THEM FROM THE OPINION OF THEIR OWN RIGHTEOUSNESS. **1. this day**—means *this time*. The Israelites had reached the confines of the promised land, but were obliged, to their great mortification, to return. But now were they certainly to enter it. No obstacle could prevent their possession; neither the fortified defences of the town, nor the resistance of the gigantic inhabitants of whom they had received from the spies so formidable a description. **cities great and fenced up to heaven**—Oriental cities generally cover a much greater space than those in Europe; for the houses often stand apart with gardens and fields intervening. They are almost all surrounded with walls built of burnt or sun-dried bricks, about 40 ft. in height. All classes in the East, but especially the nomad tribes, in their ignorance of engineering and artillery, would abandon in despair, the idea of an assault on a walled town, which European soldiers would demolish in a few hours. **4. Speak not, saying, For my righteousness the Lord hath brought me to possess it**—Moses takes special care to guard his countrymen against the vanity of supposing that their own merits had procured them the distinguished privilege. The Canaanites were a hopelessly corrupt race, and deserved extermination; but history relates many remarkable instances in which God punished corrupt and guilty nations by the instrumentality of other people as bad as themselves. It was not for the sake of the Israelites, but for His own sake: for the promise made to their pious ancestors, and in furtherance of high and comprehensive purposes of good to the world, that God was about to give them a grant of Canaan. **7. Remember how thou provokedst the Lord**—To dislodge from their minds any presumptuous idea of their own righteousness, Moses rehearses their acts of disobedience and rebellion committed so frequently, and in circumstances of the most awful and impressive solemnity, that they had forfeited all claims to the favour of God. The candour and boldness with which he gave, and the patient submission with which the people bore, his recital of charges so discreditable to their national character, has often been appealed to as among the many evidences of the truth of this history. **8. also in Horeb**—rather, even in Horeb, where it might have been expected they would have acted otherwise. **12-29. Arise, get thee down: for the people have corrupted themselves**—With a view to humble them effectually, Moses proceeds to particularize some of the most atrocious instances of their infidelity; and he begins with the impiety of the golden calf—an impiety which, while their miraculous emancipation from Egypt, the most stupendous displays of the DivineMajestythat were exhibited on the adjoining mount, and the recent ratification of the covenant by which they engaged to act as the people of God, were fresh in memory, indicated a degree of inconstancy or debasement almost incredible. **17. I took the two tables and broke them before your eyes**—not in the heat of intemperate passion, but in righteous indignation, from zeal to vindicate the unsullied honour of God, and by the suggestion of His Spirit to intimate that the covenant had been broken, and the people excluded from the Divine favour. **18. I fell down before the Lord**—The sudden and painful reaction which this scene of Pagan revelry produced on the mind of the pious and patriotic leader can be more easily imagined than described. Great and public sins call for seasons of extraordinary humiliation, and in his deep affliction for the awful apostasy, he seems to have held a miraculous fast as long as before. **20. The Lord was very angry with Aaron to have destroyed him**—By allowing himself to be overborne by the tide of popular clamour, he became a partaker in the guilt of idolatry, and would have suffered the penalty of his sinful compliance, had not the earnest intercession of Moses on his behalf prevailed. **21. I cast the dust into the brook that descended out of the mount**—*i.e.*, the smitten rock (El Leja) which was probably contiguous to, or a part of Sinai. It is too seldom borne in mind that though the Israelites were supplied with water from this rock when they were stationed at Rephidim (Wady Feiran), there is nothing in the Scripture narrative which should lead us to suppose that the rock was in the im-

fathers to love them, and he chose their seed after them, *even* you above all people, as *it is* this day.

16 Circumcise therefore ʳ the foreskin of your heart, and be no more stiff-necked.

17 For the LORD your God *is* ˢ God of gods, and ᵗ Lord of lords, a great God, a mighty, and a terrible, ᵘ regardeth not persons, nor taketh reward:

18 He ᵛ doth execute the judgment of the fatherless and widow, and loveth the stranger, in giving him food and raiment.

19 Love ye therefore the stranger: for ye were strangers in the land of Egypt.

20 Thou ʷ shalt fear the LORD thy God; him shalt thou serve, and to him shalt thou cleave, ˣ and swear by his name.

21 He ʸ *is* thy praise, and he *is* thy God, that hath done for thee these great and terrible things which thine eyes have seen.

22 Thy fathers went down into Egypt with threescore and ten persons; and now the LORD thy God hath made thee as the stars of heaven for multitude.

CHAPTER XI.

1 An exhortation to obedience. 18 A careful study is required in God's words. 26 A blessing and a curse is set before them.

THEREFORE thou shalt love the LORD thy God, and ᵃ keep his charge, and his statutes, and his judgments, and his commandments, alway.

2 And know ye this day: for *I speak* not with your children which have not known, and which have not seen the chastisement of the LORD your God, his greatness, his mighty hand, and his stretched-out arm,

3 And his miracles, and his acts, which he did in the midst of Egypt unto Pharaoh the king of Egypt, and unto all his land;

4 And what he did unto the army of Egypt, unto their horses, and to their chariots; how he made the water of the Red sea to overflow them, as they pursued after you, and how the LORD hath destroyed them unto this day;

5 And what he did unto you in the wilderness, until ye came into this place;

6 And ᵇ what he did unto Dathan and Abiram, the sons of Eliab, the son of Reuben: how the earth opened her mouth, and swallowed them up, and their households, and their tents, and all the ¹ substance that ² *was* in their possession, in the midst of all Israel;

7 But your eyes have seen all the great acts of the LORD which he did.

8 Therefore shall ye keep all the commandments which I command you this day, that ye may ᶜ be strong, and go in and possess the land whither ye go to possess it;

9 And ᵈ that ye may prolong *your* days in the land which the LORD sware unto your fathers to give unto them, and to their seed, ᵉ a land that floweth with milk and honey.

10 ¶ For the land, whither thou goest in to possess it, *is* not as the land of Egypt, from whence ye came out, ᶠ where thou sowedst thy seed, and wateredst *it* with thy foot, as a garden of herbs:

11 But ᵍ the land, whither ye go to possess it, *is* a land of hills and valleys, *and* drinketh water of the rain of heaven:

12 A land which the LORD thy God ³ careth for: ʰ the eyes of the LORD thy God *are* always upon it, from the beginning of the year even unto the end of the year.

13 ¶ And it shall come to pass, if ye shall hearken ⁱ diligently unto my commandments which I command you this day, to love ʲ the LORD your God, and to serve him with all your heart and with all your soul,

14 That ᵏ I will give *you* the rain of your land in his due season, ˡ the first rain, and the latter rain, that thou mayest gather in thy corn, and thy wine, and thine oil.

15 And ᵐ I will ⁴ send grass in thy fields for thy cattle, that thou mayest ⁿ eat, and be full.

16 Take heed to yourselves, ᵒ that your heart be not deceived, and ye turn aside, and serve other gods, and worship them;

17 And *then* ᵖ the LORD'S wrath be kindled against you, and he ᵠ shut up the heaven, that there be no rain, and that the land yield not her fruit; and *lest* ye perish quickly from off the good land which the LORD giveth you.

18 ¶ Therefore shall ye lay up these my words in your heart and in your soul, and bind them for a sign upon your hand, that they may be as frontlets between your eyes.

19 And ye shall ʳ teach them your children, speaking of them when thou sittest in thine house, and when thou walkest by the way, when thou liest down, and when thou risest up.

20 And thou shalt write them ˢ upon the door posts of thine house, and upon thy gates:

21 That ᵗ your days may be multiplied, and the days of your children, in the land which the LORD sware unto your fathers to give them, ᵘ as the days of heaven upon the earth.

22 ¶ For if ᵛ ye shall diligently keep all these commandments which I command you, to do them, to love the LORD your God, to walk in all his ways, and to cleave unto him;

23 Then will the LORD ʷ drive out all these nations from before you, and ye shall ˣ possess greater nations and mightier than yourselves.

24 Every ʸ place whereon the soles of your feet shall tread shall be yours: ᶻ from the wilderness and Lebanon, from the river, the river Euphrates, even unto the uttermost sea, shall your coast be.

25 There ᵃ shall no man be able to stand before you: *for* the LORD your God shall lay ᵇ the fear of you and the dread of you upon all the land that ye shall tread upon, as ᶜ he hath said unto you.

26 ¶ Behold, ᵈ I set before you this day a blessing and a curse;

27 A ᵉ blessing, if ye obey the commandments of the LORD your God, which I command you this day:

28 And a ᶠ curse, if ye will not obey the commandments of the LORD your God, but turn aside out of the way which I command you this day, to go after other gods, which ye have not known.

29 And it shall come to pass, when the LORD thy God hath brought thee in unto the land whither thou goest to possess it, that thou shalt put ᵍ the blessing upon mount Gerizim, and the curse upon mount Ebal.

30 *Are* they not on the other side Jordan, by the way where the sun goeth down, in the land of the Canaanites, which dwell in

mediate neighbourhood of that place (see on Ex. 17. 5, 6,). The water on this smitten rock was probably the brook that descended from the mount. The water may have flowed at the distance of many miles from the rock, as the winter torrents do now through the Wadis of Arabia Petræa (Ps. 78. 15, 16.). And the rock may have been smitten at such a height, and at a spot bearing such a relation to the Sinaitic valleys, as to furnish in this way supplies of water to the Israelites during the journey from Horeb by the way of Mount Seir and Kadesh-Barnea (ch. 1. 1, 2.). On this supposition new light is, perhaps, cast on the figurative language of the apostle, when he speaks of "the rock following" the Israelites (1 Cor. 10. 4.). (WILSON'S LAND OF THE BIBLE.] 25. Thus I fell down before the Lord, as I fell at the first—After the enumeration of various acts of rebellion, he had mentioned the outbreak at Kadesh-Barnea, which, on a superficial reading of this verse, would seem to have led Moses to a third and protracted season of humiliation. But on a comparison of this passage with Numbers, 14. 5, the subject and language of this prayer shew that only the second act of intercession (v. 18,) is now described in fuller detail.

CHAPTER X.

Ver. 1-22. GOD'S MERCY IN RESTORING THE TWO TABLES. 1. at that time the Lord said unto me—It was when God had been pacified through the intercessions of Moses with the people who had so greatly offended Him by the worship of the golden calf. The obedient leader executed the orders he had received as to the preparation both of the hewn stones, and the ark or chest, in which those sacred archives were to be laid. 3. I made an ark of Shittim wood—It appears, however, from Exodus, 37. 1, that the ark was not framed till his return from the Mount, or most probably, he gave instructions to Bezaleel, the artist employed on the work, before he ascended the mount,— that, on his descent, it might be finished, and ready to receive the precious deposit. 4, 5. he wrote on the tables according to the first writing—i.e., not Moses, who under the divine direction acted as amanuensis, but God himself who made this inscription a second time with His own hand, to testify the importance He attached to the ten commandments. Different from other stone monuments of antiquity, which were made to stand upright and in the open air, those on which the Divine law was engraven were portable, and designed to be kept as a treasure. Josephus says that each of the tables contained five precepts. But the tradition generally received, both amongst Jewish and Christian writers is, that one table contained four precepts, the other six. there they be, as the Lord commanded me—Here is another minute, but important circumstance, the public mention of which at the time attests the veracity of the sacred historian. 6-9. The children of Israel took their journey— So sudden a change from a spoken discourse to a historical narrative, has greatly puzzled the most eminent Biblical scholars, some of whom reject the parenthesis as a manifest interpolation. But it is found in the most ancient Hebrew MSS., and, believing that all contained in this book was given by inspiration, and is entitled to profound respect, we must receive it as it stands, although acknowledging our inability to explain the insertion of these encampment details in this place. There is another difficulty in the narrative itself. The stations which the Israelites are said successively to have occupied, are enumerated here in a different order from Numbers, 33. 31. That the names of the stations in both passages are the same there can be no doubt; but, in Numbers, they are probably mentioned in reference to the *first* visit of the Hebrews during the long wandering southwards, before their return to Kadesh the second time; while here they have a reference to the *second* passage of the Israelites, when they again marched south, in order to compass the land of Edom. It is easy to conceive that Mosera Hor and the wells of Jaakan might lie in such a direction that a nomadic horde might, in different years, at one time take the former *first* in their way, and at another time the latter. [ROB.] 10-22. Moses here resumes his address, and having made a passing allusion to the principal events in their history, concludes by exhorting them to fear the Lord and serve Him faithfully. 16. Circumcise the foreskin of your heart— Here he teaches them the true and spiritual meaning of that rite, as was afterwards more strongly urged by Paul, (Rom. 2. 25, 29,) and should be applied by us to our baptism, which is "not the putting away of the filth of the flesh, but the answer of a good conscience toward God."

CHAPTER XI.

Ver. 1-32. AN EXHORTATION TO OBEDIENCE. 1. Therefore thou shalt love the Lord and keep his charge—The reason of the frequent repetition of the same or similar counsels is to be traced to the infantine character and state of the church, which required line upon line, and precept upon precept. Besides, the Israelites were a headstrong and perverse people, impatient of control, prone to rebellion, and, from their long stay in Egypt, so violently addicted to idolatry, that they ran imminent risk of being seduced by the religion of the country to which they were going, which, in its characteristic features, bore a strong resemblance to that of the country they had left. 2-9. I speak not to your children which have not known, but your eyes have seen—Moses is here giving a brief summary of the marvels and miracles of awful judgment which God had wrought in effecting their release from the tyranny of Pharoah, as well as those which had taken place in the wilderness; and he knew that he might dwell upon these, for he was addressing many who had been witnesses of these appalling incidents. For it will be remembered that the divine threatening that they should die in the wilderness, and its execution extended only to males from 20 years and upward, who were able to go forth to war. No males under 20 years of age, no females, and none of the tribe of Levi, were objects of the denunciation (see Num. 14. 28-30; 16. 49.). There might, therefore, have been many thousands of the Israelites at that time of whom Moses could say, "your eyes have seen all the great acts which He did;" and with regard to those, the historic review of Moses was well calculated to stir up their minds to the duty and advantages of obedience. 10-12. For the land whither thou goest . . . is not as the land of

the champaign over against Gilgal, beside the plains of Moreh?

31 For ye shall pass over Jordan to go in to possess the land which the Lord your God giveth you, and ye shall possess it, and dwell therein.

32 And ye shall observe to do all the statutes and judgments which I set before you this day.

CHAPTER XII.

1 Monuments of idolatry are to be destroyed. 5 The place of God's service is to be kept. 16, 23 Blood forbidden. 17, 20, 26 Holy things to be eaten in the holy place.

THESE *are* the statutes and judgments which ye shall observe to do in the land which the Lord God of thy fathers giveth thee to possess it, *a* all the days that ye live upon the earth.

2 Ye *b* shall utterly destroy all the places wherein the nations which ye shall ¹ possess served their gods, *c* upon the high mountains, and upon the hills, and under every green tree:

3 And *d* ye shall ² overthrow their altars, and break their pillars, and burn their groves with fire; and ye shall hew down the graven images of their gods, and destroy the *e* names of them out of that place.

4 Ye shall not do so unto the Lord your God.

5 But unto the place which the Lord your God shall *f* choose out of all your tribes to put his name there, *even* unto his habitation shall ye seek, and thither thou shalt come:

6 And *g* thither ye shall bring your burnt offerings, and your sacrifices, *h* and your tithes, and heave offerings of your hand, and your vows, and your free-will offerings, and the firstlings of your herds and of your flocks:

7 And *i* there ye shall eat before the Lord your God, and *j* ye shall rejoice in all that ye put your hand unto, ye and your households, wherein the Lord thy God hath blessed thee.

8 Ye shall not do after all *the things* that we do here this day, every man whatsoever *is* right in his own eyes.

9 For ye are not as yet come to the rest and to the inheritance which the Lord your God giveth you.

10 But *when* ye go over Jordan, and dwell in the land which the Lord your God giveth you to inherit, and *when* he giveth you rest from all your enemies round about, so that ye dwell in safety;

11 Then there shall be *k* a place which the Lord your God shall choose to cause his name to dwell there: thither shall ye bring all that I command you; your burnt offerings, and your sacrifices, your tithes, and the heave offering of your hand, and all ³ your choice vows which ye vow unto the Lord:

12 And ye shall rejoice before the Lord your God, ye, and your sons, and your daughters, and your men-servants, and your maid-servants, and the Levite that *is* within your gates; forasmuch as *l* he hath no part nor inheritance with you.

13 Take *m* heed to thyself that thou offer not thy burnt offerings in every place that thou seest:

14 But in the place which the Lord shall choose in one of thy tribes, there thou shalt offer thy burnt offerings, and there thou shalt do all that I command thee.

15 Notwithstanding thou mayest kill and eat flesh in all thy gates, *n* whatsoever thy soul lusteth after, according to the blessing of the Lord thy God which he hath given thee: the unclean and the clean may eat thereof, *o* as of the roebuck, and as of the hart.

16 Only *p* ye shall not eat the blood; ye shall pour it upon the earth as water.

17 ¶ Thou mayest not eat within thy gates the tithe of thy corn, or of thy wine, or of thy oil, or the firstlings of thy herds, or of thy flock, nor any of thy vows which thou vowest, nor thy free-will offerings, or heave offering of thine hand:

18 But *q* thou must eat them before the Lord thy God in the place which the Lord thy God shall choose, thou, and thy son, and thy daughter, and thy man-servant, and thy maid-servant, and the Levite that is within thy gates: and thou shalt *r* rejoice before the Lord thy God in all that thou puttest thine hands unto.

19 Take *s* heed to thyself that thou forsake not the Levite ⁴ as long as thou livest upon the earth.

20 ¶ When the Lord thy God shall enlarge thy border, *t* as he hath promised thee, and thou shalt say, I will eat flesh, (because thy soul longeth to eat flesh,) thou mayest eat flesh, whatsoever thy soul lusteth after.

21 If the place which the Lord thy God hath chosen to put his name there be too far from thee, then thou shalt kill of thy herd and of thy flock, which the Lord hath given thee, as I have commanded thee, and thou shalt eat in thy gates whatsoever thy soul lusteth after.

22 Even as the roebuck and the hart is eaten, so thou shalt eat them; the unclean and the clean shall eat *of* them alike.

23 Only ⁵ be sure that thou eat not the blood: *u* for the blood *is* the life; and thou mayest not eat the life with the flesh.

24 Thou shalt not eat it; thou shalt pour it upon the earth as water.

25 Thou shalt not eat it; *v* that it may go well with thee, and with thy children after thee, *w* when thou shalt do *that which is* right in the sight of the Lord.

26 Only thy *x* holy things which thou hast, and *y* thy vows, thou shalt take, and go unto the place which the Lord shall choose:

27 And *z* thou shalt offer thy burnt offerings, the flesh and the blood, upon the altar of the Lord thy God: and the blood of thy sacrifices shall be poured out upon the altar of the Lord thy God, and thou shalt eat the flesh.

28 Observe and hear all these words which I command thee, that *a* it may go well with thee, and with thy children after thee for ever, when thou doest *that which is* good and right in the sight of the Lord thy God.

29 ¶ When *b* the Lord thy God shall cut off the nations from before thee, whither thou goest to possess them, and thou ⁶ succeedest them, and dwellest in their land;

30 Take heed to thyself that thou be not snared ⁷ by following them, after that they be destroyed from before thee; and that thou enquire not after their gods, saying,

Egypt—The physical features of Palestine present a striking contrast to those of the land of bondage. A widely extending plain forms the cultivated portion of Egypt, and on the greater part of this low and level country rain never falls. This natural want is supplied by the annual overflow of the Nile, and by artificial means from the same source, when the river has receded within its customary channel. Close by the bank, the process of irrigation is very simple. The cultivator opens a small sluice on the edge of the square bed in which seed has been sown, making drill after drill; and when a sufficient quantity of water has poured in, he shuts them up with his foot. Where the bank is high, the water is drawn up by hydraulic engines, of which there are three kinds used, of different power, according to the subsidence of the stream. The water is distributed in small channels or earthen conduits, simple in construction, worked by the foot, and formed with a mattock by the gardener who directs their course, and which are banked up or opened, as occasion may require, by pressing in the soil with the foot. Thus was the land watered in which the Israelites had dwelt so long. Such vigilance and laborious industry would not be needed in the promised land, for instead of being visited only at one brief season, and left during the rest of the year under a withering blight, every season it would enjoy the benign influences of a genial climate; the hills would attract the frequent clouds, and, in the refreshing showers, the blessing of God would specially rest upon the land. A land which ... careth for—*i.e.*, watering it as it were with his own hands, without human aid or mechanical means. **14.** The first rain and the latter rain—The early rain commenced in autumn, *i.e.*, chiefly during the months of September and October, while the latter rain fell in the spring of the year, *i.e.*, during the months of March and April. It is true that occasional showers fell all the winter; but, at the autumnal and vernal seasons, they were more frequent, copious, and important; for the early rain was necessary, after a hot and protracted summer, to prepare the soil for receiving the seed; and the latter rain, which shortly preceded the harvest, was of the greatest use in invigorating the languishing powers of vegetation (Jer. 5, 24; Joel, 11. 23; Am. 4. 7; Jam. 5. 7.). **15-17.** I will send grass—Undoubtedly the special blessing of the former and the latter rain was one principal cause of the extraordinary fertility of Canaan in ancient times. That blessing was promised to the Israelites as a temporal reward for their fidelity to the national covenant. It was threatened to be withdrawn on their disobedience or apostacy; and most signally is the execution of that threatening seen in the present sterility of Palestine. Mr. Lowthian, an English farmer, who was struck during his journey from Joppa to Jerusalem by not seeing a blade of grass, where even in the poorest localities of Britain, some wild vegetation is found, directed his attention particularly to the subject, and pursued the enquiry during a month's residence in Jerusalem, where he learned that a miserably small quantity of milk is daily sold to the inhabitants at a dear rate, and that chiefly ass's milk. "Most clearly," says he, "did I perceive that the barrenness of large portions of the country was owing to the cessation of the early and latter rain, and that the absence of grass and flowers made it no longer the land *v.* 9,) flowing with milk and honey." **18-25.** lay up these my words, bind them—(see on ch. 6, 8.). every place ... shall be yours—not as if the Jews should be lords of the world, but of every place within the promised land. It should be granted to them, and possessed by them, on conditions of obedience—from the wilderness—the Arabah on the south; Lebanon—the northern limit; Euphrates— their boundary on the east; their grant of dominion extended so far, and the right was fulfilled to Solomon. uttermost sea—the Mediterranean. **26-32.** Behold I set before you this day, a blessing and a curse—(See on ch. 27. 11.).

CHAPTER XII.

Ver. 1.-4. MONUMENTS OF IDOLATRY TO BE DESTROYED. **1.** These are the statutes and judgments, &c.—Having in the preceding chapter inculcated upon the Israelites the general obligation to fear and love God, Moses here enters into a detail of some special duties they were to practise on their obtaining possession of the promised land. **2.** Ye shall utterly destroy all the places wherein the nations serve their gods—This divine command was founded on the tendencies of human nature: for to remove out of sight everything that had been associated with idolatry that it might never be spoken of, and no vestige of it remain, was the only effectual way to keep the Israelites from temptations to it. It is observable that Moses does not make any mention of temples, for such buildings were not in existence at that early period. The "places" chosen as the scene of heathen worship were situated either on the summit of a lofty mountain, or on some artificial mound, or in a grove, planted with particular trees, such as oaks, poplars, and elms Is. 57. 5-7; Hos. 4. 13.). The reason for the selection of such sites was both to secure retirement and to direct the attention upward to heaven; and the "place" was nothing else than a consecrated enclosure, or at most, a canopy or screen from the weather. **3.** overthrow their altars—Piles of turf or small stones. break their pillars—Before the art of sculpture was known, the statues of idols were only rude blocks of coloured stones. **5-15.** unto the place which the Lord shall choose out of, &c.—They were forbidden to worship either in the impure superstitious manner of the heathen, or in any of the places frequented by them. A particular place for the general rendezvous of all the tribes would be chosen by God himself; and the choice of one common place for the solemn rites of religion was an act of divine wisdom, for the security of the true religion; it was admirably calculated to prevent the corruption which would otherwise have crept in from their frequenting groves and high hills,—to preserve uniformity of worship, and keep alive their faith in Him to whom all their sacrifices pointed. The place was successively Mizpeh, Shiloh, and especially Jerusalem; but in all the references made to it by Moses, the name is never mentioned; and this studied silence was maintained partly lest the Canaanites within whose territories it lay, might have concentrated their

How did these nations serve their gods? even so will I do likewise.

31 Thou ^c shalt not do so unto the Lord thy God: for every ^g abomination to the Lord which he hateth have they done unto their gods; for ^d even their sons and their daughters they have burnt in the fire to their gods.

32 What thing soever I command you, observe to do it: ^e thou shalt not add thereto, nor diminish from it.

CHAPTER XIII.

1 Enticers to idolatry to be stoned to death, 6 without regard to nearness of relation. 12 Idolatrous cities not to be spared.

IF there arise among you a prophet, or a dreamer of dreams, ^a and giveth thee a sign or a wonder,

2 And ^b the sign or the wonder come to pass, whereof he spake unto thee, saying, Let us go after other gods, which thou hast not known, and let us serve them;

3 Thou shalt not hearken unto the words of that prophet, or that dreamer of dreams: for the Lord your God ^c proveth you, to know whether ye love the Lord your God with all your heart and with all your soul.

4 Ye shall ^d walk after the Lord your God, and fear him, and keep his commandments, and obey his voice, and ye shall serve him, and cleave unto him.

5 And ^e that prophet, or that dreamer of dreams, shall ^f be put to death; because he hath ¹ spoken to turn *you* away from the Lord your God, which brought you out of the land of Egypt, and redeemed you out of the house of bondage, to thrust thee out of the way which the Lord thy God commanded thee to walk in: ^g so shalt thou put the evil away from the midst of thee.

6 ¶ If thy brother, the son of thy mother, or thy son, or thy daughter, or ^h the wife of thy bosom, or thy friend, which *is* as thine own soul, entice thee secretly, saying, Let us go and serve other gods, which thou hast not known, thou, nor thy fathers;

7 *Namely*, of the gods of the people which *are* round about you, nigh unto thee, or far off from thee, from the one end of the earth even unto the *other* end of the earth;

8 Thou shalt ⁱ not consent unto him, nor hearken unto him; neither shall thine eye pity him, neither shalt thou spare, neither shalt thou conceal him:

9 But thou shalt surely kill him; ^j thine hand shall be first upon him to put him to death, and afterwards the hand of all the people.

10 And thou shalt stone him with stones, that he die; because he hath sought to thrust thee away from the Lord thy God, which brought thee out of the land of Egypt, from the house of ² bondage.

11 And ^k all Israel shall hear, and fear, and shall do no more any such wickedness as this is among you.

12 ¶ If ^l thou shalt hear say in one of thy cities, which the Lord thy God hath given thee to dwell there, saying,

13 *Certain* men, ³ the children of Belial, are ^m gone out from among you, and have withdrawn ⁿ the inhabitants of their city, saying, Let us go and serve other gods, which ye have not known;

14 Then shalt thou enquire, and make search, and ask diligently; and, behold, *if it be* truth, *and* the thing certain, *that* such abomination is wrought among you;

15 Thou shalt surely smite the inhabitants of that city with the edge of the sword, ^o destroying it utterly, and all that *is* therein, and the cattle thereof, with the edge of the sword.

16 And thou shalt gather all the spoil of it into the midst of the street thereof, and shalt burn with fire the city, and all the spoil thereof every whit, for the Lord thy God; and it shall be ^p an heap for ever; it shall not be built again.

17 And ^q there shall cleave nought of the cursed thing to thine hand: that the Lord may ^r turn from the fierceness of his anger, and show thee mercy, and have compassion upon thee, and multiply thee, ^s as he hath sworn unto thy fathers;

18 When thou shalt hearken to the voice of the Lord thy God, ^t to keep all his commandments which I command thee this day, to do *that which is* right in the eyes of the Lord thy God.

CHAPTER XIV.

1 God's children must not disfigure themselves in mourning. 3 What may be eaten, and what not, 4 of beasts, 9 of fishes, 11 of fowls. 22 Tithes of divine service. 28 The third year's tithe of alms and charity.

YE *are* ^a the children of the Lord your God. ^b Ye shall not cut yourselves, nor make any baldness between your eyes for the dead.

2 For ^c thou *art* an holy people unto the Lord thy God, and the Lord hath chosen thee to be a peculiar people unto himself, above all the nations that *are* upon the earth.

3 ¶ Thou ^d shalt not eat any abominable thing.

4 These ^e are the beasts which ye shall eat The ox, the sheep, and the goat,

5 The hart, and the roebuck, and the fallow deer, and the wild goat, and the ¹ pygarg, and the wild ox, and the chamois.

6 And every beast that parteth the hoof, and cleaveth the cleft into two claws, *and* cheweth the cud among the beasts, that ye shall eat.

7 Nevertheless these ye shall not eat of them that chew the cud, or of them that divide the cloven hoof; *as* the camel, and the hare, and the coney: for they chew the cud, but divide not the hoof; *therefore* they *are* unclean unto you,

8 And the swine, because it divideth the hoof, yet cheweth not the cud, it *is* unclean unto you: ye shall not eat of their flesh, nor touch their dead carcase.

9 ¶ These ye shall eat of all that *are* in the waters: all that have fins and scales shall ye eat:

10 And whatsoever hath not fins and scales ye may not eat; it *is* unclean unto you.

11 ¶ *Of* all clean birds ye shall eat.

12 But ^f these *are they* of which ye shall not eat: the eagle, and the ossifrage, and the osprey,

13 And the glede, and the kite, and the vulture after his kind,

14 And every raven after his kind,

15 And the owl, and the night hawk, and the cuckoo, and the hawk after his kind,

16 The little owl, and the great owl, and the swan,

forces to frustrate all hopes of obtaining it : partly lest the desire of possessing a place of such importance might have become a cause of strife or rivalry amongst the Hebrew tribes, as about the appointment to the priesthood (Num. 16.). 7. There ye shall eat before the Lord—Of the things mentioned (v. 6.); but of course, none of the parts assigned to the priests before the Lord—in the place where the sanctuary should be established, and in those parts of the Holy City which the people were at liberty to frequent and inhabit. 12. Ye shall rejoice—ye, your sons, and your daughters, &c.—Hence it appears, that although males only were commanded to appear before God at the annual solemn feasts (Ex. 23. 17.), the women were allowed to accompany them (1 Sam. 1. 3-23.). 15. Notwithstanding thou mayest kill and eat flesh in all thy gates— Every animal designed for food, whether ox, goat, or lamb, was during the abode in the wilderness ordered to be slain as a peace offering at the door of the tabernacle; its blood to be sprinkled, and its fat burnt upon the altar by the priest. The encampment, being then round about the altar, made this practice, appointed to prevent idolatry, easy and practicable. But on the settlement in the promised land, the obligation to slay at the tabernacle was dispensed with, and the people left at liberty to prepare their meat in their cities or homes, according to the blessing which the Lord hath given thee—*i. e.*, the style of living should be accommodated to one's condition and means—profuse and riotous indulgence can never secure the divine blessing, the unclean and the clean—The unclean here are those who were under some slight defilement, which, without excluding them from society, yet debarred them from eating any of the sacred meats (Lev. 7. 20.). They were at liberty freely to partake of common articles of food. roebuck —the gazelle. hart—The Syrian deer (cervus barbatus) is a species between our red and fallow deer, distinguished by the want of abis-antler, or second branch on the horns, reckoning from below, and for a spotted livery which is effaced only in the third or fourth year. [BIB. CYC.]

16-25. BLOOD PROHIBITED. Ye shall not eat the blood; ye shall pour it upon the earth as water—The prohibition against eating or drinking blood as an unnatural custom accompanied the announcement of the divine grant of animal flesh for food. Gen. 9. 4.), and the prohibition was repeatedly renewed by Moses with reference to the great objects of the law (Lev. 17. 4,), the prevention of idolatry, and the consecration of the sacrificial blood to God. In regard, however, to the blood of animals slain for food, it might be shed without ceremony, and poured on the ground as a common thing like water,—only for the sake of decency, as well as for preventing all risk of idolatry, it was to be covered over with earth (Lev. 17. 13,) in opposition to the practice of heathen sportsmen who left it exposed as an offering to the god of the chase. 22-28. Even as the roebuck and the hart is eaten, so thou shalt eat, &c.—Game when procured in the wilderness had not been required to be brought to the door of the tabernacle. The people were now to be as free in the killing of domestic cattle as of wild animals. The permission to hunt and use venison for food was doubtless a great boon to the Israelites, not only in the wilderness, but on their settlement in Canaan, as the mountainous ranges of Lebanon, Carmel, and Gilead, on which deer abounded in vast numbers, would thus furnish them with a plentiful and luxurious repast. 26-32. HOLY THINGS TO BE EATEN IN THE HOLY PLACE. 26. Only thy holy things which thou hast—The tithes mentioned (v. 17,) are not to be considered ordinary tithes which belonged to the Levites, and of which private Israelites had a right to eat; but they are other extraordinary tithes or gifts, which the people carried to the sanctuary to be presented as peace offerings, and on which, after being offered, and the allotted portion given to the priest, they feasted with their families and friends (Lev. 27. 30.). 29-32. Take heed to thyself that thou be not snared—saying how did these nations serve their gods—The Israelites, influenced by superstitious fear, too often endeavoured to propitiate the deities of Canaan. Their Egyptian education had early impressed that bugbear notion of a set of local deities, who expected their dues of all who came to inhabit the country which they honoured with their protection, and severely resented the neglect of payment in all new-comers. [WARB.] Taking into consideration the prevalence of this idea among them, we see that against an Egyptian influence was directed the full force of the wholesome caution with which this chapter closes.

CHAPTER XIII.

Ver. 1-5. ENTICERS TO IDOLATRY TO BE PUT TO DEATH. 1. If there arise amongst you a prophet—The special counsels which follow arose out of the general precept contained in the last verse of the preceding chapter; and the purport of them is, that every attempt to seduce others from the course of duty which that divine standard of faith and worship prescribes must not only be strenuously resisted, but the seducer punished by the law of the land. This is exemplified in three cases of enticement to idolatry. a prophet—*i.e.*, some notable person laying claim to the character and authority of the prophetic office (Num. 12. 6; 1 Sam. 10. 6,), performing feats of dexterity or power in support of his pretensions, or even predicting events which occurred as he foretold; as, for instance, an eclipse which a knowledge of natural science might enable him to anticipate (or, as Caiaphas, Jo. 18. 14.). Should the aim of such a one be to seduce the people from the worship of the true God, he is an impostor, and must be put to death. No prodigy, however wonderful, no human authority, however great, should be allowed to shake their belief in the divine character and truth of a religion so solemnly taught and so awfully attested (cf. Gal. 1. 8.). The modern Jews appeal to this passage as justifying their rejection of Jesus Christ. But he possessed all the characteristics of a true prophet, and he was so far from alienating the people from God and his worship, that the grand object of his ministry was to lead to a purer, more spiritual and perfect, observance of the law.

6-18. WITHOUT REGARD TO NEARNESS OF RELATION. 6. If thy brother—This term

17 And the pelican, and the gier eagle, and the cormorant,
18 And the stork, and the heron after her kind, and the lapwing, and the bat.
19 And every creeping thing that flieth is unclean unto you: they shall not be eaten.
20 *But of* all clean fowls ye may eat.
21 ¶ Ye *u* shall not eat *of* any thing that dieth of itself: thou shalt give it unto the stranger that *is* in thy gates, that he may eat it; or thou mayest sell it unto an alien: for thou *art* an holy people unto the LORD thy God. *h* Thou shalt not seethe a kid in his mother's milk.
22 Thou *i* shalt truly tithe all the increase of thy seed, that the field bringeth forth year by year.
23 And thou shalt eat before the LORD thy God, in the place which he shall choose to place his name there, the tithe of thy corn, of thy wine, and of thine oil, and the firstlings of thy herds and of thy flocks; that thou *j* mayest learn to fear the LORD thy God always.
24 And if the way be too long for thee, so that thou art not able to carry it; *or k* if the place be too far from thee, which the LORD thy God shall choose to set his name there, when the LORD thy God hath blessed thee:
25 Then shalt thou turn *it* into money, and bind up the money in thine hand, and shalt go unto the place which the LORD thy God shall choose:
26 And thou shalt bestow that money for whatsoever thy soul lusteth after, for oxen, or for sheep, or for wine, or for strong drink, or for whatsoever thy soul ² desireth: and thou shalt eat there before the LORD thy God, and thou shalt rejoice, thou, and thine household,
27 And *l* the Levite that *is* within thy gates; thou shalt not forsake him; for *m* he hath no part nor inheritance with thee.
28 ¶ At *n* the end of three years thou shalt bring forth all the tithe of thine increase the same year, and shalt lay *it* up within thy gates:
29 And the Levite, (because he hath no part nor inheritance with thee,) and *o* the stranger, and the fatherless, and the widow, which *are* within thy gates, shall come, and shall eat and be satisfied; that the *p* LORD thy God may bless thee in all the work of thine hand which thou doest.

CHAPTER XV.

1 *The seventh year a year of release for the poor: 7 it must be no hinderance to lending or giving.* 12 *Of Hebrew servants' freedom.* 19 *All firstling males of cattle to* ¹ *be sanctified unto the Lord.*

AT the end of ³ *every* seven years thou shalt make a ⁴ release.
2 And this *is* the manner of the release: Every ¹ creditor that lendeth *ought* unto his neighbour shall release *it*; he shall not exact *it* of his neighbour, or of his brother; because it is called the LORD's release.
3 Of *b* a foreigner thou mayest exact *it* again: but *that* which is thine with thy brother thine hand shall release;
4 ² Save when there shall be no poor among you; *c* for the LORD shall greatly bless thee in the land which the LORD thy God giveth thee *for* an inheritance to possess it:
5 Only if thou carefully hearken unto the voice of the LORD thy God, to observe to do all these commandments which I command thee this day.
6 For the LORD thy God blesseth thee, as he promised thee: and thou shalt lend unto many nations, but thou shalt not borrow; and *d* thou shalt reign over many nations, but they shall not reign over thee.
7 ¶ If there be among you a poor man of one of thy brethren within any of thy gates in thy land which the LORD thy God giveth thee, *e* thou shalt not harden thine heart, nor shut thine hand from thy poor brother;
8 But *f* thou shalt open thine hand wide unto him, and shalt surely lend him sufficient for his need, *in that* which he wanteth.
9 Beware that there be not a ³ thought in thy ⁴ wicked heart, saying, The seventh year, the year of release, is at hand; and thine *g* eye be evil against thy poor brother, and thou givest him nought; and *h* he cry unto the LORD against thee, and *i* it be sin unto thee.
10 Thou shalt surely give him, and *j* thine heart shall not be grieved when thou givest unto him: because that *k* for this thing the LORD thy God shall bless thee in all thy works, and in all that thou puttest thine hand unto.
11 For the poor shall never cease out of the land: therefore I command thee, saying, Thou shalt open thine hand wide unto thy brother, to thy poor, and to thy needy, in thy land.
12 ¶ *And l* if thy brother, an Hebrew man, or an Hebrew woman, be sold unto thee, and serve thee six years, then in the seventh year thou shalt let him go free from thee.
13 And when thou sendest him out free from thee, thou shalt not let him go away empty:
14 Thou shalt furnish him liberally out of thy flock, and out of thy floor, and out of thy wine-press: *of that* wherewith the LORD thy God hath *m* blessed thee thou shalt give unto him.
15 And thou shalt remember that thou wast a bondman in the land of Egypt, and the LORD thy God redeemed thee: therefore I command thee this thing to-day.
16 And it shall be, *n* if he say unto thee, I will not go away from thee; (because he loveth thee and thine house, because he is well with thee;)
17 Then thou shalt take an awl, and thrust *it* through his ear unto the door, and he shall be thy servant for ever. And also unto thy maid-servant thou shalt do likewise.
18 It shall not seem hard unto thee when thou sendest him away free from thee; for he hath been worth *o* a double hired servant to thee, in serving thee six years; and the LORD thy God shall bless thee in all that thou doest.
19 ¶ All *p* the firstling males that come of thy herd and of thy flock thou shalt sanctify unto the LORD thy God: thou shalt do no work with the firstling of thy bullock, nor shear the firstling of thy sheep:
20 Thou *q* shalt eat *it* before the LORD thy God year by year in the place which the LORD shall choose, thou and thy household.
21 And *r* if there be any blemish therein, *as if it be* lame, or blind, *or have* any ill blemish, thou shalt not sacrifice it unto the LORD thy God.
22 Thou shalt eat it within thy gates:

being applied very loosely in all Eastern countries (Gen. 20. 13,), other expressions are added to intimate that no degree of kindred, however intimate, should be allowed to screen an enticer to idolatry; to conceal his crime, or protect his person; piety and duty must overcome affection or compassion, and an accusation must be lodged before a magistrate. 9. thou shalt kill him—not hastily, or in a private manner, but after trial and conviction; and his relative, as informer, was to cast the first stone. (See on ch. 17. 7; Acts, 7. 58.) It is manifest that what was done in secret could not be legally proved by a single informer; and hence Jewish writers say, that spies were set in some private part of the house, to hear the conversation and watch the conduct of a person suspected of idolatrous tendencies. 12-18. certain men, the children of Belial—lawless, designing demagogues (Jud. 19. 22; 1 Sam. 1. 16; 25. 25,), who abused their influence to withdraw the inhabitants of the city to idol-worship. 14. Then shalt thou inquire—*i.e.*, the magistrate, to whom it officially belonged to make the necessary investigation; and, in the event of the report proving true, the most summary proceedings were to be commenced against the apostate inhabitants. The law in this chapter has been represented as stern and sanguinary, but it was in accordance with the national constitution of Israel. God being their king, idolatry was treason, and a city turned to idols put itself into a state, and incurred the punishment, of rebellion. 16. it shall not be built again—Its ruins shall be a permanent monument of the divine justice, and a beacon for the warning and terror of posterity. 17. There shall cleave nought of the cursed thing—No spoil shall be taken from a city thus solemnly devoted to destruction. Every living creature must be put to the sword—everything belonging to it reduced to ashes—that nothing but its infamy may remain.

CHAPTER XIV.

Ver. 1, 2. GOD'S PEOPLE MUST NOT DISFIGURE THEMSELVES IN MOURNING. 1. Ye shall not cut yourselves—It was a common practice of idolaters, both on ceremonious occasions of their worship (1 Kin. 18. 28,), and at funerals (cf. Jer. 16. 6; 41. 5, to make ghastly incisions on their faces, and other parts of their persons, with their finger nails or sharp instruments. The making a large bare space between the eyebrows was another heathen custom in honour of the dead (see on Lev. 19. 27, 28; 21. 5.. Such indecorous and degrading usages, being extravagant and unnatural expressions of hopeless sorrow (1 Thess. 4, 13,) were to be carefully avoided by the Israelites, as derogatory to the character, and inconsistent with the position of those who were the people of God.

3-21. WHAT MAY BE EATEN, AND WHAT NOT. Thou shalt not eat any abominable thing—*i.e.*, anything forbidden as unclean (see on Lev. 11.). Of BEASTS. 4-8. The hart—(see on ch. 12. 15.). fallow deer—the Hebrew word Jachmur, so rendered, does not represent the fallow deer, which is unknown in Western Asia, but an antelope (Oryx Leucoryx,), called by the Arabs Jazmar. It is of a white colour, black at the extremities, and a bright red on the thighs. It was used at Solomon's table. wild goat—The word akko is different from that commonly used for a wild goat. (1 Sam. 24. 2; Ps. 104. 18; Prov. v. 19,) and it is supposed to be a goat-deer, having the body of a stag, but the head, horns, and beard of a goat. An animal of this sort is found in the East, and called Lerwee. [SHAW'S TRAV.] Pygarg—a species of antelope (Oryx Addax) with white buttocks, wreathed horns two feet in length, and standing about three feet seven inches high at the shoulders. It is common in the tracts which the Israelites had frequented. [SHAW.] wild ox—supposed to be the Nubian Oryx, which differs from the Oryx Leucoryx formerly mentioned by its black colour; and it is, moreover, of larger stature, and a more slender frame, with longer and more curved horns. It is called *Bekkar-El-Wash* by the Arabs. chamois—rendered by the Sept. Cameleopard, but, by others who rightly judge it must have been an animal more familiar to the Hebrews, it is thought to be the Kebsch (ovis Tragelaphus,), rather larger than a common sheep, covered not with wool, but with reddish hair—a Syrian sheep-goat. Of BIRDS. 11-20. Of all clean birds ye shall eat—(see on Lev. 11. 21.). 13. glede—thought to be the same as that rendered *Vulture* (Lev. 11. 14.). the cuckow—more probably the sea-gull. the swan—rather the goose (Mich.). gier-Eagle—The Hebrew word *Rachemah* is manifestly identical with *Rachamah*, the name which the Arabs give to the common vulture of Western Asia and Egypt. (Neophron Percnopterus.). cormorant—rather the *Plungeon*; a sea-fowl. the lapwing—the upupa or hoop; a beautiful bird, but of the most unclean habits. 21. Thou shalt not eat any thing that dieth of itself—(see on Lev. 17. 15; 22. 8.). thou shalt give it unto the stranger—not a proselyte, for he, as well as an Israelite, was subject to this law; but a heathen traveller or sojourner. thou shalt not seethe a kid—This is the third place in which the prohibition is repeated. It was pointed against an annual pagan ceremony (see on Ex. 23. 19; 34. 26.). 22-27. Thou shalt truly tithe all the increase of thy seed—The dedication of a tenth part of the year's produce in every thing was then a religious duty. It was to be brought as an offering to the sanctuary; and, where distance prevented its being taken in kind, it was by this statute convertible into money. 28-29. At the end of three years, the Levite shall come, &c.—The Levites having no inheritance like the other tribes, the Israelites were not to forget them, but honestly to tithe their increase. Besides the tenth of all the land produce, they had forty-eight cities, with the surrounding grounds, "the best of the land," and a certain proportion of the sacrifices as their allotted perquisites. They had, therefore, if not an affluent, yet a comfortable and independent, fund for their support.

CHAPTER XV.

Ver. 1-19. THE SEVENTH YEAR A YEAR OF RELEASE FOR THE POOR, 1. at the end of every year—During the last of the seven, *i.e.*, the Sabbatical year (Ex. 21, 2; 23. 11; Lev. 25. 4; Jer. 34. 14.). 2. Every creditor ... shall release it—not by an absolute discharge of the debt, but by passing over that year without exacting payment. The relief was temporary and peculiar to that year, during which there was a total suspension of agricultural labour. he shall not exact it

the unclean and the clean *person* shall eat it alike, as the roebuck, and as the hart.

23 Only thou shalt not eat the blood thereof; thou shalt pour it upon the ground as water.

CHAPTER XVI.

1 *The feast of the passover, 9 of weeks, 13 of tabernacles. 18 Of judges, and of justice. 21 Groves and images forbidden.*

OBSERVE the *a* month of Abib, and keep the *b* passover unto the LORD thy God: for in the month of Abib the LORD thy God brought thee forth out of Egypt by night.

2 Thou shalt therefore sacrifice the passover unto the LORD thy God, of the flock and *c* the herd, in the place which the LORD shall choose to place his name there.

3 Thou *d* shalt eat no leavened bread with it: seven days shalt thou eat unleavened bread therewith, *even* the bread of affliction; (for thou camest forth out of the land of Egypt in haste:) that thou mayest remember the day when thou camest forth out of the land of Egypt all the days of thy life.

4 And there shall be no leavened bread seen with thee in all thy coasts seven days; neither *e* shall there *any thing* of the flesh, which thou sacrificedst the first day at even, remain all night until the morning.

5 Thou mayest not ¹ sacrifice the passover within any of thy gates, which the LORD thy God giveth thee:

6 But at the place which the LORD thy God shall choose to place his name in, there thou shalt sacrifice the passover at *f* even, at the going down of the sun, at the season that thou camest forth out of Egypt.

7 And thou shalt *g* roast and eat *it h* in the place which the LORD thy God shall choose: and thou shalt turn in the morning, and go unto thy tents.

8 Six days thou shalt eat unleavened bread: and *i* on the seventh day *shall be* a *g* solemn assembly to the LORD thy God: thou shalt do no work *therein.*

9 ¶ Seven *j* weeks shalt thou number unto thee: begin to number the seven weeks from *such time as* thou beginnest *to put* the sickle to the corn.

10 And thou shalt keep the feast of weeks unto the LORD thy God with ³ a tribute of a free-will offering of thine hand, which thou shalt give *unto the LORD thy God,* according *k* as the LORD thy God hath blessed thee:

11 And thou shalt rejoice before the LORD thy God, thou, and thy son, and thy daughter, and thy man-servant, and thy maid-servant, and the Levite that *is* within thy gates, and *l* the stranger, and the fatherless, and the widow, that *are* among you, in the place which the LORD thy God hath chosen to place his name there.

12 And *m* thou shalt remember that thou wast a bondman in Egypt: and thou shalt observe and do these statutes.

13 ¶ Thou *n* shalt observe the feast of tabernacles seven days, after that thou hast gathered in thy *4* corn and thy wine:

14 And *o* thou shalt rejoice in thy feast, thou, and thy son, and thy daughter, and thy man-servant, and thy maid-servant, and the Levite, the stranger, and the fatherless, and the widow, that *are* within thy gates.

15 Seven days shalt thou keep a solemn feast unto the LORD thy God in the place which the LORD shall choose: because the LORD thy God shall bless thee in all thine increase, and in all the works of thine hands, therefore thou shalt surely rejoice.

16 ¶ Three times in a year shall all thy males appear before the LORD thy God in the place which he shall choose; in the feast of unleavened bread, and in the feast of weeks, and in the feast of tabernacles: and they shall not appear before the LORD empty:

17 Every man *shall give b* as he is able, according to the blessing of the LORD thy God which he hath given thee.

18 ¶ Judges and officers shalt thou make thee in all thy gates, which the LORD thy God giveth thee, throughout thy tribes: and they shall judge the people with just judgment.

19 Thou *p* shalt not wrest judgment; thou *q* shalt not respect persons, *r* neither take a gift: for a gift doth blind the eyes of the wise, and pervert the *6* words of the righteous.

20 ¹ That which is altogether just shalt thou follow, that thou mayest *d* live, and inherit the land which the LORD thy God giveth thee.

21 Thou *s* shalt not plant thee a grove of any trees near unto the altar of the LORD thy God, which thou shalt make thee.

22 Neither shalt thou set thee up any *g* image; which the LORD thy God hateth.

CHAPTER XVII.

1 *Things sacrificed must be sound. 2 Idolaters must be slain. 8 The priests and judges to determine controversies. 14 The election and duty of a king.*

THOU shalt not sacrifice unto the LORD thy God any bullock or ¹ sheep wherein is blemish, *or* any evil-favouredness: for that *is* an abomination unto the LORD thy God.

2 ¶ If there be found among you, within any of thy gates which the LORD thy God giveth thee, man or woman, that hath wrought wickedness in the sight of the LORD thy God, in transgressing his covenant,

3 And hath gone and served other gods, and worshipped them, either *a* the sun, or moon, or any of the host of heaven, *b* which I have not commanded;

4 And it be told thee, and thou hast heard *of it,* and enquired diligently, and, behold, *it is* true, *and* the thing certain, *that* such abomination is wrought in Israel;

5 Then shalt thou bring forth that man or that woman, which have committed that wicked thing, unto thy gates, *even* that man or that woman, and *c* shalt stone them with stones, till they die.

6 At *d* the mouth of two witnesses, or three witnesses, shall he that is worthy of death be put to death: *but* at the mouth of one witness he shall not be put to death.

7 The hands of the witnesses shall be first upon him to put him to death, and afterward the hands of all the people. So thou shalt put the evil away from among you.

8 ¶ If there arise a matter too hard for thee in judgment, *f* between blood and blood, between plea and plea, and between stroke and stroke, *being* matters of controversy, within thy gates; then shalt thou

of his brother—*i.e.*, an Israelite, so called in opposition to a stranger or foreigner. the Lord's release—The reason for acquitting a debtor at that particular period proceeded from obedience to the command, and a regard to the honour, of God; an acknowledgment of holding their property of Him, and gratitude for His kindness. 3. Of a foreigner thou mayest ex ct it—Admission to all the religious privileges of the Israelites was freely granted to heathen proselytes, though this spiritual incorporation did not always imply an equal participation of civil rights and privileges (Lev. 25. 44; Jer. 34. 14; cf. 1 Chr. 22. 2; 2 Chr. 2. 17.). 4. save when there shall be no poor man among you—Apparently a qualifying clause added to limit the application of the foregoing statement; so that "the brother" to be released pointed to a *poor* borrower, whereas it is implied that if he were rich, the restoration of the loan might be demanded even during that year. But the words may properly be rendered (as on marg.) to the *end, in order that there may be no poor among you*—*i.e.*, that none be reduced to inconvenient straits and poverty by unseasonable exaction of debts, at a time when there was no labour and no produce, and that all may enjoy comfort and prosperity, which will be the case through the special blessing of God on the land, provided they are obedient. 7-11. If there be a poor man, thou shalt not harden thine heart—Lest the foregoing law should prevent the Israelites lending to the poor, Moses here admonishes them against so mean and selfish a spirit, and exhorts them to give in a liberal spirit of charity and kindness, which will secure the divine blessing, Rom. 12. 8; 2 Cor. 9. 7.). 11. For the poor shall never cease—Although every Israelite on the conquest of Canaan, became the owner of property, yet in the providence of God who foresaw the event, it was permitted, partly as a punishment of disobedience, and partly for the exercise of benevolent and charitable feelings, that "the poor should never cease out of the land." HEBREW SERVANTS' FREEDOM. 12-18. If thy brother be sold—The last extremity of an insolvent debtor, when his house or land was not sufficient to cancel his debt, was to be sold as a slave with his family (Lev. 25. 39; 2 Kin. 4. 1; Neh. 5. 1-13; Job, 24. 9; Matt. 18. 25.). The term of servitude could not last beyond six years; they obtained their freedom either after six years from the time of their sale, or before the end of the seventh year; and at the year of jubilee, such slaves were emancipated, although their six years of service were not completed. 13-15. Thou shalt not let him go empty—a seasonable and wise provision for enabling a poor unfortunate to regain his original status in society, and the motive urged for his kindness and humanity to the Hebrew slave, was the remembrance that the whole nation was once a degraded and persecuted band of helots in Egypt. Thus kindness towards their slaves, unparalleled elsewhere in those days, was inculcated by the Mosaic law; and in all their conduct towards persons in that reduced condition, leniency and gentleness were enforced by an appeal which no Israelite could resist. 16-17. If he say I will not go away—If they declined to avail themselves of the privilege of release, and chose to remain with their master, then by a peculiar form of ceremony, they became a party to the transaction, voluntarily sold themselves to their employer and continued in his service till death. 18. worth a double-hired servant—*i.e.*, he is entitled to double wages, because his service was more advantageous to you, being both without wages and for a length of time, whereas hired servants were engaged yearly (Lev. 25. 53,) or at most for three years (Is. 16. 14.). 19. All the firstling males . . . thou shalt sanctify—(See on Ex. 22. 30.). thou shalt do no work with the firstling of thy bullock—*i. e.*, the second firstlings (see on ch. 12. 17, 18; 14. 23.).

CHAPTER XVI.

Ver. 1-22. THE FEAST OF THE PASSOVER. 1. Observe the month of Abib—or first-fruits. It comprehended the latter part of our March and the beginning of April. Green ears of the barley, which were then filled, were offered as first-fruits, on the second day of the Passover. brought thee out of Egypt by night—This statement is apparently at variance with the prohibition, (Ex. 12. 22,) as well as with the recorded fact that their department took place in the *morning* (Ex. 13. 3; Num. 33. 3.). But it is susceptible of easy reconciliation. Pharaoh's permission, the first step of emancipation, was extorted during night, the preparations for departure commenced, the rendezvous at Rameses made, and the march entered on in the morning. 2. Thou shalt sacrifice the Passover—not the paschal lamb, which was strictly and properly the Passover. The whole solemnity is here meant, as is evident from the mention of the additional victims that required to be offered on the subsequent days of the feast (Nu. 28. 18, 19; 2 Chr. 35. 8, 9,), and from the allusion to the continued use of unleavened bread for seven days, whereas the Passover itself was to be eaten at once. The words before us are equivalent to " thou shalt observe the feast of the Passover." unleavened bread—a sour, unpleasant, unwholesome kind of bread, designed to be a memorial of their Egyptian misery, and of the haste with which they departed, not allowing time for their morning dough to ferment. 5, 6. Thou mayest not sacrifice, within any of thy gates—The Passover was to be observed nowhere but in the court of the tabernacle or temple, as it was not a religious feast or sacramental occasion merely, but an actual sacrifice (Ex. 12. 27; 23. 18; 34. 25,). The blood had to be sprinkled on the altar and in the place where the true Passover was afterwards to be sacrificed for us at even, at the going down of the sun—lit. between the evenings. at the season—*i.e.*, the month and day, though not perhaps the precise hour. The immense number of victims that had to be immolated on the eve of the Passover, *i.e.*, within a space of four hours, has appeared to some writers a great difficulty. But the large number of officiating priests, their dexterity and skill in the preparation of the sacrifices, the wide range of the court, the extraordinary dimensions of the altar of burnt-offering and orderly method of conducting the solemn ceremonial, rendered it easy to do that in a few hours, which would otherwise have required as many days. 7. thou shalt roast—(See on Ex. 12. 8; cf. 2 Chr. 35. 13.). thou shalt turn in the morning and go

arise, *and get thee up into the place which the Lord thy God shall choose;

9 And *thou shalt come unto the priests the Levites, and *unto the judge that shall be in those days, and enquire; *and they shall shew thee the sentence of judgment:

10 And thou shalt do according to the sentence, which they of that place which the Lord shall choose shall shew thee; and thou shalt observe to do according to all that they inform thee:

11 According to the sentence of the law which they shall teach thee, and according to the judgment which they shall tell thee, thou shalt do: thou shalt not decline from the sentence which they shall shew thee, *to* the right hand, nor *to* the left.

12 And *the man that will do presumptuously, and *will not hearken unto the priest that *standeth to minister there before the Lord thy God, or unto the judge, even that man shall die: and thou shalt put away the evil from Israel.

13 And all the people shall hear, and fear, and do no more presumptuously.

14 ¶ When thou art come unto the land which the Lord thy God giveth thee, and shalt possess it, and shalt dwell therein, and shalt say, *I will set a king over me, like *as all the nations that *are* about me;

15 Thou shalt in any wise set *him* king over thee whom the Lord thy God shall choose; one *from among thy brethren shalt thou set king over thee: thou mayest not set a stranger over thee, which *is* not thy brother.

16 But he shall not multiply *horses to himself, nor cause the people *to return to Egypt, to the end that he should multiply horses: forasmuch as *the Lord hath said unto you, *Ye shall henceforth return no more that way.

17 Neither shall he multiply wives to himself, that *his heart turn not away: neither shall he greatly *multiply to himself silver and gold.

18 And *it shall be, when he sitteth upon the throne of his kingdom, that he shall write him a copy of this law in a book, out of *that which is before the priests the Levites:

19 And *it shall be with him, and he shall read therein all the days of his life: that he may learn to fear the Lord his God, to keep all the words of this law and these statutes, to do them:

20 That his heart be not lifted up above his brethren, and that he *turn not aside from the commandment, *to* the right hand or *to* the left: to the end that he may prolong *his* days in his kingdom, he, and his children, in the midst of Israel.

CHAPTER XVIII.

1 The Lord is the priests' and the Levites' inheritance. 9 The abominations of the nations are to be avoided. 15 Christ the Prophet is to be heard. 20 The presumptuous prophet is to die.

THE priests the Levites, *and* all the tribe of Levi, shall have no part nor inheritance with Israel: they *shall eat the offerings of the Lord made by fire, and his inheritance.

2 Therefore shall they have no inheritance among their brethren: the Lord *is* their inheritance, as he hath said unto them.

3 ¶ And this shall be the priest's due from the people, from them that offer a sacrifice, whether *it be* ox or sheep; and *they shall give unto the priest the shoulder, and the two cheeks, and the maw.

4 The *first-fruit also* of thy corn, of thy wine, and of thine oil, and the first of the fleece of thy sheep, shalt thou give him.

5 For the Lord thy God hath chosen him out of all thy tribes, *to stand to minister in the name of the Lord, him and his sons for ever.

6 ¶ And if a Levite come from any of thy gates out of all Israel, where he *sojourned, and come with all the desire of his mind unto the place which the Lord shall choose;

7 Then he shall minister in the name of the Lord his God, as all his brethren the Levites *do*, which stand there before the Lord.

8 They shall have like *portions to eat, besides that which cometh of the sale of his patrimony.

9 ¶ When thou art come into the land which the Lord thy God giveth thee, *thou shalt not learn to do after the abominations of those nations.

10 There shall not be found among you any one that maketh his son or his daughter to pass through the fire, *or that useth divination, or an observer of times, or an enchanter, or a witch,

11 Or a charmer, or a consulter with familiar spirits, or a wizard, or a necromancer.

12 For all that do these things *are* an abomination unto the Lord: and *because of these abominations the Lord thy God doth drive them out from before thee.

13 Thou shalt be perfect with the Lord thy God.

14 For these nations, which thou shalt possess, hearkened unto *observers of times, and unto diviners: but as for thee, the Lord thy God hath not suffered thee so *to do*.

15 ¶ The *Lord thy God will raise up unto thee a Prophet from the midst of thee, of thy brethren, like unto me; unto him ye shall hearken;

16 According to all that thou desiredst of the Lord thy God in Horeb, in the day of the assembly, saying, Let me not hear again the voice of the Lord my God, neither let me see this great fire any more, that I die not.

17 And the Lord said unto me, They have well *spoken that* which they have spoken.

18 I will raise them up a Prophet from among their brethren, like unto thee, and will *put my words in his mouth; *and he shall speak unto them all that I shall command him.

19 And *it shall come to pass, that whosoever will not hearken unto my words which he shall speak in my name, I will require *it* of him.

20 But *the prophet which shall presume to speak a word in my name, which I have not commanded him to speak, or *that shall speak in the name of other gods, even that prophet shall die.

21 And if thou say in thine heart, How shall we know the word which the Lord hath not spoken?

22 When *a prophet speaketh in the name of the Lord, if the thing follow not, nor come to pass, that *is* the thing which the Lord hath not spoken, *but* the prophet hath spoken it presumptuously: thou shalt not be afraid of him.

unto thy tents—The sense of this passage, on the first glance of the words, seems to point to the morning after the first day—the Passover eve. Perhaps, however, the divinely-appointed duration of this feast, the solemn character and important object, the journey of the people from the distant parts of the land to be present, and the recorded examples of their continuing all the time (2 Chr. 30. 21; 35. 17,), (though these may be considered extraordinary, and therefore exceptional occasions,) may warrant the conclusion that the leave given to the people to return home was to be on the morning after the completion of the seven days. 9-12. Seven weeks shalt thou number—The feast of weeks, or a WEEK OF WEEKS; the feast of Pentecost (see on Ex. 34. 22; Lev. 23. 10; Acts, 2. 1.). As on the second day of the Passover, a sheaf of new barley, reaped on purpose was offered: so on the second day of Pentecost a sheaf of new wheat was presented as first-fruits (Ex. 23. 16; Nu. 28. 26,), a free-will spontaneous tribute of gratitude to God for his temporal bounties. This feast was instituted in memory of the giving of the law, that spiritual food by which man's soul is nourished (Deut. 8. 3.). 13-17. Thou shalt observe the feast, &c.—(See on Ex. 23. 16; Lev. 23. 34; Nu. 29. 12.). Various conjectures have been formed to account for the appointment of this feast at the conclusion of the whole harvest; some imagine that it was designed to remind the Israelites of the time when they had no corn fields to reap, but were daily supplied with manna; others think that it suited the convenience of the people better than any other period of the year for dwelling in booths; others that it was the time of Moses' second descent from the Mount; while a fourth class are of opinion that this feast was fixed to the time of the year when the word was made flesh and dwelt; lit., tabernacled amongst us (Jo. 1. 14,), Christ being actually born at that season. in all the works of thine hands... rejoice—i.e., praising God with a warm and elevated heart. According to Jewish tradition, no marriages were allowed to be celebrated during these great festivals: that no personal or private rejoicings might be mingled with the demonstrations of public and national gladness. 16. all thy males—No command was laid on women to undertake the journeys, partly from regard to the natural weakness of their sex, and partly to their domestic cares. 18 20. Judges and officers—these last meant heralds or bailiffs, employed in executing the sentence of their superiors. in all thy gates—The gate was the place of public resort among the Israelites and other Eastern people, where business was transacted and causes decided. The Ottoman Porte derived its name from the administration of justice at its gates. 21. Thou shalt not plant thee a grove—a grove has in Scripture a variety of significations —a group of overshadowing trees, or a grove adorned with altars dedicated to a particular deity, or a wooden image in a grove (Judges, 6. 25; 2 Kings, 23. 4-6.). They might be placed near the earthen and temporary altars erected in the wilderness, but they could not exist either at the tabernacle or temples. They were places, which, with their usual accompaniments, presented strong allurements to idolatry, and therefore the Israelites were prohibited from planting them. 22. neither shalt thou set up any image—erroneously rendered so for "pillar;" pillars of various kinds, and materials of wood or stone were erected in the neighbourhood of altars. Sometimes they were conical or oblong, at other times they served as pedestals for the statues of idols. A superstitious reverence was attached to them, and hence they were forbidden.

CHAPTER XVII.

Ver. 1. THINGS SACRIFICED MUST BE SOUND. 1. any bullock or sheep wherein is blemish—under the name of bullock were comprehended bulls, cows, and calves; under that of sheep, rams, lambs, kids, he and she goats. An ox, from mutilation, was inadmissible. The qualities required in animals destined for sacrifice are described (Ex. 12. 5; Lev. 1. 3.).

2. IDOLATORS MUST BE SLAIN. 2-7. any man or woman that hath wrought wickedness—The grand object contemplated in choosing Israel was to preserve the knowledge and worship of the one true God, and hence idolatry of any kind, whether of the heavenly bodies or in some grosser form, is called "a transgression of His covenant." No rank nor sex could palliate this crime. Every reported case, even a flying rumour of the perpetration of so heinous an offence was to be judicially examined, and if proved by the testimony of competent witnesses, the offender was to be taken without the gates and stoned to death, the witnesses casting the first stone at him. The object of this special arrangement was partly to deter the witnesses from making a rash accusation by the prominent part they had to act as executioners, and partly to give a public assurance that the crime had met its due punishment.

8-13. THE PRIESTS AND JUDGES TO DETERMINE CONTROVERSIES. 8-13. if there arise a matter too hard for thee—In all civil or criminal cases, where there was any doubt or difficulty in giving a decision, the local magistrates were to submit them by reference to the tribunal of the Sanhedrim—the supreme council, which was composed partly of civil and partly of ecclesiastical persons. "The priests and Levites,"—should rather be "the priests—the Levites;" i.e., the Levitical priests, including the High priest, who were members of the legislative assembly; and who, as forming one body, are called "the judge." Their sittings were held in the neighbourhood of the sanctuary, because in great emergencies the High priest had to consult God by Urim (Nu. 27. 21.). From their judgment there was no appeal; and if a person were so perverse and refractory as to refuse obedience to their sentences, his conduct as inconsistent with the maintenance of order and good government was then to be regarded and punished as a capital crime.

14-20. THE ELECTION AND DUTY OF A KING. 14-20. When ye shall say, I will set a king over me—In the following passage Moses *prophetically* announces a revolution which should occur at a later period in the national history of Israel. No sanction nor recommendation was indicated; on the contrary, when the popular clamour had effected that constitutional change on the Theocracy by the appointment of a king, the divine disapproval was expressed in the

CHAPTER XIX.

1 *Of the cities of refuge.* 14 *The land-mark is not to be removed.* 15 *Two witnesses required.* 16 *Punishment of a false witness.*

WHEN the Lord thy God hath cut off the nations, whose land the Lord thy God giveth thee, and thou ¹ succeedest them, and dwellest in their cities, and in their houses;

2 Thou ᵃ shalt separate three cities for thee in the midst of thy land, which the Lord thy God giveth thee to possess it.

3 Thou shalt prepare thee a way, and divide the coasts of thy land, which the Lord thy God giveth thee to inherit, into three parts, that every slayer may flee thither.

4 ¶ And this *is* the case of the slayer which shall flee thither, that he may live: Whoso killeth his neighbour ignorantly, whom he hated not ² in time past;

5 As when a man goeth into the wood with his neighbour to hew wood, and his hand fetcheth a stroke with the ax to cut down the tree, and the ³ head slippeth from the ⁴ helve, and ⁵ lighteth upon his neighbour, that he die; he shall flee unto one of those cities, and live:

6 Lest the avenger of the blood pursue the slayer, while his heart is hot, and overtake him, because the way is long, and ⁶ slay him; whereas he *was* not worthy of death, inasmuch as he hated him not ⁷ in time past.

7 Wherefore I command thee, saying, Thou shalt separate three cities for thee.

8 And if the Lord thy God ᵇ enlarge thy coast, as he hath sworn unto thy fathers, and give thee all the land which he promised to give unto thy fathers;

9 If thou shalt keep all these commandments to do them, which I command thee this day, to love the Lord thy God, and to walk ever in his ways; ᶜ then shalt thou add three cities more for thee, besides these three:

10 That innocent blood be not shed in thy land, which the Lord thy God giveth thee *for* an inheritance, and *so* blood be upon thee.

11 ¶ But if ᵈ any man ᵉ hate his neighbour, and lie in wait for him, and rise up against him, and smite him ⁸ mortally that he die, and fleeth into one of these cities;

12 Then the elders of his city shall send and fetch him thence, and deliver him into the hand of the avenger of blood, that he may die.

13 Thine eye shall not pity him: ᶠ but thou shalt put away *the guilt of* innocent blood from Israel, that it may go well with thee.

14 ¶ Thou ᵍ shalt not remove thy neighbour's land-mark, which they of old time have set in thine inheritance, which thou shalt inherit in the land that the Lord thy God giveth thee to possess it.

15 ¶ One ʰ witness shall not rise up against a man for any iniquity, or for any sin, in any sin that he sinneth: at the mouth of two witnesses, or at the mouth of three witnesses, shall the matter be established.

16 If a false witness ⁱ rise up against any man, to testify against him ⁹ *that which is* wrong;

17 Then both the men, between whom the controversy *is*, shall stand before the Lord, before the priests and the judges, which shall be in those days;

18 And the judges shall make diligent inquisition: and, behold, *if* the witness *be* a false witness, *and* hath testified falsely against his brother;

19 Then ʲ shall ye do unto him as he had thought to have done unto his brother: so shalt thou put the evil away from among you.

20 And ᵏ those which remain shall hear, and fear, and shall henceforth commit no more any such evil among you.

21 And thine eye shall not pity; *but* ˡ life *shall go* for life, eye for eye, tooth for tooth, hand for hand, foot for foot.

CHAPTER XX.

1 *The priest's exhortation to encourage the people to battle.* 10 *How to use the cities that accept or refuse the proclamation of peace.* 16 *What cities must be devoted.*

WHEN thou goest out to battle against thine enemies, and seest ᵃ horses and chariots, *and* a people more than thou, be not afraid of them: for the Lord thy God is ᵇ with thee, which brought thee up out of the land of Egypt.

2 And it shall be, when ye are come nigh unto the battle, that the priest shall approach and speak unto the people,

3 And shall say unto them, Hear, O Israel; ye approach this day unto battle against your enemies: let not your hearts ¹ faint; fear not, and do not ² tremble, neither be ye terrified because of them;

4 For the Lord your God *is* he that goeth with you, ᶜ to fight for you against your enemies, to save you.

5 ¶ And the officers shall speak unto the people, saying, What man *is there* that hath built a new house, and hath not ᵈ dedicated it? let him go and return to his house, lest he die in the battle, and another man dedicate it.

6 And what man *is he* that hath planted a vineyard, and hath not yet ³ eaten of it? let him also go and return unto his house, lest he die in the battle, and another man eat of it.

7 And ᵉ what man *is there* that hath betrothed a wife, and hath not taken her? let him go and return unto his house, lest he die in the battle, and another man take her.

8 And the officers shall speak further unto the people, and they shall say, ᶠ What man *is there that is* fearful and faint-hearted? let him go and return unto his house, lest his brethren's heart ⁴ faint as well as his heart.

9 And it shall be, when the officers have made an end of speaking unto the people, that they shall make captains of the armies ᵇ to lead the people.

10 ¶ When thou comest nigh unto a city to fight against it, ᵍ then proclaim peace unto it.

11 And it shall be, if it make thee answer of peace, and open unto thee, then it shall be, *that* all the people *that is* found therein shall be ʰ tributaries unto thee, and they shall serve thee.

12 And if it will make no peace with thee, but will make war against thee, then thou shalt besiege it:

13 And when the Lord thy God hath delivered it into thine hands, ⁱ thou shalt smite every male thereof with the edge of the sword:

14 But the women, and the little ones,

most unequivocal terms (1 Sam. 8. 7.). Permission at length was granted, God reserving to himself the nomination of the family and the person who should be elevated to the regal dignity (1 Sam. 9. 16; 10. 24; 16. 12; 1 Chr. 28. 4.). In short, Moses, foreseeing that his ignorant and fickle countrymen, insensible to their advantages as a peculiar people, would soon wish to change their constitution and be like other nations, provides to a certain extent for such an emergency, and lays down the principles on which a king in Israel must act. He was to possess certain indispensable requisites; he was to be an Israelite, of the same race and religion, to preserve the purity of the established worship, as well as be a type of Christ, a spiritual king, one of their brethren. **15.** thou mayest not set a stranger *i.e.*, by their free and voluntary choice. But God, in the retributions of His providence, did allow foreign princes to usurp the dominion (Jer. 38.17; Matt.22.17.). **16.** He shall not multiply horses—The use of these animals was not absolutely prohibited, nor is there any reason to conclude that they might not be employed as part of the state equipage. But the multiplication of horses would inevitably lead to many evils, to increased intercourse with foreign nations, especially with Egypt, to the importation of an animal to which the character of the country was not suited, to the establishment of an Oriental military despotism, to proud and pompous parade in peace, to a dependence upon Egypt in time of war, and a consequent withdrawal of trust and confidence in God (2 Sam. 8. 4; 1 Ki. 10. 26; 2 Chr. 1. 16; 9. 28; Is. 31. 3.). **17.** Neither shall he multiply wives—There were the strongest reasons for recording an express prohibition on this point, founded on the practice of neighbouring countries in which polygamy prevailed, and whose kings had numerous harems: besides the monarch of Israel was to be absolutely independent of the people, and had nothing but the divine law to restrain his passions. The mischievous effects resulting from the breach of this condition were exemplified in the history of Solomon and other princes who, by trampling on the restrictive law, corrupted themselves as well as the nation. neither shall he multiply silver and gold—*i.e.*, the the kings were forbidden to accumulate money for private purposes. **18-20.** he shall write him a copy—The original scroll of the ancient Scriptures was deposited in the sanctuary under the strict custody of the priests (see on ch. 31. 26; 2 Ki. 22. 8.). Each monarch, on his accession, was to be furnished with a true and faithful copy, which he was to keep constantly beside him, and daily peruse it, that his character and sentiments being cast into its sanctifying mould, he might discharge his royal functions in the spirit of faith and piety, of humility and a love of righteousness. that he may prolong his days, he and his children in his kingdom—From this it appears that the crown in Israel was to be hereditary, unless forfeited by personal crime.

CHAPTER XVIII.

Ver. 1-8. THE LORD IS THE PRIESTS' AND THE LEVITES' INHERITANCE. **1.** The priests, the Levites shall eat the offerings—As the tribe of Levi had no inheritance allotted them like the other tribes, but were wholly consecrated to the priestly office, their maintenance was to arise from tithes, first-fruits, and certain portions of the oblations presented on the altar, which God having by express appointment reserved to himself, made over, after being offered to His ministers. **3.** This shall be the priests' due from the people—All who offered sacrifices of thanksgiving or peace-offerings (Lev. 7. 31-33,) were ordered to give the breast and shoulder as perquisites to the priests. Here "the two cheeks" or head, and "the maw" or stomach, deemed anciently a great dainty, are specified. But whether this is a new injunction, or a repetition of the old, with the supplement of more details, it is not easy to determine. **6-8.** If a Levite..come with all the desire of his mind—It appears that the Levites served in rotation from the earliest times; but, from their great numbers, it was only at distant intervals they could be called into actual service. Should any Levite, however, under the influence of eminent piety, resolve to devote himself wholly and continually to the sacred duties of the sanctuary, he was allowed to realize his ardent wishes; and as he was admitted to a share of the work, so also to a share of the remuneration. Though he might have a private property, that was to form no ground for withholding or even diminishing his claim to maintenance like the other ministering priests. The reason or principle of the enactment is obvious (1 Cor. 9. 13.). At the same time, while every facility was afforded for the admission of such a zealous and self-denying officer, this admission was to be in an orderly manner: he was to minister "as all his brethren," *i.e.*, a Gershonite with Gershonites; a Merarite with Merarites; so that there might be no derangement of the established courses.

9-14. THE ABOMINATIONS OF THE NATIONS ARE TO BE AVOIDED. **9-14.** Thou shalt not learn to do after the abominations of those nations—(See on Lev. 18. 21; 19. 26-31; 20. 6.). In spite of this express command, the people of Canaan, especially the Philistines, were a constant snare and stumbling-block to the Israelites, on account of their divinations and superstitious practices.

15-19. CHRIST THE PROPHET IS TO BE HEARD. **15-19.** The Lord thy God will raise up unto thee a prophet—The insertion of this promise in connection with the preceding prohibition, might warrant the applicat on which some make of it, to that order of true prophets whom God commissioned in unbroken succession to instruct, to direct, and warn His people; and in this view the purport of it is, "there is no need to consult with diviners and soothsayers, as I shall afford you the benefit of divinely-appointed prophets, for judging of whose credentials a sure criterion is given" (*vs.* 20-22.). But the prophet here promised was pre-eminently the Messiah, for He alone was "like unto Moses (see on ch. 34. 10.) in his Mediatorial character; in the peculiar excellence of his ministry; in the number, variety, and magnitude of his miracles; in his close and familiar communion with God; and in His being the author of a new dispensation of religion." This prediction was fulfilled 1500 years afterwards, and was expressly applied to Jesus Christ by Peter (Ac. 3. 22, 23.), and by Stephen (Ac. 7. 37.). **19.** whosoever will not hearken, I will require it of him—The

and ⁱ the cattle, and all that is in the city, even all the spoil thereof, shalt thou ⁶ take unto thyself: and ᵏ thou shalt eat the spoil of thine enemies, which the LORD thy God hath given thee.

15 Thus shalt thou do unto all the cities *which are* very far off from thee, which *are* not of the cities of these nations.

16 But ˡ of the cities of these people, which the LORD thy God doth give thee *for* an inheritance, thou shalt save alive nothing that breatheth:

17 But thou shalt utterly destroy them; *namely*, the Hittites, and the Amorites, the Canaanites, and the Perizzites, the Hivites, and the Jebusites; as the LORD thy God hath commanded thee:

18 That ᵐ they teach you not to do after all their abominations, which they have done unto their gods; so should ye ⁿ sin against the LORD your God.

19 ¶ When thou shalt besiege a city a long time, in making war against it to take it, thou shalt not destroy the trees thereof by forcing an ax against them: for thou mayest eat of them, and thou shalt not cut them down (⁷ for the tree of the field is man's *life*,) ⁸ to employ *them* in the siege:

20 Only the trees which thou knowest that *they* be not trees for meat, thou shalt destroy and cut them down; and thou shalt build bulwarks against the city that maketh war with thee, until ⁹ it be subdued.

CHAPTER XXI.

1 *The expiation of uncertain murder.* 10 *The usage of a captive taken to wife.* 15 *The first-born is not to be disinherited upon private affection.* 18 *A stubborn son to be stoned to death.*

IF one be found ᵃ slain in the land which the LORD thy God giveth thee to possess it, lying in the field, *and* it be not known who hath slain him;

2 Then thy elders and thy judges shall come forth, and they shall measure unto the cities which *are* round about him that is slain.

3 And it shall be, *that* the city which *is* next unto the slain man, even the elders of that city shall take an heifer, which hath not been wrought with, *and* which hath not drawn in the yoke;

4 And the elders of that city shall bring down the heifer unto a rough valley, which is neither eared nor sown, and shall strike off the heifer's neck there in the valley:

5 And the priests the sons of Levi shall come near; (for ᵇ them the LORD thy God hath chosen to minister unto him, and to bless in the name of the LORD; and ᶜ by their ¹ word shall every controversy and every stroke be *tried*.)

6 And all the elders of that city, that *are* next unto the slain *man*, ᵈ shall wash their hands over the heifer that is beheaded in the valley:

7 And they shall answer and say, ᵉ Our hands have not shed this blood, neither have our eyes seen *it*.

8 Be merciful, O LORD, unto thy people Israel, whom thou hast redeemed, ᶠ and lay not innocent blood ² unto thy people of Israel's charge. And the blood shall be forgiven them.

9 So ᵍ shalt thou put away the *guilt of* innocent blood from among you, when thou shalt do *that* which *is* right in the sight of the LORD.

B. C. 1451.

CHAP. 20.
j Josh. 8. 2.
6 spoil.
k Josh. 22. 8.
l Nu. 21. 2, 3, 35.
Nu. 33. 52.
ch. 7. 1, 2.
Josh. 11. 14.
ᵐ ch. 7. 4.
ch. 12. 30, 31.
ch. 18. 9.
1 Cor. 15. 33.
ⁿ Ex. 23. 33.
7 Or, for, O man, the tree of the field is to be employed in the siege.
8 to go from before thee.
9 it come down.

CHAP. 21.
a Ps. 9, 12.
Pro. 28. 17.
b 1 Chr. 23. 13.
c ch. 17. 8, 9.
1 mouth.
d Ps. 19. 12.
Mat. 27. 24.
e 2 Sa. 3. 13.
f Jonah 1. 14.
2 in the midst.
g ch. 19. 13.
h 2 Chr. 32. 8.
Josh. 21. 44.
3 make, or, dress, or, suffer to grow.
i Ps. 45. 10.
j Gen. 34. 2.
Judg. 19. 24.
k Gen. 29. 33.
l 2 Chr. 11. 19.
ᵐ 1 Chr. 5. 1.
4 that is found with him.
ⁿ Gen. 49. 3.
o Gen. 25. 31.
p Ex. 20. 12.
Lev. 19. 3.
Pro. 1. 8.
Pro. 15. 5.
Pro. 20. 20.
Eph. 6. 1.
q ch. 19. 19.
r ch. 13. 11.
s ch. 22. 20.
Acts 23. 29.
t Josh. 8. 29.
John 19. 31.
ᵘ Gal. 3. 13.
5 the curse of God.
Nu. 25. 4.
2 Sa. 21. 6.
v Lev. 18. 25.
Nu. 35. 34.

CHAP. 22.
a Ex. 23. 4.
Ro. 12. 10.
2 Pet. 1. 7.
1 Joh. 3. 15.
1 John 4. 21.
b Pro. 27. 10.
Zech. 7. 9.

10 ¶ When thou goest forth to war against thine enemies, and the ʰ LORD thy God hath delivered them into thine hands, and thou hast taken them captive,

11 And seest among the captives a beautiful woman, and hast a desire unto her, that thou wouldest have her to thy wife;

12 Then thou shalt bring her home to thine house; and she shall shave her head, and ³ pare her nails;

13 And she shall put the raiment of her captivity from off her, and shall remain in thine house, and ⁱ bewail her father and her mother a full month: and after that thou shalt go in unto her, and be her husband, and she shall be thy wife.

14 And it shall be, if thou have no delight in her, then thou shalt let her go whither she will; but thou shalt not sell her at all for money, thou shalt not make merchandise of her, because thou ʲ hast humbled her.

15 ¶ If a man have two wives, one beloved, and ᵏ another hated, and they have born him children, *both* the beloved and the hated; and *if* the first-born son be hers that was hated;

16 Then it shall be, ˡ when he maketh his sons to inherit *that* which he hath, *that* he may not make the son of the beloved first-born before the son of the hated, which *is* indeed the first-born:

17 But he shall acknowledge the son of the hated *for* the first-born, ᵐ by giving him a double portion of all ⁴ that he hath: for he *is* ⁿ the beginning of his strength: the ᵒ right of the first-born *is* his.

18 ¶ If a man have a stubborn and rebellious son, which will not obey the voice of his ᵖ father, or the voice of his mother, and *that*, when they have chastened him, will not hearken unto them;

19 Then shall his father and his mother lay hold on him, and bring him out unto the elders of his city, and unto the gate of his place;

20 And they shall say unto the elders of his city, This our son *is* stubborn and rebellious, he will not obey our voice; he *is* a glutton and a drunkard.

21 And all the men of his city shall stone him with stones, that he die: ᵠ so shalt thou put evil away from among you; ʳ and all Israel shall hear, and fear.

22 ¶ And if a man have committed a sin worthy ˢ of death, and he be to be put to death, and thou hang him on a tree;

23 His ᵗ body shall not remain all night upon the tree, but thou shalt in any wise bury him that day; (for ᵘ he that is hanged *is* ⁵ accursed of God;) that ᵛ thy land be not defiled, which the LORD thy God giveth thee *for* an inheritance.

CHAPTER XXII.

1 *Of humanity toward brethren.* 5 *The sex to be distinguished by apparel.* 9 *Confusion to be avoided.* 12 *Adultery to be punished with death.* 23 *Of rape.* 28 *Of fornication.* 30 *Incest forbidden.*

THOU ᵃ shalt not see thy brother's ox or his sheep go astray, and ᵇ hide thyself from them: thou shalt in any case bring them again unto thy brother.

2 And if thy brother *be* not nigh unto thee, or if thou know him not; then thou shalt bring it unto thine own house, and it shall be with thee until thy brother seek

CHAPTER XIX.

Ver. 1-13. OF THE CITIES OF REFUGE. 2. Thou shalt separate three cities in the midst of the land—Goelism, or the duty of the nearest kinsman to avenge the death of a slaughtered relative, being the consuetudinary law of that age, as it still is among the Arabs and other people of the East, Moses incorporated it in an improved form with his legislative code. For the protection of the unintentional homicide, he provided certain cities of refuge;—three had been destined for this purpose on the East of Jordan (ch. 4. 41; Nu. 35. 11,); three were to be invested with the same privilege on the west of that river when Canaan should be conquered, in the midst of the land—in such a position that they would be conspicuous and accessible, and equi-distant from the extremities of the land and from each other. **3.** Thou shalt prepare thee a way—The roads leading to them were to be kept in good condition, and the brooks or rivers to be spanned by good bridges; the width of the roads was to be 32 cubits; and at all the cross roads, sign-posts were to be erected with the words, *Mekeleth, Mekeleth,* "refuge, refuge," painted on them. divide the coasts of thy land into three parts—the whole extent of the country from the south to the north; the three cities on each side of Jordan were opposite to each other "as two rows of vines in a vineyard" (see on Josh. 20. 7, 8,). **6.** Lest the avenger of blood pursue the slayer, while his heart is hot—This verse is a continuation of the third (for vs. 4, 5, which are explanatory, are in a parenthetical form), and the meaning is, that if the kinsman of a person inadvertently killed, should, under the impulse of sudden excitement, and without inquiring into the circumstances, inflict summary vengeance on the homicide, however guiltless, the law tolerated such an act; it was to pass with impunity. But to prevent such precipitate measures, the cities of refuge were established for the reception of the homicide, that "innocent blood might not be shed in thy land" (v. 10.). In the case of premeditated murder (vs. 11, 12,) they afforded no immunity; but, if it was only manslaughter, the moment the fugitive was within the gates, he found himself in a safe asylum (Num. 35. 26-28; Josh. 20. 6,). **8, 9.** And if the Lord enlarge thy coast—Three additional sanctuaries were to be established in the event of their territory extending over the country from Hermon and Gilead to the Euphrates. (See on Gen. 15. 18; Ex. 23. 31.) But it was obscurely hinted that this last provision would never be carried into effect, as the Israelites would not fulfil the conditions, viz., "that of keeping the commandments, to love the Lord, and walk ever in his ways." In point of fact, although that region was brought into subjection by David and Solomon, we do not find that cities of refuge were established; because those sovereigns only made the ancient inhabitants tributary, instead of sending a colony of Israelites to possess it. The privilege of sanctuary cities, however, was given only for Israelites; and besides, that conquered territory did not remain long under the power of the Hebrew kings.

14. THE LAND-MARK IS NOT TO BE REMOVED. 14. Thou shalt not remove thy neighbour's land-mark—The state of Palestine in regard to enclosures is very much the same now as it has always been. Though gardens and vineyards are surrounded by dry stone walls or hedges of prickly-pear, the boundaries of arable fields are marked by nothing but by a little trench, a small cairn, or a single erect stone, placed at certain intervals. It is manifest that a dishonest person could easily fill the gutter with earth, or remove these stones a few feet without much risk of detection, and enlarge his own field by a stealthy encroachment on his neighbour's. This law, then, was made to prevent such trespasses.

15. TWO WITNESSES REQUIRED. 15. One witness shall not arise. The following rules to regulate the admission of testimony in public courts, are founded on the principles of natural justice. A single witness shall not be admitted to the condemnation of an accused person. PUNISHMENT OF A FALSE WITNESS. **16-21.** But if convicted of perjury, it will be sufficient for his own condemnation, and his punishment shall be exactly the same as would have overtaken the object of his malignant prosecution (see on Ex. 21. 24; Lev. 24. 20.).

CHAPTER XX.

Ver. 1-20. THE PRIESTS' EXHORTATION TO ENCOURAGE THE PEOPLE TO BATTLE. 1. When thou goest out to battle against thine enemies—In the approaching invasion of Canaan, or in any just and defensive war, the Israelites had reason to expect the presence and favour of God. **2.** the priest shall approach and speak unto the people—Jewish writers say that there was a war priest appointed by a special ceremonial to attend the army. It was natural that the solemn objects and motives of religion should have been applied to animate patriotism, and give additional impulse to valour; other people have done this. But in the case of Israel, the regular attendance of a priest on the battlefield was in accordance with their Theocratic government, in which everything was done directly by God through his delegated ministers. It was the province of this priest to sound the trumpets (Num. 10. 9; 31. 6,), and he had others under him who repeated at the head of each battalion the exhortations which he addressed to the warriors in general. The speech (vs. 3, 4,) is marked by a brevity and expressiveness admirably suited to the occasion, viz., when the men were drawn up in line. **4.** Your God is he that goeth with you—according to Jewish writers, the ark was always taken into the field of combat. But there is no evidence of this in the sacred history; and it must have been a sufficient ground of encouragement to be assured that God was on their side. **5.** the officers shall speak unto the people—lit., *Shoterim,* who are called "scribes" or "overseers" (Ex. 5. 6.). They might be keepers of the muster-roll, or perhaps rather military heralds, whose duty it was to announce the orders of the generals (2 Chr. 26. 11.). This proclamation (vs. 5, 8,) must have been made previous to the priest's address, as great disorder and inconvenience must have been occasioned if the serried ranks were broken by the departure of those to whom the privilege was

after it, and thou shalt restore it to him again.

3 In like manner shalt thou do with his ass; and so shalt thou do with his raiment; and with all lost thing of thy brother's, which he hath lost, and thou hast found, shalt thou do likewise: thou mayest not hide thyself.

4 ¶ Thou shalt not see thy brother's ass or his ox fall down by the way, and hide thyself from them: thou shalt surely help him to lift *them* up again.

5 ¶ The ᶜwoman shall not wear that which pertaineth unto a man, neither shall a man put on a woman's garment: for all that do so *are* abomination unto the LORD thy God.

6 ¶ If a bird's nest chance to be before thee in the way in any tree, or on the ground, *whether they be* young ones or eggs, and the dam sitting upon the young, or upon the eggs, ᵈ thou shalt not take the dam with the young:

7 *But* thou shalt in any wise let the dam go, and take the young to thee; ᵉ that it may be well with thee, and *that* thou mayest prolong *thy* days.

8 ¶ When thou buildest a new house, then thou shalt make a battlement for thy roof, that thou bring not blood upon thine house, if any man fall from thence.

9 ¶ Thou ᶠ shalt not sow thy vineyard with divers seeds; lest the ¹ fruit of thy seed which thou hast sown, and the fruit of thy vineyard, be defiled.

10 ¶ Thou ᵍ shalt not plow with an ox and an ass together.

11 ¶ Thou ʰ shalt not wear a garment of divers sorts, *as* of woollen and linen together.

12 ¶ Thou shalt make thee ⁱ fringes upon the four ² quarters of thy vesture, wherewith thou coverest *thyself*.

13 ¶ If any man take a wife, and ʲ go in unto her, and hate her,

14 And give occasions of speech against her, and bring up an evil name upon her, and say, I took this woman, and when I came to her I found her not a maid:

15 Then shall the father of the damsel, and her mother, take and bring forth *the tokens of* the damsel's virginity unto the elders of the city in the gate:

16 And the damsel's father shall say unto the elders, I gave my daughter unto this man to wife, and he hateth her;

17 And, lo, he hath given occasions of speech against her, saying, I found not thy daughter a maid; and yet these *are the tokens of* my daughter's virginity. And they shall spread the cloth before the elders of the city.

18 And ᵏ the elders of that city shall take that man and chastise him;

19 And they shall amerce him in an hundred *shekels* of silver, and give *them* unto the father of the damsel, because he hath brought up an evil name upon a virgin of Israel: and she shall be his wife; he may not put her away all his days.

20 But if this thing ˡ be true, *and the tokens of* virginity be not found for the damsel;

21 Then they shall bring out the damsel to the door of her father's house, and the men of her city shall stone her with stones that she die; because she hath ᵐ wrought folly in Israel, to play the whore in her

B. C. 1451.

CHAP. 22.
ᶜ 1 Cor. 14. 40.
ᵈ Lev. 22. 28.
Neh. 9. 6.
Ps. 36. 6.
Ps. 145. 9.
Pro. 12. 10.
Mat. 10. 29.
Lu. 12. 6.
ᵉ ch. 4. 40.
ᶠ Lev. 19. 19.
¹ fulness of thy seed.
ᵍ 2 Cor. 6. 14, 15, 16.
ʰ Lev. 19. 19.
ⁱ Nu. 15. 38.
Mat. 23. 5.
² wings.
ʲ Gen. 29. 21.
Judg. 15. 1.
ᵏ Ex. 13. 21.
Deut. 1. 9-18.
Ro. 13. 4.
ˡ ch. 17. 4.
ᵐ Gen. 34. 7.
Judg. 20. 6, 10.
2 Sam. 13. 12, 13.
ⁿ ch. 13. 5.
ᵒ Lev. 20. 10.
Pro. 6. 22.
Mal. 3. 5.
Mat. 5. 27, 28.
John 8. 5.
1 Cor. 6. 9.
Heb. 13. 4.
ᵖ Mat. 1. 18, 19.
ᵠ ch. 21. 14.
³ Or, take strong hold of her.
2 Sam. 13. 14.
ʳ Ex. 22. 16, 17.
ˢ Lev. 18. 8.
Lev. 20. 11.
ch. 27. 20.
1 Cor. 5. 1.
ᵗ Gen. 9. 22-27.
Ezek. 16. 8.

CHAP. 23.
ᵃ Neh. 13. 1, 2.
ᵇ ch. 2. 29.
Gen. 14. 18.
Mat. 10. 40, 42.
Mat. 25. 41-46.
ᶜ Num. 22. 5, 6.
Josh. 24. 9.
ᵈ Pro. 26. 2.
ᵉ Ezra 9. 12.
¹ good.
ᶠ Gen. 25. 24, 25, 26.
Obad. 10. 12.
ᵍ Ex. 22. 21.
Ex. 23. 9.
ch. 10. 19.
Lev. 19. 34.

father's house: ⁿ so shalt thou put evil away from among you.

22 ¶ If ᵒ a man be found lying with a woman married to an husband, then they shall both of them die, *both* the man that lay with the woman, and the woman: so shalt thou put away evil from Israel.

23 If a damsel *that is* a virgin be ᵖ betrothed unto an husband, and a man find her in the city, and lie with her;

24 Then ye shall bring them both out unto the gate of that city, and ye shall stone them with stones that they die; the damsel, because she cried not, *being* in the city; and the man, because he hath humbled ᵠ his neighbour's wife: so thou shalt put away evil from among you.

25 ¶ But if a man find a betrothed damsel in the field, and the man ³ force her, and lie with her: then the man only that lay with her shall die:

26 But unto the damsel thou shalt do nothing; *there is* in the damsel no sin *worthy* of death: for as when a man riseth against his neighbour, and slayeth him, even so *is* this matter:

27 For he found her in the field, *and* the betrothed damsel cried, and *there was* none to save her.

28 ¶ If ʳ a man find a damsel *that is* a virgin, which is not betrothed, and lay hold on her, and lie with her, and they be found;

29 Then the man that lay with her shall give unto the damsel's father fifty *shekels* of silver, and she shall be his wife; because he hath humbled her, he may not put her away all his days.

30 ¶ A ˢ man shall not take his father's wife, nor ᵗ discover his father's skirt.

CHAPTER XXIII.

1 *Who may and who may not enter into the congregation.* 9 *Uncleanness to be avoided in the host.* 15 *Of the fugitive servant;* 17 *of filthiness;* 18 *of abominable sacrifices;* 21 *of vows;* 24 *of trespasses.*

HE that is wounded in the stones, or hath his privy member cut off, shall not enter into the congregation of the LORD.

2 A bastard shall not enter into the congregation of the LORD: even to his tenth generation shall he not enter into the congregation of the LORD.

3 An ᵃ Ammonite or Moabite shall not enter into the congregation of the LORD; even to their tenth generation shall they not enter into the congregation of the LORD for ever:

4 Because ᵇ they met you not with bread and with water in the way, when ye came forth out of Egypt; and ᶜ because they hired against thee Balaam the son of Beor of Pethor of Mesopotamia, to curse thee.

5 Nevertheless the LORD thy God would not hearken unto Balaam; but the LORD thy God turned the ᵈ curse into a blessing unto thee, because the LORD thy God loved thee.

6 Thou ᵉ shalt not seek their peace nor their ¹ prosperity all thy days for ever.

7 Thou shalt not abhor an Edomite; ᶠ for he *is* thy brother: thou shalt not abhor an Egyptian, because ᵍ thou wast a stranger in his land.

8 The children that are begotten of them shall enter into the congregation of the LORD in their third generation.

9 ¶ When the host goeth forth against

granted. Four grounds of exemption are expressly mentioned:—1. The dedication of a new house which, as in all Oriental countries still, was an important event, and celebrated by festive and religious ceremonies; (Neh. 12, 27,) exemption for a year. 2. The planting of a vineyard. The fruit of the first three years being declared unfit for use, and the first fruits producible on the fourth, the exemption in this case lasted at least four years. 3. The betrothal of a wife, which was always a considerable time before marriage. It was deemed a great hardship to leave a house unfinished, a new property half cultivated, and a recently contracted marriage; and the exemptions allowed in these cases were founded on the principle that a man's heart being deeply engrossed with something at a distance, he would not be very enthusiastic in the public service. 4. The ground of exemption was cowardice. From the composition of the Israelitish army, which was an irregular militia, all above twenty years being liable to serve, many, totally unfit for war, must have been called to the field; and it was therefore a prudential arrangement to rid the army of such unwarlike elements—persons who could render no efficient service, and the contagion of whose craven spirit might lead to panic and defeat. 9. they shall make captains—*i.e.*, when the exempted parties have withdrawn, the combatants shall be ranged in order of battle. 10-20. when thou comest nigh unto a city to fight against it —An important principle is here introduced into the war-law of Israel regarding the people they fought against, and the cities they besieged. With "the cities of those people which God doth give thee" in Canaan, it was to be a war of utter extermination (*vs.* 17, 18.). But when on a just occasion, they went against other nations, they were first to make a proclamation of peace, which, if allowed by a surrender, the people would become dependent, and, in the relation of tributaries, the conquered nations would receive the highest blessings from alliance with the chosen people; they would be brought to the knowledge of Israel's God and of Israel's worship, as well as a participation of Israel's privileges. But if the besieged city refused to capitulate and be taken, a universal massacre was to be made of the males, while the women and children were to be preserved and kindly treated (*vs.* 13, 14.). By this means a provision was made for a friendly and useful connection being established between the captors and the captives; and Israel, even through her conquest, would prove a blessing to the nations. 19. Thou shalt not destroy the fruit trees thereof—In a protracted siege, wood would be required for various purposes, both for military works and for fuel. But fruit-bearing trees were to be carefully spared; and, indeed, in warm countries like India, where the people live much more on fruit than we do, the destruction of a fruit tree is considered a sort of sacrilege. 20. thou shalt build bulwarks against the city—It is evident that some sort of military engines were intended; and accordingly we know, that in Egypt, where the Israelites learnt their military tactics, the method of conducting a siege was by throwing up banks, and making advances with moveable towers, or with the testudo. [WILK.]

CHAPTER XXI.
Ver. 1-9. EXPIATION OF UNCERTAIN MURDER. 1. If one be found slain lying in the field—The ceremonies here ordained to be observed on the discovery of a slaughtered corpse shew the ideas of sanctity which the Mosaic law sought to associate with human blood, the horror which murder inspired, as well as the fears that were felt lest God should avenge it on the country at large, and the pollution which the land was supposed to contract from the effusion of innocent, unexpiated blood. According to Jewish writers, the Sanhedrim, taking charge of such a case, sent a deputation to examine the neighbourhood, and, they having reported which was the nearest town to the spot where the body was found, an order was issued by their supreme authority to the elders or magistrates of that town, to provide the heifer at the civic expense, and go through the appointed ceremonial. The engagement of the public authorities in the work of expiation, the purchase of the victim heifer, the conducting it to a "rough valley" which might be at a considerable distance, and which, as the original implies, was a wady, a perennial stream, in the waters of which the polluting blood would be wiped away from the land, and a desert withal, incapable of cultivation: the washing of the hands, which was an ancient act symbolical of innocence; the whole of the ceremonial was calculated to make a deep impression on the Jewish, as well as on the Oriental mind generally, to stimulate the activity of the magistrates in the discharge of their official duties; to lead to the discovery of the criminal, and the repression of crime.

10-23. THE TREATMENT OF A CAPTIVE TAKEN TO WIFE. 10-14. When thou goest to war and seest among the captives a beautiful woman—According to the war customs of all ancient nations, a female captive became the slave of the victor, who had the sole and unchallengeable control of right to her person. Moses improved this existing usage by special regulations on the subject. He enacted that, in the event of her master being captivated by her beauty, and contemplating a marriage with her, a month should be allowed to elapse, during which her perturbed feelings might be calmed, her mind reconciled to her altered condition, and she might bewail the loss of her parents now to her the same as dead. A month was the usual period of mourning with the Jews, and the circumstances mentioned here were the signs of grief—the shaving of the head—the not paring, but *lit.*, doing, *i.e.,* allowing the nails to grow uncut, the putting off her gorgeous dress in which ladies on the eve of being captured, arrayed themselves to be the more attractive to their captors. The delay was full of humanity and kindness to the female slave, as well as a prudential measure to try the strength of her master's affections. If his love should afterwards cool, and he become indifferent to her person, he was not to lord it over her, neither to sell her in the slave-market, nor retain her in a subordinate condition in his house; but she was to be free to go where her inclinations led her. 15-17. If a man have two wives, one beloved, the other hated—In the original and all other translations, the words

thine enemies, then keep thee from every wicked thing.

10 If there be among you any man that is not clean, by reason of uncleanness that chanceth him by night, then shall he go abroad out of the camp, he shall not come within the camp:

11 But it shall be, when evening cometh on, he shall wash *himself* with water: and when the sun is down, he shall come into the camp again.

12 Thou shalt have a place also without the camp, whither thou shalt go forth abroad:

13 And thou shalt have a paddle upon thy weapon; and it shall be, when thou wilt ease thyself abroad, thou shalt dig therewith, and shalt turn back and cover that which cometh from thee:

14 For the LORD thy God walketh in the midst of thy camp, to deliver thee, and to give up thine enemies before thee; therefore shall thy camp be holy: that he see no unclean thing in thee, and turn away from thee.

15 ¶ Thou shalt not deliver unto his master the servant which is escaped from his master unto thee:

16 He shall dwell with thee, even among you, in that place which he shall choose in one of thy gates, where it liketh him best: thou shalt not oppress him.

17 ¶ There shall be no whore of the daughters of Israel, nor a sodomite of the sons of Israel.

18 Thou shalt not bring the hire of a whore, or the price of a dog, into the house of the LORD thy God for any vow: for even both these *are* abomination unto the LORD thy God.

19 ¶ Thou shalt not lend upon usury to thy brother; usury of money, usury of victuals, usury of any thing that is lent upon usury:

20 Unto a stranger thou mayest lend upon usury; but unto thy brother thou shalt not lend upon usury: that the LORD thy God may bless thee in all that thou settest thine hand to in the land whither thou goest to possess it.

21 ¶ When thou shalt vow a vow unto the LORD thy God, thou shalt not slack to pay it: for the LORD thy God will surely require it of thee; and it would be sin in thee.

22 But if thou shalt forbear to vow, it shall be no sin in thee.

23 That which is gone out of thy lips thou shalt keep and perform; even a freewill offering, according as thou hast vowed unto the LORD thy God, which thou hast promised with thy mouth.

24 ¶ When thou comest into thy neighbour's vineyard, then thou mayest eat grapes thy fill at thine own pleasure; but thou shalt not put any in thy vessel.

25 When thou comest into the standing corn of thy neighbour, then thou mayest pluck the ears with thine hand; but thou shalt not move a sickle unto thy neighbour's standing corn.

CHAPTER XXIV.

1 *Of divorce;* 6, 10 *of pledges;* 7 *of men-stealers;* 8 *of leprosy.* 14 *The hire of a servant to be given.* 17 *Of justice,* 19 *of charity.*

WHEN a man hath taken a wife, and married her, and it come to pass that she find no favour in his eyes, because he hath found some uncleanness in her; then let him write her a bill of divorcement, and give *it* in her hand, and send her out of his house.

2 And when she is departed out of his house, she may go and be another man's wife.

3 And *if* the latter husband hate her, and write her a bill of divorcement, and giveth *it* in her hand, and sendeth her out of his house; or if the latter husband die, which took her *to be* his wife;

4 Her former husband, which sent her away, may not take her again to be his wife, after that she is defiled; for that *is* abomination before the LORD: and thou shalt not cause the land to sin, which the LORD thy God giveth thee *for* an inheritance.

5 ¶ When a man hath taken a new wife, he shall not go out to war, neither shall he be charged with any business: *but* he shall be free at home one year, and shall cheer up his wife which he hath taken.

6 ¶ No man shall take the nether or the upper millstone to pledge: for he taketh *a man's* life to pledge.

7 ¶ If a man be found stealing any of his brethren of the children of Israel, and maketh merchandise of him, or selleth him; then that thief shall die; and thou shalt put evil away from among you.

8 ¶ Take heed in the plague of leprosy, that thou observe diligently, and to do according to all that the priests the Levites shall teach you: as I commanded them, so ye shall observe to do.

9 Remember what the LORD thy God did unto Miriam by the way, after that ye were come forth out of Egypt.

10 ¶ When thou dost lend thy brother any thing, thou shalt not go into his house to fetch his pledge.

11 Thou shalt stand abroad, and the man to whom thou dost lend shall bring out the pledge abroad unto thee.

12 And if the man *be* poor, thou shalt not sleep with his pledge:

13 In any case thou shalt deliver him the pledge again when the sun goeth down, that he may sleep in his own raiment, and bless thee: and it shall be righteousness unto thee before the LORD thy God.

14 ¶ Thou shalt not oppress an hired servant *that is* poor and needy, *whether he be* of thy brethren, or of thy strangers that *are* in thy land within thy gates:

15 At his day thou shalt give *him* his hire, neither shall the sun go down upon it; for he *is* poor, and setteth his heart upon it: lest he cry against thee unto the LORD, and it be sin unto thee.

16 The fathers shall not be put to death for the children, neither shall the children be put to death for the fathers: every man shall be put to death for his own sin.

17 ¶ Thou shalt not pervert the judgment of the stranger, nor of the fatherless; nor take a widow's raiment to pledge:

18 But thou shalt remember that thou wast a bondman in Egypt, and the LORD thy God redeemed thee thence: therefore I command thee to do this thing.

19 ¶ When thou cuttest down thine harvest in thy field, and hast forgot a sheaf in the field, thou shalt not go again to fetch it: it shall be for the stranger, for the

are rendered "have had," referring to events that have already taken place; and that the "had" has, by some mistake, been omitted in our version, seems highly probable from the other verbs being in the past tense—" hers that was hated," not " hers that is hated," evidently intimating that she (the first wife) was dead at the time referred to. Moses, therefore, does not here legislate upon the case of a man who has two wives at the same time, but on that of a man who has married twice in succession, the second wife after the decease of the first; and there was an obvious necessity for legislation in these circumstances; for the first wife, who was hated, was dead, and the second wife, the favourite, was alive; and with the feelings of a stepmother, she would urge her husband to make her own son the heir. This case has no bearing upon polygamy, which there is no evidence that the Mosaic code legalized. 18-21. If a man have a stubborn and rebellious son—A severe law was enacted in this case. But the consent of both parents was required as a prevention of any abuse of it; for it was reasonable to suppose that they would not both agree to a criminal information against their son, except from absolute necessity, arising from his inveterate and hopeless wickedness; and, in that view, the law was wise and salutary, as such a person would be a pest and nuisance to society. The punishment was that to which blasphemers were doomed; for parents are considered God's representatives, and invested with a portion of his authority over their children. 22, 23. If a man have committed a sin, and thou hang him on a tree—hanging was not a Hebrew form of execution—gibbeting is meant—but the body was not to be left to rot, or be a prey to ravenous birds: it was to be buried "that day," either because the stench in a hot climate would corrupt the air, or the spectacle of an exposed corpse bring ceremonial defilement on the land.

CHAPTER XXII.

Ver. 1-4. OF HUMANITY TOWARD BRETHREN. 1. Thou shalt not see thy brother's ox, &c.—"Brother" is a term of extensive application, comprehending persons of every description; not a relative, neighbour, or fellow-countryman only, but any human being, known or unknown, a foreigner, and even an enemy (Ex. 23. 4.). The duty inculcated is an act of common justice and charity, which, while it was taught by the law of nature, was more clearly and forcibly enjoined in the law delivered by God to His people. Indifference or dissimulation in the circumstances supposed, would not only be cruelty to the dumb animals, but a violation of the common rights of humanity; and therefore the dictates of natural feeling, and still more the authority of the divine law enjoined, that the lost or missing property of another should be taken care of by the finder, till a proper opportunity occurred of restoring it to the owner. 5-12. THE SEX TO BE DISTINGUISHED BY APPAREL. 5. The woman shall not wear that which pertaineth to man—Though disguises were assumed at certain times in heathen temples, it is probable that a reference was made to unbecoming levities practised in common life. They were properly forbidden; for the adoption of the habiliments of the one sex by the other is an outrage on decency, obliterates the distinctions of nature by fostering softness and effeminacy in the man, impudence and boldness in the woman, as well as levity and hypocrisy in both; and, in short, opens the door to an influx of so many evils, that all who wear the dress of another sex are pronounced "an abomination unto the Lord." 6, 7. If a bird's nest chance to be before thee—This is a beautiful instance of the humanizing spirit of the Mosaic law, in checking a tendency to wanton destructiveness, and encouraging a spirit of kind and compassionate tenderness to the tiniest creatures. But there was wisdom as well as humanity in the precept; for, as birds are well known to serve important uses in the economy of nature, the extirpation of a species, whether of edible or ravenous birds, must in any country be productive of serious evils. But Palestine, in particular, was situated in a climate which produced poisonous snakes and scorpions; and between deserts and mountains from which it would have been overrun with them, as well as immense swarms of flies, locusts, mice, and vermin of various kinds, if the birds which fed upon them were extirpated. [MICH.] Accordingly, the counsel given in this passage was wise as well as humane, to leave the hen undisturbed for the propagation of the species, while the taking of the brood occasionally was permitted as a check to too rapid an increase. 8. thou shalt make a battlement for thy roof—The tops of houses in ancient Judea, as in the East still, were flat, being composed of branches or twigs laid across large beams, and covered with a cement of clay or strong plaster. They were surrounded by a parapet breast high; for as in summer the roof is a favourite resort for coolness, accidents would frequently happen from persons incautiously approaching the edge and falling into the street or court; hence it was a wise and prudent precaution in the Jewish legislator to provide, that a stone balustrade or timber railing round the roof should form an essential part of every new house. 9. Thou shalt not sow thy vineyard with divers seeds—(See on Lev. 19. 19.). 10. Thou shalt not plow with an ox and an ass together—Whether this association, like the mixture of seeds, had been dictated by superstitious motives, and the prohibition was symbolical, designed to teach a moral lesson (2 Cor. 6. 14,) may or may not have been the case. But the prohibition prevented a great inhumanity still occasionally practised by the poorer sort in Oriental countries. An ox and ass being of different species, and of very different characters, cannot associate comfortably, nor unite cheerfully in drawing a plough or a waggon. The ass being much smaller and his step shorter, there must be an unequal and irregular draught. Besides, the ass, from feeding on coarse and poisonous weeds, has a fœtid breath, which its yoke-fellow seeks to avoid, not only as poisonous and offensive, but producing leanness, or, if long continued, death; and hence, it has been observed always to hold away its head from the ass, and to pull only with one shoulder. 11. thou shalt not wear a garment of divers sorts—The essence of the crime (Zeph. 1. 8,) consisted, not in wearing a woollen and a linen robe, but in the two stuffs being woven together,

fatherless, and for the widow: that the Lord thy God may bless thee in all the work of thine hands.

20 When thou beatest thine olive tree, thou shalt not go over the boughs again: it shall be for the stranger, for the fatherless, and for the widow.

21 When thou gatherest the grapes of thy vineyard, thou shalt not glean it afterward: it shall be for the stranger, for the fatherless, and for the widow.

22 And thou shalt remember that thou wast a bondman in the land of Egypt: therefore I command thee to do this thing.

CHAPTER XXV.

1 Stripes must not exceed forty. 4 The ox is not to be muzzled. 5 Of raising seed unto a brother: 11 of the immodest woman: 13 of unjust weights. 17 The memory of Amalek is to be blotted out.

IF there be a controversy between men, and they come unto judgment, that the judges may judge them; then they shall justify the righteous, and condemn the wicked.

2 And it shall be, if the wicked man be worthy to be beaten, that the judge shall cause him to lie down, and to be beaten before his face, according to his fault, by a certain number.

3 Forty stripes he may give him, and not exceed: lest, if he should exceed, and beat him above these with many stripes, then thy brother should seem vile unto thee.

4 ¶ Thou shalt not muzzle the ox when he treadeth out *the corn.*

5 ¶ If brethren dwell together, and one of them die, and have no child, the wife of the dead shall not marry without unto a stranger: her husband's brother shall go in unto her, and take her to him to wife, and perform the duty of an husband's brother unto her.

6 And it shall be, *that* the first-born which she beareth shall succeed in the name of his brother *which is* dead, that his name be not put out of Israel.

7 And if the man like not to take his brother's wife, then let his brother's wife go up to the gate unto the elders, and say, My husband's brother refuseth to raise up unto his brother a name in Israel, he will not perform the duty of my husband's brother.

8 Then the elders of his city shall call him, and speak unto him: and *if* he stand *to it,* and say, I like not to take her,

9 Then shall his brother's wife come unto him in the presence of the elders, and loose his shoe from off his foot, and spit in his face, and shall answer and say, So shall it be done unto that man that will not build up his brother's house.

10 And his name shall be called in Israel, The house of him that hath his shoe loosed.

11 ¶ When men strive together one with another, and the wife of the one draweth near for to deliver her husband out of the hand of him that smiteth him, and putteth forth her hand, and taketh him by the secrets:

12 Then thou shalt cut off her hand, thine eye shall not pity *her.*

13 ¶ Thou shalt not have in thy bag divers weights, a great and a small.

14 Thou shalt not have in thine house divers measures, a great and a small.

15 *But* thou shalt have a perfect and just weight, a perfect and just measure shalt

thou have: that thy days may be lengthened in the land which the Lord thy God giveth thee.

16 For all that do such things, *and* all that do unrighteously, *are* an abomination unto the Lord thy God.

17 ¶ Remember what Amalek did unto thee by the way, when ye were come forth out of Egypt;

18 How he met thee by the way, and smote the hindmost of thee, *even* all *that were* feeble behind thee, when thou *wast* faint and weary; and he feared not God.

19 Therefore it shall be, when the Lord thy God hath given thee rest from all thine enemies round about, in the land which the Lord thy God giveth thee *for* an inheritance to possess it, *that* thou shalt blot out the remembrance of Amalek from under heaven; thou shalt not forget it.

CHAPTER XXVI.

1 The confession of him that offereth the basket of first-fruits. 12 The third year's tithes. 16 The covenant between God and the people.

AND it shall be, when thou *art* come in unto the land which the Lord thy God giveth thee *for* an inheritance, and possessest it, and dwellest therein,

2 That thou shalt take of the first of all the fruit of the earth, which thou shalt bring of thy land that the Lord thy God giveth thee, and shalt put it in a basket, and shalt go unto the place which the Lord thy God shall choose to place his name there.

3 And thou shalt go unto the priest that shall be in those days, and say unto him, I profess this day unto the Lord thy God, that I am come unto the country which the Lord sware unto our fathers for to give us.

4 And the priest shall take the basket out of thine hand, and set it down before the altar of the Lord thy God.

5 And thou shalt speak and say before the Lord thy God, A Syrian ready to perish *was* my father; and he went down into Egypt, and sojourned there with a few, and became there a nation, great, mighty, and populous:

6 And the Egyptians evil entreated us, and afflicted us, and laid upon us hard bondage:

7 And when we cried unto the Lord God of our fathers, the Lord heard our voice, and looked on our affliction, and our labour, and our oppression;

8 And the Lord brought us forth out of Egypt with a mighty hand, and with an outstretched arm, and with great terribleness, and with signs, and with wonders;

9 And he hath brought us into this place, and hath given us this land, *even* a land that floweth with milk and honey.

10 And now, behold, I have brought the first-fruits of the land which thou, O Lord, hast given me. And thou shalt set it before the Lord thy God, and worship before the Lord thy God:

11 And thou shalt rejoice in every good thing which the Lord thy God hath given unto thee, and unto thine house, thou, and the Levite, and the stranger that *is* among you.

12 ¶ When thou hast made an end of tithing all the tithes of thine increase the third year, *which is* the year of tithing,

according to a favourite superstition of ancient idolators (see on Lev. 19. 19.). 12. thou shalt not make thee fringes upon the four quarters—or, according to some eminent Biblical interpreters, *tassels on the coverlet of the bed.* The precept is not the same as Num. 15. 38. 13-30. If a man take a wife, &c.— The regulations that follow might be imperatively needful in the *then* situation of the Israelites; and yet, it is not necessary that *we* should curiously and impertinently inquire into them. So far was it from being unworthy of God to leave such things upon record, that the enactments must heighten our admiration of His wisdom and goodness in the management of a people so perverse and so given to irregular passions. Nor is it a better argument that the Scriptures were not written by inspiration of God to object, that this passage, and others of a like nature, tend to corrupt the imagination, and will be abused by evil-disposed readers, than it is to say that the sun was not created by God, because its light may be abused by wicked men as an assistant in committing crimes which they have meditated. [HORNE.]

CHAPTER XXIII.

Ver. 1-25. WHO MAY AND WHO MAY NOT ENTER INTO THE CONGREGATION. 1. He that is wounded, &c. shall not enter into the congregation of the Lord—"To enter into the congregation of the Lord" means either admission to public honours and offices in the Church and State of Israel, or, in the case of foreigners' incorporation with that nation by marriage. The rule was, that strangers and foreigners, for fear of friendship or marriage connexions with them leading the people into idolatry, were not admissable till their conversion to the Jewish faith. But this passage describes certain limitations of the general r le. The following parties were excluded from the full rights and privileges of citizenship:—1st, Eunuchs—it was a very ancient practice for parents in the east by various arts to mutilate their chi dren, with a view of training them for service in the houses of the great. 2d, Bastards—such an indelible stigma in both these instances was designed as a discouragement to practices that were disgraceful, but too common from intercourse with foreigners. The word rendered "bastard," however, is by some supposed to mean a "stranger" (Zech. 9. 6.) 3d, Ammonites and Moabites were excluded —for without provocation they combined to engage a soothsayer to curse the Israelites; and further endeavoured, by ensnaring them into the guilt and licentious abominations of idolatry, to seduce them from their allegiance to God, and thereby make them forfeit the privileges of their national covenant. The offence of the Ammonites and Moabites was an aggravated one. It was not only a denial of common hospitality and kindness to strangers and pilgrims; but it was a scheme of premeditated villany, indicating deep malice and inextinguishable hatred. Their exclusion, therefore, as avowed public enemies, was perpetual and immutable. even to the tenth generation shall they not enter—Many eminent writers think that this law of exclusion was applicable only to males; at all events that a definite is used for an indefinite number (Neh. 13.1.). As God cannot do evil, the declaration must be considered not to foster enmity against the people (Ruth, 4.10; 2 Ki. 10.2,), but against their crime. And it was the more necessary to make it at this time, as many of the Israelites being established on the east side of Jordan in the immediate neighhood of those people, God raised this partition-wall between them to prevent the consequences of evil communications. 4th, More favour was to be shewn to Edomites and Egyptians—to the former from their near relationship to Israel; and to the latter, from their early hospitalities to the family of Jacob as well as the many acts of kindness rendered them by private Egyptians at the Exodus (Ex. 12. 36.). The grandchildren of Edomite or Egyptian proselytes were declared admissible to the full rights of citizenship as native Israelites; and by this remarkable provision, God taught His people a practical lesson of generosity and gratitude for special deeds of kindness, to the forgetfulness of all the persecution and ill services sustained from those two nations. 9-14. When the host goest forth—keep thee from every wicked thing —From theft, violence, licentiousness, and all the excesses incident to life in a camp (Luke, 3. 14.). Cleanliness being indispensably necessary, the strictest sanitary regulations are always enforced by those who have charge of a large body of men; the first appearance of disease is watched—precautions are taken to prevent the spread of infection. But in warm climates something more is requisite; constant care in the removal of foul and foetid matter; and accordingly Turkish soldiers are said to carry an implement similar to that with which every Israelite was enjoined to furnish himself. In the case of the Israelites, cleanliness was the more imperative, that their heavenly king was present in the camp (v. 14, whence some think that the ark was carried with them in their wars); and moreover, cleanliness was symbolical of the moral purity to which God was training them. 15, 16. Thou shalt not deliver unto his master the servant which has escaped —Evidently a servant of the Canaanites or some of the neighbouring people, who was driven by tyrannical oppression, or induced, with a view of embracing the true religion to take refuge in Israel. 19, 20. Thou shalt not lend upon usury to thy brother ... Unto a stranger—The Israelites being employed chiefly in the culture of the soil and the rearing of cattle, would have little occasion to borrow except for personal use through temporary want and poverty. They lived in a simple state of society, and hence they were encouraged to lend to each other in a friendly way, without any hope of gain. But the case was different with foreigners, who, engaged in trade and commerce—borrowed to enlarge their capital and might reasonably be expected to pay interest on their loans. Besides, the distinction was admirably conducive to keeping the Israelites separate from the rest of the world. 21, 22. When thou vowest a vow—See on Num. 30. 2,). 24, 25. When thou comest into thy neighbour's vineyard—Vineyards, like corn-fields mentioned in the next verse, were often unenclosed. In vine-growing countries grapes are amazingly cheap; and we need not wonder, therefore, that all within reach of a passenger's arm was free,—the quantity plucked was a loss never felt by the proprietor, and it

and hast given it unto the Levite, the stranger, the fatherless, and the widow, that they may eat within thy gates, and be filled;

13 Then thou shalt say before the LORD thy God, I have brought away the hallowed things out of mine house, and also have given them unto the Levite, and unto the stranger, to the fatherless, and to the widow, according to all thy commandments which thou hast commanded me: I have not transgressed thy commandments, *n* neither have I forgotten them:

14 I *o* have not eaten thereof in my mourning, neither have I taken away ought thereof for any unclean use, nor given ought thereof for the dead: but I have hearkened to the voice of the LORD my God, and have done according to all that thou hast commanded me.

15 Look *p* down from thy holy habitation, from heaven, and bless thy people Israel, and the land which thou hast given us, as thou swarest unto our fathers, a land that floweth with milk and honey.

16 ¶ This day the LORD thy God hath commanded thee to do these statutes and judgments: thou shalt therefore keep and do them with all thine heart, and with all thy soul.

17 Thou hast *q* avouched the LORD this day to be thy God, and to walk in his ways, and to keep his statutes, and his commandments, and his judgments, and to hearken unto his voice:

18 And *r* the LORD hath avouched thee this day to be his peculiar people, as he hath promised thee, and that thou shouldest keep all his commandments;

19 And to make thee *s* high above all nations which he hath made, in praise, and in name, and in honour; and that thou mayest be *t* an holy people unto the LORD thy God, as he hath spoken.

CHAPTER XXVII.

1 The people are to write the law upon stones, and to build an altar of whole stones. 11 The tribes divided on Gerizim and Ebal. 14 The curses pronounced on Ebal.

AND Moses with the elders of Israel commanded the people, saying, Keep all the commandments which I command you this day.

2 And it shall be on the day *a* when ye shall pass over Jordan unto the land which the LORD thy God giveth thee, that *b* thou shalt set thee up great stones, and plaster them with plaster.

3 And thou shalt write upon them all the words of this law, when thou art passed over, that thou mayest go in unto the land which the LORD thy God giveth thee, a land that floweth with milk and honey; as the LORD God of thy fathers hath promised thee.

4 Therefore it shall be when ye be gone over Jordan, that ye shall set up these stones, which I command you this day, *c* in mount Ebal, and thou shalt plaster them with plaster.

5 And there shalt thou build an altar unto the LORD thy God, an altar of stones: thou *d* shalt not lift up any iron tool upon them.

6 Thou shalt build the altar of the LORD thy God of whole stones; and thou shalt offer burnt offerings thereon unto the LORD thy God:

B. C. 1451.

CHAP. 26.
n Ps. 119. 141, 153, 176.
o Lev. 7. 20. Lev. 21. 1, 11.
Hos. 9. 4.
p 2 Chr. 6. 26, 27.
Is. 63. 15.
Zech. 2. 13.
q Ex. 20. 19.
Ex. 6. 7.
Ex. 19. 5.
ch. 7. 6.
ch. 14. 2.
ch. 28. 9.
s ch. 4. 7, 8.
ch. 28. 1.
Psalm 148. 14.
t Ex. 19. 6.
ch. 7. 6.
ch. 28. 9.
1 Pet. 2. 9.

CHAP. 27.
a Josh. 4. 1.
b Josh. 8. 32.
c ch. 11. 29.
Josh. 8. 30.
d Ex. 20. 25.
Josh. 8. 31.
e Hab. 2. 2.
f ch. 11. 29.
Judg. 9. 7.
1 for a cursing.
g ch. 33. 10.
Dan. 9. 11.
h Ex. 20. 4, 23.
Ex. 34. 17.
Lev. 19. 4.
Lev. 26. 1.
ch. 4. 16, 23.
Is. 44. 9.
Hos. 13. 2.
i Nu. 5. 22.
Jer. 11. 5.
1 Cor. 14. 16.
j Ex. 20. 12.
Lev. 19. 3.
k Pro. 22. 28.
l Lev. 19. 14.
m Ex. 22. 21.
ch. 10. 18.
Mal. 3. 5.
n Lev. 18. 8.
1 Cor. 5. 1.
o 2 Sa. 13. 1.
p Lev. 24. 17.
Num. 35. 31.
q Exod. 23. 7, 8.
ch. 10. 17.
ch. 10. 19.
Ps. 15. 5.
Ezek. 22. 12.
r Ps. 119. 21.
Jer. 11. 3.
Gal. 3. 10.

CHAP. 28.
a Ex. 15. 26.
Lev. 26. 3.
Is. 55. 2.
b 1 Chr. 14. 2.
Pro. 14. 34.
Ro. 2. 10.
c Zech. 1. 6.

7 And thou shalt offer peace offerings, and shalt eat there, and rejoice before the LORD thy God.

8 And thou shalt write upon the stones all the words of this law *e* very plainly.

9 ¶ And Moses and the priests the Levites spake unto all Israel, saying, Take heed, and hearken, O Israel; this day thou art become the people of the LORD thy God.

10 Thou shalt therefore obey the voice of the LORD thy God, and do his commandments and his statutes, which I command thee this day.

11 ¶ And Moses charged the people the same day, saying,

12 These shall stand *f* upon mount Gerizim to bless the people, when ye are come over Jordan; Simeon, and Levi, and Judah, and Issachar, and Joseph, and Benjamin:

13 And these shall stand upon mount Ebal to curse; Reuben, Gad, and Asher, and Zebulun, Dan, and Naphtali.

14 ¶ And *g* the Levites shall speak, and say unto all the men of Israel with a loud voice,

15 Cursed *h* be the man that maketh any graven or molten image, an abomination unto the LORD, the work of the hands of the craftsman, and putteth it in a secret place. *i* And all the people shall answer and say, Amen.

16 Cursed *j* be he that setteth light by his father or his mother. And all the people shall say, Amen.

17 Cursed *k* be he that removeth his neighbour's land-mark. And all the people shall say, Amen.

18 Cursed *l* be he that maketh the blind to wander out of the way. And all the people shall say, Amen.

19 Cursed *m* be he that perverteth the judgment of the stranger, fatherless, and widow. And all the people shall say, Amen.

20 Cursed *n* be he that lieth with his father's wife; because he uncovereth his father's skirt. And all the people shall say, Amen.

21 Cursed be he that lieth with any manner of beast. And all the people shall say, Amen.

22 Cursed *o* be he that lieth with his sister, the daughter of his father, or the daughter of his mother. And all the people shall say, Amen.

23 Cursed be he that lieth with his mother-in-law. And all the people shall say, Amen.

24 Cursed *p* be he that smiteth his neighbour secretly. And all the people shall say, Amen.

25 Cursed *q* be he that taketh reward to slay an innocent person. And all the people shall say, Amen.

26 Cursed *r* be he that confirmeth not all the words of this law to do them. And all the people shall say, Amen.

CHAPTER XXVIII.

1 The blessings for obedience. 15 The curses for disobedience.

AND it shall come to pass, *a* if thou shalt hearken diligently unto the voice of the LORD thy God, to observe and to do all his commandments which I command thee this day, that the LORD thy God will set thee *b* on high above all nations of the earth:

2 And all these blessings shall come on thee, and *c* overtake thee, if thou shalt

CHAPTER XXIV.

Ver. 1-22. OF DIVORCES. 1. it come to pass that she find no favour in his eyes—It appears that the practice of divorces was at this early period very prevalent amongst the Israelites, who had in all probability become familiar with it in Egypt [LANE], where too great facilities, and that on the most frivolous pretexts, have always existed to the dissolution of the nuptial tie. The usage being too deep-rooted to be soon or easily abolished, was tolerated by Moses (Matt. 19. 8,), but it was accompanied under the law with two conditions, which were calculated greatly to prevent the evils incident to the permitted system, viz.—1st, That the act of divorcement was to be certified on a written document, the preparation of which, with legal formality, would afford time for reflection and repentance; and 2d, That, in the event of the divorced wife being married to another husband, she could not, on the termination of that second marriage, be restored to her first husband, however desirous he might be to receive her. In the circumstances of the Israelitish people, this law of divorce was of great use in preserving public morals, and promoting the comfort and permanence of married life. 5. When a man hath taken a new wife, he shall not go to war—This law of exemption was founded on good policy, and was favourable to matrimony, as it afforded a full opportunity for the affections of the newly married pair being more firmly engaged, and it diminished or removed occasions for the divorces just mentioned. 6. No man shall take the nether or the upper millstone—The "upper" stone being concave, covers the "nether" like a lid; and it has a small aperture, through which the corn is poured, as well as a handle by which it is turned. The propriety of the law prohibiting either being taken was founded on the custom of grinding corn every morning for daily consumpt. If either of the stones, therefore, which composed the handmill was wanting, a person would be deprived of his necessary provision; and as there was no other means of preparing it, all rational prospect of subsistence, no less than of paying his debts, was taken away. 7. If a man be found stealing any of his brethren—(See on Ex. 21. 16.). 8, 9. Take heed in the plague of leprosy—(See on Lev. 13. 14. . Avoid all occasion of contracting that dreadful disease, especially in the way of punishment for disobedience, like Miriam. But in the event of being overtaken by it, be implicitly subject to the counsels and instructions of the Levites, who were divinely directed what remedies to prescribe. 10-13. When thou dost lend thy brother any thing—The course recommended was, in kind and considerate regard, to spare the borrower's feelings, by not exposing the poverty of his house, or affording an opportunity for the creditor to shew insolvency. In the case of a poor man who had pledged his cloak, it was to be restored before night, as the poor in Eastern countries have commonly no other covering for wrapping themselves in when they go to sleep than the hyke or plaid they have worn during the day. 14, 15. Thou shalt not oppress a hired servant that is poor and needy—Hired servants in the East are paid every day. No one works after the sun goes down, even in winter. The wages are given at the close of the day; and for a master to defraud the labourer of his hire, or to withhold it wrongfully for a night, might have subjected a poor man with his family to suffering, and was therefore an injustice to be avoided (Lev. 19. 13.). 16-18. The fathers shall not be put to death for the children—God, the sovereign author and proprietor of life, may, in certain circumstances, command this penalty: but the rule was addressed for the guidance of earthly magistrates, and it established the equitable principle that none should be responsible for the crimes of others, and that impartial justice should be blended with mercy in all their decisions. 19-22. When thou cuttest down thine harvest —The grain pulled up by the roots, or cut down with a sickle was laid in loose sheaves; the fruit of the olive was obtained by striking the branches with long poles, and the grape clusters, severed by a hook, were gathered in the hands of the vintager. Here is a beneficent provision for the poor, who were to participate in the general joy at the crowning of the year with the divine goodness. Every forgotten sheaf in the harvest-field was to lie; the olive tree was not to be beaten a second time; nor gleaning grapes to be gathered in order that in collecting what remained, the hearts of the stranger, the fatherless, and the widow might be gladdened by the bounty of Providence.

CHAPTER XXV.

Ver. 1-19. STRIPES MUST NOT EXCEED FORTY. 2. worthy to be beaten—In judicial sentences, which awarded punishment short of capital, scourging was the most common form in which they were executed. The amount of stripes was of course proportioned to the nature or aggravations of the offence; and from the criminal being "caused to lie down," the Hebrew mode of inflicting them seems to have been precisely the same as the Egyptian bastinado, which was applied to the bared back of the culprit, who was stretched flat on the ground, his hands and feet being held by attendants. The Mosaic law, however, introduced two important restrictions, viz.—1st, That the punishment should be inflicted in presence of the judge, instead of being dealt with in private by some heartless official; and 2d, That the maximum amount of it should be limited to forty stripes, instead of being awarded according to the arbitrary will or passion of the magistrate, who, like Turkish or Chinese rulers, often apply the stick till they cause death or lameness for life. Of what the scourge consisted at first, whether a single stick or a bundle of twigs, we are not informed; but in later times, when the Jews were exceedingly scrupulous in adhering to the letter of the law, and, for fear of miscalculation, were desirous of keeping within the prescribed limit, it was formed of three cords, terminating in leathern thongs, and thirteen strokes of this counted thirty-nine (2 Cor. 11. 24.). 4. Thou shalt not muzzle the ox when he treadeth out the corn—In Judea, as in modern Syria and Egypt, the larger grains, wheat, barley, and rice, were not thrashed, but beaten out by the feet of oxen, which, yoked together, trode round day after day the wide open spaces which form the thrashing floors,

The blessings for obedience.   DEUTERONOMY, XXVIII.   *The curses for disobedience.*

hearken unto the voice of the LORD thy God.

3 Blessed ^d shalt thou *be* in the city, and blessed *shalt* thou *be* ^e in the field.

4 Blessed *shall be* ^f the fruit of thy body, and the fruit of thy ground, and the fruit of thy cattle, the increase of thy kine, and the flocks of thy sheep.

5 Blessed *shall be* thy basket and thy ¹ store.

6 Blessed ^g shalt thou *be* when thou comest in, and blessed *shalt* thou *be* when thou goest out.

7 The LORD ^h shall cause thine enemies that rise up against thee to be smitten before thy face: they shall come out against thee one way, and flee before thee seven ways.

8 The LORD shall ⁱ command the blessing upon thee in thy ² storehouses, and in all that thou ^j settest thine hand unto; and he shall bless thee in the land which the LORD thy God giveth thee.

9 The ^k LORD shall establish thee an holy people unto himself, as he hath sworn unto thee, if thou shalt keep the commandments of the LORD thy God, and walk in his ways.

10 And all people of the earth shall see that thou art ^l called by the name of the LORD; and they shall be afraid of thee.

11 And ^m the LORD shall make thee plenteous ³ in goods, in the fruit of thy ⁴ body, and in the fruit of thy cattle, and in the fruit of thy ground, in the land which the LORD sware unto thy fathers to give thee.

12 The LORD ⁿ shall open unto thee his good treasure, the heaven to give the rain unto thy land in his season, and to bless all the work of thine hand: and thou shalt lend unto many nations, and thou shalt not borrow.

13 And the LORD shall make thee the head, and not the tail; and thou shalt be above only, and thou shalt not be beneath; if that thou hearken unto the commandments of the LORD thy God, which I command thee this day, to observe and to do *them:*

14 And ^o thou shalt not go aside from any of the words which I command thee this day, *to* the right hand or *to* the left, to go after other gods to serve them.

15 ¶ But it shall come to pass, ^p if thou wilt not hearken unto the voice of the LORD thy God, to observe to do all his commandments and his statutes, which I command thee this day, that all these curses shall come upon thee, and overtake thee:

16 Cursed *shalt* thou *be* in the city, and cursed *shalt* thou *be* in the field.

17 Cursed *shall be* thy basket and thy store.

18 Cursed *shall be* the fruit of thy body, and the fruit of thy land, the increase of thy kine, and the flocks of thy sheep.

19 Cursed *shalt* thou *be* when thou comest in, and cursed *shalt* thou *be* when thou goest out.

20 The LORD shall send upon thee ^q cursing, ^r vexation, and ^s rebuke, in all that thou settest thine hand unto ⁵ for to do, until thou be destroyed, and until thou perish quickly; because of the wickedness of thy doings, whereby thou hast forsaken me.

21 The LORD shall make ^t the pestilence cleave unto thee, until he have consumed thee from off the land whither thou goest to possess it.

22 The ^u LORD shall smite thee with a consumption, and with a fever, and with an inflammation, and with an extreme burning, and with the ⁶ sword, and with blasting, and with mildew; and they shall pursue thee until thou perish.

23 And thy heaven that *is* over thy head shall be brass, and the earth that *is* under thee *shall be* iron.

24 The LORD shall make the rain of thy land powder and dust: from heaven shall it come down upon thee, until thou be destroyed.

25 The ^v LORD shall cause thee to be smitten before thine enemies: thou shalt go out one way against them, and flee seven ways before them; and ^w shalt be ⁷ removed into all the kingdoms of the earth.

26 And thy carcase shall be meat unto all fowls of the air, and unto the beasts of the earth, and no man shall fray *them* away.

27 The LORD will smite thee with ^x the botch of Egypt, and with ^y the emerods, and with the scab, and with the itch, whereof thou canst not be healed.

28 The LORD shall smite thee with madness, and blindness, and astonishment of heart:

29 And thou shalt grope at noon-day, as the blind gropeth in darkness, and thou shalt not prosper in thy ways: and thou shalt be only oppressed and spoiled evermore, and no man shall save *thee.*

30 Thou ^z shalt betroth a wife, and another man shall lie with her: thou shalt build an house, and thou shalt not dwell therein: thou shalt plant a vineyard, and shalt not ⁸ gather the grapes thereof.

31 Thine ox *shall be* slain before thine eyes, and thou shalt not eat thereof: thine ass *shall be* violently taken away from before thy face, and ⁹ shall not be restored to thee: thy sheep *shall be* given unto thine enemies, and thou shalt have none to rescue *them.*

32 Thy sons and thy daughters *shall be* given unto another people, and thine eyes shall look, and fail *with longing* for them all the day long: and *there shall be* no might in thine hand.

33 The ^a fruit of thy land, and all thy labours, shall a nation which thou knowest not eat up: and thou shalt be only oppressed and crushed alway:

34 So that thou shalt be mad for the sight of thine eyes which thou shalt see.

35 The LORD shall smite thee in the knees, and in the legs, with a sore botch that cannot be healed, from the sole of thy foot unto the top of thy head.

36 The LORD shall ^b bring thee, and ^c thy king which thou shalt set over thee, unto a nation which neither thou nor thy fathers have known; and ^d there shalt thou serve other gods, wood and stone.

37 And thou shalt become ^e an astonishment, a proverb, ^f and a by-word, among all nations whither the LORD shall lead thee.

38 Thou ^g shalt carry much seed out into the field, and shalt gather *but* little in; for the ^h locust shall consume it.

39 Thou shalt plant vineyards, and dress *them,* but shalt neither drink *of* the wine, nor gather *the grapes;* for the worms shall eat them.

The animals were allowed freely to pick up a mouthful, when they chose to do so; a wise as well as humane regulation, introduced by the law of Moses, as it would have been not only great cruelty, but have produced a dispiriting effect on the cattle, to be trampling, as was the primitive practice, with a bag on their mouths, or their necks bound up a whole day, amid heaps of grain, while they were under irksome restraint from touching the grain or the straw (cf. 1 Cor. 9. 9; 1 Tim. 5. 17, 18.). 5-10. her husband's brother shall take her to wife—This usage existed before the age of Moses (Gen. 38. 8,), and seems to have originated in patriarchal times for preserving the name and honours of the eldest son—the chieftain of the family. But the Mosaic law rendered the custom obligatory (Matt. 22. 25,) on younger brothers, or the nearest kinsman, to marry the widow, (Ruth. 4. 4,), by associating the natural desire of perpetuating a brother's name, with the preservation of property in the Hebrew families and tribes. No betrothal was necessary nor marriage ceremonies observed; it was a succession by divine right to the wife, with all the possessions of the deceased to the child, who would be the heir. In the event of the younger brother declining to comply with the law, the widow brought her claim before the authorities of the place at a public assembly (the gate of the city,), and he having declared his refusal, she was ordered to loose the thong of his shoe—a sign of degradation—following up that act by spitting on the ground—the strongest expression of ignominy and contempt amongst Eastern people. The shoe was kept by the magistrate as an evidence of the transaction, and the parties separated. 13-16. Thou shalt not have divers weights—*lit.*, "a stone and a stone"—a just and false or a light and heavy one. Weights were anciently made of stone, and the facility for procuring stones apparently, though not exactly, similar, gave much occasion to fraud. bag—the leathern pouch in which the weights were kept. Stones are frequently used still by Eastern shop-keepers and traders, who take them out of the bag and put them in the balance. The man who is not cheated by the trader and his bag of divers weights must be blessed with more acuteness than most of his fellows [ROBERTS.] cf. Pro. 16. 11; 20. 10.). 14. divers measures—*lit.*, "an ephah and an ephah," which was the common and standard measure in Israel. 17-19. Remember what Amalek did—This cold-blooded and dastardly atrocity is not narrated in the previous history (Ex. 17. 14.). It was an unprovoked outrage on the laws of nature and humanity, as well as a daring defiance of that God who had so signally shewn His favour towards Israel (see on 1 Sam. 15.; 27. 8; 30.).

CHAPTER XXVI.

Ver. 1-15. THE CONFESSION OF HIM THAT OFFERETH THE BASKET OF FIRST-FRUITS. 2. Thou shalt take of the first of all the fruit—The Israelites in Canaan being God's tenants at will, the entire produce of the land was His, and as holding of Him, they were required to give Him tribute in the form of first-fruits and tithes. No Israelite was at liberty to use any productions of his fields, until he had presented the required offering. The terms of the law (v. 1,) seem to restrict the obligation to Canaan proper: but the duty was considered equally binding on those who resided on the East of Jordan. The tribute began to be exigible after the settlement in the promised land, and it was yearly repeated at one of the great feasts—the first-fruits of barley at the Passover (Lev. 2. 14; 23. 10,); of wheat at Pentecost (Lev. 23. 15; Nu. 28. 26; ch. 16. 9,); and those of other fruits as they ripened. Every master of a family carried it on his shoulders in a little basket of osier, peeled willow, or palm leaves, and brought it to the sanctuary. 5. Thou shalt speak and say before the Lord thy God—the act of presentation was accompanied by a formal expression of devout acknowledgment, A Syrian ready to perish was my father—rather, a wandering Syrian. The ancestors of the Hebrews were nomad shepherds, either Syrians by birth as Abraham, or by long residence as Jacob; and when, out of deep degradation and prolonged persecution, they were led through a succession of marvellous experiences, till they were established as a nation in the possession of the promised land; it was to God's unmerited goodness they were indebted for their distinguished privileges, and in token of gratitude they brought this basket of first-fruits. 11. thou shalt rejoice—either taking the comfortable use of the possessions which God had given them, or rather, as the context indicates, feasting with their friends and the Levites, who were invited on such occasions to share in the cheerful festivities that followed oblations (ch. 12. 7; 16. 10-15.). 12-15. When thou hast made an end of tithing... the third year—Among the Hebrews there were two tithings. The first was appropriated to the Levites (Nu. 18. 21.). The second being the tenth of what remained was brought to Jerusalem in kind; or if that was found inconvenient, it was converted into money, and the owner on arriving in the capital, purchased sheep, bread, and oil, which afforded a feast to his family and the Levites (ch. 14. 22. 23.). This was done for two years together. But this second tithing was eaten at home and distributed amongst the poor of the place at discretion (ch. 14. 28, 29.). 13. Thou shalt say before the Lord thy God—This was a solemn and conscientious declaration that nothing which should be devoted to the Divine service had been secretly reserved for personal use. 14. I have not eaten thereof in my mourning—in a season of sorrow, which brought defilement on sacred things; according to a second class of commentators,—"I have not eaten thereof, under a pretence of poverty, and grudging to give any away to the poor;" according to a third class, the words expressed a repudiation of an idolatrous custom of the Egyptians, who, in offering their first-fruits to Isis, invoked that deity in mournful strains. neither, for any unclean use—*i.e.*, any common purpose, different from what God had appointed, and which would have been a desecration of it. nor given ought thereof for the dead—on any funeral service, or, as some refer the words, to an *idol*, which is a dead thing—a lifeless image, or a hero deified after his decease.

CHAPTER XXVII.

Ver. 1-10. THE PEOPLE ARE TO WRITE THE LAW UPON STONES. 1. Keep all the

40 Thou shalt have olive trees throughout all thy coasts, but thou shalt not anoint *thyself* with the oil; for thine olive shall cast *his fruit*.

41 Thou shalt beget sons and daughters, but ¹⁰ thou shalt not enjoy them; for 'they shall go into captivity.

42 All thy trees and fruit of thy land shall the locust ¹¹ consume.

43 The stranger that *is* within thee shall get up above thee very high, and thou shalt come down very low.

44 He shall lend to thee, and thou shalt not lend to him; *ʲ* he shall be the head, and thou shalt be the tail.

45 Moreover all these curses shall come upon thee, and shall pursue thee, and overtake thee, till thou be destroyed; because thou hearkenedst not unto the voice of the LORD thy God, to keep his commandments and his statutes which he commanded thee:

46 And they shall be upon thee ᵏ for a sign, and for a wonder, and upon thy seed for ever.

47 Because ˡ thou servedst not the LORD thy God with joyfulness, and with gladness of heart, for the abundance of all *things;*

48 Therefore shalt thou serve thine enemies, which the LORD shall send against thee, in hunger, and in thirst, and in nakedness, and in want of all *things:* and he ᵐ shall put a yoke of iron upon thy neck, until he have destroyed thee.

49 The ⁿ LORD shall bring a nation against thee from far, from the end of the earth, as ᵒ *swift* as the eagle flieth; a nation whose tongue thou shalt not ¹² understand;

50 A nation ¹³ of fierce countenance, which ᵖ shall not regard the person of the old, nor show favour to the young:

51 And he shall ᑫ eat the fruit of thy cattle, and the fruit of thy land, until thou be destroyed; which *also* shall not leave thee *either* corn, wine, or oil, *or* the increase of thy kine, or flocks of thy sheep, until he have destroyed thee.

52 And he shall ʳ besiege thee in all thy gates, until thy high and fenced walls come down, wherein thou trustedst, throughout all thy land; and he shall besiege thee in all thy gates, throughout all thy land, which the LORD thy God hath given thee.

53 And ˢ thou shalt eat the fruit of thine own ¹⁴ body, the flesh of thy sons and of thy daughters, which the LORD thy God hath given thee, in the siege, and in the straitness, wherewith thine enemies shall distress thee:

54 So that the man that *is* tender among you, and very delicate, his eye shall be evil toward his brother, and toward the wife of his bosom, and toward the remnant of his children which he shall leave:

55 So that he will not give to any of them of the flesh of his children whom he shall eat: because he hath nothing left him in the siege, and in the straitness, wherewith thine enemies shall distress thee in all thy gates.

56 The tender and delicate woman among you, which would not adventure to set the sole of her foot upon the ground for delicateness and tenderness, her eye shall be evil toward the husband of her bosom, and toward her son, and toward her daughter.

57 And ᵗ toward her ¹⁵ young one that cometh out from between her feet, and toward her children which she shall bear: for

B. C. 1451.

CHAP. 28.
10 they shall not be thine.
ᵢ Jer. 32. 28.
11 Or, possess.
ⱼ Lam. 1. 5.
ᵏ Is. 8. 18.
Ezek. 5. 15.
Ezek. 14. 8.
ˡ Neh. 9. 36, 36, 37.
ᵐ Jer. 28. 14.
ⁿ Jer. 5. 15.
Jer. 6. 22, 23.
Lu. 19. 43.
ᵒ Jer. 48. 40.
Jer. 49. 22.
Lam. 4. 19.
Ezek. 17. 3.
Hos. 8. 1.
12 hear.
13 strong of face.
Pro. 7. 13.
Ec. 8. 1.
Dan. 8. 23.
ᵖ 2 Chr. 36. 17.
Is. 47. 6.
ᑫ Le. 1. 7.
Is. 62. 8.
ʳ 2 Ki. 25. 1.
ˢ Lev. 26. 29.
2 Ki. 6. 28, 29.
Jer. 19. 9.
Lam. 2. 20.
Lam. 4. 19.
Lu. 21. 23.
14 belly.
ᵗ Lam. 4. 10.
15 afterbirth.
ᵘ Ex. 6. 3.
ᵛ Ps. 83. 18.
Is. 42. 8.
Phil. 2. 10.
ʷ Dan. 9. 12.
2 Chr. 21. 12-15.
16 cause to ascend.
ˣ Neh. 9. 23.
ʸ Jer. 32. 41.
ᶻ Pro. 1. 26.
Is. 1. 24.
ᵃ Lev. 26. 33.
Neh. 1. 8.
Jer. 16. 13.
ᵇ Amos 9. 4.
ᶜ Lev. 26. 36.
ᵈ Job 7. 4.
ᵉ Jer. 44. 7.
Hos. 8. 13.
Hos. 9. 3.
Fulfilled at the destruction of Jerusalem by the Romans, A.D. 79.

CHAP. 29.
ᵃ ch. 4. 34.
ch. 7. 19.
ᵇ Is. 6. 9.
Is. 63. 17.
John 8. 43.
Acts 28. 26.
Ephes. 4. 18.
² Thess. 2. 11.

she shall eat them for want of all *things* secretly in the siege and straitness, wherewith thine enemy shall distress thee in thy gates.

58 If thou wilt not observe to do all the words of this law that are written in this book, that thou mayest fear ᵘ this glorious and fearful ᵛ name, THE LORD THY GOD;

59 Then the LORD will make thy plagues ʷ wonderful, and the plagues of thy seed, *even* great plagues, and of long continuance, and sore sicknesses, and of long continuance.

60 Moreover he will bring upon thee all the diseases of Egypt, which thou wast afraid of; and they shall cleave unto thee:

61 Also every sickness, and every plague, which *is* not written in the book of this law, them will the LORD ¹⁶ bring upon thee, until thou be destroyed.

62 And ye shall be left few in number, whereas ye were ˣ as the stars of heaven for multitude; because thou wouldest not obey the voice of the LORD thy God.

63 And it shall come to pass, *that* as the LORD ʸ rejoiced over you to do you good, and to multiply you; so the LORD ᶻ will rejoice over you to destroy you, and to bring you to nought; and ye shall be plucked from off the land whither thou goest to possess it.

64 And the LORD ᵃ shall scatter thee among all people, from the one end of the earth even unto the other; and there thou shalt serve other gods, which neither thou nor thy fathers have known, *even* wood and stone.

65 And ᵇ among these nations shalt thou find no ease, neither shall the sole of thy foot have rest: ᶜ but the LORD shall give thee there a trembling heart, and failing of eyes, and sorrow of mind:

66 And thy life shall hang in doubt before thee; and thou shalt fear day and night, and shalt have none assurance of thy life:

67 In ᵈ the morning thou shalt say, Would God it were even! and at even thou shalt say, Would God it were morning! for the fear of thine heart wherewith thou shalt fear, and for the sight of thine eyes which thou shalt see.

68 And the LORD ᵉ shall bring thee into Egypt again with ships, by the way whereof I spake unto thee, Thou shalt see it no more again: and there ye shall be sold unto your enemies for bondmen and bondwomen, and no man shall buy *you.*

CHAPTER XXIX.

1 *An exhortation to obedience.* 10 *The people are all presented before the Lord to enter into his covenant.* 18 *The great wrath on him that flattereth himself in his wickedness.*

THESE *are* the words of the covenant which the LORD commanded Moses to make with the children of Israel in the land of Moab, besides the covenant which he made with them in Horeb.

2 ¶ And Moses called unto all Israel, and said unto them, Ye have seen all that the LORD did before your eyes in the land of Egypt unto Pharaoh, and unto all his servants, and unto all his land;

3 The ᵃ great temptations which thine eyes have seen, the signs, and those great miracles:

4 Yet ᵇ the LORD hath not given you an

153

commandments which I command you this day—This chapter should have commenced at verse 16 of the preceding one, for there Moses enters on the concluding part of the discourse which he pronounced on the plains of Moab; and having put the people in remembrance of the national covenant which had been mutually established between the Lord and Israel, by which He chose them for His people, and they engaged to serve Him as their God, he proceeds to found on that solemn transaction a general, but earnest exhortation to obedience. Moses was surrounded, while giving this address, by the elders, or principal authorities in Israel, who by their presence, gestures, or audible declaration, not only approved of its strain, but united with him in enforcing fidelity to the divine service. Some further means, however, were thought necessary to promote the remembrance and observance of the divine laws. 2. It shall be on the day when ye shall pass over Jordan—day is often put for time; and the meaning is "about the time," for it was not till some days after the passage, that the following instructions were acted upon. thou shalt set thee up great stones, and plaster them with plaster. These stones were to be taken in their natural state, unhewn, and unpolished—the occasion on which they were used not admitting of long or elaborate preparation; and they were to be daubed over with paint or white wash, to render them more conspicuous. Stones and even rocks are seen in Egypt and the peninsula of Sinai, containing inscriptions made 3000 years ago, in paint or plaister, of which, owing to the serenity of the climate, the coating is as firm and the colour as fresh, as if it had been put on yesterday. The sphinx is covered with inscriptions in black paint, upon the red surface of the statue. By some similar method, or, as some suppose, by the letters being in relievo, while the spaces were filled up by paint or mortar, those stones may have been inscribed, and it is most probable that Moses learned the art from the Egyptians. 3. Thou shalt write upon them all the words of this law—not certainly the whole five books of Moses, nor even the abridgement of it given in this book of Deuteronomy. It might be, as some think, the Decalogue; but a greater probability is, that it was "the blessings and curses" which comprised in fact an epitome of the law (Josh. 8. 34.). 5-10. there shalt thou build an altar . . . of whole stones—The stones were to be in their natural state, as if a chisel would communicate pollution to them. It is not certain whether the same stones formed the monument, on the sides of which the words of the law were inscribed, as well as the altar on which the victims were sacrificed that signalised its renewed ratification. At all events, the stony pile was so large as to contain all the conditions of the covenant, so elevated as to be visible to the whole congregation of Israel; and the religious ceremonial performed on the occasion was solemn and impressive: consisting first, of the elementary worship needed for sinful men; and secondly, of the peace-offerings, or lively, social feasts, that were suited to the happy people, whose God was the Lord. There were thus, the law which condemned, and the typical expiation—the two great principles of revealed religion.

11-13. THE TRIBES DIVIDED ON GERIZIM AND EBAL. 11-13. these shall stand upon mount Gerizim . . . these shall stand upon mount Ebal—Those long rocky ridges lay in the province of Samaria, and the peaks referred to were near Shechem (Nablous), rising in steep precipices, to the height of about 800 feet, and separated by a green, well-watered valley, of about 500 yards wide. The adjoining sides of the two mounts give to the valley an air of pleasant, and, at the same time, of complete seclusion. The people of Israel were here divided into two parts. On mount Gerizim (now Jebel-et-Tur) were stationed the descendants of Rachel and Leah, the two principal wives of Jacob, and to them was assigned the most pleasant and honourable office of pronouncing the benedictions; while on the twin hill of Ebal (now Imad-el-Deen) were placed the posterity of the two secondary wives, Zilpah and Bilhah, with those of Reuben, who had lost the primogeniture, and Zebulun, son of Leah, youngest son; to them were committed the necessary but painful duty of pronouncing the maledictions. Thus one-half the Hebrew people were ranged on the one hill, which seems well suited to be the mount of Blessing, as it smiles still with verdure and olives; and the other half on the opposite Ebal, a bare, rugged, and desolate hill, to hear the law rehearsed (see on Judg. 9. 7.). The ceremony might have taken place on the lower spurs of the mountains, where they approach more closely to each other; and although the account given here of the proceedings is very brief, the curses only being recorded, the course observed was as follows:—Amid the silent expectations of the solemn assembly, the priests standing round the ark in the valley below, said aloud, looking to Gerizim, "Blessed is the man that maketh not any graven image," when the people ranged on that hill responded in full simultaneous shouts of "Amen;" then turning round to Ebal, they cried, "Cursed is the man that maketh any graven image;" to which those that covered the ridge answered, "Amen." The same course at every pause was followed with all the blessings and curses (see on Josh. 8, 33, 34.). These blessings and curses attendant on disobedience to the divine will, which had been revealed as a law from heaven, be it observed, are given in the form of a *declaration*, not a *wish*, as the words should be rendered, "Cursed is he," and not "Cursed be he."

CHAPTER XXVIII.

Ver. 1-68. THE BLESSINGS FOR OBEDIENCE. 1. if thou shalt hearken diligently unto the voice of the Lord thy God—In this chapter the blessings and curses are enumerated at length, and in various minute details, so that on the first entrance of the Israelites into the land of promise, their whole destiny was laid before them, as it was to result from their obedience or the contrary. 2. All these blessings shall come on thee—their national obedience was to be rewarded by extraordinary and universal prosperity. 3 in the city and in the field—whether living in town or country; whether engaged in trade or agriculture. 5. thy basket and thy store—the word "store" is rendered "kneading-trough (Ex. 12. 34.), so that the meaning is, there will be plenty of fruit for the basket,

heart to perceive, and eyes to see, and ears to hear, unto this day.

5 And ^c I have led you forty years in the wilderness: your clothes are not waxen old upon you, and thy shoe is not waxen old upon thy foot.

6 Ye ^d have not eaten bread, neither have ye drunk wine or strong drink: that ye might know that I am the LORD your God.

7 And when ye came unto this place, Sihon ^e the king of Heshbon, and Og the king of Bashan, came out against us unto battle, and we smote them:

8 And we took their land, and ^f gave it for an inheritance unto the Reubenites, and to the Gadites, and to the half tribe of Manasseh.

9 Keep ^g therefore the words of this covenant, and do them, that ye may prosper in all that ye do.

10 ¶ Ye stand this day all of you before the LORD your God; your captains of your tribes, your elders, and your officers, with all the men of Israel,

11 Your little ones, your wives, and thy stranger that is in thy camp, from ^h the hewer of thy wood unto the drawer of thy water;

12 That thou shouldest ¹ enter into covenant with the LORD thy God, and ⁱ into his oath, which the LORD thy God maketh with thee this day;

13 That he may establish thee to-day for a people unto himself, and that he may be unto thee a God, as he hath said unto thee, and as he hath sworn unto thy fathers, to Abraham, to Isaac, and to Jacob.

14 Neither with you only ^j do I make this covenant and this oath;

15 But with him that standeth here with us this day before the LORD our God, ^k and also with him that is not here with us this day:

16 (For ye know how we have dwelt in the land of Egypt; and how we came through the nations which ye passed by;

17 And ye have seen their abominations, and their ² idols, wood and stone, silver and gold, which were among them:)

18 Lest there should be among you man, or woman, or family, or tribe, whose heart turneth away this day from the LORD our God, to go and serve the gods of these nations; ^l lest there should be among you a root that beareth ³ gall and wormwood;

19 And it come to pass, when he heareth the words of this curse, that he bless himself in his heart, saying, ^m I shall have peace, though I walk ⁿ in the ⁴ imagination of mine heart, ^o to add ⁵ drunkenness to thirst:

20 The ^p LORD will not spare him, but then ^q the anger of the LORD and ^r his jealousy shall smoke against that man, and all the curses that are written in this book shall lie upon him, and the LORD shall blot out his name from under heaven.

21 And the LORD ^s shall separate him unto evil out of all the tribes of Israel, according to all the curses of the covenant that ⁶ are written in this book of the law:

22 So that the generation to come of your children that shall rise up after you, and the stranger that shall come from a far land, shall say, when they see the plagues of that land, and the sicknesses ⁷ which the LORD hath laid upon it;

B.C. 1451.

CHAP. 29.
^c ch. 1. 3.
ch. 8. 2.
^d Ex. 16. 12.
Ps. 72. 24.
^e Nu. 21. 23.
^f Nu. 32. 33.
^g Josh. 1. 7.
1 Ki. 2. 3.
^h Josh. 9. 21.
1 pass.
ⁱ Neh. 10. 29.
^j Jer. 31. 31.
Heb. 8. 7, 8.
^k Acts 2. 39.
1 Cor. 7. 14.
2 dungy gods.
^l Heb. 12. 15.
3 rosh, or, a poisonful herb.
^m Ps. 14. 1.
ⁿ Nu. 15. 39.
Ez. 11. 9.
4 Or, stubbornness.
Jer. 7. 24.
^o Is. 30. 1.
5 the drunken to the thirsty.
^p Ezek. 14. 7.
^q Ps. 74. 1.
^r Ps. 79. 5.
Ezek 23. 25.
^s Mat. 24. 51.
6 is written.
7 wherewith the LORD hath made it sick.
^t Jer. 17. 6.
Zeph. 2. 9.
^u Gen. 19. 24.
^v 1 Ki. 9. 8.
Jer. 22. 8.
8 Or, who had not given to them any portion.
9 divided.
^w Ps. 11. 6.
Dan. 9. 11.
^x 2 Chr. 7. 20.
Ps. 52. 5.
Pro. 2. 22.
^y Acts 1. 7.
^z Ps. 19. 7.
Lu. 16. 29.
John 5. 39.
Acts 17. 11.
2 Tim. 3. 16.

CHAP. 30.
^a Lev. 26. 40.
^b ch. 28.
^c 1 Kin. 8. 47, 48.
^d Neh. 1. 9.
Is. 55. 7.
Lam. 3. 40.
Joel 2. 12.
^e Psalm 106. 45.
Ps. 126. 1, 4.
Jer. 29. 14.
Lam. 3. 22.
^f Ps. 147. 2.
Jer. 32. 37.
Ezek. 34. 13.
^g ch. 28. 64.
Neh. 1. 9.
^h ch. 10. 16.
Ezr. 11. 19.
ⁱ ch. 29. 11.
^j Jer. 32. 41.

23 And that the whole land thereof is brimstone, ^t and salt, and burning, that it is not sown, nor beareth, nor any grass groweth therein, ^u like the overthrow of Sodom, and Gomorrah, Admah, and Zeboim, which the LORD overthrew in his anger, and in his wrath;

24 Even all nations shall say, ^v Wherefore hath the LORD done thus unto this land? what meaneth the heat of this great anger?

25 Then men shall say, Because they have forsaken the covenant of the LORD God of their fathers, which he made with them when he brought them forth out of the land of Egypt;

26 For they went and served other gods, and worshipped them, gods whom they knew not, and ⁸ whom he had not ⁹ given unto them:

27 And the anger of the LORD was kindled against this land, ^w to bring upon it all the curses that are written in this book:

28 And the LORD ^x rooted them out of their land in anger, and in wrath, and in great indignation, and cast them into another land, as it is this day.

29 The ^y secret things belong unto the LORD our God: but ^z those things which are revealed belong unto us and to our children for ever, that we may do all the words of this law.

CHAPTER XXX.

1 Great mercies promised unto the penitent. 11 The commandment is manifest. 15 Death and life are set before the Israelites.

AND ^a it shall come to pass, when ^b all these things are come upon thee, the blessing and the curse, which I have set before thee, and ^c thou shalt call them to mind among all the nations whither the LORD thy God hath driven thee,

2 And shalt ^d return unto the LORD thy God, and shalt obey his voice, according to all that I command thee this day, thou and thy children, with all thine heart, and with all thy soul;

3 That ^e then the LORD thy God will turn thy captivity, and have compassion upon thee, and will return and ^f gather thee from all the nations, whither the LORD thy God hath scattered thee.

4 If ^g any of thine be driven out unto the outmost parts of heaven, from thence will the LORD thy God gather thee, and from thence will he fetch thee:

5 And the LORD thy God will bring thee into the land which thy fathers possessed, and thou shalt possess it; and he will do thee good, and multiply thee above thy fathers.

6 And ^h the LORD thy God will circumcise thine heart, and the heart of thy seed, to love the LORD thy God with all thine heart, and with all thy soul, that thou mayest live.

7 And the LORD thy God will put all these curses upon thine enemies, and on them that hate thee, which persecuted thee.

8 And thou shalt return, and obey the voice of the LORD, and do all his commandments, which I command thee this day.

9 And ⁱ the LORD thy God will make thee plenteous in every work of thine hand, in the fruit of thy body, and in the fruit of thy cattle, and in the fruit of thy land, for good: for the LORD will again ^j rejoice over thee for good, as he rejoiced over thy fathers;

Blessings for Obedience. DEUTERONOMY, XXVIII. *Curses for Disobedience.*

and meal for the kneading-trough; an abundant supply of all the necessaries and comforts of life. 6. when thou comest in, and when thou goest out—they should have pleasant and prosperous journeys when they required to travel, and should return home in happiness and safety. 7. flee before thee seven ways—i.e., in various directions, as always happens in a rout. 10. called by the name of the Lord—i.e., are really and actually His people (ch. 14. 1; 26. 18.). 11. The Lord shall make thee plenteous in goods—Beside the natural capabilities of Canaan, and the division of tribes, which insured the cultivation of every spot,—even the sides of the mountains, its extraordinary fruitfulness, and the number of its inhabitants were traceable to the special blessing of heaven, which that favoured people for ages enjoyed. 12. The Lord shall open unto thee his good treasure—The seasonable supply of the early and latter rain was one of the principal means by which their land was so uncommonly fruitful. thou shalt lend unto many nations, and shalt not borrow—i.e., thou shalt be in such affluent circumstances, as to be capable, out of thy superfluous wealth, to give aid to thy poorer neighbours. 13, 14. the head and not the tail—an Oriental form of expression, indicating the possession of independent power and great dignity and acknowledged excellence (Isa. 9. 14; 19. 15.). This high condition was realised in the reigns of David and Solomon, and it would have been longer maintained had the Israelites adhered to the conditions of their covenant with God. The detail of blessings comprehends the possession of everything necessary for a people's happiness,—health and wealth, security from external disturbance, and prosperity in all their internal concerns. They are exclusively temporal blessings, such as were calculated to engage the interest of a people like the Israelites, and were suited to the character of their dispensation. But at all times they are included among the benefits held out by the gospel itself (1 Tim. 4. 8.; they form powerful incentives to obedience. 15. But if thou wilt not hearken unto the voice of the Lord—Curses that were to follow them in the event of disobedience are now enumerated, and they are almost exact counterparts to the blessings which were described in the preceding context, as the reward of a faithful adherence to the covenant. The parallel is observed in the particulars specified (vs. 16 19,); and the special blessing of heaven in all their undertakings promised to faithful and continued obedience, is substituted by an unmitigated curse (v. 20,) overhanging them in every situation. 21. pestilence—some fatal epidemic; there is no reason, however, to think that the plague, which is the great modern scourge of the East, is referred to. 22. a consumption—a wasting disorder; but the European phthisis is almost unknown in Asia, fever, inflammation. extreme burning—(fever is rendered "burning ague" Lev. 26. 16,), and the others mentioned along with it, evidently point to those febrile affections which are of malignant character and great frequency in the East. the sword—rather "dryness,"—the effect on the human body of such violent disorders. blasting and mildew—two atmospheric influences fatal to grain. A hot or scorching wind, before the harvest is ripe, is one of the most disastrous occurrences that can take place in Palestine. 23. heaven ... brass ... earth ... iron—strong Oriental figures used to describe the effects of long-continued drought. But the language is limited to Judea: "the heaven that is over thy head, the earth that is under thee,"—i.e., while the clouds may carry vapour and moisture to other regions, there shall be none in Judea; and this want of regular and seasonable rain is allowed by the most intelligent observers, to be one great cause of the present sterility of Palestine. 24. the rain of thy land powder and dust—An allusion probably to the dreadful effects of tornadoes in the East, which, raising the sand in immense twisted pillars, and driving them along with the fury of a tempest, darken the heavens and envelop caravans and armies in a stifling deluge of dust. To this species of rain Moses was no stranger; he had seen it and felt its effects in the sandy deserts of Arabia, and he places it among the curses that were in subsequent ages to punish the apostacy of the Israelites. These shifting sands are most destructive to cultivated lands; and in consequence of their encroachment many once fertile regions of the East are now barren deserts. 27. the botch of Egypt—a troublesome eruption, marked by red pimples to which, at the rising of the Nile, the Egyptians are subject. emerods—fistula or piles. scab—scurvy. itch—the disease commonly known by that name; but it is far more malignant in the East than is ever witnessed in our part of the world. 28. madness, blindness, and astonishment of heart—they would be bewildered and paralyzed with terror at the extent of their calamities. 29-33. thou shalt grope at noonday—a general description of the painful uncertainty in which they would live. During the middle ages the Jews were considered everywhere a legitimate prey—their most valuable possessions liable at any time to be seized by rapacious violence; their lives in continual jeopardy, so that they were driven from society into hiding places which they were afraid to leave, not knowing from what quarter they might be assailed, and their children dragged into captivity, from which no friend could rescue, and no money ransom them. 35. the Lord shall smite thee in the knees and in the legs—this is an exact description of elephantiasis, a horrible disease, something like leprosy, which covers the body with a foul and ulcerous skin—attacks particularly the lower extremities, which are covered with tumours that degenerate into loathsome and incurable sores. 36. The Lord shall bring thee and thy king—This shows how wide-spread would be the range of the national calamity, which even the monarch, with all his guards and means of protection, should not escape; and at the same time how hopeless, when he who should have been their defender shared the captive fate of his subjects. there shalt thou serve other gods, wood and stone—The Hebrew exiles, with some honourable exceptions, were seduced, or compelled into idolatry in the Assyrian and Babylonish captivities (Jer. 44. 17-19.). Thus, the sin to which they had too often betrayed a perverse fondness, a deep-rooted propensity,—became their punishment and their misery. 37. thou shalt

10 If thou shalt hearken unto the voice of the LORD thy God, to keep his commandments and his statutes *which are* written in this book of the law, *and* if thou turn unto the LORD thy God with all thine heart, and with all thy soul.

11 ¶ For this commandment which I command thee this day, *it is* not hidden from thee, neither *is* it far off:

12 It *is* not in heaven, that thou shouldest say, Who shall go up for us to heaven, and bring it unto us, that we may hear it, and do it?

13 Neither *is* it beyond the sea, that thou shouldest say, Who shall go over the sea for us, and bring it unto us, that we may hear it, and do it?

14 But the word *is* very nigh unto thee, in thy mouth, and in thy heart, that thou mayest do it.

15 ¶ See, I have set before thee this day life and good, and death and evil;

16 In that I command thee this day to love the LORD thy God, to walk in his ways, and to keep his commandments and his statutes, and his judgments, that thou mayest live and multiply: and the LORD thy God shall bless thee in the land whither thou goest to possess it.

17 But if thine heart turn away, so that thou wilt not hear, but shalt be drawn away, and worship other gods, and serve them;

18 I denounce unto you this day, that ye shall surely perish, *and that* ye shall not prolong *your* days upon the land whither thou passest over Jordan to go to possess it.

19 I call heaven and earth to record this day against you, *that* I have set before you life and death, blessing and cursing: therefore choose life, that both thou and thy seed may live;

20 That thou mayest love the LORD thy God, *and* that thou mayest obey his voice, and that thou mayest cleave unto him; for he *is* thy life, and the length of thy days: that thou mayest dwell in the land which the LORD sware unto thy fathers, to Abraham, to Isaac, and to Jacob, to give them.

CHAPTER XXXI.

1 *Moses encourageth the people, and Joshua;* 9 *he delivers the law to the priests, to read it every seventh year to the people.* 19 *God giveth Moses a song to testify against the people.* 23 *Joshua receiveth a charge.*

AND Moses went and spake these words unto all Israel.

2 And he said unto them, I *am* an hundred and twenty years old this day; I can no more go out and come in: also the LORD hath said unto me, Thou shalt not go over this Jordan.

3 The LORD thy God, he will go over before thee, *and* he will destroy these nations from before thee, and thou shalt possess them: *and* Joshua, he shall go over before thee, as the LORD hath said.

4 And the LORD shall do unto them as he did to Sihon and to Og, kings of the Amorites, and unto the land of them, whom he destroyed.

5 And the LORD shall give them up before your face, that ye may do unto them according unto all the commandments which I have commanded you.

6 Be strong, and of a good courage, fear not, nor be afraid of them: for the LORD thy God, he *it is* that doth go with thee; he will not fail thee, nor forsake thee.

7 ¶ And Moses called unto Joshua, and said unto him in the sight of all Israel, Be strong, and of a good courage: for thou must go with this people unto the land which the LORD hath sworn unto their fathers to give them; and thou shalt cause them to inherit it.

8 And the LORD, he *it is* that doth go before thee; he will be with thee, he will not fail thee, neither forsake thee: fear not, neither be dismayed.

9 ¶ And Moses wrote this law, and delivered it unto the priests the sons of Levi, which bare the ark of the covenant of the LORD, and unto all the elders of Israel.

10 And Moses commanded them, saying, At the end of *every* seven years, in the solemnity of the year of release, in the feast of tabernacles,

11 When all Israel is come to appear before the LORD thy God in the place which he shall choose, thou shalt read this law before all Israel in their hearing.

12 Gather the people together, men, and women, and children, and thy stranger that *is* within thy gates, that they may hear, and that they may learn, and fear the LORD your God, and observe to do all the words of this law:

13 And *that* their children, which have not known *any thing,* may hear, and learn to fear the LORD your God, as long as ye live in the land whither ye go over Jordan to possess it.

14 ¶ And the LORD said unto Moses, Behold, thy days approach that thou must die: call Joshua, and present yourselves in the tabernacle of the congregation, that I may give him a charge. And Moses and Joshua went, and presented themselves in the tabernacle of the congregation.

15 And the LORD appeared in the tabernacle in a pillar of a cloud: and the pillar of the cloud stood over the door of the tabernacle.

16 ¶ And the LORD said unto Moses, Behold, thou shalt sleep with thy fathers; and this people will rise up, and go a whoring after the gods of the strangers of the land whither they go *to be* among them, and will forsake me, and break my covenant which I have made with them.

17 Then my anger shall be kindled against them in that day, and I will forsake them, and I will hide my face from them, and they shall be devoured, and many evils and troubles shall befall them; so that they will say in that day, Are not these evils come upon us, because our God *is* not among us?

18 And I will surely hide my face in that day for all the evils which they shall have wrought, in that they are turned unto other gods.

19 Now therefore write ye this song for you, and teach it the children of Israel: put it in their mouths, that this song may be a witness for me against the children of Israel.

20 For when I shall have brought them into the land which I sware unto their fathers, that floweth with milk and honey; and they shall have eaten and filled themselves, and waxen fat; then will they turn unto other gods, and serve them, and provoke me, and break my covenant.

become an astonishment, a proverb, and a byeword among all nations—Other people should wonder at their great and protracted calamities. The annals of almost every nation, for 1800 years, afford abundant proofs that this has been, as it still is, the case; the very name of Jew being a universally recognised term for extreme degradation and wretchedness, and is often applied by passionate people in derision, "*you Jew.*" 49. the Lord shall bring a nation against thee from far—The predictions in this and the subsequent verses are usually referred to the invasion of the Romans, and certainly the course of that destructive war answers with literal exactness to the prophetic intimations in this passage—"they came from far;" the soldiers of the invading army were taken from France, Spain, and Britain,—then considered "the end of the earth." Julius Severus, the commander, afterwards Vespasian and Hadrian, left Britain for the scene of contest. Morever, the ensign on the standards of the Roman army was an eagle; and the dialects spoken by the soldiers of the different nations that composed that army were altogether unintelligible to the Jews. 50. A nation of fierce countenance—A just description of the Romans who were not only bold and unyielding, but ruthless and implacable; sparing, as Josephus expressly records, neither age, nor condition, nor sex. 51. he shall eat the fruit of thy cattle, &c.—the ravages of an invading army are in all cases disastrous; but so great and dreadful were the excesses committed by the Romans, from the time they entered Judea, that, according to the Jewish historian, every district of the country through which they passed was strewed with the wrecks of their devastations. 52. He shall besiege thee until thy high and fenced walls come down—All the fortified places to which the people bet ok themselves for safety, were burnt or demolished, and the walls of Jerusalem itself razed to the ground. 53-57. thou shalt eat the fruit of thine own body—(See on 2 Ki. 6. 29; Lam. 4. 10.). Such were the dreadful extremities to which the inhabitants during the siege were reduced, that, according to the testimony of Josephus, many women sustained a wretched existence by eating the flesh of their own children. Parental affection was extinguished, and the nearest relatives were jealously avoided lest they should discover and demand a share of the revolting viands. 62. ye shall be few in number—Notwithstanding the teeming population of ancient Judea, there has been ever since the destruction of Jerusalem only an inconsiderable remnant of Jews existing in that land. This diminution took place at an early period; for according to Josephus, 1,100,000 persons died by famine, pestilence, and other causes, at the time of the siege; and more than 90,000 were carried captives by the Romans. In the subsequent war of Hadrian, 580,000 were slain and destroyed through various causes. Ever since, Palestine has been in the hands of many successive masters; but all have been equally hostile to the Jewish race; comparatively few have remained in that country; those who did so were aliens in the land of their fathers; and of all classes of the inhabitants, they are the most degraded and miserable beings, dependent for their support on contributions from Europe. 63. ye shall be plucked from off the land—Hadrian issued a proclamation, forbidding any Jews to reside in Judea, or even to appr ach its confines. 64. The Lord shall scatter thee among all people—There is, perhaps, not a country in the world where Jews are not to be found. But for centuries they underwent every species of public and private persecution; they have nowhere acquired a settlement, and although they are in some European States admitted to the privileges of citizenship, those "tribes of the wandering foot and weary breast" are always looked upon as foreigners, whose wishes and destiny are associated with another land. Who that looks on this condition of the Hebrews is not filled with awe, when he considers the fulfilment of this prophecy? 68. The Lord shall bring thee into Egypt again with ships—The accomplishment of this prediction took place under Titus, when, according to Josephus, multitudes of Jews were transported in ships to the land of the Nile and sold as slaves. Those above seventeen years of age were despatched to various parts of the Roman Empire, to be employed in the public works, or doomed to fight with wild beasts in the amphitheatres. Those under seventeen were exposed as slaves in such numbers and such abject circumstances, that the market was glutted with them. Thirty were offered for a trifle, and it was often difficult to find a purchaser. These curses have been dreadfully fulfilled on apostate Israel, and of this every Jew of every subsequent age has been a living memorial. "Here, then, are instances of prophecies delivered above 3,000 years ago; and yet, as we see, being fulfilled in the world at this very time; and what stronger proofs can we desire of the divine legation of Moses? How these instances may affect others I know not; but, for myself, I must acknowledge, they not only convince, but amaze and astonish me beyond expression; they are truly, as Moses foretold (*vs.* 45, 46, they would be, a sign and a wonder for ever." [BISHOP NEWTON.]

CHAPTER XXIX.

Ver. 1-9. AN EXHORTATION TO OBEDIENCE. 1. These are the words of the covenant—Whether this verse be considered a conclusion to what is contained in the preceding chapters, or a preface to what is to follow, is of no importance to determine; the discourse of Moses is continued, and the subject of that discourse was Israel's covenant with God—the privileges it conferred, and the obligations it imposed, beside the covenant which he made with them in Horeb—It was substantially the same; but it was renewed now, in different circumstances. They had violated its conditions. Moses rehearses them; and, as he was about to die, gives them a clear and full explanation of it, that they might have a better knowledge of its conditions, and be more disposed to comply with them. 2. Moses called unto all Israel, Ye have seen all that the Lord did, &c.—This appeal to the experience of the people, though made generally, was applicable only to that portion of them who had been very young at the period of the Exodus, and who remembered the marvellous transactions that preceded and followed that era. Yet, alas! those wonderful events made no good impression upon

21 And it shall come to pass, when many evils and troubles are befallen them, that this song shall testify against them as a witness; for it shall not be forgotten out of the mouths of their seed: for I know their imagination which they go about, even now, before I have brought them into the land which I sware.

22 Moses therefore wrote this song the same day, and taught it the children of Israel.

23 And he gave Joshua the son of Nun a charge, and said, Be strong, and of a good courage: for thou shalt bring the children of Israel into the land which I sware unto them: and I will be with thee.

24 ¶ And it came to pass, when Moses had made an end of writing the words of this law in a book, until they were finished,

25 That Moses commanded the Levites, which bare the ark of the covenant of the LORD, saying,

26 Take this book of the law, and put it in the side of the ark of the covenant of the LORD your God, that it may be there for a witness against thee.

27 For I know thy rebellion, and thy stiff neck: behold, while I am yet alive with you this day, ye have been rebellious against the LORD; and how much more after my death!

28 Gather unto me all the elders of your tribes, and your officers, that I may speak these words in their ears, and call heaven and earth to record against them.

29 For I know that after my death ye will utterly corrupt yourselves, and turn aside from the way which I have commanded you; and evil will befall you in the latter days; because ye will do evil in the sight of the LORD, to provoke him to anger through the work of your hands.

30 And Moses spake in the ears of all the congregation of Israel the words of this song, until they were ended.

CHAPTER XXXII.

1 Moses' song, which sets forth the perfections of God; 44 the people exhorted to set their hearts upon it. 48 God sends him up to mount Nebo, to see the land, and die.

GIVE ear, O ye heavens, and I will speak; and hear, O earth, the words of my mouth.

2 My doctrine shall drop as the rain, my speech shall distil as the dew, as the small rain upon the tender herb, and as the showers upon the grass:

3 Because I will publish the name of the LORD: ascribe ye greatness unto our God.

4 He is the Rock, his work is perfect: for all his ways are judgment: a God of truth, and without iniquity, just and right is he.

5 They have corrupted themselves, their spot is not the spot of his children: they are a perverse and crooked generation.

6 Do ye thus requite the LORD, O foolish people and unwise? is not he thy father that hath bought thee? hath he not made thee, and established thee?

7 Remember the days of old, consider the years of many generations: ask thy father, and he will show thee; thy elders, and they will tell thee.

8 When the Most High divided to the nations their inheritance, when he separated the sons of Adam, he set the bounds of the people according to the number of the children of Israel:

9 For the LORD's portion is his people; Jacob is the lot of his inheritance.

10 He found him in a desert land, and in the waste howling wilderness; he led him about, he instructed him, he kept him as the apple of his eye.

11 As an eagle stirreth up her nest, fluttereth over her young, spreadeth abroad her wings, taketh them, beareth them on her wings;

12 So the LORD alone did lead him, and there was no strange god with him.

13 He made him ride on the high places of the earth, that he might eat the increase of the fields; and he made him to suck honey out of the rock, and oil out of the flinty rock;

14 Butter of kine, and milk of sheep, with fat of lambs, and rams of the breed of Bashan, and goats, with the fat of kidneys of wheat; and thou didst drink the pure blood of the grape.

15 But Jeshurun waxed fat, and kicked: thou art waxen fat, thou art grown thick, thou art covered with fatness: then he forsook God which made him, and lightly esteemed the Rock of his salvation.

16 They provoked him to jealousy with strange gods, with abominations provoked they him to anger.

17 They sacrificed unto devils, not to God; to gods whom they knew not, to new gods that came newly up, whom your fathers feared not.

18 Of the Rock that begat thee thou art unmindful, and hast forgotten God that formed thee.

19 And when the LORD saw it, he abhorred them, because of the provoking of his sons and of his daughters.

20 And he said, I will hide my face from them, I will see what their end shall be: for they are a very froward generation, children in whom is no faith.

21 They have moved me to jealousy with that which is not God; they have provoked me to anger with their vanities: and I will move them to jealousy with those which are not a people; I will provoke them to anger with a foolish nation.

22 For a fire is kindled in mine anger, and shall burn unto the lowest hell, and shall consume the earth with her increase, and set on fire the foundations of the mountains.

23 I will heap mischiefs upon them; I will spend mine arrows upon them.

24 They shall be burnt with hunger, and devoured with burning heat, and with bitter destruction: I will also send the teeth of beasts upon them, with the poison of serpents of the dust.

25 The sword without, and terror within, shall destroy both the young man and the virgin, the suckling also with the man of grey hairs.

26 I said, I would scatter them into corners, I would make the remembrance of them to cease from among men:

27 Were it not that I feared the wrath of the enemy, lest their adversaries should behave themselves strangely, and lest they should say, Our hand is high, and the LORD hath not done all this.

them (v. 4.). They were strangers to that grace of wisdom which is liberally given to all who ask it; and their insensibility was all the more inexcusable that so many miracles had been performed which might have led to a certain conviction of the presence and the power of God with them. The preservation of their clothes and shoes, the supply of daily food and fresh water; these, continued without interruption or diminution during so many years' sojourn in the desert, were miracles which unmistakeably proclaimed the immediate hand of God, and were performed for the express purpose of training them to a practical knowledge of, and habitual confidence in, Him. Their experience of this extraordinary goodness and care, together with their remembrance of the brilliant successes by which, with little exertion or loss on their part, God enabled them to acquire the valuable territory on which they stood, is mentioned again to enforce a faithful adherence to the covenant, as the direct and sure means of obtaining its promised blessings. **10-29. Ye stand this day all of you, before the Lord**—The whole congregation of Israel, of all ages and conditions, all—young as well as old; menials as well as masters; native Israelites as well as naturalized strangers; all were assembled before the tabernacle to renew the *Sinaitic* covenant. None of them were allowed to consider themselves as exempt from the terms of that national compact, lest any lapsing into idolatry might prove a root of bitterness, spreading its noxious seed and corrupt influence all around (cf. Heb. 12. 15,). It was of the greatest consequence thus to reach the heart and conscience of every one, for some might delude themselves with the vain idea, that by taking the oath (v. 12,) by which they engaged themselves in covenant with God, they would secure its blessings; and even though they should not rigidly adhere to His worship and commands, but follow the devices and inclinations of their own hearts, yet that He would wink at such liberties and not punish them. It was of the greatest consequence to impress all with the strong and abiding conviction, that while the covenant of grace had special blessings belonging to it, it at the same time had curses in reserve for transgressors; the infliction of which would be as certain, as lasting and severe. This was the advantage contemplated in the law being rehearsed a second time. The picture of a once rich and flourishing region, blasted and doomed in consequence of the sins of its inhabitants, is very striking, and calculated to awaken awe in every reflecting mind. Such is, and long has been, the desolate state of Palestine; and, in looking at its ruined cities, its blasted coast, its naked mountains, its sterile and parched soil—all the sad and unmistakeable evidences of a land lying under a curse, numbers of travellers from Europe, America, and the Indies—"strangers from a far country" (v. 22,), in the present day see that the Lord has executed his threatening. Who can resist the conclusion that it has been inflicted "because the inhabitants had forsaken the covenant of the Lord God of their fathers, and the anger of the Lord was kindled against this land, to bring upon it all the curses that are written in this book?" **29. The secret things belong unto the Lord**—This verse has no apparent connection with the thread of discourse; and it is thought to have been said in answer to the looks of astonishment or the words of inquiry, whether they would be ever so wicked, as to deserve such punishments. The recorded history of God's providential dealings towards Israel presents a wonderful combination of "goodness and severity." There is much of it involved in mystery too profound for our limited capacities to fathom; but, from the comprehensive wisdom displayed in those parts which have been made known to us, we are prepared to enter into the full spirit of the apostles' exclamation, how unsearchable are His judgments (Rom. 11. 33.).

CHAPTER XXX.

Ver. 1-10. GREAT MERCIES PROMISED UNTO THE PENITENT. 2, 3. When all these things are come upon thee, and thou shalt return... then the Lord shall turn thy captivity—The hopes of the Hebrew people are ardently directed to this promise, and they confidently expect that God, commiserating their forlorn and fallen condition, will yet rescue them from all the evils of their long dispersion. They do not consider the promise as fulfilled by their restoration from the captivity in Babylon, for Israel was not then scattered in the manner here described —"among all the nations," "unto the utmost parts of heaven" (v. 4,); and when God recalled them from that bondage, all the Israelites were not brought back, they were not multiplied above their fathers (v. 5,), nor were their hearts and those of their children circumcised to love the Lord (v. 6.). It is not, therefore, of the Babylonish captivity, that Moses was speaking in this passage; it must be of the dispersed state to which they have been doomed for 1800 years. This prediction may have been partially accomplished on the return of the Israelites from Babylon; for, according to the structure and design of Scripture prophecy, it may have pointed to several similar eras in their national history; and this view is sanctioned by the prayer of Nehemiah (Neh. 1. 8, 9.). But undoubtedly it will receive its full and complete accomplishment in the conversion of the Jews to the Gospel of Christ. At the restoration from the Babylonish captivity, that people were changed in many respects for the better. They were completely weaned from sensible idolatry; and this outward reformation was a prelude of the higher attainments they are destined to reach in the age of Messiah, "when the Lord God will circumcise their hearts and the hearts of their seed to love the Lord." The course pointed out seems clearly to be this: that the hearts of the Hebrew people shall be circumcised Col. 2. 2,); in other words, by the combined influences of the Word and Spirit of God, their hearts will be touched and purified from all their superstition and unbelief; they will be converted to the faith of Jesus Christ as their Messiah—a spiritual deliverer, and the effect of their conversion will be that they will return and obey the voice (the Gospel, the Evangelical law) of the Lord. The words may be interpreted either wholly in a spiritual sense John, 11. 51, 52,), or as many think, in a literal sense also (Rom. 11.). They will be recalled from all places of the dispersion to their own land, and enjoy the highest prosperity. The mer-

28 For they *are* a nation void of counsel, neither *is there any* understanding in them.
29 Oh *b* that they were wise, *that* they understood this, *that* they would consider their latter end!
30 How should *c* one chase a thousand, and two put ten thousand to flight, except their Rock *d* had sold them, and the LORD had shut them up?
31 For their rock *is* not as our Rock, even *e* our enemies themselves *being* judges.
32 For their vine [14] *is* of the vine of Sodom, and of the fields of Gomorrah: their grapes *are* grapes of gall, their clusters *are* bitter:
33 Their wine *is* the poison of dragons, and the cruel venom of asps.
34 *Is* not this *f* laid up in store with me, *and* sealed up among my treasures?
35 To *g* me *belongeth* vengeance and recompence; their foot shall slide in *due* time: for the day of their calamity *is* at hand, and the things that shall come upon them make haste.
36 For the LORD shall judge his people, and *h* repent himself for his servants, when he seeth that *their* [15] power is gone, and *there is* none shut up, or left.
37 And he shall say, *i* Where *are* their gods, *their* rock in whom they trusted;
38 Which did eat the fat of their sacrifices, *and* drank the wine of their drink offerings? let them rise up and help you, *and* be [16] your protection.
39 See now that I, *even* I, *am* he, and *there* is no god with me: *k* I kill, and I make alive; I wound, and I heal: neither *is there any* that can deliver out of my hand.
40 For *l* I lift up my hand to heaven, and say, I live for ever.
41 If I whet my glittering sword, and mine hand take hold on judgment, I will render vengeance to mine enemies, and will reward them that hate me.
42 I will make mine arrows drunk with blood, and my sword shall devour flesh; *and that* with the blood of the slain and of the captives, from the beginning of *m* revenges upon the enemy.
43 [17] Rejoice, *n* O ye nations, *with* his people; for he will *o* avenge the blood of his servants, and will render vengeance to his adversaries, and *p* will be merciful unto his land, *and* to his people.
44 ¶ And Moses came and spake all the words of this song in the ears of the people, he and [18] Hoshea the son of Nun.
45 And Moses made an end of speaking all these words to all Israel:
46 And he said unto them, Set your hearts unto all the words which I testify among you this day, which ye shall command your children to observe to do, all the words of this law.
47 For it *is* not a vain thing for you; because *q* it *is* your life: and through this thing ye shall prolong *your* days in the land whither ye go over Jordan to possess it.
48 ¶ And *r* the LORD spake unto Moses that selfsame day, saying,
49 Get thee up into this mountain Abarim, *unto* mount Nebo, which *is* in the land of Moab, that *is* over against Jericho, and behold the land of Canaan, which I give unto the children of Israel for a possession.

50 And die in the mount whither thou goest up, and be gathered unto thy people; as Aaron thy brother died in mount Hor, and was gathered unto his people:
51 Because *s* ye trespassed against me among the children of Israel at the waters of [19] Meribah-Kadesh, in the wilderness of Zin; because ye sanctified me not in the midst of the children of Israel.
52 Yet thou shalt see the land before *thee*; but thou shalt not go thither unto the land which I give the children of Israel.

CHAPTER XXXIII.

1 *The majesty of God.* 4 *The blessings of the twelve tribes.* 26 *The excellency of Israel.*

AND this *is* *a* the blessing wherewith Moses the man of God blessed the children of Israel before his death.
2 And he said, *b* The LORD came from Sinai, and rose up from Seir unto them; he shined forth from mount Paran, and he came with *c* ten thousands of saints: from his right hand *went* [1] a fiery law for them.
3 Yea, *d* he loved the people; *e* all his saints *are* in thy hand: and they *f* sat down at thy feet; *every one* shall receive of thy words.
4 Moses *g* commanded us a law, *even* the inheritance of the congregation of Jacob.
5 And he was *h* king in Jeshurun, when the heads of the people *and* the tribes of Israel were gathered together.
6 ¶ Let Reuben live, and not die; and let *not* his men be few.
7 ¶ And this *is the blessing* of Judah: and he said, Hear, LORD, the voice of Judah, and bring him unto his people: *i* let his hands be sufficient for him; and be thou an help *to him* from his enemies.
8 ¶ And of Levi he said, *j* Let thy Thummim and thy Urim *be* with thy holy one, whom thou didst prove at Massah, *and with* whom thou didst strive at the waters of Meribah;
9 Who said unto his *k* father and to his mother, I have not seen him; *l* neither did he acknowledge his brethren, nor knew his own children: for *m* they have observed thy word, and kept thy covenant.
10 [2] They shall teach Jacob thy judgments, and Israel thy law: [3] they shall put incense *before thee*, *n* and whole burnt sacrifice upon thine altar.
11 Bless, LORD, his substance, and *o* accept the work of his hands: smite through the loins of them that rise against him, and of them that hate him, that they rise not again.
12 ¶ *And* of Benjamin he said, The beloved of the LORD shall dwell in safety by him; *and the LORD* shall cover him all the day long, and he shall dwell between his shoulders.
13 ¶ And of Joseph he said, *p* Blessed of the LORD *be* his land, for the precious things of heaven, for *q* the dew, and for the deep that coucheth beneath,
14 And for the precious fruits *brought forth* by the sun, and for the precious things [5] put forth by the [6] moon,
15 And for the chief things of the ancient mountains, and for the precious things *r* of the lasting hills,
16 And for the precious things of the earth and fulness thereof, and *for* the good will of *s* him that dwelt in the bush: let *the blessing* come upon the head of Joseph,

them—war, famine, pestilence (Ps. 77. 17,), are called in Scripture the arrows of the Almighty. 29. O that they would consider their latter end—the terrible judgments, which, in the event of their continued and incorrigible disobedience, would impart so awful a character to the close of their national history. 32. vine of Sodom . . . grapes of gall—This fruit, which the Arabs call "Lot's Sea Orange," is of a bright yellow colour, and grows in clusters of three or four. When mellow, it is tempting in appearance, but on being struck, explodes like a puff-ball, consisting of skin and fibre only. 44-47. Moses spake all the words of his song in the ears, &c.—It has been beautifully styled "the Song of the Dying Swan." [LOWTH.] It was designed to be a national anthem, which it should be the duty and care of magistrates to make well known by frequent repetition, to animate the people to right sentiments towards a steadfast adherence to His service. 48-51. Get thee up and die, because ye trespassed at Meribah—(See on Num. 20. 12.). 52. Thou shalt see the land, but shalt not go thither— Num. 27. 12.). Notwithstanding so severe a disappointment, not a murmur or complaint escapes his lips; he is not only resigned but acquiescing; and in the near prospect of his death, he pours forth the feelings of his devout heart in sublime strains and eloquent blessings.

CHAPTER XXXIII.

Ver. 1-28. THE MAJESTY OF GOD. 1. Moses, the man of God—This was a common designation of a prophet 1 Sam. 2. 27; 9. 6,), and it is here applied to Moses, when, like Jacob, he was about to deliver ministerially before his death, a prophetic benediction to Israel. 2-4. The Lord came—under a beautiful metaphor, borrowed from the dawn and progressive splendour of the sun, the Majesty of God is sublimely described as a divine light which appeared in Sinai, and scattered its beams on all the adjoining region in directing Israel's march to Canaan. In these descriptions of a *theophania*, God is represented as coming from the south, and the allusion is in general to the thunderings and lightnings of Sinai; but other mountains in the same direction are mentioned with it. The location of Seir was on the East of the Ghor; Mount Paran was either the chain on the west of the Ghor, or rather the mountains on the southern border of the desert towards the peninsula. [ROB.] (cf. Jud. 5. 4, 5; Ps. 68. 7, 8; Hab. 3. 3.), ten thousand saints—rendered by some, "with the ten thousand of Kadesh," or perhaps better still, "from Meribah-Kadesh." [EWALD.] 2.). a fiery law—so called both because of the thunder and lightning which accompanied its promulgation (Ex. 19. 16-18; ch. 4. 11.), and of the fierce unrelenting curse denounced against the violation of its precepts (2 Cor. 3. 7-9.). Notwithstanding those awe-inspiring symbols of Majesty that were displayed on Sinai, the law was really given in kindness and love (v. 3,) as a means of promoting both the temporal and eternal welfare of the people; and it was "the inheritance of the congregation of Jacob," not only from the hereditary obligation under which that people were laid to observe it, but from its being the grand distinction, the peculiar privilege of the nation. 6. Let Reuben live and not die—Although deprived of the honour and privileges of primogeniture, he was still to hold rank as one of the tribes of Israel. He was more numerous than several other tribes (Num. 1. 21; 2. 11,), yet gradually sunk into a mere nomadic tribe, which had enough to do merely "to live and not die." Many eminent Biblical scholars, resting on the most ancient and approved manuscripts of the Septuagint, consider the latter clause as referring to Simeon; "and Simeon, let his men be few," a reading of the text which is in harmony with other statements of Scripture respecting this tribe (Num. 25. 6-14; 1. 23; 26. 14; Josh. 19. 1.). 7. This is the blessing of Judah—Its general purport points to the great power and independence of Judah, as well as its taking the lead in all military expeditions. 8-10. Of Levi he said—The burden of this blessing is the appointment of the Levites to the dignified and sacred office of the priesthood (Lev. 10. 11; ch. 22. 8; 17. 8-11,); a reward for their zeal in supporting the cause of God, and their unsparing severity in chastising even their nearest and dearest relatives who had participated in the idolatry of the molten calf (Ex. 32. 26-28; cf. Mal. 2. 4-6.). 12. Of Benjamin he said—A distinguishing favour was conferred on this tribe in having its portion assigned near the temple of God. between his shoulders—*i.e.*, on his sides or borders. Mount Zion, on which stood the city of Jerusalem, belonged to Judah; but Mount Moriah, the site of the sacred edifice, lay in the confines of Benjamin. 13-17. of Joseph he said—The territory of this tribe, diversified by hill and dale, wood and water would be rich in all the productions—olives, grapes, figs, &c., that are reared in a mountainous region as well as in the grain and herbs that grow in the level fields. "The firstling of the bullock and the horns of the unicorn" (rhinoceros), indicate glory and strength, and it is supposed that under these emblems were shadowed forth the triumphs of Joshua and the new kingdom of Jeroboam, both of whom were of Ephraim (cf. Gen. 48. 20.). 18, 19. Zebulun, rejoice in thy going out—on commercial enterprises and voyages by sea, and Issachar in thy tents—preferring to reside in their maritime towns. shall suck of the abundance of the sea and treasures hid in the sand—Both tribes should traffic with the Phœnicians in gold and silver, pearl and coral, especially in *murex*, the shell-fish that yielded the famous Tyrian dye, and in glass, which was manufactured from the sand of the river Belus, in their immediate neighbourhood. 20, 21. Of Gad he said—Its possessions were larger than they would have been had they lain west of Jordan; and this tribe had the honour of being settled by Moses himself in the first portion of land conquered. In the forest region, south of the Jabbok, "he dwelt as a lion" (cf. Gen. 30. 11; 49. 19.). Notwithstanding, they faithfully kept their engagement to join the "heads of the people" in the invasion of Canaan. 22. Dan is a lion's whelp—His proper settlement in the south of Canaan being to small, he by a sudden and successful irruption, established a colony in the northern extremity of the land. This might well be described as the leap of a young lion from the hills of Bashan. 23. of Naphtali he said—The plea-

and upon the top of the head of him *that was* separated from his brethren.

17 His glory *is like* the firstling of his bullock, and his horns *are like* the horns of ⁷ unicorns: with them *ᵗ* he shall push the people together to the ends of the earth: and they *are* the ten thousands of Ephraim, and they *are* the thousands of Manasseh.

18 ¶ And of Zebulun he said, Rejoice, Zebulun, in thy going out; and, Issachar, in thy tents.

19 They shall *ᵘ* call the people unto the mountain; there *ᵛ* they shall offer sacrifices of righteousness: for they shall suck *of* the abundance of the seas, and *of* treasures hid in the sand.

20 ¶ And of Gad he said, Blessed *be* he that *ʷ* enlargeth Gad: he dwelleth as a lion, and teareth the arm with the crown of the head.

21 And *ˣ* he provided the first part for himself, because there, *in* a portion of the lawgiver, *was he* ⁸ seated; and *ʸ* he came with the heads of the people, he executed the justice of the LORD, and his judgments with Israel.

22 ¶ And of Dan he said, Dan *is* a lion's whelp: *ᶻ* he shall leap from Bashan.

23 ¶ And of Naphtali he said, O Naphtali, satisfied with favour, and full with the blessing of the LORD; *ᵃ* possess thou the west and the south.

24 ¶ And of Asher he said, Let Asher *be* blessed with children; let him be acceptable to his brethren, and let him *ᵇ* dip his foot in oil.

25 ⁹ Thy shoes *shall be* iron and brass; and as thy days, *so shall* thy strength *be*.

26 ¶ *There is ᶜ* none like unto the God of Jeshurun, *ᵈ who* rideth upon the heaven in thy help, and in his excellency on the sky.

27 The eternal God *is thy ᵉ* refuge, and underneath *are* the everlasting arms: and he shall thrust out the enemy from before thee; and shall say, Destroy *them*.

28 Israel *ᶠ* then shall dwell in safety alone: the fountain of Jacob *shall be* upon a land of corn and wine; also his heavens shall drop down dew.

29 Happy *ᵍ art* thou, O Israel: *ʰ* who *is* like unto thee, O people saved by the LORD, the shield of thy help, and who *is* the sword

B. C. 1451.

CHAP. 33.
⁷ an unicorn.
c 1 Kin. 22. 11.
Ps. 44. 5.
ᵘ Is. 2. 3.
ᵛ Ps. 4. 5.
ʷ Josh. 13. 10.
1 Chr.12.8.
ˣ Nu. 32. 16.
8 cieled.
ʸ Josh. 4. 12.
ᶻ Josh. 19. 47.
Judg.18.27.
ᵃ Josh. 19. 32.
ᵇ Job 29. 5.
9 Or, Under thy shoes shall be iron.
ᶜ Ez. 15. 11. Ps. 86. 8. Jer. 10. 6.
ᵈ Ps. 68. 4, 33, 34. Ps. 104. 3. Hab. 3. 8.
ᵉ Ps. 90. 1.
ᶠ Nu. 23. 9. Jer. 23. 6. Jer. 33. 16.
ᵍ Ps. 144. 15.
ʰ 2 Sam. 7. 23.
10 Or, shall be subdued.

CHAP. 34.
1 Or, the hill.
ᵃ Josh. 19. 40-48. Judges 18. 28.
ᵇ ch. 11. 24.
ᶜ Judg. 1. 16. Judg. 3. 13.
ᵈ Josh. 1.1,2.
ᵉ Jude 9.
ᶠ ch. 31. 2.
ᵍ Josh. 14. 10.
2 moisture fled.
ʰ Gen. 50. 3.
ⁱ Is. 11. 2. Dan. 6. 3.
ʲ Num. 27. 18.

of thy excellency! and thine enemies ¹⁰ shall be found liars unto thee; and thou shalt tread upon their high places.

CHAPTER XXXIV.

1 *Moses from mount Nebo vieweth the land:* 5 *his death and burial:* 7 *his age:* 8 *thirty days' mourning for him;* 9 *Joshua succeedeth him.* 10 *The praise of Moses.*

AND Moses went up from the plains of Moab unto the mountain of Nebo, to the top of ¹ Pisgah, that *is* over against Jericho. And the LORD showed him all the land of Gilead, *ᵃ* unto Dan,

2 And all Naphtali, and the land of Ephraim, and Manasseh, and all the land of Judah, *ᵇ* unto the utmost sea,

3 And the south, and the plain of the valley of Jericho, *ᶜ* the city of palm trees, unto Zoar.

4 And the LORD said unto him, This *is* the land which I sware unto Abraham, unto Isaac, and unto Jacob, saying, I will give it unto thy seed: I have caused thee to see *it* with thine eyes, but thou shalt not go over thither.

5 ¶ So *ᵈ* Moses the servant of the LORD died there in the land of Moab, according to the word of the LORD.

6 And he buried him in a valley in the land of Moab, over against Beth-peor: but no *ᵉ* man knoweth of his sepulchre unto this day.

7 ¶ And *ᶠ* Moses *was* an hundred and twenty years old when he died: *ᵍ* his eye was not dim, nor his ² natural force abated.

8 ¶ And the children of Israel wept for Moses in the plains of Moab *ʰ* thirty days: so the days of weeping *and* mourning for Moses were ended.

9 ¶ And Joshua the son of Nun was full of the *ⁱ* spirit of wisdom; for *ʲ* Moses had laid his hands upon him: and the children of Israel hearkened unto him, and did as the LORD commanded Moses.

10 ¶ And there arose not a prophet since in Israel like unto Moses, whom the LORD knew face to face,

11 In all the signs and the wonders which the LORD sent him to do in the land of Egypt to Pharaoh, and to all his servants, and to all his land,

12 And in all that mighty hand, and in all the great terror which Moses showed in the sight of all Israel.

THE
BOOK OF JOSHUA.

CHAPTER I.

1 *The Lord appoints Joshua to succeed Moses.* 3 *Extent of the promised land.* 5 *God promises to assist Joshua.* 10 *Joshua prepares the people to pass over Jordan.*

NOW after the death of Moses the servant of the LORD it came to pass, that the LORD spake unto Joshua the son of Nun, Moses' *ᵇ* minister, saying,

2 Moses *ᵇ* my servant is dead; now therefore arise, go over this Jordan, thou, and all this people, unto the land which I do give to them, *even* to the children of Israel.

3 Every *ᶜ* place that the sole of your foot

B. C. 1451.

CHAP. 1.
ᵃ Deu. 1. 38.
ᵇ Deu. 34. 5.
ᶜ Deu. 11. 24.
ᵈ Gen. 15.18. Nu. 34. 3.
ᵉ Deu. 7. 24.
ᶠ Ex. 3. 12.
ᵍ Deu. 31. 6.
1 Or, thou shalt cause this people to inherit the land.

shall tread upon, that have I given unto you, as I said unto Moses.

4 From *ᵈ* the wilderness and this Lebanon, even unto the great river, the river Euphrates, all the land of the Hittites, and unto the great sea toward the going down of the sun, shall be your coast.

5 There *ᵉ* shall not any man be able to stand before thee all the days of thy life: as *ᶠ* I was with Moses, *so* I will be with thee: I *ᵍ* will not fail thee, nor forsake thee.

6 Be strong and of a good courage: for ¹ unto this people shalt thou divide for an

sant and fertile territory of this tribe lay to "the west," on the borders of lakes Merom and Chinnereth, and to "the south" of the northern Danites. **24, 25.** of Asher he said— The condition of this tribe is described as combining all the elements of earthly felicity—dip his foot in oil—These words allude either to the process of extracting the oil by foot presses, or to his district as particularly fertile, and adapted to the culture of the olive. shoes of iron and brass —These shoes suited his rocky coast from Carmel to Sidon. Country people as well as ancient warriors, had their lower extremities protected by metallic greaves (1 Sam. 17. 6; Eph. 6. 15,), and iron-soled shoes. **26-29.** There is none like unto the God of Jeshurun— The chapter concludes with a congratulatory address to Israel on their peculiar happiness and privilege in having Jehovah for their God and protector. who rideth upon the heavens in thy help—an evident allusion to the pillar of cloud and fire, which was both the guide and shelter of Israel. **28.** the fountain of Jacob—the posterity of Israel shall dwell in a blessed and favoured land.

CHAPTER XXXIV.

Ver. 1-12. MOSES FROM MOUNT NEBO VIEWETH THE LAND. **1.** Moses went up from the plains of Moab—This chapter appears from internal evidence to have been written subsequently to the death of Moses, and it probably formed, at one time, an introduction to the book of Joshua. unto the mountain of Nebo, to the top of Pisgah—*lit.*, the head or summit of *the Pisgah*,—*i.e.*, the height (cf. Num. 23. 14; ch. 3. 17-27; 4. 49.). The general name given to the whole mountain range east of Jordan, was Abarim (cf. ch. 32. 49,), and the peak to which Moses ascended was dedicated to the heathen Nebo, as Balaam's standing place had been consecrated to Peor. Some modern travellers have fixed on Jebel-Attarus, a high mountain south of the Jabbok (Zurka), as the Nebo of this passage. [BUCKHARDT, SEETZEN, &c.] But it is situated too far north for a height which, being described as "over against Jericho," must be looked for above the last stage of the Jordan. the Lord showed him all the land of Gilead—That pastoral region was discernible at the northern extremity of the mountain-line on which he stood, till it ended, far beyond his sight, in Dan. Westward, there were on the horizon, the distant hills of "all Naphtali." Coming nearer was "the land of Ephraim and Manasseh." Immediately opposite was "all the land of Judah," a title at first restricted to the portion of this tribe, beyond which were "the utmost sea" (the Mediterranean) and the Desert of the "South." These were the four great marks of the future inheritance of his people, on which the narrative fixes our attention. Immediately below him was "the circle" of the plain of Jericho, with its oasis of palm trees; and far away on his left, the last inhabited spot before the great Desert "Zoar." The foreground of the picture alone was clearly discernible. There was no miraculous power of vision imparted to Moses. That he should see all that is described is what any man could do, if he attained sufficient elevation. The atmosphere of the climate is so subtile and free from vapour, that the sight is carried to a distance of which the beholder, who judges from the more dense air of Europe, can form no idea. [VERE MONRO.] But between him and that "good land" the deep valley of the Jordan intervened; "he was not to go over thither." **5.** So Moses died—After having governed the Israelites forty years. **6.** he buried him—or, "he was buried in a valley," *i.e.*, a ravine or gorge of the Pisgah. Some think that he entered a cave and there died, being according to an ancient tradition of Jews and Christians, buried by angels (Jude, 9; Nu. 21. 20.). no man knoweth of his sepulchre unto this day—This concealment seems to have been owing to a special and wise arrangement of Providence, to prevent its being ranked among "Holy places," and made the resort of superstitious pilgrims or idolatrous veneration, in after ages. **8.** wept for Moses thirty days—seven days was the usual period of mourning, but for persons of high rank or official eminence, it was extended to thirty (Gen. 50. 3-10; Nu. 20. 29.). **9.** Joshua was full of the spirit of wisdom—He was appointed to a peculiar and extraordinary office; he was not the successor of Moses, for he was not a prophet or civil ruler, but the general or leader, called to head the people in the war of invasion, and the subsequent allocation of the tribes, **10-12.** there arose not a prophet since—In whatever light we view this extraordinary man, the eulogy pronounced in these inspired words will appear just. No Hebrew prophet or ruler equalled him in character, official dignity as well as knowledge of God's will and opportunities of announcing it.

THE BOOK OF JOSHUA.

CHAPTER I.

Ver. 1-18. THE LORD APPOINTS JOSHUA TO SUCCEED MOSES. **1.** Now after the death of Moses—Joshua having been already appointed and designated leader of Israel Nu. 27, 18-23,), in all probability assumed the reins of government *immediately* "after the death of Moses." the servant of the Lord— this was the official title of Moses, as invested with a special mission to make known the will of God; and it conferred great honour and authority. the Lord spake—probably during the period of public mourning, and either by a direct revelation to the mind of Joshua, or by means of Urim and Thummim (Num. 27. 21.). This first communication gave a pledge that the Divine instructions which, according to the provisions of the Theocracy, had been imparted to Moses, would be continued to the new leader, though God might not perhaps speak to him "mouth to mouth" (Nu. 12.

inheritance the land which I sware unto their fathers to give them.

7 Only be thou strong and very courageous, that thou mayest observe to do according to all the law ʰ which Moses my servant commanded thee: turn not from it to the right hand or to the left, that thou mayest ² prosper whithersoever thou goest.

8 This ⁱ book of the law shall not depart out of thy mouth; but ʲ thou shalt meditate therein day and night, that thou mayest observe to do according to all that is written therein: for ᵏ then thou shalt make thy way prosperous, and then thou shalt ³ have good success.

9 Have not I commanded thee? Be strong and of a good courage; ˡ be not afraid, neither be thou dismayed: for the LORD thy God is with thee whithersoever thou goest.

10 ¶ Then Joshua commanded the officers of the people, saying,

11 Pass through the host, and command the people, saying, Prepare you victuals; for ᵐ within three days ye shall pass over this Jordan, to go in to possess the land, which the LORD your God giveth you to possess it.

12 ¶ And to the Reubenites, and to the Gadites, and to half the tribe of Manasseh, spake Joshua, saying,

13 Remember ⁿ the word which Moses the servant of the LORD commanded you, saying, The LORD your God hath given you rest, and hath given you this land.

14 Your wives, your little ones, and your cattle, shall remain in the land which Moses gave you on this side Jordan; but ye shall pass before your brethren ⁴ armed, all the mighty men of valour, and help them;

15 Until the LORD have given your brethren rest, as he hath given you, and they also have possessed the land which the LORD your God giveth them: ᵒ then ye shall return unto the land of your possession, and enjoy it, which Moses the LORD'S servant gave you on this side Jordan toward the sun-rising.

16 ¶ And they answered Joshua, saying, All that thou commandest us we will do, and whithersoever thou sendest us we will go.

17 According as we hearkened unto Moses in all things, so will we hearken unto thee: only the LORD thy God ᵖ be with thee, as he was with Moses.

18 Whosoever he be that doth rebel against thy commandment, and will not hearken unto thy words in all that thou commandest him, he shall be put to death: only be strong and of a good courage.

CHAPTER II.

1 *Rahab receives and conceals the two spies sent from Shittim:* 8 *the covenant between her and them:* 23 *their return and report to Joshua.*

AND Joshua the son of Nun ¹ sent ᵃ out of Shittim two men to spy secretly, saying, Go view the land, even Jericho. And they went, and ᵇ came into an harlot's house, named ᶜ Rahab, and ² lodged there.

2 And ᵈ it was told the king of Jericho, saying, Behold, there came men in hither to-night of the children of Israel to search out the country.

3 And the king of Jericho sent unto Rahab, saying, Bring forth the men that are come to thee, which are entered into thine house: for they be come to search out all the country.

4 And ᵉ the woman took the two men, and hid them, and said thus, There came men unto me, but I wist not whence they *were*:

5 And it came to pass, *about the time* of shutting of the gate, when it was dark, that the men went out: whither the men went I wot not: pursue after them quickly; for ye shall overtake them.

6 But ᶠ she had brought them up to the roof of the house, and hid them with the stalks of flax, which she had laid in order upon the roof.

7 And the men pursued after them the way to Jordan unto the fords: and as soon as they which pursued after them were gone out, they shut the gate.

8 ¶ And, before they were laid down, she came up unto them upon the roof;

9 And she said unto the men, I know that the LORD hath given you the land, and that your ᵍ terror is fallen upon us, and that all the inhabitants of the land ³ faint because of you.

10 For we have heard how the LORD dried ʰ up the water of the Red sea for you, when ye came out of Egypt; and ⁱ what ye did unto the two kings of the Amorites, that *were* on the other side Jordan, Sihon and Og, whom ye utterly destroyed.

11 And as soon as we had ʲ heard *these things,* ᵏ our hearts did melt, neither ⁴ did there remain any more courage in any man, because of you: for ˡ the LORD your God, he *is* God in heaven above, and in earth beneath.

12 Now therefore, I pray you, ᵐ swear unto me by the LORD, since I have showed you kindness, that ye will also show kindness unto ⁿ my father's house, and give me a true token:

13 And *that* ye will save alive my father, and my mother, and my brethren, and my sisters, and all that they have, and deliver our lives from death.

14 And the men answered her, Our life ⁵ for yours, if ye utter not this our business. And it shall be, when the LORD hath given us the land, that ᵒ we will deal kindly and truly with thee.

15 Then she ᵖ let them down by a cord through the window; for her house *was* upon the town wall, and she dwelt upon the wall.

16 And she said unto them, Get you to the mountain, lest the pursuers meet you; and hide yourselves there three days, until the pursuers be returned: and afterward may you go your way.

17 And the men said unto her, We *will be* blameless ᵠ of this thine oath which thou hast made us swear:

18 Behold, *when* we come into the land, thou shalt bind this line of scarlet thread in the window which thou didst let us down by: ʳ and thou shalt ⁶ bring thy father, and thy mother, and thy brethren, and all thy father's household, home unto thee.

19 And it shall be, *that* whosoever shall go ˢ out of the doors of thy house into the street, his blood *shall be* upon his head, and we *will be* guiltless: and whosoever shall be with thee in the house, ᵗ his blood *shall be* on our head, if *any* hand be upon him.

20 And if thou utter this our business,

8. Joshua—The original name, Oshea (Nu. 13. 8,), which had been according to Eastern usage changed like those of Abram and Sarai (Gen. 17, 5-15,) into Jehoshua or Joshua, i.e., God's salvation, was significant of the services he was to render, and typified those of a greater Saviour Heb. 4. 8,). Moses' minister—i.e., his official attendant, who, from being constantly employed in important services, and early initiated into the principles of the government, would be well trained for undertaking the leadership of Israel. **2-9.** Now, therefore, arise, go over this Jordan—Joshua's mission was that of a military leader. This passage records his call to begin the work, and the address contains a literal repetition of the promise made to Moses (Deu. 11. 24, 25; 31. 6-8; 23,). **3, 4.** Every place ... have I given you—meaning, of course, not universal dominion, but only the territory comprised within the boundaries here specified see on Deu. 19. 8, 9.). all the land of the Hittites—These occupied the southern extremities, and were the dominant tribe, of Canaan. Their superior power, and the extent of their dominions, are attested by the mention of them under the name of Khita, on the Assyrian inscriptions, and still more frequently on the Egyptian inscriptions of the 18th and 19th Dynasties. What life and encouragement must have been imparted to Joshua by the assurance that his peop e who had been overwhelmed with fear of that gigantic race, were to possess "all the land of the Hittites?" **5-9.** There shall not any be able to stand before thee —Canaan was their's by a divine grant; and the renewed confirmation of that grant to Joshua when about to lead the people into it, intimated not only a certa n, but an easy conquest. It is remarkable, however, that his courage and hope of victory was made to depend see on Deu. 17. 19,) on his firm and inflexible adherence to the law of God, not only that regarding the extirpation of the Canaanites, but the whole divine code. **10-18.** Then Joshua commanded the officers of the people—These were the Shoterim (see on Ex. 5. 6; Deu. 20. 5,). prepare you victuals—not manna, which, though it still fell, would not keep; but corn, sheep, and articles of food procurable in the conquered countries. for within three days ye shall pass over this Jordan—(i.e., the third day according to *Heb.* idiom)—the time allotted for getting ready ere the encampment in Abel-Shittim b oke up, and they removed to the desert bank of the river where no victuals could be got. At the same time Joshua himself convened the 2½ tribes which had settled East of Jordan, to remind them of their engagement Num. 32. 1-42,); to assist their brethren in the conquest of Western Canaan. Their readiness to redeem their p.edge, and the terms in which they answered the appeal of Joshua, displayed to great advantage their patriotic and pious feelings at so interesting a crisis. ye shall pass "armed"—i.e., officered or marshalled under five leaders in the old and approved caravan order (see on Ex. 13. 18.). all the mighty men of valour—The words are not to be interpreted strictly as meaning the whole, but only the flower or choice of the fighting men (see on ch. 4. 12, 13.).

CHAPTER II.

Ver. 1-7. RAHAB RECEIVES AND CONCEALS THE TWO SPIES. **1.** Joshua sent two men to spy secretly—Faith is manifested by an active persevering use of means (Jam. 2. 22,); and accordingly Joshua, while confiding in the accomplishment of the Divine promise (ch. 1. 3,) adopted every precaution which a skilful general could think of to render his first attempt in the invasion of Canaan successful. Two spies were despatched to reconnoitre the country, particularly in the nei.hbourhood of Jericho; for in the prospect of investing that place, it was desirable to obtain full information as to its site, its approaches, the character and resources of its inhabitants. This mission required the strictest privacy, and it seems to have been studiously concealed from the knowledge of the Israelites themselves, lest any unfavourable or exaggerated report, publicly circulated, might have dispirited the people, as that of the spies did in the days of Moses. Jericho—Some derive this name from a word signifying "*new moon,*" in reference to the crescent-like plain in which it stood, formed by an amphitheatre of hills; others from a word signifying "*its scent,*" on account of the fragrance of the balsam and palm trees in which it was embosomed. Its site was long supposed to be represented by the small mud-walled hamlet Er-Riha; but recent researches have fixed on a spot about half-an-hour's journey westward, where large ruins exist, and about six or eight miles distant from the Jordan. It was for that age a strongly-fortified town, the key of the Eastern pass through the deep ravine, now called Wady-Kelt, into the interior of Palestine. they came into an harlot's house—Many expositors, desirous of removing the stigma of this name from an ancestress of the Saviour (Matt. 1. 5,), have called her a hostess or tavern-keeper. But scriptural usage (Lev. 21. 7-14; Deu. 23. 18; Jud. 11. 1; 1 Ki. 3. 16,). the authority of the Septuagint, followed by the apostles (Heb. 11. 31; Jam. 2. 25,) and the immemorial style of Eastern Khans, which are never kept by women, establish the propriety of the term employed in our version. Her house was probably recommended to the spies by the convenience of its situation, without any knowledge of the character of the inmates. But a divine influence directed them in the choice of that lodging-place. **2, 3.** It was told to the king—By the sentinels who at such a time of threatened invasion would be posted on the Eastern frontier, and whose duty required them to make a strict report to head-quarters of the arrival of all strangers. **4-6.** The woman took the two men and hid them—*lit.* him, *i.e.*, each of them in separate places, of course previous to the appearance of the royal messengers, and in anticipation of a speedy search after her guests. According to Eastern manners, which pay an almost superstitious respect to a woman's apartment, the royal messengers did not demand admittance to search, but asked her to bring the foreigners out. **6.** she had ... hid them with the stalks of flax— Flax, with other vegetable productions, is at a certain season spread out in the flat roofs of Eastern houses to be dried in the sun; and after lying awhile, it is piled up in numerous little stacks, which, from the luxuriant growth of the flax, rise to a height of 3 or 4 feet. Behind some of these stacks

then we will be quit of thine oath which thou hast made us to swear.

21 And she said, According unto your words, so be it. And she sent them away, and they departed: and she bound the scarlet line in the window.

22 And they went, and came unto the mountain, and abode there three days, until the pursuers were returned: and the pursuers sought *them* throughout all the way, but found *them* not.

23 So the two men returned, and descended from the mountain, and passed over, and came to Joshua the son of Nun, and told him all *things* that befell them:

24 And they said unto Joshua, Truly the LORD hath delivered into our hands all the land; for even all the inhabitants of the country do faint because of us.

CHAPTER III.

1 *Joshua comes to Jordan.* 7 *The Lord encourages him.* 9 *Joshua encourages the people.* 14 *The waters of Jordan are divided.*

AND Joshua rose early in the morning; and they removed from Shittim, and came to Jordan, he and all the children of Israel, and lodged there before they passed over.

2 And it came to pass after three days, that the officers went through the host;

3 And they commanded the people, saying, When ye see the ark of the covenant of the LORD your God, and the priests the Levites bearing it, then ye shall remove from your place, and go after it.

4 Yet there shall be a space between you and it, about two thousand cubits by measure: come not near unto it, that ye may know the way by which ye must go: for ye have not passed this way heretofore.

5 And Joshua said unto the people, Sanctify yourselves: for to-morrow the LORD will do wonders among you.

6 And Joshua spake unto the priests, saying, Take up the ark of the covenant, and pass over before the people. And they took up the ark of the covenant, and went before the people.

7 ¶ And the LORD said unto Joshua, This day will I begin to magnify thee in the sight of all Israel, that they may know that, as I was with Moses, so I will be with thee.

8 And thou shalt command the priests that bear the ark of the covenant, saying, When ye are come to the brink of the water of Jordan, ye shall stand still in Jordan.

9 ¶ And Joshua said unto the children of Israel, Come hither, and hear the words of the LORD your God.

10 And Joshua said, Hereby ye shall know that the living God is among you, and that he will without fail drive out from before you the Canaanites, and the Hittites, and the Hivites, and the Perizzites, and the Girgashites, and the Amorites, and the Jebusites.

11 Behold, the ark of the covenant of the Lord of all the earth passeth over before you into Jordan.

12 Now therefore take you twelve men out of the tribes of Israel, out of every tribe a man.

13 And it shall come to pass, as soon as the soles of the feet of the priests that bear the ark of the LORD, the Lord of all the earth, shall rest in the waters of Jordan, *that* the waters of Jordan shall be cut off from the waters that come down from above; and they shall stand upon an heap.

14 ¶ And it came to pass, when the people removed from their tents, to pass over Jordan, and the priests bearing the ark of the covenant before the people;

15 And as they that bare the ark were come unto Jordan, and the feet of the priests that bare the ark were dipped in the brim of the water, (for Jordan overfloweth all his banks all the time of harvest,)

16 That the waters which came down from above stood *and* rose up upon an heap very far from the city Adam, that *is* beside Zaretan: and those that came down toward the sea of the plain, *even* the salt sea, failed, *and* were cut off; and the people passed over right against Jericho.

17 And the priests that bare the ark of the covenant of the LORD stood firm on dry ground in the midst of Jordan, and all the Israelites passed over on dry ground, until all the people were passed clean over Jordan.

CHAPTER IV.

1 *Twelve stones taken for a memorial out of Jordan:* 9 *twelve other stones set up in the midst thereof.* 10 *The people pass over.* 14 *God magnifies Joshua.*

AND it came to pass, when all the people were clean passed over Jordan, that the LORD spake unto Joshua, saying,

2 Take you twelve men out of the people, out of every tribe a man,

3 And command ye them, saying, Take you hence out of the midst of Jordan, out of the place where the priests' feet stood firm, twelve stones; and ye shall carry them over with you, and leave them in the lodging place where ye shall lodge this night.

4 Then Joshua called the twelve men, whom he had prepared of the children of Israel, out of every tribe a man:

5 And Joshua said unto them, Pass over before the ark of the LORD your God into the midst of Jordan, and take you up every man of you a stone upon his shoulder, according unto the number of the tribes of the children of Israel:

6 That this may be a sign among you, *that* when your children ask their fathers in time to come, saying, What mean ye by these stones?

7 Then ye shall answer them, That the waters of Jordan were cut off before the ark of the covenant of the LORD; when it passed over Jordan, the waters of Jordan were cut off: and these stones shall be for a memorial unto the children of Israel for ever.

8 And the children of Israel did so as Joshua commanded, and took up twelve stones out of the midst of Jordan, as the LORD spake unto Joshua, according to the number of the tribes of the children of Israel, and carried them over with them unto the place where they lodged, and laid them down there.

9 And Joshua set up twelve stones in the midst of Jordan, in the place where the feet of the priests which bare the ark of the covenant stood: and they are there unto this day.

10 ¶ For the priests which bare the ark stood in the midst of Jordan, until every

Rahab concealed the spies, the time of shutting the gates—the gates of all Oriental cities are closed at sunset, after which there is no possibility either of admission or egress. the men went out—This was a palpable deception. But, as lying is a common vice among heathen people, Rahab was probably unconscious of its moral guilt, especially as she resorted to it as a means for screening her guests; and she might deem herself bound to do it by the laws of Eastern hospitality, which make it a point of honour to preserve the greatest enemy, if he has once eaten one's salt. Judged by the divine law, her answer was a sinful expedient; but her infirmity being united with faith, she was graciously pardoned and her service accepted (Ja. 2. 25.). 7. The men pursued after them the way to Jordan unto the fords—That river is crossed at several well known fords. The first and second immediately below the sea of Galilee; the third and fourth immediately above and below the pilgrims' bathing place, opposite Jericho. as soon as they were gone... shut the gate—This precaution was to ensure the capture of the spies, should they have been lurking in the city.

8-21. THE COVENANT BETWEEN HER AND THEM. 8-13. She came up unto them to the roof and said—Rahab's dialogue is full of interest, as showing the universal panic and consternation of the Canaanites on the one hand ch. 24. 11; Deu. 2. 25,), and her strong convictions on the other, founded on a knowledge of the divine promise; and the stupendous miracles that had opened the way of the Israelites to the confines of the promised land. She was convinced of the supremacy of Jehovah, and her earnest stipulations for the preservation of her relatives amid the perils of the approaching invasion, attest the sincerity and strength of her faith. 14. The men answered, Our life for yours—This was a solemn pledge—a virtual oath, though the name of God is not mentioned; and the words "if ye utter not this our business," were added, not as a condition of their fidelity, but as necessary for her safety, which might be endangered if the private agreement was divulged. 15. Her house was on the wall—In many Oriental cities houses are built on the walls with overhanging windows; in others the town wall forms the back wall of the house, so that the window opens into the country. Rahab's was probably of this latter description, and the cord or rope sufficiently strong to bear the weight of a man. 16-21. She said—rather "she had said," for what follows must have been part of the previous conversation. Go, get you to the mountain—A range of white limestone hills extends on the north, called Quarantania now Jebel-Karantul), rising to a height of from 1200 to 1500 feet, and the sides of which are perforated with caves. Some one peak adjoining, was familiarly known to the inhabitants as "the mountain." The prudence and propriety of the advice to flee in that direction rather than to the ford, were made apparent by the sequel. 21. She bound the scarlet line in the window—Probably soon after the departure of the spies. It was not formed, as some suppose, into net-work, as a lattice, but simply to hang down the wall. Its red colour made it conspicuous, and it was thus a sign and pledge of safety to Rahab's house, as the bloody mark on the lintels of the houses of the Israelites in Egypt to that people.

CHAPTER III.

Ver. 1-6. JOSHUA COMES TO JORDAN. 1. Joshua rose early in the morning—i.e., on the day following that on which the spies had returned with their encouraging report, the camp was broken up in "Shittim," the acacia groves) and removed to the Eastern bank of the Jordan. The duration of their stay is indicated (v. 2,), being according to Heb. reckoning only one entire day, including the evening of arrival and the morning of the passage; and such a time would be absolutely necessary for so motley an assemblage of men, women, and children, with all their gear and cattle to make ready for going into an enemy's country. 2-4. the officers went through the host, and commanded the people—The instructions given at this time and in this place were different from those described ch. 1. 11). when ye see the ark, &c.—The usual position of the ark, when at rest, was in the centre of the camp; and, during a march, in the middle of the procession. On this occasion it was to occupy the van, and be borne not by the Kohathite Levites, but the priests, as on all solemn and extraordinary occasions (cf. Nu. 4. 15; ch. 6. 6; 1 Ki. 8. 3-0.). then ye shall go after it, yet there shall be a space between it and you—These instructions refer exclusively to the advance into the river. The distance which the people were to keep in the rear of the ark was nearly a mile; had they crowded too near the ark, the view would have been intercepted, and this intervening space, therefore, was ordered, that the chest containing the sacred symbols might be distinctly visible to all parts of the camp, and be recognized as their guide in the untrodden way. 5. Joshua said unto the people—rather "had said," for as he speaks of "to-morrow," the address must have been made previous to the day of crossing, and the sanctification was in all probability the same as Moses had commanded before the giving of the law, consisting of an outward cleansing (Ex. 19, 10-15,) preparatory to that serious and devout state of mind with which so great a manifestation should be witnessed. 6. Joshua spake unto the priests—This order to the priests would be given privately, and involving as it did an important change in the established order of march, it must be considered as announced in the name and by the authority of God. Moreover, as soon as the priests stepped into the waters of Jordan they were to stand still. The ark was to accomplish what had been done by the rod of Moses.

7, 8. THE LORD ENCOURAGETH JOSHUA. 7, 8. The Lord said to Joshua, this day will I magnify thee—Joshua had already received distinguished honours (Ex. 24. 13; Deu. 31. 7.). But a higher token of the divine favour was now to be publicly bestowed on him, and evidence given in the same unmistakeable manner, that his mission and authority were from God as was of Moses (Ex. 14. 31.).

9-13. JOSHUA ENCOURAGETH THE PEOPLE. 9-13. Come hither and hear the words of the Lord—It seems that the Israelites had no intimation how they were to cross the river till shortly before the event. The premonitory address of Joshua, taken in connection

thing was finished that the LORD commanded Joshua to speak unto the people, according to all that Moses commanded Joshua: and the people hasted and passed over.

11 And it came to pass, when all the people were clean passed over, that the ark of the LORD passed over, and the priests, in the presence of the people.

12 And the children of Reuben, and the children of Gad, and half the tribe of Manasseh, passed over armed before the children of Israel, as Moses spake unto them:

13 About forty thousand prepared for war passed over before the LORD unto battle, to the plains of Jericho.

14 ¶ On that day the LORD magnified Joshua in the sight of all Israel; and they feared him, as they feared Moses, all the days of his life.

15 ¶ And the LORD spake unto Joshua, saying,

16 Command the priests that bear the ark of the testimony, that they come up out of Jordan.

17 Joshua therefore commanded the priests, saying, Come ye up out of Jordan.

18 And it came to pass, when the priests that bare the ark of the covenant of the LORD were come up out of the midst of Jordan, *and* the soles of the priests' feet were lifted up unto the dry land, that the waters of Jordan returned unto their place, and flowed over all his banks, as *they did* before.

19 ¶ And the people came up out of Jordan on the tenth *day* of the first month, and encamped in Gilgal, in the east border of Jericho.

20 And those twelve stones, which they took out of Jordan, did Joshua pitch in Gilgal.

21 And he spake unto the children of Israel, saying, When your children shall ask their fathers in time to come, saying, What *mean* these stones?

22 Then ye shall let your children know, saying, Israel came over this Jordan on dry land.

23 For the LORD your God dried up the waters of Jordan from before you, until ye were passed over, as the LORD your God did to the Red sea, which he dried up from before us, until we were gone over:

24 That all the people of the earth might know the hand of the LORD, that it *is* mighty; that ye might fear the LORD your God for ever.

CHAPTER V.

1 *The Canaanites afraid.* 2 *Circumcision is renewed.* 10 *The passover kept at Gilgal.* 13 *An Angel appears to Joshua.*

AND it came to pass, when all the kings of the Amorites, which *were* on the side of Jordan westward, and all the kings of the Canaanites, which *were* by the sea, heard that the LORD had dried up the waters of Jordan from before the children of Israel, until we were passed over, that their heart melted, neither was there spirit in them any more, because of the children of Israel.

2 ¶ At that time the LORD said unto Joshua, Make thee sharp knives, and circumcise again the children of Israel the second time.

3 And Joshua made him sharp knives, and circumcised the children of Israel at the hill of the foreskins.

4 And this *is* the cause why Joshua did circumcise: All the people that came out of Egypt, *that were* males, *even* all the men of war, died in the wilderness by the way, after they came out of Egypt.

5 Now all the people that came out were circumcised; but all the people *that were* born in the wilderness by the way as they came forth out of Egypt, *them* they had not circumcised.

6 For the children of Israel walked forty years in the wilderness, till all the people *that were* men of war, which came out of Egypt, were consumed, because they obeyed not the voice of the LORD: unto whom the LORD sware that he would not show them the land which the LORD sware unto their fathers that he would give us, a land that floweth with milk and honey.

7 And their children, *whom* he raised up in their stead, them Joshua circumcised: for they were uncircumcised, because they had not circumcised them by the way.

8 And it came to pass, when they had done circumcising all the people, that they abode in their places in the camp till they were whole.

9 And the LORD said unto Joshua, This day have I rolled away the reproach of Egypt from off you. Wherefore the name of the place is called Gilgal unto this day.

10 ¶ And the children of Israel encamped in Gilgal, and kept the passover on the fourteenth day of the month at even in the plains of Jericho.

11 And they did eat of the old corn of the land on the morrow after the passover, unleavened cakes, and parched *corn* in the selfsame day.

12 ¶ And the manna ceased on the morrow after they had eaten of the old corn of the land; neither had the children of Israel manna any more; but they did eat of the fruit of the land of Canaan that year.

13 ¶ And it came to pass, when Joshua was by Jericho, that he lifted up his eyes and looked, and, behold, there stood a man over against him with his sword drawn in his hand: and Joshua went unto him, and said unto him, *Art* thou for us, or for our adversaries?

14 And he said, Nay; but *as* captain of the host of the LORD am I now come. And Joshua fell on his face to the earth, and did worship, and said unto him, What saith my Lord unto his servant?

15 And the captain of the LORD's host said unto Joshua, Loose thy shoe from off thy foot; for the place whereon thou standest *is* holy. And Joshua did so.

CHAPTER VI.

1 *Jericho shut up.* 8 *The city compassed six days.* 20 *The walls fall down.* 22 *Rahab is saved.* 26 *The rebuilder of Jericho cursed.*

NOW Jericho was straitly shut up because of the children of Israel: none went out, and none came in.

2 And the LORD said unto Joshua, See, I have given into thine hand Jericho, and the king thereof, *and* the mighty men of valour.

3 And ye shall compass the city, all ye men of war, *and* go round about the city once. Thus shalt thou do six days.

4 And seven priests shall bear before the ark seven trumpets of rams' horns: and

with the miraculous result exactly as he had described it, would tend to increase and confirm their faith in the God of their fathers as not a dull, senseless, inanimate thing like the idols of the nations, but a Being of life, power, and activity to defend them and work for them.

14. **The Waters of Jordan are Divided.** 14. And it came to pass, &c.—To understand the scene described we must imagine the band of priests with the ark on their shoulders, standing on the depressed edge of the river, while the mass of the people were at a mile's distance. Suddenly the whole bed of the river was dried up; a spectacle the more extraordinary that it took place in the time of harvest, corresponding to our April or May,—when "the Jordan overfloweth all its banks." The original words may be more properly rendered "fills all its banks," its channel, snow-fed from Lebanon, is at its greatest height—brim full: a translation which gives the only true description of the state of Jordan in harvest as observed by modern travellers. The river about Jericho is, in ordinary appearance, about 50 or 60 yards in breadth. But as seen in harvest, it is twice as broad; and in ancient times, when the hills on the right and left were much more drenched with rain and snow than since the forests have disappeared, the river must, from a greater accession of water, have been broader still than at harvest time in the present day. 16. the waters which came down from above—*i.e.*, the Sea of Galilee "stood and rose up in a heap," a firm, compact barrier (Ex. 15. 8; Ps. 78. 13, "very far," high up the stream; "from the city Adam, that is beside Zaretan," near mount Sartabeh, in the northern part of the Ghor (1 Ki. 7. 46,; *i.e.*, a distance of thirty miles from the Israelitish encampment; and "those that came down towards the sea of the desert"—the Dead Sea—failed and were cut off Ps. 114. 2, 3.,. The river was thus dried up as far as the eye could reach. This was a stupendous miracle; Jordan takes its name, "the Descender," from the force of its current, which, after passing the Sea of Galilee, becomes greatly increased as it plunges through twenty-seven "horrible rapids and cascades," besides a great many lesser, through a fall of 1000 feet, averaging from four to five miles an hour. [Lynch.] When swollen "in time of harvest," it flows with a vastly accelerated current. the priests and all the Israelites passed on dry ground—the river about Jericho has a firm pebbly bottom on which the host might pass without inconvenience when the water was cleared off. right against Jericho—The exact spot is unknown; but it cannot be that fixed by Greek tradition—the pilgrims' bathing-place —both because it is too much to the north, and the Eastern banks are there sheer precipices of 10 or 15 feet high.

CHAPTER IV.

Ver. 1-8. **Twelve Stones taken for a Memorial out of Jordan.** 1, 2. The Lord spake unto Joshua, Take you twelve men—each representing a tribe; they had been previously chosen for this service (ch. 3. 12,), and the repetition of the command is made here solely to introduce the account of its execution. Though Joshua had been divinely instructed to erect a commemorative pile, the representatives were not apprised of the work they were to do till the time of the passage. 4, 5. Jeshua called the twelve men— They had probably, from a feeling of reverence, kept back, and were standing on the eastern bank. They were now ordered to advance, and picking up each a stone, probably as large as he could carry, from around the spot "where the priests stood," pass over before the ark, and deposit the stones in the place of next encampment (*vs.* 19, 20,', viz., Gilgal. 6, 7. that this may be a sign among you—The erection of cairns, or huge piles of stones, as monuments of remarkable incidents, has been common amongst all people, especially in the early and rude periods of their history. They are the established means of perpetuating the memory of important transactions, especially amongst the nomadic people of the East; and although there be no inscription engraven on them, the history and object of such simple monuments are traditionally preserved from age to age. Similar was the purpose contemplated by the conveyance of the twelve stones to Gilgal: it was that they might be a standing record to posterity of the miraculous passage of the Jordan. 8. the children of Israel did so—that is, it was done by their twelve representatives.

9. **Twelve Stones set up in the midst of Jordan.** 9. Joshua set up twelve stones in the place where the feet of the priests stood—In addition to the memorial just described, there was another memento of the miraculous event, a duplicate of the former, set up in the river itself, on the very spot where the ark had rested. This heap of stones might have been a large and compactly-built one, and visible in the ordinary state of the river. As nothing is said whence these stones were got, some have imagined that they might have been gathered in the adjoining fields, and deposited by the people as they passed the appointed spot. they are there unto this day—at least 20 years after the event, if we reckon by the date of this history (ch. 24. 26,), and much later, if the words in the latter clause were inserted by Samuel or Ezra.

10-13. **The People pass over.** 10. the priests who bare the ark stood in the midst of Jordan—This position was well calculated to animate the people, who probably crossed *below* the ark, as well as to facilitate Joshua's execution of the minutest instructions respecting the passage (Num. 27. 21-23.). The unfaltering confidence of the priests contrasts strikingly with the conduct of the people, who "hasted and passed over." Their faith, like that of many of God's people, was, through the weakness of nature, blended with fears. But perhaps their "haste" may be viewed in a more favourable light, as indicating the alacrity of their obedince, or it might have been enjoined, in order that the whole multitude might pass in one day. 11. their ark ... passed over, and the priests in the presence of the people—The ark is mentioned as the efficient cause; it had been the first to move—it was the last to leave; and its movements arrested the deep attention of the people, who probably stood on the opposite bank, wrapt in admiration and awe of this closing scene. It was a great miracle, greater even than the passage of the Red Sea in this respect: that, admitting the fact, there is no possibility of rational-

Jericho is besieged,   JOSHUA, VII.   *taken, and destroyed.*

the seventh day ye shall compass the city seven times, and *e* the priests shall blow with the trumpets.

5 And it shall come to pass, that when they make a long *blast* with the ram's horn, *and* when ye hear the sound of the trumpet, all the people shall shout with a great shout; and the wall of the city shall fall down ² flat, and the people shall ascend up every man straight before him.

6 ¶ And Joshua the son of Nun called the priests, and said unto them, Take up the ark of the covenant, and let seven priests bear seven trumpets of rams' horns before the ark of the LORD.

7 And he said unto the people, Pass on, and compass the city, and let him that is armed pass on before the ark of the LORD.

8 ¶ And it came to pass, when Joshua had spoken unto the people, that the seven priests bearing the seven trumpets of rams' horns passed on *d* before the LORD, and blew with the trumpets: and the ark of the covenant of the LORD followed them.

9 And the armed men went before the priests that blew with the trumpets, *e* and the ³ rereward came after the ark, *the priests* going on, and blowing with the trumpets.

10 And Joshua had commanded the people, saying, Ye shall not shout, nor ⁴ make any noise with your voice, neither shall *any* word proceed out of your mouth, until the day I bid you shout; then shall ye shout.

11 So the ark of the LORD compassed the city, going about *it* once: and they came into the camp, and lodged in the camp.

12 ¶ And Joshua rose early in the morning, *f* and the priests took up the ark of the LORD.

13 And seven priests bearing seven trumpets of rams' horns before the ark of the LORD *g* went on continually, and blew with the trumpets: and the armed men went before them; but the rereward came after the ark of the LORD, *the priests* going on, and blowing with the trumpets.

14 And the second day they compassed the city once, and returned into the camp: so they did six days.

15 And it came to pass on the seventh day, that they rose early, about the dawning of the day, and compassed the city after the same manner seven times: only on that day they compassed the city seven times.

16 And it came to pass at the seventh time, when the priests blew with the trumpets, Joshua said unto the people, *h* Shout; for the LORD hath given you the city.

17 And the city shall be ⁵ accursed, *even* it, and all that *are* therein, to the LORD: only Rahab the harlot shall live, she and all that *are* with her in the house, *i* because she hid the messengers that we sent.

18 And ye, *j* in any wise keep *yourselves* from the accursed thing, lest ye make *yourselves* accursed, when ye take of the accursed thing, and make the camp of Israel a curse, *k* and trouble it.

19 But all the silver, and gold, and vessels of brass and of iron, *are* ⁶ consecrated unto the LORD: they shall come into the treasury of the LORD.

20 So the people shouted when *the priests* blew with the trumpets: and it came to pass, when the people heard the sound of the trumpet, and the people shouted with a great shout, that *l* the wall fell down

7 flat, so that the people went up into the city, every man straight before him, and they took the city.

21 And they *m* utterly destroyed all that *was* in the city, both man and woman, young and old, and ox, and sheep, and ass, with the edge of the sword.

22 But Joshua had said unto the two men that had spied out the country, Go into the harlot's house, and bring out thence the woman, and all that she hath, *n* as ye sware unto her.

23 And the young men that were spies went in, and brought out Rahab, *o* and her father, and her mother, and her brethren, and all that she had; and they brought out all her ⁸ kindred, and left them without the camp of Israel.

24 And they burned the city with fire, and all that *was* therein: only the silver, and the gold, and the vessels of brass and of iron, they put into the treasury of the house of the LORD.

25 And Joshua saved Rahab the harlot alive, and her father's household, and all that she had; and *p* she dwelleth in Israel *even* ⁹ unto this day; because she hid the messengers which Joshua sent to spy out Jericho.

26 ¶ And Joshua adjured *them* at that time, saying, *q* Cursed *be* the man before the LORD that riseth up and buildeth this city Jericho: he shall lay the foundation thereof in his first-born, and in his youngest *son* shall he set up the gates of it.

27 So *r* the LORD was with Joshua; and his *s* fame was *noised* throughout all the country.

CHAPTER VII.

1 *Achan's trespass.* 2 *The Israelites smitten at Ai.* 6 *Joshua's complaint:* 10 *God instructs him what to do.* 16 *Achan taken by lot:* 19 *his confession:* 24 *he and all that he had destroyed in the valley of Achor.*

BUT the children of Israel committed a trespass in the accursed thing: *a* for 1 Achan, the son of Carmi, the son of 2 Zabdi, the son of Zerah, of the tribe of Judah, took of the accursed thing: and the anger of the LORD was kindled against the children of Israel.

2 And Joshua sent men from Jericho to Ai, which *is* beside Beth-aven, on the east side of Beth-el, and spake unto them, saying, Go up and view the country. And the men went up and viewed Ai.

3 And they returned to Joshua, and said unto him, Let not all the people go up; but let ³ about two or three thousand men go up and smite Ai; *and* make not all the people to labour thither; for they *are* but few.

4 So there went up thither of the people about three thousand men: *b* and they fled before the men of Ai.

5 And the men of Ai smote of them about thirty and six men: for they chased them *from* before the gate *even* unto Shebarim, and smote them ⁴ in the going down: wherefore *c* the hearts of the people melted, and became as water.

6 ¶ And Joshua *d* rent his clothes, and fell to the earth upon his face before the ark of the LORD until the eventide, he and the elders of Israel, and *e* put dust upon their heads.

B. C. 1451.

CHAP. 6.
c Nu. 10. 8.
² under it.
d That is, before the ark. ch. 4. 13.
e Nu. 10. 25.
³ gathering host.
⁴ make your voice to be heard.
f Deu. 31. 25.
g Gal. 6. 9.
h Judges 7. 20.
2 Chr. 13. 14.
⁵ Or, devoted.
Lev. 27. 28.
Mic. 4. 13.
i ch. 2. 4.
Mat. 10. 41.
j Deu. 7. 26.
Deu. 13. 17.
ch. 7. 1, 11, 12.
Is. 52. 11.
Ro. 12. 9.
2 Cor. 6. 17.
Eph. 5. 11.
1 Thess. 5. 22.
k ch. 7. 25.
1 Kin. 18. 17, 18.
Jonah 1. 12.
⁶ holiness.
l Heb. 11. 30.
⁷ under it.
m Deu. 7. 2.
n ch. 2. 14.
Heb. 11. 31.
o ch. 2. 13.
⁸ families.
p Mat. 1. 5.
q B.C. 1427.
r 1 Kin. 16. 34.
Mal. 1. 4.
r ch. 1. 5.
s ch. 9. 1, 3.
1 Sa. 2. 30.

CHAP. 7.
a ch. 22. 20.
1 1 Chr. 2. 7, Achar.
2 Or, Zimri, 1 Chr. 2. 6.
³ about two thousand men, or about three thousand men.
b Lev. 26. 17.
Deu. 28. 25.
⁴ Or, in Morad.
c ch. 2. 9, 11.
Lev. 26. 36.
Ps. 22. 14.
d Gen. 37. 29.
e 1 Sam. 4. 12.
2 Sa. 1. 2.
2 Sam. 13. 19.
Neh. 9. 1.
Job 2. 12.

istic insinuations as to the influence of natural causes in producing it, as have been made in the former case. **12, 13.** The children of Reuben ... passed over armed before the children of Israel—There is no precedency to the other tribes indicated here; for there is no reason to suppose that the usual order of march was departed from; but these are honourably mentioned to show that, in pursuance of their engagement (ch. 1. 16-18,), they had sent a complement of fighting men to accompany their brethren in the war of invasion. into the plains of Jericho—That part of the Araba or Ghor, on the west, is about seven miles broad from the Jordan to the mountain entrance at Wady-Kelt. Though now desert, this valley was in ancient times richly covered with wood—an immense palm forest, 7 miles long, surrounded Jericho.

14-24. GOD MAGNIFIES JOSHUA. 14-17. On that day the Lord magnified Joshua—It appeared clear, from the chief part he acted, that he was the divinely-appointed leader: for even the priests did not enter the river, or quit their position, except at his command; and thenceforward his authority was as firmly established as that of his predecessor. **18.** The priests who bare the ark were come out of the midst of Jordan—Their crossing, which was the final act, completed the evidence of the miracle; for then, and not till then, the suspended laws of nature were restored, the waters returned to their place, and the river flowed with as full a current as before. **19.** The people came out of Jordan on the tenth day of the first month—*i.e.*, the month Nisan, four days before the Passover, and the very day when the Paschal Lamb required to be set apart. the providence of God having arranged that the entrance into the promised land should be at the Feast. and encamped in Gilgal—the name is here given by anticipation see on ch. 5. 9.). It was a tract of land, according to Josephus, 50 stadia (6¼ miles) from Jordan, and 10 stadia (1¼ miles) from Jericho at the eastern outskirts of the palm forest, now supposed to be the spot occupied by the village Riha. **20-24.** Those twelve stones did Joshua pitch—probably to render them more conspicuous, they might be raised on a foundation of earth or turf; and the pile was designed to serve a double purpose—that of impressing the heathen with a sense of the omnipotence of God, while at the same time it would teach an important lesson in religion to the young and rising Israelites in after ages.

CHAPTER V.

Ver. 1. THE CANAANITES AFRAID. 1. the kings of the Amorites ... and Canaanites by the sea—Under the former designation were included the people who inhabited the mountainous region, and under the latter those who were on the sea-coast of Palestine. their heart melted—They had probably reckoned on the swollen river interposing for a time a sure barrier of defence. But seeing it had been completely dried up, they were completely paralysed by so incontestible a proof that God was on the side of the invaders. In fact, the conquest had already begun in the total prostration of spirit among the native chiefs. "Their heart melted," but unhappily not into faith and penitent submission.

2-12. CIRCUMCISION IS RENEWED. 2. At that time—on the encampment being made after the passage. the Lord said unto Joshua, make thee sharp knives—Stone knives, collect and make them ready. Flints have been used in the early times of all people: and although the use of iron was known to the Hebrews in the days of Joshua, probably the want of a sufficient number of metallic implements dictated the employment of flints on this occasion (cf. Ex. 4. 25.) circumcise again ... the second time—*lit.*, return and circumcise. The command did not require him to repeat the operation on those who had undergone it, but to resume the observance of the rite, which had been long discontinued. The language, however, evidently points to a general circumcising on some previous occasion, which, though unrecorded, must have been made before the celebration of the Passover at Sinai (cf. Ex. 12. 48; Num. 9. 5,), as a mixed multitude accompanied the camp. "The second time" of general circumcising was at the entrance into Canaan. **3.** at the hill—Probably one of the argillaceous hills that form the highest terrace of the Jordan, or a rising ground at the palm forest. **4-7.** this is the cause why Joshua did circumcise—The omission to circumcise the children born in the wilderness might have been owing to the incessant movements of the people; but it is most generally thought that the true cause was a temporary suspension of the covenant with the unbelieving race who, being rejected of the Lord, were doomed to perish in the wilderness, and whose children had to bear the iniquity of their fathers (Num. 14. 33,), though, as the latter were to be brought into the promised land, the covenant would be renewed with them. **8.** when they had done circumcising all the people—As the number of those born in the wilderness and uncircumcised must have been immense, a difficulty is apt to be felt how the rite could have been performed on such a multitude in so short a time. But it has been calculated that the proportion between those already circumcised (under twenty when the doom was pronounced,), and those to be circumcised, was one to four, and consequently the whole ceremony could easily have been performed in a day. Circumcision being the sign and seal of the covenant, its performance was virtually an infeoffment in the promised land, and its being delayed till their actual entrance into the country was a wise and gracious act on the part of God, who postponed this trying duty till the hearts of the people, animated by the recent astonishing miracle, were prepared to obey the Divine will. they abode ... till they were whole—It is calculated that, of those who did not need to be circumcised, more than 50,000 were left to defend the camp, if an attack had been then made upon it. **9.** rolled away the reproach of Egypt—The taunts industriously cast by that people upon Israel as *nationally* rejected by God by the cessation of circumcision, and the renewal of that rite was a practical announcement of the restoration of the covenant. [KEIL.] Gilgal—No trace either of the name or site is now to be found; but it was about 2 miles from Jericho [JOSEPHUS,], and well suited for an encampment, by the advantages of shade and water. It was the first place pronounced "holy" in the Holy Land (*v.* 15.). **10.** kept the passover

7 And Joshua said, Alas, O Lord God, wherefore *f* hast thou at all brought this people over Jordan, to deliver us into the hand of the Amorites, to destroy us? would to God we had been content and dwelt on the other side Jordan!

8 O Lord, what shall I say, when Israel turneth their 5 backs before their enemies!

9 For the Canaanites and all the inhabitants of the land shall hear *of it*, and shall environ us round, and *g* cut off our name from the earth: and *h* what wilt thou do unto thy great name?

10 ¶ And the Lord said unto Joshua, Get thee up; wherefore *o* liest thou thus upon thy face?

11 Israel hath sinned, and they have also transgressed my covenant which I commanded them; *i* for they have even taken of the accursed thing, and have also stolen, and *j* dissembled also, and they have put *it* even among their own stuff.

12 Therefore *k* the children of Israel could not stand before their enemies. *but* turned *their* backs before their enemies, because they *l* were accursed: neither will I be with you any more, except ye destroy the accursed from among you.

13 Up, *m* sanctify the people, and say, Sanctify *n* yourselves against to-morrow: for thus saith the Lord God of Israel, *There is* an accursed thing in the midst of thee, O Israel: thou canst not stand before thine enemies, until ye take away the accursed thing from among you.

14 In the morning therefore ye shall be brought according to your tribes: and it shall be, *that* the tribe which *o* the Lord taketh shall come according to the families *thereof;* and the family which the Lord shall take shall come by households; and the household which the Lord shall take shall come man by man.

15 And *p* it shall be, *that* he that is taken with the accursed thing shall be burnt with fire, he and all that he hath: because he hath transgressed the covenant of the Lord, and because he *q* hath wrought 7 folly in Israel.

16 ¶ So Joshua rose up early in the morning, and brought Israel by their tribes; and the tribe of Judah was taken:

17 And he brought the family of Judah; and he took the family of the Zarhites: and he brought the family of the Zarhites man by man; and Zabdi was taken:

18 And he brought his household man by man; and *r* Achan, the son of Carmi, the son of Zabdi, the son of Zerah, of the tribe of Judah, was taken.

19 And Joshua said unto Achan, My son, give. *s* I pray thee, glory to the Lord God of Israel, *t* and make confession unto him; and tell me now what thou hast done; hide it not from me.

20 And Achan answered Joshua, and said, Indeed I have sinned against the Lord God of Israel, and thus and thus have I done:

21 When I saw among the spoils a goodly Babylonish garment, and two hundred shekels of silver, and a 8 wedge of gold of fifty shekels weight, then I *u* coveted them, and took them; and, behold, they *are* hid in the earth in the midst of my tent, and the silver under it.

22 So Joshua sent messengers, and they ran unto the tent; and, behold, *it was* hid in his tent, and the silver under it.

23 And they took them out of the midst of the tent, and brought them unto Joshua, and unto all the children of Israel, and 9 laid them out before the Lord.

24 And Joshua, and all Israel with him, took Achan the son of Zerah, and the silver, and the garment, and the wedge of gold, and his sons, and his daughters, and his oxen, and his asses, and his sheep, and his tent, and all that he had: and they brought them unto *v* the valley of Achor.

25 And Joshua said, *w* Why hast thou troubled us? the Lord shall trouble thee this day. *x* And all Israel stoned him with stones, and burned them with fire, after they had stoned them with stones.

26 And they *y* raised over him a great heap of stones unto this day. So *z* the Lord turned from the fierceness of his anger. Wherefore the name of that place was called, *a* The valley of 10 Achor, unto this day.

CHAPTER VIII.

1 *God encourages Joshua.* 3 *The stratagem whereby Ai was taken.* 29 *The king thereof hanged.* 30 *Joshua builds an altar, writes the law on stones, and pronounces blessings and cursings.*

AND the Lord said unto Joshua, *a* Fear not, neither be thou dismayed: take all the people of war with thee, and arise, go up to Ai: see, *b* I have given into thy hand the king of Ai, and his people, and his city, and his land:

2 And thou shalt do to Ai and her king as thou didst unto *c* Jericho and her king: only *d* the spoil thereof, and the cattle thereof, shall ye take for a prey unto yourselves: lay thee an ambush for the city behind it.

3 ¶ So Joshua arose, and all the people of war, to go up against Ai: and Joshua chose out thirty thousand mighty men of valour, and sent them away by night.

4 And he commanded them, saying, Behold, *e* ye shall lie 1 in wait against the city, *even* behind the city: go not very far from the city, but be ye all ready:

5 And I, and all the people that *are* with me, will approach unto the city: and it shall come to pass, when they come out against us, as at the first, that *f* we will flee before them,

6 (For they will come out after us.) till we have 2 drawn them from the city; for they will say, They flee before us, as at the first: therefore we will flee before them.

7 Then ye shall rise up from the ambush, and seize upon the city: for the Lord your God will deliver it into your hand.

8 And it shall be, when ye have taken the city, *that* ye shall set the city on fire: according to the commandment of the Lord shall ye do. *g* See, I have commanded you.

9 Joshua therefore sent them forth: and they went to lie in ambush, and abode between Beth-el and Ai, on the west side of Ai: but Joshua lodged that night among the people.

10 And Joshua *h* rose up early in the morning, and numbered the people, and went up, he and the elders of Israel, before the people to Ai.

11 And all the people, *even the people* of war that *were* with him, went up, and

on the fourteenth day at even—The time fixed by the law see Ex. 12. 18; Lev. 23. 5. Num. 28. 16.'. Thus the national existence was commenced by a solemn act of religious dedication. 11, 12. they did eat old corn—Found in store-houses of the inhabitants who had fled into Jericho, parched corn—New grain (see on Lev. 23. 10,), probably lying in the fields. Roasted—a simple and primitive preparation, much liked in the East. This abundance of food led to the discontinuance of the manna; and the fact of its then ceasing, viewed in connection with its seasonable appearance in the barren wilderness, is a striking proof of its miraculous origin.
13-15. AN ANGEL APPEARS TO JOSHUA. 13. When Joshua was by Jericho—in the immediate vicinity of that city, probably engaged in surveying the fortifications, and in meditating the best plan of a siege, there stood a man with a sword drawn—It is evident from the strain of the context that this was not a mere vision, but an actual appearance; the suddenness of which surprised, but did not daunt, the intrepid leader. 14. the host of the Lord—either the Israelitish people (Ex. 7. 4; 12. 41; Isa. 55. 4,), or the angels (Ps. 148. 2,', or both included, and the Captain of it was the angel of the covenant, whose visible manifestations were varied according to the occasion. His attitude of equipment betokened his approval of, and interest in, the war of invasion. Joshua fell on his face, and did worship—The adoption by Joshua of this absolute form of prostration, demonstrates the sentiments of profound reverence with which the language and majestic bearing of the stranger inspired him. The real character of this personage was disclosed by His accepting the homage of worship (cf. Ac. 10. 25, 26; Rev. 19. 10,), and still further in the command, "Loose thy shoe from off thy foot." (Ex. 3. 5.)

CHAPTER VI.

Ver. 1-7. JERICHO SHUT UP. 1. Now Jericho was straitly shut up—This verse is a parenthesis introduced to prepare the way for the directions given by the Captain of the Lord's host. See, I have given into thine hand—the language intimates that a purpose already formed was about to be carried into immediate execution; and that, although the king and inhabitants of Jericho were fierce and experienced warriors who would make a stout and determined resistance, the Lord promised a certain and easy victory over them. 3-5. Ye shall compass the city, &c.—Directions are here given as to the mode of procedure. *Heb.*, "horns of jubilee;" *i.e.*, the bent or crooked trumpets with which the jubilee was proclaimed. It is probable that the horns of this animal were used at first; and that afterwards, when metallic trumpets were introduced, the primitive name, as well as form of them, was traditionally continued. The design of this whole proceeding was obviously to impress the Canaanites with a sense of the Divine Omnipotence—to teach the Israelites a memorable lesson of faith and confidence in God's promises, and to inspire sentiments of respect and reverence for the ark, as the symbol of His presence. The length of time during which those circuits were made tended the more intensely to arrest the attention, and to deepen the impressions, both of the Israelites and the enemy. The number seven was among the Israelites the symbolic seal of the covenant between God and their nation. [KEIL, HENG.] 6, 7. Joshua called the priests—The pious leader, whatever military preparations he had made, surrendered all his own views at once and unreservedly, to the declared will of God.

8-19. THE CITY COMPASSED SIX DAYS. 8-11. passed on before the Lord—before the ark, called "the ark of the covenant," for it contained the tables on which the covenant was inscribed. The procession was made in deep and solemn silence, conformably to the instructions given to the people by their leader at the outset, that they were to refrain from all acclamation and noise of any kind, until he should give them a signal. It must have been a strange sight; no mount was raised, no sword drawn, no engine planted, no pioneers undermining—here were armed men, but no stroke given; they must walk and not fight. Doubtless the people of Jericho made themselves merry with the spectacle. [BP. HALL.] 12-14. Joshua rose early in the morning—The second day's procession seems to have taken place in the morning. In all other respects down, even to the smallest details, the arrangements of the first day continued to be the rule followed on the other six. 15. On the seventh day they rose early, about the dawning of the day—On account of the seven circuits they had to make that day. It is evident, however, that the milita only of the Israelites had been called to the march—for it is inconceivable that two millions of people could have gone so frequently round the city in a day. 16. it came to pass at the seventh time—This delay brought out their faith and obedience in so remarkable a manner, that it is celebrated by the apostle Heb. 11. 30.). 17-19. the city shall be accursed—See on Lev. 27. 28. 29.). The *cherem* or anathema, was a devotion to utter destruction (Deu. 7.2; 20. 17; 1 Sam. 15. 3.). When such a ban was pronounced against a hostile city, the men and animals were killed—no booty was allowed to be taken; the ido s and all the precious ornaments on them were to be burned (Deu. 7. 25; cf. 1 Chron. 14.12.); every thing was either to be destroyed, or consecrated to the sanctuary. Joshua pronounced this ban on Jericho, a great and wealthy city, evidently by Divine direction, and the severity of the doom, accordant with the requirements of a law which was holy, just, and good, was justified not only by the fact of its inhabitants being part of a race who had filled up their iniquities, but by their resisting the light of the recent astonishing miracle at the Jordan. Besides, as Jericho seems to have been defended by re-inforcements from all the country (ch. 24.11.), its destruction would paralyze all the rest of the devoted people, and thus tend to facilitate the conquest of the land; showing, as so astounding a military miracle did, that it was done, not by man, but by the power, and through the anger of God. 18. in any wise keep yourselves from the accursed thing—Generally they were left at liberty to take the spoil of other cities that were captured (Deu. 2. 35; 3. 7; ch. 8. 27.). But this, as the first-fruits of Canaan, was made an exception; nothing was to be spared but Rahab and those in her house. A violation of these stringent orders would not only render the guilty persons obnoxious the curse,

drew nigh, and came before the city, and pitched on the north side of Ai: now *there was* a valley between them and Ai.

12 And he took about five thousand men, and set them to lie in ambush ⁱ between Beth-el and Ai, on the west side ³ of the city.

13 And when they had set the people, *even* all the host that *was* on the north of the city, and ⁴ their liers in wait on the west of the city, Joshua went that night into the midst of the valley.

14 And it came to pass, when the king of Ai saw *it*, that they hasted, and rose up early, and the men of the city went out against Israel to battle, he and all his people, at a time appointed, before the plain: but he wist ʲ not that *there were* liers in ambush against him behind the city.

15 And Joshua and all Israel ᵏ made as if they were beaten before them, and fled ˡ by the way of the wilderness.

16 And all the people that *were* in Ai were called together to pursue after them: and they pursued after Joshua, and were drawn ᵐ away from the city.

17 And there was not a man left in Ai or Beth-el that went not out after Israel: and they left the city open, and pursued after Israel.

18 And the LORD said unto Joshua, Stretch out the spear that *is* in thy hand toward Ai; for ⁿ I will give it into thine hand. And Joshua stretched out the spear that *he had* in his hand toward the city.

19 And the ambush arose quickly out of their place, and they ran as soon as he had stretched out his hand; and they entered into the city, and took it, and hasted and set the city on fire.

20 And when the men of Ai looked behind them, they saw, and, behold, the smoke of the city ascended up to heaven, and they had no ⁵ power to flee this way or that way: and the people that fled to the wilderness turned back upon the pursuers.

21 And when Joshua and all Israel saw that the ambush had taken the city, and that the smoke of the city ascended, then they turned again, and slew the men of Ai.

22 And the other issued out of the city against them; so they were in the midst of Israel, some on this side, and some on that side: and they smote them, so that they let ᵒ none of them remain or escape.

23 And the king of Ai they took alive, and brought him to Joshua.

24 And it came to pass, when Israel had made an end of slaying all the inhabitants of Ai in the field, in the wilderness wherein they chased them, and when they were all fallen on the edge of the sword, until they were consumed, that all the Israelites returned unto Ai, and smote it with the edge of the sword.

25 And *so* it was, *that* all that fell that day, both of men and women, *were* twelve thousand, *even* all the men of Ai.

26 For Joshua drew not his hand back, wherewith he stretched out the spear, until he had utterly destroyed all the inhabitants of Ai.

27 Only ᵖ the cattle, and the spoil of that city, Israel took for a prey unto themselves, according unto the word of the LORD which he commanded Joshua.

28 And Joshua burnt Ai, and made it ᑫ an heap for ever, *even* a desolation unto ʳ this day.

29 And ˢ the king of Ai he hanged on a tree until eventide: ᵗ and as soon as the sun was down, Joshua commanded that they should take his carcase down from the tree, and cast it at the entering of the gate of the city, and ᵘ raise thereon a great heap of stones, *that remaineth* unto this day.

30 ¶ Then Joshua ᵛ built an altar unto the LORD God of Israel ʷ in mount Ebal,

31 As Moses the servant of the LORD commanded the children of Israel, as it is written in the ˣ book of the law of Moses, an altar of whole stones, over which no man hath lift up *any* iron: and ʸ they offered thereon burnt offerings unto the LORD, and sacrificed peace offerings.

32 And ᶻ he wrote there upon the stones a copy of the law of Moses, which he wrote in the presence of the children of Israel.

33 And all Israel, and their elders, and officers, and their judges, stood on this side the ark and on that side before the priests the Levites, ᵃ which bare the ark of the covenant of the LORD, as well ᵇ the stranger, as he that was born among them; half of them over against mount Gerizim, and half of them over against mount Ebal; as ᶜ Moses the servant of the LORD had commanded before, that they should bless the people of Israel.

34 And afterward ᵈ he read all the words of the law, ᵉ the blessings and cursings, according to all that is written in the book of the law.

35 There was not a word of all that Moses commanded, which Joshua read not before all the congregation of Israel, ᶠ with the women, and the little ones, and the strangers ᵍ that ⁶ were conversant among them.

CHAPTER IX.

1 *The kings combine against Israel.* 3 *The Gibeonites, obtaining a league by craft,* 16 *are condemned to perpetual bondage.*

AND it came to pass, when all the kings which *were* on this side Jordan, in the hills, and in the valleys, and in all the coasts of ᵃ the great sea over against Lebanon, ᵇ the Hittite, and the Amorite, the Canaanite, the Perizzite, the Hivite, and the Jebusite, heard *thereof*;

2 That they ᶜ gathered themselves together, to fight with Joshua and with Israel, with one ¹ accord.

3 ¶ And when the inhabitants of ᵈ Gibeon heard ᵉ what Joshua had done unto Jericho and to Ai,

4 They did work wilily, and went and made as if they had been ambassadors, and took old sacks upon their asses, and ᶠ wine bottles, old, and rent, and bound up;

5 And old shoes and clouted upon their feet, and old garments upon them; and all the bread of their provision was dry *and* mouldy.

6 And they went to Joshua ᵍ unto the camp at Gilgal, and said unto him, and to the men of Israel, We be come from a far country: now therefore make ye a league with us.

7 And the men of Israel said unto ʰ the Hivites, Peradventure ye dwell among us; and ⁱ how shall we make a league with you?

8 And they said unto Joshua, ʲ We are

but entail distress and adversity upon all Israel, by provoking the divine displeasure. These were the instructions given, or repeated (Deu. 13. 17; 7. 26.), previously to the last act of the siege.

20, 21. THE WALLS FALL DOWN. 20. So the people shouted when the priests blew—Towards the close of the seventh circuit, the signal was given by Joshua, and on the Israelites raising their loud war-cry, the walls fell down, doubtless burying multitudes of the inhabitants in the ruins, while the besiegers, rushing in, consigned every thing animate and inanimate to indiscriminate destruction. (Deu. 20. 16, 17.) Jewish writers mention it as an immemorial tradition, that the city fell on the Sabbath. It should be remembered that the Canaanites were incorrigible idolators, addicted to the most horrible vices, and that the righteous judgment of God might sweep them away by the sword, as well as by famine or pestilence. There was mercy mingled with judgment in employing the sword as the instrument of punishing the guilty Canaanites, for while it was directed against one place, time was afforded for others to repent.

22-25. RAHAB IS SAVED. 22, 23. Joshua said, Go into the harlot's house—it is evident that the town walls were not demolished universally, at least all at once, for Rahab's house was allowed to stand until her relatives were rescued according to promise, were left without the camp of Israel—a temporary exclusion, in order that they might be cleansed from the defilement of their native idolatries, and gradually trained for admission into the society of God's people. 24. Burned the city and all therein—except the silver, gold, and other metals, which, as they would not burn, were added to the treasury of the sanctuary. 25. Rahab dwelleth in Israel unto this day—a proof that this book was written not long after the events related.

26, 27. THE REBUILDER OF JERICHO CURSED. 26. Joshua adjured them at that time—i.e., imposed upon his countrymen a solemn oath, binding on themselves as well as their posterity, that they would never rebuild that city. Its destruction was designed by God to be a permanent memorial of His abhorrence of idolatry, and its attendant vices. Cursed be the man that riseth up—i.e., makes the daring attempt to build. He shall lay the foundation in his first-born, &c.—shall become childless—the first beginning being marked by the death of his eldest son, and his only surviving child dying at the time of its completion. This curse was accomplished 550 years after its denunciation (See on 1 Ki. 16. 34.).

CHAPTER VII.

Ver. 1. ACHAN'S TRESPASS. 1. The children of Israel committed a trespass in the accursed thing—There was one transgressor against the *cherem*, or ban, on Jericho, and his transgression brought the guilt and disgrace of sin upon the whole nation. Achan, called afterwards Achar (trouble) (1 Chr. 2. 7.. Zabdi, or Zimri (1 Chr. 2. 6.). Zerah, or Zarah, son of Judah and Tamar (Gen. 38. 30.). His genealogy is given probably to show that from a parentage so infamous the descendants would not be carefully trained in the fear of God.

2-26. THE ISRAELITES SMITTEN AT AI. 2. Joshua sent men from Jericho to Ai—after the sacking of Jericho, the next step was to penetrate into the hills above. Accordingly, spies went up the mountain-pass to view the country. The precise site of Ai or Hai is indicated with sufficient clearness (Gen. 12. 8; 13. 3,), and has been recently discovered in an isolated Tell, called by the natives Tell-el-hajar, "the Mount of Stones," at two miles, or thirty-five minutes' distance, east-south-east, from Bethel. [VAN DE VELDE.] Bethaven—("house of vanity,") a name afterwards given derisively (Hos. 4. 15; 5. 8; 10. 5;) on account of its idolatries to Bethel, "house of God." But here referred to another place, about six miles east of Bethel, and three north of Ai. 3. Let not all the people go up, for they are but few—As the population of Ai amount'd to 1200 (ch. 8. 25,) it was a considerable town; though in the hasty and distant reconnoitre made by the spies, it probably appeared small in comparison of Jericho, and this may have been the reason of their proposing so small a detachment to capture it. 4, 5. They fled before the men of Ai—An unexpected resistance, and the loss of thirty-six of their number, diffused a panic, which ended in an ignominious rout. Chased them . . . even unto Shebarim—i.e., unto the "breakings" or "fissures" at the opening of the passes. and smote them in the going down—i.e., the declivity or slope of the deep rugged adjoining wady. wherefore the hearts of the people melted.—It is evident that the troops engaged were a tumultuary, undisciplined band, no better skilled in military affairs than the Bedouin Arabs, who bec me disheartened and flee on the loss of ten or fifteen men. But the consternation of the Israelites arose from another cause—the evident displeasure of God who withheld that aid on which they had confidently reckoned. 6-9. Joshua rent his clothes and fell . . . before the ark, he and the elders—It is evident, from those tokens of humiliation and sorrow, that a solemn fast was observed on this occasion. The language of Joshua's prayer is thought by many to savour of human infirmity, and to be wanting in that reverence and submission he owed to God. But, although apparently breathing a spirit of bold remonstrance and complaint, it was in reality the effusion of a deeply humbled and afflicted mind, expressing his belief that God could not, after having so miraculously brought His people over Jordan into the promised land, intend to destroy them, to expose them to the insults of their triumphant enemies, and bring reproach upon his own name for inconstancy or unkindness to His peop e, or inability to resist their enemies. Unable to understand the cause of the present calamity he owned the hand of God. 10-15. the Lord said, Get thee up—The answer of the divine oracle was to this effect:—the crisis is owing not to unfaithfulness in Me, but sin in the people. The conditions of the covenant have been violated by the reservation of spoil from the doomed city, wickedness, emphatically called folly, has been committed in Israel, (Ps. 14. 1,) and dissimulation, with other aggravations of the crime, continues to be practised. The people are liable to destruction equally with the accursed nations of Canaan (Deut. 7. 26.). Means must, without delay, be taken to discover and punish the perpetrator of

thy servants. And Joshua said unto them, Who *are* ye? and from whence come ye?

9 And they said unto him, *k* From a very far country thy servants are come because of the name of the LORD thy God: for we have *l* heard the fame of him, and all that he did in Egypt,

10 And *m* all that he did to the two kings of the Amorites, that *were* beyond Jordan, to Sihon king of Heshbon, and to Og king of Bashan, which *was* at Ashtaroth.

11 Wherefore our elders and all the inhabitants of our country spake to us, saying, Take victuals ² with you for the journey, and go to meet them, and say unto them, We *are* your servants: therefore now make ye a league with us.

12 This our bread we took hot *for* our provision out of our houses on the day we came forth to go unto you: but now, behold, it is dry, and it is mouldy:

13 And these bottles of wine which we filled *were* new; and, behold, they be rent: and these our garments and our shoes are become old by reason of the very long journey.

14 And ³ the men took of their victuals, and *n* asked not *counsel* at the mouth of the LORD.

15 And Joshua *o* made peace with them, and made a league with them, to let them live: and the princes of the congregation sware unto them.

16 ¶ And it came to pass, at the end of three days after they had made a league with them, that they heard that they *were* their neighbours, and *that* they dwelt among them.

17 And the children of Israel journeyed, and came unto their cities on the third day. Now their cities *were* *p* Gibeon, and Chephirah, and Beeroth, and Kirjath-jearim.

18 And the children of Israel smote them not, *q* because the princes of the congregation had sworn unto them by the LORD God of Israel. And all the congregation murmured against the princes.

19 But all the princes said unto all the congregation, We have sworn unto them by the LORD God of Israel: now therefore we may not touch them.

20 This we will do to them; we will even let them live, lest *r* wrath be upon us, because of the oath which we sware unto them.

21 And the princes said unto them, Let them live; but let them be *s* hewers of wood and drawers of water unto all the congregation; as the princes had promised them.

22 ¶ And Joshua called for them, and he spake unto them, saying, Wherefore have ye beguiled us, saying, We *are* very far from you; when ye dwell among us?

23 Now therefore ye *are* *t* cursed; and there shall ⁴ none of you be freed from being bondmen, and hewers of wood and drawers of water for the house of my God.

24 And they answered Joshua, and said, Because it was certainly told thy servants, how that the LORD thy God *u* commanded his servant Moses to give you all the land, and to destroy all the inhabitants of the land from before you, therefore *v* we were sore afraid of our lives because of you, and have done this thing.

25 And now, behold, we *are* *w* in thine

B. C. 1451.

CHAP. 9.
k Deu. 20. 15.
l Ex. 15. 14.
Josh. 2. 10.
m Num. 21. 24, 33.
2 in your hand.
3 Or, they received the men by reason of their victuals.
n Nu. 27. 21. Judg. 1. 1. 1 Sam. 22. 10.
1 Sam. 23. 10, 11.
1 Sa. 30. 8.
2 Sa. 2. 1.
2 Sam. 5. 19.
Is. 30. 1, 2.
o 2 Sa. 21. 2.
p ch. 18. 25.
Ezra 2. 25.
q Ps. 15. 4.
r 2 Sa. 21. 1.
Ezek. 17. 13, 15, 18, 19.
Zech. 5. 3, 4.
Mal. 3. 5.
s Deu. 29. 11.
t Gen. 9. 25.
4 not be cut off from you.
u Ex. 23. 32. Deut. 7. 1, 2.
v Ex. 15. 14.
w Gen. 16. 6.
5 gave, or, delivered to be.
1 Chr. 9. 2.
Ezra 9. 20.
x Deu. 12. 5.

CHAP. 10.
a ch 6. 21.
b ch. 8. 22.
c ch. 9. 15.
d Ex. 15. 14, 15, 16.
Deut. 11. 25.
1 cities of the kingdom.
e Gen. 23. 2. Nu. 13. 22.
f ch. 9. 15.
g ch. 9. 2.
h ch. 5. 10.
i ch. 8. 1.
j ch. 11. 6.
Judg. 4. 14.
k ch. 1. 5.
l Judg. 4. 15.
1 Sa. 7. 10, 12.
Ps. 18. 14.
Is. 28. 21.
2 Chr. 14. 12.
m ch. 16. 3. 5.
n ch. 15. 35.
o Ps. 18. 13, 14.
Ps. 77. 17.
Is. 30. 30.
Rev. 16. 21.

hand: as it seemeth good and right unto thee to do unto us, do.

26 And so did he unto them, and delivered them out of the hand of the children of Israel, that they slew them not.

27 And Joshua ⁵ made them that day hewers of wood and drawers of water for the congregation, and for the altar of the LORD, even unto this day, *x* in the place which he should choose.

CHAPTER X.

1 *Five kings war against Gibeon; 6 Joshua rescues it. 10 God fights against them with hailstones. 12 The sun and moon stand still at the word of Joshua. 26 The five kings hanged. 28 Seven more kings conquered. 40 Joshua's return.*

NOW it came to pass, when Adoni-zedek king of Jerusalem had heard how Joshua had taken Ai, and had utterly destroyed it; *a* as he had done to Jericho and her king, so he had done to *b* Ai and her king; and *c* how the inhabitants of Gibeon had made peace with Israel, and were among them;

2 That they *d* feared greatly, because Gibeon *was* a great city, as one of the ¹ royal cities, and because it *was* greater than Ai, and all the men thereof *were* mighty.

3 Wherefore Adoni-zedek king of Jerusalem sent unto Hoham king of *e* Hebron, and unto Piram king of Jarmuth, and unto Japhia king of Lachish, and unto Debir king of Eglon, saying,

4 Come up unto me, and help me, that we may smite Gibeon: *f* for it hath made peace with Joshua and with the children of Israel.

5 Therefore the five kings of the Amorites, the king of Jerusalem, the king of Hebron, the king of Jarmuth, the king of Lachish, the king of Eglon, *g* gathered themselves together, and went up, they and all their hosts, and encamped before Gibeon, and made war against it.

6 ¶ And the men of Gibeon sent unto Joshua *h* to the camp to Gilgal, saying, Slack not thy hand from thy servants; come up to us quickly, and save us, and help us: for all the kings of the Amorites that dwell in the mountains are gathered together against us.

7 So Joshua ascended from Gilgal, he, and *i* all the people of war with him, and all the mighty men of valour.

8 ¶ And the LORD said unto Joshua, *j* Fear them not: for I have delivered them into thine hand; *k* there shall not a man of them stand before thee.

9 Joshua therefore came unto them suddenly, *and* went up from Gilgal all night.

10 And the LORD *l* discomfited them before Israel, and slew them with a great slaughter at Gibeon, and chased them along the way that goeth up *m* to Beth-horon, and smote them to *n* Azekah, and unto Makkedah.

11 And it came to pass, as they fled from before Israel, *and* were in the going down to Beth-horon, *o* that the LORD cast down great stones from heaven upon them unto Azekah, and they died: *they were* more which died with hailstones than *they* whom the children of Israel slew with the sword.

12 ¶ Then spake Joshua to the LORD in the day when the LORD delivered up the Amorites before the children of Israel, and

this trespass, that Israel may be released from the ban, and things be restored to their former state of prosperity. **16-18.** So Joshua rose early, and brought Israel by tribes —*i. e.,* before the tabernacle. The lot being appealed to (Pro. 16. 33.), he proceeded in the enquiry from heads of tribes to heads of families, and from heads of households in succession to one family and to particular persons in that family, until the criminal was found to be Achan, who, on Joshua's admonition, confessed the fact of having secreted for his own use, in the floor of his tent, spoil both in garments and money. How dreadful must have been his feelings when he saw the slow but certain process of discovery (Num. 32. 23.). **19.** Joshua said, My son, give glory to God—a form of adjuration to tell the truth. **20.** A goodly Babylonish garment—lit., a mantle of Shinar. The plain of Shinar was in early times celebrated for its gorgeous robes, which were of brilliant and various colours, generally arranged in figured patterns, probably resembling those of modern Turkey carpets, and the colours were either interwoven in the loom or embroidered with the needle. 200 shekels of silver—equivalent to £22 10s. sterling, according to the old Mosaic shekel, or the half of that sum, reckoning by the common shekel. A wedge of gold—lit., an ingot or bar in the shape of a *tongue*. **22, 23.** Joshua sent messengers, and they ran unto the tent—from impatient eagerness not only to test the truth of the story, but to clear Israel from the imputation of guilt. Having discovered the stolen articles, they laid them out before the Lord, "as a token of their belonging to Him" on account of the ban. **24-26.** Joshua and all Israel with him, took Achan—himself with his children and all his property, cattle as well as moveables, were brought into one of the long broad ravines that open into the Ghor, and after being stoned to death (Num. 15. 30-35,), his corpse, with all belonging to him, was consumed to ashes by fire. "All Israel" were present, not only as spectators, but active agents, as many as possible, in inflicting the punishment—thus testifying their abhorrence of the sacrilege, and their intense solicitude to regain the divine favour. As the divine law expressly forbade the children to be put to death for their fathers' sins (Deut. 24. 16,), the conveyance of Achan's "sons and daughters" to the place of execution might be only as spectators, that they might take warning by the parental fate; or, if they shared his punishment (ch. 22, 20.), they had probably been accomplices in his crime, and, indeed, he could scarcely have dug a hole within his tent without his family being privy to it. They raised over him a great heap of stones—It is customary to raise *cairns* over the graves of criminals or infamous persons in the East still called, The Valley of Achor (trouble) unto this day—So painful an episode would give notoriety to the spot, and it is more than once noticed by the sacred writers of a later age (Is. 65. 10; Hos. 2. 15.).

CHAPTER VIII.

Ver. 1-28. GOD ENCOURAGETH JOSHUA. **1.** The Lord said unto Joshua, Fear not—By the execution of justice on Achan, the Divine wrath was averted, the Israelites were re-assured, defeat was succeeded by victory; and thus the case of Ai affords a striking example of God's disciplinary government, in which chastisements for sin are often made, to pave the way for a bestowment of those temporal benefits, which, on account of sin, have been withdrawn, or withheld for a time. Joshua, who had been greatly dispirited, was encouraged by a special communication promising him (see ch. 1. 6; Deu. 31. 6-8.) success in the next attempt, which, however, was to be conducted on different principles. take all the people of war with thee, and arise, go up to Ai—The number of fighting men amounted to 600,000, and the whole force was ordered on this occasion, partly because the spies, in their self-confidence, had said that a few were sufficient to attack the place (ch. 7. 3.), partly to dispel any misgivings which the memory of the late disaster might have created, and partly that the circumstance of the first spoil obtained in Canaan being shared amongst all, might operate both as a reward for obedience in refraining from the booty of Jericho, and as an incentive to future exertions. (Deu. 6. 10.) The rest of the people, including the women and children, remained in the camp at Gilgal. Being in the plains of Jericho, it was an ascent to Ai, which was on a hill. I have given into thy hand .... lay an ambush for the city—God assured him of its capture, but allowed him to follow his own tactics in obtaining the possession. **3-28.** So Joshua ... chose out thirty thousand men of valour—Joshua despatched 30,000 men under covert of night, to station themselves at the place appointed for the ambuscade. Out of this number a detachment of 5000 were sent forward to conceal themselves in the immediate precincts of the town, in order to seize the first opportunity of throwing themselves into it. **4.** behind the city—is rendered (v. 9,) "on the west of Ai." between Beth-el and Ai—Beth-el, though lying quite near, in the direction of west by north, cannot be seen from Tell-el-hajar; two rocky heights rise between both places, in the wady El-Murogede, just as the laying of an amb sh to the west of Ai would require. [VANDE VELDE, ROB.] **10.** Joshua numbered the people—*i.e.*, the detachment of liers-in-wait; he did this, to be furnished with clear evidence afterwards, that the work had been done without any loss of men, whereby the people's confidence in God would be strengthened, and encouragement given them to prosecute the war of invasion with vigour. he and the elders of Israel—the chief magistrates and rulers, whose presence and official authority were necessary to ensure that the cattle and spoil of the city might be equally divided betwixt the combatants and the rest of the people (Nu. 31. 27.)—a military rule in Israel, that would have been very liable to be infringed, if an excited soldiery, eager for booty, had been left to their own will. **11-14.** There was a valley (*lit., the* valley,) between them and Ai. Joshua went that night into the midst of the valley—The deep and steep-sided glen to the north of Tell-el-hajar, into which one looks down from the Tell, fully agrees with this account. [VANDE VELDE.] Joshua himself took up his position on the north side of "the ravine"—the deep chasm of the wady El-Murogede, "*that* night"—means, while it was dark, probably after midnight, or very early in the morning. (Jo. 20. 1.) The king

he said in the sight of Israel, ^{p} Sun, ^{2} stand thou still upon Gibeon; and thou, Moon, in the valley of ^{q} Ajalon!

13 And the sun stood still, and the moon stayed, until the people had avenged themselves upon their enemies. ^{r} *Is* not this written in the book of ^{3} Jasher? So the sun stood still in the midst of heaven, and hasted not to go down about a whole day.

14 And there was ^{s} no day like that before it or after it, that the LORD hearkened unto the voice of a man: for ^{t} the LORD fought for Israel.

15 ¶ And Joshua returned, and all Israel with him, unto the camp to Gilgal.

16 But these five kings fled, and hid themselves in a cave at Makkedah.

17 And it was told Joshua, saying, The five kings are found hid in a cave at Makkedah.

18 And Joshua said, Roll great stones upon the mouth of the cave, and set men by it for to keep them:

19 And stay ye not, *but* pursue after your enemies, and ^{4} smite the hindmost of them; suffer them not to enter into their cities: for the LORD your God hath delivered them into your hand.

20 And it came to pass, when Joshua and the children of Israel had made an end of slaying them with a very great slaughter, till they were consumed, that the rest *which* remained of them entered into fenced cities.

21 And all the people returned to the camp to Joshua at Makkedah in peace: ^{u} none moved his tongue against any of the children of Israel.

22 Then said Joshua, Open the mouth of the cave, and bring out those five kings unto me out of the cave.

23 And they did so, and brought forth those five kings unto him out of the cave, the king of Jerusalem, the king of Hebron, the king of Jarmuth, the king of Lachish, *and* the king of Eglon.

24 And it came to pass, when they brought out those kings unto Joshua, that Joshua called for all the men of Israel, and said unto the captains of the men of war which went with him, Come near, ^{v} put your feet upon the necks of these kings. And they came near, and put their feet upon the necks of them.

25 And Joshua said unto them, ^{w} Fear not, nor be dismayed; be strong, and of good courage: for ^{x} thus shall the LORD do to all your enemies against whom ye fight.

26 And afterward Joshua smote them, and slew them, and hanged them on five trees: and they ^{y} were hanging upon the trees until the evening.

27 And it came to pass at the time of the going down of the sun, *that* Joshua commanded, and they ^{z} took them down off the trees, and cast them into the cave wherein they had been hid, and laid great stones in the cave's mouth, *which remain* until this very day.

28 ¶ And that day Joshua took Makkedah, and smote it with the edge of the sword, and the king thereof he utterly destroyed, and all the souls that *were* therein; he let none remain: and he did to the king of Makkedah ^{d} as he did unto the king of Jericho.

B. C. 1451.

CHAP. 10.
p Is. 28. 21.
Hab. 3. 11.
2 be silent.
q Judg. 12. 12.
r 2 Sam. 1. 18.
3 Or, the upright?
s Is. 38. 8.
t Deu. 1. 30.
4 cut off the tail.
u Ex. 11. 7.
v Psalm 107. 40.
Ps. 110. 5.
Psalm 149. 8, 9.
Is. 26. 5, 6.
Mal. 4. 3.
w Deut. 31. 6, 8.
ch. 1. 9.
x Deu. 3. 21.
Deu. 7. 19.
y ch 8. 29.
Psalm 149. 7-9.
z Deut. 21. 23.
ch. 8. 29.
a ch. 6. 21.
b ch. 15. 42.
ch. 21. 13.
2 Kin. 8. 22.
2 Ki. 19. 8.
c 2 Kin. 14. 19.
Micah 1. 13.
d ch. 16. 3, 10.
Judges 1. 29.
1 Kings 9. 16, 17.
1 Chr.20.4.
5 pulled down.
Job 19. 10.
2 Cor. 4. 9.
e Nu. 13. 22.
ch. 14. 13.
ch. 15. 13.
Judg. 1. 10.
2 Sam. 5. 1, 4.
f ch. 15. 15.
g ch. 15. 21-63.
h Gen. 20. 16, 17.
i Num. 13. 17, 26.
Nu. 32. 8.
j Gen. 10. 19.
Deut. 2. 23.
Judg. 16. 1.
Amos 1. 6.
Zeph. 2. 4.
Zech. 9. 5.
Acts 8. 26.
k ch. 11. 16.
l Ps. 44. 2.
Ps. 80. 8.
Is. 43. 4.

CHAP. 11.
a Judg. 4. 2.
Ps. 2. 1, 2.
Ps.83.1-18.
b ch. 10. 3.
ch. 19. 15.

29 Then Joshua passed from Makkedah, and all Israel with him, unto ^{b} Libnah, and fought against Libnah:

30 And the LORD delivered it also, and the king thereof, into the hand of Israel; and he smote it with the edge of the sword, and all the souls that *were* therein: he let none remain in it; but did unto the king thereof as he did unto the king of Jericho.

31 ¶ And Joshua passed from Libnah, and all Israel with him, unto ^{c} Lachish, and encamped against it, and fought against it:

32 And the LORD delivered Lachish into the hand of Israel, which took it on the second day, and smote it with the edge of the sword, and all the souls that *were* therein, according to all that he had done to Libnah.

33 ¶ Then Horam king of ^{d} Gezer came up to help Lachish; and Joshua smote him and his people, until he had left him none remaining.

34 ¶ And from Lachish Joshua passed unto Eglon, and all Israel with him; and they encamped against it, and fought against it:

35 And they took it on that day, and smote it with the edge of the sword; and all the souls that *were* therein he utterly ^{5} destroyed that day, according to all that he had done to Lachish.

36 And Joshua went up from Eglon, and all Israel with him, unto ^{e} Hebron; and they fought against it:

37 And they took it, and smote it with the edge of the sword, and the king thereof, and all the cities thereof, and all the souls that *were* therein; he left none remaining, according to all that he had done to Eglon, but destroyed it utterly, and all the souls that *were* therein.

38 ¶ And Joshua returned, and all Israel with him, to ^{f} Debir, and fought against it:

39 And he took it, and the king thereof, and all the cities thereof; and they smote them with the edge of the sword, and utterly destroyed all the souls that *were* therein; he left none remaining: as he had done to Hebron, so he did to Debir, and to the king thereof; as he had done also to Libnah, and to her king.

40 ¶ So Joshua smote ^{g} all the country of the hills, and of the south, and of the vale, and of the springs, and all their kings: he left none remaining, but utterly destroyed all that breathed, as the LORD God of Israel ^{h} commanded.

41 And Joshua smote them from ^{i} Kadeshbarnea even unto ^{j} Gaza, ^{k} and all the country of Goshen, even unto Gibeon.

42 And ^{l} all these kings and their land did Joshua take at one time, because the LORD God of Israel fought for Israel.

43 And Joshua returned, and all Israel with him, unto the camp to Gilgal.

CHAPTER XI.
1 *Divers kings overcome at the waters of Merom.* 10 *Hazor is taken and burnt.* 21 *The Anakims cut off.* 23 *The land subdued.*

AND it came to pass, when ^{a} Jabin king of Hazor had heard *those things*, that he sent ^{b} to Jobab king of Madon, and to the king of Shimron, and to the king of Achshaph,

2 And to the kings that *were* on the north of the mountains, and of the plains south

of Ai, in the early dawn, rouses his slumbering subjects, and makes a hasty sally with all his people who were capable of bearing arms, once more to surprise and annihilate them. at a time appointed—either an hour concocted between the king and people of Ai, and those of Beth-el, who were confederates in this enterprise, or perhaps they had fixed on the same time of day, as they had fought successfully against Israel on the former occasion, deeming it a lucky hour (Ju. 20. 38.) but he wist not that there were liers in ambush. It is evident that this king and his subjects were little experienced in war, otherwise they would have sent out scouts to reconnoitre the neighbourhood; at all events, would not have left their town wholly unprotected and open. Perhaps an ambuscade may have been a war stratagem hitherto unknown in that country, and amongst that people. 15-17. Joshua and all Israel made as if they were beaten before them—the pretended flight in the direction of the wilderness—*i. e.*, south-east, into the Ghor, the desert valley of the Jordan, decoyed all the inhabitants of Ai out of the city, while the people of Beth-el hastened to participate in the expected victory. It is supposed by some, from "the city," and not "cities," being spoken of, that the effective force of Beth-el had been concentrated in Ai, as the two places were closely contiguous, and Ai the larger of the two. See on ch. 12. 16.) It may be remarked, however, that the words, "or Beth-el," are not in the Sept., and are rejected by some eminent scholars, as an interpolation not found in the most ancient MSS. 18-25. Joshua stretched out the spear —the uplifted spear had probably a flag, or streamer on it, to render it the more conspicuous from the height where he stood. At the sight of this understood signal, the ambush nearest the city, informed by their scouts, made a sudden rush, and took possession of the city, telegraphing to their brethren, by raising a smoke from the walls. Upon seeing this, the main body, who had been feigning a flight, turned round at the head of the pass upon their pursuers, while the 25,000 issuing from their ambuscade, fell upon their rear. The Aites surprised, looked back, and found their situation now desperate. 23. the king of Ai they took alive—to be reserved for a more ignominious death, as a greater criminal in God's sight than his subjects. In the mingled attack from before and behind, the whole men of Ai were massacred. all the Israelites returned unto Ai, and smote it with the edge of the sword—the women, children, and old persons left behind, amounting, in all, to 12,000 people. Joshua drew not his hand back— Perhaps, from the long continuance of the posture, it might have been a means appointed by God, to animate the people, and kept up in the same devout spirit as Moses had shewn, in lifting up his hands, until the work of slaughter had been completed—the ban executed. (See on Ex. 17. 11, 12.) 28. Joshua burnt Ai, and made it an heap for ever— "for ever" often signifies a long time. (Gen. 6. 3.) One of the remarkable things, with regard to the Tell we have identified with Ai is its name; the Tell, of the heap of stones; a name which to this day remains. [VANDE VELDE.] 29. THE KING HANGED. 29. The king of Ai he hanged on a tree—*i. e.*, gibbetted. In ancient, and particularly Oriental wars, the chiefs, when taken prisoners, we e usually executed. The Israelites were obliged, by the divine law, to put them to death. The execution of the king of Ai would tend to facilitate the conquest of the land, by striking terror into the other chiefs, and making it appear a judicial process, in which they were inflicting the vengeance of God upon his enemies. take his carcase down, ... and raise thereon a great heap of stones—It was taken down at sunset, according to the Divine command (Deu. 21. 23.), and cast into a pit dug "at the entering of the gate," because that was the most public place. An immense cairn was raised over his grave—an ancient usage, still existing in the East, whereby is marked the sepulchre of persons whose memory is infamous.

30, 31. JOSHUA BUILDS AN ALTAR. 30, 31. Then Joshua built an altar ... in mount Ebal—(See on Deu. 27. 1, 2.). This spot was little short of twenty miles from Ai. The march through a hostile country, and the unmolested performance of the religious ceremonial observed at this mountain, would be greatly facilitated, through the blessing of God, by the disastrous fall of Ai. The solemn duty was to be attended to at the first convenient opportunity after the entrance into Canaan (Deu. 27. 2.; and with this view Joshua seems to have conducted the people through the mountainous region that intervened, though no details of the journey have been recorded. Ebal was on the north, opposite to Gerizim, which was on the south side of the town Sichem. (Nablous.) built an altar of whole stones — according to the instructions given to Moses. (Ex. 20, 25; Deu. 27. 5.) over which no man hath lifted up any iron—*i. e.*, iron tool. The reason of this was, that every altar of the true God ought properly to have been built of earth (Ex. 20. 24.); and if it was constructed of stone, rough unhewn stones were to be employed, that it might retain both the appearance and nature of earth, since every bloody sacrifice was connected with sin and death, by which man, the creature of earth, is brought to earth again. [KEIL.] they offered thereon burnt offerings ... and sacrificed peace offerings—This had been done when the covenant was established (Ex. 24. 5.); and by the observance of these rites (Deu. 27. 6.), the covenant was solemnly renewed —the people were reconciled to God by the burnt offering, whilst, by this feast accompanying the peace, or thank offering, a happy communion with God was enjoyed by all the families in Israel. 32. he wrote there upon the stones a copy of the law—(See on Deu. 27. 2-8.); *i. e.* the blessings and curses of the law. Some think that the stones which contained this inscription, were the stones of the altar; but this verse seems rather to indicate that a number of stone pillars were erected alongside of the altar, and on which, after they were plastered, this duplicate of the law was inscribed. 33. all Israel ... stood on this side the ark and on that side—One-half of Israel was ranged on Gerizim, and the other half on Ebal—along the sides and base of each. before the priests and Levites—in full view of them. 34. afterward he read the law— caused the priests or Levites to read it. (Deu. 27. 14.) Persons are often said in Scripture to do that, which they only com-

of Chinneroth, and in the valley, and in the borders of Dor on the west.

3 And to the Canaanite on the east and on the west, and to the Amorite, and the Hittite, and the Perizzite, and the Jebusite in the mountains, and to the Hivite under Hermon in the land of Mizpeh.

4 And they went out, they and all their hosts with them, much people, even as the sand that is upon the sea-shore in multitude, with horses and chariots very many.

5 And when all these kings were met together, they came and pitched together at the waters of Merom, to fight against Israel.

6 ¶ And the LORD said unto Joshua, Be not afraid because of them: for to-morrow, about this time, will I deliver them up all slain before Israel: thou shalt hough their horses, and burn their chariots with fire.

7 So Joshua came, and all the people of war with him, against them by the waters of Merom suddenly; and they fell upon them.

8 And the LORD delivered them into the hand of Israel, who smote them, and chased them unto great Zidon, and unto Misrephoth-maim, and unto the valley of Mizpeh eastward; and they smote them, until they left them none remaining.

9 And Joshua did unto them as the LORD bade him: he houghed their horses, and burnt their chariots with fire.

10 ¶ And Joshua at that time turned back, and took Hazor, and smote the king thereof with the sword: for Hazor beforetime was the head of all those kingdoms.

11 And they smote all the souls that were therein with the edge of the sword, utterly destroying them: there was not any left to breathe: and he burnt Hazor with fire.

12 And all the cities of those kings, and all the kings of them, did Joshua take, and smote them with the edge of the sword, and he utterly destroyed them, as Moses the servant of the LORD commanded.

13 But as for the cities that stood still in their strength, Israel burned none of them, save Hazor only; that did Joshua burn.

14 And all the spoil of these cities, and the cattle, the children of Israel took for a prey unto themselves; but every man they smote with the edge of the sword, until they had destroyed them, neither left they any to breathe.

15 As the LORD commanded Moses his servant, so did Moses command Joshua, and so did Joshua; he left nothing undone of all that the LORD commanded Moses.

16 So Joshua took all that land, the hills, and all the south country, and all the land of Goshen, and the valley, and the plain, and the mountain of Israel, and the valley of the same;

17 Even from the mount Halak, that goeth up to Seir, even unto Baal-gad in the valley of Lebanon, under mount Hermon: and all their kings he took, and smote them, and slew them.

18 Joshua made war a long time with all those kings.

19 There was not a city that made peace with the children of Israel, save the Hivites, the inhabitants of Gibeon: all other they took in battle.

20 For it was of the LORD to harden their hearts, that they should come against Israel in battle, that he might destroy them utterly, and that they might have no favour, but that he might destroy them, as the LORD commanded Moses.

21 ¶ And at that time came Joshua, and cut off the Anakims from the mountains, from Hebron, from Debir, from Anab, and from all the mountains of Judah, and from all the mountains of Israel: Joshua destroyed them utterly with their cities.

22 There was none of the Anakims left in the land of the children of Israel: only in Gaza, in Gath, and in Ashdod, there remained.

23 So Joshua took the whole land, according to all that the LORD said unto Moses; and Joshua gave it for an inheritance unto Israel according to their divisions by their tribes. And the land rested from war.

CHAPTER XII.

1 *The two kings whose countries Moses took and disposed of.* 7 *The one and thirty kings on the west side of Jordan which Joshua smote.*

NOW these are the kings of the land, which the children of Israel smote, and possessed their land on the other side Jordan toward the rising of the sun, from the river Arnon unto mount Hermon, and all the plain on the east:

2 Sihon king of the Amorites, who dwelt in Heshbon, and ruled from Aroer, which is upon the bank of the river Arnon, and from the middle of the river, and from half Gilead, even unto the river Jabbok, which is the border of the children of Ammon;

3 And from the plain to the sea of Chinneroth on the east, and unto the sea of the plain, even the salt sea on the east, the way to Beth-jeshimoth; and from the south, under Ashdoth-pisgah:

4 And the coast of Og king of Bashan, which was of the remnant of the giants, that dwelt at Ashtaroth and at Edrei,

5 And reigned in mount Hermon, and in Salcah, and in all Bashan, unto the border of the Geshurites and the Maachathites, and half Gilead, the border of Sihon king of Heshbon.

6 Them did Moses the servant of the LORD and the children of Israel smite: and Moses the servant of the LORD gave it for a possession unto the Reubenites, and the Gadites, and the half tribe of Manasseh.

7 ¶ And these are the kings of the country which Joshua and the children of Israel smote on this side Jordan on the west, from Baal-gad in the valley of Lebanon even unto the mount Halak, that goeth up to Seir; which Joshua gave unto the tribes of Israel for a possession according to their divisions;

8 In the mountains, and in the valleys, and in the plains, and in the springs, and in the wilderness, and in the south country; the Hittites, the Amorites, and the Canaanites, the Perizzites, the Hivites, and the Jebusites:

9 The king of Jericho, one; the king of Ai, which is beside Beth-el, one;

10 The king of Jerusalem, one; the king of Hebron, one;

11 The king of Jarmuth, one; the king of Lachish, one;

mand to be done. 35. There was not a word ... which Joshua read not—It appears that a much larger portion of the law was read on this occasion, than the brief summary inscribed on the stones; and this must have been the essence of the law as contained in Deuteronomy. (Deu. 4, 44; 6. 9; 27. 8.) It was not written on the stones, but on the plaster. The immediate design of this rehearsal was attained by the performance of the act itself; it only related to posterity, in so far as the record of the event would be handed down in the Book of Joshua, or the documents which form the ground-work of it. [HENG.] Thus faithfully did Joshua execute the instructions given by Moses. How awfully solemn must have been the assemblage and the occasion. The eye and the ear of the people being both addressed, it was calculated to leave an indelible impression; and with spirits elevated by their brilliant victories in the land of promise, memory would often revert to the striking scene on mounts Ebal and Gerizim, and in the vale of Sychar.

CHAPTER IX.

Ver. 1-29. THE KINGS COMBINE AGAINST ISRAEL. 1. all the kings which were on this side—*i.e.*, the western side of Jordan—in the hills, the valleys, and all the coasts of the great sea—This threefold distinction marks out very clearly a large portion of Canaan. The first designates the hill country, which belonged afterwards to the tribes of Judah and Ephraim: the second, all the low country from Carmel to Gaza; and the third, the shores of the Mediterranean, from the Isthmus of Tyre to the plain of Joppa. As for the tribes mentioned, see on ch. 3. 10. heard (thereof) — that is, of the sacking of Jericho and Ai, as well as the rapid advance of the Israelites into the interior of the country. 2. they gathered themselves together to fight, with one accord—although divided by separate interests, and often at war with each other, a sense of common danger prompted them to suspend their mutual animosities, that by their united forces they might prevent the land from falling into the hands of foreign masters.

3-15. THE GIBEONITES OBTAIN A LEAGUE BY CRAFT. 3-15. when the inhabitants of Gibeon heard—this town, as its name imports, was situated on a rocky eminence, about six miles north-west from Jerusalem, where the modern village of El-Jib now stands; it was the capital of the Hivites, and a large important city (ch. 10, 2.). It seems to have formed, in union, with a few other towns in the neighbourhood, a free independent state (v. 17,), and to have enjoyed a republican government (v. 11.). they did work wilily—they acted with dexterous policy, seeking the means of self-preservation, not by force, which, they were convinced, would be unavailing, but by artful diplomacy. took old sacks upon their asses—Travellers in the East transport their luggage on beasts of burden; the poorer sort stow all their necessaries, food, clothes, utensils together, in a woollen or hair-cloth sack, laid across the shoulders of the beast they ride upon. Wine bottles, old, rent, and bound up—Goat-skins, which are better adapted for carrying liquor, of any kind, fresh and good, than either earthenware, which is porus, or metallic vessels, which are soon heated by the sun. These skin bottles are liable to be rent when old and much used; and there are various ways of mending them, by inserting a new piece of leather, or by gathering together the edges of the rent and sewing them in the form of a purse, or by putting in a round flat splinter of wood into the hole. old shoes clouted—Those who have but one ass or mule for themselves and baggage, frequently dismount, and walk—a circumstance which may account for the worn shoes of the pretended travellers. bread dry and mouldy—This must have been that commonly used by travellers—a sort of biscuit made in the form of large rings, about an inch thick, and four or five inches in diameter. Not being so well baked as our biscuits, it becomes hard and mouldy from the moisture left in the dough. It is usually soaked in water previous to being used. 6-14. they went to Joshua unto the camp at Gilgal—Arrived at the Israelitish head-quarters, the strangers obtained an interview with Joshua and the elders, to whom they opened their business. peradventure ye dwell among us—The answer of the Israelites implied that they had no discretion, that their orders were imperative, and that if the strangers belonged to any of the native tribes, the idea of an alliance with them was unlawful, since God had forbidden it, Ex. 23.32; 34.12; Deut. 7. 2. 9. from a very far country . . . because of the name of the Lord thy God—They pretended to be actuated by religious motives in seeking to be allied with his people. But their studied address is worthy of notice in appealing to instances of God's miraculous doings at a distance, while they pass by those done in Canaan, as if the report of these had not yet reached their ears. 14, 15. the men took their victuals—the mouldy appearance of their bread was, after examination, accepted as guaranteeing the truth of the story, and in this precipitate conclusion, the Israelites were guilty of excessive credulity and culpable negligence, in not asking by the high priest's Urim and Thummim the mind of God, before entering into the alliance. It is not clear, however, that had they applied for divine direction they would have been forbidden to spare and connect themselves with any of the Canaanite tribes who renounced idolatry and embraced and worshipped the true God. At least, no fault was found with them for making a covenant with the Gibeonites; while, on the other hand, the violation of it was severely punished (2 Sam. 21. 1; and ch. 11. 19, 20. 16, 17. at the end of three days, they heard that they were neighbours—This information was obtained in their further progress through the country; for as v. 17 should be rendered, "when the children of Israel journeyed they came to their cities." Gibeon was about eighteen or twenty miles from Gilgal. *Chephirah*, ch. 18. 26; Ezra, 2. 25; Neh. 7. 29.). Beeroth (2 Sam. 4. 2.), now *El Berich*, about twenty minutes' distance from El Jib (Gibeon.). Kirjath-jearim, "the city of forests," now Kuryet-el-Enab. [ROB]. 18-27. the children of Israel smote them not—The moral character of the Gibeonites' stratagem was bad. The princes of the congregation did not vindicate either the expediency or the lawfulness of the connexion they had formed, but they felt the solemn obligations of their oath; and, although the popular clamour was loud against them, caused either by disappoint-

12 The king of Eglon, one; the king of Gezer, one;
13 The king of Debir, one; the king of Geder, one;
14 The king of Hormah, one; the king of Arad, one;
15 The king of Libnah, one; the king of Adullam, one;
16 The king of Makkedah, one; the king of Beth-el, one;
17 The king of Tappuah, one; *o* the king of Hepher, one;
18 The king of Aphek, one; the king of ³ Lasharon, one;
19 The king of Madon, one; the king of Hazor, one;
20 The king of *p* Shimron-meron, one; the king of Achshaph, one;
21 The king of Taanach, one; the king of Megiddo, one;
22 The *q* king of Kedesh, one; the king of Jokneam of Carmel, one;
23 The king of Dor in the coast of Dor, one; the king of *r* the nations of Gilgal, one;
24 The king of Tirzah, one: all the kings thirty and one.

CHAPTER XIII.

2 Bounds of the land not yet conquered. 15 The two tribes and half, and tribe of Levi, excepted. 22 Balaam slain.

NOW Joshua *a* was old *and* stricken in years; and the LORD said unto him, Thou art old *and* stricken in years, and there remaineth yet very much land ¹ to be possessed.
2 This *b* is the land that yet remaineth: all *c* the borders of the Philistines, and all *d* Geshuri,
3 From *e* Sihor, which *is* before Egypt, even unto the borders of Ekron northward, *which* is counted to the Canaanite: *f* five lords of the Philistines; the Gazathites, and the Ashdothites, the Eshkalonites, the Gittites, and the Ekronites; also *g* the Avites:
4 From the south, all the land of the Canaanites, and ² Mearah that *is* beside the Sidonians, *h* unto Aphek, to the borders of the *i* Amorites:
5 And the land of *j* the Giblites, and all Lebanon, toward the sun-rising, *k* from Baal-gad under mount Hermon unto the entering into Hamath:
6 All the inhabitants of the hill country from Lebanon unto *l* Misrephoth-maim, and all the Sidonians, them *m* will I drive out from before the children of Israel: only divide *n* thou it by lot unto the Israelites for an inheritance, as I have commanded thee.
7 Now therefore divide this land for an inheritance unto the nine tribes, and the half tribe of Manasseh,
8 With whom the Reubenites and the Gadites have received their inheritance, which *o* Moses gave them, beyond Jordan eastward, *even* as Moses the servant of the LORD gave them;
9 From Aroer, that *is* upon the bank of the river Arnon, and the city that *is* in the midst of the river, *p* and all the plain of Medeba unto Dibon;
10 And all the cities of Sihon king of the Amorites, which reigned in Heshbon, unto the border of the children of Ammon;
11 And *q* Gilead, and the border of the Geshurites and Maachathites, and all mount Hermon, and all Bashan unto Salcah;
12 All the kingdom of Og in Bashan, which reigned in Ashtaroth and in Edrei, who remained of *r* the remnant of the giants: *s* for these did Moses smite, and cast them out.
13 Nevertheless the children of Israel expelled not the Geshurites, nor the Maachathites; but the Geshurites and the Maachathites dwell among the Israelites until this day.
14 Only *t* unto the tribe of Levi he gave none inheritance; the sacrifices of the LORD God of Israel made by fire *are* their inheritance, as he said unto them.
15 ¶ And Moses gave unto the tribe of the children of Reuben *inheritance* according to their families.
16 And their coast was *u* from Aroer, that *is* on the bank of the river Arnon, *v* and the city that *is* in the midst of the river, and all the plain by Medeba;
17 Heshbon, and all her cities that *are* in the plain; Dibon, and ³ Bamoth-baal, and Beth-baal-meon,
18 And *w* Jahaza, and Kedemoth, and Mephaath,
19 And *x* Kirjathaim, and Sibmah, and Zareth-shahar in the mount of the valley,
20 And Beth-peor, and *y* Ashdoth-pisgah, and Beth-jeshimoth,
21 And *z* all the cities of the plain, and all the kingdom of Sihon king of the Amorites, which reigned in Heshbon, *a* whom Moses smote *a* with the princes of Midian, Evi, and Rekem, and Zur, and Hur, and Reba, *which were* dukes of Sihon, dwelling in the country.
22 ¶ Balaam *b* also the son of Beor, the *c* soothsayer, did the children of Israel slay with the sword among them that were slain by them.
23 And the border of the children of Reuben was Jordan, and the border *thereof*. This *was* the inheritance of the children of Reuben after their families, the cities and the villages thereof.
24 ¶ And Moses gave *inheritance* unto the tribe of Gad, *even* unto the children of Gad according to their families.
25 And *c* their coast was Jazer, and all the cities of Gilead, *d* and half the land of the children of Ammon, unto Aroer that *is* before *e* Rabbah;
26 And from Heshbon unto Ramath-mizpeh, and Betonim; and from Mahanaim unto the border of Debir;
27 And in the valley, Beth-aram, and Beth-nimrah, *f* and Succoth, and Zaphon, the rest of the kingdom of Sihon king of Heshbon, Jordan and *his* border, *even* unto the edge *g* of the sea of Chinnereth on the other side Jordan eastward.
28 This *is* the inheritance of the children of Gad after their families, the cities, and their villages.
29 ¶ And Moses gave *inheritance* unto the half tribe of Manasseh: and *this* was the *possession* of the half tribe of the children of Manasseh by their families.
30 And their coast was from Mahanaim, all Bashan, all the kingdom of Og king of Bashan, and *h* all the towns of Jair, which *are* in Bashan, threescore cities:
31 And half Gilead, and *i* Ashtaroth, and Edrei, cities of the kingdom of Og in

ment at losing the spoils of Gibeon, or by displeasure at the apparent breach of the divine commandment, they determined to adhere to their pledge; "because they had sworn by the Lord God of Israel." The Israelitish princes acted conscientiously; they felt themselves bound by their solemn promise, but to prevent the disastrous consequences of their imprudent haste, they resolved to degrade the Gibeonites to a servile condition as a means of preventing their people from being ensnared into idolatry, and thus acted up, as they thought, to the true spirit and end of the law. hewers of wood and drawers of water—The menials who performed the lowest offices and drudgery in the sanctuary; whence they were called Nethinims (1 Chr. 9. 2; Ezra, 2. 43; 8. 20.); *i. e.*, given, appropriated. Their chastisement thus brought them into the possession of great religious privileges. (Ps. 84. 10.)

CHAPTER X.

Ver. 1-5. FIVE KINGS WAR AGAINST GIBEON. 1. Adoni-zedek—"lord of righteousness,"—nearly synonymous with Melchizedec, "king of righteousness." These names were common titles of the Jebusite kings. Jerusalem—The original name, "Salem" (Gen. 14. 18; Ps. 76. 2,) was superseded by that here given, which signifies "a peaceful possession," or, "a vision of peace," in allusion, as some think, to the strikingly symbolic scene (Gen. 22. 14,) represented on the mount, whereon that city was afterwards built. inhabitants of Gibeon . . . were amongst them—*i. e.*, the Israelites—had made an alliance with that people, and acknowledging their supremacy, were living on terms of friendly intercourse with them. 2. they feared greatly—The dread inspired by the rapid conquests of the Israelites, had been immensely increased by the fact of a state so populous and so strong as Gibeon having found it expedient to submit to the power and the terms of the invaders, as one of the royal cities—although itself a republic (ch. 9. 3.), it was large and well fortified, like those places in which the chiefs of the country usually established their residence. 3. wherefore Adoni-zedek sent, saying, Come up unto me, and help me—A combined attack was meditated on Gibeon, with a view not only to punish its people for their desertion of the native cause, but by its overthrow to interpose a barrier to the farther inroads of the Israelites. This confederacy among the mountaineers of Southern Palestine was formed and headed by the king of Jerusalem, because his territory was most exposed to danger, Gibeon being only six miles distant, and because he evidently possessed some degree of pre-eminence over his royal neighbours. 5. the five kings of the Amorites—The settlement of this powerful and warlike tribe lay within the confines of Moab; but having also acquired extensive possessions on the south-west of the Jordan, their name, as the ruling power, seems to have been given to the region generally (2 Sam. 21. 2,), although Hebron was inhabited by Hittites or Hivites (ch. 11. 19, , and Jerusalem by Jebusites (ch. 15. 63.).

6-9. JOSHUA RESCUES IT. 6-8. the men of Gibeon sent unto Joshua—Their appeal was urgent, and their claim to protection irresistible, on the ground, not only of kindness and sympathy, but of justice. In attacking the Canaanites, Joshua had received from God a general assurance of success (ch. 1. 5. . But the intelligence of so formidable a combination among the native princes seems to have depressed his mind with the anxious and dispiriting idea, that it was a chastisement for the hasty and inconsiderate alliance entered into with the Gibeonites. It was evidently to be a struggle for life and death not only to Gibeon, but to the Israelites. And in this view the divine communication that was made to him was seasonable and animating. He seems to have asked the counsel of God, and received an answer, before setting out on the expedition. 9. Joshua therefore came upon them suddenly—This is explained in the following clause, where he is described as having accomplished, by a forced march of picked men, in one night, a distance of twenty-six miles, which, according to the slow pace of Eastern armies and caravans, had formerly been a three days' journey (ch. 9. 17.).

10, 11. GOD FIGHTS AGAINST THEM WITH HAILSTONES. 10, 11. The Lord discomfited them—*Heb.*, terrified, confounded the Amorite allies, probably by a fearful storm of lightning and thunder. So the word is usually employed (1 Sam. 7. 10; Ps. 18. 13; 144. 6. . and slew them with a great slaughter at Gibeon—This refers to the attack of the Israelites upon the besiegers. It is evident that there had been much hard fighting around the heights of Gibeon, for the day was far spent ere the enemy took to flight. chased them along the way that goeth up to Beth-horon—*i. e.*, the House of Caves, of which there are still traces existing. There were two contiguous villages of that name, upper and nether. Upper Beth-horon was nearest Gibeon—about ten miles distant, and approached by a gradual ascent through a long and precipitous ravine. This was the first stage of the flight. The fugitives had crossed the high ridge of Upper Beth-horon, and were in full flight down the descent to Beth-horon the Nether. The road between the two places is so rocky and rugged, that there is a path made by means of steps cut in the rock. [ROB.] Down this pass Joshua continued his victorious rout. Here it was that the Lord interposed, assisting his people by means of a storm, which, having been probably gathering all day, burst with such irresistible fury, that "they were more which died with hailstones, than they whom the children of Israel slew with the sword." The oriental hail storm is a terrific agent; the hailstones are masses of ice, large as walnuts, and sometimes as two fists; their prodigious size, and the violence with which they fall, make them always very injurious to property, and often fatal to life. The miraculous feature of *this* tempest, which fell on the Amorite army, was the entire preservation of the Israelites from its destructive ravages.

12-15. THE SUN AND MOON STAND STILL AT THE WORD OF JOSHUA. 12-15. Then spake Joshua to the Lord . . . Sun, stand still, and thou, Moon—The inspired author here breaks off the thread of his history of this miraculous victory, to introduce a quotation from an ancient poem, in which the mighty acts of that day were commemorated. The passage, which is parenthetical, contains a poetical description of the victory which was

Bashan, *were pertaining* unto the children of Machir the son of Manasseh, *even* to the one half of the children of Machir by their families.

32 These *are the countries* which Moses did distribute for inheritance in the plains of Moab, on the other side Jordan, by Jericho, eastward.

33 But *j* unto the tribe of Levi Moses gave not *any* inheritance; *k* the LORD God of Israel *was* their inheritance, as he said unto them.

CHAPTER XIV.

1 *The nine tribes and an half to have their inheritance by lot.* 6 *Caleb by privilege requireth and obtaineth Hebron.*

AND these *are the countries* which the children of Israel inherited in the land of Canaan, *a* which Eleazar the priest, and Joshua the son of Nun, and the heads of the fathers of the tribes of the children of Israel, distributed for inheritance to them.

2 By *b* lot *was* their inheritance, as the LORD commanded by the hand of Moses, for the nine tribes, and *for* the half tribe.

3 For *c* Moses had given the inheritance of two tribes and an half tribe on the other side Jordan: but unto the Levites he gave none inheritance among them.

4 For *d* the children of Joseph were two tribes, Manasseh and Ephraim: therefore they gave no part unto the Levites in the land, save cities to dwell *in*, with their suburbs for their cattle and for their substance.

5 As *e* the LORD commanded Moses, so the children of Israel did, and they divided the land.

6 ¶ Then the children of Judah came unto Joshua in Gilgal: and Caleb the son of Jephunneh the *f* Kenezite said unto him, Thou knowest *g* the thing that the LORD said unto Moses the man of God concerning me and thee *h* in Kadesh-barnea.

7 Forty years old *was* I when Moses the servant of the LORD sent me from Kadesh-barnea to espy out the land; and I brought him word again as *it was* in mine heart.

8 Nevertheless my brethren that went up with me made the heart of the people melt: but I wholly *i* followed the LORD my God.

9 And Moses sware on that day, saying, Surely *j* the land *k* whereon thy feet have trodden shall be thine inheritance, and thy children's for ever, because thou hast wholly followed the LORD my God.

10 And now, behold, the LORD hath kept me alive, *l* as he said, these forty and five years, even since the LORD spake this word unto Moses, while *the children of* Israel I wandered in the wilderness: and now, lo, I am this day fourscore and five years old.

11 As *m* yet I am as strong this day as I *was* in the day that Moses sent me: as my strength *was* then, even so is my strength now, for war, both *n* to go out, and to come in.

12 Now therefore give me this mountain, whereof the LORD spake in that day; for thou heardest in that day how the Anakims *were* there, and *that* the cities *were* great and fenced: *o* if so be the LORD *will be* with me, then *p* I shall be able to drive them out, as the LORD said.

13 And Joshua *q* blessed him, *r* and gave unto Caleb the son of Jephunneh Hebron for an inheritance.

14 Hebron therefore became the inheritance of Caleb the son of Jephunneh the Kenezite unto this day, because that he wholly followed the LORD God of Israel.

15 And *s* the name of Hebron before *was* Kirjath-arba; *which Arba was* a great man among the Anakims. *t* And the land had rest from war.

CHAPTER XV.

1 *Borders of the lot of Judah.* 13 *Caleb's portion and conquest.* 16 *Othniel, for his valour, hath Achsah to wife.* 21 *Cities of Judah.* 63 *The Jebusites not conquered.*

THIS then was the lot of the tribe of the children of Judah by their families; *a* even to the border of Edom the *b* wilderness of Zin southward *was* the uttermost part of the south coast.

2 And their south border was from the shore of the salt sea, from the ¹ bay that looketh southward:

3 And it went out to the south side to ²Maaleh-acrabbim, and passed along to Zin, and ascended up on the south side unto Kadesh-barnea, and passed along to Hezron, and went up to Adar, and fetched a compass to Karkaa:

4 *From thence* it passed *c* toward Azmon, and went out unto *d* the river of Egypt; and the goings out of that coast were at the sea: this shall be your south coast.

5 And the east border *was* the salt sea, *even* unto the end of Jordan: and *their* border in the north quarter *was* from the bay of the sea at the uttermost part of Jordan:

6 And the border went up to Beth-hogla, and passed along by the north of Beth-arabah; and the border went up *e* to the stone of Bohan the son of Reuben:

7 And the border went up toward Debir from *f* the valley of Achor, and so northward, looking toward Gilgal, that *is* before the going up to Adummim, which *is* on the south side of the river: and the border passed toward the waters of En-shemesh, and the goings out thereof were at ³ En-rogel:

8 And the border went up *g* by the valley of the son of Hinnom unto the south side of the *h* Jebusite; the same *is* Jerusalem: and the border went up to the top of the mountain that *lieth* before the valley of Hinnom westward, which is at the end *i* of the valley of ⁴ the giants northward:

9 And the border was drawn from the top of the hill unto the fountain of the water of Nephtoah, and went out to the cities of mount Ephron; and the border was drawn to *j* Baalah, which is *k* Kirjath-jearim:

10 And the border compassed from Baalah westward unto mount Seir, and passed along unto the side of mount Jearim, which is Chesalon, on the north side, and went down to Beth-shemesh, and passed on to *l* Timnah:

11 And the border went out unto the side of Ekron *m* northward: and the border was drawn to Shicron, and passed along to mount Baalah, and went out unto Jabneel; and the goings out of the border were at the sea.

12 And the west border *was* ⁿ to the great sea, and the coast *thereof*. This *is* the coast of the children of Judah round about according to their families.

13 ¶ And *o* unto Caleb the son of Jephunneh he gave a part among the children of

miraculously gained by the help of God, and forms an extract from "the book of Jasher," *i.e.*, "the upright"—an anthology, or collection of national songs, in honour of renowned and eminently pious heroes. The language of a poem is not to be literally interpreted, and therefore, when the sun and moon are personified, addressed as intelligent beings, and represented as standing still, the explanation is, that the light of the sun and moon was supernaturally prolonged by the same laws of refraction and reflection that ordinarily cause the sun to appear above the horizon, when he is in reality below it. [KEIL. BUSH.] Gibeon (a hill,) was now at the back of the Israelites, and the height would soon have intercepted the rays of the setting sun. The valley of Ajalon (stags,) was before them, and so near, that it was sometimes called "the valley of Gibeon." (Is. 28. 21.) It would seem, from *v.* 14, that the command of Joshua was in reality a prayer to God for the performance of this miracle; and that, although the prayers of eminently good men like Moses often prevailed with God, never was there on any other occasion so astonishing a display of divine power made in behalf of his people, as in answer to the prayer of Joshua. Ver. 15 is the end of the quotation from Jasher; and it is necessary to notice this, as the fact described in it is recorded in due course, and the same words, by the sacred historian. *v.* 43.

16-27. THE FIVE KINGS HANGED. 16-27. these five kings hid themselves in a cave (*Heb.*, the cave,) at Makkedah—The pursuit was continued, without interruption, to Makkedah, at the foot of the western mountains, where Joshua seems to have halted with the main body of his troops, while a detachment was sent forward to scour the country in pursuit of the remaining stragglers, a few of whom succeeded in reaching the neighbouring cities. The last act, probably the next day, was the disposal of the prisoners, among whom the five kings were consigned to the infamous doom of being slain (Deu. 20. 16, 17,), and then their corpses suspended on five trees till the evening. 24. put your feet upon the necks of these kings—not as a barbarous insult, but a symbolical action, expressive of a complete victory (Deu. 33. 29; Ps. 110. 5; Mal. 4, 3.).

28-42. SEVEN MORE KINGS CONQUERED. 28-42. that day Joshua took Makkedah—In this and the following verses is described the rapid succession of victory and extermination which swept the whole of Southern Palestine into the hands of Israel. "All those kings and their land Joshua take *at one time*, because the Lord God of Israel fought for Israel. And Joshua returned, and all Israel with him, to the camp at Gilgal."

CHAPTER XI.

Ver. 1-9. DIVERS KINGS OVERCOME AT THE WATERS OF MEROM. 1-9. And it came to pass, when Jabin ... had heard those things—The scene of the sacred narrative is here shifted to the north of Canaan, where a still more extensive confederacy was formed among the ruling powers, to oppose the further progress of the Israelites. Jabin ("the Intelligent,"), which seems to have been a hereditary title (Ju. 4. 2.), took the lead, from Hazor being the capital of the northern region (*v.* 10.). It was situated on the borders of lake Merom. The other cities mentioned must have been in the vicinity, though their exact position is unknown. 2. the kings on the mountains—the antilibanus district. the plains south of Chinneroth—the northern part of the Arabah, or valley of the Jordan. the valley—the low and level country, including the plain of Sharon. borders of Dor on the west—the hi h-lands of Dor, reaching to the town of Dor, on the Mediterranean coast, below Mount Carmel. 3. the Canaanite on the east and on the west—a particular branch of the Canaanitish population who occupied the western bank of the Jordan as far northward as the sea of Galilee, and also the coasts of the Mediterannean Sea. under Hermon—now Jebel-es-sheikh was the northern boundary of Canaan on the east of the Jordan. land of Mizpeh—now Cole-Syria. 4, 5. they went out as the sand upon the sea-shore in multitude—The chiefs of these several tribes were summoned by Jabin, being all probably tributary to the kingdom of Hazor; and their combined forces, according to Josephus, amounted to 300,000 infantry, 10,000 cavalry, and 20,000 war-chariots. with horses and chariots very many—The war-chariots were probably like those of Egypt, made of wood, but nailed and tipped with iron. These appear for the first time in the Canaanite war, to aid this last determined struggle against the invaders; and "it was the use of these which seems to have fixed the place of rendezvous by the lake Merom (now Huleh,), along whose level shores they could have full play for their force." A host so formidable in numbers, as well as in military equipments, was sure to alarm and dispirit the Israelites. Joshua, therefore, was favoured with a renewal of the divine promise of victory *v.* 6,), and thus encouraged, he, in the full confidence of faith, set out to face the enemy. to-morrow about this time—As it was impossible to have marched from Gilgal to Merom in one day, we must suppose Joshua already moving northward, and within a day's distance of the Canaanite camp, when the Lord gave him this assurance of success. With characteristic energy he made a sudden advance, probably during the night, and "on the morrow fell" upon them like a thunderbolt, when scattered along the rising grounds (Sept.,), before they had time to rally on the plain. In the sudden panic "the Lord delivered them into the hand of Israel, who smote them, and chased them." The rout was complete, some went westward over the mountains, above the gorge of the Leontes, to Sidon and Misrephoth-Maim (glass-smelting houses,), in its neighbourhood, and others eastward to the plain of Mizpeh. they left none remaining—of those whom they overtook. All those who fell into their hands alive were slain. 9. Joshua did as the Lord *v.* 6,) bade him—Houghing the horses is done by cutting the sinews and arteries of their hinder legs, so that they not only become hopelessly lame, but bleed to death. The reasons for this special command were, that the Lord designed to lead the Israelites to trust in Him, not in military resources (Ps. 20. 7,): to shew that in the land of promise there was no use of horses; and, finally, to discourage their travelling, as they were to be an agricultural not a trading people. 11 he

Judah, according to the commandment of the LORD to Joshua, even the city of Arba the father of Anak, which city is Hebron.

14 And Caleb drove thence the three sons of Anak, Sheshai, and Ahiman, and Talmai, the children of Anak.

15 And he went up thence to the inhabitants of Debir: and the name of Debir before was Kirjath-sepher.

16 And Caleb said, He that smiteth Kirjath-sepher, and taketh it, to him will I give Achsah my daughter to wife.

17 And Othniel the son of Kenaz, the brother of Caleb, took it: and he gave him Achsah his daughter to wife.

18 And it came to pass, as she came unto him, that she moved him to ask of her father a field: and she lighted off her ass; and Caleb said unto her, What wouldest thou?

19 Who answered, Give me a blessing; for thou hast given me a south land; give me also springs of water. And he gave her the upper springs, and the nether springs.

20 This is the inheritance of the tribe of the children of Judah according to their families.

21 ¶ And the uttermost cities of the tribe of the children of Judah toward the coast of Edom southward were Kabzeel, and Eder, and Jagur,

22 And Kinah, and Dimonah, and Adadah,

23 And Kedesh, and Hazor, and Ithnan,

24 Ziph, and Telem, and Bealoth,

25 And Hazor, Hadattah, and Kerioth, and Hezron, which is Hazor,

26 Amam, and Shema, and Moladah,

27 And Hazar-gaddah, and Heshmon, and Beth-palet,

28 And Hazar-shual, and Beer-sheba, and Bizjothjah,

29 Baalah, and Iim, and Azem,

30 And Eltolad, and Chesil, and Hormah,

31 And Ziklag, and Madmannah, and Sansannah,

32 And Lebaoth, and Shilhim, and Ain, and Rimmon: all the cities are twenty and nine, with their villages:

33 And in the valley, Eshtaol, and Zoreah, and Ashnah,

34 And Zanoah, and En-gannim, Tappuah, and Enam,

35 Jarmuth, and Adullam, Socoh, and Azekah,

36 And Sharaim, and Adithaim, and Gederah, and Gederothaim; fourteen cities with their villages:

37 Zenan, and Hadashah, and Migdalgad,

38 And Dilean, and Mizpeh, and Joktheel,

39 Lachish, and Bozkath, and Eglon,

40 And Cabbon, and Lahmam, and Kithlish,

41 And Gederoth, Beth-dagon, and Naamah, and Makkedah; sixteen cities with their villages:

42 Libnah, and Ether, and Ashan,

43 And Jiphtah, and Ashnah, and Nezib,

44 And Keilah, and Achzib, and Mareshah; nine cities with their villages:

45 Ekron, with her towns and her villages:

46 From Ekron even unto the sea, all that lay near Ashdod, with their villages:

47 Ashdod with her towns and her villages, Gaza with her towns and her villages, unto the river of Egypt, and the great sea, and the border thereof:

48 And in the mountains, Shamir, and Jattir, and Socoh,

49 And Dannah, and Kirjath-sannah, which is Debir,

50 And Anab, and Eshtemoh, and Anim,

51 And Goshen, and Holon, and Giloh; eleven cities with their villages:

52 Arab, and Dumah, and Eshean,

53 And Janum, and Beth-tappuah, and Aphekah,

54 And Humtah, and Kirjath-arba, which is Hebron, and Zior; nine cities with their villages:

55 Maon, Carmel, and Ziph, and Juttah,

56 And Jezreel, and Jokdeam, and Zanoah,

57 Cain, Gibeah, and Timnah; ten cities with their villages:

58 Halhul, Beth-zur, and Gedor,

59 And Maarath, and Beth-anoth, and Eltekon; six cities with their villages:

60 Kirjath-baal, which is Kirjath-jearim, and Rabbah; two cities with their villages:

61 In the wilderness, Beth-arabah, Middin, and Secacah,

62 And Nibshan, and the city of Salt, and En-gedi; six cities with their villages.

63 ¶ As for the Jebusites, the inhabitants of Jerusalem, the children of Judah could not drive them out: but the Jebusites dwell with the children of Judah at Jerusalem unto this day.

CHAPTER XVI

1 *The general borders of the sons of Joseph.* 5 *The borders of the inheritance of Ephraim.* 10 *The Canaanites not conquered.*

AND the lot of the children of Joseph fell from Jordan by Jericho, unto the water of Jericho on the east, to the wilderness that goeth up from Jericho throughout mount Beth-el,

2 And goeth out from Beth-el to Luz, and passeth along unto the borders of Archi to Ataroth,

3 And goeth down westward to the coast of Japhleti, unto the coast of Beth-horon the nether, and to Gezer: and the goings out thereof are at the sea.

4 So the children of Joseph, Manasseh and Ephraim, took their inheritance.

5 ¶ And the border of the children of Ephraim according to their families was thus: even the border of their inheritance on the east side was Ataroth-adar, unto Beth-horon the upper;

6 And the border went out toward the sea to Michmethah on the north side; and the border went about eastward unto Taanath-shiloh, and passed by it on the east to Janohah;

7 And it went down from Janohah to Ataroth, and to Naarath, and came to Jericho, and went out at Jordan.

8 The border went out from Tappuah westward unto the river Kanah; and the goings out thereof were at the sea. This is the inheritance of the tribe of the children of Ephraim by their families.

9 And the separate cities for the children of Ephraim were among the inheritance of the children of Manasseh, all the cities with their villages.

10 And they drave not out the Canaanites that dwelt in Gezer; but the Canaanites dwell among the Ephraimites unto this day, and serve under tribute.

burnt Hazor with fire—calmly and deliberately, doubtless, according to divine direction. **13. as for the cities that stood still in their strength**—*lit.*, "on their heaps." It was a Phœnician custom to build cities on heights, natural or artificial. [HENG.] **16. So Joshua took all the land**—Here follows a general view of the conquest. The division of the country there into five parts; viz., the hills, the land of Goshen, *i.e.*, a pastoral land near Gibeon (ch. 10. 41,); the valley, the plains, the mountains of Israel, *i.e.*, Carmel, rests upon a diversity of geographical positions, which is characteristic of the region. **17. from the mount Halak** (*Heb.*, the smooth mountain,) **that goeth up to Seir**—an irregular line of white naked hills, about eighty feet high, and seven or eight geographical miles in length, that cross the whole Ghor, eight miles south of the Dead Sea, probably "the ascent of Akrabbim." [ROB.] **unto Baal-gad in the valley of Lebanon**—the city or temple of the God of Destiny, in Baalbec. **23. So Joshua took the whole land**—The battle of the lake of Merom was to the north what the battle of Beth-horon was to the south; more briefly told, but less complete in its consequences; but still the decisive conflict by which the whole northern region of Canaan fell into the hands of Israel. [STANLEY.]

CHAPTER XII.

Ver. 1-6. THE TWO KINGS WHOSE COUNTRIES MOSES TOOK AND DISPOSED OF. **1. Now these are the kings of the land on the other side Jordan**—This chapter contains a recapitulation of the conquests made in the promised land, with the additional mention of some places not formerly noticed in the sacred history. The river Arnon on the south, and Mount Hermon on the north, were the respective boundaries of the land acquired by the Israelites beyond Jordan (see on Num. 21. 21; Deu. 2. 36; 3. 6-16.).

7-24. THE ONE-AND-THIRTY KINGS ON THE WEST SIDE OF JORDAN, WHICH JOSHUA SMOTE. **7. Baal-gad even unto Halak**—see on ch. 11. 17. A list of thirty-one chief towns is here given, and, as the whole land contained a superficial extent of only fifteen miles in length, by fifty in breadth, it is evident that these capital cities belonged to petty and insignificant kingdoms. With a few exceptions, they were not the scenes of any important events recorded in the sacred history, and therefore do not require a particular notice.

CHAPTER XIII.

Ver. 1-33. BOUNDS OF THE LAND NOT YET CONQUERED. **1. Now Joshua was old and stricken in years**—He was probably above a hundred years old; for the conquest and survey of the land occupied about seven years, the partition one; and he died at the age of 110 years (ch. 24. 29.). The distribution, as well as the conquest of the land, was included in the mission of Joshua; and his advanced age supplied a special reason for entering on the immediate discharge of that duty—viz., of allocating Canaan amongst the tribes of Israel, not only the parts already won, but those also which were still to be conquered. **2 6. This is the land that yet remaineth**—*i.e.*, to be acquired. This section forms a parenthesis, in which the historian briefly notices the districts yet unsubdued—viz., first, the whole country of the Philistines—a narrow tract stretching about sixty miles along the Mediterranean coast, and that of the Geshurites to the south of it (1 Sam. 27. 8.). Both included that portion of the country "from Sihor which is before Egypt," a small brook near El-Arish, which on the east was the southern boundary of Canaan, "to Ekron," the most northerly of the five chief lordships or principalities of the Philistines. also how Avites: from (on) the south—The two clauses are thus connected in the Sept., and many other versions. On being driven out (Deu. 2. 23,), they established themselves in the south of Philistia. The second division of the unconquered country comprised all the land and Mearah (the cave) that is beside the Sidonians—a mountainous region of Upper Galilee, remarkable for its caves and fastnesses, eastward unto Aphek (now Afka) in Lebanon, to the borders of the Ammonites—a portion of the north-eastern territory that had belonged to Og. The third district that remained unsubdued was, **5. all the land of the Giblites**—their capital was Gebal or Bylbos (*Gr.*) on the Mediterranean, forty miles north of Sidon. all Lebanon towards the sunrising—*i.e.*, Antilibanus; the eastern ridge, which has its proper termination in Hermon. entering in of Hamath—the valley of Baalbec. **6, 7. all the inhabitants of the hill country from Lebanon unto Misrephoth-maim** —(see on ch. 11. 8.), that is, "all the Sidonians and Phœnicians." **them will I drive out**—The fulfilment of this promise was conditional. In the event of the Israelites proving unfaithful or disobedient, they would not subdue the districts now specified, and, in point of fact, the Israelites never possessed them, though the inhabitants were subjected to the power of David and Solomon. **only divide thou it by lot**—The parenthetic section being closed, the historian here resumes the main subject of this chapter—the order of God to Joshua to make an immediate allotment of the land. The method of distribution by lot was, in all respects, the best that could have been adopted, as it prevented all ground of discontent, as well as charges of arbitrary or partial conduct on the part of the leaders; and its being announced in the life of Moses (Num. 33. 54.), as the system according to which the allocations to each tribe should be made, was intended to lead the people to the acknowledgment of God as the proprietor of the land, and having the entire right to its disposal. Moreover, a solemn appeal to the lot showed it to be the dictate, not of human, but divine wisdom. It was used, however, only in determining the part of the country where a tribe was to be settled—the extent of the settlement was to be decided on a different principle (Num. 26. 54), and what proves the overruling control of God, each tribe received the possession predicted by Jacob (Gen. 49,) and by Moses (Deu. 33.). **8. with whom**—*Heb.* "him." The antecedent is evidently to Manasseh, not, however, the half tribe just mentioned, but the other half; for the historian, led, as it were, by the sound of the word, breaks off to describe the possessions beyond Jordan already assigned to Reuben, Gad, and the half of Manasseh (see on Num. 32; Deu. 3. 8-17.). It may be proper to remark that it was wise to put these boundaries on record, as, in case of any misunderstanding or dispute arising about the exact

CHAPTER XVII.

1 Lot of Manasseh; 7 his coast. 12 Canaanites not driven out. 14 The children of Joseph sue for another lot.

THERE was also a lot for the tribe of Manasseh; for he was the *a* first-born of Joseph: to wit, for *b* Machir, the first-born of Manasseh, the father of Gilead: because he was a man of war, therefore he had *c* Gilead and Bashan.

2 There was also a lot for *d* the rest of the children of Manasseh by their families: for *e* the children of ¹ Abiezer, and for the children of Helek, and for the children of Asriel, and for the children of Shechem, and *f* for the children of Hepher, and for the children of Shemida: these were the male children of Manasseh the son of Joseph by their families.

3 ¶ But *g* Zelophehad, the son of Hepher, the son of Gilead, the son of Machir, the son of Manasseh, had no sons, but daughters: and these are the names of his daughters, Mahlah, and Noah, Hoglah, Milcah, and Tirzah.

4 And they came near before *h* Eleazar the priest, and before Joshua the son of Nun, and before the princes, saying, *i* The LORD commanded Moses to give us an inheritance among our brethren. Therefore, according to the ² commandment of the LORD, he gave them an inheritance among the brethren of their father.

5 And there fell ten portions to Manasseh, besides the land of Gilead and Bashan, which were on the other side Jordan;

6 Because the daughters of Manasseh had an inheritance among his sons: and *j* the rest of Manasseh's sons had the land of Gilead.

7 ¶ And the coast of Manasseh was from Asher to Michmethah, that lieth before Shechem; and the border went along on the right hand unto the inhabitants of En-tappuah.

8 Now Manasseh had the land of ³ Tappuah: but *k* Tappuah on the border of Manasseh belonged to the children of Ephraim:

9 And the coast descended *l* unto the ⁴ river Kanah, southward of the river: these *m* cities of Ephraim are among the cities of Manasseh: the coast of Manasseh also was on the north side of the river, and the outgoings of it were at the sea:

10 Southward it was Ephraim's, and northward it was Manasseh's, and the sea is his border; and they met together in Asher on the north, and in Issachar on the east.

11 And *n* Manasseh had in Issachar and in Asher, *o* Beth-shean and her towns, and Ibleam and her towns, and the inhabitants of Dor and her towns, and the inhabitants of En-dor and her towns, and the inhabitants of Taanach and her towns, and the inhabitants of Megiddo and her towns, even three countries.

12 Yet *p* the children of Manasseh could not drive out the inhabitants of those cities; but the Canaanites would dwell in that land.

13 Yet it came to pass, when the children of Israel were waxen strong, that they put the Canaanites to ⁵ tribute; but *q* did not utterly drive them out.

14 ¶ And *r* the children of Joseph spake unto Joshua, saying, Why hast thou given me but *s* one lot and one portion to inherit, seeing I am *t* a great people, forasmuch as the LORD hath blessed me hitherto?

15 And Joshua answered them, If thou be a great people, then get thee up to the wood country, and cut down for thyself there in the land of the Perizzites and of the ⁶ giants, if mount Ephraim be too narrow for thee.

16 And the children of Joseph said, The hill is not enough for us: and all the Canaanites that dwell in the land of the valley have *u* chariots of iron, both they who are of Beth-shean and her towns, and they who are *v* of the valley of Jezreel.

17 And Joshua spake unto the house of Joseph, even to Ephraim and to Manasseh, saying, Thou art a great people, and hast great power: thou shalt not have one lot only:

18 But the mountain shall be thine; for it is a wood, and thou shalt cut it down: and the outgoings of it shall be thine: for thou shalt drive out the Canaanites, *w* though they have iron chariots, and though they be strong.

CHAPTER XVIII.

1 The tabernacle is set up at Shiloh. 2 The remainder of the land is described, 10 and divided by lot. 11 The lot and border of Benjamin. 21 Their cities.

AND the whole congregation of the children of Israel assembled together *a* at Shiloh, and *b* set up the tabernacle of the congregation ¹ there. And the land was subdued before them.

2 And there remained among the children of Israel seven tribes, which had not yet received their inheritance.

3 And Joshua said unto the children of Israel, *c* How long are ye slack to go to possess the land, which the LORD God of your fathers hath given you?

4 Give out from among you three men for each tribe: and I will send them, and they shall rise and go through the land, and describe it according to the inheritance of them; and they shall come again to me.

5 And they shall divide it into seven parts: Judah *d* shall abide in their coast on the south, and *e* the house of Joseph shall abide in their coasts on the north.

6 Ye shall therefore describe the land into seven parts, and bring the description hither to me, *f* that I may cast lots for you here before the LORD our God.

7 But *g* the Levites have no part among you; for the priesthood of *h* the LORD is their inheritance: *i* and Gad, and Reuben, and half the tribe of Manasseh, have received their inheritance beyond Jordan on the east, which Moses the servant of the LORD gave them.

8 ¶ And the men arose, and went away: and Joshua charged them that went to describe the land, saying, Go and walk through the land, and describe it, and come again to me, that I may here cast lots for you before the LORD in Shiloh.

9 And the men went and passed through the land, and described it by cities into seven parts in a book, and came again to Joshua to the host at Shiloh.

10 And Joshua cast *j* lots for them in Shiloh before the LORD: and there Joshua divided the land unto the children of Israel according to their divisions.

limits of each district or property, an appeal could always be made to this authoritative document, and a full knowledge as well as grateful sense obtained of what they had received from God (Ps. 16. 5, 6.).

CHAPTER XIV.

Ver. 1-5. THE NINE TRIBES AND A-HALF TO HAVE THEIR INHERITANCE BY LOT. 1. These are the countries which the children of Israel inherited in the land of Canaan—This chapter forms the introduction to an account of the allocation of the land west of Jordan, or Canaan proper, to the nine tribes and a-half. It was also made by lot in presence of a select number of superintendants, appointed according to divine directions given to Moses (see on Num. 34. 16-29.). In every thing pertaining to civil government, and even the division of the land, Joshua was the acknowledged chief. But in a matter to be determined by lot, a solemn appeal was made to God, and hence Eleazar, as high priest, is named before Joshua. 4. The children of Joseph were two tribes—As two and a-half tribes were settled on the east of Jordan, and the Levites had no inheritance assigned them in land, there would have been only eight tribes and a-half to provide for. But Ephraim and Manasseh, the two sons of Joseph, had been constituted two tribes (Gen. 48. 5,), and although Levi was excluded, the original number of the tribes of Israel was still preserved. 5. the children of Israel divided the land—*i.e.*, they made the preliminary arrangements for the work. A considerable time was requisite for the survey and measurement.

6-15. CALEB BY PRIVILEGE REQUIRETH AND OBTAINETH HEBRON. 6-11. then the children of Judah came to Joshua in Gilgal; and Caleb said—This incident is recorded here, because it occurred while the preparations were being made for casting the lots, which, it appears, were begun in Gilgal. The claim of Caleb to the mountains of Hebron as his personal and family possessions, was founded on a solemn promise of Moses, forty-five years before (Num. 14. 24; Deu. 1. 36,), to give him that land on account of his fidelity. Being one of the nominees appointed to preside over the division of the country, he might have been charged with using his powers as a commissioner to his own advantage, had he urged his request in private; and therefore he took some of his brethren along with him as witness of the justice and propriety of his conduct. 12. give me this mountain—this highland region. for thou heardest in that day how the Anakims were there—The report of the spies who tried to kindle the flame of sedition and discontent, related chiefly to the people and condition of this mountain district, and hence it was promised as the reward of Caleb's truth, piety, and faithfulness. 13, 14. Joshua blessed him, and gave Hebron—Joshua, who was fully cognizant of the whole circumstances, not only admitted the claim, but in a public and earnest manner prayed for the divine blessing to succour the efforts of Caleb in driving out the idolatrous occupiers. 15. Kirjath-Arba—*i.e.*, the city of Arba—a warrior among the native race remarkable for strength and stature. the land had rest from war—Most of the kings having been slain and the natives dispirited, there was no general or systematic attempts to resist the progress and settlement of the Israelites.

CHAPTER XV.

Ver. 1-12. BORDERS OF THE LOT OF JUDAH. 1. This then was the lot of the tribe of Judah—In what manner the lot was drawn on this occasion the sacred historian does not say; but it is probable that the method adopted was similar to that described in ch. 18. Though the general survey of the country had not been completed, some rough draught or delineation of the first conquered part must have been made, and satisfactory evidence obtained, that it was large enough to furnish three cantons, before all the tribes cast lots for them; and they fell to Judah, Ephraim, and the half-tribe of Manasseh. The lot of Judah came first, in token of the pre-eminence of that tribe over all the others; and its destined superiority thus received the visible sanction of God. The territory assigned to it as a possession, was large and extensive, being bounded on the south by the wilderness of Zin, and the southern extremity of the Salt Sea Num. 34. 3-5,); on the east, by that sea, extending to the point where it receives the waters of the Jordan; on the north, by a line drawn nearly parallel to Jerusalem, across the country, from the northern extremity of the Salt Sea to the southern limits of the Philistine territory, and to the Mediterannean; and on the west this sea was its boundary, as far as Sihor (Wady El-Arish,). 2. the bay—*Heb.*, the "tongue." It pushes its waters out in this form to a great distance. [ROB.] 3. Maaleh-acrabbim—*Heb.*, the ascent of Scorpions; a pass in the "bald mountain" (see on ch. 11. 17,), probably much infested by these venemous reptiles. 5. the end—*i.e.*, the mouth of the Jordan. 6. Beth-hogla—now *Ain* Hadjla, a fine spring of clear and sweet water, at the northern extremity of the Dead Sea, about two miles from the Jordan. [ROB.] Beth-arabah—the house, or place of solitude, in the desert of Judah (v. 61.). stone of Bohan the son of Reuben—the sepulchral monument of a Reubenite leader, who had been distinguished for his bravery, and had fallen in the Canaanite war. 7. Achor—(see on ch. 7. 26.). Adummim—a rising ground in the wilderness of Jericho, on the south of the little brook that flowed near Jericho (ch. 16. 1.). En-shemesh—the fountain of the sun; "either the present well of the apostle, below Bethany, on the road to Jericho, or the fountain near to St. Saba." [ROB.] Enrogel—the fuller's fountain, on the south-east of Jerusalem, below the spot where the valley of Jehoshaphat and Hinnom unite.

13-15. CALEB'S PORTION AND CONQUEST. 13. unto Caleb he gave a part—(see on ch. 14. 6-15.). 14. Drove out from thence the three sons of Anak—rather three chiefs of the Anakim race. This exploit is recorded to the honour of Caleb, as the success of it was the reward of his trust in God. 15. Debir—oracle. Its former name, Kirjath-sepher, signifies "city of the book," being, probably, a place where public registers were kept.

16-20. OTHNIEL, FOR HIS VALOUR, HATH ACHSAH TO WIFE. 16-20. He that smiteth—This offer was made as an incentive to youthful bravery (see on 1 Sam. 17, 25,); and the prize was won by Othniel, Caleb's *younger* brother (Ju. 1. 13; 3. 9.). This was the occasion of drawing out the latent energies of

11 ¶ And the lot of the tribe of the children of Benjamin came up according to their families: and the coast of their lot came forth between the children of Judah and the children of Joseph.

12 And *k* their border on the north side was from Jordan; and the border went up to the side of Jericho on the north side, and went up through the mountains westward; and the goings out thereof were at the wilderness of Beth-aven.

13 And the border went over from thence toward Luz, to the side of Luz, *l* which *is* Beth-el, southward; and the border descended to Ataroth-adar, near the hill that *lieth* on the south side *m* of the nether Beth-horon.

14 And the border was drawn *thence*, and compassed the corner of ² the sea southward, from the hill that *lieth* before Beth-horon southward; and the goings out thereof were at *n* Kirjath-baal, which *is* Kirjath-jearim, a city of the children of Judah: this *was* the west quarter.

15 And the south quarter *was* from the end of Kirjath-jearim, and the border went out on the west, and went out to *o* the well of waters of Nephtoah;

16 And the border came down to the end of the mountain that *lieth* before *p* the valley of the son of Hinnom, *and* which *is* in the valley of ³ the giants on the north, and descended to the valley of Hinnom, to the side of Jebusi on the south, and descended to ⁴ En-rogel,

17 And was drawn from the north, and went forth to En-shemesh, and went forth toward Geliloth, which *is* over against the going up of Adummim, and descended to the *q* stone of Bohan the son of Reuben,

18 And passed along toward the side over against ⁵ Arabah northward, and went down unto Arabah;

19 And the border passed along to the side of Beth-hoglah northward: and the outgoings of the border were at the north ⁶ bay of the salt sea at the south end of Jordan: this *was* the south coast.

20 And Jordan was the border of it on the east side. This *was* the inheritance of the children of Benjamin, by the coasts thereof round about, according to their families.

21 Now the cities of the tribe of the children of Benjamin according to their families were *r* Jericho, and *s* Beth-hoglah, and the valley of Keziz,

22 And Beth-arabah, and Zemaraim, and Beth-el,

23 And Avim, and Parah, and Ophrah,

24 And Chephar-haammonai, and Ophni, and *t* Gaba; twelve cities with their villages:

25 Gibeon, and Ramah, and Beeroth,

26 And Mizpeh, and Chephirah, and Mozah,

27 And Rekem, and Irpeel, and Taralah,

28 And *u* Zelah, Eleph, and *v* Jebusi, which *is* Jerusalem, Gibeath, *and* Kirjath; fourteen cities with their villages. This *is* the inheritance of the children of Benjamin *w* according to their families.

CHAPTER XIX.

1 *The lot of Simeon*, 10 *of Zebulun*, 17 *of Issachar*, 24 *of Asher*, 32 *of Naphtali*, 40 *and of Dan.* 49 *The children of Israel give an inheritance to Joshua.*

AND the second lot came forth to Simeon, *even* for the tribe of the children of Simeon according to their families: and their inheritance was *a* within the inheritance of the children of Judah.

2 And *b* they had in their inheritance *c* Beer-sheba, and Sheba, and *d* Moladah,

3 And Hazar-shual, and Balah, and Azem,

4 And *e* Eltolad, and Bethul, and Hormah,

5 And Ziklag, and Beth-marcaboth, and Hazar-susah,

6 And Beth-lebaoth, and Sharuhen; thirteen cities and their villages:

7 Ain, Remmon, and Ether, and Ashan; four cities and their villages:

8 And all the villages that *were* round about these cities to Baalath-beer, Ramath of the south. This *is* the inheritance of the tribe of the children of Simeon according to their families.

9 Out of the portion of the children of Judah *was* the inheritance of the children of Simeon: for the part of the children of Judah was too much for them: therefore the children of Simeon had their inheritance within the inheritance of them.

10 ¶ And the third lot came up for the children of Zebulun according to their families: and the border of their inheritance was unto Sarid:

11 And their border went up toward *f* the sea, and Maralah, and reached to Dabbasheth, and reached to the river that *is* before *g* Jokneam;

12 And turned from Sarid eastward toward the sun-rising unto the border of Chisloth-tabor, and then goeth out to Daberath, and goeth up to Japhia,

13 And from thence passeth on along on the east to Gittah-hepher, to Ittah-kazin, and goeth out to Remmon-méthoar, to Neah;

14 And the border compasseth it on the north side to Hannathon: and the outgoings thereof are in the valley of Jiphthah-el:

15 And *h* Kattath, and Nahallal, and *i* Shimron, and Idalah, and Beth-lehem: twelve cities with their villages.

16 This *is j* the inheritance of the children of Zebulun according to their families, these cities with their villages.

17 ¶ *And* the fourth lot came out to Issachar, for the children of Issachar according to their families.

18 And their border was toward *k* Jezreel, and Chesulloth, and *l* Shunem,

19 And Haphraim, and Shihon, and Anaharath,

20 And Rabbith, and Kishion, and Abez,

21 And *m* Remeth, and En-gannim, and En-haddah, and Beth-pazzez;

22 And the coast reacheth to *n* Tabor, and Shahazimah, and Beth-shemesh; and the outgoings of their border were at Jordan; sixteen cities with their villages.

23 This *is* the inheritance of the tribe of the children of Issachar according to their families, the cities and their villages.

24 ¶ And the fifth lot came out for the tribe of the children of Asher according to their families.

25 And their border was *o* Helkath, and Hali, and Beten, and Achshaph,

26 And Alammelech, and Amad, and Misheal; and reacheth to *p* Carmel westward, and to Shihor-libnath;

27 And turneth toward the sun-rising to Beth-dagon, and reacheth to Zebulun, and to the valley of Jiphthah-el toward the north side of Beth-emek, and Neiel, and goeth out to *q* Cabul on the left hand,

him who was destined to be the first judge in Israel. 18. as she came unto him—*i.e.*, when about to remove from her father's to her husband's house. She suddenly alighted from her travelling equipage—a mark of respect to her father, and a sign of making some request. She had urged Othniel to broach the matter, but he not wishing to do what appeared like evincing a grasping disposition, she resolved herself to speak out, and taking the advantage of the parting scene, when a parent's heart was likely to be tender, begged that, as her marriage portion consisted of a field which, having a southern exposure, was comparatively an arid and barren waste, he would add the adjoining one, which abounded in excellent springs. The request being reasonable, was granted; and the story conveys this important lesson in religion, that if earthly parents are ready to bestow on their children that which is good, much more will our heavenly Father give every necessary blessing to them who ask him.

21-63. CITIES OF JUDAH. 21-33. the uttermost cities—There is given a list of cities within the tribal territory of Judah, arranged in four divisons, corresponding to the districts of which it consisted—the cities in the southern part (21-32,)—those in the low lands (33-47,), and those in the high lands (48-60,)—those in the desert (61, 62.). The best idea of the relative situation of these cities will be got from looking at the map.

CHAPTER XVI.

Ver. 1-4. THE GENERAL BORDERS OF THE SONS OF JOSEPH. 1. The lot of the children of Joseph fell—*Heb.*, went forth, referring either to the lot as drawn out of the urn, or to the tract of land thereby assigned. The first four verses describe the territory allotted to the family of Joseph, in the rich domains of central Palestine. It was drawn in one lot, that the brethren might be contiguously situated; but it was afterwards divided. The southern boundary only is described here, that on the north being irregular and less defined (ch. 17. 10, 11,), is not mentioned. mount Beth-el—the ridge south of Beth-el. water of Jericho (2 Ki. 2. 19,)—at the point of its junction with the Jordan. Having described the position of Joseph's family generally, the historian proceeds to define the territory; first, of Ephraim.

5-9. THE BORDERS OF THE INHERITANCE OF EPHRAIM. 5-9. the border of their inheritance was Ataroth-adar—Ataroth-adar (now Atara), four miles south of Jetta [ROB.], is fixed on as a centre, through which a line is drawn from upper Beth-horon to Michmethah, shewing the western limit of their actual possessions. The tract beyond that line to the sea was still unconquered. 6, 7. Michmethah on the north side—The northern boundary is traced from this point eastward to the Jordan. 8. from Tappuah westward unto the river Kanah—it is retraced from east to west, to describe the prospective and intended boundary, which was to reach to the sea. Kanah (reedy,) flows into the Mediteranean. 9. separate cities were among the inheritance of Manasseh—(ch. 17. 9.), because it was found that the tract allotted to Ephraim was too small in proportion to its population and power. 10. Drove not out the Canaanites . . . serve under tribute—This is the first mention of the fatal policy of the Israelites, in ne-glecting the divine command (Deu. 20. 16,) to exterminate the idolators.

CHAPTER XVII.

Ver. 1-6. LOT OF MANASSEH. 1. There was also a lot for the tribe of Manasseh—Ephraim was mentioned, as the more numerous and powerful branch of the family of Joseph (Gen. 48. 19, 20,); but Manasseh still retained the right of primogeniture, and had a separate inheritance assigned. Machir—his descendants. the father of Gilead—though he had a son of that name (Nu. 26. 29; 27. 1,); yet, as is evident from the use of the *Heb.* article, reference is made, not to the person, but the province of Gilead. Father here means lord or possessor of Gilead; and this view is confirmed by the fact, that it was not Machir, but his descendants, who subdued Gilead and Bashan (Nu. 32. 41; Deu. 3. 13-15,). These Machirites had their portion on the east side of Jordan. The western portion of land, allotted to the tribe of Manasseh, was divided into ten portions, because the male descendants who had sons, consisted of five families, to which, consequently, five shares were given; and the sixth family, viz., the posterity of Hepher, being all females, the five daughters of Zelophehad were, on application to the valuators, endowed each with an inheritance in land (see on Nu. 27. 1.).

7-11. THIS COAST. 7-11. the coast of Manasseh was from Asher to Michmethah—the southern boundary is here traced from the east. Asher (now Yasir,), the starting point, was a town fifteen Roman miles east of Sichem, and anciently a place of importance. 9. the coast descended unto the river Kanah, southward of the river—The line which separated the possessions of the two brothers from each other ran to the south of the stream, and thus the river was in the territory of Manasseh; but the cities which were upon the river, though all were within the limits of Manasseh's possessions, were assigned partly to Ephraim, and partly to Manasseh; those on the south side being given to the former; those upon the north to the latter. [KEIL.] It appears (*v.* 10,) that Manasseh was still further interlaced with other neighbouring tribes. Beth-shean and her towns—*Gr.*, Scythopolis (now Beisan,), in the valley of the Jordan, towards the east end of the plain of Jezreel. "Beth-shean" means "house of rest;" so called from its being the halting-place for caravans travelling between Syria or Midian, and Egypt, and the great station for the commerce between these countries for many centuries. Ibleam and her towns—in the neighbourhood of Megiddo (2 Ki. 9. 27.). the inhabitants of Dor and her towns—(now Tantoura), anciently a strong fortress; a wall of wild precipitous rock defended the shore fortifications against attack from the land side. En-dor and her towns—situated on a rocky eminence, four Roman miles south of Tabor. three countries—districts or provinces. It is computed that Manasseh possessed in Asher and Issachar portions of ground to the extent of more than 200 square miles. Taanach and Megiddo—These were near to each other, and they are generally mentioned in Scripture together. They were both royal and strongly fortified places (see on Ju. 1. 27.).

12, 13. CANAANITES NOT DRIVEN OUT. 12, 13. Manasseh could not drive out the in-

28 And Hebron, and Rehob, and Hammon, and *Kanah, *even unto great Zidon;
29 And *then* the coast turneth to Ramah, and to the strong city ¹ Tyre; and the coast turneth to Hosah; and the outgoings thereof are at the sea from the coast to ᵗAchzib;
30 Ummah also, and Aphek, and Rehob: twenty and two cities with their villages.
31 This *is* the inheritance of the tribe of the children of Asher according to their families, these cities with their villages.
32 ¶ The sixth lot came out to the children of Naphtali, *even* for the children of Naphtali according to their families.
33 And their coast was from Heleph, from Allon to Zaanannim, and Adami, Nekeb, and Jabneel, unto Lakum; and the outgoings thereof were at Jordan:
34 And *then* ᵘ the coast turneth westward to Aznoth-tabor, and goeth out from thence to Hukkok, and reacheth to Zebulun on the south side, and reacheth to Asher on the west side, and to Judah upon Jordan toward the sun-rising.
35 And the fenced cities *are* Ziddim, Zer, and ᵛHammath, Rakkath, and ʷChinnereth,
36 And Adamah, and Ramah, and Hazor,
37 And Kedesh, and Edrei, and En-hazor,
38 And Iron, and Migdal-el, Horem, and Beth-anath, and Beth-shemesh; nineteen cities with their villages.
39 This *is* the inheritance of the tribe of the children of Naphtali according to their families, the cities and their villages.
40 ¶ *And* the seventh lot came out for the tribe of the children of Dan according to their families.
41 And the coast of their inheritance was ˣZorah, and Eshtaol, and Ir-shemesh,
42 And ʸShaalabbin, and Ajalon, and Jethlah,
43 And Elon, and Thimnathah, and Ekron,
44 And Eltekeh, and Gibbethon, and Baalath,
45 And Jehud, and Bene-berak, and Gath-rimmon,
46 And Me-jarkon, and Rakkon, with the border ²before ³Japho.
47 And ᶻ the coast of the children of Dan went out *too little* for them: therefore the children of Dan went up to fight against Leshem, and took it, and ᵃsmote it with the edge of the sword, and possessed it, and dwelt therein, and called Leshem, ᵇDan, after the name of Dan their father.
48 This ᶜ *is* the inheritance of the tribe of Dan according to their families, these cities with their villages.
49 ¶ When they had made an end of dividing the land for inheritance by their coasts, the children of Israel gave an inheritance to Joshua the son of Nun among them:
50 According to the word of the LORD, they gave him the city which he asked, *even* ᵈ Timnath-serah ᵉ in mount Ephraim: and he built the city, and dwelt therein.
51 These ᶠ *are* the inheritances, which Eleazar the priest, and Joshua the son of Nun, and the heads of the fathers of the tribes of the children of Israel, divided for an inheritance by lot ᵍ in Shiloh before the LORD, at the door of the tabernacle of the congregation. So they made an end of dividing the country.

173

B. C. 1444.

CHAP. 19.
ʳ John 2. 1, Cana.
ˢ ch. 11. 8.
ᵗ Judg. 1. 31.
1 Tsor, that is, The rock.
2 Sam. 5. 11.
ᵘ Gen. 33. 5. Judg. 1. 31. Mic. 1. 14.
ᵛ Deut. 33. 23.
ʷ Gen. 10.18. Nu. 13. 21. 1 Kin. 8. 65.
ˣ Deu. 3. 17. Mark 5.53.
ʸ Judg. 13. 2.
ʸ Judg. 1. 35.
2 Or, over against.
3 Or, Joppa. Ezra 3. 7.
2 Chr. 2. 16.
Jonah 1. 3.
ᵃ Acts 9. 36.
ᵇ Judg. 18. 1.
ᶜ Gen. 49.17.
ᵈ Judg. 18. 29.
ᵉ Nu. 26. 54. Acts 17.26.
ᵈ ch. 24. 30.
ᵉ 1 Chr. 7. 24.
ᶠ Nu. 34. 17. ch. 14. 1.
ᵍ ch. 18. 1, 10.

CHAP. 20.
ᵃ Ex. 21. 13. Nu. 35. 6, 11, 14. Deut. 19. 2, 9.
ᵇ Deut. 21. 19. Ruth 4.1,2. Job 5. 4. Jer. 38. 7.
1 gather.
Ps. 26. 9.
ᶜ Nu. 35. 12. ᵈ Num. 35. 12, 25.
2 sanctified.
ᵉ ch. 21. 32. 1 Chr. 6. 76.
ᶠ ch. 21. 21. 2 Chr. 10. 1.
ᵍ ch. 14. 15. ch. 21. 11, 13.
ʰ Luke 1. 39.
ⁱ Deu. 4. 43. ch. 21. 36. 1 Chr. 6. 78.
ʲ ch. 21. 38. 1 Ki. 22. 3.
ᵏ ch. 21. 27.
ˡ Nu. 35. 15.

CHAP. 21.
ᵃ ch. 14. 1. ch. 17. 4.
ᵇ ch. 18. 1.
ᶜ Nu. 35. 2.
ᵈ ch. 24. 33.

CHAPTER XX.

1 *The Lord commands, 7 and the Israelites appoint by name, six cities of refuge.*

THE LORD also spake unto Joshua, saying,
2 Speak to the children of Israel, saying, Appoint ᵃ out for you cities of refuge, whereof I spake unto you by the hand of Moses:
3 That the slayer that killeth *any* person unawares *and* unwittingly may flee thither: and they shall be your refuge from the avenger of blood.
4 And when he that doth flee unto one of those cities shall stand at the entering of the ᵇ gate of the city, and shall declare his cause in the ears of the elders of that city, they shall ¹ take him into the city unto them, and give him a place, that he may dwell among them.
5 And ᶜ if the avenger of blood pursue after him, then they shall not deliver the slayer up into his hand; because he smote his neighbour unwittingly, and hated him not beforetime.
6 And he shall dwell in that city, ᵈ until he stand before the congregation for judgment, *and* until the death of the high priest that shall be in those days: then shall the slayer return, and come unto his own city, and unto his own house, unto the city from whence he fled.
7 ¶ And they ²appointed ᵉ Kedesh in Galilee in mount Naphtali, and ᶠ Shechem in mount Ephraim, and ᵍ Kirjath-arba, which *is* Hebron, in ʰ the mountain of Judah.
8 And on the other side Jordan by Jericho eastward, they assigned ⁱ Bezer in the wilderness upon the plain out of the tribe of Reuben, and ʲ Ramoth in Gilead out of the tribe of Gad, and ᵏ Golan in Bashan out of the tribe of Manasseh.
9 These ˡ were the cities appointed for all the children of Israel, and for the stranger that sojourneth among them, that whosoever killeth *any* person at unawares might flee thither, and not die by the hand of the avenger of blood, until he stood before the congregation.

CHAPTER XXI.

1 *Eight and forty cities given by lot out of the other tribes unto the Levites. 9 The cities of the priests. 43 God gave them rest.*

THEN came near the heads of the fathers of the Levites unto ᵃ Eleazar the priest, and unto Joshua the son of Nun, and unto the heads of the fathers of the tribes of the children of Israel;
2 And they spake unto them at ᵇ Shiloh in the land of Canaan, saying, ᶜ The LORD commanded by the hand of Moses to give us cities to dwell in, with the suburbs thereof for our cattle.
3 And the children of Israel gave unto the Levites out of their inheritance, at the commandment of the LORD, these cities and their suburbs.
4 And the lot came out for the families of the Kohathites: and the children of Aaron the priest, *which were* of the Levites, ᵈ had by lot out of the tribe of Judah, and out of the tribe of Simeon, and out of the tribe of Benjamin, thirteen cities.
5 And the rest of the children of Kohath *had* by lot out of the families of the tribe

habitants of those cities—indolence, a love of ease; perhaps a mistaken humanity, arising f. om a disregard or forgetfulness of the divine command, a decreasing principle of faith and zeal in the service of God, were the causes of their failure.

14-18. The Children of Joseph Sue for Another Lot. 14-18. The children of Joseph spake unto Joshua—The two tribes join in laying a complaint before the leader, as to the narrow boundaries of their allotment, and its insufficiency to be the residence of tribes so vastly increased. But Joshua's answer was full of wisdom as well as patriotism. Knowing their character, he treated them accordingly, and sarcastically turned all their arguments against themselves. Thus he rebuked their unbelief and cowardice. Mount Ephraim—called so here by anticipation. The Gilboa range between Beth-shean and the plain of Jezreel is meant, anciently covered with an extensive forest. iron cnariots—unusually strengthened with that metal, and perhaps armed with projecting scythes.

CHAPTER XVIII.

Ver. 1. The Tabernacle set up at Shiloh. 1. the whole congregation assembled together at Shiloh—The main body of the Israelites had been diminished by the separation of the three tribes, Judah, Ephraim, and Manasseh into their respective allotments, and the country having been in a great measure subdued, the camp was removed to Shiloh—now Seilun. It was twenty or twenty-five miles north of Jerusalem, twelve north of Bethel, and ten south of Shechem, and embosomed in a rugged and romantic glen. This sequestered spot in the heart of the country might have been recommended by the dictates of convenience; there the allotment of the territory could be most conveniently made, north, south, east, and west, to the different tribes. But "the tabernacle of the congregation was also set up there," and its removal therefore must have been made or sanctioned by divine intimation (Deu. 12. 11.). It remained in Shiloh for more than 300 years (1 Sam. 4. 1-11.).

2-9. The Remainder of the Land Described. 2. there remained seven tribes which had not yet received their inheritance—The selection of Shiloh for the seat of worship, together with the consequent removal of the camp thither, had necessarily interrupted the casting of lots, which was commenced by fixing localities for the tribes of Judah and Joseph. Various causes led to a long delay in resuming it. The satisfaction of the people with their change to so pleasant and fertile a district, their preference of a nomad life, a love of ease, and reluctance to renew the war, seem to have made them indifferent to the possession of a settled inheritance. But Joshua was too much alive to the duty laid on him by the Lord to let matters continue in that state; and accordingly, since a general conquest of the land had been made, he resolved to proceed immediately with the lot, believing that when each tribe should receive its inheritance, a new motive would arise to lead them to exert themselves in securing the full possession. **3.** how long are ye slack to go to possess the land—This reproof conveys an impression that the seven tribes were dilatory to a criminal extent. **4-9.** give out from among you three men for each tribe—Though the lot determined the part of the country where each tribe was to be located, it could not determine the extent of territory which might be required; and the dissatisfaction of the children of Joseph with the alleged smallness of their possession, gave reason to fear that complaints might arise from other quarters, unless precautions were taken to make a proper distribution of the land. For this purpose a commission was given to twenty-one persons—three chosen from each of the seven tribes which had not yet received their inheritance, to make an accurate survey of the country. "They went and passed through the land and described it by cities in seven parts in a book" (v. 9); dividing the land according to its value, and the worth of the cities which it contained, into seven equal portions. This was no light task to undertake. It required learning and intelligence which they or their instructors had, in all probability, brought with them out of Egypt. Accordingly, Josephus says that the survey was performed by men expert in geometry. And, in fact, the circumstantial account which is given of the boundaries of each tribe and its situation, well proves it to have been the work of no mean or incompetent hands. **10. Divided by Lot. 10.** Joshua cast lots for them in Shiloh before the Lord—before the tabernacle, where the divine presence was manifested, and which associated with the lot the idea of divine sanction. **11.** the lot of Benjamin came up—It has been supposed that here were two urns or vessels, from which the lots were drawn; one containing the names of the tribes; the other containing those of the seven portions; and that the two were drawn out simultaneously. between the children of Judah and the children of Joseph—Thus the prophecy of Moses respecting the inheritance of Benjamin was remarkably accomplished (see on Deu. 33. 12.).

CHAPTER XIX.

Ver. 1-9. The Lot of Simeon. 1. the second lot came forth to Simeon—The next lot that was drawn at Shiloh, giving the tribe of Simeon his inheritance within the territory, which had been assigned to that of Judah. The knowledge of Canaan possessed by the Israelites, when the division of the land commenced, was but very general, being derived from the rapid sweep they had made over it during the course of conquest; and it was on the ground of that rough survey alone, that the distribution proceeded, by which Judah received an inheritance. Time showed that this territory was too large (v. 9,), either for their numbers, however great, to occupy, and their arms to defend, or too large in proportion to the allotments of the other tribes. Justice therefore required, what kind and brotherly feeling readily dictated, a modification of their possession, and a part of it was appropriated to Simeon. By thus establishing it within the original domain of another tribe, the prophecy of Jacob in regard to Simeon was fulfilled (Gen. 49. 7,); for from its boundaries being not traced, there is reason to conclude that its people were divided and dispersed among those of Judah; and though one group of its cities named 2-6,) give the idea of a compact district, as it is usually represented by mapmakers, the other group (7, 8,) were situated, two in the south, and two elsewhere, with tracts of the country around them.

of Ephraim, and out of the tribe of Dan, and out of the half tribe of Manasseh, ten cities.

6 And the children of Gershon *had* by lot out of the families of the tribe of Issachar, and out of the tribe of Asher, and out of the tribe of Naphtali, and out of the half tribe of Manasseh in Bashan, thirteen cities.

7 The children of Merari by their families *had* out of the tribe of Reuben, and out of the tribe of Gad, and out of the tribe of Zebulun, twelve cities.

8 And *e* the children of Israel gave by lot unto the Levites these cities with their suburbs, *f* as the Lord commanded by the hand of Moses.

9 ¶ And they gave out of the tribe of the children of Judah, and out of the tribe of the children of Simeon, these cities which are *here* [1] mentioned by name,

10 Which the children of Aaron, *being* of the families of the Kohathites, *who were* of the children of Levi, had: for theirs was the first lot.

11 And *g* they gave them [2] the city of Arba the father of *h* Anak, which *city is* Hebron, *i* in the hill *country* of Judah, with the suburbs thereof round about it.

12 But *j* the fields of the city, and the villages thereof, gave they to Caleb the son of Jephunneh for his possession.

13 Thus *k* they gave to the children of Aaron the priest *l* Hebron with her suburbs, *to be* a city of refuge for the slayer; and *m* Libnah with her suburbs,

14 And *n* Jattir with her suburbs, *o* and Eshtemoa with her suburbs,

15 And *p* Holon with her suburbs, *q* and Debir with her suburbs,

16 And *r* Ain with her suburbs, *s* and Juttah with her suburbs, *and t* Beth-shemesh with her suburbs; nine cities out of those two tribes.

17 And out of the tribe of Benjamin, Gibeon *u* with her suburbs, *v* Geba with her suburbs,

18 Anathoth with her suburbs, and *w* Almon with her suburbs; four cities.

19 All the cities of the children of Aaron, the priests, *were* thirteen cities with their suburbs.

20 ¶ And *x* the families of the children of Kohath, the Levites which remained of the children of Kohath, even they had the cities of their lot out of the tribe of Ephraim.

21 For they gave them *y* Shechem with her suburbs in mount Ephraim, *to be* a city of refuge for the slayer; and *z* Gezer with her suburbs,

22 And Kibzaim with her suburbs, and Beth-horon with her suburbs; four cities.

23 And out of the tribe of Dan, Eltekeh with her suburbs, Gibbethon with her suburbs,

24 Aijalon with her suburbs, Gath-rimmon with her suburbs; four cities.

25 And out of the half tribe of Manasseh, Taanach with her suburbs, and Gath-rimmon with her suburbs; two cities.

26 All the cities *were* ten with their suburbs for the families of the children of Kohath that remained.

27 ¶ And *z* unto the children of Gershon, of the families of the Levites, out of the *other* half tribe of Manasseh, *they* gave Golan *a* in Bashan with her suburbs, *to be* a city of refuge for the slayer; and *b* Beeshterah with her suburbs; two cities.

28 And out of the tribe of Issachar, Kishon with her suburbs, Dabareh with her suburbs,

29 Jarmuth with her suburbs, En-gannim with her suburbs; four cities.

30 And out of the tribe of Asher, Mishal with her suburbs, Abdon with her suburbs,

31 Helkath with her suburbs, and Rehob with her suburbs; four cities.

32 And out of the tribe of Naphtali, Kedesh *b* in Galilee with her suburbs, *to be* a city of refuge for the slayer; and Hamothdor with her suburbs, and Kartan with her suburbs; three cities.

33 All the cities of the Gershonites according to their families *were* thirteen cities with their suburbs.

34 ¶ And *c* unto the families of the children of Merari, the rest of the Levites, out of the tribe of Zebulun, Jokneam with her suburbs, and Kartah with her suburbs,

35 Dimnah with her suburbs, Nahalal with her suburbs; four cities.

36 And out of the tribe of Reuben, *d* Bezer with her suburbs, and Jahazah with her suburbs,

37 Kedemoth with her suburbs, and Mephaath with her suburbs; four cities.

38 And out of the tribe of Gad, *e* Ramoth in Gilead with her suburbs, *to be* a city of refuge for the slayer; and *f* Mahanaim with her suburbs,

39 Heshbon with her suburbs, Jazer with her suburbs; four cities in all.

40 So all the cities for the children of Merari, by their families, which were remaining of the families of the Levites, were by their lot twelve cities.

41 All *g* the cities of the Levites within the possession of the children of Israel *were* forty and eight cities with their suburbs.

42 These cities were every one with [4] their suburbs round about them: thus *were* all these cities.

43 ¶ And the Lord gave unto Israel *h* all the land which he sware to give unto their fathers; and they possessed it, and dwelt therein.

44 And *i* the Lord gave them rest round about, according to all that he sware unto their fathers: and *j* there stood not a man of all their enemies before them; the Lord delivered all their enemies into their hand.

45 There *k* failed not ought of any good thing which the Lord had spoken unto the house of Israel; all came to pass.

CHAPTER XXII.

1 *Joshua dismisses the two tribes and half with a blessing:* 10 *they build the altar of testimony in their journey:* 11 *contention thereupon.* 30 *The deputies satisfied.*

THEN Joshua called the Reubenites, and the Gadites, and the half tribe of Manasseh,

2 And said unto them, Ye have kept *a* all that Moses the servant of the Lord commanded you, *b* and have obeyed my voice in all that I commanded you:

3 Ye have not left your brethren these many days unto this day, but have kept the charge of the commandment of the Lord your God.

10-16. OF ZEBULUN. 10-14. the third lot came up for the children of Zebulun—The boundaries of the possession assigned to them extended from the Lake of Cinneroth (Sea of Galilee) on the east, to the Mediterranean on the west; for although they do not seem at first to have touched on the western shore— a part of Manasseh running north into Asher— (ch. 17. 10), they afterwards did, according to the prediction of Moses (Deu. 33. 19.). The extent from south to north cannot be very exactly traced; the sites of many of the places through which the boundary line is drawn being unknown. Some of the cities were of note.

17-23. OF ISSACHAR. 17-20. the fourth lot came out to Issachar—Instead of describing the boundaries of this tribe, the inspired historian gives a list of its principal cities. These cities are all in the eastern part of the plain of Esdraelon.

24-31. OF ASHER. 24-31. the fifth lot came out for the tribe of the children of Asher—The western boundary is traced from north to south through the cities mentioned; the site of which, however, is unknown. to Carmel and Shihor-libnath—*i. e.*, the black or muddy river; probably the Nahr Belka, below Dor (Tantoura.); for that town belonged to Asher (ch. 17. 10.). Thence the boundary line turned eastward to Beth-dagon, a town at the junction of Zebulun and Naphtali, and ran northwards as far as Cabul, with other towns, amongst which is mentioned (v. 28,) "great Zidon," so called on account of its being even then the flourishing metropolis of the Phœnicians. Though included in the inheritance of Asher, this town was never possessed by them Ju. 1. 31.). 29. and then the coast turneth to Ramah—now El-Hamra, which stood where the Leontes (Litany,) ends its southern course and flows westward. and to the strong city Tyre—the original city appears to have stood on the main land, and was well fortified. From Tyre the boundary ran to Hosah, an inland town; and then passing the unconquered district of Achzib (Ju. 1. 31,), terminated at the sea-coast.

32-39. OF NAPHTALI. 32-39. the sixth lot came out to the children of Naphtali—Although the cities mentioned have not been discovered, it is evident, from Zaanannim, which is by Kedesh, *i.e.*, on the north-west of Lake Merom (Ju. 4. 11,), that the boundary described *v.* 34,) ran from the south-west towards the north-east, up to the sources of the Jordan. Aznoth-tabor—on the east of Tabor towards the Jordan, for the border ran thence to Hukkok, touching upon that of Zebulun; and as the territory of Zebulun did not extend as far as the Jordan, Aznoth-tabor and Hukkok must have been border towns on the line which separated Napthali from Issachar. to Judah upon Jordan toward the sun-rising—The sixty cities, Havoth-jair, which were on the eastern side of the Jordan, opposite Naphtali, were reckoned as belonging to Judah, because Jair, their possessor, was a descendant of Judah (1 Chr. 2. 4-22.) [KEIL.]

40-48. OF DAN. 40-46. the seventh lot came out for the tribe of Dan—It lay on the west of Benjamin, and consisted of portions surrendered by Judah and Ephraim. Its boundaries are not stated, as they were easily distinguishable from the relative position of Dan to the three adjoining tribes. **47.** the children of Dan went out to fight—The Danites finding their inheritance too small, meditated enlarging its boundaries by the sword; and having conquered Leshem (Laish,), planted a colony there, calling the new settlement by the name of Dan (see on Judg. 18.).

49-51. THE CHILDREN OF ISRAEL GIVE AN INHERITANCE TO JOSHUA. 49-51. they gave him the city which he asked—It was most proper that the great leader should receive an inheritance suited to his dignity, and as a reward for his public services. But the gift was not left to the spontaneous feelings of a grateful people. It was conferred, "according to the word of the Lord"—probably an unrecorded promise, similar to what had been made to Caleb (ch. 14. 9.). Timnath-serah—or Heres, on mount Gaash (Ju. 2. 9.). Joshua founded it, and was afterwards buried there (ch. 24. 30.). **51.** These are the inheritances—This verse is the formal close of the section which narrates the history of the land distribution; and to stamp it with due importance, the names of the commissioners are repeated, as well as the spot where so memorable a transaction took place.

CHAPTER XX.

Ver. 1-6. THE LORD COMMANDS THE CITIES OF REFUGE. 1. the Lord spake unto Joshua. Appoint out for you cities of refuge—(see Nu. 35. 9-28; Deu. 19. 1-13.). The command here recorded was given on their going to occupy their allotted settlements. The sanctuaries were not temples or altars, as in other countries, but inhabited cities; and the design was not to screen criminals, but only to afford the homicide protection from the vengeance of the deceased's relatives, until it should have been ascertained whether the death had resulted from accident and momentary passion, or from premeditated malice. The institution of the cities of refuge, together with the rules prescribed for the guidance of those who sought an asylum within their walls, was an important provision, tending to secure the ends of justice as well as of mercy. **4.** he that doth flee .. shall stand at the entering of the gate of the city—It was the place of public resort; and on arriving there he related his tale of distress to the elders, who were bound to give him shelter and the means of support, until the local authorities (*v.* 6,) having carefully investigated the case, should have pronounced the decision. If found guilty, the man-slayer was surrendered to the blood-avenger: if extenuating circumstances appeared, he was to remain in the city of refuge, where he would be safe from the vindictive feelings of his pursuers; but he forfeited the privilege of immunity the moment he ventured beyond the walls, until the death of the high priest—his death secured the complete deliverance of the man-slayer from his sin, only because he had been anointed with the holy oil (Nu. 35. 25.), the symbol of the Holy Ghost; and thus the death of the earthly High priest became a type of that of the heavenly One; Heb. 9. 14, 15.).

7-9. THE ISRAELITES APPOINT BY NAME THE CITIES OF REFUGE. 7-9. they appointed cities—There were six; three on the west, and three on the east of Jordan. In the first instance, they were a provision of the criminal law of the Hebrews, necessary in the circumstances of that people (see on Nu. 35. 9-15; Deu. 19.); and at the same time they were

4 And now the LORD your God hath given rest unto your brethren, as he promised them: therefore now return ye, and get you unto your tents, *and* unto the land of your possession, ᶜ which Moses the servant of the LORD gave you on the other side Jordan.

5 But ᵈ take diligent heed to do the commandment and the law, which Moses the servant of the LORD charged you, ᵉ to love the LORD your God, and to walk in all his ways, and to keep his commandments, and to cleave unto him, and to serve him with all your heart, and with all your soul.

6 So Joshua ᶠ blessed them, and sent them away; and they went unto their tents.

7 ¶ Now to the *one* half of the tribe of Manasseh Moses had given *possession* in Bashan; ᵍ but unto the *other* half thereof gave Joshua among their brethren on this side Jordan westward. And when Joshua sent them away also unto their tents, then he blessed them,

8 And he spake unto them, saying, Return with much riches unto your tents, and with very much cattle, with silver, and with gold, and with brass, and with iron, and with very much raiment: ʰ divide the spoil of your enemies with your brethren.

9 And the children of Reuben, and the children of Gad, and the half tribe of Manasseh, returned, and departed from the children of Israel out of Shiloh, which *is* in the land of Canaan, to go unto ⁱ the country of Gilead, to the land of their possession, whereof they were possessed, according to the word of the LORD by the hand of Moses.

10 ¶ And when they came unto the borders of Jordan, that *are* in the land of Canaan, the children of Reuben, and the children of Gad, and the half tribe of Manasseh, built there an altar by Jordan, a great altar to see to.

11 ¶ And the children of Israel ʲ heard say, Behold, the children of Reuben, and the children of Gad, and the half tribe of Manasseh, have built an altar over against the land of Canaan, in the borders of Jordan, at the passage of the children of Israel.

12 And when the children of Israel heard *of it,* ᵏ the whole congregation of the children of Israel gathered themselves together at Shiloh, to go up to war against them.

13 And the children of Israel ˡ sent unto the children of Reuben, and to the children of Gad, and to the half tribe of Manasseh, into the land of Gilead, ᵐ Phinehas the son of Eleazar the priest,

14 And with him ten princes, of each ¹ chief house a prince throughout all the tribes of Israel; and ⁿ each one *was* an head of the house of their fathers among the thousands of Israel.

15 And they came unto the children of Reuben, and to the children of Gad, and to the half tribe of Manasseh, unto the land of Gilead, and they spake with them, saying,

16 Thus saith the whole congregation of the LORD, What trespass *is* this that ye have committed against the God of Israel, to turn away this day from following the LORD, in that ye have builded you an altar, ᵒ that ye might rebel this day against the LORD?

17 *Is* the iniquity ᵖ of Peor too little for us, from which we are not cleansed until this day, although there was a plague in the congregation of the LORD,

18 But that ye must turn away this day from following the LORD? and it will be, *seeing* ye rebel to-day against the LORD, that to-morrow ᵠ he will be wroth with the whole congregation of Israel.

19 Notwithstanding, if the land of your possession *be* unclean, *then* pass ye over unto the land of the possession of the LORD, wherein ʳ the LORD's tabernacle dwelleth, and take possession among us; but rebel not against the LORD, nor rebel against us, in building you an altar besides the altar of the LORD our God.

20 Did ˢ not Achan the son of Zerah commit a trespass in the accursed thing, and wrath fell on all the congregation of Israel? and that man perished not alone in his iniquity.

21 ¶ Then ᵗ the children of Reuben, and the children of Gad, and the half tribe of Manasseh, answered and said unto the heads of the thousands of Israel,

22 The LORD ᵘ God of gods, the LORD God of gods, he ᵛ knoweth, and Israel he shall know; if *it be* in rebellion, or if in transgression against the LORD, (save us not this day,)

23 That we have built us an altar to turn from following the LORD, or if to offer thereon burnt offering or meat offering, or if to offer peace offerings thereon, let the LORD himself ʷ require *it;*

24 And if we have not *rather* done it for fear of *this* thing, saying, ² In time to come your children might speak unto our children, saying, What have ye to do with the LORD God of Israel?

25 For the LORD hath made Jordan a border between us and you, ye children of Reuben and children of Gad; ye have no part in the LORD: so shall your children make our children cease from fearing the LORD.

26 Therefore we said, Let us now prepare to build us an altar, not for burnt offering, nor for sacrifice:

27 But *that it may be* ˣ a witness between us and you, and our generations after us, that we might ʸ do the service of the LORD before him with our burnt offerings, and with our sacrifices, and with our peace offerings; that your children may not say to our children in time to come, Ye have no part in the LORD.

28 Therefore said we, that it shall be, when they should *so* say to us or to our generations in time to come, that we may say *again,* Behold the pattern of the altar of the LORD, which our fathers made, not for burnt offerings, nor for sacrifices; but it *is* a witness between us and you.

29 God forbid that we should rebel against the LORD, and turn this day from following the LORD, ᶻ to build an altar for burnt offerings, for meat offerings, or for sacrifices, besides the altar of the LORD our God that *is* before his tabernacle.

30 ¶ And when Phinehas the priest, and the princes of the congregation, and heads of the thousands of Israel which *were* with him, heard the words that the children of Reuben, and the children of Gad, and the children of Manasseh spake, ³ it pleased them.

designed also typically to point out the sinner's way to Christ (Heb. 6. 18.).

CHAPTER XXI.

Ver. 1-8. EIGHT AND FORTY CITIES GIVEN BY LOT OUT OF THE OTHER TRIBES UNTO THE LEVITES. 1. Then came near the heads of the fathers of the Levites—the most venerable and distinguished members of the three Levitical families who, on behalf of their tribe, applied for the special provision that had been promised them to be now awarded (see on Num. 35. 1-5.). Their inheritance lay within the territory of every tribe. It was assigned in the same place and manner, and by the same commissioners as the other allotments; and while the people, knowing the important duties they were to perform, are described (v. 3,) as readily conceding this "peculiar" to them: it had most probably been specified and reserved for their use, while the distribution of the land was in progress. 4-8. the lot came out for the families of the Kohathites—The Levites were divided into Kohathites, Gershonites, and Merarites. Among the former the family of Aaron were exclusively appointed to the priesthood, and all the rest were ranked in the common order of Levites. The first lot was drawn by the Kohathites; and the first of their's again by the priests, to whom thirteen cities were granted, and ten to the rest of the Kohathites (v. 5.); thirteen to the Gershonites (v. 6.), and twelve to the Merarites (v. 7.).

9-42. THE CITIES OF THE PRIESTS. 9-40. they gave these cities which are mentioned by name—It was overruled by the unerring providence of the divine lawgiver, that the cities of the priests lay within the territories of Judah and Benjamin; and this was a provision, the admirable wisdom and propriety of which was fully manifested on the schism that took place in the reign of Rehoboam. 41. all the cities of the Levites were forty and eight cities with their suburbs—This may appear too great a proportion compared with those of the other tribes. But it must be borne in mind, that the list given here contains the names of every Levitical city see on 1 Chr. 6. 39-66); whereas, only those cities of the other tribes are mentioned, which lay on the frontier or along the boundary line. Besides, the Levites were not the exclusive inhabitants of those forty-eight cities; for there must have been also a considerable number of people kept there to cultivate the glebe lands and tend the cattle. Still further, the Levitical cities had nothing but "their suburbs—a limited circuit of ground—round about them;" whereas the other cities in Israel possessed a group of independent villages (see chaps. 17. 18. 19.).

43-45. GOD GAVE THEM REST. 43-45. The Lord gave unto Israel all the land—This is a general winding up of the history from ch. 13. which narrates the occupation of the land by the Israelites. All the promises made, whether to the people or to Joshua ch. 1. 5.), had been, or were in the course of being fulfilled; and the recorded experience of the Israelites (v. 45.) is a ground of hope and confidence to the people of God in every age, that all other promises made to the Church will, in due time, be accomplished.

CHAPTER XXII.

Ver. 1-9. JOSHUA DISMISSES THE TWO TRIBES AND A-HALF WITH A BLESSING. 1. then Joshua called the Reubenites and the Gadites, and the half tribe of Manasseh—The general war of invasion being ended, and the enemy being in so dispirited and isolated a condition, that each tribe, by its own resources, or with the aid of its neighbouring tribe, was able to repress any renewed hostilities;—the auxiliary Israelites from the eastern side of the Jordan were now discharged from service. Joshua dismissed them with high commendations of their fidelity, and earnest admonitions to cultivate perpetual piety in life. The redundancy of the language is remarkable, and shows how important, in the judgment of the venerable leader, a steadfast observance of the divine law was to personal happiness, as well as national prosperity. 3. ye have not left your brethren these many days—For the space of seven years. 4-7. get ye unto your tents—i.e., home; for their families had been left in fortified towns (Num. 32. 17.). 8. much riches—In cattle, clothes, and precious metals. divide the spoil of your enemies with your brethren—see on Num. 31. 25-39.

10. THEY BUILD THE ALTAR OF TESTIMONY ON THEIR JOURNEY. 10. when they came unto the borders of Jordan, that are in the land of Canaan—This altar was probably an immense pile of stones and earth. The generality of our translators suppose that it was reared on the banks of the Jordan, within the limits of Canaan proper. But a little closer examination seems to make the conclusion irresistible that its position was on the eastern side of the river, for these two reasons; first, because it is said (v. 11) to have been built "over against," or in the sight of the land of Canaan—not within it; and secondly, because the declared motive of the trans-Jordanic Israelites in erecting it was to prevent their brethren in Canaan ever saying, "in time to come, What have ye to do with the Lord God of Israel? For the Lord hath made Jordan a barrier between us and you," &c. Such a taunt would be obviously prevented, or confuted by the two tribes and a-half having on the eastern side of Jordan, within their own land, a facsimile of the altar at Shiloh, as a witness they acknowledged the same God, and practised the same rites of worship as the brethren in Canaan.

11-29. CONTENTION THEREUPON. 11-29. and the children of Israel heard say—Fame speedily spread intelligence of what the trans-Jordanic tribes had done. The act being suspected of some idolatrous design, the whole tribes rose in a mass, and repairing to the tabernacle at Shiloh, resolved to declare war against the two tribes and a-half as apostates from God. On calmer and more mature considerations, however, they determined, in the first instance, to send a deputation consisting of the son of the high priest, and ten eminent persons from each tribe to make inquiry into this rumoured rebellion against God (Deu. 13. 13-15.). The quality of the deputies evinced the deep solicitude that was felt on the occasion to maintain the purity of the divine worship throughout Israel. In the presumptive belief that the two tribes and a-half had really built an altar, the deputies expressed astonishment at their so soon falling into such a heinous crime as that of violating the unity of divine worship (Ex. 20. 24; Lev. 17. 8, 9; Deu. 12. 5-13,), re-

31 And Phinehas the son of Eleazar the priest said unto the children of Reuben, and to the children of Gad, and to the children of Manasseh, This day we perceive that the LORD is ᵃ among us, because ye have not committed this trespass against the LORD: ᵈ now ye have delivered the children of Israel out of the hand of the LORD.

32 And Phinehas the son of Eleazar the priest, and the princes, returned from the children of Reuben, and from the children of Gad, out of the land of Gilead, unto the land of Canaan, to the children of Israel, and brought them word again.

33 And the thing pleased the children of Israel; and the children of Israel ᵇ blessed God, and did not intend to go up against them in battle, to destroy the land wherein the children of Reuben and Gad dwelt.

34 And the children of Reuben and the children of Gad called the altar 5 *Ed:* for it *shall* be a witness between us that the LORD *is* God.

CHAPTER XXIII.

1 *Joshua's exhortation before his death,* 3 *by former benefits,* 5 *by promises,* 12 *and by threatenings, in case of disobedience.*

AND it came to pass, a long time after that the LORD ᵃ had given rest unto Israel from all their enemies round about, that Joshua ᵇ waxed old *and* ¹ stricken in age.

2 And Joshua ᶜ called for all Israel, *and* for their elders, and for their heads, and for their judges, and for their officers, and said unto them, I am old *and* stricken in age:

3 And ye have seen all that the LORD your God hath done unto all these nations because of you: for the LORD your God *is* he that hath fought for you.

4 Behold, I have divided unto you by lot these nations that remain, to be an inheritance for your tribes, from Jordan, with all the nations that I have cut off, even unto the great sea ² westward.

5 And the LORD your God, ᵈ he shall expel them from before you, and drive them from out of your sight; and ye shall possess their land, ᵉ as the LORD your God hath promised you.

6 Be ye therefore very courageous to keep and to do all that is written in the book of the law of Moses, ᶠ that ye turn not aside therefrom *to* the right hand or *to* the left;

7 That ye ᵍ come not among these nations, these that remain among you; neither make ʰ mention of the name of their gods, nor cause to swear *by them*, neither serve them, nor bow yourselves unto them:

8 ʲ But cleave unto the LORD your God, as ye have done unto this day.

9 ᵏ For the LORD hath driven out from before you great nations and strong: but *as for* you, ⁱ no man hath been able to stand before you unto this day.

10 One ʲ man of you shall chase a thousand: for the LORD your God, he *it is* that fighteth for you, as he hath promised you.

11 Take good heed therefore unto ᵇ yourselves, that ye love the LORD your God.

12 Else if ye do in any wise ᵏ go back, and cleave unto the remnant of these nations, *even* these that remain among you, and

176

B. C. 1444.

CHAP. 22.
ᵃ Lev. 26. 11, 12.
1 Cor. 14. 25.
2 Chr. 15. 2.
Zech. 8. 23.
4 then.
ᵇ 1 Chr. 29. 20.
Neh. 8. 6.
Dan. 2. 19.
Lu. 2. 28.
5 That is, a witness.
ch. 24. 27.

CHAP. 23.
ᵃ ch. 21. 44.
ch. 22. 4.
ᵇ ch. 13. 1.
1 come into days.
ᶜ Deu. 31. 28.
ch. 24. 1.
1 Chr. 28. 1.
2 at the sunset.
ᵈ Ex. 23. 30.
ᵉ Nu. 33. 53.
ᶠ Deu. 5. 32.
ᵍ Pro. 4. 14.
Eph. 5. 11.
ʰ Nu. 32. 38.
Ps. 16. 4.
Jer. 5. 7.
Zeph. 1. 5.
3 Or, For if ye will cleave.
4 Or, then the LORD will drive.
ⁱ ch. 1. 5.
ʲ Judg. 3. 31.
5 your souls.
ᵏ Heb. 10. 38.
2 Pet. 2. 20.
ˡ Judg. 2. 3.
ᵐ 1 Ki. 11. 4.
ⁿ Ecclcs. 12. 3-7.
Heb. 9. 27.
Heb. 11. 13.
ᵒ Lu. 21. 33.
ᵖ Deu. 28. 63.
ᵠ Lev. 26. 16.
Deut. 28. 15, 16.

CHAP. 24.
ᵃ Gen. 35. 4.
ᵇ ch. 23. 2.
ᶜ 1 Sam. 10. 19.
ᵈ Gen. 11. 26.
ᵉ Gen. 31. 53.
ᶠ Acts 7. 2, 3.
ᵍ Ps. 127. 3.
ʰ Gen. 36. 8.
Deu. 2. 6.
Acts 17. 26.
ⁱ Ex. 3. 10.
ʲ Ex. 7. 1.
Ex. 8. 1.
Ex. 9. 1.
Ex. 10. 1.
Ex. 12. 1.
ᵏ Ex. 12. 37, 51.
ˡ Ex. 14. 9.
ᵐ Num. 21. 21, 33.
Deut. 2. 32.
Deu. 3. 1.

shall make marriages with them, and go in unto them, and they to you:

13 Know for a certainty that ˡ the LORD your God will no more drive out *any of* these nations from before you; ᵐ but they shall be snares and traps unto you, and scourges in your sides, and thorns in your eyes, until ye perish from off this good land which the LORD your God hath given you.

14 And, behold, this day ⁿ I *am* going the way of all the earth: and ye know in all your hearts, and in all your souls, that ᵒ not one thing hath failed of all the good things which the LORD your God spake concerning you; all are come to pass unto you, *and* not one thing hath failed thereof.

15 Therefore ᵖ it shall come to pass, *that* as all good things are come upon you, which the LORD your God promised you; so shall the LORD bring upon you ᵠ all evil things, until he have destroyed you from off this good land which the LORD your God hath given you.

16 When ye have transgressed the covenant of the LORD your God, which he commanded you, and have gone and served other gods, and bowed yourselves to them; then shall the anger of the LORD be kindled against you, and ye shall perish quickly from off the good land which he hath given unto you.

CHAPTER XXIV.

1 *Joshua, assembling the tribes,* 2 *relates God's benefits:* 14 *he renews the covenant between God and them:* 29 *his age and death.* 33 *Eleazar dies.*

AND Joshua gathered all the tribes of Israel to ᵃ Shechem, and ᵇ called for the elders of Israel, and for their heads, and for their judges, and for their officers; and they ᶜ presented themselves before God.

2 And Joshua said unto all the people, Thus saith the LORD God of Israel, ᵈ Your fathers dwelt on the other side of the flood in old time, *even* Terah, the father of Abraham, and the father of Nahor: and they ᵉ served other gods.

3 And ᶠ I took your father Abraham from the other side of the flood, and led him throughout all the land of Canaan, and multiplied his seed, and ᵍ gave him Isaac.

4 And I gave unto Isaac Jacob and Esau: and I gave unto ʰ Esau mount Seir, to possess it; but Jacob and his children went down into Egypt.

5 I ⁱ sent Moses also and Aaron, and ʲ I plagued Egypt, according to that which I did among them: and afterward I brought you out.

6 And I ᵏ brought your fathers out of Egypt: and ye came unto the sea; ˡ and the Egyptians pursued after your fathers with chariots and horsemen unto the Red sea.

7 And when they cried unto the LORD, he put darkness between you and the Egyptians, and brought the sea upon them, and covered them; and your eyes have seen what I have done in Egypt: and ye dwelt in the wilderness a long season.

8 And I brought you into the land of the Amorites, which dwelt on the other side Jordan; ᵐ and they fought with you: and I gave them into your hand, that ye might possess their land; and I destroyed them from before you

minded their Eastern brethren of the disastrous consequences that were entailed on the nation at large by the aposta-y at Peor, and by the sin of Achan, and finally exhorted them, if they felt the want of the tabernacle and altar, and repented of their rash choice in preferring worldly advantages to religious privileges, to remove to the western side of the Jordan, where the whole tribes would form a united and obedient community of worshippers. 21. then the children of Reuben, &c., answered—repudiating, in the strongest terms, the alleged crime, and deponing that so far from entertaining the intention imputed to them, their only object was to perpetuate the memory of their alliance with Israel, and their adherence to the worship of Israel's God.

30-34. THE DEPUTIES SATISFIED. 30-34. it pleased them—The explanation not only gave perfect satisfaction to the deputies, but elicited from them expressions of unbounded joy and thankfulness. "This day we perceive that the Lord is among us," i.e., by his gracious presence and preventing goodness, which has kept you from falling into the suspected sin, and rescued the nation from the calamity of a fratricidal war or providential judgments. This episode reflects honour upon all parties, and shows that piety and zeal for the honour and worship of God animated the people that entered Canaan to an extent far beyond what was exemplified in many other periods of the history of Israel.

CHAPTER XXIII.

Ver. 1, 2. JOSHUA'S EXHORTATION BEFORE HIS DEATH. 1. a long time after the Lord had given rest unto Israel—about fourteen years after the conquest of Canaan, and seven after the distribution of that country among the tribes. 2. called for all Israel—the clause which follows seems to restrict this general expression as applicable only to the officers and representatives of the people. The place of assembly was most probably Shiloh. The occasion of convening it was the extreme age and approaching death of the venerable leader; and the purport of this solemn address was to animate the chosen people and their posterity to a faithful and unswerving continuance in the faith and worship of the God of Israel.

3. BY FORMER BENEFITS. Ye have seen all that the Lord your God hath done for you—The modesty and humility of Joshua are remarkably displayed at the commencement of this address. Sinking all thoughts of his personal services, he ascribed the subjugation and occupation of Canaan entirely to the favouring presence and aid of God; and in doing so, he spoke not more piously than truly. This had been promised (Deu. 1. 30; 3. 22,); and the reality of the divine aid was seen in the rapid overthrow of the Canaanites, which had already led to the division of the whole land amongst the tribes.

5-11. BY PROMISES. 5-11. The Lord your God, he shall expel them from before you, &c.—The actual possessions which God had given were a pledge of the complete fulfilment of His promise in giving them the parts of the country still unconquered. But the accomplishment of the divine promise depended on their inviolable fidelity to God's law—on their keeping resolutely aloof from all familiar intercourse and intimate connexions with the Canaanites, or in any way partaking of their idolatrous sins. In the event of their continuing in steadfast adherence to the cause of God, as happily distinguished the nation at that time, His blessing would secure them a course of briliant and easy victories (Lev. 26. 7; Deu. 28. 7; 32. 30. . 11. Take good heed, therefore, that ye love the Lord your God—The sum of his exhortation is comprised in the love of God, which is the end or fulfilment of the law (Deu. 6. 5; 11. 13; M. 22. 37.).

12. BY THREATENINGS IN CASE OF DISOBEDIENCE. 12. Else if ye do in any wise go back, and cleave to the remnant of those nations—By "going back" is meant transgression of the divine law; and as marriage connexions with the idolatrous Canaanites would present many and strong temptations to transgress it, these were strictly prohibited (Ex 34. 12-16; Deu. 7. 3.). With his eye, as it were, upon those prohibitions, Joshua threatens them with the certain withdrawal of the divine aid in the further expulsion of the Canaanites; a threat founded on Ex. 23. 33; Nu. 33. 55; Deu. 7. 16.

CHAPTER XXIV.

Ver. 1. JOSHUA ASSEMBLING THE TRIBES. 1. Joshua gathered all the tribes of Israel to Shechem—Another and final opportunity of dissuading the people against idolatry is here described as taken by the aged leader, whose solicitude on this account arose from his knowledge of the extreme readiness of the people to conform to the manners of the surrounding nations. This address was made to the representatives of the people convened at Shechem, and which had already been the scene of a solemn renewal of the covenant (ch. 8. 30, 35.). The transaction now to be entered upon being in principle and object the same, it was desirable to give it all the solemn impressiveness which might be derived from the memory of the former ceremonial, as well as from other sacred associations of the place (Gen. 12. 6, 7; 33. 18-20; 35. 2-4.). they presented themselves before God—It is generally assumed that the ark of the covenant had been transferred on this occasion to Shechem; as on extraordinary emergencies it was for a time removed (Jud. 20. 1-18; 1 Sam. 4. 3; 2 Sam. 15. 24.). But the statement, not necessarily implying this, may be viewed as expressing only the religious character of the ceremony. [HENG.]

2-13. RELATES GOD'S BENEFITS. 2-13. Joshua said unto the people — His address briefly recapitulated the principal proofs of the divine goodness to Israel from the call of Abraham to their happy establishment in the land of promise; and showed them that they were indebted for their national existence as well as their peculiar privileges, not to any merits of their own, but to the free grace of God. on the other side of the flood—The Euphrates, viz., at Ur. Terah, the father of Abraham, and Nahor—see on Gen. 11. 27.). Though Terah had three sons, Nahor only is mentioned with Abraham, as the Israelites were descended from him on the mother's side through Rebekah and her nieces, Leah and Rachel. served other gods—Conjoining, like Laban, the traditional knowledge of the true God with the domestic use of material images (Gen. 31. 19, 34.). 3. took your father Abraham—It was an irresistible impulse of divine grace which led the patriarch to leave his country and rela-

The covenant with God renewed.   JOSHUA, XXIV.   *The death of Joshua.*

9 Then ⁿ Balak the son of Zippor, king of Moab, arose, and warred against Israel, and ^o sent and called Balaam the son of Beor to curse you:

10 But ^p I would not hearken unto Balaam; therefore ^q he blessed you still: so I delivered you out of his hand.

11 And ye went over Jordan, and came unto Jericho: and the men of Jericho fought against you, the Amorites, and the Perizzites, and the Canaanites, and the Hittites, and the Girgashites, the Hivites, and the Jebusites; and I delivered them into your hand.

12 And ^r I sent the hornet before you, which drave them out from before you, *even* the two kings of the Amorites; *but* not ^s with thy sword, nor with thy bow.

13 And I have given you a land for which ye did not labour, and ^t cities which ye built not, and ye dwell in them; of the vineyards and oliveyards which ye planted not do ye eat.

14 ¶ Now ^u therefore fear the LORD, and serve him in ^v sincerity and in truth: and put ^w away the gods which your fathers served on the other side of the flood, and in ^x Egypt; and serve ye the LORD.

15 And if it seem evil unto you to serve the LORD, choose you this day whom ye will serve; whether the gods which your fathers served, that *were* on the other side of the flood, or ^y the gods of the Amorites, in whose land ye dwell: ^z but as for me and my house, we will serve the LORD.

16 And the people answered and said, God forbid that we should forsake the LORD, to serve other gods;

17 For the LORD our God, he *it is* that brought us up and our fathers out of the land of Egypt, from the house of bondage, and which did those great signs in our sight, and preserved us in all the way wherein we went, and among all the people through whom we passed:

18 And the LORD drave out from before us all the people, even the Amorites which dwelt in the land: *therefore* will we also serve the LORD; for he *is* our God.

19 And Joshua said unto the people, ^a Ye cannot serve the LORD: for he *is* an ^b holy God; he *is* a jealous God; ^c he will not forgive your transgressions nor your sins.

20 If ^d ye forsake the LORD, and serve strange gods, ^e then he will turn and do you hurt, and consume you, after that he hath done you good.

21 And the people said unto Joshua, Nay, but we will serve the LORD.

22 And Joshua said unto the people, Ye *are* witnesses against yourselves that ^f ye have chosen you the LORD, to serve him. And they said, *We are* witnesses.

23 Now therefore ^g put away, *said he,* the strange gods which *are* among you, and incline your heart unto the LORD God of Israel.

24 And the people said unto Joshua, The LORD our God will we serve, and his voice will we obey.

25 So Joshua ^h made a covenant with the people that day, and set them a statute and an ordinance in Shechem.

26 And Joshua ⁱ wrote these words in the book of the law of God, and took ^j a great stone, and ^k set it up there under an oak that *was* by the sanctuary of the LORD.

27 And Joshua said unto all the people, Behold, this stone shall be ^l a witness unto us; for ^m it hath heard all the words of the LORD which he spake unto us: it shall be therefore a witness unto you, lest ye deny your God.

28 So Joshua let the people depart, every man unto his inheritance.

29 ¶ And it came to pass after these things, that Joshua the son of Nun, the servant of the LORD, died, *being* an hundred and ten years old.

30 And they buried him in the border of his inheritance in ⁿ Timnath-serah, which *is* in mount Ephraim, on the north side of the hill of Gaash.

31 And ^o Israel served the LORD all the days of Joshua, and all the days of the elders that ¹ overlived Joshua, and which had known all the works of the LORD, that he had done for Israel.

32 ¶ And ^p the bones of Joseph, which the children of Israel brought up out of Egypt, buried they in Shechem, in a parcel of ground ^q which Jacob bought of the sons of Hamor the father of Shechem, for an hundred ² pieces of silver: and it became the inheritance of the children of Joseph.

33 ¶ And Eleazar the son of Aaron died; and they buried him in a hill *that pertained to* Phinehas his son, which was given him in mount Ephraim.

tives, to migrate to Canaan, and live a "stranger and pilgrim" in that land. 4. gave unto Esau mount Seir—(see on Gen. 36. 8, 9.). In order that he might be no obstacle to Jacob and his posterity being the exclusive heirs of Canaan. 12. sent the hornet—A particular species of wasp which swarms in warm countries, and sometimes assumes the scourging character of a plague, or, as many think, it is a figurative expression for uncontrollable terror (Ex. 23. 27, : 8.). 14-28. Now therefore fear the Lord, and serve him in sincerity and truth—After having enumerated so many grounds for national gratitude, Joshua calls on them to declare, in a public and solemn manner, whether they will be faithful and obedient to the God of Israel. He avowed this to be his own unalterable resolution, and urges them, if they were sincere in making a similar avowal, "to put away the strange gods that were among them"—a requirement which seems to imply that some were suspected of a strong hankering for, or concealed practise of the idolatry, whether in the form of Zabaism—the fire-worship of their Chaldean ancestors, or the grosser superstitions of the Canaanites. 26. Joshua wrote these words in the books of the law of God—Registered the engagements of that solemn covenant in the book of sacred history. took a great stone—According to the usage of ancient times to erect stone pillars as monuments of public transactions. set it up under an oak—Or terebinth, in all likelihood, the same as that at the root of which Jacob buried the idols, and charms found in his family, that was by the sanctuary of the Lord — Either the spot where the ark had stood, or else the place around, so called from that religious meeting as Jacob named Bethel the house of God.

14-33. HIS AGE AND DEATH. 29, 30. Joshua died—Lightfoot computes that he lived seventeen, others twenty-seven years after the entrance into Canaan. He was buried, according to the Jewish practice, within the limits of his own inheritance. The eminent public services he had long rendered to Israel, and the great amount of domestic comfort and national prosperity he had been instrumental in diffusing among the several tribes, were deeply felt—were universally acknowledged; and a testimonial in the form of a statue or obelisk would have been immediately raised to his honour, in all parts of the land, had such been the fashion of the times. The brief but noble epitaph by the historian is, Joshua "the servant of the Lord." 31. Israel served the Lord all the days of Joshua—The high and commanding character of this eminent leader, had given so decided a tone to the sentiments and manners of his contemporaries, and the memory of his fervent piety and many virtues, continued so vividly impressed on the memories of the people, that the sacred historian has recorded it to his immortal honour. "Israel served the Lord all the days of Joshua, and all the days of the elders that overlived Joshua. 32. the bones of Joseph—They had carried these venerable relics with them in all their migrations through the desert, and deferred the burial, according to the dying charge of Joseph himself, till they arrived in the promised land. The sarcophagus, in which his mummied body had been put, was brought thither by the Israelites, and probably buried when the tribe of Ephraim had obtained their settlement, or at the solemn convocation described in this chapter. in a parcel of ground which Jacob bought for a hundred pieces of silver—*Kesitah*, translated "piece of silver," is supposed to mean a lamb, the weights being in the form of lambs or kids, which were, in all probability, the earliest standard of value among pastoral people. The tomb that now covers the spot is a Mahommedan *Welce*, but there is no reason to doubt that the precious deposit of Joseph's remains may be concealed there at the present time. 33. Eleazar ... died, and they buried him in mount Ephraim—The sepulchre is at the modern village Awertah, which, according to Jewish travellers, contains the graves also of Ithamar, the brother of Phinehas, the son of Eleazar. [VAN DE VELDE.]

www.ingramcontent.com/pod-product-compliance
Lightning Source LLC
Chambersburg PA
CBHW032358230426
43672CB00007B/739